□□□

THE WRITER'S HANDBOOK

□□□

The Writer's Handbook

Edited by

SYLVIA K. BURACK

Editor, The Writer

Publishers THE WRITER, INC. Boston

CONTENTS

BACKGROUND FOR WRITERS

HOW TO WRITE—TECHNIQUES

General Fiction

Background
for Writers

❏ 1

TOOLS OF THE WRITER'S TRADE

BY CHRISTOPHER SCANLAN

IN SHAKESPEARE'S TIME, ITINERANT ACTORS WHO TOOK THEIR PLAYS from village to town carried bags bulging with the tools of their art—scraps of costume, props, jars of paint. A writer's tools can be every bit as colorful and creative, and they won't take up as much room. Rummage through your memory and imagination to see if you find long-forgotten tools you can dust off.

Here are the tools I found and use: a tightrope, a net, a pair of shoes, a loom, six words, an accelerator pedal, and a time clock.

A tightrope

Take a risk with your writing every day. Submit to the magazine of your dreams. Conceive the next Great American Novel. The risks I've taken as a writer—pitching an ambitious project, calling for an interview with a reputed mobster, sending a short story back out in the mail the day it returned in my self-addressed envelope—have opened new doors and, more important, encouraged me to take other risks. Stretch an imaginary tightrope above your desk and walk across it every day.

A net

The best writers I know cast trawler's nets on stories. And they cast them wide and deep. They'll interview ten people, listening and waiting, to get the one quote that sums up the theme. They'll spend hours trolling for the anecdote that reveals the story. They'll sift through records and reports, looking for the one specific that explains the universal or the detail that captures the person or conveys the setting. I once wrote a story about a family in Utah whose daughter was a suspected victim of serial murderer Ted Bundy. During my visit, I noticed that a light switch next to the front door had a piece of tape over it so no one could turn it off. When I asked about it, the mother said she always left the light on until her daughter came home. The light had been burning for twelve years, a symbol of one family's unending grief.

A pair of shoes

Empathy, an ability to feel what another person feels, may be the writer's most important tool. Empathy is different from sympathy: It's one thing to feel sorry for a rape victim; it's another to imagine and write persuasively to recreate the constant terrors and distrust sown in the victim's mind. To write about a young widow in my story "School Uniform," I had to imagine the problems of a woman coping with her own grief and that of her children:

> After the funeral, Maddy had made sure that each child had something of Jim's. It was torture to handle his things, but she spread them out on their bed one night after the children were asleep and made choices. Anna draped his rosary from the mirror on her makeup table; Martin kept his paper route money secured in his father's silver money clip. Brian filled the brass candy dish that Jim used as an ashtray with his POGS and Sega Genesis cartridges. Daniel kept his baseball cards in Jim's billfold. There were days she wished she could have thrown everything out, and had she been alone, she might have moved away, started somewhere fresh with nothing to remind her of what had been, all she had lost when he died, leaving her at 38 with four children. And on nights like this, when there was trouble with Daniel, again, she wanted to give up.

When you write about a character, try to walk in that person's shoes.

A loom

Writers, like all artists, help society understand the connections that bind us. They identify patterns. Raymond Carver said, "writing is just a process of connections. Things begin to connect. A line here, a word here." Are you weaving connections in your stories? In your reading? In your life? Are you asking yourself what line goes to what line, and what makes a whole? "Only connect!" urged E.M. Forster. Turn your computer into a loom that weaves stories.

Six words

Thinking is the hardest part about writing and the one writers are likeliest to bypass. When I'm writing nonfiction, I try not to start writing until I've answered two questions: "What's the news?" and "What's the story?" Whatever the genre—essay, article or short story—effective writing conveys a single dominant message. To discover that theme or focus, try to sum up your story in six words, a phrase that captures the tension of the story. For a story about a teenage runaway hit by a train and rescued by another teen, my six words are "Lost, Then Found, On the Tracks." Why six words? No reason, except that in discipline, there is freedom.

An accelerator pedal

Free writing is the writer's equivalent of putting the pedal to the metal. I often start writing workshops by asking participants to write about "My Favorite Soup." It loosens the fingers, memory, and imagination. I surprised myself recently by describing post-Thanksgiving turkey soup:

> Most holidays have a "Do Not Resuscitate" sign on them. At the end of Christmas everybody vows that next year will be different, we'll pick names, not buy for everybody. It's too expensive, too time-consuming. But turkey soup puts a holiday on a respirator for a few more days of life, enough time to remember and savor the memories of the family around the table.

Speeding on a highway is a sure-fire route to an accident, but doing it on the page or computer screen creates an opportunity for fortunate accidents—those flashes of unconscious irony or insight that can trigger a story or take you and your readers deeper into one.

A time clock

Writers write. It's that simple—and that hard. If you're not writing regularly and for *at least* 15 minutes before your day job, then you're not a writer. Many times I resist; the writing is terrible, I'm too tired, I have no ideas, and then I remember that words beget other words. I stifle my whining and set to work, just for a little while, I tell myself. Almost always, I discover writing I had never imagined before I began, and those are the times I feel most like a writer. Put an imaginary time clock on your desk, right next to your computer. Punch in.

❑ 2

BREAKING THE RULES

BY ALISON SINCLAIR

HANDS UP, EVERYONE WHO HAS EVER BEEN TOLD, "WRITE WHAT YOU KNOW."

Hands up, everyone who has heard, "Show, Don't Tell."

If there's a writer who hasn't heard either at some point early in his or her career, I'd consider that person fortunate indeed.

(They've surely heard the third—Stand up, please, anyone who hasn't—"You'll Never Make a Living at It!")

Though intolerant of abusers of the common apostrophe, I am a tender-hearted soul. I will not advocate the slaughtering of sacred cows, even in metaphor, but I would advocate firmly turning them out to pasture. Here's why.

1) Writers should *not* be urged to write what they know. They should be urged to write what they care about, care about passionately, argumentatively, gracelessly, if need be. Knowledge can be acquired, whether through books, the world wide web, or stoking or stroking an expert. (People love to talk about their own personal passions.) Knowledge can be acquired in the absence of caring. Ask any diligent student working just for a grade, or a responsible adult making a living in a job he or she dislikes. But caring, unlike knowledge, cannot be acquired at second hand. Knowledge gives writing authority—I cannot dispute that—but caring gives writing life.

A few years ago, in Canada, where I now live, and in particular amongst the community of women writers, there came a call that women of the majority culture (i.e., white) should not impersonate, in writing, minority characters. It was an act of appropriation. In one respect, I could see the justice of it, that the way would be cleared for writers from minorities to speak in their own voice. In another, I could see that it struck at the fundamental nature of writing. By raising "write what you know (and *only* what you know)" to a formal imperative, the imaginative projection of experience unalike one's own—experience not known but imagined—was denied. The controversy has settled, but I remember it, the questions it raised about balancing social justice and imaginative liberties, and the threat I felt it posed to the life of the imagination.

2) Every writing book somewhere says, "Show, don't tell." That phrase should come with a health warning: "Keep out of reach of novices." Like cellophane wrapping, it can suffocate. As many beginning writers do, I believed it. In my first novel, a character went out to meet a woman about whom he'd heard a great deal. So he got out bed, got dressed, went downstairs, had a conversation with other people in the house, and he was given an errand, which he did, which led to another conversation, and he walked downhill. I described everything he saw on the way, and ten pages on he finally met her. It was a good meeting, if I say so myself, but when the book was accepted (not, I suspect, for what I had done, but for what the editor thought I might yet do), the editor decreed CUT. And cut I did. I discovered, under her rigorous tutelage, that you show only what you absolutely have to, tell what you can't avoid, and leave the rest out. The final version of that chapter had my couple face to face in two-and-a-half pages. They went on to have a turbulent though happy life together (most of it long after the final line of the book because that had nothing to do with the problem set up in the first chapter). Paragraphs and paragraphs of "showing" were dispensed with in a few sentences or even words. And the book was by far the better for it.

Even in a 150,000-word novel, there is no space for "show," no scenes that can be given over to "I just wanted to show that this society was egalitarian." If these things are part of the story, they will be revealed through the action. If they are not, they are irrelevant; they can be narrated, briefly, or left out. "Tell" is a powerful tool for keeping minor matters in their place.

3) There are any number of Rules propounded for writers (which in itself is probably a reflection of Maugham's Three Rules, noted below. Nothing generates regulation like uncertainty): ONE MUST WRITE ONE THOUSAND WORDS EVERY DAY (honored more in the breach than in the observance; writers have lives, too). NEVER START A NOVEL WITH DIALOGUE (did anybody tell Tolstoy?). DO NOT TALK ABOUT YOUR WRITING; YOU'LL TALK IT OUT; or alternatively, IF YOU CAN'T TELL

SOMEONE ELSE YOUR PLOT, IT'S NO GOOD. NOVELS ABOUT (fill in the blank) DO NOT SELL, etc.

For every writer who swears by a Rule, there is one as good, as successful, as sagacious and temperate, who breaks it. For myself, I believe in Somerset Maugham's Three Rules, Le Guin's Advice, and Granny Weatherwax's Principle. Maugham observed that there were Three Rules of Writing; unfortunately, no one knows what they are. Le Guin's Advice (from *The Language of the Night*): "No matter how any story begins, it ends typed in good, clear, black text on one side of white paper, with name and address on each page."*

Granny Weatherwax's Principle is: "When you break the rules, break 'em good and hard."†

---

*This predates the electronic age. Things have become more complicated since, so this rule should be amended to: Read submission instructions in the latest issue.

†Granny Weatherwax is a witch (Terry Pratchett's *Wyrd Sisters*).

❑ 3

FACING UP TO TIME

BY ELIZABETH YATES

IT WAS A STARTLING QUESTION, AND IT CAME FROM A FOURTH-GRADER in a small group of children who had come to talk with me about writing: "Has aging improved your writing?" I had to think for a moment. The other questions had been fairly routine: How long does it take to write a book? What can I do when I get stuck in the middle? Where do I get an idea? But this was one directed at me, where I am now, even before that, the years of apprenticeship and the long years of work with their richness and their agony, even up to this very moment. Thinking back I found my answer, and it was unequivocal: "Yes, because life is a learning process, and the longer we live, the more we become aware of this."

I wanted to give these children an instance, so I told them of the time when an idea had come to me with such insistency that I had to act on it. It could not be shelved, or put away in a notebook. It was when I was standing by the stone that marked the grave of Amos Fortune in the old cemetery in Jaffrey, New Hampshire. Reading the eloquent though brief words about a man whose life spanned from Africa in 1715 to America in 1801, I wanted to know more, to find the story within those lines. The idea took hold of me, or I of it, and I knew that nothing must keep me from following it. A line of William Blake's came to mind: "He who kisses the joy as it flies/Lives in eternity's sunrise." Months of research were before me, months of work, the writing and then the careful revision, but finally when the words looked up at me from the page, I felt right about them. So, more than ever, I want to take hold of the idea that grips me, not because time may be running out on me, but because of the marvelous freshness.

Something else I have been learning has to do with the aptness of words. There are times when the one I think I want won't come to mind, so I leave a blank and decide to return to it when the flow of creativity has run itself out. James Barrie in *Sentimental Tommie* tells of a small boy in school (I'm sure it was Barrie himself) when the class was writing essays, and the word he wanted eluded him. Trying to find it, he forgot about time, but the clock did not, and when the hour was up, the boy had little on his page. However, much later he did find the word and returned to tell it to the teacher. I leave a blank, and when I get back with time to search the treasure trove of words tucked away in my mind, I come upon the one I want. I fill in the blank with it and smile inwardly, for it is right, so much better than the one I might hastily have used. Startling in its aptness, I cherish it and add it to my immediate store of words, but not until I have gone to my faithful *Webster's Collegiate* to confirm the meaning. Am I really right? Oh, dear delight, I am righter than right!

"Have you ever regretted anything you've written?" came the next question. Again, I sent my mind back over the years and their books. The answer was at hand, and it was *No,* for I have had a rule with myself that nothing ever leaves my desk unless it is the best I can do at the time with the material I have. Then I go back to Amos Fortune as an example.

The idea that took hold of me as I stood by that stone in the old churchyard and that became the book *Amos Fortune, Free Man* was written in 1949 and published a year later. All the pertinent, reliable material that I could find went into the book and became the story. It could not be a biography but an account of a man's life, with facts assured and some imaginative forays based on the temper of the times. The research, the writing, was done long before the Civil Rights upheavals of the 60's. I might today write a very different story, but that was then.

The final question, "How will I know when to stop?," was one that I did not have to search my mind to answer. "When you have said what you wanted to say and feel satisfied." I could see in these children's faces that they wanted me to go further. "Your story may take many pages, or not so many, but stop when you have told the story you set out to tell and are pleased with it, for you are the one who must be pleased." In my own thinking, I recalled words of Sydney Cox in his small book, *Indirections,* which, for me, says everything that needs to be said about writing: ". . . the end of a story should leave the reader with an upward impulse and a kind of peace."

Often a P.S. can be the most important part of a letter, and I had one for the children. It is something I have always known but not always heeded. It is listening to my inner voice, and I find myself giving it more and more attention. So, I am still learning.

❏ 4

Doing It for Love

By Erica Jong

Despite all the cynical things writers have said about writing for money, the truth is we write for love. That is why it is so easy to exploit us. That is also why we pretend to be hard-boiled, saying things like "No man but a blockhead ever wrote except for money" (Samuel Johnson). Not true. No one but a blockhead ever wrote except for love.

There are plenty of easier ways to make money. Almost anything is less labor-intensive and better paid than writing. Almost anything is safer. Reveal yourself on the page repeatedly, and you are likely to be rewarded with exile, prison or neglect. Ask Dante or Oscar Wilde or Emily Dickinson. Scheme and betray, and you are likely to be rewarded with wealth, publicity and homage. Tell the truth, and you are likely to be a pariah within your family, a semi-criminal to authorities and damned with faint praise by your peers. So why do we do it? Because saying what you think is the only freedom. "Liberty," said Camus, "is the right not to lie."

In a society in which everything is for sale, in which deals and auctions make the biggest news, doing it for love is the only remaining liberty. Do it for love and you cannot be censored. Do it for love and you cannot be stopped. Do it for love and the rich will envy no one more than you. In a world of tuxedos, the naked man is king. In a world of bookkeepers with spreadsheets, the one who gives it away without counting the cost is God.

I seem to have known this from my earliest years. I never remember a time when I didn't write. Notebooks, stories, journals, poems—the act of writing always made me feel centered and whole. It still does. It is my meditation, my medicine, my prayer, my solace. I was lucky enough to learn early (with my first two books of poetry and my first novel) that if you are relentlessly honest about what you feel and fear,

11

you can become a mouthpiece for something more than your own feelings. People are remarkably similar at the heart level—where it counts. Writers are born to voice what we all feel. That is the gift. And we keep it alive by giving it away.

It is a sacred calling. The writers I am most drawn to understand it as such: Thomas Merton, Pablo Neruda, Emily Dickinson. But one doesn't always see the calling clearly as one labors in the fields of love. I often find myself puzzling over the choices a writer is given. When I am most perplexed, I return to my roots: poetry. The novel is elastic: It allows for social satire, cooking, toothbrushes, the way we live now. Poetry, on the contrary, boils down to essences. I feel privileged to have done both.

And I am grateful to have found my vocation early. I was also blessed to encounter criticism early. It forced me to listen to my inner voice, not the roar of the crowd. This is the most useful lesson a writer can learn.

Lately, we keep hearing dire warnings about the impending death of the novel. As one who has written frankly autobiographical fiction (*Fear of Flying*), historical fiction (*Fanny, Serenissima* or *Shylock's Daughter*) and memoir (*Fear of Fifty* and *The Devil at Large*), I think I've begun to understand how the process of making fiction differs from that of making memoir. A memoir is tethered to one's own experience in a particularly limiting way: The observing consciousness of the book is rooted in a real person. That person may be fascinating, but he or she can never be as rich and subtle as the characters that grow out of aspects of the author. In the memoir, the "I" dominates. In the novel, the "I" is made up of many "I"s. More richness is possible, more points of view, deeper imitation of life.

When I finished *Fear of Fifty*, I felt I had quite exhausted my own life and might never write another book. What I eventually discovered was that the process had actually liberated me. Having shed my own autobiography, I now felt ready to invent in a new way. I wanted to write a novel about the 20th century and how it affected the lives of women. I wanted to write a novel about a Jewish family in the century that nearly saw the destruction of the Jewish people.

I began by reading history and literature for a year. And when I started to write again, it was in the voice of a woman who might have been my great-grandmother. Liberated from my place and time, I found myself inventing a woman's voice quite different from my own. But as I began to fashion this alternate family history, I found myself at play in the fields of my imagination. Characters sprang up like mushrooms after the rain. I couldn't wait to get to work in the morning to see what I thought and who was going to embody it.

Eventually I found I had four heroines, born in different decades, and that they were all mothers and daughters. Each had a distinctive voice and way of looking at the world. Each was me and not me.

Graham Greene once said, "The more the author knows of his own character the more he can distance himself from his invented characters and the more room they have to grow in."

That seems to me precisely right. A novelist's identity is fixed. Her character, however, can fly.

A character may even access some deep memory in the writer's brain that seemed lost forever. Fictional characters excavate real memories. Flaubert, after all, claimed to be Emma Bovary and gave her his restlessness and discontent. In some ways an author may be freer to expose himself in a character unlike himself. There is liberty behind a mask. The mask may become the condition for speaking the truth.

The line between novel and autobiography has never been as blurry as it is in our century. And this is probably a good thing. The novel endures because it mimics truth. So if we find truths in autobiography in our age, even fiction will come to mimic that genre. And genres themselves matter less and less. The most enduring books of the modern era are, like *Ulysses,* full of exposition, narrative, dramatic writing and even poetry.

As a reader, I want a book to kidnap me into its world. Its world must make my so-called real world seem flimsy. Its world must lure me to return. When I close the book, I should feel bereft.

How rare this is and how grateful I am to find it. The utter trust that exists between reader and author is like the trust between lovers. If I feel betrayed by the author, I will never surrender to him or her again.

That trust is why it is so hard to start a new book. You must find the right voice (or voices) for the timbre that can convince the reader to give himself up to you. Sometimes it takes years to find the tone of voice that unlocks the story.

The books we love best kidnap us with the first line. "Whether I shall turn out to be the hero of my own life, or whether that station will be held by anybody else, these pages must show" (*David Copperfield*). "You don't know about me, without you have read a book by the name of *The Adventures of Tom Sawyer,* but that ain't no matter" (*Huckleberry Finn*). It's not only the question of an arresting opening—the writer's best trick—but of letting the main character's quirks show, too. I tried it myself in *Fear of Flying:* "There were 117 analysts on the Pan Am flight to Vienna, and I'd been treated by at least six of them." And it's easier to do in the first person than in the third.

But as I said in the beginning, you must do it for love. If you do it for money, no money will ever be enough, and eventually you will start imitating your first successes, straining hot water through the same old teabag. It doesn't work with tea, and it doesn't work with writing. You must give all you have and never count the cost. ("Sit down at the typewriter and open a vein," as Red Smith said.)

Every book I have written has subsumed all the struggles of the years in which I wrote it. I don't know how to hold back. Editing comes only after the rush of initial feeling. I end up cutting hundreds of pages sometimes. But in the writing process, I let it all hang out. Later I and my editor chop.

Generosity is the soul of writing. You write to give something. To yourself. To your reader.

□ 5

WHAT EMILY DICKINSON KNEW

BY HELEN MARIE CASEY

IF THERE'S ONE THING EMILY DICKINSON KNEW FOR SURE, IT WAS what a good poem should do. "If I feel physically as if the top of my head were taken off, I know that is poetry," she wrote.

Dickinson was attempting to describe for her sister-in-law the power of poetry to envelop and even to devastate the reader (or listener). Her physical description was an effort to convey that successful poems are not effete passages or bookish exercises; they are chillingly annihilating. They have the power to alter us irrevocably.

Poetry, the Belle of Amherst knew, is that form of communication in which words are never simple equivalents of experience or perception. The words themselves, the words as words, have a life as sounds, as images, as the means for generating a series of associations.

Contemporary poet and critic Ann Lauterbach claims that "For poets, the world is apprehended *as* language . . . Every object in the world is simultaneously itself and its word." It is impossible to put too much weight on the importance of each individual word. Yet, paradoxically, poetry is that art form in which what is unsaid is often as important—or more important—than what is said. And, to the bewilderment of some, it is a literary genre in which the voice, the tone, the texture, and the poetic form—that is, the way of saying what the poem is saying—are also fundamental parts of what is being said.

Poets are certainly not the only writers to concern themselves with the simultaneous life of language as symbol *and* as nonreferential but it is poets who most seem to insist on seeing and hearing words as if each is a multi-faceted gem that has, in the hands of the skillful artist, the capacity to resonate and to go in multiple directions at once.

Take, for example, the lines that begin the Wallace Stevens poem, "The Course of a Particular":

> Today the leaves cry, hanging on branches swept by wind,
> Yet the nothingness of winter becomes a little less.
> It is still full of icy shades and shapen snow.

Syntactically, the lines are constructed like direct prose statements. Yet, we know that leaves do not, in fact, cry. We recognize that we are dealing with language used imaginatively, language used to do something other than simply deliver a message.

We recognize immediately that mood will be part of what we derive from the poem and that the images—*wind, winter, icy shades, snow, leaves crying*—will be part of the way the poem says what it wants to say.

We recognize in words like *still, shades,* and *shapen snow,* a recurrent "s" sound. Looking back over the first two lines we hear additional "s" sounds in the endings of the words *leaves, branches, nothingness, becomes, less,* and *shades.*

The repetition of "win" in *wind* and *winter* is the repetition of a sound that requires us to blow out as wind itself blows.

In poetry, the sounds, shadings, color, and associative values of the words are every bit as important as the specific denotative meanings. This does not mean that the language of poetry is imprecise. On the contrary, there is absolutely nothing arbitrary about a poet's choice of vocabulary or about the manner in which the poet arranges and juxtaposes the words selected. There is nothing superfluous in poems that work.

The reason many readers keep their distance from poetry is probably best captured by the observation of a student who wrote, "The trouble with poems is they start out to be about one thing, and then they end up being about something else." What the student understood is that part of the magic of poetry is its ability to sustain multiple levels of meaning, to be at once literally what it seems to be and also to exist, because of the power of suggestion, on a figurative level. What is frustrating to her is the richness and texture of a successful poem. What she thinks she would like is a straightforward description in which everything is laid out clearly.

It is the misperception that poems ought to be easy to apprehend that leads so many beginning poets to mistrust the powers of allusion and suggestion and to err by telling all. They bore readers and deny them the thrill of discovery. In addition, they often believe that ambiguity is some kind of writing sin and fail to see that, in fact, intentional ambiguity can be the source of irony, humor, foreboding, and thematic weight in a poem.

If there were a single question that might be a productive spring-board to the creation of richer poems, it might well be this: Have I wholly engaged the imagination of my readers by creating the path we shall traverse together and then purposefully stopped short on it, allowing the reader to go on without me?

There is, of course, no single solution to the question of how to write effectively, but I am inclined to trust Marianne Moore's observation in her poem, "Bowls": "Only so much colour shall be revealed as is necessary to the picture."

❑ 6

REWRITING

By Lucian K. Truscott IV

I SUPPOSE THE TERM "REWRITING" COMES FROM MY YEARS AS A JOUR-nalist, but I think the notion of rewriting instead of mere revision also sums up my attitude about going at the work you have just done. I don't look at a second draft as revision. I look at it as doing the whole damn thing again.

I've lived in Hollywood for almost seven years now and have worked steadily writing screenplays ever since. I have learned a thing or two about rewriting from working under contract to the major studios. The way it works is this: You come up with an idea for a movie; you go around to various producers and/or studio executives and you pitch the idea, and if you're really, really, *really* lucky, somebody bites, you get a contract for a screen play, and you write the thing. You hand it in and wait a couple of weeks. They call you in for a meeting, and one of the executives says something like this (actually said to me in a meeting with a major studio executive): "You know the dead girl on page 18? She was incredibly sexy, and I think she'd make a great lead character. Don't you think we could have her solve the murder, and have somebody else get killed?"

Now if they insist on something like that, what you end up with is not *revision* but *rewriting,* which has been incredibly instructive to my life as a novelist.

I have learned one thing of immeasurable value in Hollywood: If a work can withstand such an elemental question as the one above, it can withstand anything. So, after a couple of years in the trenches, I concluded that the studio executives were not the only ones who could ask hard questions or raise outrageous points about my work.

So could I.

In this way, I learned to be my own worst critic. I started out doing it with screenplays, but the process bled naturally into work on novels.

You sit down and write a first draft, and you give it a rest for awhile— say a month or two, if you've got the time; if not, a week or two might suffice. Then you get back into the things and start to ask yourself hard questions: What is it that *works* about this piece, and what is it that *doesn't* work?

If you go at it hard enough, you'll come up with something, and having identified an element or two that doesn't work, you then throw out what doesn't work and start something new.

This can be quite a shock if you figure out that the crux of the movie or the book just isn't holding up, because that means you are very definitely going to be doing some rewriting and not mere revision.

This happened to me when I began working on rewriting my most recent novel, *Full Dress Gray,* the sequel to my first novel, *Dress Gray.* Because we were on a tight publication deadline, the publisher notified me that I would have to complete a second draft within two months. I sat down and started and went at it eight to ten hours a day. The first 102 pages were O.K. But from page 103 on, I ended up writing what amounted to an entirely new book, and by this I mean, everything got shifted around, nothing in the story ended up in the same sequence as in the first draft, new characters were created, and characters who had been minor players blossomed into superstars. In fact, the daughter of they guy who had been the main character started asserting herself and ended up taking over the book.

What I learned from rewriting movies is to let it happen. It's a bit daunting at first to look at 600 pages of manuscript and realize that every page from 102 to 702 is going to change, but the best thing to do is just let it rip. I have found when you ask yourself the hard ques- tions the answers start coming, and when you let the answers take over, you are well on your way to making the novel everything it can be. When you start second-guessing yourself and try to protect what you have done too much, then you get in the way of your own creative energies and run the risk of defending the status quo at the cost of allowing something new and wonderful to be born.

There's one other thing I have learned writing movies, what I'd call the portability of scenes—in the case of novels, sometimes entire *chapters.* Just because you write chapter 15 after chapter 14 doesn't mean that it couldn't become chapter 12 when you're rewriting some- where down the line. In my rewrite of *Full Dress Gray* my editor spied a fault of logic in the story. Something that was explained in one way by the main characters about halfway through the book was again explained by a doctor one chapter later. So I exchanged the chapters, had the doctor make the discovery and explain the medical reasons for the event. In the next chapter, by changing about three sentences, I had the main characters reacting to this news and putting their own spin on it.

Of course in a movie, scenes can be much more discrete, self-contained, but there is a tendency in telling a story in the prose of a novel to believe that once your tale has been written, the sequence shouldn't be terribly disturbed in revision.

Balderdash. Rewrite the thing. Give it an entirely different order if for no other reason than just to see if you can do it. But better still, ask the difficult questions...what *works* and what *doesn't* work, and having learned the answers, go ahead and tell the tale another way.

❑ 7

CONFESSIONS OF A
LAZY RESEARCHER

BY NANCY SPRINGER

I LOATHE RESEARCH. ALL THROUGH SCHOOL I KNEW I COULD NEVER be a writer, because writers are supposed to love research, and I detest it. I *hate* digging for picky little facts! I want to tell stories; I don't want to worry about the *details!* My aversion to research paralyzed me so badly that I didn't start writing novels until I had a brain spasm in which I thought that I wouldn't have to worry about research if I wrote fantasy. (Wrong!) Since then I have published realistic novels for children and young adults, horror, mainstream, mystery, some nonfiction. Of necessity, I've learned to handle research. Want to know how? The lazy way, that's how.

The Internet, you're thinking? Nope. I surf not, nor have I yet set foot on the Information Super-Highway. I spend quite enough of my time hunched in front of a computer screen. Anyway, all the techno-hoopla annoys me. I'm contrary by nature; this trait has served me well as a fiction writer.

So, you're thinking, she spends of lot of time in the library. Not me. The air always seems gray in a library. And the book I need is always out, or the copy is missing, or it's at another library, and anyway, you can't keep the books long enough. Once every month or two I might venture into the library for something.

So how do I research? In a sense, my whole life is research: to try to pay attention, to be observant. The kinds of information you need for fiction writing you can't find in reference books—smells, textures, color nuances, slang, dialect, jokes, bumper stickers, tattoos, the taste of fast food. . . . Most of what you need to know, you learn best in your everyday life. I keep notebooks to help me remember what I have learned. Nothing's a total waste, not even visiting Aunt Marge; you might use her flamingo lamps in a book sometime. Moreover, being a writer gives you a great excuse to do fun things: horseback camping, scuba diving in a quarry, painting your body blue—whatever. Being a writer gives you all the more reason to have a life.

To supplement real life as research, I read nonfiction for pleasure. The more I write fiction, the more I hunger for intriguing, quirky non-fiction, and my taste in pleasure reading has become so esoteric it's almost pathological. I browse and prowl, I haunt book sales and yard sales and used bookstores. (I can never find the kind of book I want in a chain bookstore.) When everybody is saying, "I just want to read *Women Who Run With the Wolves*," I won't go near it. Instead, I read a book called *Frogs: Their Wonderful Wisdom, Follies and Foibles, Mysterious Powers, Strange Encounters, Private Lives, Symbolism & Meaning,* by Gerald Donaldson, and two books with frog themes eventually result.

At the time I read my finds, I have no idea how I will use them, if ever. It doesn't matter. I am reading for fun. Other favorite finds: *The Encyclopedia of Bad Taste,* by Jane and Michael Stern; *Big Hair: A Journey into the Transformation of Self,* by Grant McCracken; and *The Book of Weird* (formerly *The Glass Harmonica*), by Barbara Ninde Byfield.

Other than this sort of goofing off, I do no research at all before I start to write a book. None.

I have my reasons for doing as little research as possible. One is financial. Time is money; I need to earn a living; I want to spend my work time writing, not researching. But the main reason I don't research before writing is simply that ideas don't stay fresh forever. When I get a book idea, I want to run with it, not diddle around gathering a lot of facts I might not even read.

When I'm ready with the idea for my next book, I sit down and write. As I write, I come up against research questions, of course. A lot of them I can finesse; over the years I've discovered that "facts" are not nearly as solid as I used to think—such as what kids wear, for instance, if I'm writing a YA. Ask ten different kids, and you'll get ten different answers, so I just ask one kid, my own, and let it go at that.

I take care of a lot of my research by yelling downstairs—my husband will tell me what model car the prospering pediatrician ought to drive this year. Other times, I might have to grab a book—over the years I have acquired a motley assortment of dictionaries and encyclopedias—or I might need to call that wonderful person, the reference librarian. Sometimes, though seldom, I have to write myself a note to verify something when I get time. Only very occasionally do I actually have to stop writing until I clear something up. Even then, the stoppage is usually only for a day, as compared to the three to six months a lot of writers spend on research before writing. In my not-so-humble opinion, there's a lot to be said for writing the book first, thereby finding out what you *really* need to find out. As a kind of fringe benefit, this method forces me to abide by that classic fiction-writing rule: Write What You Know.

After I finish the first draft, it usually takes me no more than a few days to get answers to any questions that might have come up, usually by means of that time-honored ploy of the lazy researcher: I ask somebody who is likely to know. For instance, with a question about guns, I call my brother, the ex-cop and quondam gunsmith. Chatting with him for ten minutes or so is a lot more pleasant and less time-consuming than reading a bunch of gun books. For a question about secondary sexual characteristics of turtles, I call a friend who's a naturalist. For medical questions, my sister-in-law the physician, et cetera . . . . The only drawback to this method is that sometimes it's hard to get the information you really need. Normal people don't think like writers, so even when you're asking a specific question—what color are toad guts?—they manage to give you a vague answer. For this reason, I often call fellow writers with research questions in their areas of expertise, and I find them much better than my sister-in-law at giving me the information I need.

Doing my research this way, I haven't spent an extra moment peering into a bilious computer screen. Instead, I have had an interesting conversation with a real human being.

That's how I handle my research, and I love it. I've published thirty books doing research this way. You might argue that I could write bigger books and make more money if I did more research, and you might be right. But I'm contrary: I'd rather write my books my way, and besides, I'd rather have a life.

❏ 8

THE STATUE IN THE SLAB

BY EDITH PEARLMAN

I AM NOT ONE OF THOSE LUCKY WRITERS INTO WHOSE EARS A THRILL-ing tale is confided on a train, in front of whose eyes an anguished romance is enacted at a seaside hotel. My fictions begin as fragments, more irritating than inspiring. For instance: I find myself thinking of elderly Manhattan widows in apartments, resentfully growing frail. Or: In a dream a lost child and her mysteriously damaged younger sister, reunited, exchange a few surreal words. Also: I notice a patient waiting outside an X-ray office, shivering in his johnny. He is ignored by the surly attendant, who resembles a South American general.

No story yet—only pebbles in my shoe.

Standing at a distance from my desk, I glower. Then the ghost of Michelangelo taps me on the shoulder. Michelangelo claimed that he didn't create his statues but rather, released them. Find a slab of marble, he told younger artists; then take away everything that *isn't* the statue.

I need a slab of marble. And I can't order it from Carrara. I have to build it, myself, around one of those damned pebbles.

This slab, which will later be ruthlessly hacked at, must be first made pretty big. It must contain a believable city or village—I've set my tales all over the world. It must contain buildings with doors, roofs, back stairs—my stories have played themselves out in a tobacco shop, a soup kitchen, a museum, a pharmacy; in houses and lonely flats. The slab must hold history, and perhaps a vision of the future. Inside the slab lurk characters and their children and their handkerchiefs and their Uzis.

So I read. I read about the streets my characters walk in and the wars they endure; about the work they do; about the diseases hiding in their bodies; about the pills they crave and the drink they can't leave alone.

And I play. For the sake of one story, I lost innumerable games of chess. For the sake of another, I spent a week using my left hand only.

And I write. Sentences, paragraphs, pages; reminders on three-by-five cards; a string of adjectives on the back of a charge receipt. I arrange and rearrange my characters' biographies, and also their rooms. I imagine their fantasies and I dream their dreams. I turn them toward each other and then transcribe their stunned declarations of love, their helpless lies. I design their wardrobes, and I equip them with hobbies (more reading!) and enemies and possessions. This material will continue to pile up. Not a comma will be discarded until the story is finished, revised, ripped into pieces, begun again, finished again, revised again, submitted again *and* again, finally published. My manual typewriter does not know how to delete. My wastebasket holds pussy willows, not crumpled papers. My folders stretch and eventually split open; still, the dossier expands. Nothing leaves this room! That diamond pin which in an early draft seems too flashy for the heroine may, in the final draft, illuminate the entire story. That excessive metaphor, mercilessly pared, may become not only apt but irreplaceable.

What a mound of pages! At last it resembles a slab of marble. I walk around it, riffle silently through it—and, when I'm lucky, my tale's contour and its hinted truth reveal themselves in the depths of the slab. An elderly widow, visited wearily by her children one by one, will decide to leave her home: Independence can be cruelty. The lost child, before she finds her way back to her family, will foresee that her future is inseparable from her afflicted sister's: in chance begins responsibility. The X-ray technician, rattling on to a stranger about his bedeviled country, will learn from his own words and his own omissions the nature of loyalty: flexible as a snake.

The story cannot be as dense as the slab of details I've constructed. No reader wants to know the name of the coffee shop the widow visits daily; or the etiology of the condition of the younger sister; or the succession of rulers in the country the X-ray technician has fled. These chunks of information would only encumber a short story.

But *I* know the chunks of information. I designed the coffee shop and installed its tolerant proprietor; my widow loves what she must leave. I read a shelf of books about the younger sister's affliction; her sweet face is properly vacant, her gestures properly vague. I invented the corrupt regimes that the X-ray technician refers to only by their soubriquets—The Coffee Revolution, The Month of the Colonels.

Now I chip away at whatever is not necessary, and polish and repolish what's left—leaving, I hope, characters who are affecting and a situation that is tense and a resolution that is satisfying.

What a mess, this way of writing. It is lengthy and indirect; it ignores the notion that art is a free expression of self; it slams the door on autobiography; it leaves shards all over the floor.

On the other hand, efficiency is a third-rate virtue. Self-expression is often self-indulgence, best kept in firm check. Autobiography knows all too well how to creep in through the keyhole. And those shards—sometimes they lodge like pebbles in my shoe, and become the centers of new slabs to be doggedly built up and then doggedly reduced, until all that is left is the story.

❑ 9

SERENDIPITY AND THE WRITER

BY C. J. NEWTON

> serendipity, *n*. [coined by Horace Walpole (c. 1754) after his tale *The Three Princes of Serendip* (i.e. Ceylon), who made such discoveries.] an apparent aptitude for making fortunate discoveries accidentally.
> —*Webster's Dictionary of the English Language, Unabridged*

RECENTLY WHEN DISCUSSING MY WRITING WITH A FRIEND I sketched out my plans to finish one novel and start another, and gave specific dates for each stage. My friend was rather surprised at this "conscious control" of creativity. After we spoke, I realized that a writer must combine rational structure and method—for example, writing at a certain hour every day, or committing to write so many words per week—with the unplanned, magical side of writing that so often surprises us. We need to be open to serendipity.

The unsummoned inspirational component of writing is a subject for research by psychologists, a source of wonder for those who see it happen, and a mystery frequently to writers ourselves. I am not recommending that you dissect every creative experience. However, it can be useful to look at the circumstances that led to your inspiration, to the particular time and place at which the sudden torrent of associations, images, and dialogues opened like a cloudburst. You may find the influence of serendipity.

In my own case serendipity prompted me to visit a town, which inspired a novel, which led to another novel, which led to my first fiction sale.

For years while living in San Francisco I "intended" to visit Half Moon Bay, about 30 miles south. After eight years of intending, I drove there one evening on a twisting road through groves of eucalyptus trees. Through a clearing, I beheld the Pacific Ocean, and a rich small town. In a flash I *felt* a mystery novel—characters, settings, and plot outline—set there. I still can't explain it.

Here is the serendipitous part. Half Moon Bay has a Portuguese community that sponsors a picturesque annual parade. As I subsequently researched the town for my mystery, I became interested in Portugal's history.

And later, when I wanted to write a novel satirizing attorneys, I was able to apply my knowledge of Portuguese names, references, and culture in a convincing depiction of a fictional republic founded by Portugal in Central America. The result was *Costa Azul,* which I wrote after the mystery (but which found a publisher first). Half Moon Bay was a "fortunate discovery" indeed.

Travel

If you can afford it, travel to faraway places is very stimulating. Hearing French spoken on the busy streets of Montreal, seeing otherwise-modern people in Montevideo enjoying *maté* tea made from traditional gourds, hiking cobblestoned streets in Lisbon, passing café patrons who may be lovers, spies, or solid civil servants—all these can add fuel to your creative fire.

Adventure can be as close as your neighboring town. Like most teenagers I yearned to escape from my hometown for more exciting places. Yet I wasn't far from New Windsor, New York, the site of George Washington's last winter as Continental commander. Less famous than Valley Forge, the New Windsor Cantonment offered high drama as Washington battled his final enemies, and intrigue and boredom, as he waited to sign the Treaty of Paris that ended the war. I felt that this would be a perfect setting for a historical novel.

Take a new look at your neighboring towns. You may find rich material for historical or contemporary fiction.

Getting there

Tour Books from the American Automobile Association are great resources. Free to members, they include richly informative descriptions of overlooked gems like local museums and historical houses, complete with opening hours and admission prices.

Use public transportation. Once you accept the waiting as constructive idleness—a gift of time when you are free to let your mind wander or compose—you may actually enjoy the journey as much as the destination. It is pleasurable to leave the driving to the bus or train driver, and to look out the window. If public transportation is not practical, then drive to a reasonable point and walk the rest of the way. You'll gain many impressions exploring the site on foot. Always bring a notebook to record them.

Feeding your creativity

Here is an outline for using an excursion to feed your creativity:

1. Carefully observe the physical look of the place: the grade of descent to a beach, or, in an urban setting, the names of streets and the architecture.

2. As an exercise, narrate your own movements. Try a first-person point of view, then switch to third person to describe your actions from the outside.

3. Observe people buying, selling, fishing, talking on cell phones, cutting hair, or unloading trucks. File them as background to your fictional construction.

4. Sketch a fictional character and motive for his or her being there, and walk the character through a few scenes.

5. Collect brochures and newspapers. Visit local bookstores, libraries, and museums.

6. If possible, travel home by a different route from the one you took to get there.

By varying your routine journeys, you can stimulate that part of your mind where inspiration visits. All roads can lead to serendipity.

❑ 10

THE JOURNEY INWARD

BY KATHERINE PATERSON

"DO YOU KEEP A JOURNAL?" NO, I ANSWER A BIT RED-FACED, BECAUSE I know that *real* writers keep voluminous journals so fascinating that the world can hardly wait until they die to read the published versions. But it's not quite true. I do make journal-like entries in used schoolgirl spiral notebooks, on odd scraps of paper, in fairly anonymous computer files. These notations are all so embarrassing that I am hoping for at least a week's notice to hunt them down and destroy all the bits and pieces before my demise.

I write these entries, you see, only when I can't write what I want to write. If they were collected and published, the reader could logically conclude that I was not only totally inept as a writer but that I lacked integration of personality at best, and at worst, was dangerously depressed.

If I had kept a proper journal, these neurotic passages would be seen in context, but such is not the case. If my writing is going well, why would I waste time talking about it? I'd be doing it. So if these notes survive me, they will give whatever segment of posterity might happen upon them a very skewed view of my mental state.

The reason I am nattering on about this is that I have come to realize that I am not alone. As soon as my books (after years of struggle) began to be published, I started to get questions from people that I had trouble answering in any helpful way: "Do you use a pen and pad or do you write on a typewriter?" (Nowadays, "computer" is always included in this question, but I'm talking about twenty years ago.)

"Whatever works," I'd say. Which was true. Sometimes I wrote first drafts by hand, sometimes on the typewriter; often I'd switch back and forth in an attempt to keep the flow going. The questioner would thank me politely, but, looking back, I know now that I had failed her.

"Do you have a regular schedule everyday or do you just write when you feel inspired?" the person would ask earnestly. I am ashamed to say, I would often laugh at this. "If I wrote only when I was inspired," I'd say, "I'd write about three days a year. Books don't get written in three days a year."

Occasionally, the question (and now, I know, all these were the same question) would be framed more baldly. "How do you begin?" "Well," I would say, "you sit down in front of the typewriter, roll in a sheet of paper and . . ."

If I ever gave any of you one of those answers, or if any other writer has ever given you similar tripe, I would like to apologize publicly. I was asked, in whatever disguise, a truly important question, and I finessed the answer into a one-liner.

How *do* you begin? It is not an idle or trick question. It is a cry from the heart.

I know. That's what all those aborted journal notes are about. They are the cry when I simply cannot begin. When no inspiration ever comes, when neither pen, nor pencil, nor typewriter, nor state-of-the-art computer can unloose what's raging about inside me.

So what happens? Well, something must. I've begun and ended over and over again through the years. There are several novels out there with my name on the cover. Somehow I figured out how to begin. Once the book is finished, the memory of the effort dims—until you're trying to begin the next one.

Well, I'm there now. I have to begin again. What have I done those other times? How have I gotten from that feeling of stony hopelessness? How do I break through that barrier as hard as sunbaked earth to the springs of creativity?

Sometimes, I know, I have a conversation with myself on paper:

What's the matter?

What do you mean "what's the matter?" You know perfectly well. I want to write, but I can't think of a thing to say.

Not a single thing?

Not a single thing worth saying.

You're scared what you might say won't be up to snuff? Scared people might laugh at you? Scared you might despise yourself?

Well, it is scary. How do I know there's still anything in here?

You don't. You just have to let it flow. If you start judging, you'll cut off the flow—you've already cut off the flow from all appearances—before it starts.

Grump.

Ah yes, we never learn, do we? Whatever happened to that wonderful idea of getting up so early in the morning that the critic in you was still asleep?

How do I know it will work this time?

You won't know if you don't try. But then, trying is risky, and you do seem a bit timid to me.

You don't know what it's like pouring out your guts to the world.

I don't?

Well, you don't care as much as I do.

Of course I do. I just happen to know that it is so important to my psychic health to do this that I'm willing to take the risk. You, my friend, seem to want all the creative juices inside you to curdle and poison the whole system.

You're nothing but a two-bit psychologist.

Well, I've been right before.

But how do I begin?

I don't know. Why don't we just get up at five tomorrow, come to the machine and type like fury for an hour and see what happens? Could be fun. Critic won't be up, and we won't ever have to show anybody what we've done.

Now you understand why I have to burn this stuff before I die. My posthumous reputation as a sane person of more than moderate intelligence hangs in the balance. But living writers, in order to keep writing, have to forget about posthumous reputations. We have to become, quite literally, like little children. We have to remember our early griefs and embarrassments. Talk aloud to ourselves. Make up imaginary companions. We have to play.

Have you ever watched children fooling with play dough or fingerpaint? They mess around to see what will emerge, and they fiddle with what comes out. Occasionally, you will see a sad child, one that has decided beforehand what he wants to do. He stamps his foot because the picture on the page or the green blob on the table falls short of the vision in his head. But he is, thankfully, a rarity, already too concerned with adult approval.

The unspoiled child allows herself to be surprised with what comes out of herself. She takes joy in the material, patting it and rolling it and shaping it. She is not too quick to name it. And, unless some grownup interferes, she is not a judge but a lover of whatever comes from her heart through her hands. This child knows that what she has created is marvelous simply because she has made it. No one else could make this wonderful thing because it has come out of her.

What treasures we have inside ourselves—not just joy and delight but also pain and darkness. Only I can share the treasures of the human spirit that are within me. No one else has *these* thoughts, *these* feelings, *these* relationships, *these* experiences, *these* truths.

How do I begin? You could start, as I often do, by talking to yourself. The dialogue may help you understand what is holding you back. Are you afraid that deep down inside you are really shallow? That when you take that dark voyage deep within yourself, you will find there is no treasure to share? Trust me. There is. Don't let your fear stop you. Begin early in the morning before that critical adult within wakes up. Like a child, pour out what is inside you, not listening to anything but the stream of life within you. Read Dorothea Brande's classic *On Becoming a Writer,* in which she suggests that you put off for several days reading what you have written in the wee hours. Then when you do read it you may discern a repeated theme pointing you to what you want to begin writing about.

Begin, Anne Lamott suggests in her wonderful book *Bird by Bird,* in the form of a letter. Tell your child or a trusted friend stories from your past. Exploring childhood is almost always an effective wedge into what's inside you. And didn't you mean to share those stories with your children someday anyhow?

While I was in the midst of revising this article, my husband happened to bring home Julia Cameron's book, *The Artist's Way.* Cameron suggests three pages of longhand every morning as soon as you get up. I decided to give the "morning pages" a try and heartily recommend the practice, though these pages, too, will need to be destroyed before I die.

When I was trying to begin the book which finally became *Flip-Flop Girl* (and you should see the anguished notes along the way!), I just began writing down the name of every child I could remember from the fourth grade at Calvin H. Wiley School. Sometimes I appended a note that explained why that child's name was still in my head. Early-

morning exercises explored ways the story might go, and I rejected
most of them, but out of those fourth-grade names and painful be-
trayals a story began to grow. Judging from the notes, it was over a
year in developing and many more months in the actual writing. But
I did begin, and I did finish. There's a bit of courage for the next
journey inward.

Now it's your turn. Bon voyage.

❑ 11

An Idea Is Only the Bait

By Madonna Dries Christensen

Where do writers get their ideas? The short answer is: Ideas are everywhere and anywhere. William Styron says he dreamed about a woman with a number tattooed on her arm. He put aside the book he was having trouble writing and wrote *Sophie's Choice.*

Wherever ideas come from, they are only the bait. Because writers are curious and have an innate sense of imagination, they grab bait and let it lead them to plot, characters, point of view, and dialogue. The bait may end up as the title for a story, the beginning, middle, or end.

Writers have a keen awareness of their immediate surroundings and of those they remember. The people you observe become the ingredients for composite characters. No matter what else you are doing, you can be gleaning bits and pieces from what you see, hear, touch, taste, and smell.

The earthy smell of apples at the produce stand inspired my first published piece, "Simply Delicious." The fragrance of four o'clocks wafting from my husband's garden took me back to childhood, to my mother's window box. Out of that evoked memory came "Collected Scents," published in the anthology *Poems from Farmers Valley.*

Remembering the cloying smell and horrible taste of cod liver oil, I wrote, "It's Good for You," a humor piece on this "cure-all" of the 1940s. After hearing Bob Dylan mumble a song and unable to understand even one word, I wrote "With a Song in My Heart," a look at the generation gap in music.

Entering an old library in my hometown in Iowa, I was embraced by a distinctive essence so familiar that, had I been led blindfolded into the building, I would have known I was in my childhood library. A compatible blend of old books, book binding paste, newspaper ink, furniture oil, floor wax, and the dry, dusty odor steam radiators emit gave the library this inviting aromatic charm. I published "Guardian of the Books" as a reminiscence about the small-town library and its librarian. I expanded on the idea with a piece about my hometown, "I Still Call it Home," for the anthology *Where the Heart Is: A Celebration of Home.*

On a visit to my ancestral farm in Wisconsin, I stood alone in the doorway of the cavernous dilapidated barn, wrapped in the silence of the countryside. From nearby, the present owner's pronounced European accent helped me conjure up the presence of my German paternal great-grandfather and his family. These benevolent ghosts led me through a typical day at the farm as it had been one hundred years earlier. The energy from that imagined excursion and those spectral images led me to write "Sojourner in the Past" for *The Wind-Mill,* a genalogy magazine.

Family histories hold a treasure trove of stories. In 1951, my mother, who worked in a café, cooked supper for Henry Fonda and the stage cast of *Mr. Roberts,* who were stranded in town during a snowstorm. I published that story, "The Prince Dined at the Palace," as nonfiction and in a fictionalized version.

"The Last Dance" came from my family history. Published first in *Catholic Digest,* it tells of four sisters and their widowed mother, all of whom became nuns on the same day. The sisters were members of an all-girl band that was so popular in the 1930s, it was featured in *Billboard* and *Variety.*

With only scant information from two obituaries, I fictionalized a family event into a twice-published story, "Prairie Fire." It links my maternal great-grandfather's death in 1909 with that of his young daughter's death seventeen years earlier. Both were struck and killed by lightning.

Conversations with friends or strangers have yielded many ideas. Remarks about my given name, now so recognizable, provided anecdotes for "The Fame of the Name." A writer's comment about writers not being paid for their work prompted me to write "A Penny for Your Prose," about the pros and cons of paying and nonpaying markets. A remark by a man in my writer's group and an aside by another writer gave me an idea for a humor piece. One writer told me about her adoption in 1917 after being sent to Minnesota on the Orphan Train. I fictionalized her experience in "The End Game," for the literary journal *Thema.*

It's a cliché, but true; writers write what they know. They can't avoid it. Human beings are who they are because of what they know, what they've experienced thus far. Writers tap into what they know, explore it, and try to explain it to themselves and others through writing.

Much of my work is based in the Midwest. Born and raised there, I know the people, the climate, the flora and fauna. The Midwest gives me my sense of place. Some of my fiction is written in the voice of children of the Depression years. I know those times; I know the children and their parents.

What writers don't know, they can learn. When I read Barbara Anton's novel *Egrets to the Flames,* I was impressed with her knowledge of the Florida sugar cane industry. I asked if she'd grown up on a sugar cane plantation. She said no, she'd researched the subject.

You can find ideas in writers magazines about contests and anthologies that solicit material on specific subjects. Even if you don't submit to these publications, you can use the idea. Ideas cannot be copyrighted. The journal *Thema* sets the theme for each issue. I would not have written any of the ten stories I've had published in *Thema* without a head start, the given idea.

Familiarize yourself with local and regional periodicals and the type of material they use. Some newspapers have a regular column featuring local writers; others solicit material on specific subjects, holidays, or anniversaries of local events. Every community has stories waiting to be told; you need only scan the paper for items about anniversaries of historical events and interesting places or people.

Writers are insatiable readers. Reading generates ideas, ideas generate writing. A word, a phrase, a picture can stoke the fires of your imagination. A haunting picture of a little immigrant girl at Ellis Island, combined with a *Thema* premise, led me to write and publish *In Mama's Footsteps.*

My first writing instructor advised, "Save articles and stories by writers whose work you admire or whose subject interests you. The clippings will provide ideas for stories of your own." She was right. Sifting through my collection triggers enough ideas to take me to the year 2000. Come to think of it, why stop there? The possibilities are endless for stories about that coming event.

❑ 12

THE CREATIVE POWER OF DOING NOTHING

BY COLLEEN MARIAH RAE

LET'S SAY YOU'VE BEEN WORKING ON A STORY. IT'S COMING, BUT IT'S not coming fast enough. What will speed things up? Surprisingly: *Doing nothing*. Now's the time to turn to your unconscious and to let it do the work for you.

This is often the hardest part of the writing process but an essential part of the creative process. For a week, allow the unconscious to do its work. And, paradoxically, without any conscious effort on your part, your creative product will grow.

The trick is to do nothing long enough for the work to come to fruition in your unconscious. But because this is hard, what follow are some tips for *what to do when you're doing nothing;* and *how to do nothing so effectively that your story will pop from you full-blown.*

So, for the first tip: *What to do when you're doing nothing*.

It's always important to know where you're going, if you have any hope of reaching your goal. Here, the goal's a finished story that pops like Athena from the head of Zeus, and the only way to achieve this is through doing things that unclutter the unconscious sufficiently to allow it to devote full-time to the job.

This is the time to cook, build a model, swim, play chess, hike, paint, play music, or repair a toaster—whatever it is that puts you into that "time out of time state," where you lose all track of time. What you're looking for are activities that allow you to *immerse* yourself in an experience without thought. Whatever takes you away from the ceaseless round of chatter unclutters the unconscious. What works for you? Include it in your day, every day, because each day takes you through the same cycle of creativity in an abbreviated way.

For me, painting is the best "immersion" activity. I can so lose myself in the process that when I stop, I discover surprisingly that hours have passed. While I'm painting, I'm not thinking. But I'm not floating in a sea of no-thought: I'm doing what Aldous Huxley thought so important he had birds in his fictional country in *Island* crying "Attention, attention, attention." I am focused in on what I'm doing with a highly concentrated attention.

So that's what to do when you're doing nothing: anything that allows you to immerse yourself fully in the activity and at the same time challenges you enough, but not too much. Do anything, that is, but write. During this stage of the process, do anything but write—even one word. And, don't tell your story to anyone. Telling it will dissipate the energy. Keeping your story inside creates a pressure-cooker sensation—eventually you will feel as though you're going to explode if you can't let your story out. And that's the sensation you're aiming for.

Now for the second tip: *How to do nothing so effectively that your story will pop from you full-blown.* This is often the most fun, because it isn't so "hands-off" as immersion. You can really feel you're doing something to work with your unconscious—even though you *are* letting go and trusting the unconscious to do the work for you. I call this *active incubation,* because you're building bridges between the conscious and the unconscious mind.

One of these bridges you probably know well: How often have you said, "Let me sleep on it"? It's one of the best problem-solving tools we have. And it works for writing so well that I've come to believe that I couldn't write a darn thing worth publishing if I couldn't sleep on it. I'll go to sleep unclear of how to proceed in a story and wake in the morning with the answer.

You can also build bridges during your waking hours. Either way, it's still the same process: You have to silence your analytical mind long enough to let the unconscious speak. You have probably had a few such experiences: Names you couldn't remember an hour before come to you as soon as you get into the mind-numbing rhythm of vacuuming, or as you're washing the car, you recall what it is you forgot to buy at the store.

I make use of active incubation every day I write. I don't take a shower until I get stuck in my writing stint for the day, because invariably it's in the shower that ideas pop up. My writing journals are filled with "shower thought" notations.

Other things that shift me from that "stuck" analytical place also include water: I love to sit by a waterfall or any running water—even the fountains in shopping malls will do. Find your own. Some writers get unstuck sitting by a fire; some with candlelight; some while they meditate. Others can't write if they aren't driving. One of my students puts Grieg on the car stereo and drives across the desert, preferably during lightning storms. Any activity that stops analytical thought lets inspiration surface. And just a suggestion: Always keep a small notebook with you, so you won't forget your breakthroughs—write them down!

But there's more to active incubation than just getting out of your own way. This is the time to work actively with your unconscious. One way to do that is through what I call a "nightly recap." Lie in bed in the dark and try to visualize your story as clearly as possible; let all the details come alive for you. Summon the smells, tastes, textures, emotions, sounds. Make them as vivid as you can. You may find yourself in a state similar to Robert Louis Stevenson's, who was thrashing about in his bed one night, greatly alarming his wife. She woke him up, infuriating Stevenson, who yelled, "I was dreaming a fine bogey tale!" The nightmare from which he had been unwillingly awakened was the premise for *Dr. Jekyll and Mr. Hyde*.

When you wake in the morning after such a night, don't get out of bed. Stay there, moving only to pick up your already open notebook and uncapped pen. Write without thinking—anything about your story that comes to mind. Write for at least five minutes before you get up. Then close your notebook without reading what you've written. You'll read it later—when this period of doing nothing comes to an end. To read it too soon flips you into analytical thought.

"Silent movies" is another technique that helps build the pressure. Set a timer for ten minutes, and then sit without thinking until the timer rings. If thoughts do come, just let them move through your mind; don't hold onto them. Stay still. For the next ten minutes, see your story as a movie in your mind. Make it as vivid as you can; flesh out the details. Go back and forth, back and forth. Stop the projector, reverse the film, run it forward again. See it more and more clearly each time it reels by. Watch, but do not let yourself write—no matter how strong the urge.

Finally, for the last ten minutes, sit quietly without consciously thinking, until your urge to write is so strong that you just can't resist it. Then, and only then, pick up your pen and write.

Make these silent movies as often as you can during the days of this period of doing nothing. If you can't spend a full 30 minutes on it, cut back to five-minute segments. Remember: Don't read anything you write.

There's another aspect to this part of the creative process that's often given short shrift: solitude. Give yourself time alone each day, even if it's only to take a walk. A quiet walk alone can help your writing more than you'll ever know.

What if you do all this, and no story seems ready to pop into your head? In his autobiography, *Education of a Wandering Man,* Louis L'Amour said,

> There are so many wonderful stories to be written, and so much material to be used. When I hear people talking of writer's block, I am amazed. Start writing, no matter about what. The water does not flow until the faucet is turned on. You can sit and look at a page for a long time and nothing will happen. Start writing, and it will.

That's every writer's secret: not waiting for the muse. Give yourself a week at most to do nothing, then sit down to write.

Set yourself a schedule, and give yourself a goal. When I was writing fiction full-time, my writing hours were 7:00 a.m. till noon. My goal was to write five pages per day. Sometimes I finished the five pages *before* noon, and then I was free to stop. Sometimes I finished the five pages by noon, but even if I hadn't, I still stopped. It's a goal, not a stick.

When your writing is coming easily, it feels too good to stop. I rarely would stop if I had finished my five pages before noon, for instance. But I always remembered advice that came from a *Paris Review* interview with Ernest Hemingway. Although he wrote only in the morning, he said he would make a point of stopping before he'd written everything that was in him that day to write. It's great advice. If you know what's going to happen in the next scene, it'll prime your pump the following day.

Become aware of your own pattern. You may work best doing 16-hour-a-day stints for three weeks straight. Or you may find you can write only one hour a day without exhausting yourself. So schedule an hour and set a goal of a page a day. Even if you write only five pages a week, you'll still have produced 260 pages in one year. That's a whole book! The important thing is to find your own pattern—and then make it a habit. Good habits are just as hard to break as bad ones.

Rollo May's message in *The Courage to Create* is that for the creative person, fear never goes away. How can it? When we're working with the unconscious, as we must do in writing fiction, we walk up to the abyss every day and jump in. A very scary process! Allow yourself time to sharpen pencils or stare out the window for ten minutes or so before you start. After that, stay in your chair until your allotted hours are up, whether you've written anything or not. You'll find that the sheer boredom of doing nothing is often a catalyst to a remarkable gush of words.

□ 13

A Writer's Immortality

By Elissa Ely

I FOUND THE RECIPE BOOK IN A CABIN ON AN ISLAND OFF THE COAST of northern Maine. It was sandwiched between a pamphlet on edible plants and a bottle of insect repellent that could have told a few tales. I thought it was a handful of papers folded in half and forgotten. But it was a book. When I opened it, I heard the ring of a typewriter carriage at the end of the first yellow line.

The book was published in 1956 by the few dozen islanders who lived there year-round. The front page explained that profits were donated to the local library, which had been built 30 years earlier in memory of two children who had drowned off some cove rocks. The second page was a list of island contributors; those salty cooks themselves. There were asterisks by the names of those who had died before the book went to print.

Without further preface, the recipes begin on the third page. Each is signed. No space is wasted. The longest section ("Fish") is a stiff required course. Instructions for chowder are given without any pronouns; boiling a halibut is all business; fried mussels are dispensed with in two sentences ("Remove from shells. Fry."). A single name ends many of the recipes; some reluctant lobsterman, I presumed, egged into telegraphic authorship by his wife, the chairman of the library committee.

About halfway through Fish, the lobsterman suddenly pulls off his rubber boots. It's like when other men pull off their ties. Without explanation, he begins to loosen up. He adds prefaces and postscripts. Commentaries come thick and fast. At first they are understated and reasonable. Introducing Paella, he writes that the efforts required are "Good for when the fog comes in and stays a while." After an unappetizing recipe for Cod Tongues and Bisquik, he adds, "Not recommended by Wife." Of a tomato-based soup: "No New Englander would

43

be caught eating this as a chowder." Then he starts to go wild. It is a little startling. His recipe for fish with walnuts is exuberant: one cup of nut meats must be broken with a hammer "so you can take good aim." On testing the doneness of a fish fillet, "take 'em out when the middle looks proud of itself." And finally, having warmed completely toward me, his unknown (and possibly his only) future reader, he offers this advice: "For those who find mackerel too rich in fats: Fry the fish in butter and forget your past aversions."

Forty years after he typed and signed the recipes, and quite possibly after he was no longer alive, I was shocked by his sudden expansiveness. It seemed so unlike the him I had read and accepted at the beginning. It was as if, by the end of Fish, he had gone naked, caught up in the delirium of happy self-exposure. I couldn't imagine what had caused it.

The question baffled me during island walks. Evenings on the porch, I reread the recipes. I thought of stealing the book and bringing it back to Boston for further scrutiny, even though that would have done nothing for the island library fund. But finally, late one night, the light went on.

It was those asterisks on Page 2, the contributor's page, beside the names of the dead. An asterisk was not easy to make on a manual typewriter 40 years ago. It required lifting the typewriter bar, pulling the paper up slightly but evenly when hitting the star key, then lowering the paper to exactly where it was.

On Page 2, asterisks, laboriously made, honored those who did not live long enough to have the pleasure of being known in print.

This is the key: the pleasure of being known in print. Even in a place where the ferry comes three times a week and readers are severely limited, being known in print matters; it is the assurance of an existence beyond the constraints of time.

When written thoughts are read, they take on worth beyond their thinking. It is a moment of mattering, in a world where we all want to matter.

I believe this is what happens to my taciturn lobsterman as he writes the Fish section of a recipe book on a remote island. He realizes that he is not muttering to his solitary self on the high seas: What he writes will be read by someone else. He does not know who it is, but some stranger is going to associate him with his words. That stranger will form an opinion of him. And that opinion, though he will never know what it is, matters to him. He cares to make himself transparent for viewing. He cares to be known.

On the ferry home, I listened aimlessly to conversations around me. One eye was on the receding island; the other squinted stoically toward the mainland. Two women sat on the next bench. They had arrived separately, but in their last moments, with the ferry churning, they were coming to know each other. They would never meet again. They got down to the business of essentials.

"I'm a novelist," one said.

"Isn't that amazing?" cried the other. "I am, too."

❏ 14

Rhetorically Speaking

By LouAnne Johnson

I PEEKED IN THE WINDOW. THIRTY FRESHMAN HONOR STUDENTS SAT waiting, pens poised above their brand-new notebooks. They were ready. I wasn't sure I was, but I decided to go ahead and give my plan a shot. If they got it, fine. If they didn't, I'd think of something.

"Good morning, ladies and gentlemen!" I shouted as I marched across the floor and slammed my briefcase down on the instructor's desk. Silence. "As you know," I went on, "this is an honors level composition course. You are here because you have high grade-point averages, and your high school teachers think you are good writers. Perhaps you are. I intend to find out." One boy in the back of the room put his head down on his desk. I ignored him.

"My name is Miss Johnson. I've been a writer for the past thirty years. I am also a former officer of the United States Marine Corps. I'm not used to taking any crap, and I don't intend to take any from you. If you expect to get an A in this course, you're going to have to earn it. If you aren't ready to work, the door is open. Make your choice, and make it now."

I could tell from their expressions, and their glances toward the door, that every student in the class wanted to leave. But they were smart kids, smart enough to know that walking out of a required course on the first day of college would not be an intelligent move. They sat still. Without saying anything further, I made a quick turnabout and marched out of the room, letting the door slam behind me. Before they had a chance to recover, I swung the door open again and sashayed daintily back inside.

"Hi," I said, as I giggled and patted my hair. "My name is, like, LouAnne, and I'm, like, your instructor, and I want everything to be, like, really cool, so everybody can, like, express himself or herself without, like, being afraid of any put-downs or anything. Oka-a-ay?"

The boy who had put his head down on the desk during my drill sergeant routine sat up straight and glanced at the girl beside him. She raised her eyebrows and shrugged. A few small smiles showed me that some of the students were starting to catch on. But most of them sat, staring at me, clearly confused. I giggled again and ran out of the room.

The third time I opened the door, I walked in and smiled pleasantly. "Good morning. I am your instructor. My name is LouAnne Johnson, and I hope that we will accomplish two things in this class. Number one, we will meet the requirements for this course. Number two, you will actually learn something about writing."

I picked up a marker and drew two vertical lines, dividing the white board behind me into thirds. I labeled the sections #1, #2 and #3, then asked the class members to vote which of my three different introductions represented "the real Miss Johnson." I recorded their votes on the board. The boy in the back voted for #1, but the rest of the class voted for #3.

"Why did you pick the third one?" I asked. "Anybody? Just speak up."

"I could just tell," one young woman said.

"You seemed real," somebody added from the far corner. "Genuine."

"But why?" I insisted. "Can somebody try to explain it?"

There was such a long silence that I almost gave up. Then a young man in the front row adjusted his glasses and cleared his throat. "I believe there was some element in your voice that matched the expression on your face and the look in your eye. They all matched, so to speak. I didn't sense any incongruity."

"Thank you very much," I said, and I meant it. His explanation was even better than the one I had planned. "Just as you can sense that a person is pretending, acting insincerely, you can also sense dishonesty in writing. I'm sure you've all read pretentious prose that put you off because it tried to impress you. And it's quite likely that you've thrown down some article or essay you'd started to read that may have contained a brilliant idea, but was so poorly presented and illogically organized that it wasn't worth the effort it would have taken to read it." A few nods encouraged me to continue.

"When you write compositions for me, don't try to sound like a textbook, or your high school English teacher, or your favorite author. While I'd encourage you to use techniques and writing styles that you admire, I don't mean for you to try to copy them. Learn how to use them; make them your own. Write in your own voice. Each of you has a particular combination of vocabulary, tone of voice, facial expressions and gestures that creates a distinct, individual personality when you express your ideas during a conversation. But when you write, you can rely only on language—word choice, sentence style, punctuation—to communicate your personality."

It worked. They got it. Instead of deluging me with the standard five-paragraph essay, written entirely in passive voice, using the longest possible words, these students learned to use language either to show or hide their personalities, depending upon the assignment. To project a sense of objectivity in her research paper, for example, one young woman, Suzette, chose relatively formal language and complex sentence structure:

> College campuses can be misleading, with their tree-lined walkways, stately lecture halls, and dormitories. Statistics have repeatedly demonstrated that America's colleges and universities are not the safe havens many parents believe them to be.

Later, Suzette wrote a personal essay on the same topic, but the voice was completely different.

> My parents think I'm safe here at NMSU. They don't know about the date rapes and muggings. And I'm not going to tell them. They would just worry about me, because they don't realize how much the whole world has changed since they went to college.

In this essay, colloquial phrases, first-person voice, and simpler sentence structure gave a good sense of Suzette's personality and attitude: She's young and scared, but she's determined to be independent.

Although all of my students agreed that finding their own voices was necessary, some of them needed extra time and practice before they finally "got it right." One young man became frustrated when his peer critique group pronounced that he was almost, but not quite, there.

"How do they know whether it's my voice or not?" he challenged me.

"Other people can critique your writing for form and content," I said, "but no one else can know whether you have said what you wanted to say, whether the message the reader receives is the one you meant to send."

"How will I know when it's right?" he asked.

I was tempted to say, "How do you know when you're in love?" But I realized that my voice might not be the one this particular student needed to hear. So I quoted from journalist Marya Mannes's essay, "How Do You Know It's Good?" Mannes's answer? "When you begin to detect the difference between freedom and sloppiness, between serious experimentation and egotherapy, between skill and slickness, between strength and violence, you are on your way. . . ."

My student frowned for a moment, digesting this new idea, then smiled. "Why didn't you say that before?"

❑ 15

KEEP YOUR WRITING ON TRACK

BY GENIE DICKERSON

"WHAT IS THE USE OF WRITING WHEN YOU ARE ON THE WRONG road?" said English writer and naturalist John Ray. A wrong turn—a seeming shortcut—may detour us and prove fatal to our writing.

Detour 1: Writers clubs, classes, and conferences. *Rationalization:* I always get fired up about writing by these groups, and I pick up pointers. *Rebuttal:* A little fire goes a long way. If social activities cut into your writing time, you have been sidetracked and may find it wise to return to the main road. As for picking up pointers from other writers, only firsthand experience will teach you which pointers are valid.

Detour 2: A book as first project. *Rationalization:* The money and satisfaction are in books. *Rebuttal:* Except for big-selling books, magazine writing offers writers more money, more readers, more contact with editors, as well as greater opportunities for developing your writing skills. For an inexperienced writer, the trap in writing a book first is procrastination. Magazine and newspaper work require all facets to be completed in a timely manner. With a book, it's easy to put off less-fun tasks.

Detour 3: Looking for an agent. *Rationalization:* A writer needs an agent to sell writing. *Rebuttal:* The search may be unnecessary. Virtually all novices start selling their writing without agents. After writers have sold work on their own, they find that agents are more receptive to them.

Detour 4: The presumption that editors have time to read every word sent to them. *Rationalization:* My piece will sell on the basis of the beautiful last paragraph. *Rebuttal:* Editors and other readers are not inclined to drag themselves through slow material. Discounting the importance of a gripping lead is a dead end.

Detour 5: Co-authoring. *Rationalization:* I'm not sure enough of my ability to write something by myself. *Rebuttal:* Unless both authors are good workers and contribute complementary skills to the project, the partnership will produce nothing but false hopes.

Detour 6: Dependence on computer spelling and grammar checkers. *Rationalization:* I don't have time to waste on boring details—the computer can do it for me. *Rebuttal:* Spelling and grammar checkers miss a lot. Spelling and grammar are what make up English. Don't let computer aids replace what you need to know. Computers can flag typographical errors, but total dependence on spelling and grammar checkers is the wrong route.

Detour 7: Asking friends to read and comment on your unpublished writing. *Rationalization:* Even if my friends aren't experts, they can make comments like ordinary readers. *Rebuttal:* Unless your friends read your type of writing, they may not be the best judges of the salability of your manuscripts. Worse, they may flatter you or shoot you down, misleading you on the quality of your work.

Detour 8: Writer's block. *Rationalization:* I sit down at the computer but can't think of anything to write. *Rebuttal:* A sure barrier to Easy Street. Ignore the block, and jot down whatever you have done or talked about or thought up in the previous 24 hours. Publications buy essays about neighborhood walks, humorous pieces about incidents at the grocery store, and how-to articles about pulling weeds. Thoughts sell, just about any thoughts that are well presented. Once you begin to write, the creative change of pace will energize you to develop your thoughts.

Detour 9: Letterhead stationery, business cards, bumper stickers, and T-shirts that say "Writer." *Rationalization:* They define me as a serious professional. *Rebuttal:* Are you hornswoggling yourself? Are the stationery, business cards, bumper stickers, and what you wear more for convenience and fun?

Detour 10: Overemphasis on creativity. *Rationalization:* The more literary and creative your writing is, the less smooth, clear and logical it needs to be. *Rebuttal:* Writing is, above all, communication. If people have to exert themselves to understand a piece of writing, they won't read (or buy) it.

Detour 11: Treasure hunt. *Rationalization:* I refuse to write for small publications. Why should I do a piece for $25 when other writers get $2,500 from glossier magazines for the same amount of work? *Rebuttal:* Everyone starts at the beginning.

Detour 12: Lost in research. *Rationalization:* I love hunting for background facts. *Rebuttal:* Research can be a form of procrastination. Once you find the information you need, you can return to the drawing board, which is more fun anyway.

Detour 13: Computer roadblock. *Rationalization:* I have to get my new word processor up and running before I can write. *Rebuttal:* Dust off your typewriter, and use it. Or do rough drafts by hand. Conquer your computer after you get at least some writing done.

Detour 14: Avoid submitting manuscript. *Rationalizations:* a) Publishers won't pay me, a beginner, enough to cover my time. b) My work isn't good enough to submit yet. c) I don't need to see my byline in print in order to be a writer. d) Researching markets takes too much time. e) Contemporary literature isn't very good, so editors wouldn't recognize or appreciate my writing. f) I submitted a few things, but they were rejected. *Rebuttal:* Despite imperfections, the best way to improve your writing and develop into a professional is to submit your manuscripts frequently to editors. By saying yes or no, and often with specific helpful comments, editors are our best teachers. Inventors work much the same way as writers do, by trial and error, and experimentation with modifications. And who knows? You just might earn that $2,500 on your first manuscript submission.

Detour 15: Not including an SASE with submissions. *Rationalization:* Stamps are expensive, and editors ought to pay for half of the cost of submissions. Why would I want my manuscript returned? If the editor doesn't buy my story, I can run off a fresh copy on my printer. *Rebuttal:* Publishers don't believe they owe free lancers anything. Most editors will not read or return a manuscript if you don't enclose a stamped return envelope. Send an SASE to make sure the editor received your piece, to show professionalism, and to invite helpful comments from the editor. To economize on manuscripts mailed flat, enclose a business-size SASE (#10) and a note saying that you don't need your manuscript returned.

To succeed as a writer, you must stay on track. Every writer needs self-discipline. Detours are paved with rationalizations, but common sense keeps writers on the main road.

❑ 16

A GUIDE TO DEALING WITH REJECTIONS

BY FRED HUNTER

ALL OF YOUR FAVORITE AUTHORS, ALL BEST-SELLING AUTHORS, AND all of the authors you love who have not yet been discovered by the general public have two things in common: Their work has at one time been rejected, and they've managed to go beyond that rejection to earn their respective places in the literary spectrum.

Rejection is an unfortunate fact of life for writers, and it's never easy to take. Although it's true that all writers suffer rejection, that fact can seem like little more than a useless bromide to a writer who's just opened his mail to find a form letter saying, "don't call us, we'll call you" (and believe it or not, I've actually received one that said that).

When I finished writing my first mystery, *Presence of Mind,* I decided that instead of using an agent I would attempt to sell the book myself. I put together cover letters and samples (the first three chapters) and sent them to ten publishers at a time until the book was accepted. I was very fortunate in that it sold to one of the first five publishers to whom it was sent, but by the time that happened I had sent out thirty samples, so for over a year afterward I was still receiving rejections for a book that was already accepted for publication. This gave me the unique luxury of being able to take an objective look at the business of rejection. Even though rejection letters are rarely personalized, from the editors who have taken the time to offer comments I've gleaned a few hints on how to handle rejection.

• **Editors are people**

Although writers often think of editors as unfeeling ogres, they really are basically just people with particular tastes who select books much the way any other reader would. It helps to think of how you read novels: When you're reading a book by a new author, even one that was recommended to you, you will either like or dislike the book, and your gut feeling will help you decide whether or not you will ever revisit that author's work.

Writers would like to think that editors can go beyond their personal taste and objectively recognize fine writing, and I have news for you: They do. But they will still rarely buy a book that doesn't appeal to them personally, any more than you would.

One rejection letter I received particularly illustrates this. It said, "Your writing is better than 90% of what crosses my desk . . . but I found the detective too smug (in the same way that Hercule Poirot is, and I didn't like him, either)." I hardly needed to point out to this editor how well the Poirot books have sold; she certainly knew that. The fact remained that my style just didn't appeal to that editor. It was comforting, though, to know that she wouldn't have bought Agatha Christie, either.

To give you an idea of how subjective editorial reactions are, I received one rejection letter that said, "There's too much character development in this book, and not enough plot," while another editor commenting on the same manuscript said, "The plot is very strong, but I thought the characters were a bit thin."

The fact that the responses of different editors are often so contradictory points up how important it is that you are satisfied with your own work, and that you have faith in it before submitting it. Obviously, it would be foolhardy to attempt to rewrite your manuscript based on the comments of one editor; however, if three editors tell you, "This manuscript is too wordy," I would do some heavy cutting before sending it out again.

• Rejection is part of a writer's life

Carolyn Hart, author of several award-winning mystery novels, says, "To be a writer, you have to be willing to fail. Even exceptional writers have their work rejected." Once you've completed your masterpiece, you've left the artistic part of writing and entered the business side, and it's best to approach it as you would any other business. You're a salesman, and your product is your work. As with any other product, some will buy it, some won't. It's O.K. to be disappointed when you don't make a sale to a particular editor, but you shouldn't be devastated. An editor will not buy a product that he doesn't believe he can sell to his audience. But there's always another editor and another audience.

• Always be working on something else

Start writing your next piece the minute you drop your current completed manuscript in the mailbox. Barbara D'Amato, author of the popular Cat Marsala mysteries, says, "I know many otherwise sane people who will write something, send it off, and then wait and wait and wait for it to be accepted somewhere before starting on something else. You have to start your next book right away, otherwise you're putting all your emotional stock in one thing."

Madeleine L'Engle, the highly esteemed author of both fiction and nonfiction, suffered a ten-year stretch of not being able to get her work published *after* the success of her earlier novels. She writes very candidly about that decade of rejection in her book *A Circle of Quiet.* During that period she continued to write, eventually going on to win the Newbery Medal for *A Wrinkle in Time.*

Far from finding these examples discouraging, writers should realize how large a role perseverance plays in the business of getting published. In my own work, even though I had some early success, I wasn't quite so fortunate when I tried to launch my second series. I submitted the first book in the series to publisher after publisher for almost two years before it was accepted. Even with a track record, I still had to find an editor who liked the book enough to take a chance on it. By the time the first book was sold, I'd completed the second and started the third. I found continuing to write was infinitely preferable to sitting at home developing ulcers.

But how do you go on writing without the encouragement of success? You must focus on the writing itself, not on the possible rewards. It's like the old joke about the restaurant with no prices on the menu: If you have to ask the price, you can't afford to eat there. Similarly, if your goal as a writer is anything other than the work itself, you can't afford to be one.

• Never give up

"I like to think it's a fortuitous world," says Carolyn Hart. "You can be an excellent writer and still fail, but you should never, never give up, because you never know when things will turn around—and the only way for that to happen is to keep writing."

Keep believing that things will turn around. Though it may take years, you *will* eventually find that editor who falls in love with your work . . . but that editor will never get to see your work if you allow rejections to make you give up along the road.

Disraeli said it better than anyone else: "The secret of success is constancy of purpose."

I wish I'd written that.

❑ 17

MYTHS OF THE WRITING LIFE

BY JAMES A. RITCHIE

RECENTLY I'VE FOUND THAT MANY OF THE OLD TRIED AND TRUE rules of fiction writing, and the writing life in general, have come under attack. So I think it's time to set the record straight.

Myth: You don't have to write everyday.

Fact: Well, no, you don't. You don't have to write at all. There probably isn't a soul in the world who will care if you never write another word.

And, yes it is possible to sell a few short stories, a few articles, a little of this and a pinch of that, if you write only on Saturday, or during the full moon, or whenever the mood hits. You may even legitimately call yourself a writer—small "w"—by working in this manner.

But unless you work at least five or six days a week, no excuses, you will never be able to call yourself a Professional Writer, meaning a writer who earns a living from writing fiction. And because writing, like playing the violin, requires hundreds and thousands of hours of practice to get right, you will never develop your talent to the fullest unless you write nearly everyday.

Even if you succeed financially, the first million or so words you write will screech and jangle the nerves as will a violin played by a rank beginner.

And anyone who tells you otherwise is a dilettante, a dabbler.

Myth: Procrastination is no more than your subconscious telling you the story isn't ready to be written.

Fact: No, procrastination is your way of telling the world you're too lazy and too soft to stick it out when the writing gets tough. Good writing is always difficult, always hard work. Anytime the words are flowing too easily you'd better look at your hole card.

Unless, when you're old and gray, you're certain you'll be content looking back and realizing you published only a tiny fraction of what you might have, and that most of it was mediocre at best, get over the notion that procrastination is ever a good thing.

Myth: It isn't the writing that matters, it's the act of creating, and since a writer works all the time, you're creating even when you're fishing, crocheting, or watching a football game, as long as you're *thinking* about writing.

Fact: Horse hockey. There may be some truth to the statement that a writer works all the time, but it's only at the keyboard that a writer creates anything.

At best, the work a writer does in his or her mind between stints at the keyboard is only planning to create. It's easy to justify anything, but justified or not, I can guarantee Joe Blow, that writer down the street with half your talent but twice your drive, is going to succeed much sooner that you do if you buy into this one.

Myth: It's the editor's job to fix my bad grammar (style, paragraph, plot line, etc.).

Fact: Why should he? I was once—briefly and small time—an editor. I quickly learned two things. One: many, many would-be writers expect editors to do everything, from correcting horrific spelling to transcribing handwritten manuscripts, to teaching them how to write basic English.

An editor's job is actually pretty simple when it comes to manuscripts: Keep the ones good enough to publish and reject the others. That's all there is to it.

Yes, once an editor finds a good story, one that really could see publication as is, he or she will say, "Now, let's see what we can do to make this story even better."

But, that's it. Editors should not be expected to rewrite, correct grammar or spelling (except for an occasional typo), or give writing lessons. And they do not ever read handwritten manuscripts.

I also learned that editors do not enjoy rejecting stories. Editors, in fact, love finding stories good enough to publish. So don't blame the editor if you receive a rejection slip instead of an acceptance letter.

Myth: You can't get an agent until you've been published, and you can't get published until you have an agent.

Fact: This one is nonsense. Agents are in the business of finding new, publishable writers. It's how agents, at least reputable agents, earn their money. But the key word is *publishable*. Almost all agents read queries, and so do many publishers.

Myth: Big name writers get such large advances there's no money left over for the rest of us.

Fact: There's a grain of truth in this, but there is a reason for it. Simply, big name writers get big bucks because they write big novels that sell in big numbers.

But remember that just about every big name writer out there was once an obscure, unpublished writer who earned very little or nothing. They may even have believed the same myth.

Instead of wasting energy griping about how much money somebody else makes, study what she does and how she does it. Then, one of these days, you may pull down huge advances while others gripe about you.

Myth: You must have a college education to be a professional writer.

Fact: I hope not. I dropped out of school in the eighth grade. I did take a G.E.D. test years later, but that's it. I tried college for a few months, quickly realized my time would be much better spent writing, and dropped out without taking a single writing course.

And I'm now working on my sixth novel.

Myth: A would-be fiction writer shouldn't read other people's fiction because it will unduly influence his own writing.

Fact: If you don't read other people's fiction, and lots of it, you will never, ever succeed as a writer. Period.

You *want* to be influenced. In the early stages of your career, and even when you're established, studying other writers, and imitating their style, is exactly how you learn to write well yourself. There is no other way. So read everything, and read often.

Myth: Writing fiction is an art, and rewriting only obscures the artist's spontaneous vision.

Fact: Yes, writing fiction is an art. But it's also a craft. Failure to rewrite will guarantee that the artist's vision will never be seen by anyone except those unfortunate friends and family members forced to read it.

How much rewriting is enough? Beats me. Dean Koontz claims to rewrite each page an average of 26 times. Ernest Hemingway is said to have rewritten *A Farewell to Arms* 39 times.

My own rule is to rewrite until it's either as good as I can get it, or until I'm so sick of the process I can't take it any more. As Hemingway explained in an interview, you rewrite until you get the words right, then you stop.

The competition is fierce. Getting the words "almost right" isn't going to get you anything except rejection slips to paper your office walls.

Myth: You must be certifiably insane to be a fiction writer.

Fact: All right, so this one is true.

❏ 18

THE WORD POLICE

BY BETH LEVINE

IT'S SUNDAY NIGHT AND THE SMELL OF CHINESE FOOD HANGS LOW over the city. Two figures are poised outside of a neon-lit overpriced specialty food store.

"Look, Joe, here's another one: 'Gormet Pastries,'" Lisa observes.

"Don't these people have any respect for the law? Let's take him in," Joe sighs, exasperated.

Joe pulls down on his snap brim hat. He and Lisa (and that's *Lisa;* not Leesa, Lysa, or Lise), a woman with determinedly clicking high heels, enter the aforementioned "Gormet Pastries."

The owner, a member of the I-Dress-Only-In-Black-And-Not-Be-cause-It's-Slimming tribe, eyes them disdainfully. "Can I help you?" he asks faintly.

"Are you the proprietor of . . . *Gourmet* Pastries?" Lisa inquires, annoyed. This jerk can't spell and he's looking down on *her?*

"Yes. Is there a problem?"

The couple looks at each other meaningfully before whipping out their pocket-sized New Webster's Dictionaries.

"Word Police," Joe says with a penetrating stare. The owner turns pale, and his eyes start to dart around the store. Joe points to the back of the sign in the window and sure enough, there is *GORMET* in all its purple shame. The owner pales. "I . . . uh . . . guess I never noticed," he stammers.

"No, you people never do!" Joe exclaims. "Don't you ever *proof* things before shelling out your money? Day after day, you come in here and you never *noticed* a sign three feet high?"

Lisa puts her hand on his arm. "Easy, Joe," she says quietly. Turning to the owner, she asks, "What's your name, buddy?"

"Lonnee. L O N N . . ." He stops when he sees Joe and Lisa's faces turn pale. They are looking at a sign behind the counter that reads *Baking Done on Premise.*

"What is that?" Joe asks curtly. "You bake with the hope that it might come out right?" Lonnee looks confused, as Joe begins to tie two copies of *The Chicago Manual of Style* to Lonnee's wrists. The three begin to shuffle to the door, while Lisa reads him his rights.

"You have the right to remain silent—something we prefer, actually. You have the right to remain literate. In the absence of this ability, you have the right to an English professor, which the court will provide."

Lonnee raises his head in defiance. "Ha! I just catered an affair for Edwin Newman; he'll defend me! He owes me!"

"I don't think so. The man has principles—and that's *ples* not *pals,*" snaps Joe. He sadly shakes his head and looks at Lisa. "Pathetic, isn't it?"

As they pass, the customers of the soon-to-be renamed Gourmet Pastries watch in open-mouthed horror. "He seemed to pay such attention to details. Who knew?" says one.

A mother looks down at her ashen-faced 10-year-old son. "See, sonny? He probably cheated his way through spelling class, too. Thought he could get away with it. See? It always catches up to you." The boy bursts into tears. (When he grows up, he will produce an Academy Award-winning documentary on his experiences, "Scared Grammatical.")

Later, Joe and Lisa emerge from the New York Public Library as the former owner of Gormet Pastries is bundled off into a library bus.

"What a dope," says Joe. "I'm glad they threw the book at him, not that he could read it. Imagine—dragging Edwin Newman's name into it!"

"Let's go get a cup of coffee," says Lisa. She takes Joe's arm, and they proceed to Bagels 'N Stuff. Joe balks when he sees the sign.

Lisa reassures him, "Well, it's a little cutesy, but I think colloquially it's correct." Joe stares at her intently as they enter the restaurant.

Ten minutes later, the two are relaxing in a booth.

"How'd you get into this crazy business, Joe?" Lisa asks meditatively.

"I started as a copy editor at a book publisher. I loved the job, but then to save money, the publisher . . ." Lisa leans over and pats his hand. Joe bravely continues, "The publisher started allowing books to go to press with *Britishisms* intact so they wouldn't have to spend money to reset type. *Colour* instead of *color,* that sort of thing. I said no. This far I will bend and no further.

"Turns out my boss used to work for McDonald's and was the one responsible for 'Over 5 billion sold,' not even knowing it should be 'More than 5 billion.' He was that sloppy. So he fired me! That's when I realized my true vocation: Cleaning up this ungrammatical city of ours."

Lisa sighs. "Sometimes I wonder if it really does matter."

Joe spills his coffee. "What? How can you possibly say that?"

"Oh, *more than, over. Gourmet* with or without a u, does it really amount to," she pauses before uttering the cliché, "a hill of beans?"

Now it's Joe's turn to reach for her hand. "Don't burn out on me now, baby. It happens to others, but not to us. It's in our blood."

Lisa's eyes well up. "I can't take it anymore. Everywhere I go—the bank, the sandwich shops, dry cleaners—there are typos everywhere. I went to buy a co-op, but when I saw the awning said 'Two Fourty,' I couldn't do it. I have no friends, because I'm always correcting them. Countermen hate me, because I'm forever pointing out that it's ice*d* tea, not *ice* tea. And don't even talk to me about apostrophes; they show up everywhere but where they are supposed to. Joe," Lisa's tears spill out, "I want to be like other people. I want to be sloppy."

Joe takes his hand away. "But we can't be like other people. We're a breed. We're . . . The Word Police. If we slip, it's the end of the civilized world, the demise of the society of Safire and Newman and Webster. It means the Lonnees and McDonald's of the world win."

Restlessly, Joe taps the end of his pencil on the tabletop. "Language defines what we can think," he continues. "I believe undisciplined, careless writing makes for undisciplined, careless thinking. How can you formulate ideas without appropriate tools—clarity, attention to detail? Without them, the world's thinking becomes muddled and unin-formed. The mind is a muscle. Use it or lose it."

"We could go away, Joe," Lisa says plaintively through her sobs. "We could go to France. We don't speak French, so we'd never know when something was incorrect."

"Sorry, Lisa, I can't turn my back on murderers of the mother tongue. I need the facts, ma'am." Joe gives Lisa a despairing look, and then throws a dollar on the table. Coat collar up, hat brim pulled down, he sadly leaves Lisa and Bagels 'N Stuff behind, but not before point-ing out to the amazed proprietor that *decaffeinated* has two Fs in it.

"I'll let you off with a warning this time," he says, exiting to chase a passing exterminator's truck with *MICES, TERMITES AND ROACHES* written on the side.

Back at the table, Lisa watches him go and says softly to herself, "I'll miss ya, Joe. Paris would of been swell." She shudders after mouthing the foul words of her new world. Picking up her decafeinated coffee, she drinks the bitter cup.

How To Write—
Techniques

❑ GENERAL FICTION

❑ 19

THE MANY HATS OF A FICTION WRITER

BY MADELEINE COSTIGAN

AS A FICTION WRITER TODAY, YOU WEAR MANY HATS. YOU'RE YOUR own boss, your own editor, and probably your own agent. When you play so many roles how do you keep them all in balance? It isn't easy, but it can be done.

1. Be a realistic boss.

You have to take yourself seriously as a writer before you can expect anyone else to take you seriously. Establish professional work habits early on, and believe in yourself enough to stick to them. Even if your office is a corner of the basement or an alcove under the eaves, do everything you can to make it as user-friendly as possible. Something wonderful is happening here.

Write every day. The more you write, the more fluent your writing will become. In the beginning you may be writing around what you want to say instead of getting to the core. Keep writing. The route may be circuitous but after you zero in on what you truly want to say, you'll see that during all those false starts and detoured storylines, you weren't wasting time, as you feared. You were developing as a writer, developing a discerning eye and ear, finding your own voice, learning to respect self-imposed deadlines.

You may be the only person who knows you're working when you're doing what your grandmother would call woolgathering, but who else needs to know? Alice Munro says that when her family sees her staring at the wall, she tells them she's thinking, even though she knows she's somewhere between thinking and a trancelike state. Toni Morrison refers to entering a space she can only call nonsecular. Every writer has such moments of reaching deeper and deeper levels of concentration, and whatever label you use to describe what you're doing, you soon learn that during such moments answers frequently come to nagging problems that days of writing won't solve. That's part of the mystery of writing fiction.

Some days you may become so immersed in your work that you lose all sense of time; there are those who might say all sense. For some writers the best course is to work until the vein is exhausted. Ernest Hemingway liked to stop when he knew what was going to happen next. Choose the method that suits you.

Other days nothing you write seems to work. Here's where keeping a notebook can be useful. Not only does it get you into the habit of writing every day, but while browsing through it you may come across a scene written at random, or a snatch of conversation that regenerates your enthusiasm for the work-in-progress, and changes your perspective. For me, it has always been fascinating to see how unrelated bits and pieces can meld to form a symmetrical whole.

In the beginning, you really need professional reaction to your work, but that's when it's most difficult to get. A plain rejection slip tells you nothing. If possible, join a local writers' group or go to a writers' conference. It can be most illuminating to listen to other writers discuss your work, and, if you've done your homework, probably not nearly so painful as you fear. The company of other writers can be wonderfully sustaining and exhilarating throughout your writing life.

2. Be a tough editor.

The first time you submit a story to a magazine you're competing with professionals. Most new writers send work out too soon. The hope is that it will quickly find a home at a top magazine. When instead, it meets with rejection, the writer may easily become discouraged. It may be that what you had hoped was a well-turned short story is actually a first draft. While a first draft is not finished work, it is tangible, concrete, and best of all, something to revise. Sidney Sheldon says he writes as many as a dozen drafts.

Take your story scene by scene and put it to the test: Does each scene unfold naturally, move the story forward? If a scene is static, work on it until it crystallizes. One way to do this may be to get your characters talking.

Or it may be that a scene is unnecessary. What you really need is a smooth transition. Sometimes beginning writers include a scene because they don't know how to get a character from here to there without explaining. When you find yourself having difficulty getting a character from the telephone to the agreed-upon meeting, you might well consider skipping the interim scene.

Is your opening compelling? If you were reading a story while standing at the airport magazine rack, waiting for your plane to be called, would you be unable to put the magazine back after reading only the first few lines? Toni Morrison has said that her favorite opening line is from *Tar Baby: He thought he was safe.* He isn't safe. Why isn't he? With five short words Toni Morrison has involved the reader in her character's dilemma.

Is your language fresh? Or cliché bound?

Reading fine writing is a good way to develop your ear for the precise word. What a difference if instead of writing, *They persevered in their conversation,* Jane Austen had chosen a different verb.

Is your setting an integral part of the story? Is it reader oriented? Offer a few telling details and the reader will extrapolate. In a story that takes place in a school building, mentioning the scarred, pitted lockers or the smell of linseed oil may be enough to suggest authenticity. In a different school, the sight of students hunched at computer terminals or passing through metal detectors might do it.

Are your characters real? Does your reader know and care about them? Many writers work with the contrast between a character's thoughts and words to reveal a character. When I was writing "A Small But Perfect Crime," I used this technique. Harold Burgoyne, principal of Howell Middle School has discovered that Charlie Patch, son of Burgoyne's cardiologist, has been vandalizing the school. The following conversation takes place between Bur-goyne and Karl Webb, a teacher at the school:

"Fraley is steamed over the vandalism," Burgoyne said. "It's ruining our image."

Image was the stuff of life to Burgoyne. "Vandalism can't be tolerated," Karl said, waiting for Burgoyne to show his hand.

"I've never considered Charlie to be Howell Middle School material," Burgoyne continued. "We've got to finesse this one, Webb. Sending Charlie to the youth center would be a grave mistake. Keeping him here is not in the best interest of Howell." Burgoyne's watery blue eyes gave Karl a searching look. "You know how dedicated I am to this school's best interest?"

"Indeed." To himself, Karl called the language he spoke to Burgoyne, 'pedageese.'

Burgoyne leaned forward, his hands taut. "Charlie Patch is a year older than his classmates. It would be helpful to all concerned if two of his teachers recommended that Charlie be skipped into Jefferson High, where it won't be quite so easy for him to dominate the other students. I'm counting on your recommendation, Webb, and Ira Carpenter's as well."

"Brilliant," Karl said.

Does your dialogue ring true? It may be that your character says what a real person would say in a given situation, but that isn't a sufficient test for good dialogue. True, your dialogue should create the illusion of real speech, but it should also advance the plot, economically characterize, or evoke an emotional response from the reader. It must also be much shorter than real conversation.

Try listening with even more concentration than you give to talking. You want more than the gist of what you're hearing. Listen for cadence, word order, flavor, figures of speech, all the revelations each of us makes on a daily basis. And then write in your notebook whatever strikes you as useful.

Do you have a good title?

Many editors consider a title to be an editorial decision. They know their readers and what will attract those readers. Sometimes a title has to fit with an illustration, and must be changed because of space limitations. Even though it may be discarded, you still need an intriguing title for your work. It's the first thing the editor sees.

3. Be a tireless agent.

Many major magazines have stopped publishing fiction. Very few literary agents today handle short stories. It's up to you to place your own work.

First, do some research at the library. Read several issues of any magazine you think might find your story suitable. Skimming only one issue can be misleading and cause you to waste time and postage.

List the magazines according to your order of preference, making sure you've chosen the appropriate editor's name from the masthead. What's in a name? Maybe the difference between acceptance and rejection. You don't want to address your manuscript in the generic, or risk mailing it off to the magazine trusting that someone there will route it to the proper person. It's too easy for that someone to whip out a rejection slip and send your story winging back.

Not all magazines, particularly literary journals, are available at the local library or bookstore. Study writers' magazines for information about these and send for sample copies. While literary magazines offer little financial compensation for your work, they are valuable showcases, read by publishers, editors, and agents.

How long should you wait to hear from an editor concerning the fate of your story? I used to advise six weeks, but I now think three months is more realistic. Before a manuscript is accepted it is usually read by several editors. Very few editors can afford to read in the course of the business day; they do most of their manuscript reading after hours.

And yes, there are gradations of rejections. The most disappointing is the plain rejection slip. Even a handwritten note is encouraging.

A signed letter from an editor indicates more interest. And a detailed letter referring to your story's strengths and weaknesses demonstrates thoughtful consideration.

Close, but no cigar, you may think. Think again. You are now being taken seriously as a writer. Several people on the editorial staff have probably read your story, seen its merit, and passed it on to the editor who wrote to you. Editors do not have time to write letters to writers unless they see promise and real talent in the manuscript.

Now it's your turn to accept and reject. If you find more than one editor making the same criticism, take the editors' words to heart and rework the story accordingly. Incorporate the suggestions you find worthwhile. Those that seem irrelevant, file for later review. You can always throw them away after you sell the story. Like a good stew, criticism is best evaluated after it simmers a while.

When an editor expresses an interest in seeing more of your work, respond with a new story in a timely manner. This story may meet with acceptance—which is why it's so very important to work on something new while you're waiting. Which brings us back to being a realistic boss.

□ 20

SAGGING MIDDLES AND DEAD ENDS

BY SID FLEISCHMAN

THROUGHOUT A LONG WRITING LIFE, I HAVE HAD MY PROBLEMS WITH middles and endings—TO SAY nothing of beginnings. I have never written a story in which the rain didn't fall somewhere along the way. But there is a sunny side to this weather. In solving a gnarly story problem I find that inevitably I run into fresh scenes I wouldn't otherwise have thought of.

In this regard, story problems (I tell myself while beating my head against the wall) are the writer's best friend. I am, in fact, always suspicious of a story that comes dancing out of the computer without any trips or falls.

Well, what does one do when the middle of a story begins to sag? I experienced this in the first novel I ever wrote—a long-forgotten detective novel.

About a third of the way along, I could feel the story tension go slack. I was too inexperienced to know what to do, so I impulsively killed off another character. That brightened up the story wonderfully! The incident brought to my attention what a powerful ploy it is to add something new to a story in trouble. More than once this sort of CPR has kept one of my novels alive and kicking. A stranger turns up. A storm blows in. A villain appears. A character disappears. Something, something new. I know a prominent author who, feeling her story becalmed, burned down the character's house. That livened things up.

But looking for a new element is not the only area I turn my mind to these days. When the story battery goes dead, I immediately reexamine the opening chapters to see if I have made a wrong move somewhere. Often, even a slight change in relationships will act like a jumper cable and revive the tale. The technique is much like giving a slight shake to a kaleidoscope, for a different story pattern will inevitably reveal itself.

Let me cite personal examples of these solutions.

When I began a children's novel, *Humbug Mountain* (Dell), I was working with the idea of doing a Robinson Crusoe or Swiss Family Robinson survival tale set on the vast frontier of what once was called The Great American Desert.

I established a family, traveling up the Missouri River to the Dakota boom town of Humbug Mountain. When my characters arrive, they see nothing but weathered real estate stakes in the ground and a beached old river boat. The town went bust before it could boom. The characters were "shipwrecked" on the prairie, and I had my Swiss Family Robinson set up.

Or did I? The story turned to ashes. The next chapter simply wouldn't write. I considered having the kids catch a catfish for supper, but that would not exactly be a show stopper. Why, I muttered to myself, didn't the family just wait out the next river boat and hurry back to civilization?

They couldn't, *only* because if they did I'd have to throw away several dazzling chapters. They dazzled me, at any rate.

Instead, I threw out Robinson Crusoe and I turned to something new. I brought onstage a couple of ghastly villains. When the kids are exploring the dead old river boat, they sense that someone else is aboard. They are right, and they soon come face to face with Shagnasty John and the Fool Killer, two unwashed nightmares hiding from the law. From that point on, the story took off like a runaway horse, and went on to become a finalist for the National Book Awards.

The stranger need not be a villain, as I was to discover when trying to write a picture book story, *The Scarebird* (Greenwillow).

I set up a strong but tender story about an isolated old man and a scarecrow he puts up. He begins to talk to it, to clothe it against the winds and stormy weather, and even to mumble through a game of checkers with it.

Suddenly, I was in quicksand. What do I do with the situation? Nothing wanted to happen next. The story had become a still life. I don't remember how long I wandered around in the dark before the obvious occurred to me. Why not bring on a stranger? What would happen?

I introduced a farmhand down on his luck and looking for work. Little by little, Lonesome John gives the unwelcome young man the scarebird's hat against the blazing sun. On other days, he takes pity and gives the young man the scarebird's shoes and then its gloves against the thorny brambles. The scarebird is transformed, day by day and bit by bit, into a living being—with whom finally we see the old man play a real game of checkers.

To a writer who feels locked and bolted to an outline, the ability to turn on a dime, to change a key story element, may give one the vapors. But with a project in trouble, one has no choice but to look the outline in its bloodshot eyes—and to revise it as necessary. Only this sort of flexibility will spare the reader, who cares nothing about outlines or preliminary inspirations, from sagging middles or dead ends.

Endings require a different sort of acrobatics. It's too late in the story to lay in new backflips. One must work with what's already on paper.

My endings grow organically out of materials I established early— and as often as not, *quite by accident.* By that I mean I don't see ahead how important marginal details or props will prove to be at the end.

Early in *The 13th Floor* (Greenwillow), a time travel novel, my main character, Buddy, is seen practicing Spanish with a small tape recorder for a school test. It was a passing detail; I absolutely had no further plans for it. But it reappeared, as surprising to me as a jack-in-the-box.

Just before the final curtain Buddy sees a chance to shove the tape recorder down the throat of a freshly-caught fish. The gasping cod starts talking in Spanish, the 17th-century villain jumps out of his buckle shoes, and in the confusion my lead characters are able to make a final escape.

If I hadn't so casually introduced the pocket tape recorder early on, I still might be hunting for an ending to *The 13th Floor.* Props have been lifesavers for me.

A marginal detail gave me the ending for a gold rush novel, *By the Great Horn Spoon!* (Little, Brown). I had read that ships rounding the Horn were often boarded by stray cats in the seaports of South America. I slipped this in as little more than local color. To my immense surprise, the cats popped up importantly at the end.

While my characters, young Jack and his butler, Praiseworthy, store up a few pouches of gold dust, they lose everything in a boat explosion. But wait! What about those Peruvian cats breeding aboard the now abandoned ship in the bay? I'd read that San Francisco was overrun with rats and that cats were worth their weight in gold. Jack and Praiseworthy strike it rich, at last, by selling Peruvian cats. Happy last-minute thought! Those felines have been continuously in print for almost thirty-five years.

As I never plot my endings in advance (I don't want to know how things turn out; that's why I write the story), I seem always to be glancing back over my shoulder for the ending.

In *Jim Ugly* (Greenwillow), I had no dramatic curtain until I recalled the chicken ranch I had introduced only for background early on. Why couldn't the chickens have pecked up the hidden diamonds—and then gotten loose across the Nevada landscape?

They could, they did, and I had the comic ending I'd been searching for.

Every story problem that it is possible to have, together with these solving techniques, came into play in my recent novel, *Bandit's Moon* (Greenwillow). The story is about a girl, Annyrose, who attaches herself to the legendary California highwayman of the last century, Joáquin Murieta.

Posters were nailed to the trees all over California offering a reward for the head of Joáquin. The posters didn't say Joáquin Murieta. Just Joáquin.

Now, there were plenty of honest Joáquins, a fairly common Mexican name, and alas, a few of them were strung up in hasty error.

That, I thought, would be my story. I'd have Annyrose become involved with the wrong Joáquin, an innocent man destined for a hanging tree.

A couple of chapters in, and I felt I was up to my eyebrows in marshmallows.

So I gave the kaleidoscope a slight turn. What if Annyrose becomes involved, instead, with the real Joáquin? Say he saves her life and becomes her friend and protector, bandit or not. And then, what if, what if—what if she learns that in the past he has killed her father or brother or someone close? Sudden hatred would drive her to turn him in, wouldn't it?

I started the novel from scratch again. I could feel so much story tension I needed tranquilizers. But I hit a sudden sag in the middle. I needed something new to happen. I brought in a stranger, a Chilean, a Joáquin impostor, and wrote a scene in which he tries to hold up the real Joáquin. I never expected to see the impostor again. I was wrong.

As the pages of *Bandit's Moon* piled up I began to worry in earnest about the final curtain ahead. I was unable to come up with a dramatic scene to wrap up the story.

Eyes fixed firmly over my shoulder, I reexamined my opening moves. My eyes lit on a passing detail.

As I wanted my heroine and her older brother to be penniless, I established in the first chapter that his pocket had been picked: His money and papers were gone. I had no further plans for the incident.

But I now saw how perfectly it could become part of the ending. I had already written that Annyrose, now separated from her brother, reads in the paper that he had been shot during a stagecoach holdup at the hands of the legendary bandit. In tears, she turns in her friend, Joáquin.

But what about the pickpocket lurking in the first chapter? Why couldn't he be misidentified because of the stolen papers in his pocket? What if *he* were the one killed in the stagecoach holdup? I could then bring the brother back to life in the end. Seeing him alive, Annyrose would realize that she had turned in her great friend Joáquin—by mistake.

Now I had a gutsy end scene.

And remember that Chilean impostor, that throwaway character I had introduced to fix a sag in the middle of the story?

I won't tell you how *he* turns up in the end. But count on it.

Don't underestimate the power of props and minor details, of kaleidoscopes and strangers and villains and jack-in-the-boxes. I couldn't write my books without them.

❏ 21

MATTERS OF FACT:
FICTION WRITERS AS RESEARCHERS

BY SHARON OARD WARNER

A FEW INTERESTING FACTS ON HONEY BEES:

1. Worker bees irritate the queen to prepare her to fly. She has to lose a little weight before she can take to the air.
2. The queen flies only once, going a distance of seven or eight miles so as not to mate with her brothers.
3. Mating occurs in the air, and after the act is completed, the drone dies and falls to the ground. (I could make all sorts of wise cracks here, but I'll refrain.)

This is the first use I've had for a whole legal pad full of notes I took in a beekeeping class a few summers ago. I registered for the class because I intended to write about a beekeeper, and to that end, I took faithful notes. More than two years have passed, and my beekeeper has yet to show himself. I do have firm possession of a radiologist who reads tarot cards, and I'm hoping to give her the beekeeper for a husband. As of this morning, she has yet to embrace him, but I'm optimistic about working it out. I intend to use some of this material on bees, but it's obvious that I'm not going to do all of it justice. If you need a stray bee fact or two, you're welcome to the above. Interesting though these facts are, I doubt that I'll find a place for them.

A few additional facts:

1. Bees don't like carbon dioxide, so when you work with them, be sure to breathe out the side of your mouth. (Try doing that, just to see how it feels.)
2. When a bee stings, she will die, but in the process she'll leave a "mad bee" smell on your skin, a smell that makes other bees want to sting you as well.
3. The mad bee smell is easy to identify: It smells for all the world like bananas with a little solvent mixed in.

Keep your hands off these facts. I can almost guarantee I'll use them sooner or later, and probably sooner. These are the kinds of facts that authenticate character and offer opportunities to advance a plot. They're active facts that carry a sensory charge. Let me show you what I mean: Once the radiologist acquiesces and agrees to be married to the beekeeper, one of the first things he'll do is lumber out to the hives and check on his bees. Maybe he has someone else with him, his daughter Sophie say, and he'll tell her a little about how to handle the combs. Already, I can predict that Sophie will insist on getting stung. She's that sort of girl. And there we have it: the "mad bee" smell all over Sophie, enticing the other bees to sink their stingers into the soft skin of her upper arm and to swarm menacingly about her face. "Get away, Sophie!" her father will yell, wresting the comb from her hands. But Sophie will refuse because she's sixteen and more hormones than good sense.

This one little scene requires more facts than might be readily apparent. The three I've listed will launch the scene, but they won't complete it. Almost immediately, others will be necessary. Without them, the scene will lose steam, and the plot will stall. As it turns out, fiction and fictional characters take their vitality from facts, from real-life detail, which means that writers of fiction are in the business of research. We're fact hoarders—accumulating, sorting, and storing details that give our stories life.

Some of the fact-finding is rather mundane, but research need not be dull. The beekeeping class and my trip to the beekeeper's house to "handle" the bees were recent highlights. (No, I did not get stung while I held the combs, nor did I wear gloves or a veil. Are you impressed? Well, you shouldn't be. These were gentle bees.) I think of this early research as a sort of "grounding" because I use these facts to situate my main characters in their milieu. Where do these people I'm writing about live? In which city, on what street, in this house or that? What do they do for a living? What are their hobbies, besides beekeeping, of course? Their fears? Their joys? To answer these questions, it's necessary to leave the computer and enter the world.

Sometimes, these forays take me only as far as the local library or bookstore. Books, newspapers, and magazines often provide sufficient information. For instance, I recently bought a book called *Beekeeping,* which advertises itself as a "Complete Owner's Manual," all you need to be a beekeeper or to create one. Like everything else, it's not what it claims to be, but it will answer some of my questions. What sort of questions? Well, here's one: To write the scene where stubborn Sophie invites a bee sting, I need to know the season, and the decision can't be arbitrary. From my bee class, I learned that bees winter, a state akin to hibernation, and that wintering lasts longer in certain areas of the country than in others. The farther north you live, the trickier this wintering process can be, but I digress.

And digress again: It's important to know facts, yes, but it's just as important to recognize when enough is enough. Lengthy and in-depth research carries its own liabilities. Think about it. Having spent time, energy and *el dinero* on acquiring precious facts, how likely are you to squander them? Not bloody likely. Which leads perfectly good writers to stuff their narratives with tangential information, just to justify that expensive tome on medieval bedroom practices or the weekend trip to Amarillo for local color. Don't overdo it; that's my advice. I almost quit reading that wonderful novel *Snow Falling on Cedars* for exactly this reason. There's only so much I want to know about fishing boats, and David Guterson tested my patience more than once. (I realize he won the PEN Faulkner and all, but no one is perfect.)

But don't let's go to Puget Sound, beautiful though it is. Let's stay in arid Albuquerque with the beekeeper. He lives right in town with me, in the North Valley, on the other side of the Rio Grande. So we've established place. What about the season? Checking my handy-dandy beekeeping book, I note that by mid-April the hive will be quite active. The desert is blooming, and nectar is plentiful. (Before I write this scene, I'll need to know exactly which plants bloom in April in Albuquerque, because the beekeeper is not only concerned with his insects; he's also concerned with their food sources. Lumbering out to check the hive, he'll be thinking about goldenrod, prickly pear, and Palmer lupine.) By April, the old bees that wintered over are dying off, and the young bees are taking their place. The brood nest will have swelled to six to eight combs, providing the beekeeper with something to check. And I'm guessing that the young bees are more likely to sting. I'll have to check to make sure, but if they're anything like teenage Sophie, they're hotheaded and impulsive.

To tell the truth, Sophie is the real subject of my book, and I'll let you in on a secret not even her parents know. Sophie's pregnant. Now I've been pregnant, twice actually, so I don't need to research the various stages of pregnancy. I remember them all too well. But I've never been pregnant as a teenager, and certainly not as a teenager in 1998, and this does require some investigation. Before I began to work on this project—so far, I've written two short stories on these characters, and the stories themselves are a kind of research, a way of developing characters and familiarizing myself with the material—I read *Reviving Ophelia: Saving the Selves of Adolescent Girls.* The author, Mary Pipher, is a clinical psychologist in private practice in Lincoln, Nebraska. I also went to a reading and talk Ms. Pipher gave at a local bookstore, which proved helpful in a larger sense. It provided context and some sense of urgency. Ms. Pipher is very concerned about plight of teenage girls in the 1990s.

> Girls know they are losing themselves. One girl said, "Everything good in me died in junior high." Wholeness is shattered by the chaos of adolescence. Girls become fragments, their selves split into mysterious contradictions. They are sensitive and tenderhearted, mean and competitive, superficial and idealistic. They are confident in the morning, and overwhelmed with anxiety by nightfall. They rush through their days with wild energy and then collapse into lethargy. They try on new roles every week—this week the good student, next week the delinquent, and the next, the artist. . . . Much of their behavior is unreadable. Their problems are complicated and metaphorical—eating disorders, school phobias, and self-inflicted injuries. I need to ask again and again in a dozen different ways, "What are you trying to tell me?"

This is precisely the question I'm asking of Sophie, again and again, and the answers she provides will do much to shape the material for the novel. Thus, *Reviving Ophelia* provides me with a necessary cultural perspective, one I will certainly find useful, but this "grounding" I'm talking about is something more elemental. It's a matter of territory, of the actual earth on which a character walks.

So where does Sophie walk? Well, she walks around high school for one thing. Sophie goes to Valley High School in Albuquerque, which is, not so coincidentally, where my son goes to school as well. My son Corey is a sophomore, and Sophie is a senior, so it's not likely they'll run into one another, which is just as well because Sophie is not, as mothers say, a "good influence." She's got troubles, that girl. Still, my son's attendance at Valley is as useful to me as Ms. Pipher's book. Maybe more useful. I go to the high school frequently, and whenever I do, I take note of the place itself and of the kids who spend their days there.

Valley is one of the oldest high schools in Albuquerque. From all appearances, the main buildings date from the fifties. The campus has been maintained over the years, but in piecemeal fashion: In "senior circle," new picnic tables hunker up to crumbling cement benches. The library is now labeled the Media Center, but it houses a modest collection of moldy-looking books, not a computer in plain sight. The carpet in the Media Center is a horrible shade of puke green, and appears to have been laid down in the late sixties or early seventies when all the adults went temporarily color blind. I was around then, but still coming of age, and so I don't have to take responsibility for that carpet. At the last meeting of the Parent's Advisory Council—yes, I'm a member—the principal, a gracious and energetic man named Toby Herrera, voiced his hope that the carpet would soon be replaced. We all nodded vigorously and tried not to look down.

At an earlier meeting this year, Mr. Herrera happened to mention that Albuquerque has a high school specifically designed for pregnant teens. (Is this a step forward or backward? I can't decide.) The school is called New Futures, and the facility includes counseling for new and expectant mothers as well as on-site day care. When Mr. Herrera mentioned this school, I thought of Sophie, for whom New Futures will be an option, and I also thought of my own high-school career, when the girls who got pregnant had no options whatsoever. By and large, they did not have abortions, unless they crossed the border into Mexico—we're talking pre-Roe vs. Wade here—and they did not stay in school. What they did do, I suppose, was to get married, if the boy in question had the presence of mind or the generosity to propose, or else they slipped away to a home for unwed mothers in Fort Worth. I used to hear girls whisper about that place. It might have been, might still be, a humane and cheerful alternative to living at home or jumping off a cliff; I don't know. But at the time, it seemed a sort of prison where everything was stripped away, first your identity, your family and your friends, and finally, your baby, as well.

But Sophie lives in a different world, and it's one I need to know about. As Mr. Herrera was quick to point out, pregnant girls can choose to go to school at New Futures or they can stay at their home school. In other words, Sophie can continue to attend Valley, and knowing Sophie, I imagine that's what she'll do. Of course, that decision will simplify my research tasks a bit because it means I won't have to scout out New Futures. One of the most important aspects of this "grounding" is to gain a firm sense of place, and here we're talking about everything from the time period to the city to the weather.

Naturally, Sophie blames her several bee stings on Daddy, then runs sobbing into the house. Ahh, yes, the house. What color is the back door Sophie slams behind her? And is her room at the front of the house or the back? For me, identifying home is one of the most important early research tasks. Before I can accomplish much in the way of characterization and plot, I must know where my characters live, and by this, I mean a particular house with particular windows that look out on particular plants and alleys and streets. Imagining the house does not work for me. It's too ephemeral—made-up people in a made-up house. The walls begin to waver and shift before my eyes, the kitchen to slide from one end of the house to the other, the garage to attach then unattach. Just where did I put that third bedroom, I wonder, and what was on the walls? Sooner or later, the occupants feel a tremor beneath their feet; they're threatened with imaginary collapse. Everything has its limits, you see, my imagination included.

So where to find a real house? My own doesn't work. I live there, my husband and children live there. We don't have room for a fictional family, and besides, they're bound to have entirely different tastes from mine. They're better housekeepers; they find time to dust thoroughly and not just swipe at the surfaces of things. Or maybe they're worse: Maybe pet hair gathers in the corners of the rooms, and dirty plates and coffee cups collect beside the bed and on top of the toilet tank. What I need, you see, is somebody else's home, full of furniture and magazines and knick knacks, but without occupants. A ready-made set.

For my first novel, I had a piece of luck. My family was in Austin, Texas, for the holidays, which is where the novel takes place, and my husband and I spent New Year's Eve with a friend who just happened to be house-sitting for an entire year. So there we were, drinking a little wine and listening to The Gypsy Kings, my husband and his friend Mark discussing, yawn, the University of Texas basketball team. An hour passed, and they moved on to the Dallas Cowboys. To keep from nodding off, I got up and had a look around. I took note of the flamingoes in the study, a whole motley crew of flamingoes—plastic ones, metal ones, and a wooden flamingo that swung from the ceiling. I puzzled over a small black and white TV on the counter in the bathroom, and the red tile floor in the kitchen. I peered out the bedroom windows and weighed myself on the scales. Nosy, you say. Yes, you're absolutely right, but I didn't open the medicine chest or any of the drawers. I didn't try on clothes, like the main character in Raymond Carver's story, "Neighbors." I just made a leisurely stroll around the premises. Later, when the characters in my first novel took up residence in this house, I had only to turn on The Gypsy Kings to bring it all back. Perfect.

For the second novel, I had to take action. No gift houses this time around. So I "feigned" and pretended to be a potential home buyer. Dragging my husband along to make it look good, I scouted several houses. I had ideas about where the beekeeper and his family would live. For one thing, I wanted them to reside in the North Valley, because I like it there, and because Sophie is already enrolled at Valley High School. She has friends there. We wouldn't want to move her at this late date. And the beekeeper requires land with flowering plants around his house, as well as a nearby water source. Bees have to drink.

Beforehand, I studied newspaper ads, choosing houses for description, location, price, and size. All these houses were occupied and previously owned. In each case, a real estate person was hosting an open house, so no one would be inconvenienced. The first houses we saw were all wrong. In a strange turn of events, we happened to go to a house which was the scene of a terrible murder, a story that had been on the news and in the papers for weeks, a death befitting a Dostoevsky novel. I won't go into details, as they will plunge you into despair. The real estate agent, who was clearly ill at ease, referred to the crime obliquely, mentioning it to us in order to be "up front." He'd been ordered by the court to sell the house, he said. What could he do? Indeed, I thought. His situation deserved its own novel. Before, the house had seemed dreary, broken up in odd ways, old and neglected. But afterwards, it seemed more than gloomy; it seemed downright haunted. Naturally, my husband and I hightailed it out of there, retreating to the car where we sat in shock for a few minutes before pulling slowly away, leaving the real estate agent to pace back and forth in the family room, an honest man who would surely be trapped in this tragic house for countless Sundays to come.

Quite naturally, we were tempted to abandon house hunting, for that day anyway, but we decided to forge on, and now I'm glad we did.

The third house was perfect, or close to perfect, more expensive than
the house I imagined for Sophie and her parents, but otherwise ideal.
I took away a real estate brochure that I covered with notes. Here's
the realtor's description: "This wonderful custom adobe home offers
a quiet private retreat with views, Northern New Mexico decor, and
room for horses." Or bees, lots of bees. The house is situated on 1.3
acres. It's a territorial style home with a pitched metal roof, a long
front porch, brick floors and window ledges, vigas, latillas, and tile
accents. (Live in Albuquerque for a few years, and you'll be able to
sling these terms, too.) The house is shaped in an L; one wing is
eighteen years old, the other only seven, but it was constructed to look
old. The upstairs windows offer a view of the bosque, which is Spanish
for woods. Whenever you see the bosque, you know the river is close
by. Beyond the bosque, two inactive volcanoes rise like the humps of
a camel's back. You want to move there, right? So did I, but I didn't
have an extra $332,500. Yep, that was the asking price.

Though I can't have the house in reality, I've taken possession of it
in my imagination. Sophie and her parents live there, and in order to
give the family the financial wherewithal to afford this little hacienda
in the midst of the city, I gave the mother, Peggy, a career that would
bring in the big bucks, or at least the medium-sized bucks. Hence, her
job as a radiologist. Actually, my reasons for making her a radiologist
are a bit more complicated. I imagine Peggy to be a woman of extraordinary insight, someone who can see into people, very nearly a
psychic.

Not surprisingly, Peggy's profession and her interest in tarot cards
were suggested to me by some of the paraphernalia I noted in the
house. The back upstairs bedroom was occupied by a young woman
named Zoe (test papers in evidence), whose interests in Buddhism and
acupuncture were also on display. An altar stood at one end of the
room, and among the books on Zoe's desk was *The Book of Shiatsu*
as well as a plastic body model for both the meridianal and extraordinary points. I made notes quickly because my husband insisted we
not linger. He had compunctions about my nosiness, but I maintain
that I did no one any harm, and again, I only looked at the things that
were out in the open. Already, I've altered the particulars. Peggy is
not a Buddhist, nor does she do acupuncture. But she does concern
herself with what can't be seen on the surface, and it was Zoe's room
that put this idea in my head. Thank you, Zoe.

But nothing comes free. I know about tarot cards because I took a class when I was seventeen and intent on the future. I still have the cards and the books. But here's a piece of research I have yet to do. I have to learn about the daily life of a radiologist: hours, tasks, and so forth. Having been to one fairly recently, I have a general sense of what radiologists do, but I need to know a great deal more. Already, I've lined up a lunch date with an acquaintance who used to work for a group of radiologists. And I have library sources. That won't be enough, of course, but it will get me started. The task is to find out how radiologists *think*, how they integrate their work in their day to day lives. Because radiologists aren't just radiologists at work. Like the rest of us, they carry their work away with them, and use it to understand the world.

The same is true for writers, of course, and for visual artists, photographers, assistant principals, day care workers, police officers, and doctors. A few years back, I asked my gynecologist so many questions about abortion that he quipped I could write off the visit as research, which, not so coincidentally, is exactly what it was.

Fiction writers are researchers. We can't help it. It's part and parcel of who we are. In restaurants, we crane our heads to listen to conversations taking place around us; we note accents and idiosyncratic speech patterns. At the mall, we stare at the strangers milling about, all of them people with homes to go to, children to care for, lives to lead. They have secrets these strangers, and we imagine what they are. It turns out that research isn't a distinct process, something with a beginning and end. It's ongoing, part and parcel of our lives. It is, in some sense, *our* secret.

One more interesting bee fact:

When working with bees, wear white or light-colored clothing. Bees are attracted to red and black.

They're bees, you see. They can't help it.

❑ 22

MAKE YOUR MINOR CHARACTERS WORK FOR YOU

BY BARNABY CONRAD

HOW DO WE KNOW THAT SCARLETT O'HARA IS CATNIP TO MEN?

The Tarleton twins *show* us in the first scene of *Gone With the Wind* by their adulation of her. The author doesn't tell us—she has minor characters do it for her.

In *The Godfather,* Mario Puzo doesn't *tell* us that Don Corleone is powerful and ruthless and lives outside the law, he shows us. In the very first chapter, the author skillfully establishes the eponymous Godfather's character and position by giving us brief vignettes of three minor characters in deep trouble: the wronged undertaker, Amerigo Bonasera; the washed-up crooner, John Fontaine; and an anguished father, the baker Nazorine. Who do they decide is the only person to come up with illegal solutions to their woes? Don Corleone. And in the next sequence we see them reverently approach the Don himself with their pleas and see him solve their problems savagely. And later that day, we hear Kay, another minor figure, speaking to Michael, the Don's son:

Kay said thoughtfully, "Are you sure you're not jealous of your father? Everything you've told me about him shows him doing something for other people. He must be good-hearted." She smiled wryly. "Of course, his methods are not exactly constitutional."

How much more convincing this method is than if the author himself had ticked off a list of the Don's characteristics and background information.

Never fail to use your secondary characters wherever possible to characterize your protagonist and to further your plot.

What would Detective Steve Carella, of Ed McBain's many books about the 87th precinct, do without Meyer Meyer and the other minor characters who illuminate his lively pages? And in Nelson DeMille's bestseller, *Plum Island,* Detective John Corey goes from minor character to minor character, each with his or her own life and agenda, until he finally uncovers the identity of the murderer.

Books about criminal activities usually lean heavily on secondary characters. In *Silent Witness,* Richard North Patterson's bestseller, the young attorney depends greatly on his old mentor's advice—and so do the readers—to find out necessary information of a technical nature about the murder:

Saul gave him a sour smile. "Don't you find it a little funny that we're the ones having this conversation?"

"I stopped laughing about an hour ago, Saul. When Stella Marz told me about the blood on Sam's steering wheel."

Saul's smile vanished. "There are a thousand possible explanations, my son. Even if it's hers. They can't convict on that."

"I know. But that's not enough to make me feel better."

Saul reached for the bottle, pacing himself a pre cise two inches, neat, in a tumbler.

Some secondary characters are dead before the story even starts, viz., the ghost of Hamlet's father; Mrs. Maximilian de Winters in Daphne Du Maurier's classic novel, *Rebecca;* and the writer Terry O'Neal in Olivia Goldsmith's 1996 novel *The Bestseller.*

What would playwrights have done over the years without minor characters? The curtain goes up:

BUTLER (*Dusting the furniture*): We've best get this parlour spick and span wot wif the young master comin' 'ome from the war!

MAID (*Arranging some flowers*): And 'im bringin' 'ome some French floozie he wants to marry and the missus sayin' over m'dead body and all.

Just as the playwrights did and do (and, one hopes, more subtly than the above example), so can novelists and short story writers use minor charac ters to let the readers in on who the protagonists are and what their problem is.

Homer knew the significant role minor characters could play. In *The Iliad,* the soldiers are grumbling about the war; they've been in Troy ten long years, and they want to go back home to Greece. This is the only war in history where both sides knew *exactly* what they were fighting for—Helen of Troy—but the soldiers are battle-weary and homesick. Then radiant Helen walks by. Wow! The men stare at her unbelievable beauty, then grab their weapons enthusiastically and charge back into the fight, home and hearth forgotten.

Now we have been made to believe that Helen is indeed the most beautiful creature in the world in a way that all the adjectives in the dictionary could not accomplish.

Which would convince you more of a character's goodness? Consider the following:

Old Daniel Badger seemed a cold aloof man, but actually he was quite kind and did many nice things for people in town.

Or do you prefer this:

When Daniel Badger shuffled out of the barber shop, Max growled, "Old sourpuss!"
"Yeah?" said Bill. "When my little girl took sick with cancer last year I got an anonymous check in the mail for five grand for the treatment. Saved her life. Just found out yesterday—my son works in the bank—he told me who sent it. Old man Badger! And I barely know the guy."

Of course, the second is more convincing because no conniving, manipulative writer told you about Badger; you just happened to overhear it at the barber shop.

Secondary characters can be invaluable in describing your main character's looks. The narrator of F. Scott Fitzgerald's classic, *The Great Gatsby,* is a minor player in the story, but is important in helping us *see* the people and events. Here we get our first look at the protagonist:

He smiled understandingly—much more than understandingly. It was one of those rare smiles with a quality of eternal reassurance in it, that you may come across four or five times in life. It faced—or seemed to face—the whole eternal world for an instant, and then concentrated on *you* with an irresistible prejudice in your favor. It understood you just as far as you wanted to be understood, believed in you as you would like to believe in yourself, and assured you that it had precisely the impression of you that, at your best, you hoped to convey. Precisely at that point it vanished—and I was looking at an elegant young roughneck, a year or two over thirty, whose elaborate formality of speech just missed being absurd.

The narrator in *Gatsby* also serves as sort of a Greek chorus, briefly summing up the meaning of the novel, and ending with the lovely line:

"So we beat on, boats against the current, borne back ceaselessly into the past."

In this way, a minor character can perform a valuable function for the author, subtly expressing some final thought or emotion for the reader. In my novel *Matador,* when the hero dies, a very minor character, Cascabel, a banderillero, sums up the tragedy and the heartlessness of the crowd—"the only beast in the arena," as Blasco Ibañez wrote in *Blood and Sand:*

"More and more," said Cascabel dully, the tears spilling down his face. "They kept demanding more and more—and more was his life, so he gave it to them."

Sometimes minor characters achieve a life of their own, "pad their parts," and become pivotal in the plot even to the point of altering the outcome of the story. Such a character is the oily Uriah Heep in Dickens's *David Copperfield;* the murderer in Joseph Kanon's bestseller, *Los Alamos;* and many characters in Elmore Leonard's books.

So take care with your minor characters; as factors in your story they can be *major.* Be sure to invest them with human idiosyncrasies, foibles, and agendas of their own. They can enhance your main characters, provide your plot with unanticipated twists, and let your readers know that they are in the hands of a professional writer.

❑ 23

THE PLOT THICKENS

BY BARBARA SHAPIRO

SOME WRITERS CAN SIT DOWN AND BEGIN A NOVEL WITHOUT KNOW-ing where it will end, trusting in the process to bring their story to a successful conclusion. I'm not that trusting. And I'm not that brave. I don't have the guts to begin a book until I know there *is* an end— and a middle, too. I need to have a rough outline that allows me to believe my idea might someday be transformed into a successful novel. Some writers need a working title; I need a working plot.

A substantial segment of the writing community turns its collective nose up at the mere mention of the word "plot"—particularly if that plot is devised before writing has begun. "Plot is not what novels are about," they claim. "Novels are about feelings and characters and ideas. Plot is for TV movies." Novels *are* about feelings and characters and ideas, but novels are, above all else, stories, and it is through the story that the characters' feelings and the author's ideas are revealed. A handy equation is: Story equals plot equals novel. But what exactly *is* a story?

A story is a tale with a beginning, a middle, and an end. It's a quest. Your protagonist goes after something she wants very badly— something she gets, or doesn't get, by the end. Whether it's returning to Kansas (Dorothy in *The Wizard of Oz*) or killing the witch ("Hansel and Gretel"), this journey is the story, the plot, the means by which your characters' strengths and weaknesses are unveiled, his or her lessons learned. It is the trip you and your protagonist and your reader all make together.

All human beings have the same features, yet the magic of the human race is that we all look different. The same holds true for plot. While the specifics of your plot are unique, there is an underlying structure that it shares with other stories—and it is this structure that you can use to develop your working plot.

94

Human beings have been telling stories and listening to stories as long as there have been human beings, and there is a structure to these stories. Tell the story without the right structure and risk losing your listeners. Find this structure, and your job as a novelist will be easier; you will understand your readers' expectations and be able to meet them. Follow this plot structure and add your own voice, your own words, your own creativity, and you will have a unique novel that works.

Discovering and understanding the underlying structure of the novel will help you develop your working plot even before you begin writing. It will get you moving by assuring you that you are on the right path. In my career, I have used this concept to come up with a number of tricks to help me discover where my novel is going—and to get myself going. These tricks can be translated into four exercises: (1) classical structure; (2) plot statement; (3) the disturbance; and (4) the crisis.

Step 1: Classical structure

There is a long-running argument among writers as to exactly how many different stories there are. Some say there are an infinite number, some say there are 47 or 36 or 103, and others say there is only one. I am a member of the "only one story" school. I believe this one story is the skeleton upon which almost all successful novels are hung—this story *is* the underlying structure. If I can figure out how *my* story hangs on this skeleton, I can begin to move forward. This is how the story goes:

There once was a woman who had a terrible problem enter her life (*the disturbance*). She decided that she was going to solve/get rid of her problem so she devised a plan (*goal*). But whenever she put this plan into action, everything around her worked against her (*conflicts*) until the problem had grown even worse and she seemed even further then ever from reaching her goal. At this darkest moment (*crisis*), the woman made a decision based on who she was and what she had learned in the story. Through this decision and the resulting action (*climax*), her problem was resolved (*resolution*) in either a positive (*happy ending*) or negative way (*unhappy ending*).

The first step to understanding and using story structure is to break the classic story into its component parts. The key elements are: the disturbance; the goal; the conflicts; the crisis; the climax—the sacrifice and the unconscious need filled from the backstory; and the resolution. Once this is clear to you, then you can transpose these components into your particular story. To accomplish this, ask yourself the following five questions:

What is the disturbance? Some terrible or wonderful or serendipitous event that comes into your protagonist's life, upsets her equilibrium and causes her to develop a goal that propels her through your story. A tornado, for instance.

What is the protagonist's goal? To get out of Oz and return to Kansas.

What are some of the conflicts that stand in her way? The key to creating a successful story is putting obstacles in your protagonist's path—external, internal, and interpersonal. Create opposition and frustration to force her to fall back on who she is, and what she knows, to overcome the hurdles you have created. No hurdles, no conflict, no story. Conflict is what moves your story forward and what develops your protagonist's character.

What specific crisis will she face in the end?

How will she resolve this crisis?

Once you have answered these questions, you will have the skeletal outline for a story that is the basis for almost every successful novel written, and you may find you are ready to begin. If this is the case, dive right in. Unfortunately, for me, this is not enough. I need to do a bit more.

Step 2: Plot statement
A plot statement is a one-sentence, high-concept summary of the set-up of your story. It is what you might pitch to a producer to whom you were trying to sell a movie—or to an agent to whom you are trying to sell a book. To write this statement all you need to know is your protagonist, the disturbance, his goal, and what is at stake.

"Dorothy Gale (protagonist) must find her way home (goal/stakes) after a tornado blows her into the strange land (disturbance) full of evil witches and magical wizards," is the plot statement for Frank Baum's *The Wizard of Oz*.

"Jay Gatsby (protagonist) must win back the love of Daisy Buchanan (goal) to give meaning to his meaningless life (stakes) after he buys a mansion across the water from the one in which Daisy lives (disturbance)," is the plot statement for F. Scott Fitzgerald's *The Great Gatsby*.

"Delia Grinstead (protagonist) must create a new life for herself (goal/stakes) after she impulsively walks away from her three children and long-term marriage," is the plot statement for Anne Tyler's *Ladder of Years*.

"Suki Jacobs (protagonist) must discover what really happened on the night Jonah Ward was killed (goal) before her teenage daughter is arrested for a murder she didn't commit (stakes), but that she did predict (disturbance)," is the plot statement for my latest book, *Blind Spot*.

What's the plot statement for yours?

Step 3: The disturbance

Although you already have a rough idea of what the disturbance of your story is, it is useful to make it more specific. This isn't just any disturbance: It is a particular event that begins the action of your particular story, throws your protagonist into turmoil, and forces her to devise a specific goal that will place her on the path that will lead her to *her* crisis. It is the "particular" aspect of these events that makes your story unique. To discover your disturbance—and, in many ways, your character—ask yourself the following question: "What is the worst thing that can happen to my protagonist, but will ultimately be the best thing that could happen to her?"

What does your protagonist need to learn? Her lesson is your readers' lesson: It is the theme of your book. What life lesson do you want to teach? Once you have answered these questions, you will be able to develop a character whose story resonates to your theme—a character whose backstory reflects what she needs to learn and whose journey within your story teaches it to her.

The disturbance in my second book, *Blameless,* occurs when Dr. Diana Marcus' patient, James Hutchins, commits suicide. It is the worst thing for Diana because it tears her life apart:

She begins to question herself as a psychologist.

A wrongful death and malpractice suit is filed by the Hutchins family, jeopardizing Diana's teaching position and practice as a psychologist.

She is publicly humiliated when the media disclose her unprofessional behavior.

Her husband Craig becomes suspicious, and their marriage is jeopardized.

Diana's inability to save James mirrors her childhood tragedy when she was unable to save her younger sister, and taps into all of her deepest insecurities.

This all sounds pretty terrible, but, like life, it's not all bad. James' death is also a good thing for Diana, because it forces her to face her tragic flaws and try to correct them:

She acknowledges her professional mistakes, making her a better therapist.
She and her husband rediscover their relationship.
She learns that she cannot cure everyone.
She forgives herself for her sister's death.

In order to come up with this disturbance, I had to delve deeply into Diana's present life and develop a past for her that would create a character who needed to learn this lesson. This process deepened both Diana and my plot.

How is your disturbance the best and worst thing that could happen to your protagonist?

Step 4: The crisis

The crisis of your novel is the major decision point for your protagonist. It reveals who she really is and what the experience has taught her. Its seeds are in the disturbance, and all the conflicts lead inexorably to this specific crisis, this specific decision and its specific resolution. But the decision can't be a simple one. If the choice is too easy, your reader will be unsatisfied. Therefore, you must create a decision that has both good and bad consequences, that has both gains and sacrifices, so that your reader will not know which choice your protagonist will make. To determine the crisis in your story, ask yourself the following questions:

What is the event that precipitates the crisis?
What is the decision the protagonist must make?
What does she learn in the decision-making process?
How does the decision reveal who she is (the backstory)?
How does her decision reflect on what happened to her in this story?
What does she lose in the decision (the sacrifice)?
What does she gain from her decision?
How is the decision turned into action?
How does the decision resolve the plot?

When I was developing the plot for *Blameless,* I asked myself the above questions and came up with these answers:

James shows up at Diana's apartment and holds a gun to his head; he tells her that if she tells him not to shoot himself, he won't.

Diana must decide whether to stop James from killing himself.

Diana learns that everyone cannot be saved, that she cannot save everyone, and she is not responsible for James.

Diana overcomes her belief that it is her mission to save everyone, realizes that she is not responsible for her sister's death, and ultimately forgives herself for it.

Diana struggles with her need to control her career, her marriage, her patients, and herself.

James will be dead, and she will be responsible for not stopping him.

A dangerous murderer will be dead, and Diana will remove the threat to herself and her unborn baby.

Diana doesn't say anything, and James blows his brains out.

James really is dead, and Diana is cleared of his murder.

So if you aren't as brave a writer as you'd like to be—or if that mythical muse just won't appear—try these four exercises. You just might discover that you aren't that cowardly after all. And that novel might just get finished.

❑ 24

Seven Keys to Effective Dialogue

By Martin Naparsteck

Good dialogue makes characters in a story sound like real people talking, yet no one I know talks like a character, even in the best novels. This seeming contradiction can be explained by examining the seven attributes of good dialogue.

1. **Every voice is unique.**

In my novel *A Hero's Welcome,* Culver and Mabel talk:

> "Hi," she said softly.
> "Hi."
> "You feeling better?"
> "Yeah."
> "You had too much to drink."
> "I know."
> "Maybe you should go back to your room and sleep it off."
> "I would miss the party."
> "It's not much fun anyway."
> "Maybe I should have some coffee?"

Although both characters are products of middle-class, Eastern America, they are individuals, and I tried to keep that in mind. I tried to reflect Mabel's caring for Culver's condition and to capture Culver's condition—near-drunkenness—and a desire to continue the conversation. She speaks in longer sentences and controls the subject; he often speaks in incomplete sentences and only in response to her verbal initiatives. The differences may be subtle, but readers are unlikely to confuse who is speaking, despite the lack of attribution. Any time you have two or more characters speaking, make their rhythms differ. Some can speak staccato, some can speak with flow, some can use profanity, others can use big and fancy words. Assign a different voice to each character.

2. **Don't make speeches.**

Unless your character is running for president or teaching a literature class or is pompous, don't let him rant on for more than three or four sentences without being interrupted by another character. In my novel *War Song,* Fernandez says,

"In case you never heard, war is hell. War is hell. Some people got to get killed so others can live in freedom. I know that might sound corny to you, but if enough people believed it this world would be a lot better off."

Then he's cut off by a character who finds his little speech pompous.

In real life we don't usually tolerate being lectured at. Sitting in a classroom or in a church, we might have to, but not always even then. We prefer a chance to respond. In a bar or a living room, we're likely to respond with our own opinion before the speaker gets too carried away. Your characters should display the same intolerance.

3. Authors are not tape recorders.

In "Deep in the Hole," a short story published in *Aethlon,* I have Mickey, a member of his college's baseball team, say to his literature professor, "I have a game on Wednesday and I wonder if it would be all right if I skipped the class. I can read all the. . . ." Because it's a highly autobiographical story, and because I was tremendously awkward in speech in the late 60's, I feel certain the real-life dialogue this bit of fiction is based upon went something like this: "Eh, I have, eh, you know, a game on Wednesday and I, eh, wonder, would it be, eh, all right. . . ." All those "ehs" and that "you know" may be O.K. for a sentence or two, but for a whole story it would not only annoy most readers, but would distract them to the point of losing them. A fiction writer is not a journalist, and he has no obligation to act like a stenographer or a tape recorder. The idea is to capture both the essence and the underlying emotion of what's said, not to reproduce a transcript.

4. People tell more little lies than big ones.

Probably most people who commit a murder will tell the police they didn't do it. Big lies are part of life and should be part of stories. But most of us don't get that much opportunity to tell big lies (most of us will never be asked by the police if we committed a murder). But smaller lies are part of our everyday conversations. In my *Ellery Queen* short story, "The 9:13," two men are alone in a train station, and one tells the other his name is Thunder, but two pages later he says:

"My name ain't Thunder."
"What?"
"My name ain't Thunder."
"No?"
"No, it ain't."
"Oh."
"Ain't you curious what it is?"
Joe stammered a bit.
"It's Eddie."
"I—I see."
"Ain't you curious why I told ya it was Thunder?"
"Yes, I suppose so. Why?"
"Why what?"
"Why did you tell me your name was Thunder?"
"I ain't gonna tell ya."

Eddie's lie has no real purpose, but the fact that he chose to tell this particular lie in this particular manner reveals something about his character. Not everyone's playfulness is malevolent. Have your characters lie about small things in a manner that reveals who they are.

5. Dialogue is made up of monologues.

When someone is speaking to you, consider how you typically devote part of your attention to what she's saying, but you are also focused on what you're going to say when it's your turn to speak. In "Getting Shot," a short story of mine published in *Mississippi Review,* a soldier who has been wounded in Vietnam is told by his lieutenant:

"You're gonna get a Purple Heart out of this. What do you think about that?"
"Not much." I'm smiling like a teenage kid just got his first lay, and the Louey, he knows it.
He pats my right shoulder. "Sure, sure." He adds, "Sure."

Although the narrator responds to what the lieutenant has said, he clearly has something else on his mind, part of which reflects the false bravado he assumes the situation requires. The lieutenant, while detecting that and playing along, uses a bit of staccato speech to end that portion of the conversation so he can move on to other things.

6. Every word in dialogue represents a choice.

Every word you ever spoke in your life represented a choice. You could have chosen to be silent. You could have used another word. Consider this bit of dialogue (from *War Song*): "Don't you wanna go home?" It could have been, "Do you not desire to return to your home?" Or, "Have you no desire to go home again?" The choice is based on who the character is. One test that works for me is to write the same bit of dialogue a dozen or more times, at least in my mind, sometimes on my computer screen, and then, only then, to decide which is most appropriate for a particular character under this particular circumstance. Chances are the first words you choose are not the ones that best reflect the character. As with all other writing, nothing improves dialogue like rewriting.

7. All dialogue should reveal character and/or advance plot.

I have never included a piece of dialogue like this in any story I've ever written (thank the great muse):

> He told me how to get to Salt Lake City from Logan.
> "Take Valley West Highway until you come to the Interstate 15 interchange and proceed on to the interstate, going south, for about 90 miles, and when you come to the exit marked 600 north, get off and follow the signs to downtown." Thanks to his accurate and detailed directions I found my way to Salt Lake City safely.

Any dialogue that simply exchanges information between characters (who was the 26th president of the U.S., what does antidisestablishment mean) is static. Stories need to move forward. Just as you never need to say the character walked to the other side of the room (unless it's the first time this guy has walked in 10 years), you never need to reveal how someone learned the directions from here to there. Just assume, as your readers will, that there are some bits of conversation we know take place in real life but which are far too boring to include in a story.

But do let a character say, "You're fired," even though it reveals a bit of information the listener didn't know, because it changes the life of the poor guy. If the dialogue doesn't change the listener's life, no matter how slightly, or help us better understand who the speaker is, leave it out.

Each of the first six examples I've given help make the speakers sound like real people. But only the seventh one is likely to reflect accurately a real bit of conversation. And that's the one you should never use.

❏ 25

THE NOVEL—YOU DO IT YOUR WAY, I'LL DO IT MINE

BY DOROTHY UHNAK

I ADMIT TO BEING AN ECCENTRIC WRITER. I'VE YET TO MEET ANOTHER writer who works as I do, so don't consider this an instructional article. But do take from it whatever methods will serve you best. And don't permit *anyone* to tell you that *your method* of working is wrong. It is the work itself that counts.

Years ago, as a fairly accomplished knitter, I undertook to copy a very complicated Irish-fisherman quilt. It contained at least seven different patterns: twists and cables and popcorns and secret family weaves. Looking at the picture of the quilt in question, I stopped cold. Never, not in a million years, could I do this. It then occurred to me, you don't knit a whole quilt all at once. One stitch at a time; one line at a time; one pattern at a time.

Maybe this isn't a very good analogy for writing a novel, but after all, we do write one word at a time, one line at a time, one paragraph and one page at a time. The unifying force of all the pieces, in the novel as in the quilt, draws the whole thing together.

The unifying force in my novels has always been the characters. I care about their growth or regression, about the circumstances that change them and move them through the story, much as life molds and shapes each of us.

What I must know, absolutely, before I start a novel is who each character is at the beginning and who he will be at the end. I'm never really sure how the characters will get from the first place to the last, but I am positive where they will end up.

The Ryer Avenue Story (St. Martin's Press, 1993) had six characters not of equal importance but essential, since the story belonged to all of them. We meet them as children, 11- and 12-year-olds. What I knew about them was simple. They lived and played together on the Avenue

104

in the Bronx where I grew up. In middle age, all five boys and one girl were successful, accomplished people, some more than others. They moved in life from when we meet them on the street of a cold snowy night until they are confronted in mid-life with a problem set in motion when they were kids.

The first thing I had to know about these people was what they looked and sounded like. My characters have to be named absolutely on target. Megan Magee could not be Mary Reardon; Danny DeAngelo could not be Bobby Russelli. They become as real to me as people I actually know and speak to day after day. (You wouldn't want to address your best friend Sally as Luanne, would you?)

Here is my first eccentricity: I work on a standard Hermes 45 typewriter. I have three machines carefully stored away—don't ask how one gets ribbons—you remember ribbons? No? Well, anyway—I don't go near my heavy, trusty machine for quite a while.

First, I research as meticulously as possible in order to know the world in which my people live. For Ryer Avenue, I used the neighborhood where I was born and raised. But I never did go to their Catholic school (St. Simon Stock in the Bronx). Some of my friends did, and I absorbed their stories, peeked through their school windows and stole into their church when I was a child. I didn't know why I did these things until years later: It was material I would need to draw on one day.

To describe accurately a scene in the death camps of WWII, I read almost more than my mind could hold of horror stories. There is no way I could write substantially about any of this. But I had the good fortune of talking with an older friend who told me he had been one of the young American lieutenants in the advanced group entering the death camps and opening them up for our troops. He lent me that part of his life in one long, dark, horrible conversation, during which we left our cake uneaten and the coffee cold. He gave me this part of himself to use in my novel, and later when he read the book, he said I had made him nicer than he really was, but I don't think so.

In my Ryer Avenue story, one of my characters becomes a big shot in the movie industry; one a leading light of the church; one a promising, rising politician; the woman becomes a psychiatrist. Each area had to be researched. If Gene O'Brien was to work in the Vatican, I needed to be very sure I knew what his physical surroundings would be and what his daily routines would encompass. I consult my research notes until I'm thoroughly familiar with the material and can place my people in an environment formerly alien to me.

Before setting one word on paper, I had to visualize scenes that would define each character as a child: Megan in the classroom; Dante in his father's shoe repair shop; Eugene at church; Willie losing himself in the world of movies. Since the novel begins in the childhood of my characters, I walked around with each kid in my head, one at a time. I needed to know how the characters looked, sounded, acted, reacted, what they showed of themselves and what they hid. Only then did I sit, fingers on the trusty faithful noisy Hermes 45 keys, and pound out the chapters, one at a time.

I have the whole scene completely worked out before I begin to work: no notes (except for background research), just a scene that comes as I walk, rest, stare blankly at TV, even as I read a book by another writer. When I place the character in the scene, he or she knows how to move, what to think, what to say. By this time, I can hear each individual voice. No character sounds exactly like any other. They may all use certain phrases, expressions, and expletives, but each voice belongs only to the speaker.

Sometimes the scene I'm describing leads directly to the next scene, sometimes not. There are times when I get a whole chapter down on paper; other times, only two or three pages. And then I walk away. I've been known to work for fifteen minutes at a stretch or for ten hours. It is the story going on in my head that dictates my working hours. No nine-to-five for me!

The creative work for me is not done at the typewriter. It's done through all the long hours of listening, imagining, getting to know and trust my characters as they move through their lives toward the resolutions I know they must reach. Sometimes, I am surprised by the routes they take, the diversions they encounter.

One time when I was working on a television script, my producer called to ask about Act Five. I told him it was terrific; worked out exactly right. He asked me to send it to him. One problem—I hadn't typed it. I buckled down and did the annoying job of putting words to paper.

I don't wait for "inspiration," unless inspiration can be described as continuous, uninterrupted thinking, living with the story, and the fictional people who are taking on their own lives. With this strange method of working, I accomplish more than if I sat down at a given hour and stayed put for four or five hours, without knowing what I was going to write. I usually wait until the scene, chapter, or event is practically bursting from my head—then I form the scene into words on paper.

This process occurs during the first draft. I do go over every page before beginning a new session. I make my notations; slash things out and cram things in. I usually try to stop work when I have a strong feeling about what will come next; save it, walk it, think it, let it have free flow until the pictures, words, and actions must absolutely be on paper.

My working habits on the second draft are more typical of other writers', and I work long hours. I change, rewrite, or leave untouched pages and pages of the manuscript. I see where a character has taken over and where he or she shouldn't have; where I have interfered when I shouldn't have.

In the second draft, sometimes incredible moments happen when I find myself reworking something I hadn't intended to, and the descriptions and conversations soar. I feel myself to be the medium by which the story is told. I just write what I feel I'm supposed to write. Magic. Sometimes it's absolutely wonderful. (Sometimes it isn't!)

In my novel, *Codes of Betrayal,* a very strange thing happened. My heroine, Laura Santangelo, comes into her apartment, stunned and angry to find one Richie Ventura sitting on her couch, his feet up on her coffee table. The chapter ends with Laura saying, "Richie, what the hell are *you* doing here?"

I didn't know what he was doing there. I hadn't a clue. I just instinctively felt his presence was absolutely necessary. I had to let my mind flow to find the logic for the scene. I would not invent some fraudulent reason just because I liked the slam-bang last sentence in that chapter. I skipped ahead, did a few chapters, and suddenly it came to me: Richie was in her apartment for a very specific reason, and he had a very valid excuse to offer Laura. I backtracked and let them work it out.

One thing my publisher asked me to do with that novel was to give him an outline of the last half of the book. I told him it was impossible; the work would proceed step by step from what came before. He insisted; I wrote an outline. It was cold, bloodless, meaningless. The characters were sticks with wooden personalities. If I had followed it, my book would have sunk. My publisher returned the outline and said, "I guess you don't do outlines."

A very strange thing happens when I finish a book. I send it off to a woman who puts it on her computer to get it into wonderful-looking condition. It goes to the publisher who loves it and makes a few suggestions here and there. Then I handle the three-hundred-plus-page manuscript, all neatly and professionally typed, and have the eerie feeling that I didn't write this book, that I didn't put in any *real* time. I didn't work hours and days in my little workroom. I feel that I started at the sea down the hill from our house; I walked the dogs and the cats; I stared at the television; I knitted; I read books. When and how did that book get written?

At that point, I have to just let the whole thing go. It's out of my hands. It belongs to others now. I need to get free of all emotion about it. Yes, I did write it; yes, I did work hard on it; yes, I did agonize and complain and question myself and my talent and the worth of the story itself. Yes, I did actually write it, if in my own particularly eccentric way.

I've knitted only one Irish quilt, but I have written ten novels, so I guess I just keep at it, one word at a time, one line at a time, one paragraph, one page and chapter at a time.

The big problem now is the very beginning of the search for the next group of people, floating around, trying to get my attention. Or rather, trying to take over my life, body, and soul. You do it your way, I'll do it mine.

❑ 26

BRINGING YOUR
SETTINGS TO LIFE

BY MOIRA ALLEN

GOD, IT'S BEEN SAID, IS IN THE DETAILS. SO, TOO, IS MUCH OF THE work of a writer. Too little detail leaves your characters wandering through the narrative equivalent of an empty stage. Too much, and you risk the tombstone effect: gray blocks of description that tempt the reader to skip and skim, looking for action.

To set your stage properly, it's important to choose the most appropriate, vivid details possible. It's equally important, however, to present those details in a way that will engage your reader. The following techniques can help you keep your reader focused both on your descriptions and on your story.

Reveal setting through motion

Few people walk into a room and instantly absorb every detail of their surroundings. Often, however, we expect the reader to do just that by introducing a scene with a block of text that completely halts the action.

As an alternative, let your description unfold as the character moves through the scene. Ask yourself which details your character would notice immediately and which might register more slowly.

Suppose, for example, that your heroine, a secretary of humble origins, has just entered the mansion of a millionaire. What would she notice first? How would she react to her surroundings?

Let her observe how soft the rich Persian carpet feels underfoot, how it muffles her footfalls, how she's almost tempted to remove her shoes. Does she recognize any of the masterpieces on the walls, or do they make her feel even more out of place because she doesn't know a Cezanne from a Monet? Don't tell readers the sofa is soft until she actually sinks into it. Let her smell the leather cushions, mingling with the fragrance of hothouse flowers filling a cut-crystal vase on a nearby table.

Use active verbs to set the scene—but use them wisely. Don't inform the reader that "a heavy marble table dominated the room"; force your character to detour around it. Instead of explaining that "light glittered and danced from the crystal chandelier," let your character blink, dazzled by the prismatic display.

"Walking through" a description breaks the details into small nuggets and scatters them throughout the scene, so the reader never feels overwhelmed or bored. However, doing this raises another important question: Which character should do the walking?

Reveal setting through a character's level of experience

What your character knows will directly influence what she sees. Suppose, for example, that your humble secretary really doesn't know a Cezanne from a Monet, or whether the carpet is Persian or Moroccan. Perhaps she doesn't even know whether it's wool or polyester. If these details are important, how can you convey them?

You could, of course, introduce the haughty owner of the mansion and allow him to reveal your heroine's ignorance. Or, you could write the scene entirely from the owner's perspective. Keep in mind, however, that different characters will perceive the same surroundings in very different ways, depending on the character's familiarity (or lack of familiarity) with the setting.

Imagine, for example, that you're describing a stretch of windswept coastline from the perspective of a fisherman who has spent his entire life in the region. What would he notice? From the color of the sky or changes in the wind, he might make deductions about the next day's weather and sailing conditions. When he observes seabirds wheeling against the clouds, they are not "gulls" to him, but terns and gannets and petrels—easily identified by his experienced eye by the shape of their wings or pattern of their flight.

Equally important, however, are the things he might not notice. Being so familiar with the area, he might pay little attention to the fantastic shapes of the rocks, or the gnarled driftwood littering the beach. He hardly notices the bite of the wind through his cable-knit sweater or the tang of salt in the air, and he's oblivious to the stench of rotting kelp-mats that have washed ashore.

Now suppose an accountant from the big city is trudging along that same beach. Bundled up in the latest Northwest Outfitters down jacket, he's still shivering—and can't imagine why the fisherman beside him, who isn't even wearing a sweater, isn't freezing to death. He keeps stumbling over half-buried pieces of driftwood and knows that the sand is ruining his Italian loafers. From the way the waves pound against the beach, it's obvious a major storm is brewing. The very thought of bad weather makes him nauseous, as does the stench of rotting sea-weed (he doesn't think of it as "kelp") and dead fish.

Each of these characters' perceptions of the beach will be profoundly influenced by his background and experience. Bear in mind, however, that "familiar" doesn't imply a positive outlook, nor is the "unfamiliar" necessarily synonymous with "negative." Your accountant may, in fact, regard the beach as an idyllic vacation spot—rugged, romantic, iso-lated, just the place to make him feel as if he's really getting in touch with nature and leaving the rat race of the city behind. The fisherman, on the other hand, may loathe the ocean, feeling trapped by the whims of the wind and weather that he must battle each day for his livelihood. This bring us to the next point.

Reveal setting through the mood of your character

What we see is profoundly influenced by what we feel. The same should be true for our characters. Filtering a scene through a charac-ter's feelings can profoundly influence what the reader "sees." Two characters, for example, could "see" exactly the same setting, yet per-ceive it in opposite ways.

Suppose, for example, that a motorist has strolled a short distance into an archtypical stretch of British moorland. Across a stretch of blossoming gorse, she sees ruins of some ancient watch tower, now little more than a jumble of stones crowning the next hill (or "tor," as her guidebook puts it).

The temptation is irresistible. Flicking at dandelion heads with her walking stick, our intrepid motorist hikes up the slope, breathing in the scents of grass and clover, admiring the lichen patterns on the gray granite boulders. At last, warmed by the sun and her exertions, she leans back against a rock and watches clouds drift overhead like fuzzy sheep herded by a gentle wind. A falcon shrills from a nearby hollow, its cry a pleasant reminder of how far she has come from the roar and rumble of the city.

A pleasant picture? By now, your reader might be considering travel arrangements to Dartmoor. But what if your motorist is in a different mood? What if her car has broken down, and she has been unable to find help? Perhaps she started across the moor because she thought she saw a house or hut, but was dismayed to find that it was only a ruin, and a creepy one at that. The tower's scattered stones, half-buried in weeds and tangled grasses, remind her of grave markers worn faceless with time. Its silent emptiness speaks of secrets, of desolation that welcomes no trespassers. Though the sun is high, scudding clouds cast a pall over the landscape, and the eerie, lonesome cry of some unseen bird reminds her just how far she has strayed from civilization.

When this traveler looks at the gorse, she sees thorns, not blossoms. When she looks at clouds, she sees no faithful shapes, only the threat of rain to add to her troubles. She wants to get out of this situation, while your reader is on the edge of his seat, expecting something far worse than a creepy ruin to appear on this character's horizon!

Reveal setting through the senses

A character's familiarity with a setting and his or her emotional perception of that setting will influence and be influenced by the senses. Our stranded motorist, for example, may not notice the fragrance of the grass, but she will be keenly aware of the cold wind. Our accountant notices odors the fisherman ignores, while the fisherman detects subtle variations in the color of the sky that are meaningless to the accountant.

Different sensory details evoke different reactions. For example, people process visual information primarily at the cognitive level: We make decisions and take action based on what we see. When writers describe a scene in terms of visual observations, they are appealing to the reader's intellect.

Emotions, however, are often affected by what we hear. Think of the effects of a favorite piece of music, the sound of a person's voice, the whistle of a train. In conversation, tone of voice is a more reliable indicator of mood and meaning than words alone. Sounds can make us shudder, shiver, jump—or relax and smile. Scenes that include sounds—fingers scraping a blackboard, the distant baying of a hound—are more likely to evoke an emotional response.

Smell has the remarkable ability to evoke memories. While not everyone is taken back to childhood by "the smell of bread baking," we all have olfactory memories that can trigger a scene, a recollection of an event or person. Think of someone's perfume, the smell of new-car leather, the odor of wet dog. Then describe that smell so that your reader is *there*.

Touch evokes a sensory response. Romance writers know they'll get more mileage out of writing "he trailed his fingertips along her spine" than "he whispered sweet nothings in her ear." The first can evoke a shiver of shared sensory pleasure; the second is just words. Let your reader feel the silkiness of a cat's fur, the roughness of castle stones, the prickly warmth of your hero's flannel shirt beneath his lover's fingertips. Let your heroine's feet ache, let the wind raise goosebumps on her flesh, let the gorse thorns draw blood.

Finally, there is taste, which is closely related to smell in its ability to evoke memories. Taste, however, is perhaps the most difficult to incorporate into a setting; often, it simply doesn't belong there. Your heroine isn't going to start licking the castle stones, and it isn't time for lunch. "Taste" images should be used sparingly and appropriately, or you may end up with a character who seems more preoccupied with food than with the issues of the story.

The goal of description is to create a well-designed set that provides the perfect background for your characters—a setting that *stays* in the background, without overwhelming the scene or interrupting the story. In real life, we explore our surroundings through our actions, experience them through our senses, understand (or fail to understand) them through our knowledge and experience, and respond to them through our emotions. When your characters do the same, readers will keep turning pages—and not just because they're waiting for something interesting to happen!

❑ 27

TURNING YOUR EXPERIENCE INTO FICTION

BY EDWARD HOWER

"THAT WOULD MAKE A GOOD STORY—YOU OUGHT TO WRITE IT!" HOW many times have you heard people say this, after you've told them about some interesting experience?

But if you're like me, you may not *want* to write directly about yourself, except perhaps in your private journal. This doesn't mean, however, that your own life can't be used as material for fiction. Using your own experiences as starting places for stories or novels gives your work an authenticity that made-up adventures may lack. A great many fiction writers have mined their own pasts—some of them over and over throughout their careers.

Advantages of starting with yourself

Writing stories that are similar to real-life occurrences allows you to relive and to re-examine your life. In fiction, you can explore all the might-have-beens of your past. You can experience the loves that didn't quite happen but that might have proved blissful or (more interestingly) disastrous in tragic or amusing ways. You can delve into your worst fears, describing what might have happened if you hadn't been so careful about trusting strangers or about avoiding life's dark alleys.

And by creating characters similar to yourself and to people you've known, you can get a perspective on your past that couldn't come from direct, analytic examination. One of the most gratifying experiences I had in writing my last novel was getting to know my family all over again in ways I'd never previously considered. Some anger resurfaced, but so did a lot of compassion. And I finally got a kind of closure on my sometimes painful childhood that had eluded me before.

I've emphasized writing about the past here rather than about the

114

present. This is because I think it's a lot more productive to deal with material from which you have psychic distance.

Selective memory can produce interesting, emotionally charged material for fiction. Recent events, however, are hard to deal with creatively. Immediate reality intrudes, and issues unresolved in life resist resolution in fiction.

Searching your life

Here's an exercise I used while I was writing my semi-autobiographical novel, *Night Train Blues*. I've frequently given the exercise to students in my creative writing workshops, too. It's designed to help retrieve buried memories and then transform them into usable images, characters, and episodes for stories or longer fiction.

First, decide on a period in your life you'd like to write about. A year in your past in which emotionally intense experiences happened is often the best one. This doesn't mean that the events need to be melodramatic. Small traumas and triumphs often make the best material for fiction, especially if they involve people you've had strong feelings about. Events that caused you to change your attitude toward yourself and other people are especially good. For this reason, many writers choose a period from childhood or adolescence—the times of many emotional changes.

Start the exercise in a quiet place, alone. Get comfortable, close your eyes, and take slow deep breaths. Now imagine yourself going home during the time period you've chosen. Picture yourself approaching the place where you lived. Imagine entering it. What do you see . . . hear . . . smell? Go into the next room. What's there? Now go into the room in which you kept your personal possessions. Stand in the middle of the floor and look around. What do you see . . . hear . . . smell? Now go to some object that was especially precious to you. Hold it. Feel it. Turn it around. Get to know it again with as many senses as possible. Then ask yourself: Why did I choose this object?

As soon as you're ready, open your eyes and start writing as fast as you can. First describe the object in great detail. If you want to discuss people and events associated with it, that's fine, too. Finally, write about the object's importance to you. You might give yourself ten to fifteen minutes for the entire exercise. Don't edit what you write. Don't even pause to look back over it—fill as much paper as you can. If you write fast, you'll fill at least a page, probably more.

When I did this exercise, the object I found was an old wooden radio with a cloth dial and an orange light that glowed behind it. I mentally ran my fingers over its smooth, rounded surfaces. I put my nose up to it and smelled the dusty cloth warmed by the pale bulb behind it. I twisted the dial, and listened to my favorite childhood stations.

Thinking about the radio's meaning for me, I remembered the warm relationship I'd had with the person who gave it to me. The radio also re-acquainted me with country songs I later came to associate with an important character in my novel, my young hero's wandering older brother. So I gave my fictional narrator a radio similar to the one I'd had, and I let him find solace in its music, too.

My students have also come up with radios given to them by important people in their lives. Dolls and stuffed animals, sports equipment, pictures, china figurines, tools, articles of clothing—all have been highly evocative objects that eventually radiated emotions not only for the writers but for their fictional characters as well. Cars, records, and clothes were important items for people returning to adolescence. Each freshly-recalled object resonated with feelings about rebellion, first love, and newfound freedoms.

Transforming truth into fiction

Now it's time to turn this object into the central image of a story or novel chapter. Write "If this were fiction . . ." at the top of a page. Give yourself a different name. You are now a fictional character, one who resembles you but who will gradually develop his or her own personality as you continue working.

Then jot down some answers to these questions:

Character development
1. What does the choice of this object tell about the character (A—"you") who chose it?
   • Who is A? Describe this person quickly.

2. Imagine that another character (B) gave A the object.
   • Who is B? Describe B quickly.
   • What is B's relationship to A?

3. Imagine that yet another character (C) wants the object.
   • Who is C? Describe C quickly.
   • What is C's relationship to B and A?

When trying to imagine B and C, you might choose people from your own life or people like them who might have given you the object or might have coveted it. Characters often come from composites of several people you knew—the physical attributes of one person, the voice of another, the sense of humor or the mannerisms of another.

One way to get to know characters not modeled after yourself is to start the visualization exercise again, this time treating someone you knew as you did the object in the previous exercise. Follow the person around in your visualization, observing and listening closely. Then write a fast page or two about what you discovered.

Another good way to understand a character is to make lists of his or her attributes and preferences. Jot down his or her favorite clothes, food, TV show, brand of car, breed of dog, film hero, period in history, childhood memory, and so forth. Say what religious, political, and ethical beliefs the character has. Expand the list until you feel you know as much about this fictional person as you do about your best friend. You may not use much of this material in the actual story, but it gives you the background of the character that you need in order to write with authority.

Plot development

The treasured object can give you some ideas about what storyline to follow. Try answering these questions:

1. **A and the object**
   - Why does A treasure it? What will A do with it?
   - What problems might result from his having it?
2. **B and the object**
   - Where did B get the object? Why did B give it to A?
   - What problems might result from B giving it to A?
3. **C and the object**
   - Why does C want the object?
   - What problems might result from C trying to get it?

All plots involve conflicts—thus the emphasis on problems. Once you've listed some conflicts, choose one that interests you and try answering some more questions:

1. What events might foreshadow this conflict?
2. What dramatic action might result from this conflict?
3. How might the conflict be resolved?

By this time, you've probably discovered that although the story has ostensibly been about an object, it's really about people. One is a central character who probably resembles you in some ways, and one or more other characters are based—closely or loosely, it doesn't matter—on people you've known.

Deciding on a setting

To become familiar with your fictional locale, try closing your eyes and visualizing the place where you found the object in the original exercise. Observe the details of the room, the sounds you hear from the other rooms, and the view from the windows. Then, as if you were a bird, fly out a window to observe the neighborhood, the town or city, the county or region. Pay attention to details—the clothes people are wearing, the kinds of cars in the streets, the signs in shop windows. Smell the smells. Listen to the sounds of life. Feel the energy given off by ball parks, bars, beaches, playgrounds, political rallies. After you've flown around for a while, return to your region . . . neighborhood . . . dwelling . . . and room—for a last look-around.

Then start writing as fast as you can about things you've discovered on your journey. You might want to draw a quick map with concentric circles radiating out from your own small world. You don't need to include everything you found—this isn't a memory test. But do go into detail about discoveries that stand out sharply. Be aware that the best details of a setting give off strong emotions, providing atmosphere for your characters to move around in. The way they respond to their environment will help define who they are and what they do.

Development of a theme

To get a grip on the story's meaning, it will be helpful to go back to the treasured object at least one more time and answer these questions:

1. How does the object resemble
   - You
   - character A
   - character B and/or C

2. What effect does the object have on the relationship
   - between A and B
   - between B and C
   - between A and C

Again, you'll probably discover that whatever your story means, it has to do with people developing relationships with each other, entering into conflicts, and trying to find resolutions to them. The treasured object may fade in importance by the time you've finished the story's last draft. But it will have served its purpose.

Truth and invention

What if the characters and plot of your fiction closely resemble real people and/or events that have actually occurred? Does it matter?

I don't think it does. If you use the *techniques* of fiction-writing—characterization, plot, conflict, dialogue, description, and so on—then what you'll have at the end will be fiction, regardless of its source.

But you may still find that similarities between your life and your fiction inhibit your creative writing. You might also worry that readers who know you could be disturbed by what you write. In this case, you can do what a great many authors have done throughout history (sometimes on the advice of their attorneys)—make alterations in their fiction to avoid resemblances to actual people, places, and events.

• With characters, change one or more of these attributes: size, shape, hair color, accent, nationality, clothes
• Change the story's setting to a different region
• Move the story backward or forward in time

Having made these changes, you'll probably have to change other details of the fictional work in order to fit in the new material. This in itself can become part of the creative process, helping you to imagine more and remember less. At the end, even those who know you best may not be clear about what you've recalled and what you've made up. And you may not be sure, yourself.

If this happens, you may be certain you've moved from autobiography to fiction—one of the most interesting and satisfying ways in which your writing can develop.

□ 28

DIALOGUE AND CHARACTERIZATION

BY MAYA KAATHRYN BOHNHOFF

"SHOW, DON'T TELL" IS ONE OF THE FIRST RULES OF THE FICTIONAL road, yet one of the hardest to master. How do you show the reader your protagonist is strong-minded to the point of being argumentative or that your heroine tends to bite off more than she can chew? Yes, you could just *say* it: "Justin was strong-minded to the point of being argumentative." "Matilda had a tendency to bite off more than she could chew." But these statements are meaningless if Justin doesn't insist on his own way of doing things or Matilda doesn't constantly try to overreach her abilities.

Before you can either tell or show the reader anything about your characters, you must know them yourself: their history, their educational level, their loves and hates and foibles. You must know how they feel about life, the universe, everything.

The puppet master

Knowing these things, you must be able to portray your characters as individuals, which means that they should be distinctive. Further, the reader should never see the "strings" by which you, the writer, are manipulating the characters. Your heroine is strong-willed, savvy self-assured . . . until a scene requires her to whine and grovel. So she whines and grovels. You are playing (evil laughter) the puppet master.

Like a real human being, a fictional character must seem to be the product of both nature and nurture. Some of the best moments of high drama, in real life and in literature, occur when flawed human beings do incredible things. By having a character's flaws imposed from *outside* the story by the (evil laughter) puppet master, you rob yourself and your reader of this drama.

If you really *need* this character to whine and grovel at this point, let the weakness come from *inside,* and show the reader the genesis of

120

that weakness. Perhaps you can have your strong-willed, savvy, young protagonist be weakened by grief over the loss of a loved one. This weakness is contrary to her self-image, which in turn makes her angry at herself and the universe, and results in guilt. These forces can make a normally rock-solid personality resemble gelatin. This character's greatest struggle may be to rediscover herself, and she may be less than consistent as she goes about it.

"I'm wounded!" she said lightly.

Dialogue is, at once, one of the most essential tools of characterization and one of the easiest ways to undermine it.

The title line of this section was in a manuscript I was given at a writer's conference some years back. In the context of this story, the coupling of this exclamation with an inappropriate modifier suggested that the speaker had ceased to have a human appreciation of pain. Since this was not the case, it made the narrative voice (and hence the writer) seem unreliable.

"You're so smart!" he snorted wryly.

They call it "said-book-ism": People *snort* and *exhort* when perhaps they ought to just *say* something. Snorts are fine once in a while, but unwatched, they proliferate like March hares.

A close companion of said-book-ism is "adverbitis," which can affect both dialogue and action. Mark Twain is supposed to have said, "If you see an adverb, kill it." Extreme, but some stories have led me to suggest that if the writer cut about three-quarters of the adverbs, the manuscript would improve dramatically.

In the kitchen, he found Constance preparing their meal. He watched her QUIETLY. He found that he was still anxious and closed his eyes TIGHTLY and sighed LOUDLY.

Constance jumped. "Jerrod!" she cried ANXIOUSLY.

"I'm sorry, Constance." Jerrod smiled NERVOUSLY.

The adverbs here disrupt the dialogue and produce shallow characterization. We know these people are nervous or anxious, but couched in weak adverbs instead of strong verbs their anxiety is barely felt.

Here's the same passage, reworded:

Constance was in the kitchen preparing a simple meal. He watched her in silence for a moment, anxiety digging pitons into the wall of his stomach. What he meant as a cleansing breath came out as a melodramatic sigh.

Constance jumped and turned to face him. "Jerrod!"
His smile dried and set on his lips. "I'm sorry, Constance."

Using mountain-climbing gear to evoke a mental image of anxiety for the reader conveys much more than "he said anxiously." It's through dialogue, thought, and action that your reader knows your characters and gauges their feelings. If these essentials are not fully formed, your characters will not be fully formed. If your dialogue lacks emotional depth, so will your characters. Strong verbs are better tools for building depth into dialogue than are weak verbs qualified by adverbs.

I challenge thee to a duel (of words).

Poorly constructed dialogue can reduce reader comprehension, hamper pacing, and make characters seem like bad high school actors flogging their way through scenes in which no one understands his lines or motivation. Worse, it may seem as if the lines have been forgotten altogether and the characters have resorted to ad-libbing without listening to each other.

Here's an example:

JERROD: "Constance, I'd like you to meet my friend, Peter Harrar."
CONSTANCE: "I'm glad to meet you."
PETER: "The pleasure is all mine, my lady. (*He tries to read her mind.*) Oh, that was dumb!"
JERROD: "I agree!"
PETER: "I apologize, my lady."
CONSTANCE: "No need, sir."
JERROD: "What's the matter, Peter? Forget that she's a level five Psi?"
PETER: "One of these days, friend! Would it be too rude just to bow?"
CONSTANCE: "No . . . no. I don't think so."
JERROD: "Don't you think you're overdoing it a bit?"
PETER: "No, I don't think so."
CONSTANCE: "I don't think so either. Leave him alone, Jerrod. At least he knows the meaning of the word respect."
JERROD: "Him???"
PETER: "Yeah, me."

What's wrong with this conversation? Simply that it's not a conversation—it's a duel (or the three-participant equivalent). It's also repetitive, trivial, and long.

The original scene staggered under the weight of stage business that seemed to exist only to give the characters something to do with their bodies. When I stripped away all the aimless movement that accompanied this dialogue, what was left was a barrage of small talk that took up several pages and failed either to advance the story or reveal character.

"It is a matter of life and death!"

Avoiding the use of contractions in an academic paper or essay may be a good idea, but in fictional dialogue it is a bad idea simply because real people generally do use contractions in their speech.

"I have to talk to Matilda." Justin tried not to let his desperation show.
"She is not receiving visitors," the guard told him.
Justin balled his fists against the desire to use them. "This cannot wait. I have got to speak to her. I am telling you-it is a matter of life and death."

The lack of contractions here stiffens the prose and removes any urgency from the scene. Ultimately, poor Justin does not come across as a man desperate to see his beloved. The narration—his suppressed desperation, his desire to manhandle the guard—is at odds with the preciseness of the dialogue. Desperate people are not precise in their speech. They're, well, desperate.

Will the real Dinsdale please speak up?

Speech and thoughts should reveal character, show strength or weakness; truth, falsehood or ambiguity. They must seem like thoughts the readers have or, at the very least, thoughts they can imagine others could have. Also, the words a writer uses should be those that readers imagine a particular character would use.

If a character is supposed to be callous, then the words he uses should reveal his callousness.

Ariel followed Dinsdale down the long, dark flight of stairs. At the top of the third landing, she slipped and fell.
Below her, Dinsdale stopped and glanced back over his shoulder. "What's the matter?" he asked callously. Good God, she might have broken her neck!

Dinsdale's dialogue could just as easily have read: *"What's the matter?" he asked fearfully.*

The only difference between Dinsdale's being a rogue or a gentleman is in the adverb chosen to modify "asked." This should raise a few red flags.

Let's try a different approach:

Ariel followed Dinsdale down the long, dark flight of stairs. At the top of the third landing she slipped and fell.

Below her, Dinsdale stopped and glanced back over his shoulder. Hell, he thought, she might have broken her neck and stuck him with having to dispose of the body. "Trying to reach the bottom more quickly, my lady?" he asked.

I don't have to tell you that Dinsdale spoke callously; his thoughts and words are snide and uncaring. They make even a simple glance over the shoulder seem heartless. An acid test for dialogue, then, might be to ask: If I strip away all modifiers, what do these words tell me about the character?

Get real!

You have to develop an ear for dialogue. You can do several things when you write dialogue to make it sound real:

• *Strip away all stage business and action.* Try to write dialogue as if you were eavesdropping in the dark. No movement, just people talking.

• *Read your dialogue aloud to see what it sounds like if spoken by a real person.* Imagine your characters in a real-life situation, saying these words.

• *Ask if everything you've written is necessary.* Does it advance the plot or reveal character? Real people "um" and "uh" and "y'know" their way through life, and they indulge in conversations that wander. Fictional characters can't afford those luxuries.

• *"Run the scene" in your mind and put in the action and atmosphere only after you're satisfied that the words work.* If necessary, modify the pacing of the dialogue to work with the action.

Obviously, there are other ways to make your dialogue realistic. Here are a few of them:

Get your plot straight. If you don't know where your characters are going or where they've been, it will be reflected in what they say. Don't contradict yourself or your characters. Make sure the plot is convincing, that the elements are clear and flow logically. Then, cut any elements that don't advance the plot, develop or reveal character, or give the reader necessary information. A single plot flaw can make your entire story unravel.

Establish a definite point of view. You may wish to write dialogue from one character's viewpoint, allowing the viewpoint character's thoughts to reveal to the reader who he is.

Watch the pace. If the pacing of a scene is off, the gist of conversations can be lost, and important clues about character missed. Don't let "stage business" get in the way of dialogue. We don't need to know whether a character brandished his revolver in his left or right hand. Nor, once informed of a fact, do we need to be reminded of it every time he speaks.

Tighten your prose. Good dialogue can be the very embodiment of the phrase "elegant in its simplicity." Unless you've created a character who is known by his very penchant for tangled phrases, keep the dialogue as direct as possible. The purpose of speech is communication: Characters communicate with each other and through your characters, *you* communicate with your reader.

Know your characters. Learn who they are, then introduce them to the reader. Put words in their mouths that will make us like or dislike them (depending on their roles in your story), but their words must, above all, make us *care* what happens to them for better or worse. Above all, don't pull their strings. Give them distinctive personalities and motivation, put them in a situation, then stand back and watch what they do and listen to what they say.

There's a story in that.

❏ 29

Using *Real* People in Your Stories

By Eileen Herbert Jordan

WHEN HENRY JAMES DESCRIBED HIS WRITING METHODS, HE WROTE of how fitting he had found it to place a willful heroine in the gardens of an estate he had long admired, and thus capture her, thereby introducing his readers to Isabel Archer in *Portrait of a Lady*. That may have been fine for Henry James, but it's not going to help you much. Your story is about your willful mother-in-law, who doesn't want to be captured in print, and no matter where you place her, when she reads your story, she's not going to like it, and God knows what it will do to your family relationships!

There isn't a writer, dead or alive, who has not had this problem. In fact, through the years there has been so much conflict between writers and those they write about (or those who *think* they are written about) that I don't presume to come up with a solution. But a few things *have* worked for me when I have had an idea for a story and been stopped by the thought, *Oh, I can't say that about her—she'll never speak to me again. . . .* a thought that has stopped me a lot. And it's no wonder—the dilemma is very real.

If all good writing comes from life—and I believe it does—and we fail to tap the source, we end with cardboard figures whose every move is unreal, and whose story is usually unpublishable. Still, in the world we live in, most of us are not misogynists (or man haters, either); in fact, we court approval and dislike living in alienation. Yet writing is what we do, the thing that defines us, and we have to do it the best we can.

Writing instructors are fond of suggesting that the psyches of two or three people we know can be mingled to produce one in a story. Like many similar suggestions, this one *doesn't* work more often that it *does,* and at best, it takes considerable skill. We are, after all, en-

126

gaged in the business of mixing the characteristics of different people—not in making soup. But before you despair, try these approaches:

Change genders. This doesn't always work, of course, but it does more often than you would think. Recall the family situations you have observed in which daughters behaved exactly as their fathers had, sons mirrored the reactions of mothers, etc. When a character's emotions and actions are not solely motivated by his gender, it is perfectly viable to make the switch and get away with it.

Do a makeover. It's often been said that inside every short, fat person there lies a tall and willowy one, yearning to be free. Well, you can do it. I have done it often and have not been found out yet, although once it did boomerang and work in reverse. I wrote a story about the romance of a friend of mine. Aware that magazines crave youth and beauty, I made my heroine younger, slimmer, taller, and quite a bit more lissome than my friend.

I also set the romance in Manhattan (it actually took place in the suburbs) because I knew the area, and I knew the sneaky magic of liaisons that begin there. The story was published, but not right away, having been rejected the first time around by an editor I knew slightly. She admitted later that the problem was she couldn't bear the thought of seeing it in print because she felt that I had invaded her privacy and written *her* story. Her reaction was a total surprise to me, and ironic, too—after all my duplicity in fashioning the characters! The second editor, without the same baggage, bought it.

Despite the above example, however, a makeover does not consist merely of a few cosmetic touches. It is a process of imbuing your protagonist with a star quality she did not have before. Most of us don't believe we are stars and never recognize ourselves as such.

Change the label. We are captives of our identity, defined by labels we have acquired, sometimes by choice, often not. We are mothers, daughters, sisters, neighbors. This can be changed. After you have explored the gender possibilities, making your mother your father, try making your neighbor your sister, your daughter your roommate, your mother your best friend. Simply take the person you know, foibles intact, and give her a new identity.

Recently, I wrote a story that I felt might not be popular with the person who inspired it. I solved the problem by identifying her at the

beginning as a grandmother. Except for the age requirement, grand-
motherhood had nothing whatsoever to do with my story, so it didn't
matter. What I did know was that the person in question was *not* a
grandmother and had no urge to become one; her eyes would glaze
over as she read the word, and she never would connect any part of
what followed with herself. I was right.

Change the skill. To many people a skill or talent is as much a part
of them as a thumbprint. So, in fact, is a lack of ability—we are all
very aware of what we *can't* do. Let me give you an example. I have
two sons, and I write about them often. But in a short story, you
should not have too many characters, or you will lose your reader in
the crowd. I write about my sons, therefore, as one person. They try
to guess who's who and sometimes succeed, but sometimes I fool
them. The main character in one of my recent stories was a dead ringer
for my younger boy, until the climax, which involved his swimming
across a lake.

"Well, Mom," he said, "this one's not me—I know that. You know
I don't swim."

Obviously, if what you are writing is totally involved with a cross-
country skier, a ballroom dancer, or the soul of a poet, you can't do
much about it. But if the skill doesn't matter to the plot, taking it away,
changing it, or, perhaps, conferring it on another character can blur
recognition with no harm done.

Don't think "Know Thyself" works for everyone. You may be surprised at the number of people who believe they could never be fooled;
they're sure they would recognize themselves—but they don't. If you
write a story that you know may expose someone, remember that—
then cross your fingers.

I know a successful writer who was determined never to exploit
friends, family, or acquaintances, and she never did until she completed a novel, reread it, and found, to her horror, that one of the main
characters was a clone of somebody she knew, a character who had
somehow slipped from the writer's unconscious onto the printed page.
Not only that, the character was not a flattering clone, either; she was
Matilda, the evil force who drove the story. And it was too late to do
anything about it—except wait and see.

That did not take long. Shortly after the book was published, at a
party, the writer gazed across the room and her eyes locked with those

of her nemesis. She stopped still and just stood there silently, racking her brains for an approach as the other woman began walking toward her. What to do?

Should she start the conversation with a burst of pleasantries, ignoring the issue?

Should she apologize right away, call writers like herself insensitive clods—and see what happens?

Should she just lie?

The woman reached her side, and grabbing her arm, she said, "I've read your novel. I couldn't put it down. It's just wonderful. . . ." There was a pause. "Just one thing . . ."

My friend swallowed hard.

"How do you ever dream up those characters? I could never do that. Or maybe I just never meet people like that. That Matilda is a monster—and so real! Congratulations!"

So she got away with it—by a stroke of sheer luck. And you may, too. For a writer it is the ideal solution to the problem, and it is not one he forgets, either. It has been almost forty years since Neil Simon's first play, *Come Blow Your Horn,* opened and he can still remember how worried he was that the character of the household head would be offensive to his father, upon whom the play was entirely based. Worried, that is, until his father came to him afterwards, shook his head and said, "I know so many men just like him."

On the other hand, Truman Capote lost all his friends when he made their identities obvious in a short story. So if you would rather take precautions, try some I have suggested. It gets easier with practice— in fact, the characters you create grow so real, you feel as if you've made new friends!

❑ 30

Novel Writing: Questions and Answers

By Sidney Sheldon

Q. *At what age did you think about becoming a writer?*

A. I began writing when I was very young. My first poem was published by a children's magazine when I was ten years old. I have always enjoyed working with language and ideas.

Q. *How long, on average, does it take you to write a novel—from idea to finished manuscript? Do you ever work on two books simultaneously?*

A. I take anywhere from a year to two years to write a novel. I may finish a draft in 3 to 4 months. I then spend the rest of the time rewriting until the manuscript is as good as I know how to make it, before the publisher ever sees a word. When I was writing TV and motion picture scripts, I used to work on 3 or 4 projects simultaneously. When I write a novel, I work only on the novel.

Q. *Do your books ever take unexpected twists as you are writing them? How far should a beginning writer follow a tangent when it presents itself in the course of writing a novel?*

A. The twists in my books are constantly surprising me. I never know what is going to happen next, since I don't work with an outline. If a beginning writer finds himself thinking about an unexpected tangent, he or she should follow it. That's the character talking.

Q. *How have your experiences and relationships with people been reflected in your novels?*

A. Some wise person once said that writers paper their walls with themselves. Everything that a writer sees or hears usually winds up in some form in his or her work. Many novels are autobiographical to a large extent. I've used incidents in my life in many of my books.

Q. *Your protagonists are morally strong individuals, and likewise, the endings of your novels leave the reader with the sense of justice having been served. How essential to modern storytelling is the element of good vs. evil?*

A. I think the element of good vs. evil goes back to the most ancient storytellers. I believe that if evil triumphs, the reader is left with a feeling of disappointment. It's like a sonata where the last chord is dissonant.

Q. *Why are so many of your main characters female? What are the options with and limitations of female and male protagonists?*

A. Most of the protagonists in my novels are females. I enjoy writing about women. I think they're more interesting than men, more complex and more vulnerable. Since my novels have an element of suspense and danger in them, vulnerability is important.

Q. *When a character completely absorbs you, do you find yourself almost chameleon-like, taking on a character's personality as you write, or shifting from one to another?*

A. The characters in my novels are very real to me while I'm writing their story, but life goes on, and I meet new characters every few years. I've had a few murderers in my books, so if I took on their personality, I'd be in real trouble!

Q. *Why do so many successful first novelists have difficulties writing their second novels?*

A. One of the reasons that some successful first novelists have problems writing their second novel is that they are intimidated, afraid that they can't live up to their first success. Some writers seem to have only one novel in them, especially if that novel is autobiographical. Carl Reiner wrote a wonderful play called *Exit Laughing*, about a playwright who wrote a smash hit and had trouble writing a second play until he moved back into the poverty-stricken life he was living when he wrote his hit play.

Q. *What tactics do you recommend for overcoming the dreaded writer's block?*

A. One of the most practical suggestions I have for trying to prevent writer's block is to end each day's work with the beginning of the following day's scene, so that when you sit down to write the next morning, your scene has already been started.

Q. *What characteristics do novels and films have in common? What has to be left out when a novel is turned into a film? What does a novel gain from being a film?*

A. Novels and films both tell stories. What has been left out when a novel is turned into a film is a lot of description, extraneous scenes, and extraneous characters. When a novel is turned into a film, it's usually wonderful publicity for the book, and will gain a wider audience for the author.

Q. *Do you write scenes in the order they will appear in the novel? Or do you write key scenes first and arrange them later?*

A. Many writers will plot out their books in advance. I read that Jerzy Kosinski used to get up in the morning and look at the huge board he had, where each scene in the book was numbered. He would then pick out the number (a love scene, a murder scene, etc.) and write the scene he was in the mood to do that day. I write my books in sequence from beginning to end.

Q. *Do you have any strong feelings about the use of flashbacks, how they should be used, or when? What devices do you use for transitions from past to present?*

A. Flashbacks are very tricky and have to be handled carefully. When you jump backward or forward in time, it is easy to confuse the reader. There are mechanical devices like asterisks and leaving extra space between paragraphs, but it is a mistake to rely solely on those methods. You have to phrase your sentences so that it is clear to the reader that you are now taking him back in time or forward in time, or that you have returned to the present. These are important guideposts, so handle them carefully.

Q. *How attentively should a beginning writer listen to his critics? How seriously do you take reviews of your work?*

A. I learned long ago never to ignore a specific criticism of my work. I used to say, "but don't you see what I meant was," but I realized that if you have to explain, it's not the reader's problem, it's your problem. As far as how seriously I take reviews of my books, it depends on the reviewer. I look for constructive criticism. I don't hold the general critical community in very high regard.

❏ 31

MAKING EVERY WORD COUNT IN YOUR STORY

BY DIANE LEFER

YEARS AGO, WHEN MY STORIES STARTED COMING BACK IN THE MAIL with written comments instead of form rejection slips, I was both elated and frustrated. "Needs tightening," I read again and again. I pictured a screwdriver and hadn't the slightest idea what these editors wanted me to do.

I didn't see anything wrong with a sentence like, *She squeezed the trigger and fired a shot from the gun held in her hand.* These days, I can't stop myself from thinking, "Well, gosh, I didn't think she fired it by licking the trigger with her tongue." But even as I now laugh at the sentence, I'm not making fun of the writer. From experience with my own writing, from reading manuscripts in slush piles, and from working with students at various stages of development, I'm convinced we pick up the habit of being long-winded because we've often won praise for it. I've isolated some of these habits to keep my students and myself alert.

The getting A's in high school English habit

George Bernard Shaw said you're not a writer till you know five synonyms for every word. That may be true, but I suggest that a writer who knows five synonyms should also know enough not to use them, because there are very few true synonyms. I can't tell you how many stories I've read in magazine slush piles in which a character makes herself a cup of coffee and then—I'm already cringing in anticipation of the language that all too often follows—*she brings the cup of hot brown liquid to her lips and savors the aromatic beverage.* Personally, I often crave a cup of coffee. I do not crave a cup of hot brown liquid!

Why do we do it? In part, because we've been taught that word repetition is bad, but in creative writing, word repetition is often good.

Repetition may create an incantatory effect. When the same word shifts its meaning slightly in the text, it may add depth to a story. There are much worse sins than using a word twice. The only caution I would advise is: if you see a word repeated again and again in a paragraph, you may be dragging out the scene, and this is place where your manuscript can be tightened or condensed. For example, when the character drinks her morning coffee, you probably don't need the details of her making it, pouring it, inhaling the aroma, and finally drinking it. Unless there's something very unusual about her coffee routine, this is a conventional scene that does not require details.

We also stretch out our sentences to show off our extensive vocabularies because substitution, euphemism, and indirect statement are stylistic features of much of the writing of earlier times. Novels considered classics have admirable features, but the language and style come from a world very different from our own. Many writers, trying to model their own writing on work they've been taught is great, end up writing in old-fashioned language that isn't natural or comfortable for them—or for their characters.

So why did your English teachers love it? Why did you get A's for writing that way? In part, because your teachers studied and respected classics, in part because such writing indicates a fascination with language that should be encouraged in a young writer. They often praised you for writing that later, as literary writers, you learned to drop or use with caution.

The creative writing rules habit

One problem I often see in manuscripts is a description of ordinary actions, such as leaving or entering rooms, presented in excruciating detail:

His thigh muscles contracted as he rose from his chair. He approached the door, placed his hand on the doorknob, the smooth surface against his right palm as his fingers grasped. He turned the knob, pushed against the wood, opening the door, and paused a moment on the threshold before walking out, turning, closing and locking the door behind him by inserting and turning the key he had at the appropriate moment removed from his pocket.

When I read such a passage, I know the writer has heard the rule, "Show, Don't Tell" so many times, she or he is afraid to summarize anything and is thinking of the rule rather than its effect. I think the show-don't-tell rule is overapplied most often in portrayals of emotion. Think of the opening sentence to Ford Maddox Ford's novel, *The Good Soldier:* "This is the saddest story I have ever heard."

The story the narrator goes on to tell certainly isn't the saddest *I* have ever heard, but I found that stark assertion irresistible as an opening. I would not have read on if the narrator had begun with a conventional show-don't-tell portrayal of sadness: *When I heard the story I'm about to tell you, my eyes clouded with tears, my throat constricted, muffled sobs and a deep sigh rose from somewhere within me, and I shuddered with the chill of the saddest feeling I had ever known.*

Obviously, this example is exaggerated, but many writers do feel they're not allowed to say, *He cried,* or *He felt sad,* but must illustrate the emotion with the wetness of tears and tightness in the throat. I'm not suggesting that emotion must always be presented through a direct statement.

One of my favorite sentences of all time comes from "The Johnstown Polka," a short story by Sharon Sheehe Stark (from *The Dealer's Yard and Other Stories,* (Morrow, 1985). It's about Francine, who years earlier lost her husband and children in the Johnstown flood and whose continuing emotional wound is invisible to those around her:

> But what they perceive as tranquility, Francine experiences as a sort of unpleasant limpness, her heart a slack muscle, as if after having delivered an outsized grief, it never quite snapped back and stubbornly holds, if not sorrow itself, then the soft shape of it.

That's the kind of line that makes me stop short. I have to put down the book. Pick it up again and reread the sentence. Which is one great advantage a story has over a movie: If you're overwhelmed, you can stop and catch your breath. The written story can't go on without you.

This sentence illustrates why I love literary fiction. Looking at this sentence, I know I can't duplicate it. But maybe I can say something else. Everyone has thoughts, feelings, ideas that truly matter. If, as writers, we're going to have something as a standard, something to strive toward, Stark's sentence is an example of what language can do. But no one, not even a literary genius, has something profound to say all the time. When you don't, spare the reader the carefully crafted restatement of what everyone already knows (e.g, tears are wet); you're better off writing, "I felt sad."

The speech and presentation habit

Many of us have experience in lecturing, giving speeches, making presentations. In this context, we learn to *Tell them what you're going to tell them, then tell them, then tell them what you've told them.*

The technique of redundancy is reinforced by TV news. The anchorperson says:

An early morning fire destroyed three buildings and left twenty families homeless in Mayberry. And now we go to Mary Jones, live on the scene. . . . Mary?
"I'm here in Mayberry, at the scene of an early morning fire that destroyed three buildings and left twenty families homeless."

Then Mary briefly interviews a man who says,

"We lost everything and we're homeless, but we're alive and that's what counts."

Then back to the anchor, who says,

"Terrible situation, all those people homeless after the fire. But they're alive, and that's what counts."

I see this pattern again and again in short stories. The writer explains in the first paragraph what the story's going to be about and what's going to happen. The last paragraph sums up the material and repeats the meaning to be drawn from it. Not only does this kill suspense, but it detracts from the meaning. A wonderful short story can't be summarized in a paragraph. There is no one single meaning or lesson readers should take from it. Of course, this problem can be easily solved by cutting the first and last paragraphs, but I find that many writers also fall into this pattern throughout the development of the story. They will often begin a scene by telling what is about to happen. Then, after presenting the interaction between characters, they won't let the moment speak for itself but will summarize it. For example:

On Sunday morning, Glenn and Linda had a fight about how much he'd had to drink at the party.
"Why did you have to get drunk at that party?" Linda asked.
"I had two drinks. Big deal. Just two drinks," Glenn said.
Linda threw up her hands in despair. She was upset over Glenn's drinking and that they were fighting about it.

Editing can solve this problem, but when there's an overall effect of redundancy, the manuscript may become tedious, and it's less likely that an editor will want to bother.

Most important, you're tightening your prose not only to improve your chances of publication; you're also doing it for your reader. Sentences that develop obvious information encourage the reader to skim. Wouldn't you rather have your readers pay attention because every word counts?

.

❑ 32

PUTTING EMOTION INTO YOUR FICTION

BY BHARTI KIRCHNER

LAUGH, SCREAM AND WEEP BEFORE YOUR KEYBOARD; MAKE YOUR reader feel. I kept this in mind when I started writing my first novel, *Shiva Dancing*. In developing characters, plot, and setting, I looked for every opportunity to make an emotional impact on the reader. Often, as I composed a sentence or paragraph, I felt the emotion myself.

Why are emotions important? Because they're more compelling than ideas, facts, and reasoning, which are the stuff of nonfiction. In fiction, the character must act from emotion, rather than from reason. And emotional truth is the reward readers hope to get from a novel. They will not turn to the next chapter or even the next page unless the material engages their emotions.

What emotions? Love and hate, joy and despair, fear and hope. Those are the significant ones to develop over a novel or chapter. But there are others—pride, timidity, shame, and humiliation—that move people and characters minute to minute, word to word.

Whether simple and understated or complex and dramatic, emotions need to be conveyed in a story, first by developing sympathetic characters. The more readers identify or sympathize with your protagonist, the more they'll feel her emotions and be curious enough to turn the page.

In the first chapter of *Shiva Dancing*, for example, seven-year-old Meena is kidnapped by bandits from her village in Rajasthan on the night of her wedding. The girl cries as she's snatched away from her mother's loving embrace by two big men on camels. Her old grandfather, who shuffled after them, looks on helplessly. This incident is meant to draw an emotional response from the reader. At the end of the chapter Meena's found by an American couple in a train far away from her village. They're about to take her to their home in New Delhi, where they're temporarily posted, when the chapter ends. The reader is likely to ask at this point: What's going to happen to Meena? Will she ever find her village? Where will she end up?

Turn to the next chapter.

If emotion is important, the question is: How do you, the writer, actually depict it on paper? And how does the reader know what that emotion is? The cardinal rule is: *Show, don't tell.* In other words, stating a mental condition directly may not convince the reader. For example:

She was anxious.

In real life, you observe someone's behavior and draw appropriate conclusions. The example below from *The Power of the Sword* by Wilbur Smith *shows* that the character is agitated:

Centaine was too keyed up to sit down. She stood in the center of the floor and looked at the pictures on the fireplace wall without actually seeing them.

You can also *show* an emotion through a character's thought. This is often effective, since a person may not reveal his true feeling in his speech. Use a simile, as Alice Hoffman does in *Second Nature:*

He just couldn't shake the feeling of dread; he was like an old woman, waiting for disaster to strike.

Notice how much more effective the above is than saying:

He was afraid.

Use physical symptoms. Readers are convinced of an emotion only when they recognize a physical reaction similar to one they've experienced themselves: a racing heart, stiff legs, or cold palms. Here's one of Meena's reactions in *Shiva Dancing,* but first a bit about the story and the scene where she finds herself.

Meena is adopted by the American couple, who raise her in San Francisco. When we meet her again, she's 35, a software techie, working for a Bay Area company. In one scene, Meena goes to a bookstore to attend a reading by Antoine Peterson, a celebrity novelist she has met briefly on one previous occasion. After the reading, he invites her for tea. Just when the chai is tasting "creamy smooth," and the tabla music has reached a crescendo, Antoine mentions his upcoming marriage to Liv and their honeymoon. Meena's reaction?

Her tea tasted cold and weak. She set her cup down, trying to keep her hand steady.

An emotion, however, is not an end in itself. Describing it in a vacuum is never enough. You have to combine facts and action with emotion to create an illusion of reality. Here's an example from *The Rest of Life* by Mary Gordon.

She gets into the train, one of the first to board. [action and fact] Everything is still and quiet. [fact] Then the train starts up with an insulting lurch. [emotion]

Though I try to bring out a character's feelings even during the first draft, I find I never catch them one hundred per cent. Revision is the perfect time to check for the following: What are the various emotional situations in which the protagonist has found herself? How does she react to the stimulus? Look for a sentence, some piece of dialogue, or a flashback where emotions can be injected. Nostalgia, a milestone in life, a return to some place previously visited, are potential sources.

In *Shiva Dancing,* Meena returns to her village after an absence of three decades. As she arrives with her driver, she notices that the thatched-roof houses have been replaced by newer buildings. She can't recognize any of the sights. She's eager to find her mother. The reader knows—but Meena doesn't—that her mother is long dead. Meena meets a schoolboy on the street and asks, in one poignant moment, about her mother:

"My mother made clothes for the kids. She embroidered their names on their baby sari. Everyone in the village came to her."
The shocking reply that comes to Meena through her driver is:
His mother buys ready-made clothes for him.

Use sizzle in your dialogue: Inane comments, yes-and-no answers might do in real life, but speech in fiction must have the effect of potential shockers. In *Shiva Dancing,* Antoine returns from a book tour and immediately goes to visit Meena at her apartment. There, he finds Carlos, a close friend of Meena's, who tells him Meena has left for India. Antoine doesn't like Carlos in the first place, and now he has the task of finding out where she is actually staying. Carlos, protective of Meena, has been unwilling up to this point to share any information about her. Finally, the outwardly polite Carlos explodes:

> "She had strong feelings for you. I've never seen Meena get so excited about a man. And what do you do? You build up her hopes, then dump her the day Liv comes back. Pardon me if I'm getting a little emotional. Meena's my friend. It hurts me to see her cut up like that."
> "I didn't mean to hurt her," Antoine said. "My situation is different now."
> "It better be."

The words used in a dialogue can be simple, but just repeating a phrase can intensify the emotion. Here's Alice Hoffman in *Second Nature:*

> "Help me up," Richard Aaron shouted over the sound of the hooves hitting against the earth. "Just help me up."

A person's words may be a smoke screen, but her voice, facial expression, and gestures can be a dead giveaway. Notice how Gail Godwin does this in *The Finishing School:*

> Her chin shot up so fast that it set in motion the crest of her feathery haircut. "Where did you hear about them?"

Another place where an emotional quality can be imparted is in the setting. *Create an atmosphere:* A dark house on a stormy night has a sinister connotation, whereas a sunny day on a beach is quite the opposite. You can make effective use of the environment to set a mood. This is equivalent to using background music in a movie to highlight the action on the screen. In this example from *Shiva Dancing,* Meena is about to attend a staff meeting at Software International Company. There's tension among her coworkers. The scene opens with a short description of the conference room:

> Sunlight streamed in through the room's only window, casting shadows of the saucerlike leaves of the potted plants on the wall *without warming the room.*

The italics is mine. When selecting from a number of details in a surrounding, pick only those elements relevant for the character, those that bring an emotional surge. Here's novelist Antoine in *Shiva Dancing* arriving in Calcutta in pursuit of Meena. He feels lonely and uncertain. Everything he sees through his taxi window on the way to the hotel is colored by his present mental condition:

Antoine's eyes watered as acrid charcoal smoke from a clay oven on the sidewalk drifted in through the open car window. Along with the smoke came the smell of freshly baked flat bread. A young woman in a yellow-orange sari browned the puffy *roti* rounds over the fire. Her deep eyes and rhythmic gestures reminded him of Meena. He yearned for fresh bread made just for him.

Use symbolism. A symbol is a habit, an object, an event, almost anything charged with a hidden meaning that stems from association. In *Shiva Dancing,* a symbol used for Meena is her thirst, which, in effect, is her longing for her desert homeland. In her San Francisco office, she always keeps a glass of water on her desk and sips from it often. The true meaning of this ritualistic habit is revealed to her only after she finally returns to her village.

"Tubewell," the boy said, pointing. He rushed to it and levered the handle until water gushed out. Meena made a cup of her hands, drank deeply and splashed the remainder on her face. As she did so, she went back in time when she was tiny. Mataji would hold a glass of well water to her mouth. This clear earth water tasted the same. She had missed it. Without knowing it, she had been thirsty all these years.

Collect "feeling" words: Avoid overusing common words, such as "loving," "calm," or "blissful." Consider cataloguing your own feelings in a notebook and using them for your characters. Here are some examples:

Animated	Exasperated
Diffident	Sated
Bubbly	Petrified
Refreshed	Crushed

Regardless of what techniques are used, ultimately it's the writer's own emotions that set the tone of a scene or piece of fiction. As a preparation for writing, it might be necessary for you to revisit an incident in the past and try to identify and relive an emotion. Or, like an actor, you might assume a new role and experience a new set of emotions. The choice of words, the length of a sentence, the pacing of paragraphs all broadcast to readers how they should feel. In general, short sentences and paragraphs heighten the drama, whereas longer, more leisurely writing gives the reader more breathing space.

Avoid sentimentality. As important as emotions are, don't overemphasize powerful ones such as loss and grief. Readers feel manipulated when presented with one misery after another. You may summarize such happenings or provide relief by using humor and insight. In general, the stronger the emotion, the more you need to restrain your passion in describing it.

To sum up, don't be afraid to transfer one or more emotional experiences of laughter, pain, or agony to your readers. They may curse you because they burned the rice, dropped their aerobics routine, and were late for work, but they won't put your book down.

□ 33

PITCH-PERFECT DIALOGUE

BY SHELBY HEARON

I'M AN INVETERATE EAVESDROPPER. NOTHING IS MORE FUN THAN GOing out for an early-morning muffin or a late-night plate of fried eggs and listening to the couple or the family in the booth behind you. A few lines of conversation, scraps of talk, and you know at once what the relationship between the people is, what the problem is, where they're coming from. All without even turning your head.

Achieving the same instant sense of "knowing all about" fictional people is more difficult. For one thing, you don't have the tone of voice, which is so revealing. In real life, the transaction—"I think I'll have the pancakes" and "I'm looking at the waffles"—can be heard with several different undertones, inflections, nuances. But on the page it's hard to convey what the listener knows is the subtext. Yet, the secret of pitch-perfect dialogue begins there: with trying to figure out what you know and how you know it when you're listening in on other lives.

Private eyes and spies provide unbeatable "eavesdropping" opportunities on the printed page. Who could confuse a character from P. D. James saying, "That was preternaturally slow," with one from Elmore Leonard asking, "Wha' took you so long?"

But in addition to these obvious clues in vocabulary and syntax, I always start on a new character by asking myself what I want to tell the reader first about the person. How to tell something is not nearly as difficult as deciding what is the crucial trait to reveal. But, say you decide to show right at the start how your character (let's take a father-type of guy) feels about his body and how he feels about authority: If you're dealing with men, you know they spend a lot of time wishing their bodies were different, and a lot of emotion on their relation to the guy in charge.

So you decide—two birds with one stone—to have your father-type in the hospital about to have his gallbladder out. He's prepped, waiting on that tight, white-sheeted bed, and in comes John Archer, abdominal surgeon.

Your man says:

"Hey, Arch, watch out when you're messing around down there below the belt you don't remove anything I may need. Ha ha."

Or he says:

"Jeez, Dr. Archer, I'm scared blue. I can't help it, look at me, I'm cold as a fish. My old man, he flat out died from this same trouble. Younger than me."

Or he says:

"Morning, John. I guess I'm as ready as I'll ever be. Maybe taking some of my gall out will make me easier to live with. I know a few who'd agree with that."

Or he says:

"Well, Doc, don't take this as lack of confidence, but my law partners, malpractice litigators par excellence, will be looking over your shoulder when you pick up that knife."

Let's take another example. Say you want to show that the way a young woman feels about her man goes right back to how she feels about her mom. So maybe you start with her having lunch with him in a public place.

She says:

"The pastrami was O.K., I don't care all that much, the corned beef probably isn't any better, but just once I'd like to order for myself. Just once I'd like to open my mouth and say exactly what I want."

Or she says:

"You're sure? Gosh, you're always paying for everything. Lunch, the trip to Cancun, that totally gorgeous pink sweater. Really, I mean it, you make me feel really special."

Or she says:

"Here, I'll read it for you. I think you left your glasses on the dashboard. You like that soup, remember? The sort of borsch. It agrees with you, you said last time."

From here, it's just a matter of a phone call to Mom, in which we overhear a few snippets of conversation, to make your point that history, at least in our love life, always repeats.

An aid to writing convincing dialogue, and one you'll unconsciously pick up when you're listening in, is to give your character her or his own special metaphors. I often do this, as an exercise, just to get new voices clearly in my head: Have each character say, "It's hot as ———," "I'm mad as ———," "It's time to ———," "No point in ———." And I always have my ear out for phrases I have never heard before. One I picked up when I moved to Vermont (writers love to move around to new places for this reason!) and I'm sure to put to use soon is: "He may not be the sharpest knife in the drawer, but ———." And almost anything can follow—"he's a true friend," "steady as night and day," "somebody you can trust," etc. I jot down every sentence like that I overhear.

Another choice the writer can make in deciding how to reveal character through dialogue is selecting who gets to say what lines. My own preference is to "cast against type," to use a film term. For example, listen to a couple fighting: One of them wants to get married, the other doesn't. One of them has been hurt to the quick by the cavalier attitude of the other. Readers will be more apt to hear the fight and really feel they have come to know these two people, if you do the unexpected. *He* wants to get married; *she* wants to play around. He's been wounded by her; she has grown tired of all the talk about commitment.

"I want marriage. I want the whole baggage. The dirty socks and pink toothbrush and recycle bins."

"Place an ad."

"Do you know how comments like that hurt? Do you have a clue how words can bruise?"

Read them with *she said* and then *he said,* then reverse it and read *he said* and *she said,* and you hear the impasse between them in a new way.

Or try a parent and child.

"I never know where you are or when you're coming home."

"Lighten up. What are my options in this burg, anyways?"

Spoken by a parent to a child, the reader doesn't really hear the words, because expected scenarios get in the way. But spoken by a twelve-year-old boy to his forty-five-year-old mother, the two lines seem fresh, and a new situation is suggested. The reader is drawn into the story.

A lot of times, real life suggests these switches on the expected. I can recall when I was a young mother, driving to the trailhead in the

Rockies to pick up my backpacking son, gone sometimes for days at a time. Then, three years ago, I went back to Aspen after a long absence, to see if I could do the day hikes I'd done years before. (To prove that if I wasn't the sharpest knife in the drawer, at least I wasn't rusty.) And there my son was, grown, driving me to the trailhead, setting a time when I had to return, checking to be sure I had a windbreaker in case of a summer storm, and proper gear. And I'm sure our conversation mirrored the ones we'd had in the past, with the roles reversed.

Go back to the thrillers I mentioned earlier. What if Elmore Leonard's guy on the lam in Florida says, "That was preternaturally slow," and P. D. James's man in London asks, "Wha' took you so long?" There would be a sense of having met someone unexpected and the surprise would engage the reader.

In my current novel, *Footprints,* I have a couple whose daughter died in a car wreck, and her heart is transplanted into a southern preacher's chest. The father (a brain scientist) is devastated; he clings to the belief his daughter is still alive, and becomes very mystical about the transplant. His wife, in turn, becomes quite scientific in her handling of loss, exploring in a cool, investigative manner the theories of what life is, what the mind or self really is, considering the transplant almost akin to Frankenstein's borrowed life.

But why not imagine you are listening to them talk over coffee in the booth behind you. What does she say to him? What does he say to her? What does the reader overhear?

□ 34

CHARACTERS THAT MOVE

BY ALYCE MILLER

WHILE CONFLICT IS CERTAINLY AT THE HEART OF ALL GOOD FICTION, one might argue that character lies at its soul. Fiction is generally only as interesting as the people in it. One famous writer said that you need just enough plot to hang your characters on. Complex, developed, animated characters versus simple, stock, static characters may well be one of the defining distinctions between literary and popular fiction. The multiple meanings of "Characters That Move" suggest several possible kinds of motion essential to presenting interesting characters: physical or emotional (as in change or revelation), as well as the evocation of emotion in the reader.

In my own reading, it is character that time and again draws me back to a story or novel, and character that lives on my mind, resurfacing and informing my memory of the work. A curious thing about fiction is that it often can approach certain truths that nonfiction can't. So what is our attraction as both readers and writers to the lives of imaginary people? And why is that some fictional characters are indelible and continue to evolve in our memory, and others are quickly forgotten?

Character may be one of the least understood and most challenging elements of fiction writing. Poets talk a lot about voice. Fiction writers talk a lot about character. Voice is often the start of a fictional character, and even in third-person narratives, the two are inseparable. Voice may begin in fragments, as in a phrase, an inflection, a question, or an observation. You might be walking down the street when something starts in your head, thoughts that don't exactly belong to you, or you hear a voice distinct from your own internal monologues. When that happens, it's time to grow quiet and listen, to allow the voice to take shape and the language to develop. And if the voice persists, pick up a pen and follow it.

This can often be a writer's introduction to a character. Ultimately, fiction is about invention, and most characters are probably composites of real and imagined people transformed through the writer's imagination. The best characters, it seems to me, are those that the writer seems to live, much like an actor inhabiting a role. Perhaps it's helpful to move away from the idea that we "write about" characters and instead that we "become them." In this way, writing has a performance aspect, even though not publicly staged. The actual process of writing is performative, with characters speaking and acting and doing, and events unfolding.

Some writers swear by writing biographies for characters or making lists of attributes. I have seen impressive numbers of pages filled by writers, with all sorts of notes about their characters. Many books on writing seem to encourage this, even offering lists of questions like, "Does your character believe in God?" or "Has your character traveled a lot?" I have never found this strategy useful and, in most cases, I believe it can be distracting—partly, I think, because the exercise isolates character from the rest of the work and treats it mechanically, as an accumulation of details. It also may encourage a kind of imposed development of the character, rather than allowing the character to unfold and reveal herself naturally. A character is much more than the sum of her parts. Imposed attributes often lead to chunky characterization.

How can you possibly know if your character believes in God, or at least not until the situation arises? And even if she does, how does that belief affect the development of the story? It may be completely unimportant. It's my sense that we discover what is important to our characters by writing, not the other way around. If we begin to impose attributes too early, we squelch other possibilities and eliminate surprises. We place a template over the story and insist it has to go a certain way, tugging and pulling it into place. Sometimes the less you know when starting out, the better; sometimes just the germ of an idea is enough to launch a piece of fiction.

Ultimately, though, you do need to know much more about your character than may end up in the story or the novel you are writing. Say, for example, your character is a doctor. In your mind you may picture what medical school the character attended, but it may not ever need to be mentioned in the story. You might add it at a certain point and then strike it, unless it serves a larger purpose beyond exposition. Or you may find yourself writing a scene that you later discover is unnecessary, but it served the important purpose of getting you closer to the character.

In his discussions of character, E.M. Forster introduced the famous terms "flat" and "round." Simply put, a flat character is often a fixed (static) or stock character, or a person we might think of as one-dimensional who generally functions in a secondary role. Charles Dickens was a master of flat characters, skilled at finding the one detail (often ironic or humorous) that defined the character. Dickens was also a master of round characters, those who are dynamic, complex, mobile, and most important, capable of some change (usually subtle). There is certainly a place for both types of characters in a work of fiction, but generally, the main characters should be in the round category: They not only exist or act, but have emotions, thoughts, mixed motives, dreams, hopes, disappointments, and, important, flaws. In other words, they are human, and they are individualized through particulars rather than painted with the broad brush of generalities.

Getting inside a character's head is essential. Even a despicable character requires empathy and understanding. There needs to be the connection that keeps the reader reading. This is different from approval. The writer's role is not to sit back and make pronouncements of moral judgment, though issues of morality may surface naturally in the course of the story. In fact, some of fiction's most notorious, wicked, or difficult characters are some of readers' favorites. For example, Humbert Humbert, Nabokov's lecherous narrator in *Lolita,* exudes charm and wit and intelligence in the telling of his first-person narrative, despite the fact that he is finally morally reprehensible. He is funny and observant, and his facility with language and word play is more than entertaining. Or consider how as readers, our attitudes toward a character change through the course of a novel or story, as we get more and more information. It has been said that a bit of the writer is in every character, and this is why characters behave in less than noble ways.

There's an old adage "write what you know," and many writers take it literally. There are many ways of "knowing." Writers are people upon whom little that goes on in the world is lost. They listen, they pay attention, they watch, they make mental notes. Many writers may not be aware of when writing stops and life begins, so intertwined the two become. In the movie *Sybil,* about the woman with multiple personalities, there is a wonderful scene in which a small child who witnesses Sybil accessing other personalities, runs home and ecstatically exclaims, "Mama, Sybil's just stuffed with people!"

Perhaps the writer is also stuffed with people, and there are no limits to what a writer can write, as long as the particulars of character are there. Often, if a writer reaches too far out of his experience (real, borrowed, or imagined), he may run into the temptation to draw on stereotypes. For example, he may start with a limited understanding of how something works in another culture or social structure, and run headlong into stereotypes. The interesting thing about stereotypes is that there is often a kernel of truth at the core, but it is a truth the observer has not adequately processed, and it becomes distorted and ultimately misunderstood or misinterpreted. Sometimes, it's sheer laziness on the part of a writer, inattention to detail, inability to absorb without judgment.

Fiction works in the territory of the imagination. It is about transformation, not transcription. Characters, therefore, even those who may be composites of real people, or based loosely on people the writer has known, become transformed through imagination and language. Part of the key to creating characters is being willing to learn. The know-it-all writer often flattens a character faster than a speeding train. Characters need room to move around; they need space to stretch their legs. Most of all, they need an attentive writer, one who is willing to take the time to observe and chronicle what is being revealed.

❑ 35

PIQUING THE READER'S CURIOSITY

BY JOAN AIKEN

ONCE WHEN I WAS SITTING IN A PACKED LONDON UNDERGROUND train, I heard the following snatch of conversation between two men who were standing close by me, but I never saw their faces among the crowd of rush-hour passengers. The first voice, the sort that alerts you at once to listen, asked, "Did I ever tell you the story of the mushroom?"

"No, what was it?" the other voice asked.

"Well, there were only two officers in charge. A couple of days before this happened they had vacuumed the parade ground. Lord, those Germans are thorough! You could have rolled out pastry on that parade ground."

"But what about the mushroom?"

"I was coming to that. There was this white flagpole in the middle of the parade ground. . . . Ah, Charing Cross, here we are."

The train stopped, the two men got out, taking with them forever the secret of what happened to the mushroom. That was about thirty years ago, but I still wake sometimes in the small hours and occupy myself with speculations as to where and in what circumstances the mushroom turned up.

Curiosity is the main characteristic that divides human beings from other animals. Of course some animals are inquisitive, too, but not to the ruinous degree that has brought the human race to its present precarious clutch on atomic development and other undesirable areas of knowledge. If only our earliest ancestor had not rubbed two sticks together and discovered how to light a campfire. . . . But here we are, congenitally inquisitive, and there is no going back. We long to find out what began it all, and what happened in the end. Ancient myths and folk tales give warnings about the perils incurred from prying into other people's business: Prometheus stealing fire from the gods; Psyche spilling hot oil from the lamp on Cupid in her eagerness to discover the identity of her nightly visitor; the terrible revelations of Bluebeard's chamber.

Magic—a dangerous force, like electricity, like radiation—is unleashed by attempts to discover what lies ahead, to divine the future, to skip all the tedious intervening chapters and turn on to the very last page. Why do we read stories? Because we long to find out what happened next. Any writer who can evoke this curiosity is sure of an audience. But how is it done? How can you keep your readers atwitter with suspense? Some authors can relate the most wonderful, hair-raising events in such a flat, disinterested manner that they might just as well be recounting the annals of the local archaeological society, while others make the most trifling event full of entertainment and surprise. The important factors are who is telling and who is listening.

One way to arouse curiosity, and a very good one, is to imply that there is a secret waiting to be revealed. What kind of secret? Well, it must be an important, a crucial one, or it would not have been kept secret in the first place. The revelation must then be postponed for as long as possible. This is a matter of judgment, for if you delay the revelation *too* long, the reader may become impatient, and close the book, or turn on to the end; or, even worse, when the disclosure comes, it comes as an anti-climax and the disappointed reader may feel that it was not worth waiting for.

Dickens was a very shrewd hand at delayed-action disclosure: A main part of his technique was to provide half a dozen subplots, each with its own mystery, so that, in *Our Mutual Friend,* for instance, there is the mystery of the dead man found in the Thames, the mystery of Silas Wegg's evil hold over Mr. Boffin, and Mr. Boffin's peculiar behavior, the involved goings-on of the Lammles and Veneerings and their financial dealings, the paranoid behavior of Bradley Headstone, and the very odd, inscrutable relationship of Fledgeby and Riah—and a wealth of other oddities. The reader is given continual short glimpses of all these strange connections, enough to whet curiosity. But it is not until well after the halfway mark of the book that any explanations are forthcoming, and, as fast as one mystery is unravelled, another is brought back, to keep the reader turning the pages until the very end. Dickens's work had to be planned in installments for serial publication, so there was an obligation to provide a cliffhanger for the end of each part.

Fiction writing in Dickens's day had undergone a total change from the tranquil pace of the eighteenth century, before the Industrial Revolution, when readers, living mostly in the country, had unlimited reading time and were prepared for a novel to begin in a leisurely manner.

Writers then had all the time in the world to convey their message, and readers could settle down comfortably for a nice peaceful three-volume reading orgy in the long lamplit winter evenings.

All this came to an abrupt end in 1859 with the publication of Wilkie Collins's *The Woman in White,* which appeared serially in *All the Year Round.* A mass audience of middle-class readers had arrived. They wanted action. Stories had to begin with a bang: the Dover coach on a foggy night brought to a halt by a lone horseman; an escaped convict confronting a terrified boy in a lonely churchyard; wills, legacies, deathbed dramas. Wilkie Collins was a master hand at a gripping beginning. The protagonist in *The Woman in White* is first seen fleeing from her persecutors across Hampstead Heath. *The Moonstone* (not actually a moonstone, but a yellow diamond) opens with the storming of Seringapatam and the theft of the jewel from the forehead of the Brahmin god.

The only problem with such a rousing start is that not every writer has the ability to maintain the tension at this pitch for the rest of the story. Wilkie Collins at his best could do so, but he was not always *at* his best, and sometimes the tension began to sag as the plot became almost too formidably complicated.

How can this kind of lapse be avoided—apart from having a simpler plot? Keep your tale peppered with odd, unexplained episodes. You can have characters behave seemingly out of character, turn nasty, be seen in unexpected places in unlikely company. Your hero, for instance, meets an old friend who greets him with a blank stare, with no sign of recognition; a faithful hound growls at his master of ten years; two old women are seen in a village street looking at photographs, and one of them suddenly shrieks in astonishment.

To keep the reader's attention focused on your hero (who is engaged in a struggle against apparently insuperable odds), it can be useful to endow him with an unexpected minor attribute that will stand him in good stead in confronting a vital crisis. He is a qualified tea-taster; or she has perfect musical pitch; he speaks ten different African languages; she is an expert on the kind of paint Velasquez used. The reader must, of course, have been previously informed of this specialized knowledge or skill, but in a passing, offhand way. If it comes as a complete surprise to the reader at the moment of crisis (he was the only man in England who could undo a particular knot), the reader could be justifiably annoyed. "Author's convenience" must be avoided at all costs. The author's real skill lies in creating the type of situation that would require the hero or heroine's unique expertise to be brought into play. There is a folk-tale model based on exactly this pattern: The hero is sent into the world on a seemingly hopeless quest, accompanied by six friends. One can run faster than anyone in the world; another is a champion archer . . . and so on. Here, of course, the pleasure for the reader lies in anticipating the triumph of the hero and his friends.

I had a good time writing my children's book, *The Whispering Mountain,* in which the hero, a short-sighted, delicate, unathletic boy, has to contend with a gang of local bullies and with a couple of London criminals. He always carries with him a tiny *Book of Knowledge,* which invariably provides him with the precise bit of know-how to meet each emergency. I happen to own such a book, and so was able to tailor the emergencies in the story to fit the information it provided. The idea, of course, is not new: I adopted it from *The Swiss Family Robinson,* in which the calmly competent mother of the family is always able to produce from her reticule the necessary ball of string, pair of pliers, or sticking plaster to deal with a problem.

Naturally, a story need not be presented on such a simplistic physical level to keep the reader's curiosity stimulated. Jane Austen arouses and maintains interest easily and spontaneously with her basic problem situations. How will the Bennets ever manage to marry off all those five daughters? How will Anne Elliot manage to endure the painful ordeal of encountering her lost lover again after eight years of heartbreak? What is the mystery attached to Jane Fairfax? Why wouldn't she go to Ireland? How will poor little Fanny Price make out when she is sent to live among those rich scornful relatives?

A tremendously important element of readability is the solid basis of the plot. A well-balanced, strong story generally has one or perhaps two crucial events in it. One, fairly early on, is to give you a foretaste of what the writer is able to provide. Charlotte Brontë whets your appetite by telling about Jane Eyre's incarceration in the Red Room and the consequent ghostly terrors. Then the story settles down to sober reality until the second explosion with the mad Mrs. Rochester in the attic. Mystery novelist Reginald Hill, in one of his Detective Dalziel mysteries, teases the aghast reader early on with a wild description of a crazed gunman and mayhem in a village street; then he rewinds the story to an earlier point of time, and so keeps readers on tenterhooks, waiting while he leads up again to the moment when all hell is going to break loose. And then he deals the expectant reader another shattering surprise.

Readers today are much more sophisticated than they used to be. They are accustomed to fictional trickery, guessing games, speeding up and slowing down of action, even unresolved questions and crises. They have only to walk along the street or into a supermarket or bookstore to see racks and racks of paperbacks and hardbacks, all screaming their messages of drama and sensationalism. But it is still possible to find a simple straight-forward story that will keep the reader breathless, attentive, and compulsively turning the pages. The novels of Sara Paretsky, Tony Hillerman, Reginald Hill, Dick Francis, and Rosamund Pilcher are good examples.

Fiction today has to compete with television, videotapes, films, rock music, virtual reality; and the horrors and crises in world news, exciting discoveries and inventions, and human deeds and misdeeds.

Sometimes a story depends for its momentum on a single character, or on the relationship between two characters. We love Character A and would like to see him on good terms with Character B, but they have always been at odds. How can an agreement between them be brought about? The relationship between Beatrice and Benedict in Shakespeare's *Much Ado About Nothing* is a fine example of such a story.

In *Little Lord Fauntleroy,* Frances Hodgson Burnett accomplishes this in a domestic setting. Character A won't love B, but B wins him over. The crusty old Earl of Dorincourt is unwillingly obliged by law to accept his unknown American grandson as his heir; how long will it take the gallant little fellow and his gentle gracious American mother to win their rightful places in the old aristocrat's rugged heart? Of course, it does not take very long, but the course of the story is pure pleasure for the reader all the way, even with the end so clearly in view.

Another heroine who achieves her end by possessing startlingly unexpected attributes and winning hearts all the way is Dorothy Gilman's

Mrs. Pollifax, a senior citizen spy. Often teamed with tough male colleagues who at first deeply mistrust and resent her, she breaches their
defenses by candor, practical good sense, humor, courage, and a touch
of mysticism that is irresistible. We all love to read about good tri-
umphing over evil, and to be given the certainty that it will do so, with
a touch of humor thrown in, is an unbeatable combination.

Unrecognized love must always command the fascinated attention
of readers, and Rebecca West makes tantalizing use of this knowledge
in her magnificent novel, *The Birds Fall Down*. In this story, the clever
but repulsive double agent Kamensky is infatuated by the teenage
heroine Laura, but she is wholly unaware of this from first to last,
believing that he intends to assassinate her. The unacknowledged duel
between them builds up to an almost intolerably suspenseful climax,
heightened by the fact that most of the other characters, Russians,
are given to immense, loquacious, red-herring monologues on every
conceivable topic, always just at the moment when some catastrophe
seems imminent, or a train is about to leave.

Virginia Woolf had an idea for a play, never actually written: "I'm
going to have a man and a woman . . . never meeting, not knowing
each other, but all the time you'll feel them coming nearer and nearer.
This will be the really exciting part, but when they *almost* meet—only
a door between—you see how they just miss." Perhaps not surprisingly, she never did put the idea into a play or story. But Mary Wesley,
in her novel, *An Imaginative Experience,* used a similar plot, except
that she does finally permit her couple to meet. This kind of scheme
for a story clearly displays that fiction is a kind of teasing game carried
on between writer and reader, a game like Grandmother's Footsteps,
in which I, the writer, try to steal up on you, the reader, without
allowing you to find out beforehand what I intend to do.

And the theme of *curiosity,* dangerous, misplaced, unwarrantable
curiosity, takes us, by way of myth and folklore, to ghost stories and
the supernatural. "A Warning to the Curious" is the title of one of
M.R. James's best-known ghost stories, and a very terrifying story it
is, yet entirely convincing. Who could resist the possibility of discovering one of the legendary three royal crowns, buried somewhere,
long ago, on the Suffolk coast "to keep off the Danes or the French or
the Germans." But the surviving crown has a ghostly guardian, and
the fate of the inquisitive rabbity young man who goes after it is very

awful indeed. All the details in this story are exactly right: the foggy, sandy countryside, and the character of Paxton, the silly young man who has dug up the crown and now wishes he hadn't. The narrator and his friend try to help, but "all the same the snares of death overtook him," James states, but then proceeds to describe a harrowing chase through the fog, poor Paxton pursued by a creature "with more bones than flesh" and a "lungless laugh." Paxton is finally found with his mouth full of sand, his teeth and jaws broken to bits. . . .

Operas have overtures, in which snatches of all the best arias are beguilingly introduced, giving the audience a taste of the pleasures to come. In the same way, the shrewd writer will, by an opening sentence, sound the *voice* of his story, suggest what is likely to happen, and so whet the reader's appetite: "The marriage wasn't going well and I decided to leave my husband," says Anne Tyler at the start of *Earthly Possessions;* "I went to the bank to get cash for the trip." And so she set the style and tempo for a wildly free-wheeling and funny plot.

Your voice can be humorous or terrifying, sad, wild, or romantic; only *you* can give it utterance, only you can lead your reader by a cobweb thread through the windings of your own particular story. What did happen to the mushroom? Each of us has his own theory as to that.

❏ 36

Storytelling, Old and New

By Elizabeth Spencer

Being a Southerner, a Mississippian, had a good deal to do, I now believe, with my ever having started to write at all, though I did not have any notion about this at the time it all began. Having had stories read to me and having listened to them being told aloud since I could understand speech, I began quite naturally as soon as I could write to fashion stories of my own. I now can see that my kind of part-country, part-small-town Southerners *believed* in stories and still remain, in my experience, unique in this regard. They believed, that is, in events and the people concerned in them, both from the near and distant past, and paid attention to getting things straight, a habit which alone can give true dignity to character, for it defeats the snap judgment, the easy answer, the label and the smear. Bible stories, thus, which were heard at home and in church, were taken literally, and though the Greek and Roman myths that were read aloud to me, along with Arthurian legend and many others, were described as "just" stories, the distinction was one I found easy to escape; maybe I did not want to make it. And we heard oral stories, too: Civil War accounts and tragic things, some relating to people we could actually see uptown almost any day. All ran together in my head at that magic time—I trace any good books I have written, or stories, right back to them.

Starting at the other end of things, however, is what the writer who daily faces the blank sheet must do: that is to say, O.K. about childhood, what about now?

From motion to repose

The work of fiction begins for the writer and reader alike, I feel, when the confusing outer show of things can be swept aside, when something happens that gives access to the dangerous secret pulse of life. What is really going on? This is the question that continually

160

tantalizes and excites. For the fiction writer, the way of getting the answer is by telling the story.

Right back to stories. You see how quick it was.

A story is a thing in itself. It has a right to be without making any apology about what it means, or how its politics and religion and pedigree and nationality may be labeled. The name of the writer can be guessed at by the stories he puts down, but the writer is not the story any more than an architect is a building. The events in a true—that is to say, real—story are a complex of many things, inexhaustibly rich, able to be circled around like a statue or made at a touch to create new patterns like a kaleidoscope. Such a story may be absorbed sensually or pondered about reasonably; it may be talked about by friends or strangers in the presence or the absence of the writer. The story should be allowed to take in all its basic wants. It may want discipline, but it may not get it, depending upon how greedy it is or how obsessed the writer is about it. A story has the curious, twofold quality of seeming all in motion and at times even in upheaval while it is being told, but when finished, of having reached its natural confines and attained repose. Many times characters seem to have life outside the story in which they engage. So much the better; the story will not question this.

A silent magnetism

Each story I have written commenced in a moment, usually unforeseen, when out of some puzzlement, bewilderment, or wonder, some response to actual happening, my total imagination was drawn up out of itself; a silent magnetism, without my willing it, had taken charge. What was it all about? It is just as well for the writer to pause here and consider. Not that the writer will take the imprint, literally, of people and event—though for some writers the main worry falls here. To me, it is rather the power of the story that one should be warned about: Don't enter that lion's cage without knowing about lions. For the writer enters alone. He may be eaten up, or mauled, or decide to get the hell out of there, but even if all goes splendidly and ends in fine form, the person who comes out is not the same one who went in.

Anyone who takes stories as an essential part of life is only recognizing the obvious. Religion, love, psychiatry, families, nations, wars and history have all become deeply mixed up with stories and so find no way to shed them without violating or even destroying their own natures. Every human being is deeply involved with at least one story—

his own. (The Southern tendency to get involved with family stories has accounted for the larger part of Southern fiction—if we add to this hunting stories and war stories, then we have just about accounted for all of it.) The present faint-hearted tone that some critics now adopt when discussing the future of fiction is surprising, for stories, being part of the primal nature of human expression, are in one way or another going to continue to be told. What disturbs us all, I believe, is the debasement of the story into something mass-made, machine-tooled, slick and false. (The lion was stuffed or drugged or doctored some way.) At its highest level, a story is a free art form, daring to explore and risk, to claim that it recognizes truth . . . and that even when inventive, what it imagines is, in terms it can splendidly determine, true.

A common note

At a level short of this highest fiction, but shared by it, many group stories exist, the bulk of which never get written down. They are told every day, repeated, embellished, continued, or allowed to die, and some are better than others; inventive and factual at once, both commonplace and myth-like, they grow among humanity like mistletoe in oaks. They are much better than average TV fare, and anyone who wants to write should start collecting everyday accounts that are passed about offices, campuses, neighborhoods, or within family situations, noticing whatever there is to be found of humor and terror, character, achievement, failure, triumph, tragedy, irony and delight. The modern theme of self-exploration with heavy emphasis on the private sexual nature and fantasy has been done to the point of weariness. Can we think of ourselves again in communion with others, in communities either small, medium or large, which may be torn apart disastrously or find a common note, an accord? One word for it maybe, is love.

□ 37

MAKING THE READER CARE

BY MARJORIE FRANCO

EMOTION, OR A STATE OF FEELING, IS SOMETHING WE ALL EXPERI-
ence, and for most of us our persistent memories are of situations or
happenings that aroused a powerful emotion. When writing a story,
the author uses a variety of emotions, trusting the reader to experience
them along with the character. The character needs to be convincing
enough to cause the reader to recall his or her own emotions, though
not necessarily the specific experience that aroused them.

A friend once told me that her brother's favorite memory of childhood was of a summer night when he and the other members of his
family stood around in the kitchen eating ice cream cones. Happiness,
no doubt, was the emotion he connected to the scene, and this simple
emotion resulted from many factors, including the summer night, the
kitchen, the cold sweetness of the ice cream on his tongue, and above
all, the sharing of pleasure with a loving family.

Although this memory from real life is different from the world of
fiction, it is an example of how we remember moments that affect
us. Our storehouse of memory continues to grow from childhood on,
providing us with ideas for characters, setting, and conflicts, which,
with the help of imagination, craft, and an appropriate tone, we weave
together to create a story we hope will make the reader care.

Not an easy task, and one that beginning writers sometimes sidestep
by having emotion occur off scene, or by simply stating it in narrative.

In *Lectures on Literature,* Vladimir Nabokov writes that memory
causes the perfect fusion of past and present; that inspiration adds a
third ingredient, the future. The writer, he believes, see the world as
the potentiality of fiction.

An observant writer once saw a woman getting off a bus, and was
so struck by something about her appearance and manner, she became
the inspiration for a character in his story.

Henry James, sitting next to a woman at a dinner party, listening to her describe an event that actually took place, began thinking along fictional lines, sowing the seeds for what would become his novella *The Aspern Papers*. Once the idea had formed in his mind, he didn't want to hear the woman's entire story, for he was already creating his own.

We may begin creating a fictional character with a real person in mind, but the end result is never a duplicate of that person, because it's impossible to get inside another person's head, no matter how well we may know him or her. But it is necessary to get inside our characters, to know their personalities, strengths and weakness, what will make them feel love, hate, joy, anger, fear and pain; what experiences will affect their lives, and how they will deal with their problems. Much of this is revealed by showing them interacting with other characters in particular situations; with scene and dialogue; and with conflict.

The idea for my story "Between Friends" (*Good Housekeeping*) began with a real person in mind, but the character of Janet quickly took on her own personality and became fictional. The protagonist, Alison, welcomes new arrival, Janet, to the neighborhood, and they become friends. The conflict begins with Janet's casual criticism of Benny, Alison's son. Gradually, it escalates to the point where Janet says, "Maybe you've put your job before the interests of your child. Maybe if you'd stayed home more things would have been better." Words are exchanged, and the friendship ends with bitter feelings on both sides.

I believe the reader can relate to this confrontation, for we have all experienced criticism, as well as the hurt and feeling of rejection that accompany it. And when the critic is a friend, we may feel doubly rejected. Alison, who has gone out of her way for Janet, feels she's been treated unfairly, just as the reader may have felt at some time, even though the situation might have been different. Here, again, I trust the reader to tap into emotions that may be latent and experience them vicariously with the character.

The climax of the story occurs when a desperate Janet comes to Alison for help. Alison is about to leave for an important job interview, but when Janet says, "It's Andy, he ate a whole bottle of aspirin," she is horrified, and putting aside their differences (as well as her interview), she immediately drives Janet and Andy to the hospital.

Here, Alison has to make a quick decision, and the one she chooses says something about her character, her sense of right and wrong. Another person, unwilling to sacrifice an important interview for someone who has treated her badly, might have called an ambulance and left Janet and her son to wait for its arrival.

In addition to trying to show insight into the main character, I was also trying to establish empathy for Janet, the antagonist. Janet has her own problems. Perhaps she regrets having given up her job to stay home with her children; perhaps her criticism of Alison is grounded in envy; and, most important of all, perhaps she feels responsible for placing her son in danger, guilty of an act of negligence, the same kind of negligence of which she had accused Alison's son. Anger, envy, and guilt are emotions that have touched us all.

In our attempt to make the reader care, I believe we must keep in mind the difference between identifying with and relating to characters. The definition of identify is "to be, or become the same." Writers who create unique characters shouldn't expect the reader to identify with them. I take the view that though there is a universality in human beings, still each of us is different in a unique way. In contrast, the definition of relate is "to have a relationship or connection," a better goal, I think, for making the reader care.

As important as characters are to a story, they would not hold the reader's attention without some form of conflict. Conflict moves the story and keeps the reader interested while waiting to discover what happens next. Conflict generates emotion and requires the character either to solve the problem or to deal with it in a satisfactory way.

In my story "Midnight Caller" (*Good Housekeeping*) Dianne, a teacher and recently divorced mother of an infant son, is receiving anonymous phone calls, usually at midnight. She lives on the second floor of a three-story building; her friend Greta lives upstairs with her teenaged son, and another friend, Hank, lives on the first floor. Safety is of great importance to Dianne: On her own, and responsible for her infant son as well as for herself, she has tried to protect herself by choosing to live near friends. When the phone calls begin, she persuades herself that her name was picked at random from the phone book; still, they represent a threat to her feeling of safety and cause her a sense of unease. Then one snowy night, with all the roads blocked, all feelings of safety vanish and unease gives way to outright fear.

"What are you wearing?" the voice on the phone says. "Is it the yellow nightgown with the ruffles, or the white one with the lace?" Slowly, as if in a dream, she touches the neck of her nightgown and runs her fingers over the yellow ruffles. She hangs up, heart pounding, wide awake after being startled out of a sound sleep, and goes to her son's room.

The setting contributes to the tension—the apartment building surrounded by snow "thick on the rooftops and the bare trees, high where it had drifted against fences in backyards"—and so does the detail: the nightgown with the ruffles, her son's room "small, shadowy and warm, smelling of baby powder and freshly washed blankets. Clean."

Dianne's desire for safety is in conflict with the outside threat, the fact that she is interacting with an unknown person. By using certain words, abstractions are made concrete: "pounding" and "startled" contrast with "warm," "baby powder," and "clean."

In the end, Dianne discovers the identity of the midnight caller. It is not Hank, her neighbor, or one of her students at school, possibilities she had considered. It is Greta's son, who has often baby-sat for her. Like Alison in the first story I mentioned, Dianne is faced with a difficult and very important decision.

In these two stories, I've tried to show how characters, conflicts, and settings can generate emotion in the reader. But the emotion expressed through the character must first be felt by the writer who uses memory, experience and observations together with creative imagination to write the story and present it with clarity so the reader will understand.

Readers don't need to have conscious memory of events in their lives that aroused certain feelings in order to imagine a fictional situation and relate to it either positively or negatively. But those feelings can be touched by the characters in a story and the events in their lives, and when that happens, readers begin to care.

❏ SPECIALIZED FICTION

❏ 38

How Real History Fits Into the Historical Novel

By Thomas Fleming

Too many writers—and not a few readers—tend to think of nonfiction and fiction as opposites—a twain that should never meet. Throughout my career, I have taken a very different approach. While I am writing a nonfiction book or article, I am constantly looking for situations, events, characters, that present an opening to the imagination.

For example, I received an assignment to write an article about the 1942 Battle of Savo Island, the disastrous naval engagement off Guadalcanal in which the Japanese inflicted a stunning defeat on the Americans. As I assembled the research, I discovered that the *USS Chicago,* the acting flagship of the American cruiser squadron, had unaccountably sailed *away* from the attacking Japanese soon after the midnight assault began. The other American cruisers were sunk. The *Chicago*'s captain was relieved of duty and later shot himself rather than face a court of inquiry.

I asked myself: What if the captain of that disgraced ship was replaced by his Annapolis roommate, his closest friend? How would the new captain handle the job? Would he investigate what had happened aboard the ship on that terrible night, and perhaps destroy his friend's career? In a flash, the plot of my novel, *Time and Tide,* leaped into my mind. I created an imaginary cruiser, the *USS Jefferson City,* which became the guilt-haunted ship. I peopled it with a crew tormented by the memory of Savo Island. As they struggled to redeem themselves and the Captain tried to redefine his relationship with his friend, who had always been the superior voice, the naval war in the Pacific unfolded around them, seen from a dramatic new perspective.

Sometimes it is a special insight into a historical character that triggers an imaginative explosion. While working on a profile of General

John J. Pershing, the American commander in World War I, I discovered that shortly before he went to France, his wife and three children were killed in a fire at the Presidio, the San Francisco army base. What did that tragedy do to the general's soul? I wondered. Did it have an impact on his conduct in France? How could that be dramatized?

What if Pershing had a close army friend who had sustained a similar loss? Enter Colonel Malvern Hill Bliss, the central character of my novel, *Over There*. He is speeding down a highway outside San Antonio, drunk and demoralized by the death of his wife and son from a terrorist machete in the Philippines. Before this opening chapter ends, Pershing has dragged Bliss out of a brothel and ordered him to prepare to depart for France with him in 24 hours. The Pershing that Bliss reveals to the reader is a very different man from the Iron General in the history books—and so is the World War that both of them fight.

My novel *Dreams of Glory* is another novel whose genesis was derived from a nonfiction book. I was writing *The Forgotten Victory,* an account of the 1780 battle of Springfield, when I came across the story of a black American soldier found in a snowdrift outside George Washington's headquarters in Morristown, with a bayonet in his chest. Washington's army was about 15% black by this time. Who had killed this man? Apparently no one ever found out.

Again, this fact exploded into a whole novel in my imagination. What if the black soldier was a spy who was killed in the intelligence war that raged between the two armies? The result was a book that reveals a dark underside of the Revolutionary struggle.

By now it should be apparent that a historical novel is not "made up." Its vitality can and should come from history itself, and the deeper its roots in reality, the better.

Another trigger to the imagination may be the discovery of a little-known set of historical facts or a situation that has relevance to our own time. I believe a prime function of the historical novel is to surprise as well as intrigue the reader.

A few years ago, I was fascinated to discover that before the American Revolution, New York City was 25% black—mostly slaves. In the 1740s the blacks concocted a plot to sack the city and hand it over to the French in exchange for their freedom.

How would this startling set of facts fit into a novel? I wanted to tell the story from the inside, retaining sympathy for the slaves, yet seeing the episode in all its complexity. What if there were someone in the conspiracy who saw it differently? I created Clara Flowers, a beautiful black woman who was captured and raised by Seneca Indians, then repatriated to the white world at seventeen. She became the main character of my recently published novel, *Remember The Morning*.

Growing up in the so-called middle ground around the Great Lakes, where whites and Indians mingled, Clara has a different view of race relations. As her role grew in my mind, I saw she could also illuminate women's experience in pre-revolutionary America. I created a Dutch woman, Catalyntie Van Vorst, with whom Clara shared her Indian captivity. Catalyntie becomes a successful merchant, not unusual among the American Dutch. Although the slave revolt strains their relationship, their early bonding as Senecas and their common identity as women enable them to continue their friendship.

To make this work, I had to learn the mores and customs of the "middle ground," the intricacies of the fur trade, the local politics of colonial New York, and the global politics of the struggle for world supremacy between Catholic France and Protestant England. It all began with the seed of my original discovery about the startling role of the blacks in New York, two hundred years before Harlem and Bedford-Stuyvesant. As good historical novels should, this book resonates in our own time, making us think about our present dilemmas in a new way.

Similarly, one of the primary insights of my twenty-five years of research into the American Revolution was the little-known fact that in some states, such as New Jersey, the struggle was a civil war. Brothers fought brothers and sisters fell in love with their brothers' or their fathers' enemies.

Swiftly, my imagination created a character who could convey this startling ambiguity. What if an ex-British officer named Jonathan Gifford married an American widow, adopted her two children, and opened a tavern on the Kings Highway in New Jersey? Into the tavern—and the story—would swirl loyalists and neutrals and ferocious rebels, eager to hang every waverer in sight. It would be especially poignant if Gifford's stepson, Kemble Stapleton, was the local Robespierre. Thus was born my novel *Liberty Tavern,* which told the story of Gifford's gradual conversion to the American cause—and Kemble's education in the complexities of Revolutionary politics.

Crucial to the success of every work of historical fiction is a thorough knowledge of the period, so that the imaginary events fit plausibly into the known history of the time. This "veracious imagination" (a term coined by English novelist George Eliot and revived by Cornell critic Cushing Stout) is a vital ingredient in meshing real history and the imaginative, symbolic events that the novelist is adding to the story. Without this background knowledge, the writer may create "improbable truths," something the father of the American historical novel, James Fenimore Cooper, felt was a primary danger in interweaving the imaginative and the real.

Achieving this fit is not as daunting as it seems at first. Rich as the historical record is, it is not so crowded with information that the creation of an imaginary character like Malvern Hill Bliss or Clara Flowers strains plausibility. On the contrary, by giving the reader a closeup of the historical experience, it may make the story even more plausible.

Real characters, such as Pershing, George Washington, Adolf Hitler, Franklin D. Roosevelt have appeared in my novels, alongside the imaginary ones. It is extremely important to present such historical figures accurately. To portray Washington as a drunk or Pershing as a coward, for instance, would be a serious violation of the novelist's historical responsibilities.

But dialogue *can* be invented for these historical figures. In my novel *Loyalties,* for instance, I have a scene in which F.D.R. reveals his pathological hatred of the German people—a little-known fact that plays a large part in the novel's plot (and was a major factor in prolonging World War II). I put words in F.D.R.'s mouth that are based on extensive research, making them not only plausible but probable.

There is another reason for grasping the great issues and inner spiritual and psychological struggles of a whole period. *Remember the Morning,* for instance, is more than the story of Clara Flowers' and Catalyntie Van Vorst's search for security and love. As the story unfolds, they both get emotionally involved with a raw young would-be soldier named Malcolm Stapleton. The growing American dissatisfaction with England's corrupt imperial control of America becomes the book's leitmotif. Out of the racial and personal turmoil in the forefront of the novel, an awakening sense of a separate American destiny emerges. The drums of the American Revolution are thudding in the distance as the story ends, adding substance and a deeper meaning to the book.

The historical novelist has to be even more selective than the historian in constructing his narrative. His goal is emotional truth—a considerable leap beyond factual truth. Historians seldom deal with personal emotions in history. In the novel, such emotions are the primary focus of the story. This means that you cannot describe every battle of World War I while writing about Bliss and Pershing in France. You have to choose one or two battles in which their inner anguish becomes visible. It means you can shift the timing of a historical event a few years in either direction in order to increase the emotional intensity—as I did with the black revolt in *Dreams of Glory.*

Perhaps the least understood role of reality in the historical novel is the way research can supply you with details that deepen and otherwise improve the story you are telling. In *Loyalties,* the main character, Berthe Von Hoffmann, an agent for the German Resistance to Hitler, is kidnapped from Madrid by her former lover, who is working for the Nazis. The American protagonist Jonathan Talbot follows them to Grenada. The imperatives of the plot require Talbot to kill the Nazi.

I found myself recoiling from a scene which was routine spy novel huggermugger. Something else was needed. In another day's research on Grenada, I discovered that inside the famed Moslem palace, the Alhambra, was a crude Spanish palace built by King Charles V. On one of its walls was an enormous painting of a column of refugees plodding into the distance. "The Expulsion of the Jews" by Emilio Sala depicted the decision of King Ferdinand and Queen Isabella to banish the Jews from Spain in 1492.

I had the ingredient I needed to create an original scene that fit perfectly into the story. While the Nazi gazes up at the painting and remarks that he hoped to persuade the Spanish government to let him bring it to Berlin, Talbot slips a silken cord around the Nazi's throat and strangles him. It was not my imagination that transformed this scene from cliché to meaningful drama; it was research—reality—fact.

More and more, I have come to think of these two sides of a historical novel as competing themes in a piece of music. Ultimately, fact can and should be woven into fiction so seamlessly, readers never stop to ask what is true in the literal sense and what is imaginative. All that should matter is the conviction that they are being taken inside events in a new revelatory, personal way. It takes hard work—but it is tremendously satisfying to write a book that engages readers' heads and hearts.

❑ 39

PARTNERS IN CRIME

BY MARCIA MULLER

LIKE MANY CRIME WRITERS, I CAME TO THE GENRE THROUGH MY love of reading, and the novels that most appealed to me were those featuring private investigators. Possibly because I don't respond well to any type of authority, I was fascinated by detectives who, unhampered by regulations and procedure, would set off down the mean streets to right wrongs, strong and unafraid. As one who had always wanted to write, I'd then dream of creating my own character who would walk those streets, strong and unafraid.

Unfortunately, almost all the fictional models at that time were male, and while I could empathize with men and understand them on an individual basis, of course I didn't know the slightest thing about actually *being* male. Thus, the character I'd dream of creating was always a woman.

By the time I'd seriously begun to consider writing a novel featuring a private investigator of my own, I'd discovered several authors who were doing excellent characterization within the framework of the crime novel. Bill Pronzini (whom I did not know at the time, but to whom I'm now married) wrote about a detective who had no name, yet I knew intimate details about him that made him more real to me than many characters *with* names. Lillian O'Donnell had created New York City policewoman Norah Mulcahaney who, in addition to a lively professional life, found time to marry; her family life provided a rich backdrop to the cases she solved.

When I sat down to write my first (never published, and quite horrible) Sharon McCone novel, I was well aware that I could create a woman who would conform to the stereotype of the hard-bitten loner with the whiskey bottle in the desk drawer. Or I could make her a camera who observed the world around her without fully reacting or interacting. Or, at the far end of the spectrum, I could create a woman who would be a fully developed individual.

Sharon McCone, I decided, was to be as close to a real person as possible. Like real people she would age, grow, change; experience joy and sorrow, love and hatred—in short, the full range of human emotions. In addition, McCone was to live within the same framework most of us do, complete with family, friends, coworkers, and lovers; each of her cases would constitute one more major event in an ongoing biography. This choice also had a practical basis. In writing crime fiction, the author frequently asks the reader to suspend disbelief in situations that are not likely to occur in real life. Private investigators do not, as a rule, solve dozens of murder cases over the course of their careers. And what few criminals they do encounter do not tend to be as clever and intelligent as their fictional counterparts. To make the story convincing to the reader, the character and day-to-day details of her life had to be firmly grounded in reality.

The choice made, I realized I hadn't a clue as to how to go about creating such an individual. I had a name: Sharon, for my college roommate; McCone, for the late John McCone, former head of the CIA (a joke, since politically Sharon is as far from any CIA employee as one can get). I also had a location, San Francisco, my adopted home city. But as for the rest . . . ?

Should I make my character like me in background, lifestyle, appearance, and spirit? Certainly not! At the time I had no job, no recognizable skills, no prospects, a failing marriage, and was afraid of my own shadow. I longed to be three or four inches taller, to be fifteen to twenty pounds lighter, to be able to eat all the ice cream I wanted and never gain an ounce. And I was vehemently opposed to making Sharon's background similar to mine, lest I fall into the trap of undisciplined autobiographical writing.

I therefore began building McCone's character by giving her a background as different from mine as I could make it. She is a native Californian; I am not. She comes from a large blue-collar family; I do not. She put herself through the University of California at Berkeley by working as a security guard; I was supported by my parents during my six years at the University of Michigan. And Sharon has exotic Native American features and long black hair, is enviably tall and slender, and can eat whatever she likes without gaining weight. Since I don't possess such qualities, I wanted to spend time with a character who did.

At the time I was developing McCone, I was participating in an informal writers' workshop that met every week; fear of having nothing to read aloud at the sessions drove me daily to the typewriter. I chose to take the suggestion of the group leader (a published author) to work up a biographical sheet on McCone, in which I fine-tuned the other details of her life: names of parents and siblings; likes and dislikes; religious and political attitudes; talents and weaknesses; even the circumstances of her first sexual experience.

By the time I'd completed the biographical sheet, McCone finally emerged as real to me. Still, it was in a form that was more like a questionnaire than a work of fiction. At this point I was forced to face the fact that the only way to develop a character fully is to write her. And write her, and write her. . . .

Anyone who claims that first manuscripts aren't simply learning exercises is either exceptionally gifted or completely deluded. My early efforts were stiff and wooden and—with the exception of McCone's narrative voice, which was the same from the very first—totally different from what eventually saw publication.

I was insecure as to how to go about constructing a mystery, and in spite of my resolve to let the events flow from character, I found the stories becoming very plot-driven. I manipulated secondary characters and their actions to fit the plot; kept elaborate charts showing what every person was doing at every moment during the story; wrote long accounts of the back story (the events that set the crime in motion). I wasted paper, time, and energy concocting cryptic clues, red herrings, and unnecessary complications. Even after my third novel manuscript was accepted for publication, I continued to fall back on stock scenes and situations: ongoing antagonism between private investigator and police; the standard body-finding scene; the obligatory talk about the case in the office of Sharon's boss.

Fortunately, through all of this, McCone came into her own as a person and also became my full partner in fictional crime. I take little credit for this; it simply happened. Writers constantly talk about how their characters "just take over," and when I hear myself doing the same, I feel vaguely embarrassed, but it *does* happen, and is vitally important to any long-running series.

My theory about this phenomenon is that knowing one's character intimately allows the writer to tap into her subconscious, which usually works far ahead of the conscious mind. The fictional character's actions and reactions often have little to do with the writer's original intention. In this area, McCone has served me well.

I first experienced her determination to be her own person while writing the second book in the series, *Ask the Cards a Question* (1982). In my previous efforts, Sharon had many analytical conversations about her cases with her boss, Hank Zahn, and they inevitably took place in his office at All Souls Legal Cooperative, the poverty law firm where she worked. A third of the way through *Cards,* it seemed time for one of these talks, so I had Sharon leave her office for Hank's. But contrary to my intentions, she detoured down the hall to the desk of the co-op's secretary, Ted, to ask him where Hank was, and in doing so, she—and I—took a look around the big Victorian that housed All Souls. What I saw was a goldmine in terms of places to set scenes and characters to play in them: There were rooms, lots of them; there were attorneys and paralegal workers and other support staff, some of whom lived there communally, and often had potlucks and parties and poker games. As in any situation where people live and work at close quarters, there was the opportunity for conflict and resolution.

Where Hank Zahn had once been the only partner who had an identity, I now began to flesh out others. A number of them became important in McCone's life. They began to demand more important roles, and soon I realized that they—as well as McCone—would determine the direction that the series as a whole would take.

The development of fully realized characters is essential to creating a strong series. Without them, the author is simply manipulating cardboard people aimed at a specific—and usually contrived—end. Eventually the writer will become bored with the artificiality of the story and lose all sense of identification with the characters. And if the writer is bored, imagine the poor reader!

Over the twenty years I've been writing the McCone series, I've made a number of choices and changes, and each of these came from within Sharon's character and her reactions and interactions with others. This involves a firm commitment on my part to remain flexible, willing to switch directions mid-stream. Initially, this was a rather frightening process, but the rewards have proved considerable.

Different facets of McCone's character have been revealed to me by her interactions with other characters. A violent confrontation with a man she considered the most evil person she'd ever encountered, and the choice she made in dealing with him, affirmed that she was unable to step over the line into pointless violence. Another confrontation, this time when the lives of people she cared about were at stake, demonstrated that she could take violent action when the circumstances justified it.

During the past four years, McCone has revealed feelings and attitudes that have dictated radical changes in the overall direction of the series—long before I considered making any. When the All Souls partners threatened to confine Sharon to a desk job (*Wolf in the Shadows*, 1993), I'd originally intended for them to work out some sort of compromise, coupled with expanding the scope of her responsibilities. At the end of the novel, I was still undecided as to the nature of that compromise. But at the beginning of the next novel in the series, *Till the Butchers Cut Him Down* (1994), McCone made the decision for me: She decided to leave the co-op and establish her own agency, while retaining offices in the house—thus permitting her to continue her association with people for whom she cared.

But only months after her new office furniture was delivered, McCone began to doubt the wisdom of her decision. As I was writing a scene in *A Wild and Lonely Place* (1995), I found her saying, "No wonder I avoided having clients come to the office. . . . Actually, a lot of things about All Souls were beginning to pale for me." Her doubts mirrored my own, which I'd scarcely confronted until that point. She decided for me that the time had come to leave All Souls; time, in fact, for All Souls to become defunct. With roots in the 1970s, it was an outmoded institution; my attempts to bring it into the 1990s with its virtues intact had failed.

But in what direction to go? And where? Certainly not a stereotypical seedy office where McCone would keep a bottle in her desk drawer. And certainly not a suite in a high-rent building; she is too frugal for that.

The answer came to me while I was walking on the Embarcadero, San Francisco's waterfront boulevard, with a friend who was talking about some people she knew who had offices in a renovated pier. I looked around, spotted the San Francisco fireboat station, and noted a space between it and Pier 24 that was almost large enough for a fictional Pier 24½. The surrounding area was an exciting one, undergoing a renaissance; artists' lofts, lively clubs, trendy restaurants, and unusual sorts of enterprises abounded. And there was also San Francisco's rich maritime history, which offered many possibilities. Immediately, Sharon McCone made the decision to move her offices to Pier 24½.

But would I be forced to abandon Hank Zahn, his wife Anne-Marie Altman, Rae Kelleher, and Ted Smalley? Of course not. The co-op had paled for Anne-Marie several books before; it would now do the same for Hank, and they would decide to form their own law firm, then ask McCone to share a suite of offices with them. As for Rae and Ted, they would need jobs when All Souls went under, so Ted would come along as office manager, Rae as the first of what McCone hoped would be many operatives. Without delay, Sharon, Hank, and Anne-Marie signed a lease for space at Pier 24½.

A long and intimate association with well-rounded characters can not only enrich a series, but also an author's life. Over the years, I've found myself moving closer to McCone in spirit. Where she was once the independent, strong, brave half of the partnership, I've now become more independent, strong, and brave myself.

It's strange but gratifying to know that my own creation has empowered me. That's what the series is all about: to entertain and inspire the reader; perhaps to make some readers think more seriously about an issue that's important to McCone and me; and to give escape and pleasure to those who buy our books.

❑ 40

THE CRAFT OF THE ESPIONAGE THRILLER

BY JOSEPH FINDER

WHEN I WAS IN MY MID-TWENTIES AND STRUGGLING TO WRITE MY first novel, *The Moscow Club,* I got to know another aspiring writer, a cynical and embittered (but very funny) man, and told him I was immersed in the research for a spy thriller I hadn't begun to write. He shook his head slowly and scowled. "That's a sign of desperation," he intoned ominously. "Research is an excuse for not writing."

This ex-friend has given up trying to write and is working at some job he despises, while I'm making a living writing novels, so I think there may be a moral here. That old dictum writers are always accosted by—"Write what you know"—is, in the espionage-thriller genre, at least, a fallacy.

Obviously, research is no substitute for good writing, good storytelling, or the ability to create flesh-and-blood characters. But even the masters of the spy novel plunge into research for the worlds they create. John le Carré (the pen name for David Cornwell) was for a short while a spy for the British secret service, but nevertheless, he assiduously researches his spy tales. In the extensive acknowledgements at the end of *The Night Manager,* he thanks numerous sources in the U.S. Drug Enforcement Agency and the U.S. Treasury, mercenary soldiers, antiques dealers, and the "arms dealers who opened their doors to me." The novel only *reads* effortlessly.

I suppose you can just make it up, but it will always show, if you do, and the spy thriller must always evoke an authentic, fully realized world. Readers want to believe that the author is an authority, an expert, an insider who's willing to let them in on a shattering secret or two.

But no one can be expert in everything. My first novel was about a CIA analyst who learns of an impending coup attempt in Moscow and

181

is drawn into the conspiracy. In the first draft, however, the hero, Charles Stone, was instead a ghostwriter for a legendary American statesman. Luckily, my agent persuaded me that no one wants to read about the exploits of a ghostwriter.

Transforming Charlie into a CIA officer took a lot of rethinking, but fortunately, I had sources: While a student at Yale, I'd been recruited by the CIA (but decided against it), and I had some friends in the intelligence community. They helped me make Charlie Stone a far more interesting, more appealing and believable character.

The best ideas, I believe, spring from real-life events, from reading newspapers and books, and from conducting interviews. Frederick Forsyth came up with the idea for his classic thriller, *The Day of the Jackal* (a fictional plot on the life of Charles de Gaulle), from his experience working as a Reuters correspondent in Paris in the early 1960s, when rumors kept circulating about assassination attempts on de Gaulle. Robert Ludlum was watching TV news in a Paris hotel when he happened to catch a report about an international terrorist named Carlos; this became the seed for one of his best novels, *The Bourne Identity.*

When I first began thinking about writing the novel that later became *The Moscow Club,* I was a graduate student at the Harvard Russian Research Center, studying the politics of the Soviet Union. I remember reading Forsyth's *The Devil's Alternative,* which concerns intrigue in the Kremlin. Why not try my hand at this? I thought. After Mikhail Gorbachev became head of the Soviet Union and began the slow-motion revolution that would eventually lead to the collapse of that empire, I began to hear bizarre rumors about attempts in Moscow to unseat Gorbachev. The rumors didn't seem so far-fetched to me. But when *The Moscow Club* came out at the beginning of 1991, I was chided for my overly active imagination. Then, in August of that year, the real thing happened: The KGB and the military banded together to try to overthrow the Gorbachev government—and suddenly, I was a prophet!

My second novel, however, was a significant departure from this political background. *Extraordinary Powers* concerns Ben Ellison, an attorney for a prestigious Boston law firm (and former clandestine operative for the CIA). He is lured into a top-secret government experiment and emerges with a limited ability to "hear" the thoughts of others. This sprang from a reference I'd come across in a study of the KGB to some highly secret programs in the U.S. and Soviet governments that attempted to locate people with telepathic ability to serve in various espionage undertakings. Whether or not one believes in ESP, the fact that such projects really do exist was irresistible to me. I sent *Extraordinary Powers* to a friend who does contract work for the CIA; he confided in me that he'd received a call from a highly placed person in a government agency who actually runs such a project and had used psychics during the Gulf War. He wanted to know whether I'd been the recipient of a leak.

With this seemingly fantastic premise at the center of my novel, it was crucially important that the world in which this plot takes place be a very real, very well-grounded one. Because I wanted the telepathy project to hew as closely to reality as possible, I spent a great deal of time talking to patent lawyers, helicopter pilots, gold experts, and even neurologists. I was relieved to get letters from a world-famous neurobiologist and from the editor of *The New England Journal of Medicine* saying that they were persuaded that such an experiment was within the realm of possibility.

In one crucial scene in *The Moscow Club,* Charlie had to smuggle a gun through airport security, but I had no idea how this might actually work, so I tracked a knowledgeable gun dealer, and after I'd convinced him I was a writer, not a criminal, he became intrigued by the scenario and agreed to help. It turned out that this fellow had a friend who used to be in the Secret Service and had actually taken a Glock pistol and got it past the metal detectors and X-ray machines in security at Washington's National Airport and onto a plane to Boston. He then showed me exactly how he'd done it, so I could write about it accurately. (I left out a few key details to foil any potential hijacker.)

Can readers tell when a scene or a detail is authentic? I believe so. I'm convinced that painstaking research can yield a texture, an atmosphere of authenticity, that average readers can feel and smell. (There will always be a few experts waiting to pounce. In *Extraordinary Powers,* I mistakenly described a Glock 19 as having a safety, and I continue to get angry letters about it.)

The longer I write, it seems, the more research I do. For my forthcoming novel, *Prince of Darkness,* whose hero is a female FBI counter-terrorism specialist, I managed to wangle official cooperation from the FBI, and I spent a lot of time talking to several FBI Special Agents. I also interviewed past and present terrorism experts for the CIA, asking them such questions as, would they really be able to catch a skilled professional terrorist—as well as some seemingly trivial ones.

Since the other main character in *Prince of Darkness* is a professional terrorist-for-hire, I thought it was important to talk to someone who's actually been a terrorist. This was not easy. In fact, it took me months to locate an ex-terrorist (through a friend of a friend) who was willing to talk. But it was worth the time and effort: My fictional terrorist is now, I think, far more credible than he'd have been if I'd simply invented him.

I've done interviews with a convicted forger for details on how to falsify a U.S. passport; with a bomb disposal expert about how to construct bombs; with an expert in satellite surveillance to help me describe authentically how the U.S. government is able to listen in on telephone conversations. I've often called upon the expertise of police homicide detectives, retired FBI agents, helicopter pilots, pathologists, even experts in embalming (or "applied arts," as they are called).

Since an important character in *Prince of Darkness* is a high-priced call girl, I spent a lot of time interviewing prostitutes, expensive call girls, and madams. As a result of this groundwork, I think this particular character is more sympathetic, more believable, than I'd have drawn her otherwise.

Because international settings are often integral parts of spy novels, I strongly believe that travel—really being there in Paris, say, or Rome, or wherever—not only can help you create plausible settings, make them look and smell and feel real, but can suggest scenes and ideas that would otherwise never occur to you. But not everyone can afford to travel (or likes to; ironically, Robert Ludlum, whose plots traverse the globe, abhors traveling). No doubt you can get by tolerably well consulting a good guidebook or two.

Gathering research material is a strange obsession, but it's by far the best part of writing thrillers. I will admit, however, that this passion can go too far. In Rome, I was pickpocketed while standing in a *gelato* shop. When I realized that my passport and all my cash and travelers checks were gone, I panicked. I searched for the perpetrator and came upon a man who looked somewhat shifty. I approached him and pleaded, in my pathetic Italian, *"Per favore, signore! Per favore!* My passport! *Per piacere!*" When the man responded by unzipping his travel bag to prove he didn't have my belongings, that he was innocent, I knew I'd found my man. I told him quietly: "Look, I'm on my honeymoon. If you give me back my passport and my money, I promise I won't turn you in."

He looked around and furtively put my passport and wallet back in my bag.

At this point any sane tourist would flee, but, I went on, "One more thing. If you'll agree to be interviewed, I won't call the police."

He looked at me as if I were out of my mind. "I'm quite serious," I said. "Let me buy you an espresso."

He sat down at a table with me as I explained that I was doing research for a novel partly set in Rome. Flattered that a writer would take an interest in his life, he began to tell me all about how he got into this line of work, about his childhood in Palermo spent snatching purses, about how he travels around Europe frequenting international gatherings of the rich and famous, how he lives in hotels and is often lonely. He explained how he spots an easy mark, how he fences passports, which travelers checks he has no interest in. He demonstrated how he picks pockets and handbags, and taught me how to make sure it never happened to me again.

Much of the information I gleaned from this pickpocket later turned up in the Italy sequence in *Extraordinary Powers.*

I'm certainly not suggesting that a committed espionage novelist must go out of his way to get his pockets picked in Rome, or consort with convicted forgers, assassins, or terrorists. But the longer I write espionage fiction, the more strongly I'm convinced that if you're going to write about unusual people and circumstances in a compelling and plausible way, there's really no substitute for firsthand experience.

❑ 41

MISTAKES TO AVOID IN WRITING MYSTERIES

BY ELEANOR HYDE

NO DOUBT YOU'VE HEARD SOME EDITOR PUBLICLY PROCLAIM THAT HE or she is looking for the good book, that true talent will out, and they'll spot it immediately. I'm sure they believe this. But in their scramble to compete out there in the marketplace, they just might miss it. Most of us know of some very talented writer (you?) whose book was over-looked while the mediocre or less was published. So what happened?

In a confidential mood, an editor once told me that he looked for reasons to turn a book down, and the sooner he found something wrong, the better. This wasn't a person who enjoyed hurting others' feelings; this was merely someone who had too many manuscripts to read and too little time in which to read them. Maybe the big book was in the pile and maybe he missed it. Possibly, a lot of editors do: Maybe in their hurry to get through that pile of manuscripts and on to the next one, the big book was bypassed because of some slip up, some inaccuracy that made the editor think the book wasn't worth wasting precious time on.

Once a manuscript is out of your hands there's nothing to be done. The book you slaved over, rewrote, cut, expanded, cut again, and re-re-rewrote; the book you got up at five in the morning to work on before the kids woke up or before you left for work; the book for which you sacrificed your weekends and vacation time; the book you neglected your nearest and dearest for is now there in some editor's office, an editor who doesn't care that the book practically caused a nervous breakdown or a divorce. Confronting that editor is a stack of floor-to-ceiling manuscripts that have to be read. From then on, what happens to your book is, alas, as much matter of luck and timing as talent. But there are some crucial things you can do before you submit your manuscript to guarantee it gets the best possible chance.

For three years I chaired the Mentor Program* for the New York region of the Mystery Writers of America, a program in which published writers (mentors) critiqued fifty manuscript pages submitted by beginners and/or unpublished writers. In reading the mentor's critiques, I saw a pattern emerge—the same errors cropping up over and over again. Following are the mistakes cited most often by the mentors—after first finding something good in the manuscript to sugar coat the pill.

Inaccuracies: The winner, or loser, hands down. In murder mysteries, which run the gamut from cozies to hard-boiled police procedurals, suspending disbelief is important, since there's a lot of disbelief to suspend. Although murders occur all too often in real life, they're still, fortunately, something we hear or read about, not something we witness firsthand.

Inaccuracies varied from the obvious to the oblivious. In the obvious, the writer lost track of some minor detail—he or she changed a character's name or age but neglected to make the changes throughout. Such inconsistencies can be confusing to the editor, who is, don't forget, reading a lot of manuscripts at once and can't waste time figuring things out. "Sloppy," the editor thinks, and goes on to the next one.

The manuscript might contain oblivious mistakes cited so often by the mentors—facts that the writer failed to check out. Maybe he or she didn't know the subject well enough to know they'd committed a blooper, or maybe the writer didn't bother looking something up. Such inaccuracy occurred when one writer had a scene set in Manhattan with a car going east on 73rd Street, a one-way street on which cars can go only west—a mistake an editor living in Manhattan would be likely to notice. I'm sure you can cite examples of some well-known writer committing a similar glaring error in a book you read recently, but well-known writers don't generally have to worry about rejection slips!

One-dimensional characters. Mentor comments: "You never physi-

---

*The Mentor Program was initiated six years ago by the New York Chapter of the Mystery Writers of America to help its unpublished members break into print. Published writers volunteer to critique fifty pages of an unpublished writer's mystery novel or short story. The program is limited to MWA members in the area covered by the New York City Chapter and to the number of published writers who volunteer for this service (approximately forty). A small fee is charged to cover mailing costs. Quite a few beginning writers have been helped by this program.

cally described Matt. All of your characters are sketched well, but 'sketched' is the operative word."

Although inaccuracies were cited most often, failure to portray a well-rounded protagonist is far more serious. This resulted when the characters strayed out of character, lost their "voice." In one manuscript, a paper boy poetically referred to a star-crammed sky and a moon perched on the tip of a church spire. "Nice image," the mentor wrote, "but not a paper boy's." It's certainly not how Mark Twain would have done it.

Some writers chose protagonists fields unfamiliar to them (for example, a newspaper journalist who had no deadlines and failed to report a murder she witnessed). It's easier and generally more effective to write about someone and something you know. But even when your main character is someone whose voice, virtues, failings, longings, quirks, and favorite food are totally unfamiliar, you can still go wrong if you commit the folly cited below by any number of mentors:

Introducing too many characters at once. When this happens, the protagonist is slighted, lost in the shuffle. Unless you're a household name, no editor is going to bother sorting people out. Often, the mentor has to ask who the main character was supposed to be. Don't overload your beginning with too many people too soon. Ask yourself, too, how important each character is to the plot. You might be surprised how many you can cut out.

Shifting viewpoint confusion. Mentor's comments: "The mixing of viewpoints in the same chapter was confusing."

"The changing of tenses and shifting of viewpoints make the narrative difficult to follow."

"Your problem is abruptly changing POV, sometimes in midsentence. You have to be good to get away with this."

For "good," read experienced. Still, switching viewpoints is something many accomplished writers avoid. All too often beginning writers rush in where experienced writers fear to tread, mainly because they don't like what they're letting themselves in for. The more difficult the technique, the more likely an inexperienced writer will be to use it. It's O.K. to experiment. Try all the techniques. Play at work. Enjoy it. Learn from it. Show it to your friends and family. But don't show it to your editor. Isaac Singer once observed that a writer's best friend was his wastebasket.

Telling instead of showing. Writer: "He had brushed disaster several times." Mentor: "How? In some of his earlier, high profile cases? About which we heard nothing?"

"Show, don't tell" is a cliché that every writer knows but sometimes ignores, including some of the mentors who cited this infraction of the rules; they just don't ignore it as often. Be concrete. Although writers will take their time to search for the right verb, they don't always bother to search for the right example, lapsing into something vague, or reaching for the nearest convenient cliché. There were times when the beginning writer went one better, or rather, one worse, and not only didn't show, but also scarcely told, as in the following:

Sidestepping the big scene. The big scene, the murder, is the pivotal point of the mystery, but, according to a number of mentors, got short shrift from certain writers, one of whom dismissed the murder in a brief paragraph but devoted a page to finding a cat in a closet.

Certainly, confronting the dramatic scene can be intimidating. The only writers I know who can plow through a dramatic scene without fear and trembling, or even a qualm, are those who have never met a cliché they didn't like. But at least they deal with the murder scene, recognize its importance. Unfortunately, many beginning writers distance themselves, their protagonist, and, consequently, the reader, from the scene by sidling up to it, taking a quick peek, and scurrying off. If the protagonist has just encountered a dead body, it comes almost as an afterthought so that there is no unique, personal reaction. Or maybe the writer dreams up some arty imagery or throws in a few clever, nightmarish details, then hurries back to safe ground to deal with a something not so emotionally challenging, something the protagonist, and the writer, can handle. Bringing off the big scene ranks up there with a great plot and good characterization.

Length of description. When description was used, it was often abused. Either it was too sketchy or too long, interfering with the action. One mentor remarked: "You give the reader information concerning the local lore, Indian names, families' politics, etc., but your protagonist is lost in all the characters. After three chapters and 9,000 words, would a casual reader—or more important, an editor—say, 'This is a great set up' or 'This book is too talky?' My gut feeling is that the response would be the latter." Another mentor put it more succinctly: "Your story slows down here—too much description. Cut."

Mistakes in dialogue. Mentor comment: "Your characters sound too much alike." Keep your dialogue in character. A school's dropout won't sound like a doctor of philosophy. Many writers give their characters distinct speech patterns, a "verbal tic," perhaps, such as an overuse of a certain word or phrase so that the reader knows immediately who is speaking. Avoid using crutch words, a dead giveaway that the writer is a beginner. Use "he said" or "she said," not "she hissed" or "he thundered." If the dialogue is apt, no explanation is needed. Another frequent fault found by mentors was dialogue crammed with so much information, it sounded unnatural. Read the dialogue out loud to see if it sounds "right." Also, in depicting a character with a distinct dialect, don't overdo it. Remember that suggestion is all.

Too many digressions. Another oft-cited mistake. A mainstream novelist might digress freely, but pace is all-important in mysteries. Stick to the subject.

Beginning too early. An error many mentors found in manuscripts. A mystery should begin near the point of attack, either when the murder occurs, or when someone ventures upon the scene of the crime. Often, this didn't happen until the third chapter. Mentors advised changing chapters three to chapter one and weaving in the previous information. Oddly enough, in no instance was the writer told to begin the book earlier.

Grammatical lapses. If the writer is in a character's head, the grammar will be loose, informal, and less than perfect, the sentence incomplete.

And, in depicting a character with little schooling, it's O.K. to break the rules of grammar. However, all too many manuscripts contained grammatical errors in straight narrative, indicating that the writer was either careless or needed a refresher course in composition.

Pronoun confusion. Although it may have been clear in some writers' minds who was doing what, the mentor didn't have a clue. It's better to risk repeating a character's name too often than to confuse the reader.

Too many modifiers. Again, an oft cited criticism. One mentor put it succinctly: "When it comes to adverbs and adjectives, less is more." Go for the active verbs.

Sloppy copy. This occurred far too often: type too light to read, creative spelling, single spacing. Don't give the editor an excuse to push your manuscript aside after all the work you've put into it.

Often, the above mistakes occur because the writer is too familiar with the material. A good idea is to have someone else read your manuscript before sending it out, preferably someone who reads a lot of mysteries.

□ 42

IDEAS IN SCIENCE FICTION

BY POUL ANDERSON

"WHERE DO YOU GET YOUR IDEAS?"

Probably every sort of writer hears this question once in a while, but science fiction writers surely more than most. In the past it often took the form, "Where do you get those crazy ideas?" but since then the field has become quite widely accepted, even respectable. Discoveries in science and advances in technology have given dazzling proof that science fiction's visions are not absurd. Meanwhile, such popular shows as "Star Trek" and *StarWars* have made many of those concepts—space travel, time travel, alien intelligences, artificial intelligences, genetic engineering, and much more—common currency.

Now, nobody claims that science fiction predicts the future or explores the universe. No "future history" has matched the actual course of events. We writers failed to anticipate a heap of developments, all the way from the Internet and its revolutionary impact, to the use of galaxies as gravitational lenses. We seized on them only as they came to pass. The few times a story has come near the mark, it's been on the shotgun principle: Put out enough different notions, and you have a chance of making an occasional hit. Moreover, a number of our standard motifs—most obviously time travel and travel faster than light—may well prove to be forever impossible.

But then, we aren't in the business of prophecy; we're storytellers. We look at the cosmos around us, wonder what this or that *might* imply, and express our thoughts in fictional, human terms.

The question "Where do you get your ideas?" is legitimate. Science fiction is preeminently a literature of ideas. The answer is: the world. Anything whatsoever may spark a story—a personal experience, something that happened to someone else, something read or seen or heard or watched on a screen, a news item, a mathematical calculation, a dream, a chance remark—anything. What counts is what you do with it. This tie to reality, however remote and unlikely it may become, is perhaps what distinguishes science fiction from fantasy. (Not that fantasy doesn't include many fine works, but it isn't what I shall be discussing.)

Admittedly, there's a lot of bad science fiction around, most conspicuously in the movies and on television, but also abundant on the newsstands and in bookstores. Characters are cardboard; plots are cookie-cutter; the underlying ideas, if any, are either ridiculous or old and worn-out, with no attempt made at the touch of originality that would freshen them a bit. We won't say more about this. If you want to write science fiction, you want it to be good, don't you?

You'll find yourself in excellent company. A significant amount of what appears in print meets high literary as well as intellectual standards while being a pleasure to read. The sheer volume of published science fiction nowadays is such that some of the good science fiction gets overlooked, lost in the pile of trash. However, some does deservedly well. Editors remain eager to discover strong new voices. In addition, although novels dominate, the science fiction (and mystery) magazines and anthologies are almost the only surviving homes for short stories. A budding writer would do well to start with them, gaining experience and reputation before making the investment of time and effort that a book requires.

First, though, you had better be reasonably familiar with the field and enjoy it. Life's too short to struggle with stuff that bores you. Also, if you don't know what's been done, you're too apt to waste your energy reinventing the wheel. Thus, "attack from outer space" is an ancient theme. Set forth baldly, it will only draw yawns. Yet it can still succeed, if the author presents unique, thought-provoking aspects. What are the aliens like? You can design interesting, hitherto unknown beings. Why are they here? After all, a technology capable of crossing interstellar space should be able to produce everything its people want at home. How do humans react? It won't be uniformly. For instance, throughout history on Earth, again and again a local faction has allied itself with foreign invaders, hoping they will crush its hated neighbors.

In my opinion, two streams run through science fiction. The first traces back to Jules Verne. It is "the idea as hero." His tales are mainly concerned with the concept—a submarine, a journey to the center of the planet, and so on. The second derives from H.G. Wells. His own ideas were brilliant, but he didn't care how implausible they might be, an invisible man or a time machine or whatever. He concentrated on the characters, their emotions and interactions.

Today, we usually speak of these two streams as "hard" and "soft" science fiction. Needless to say, they were never completely separate. Verne's characters are lively, sometimes memorable. When he chose to, Wells could write a story focused on a future development: for example, "The Land Ironclads," which foresaw the military tank. Ideally, the streams unify in a tale that meets both scientific and conventional literary standards. Though this is not exactly common, our best writers have achieved it oftener than one might think.

Indeed, not just the quantity but the diversity of current science fiction is amazing. You can find everything from the wonderfully conceived and carefully executed planets of Hal Clement to the far-flung romances of Jack Vance, from the gritty sociology of Frederick Pohl through the headlong adventure of S.M. Stirling, to the humor and sensitivity of Gordon R. Dickson—all of them, and many more, first-class reading. This is another reason for writers to know what their colleagues have been doing. It inspires.

In this short piece I can't take up the purely literary side. I'm not sure that any "how to" about it can be taught, except for advising that you experience widely, meditate on that experience, learn something about everything, and read the great works of world literature. But perhaps I can offer a few suggestions about sources of ideas and what can be accomplished by taking thought.

We begin with science and technology. You want to keep up with these fields anyway. In this day and age, I don't see how any person can be called educated who doesn't. Besides, they're boundlessly rich fountainheads of exciting story possibilities. You don't need a professional degree. Yes, Gregory Benford is a physicist who as a sideline writes novels of high literary quality; but Greg Bear is a layman whose work, equally well-written, also goes believably to the frontiers of our knowledge and beyond. We have no dearth of fascinating, authoritative books and periodicals that report from these frontiers. Prowl the bookstores and libraries; consider joining the Library of Science book club. Among magazines, I'll list *Science News, Discover, Scientific American,* and the British *New Scientist.* I subscribe to several others, too, but these four, especially the first, have the most general coverage that I know of.

All fiction deals with people. Even the rare story that has no humans in it is necessarily told from a human viewpoint. I've mentioned personal experience and the masterworks of the world as means of gaining a deeper understanding. We acquire knowledge of a more structured kind from history, anthropology, psychology, and other studies of our species. Among the benefits, we find that our twentieth-century Western civilization is not the only expression of human variousness, and probably won't be the final one. What we learn we can transmute into exotic story situations.

We can't do this mechanically. At least, attempts to generate a setting by simply changing names have had pretty dismal results. The writer's imagination must come into play, along with hard thought.

As an example of how different sources flow together, doubtless not the best but closely known to me, let me bring in my novel *The People of the Wind*. For a long time I'd wanted to write a story about a planet colonized jointly by humans and a nonhuman race. Traveling in France, I happened on the Alsatian city of Belfort. Although ethnically German, the Alsatians are fiercely patriotic French citizens. The heroic resistance of Belfort during the Franco-Prussian War caused it to be spared the annexation to Germany that the rest of the province suffered from 1871 to 1918. Ah-ha! Subjecting my planet to this kind of stress should dramatically highlight its mixed society.

In my last conversation with the late John Campbell, editor of *Analog* magazine, he tossed off the idea that post-mammalian evolution may produce a kind of biological supercharger, powered by the animal's motion and conferring tremendous cursive ability. I saw at once that this would also enable a man-sized creature with a man-sized brain to fly on a planet similar to Earth. Such a species would be satisfyingly alien to ours, but communication and cooperation were not ruled out.

These elements were a bare beginning. The planet, while habitable, would not be a copy of Earth. It would have its own characteristics and its own native life. In addition, human and nonhuman colonists would introduce plants and animals from their home worlds. Thus we'd get a mixed ecology, too. All of this needed working out in detail. Likewise did the aliens. Their anatomy had to be functional. The power of flight would basically influence their psyches. So would its energy demands; they'd be obligate carnivores, highly territorial. What social arrangements could they make? What would their languages sound like? What religions might they have? How would they and the humans influence each other? And the humans themselves wouldn't be the same as us today, when the story was set centuries in the future.

A great deal of effort went into such questions before any actual writing started, but I've seldom had more fun, and I hope the end product was interesting and vivid.

Be prepared for arguments. Science fiction readers are bright, well-informed, and good-naturedly scrappy. Thus, Larry Niven's *Ringworld* is a marvelously complete visualization of a splendid concept, a world in the form of a gigantic ring around its sun and the myriad cultures that could arise on so vast an area. It deserved the sales and awards it won. Nevertheless, several persons pointed out that he'd gotten the rotation of the Earth backward, others that the structure would be gravitationally unstable. He corrected the first mistake in a second edition. To explain how Ringworld was kept in orbit, he wrote a sequel, which naturally became more of a tour and which also was a publishing success. I too have received valuable critiques, information, and suggestions from readers—almost as much as from the conversations with my wife. Contacts like these are a major reward of writing science fiction.

Note well, Niven didn't wish tedious lectures on us. He never does. People and places come to life in the course of story events. Often a hint is enough. Robert Heinlein was an absolute master of this technique. Such casual-looking phrases as "The door dilated" or "A police car was balanced on the rooftop" throw us straight into the future. He could do this because he had very fully developed his background. He could pick and choose what items to show.

In a way, we science fiction writers are professional daydreamers. We give our readers what we have imagined. But that imagining should spring from reality, which is infinitely varied and surprising; and beneath the color, suspense, stylistic experimentation, and all else, it should make sense.

□ 43

CREATING SUSPENSE

BY SARAH LOVETT

THE GREEK PHILOSOPHER HERACLITUS, WHO WAS IN THE BUSINESS of pondering life's big questions, is often quoted, "A man's character is his fate." While you may disagree with Heraclitus when it comes to life, in fiction, plot begins with character. Desperate characters. With impossible goals. Facing forces of antagonism. In the course of writing three novels, my understanding of plot and character has evolved until both elements are inseparably intertwined in the process of creating a story.

Desperate characters

Plot begins with hungry, vulnerable characters who are desperately driven. Your protagonist steps out of the ordinary world and into the extraordinary world when she or he moves into action. Clarisse Starling in *The Silence of the Lambs* is a rookie F.B.I. agent put to the test on a serial murder investigation; Elizabeth Bennett in *Pride and Prejudice* strives to clear her family name and to overcome her own prejudice in order to find true love. Both of these literary heroines are unique and fully developed characters, and each *actively* makes choices, in motion, working toward a goal.

I spend months developing my characters and their fictional world. I make stacks of notes and fill in details of their lives, writing down questions and answers: Where were they born? What was their childhood like? Are they from lower-, middle-, or upper-class backgrounds? Are their parents alive or dead? Do they have siblings? Do they believe in God, country, and apple pie? What do they dream about? What is their work? What is their passion? Just when I think I know a character, I ask more questions.

I like to focus on my protagonist first because the *who* will affect the *what*. For example, in *Dangerous Attachments* and *Acquired Mo-*

tives, my series protagonist Sylvia Strange is a forensic psychologist who is haunted by issues of family. She needs to find out what happened to her father who abandoned her and her mother years earlier. She is estranged from her mother; she is afraid of love and commitment. Because of that, I know that Sylvia's adventures will in some way concern questions of family pathology, which also happens to be a classic motif for the crime genre. My protagonist's desperate need to know the truth leads her toward her main story goal.

Impossible, valuable goals

A worthy protagonist must be driven to reach a crucial and *almost* impossible goal. If the reader knows absolutely that the hero will succeed, ho hum. But a story becomes instantly suspenseful if the protagonist might not reach her goal. In *The Silence of the Lambs* Thomas Harris created a young and untested heroine in Clarisse Starling, and it will take incredible strength of character for her to save the killer's next victim. Jane Austen's Elizabeth Bennett is so smart and so smug she almost fails to recognize her own prejudice, thereby missing the opportunity to achieve real love.

Goals may be noble: the search for the truth or the protection of the innocent. Or, at first glance, they may be foolish and superficial: the quest for money or treasure. But if you want the reader to root for the protagonist, monetary gain must finally be used for good, for redemption, for a socially approved purpose: to save a life, or to protect the innocent, for instance. Remember, impossible, *valuable* goals.

As soon as I know where my protagonist is headed—into a secret diamond mine to recover a lost treasure, into the killer's lair to save a loved one, into a murky psyche to unravel a mystery—then I can start to imagine the mind-sets, people, and circumstances that will stand in my hero's way. These are the story's forces of antagonism, and they play a crucial role in plot and character development.

Forces of antagonism

Internal, human, and/or environmental antagonists must also be actively driven, or they must provide a powerful barrier. If the protagonist and the antagonist are worthy opponents, the story instantly gains suspenseeither force could win. These antagonistic forces will provide the ultimate test for the protagonist, and they will also tell the reader what kind of human being the protagonist truly is. In fiction—and in life—a person's accomplishments are measured against the obstacles they overcome.

Clarisse Starling is up against a deadly serial killer. She's a woman in a man's world, and she must make herself vulnerable to another dangerous killer—Hannibal "the Cannibal" Lecter—in order to reach her goal. It is Hannibal who demands to know her deepest secrets, her vulnerabilities, before he will offer clues to the killer's identity. In *The Silence of the Lambs,* Starling faces both psychic and external dangers. When the rookie FBI agent reveals herself to Hannibal, she reveals herself to the reader. In both action and thought, Starling is a hero worth rooting for.

In *Pride and Prejudice,* the forces opposing Elizabeth Bennett are those of an entire social structure—rigid and restrictive—in which women are not allowed to inherit property, and people do not marry outside their social class.

A protagonist's vulnerabilities, her weak points, should be exploited to gain reader empathy. It sounds calculated, and it is, but it works. If I have a heroine who is afraid of heights, I'll make sure she has to climb Mount Everest or swing from the Eiffel Tower in order to reach her goal. That goes double for psychological vulnerability. As a child, Sylvia Strange lost her father; as an adult, she suffers the death of a mentor and father-figure. In *Dangerous Attachments,* is she seeing the picture clearly when a prison inmate and his politically powerful father are both implicated in a family murder? Or is she prejudiced by her personal history?

Now that I have some idea of my important characters, their world, their ultimate goal and therefore, their conflicts, I need to set up a basic framework for the story.

Simple structure

A story needs a basic shape—a scaffold—the simpler the better. Divide your story into *acts*—a beginning (Act I), a middle (Act II), and an end (Act III).

Act I, the story's beginning, sets up driven characters and their valuable and almost-impossible goals. The set-up raises questions: Who is good? Who is bad? What are the goals of the protagonist and the antagonist? What drives them? Who will reach the goal first? And most important, the set-up asks the central question of the story: Will Sylvia Strange discover the killer's identity in time to prevent another death? In a highly structured class-conscious society, will Elizabeth Bennett's wit and intelligence win her true love? When these questions beg answers, they keep us in suspense.

The middle of the story, Act II, is a series of escalating conflicts between opposing forces. This section develops the story, raising the stakes. It often contains an important crisis where the protagonist's ability to reach her goal is called into deeper question.

Act III, the end of the story, is the climax, the pay-off, the big bang before the story's central question is finally resolved, before the reader knows who will ultimately win. This is where protagonist and antagonist face each other in a fight to the death—or at least to metaphorical death—where only one will be victorious.

This basic structure—these bones—should free the writer so the shape of the story doesn't get overwhelmed or lost after many drafts. Sometimes it's called the story map. Once I have a good sense of the story's basic overall structure, I can begin to break acts into chapters, chapters into scenes. This structuring tells me where to put the twists and turns that keep readers interested—and keep the story spinning.

Spin

This is what should happen to the story in a major way at the end of each act: An action should occur that sends the story into a new and surprising direction. Spin points are those moments in life when the world tilts on its axis, when what the protagonist thought she *knew* was reality is probably not reality at all.

Clarisse Starling discovers a human head preserved in a jar. This occurs at the end of Act I, spinning the story into Act II. She wonders who the man was, and who killed him—Buffalo Bill or Hannibal Lecter? This discovery spins her back to Lecter and cements their working "partnership."

At the end of Act II, Elizabeth Bennett faces disgrace as a result of her sister's illicit affair with a Colonel Wickham and the loss of contact with Mr. Darcy, the man she has grown to love deeply. In both these cases, the world has shifted, and what seemed clear before is now seen in new light.

Subplots, colliding and otherwise

Fiction, like life, has more than one strand of action occurring at one time. A good, strong subplot colliding with the main plot changes its course in the process. A subplot can also add tone and color to the story, allowing for love, identity, personal history, and the reinforcement of the story's motif. Sometimes, subplot seems to be where the unconscious mind of the story lives, while main plot is the domain of the active conscious mind. A subplot has a beginning, middle, and end, just like the main plot. It allows for a change of pace and tonal variety.

In *Pride and Prejudice,* the story of one Mr. Wickham and his wooing of and ultimate marriage to Elizabeth Bennett's sister Lydia is an example of a subplot that collides directly with the main plot. The scandal of this affair is a crucial obstacle between the heroine and the man she loves, an obstacle that tests the quality of true love.

In my novels, because I use a cast of continuing characters who inhabit the world of my protagonist, Dr. Sylvia Strange, I often use a subplot to develop secondary characters. In this way, I can also expand on thematic material and carry forward the story of Sylvia's missing father from book to book. I've also created a love interest for Sylvia, as well as a close friendship with a female penitentiary investigator.

A crisis

Every story needs a crisis, the moment at which the heroine should die or the moment at which it looks as if she will fail to achieve her goal. Somehow she survives physically, but psychologically this may be a very negative time. This is her darkest moment before the push to the final climax. Classically, this confrontation occurs midway in the story, somewhere in the second half of Act II, ending with a spin.

The Act II crisis in *The Silence of the Lambs* is a variation from the norm because the action does not center around protagonist Starling. Instead, the crisis is Hannibal Lecter's gory escape from the authorities. Although Starling is not featured in this dramatic set-piece, Lecter has left her with a gift—a clue that will lead her to Buffalo Bill in Act III.

A final death-defying climax

This is the most dangerous face-off between antagonist and protagonist. It is often a final play-out of the Act II crisis. Perhaps the heroine met the villain in the crisis, failed to defeat the villain, and faces her opponent once more in this climactic moment. This is what the entire story has been building toward.

At the climax of *Dangerous Attachments,* Sylvia Strange faces a psychotic killer who has kidnapped a young and fatherless child. She is willing to fight to the death to save the boy. Elizabeth Bennett stands up to prevailing social values personified by the imperious Lady Catherine de Bourgh. Clarisse Starling is hunted by Buffalo Bill. These climatic pay-offs have been promised from the very beginning of each story.

Until I know the story's beginning and its ending, I can't truly immerse myself in the writing process. I have to have a very good idea where my story is headed, and where my characters will end up (although events do shift as I write). I know some writers who have to write from beginning to end before they know their ending. Then they go back and rework the story. Although everyone's process is unique, it's smart to spend weeks, even months, figuring out an exciting climax before you begin the actual chapter-by-chapter or scene-by-scene writing process.

These are some basics for creating suspense with your characters and your plot. The two elements go hand in hand, character driving the story and characters affected by events in the story. It's a constant tug-of-war, an interaction that can be used to maintain suspense and pacing and to surprise the reader.

□ 44

TWILIGHT FOR HIGH NOON: TODAY'S WESTERN

BY LOREN D. ESTLEMAN

PARDON ME WHILE I INDULGE IN SOME SELF-CONGRATULATION: I WAS right. In 1981, when TV sitcoms and big-screen space operas had all but crowded out the traditional western, and Louis L'Amour's career was drawing to a close with Tom Clancy's ascendant, I went out on a limb in an article for *The Writer* Magazine and predicted the triumphant return of frontier fiction.

Only four years later, Larry McMurtry's monumental tale of a cattle drive, *Lonesome Dove,* swept to the top of *The New York Times* bestseller list and captured the Pulitzer Prize. The subsequent TV adaptation gunned down the ratings competition, saved the endangered television miniseries from extinction, and spawned three successful sequels and a regular series. In the meantime, *Dances with Wolves,* Kevin Costner's epic motion picture based on Michael Blake's acclaimed novel about a white man living with Indians, recovered its investment ten times over and took seven Academy Awards. Next in the chute was Clint Eastwood's *Unforgiven,* a grittily realistic movie about an Old West assassin, and the big winner at the Academy Awards in 1993.

The effect on Hollywood was as sudden and startling as the Gunfight at the O.K. Corral. Immediately, every major studio gave the green light to western productions that had been languishing in its story department for years. By the middle of the 1990s, more westerns were opening in the nation's theaters than at any time since the 1950s.

The pundits who had smugly announced the permanent closing of the frontier were stumped for an explanation. Writers of westerns were not.

What *Lonesome Dove, Dances with Wolves,* and *Unforgiven* have in common that set them apart from the long stream of *High Noon* imitations of decades past was a regard for authentic history. The flawed, emotionally repressed cattlemen of *Lonesome Dove* had as little in common with the heroic cowboys of 1946's *Red River* as Kevin Costner's flesh-and-blood Sioux had with the cardboard savages of the old B western; and there was certainly little of John Wayne's swagger or Gary Cooper's stoic self-sacrifice in Clint Eastwood's gunfighter, a drunken, whoring killer. They presented raw, unflinching portraits of imperfect humanity that audiences the world over recognized as genuine.

Not every entry in this spate of big-screen westerns was successful. Those that failed were dismal attempts to revive the old mythology of fast-draw contests and heroic loners with no visible means of support, dedicating their lives to the eradication of evil. Time was when these stereotypes were fresh and popular. But an increasingly sophisticated public, made cynical by real-life assassinations and corruption in high places, demands realistic characters in plausible situations.

TV documentaries such as Ken Burns's *The West,* and exhaustive revisionist histories such as Dee Brown's *Bury My Heart at Wounded Knee,* Paula Mitchell Marks's *And Die in the West,* and Evan S. Connell's *Son of the Morning Star,* have all reached wide audiences who can no longer be expected to embrace tall tales directed at readers who never ventured west of Chicago. Responding to a growing appetite for historical accuracy, a new breed of western writer is mining primary resources for people and facts that require no dramatization to attract reader interest.

Fortunately, there is no shortage of such raw material. The historical James Butler Hickok and Martha Jane Cannary were far more complex and interesting than the Wild Bill and Calamity Jane of fiction, and the thousands of less noted participants in the Westward Expansion all loom larger than life in our pampered time. Consider the haunted, burned-out expressions on the faces of those long-dead prairie wives photographed in front of their mean soddies. Yes, there were women out West; and theirs is but one of the many hundreds of tales that have yet to be told.

The traditional western is dying out, along with the readership that made it popular. Today's publishers have jettisoned the very word "western," substituting the labels "frontier fiction" and "American historical." Books herded into these categories are immediately distinguishable from their predecessors, first, by their length—100,000 words plus, as opposed to the 60,000-word horse operas of old—second, by their covers, which feature great sweeps of land and ethnically diverse casts instead of WASPish gunslingers facing off on a dusty street— third, by their reviews. *Publishers Weekly, The New York Times,* and the *Bloomsbury Review* take serious notice of these books as often now as they ignored the work of Luke Short and Ernest Haycox in the past. Today's western writers demonstrate a deeper understanding of the role of the American West in the shaping of a nation, and consequently of that nation's place in the history of the world.

As a writer, I welcome the larger canvas. In the past, I often felt constrained by the need to tell a grand story in a narrow space, and once ran afoul of an editor at Doubleday when an early entry in my Page Murdock series ran more than 300 pages in manuscript. Compare that with the freedom I felt to include this passage in Murdock's adventure, *City of Widows* (Forge, 1994):

Desert heat doesn't follow any of the standard rules. You'd expect it to be worst when the sun is straight up, but a hat will protect you from it then. When the only shade for miles is on the wrong side of the shrubbery you're using for cover, there is no hiding from that afternoon slant. I turned up my collar and unfastened my cuffs and pulled them down over the backs of my hands, but I could feel my skin turning red and shrinking under the fabric. Pinheads of sweat marched along the edge of my leather hatband and tracked down into my eyes, stinging like fire ants. The water in the canteen tasted like hot metal. I wanted the Montana snow, blue as the veins in Colleen Bower's throat with the mountain runoff coursing through it carrying shards of white ice . . .

That editor would probably have insisted I make do with the bare statement "It was hot," and get to the shooting. The end of space restrictions allows me to enlist the climate and topography of the West as characters in the plot.

One of the most significant—and progressive—developments of the new western has been the increase in women writers. Their ability to empathize with the courageous women who left behind the security of civilization to build a new life in the wilderness is largely responsible for the western's acceptance in the literary mainstream. In the past, the few women who ventured into the genre, including Dorothy M. Johnson ("The Man Who Shot Liberty Valance," "A Man Called Horse") and Willa Cather (*My Antonia, Death Comes for the Arch-*

bishop) were obliged to write from the male point of view. Successors such as Lucia St. Clair Robson, author of *Ride the Wind*, told from the perspective of Comanche captive Cynthia Ann Parker, have changed all that—to everyone's benefit.

Consider this frontier fiction staple—the showing of a notorious outlaw's corpse for profit—as transformed by Deborah Morgan in her short story "Mrs. Crawford's Odyssey" (*How the West Was Read*, Durkin Hayes, 1996), simply by adopting the point of view of the dead man's mother:

> This could not be her twenty-two-year-old son. Matthew had golden features, sunlit hair, a strong, square-set jaw. Laid out before her was an old man, bald, with flesh of a blue-white translucency, like watered-down milk. The heavily rouged cheekbones emphasized vast, dark hollows that should have been a jawline.
>
> Someone had made a terrible mistake, she was sure of it. She grabbed at that thread of hope, caught it, held it taut. This eased her, and she approached the deceased like any slight acquaintance might—respectfully, but thankful it's not one of your own. Only when she was leaning over the body did she discover death's ruse and see, unmistakably, her child.
>
> She clasped her hand over her mouth, a futile attempt to contain her emotions. Tears flowed until she believed that she would never be able to cry again.
>
> "My dear, precious boy," she said at last, "what have they done to you?"

Few male writers could write so poignantly and convincingly about a woman regarding the lifeless body of the boy to whom she gave birth.

Publishers are actively seeking women interested in tapping the rich vein of material concerning women out West. The market has rarely been so open to newcomers.

The West was settled by many different kinds of people: whites, blacks, Indians, immigrants, consumptives, heroes, and scoundrels. Bill Hotchkiss's *The Medicine Calf* and *Ammahabas* absorbingly follow the life of Jim Beckwourth, the black trapper and fur trader who became a Crow chief, and Cherokee writer Robert J. Conley (*The Dark Island, Crazy Snake*) stands at the summit of an impressive career built upon the Native American experience. In the heyday of the traditional western, such characters were regulated to secondary roles, either as villains or as comic foils.

When in my *Writer* article I first echoed Horace Greeley's advice "Go West," the necessary reference material resided only in libraries, bookstores, and county courthouses. Today, the writer with access to a computer can tap into a wealth of information on the geography, living conditions, and history of the West through the Internet. Rounding up the facts has never been so easy, but be warned: There is no longer an excuse for getting them wrong. Today's readers have the same access, and if you err, you will hear from them.

The timespan embraced by the new western is limitless. Once restricted to the bare quarter-century between the end of the Civil War in 1865 and the closing of the frontier in 1890, it now encompasses prehistoric Indian life as exemplified by the "People" series written by anthropologists W. Michael and Kathleen O'Neal Gear (*People of the Fire, People of the Silence,* and many more), and the struggles of modern westerners to come to terms with their heritage, as recounted by John L. Moore in *The Breaking of Ezra Riley.*

Freed from the tyranny of "acceptable" timeframes, I took advantage of all I had learned about the West in twenty years of researching and writing westerns to tell a fictional story based on the mysterious life of the musician who wrote the famous ballad "Jesse James." History knows nothing of this individual beyond the name he signed to his composition, so I co-opted him as representative of the itinerant modern minstrels whose music brought romance to the frontier and preserved its legend. My novel *Billy Gashade* (Forge, 1997) follows its narrator from his fateful role in the New York draft riots of 1863 to his final stint as a ghostwriter of songs for Gene Autry musicals in 1935 Hollywood:

> . . . I don't regret much. I've known some of the best and worst men of my time, survived events that sent better men than I to their graves more than half a century ago and as I was told by one of the strong, intelligent women who have charted the course of my life, I have my gift. Unlike its composer, the song I wrote fifty-three years ago grows stronger each year. A month hardly passes that I don't hear it on the radio or in a supper place with a live performer, usually at the request of one of the patrons, even if whoever sings it usually leaves out the last verse:

> > *This song was made by Billy Gashade*
> > *Just as soon as the news did arrive.*
> > *He said there was no man with the law in his hand*
> > *That could take Jesse James alive.*

The "best and worst men"—and women—of Billy's time include Jesse James, Boss Tweed, Edith Wharton, Allan Pinkerton, Oscar Wilde, George Armstrong Custer, and Greta Garbo. The liberty offered by the new western permitted me to include people and places not commonly associated with the "western," and thus to help stretch the limits; for the history of what was once dismissed as the Great American Desert is the history of America.

The mystique of the frontier has always been freedom: from restrictions, from convention, from one's past. Today, at long last, the western itself offers that same freedom, as well as the opportunity for the writer—any writer—to slap his or her brand on an exciting, expanding market. So saddle up.

□ 45

DETECTIVE NOVELS: THE PACT
BETWEEN AUTHORS AND READERS

BY IAN RANKIN

I HAD LITTLE INTEREST IN DETECTIVE STORIES UNTIL I FOUND THAT
I'd accidentally written one.

My first Inspector John Rebus novel was not meant to be a whodunit.
It was not meant to be the first book in a series that has now reached
double figures.. At the time I wrote it, I was a postgraduate student in
Edinburgh, studying literary theory and the Scottish novel. I thought
I was updating *Dr. Jekyll and Mr. Hyde,* delivering a "Scots Gothic"
for the 1980s, while also perhaps telling readers something about hidden aspects of the city of Edinburgh, aspects the tourists and day-
trippers would never see.

That was my intention. The fact that I made my central character a
policeman was (to me at the time) of little or no importance. I knew
almost nothing about policing or the mechanics of the law; in retrospect, probably no bad thing: It's easy for the would-be author to be
put off by procedure and detail, easy to be sidetracked into esoteric
research. Maybe that's why so many fictional detectives have been
amateurs (in the UK) or private eyes (in the US): These are people
who either ignore or wilfully sidestep the proper procedures for investi-
gating a murder. By using them, their authors can proceed in blissful
ignorance of the mechanics of a criminal investigation.

In the early days, my writing really did seem to descend from a
Muse, in that I depended upon a fertile imagination—and how fertile
it was! With no family life, wife or mortgage worries to get in the way,
I wrote *Knots & Crosses* in about five weeks. Because I'd already had
one novel published (*The Flood),* an agent had approached me to ask
if further novels were forthcoming. I handed her *Knots & Crosses,*
and she offered valuable suggestions for changes I should make (such
as pruning an overtangled flashback from fifty pages to a neater fifteen,

209

or so). She then found me a London publisher, and the book crept into the world without making too much fuss. (I was on book five or six before I was earning enough to even contemplate becoming a full-time writer.)

So it was back to the day job and dreams of new stories. I'd gone on to publish two spy novels before someone asked the innocent question: "Whatever happened to that Edinburgh cop of yours?" By this time, I'd discovered that *Knots & Crosses* had been classified a crime novel, and that the *genre* had not ended (as I'd assumed) with Christie and Chandler. I was now reading and enjoying crime novels, and catching up on the history of the detective story. I discovered its long and noble tradition, and that while noted for rattling good yarns, it was also capable of dealing with serious questions and the moral and psychological depth usually associated with the "literary" or "serious" novel.

I also discovered that a pact exists between mystery authors and their readers, forcing certain constraints on the author. For example, there should be no *deus ex machina,* no sudden appearance of a new character at the end of a book who would turn out to be the miscreant, no twist which the reader couldn't have been expected to be able to work out. I found that because the whodunit constantly poses questions, there have to be ways of expressing them and answering them. Thus the usefulness of the sidekick ("But gracious me, Holmes, how did you come to that astonishing conclusion?!"), or the penultimate chapter's gathering of suspects ("So you see, Madame Bouvier, you could not possibly have been in the archdeacon's antechamber at ten minutes to midnight"). In the Holmes example, the sidekick (Watson) stands for the reader and allows the detective to answer the very questions readers have been asking themselves. In the second example, the book's plot is about to be summarized and explained, and the real villain unmasked, all for the readers' edification.

The problem with such tricks, even when the reader is a willing enough accomplice, is that, to my mind, they *are* tricky, and reduce the seriousness of the crime novel, and turn it into a game, a puzzle. This is fine if the author's intention is to provide fun, entertainment, some little mental challenge to while away the hours.

But my own intentions extended further, and in my Rebus books, the detective is a loner along the lines of the American private eye. He works on the margins of the police force, eschewing sidekicks and back-up, and though written in the third person, the style of the narrative has evolved so that readers are inside the detective's head most of the time, allowing them insights into his thinking. Further, the detective is never physically described, his face and physique a blank, allowing readers to impose their own interpretation on him. In effect, he becomes *their* character.

Some critics have shrewdly commented that Rebus is not the main character in the series, that my main character is Edinburgh itself, and the country of which it is capital. But Edinburgh can "boast" only six murders a year, while Glasgow, only forty miles to the west, notches up between sixty and seventy. I've been asked why I don't write about Glasgow; wouldn't it be a more fruitful setting for a crime novel? Perhaps, but I don't *know* Glasgow. I choose to live and work in Edinburgh. It's a city that fascinates me and puzzles me, and these feelings become part of the fabric of my stories. Because *I* am fascinated by my chosen city, perhaps part of that fascination will extend to the reader which was the whole point of the series all along, even before it *became* a series. It is a cliché perhaps, but in a very real sense we are all detectives, trying to make sense of the world around us. I set up problems for Rebus, and the pleasure for the reader is in joining him on an expedition toward the various solutions. This requires a measure of holding back. *I* may know whodunit, but readers will probably be disappointed if they work it out too quickly. Premature revelation is a constant worry. One way to solve it is to be unsure yourself who your villain is. Sometimes I'm on the third or fourth draft of a book before I decide which of my cast is to be the "baddie." The first draft for me is in itself an investigation: it's only when I start to write about my characters that I begin to sense what they are capable of, and what motives they might have for committing a crime.

Just as we are all detectives, so *all* fiction is mystery fiction, setting up questions that will be answered only if we read on. Ask yourself: What makes you turn the next page? Answer: the need to find out what happens next. A story must generate tension and leave things unsaid or unexplained (until near its climax), otherwise the reader will lose interest. If there are only so many plots in fiction, there are even fewer in the detective novel, and the problems with keeping a series going are many and varied. I doubt I'd have had the guts to begin a series using the alphabet, as Sue Grafton did, in the knowledge that

twenty-five books on I'd still have to be writing about the same protagonist. How do you keep your character and your plots fresh? I've
found that it pays to have a hero with a past—and not to unlock the
door to this secret past too quickly. In *Knots & Crosses,* the plot is all
down to events that happened to Rebus during his time in the British
Army's crack SAS batallion. In future novels in the series, we learn a
little more about his army service in Northern Ireland, about his early
police cases, and about past family secrets and even boyhood mysteries.

These help add layer upon layer to the psychological make-up of the
detective, as well as providing new material for plots. But in fact plots
have never been that hard for me to find; most of them actually throw
themselves at me: Some newspaper story or overheard anecdote in a
bar will have me asking questions or railing at a miscarriage of justice.
The crime novel is the perfect vehicle for dissecting society, since in
fiction you can get away with saying things (between the lines) which,
as newspaper reporting, could get you sued. And the detective is the
perfect tool for the job, having, as he does, access to both the Establishment and society's dispossessed. In moving easily between these
two worlds (and all stops in between), the detective can uncover all
sorts of skeletons, from the personal (a character's hidden past, for
example) to the public (conspiracies in high office).

In this sense, there are no limitations to where the crime novel can
go. It may also explain why serious novels such as Don DeLillo's
Underworld (and note that title) contain their fair share of mysteries,
subterfuges, hidden identities, and murderers.

Here, then, are a few rules about the detective story, with the caveat
that rules are there to be broken by writers with a strong enough dispo-
sition:

1) No cheating. Your murderer can't turn out to be a character
you've suddenly introduced five pages from the end of the story. The
reader must be given a fair chance of solving any puzzle in your book.

2) Having said this, I must admit that some sorts of cheating are
actually expected, in that you're going to provide red herrings and false
trails galore. These can be as outlandish as you like, as long as the
reader is convinced they work within the context of the story. Note
James Ellroy's tactic of peppering his novels with real historical characters. In this way, he dupes the reader into suspending disbelief,

thinking: "That really did happen, and those people really did exist . . . so how much of the rest of this story is true?" Once you've got readers reacting that way, you've got them hooked.

3) You can keep research as minimal as you like, but your book must read as *authentic*. In other words, the reader must be hoodwinked into thinking you know what you're talking about, which isn't the same as your actually knowing what you're talking about. A little knowledge will go a long way. Conversely, writers who know too much about a subject can end up putting too much of it into their novels, slowing the story and confusing the reader. The task for the author is to know how much to put in and how much to leave out. I believe in the "less is more" principle. *Showing* is always better than *telling*. Give an example rather than a long explanation. If you have 200 pages of notes on autopsy procedure, fine, but use all of it in a novel and you'll bore the pants off everyone. An autopsy scene of a couple of paragraphs can be every bit as convicing as one of twenty pages, and you stand less risk of descending into tedium or jargon.

4) Don't strain for novelty in your central character. We all know this problem: Since all detectives are much of a muchness, how can I get mine to stand out from the herd? Well, in fact the very familiarity of a typical detective can be satisfying to readers. They're happy to work with a hero who is little more than a cipher, as long as the plot is blistering. To put meat on your hero's bones, introduce flaws and foibles, and an interesting home life. You don't need to strain after this. Don't feel the need to make your protagonist a six-foot-five Icelandic woman with poor eyesight and a box-file of homemade recipe-cards to be dispensed one per chapter. Characterization can be more subtle, and every bit as effective at delineating your detective.

5) Go read Raymond Chandler's rules. Better still, make up your own.

□ 46

DISCOVERING A STORY
IN HISTORY

BY SONIA LEVITIN

"I'M WRITING A HISTORICAL NOVEL ABOUT THE RECONSTRUCTION PE-
riod," a student told me. "I'm using my great-grandmother's Civil
War diaries."

"Wonderful," I said. "Now, what's your story?"

The student was baffled and a little insulted. Story? Hadn't she just
told me?

What she had told me was simply that she was delving into a certain
period in American history—a time filled with drama and conflict, and
she had resources at her command. What I needed to know is exactly
what any editor and every reader wants to know: What happens in
this story to make readers identify with the characters? What dangers
do they face? How do they apply courage, ingenuity, and risk to their
personal challenges? What are the stakes?

I have written various historical novels set in different periods. My
most recent, *Escape from Egypt,* is set in Biblical times and deals
with the Israelites' enslavement, exodus, and the wilderness sojourn.
Dramatic events all, but the story had to come from specific characters, all drawn boldly and vividly, to convince the reader that these
long-ago events happened to real people. Only in that way do we involve readers, make them care.

Some say that history is dry, while the novel is juicy. There is the
difference. Most writers of pure history remember the facts and forget
the people. For the novelist, the facts are the foundation, the people
are everything else.

To breathe life into history, writers must ask two questions: First,
what aspects of human endeavor never change? Second, how have
things changed since the distant past in the story?

What doesn't change is the need for people to survive, to be loved, to win the approbation of their peers, and to reach some personal/ spiritual conclusion. What do change are manners, customs, ways of thinking about the world and one's place in it. Some things go in cycles. Society moves from repression to permissiveness, back to strict control. Individuals continually battle the restrictions, which becomes the basis for many a story.

The historical novel, like any other, needs a protagonist who must battle the status quo. In my novel, *Roanoke,* protagonist William Wythers is a pauper wrongly accused of a crime. He sails for the New World to clear his name and to win fame and fortune, thus battling the status quo that relegated paupers to prison. William does not meet his goal in the ordinary sense; instead, he discovers a terrifying and captivating land. When war breaks out with the local Native Americans and most of the colonists are murdered, William survives. Why? Because he has been able to adapt to the new land, to accept change, and also (not incidentally) because he has fallen in love with a Native American girl. In a historical novel, or any novel, love can be the element that keeps the hero on course; it is the one ingredient that remains constant in a world of turmoil and change. We know the hero by what or by whom he loves, and often it is this very love (commitment) that saves him.

The hero in a historical novel must often leave his old world of conflict and conformity. Every patriot, pilgrim, and adventurer begins by stepping out of the old world and finding not only new worlds "out there" but new attitudes within. This is the universal lesson of history. Without change there is no growth.

Against this universal background, the novelist must prepare something unique and challenging, new characters with fresh faces, characters who behave boldly but in conformity with all that we know of psychology. Motivation must be clear.

In planning the plot for *Escape from Egypt,* I realized that the two primary characters, Jesse, the Israelite slave, and Jennat, the young Egyptian-Syrian concubine, must be given different lives and different motives for needing to escape from Egypt. For Jesse, it was enough that he was an Israelite whose people were ultimately released through Moses' leadership. For Jennat, however, an entirely different scenario had to be created, and it was this that became part of the plot.

Jennat and Jesse have shared a mutual attraction—forbidden love, of course. The Bible gave me the bare bones of the action: Ten plagues are unleashed upon stubborn Pharaoh. His innocent subjects suffer, too. Jennat is one of them. The final plague, the death of all the first-born of Pharaoh's subjects, gave me the perfect plot point I needed. Instead of seeing it only as part of the retribution against Pharaoh, I made this plague very personal. It provides the impetus for Jennat to leave Egypt and join the Israelites in their exodus. What happens is that Jennat's mistress loses her beloved son to the plague. Because of Jennat's association with Jesse, an Israelite, Jennat's mistress blames *her* for the death of the child and, insane with grief, tries to kill her. Jennat flees and joins the Israelites in their exodus and the wilderness adventures. Similarly, other historical events are brought into the lives of the various characters, influencing their actions, propelling the story.

Momentous events—a migration, invasion, invention, or a major catastrophe—can be the foundation for your novel. But the nuts and bolts, the action that keeps the reader turning the page, has to come from within the characters themselves, their personal struggles as they are swept away by major forces that seem to be controlling their lives.

For characters to be real, they must be in conflict. That is where the action comes in. The novelist creates conflict from every premise. The Israelites are slaves and want to escape. Or do they? In my novel, Jesse's father, a renegade and an opportunist, doesn't want to leave Egypt at all! Jesse's mother, on the other hand, is passionate about wanting to flee. Thus, Jesse is immediately plunged into conflict between the two.

Remember, the unfolding of historical events is never smooth, never easy. Among this country's westward migrants there were those who came unwillingly, resentfully. There was conflict with natives, with recalcitrant beasts, with fellow travelers, and most of all, there was conflict within.

In *The No-Return Trail,* my heroine, Nancy Kelsey, is faced with numerous conflicts, some recorded, some invented. It is the novelist's privilege to invent, as long as the facts are not overlooked. For Nancy, I invented a bossy sister-in-law and a blunt, stubborn husband, as well as a mother who grieved over her departure. None of these seems too farfetched, considering the situation. Even a few known facts can provide the seeds of conflict. For example, Nancy was the youngest in her family. As such, she would very likely be intimidated by an older in-law. Her husband was an uneducated woodsman and in later years an itinerant preacher. Certainly, he would have had a fiercely independent nature, and like other men of his day, probably spent little time romancing or sweet-talking a young wife. Thus, we can assume that Nancy longed for talk and tenderness and the companionship of other women. It is these personal reflections that make Nancy real and empathic. This personal background provides the necessary drama for the story, as Nancy sets out to be with other women but ends up the only female among thirty men who made it to California. History provides the facts; the novelist seeks out the dramatic irony that brings a story to an emotional high. For everything gained there is something lost: This is the premise of the historical novel, which, even more than the "regular" novel, imitates life.

How do we create new characters in a historical setting? My own method is, first, to immerse myself completely in the period, until I know almost instinctively what my protagonist eats for breakfast, what he hears outside the window, what smells greet him upon arising, what kind of song springs to his lips, what curses, what endearments. Because everything we say and do and think is anchored in the time and place we find ourselves.

For my *Journey to America* trilogy, I researched what was playing at the movies in the late forties, what songs were popular, the actual names of the restaurants we frequented, and even the price of an egg sandwich. On my extended calendar, I always look up the date and the day of the week, and I consult almanacs to check the weather. Why go to all that trouble? Because I know that the background I provide is as accurate as it can be, and lends veracity to the whole.

I particularly enjoy researching and using medical information in my historical novels. Everyone is interested in health and remedies. I find it amusing to note some of the outrageous "cures" that were perpetrated upon innocent patients, and also to note their abiding faith in their physicians. Probably every writer favors certain details; my personal favorites are the domestic details of housekeeping, clothing, and personal care.

In *Escape from Egypt*, the opening scene between Jennat and her mistress takes place while the latter is having her hair done. Her washstand, mirror, tiny cosmetic cups, and trays are straight out of a museum, prototypes of the things we still use today. The hairdresser inserts several hair pieces, as much tricks of the trade then as now!

Why does it matter what powders, scents, and colors women used back then? Because it makes people seem more real, more like us, engrossed in minutiae of living even while major historical events are exploding all around them. This is what makes the historical novel exciting, for while empires rise and fall, epochs emerge or end, every-day life goes on *just as if nothing were changing.*

Actual historical events are the "wall" or the structural foundation of the historical novel. Between these "walls" the characters come and go, live out the desires, compulsions, or regrets that you, the novelist, create. One character hates his father. Another is haunted by an evil memory or a damaging secret. If a character is hell-bent on proving his courage, it's a sure bet that he was once a coward, and that secret becomes a compelling part of the plot.

Of course, the outcome of actual historical events is already known. The cataclysm inevitably must occur. This creates a sense of tension in the historical novel, the inevitability of crisis known to the reader, pitted against the ignorance, complacency or apparent helplessness of the characters. Eventually the characters are forced to see and to act.

If the characters are provocative, complex, and *real,* the outcome doesn't matter as much as the journey to that outcome, because the novelist is more concerned with "how" than with "what." How do people survive tough challenges? How do they find the courage to make the right decisions? How can they go against the current of overpowering events and still come out victorious?

This is the task and the pleasure of writing the historical novel, to ponder the past, to find its truths, and then to invent new lives that will speak these truths to the reader.

❑ 47

SELLING SPECULATIVE FICTION

BY LESLIE WHAT

THE GENRE KNOWN AS SCIENCE FICTION AND FANTASY IS MUCH MORE than rocket ships, dystopias, and elves. This might explain why some critics and writers prefer to call it "the literature of the fantastic" or "speculative fiction"—SF for short. SF magazines and anthologies publish a mix of unclassifiable fiction, magical realism, urban fantasy, alternative history, high fantasy, and hard science fiction. No matter what you call it, speculative fiction is a great field for the new writer.

Editors actively seek out talent: They attend conventions; make virtual appearances on-line; teach at workshops or conferences; and read unsolicited submissions from unknowns—unceremoniously known as "slush." Leading SF magazines publish only ten to twelve of every thousand manuscripts submitted; fortunately for new writers, every editor is a reader hoping to find precious words in that mountain of paper. And there are ways to make your work stand out, at least long enough for the editor to notice your name.

My first professionally published story, "King for a Day" (*Asimov's Science Fiction*), postulated that there were so many Elvis impersonators in Hell, the *real* Elvis had a hard time finding work. In my satiric vision of the afterlife, John Lennon waited in line to see himself. The acceptance was a bit of a surprise, because I hadn't been sure if "King for a Day" was *really* science fiction. But I was sure about the important things: The story was fast-paced, original, and lively; the manuscript proofread to the best of my ability. The rest was up to the editor.

Though the creative side may be in the writing, selling fiction is business, and in business, deals can be broken by a clumsy introduction. Take time to come up with a title that creates interest and excitement in the story. A knockout line from the text might do, or a portion of a quote that has always intrigued you. Titles can mirror the concept of the story. "Designated Hater" (*Magazine of Fantasy and Science Fiction*) took its cue from the American League, but twisted the rules for the sake of the plot. "The Goddess is Alive, and Well, Living in New York City" (*Asimov's Science Fiction*) reworked a bumper sticker I saw on pre-1980 VW vans. Titles work best when they reflect both the tone and language of the story. "A Dark Fire, Burning from Within" (*Realms of Fantasy*) tells the reader not to expect one of my light-hearted pieces, while "How to Feed Your Inner Troll" (*Asimov's Science Fiction*) suggests not only an encounter with a magical being, but a satire of pop psychology.

Think of the opening paragraphs of your story as an introduction to a prospective employer. Picture yourself standing face to face with the employer while you mumble on for pages before getting down to what you both mean and want to say. Not the most effective use of time. Rambling openings can keep an editor from reading to the end and giving your work the attention it deserves.

Analyze your beginning carefully. It should:

1) Evoke a sense of time and place. A reader expects a story to take place in the here and now, unless you say otherwise. If your story is set in the Italy of 2507, mention this at the start, or offer enough clues to prevent the revelation from coming as a surprise on page six. Clues can take the form of metaphor, dialogue, or straight narrative description.

2) Establish tone and authority through voice, word choice, theme, imagery, and detail. Prove that you are in control of your story by a correct use of grammar and a healthy respect for the conventions of language.

3) Introduce major character(s), hint at ages, gender, socioeconomic background. This can be the barest introduction, to be elaborated upon throughout the story.

4) Foreshadow major story problems and introduce minor ones.

A beginning that accomplishes as much of the above as possible will increase its chances for publication. Here's an example from "Smelling of Earth, Dreaming of Sky" (*Asimov's Science Fiction*):

Sunday at church:
In his sermon, the minister preaches that the first man was made from earth.

"Adamah," he begins, "common clay begat Adam, common man." Adam of earth, who thought he knew better than God and was forced to leave Paradise.

"We all—every one of us—came from that very clay," says the minister. "With this humble beginning, the Bible teaches that not one of us is better than the rest."

I groan, disagreeing. The minister must be referring to the commoners.

This opening makes clear who the story is about, and also hints at possible conflicts. Each new piece of information builds on what has previously been established. The next few paragraphs reveal that the narrator is an angel, sent back to perform one good deed. The somber tone of the writing, the deliberate use of present tense to magnify the feelings of a character who is trapped, the angry voice coupled with the spare choice of details, suggest that she will be unlikely to fulfill her mission. (Note: The title came from an earlier work that another editor had rejected with a note, "Title great, story stinks." The truth hurt, but he was right. I kept the title, tossed the story, then wrote a better one in its place.)

Selling wonders

Gardner Dozois, the editor of *Asimov's Science Fiction,* compares himself to P. T. Barnum, who sold wonders and marvels for money. "If there's no wonder or marvel in the content of your story," says Dozois, "then it's going to be a hard sell."

Editors want stories that are interesting and entertaining, unique, and logically consistent in their own way. Read what is being published now for clues of where to send your work. Magazines like *Analog* and *Science Fiction Age* are unlikely to publish a "Gnomes on Vacation" story, while *Realms of Fantasy* might not be the first place to send a story featuring "Physicists Who Save Themselves Before the Sun Goes Nova." Of course, there are always exceptions.

Instead of trying to clone what you read, view ideas through a prism to see them in a different light. For "Mothers' Day," (*Realms of Fantasy*), I took the legend of the Pied Piper one step further. What would it *really* be like, I wondered, for a man stuck inside a cave with all those children? The resulting story was a sympathetic yet satiric look at a man living with what he *never* bargained for.

It's fine to reuse a premise if you do something different. You must take the premise where no writer has gone before. A story cannot have time travel or virtual reality as the only focus; it must use the idea as background setting, what editor Dozois calls "The furniture of plot." In "Compatibility Clause" (*Fantasy and Science Fiction*), I borrowed heavily from William Gibson, my experiences and observations at video arcades, and themes of married life. The story is about a wife (Mrs. Claus on the night before Christmas), desperate to communicate with her husband, a busy man with an addictive personality. I combined real-life tensions with a fantasy world and a science fiction gimmick to create a story.

Hard sells

You might have trouble selling what is known as a *Translation Story:* the Western set on Alpha IV, with blasters instead of shotguns, and spaceships instead of horses. As a general rule, the fantastic or scientific idea must be an integral part of the story and not put there just to set up your theme or add interest to the plot.

Other hard sells include the surprise ending: the *deus ex machina,* where the resolution occurs as if by the hand of God; the story set in virtual reality (unbeknownst to the characters, who are revealed as imaginary only at story's end); stories that take place in dreams; Adam and Eve at the end of the world; stories with joke endings. If you've written one of the above, send it out anyway, but if you get back form letter rejections, you might try changing tactics. You will not be able to sell stories based on Star Trek or any licensed characters, or stories that are spin-offs from trademarked games.

Stories about ghosts are said to be a hard sell, though I've sold several. The key to selling a ghost story might be figuring out what the ghost represents on a symbolic level, as well as knowing why the ghost is needed in the story. Little-known legends reinterpreted through your unique vision can be a source of ideas for new and inventive ghost stories. "Beside the Well" (*Bending the Landscape: Fantasy,* White Wolf Publishing 1997) was based on a Korean folk tale, but with a few unexpected twists that fit the theme of the anthology. "Clinging to a Thread" (*Fantasy and Science Fiction*) presented ghosts through their physical connection to the objects they once touched. Vampires have been done to death (sorry), but an inventive writer might come up with a way to make them fresh.

Your story must be about the day, the person, and the event—not just any day or any person who happens to be trapped in some fascinating scenario. If another person could just as easily replace the central character, if the angel is merely symbolic and could be replaced by a Western Union man, if the effect of time travel is the same as if your character just got out of jail, you'd better rethink what you've written.

Why this person? Why today? Why is THIS fantastic element necessary? In general, these questions must be answered for the story to sell. Otherwise, let yourself go wild. In the field of speculative fiction, stories are limited only by imagination.

DEFINITIONS

Cyberpunk: Combines street-smart punks with the hi-tech world of computers and neural networks.

Hard Science Fiction: SF where the scientific idea is central to the plot, conflict, and resolution in the story.

Urban Fantasy/Contemporary Fantasy: Magic in modern-day settings, also called "North American magical realism."

High Fantasy: Often set in feudal or medieval societies where magical beings reside.

Alternative History: Looking at how an alternative past would change the present.

WEB SITES OF INTEREST

1) <http://critique.org/users/critters> On-line workshop, support, critiques, advice.

2) <http://www.sff.net> Author newsgroups, marketing information, and a private on-line critique group.

3) <http://www.speculations.com> News of open anthologies, magazine guidelines.

4) <http://users.aol.com/marketlist> Marketing information.

❑ 48

PLOTTING A MYSTERY NOVEL

BY CAROLYN HART

HOW DO YOU PLOT YOUR NOVELS? THIS MAY BE THE QUESTION WRITers hear most often.

It's as if, after enjoying a particularly succulent dish, I ask a cook, "May I have that recipe?" The cook smiles, nods, offers a list of ingredients. But if I try that recipe in my own kitchen, somehow the finished dish won't be the same.

The cook's answer is quite similar to those of authors when asked how to plot. We launch into quick answers that make plotting sound, if not easy, at least quite reasonable and straightforward.

We lie. Oh, not intentionally, of course. But our answers simply don't capture the reality of plotting a novel. Plotting is never easy, rarely straightforward, and cannot be reduced to a formula.

I'm especially attuned to the deficiency of our rote answer—outline, outline, outline—because I'm presently engaged in plotting a new mystery. It should be easy, right? No. No. No!

It is terribly difficult, as all novelists know. And every novelist has an individual way of responding to the challenge. Some novelists pose that wonderful, familiar question, "What if?" Some do detailed character sketches and carefully outline every chapter. Others write a one- or two-page synopsis. We all struggle, but I truly believe there is no easy route to writing a novel. But perhaps the imperfect, tantalizing suggestions of how I forge a story will help you discover your own process.

These are the facts I must know in order to start a mystery novel:
1. The protagonist
2. The victim
3. The murderer
4. The title

The most important decision to make is who will be the main protagonist. In my Death on Demand series, it is Annie Laurance Darling, who is aided and abetted by her husband, Max. In my Henrie O series, the protagonist is retired newswoman Henrietta O'Dwyer (Henrie O) Collins. There is a world of difference between the two series, and all the differences can be traced to the personalities of the protagonists.

Annie and Max are young and enthusiastic. Annie is quite serious and intense, but she loves to laugh. She owns a mystery bookstore, and her vocation and avocation are mysteries. Max is sexy, fun and handsome, rich, easy-going and loving. He is, in fact, the kind of man women adore.

So, what do we have in the Death on Demand series? A young, eager bookstore owner who in various novels in the series falls in love, plans a murder mystery weekend, participates in a community play, gets married, teaches a class on the three great ladies of the mystery, learns about the many faces of love, celebrates the brilliance of Agatha Christie, and serves as the author liaison at a book fair. These novels also have sub-plots featuring subsidiary characters, avid reader Henny Brawley, curmudgeonly Miss Dora Brevard, and Annie's mother-in-law, unflappable, ethereal, unpredictable Laurel Darling Roethke.

In sharp contrast, Henrie O is a sixty-something, savvy, sardonic woman who has seen good and bad in a long life, has few illusions, a passion for truth, and a determination to do what she feels she must. In the first book in the series, Henri O refuses to be vanquished by either an old lover or a hurricane, and in the process of solving a murder decides that silence best serves those she loves. In the second, Henrie O saves a man unjustly accused despite the power and money arrayed against her. In my newest novel, *Death in Lovers' Lane*, Henrie O faces a hard personal decision. In discovering the murderer of a student reporter, she brings a resolution to three old unsolved crimes.

Who these people are and what they do determine the structure, tone, and objective of the books.

The Death on Demand novels are written in the third person, which makes it easy to switch viewpoints and offer the reader insights. Each book opens with a series of vignettes that give the reader an instant slice of the life of a character who will be important to the book. The recurring minor characters offer another way to entertain the reader, and that is the objective of the Death on Demand books—to entertain. Everything about their creation—the mystery bookstore, the young lovers, the subsidiary characters—is calculated to result in a good-humored novel that provides mystery lore, entertaining characters, and, hopefully, an intricate mystery.

The Henrie O mysteries are another pot of soup entirely. They are written in the first person to engage the reader totally in Henrie O's life, thoughts, and actions. I chose for her to be an older woman because I want to celebrate age and experience. In *Dead Man's Island,* Henrie O waits for an elevator . . . .

I saw my own reflection: dark hair silvered at the temples, dark eyes that have seen much and remembered much, a Roman-coin profile, a lean and angular body with an appearance of forward motion even when at rest—and the angry light in my eyes. I can't abide meanness.

The Henrie O novels are sparsely written, with quick, short, vivid sentences of a newspaper article. Henrie O wryly comments on life as she has lived and observed it, but these are not light, entertaining novels.

The differences between the two series clearly illustrate the importance of the protagonist. A book mirrors its protagonist. The choice of protagonist provides the tone, background, pace, taste, and scope of your novel.

Who will your protagonist be? A cop, a midwife, a divorcee, a lawyer? Each would make a different story out of the same facts. Is the story set in San Diego, Des Moines, Chicago, Paris, Birmingham? That depends upon the protagonist, too.

Everything else in the novel flows from the choice of the protagonist. Choose a cop, and you can have a serial killer, domestic violence, a drive-by shooting. But if you decide to create an amateur sleuth, that sleuth's vocation or avocation will determine who might be a likely murder victim.

Annie, a bookstore owner who lives on a resort island off the coast of South Carolina, is most unlikely to have contact with a murdered drug dealer. In *Death on Demand,* the victim was a mean-spirited mystery author murdered at a gathering of mystery writers in Annie's store. Victims in my other novels range from a well-to-do club woman to a love-hungry wife, to a cold, hard judge, to a crabby voyeur who snooped on the wrong night. But all of my victims grew out of Annie's world. Their existence was dictated by Annie's milieu.

Henrie O plays on a much larger stage. In *Dead Man's Island,* the story grows out of her background as a reporter, but that background can have inhabitants from diverse places. *Death in Lovers' Lane* revolves around personal responsibility and how much information is owed to society. Henrie O makes some difficult judgments, but, as she emphasizes in that book, judgments never come easy.

So, you begin to see how stories flow. The choice of a protagonist determines the background. The choice of the background determines the victim. The choice of the victim determines the murderer, because the persons involved in the victim's life make up the circle of suspects. One of the suspects will be the villain.

Villains can be flawed, likable people, or they can be horribly selfish and mean. Your choice, but this choice is once again the result of earlier choices.

In *Design for Murder,* Corinne, the victim, is the wealthy, selfish, egocentric society matron who tries to control the lives of those around her. Her circle included:
• Leighton, the charming, handsome, not-so-grieved widower
• Gail, the emotional, love-struck, frightened niece
• Bobby, the abrasive, tough, self-serving reporter
• Roscoe, the self-contained but passionate lawyer
• John, the ambitious, determined, aloof doctor
• Sybil, the lusty, willful, spoiled sybarite
• Tim, the gifted, immature, self-centered artist
• Edith, the nervous, sensitive, hardworking club woman
• Miss Dora, the eccentric, unpredictable, waspish old woman
• Lucy, Corinne's childhood friend who once loved Corinne's brother
Each person in Corinne's life—and death—evolved from Corinne's personality.

In *Death in Lovers' Lane,* the victim is a bright, beautiful student reporter, and Henrie O is her journalism professor, who insists the student find fresh facts if she intends to write about three unsolved crimes in the university town. When I was plotting the book, I knew the milieu—a university town, a campus. What kind of unsolved crimes might there be? I came up with three: the double murder of a student couple in Lovers' Lane; the shooting of a respected businessman; and the disappearance some years earlier of the dean of students.

I then had four victims: the student reporter, the lovers, the businessman, and the dean. Whom did they know? Who loved them—or hated them?

Now that you've seen how to create the characters in your novel, you may reasonably complain that this isn't a plot. No, it isn't, but you are on your way. The plot does not arrive full blown, at least, not for most writers. Some writers outline an entire novel. I am in awe of them, but most of us do not have that kind of linear skill. We begin with people. We decide the general theme. In the novel I'm plotting now, Henny Brawley is putting on a Fourth of July celebration in honor of South Carolina history, from a woman's perspective. Lt. Gen. (ret.) Charlton (Bud) Hatch insists on changing the focus to men, which puts him at cross purposes with a good portion of island society.

I know who the protagonist is: Annie.

I know who the victim is: Bud Hatch.

I know who the murderer is: (Of course, I won't tell you!)

I know who the suspects are: Henny Brawley, Bud's mistress, his next-door neighbor, an alienated stepdaughter, the director of the library, the director's lover, a librarian, a handyman.

I know the title: *Yankee Doodle Dead.* I have to have a working title when I begin a novel. It gives me a sense of reality, and it also defines the ultimate story. In *Yankee Doodle Dead,* a Yankee (Bud Hatch) comes to town and ends up dead.

So, I have a great deal, but where is the plot?

Darned if I know, and I'm not being flippant or dismissive or coy. This truthful admission is perhaps the best help I can ever offer to a new or struggling writer: All the planning in the world won't create a novel. That takes magic, and the magic happens when you write. If you figure out all the elements I've listed, you won't know how the story ends, or what's going to happen in Chapter 9, but you have enough to begin.

That's how I do it: I begin writing, and the people come to life—or death—and events occur, and I will have the great adventure of finding out who these characters are, what they are going to do, and ultimately, with them, I will—haphazardly, surprisingly, unexpectedly—reach the final chapter.

Yes, I get stuck. Sometimes everything I've written seems dull and boring, and I can't figure out how to move ahead. But if I keep on thinking about those characters, and if I sit at my computer and write, things will begin to happen. And finally I'll know that the novel exists, that it's out there, all I have to do is find it.

It isn't a straightforward process. I can't diagram it, but this is how I plot—and write—a novel. It's scary, but it's a great adventure.

❏ 49

WRITING THE SUPERNATURAL NOVEL

BY ELIZABETH HAND

I'VE ALWAYS THOUGHT THAT THE OLDEST PROFESSION WAS THAT OF storyteller—in particular, the teller of supernatural tales. A look at the cave paintings in France or Spain will show you how far back our hunger for the fantastic goes: men with the heads of beasts, figures crouching in the darkness, skulls and shadows and unblinking eyes. Take a glance at the current bestseller list, and you'll see that we haven't moved that far in the last twenty thousand years. Books by Anne Rice, Stephen King, Joyce Carol Oates, and Clive Barker, among many others, continue to feed our taste for dark wine and the perils of walking after midnight. But how to join the ranks of those whose novels explore the sinister side of town?

First, let me distinguish between supernatural fiction and its tough (and very successful) younger cousin, the horror novel. Horror novels depend heavily upon the mechanics of plot, less-than-subtle characterizations, and shock value—what Stephen King calls "going for the gross-out." In spirit and execution, they aren't that different from the "penny dreadfuls" of a century ago, crude but effective entertainments that tend to have a short shelf life. Unlike more stylized works such as *Dracula, The Turn of the Screw* or *The Shining,* most horror novels lose their ability to chill the second time around—they just don't stand up to rereading. As Edmund Wilson put it, "The only horror in these fictions is the horror of bad taste and bad art."

In the wake of Stephen King's success, the 1980's was a boom decade for horror fiction. But the market was flooded with so many books—and so many second-rate Stephen King imitators—that publishers and readers alike grew wary. With the dwindling reading public, it's far more difficult today to get a supernatural novel into print.

But the readers *are* there. And they're quite a sophisticated audience, which makes it both more challenging, and more fun, to write the sort of novel that will appeal to someone who prefers *The Vampire Lestat* to the *The Creeping Bore.*

More than other genres, supernatural fiction is defined by *atmosphere* and *characterization.* By atmosphere, I mean the author's ability to evoke a mood or place viscerally by the use of original and elegant, almost *seductive* language. Science fiction and fantasy also rely heavily upon unusual settings and wordplay, often against a backdrop of other, imagined, worlds. But the most successful supernatural novels are set in *our* world. Their narrative tension, their very ability to frighten and transport us, derives from a conflict between the macabre and the mundane, between everyday reality and the threatening *other*— whether revenant, werewolf, or demonic godling—that seeks to destroy it.

The roots of supernatural fiction lie in the gothic romances of the eighteenth and nineteenth centuries with their gloomy settings, imperiled narrators and ghostly visitations. Even today these remain potent elements. Witness Anne Rice's vampire Lestat during a perambulation about prerevolutionary Paris:

> The cold seemed worse in Paris. It wasn't as clean as it had been in the mountains. The poor hovered in doorways, shivering and hungry, the crooked unpaved streets were thick with filthy slush. I saw barefoot children suffering before my very eyes, and more neglected corpses lying about than ever before. I was never so glad of the fur-lined cape as I was then. . . .

Much of the pleasure in Rice's work comes from her detailed evocations of real, yet highly romanticized, places: New Orleans, Paris, San Francisco. It pays to have firsthand knowledge of some desirable piece of occult real estate: Readers love the thrill of an offbeat setting, but they also like recognizing familiar landmarks. So, Stephen King has staked out rural Maine as his fictional backyard. The incomparable Shirley Jackson (whose classic "The Lottery" has chilled generations of readers) also turns to New England for the horrific doings in *The Haunting of Hill House, The Bird's Nest* and *We Have Always Lived in the Castle.* Daphne du Maurier's novella "Don't Look Now" gives us a tourist couple lost amidst the winding alleys of Venice, a notion creepy enough to have inspired Ian McEwan's nightmarish *The Comfort of Strangers.* Just about any setting will do, if you can imbue it with an aura of beauty and menace. My neo-gothic novel *Waking the*

Moon takes place in that most pedestrian and bureaucratic of cities, Washington, D.C. But by counterpointing the city's workaday drabness with exotic descriptions of its lesser-known corners, I was able to suggest that an ancient evil might lurk near Capitol Hill:

> From the Shrine's bell tower came the first deep tones of the carillon calling the hour. I turned, and saw in the distance the domes and columns of the Capitol glimmering in the twilight, bone-colored, ghostly; and behind it still more ghostly buildings, their columned porticoes and marble arches all seeming to melt into the haze of green and violet darkness that descended upon them like sleep.

Style, of course, is a matter of taste and technique, and as with all writing, your most important tools should be a good thesaurus and dictionary. (Good taste in reading helps, but is probably not necessary.) A thesaurus can transform even the oldest and most unpalatable of chestnuts. "It was a dark and stormy night" becomes "Somber and tenebrous, the vespertine hour approached."

The danger, of course, is that such elevated diction easily falls into self-parody. But when well-done, it can quickly seduce the reader into believing in—well, in any number of marvelous things:

> Last night I dreamt that I woke to hear some strange, barely audible sound from downstairs—a kind of thin tintinnabulation, like those coloured-glass bird scarers which in my childhood were still sold for hanging up to glitter and tinkle in the garden breeze. I thought I went downstairs to the drawing room. The doors of the china cabinets were standing open, but all the figures were in their places—the Bow Liberty and Matrimony, the Four Seasons of Neale earthenware, the Reinecke girl on her cow; yes, and she herself—the Girl in a Swing. It was from these that the sound came, for they were weeping.

This is from Richard Adams's superb *The Girl in a Swing,* to my mind the best supernatural novel I've ever read. One of the problems in writing supernatural fiction stems from the fact that "ghost stories" are nearly always better when they are really *stories,* rather than full-length novels. Indeed, many of the classic works of dark fantasy—*The Turn of the Screw,* Charlotte Gilman's "The Yellow Wallpaper," Oliver Onions's "The Beckoning Fair One"—are novellas, a form that particularly suits the supernatural, but which is a hard sell: too short for publishers looking for meaty bestsellers, too long for a magazine market that thrives on the 5,000- to 7,000-word story. It is very difficult to sustain a high level of suspense for several hundred pages. Chapter after chapter of awful doings too often just become awful, with the "cliffhanger" effect ultimately boring the reader.

Characterization is one way of avoiding this pitfall. If your central characters are intriguing, you don't need a constant stream of ghoulish doings to hold a reader's attention. Think of Anne Rice's Lestat, whose melancholy persona has seen him through several sequels. Or the callow student narrator of Donna Tartt's *The Secret History,* a novel which has only a hint of the supernatural about it, but which is more terrifying than any number of haunted houses:

> Does such a thing as "the fatal flaw," that showy dark crack running down the middle of a life, exist outside literature? I used to think it didn't. Now I think it does. And I think that mine is this: a morbid longing for the picturesque at all costs.

The Secret History is told in the first person, as are *The Girl in a Swing,* Rice's *Vampire Chronicles,* and *Waking the Moon.* In supernatural fiction, it is not enough that the protagonist compel our interest. Readers must also be able to truly *identify* with him, to experience his growing sense of unease as his familiar world gradually crumbles in the face of some dark intruder, be it spirit or succubus. That is why the first-person narrator is so prevalent in supernatural tales. It is also why most uncanny novels feature individuals whose very *normalcy* is what sets them apart from others. Like us, they do not believe in ghosts, which makes it all the worse when a ghost actually does appear.

But "normal" does not necessarily mean "dull." Richard Papen, the narrator of *The Secret History,* is drawn into a murderous conspiracy when his college friends seek to evoke Dionysos one drunken winter night. In *The Girl in a Swing,* Alan Desland is a middle-aged bachelor whose most distinguishing characteristic is his extraordinary *niceness*—until he becomes obsessed with the beautiful Kathe, who may be the incarnation of a goddess—or of a woman who murdered her own children. And in C. S. Lewis's classic *That Hideous Strength,* an entire peaceful English village is besieged by the forces of darkness.

As with all good fiction, it is important that the central characters are *changed* by their experiences, whether for good or ill. Lazy writers often use mere physical transformations to effect this change: The heroine becomes a vampire. Or the heroine is prevented from becoming a vampire. Or the heroine is killed. Far more eerie is the plight of the eponymous hero of Peter Ackroyd's terrifying *Hawksmoor,* a police detective who finds himself drawn into a series of cult murders that took place in London churches two hundred years before:

> Hawksmoor looked for relief from the darkness of wood, stone and metal but he could find none; and the silence of the church had once again descended as he sat down upon a small chair and covered his face. And he allowed it to grow dark.

While he is very much a twentieth-century man, Nicholas Hawksmoor's unwanted clairvoyance gives him a glimpse of horrors he is unable to forget, and forever alters his perception of the power of good and evil in the world and in his work.

In many ways, the intricacies of *plot* are less central to supernatural fiction than is *pacing* (another reason why short stories usually work better than novels). A careful balance must be achieved between scenes of the ordinary and the otherworldly. Usually, a writer alternates the two, with the balance gradually tipping in favor of the unreal: Think of Dracula moving from Transylvania to London, and bringing with him a miasma of palpable evil that slowly infects all around him. In *Waking the Moon,* my heroine's involvement with the supernatural parallels her love affair in the real world. However you choose to do it, don't let the magical elements overwhelm your story completely.

Especially, don't let the Big Supernatural Payoff come too *soon.* (The only thing worse that killing off all your werewolves fifty pages before the end is penning these dreadful words: IT WAS ALL A DREAM.) Think of your novel in musical terms: You wouldn't really want to listen to one Wagnerian aria after another, would you? Well, neither would you want to read page after page of mysterious knockings, stakes through the heart, and screams at midnight.

Finally, dare to be different. Does the world really need another vampire novel? How about a lamia instead? Or an evil tree? As always, it's a good idea to be well-read in your chosen genre, so that you don't waste time and ink reinventing Frankenstein's monster. In addition to the works mentioned above, there is a wealth of terrific short supernatural fiction that can teach as well as chill you. *Great Tales of Terror and the Supernatural* (edited by Herbert A. Wise and Phyllis Fraser) is perhaps the indispensable anthology. There are also collections by great writers such as Poe, Robert Aickman, John Collier, Edith Wharton, Isak Dinesen, Sheridan Le Fanu, M. R. James, and many, many others. Jack Sullivan has written two books that I refer to constantly:

Elegant Nightmares and *Lost Souls,* classic studies of English ghost stories that can serve as a crash course on how to write elegant horror. These, along with Stephen King's nonfiction *Danse Macabre,* should put you well on your way to creating your own eldritch novel. Happy haunting!

□ 50

WHY HORROR?

BY GRAHAM MASTERTON

FEW PEOPLE UNDERSTAND THAT WRITERS ARE WRITING ALL THE time.

To think that a writer is writing only when he or she is actually hammering a keyboard is like believing that a police officer's job is "arresting people."

Even while they're not sitting down at the word processor, writers are writing in their heads. Inventing stories. Playing with words. Thinking up jokes and riddles and metaphors and similes. These days, I write both historical sagas and horror novels. Most people relish historical sagas, but I'm often asked, "Why do people like horror?"

I think they like horror novels because they depict ordinary people dealing with extraordinary threats. They like to imagine, what would *I* do if a dark shadow with glowing red eyes appeared in my bedroom at night? What would *I* do if I heard a sinister scratching inside the walls of my house? What would *I* do if my husband's head turned around 360 degrees?

I've found my inspiration for horror stories in legends from ancient cultures, and my research into how these demons came to be created by ordinary men and women is fascinating. Each of them represents a very real fear that people once felt, and often still do.

There are beguiling men who turn into evil demons. There are monsters that suck your breath when you're asleep. There are gremlins that steal children. There are horrible gorgons that make you go blind just to look at them, and vampires that drain all of the energy out of you. There are zombies who come back from the dead and torment you.

My favorite Scottish demons were the glaistigs, hideous hags who were supposed to be the ghosts of women haunting their former homes. They were frequently accompanied by a child who was called "the little plug" or "the whimperer." If you didn't leave out a bowl of milk for the glaistigs, they would suck your cows dry or drain their blood. Sometimes a glaistig would carry her little whimperer into the house, and bathe it in the blood of the youngest infant in the house, and the victim would be found dead and white in the morning.

Now, this is a legend, but you can understand what genuine fears it expresses. A woman's fear of other women intruding into her home, as in the film, *Fatal Attraction*; a man's fear of losing his livelihood; parents' fear of losing their children to malevolent and inexplicable illnesses, such as crib death. What I do is take these ancient demons, which are vivid and expressive manifestations of basic and genuine fears, and write about them in an up-to-date setting, with modern characters.

The very first horror novel I wrote was called *The Manitou*. A manitou is a Native American demon, and in this novel a 300-year-old medicine man was reborn in the present day to take his revenge on the white man. I was inspired to write that by *The Buffalo Bill Annual, 1956*.

Since then I have written books based on Mexican demons, Balinese demons, French demons and Biblical demons, two dozen in all, and I'm working on another one about the Glasgow woman who makes a pact with Satan so that her house disappears every time the rent collector calls.

I started writing horror novels at school, when I was 11. I used to read them to my friends during recess. Reading your work out loud is always invaluable training. When I met one of my old school friends only recently, he said, "I'll never forget the story you wrote about the woman with no head who kept singing 'Tiptoe Through the Tulips.' It gave me nine years of sleepless nights, and I still can't have tulips in the house."

Horror books seem to sell well all over the world, with some notable exceptions, like Germany. The French love horror, and the Poles adore it. In France, *Le Figaro* called me "Le Roi du Mal," the King of Evil. I was the first Western horror novelist to be published in Romania, home of Dracula. I received a letter from a reader this week saying, "I have to write to congratulate you on a wonderful book, rich with ideas and shining with great metaphors. Also very good printing, and excellent paper, which is appreciated here because of bathroom tissue shortage."

How extreme can you be when you write horror? As extreme, I think, as your talent and your taste permit, although gruesomeness is no substitute for skillful writing. I had several complaints about a scene in my book *Picture of Evil,* in which the hero kills two young girls with a poker. People protested my graphic description of blood spattering everywhere. In fact, I never once mentioned blood. All I said was, "He clubbed them to death like two baby seals." The reader's imagination was left to do the rest.

It is catching the mood and feel of a moment that makes your writing come to life. Most of the time you can dispense with whole realms of description if you catch one vivid image; catching those images requires thought and research. When I write historical novels, I frequently rent period costumes which my wife and I try on so I can better understand how my characters would have moved and behaved when wearing them. How do you rush to meet your lover when wearing a hobble skirt? How do you sit down with a bustle?

We also prepare food and drink from old recipes, using cookbooks by Fannie Farmer, Mrs. Beeton, and Escoffier. One of the least successful period drinks we prepared was the King's Death, drunk by King Alfonso of Spain in the Men's Bar of the Paris Ritz. The King's Death is made with wild strawberries marinated in Napoleon brandy, then topped up with half a bottle of champagne—each! We served it to some dinner party guests, and they became incoherent and had to go home.

Whether you're writing history or horror, thrillers or love stories, the most important technique is to live inside the book instead of viewing it from the outside. Your word processor or typewriter is nothing more than a key that opens the door to another world. When I'm writing, I step into that world, so that it surrounds me. So many writers as they write look only forward at the page, or screen, forgetting what's all around them.

Think of the rain on the side of your face and the wind against your back. Think of what you can hear in the distance. Think of the fragrances you can smell. Most of all, *be* all your characters: Act out their lives, act out their movements and their facial expressions, and speak their dialogue out loud. Get up from your keyboard sometimes, and do what you've imagined; then sit down and write it. The Disney artist Ward Kimball used to draw Donald Duck by making faces in the mirror. You can do the same when you're writing about the way your characters act and react.

Your best research is watching real live people living out their real lives. Watch every gesture, every nuance, listen to people's conversations and accents. Try to propel your story along at the pace that *you* would like to read it. Avoid showing off in your writing; all that does is slow down your story and break the spell you have been working so hard to conjure up. How many times has your suspension of disbelief been broken by ridiculous similes, like "her bosoms swelled like two panfuls of overboiling milk."

Two similes that really caught my attention and which I later used in novels were an old Afrikaner's description of lions roaring "like coal being delivered," and the hideous description by an Australian prisoner of war of two of his fellow prisoners being beheaded: "the blood spurted out of their necks like red walking-sticks."

To my mind, the greatest achievement in writing is to create a vivid, spectacular novel without readers being aware that they are reading at all. My ideal novel would be one that readers put down, and discover that they're still in it, that it's actually come to life.

The other day I was reading *Secrets of the Great Chefs of China,* and apart from the eel recipe, where you throw live eels into boiling water and have to clamp the lid down quickly to stop them from jumping out of the pot, the most memorable advice the book gave was, "A great chef prepares his food so that it is ready for the mouths of his guests; it is both a courtesy and a measure of his professionalism." That goes for writing, too.

□ 51

CLUES TO WRITING
A MYSTERY NOVEL

BY T. JEFFERSON PARKER

BEFORE STARTING A NEW BOOK, I MAKE A DEAL WITH MYSELF. IT doesn't involve character, atmosphere, structure, or setting. Rather, it's an agreement I make with my reader, something to keep me honest over the long haul of writing a novel.

Here are my rules when I begin.

One: Write as well as you can, never down, always up to your readers; do not pander; do not cheat; do not be dishonest. If something rings false to me, it will surely ring false to my reader, too. Treat that reader with the same respect with which you treat yourself.

Two: Make sure that what you're offering your readers is worth the several hours of reading it will take. You can make a thousand promises to your readers in the opening pages of a book, and you will have to make good on every one in a surprising, satisfying, and believable way. Deliver. After all, your pact implies that your readers will leave the novel somehow richer. Give your readers the bargain of a lifetime.

Three: Don't be afraid to entertain: You are writing popular fiction, not an instruction manual, a position paper, or an essay.

Four: Leave your readers with a feeling of something experienced, not just something read. Give them an emotional reality. Make it impossible for them simply to chuck your book into the wastebasket when they've finished reading it and grab the next one. Make your novel linger, haunt, last.

These are the self-imposed commandments I try to follow when I work. I forget them sometimes, ignore them others, amend them often. I never achieve them all perfectly.

Before I come to the point of writing, though, there is the odd fallow period during which I'm sniffing for the trail of the new book. At those times—and they may be as brief as days or as long as months—none of the above rules is relevant yet. I'm a bloodhound then, or a detective, maybe, trying to pick up the scene or the clues that will lead me to the new book. This gestation period can be brief or long, but it is generally an anxious and troubling time. When I was young and frenzied with ambition, I finished up the final draft of *Laguna Heat* on a Friday, ending roughly five years' work. The following Monday I began writing my next novel. (It was never published and probably should not have been.) Conversely, after *Summer of Fear* was finished, I took off almost half a year before finding it again.

And what is "it"? A certain scent, a smell, an emotional aroma is what you're searching for. Like many good things in life, you don't really know what it is until you find it. When you do find it—or more accurately, when it finds you—it is immediately recognizable. It's something outside you that sparks something inside you. The spark starts a fire. The fire burns for two or three years, during which time you write the book. The novel is an attempt to see what the fire leaves. It is an attempt to find something new, something born of the union between what you believed you might find, and what was actually there. If all that sounds vague, maybe I can explain.

Here's an example: After I'd finished writing *Laguna Heat,* I was sniffing around for something new. The scent hit me loud and clear one day when I was in a liquor store off Harbor Boulevard in Costa Mesa. I stood in the checkout line and there was something about the man in front of me that made me think he must be an American Vietnam War veteran. I also noticed that the clerk was a young Vietnamese woman. I stood waiting, wondering what might be going through their respective minds. What did she think of him? He of her? Could their paths possibly have crossed many years ago, in her war-torn country? Could he have fought alongside her father or brother? Against them? Could these two have actually met?

Eavesdropping shamelessly, I moved to the side just a little to watch their transaction. He stepped up to the counter, and before he could say one word, the young woman reached up to the cigarette rack above her and took out a pack of Pall Malls—soft-pack, regulars. She set them on the counter in front of him. He looked at them, then at her, then said his first words to her: "How did you know that's what I wanted?"

She smiled shyly. "Some things," she said, "I just know."

He paid and left.

Well, that's the kind of moment a novelist lives for, a moment loaded with intrigue, expectation, surprise. It connected directly with some of the things I'd been thinking about for most of my adult life—the war, what it meant to us and to them, how it changed the psyche of the republic and the face of the globe. I did not serve in Vietnam, so such questions were large, complex abstractions to me. Suddenly, they were made real, the "something" outside directly colliding with the "something" inside. I had just gotten my first whiff of the new book.

What did this tiny moment in the history of the Vietnam War have to connect with inside me? Well, all that I was. All the hours of newsreel footage of dead soldiers and body counts I had watched. All the newsprint I'd read. All the stories from friends and acquaintances who'd gone to 'Nam. All the hours of reports, synopses, analyses. All the feature films, from *Coming Home* to *Apocalypse Now* and beyond. All of the 20 years I'd been wondering about this pivotal thing in my own history. All of this fuel rushed out to meet that moment of spark— the American vet having his mind read by a young Vietnamese refugee.

Leaving that liquor store on Harbor, I knew certainly that my next book would be an attempt to deal with those things and that I would set that book in Orange County, California. Why? Because there we have a place called Little Saigon that was and is the largest enclave of Vietnamese on earth, outside of Vietnam itself. I can remember my first forays into the clubs and bars of Little Saigon, notepad in pocket, mind literally reeling at all the "material" I was discovering. It was the discovery of a large part of myself that I had known was there but had no access to before. The mystery of that encounter, the tonnage of things left unsaid in that brief moment, stayed with me for the three years of writing *Little Saigon,* and beyond.

I had another similar moment, though it was less dramatic, as I was preparing to write my fourth novel. I was sitting on a patio chair on my deck, which overlooks Laguna Canyon. It was late afternoon, then it was evening, then it was night. My wife, suffering a brain tumor, was beside me. Our dogs were sprawled around us. We had watched the light fade into sunset, experiencing each increment of the growing night. We said hardly a word. Watching anything fade was a painful correlative to what we both knew was happening to her.

As we sat there and looked out to the hillsides, Catherine noted the odd way the hills formed what looked like a supine female (torso and legs) at night, and the way the distant lights of Laguna illuminated up from her middle. Cat named her "Lady of the Canyon." For a brief moment, I was filled with a new love for this suffering young woman, and for the house in which we lived, and for the hillsides that cradled us. It was an overwhelmingly powerful love, and almost unbearably sad. And I knew that my next book would be an attempt to celebrate that love somehow. The book became *Summer of Fear,* in which crime writer Russell Monroe tries to help heal his ill wife while a murderer stalks the city around him. It is a gut-wrenching, chaotic book—confessional, tortured, and dark. But it ends in hope and redemption. In some ways, that book is a fictionalized accounting of things that we wanted to come true. Cat never got to read the ending. But the Lady of the Canyon that she had noticed is in that novel, in fact, she plays an important part.

I offer these moments to demonstrate how strangely a book can begin. The emotions that draw one to the blank page are often vague, poorly understood, ephemeral. The writing then becomes a journey of discovery rather than a mission of execution. The fire burns and what it leaves behind is the book.

❑ 52

TRICKS OF THE
WIZARD'S TRADE

BY SUSAN DEXTER

FANTASY IS THE OLDEST FORM OF LITERATURE—THE GREAT UMbrella that arches over *all* fiction. Fantasy is also a marketing category, shelved and intermingled with science fiction, wearing scaly dragons on its covers in place of shiny spaceships. Fantasy's themes spring from the collective unconscious. Fantasy is populated by archetypes and demons common to us all. Our dreams and our nightmares. Fairy tales.

It's *hard* to be original in this genre. But limits are illusions. Consider: We have but 26 letters in our alphabet. And they'd best be used in combinations readers will recognize as *words*. Now, *there's* a limit. Music? Even worse, but composers don't seem to mind that there are only so many notes to go around.

"Never been done before" may truly be impossible. But "Never been done like *that* before"? That sounds like a goal to me. *Star Wars* didn't wow the world because it was a *new* idea; it resonates with audiences because it's a very *old* story: a fairy tale, right down to the princess. Retell an old tale—do it in a fresh way, and your readers will gasp in wonder. Do it well, and you'll have editors drooling.

The first trick in a wizard's bag is this: Look at your sources of inspiration. Be a *reader,* before you begin to write. Read new fantasies. Keep up with the field. Read the classics. Comic books aren't forbidden fruit—just don't make them an exclusive diet. Read fairy tales. Read folklore. Study the magic and mythologies of many cultures. If you feed your subconscious properly, it will supply your storytelling needs.

Go to your public library. Breathe in the fresh air and book dust. Surf the Net later. No need to memorize the Dewey System to graze the shelves productively. The 200's are philosophy and religion—*all* religions. Folklore lives in the 398.2's—right next to the prettified fairy

243

tales "retold for children." You'll find original folk tales that will make
your hair stand on end and get your juices flowing. Arrowsmith's *Field
Guide to the Little People* will convince you that elves are neither
Disney critters nor the fantasy analogue of Vulcans, but beings far
more ancient and interesting. *The Golden Bough,* Frazer's study of
myth and religion, supplied the magical system my wizard Tristan used
in *The Ring of Allaire* and its two sequels. I doubt that a thousand
authors mining day and night could exhaust that book's possibilities.

Remember the hero has a *thousand* faces. If you confine your reading
to role-playing manuals, the stirring high fantasy you hope to craft will
be a pale, weak thing, a fifth-generation videotape. Recycled characters
stuck in a plot that's a copy of an imitation of Tolkien won't excite an
editor these days. Read to understand what the classic themes are.
Tolkien based *The Lord of the Rings* solidly on the northern European
mythic tradition. It's not a copy of anything, but we respond to it as
something familiar.

Fantastic elements work only if you make *reality* real. If I carelessly
give my horses "paws," will you believe what I tell you about dragons?
So think about the nuts and bolts, and don't trust Hollywood to do it
for you. Castles—where did people *live* in them? Surely everyone
wasn't born a princess. Who grows the food, does the laundry, cleans
up after the knights' horses? When you research actual medieval cultures, you'll turn up truths far stranger than anything you could *invent.*
Your characters should have real lives, with routines, habits, responsibilities. Most of us have to work for a living, and while being a princess
may be a full-time job, being an elf is not. My title character in *The
Wind-Witch* stands out from the pack of fantasy heroines: Not only is
she *not* a princess, but she has a job—two jobs: She's a farmer and a
weaver. Getting her sheep through lambing season matters just as much
to Druyan as warding off a barbarian invasion or discovering her magical talents. That makes her *real,* for all that she can literally whistle
up a storm. Readers can identify with her.

Magic was the science of its day. Science is of fairly recent origin.
Both science and magic seek to explain and control the natural world,
usually for a man's benefit. Study belief systems. Decide what suits
your story, and stick to that. Don't throw in random demons just because they sound cool. Plan your world, if you want it to work for you.

Maps are more than endpaper decorations, and you should start drawing one before you ever start writing your fantasy. Never mind your quest-bound characters: A map will keep *you*, the author, from getting lost. If the desperate ride from Castle A to Castle B takes three days, then the trip back from B to A can take *longer* once the pressure's off; but if the journey takes *less* time, you have major explaining to do. Maps can spare you such *faux pas*.

Maps can suggest plot solutions. In the real world, things are where they are for good reasons. Castles protect and are not built where there's nothing worth contesting. Towns are tied to trade; they grow where roads cross, beside safe harbors. As I began to write *The Wind-Witch*, I had established in an earlier book that my Esdragon had a cliffy coast and treacherous seas. Now I needed it to suffer an invasion—by sea. Where could the invaders strike? Well, the Eral are after plunder, so they want towns. And Esdragon's towns—as in the real-world town of Cornwall, on which I based my fictional duchy—are mostly at the mouths of the rivers that drain the upland moors and reach the sea as broad estuaries. I put rivers on my map, decided which were navigable for any distance—and *presto!* I had many places for my raiders to plunder, distant from one another, spots for Druyan to try to protect from the back of her magic-bred horse.

A primitive map has charm—perhaps one of your characters drew it—but there are tricks to convincing cartography. You can't draw a straight line without a ruler? Relax! Nobody can, and there are rather few straight lines in nature anyway. Now get yourself a real map. Any continent or bit of one will do. Put tracing paper over your selection. Pencil some outlines, imagining how the coast changes as the sea level rises—or falls. Hills become islands, islands change into peninsulas. Valleys become arms of the sea. The combination of wind and wave nibbles cliffs, isolating outcrops. It's your pick.

Change the scale. Use an island to make a continent, or vice versa. Turn your map upside down. When I designed Esdragon and Calandra, I basically used Europe—but I stood it on end, balanced on the tip of Portugal. Copy the shape of the water spot on your ceiling or the last patch of snow lingering on your sidewalk.

Study actual maps. Where do rivers flow? How do they look? Mountain ranges trap rain and alter climate. So where will your forest be? Your dry grasslands? Your band of unicorn hunters needs to cross the Dragonspike Mountains. Where are the passes? Are they open year-

round or only seasonally? The threat of being trapped by an early
winter can add drama. A map will remind you of that.

God, as Mies van der Rohe said, is in the details. As the creator of
your paper world, you have responsibilities. *You* must concern yourself
with the details, for there is no *Fodor's Guide to Middle Earth,* or
Esdragon, or your elfin kingdom. Which brings us to the Rule of
Names.

Basic rules for name use apply to all fiction. Just as you vary your
sentence lengths, so you should choose names with differing lengths
and sounds. Your names must not all begin with the same letter of the
alphabet. Characters and countries must not be easily confused with
one another. A name that brings to mind an over-the-counter remedy
will not work for your hero.

World-makers need to name *everything.* Adam got off easy doing
just the animals! I need to name kingdoms, heroes, continents, castles,
islands, mountains, rivers, lakes, gods, horses, magic swords and cats.
Unlike the author of the police procedural, I can't get my names by
stabbing a random finger into the phone book.

Names in fantasy present special pleasures and certain problems.
Names must always be apt, but you can toss off grand heroic names
without the twinge of conscience you'd feel about giving such names
to real children who'd be attending real-world schools. Remember,
though, that names are tools. They make your invented world convincing and solid, but they must evoke the feel of *your* world. You can't
just put the *Encyclopedia of Mythology* into a blender. In folkloric
tradition, names have serious power: To know a creature's true name
is to control it. That power carries over into fiction. Poorly chosen
names can strain your reader's willing suspension of disbelief until it
snaps. And then where are you?

You will be wise not to leave your naming to chance, or to the last
minute. Under the pressure of mid-paragraph, you will either heave up
a melange of x's, q's, and z's, or you'll clutch and settle for names as
bland as tapioca. Planning ahead avoids both extremes. Compile a list
of useful names.

You can keep that list in your PC or on the backs of old envelopes,
but a small notebook is the handiest. I use an address book—durably
hardbound, alphabetized pages, large enough not to be easily mislaid.
I list names down the left margins, circling those I use and noting

where. I may reuse a name from time to time, certain names being as common in Esdragon as John is in this world.

I glean and gather from sources readily available to all. Start with baby-name books. The older thebetter; you aren't after the trendy and popular. Copy whatever catches your eye. Histories of popular names offer archaic forms and less common variants. Rhisiart, in *The Wizard's Shadow,* is a name that is simply a Welsh version of Richard. The Welsh struggle to represent with their alphabet the sounds of a name they got from Norman French gives the name an exotic look.

Invent your own names. Dickens did it. Lord Dunsany was a master at it. Tolkien invented whole *languages* and took his names from them. You may enjoy playing with sounds. When I wrote *The Ring of Allaire,* I struggled for a week for a proper name for Valadan, my immortal warhorse. Wanting a proud, noble, brave name, I began with *val,* from valiant, and went on from there. Whereas Kessallia in *The Prince of Ill Luck* just popped out of my subconscious one day. Learn to spot a "keeper" like that.

Use the phone book. Use the newspaper—all those lists of engagements, weddings, obituaries. Chop off the front half of a name, or use just the ending. Stick a syllable of one name onto part of another. Minor changes yield fresh names. Switching just one letter made Robert into *Robart,* and gave Druyan's brother a familiar yet not ordinary name.

Watch movie credits. Watch the Olympics—you'll hear scads of less usual names, like Oksana, and they're *spelled* for you, right on the screen. What could be easier?

Once you have your names, use them wisely. Pick those that fit your story and its cultures. Save the rest for your next project.

The true test of imagination may be to name a cat, as Samuel Butler said. I doubt that correctly naming a dragon is far down the difficulty scale, though. World-making and myth-making are not for the fainthearted, nor the short attention span. The good news: No license is required! Only the will to do the job right—which is the *real* power behind *any* wizard's spell.

❑ Nonfiction: Articles and Books

❏ 53

SLEUTH, HUNTER, BIOGRAPHER

BY LINDA SIMON

ONE OF MY FAVORITE BIOGRAPHIES IS RICHARD HOLMES'S *FOOTSTEPS: Adventures of a Romantic Biographer.* In it, Holmes does not give us what we might expect—a chronological study of one subject—but instead, he records his own travels in search of some great British Romantic writers, including Robert Louis Stevenson, Percy Bysshe Shelley, William Wordsworth, and Mary Wollstonecraft. One admiring critic summed up the book's merits: "This exhilarating book, part biography, part autobiography, shows the biographer as sleuth and huntsman, tracking his subjects through space and time."

Not all biographies are quite as exhilarating, but the critic's words could be applied to any biographer's task: We are all part sleuth, part hunter as we travel into the past and through unfamiliar landscapes in search of our subject. For writers with boundless curiosity and a genuine respect for other people's lives, writing biography is a satisfying and illuminating project.

Your subject

Biographical subjects may be found anywhere. Your mother's uncle, the one who emigrated from Norway at the turn of the century, may be as interesting a subject as a renowned artist or statesman. A biographical subject need not be famous to the world; it is up to you, as biographer, to make that subject interesting to others. If your subject is a family member or friend, he or she may have lived a private, unheralded life—but a life no less worthy of a biography. Other subjects may have touched fame, but never achieved it for themselves. Jean Strouse, the biographer of Alice James, sister of the novelist Henry and philosopher William, coined the term "semi-private lives" to describe men and women who lived in the shadows of more famous people, but whose own lives were fairly ordinary. One of my own subjects, Alice B. Toklas, lived a "semi-private" life in comparison with her more famous companion, Gertrude Stein. And another of my subjects, Margaret Beaufort, also lived a "semi-private" life, in comparison with her more famous son, King Henry VII, and her notorious grandson, Henry VIII.

Writing about Margaret Beaufort gave me a chance to explore the lives of women in fifteenth-century England. Although Beaufort surely was a member of the aristocracy, still she shared some experiences—childbirth, for example, and widowhood—with other women of the time. Initially, I decided to write about her because she was the matriarch of the House of Tudor; but as I explored various sources, I became increasingly interested in the ways that she helped me understand the daily life of medieval women.

Margaret Beaufort, not yet sixteen, was living in Wales at the end of her first pregnancy. Her husband was in England at the time, and when labor began, she was alone, without family, in a cold, stone castle, unable to speak the language of her servants. I found a fifteenth-century gynecological manual to help me understand how young Margaret would have been cared for during childbirth. She delivered her son in a bare room, with walls a foot thick, tended by midwives who brought her strange oils and potions and who sat beside her on an oddly shaped birthing stool. Surely Margaret knew that her life—like that of all women at the time—was at risk from childbirth; and just as surely she knew that infant mortality was frighteningly high. But the birth went well: She lived and so did her son. And the thin, frail young woman quickly rallied to a newly-discovered strength when it came time to name the boy: She refused to name him after his Welsh father or grandfather, but instead insisted on a regal English name. He would be Henry, and he would be king.

Even though Margaret Beaufort was a noble woman, there were few sources available to me that gave evidence of her life and experiences, especially as a child and young wife and mother. But there were enough sources, scarce as they were, to enable me to feel confident that I could reveal the significant events and context for her life.

Make sure there are sources

As much as you may care about your subject, you cannot write a biography without sufficient historical and biographical sources. Those sources include letters, diaries, journals, interviews, memoirs, creative writing, and works of art such as paintings or films. Such sources are available in many collections—some private (in your parents' attic), some public (in libraries or museums).

The reference room of a good local or college library has many reference sources that may help you find out what material, published and unpublished, is available about your subject. Among these is the *Biography Index,* which lists references to books and more than two thousand periodicals for a wide range of subjects, including major figures in the arts, sports, science, and politics. You may also want to consult one of the many standard biographical dictionaries, such as *Dictionary of National Biography* (for British figures) or the *Dictionary of American Biography.* The *Biographical Dictionaries Master Index* can direct you to an entry about your subject in one hundred biographical dictionaries. For contemporary subjects, you may want to consult *Current Biography,* a monthly journal that began publication in 1940, offering biographical information on men and women in the news. Many public libraries subscribe to this journal and keep bound issues on their reference shelves. In addition to these general dictionaries, there are many specialized biographical dictionaries focused on gender, race, profession, or time period.

To find unpublished material about your subject (manuscripts or letters your subject may have written), you may consult directories of libraries that contain archives or manuscript collections. These directories include *American Literary Manuscripts,* the *Directory of Archives and Manuscript Repositories in the United States, and The National Union Catalog of Manuscript Collections.* Tracking down your subject in these reference books is often slow and tedious work, but it is a necessary first step in the research process.

Once you locate sources for your subject, you may be able to order photocopies of the material you need. Sometimes, however, you may need to travel to collections to do research. Before you leave on a research trip, however, it is helpful to know as precisely as possible what the library holds, what you are looking for, and how much material is available. If you plan a two-day trip and discover two weeks of reading, you will leave the library frustrated.

If your subject has been written about before, a previous biography can be invaluable in giving you a start for research. Consult the book's bibliography and notes for references to library archives. But don't stop there. Libraries are always in the process of adding to their collections. New material about your subject may have become available since the publication of books or articles. It's your job to find that new material.

Stay organized

Any researcher needs to be well-organized. For my own work, I keep notes in three places: file folders, which contain photocopies of sources; 5″ × 7″ index cards, on which I write notes taken from books or articles; and computer files, where I also keep notes from readings, interviews, and other sources. At the end of a project, I may have several drawers of file folders, hundreds and hundreds of index cards, and many computer files—far more material than will ever make its way into the finished book. But this excess is necessary so I can select what I need for a coherent and energetic narrative.

Biographers find their own way of organizing notes: Mine is to keep index cards devoted to the names of people that figure in my subject's life. Whenever someone is mentioned in a letter or book, I make an index card. When I see a reference to that person in another source, I pull out the card and take notes. In that way, I find it easy to compose small biographical sketches of the person when he or she first appears in the biography.

Other biographers may organize material chronologically or they may organize notes related to events in their subject's life. There is no right way to organize, but you need to be consistent and meticulous in both note-taking and documentation. Write down the author, title, and publication information for every published book that you use, and make sure you note the name of the library for every unpublished letter or manuscript you use. Your readers will expect careful documentation in whatever you publish. For writers who need to brush up on documentation, such reference sources as the *MLA Handbook* or the *Chicago Manual of Style* are helpful.

Keep asking questions

As a biographer, you do not serve as a conduit through which your subject tells his or her own life. Instead, you are an active questioner about that life. You are always in search of understanding why and how your subject acted, rather than merely chronicling those actions.

You are interested in relationships, in motivation, in the dimensions of your subject's personality that may have been hidden from public view.

The questions that you ask about a subject's life reflect ways of understanding human behavior that come largely from your own experiences. If, for example, you discover that your subject was a person who tried to control or manipulate the behavior of others, your own experiences with such a person will color the way you portray and understand such behavior. Some biographers also rely on psychological theory to explain behavior, bringing to their sources ideas from such famous thinkers as Freud, Jung, Karen Horney, or a host of other theorists. If you decide to take such an approach, you need to remember that your sources, however rich they are, do not provide as complete a "case history" as a psychoanalyst might glean from years of therapy sessions. Usually, it is safer to *suggest* a theorist's explanation for your subject's behavior, rather than to claim that the explanation is airtight.

Similarly, some biographers bring to their work assumptions about gender or class that reflect the work of feminist or cultural critics. You need to be careful, though, about ascribing your subject's dreams and desires to social forces or personal expectations that may or may not have been applicable at the time in which your subject lived.

Create contexts

Biographers are interested in more than the events of one person's life. They must look at the contexts—historical, cultural, and physical—in which that person lived. Every public event, of course, does not affect each person in the same way; still, the biographer needs to be aware of the history swirling around his or her subject: How did a war, an economic depression, or attitudes of racism or sexism affect the subject's life? How was the subject shaped by growing up on a farm in central Kansas, in a castle in Wales, on the city streets of nineteenth-century Manhattan? "You pick up things spending time on the native ground, taking your time, listening, poking through the old local papers," said David McCullough, biographer of Harry Truman and Theodore Roosevelt. Sometimes, though, it is not possible for a biographer to travel to that "native ground." Richard Holmes came to France in 1964 hoping to discover the landscape that Robert Louis Stevenson had traversed in 1878. In some places, the hills, the woods, and the villages seemed unchanged from the late nineteenth century;

in other places, Holmes wandered "dazed and disappointed" because sites had so greatly altered. In the end, however, armed with Stevenson's travel diary and letters, Holmes used his talents as "Baskerville Hound," as he put it, to reinvent the reality of Stevenson's life. *Footsteps* testifies to the achievement of his—and of any biographer's—goal: to enter the inner landscape of another human being's mind and feelings, and to share the adventure of that discovery with readers.

❑ 54

WRITE WHAT YOU *DON'T* KNOW

BY DONALD M. MURRAY

I DON'T KNOW WHAT TO WRITE. I SIT DOWN AND NOTHING HAPPENS. My mind is blank.

Good. That's where the best writing begins.

"But I don't have anything worth writing. No one would be interested in what I would write."

Wrong. We all have important stories to tell, but we have to begin in ignorance so that we pass through what we have said before to what we can say anew. To write well, to write what earns us readers, we need to have the courage to write what we don't yet know.

Many who want to write wait—and wait and wait—until they know all about their topic before they begin to write. Writers know—but have to keep learning—that ignorance is the beginning, not the end. Writing instructs. We write what we don't know to discover what we know that we didn't know we knew.

Here are some techniques of a writer who has taught himself to harvest ignorance, writing from not knowing to knowing:

Celebrate ignorance

I've been writing for publication for almost 60 years, and yet there are mornings when the screen is blank and the mind is blank. What I have written, thought, felt before is stripped away. I start to panic, and then I will say something that is new to me and may be new to readers, if I have the courage to confront my ignorance.

The other morning I faced the familiar but still terrifying emptiness; I started, as I usually do, with description, recording the details in the decor of the new restaurant where we ate last night. The walls and phony rafters were hung with newly manufactured antique tools. I started describing the mill in which some of those tools would have been used a hundred years or more ago.

257

This draft accelerates and takes me through the page to the looms that clattered in New England textile mills when I was a child and earlier. The words reveal a grandfather I never knew, fixing a loom, and my grandmother at the loom, carrying her firstborn, my father. I have a column about the fashionably restored mills, filled with shops, eateries, and ghosts.

Respect your difference

I was a skinny kid who was embarrassingly strange to my parents, weird to my classmates. I asked the questions no one else asked: If I could not drink milk with lobster because it was poisonous, why was my mother trying to poison me at the church picnic by demanding I eat the minister's wife's lobster bisque? What I said in class, on the playground, at dances and in the football locker room brought strange looks and set me apart.

But when I wrote, my eccentric vision of the world brought me publication. During the Korean War I kept writing editorials that were strange in form—some were very short stories, others were a former infantryman's view of military strategy—and I was awarded, to my and my family's astonishment, a Pulitzer Prize. I began to accept my difference.

Find your obsessions

School and society try to make us well rounded, equally interested in many things, but writers are obsessed with a few concerns. They have small acreage but work it over and over again for a lifetime.

We lived in my grandmother's house, and after she had her stroke I started each day of my childhood getting up first and seeing if Grandma was still alive; I did badly in school, dropping out twice before flunking out of high school; I saw infantry combat in the paratroops in World War II; I have had a lifetime fascination with the twin crafts of writing and drawing; we lost a daughter when she was 20; I am concerned with my wife's and my own aging.

There you have it. In trying to deal with these few obsessions I have published more than two dozen books, written hundreds of poems, and thousands of newspaper and magazine articles. Pay attention to what you need to understand and write your way to understanding.

Make the familiar unfamiliar

When I am bored, I stop, look, and listen to the specific, revealing details of the life swirling around me. I celebrate the life I am living with awareness—what is being done and *not* being done, what is being said and *not* being said, what has changed and what *should* be changed, what answers need questions, what solutions need problems, how people are reacting and *not* reacting to each other. The familiar world becomes unfamiliar, the ordinary extraordinary, the commonplace uncommon.

Trust accident

In writing about the eating habits in our Yankee-Scot-dull home, I was trying to list the conventional hamburger and boiled potatoes and found myself writing about my father's love for calves liver, and that led me, by accident, to his sharing more than his only child wanted to know about the women he did *not* marry, and that led me to a new understanding of his longings.

In trying to describe my mother I write a tangled sentence: "A friend is nursing his dying mother, and that brings back discomforting memories of my own mother with whom I still have strained relations, years after her death, but I have to remember she did care for my invalid grandmother—up at night, bedsores and bed pans—but it wasn't so much about love. That old woman in the bed terrified her, and, of course, I can't forget the bills her brothers folded into her hands during their weekly visits."

Two instructive accidents: The tangled sentence, which I can untangle—"Mother didn't only care for her bedridden mother out of love and Baptist duty, but for the cash pressed into her hands when her brothers visited."

Out of a bad sentence a good one. And more important, a hint of my mother's motivations that may illuminate a character in a story.

And when I typed "strained relations," it came out "stained relations." My subconscious goes to work on the "stained relations" I've had with family, friends, at work, in the neighborhood. Another fortunate accident.

Collect and connect

It is the job of the writer to collect specific information and connect it, to create patterns of meaning, to place information in a context. My most meaningful connections come when I write what I don't yet understand.

In writing about my infantry war and wondering what officers saw in me that caused them to give me so many lonely missions—delivering messages through German territory, for example—I realized I was more comfortable in the surrealistic confusion of combat war than most of my fellow soldiers. In a draft I asked myself why, and connected my childhood, where I learned to survive chaos and contradiction, with my experiences in war. That became another column.

Line—an image, a word, or fragment of language—caught out of the corner of the eye or ear, often precipitates my writing what I do not yet know. Talking to myself I hear myself say, "I was most alive among the dying and the dead," and I start to set down the contradictory feelings during combat that have grown into a poetry manuscript.

The precipitating line contains a tension that demands to be released, a contradiction, an interesting distortion, an unexpected connection, an answer without a question, an end to a story that I must begin. The line itches, and I must scratch.

Play with leads

Writing the lead—the first paragraphs of the news story that give the heart of the story first and then expand on it—was the trick that made it possible for me when I worked on rewrite, to take notes over the phone and turn out 30 or 40 stories a shift on subjects I did not understand until I wrote the stories.

Each lead is a compressed draft. It reveals the subject, the writer's attitude toward the subject, the voice, the direction, the form and order of a piece of writing. As an apprentice magazine writer I would write as many as 150 first lines, first paragraphs, first pages to discover the focus and direction, the voice and melody of what I finally learned. Now I write as many leads in my head as on paper, trying to say what I do not yet know needs to be said in ways I do not yet know it can be said. Eventually one lead points me toward where I may find the right focus and direction.

Join me tomorrow morning. Write what you don't know you know.

□ 55

CREATIVE NONFICTION WRITING

BY RITA BERMAN

WHAT IS CREATIVE NONFICTION? IS IT A NEW GENRE OF WRITING? AN oxymoron? Fictionalized facts? While it sounds like a contradiction in terms, creative nonfiction is a new description for an old skill: that of writing well-crafted salable articles. For today's market, however, nonfiction writers are allowed, even encouraged, to incorporate certain fiction techniques and to use the first-person "I."

Formerly, the formal style, using a neutral voice, is now recognized as distancing the writer from the reader, whereas writing from the first-person viewpoint can help with reader identification that is further magnified if the writer's experiences or comments resonate or connect with the reader's life. That is why seemingly ordinary concerns of everyday life, such as health, diet, sex, money, and travel can provide good potential topics for creative nonfiction. The range of creative nonfiction includes feature articles, memoirs, essays, personality profiles, travel pieces, how-to's and even contemporary, political, or other social issues pieces.

Because editors have switched from asking "just give me the facts," to "tell me a story," *how* you tell the story is where creative nonfiction comes in. In other words, the article remains nonfiction because the content is based on fact and is not created or made up, but you have more freedom in the actual writing of it. That calls for embellishing and enhancing, narrating instead of reporting, dressing up the bare facts by using fiction techniques such as setting of mood, providing description of place, expressing emotion, and often incorporating dialogue or flashbacks.

Before describing some of the fiction elements you could use, it might be helpful to review the basic structure of an article. You must catch the reader's interest in the introduction; in the next section identify your topic; in the body of the piece present your material; and close by drawing a conclusion or repeating a key point.

Your task is to write your article like a storyteller, not as a gatherer of facts. Take those facts and filter them through your eyes. Provide details so that you add to, but don't change the information you have gathered. And as you write, keep your potential readers in mind, so that you angle the story to their needs.

My article on graphology, "Unlocking Secrets in Handwriting Can Help Hiring" (*Triangle Business*), began with an opening quote from my source, Mary Gallagher, a handwriting expert:

> "Looking at how applicants cross their t's or dot their i's is one way to decide whether to hire an individual." So said Mary Gallagher, a certified graphoanalyst. More than 5,000 companies use handwriting analysis as a hiring aid. . . . Employers need the edge to know not only what the applicant projects but also what he or she is capable of doing.

Having aroused the readers' interest, a brief summary about the history of graphology came next, and then I continued with examples of what handwriting might reveal. Quotes from other people who had used Gallagher's services, including a manager who had ignored her findings, gave balance to the piece.

Framing the story

For this particular piece, I used the technique of framing the story to make a satisfactory ending: I circled around to the beginning by referring to the opening paragraph. For creative nonfiction, this is an excellent way of tying the article together, satisfying the curiosity you have aroused and leaving the reader with a resonant image of all that has gone before. You might draw a conclusion, make an evaluation, or point out a question that still needs an answer.

In this instance I ended by informing readers of how companies obtain a sample of handwriting from applicants in order to study it; they have prospective employees state in their own handwriting why they believe they are qualified for the job.

Atmosphere and mood

Specific details are highly significant in nonfiction to help the reader visualize the place or the event you are describing. They add interest and color and convey atmosphere and mood to the setting, locale, time of year, and even the weather in your article. General statements, such as, "We went to a museum, which we found interesting," fall flat without supporting detail. Use fiction techniques to describe what you saw in the museum.

Make note of your impressions and reactions as you conduct your research. Whether you are taking a tour, arriving at a new destination, or interviewing someone for a personal profile, these impressions and observations may turn out to be the lead or heart of your piece when you come to write it.

Example: In a piece about redevelopment and housing in Jamaica for *Town and Country Planning Journal,* I opened with a description of what I had seen in the drive from the airport:

> The coast road from the airport is a narrow lane overlooked by small and large estates. Plantations, old great houses, and tiny country towns dot the hillside. Snaking by resort hotels and sugar-cane fields, some of which are now being developed into housing estates, the life of the country appeared before us as we turned each bend on the main north-coast road.

Writing in first person

Your nonfiction pieces will come alive creatively when you incorporate your personal observations. Use all of your senses. Tell your readers what you tasted, saw, touched, heard. . . . By personalizing the piece, it becomes your own. No other article will have that voice— your voice.

Instead of saying that there were vendors at the site and leaving it at that, I described my encounter with them in "Spain, New and Old Faces," published in *Leader Magazine:*

> . . . As we stepped down from the bus, we were accosted by a group of women darting in front of us, each waving a lace tablecloth. Having caught our attention, they shouted prices at us in Spanish, jabbing their fingers in the air to indicate how many thousands of pesetas they wanted.
>
> To indicate that I wanted a smaller cloth, and round, I made a circle with my hands. They understood. An older woman held up a tablecloth while a young girl held up five fingers, 50,000 pesetas. I countered with two fingers. She shook her head and held up four fingers. I then showed cash—25,000 pesetas (approximately $25). She took two bills, but wanted "another finger," total of $30. No deal. I pointed to an embroidered rectangular cloth and the finger shaking started all over again. . . . I got both tablecloths for $53.

By revealing the interaction that took place, I enhanced the story and by adding color and humor, made the piece more interesting than if I had baldly stated that I spoke no Spanish, but we came to a deal.

Reveal your characters

Creative nonfiction is frequently about people. We're all curious about how other people live, what they do, and how they think. For personality profiles, draw on the external cues that you observed while doing the interview. Describe the subject's quirks, mannerisms, or appearance, what he wore, how he moved his body as he spoke. Movement can reveal and imply at the same time. "Shifting in his chair" conveys an image quite different from "settling in his chair."

Dialogue

The fiction writer makes up dialogue, but in creative nonfiction you take the dialogue from your interview notes or tapes, using direct quotes from your sources, instead of paraphrasing. This adds verbal color to your piece and encourages your readers to draw their own conclusions—an excellent way to present a controversial topic or viewpoint.

I used provocative statements about women and their reactions to conflict as my lead for a piece for *Women Executive's Bulletin:*

> Most women fear conflict—perhaps more than men fear it. . . . Many women give contradictory signals. For example, when they are under stress and trying to communicate, they often smile, unconsciously suggesting to the other person that this isn't such a serious situation, according to Dr. Ruth D. Anderson, Associate Professor of Speech Communication.

Next, I offered some significant details on how we learn to communicate:

> The communication skills we learn early in life are those that we use when we reach managerial and executive positions: to accept conflict as a normal, everyday occurrence, then to understand how to handle conflict. Think back to how your mother, or any other female authority figure in the household you grew up in, dealt with conflict. If she screamed, do you scream?

Here's another "tell me more" quote that I used for a general-interest article on buying or selling a house, a concern of many Americans:

> "The consumer has the right to bargain," said Andrew M. Barr, a real estate broker. "It isn't a rigid situation. Some houses are easier to sell than others. Why charge 6% when you can do it for 3% and sell it in a week? That's fair to the consumer and fair to us."

Published in the *Virginia Cardinal,* my article explored the sensitive topic of brokers' commission and informed the reader about available alternatives in the Washington D.C. area, the flexible fee system, or using a consumer-oriented advisory service.

Flashbacks

Flashbacks are another fiction device you might consider using to provide a change of pace. By means of the flashback you can expand your story and take the reader in a direction different from where you began. Example: "As the train drew into the station, I remembered the last time I visited London. . . ." Or, "As he spoke of his father I was remembering our first meeting, more than 20 years ago. . . ."

With this technique, you can introduce something significant from the past that has bearing on the present. To help the reader make the transition back to the present, insert a transitional phrase or word, such as "now" or "today," and continue with the present-day account.

Writing about my own experience as a temporary worker some years ago, I used a flashback to go back to when the Kelly Girl organization began in 1946, transitioning to a change of name of Kelly Temporary Services in the 1980's, then continued with more of my work experiences and ended with a forecast about the future direction of temporary work.

Know your readership

As you write, keep in mind the readers you want to reach; you need to know for whom you are writing. This calls for studying your possible markets before you commence writing, research that will be helpful when you shape the story. For example, some magazines publish only descriptive essays, while others prefer nuts-and-bolts information. After you have studied the market listings as well as writers' guidelines and read several issues of the magazine, you will know what the readers like and how to aim your articles to their preferred style.

Knowing my readership helped me slant my piece, "Pick up on the Shell Game," for *The Army, Navy, Air Force Times Magazine.* I opened with:

When Navy man Jim Wadsworth was stationed in New Guinea 30 years ago, he stooped over and picked up a shell on the beach. By that simple act, he found himself hooked on a hobby—shell collecting.

Shelling has given many military families special pleasures. Any number can play; there are no sex or age barriers. You don't have to be an expert or spend a cent, unless you want to become a professional shell collector. Shells can be traded with other collectors or bought like stamps from a dealer.

That paragraph linked the hobby of shell collecting to military families, who were the readers of this particular magazine. By focusing the angle of the story to those readers, I achieved publication.

Creative nonfiction is not a new genre, but a new description for articles based on fact but written in fictional form. Creative nonfiction uses mood, setting, descriptions of place, action, people, senses, thoughts, and feelings. It may use dialogue and flashbacks. The first-person viewpoint adds to reader identification, catches their attention. Your personal impressions and comments can help make your nonfiction unique.

□ 56

WRITING AND SELLING YOUR TRAVEL ARTICLES

BY JANET STEINBERG

DEAR ME, THE SKY IS FALLING. OR SO IT MAY SEEM TO THE MANY hopeful writers trying to break into that grossly misunderstood profession known as "Travel Writing."

To those on the outside, travel writing heretofore appeared to be an illusive magic carpet, floating you off on exciting journeys to seven continents. Sunrise in Bali . . . icebergs in Antarctica . . . pyramids along the Nile. "And," those travel-writer wannabes think, "all of this will be free, and mine for the asking, if only I write an article about it."

Those of us on the inside know better. With editors insisting that their travel writers not accept freebies, and those same editors refusing to pay the writer's expenses, we fear that the professional travel writer may well be on the way to extinction. However, until that happens, there will always be those of us dedicated to the profession who will continue to travel, continue to write about our journeys, and continue to find a way to get published.

Struggling neophytes determined to make a living in this limited field may find themselves facing instant frustration and starvation. But if you are endowed with endless stamina, insatiable curiosity, high energy, unfaltering determination, and the financial means to get you through those first lean years, you will find it a most rewarding profession.

The following tips on writing and marketing travel articles have been garnered from my two decades of travel writing experience. With allowances for individual personality, interests, and style, they should also work for the aspiring travel writer.

Open with a powerful lead: Begin your article with such a strong or catchy lead that readers can't put the article down until they've read everything you wanted to tell them. Let it paint a picture . . . arouse curiosity . . . or even anger. And don't let go until your very last paragraph takes them back to that engaging lead.

For example, one of my successful travel articles began: "I'm just wild about Harry." Playing upon the old song title, it compels readers to learn just who Harry is and what he is doing in the travel section. "I love calories! I love cholesterol! I love Fauchon!" Who or what is Fauchon? Curious readers have to read beyond this award-winning opening. "Auschwitz is the flip side of Disneyworld." This first sentence of another travel article instilled anger in some readers until they continued to read on for the explanation. But they did read on!

Anecdotes make good openers: Quote the joke that the cab driver told you, or begin with the tour guide's remark that put the entire busload of tourists into stitches.

Write as if you are talking to your best friend: Pretend you've phoned to tell your friend about the wonderful place you've just visited. Describe which sights are not to be missed and which are a waste of time and money. Tell her where to eat—in a variety of price ranges—and what dish must absolutely be tried. Go beyond the over-hyped shopping malls to the unusual boutiques that specialize in goods unique to that area. Recount with enthusiasm and delight the joys you experienced; weep for the sadness you saw. Communicate with your readers. Don't try to impress them.

Engage your readers' senses: Immerse your readers in the destination and make them eager to go there. Through your words, they should be able to *see* the Great Wall of China . . . *hear* the cacophony of sounds in the Casbah . . . *smell* the spice-laden, cow-dunged streets of India.

Write to entertain: Travelers, both real and armchair, need to be entertained as well as informed, otherwise you will lose them after the first few paragraphs. Your facts must be current and informative but not boring. If it's in-depth research your readers want, they will turn to an encyclopedia or comprehensive guidebook. Your job is that of the surrogate. Sort through the books and visit the attractions. Then write the article in a natural, readable style.

Breathe new life into the old: Make antiquity come alive as you uncover the past. Your readers might have difficulty picturing Mark Antony and Cleopatra walking along the Arcadian Way in Ephesus, Turkey. But, a mention of Charlton Heston riding down those ancient marble streets in his chariot will conjure up a myriad of images in the minds of millions of movie buffs.

Find unexplored subjects and unique angles: For the most part, travel editors are not interested in general destination pieces. When you visit a place, think of all the subjects connected to that place. Then go one step further, and look for the oft-neglected hidden treasure. Skip the overdone St. Mark's Square in Venice, Italy; instead, write about Venice's little-known ghetto. Forget the tourist-trap restaurants in the old walled city of Dubrovnik; instead, write about that secluded seafood spot a half-hour down the road. A day in Rio may be overdone for most publications, but a day on nearby Paqueta Island is new and refreshing.

Focus on the "must do's": Evaluate each destination from the viewpoint of someone who was never there. Focus on places and things your readers *must* see or do. Make them realize they may never come this way again. And, if you haven't experienced something important yourself, give them a quote from someone who has.

Be sure your articles are timely: Unless you have a regular market for your travel piece and are assured of publication, don't write about events taking place currently or in the near future. By the time an editor gets around to reading—and publishing—your story, it may be dated.

Don't write about an area that has been receiving negative publicity. A Mediterranean cruise story won't sell right after an outbreak of violence in the Gulf, nor will an Eastern European story immediately following a disaster such as the Chernobyl explosion. If Hurricane Gilbert has just devastated the Caribbean, this is not the time to submit articles about the island you visited last Christmas.

Think ahead: Jump the gun on the laggards. If a city is planning a bicentennial in two years, now is the time to query a magazine. If the local senior citizens club sponsors an annual motor coach tour for fall leafing, query seniors' magazines a year ahead to see if they'd like an on-the-coach report.

Rely on roundups: Grouping information about a subject into one article is a favorite of editors. The world's best—golf courses, tennis camps, adventure travel, honeymoon havens; the world's worst or best—restaurants, cruises, shopping, etc.

Share your travel tips: Readers want you to tell them how to travel lightly, what type of luggage you recommend, how to deal with jet lag, and what to do about nasty customs officials.

Be your own photographer: Even though you may not know a shutter from a lens, learn to take your own photos, and never travel without a camera. Presenting a complete package to an editor gives you a leading edge. Smart cameras make it easy for dumb photographers. Today's fully automatic equipment gives even amateur photographers a chance to illustrate stories with one-of-a kind shots not available from stock files. Sophisticated photographic skills, though desirable, are no longer essential. Take it from one who doesn't know a Nikon aperture from a Beethoven overture! All you need is a good eye and a smart camera.

Don't pretend to be what you're not: Sophisticated readers want travel articles by sophisticated writers. Adventurers want to read articles about trekking the Himalayas by someone who has trekked them. Leave the golf vacations to the golfers, the shopping sprees to the shoppers. Don't try to write for a publication that features a lifestyle that is totally foreign to you.

Go behind the scenes: For example, the kitchen at Air France; the flight attendants' training center at Singapore Airlines; the semi-annual sale at Harrods; the cockpit of the *Concorde;* the kennel of the *QE2;* the shop on the *Orient Express.* These are topics not likely to be overdone.

Be what you really are: Let your readers know that even travel writers have fears and emotions. "Sure," I write, "I'm afraid of sky-jackers and terrorists. Of course, I prayed when our Nepalese plane engine failed, and we turned back to Kathmandu. Certainly an outbreak of meningococcal meningitis in Delhi just prior to my trip there made me nervous. Undoubtedly, I panicked when the Chinese navy encircled our cruise ship, which had unknowingly sailed into the midst of their maneuvers. A cannon at one's porthole is most unsettling!"

Once you've assured readers that it's normal to have fears, tell them what precautions to take to alleviate those fears. Call the State Department in Washington, D.C., for security alerts; the Centers for Disease Control in Atlanta, Georgia, for medical advice.

Be humble: It's hard to be humble when you're having a grand time, but above all, don't become jaded or patronizing to your readers. Write *to* them, not *above* them. Don't try to appear as the *bon vivant* by flaunting how much you know or showing off how many places you've been. A tongue-in-cheek "snob" piece can be fun, as long as your readers are in on the joke. If you want to use foreign words, local jargon, or complicated dialects for local color or to set the mood, be sure to provide a simple translation or explanation.

Be human: Keep the human element in your writing. When you write about facilities for people with disabilities, you must include all the physical details, but don't neglect the emotional aspects—the feelings of a disabled person who has been on a cruise ship or climbed the Great Wall of China. Let your readers know how other travelers feel and have managed in spite of their disabilities.

Be fair: Advise your readers honestly of any problems or shortcomings, but don't try to build your ego by wiping the destination off the map. When I found a particular Jamaican hotel to be dirty, I wrote that "roaches romped in dresser drawers." When writing about an obviously overpriced Florida attraction, I advised "Save your money, unless a smile on your grandchild's face is worth $30." When describing the social structure of the QE2, it was difficult to state tactfully the difference between First Class and Transatlantic Class. I simply said, "leisure suits in lieu of tuxedos." Everyone understood.

Be professional: If you're going to be a travel writer, you must travel, travel, travel. And all along the way, you must pry, you must probe, and you must ask questions—and you must not give up until you get answers. Library research is fine as a *supplement* to travel, not as a *replacement.* For authenticity and credibility, let your readers know you've been to the spot about which you are writing. Describe something you ate or something you bought. Quote a local resident. Verify facts and figures that are often mixed up by local guides. Don't write from a travel brochure; readers can peruse those without your help.

Include consumer information: Your article should give a sense of place. Limit the number of dates, figures, etc., in the body of the article. Costs, documentation requirements, weather, local currency, and other service details should be relegated to an informative sidebar.

Give editors what they want: A long-term relationship with an editor is directly dependent upon the reliability of your work. Many travel writers offer readability, but fewer offer credibility. Be accurate, and always submit clean copy. No matter how enjoyable and informative your article may be, an editor will reject a messy manuscript rather than suffer eye strain trying to decipher it. And above all, spell the editor's name correctly! Whether you think it's right or not, send a query and SASE (self-addressed stamped envelope) when editors request it. Familiarize yourself with the writing style of the publication you're aiming for, and with the number of words in an average article. Editors like writers who make their jobs easier.

Think beyond the travel section: The travel sections of newspapers now rely mostly on staff writers, but you can pitch your work to other sections of the paper. Send that French restaurant piece to the food section, the Italian shopping piece to the fashion section, the Poconos piece to the weddings section, and the Smoky Mountain fish tale to the sports page. If that doesn't work, forget the traditional newspaper markets and concentrate on secondary markets, such as sports, business and trade, art, and seniors' magazines.

Work with a local travel agency: Try to convince a travel agency of the importance of a monthly newsletter or insert to go with their regular mailings. The pay for such items can be much better than that for a newspaper article—and much steadier.

Work with a local public relations firm: Though your byline might never see the light of day, the pay for travel-related press releases is much better than for newspaper articles. The same holds true for writing for the tourist offices of various cities or countries.

❑ 57

THE BUSINESS OF CRAFT WRITING

BY KATHLEEN PEELEN KREBS

IN THE PAST THREE DECADES, THE HANDCRAFT MOVEMENT HAS spawned an interest in and appreciation of fine crafts for the consumer, and big business for the artist. The proliferation of art and craft fairs in almost every town, city, state, and province across the United States and Canada is a testament to the ever-growing demand for original, handmade merchandise. The publishing world is racing to keep pace with this market, and a wide variety of books, magazines, and periodicals carry articles pertaining to craft.

As a fiber artist and basket maker for over ten years, I have contributed numerous "how-to" articles on various aspects of my craft: from locating, gathering, and preparing natural materials, to step-by-step instructions in basketry techniques, such as coiling, twining, and weaving. And selling my art through museum stores, art galleries, and fine craft fairs has inspired me to write articles on the business of craft.

Based on my experience as an artist and writer, I offer the following seven steps for entering the craft writing market:

1) *Write what you know.*
If you have ever turned a bowl, knit a sweater, crafted a candle, woven a basket, built a birdhouse, or braided a rug, you may have the how-to basics of writing about your craft. The market for craft how-to's is broad. A multitude of specialized craft publications offer techniques on quilting, knitting, woodworking and carving, embroidery, metal-smithing, ceramics, and weaving. A number of general craft magazines feature instructions on how to make anything from stained-glass lampshades to mosaic flowerpots. Home and garden magazines offer well-written articles on subjects ranging from herbal wreaths from your backyard, to building your own bent-willow garden furniture.

I have written instructions for making hats from lily leaves and mats from scented herbs. My article on drying pine needles to coil a natural

green basket was featured as a cover story for a national craft magazine, and brought me $300.

2) *Tap the children's market.*

Do you remember those beanbag squares, potato prints, and paper-
bag masks you made in second grade? Most children's magazines have
a "crafts corner" and welcome new ideas (or variations upon old ones).
This is an easy way for even crafting amateurs to enter the craft writing
market. If you have ever helped a child make a tissue-paper kite, a
newspaper mâché animal, an egg-carton caterpillar, or a felt finger
puppet, you can write an article with an original twist on your project.
An article I wrote on Southwest-style, woven newspaper baskets
earned me $250 from a national family craft magazine.

3) *Record your research.*

You have spent hours in art museums admiring antique Chinese
porcelain or seventeenth-century Japanese kimonos. You seek out contemporary expressions in wood in countless art galleries. Many fine
art and craft publications accept well-researched articles on a particular area of interest. *Fiberarts Magazine* published an article on the
sari collection of one of the last Ottoman princesses, as well as a
feature on collecting early "aloha shirts" from Hawaii. For an article
on Huichol Indian bead and yarn art published as a colorful cover
story for *Bead & Button Magazine,* I earned $375.

Read extensively in your field of interst and focus your article for a
particular publication. You may wish to call experts or collectors in
the field to add details and depth.

4) *Profile an artist.*

You are captivated by the one-of-a-kind brass door-knockers of a
local metalsmith and linger longingly over the tilework of a well-known
ceramist. Call or write the artist to request an interview, and then
query one of the art and craft publications that frequently feature artist
profiles. Ask about photo requirements.

5) *Review a crafts show.*

If you are well-informed about a particular area of craft, reviewing
an art gallery or museum show that exhibits work in your field may
prove profitable. (Shows and openings are often listed in local newspapers.) Target your market. Several craft and art publications, as well

as newspapers, accept free-lance reviews. Well-crafted impressions backed by knowledge are always acceptable.

6) *Evaluate a craft fair.*

Craft is big business, and the major venues for a majority of craft artists are the juried craft shows held throughout the United States and Canada. Professional artists and all of those concerned with the business of craft, as well as consumers of handcrafts, welcome articles evaluating and appraising these shows. There is an ever-increasing free-lance market in craft publications for such evaluations.

Visit your favorite show, noting attendance, overall quality of the artists' work, the originality and appeal of booth display. Jot down a few brief questions to ask artists or request a card and an O.K. to contact the artists after the show. Always ask permission to use an artist's name, and offer to send a copy of the article, if published. Ask how long the artist has exhibited at the show; try to find out if the show was profitable; did the artist have better wholesale or retail sales; what were the show's costs vs. profits, etc. You might also quickly interview customers, as well as show staff and promoters, asking their impressions.

7) *Offer craft business advice.*

Whether you sell your craft in galleries, gift shops, at professional craft shows, or simply through your local church or school bazaar, you know something about the business of craft. Tips on pricing, booth set-up and design, photography for jurying, advertising, bookkeeping for tax purposes, travel expenses, and sales strategies are well-received by many craft trade magazines.

Writing for the crafts market is an enjoyable way to share your professional know-how, your part-time hobby, or your special field of interest with others. The demand for well-written, informed articles has never been higher.

❑ 58

Writing Human Interest Articles

By Janet Fabyankovic and Catherine Pigora

Writing human interest articles requires having a passion for people and their unique stories. You are not only giving readers factual information, such as a person's lifestyle, tragedies, or secrets, but allowing them to see what goes on through the eyes of others. Numerous women's and religious magazines are excellent publications to target with queries of real life dramas or people narratives.

Media professionals often look to other communication sources for ideas, or draw on personal human interest stories in local or national newspapers or magazines. Recently, both print and visual media have been saturated with true-life dramas in which women or children are abused, kidnapped, acquire rare diseases or are betrayed by society, the legal system, or by men.

Many first-time writers became published when they presented accounts of how they faced and overcame adversity in columns such as "Drama in Real Life," featured in *Reader's Digest*. Mothers often become published authors when they write about their personal experiences raising a physically challenged child, surviving a marital storm, or coping with a cancer diagnosis.

It's important to find and write a chronicle that most readers can relate to, even if they haven't encountered the same situation. Although a reader may not be a grandmother who lost a grandchild when her son was divorced, she can relate to the loneliness, despair, and other similar emotions a person deals with during separation or loss.

Disaster stories provide another outlet for tales of ordinary people who become empowered with strength and courage by an extraordinary experience. If you write about a father who saved a child in an airplane crash, or a dog who rescued a baby during a fire, try to find a slant that is unique, especially if the story was covered numerous times in print and on television.

Because of their busy schedules, reporters often don't do a follow-up on original stories. Many times, incidents that occur after a heroic event have as much impact as the original piece. Or the subject may present a new perspective on the event after having time to digest it.

One teenager who risked his life saving a friend from gang violence later becomes a police dispatcher to assist with crime cases; a couple adopted a five-year-old girl whom they saved from a fire after discovering that her whole family was killed in the tragedy.

Many article writers study national trends and issues, then find a local angle that has universal appeal. With child abuse a current topic, well-written pieces that focus on a nearby shelter for battered children or a profile of an outstanding counselor may appeal to editors.

A writer may decide to collaborate with another writer, especially if both authors have a different specialty or flair that enhances an otherwise ordinary manuscript. When you face writer's block, enlisting another writer may be a good solution and add a new point of view to your piece. At an interview, two writers may have different observations or one writer may ask questions that the other might have missed or not thought of at the time.

Make sure to have a few questions jotted down for reference, but once the interview begins, don't be afraid to be spontaneous and ask spin-off questions from comments that surface in discussions. No one knows exactly what will take place during the interview. Being flexible yet professional will put the interviewee at ease. Always be considerate if a person responds with tears, anger, or a request for privacy on certain issues.

Where do you find ideas for a human interest story? Fortunately, they are easy to spot, since most people have a personal story to tell. Scan newspapers, television segments, journals, magazines, videos, or computer systems for a start. Or contact local schools, government stations, organizations, and other institutions and ask to be placed on their mailing list for releases, newsletters, and bulletins.

By perusing such publications, you may come across a story idea that could be pitched to a national magazine or journal using a different slant. For example, a feature from a hospital newsletter about a blind lady who saved a suicide victim's life on the internet was reworked and submitted to a national journal seeking accounts of emergency rescues. Written from a crisis perspective, it was immediately accepted and published.

Many writers get story ideas at bus stops, from visits to social agencies, and chats with friends or relatives. If your specialty is medical or social issues, it's imperative to develop a link with a physician or attorney. Specialized writers, such as entertainment critics, often use human interest stories as sidebars to a related article, especially when local children or adults have been involved.

After coming up with an idea, appropriate research is imperative for background, proper spellings of names and places, and additional information that will enhance your article. If your topic (such as a rare disease) is unusual and many readers may be unfamiliar with it, you should include a description of symptoms and diagnosis for its characteristics to allow medical perspective.

Once you select your subject, write an article lead that will attract the reader's attention. For example, if the story is based on an abused woman, try to create an intense, active scene as your beginning. ("As she came out of unconsciousness with blood dripping down her face, Jessica couldn't believe that the man she married only two months ago did this to her.")

Let the story unfold naturally. Remember to be patient and sensitive to the people you interview, allowing them to reveal what happened in their own way and time. Try to imagine yourself in the subject's place, and don't ask any questions that might be too upsetting, unless the person being interviewed brings up the delicate topic (or welcomes any questions.) Several writers give their interviewees the option of answering only the questions that they may feel comfortable with. Although these journalists are respected, occasionally their articles are rejected by publications that prefer a more probing approach for greater emotional impact. Obtain publication guidelines before submitting queries or articles, to determine exact editorial focus.

Capturing the mood of the story can make your article more compelling. As you describe an athlete who wins a tournament while battling the effects of leukemia, make the words active to set the pace of the event. However, if you're describing a daughter's last goodbye to her mother in a hospice, sensitivity is a must.

By spending a little extra time with the person after the interview, a writer can obtain quotes and facts that will add the extra human touch to the article. The main character must be someone whom the readers will care about and can identify with. It isn't a fast-paced, "just the facts, ma'am" piece.

Treat your subject with respect so that in revealing the story you don't offend the person who trusted you with his or her personal life. An article on suicide can be serious and poignant without being depressing. Often people grant interviews in hope of helping others prevent or cope with a similar situation. Celebrities and officials sometimes risk revealing their own or their family's weaknesses as a stepping stone to their own recovery, as in the case of Betty Ford, who helped thousands recover from addictions. Assure those you interview that you will write an inspirational, informative piece, not an exposé.

Writers who are determined to make a literary mark or spotlight a social issue may disguise themselves as a homeless lady, elderly person, or prisoner to illustrate what it's really like to "walk in their shoes." They're able to add suggestions and present possible solutions to problems that their subjects face.

Not all human interest stories are traumatic. In fact, some writers recognize that tragic stories are often too complicated or emotional for their tastes, so they concentrate on writing upbeat narratives and profiles. Their writing repertoire might include a four-year-old child who charms the audience with her singing and dancing, a farmer who makes friends with a wild pheasant, or the story behind a circus, regatta, or concert. Occasionally they may tour with symphonies, bands, police, or paramedics so they can include first-hand accounts and relevant quotes.

When you write a human interest story, a sincere concern for people combined with curiosity, good writing skills, effective research, and editing are essential to bring your views to life and intrigue an editor.

❏ 59

THE KEY TO INTERVIEWING SUCCESS

BY JOY PARISE

IF YOU WANT TO ADVANCE IN YOUR ARTICLE WRITING, INCORPORATE the opinions of outside professionals to enliven and enrich your work. If done properly, a good interview provides not only plenty of material that will add depth to an article, but also valuable ideas and sources for future projects.

The actual interview is no place for on-site training. Much of the success of an interview will depend on your behind-the-scenes preparation to make sure that your subject is enough at ease to talk freely and openly to you. With experience, you'll learn techniques that work best for you. The following are some methods that can help you on your way to interviewing success.

1. If at all possible, arrange for a face-to-face interview. While a telephone call can give you the information you need, an in-person interview will more than pay off. Eye contact with your subject will help relax him or her, and being able to describe his or her gestures, appearance, and surroundings can make your writing come alive.

Once you have phoned and arranged the interview, follow up with a note thanking the person and confirming the time and place, and enclose a simple business card, if you have one. If you'll need any specific information, photos, statistics, or phone numbers, alert your subject in your note so that he or she can have them handy. Don't send specific questions that you'll be asking. Nothing is worse than sitting down in front of the subject who reads stilted and scripted answers to you.

2. Make the most of your interviewing time, and give your subject the maximum amount of time to talk. Prepare your questions in advance so that you don't flounder. To create an atmosphere of easy conversation, don't keep the list of questions in front of you. Tuck them inside the cover of your notepad or place them discreetly to the side to peek at now and then. Be familiar enough with your questions in advance to be flexible if new material from your subject's comments and responses pops up, if your interview takes an interesting new slant, or if your prepared order doesn't work. Although your prepared questions will help keep you on course, don't be close-minded. Keep alert. You may find a whole line of discussion to pursue spontaneously.

3. Structure your questions around a preliminary outline. Try to keep the outline of your article in your mind before you go into the interview so that you ask your questions in sequence. This will make it easier later to work from your notes rather than facing a hodgepodge of information you have to organize.

When I interview someone for a feature, I structure my articles in a specific way. Drawing a picture in words of the gestures, appearance, or surroundings tells why this person is interesting enough to be written about. That's how I try to capture the readers' attention so that they will become interested enough to want to know more about this person—and keep reading.

I then go into the subject's area of expertise and give enough objective and colorful information so that readers say, "I didn't know that." (Editors often tell me that they found my articles very informative; they learned a lot.) Then I swing back to the person I'm interviewing and ask about his or her goals for the future.

Whatever your style, make a plan in advance so that you have a good idea where you want to steer your interview.

4. Dress for success. Making a good appearance begins with being on time. If you're interviewing someone important enough to be interviewed, then his or her time is important, too. Respect it.

Dress in a way to put your subject at ease. Don't underestimate this step. If you're going to a corporation, wear a suit. If you're going to a small business, try a sports jacket. If you're going to a cowboy barn, try jeans. For a sports club, neat slacks. The idea is to make your subject comfortable enough to relate to you and want to help you write a good article.

5. Let your instincts take over. If for some reason you're having a really hard time with the interview, let your subject know it. Some years ago, I was sent to cover a riding clinic at an out-of-state stable. The owner was very rude and cold. After trying to get quotes from him—to make him look good—and getting nowhere, I looked at him and lightly said, "Come on, give me a break. Help me out here." Since he knew he was being obnoxious (but was probably never called on it), he immediately tuned in and started talking.

Another time, I was asked to do an article on a whole family. The editor had tried to write a piece about them but had found them almost impossible to interview. Though they were willing to sit down with me, they found it hard to make anything other than the "name, rank, and serial number" types of comments.

When I walked into their house, to my horror I found the whole family sitting around the table. Self-conscious in front of each other, no one spoke. From the corner of the table, one person would meekly add a bit of information. I went home and waited for a few days, then phoned that person. I told him that he sounded as if he had so much background to tell me about (which he did), and I asked if I could meet with him alone so that I could write a "good" article. We met again at his house, sat under a lovely tree, and talked for an hour about the family history and their achievements in the horse world. The tree became the central symbol for the stability of the family, and the article turned out much better than I'd ever imagined it would.

Don't be afraid to ask for more if you are not getting what you need, but do so tactfully and honestly.

6. Bring a tape recorder. Be prepared to take notes to back up what's on the tape. The recorder is good for capturing the exact ways that people speak, as well as names and figures and other information that takes too much time to write. This is important in drawing a picture of your subject. Furthermore, the flow of your subject's speech as opposed to yours in your writing will help keep the rhythm of your article interesting.

A third and more subtle use of the tape recorder comes in when it is shut off. I've gotten some of my best quotes when the interview appears to be formally over and the people you're interviewing tend to relax and open up.

Once, when I was interviewing a successful professional horseman, he walked me to the door of his stable, and looking out over his forty-acre farm, he waved his arm and said, "I'm so lucky. I'm so lucky. I'm forty years old and doing what I love!"

I began the article with that gesture and those words. Since the article showed that he had attained what he had through hard work and dedication, not luck, his humility endeared him to the readers. In fact, he said he never got so much positive feedback from any other article written about him. The fact was that he was a nice guy, and it showed—particularly when the interview was "officially" over.

7. Let your subject really talk. Ask your subject what he or she thinks is important, and what he or she would like you to write. You'll be amazed!

Once when I was interviewing a man who had won at a horse show, I asked him what he would like me to say. He talked about his stable's successful breeding program—something few people knew about, although it was highly successful.

Not only did it add more information to the article, but it provided me with material for a second article on that stable—an eight-page piece I wrote the next year for a national magazine.

8. Show your appreciation. Get to your interview on time, leave on time, and be polite. Remember, you're not the important person here; the person you're interviewing is. Send a copy of your published article with a thank-you note.

9. Look inside yourself. If you're not getting a successful interview after careful preparation, then look inside. Were you sincerely interested in the person you interviewed? Dogs, horses, and kids know when someone dislikes them, but they warm up with people they know they can trust. People being interviewed do, too. Put your best foot forward, and you can't fail.

❑ 60

CREATING GREETING CARDS

BY WENDY DAGER

HAVE YOU EVER RECEIVED A GREETING CARD THAT WAS SO "YOU," IT could have been written by you? Have you ever had a brief, funny thought that would make a great T-shirt slogan, or perhaps composed a poem that brought tears to the eyes of a reader?

Using one or all of these criteria can help you break into greeting card writing, an industry that boasted $6.3 *billion* in sales last year, representing 7.4 billion greeting cards sold.

There are now approximately 1,500 greeting card companies. Although the majority of them do not accept submissions from free lancers, many are eager for writers who can provide them with fresh ideas. Just follow these simple rules, and you'll find yourself hooked on creating one-liners, poems, and words of wisdom specifically for the greeting card market.

1. Always send for guidelines. Get addresses of greeting card companies, either from *The Writer* Magazine or from the *Greeting Card Industry Directory*. (The directory is expensive, and I wouldn't advise your buying it unless you have made a few sales first.) The Greeting Card Association (1200 G Street N.W., Suite 760, Washington, D.C. 20005), which publishes the directory, is very receptive to inquiries and will send a price list of all the books, tapes, and related industry information they publish. In addition, some greeting card companies have their addresses on the backs of their cards, or the name of their city and state (so a writer can call information and get a phone number, then call the company and see if they will provide an address for free-lance submissions).

If a company does accept work from free lancers, the guidelines will tell you the required format for submissions, the style they are looking for (some even give examples of published cards), and the occasions and holidays for which they need ideas. For example, some companies may produce cards for Christmas, but not Chanukah.

2. Brainstorm! Keep pads of paper around the house so you can scribble down thoughts while you are doing chores, or invest in a voice-activated tape recorder (about $35 at discount stores) to record ideas. Make up your own worksheets. For example, for Christmas ideas (usually, a company accepts seasonal ideas for the following year right *after* the holiday), write down the many things associated with it—Santa, tree, tinsel, presents, reindeer, etc.—then try to think of them in a funny or sentimental scenario. This method can be applied to any holiday or occasion. Recall situations you've been in or things your friends or relatives have said. Are they quirky, funny, silly, romantic? Can you tighten them to create a greeting card?

3. Most companies prefer submissions on 3"x5" cards, using the following format: O indicates what's to appear on the *outside* of the card; I is for the *inside*. You can put the holiday or occasion on the topmost line of the card, as follows:

Christmas
O: What has a red suit, white beard and flies?
I: A Santa who never bathes! Merry Christmas!

Girlfriends
O: He got me an iron for my birthday, which I used right away . . .
I: He should be coming out of the coma soon.

You can also put a description of the artwork you visualize on the top line, or in parentheses after O:

Birthday
O: (photo or picture of a gorilla)
I: Happy Birthday! You're in the primate of your life!

There is no need to send a mock-up of the card, unless it is a puzzle, maze, or game. Check greeting card counters in stores for examples; these types of cards are usually directed at children.

Other greeting card companies accept submissions on 8 1/2"x11" sheets of paper (indicated in their guidelines). They might also be willing to consider faxed or E-mailed submissions, but you must first clear this with the editor. On the back of each card, put your name, address, and phone number. I recommend purchasing a self-inking stamp with this information (about $15 or less), to save time. Do *not* send simultaneous submissions. If a company rejects your ideas, then you can feel free to send them somewhere else. As a rule, do not send fewer than six or more than twenty ideas. Some companies will specify in their guidelines how many ideas (called a "batch") they will consider at one time.

Put a code number on the lower right hand corner of each submission (Birthday ideas can be B1, B2, B3, etc.; Christmas can be C1, C2, etc.), and keep track of what ideas correspond to which code numbers. Keep copies of all your submissions and the names of the companies to which you send them. A company may decide to purchase your idea C2, but, if you don't know which one they're buying, you're in trouble!

4. Expect to wait at least one month for a response, sometimes longer. After two months, send a polite follow-up letter inquiring about your submission. Enclose a self-addressed stamped envelope for their reply.

5. Greeting card companies receive hundreds of ideas a year and buy only a select few, so if you submit twenty ideas and sell one, you have beaten the odds. The company will send you a contract, indicating that they would like to purchase your idea and are buying all rights to it, which of course, means that it becomes their property. You must also attest to the fact that it is, indeed, *your* idea to sell. Read the contract carefully before signing it, then return it. Don't forget to make a copy for yourself. Generally, payment arrives thirty days or so after publication of the card, along with several samples of the finished card. It is rare, though not unheard of, for a writer to receive writing credit on the back of the card.

6. How much can you expect to be paid? Anywhere from $25 to $150 for each idea purchased, with $100 the average for a one- or two-line gag. Although not the norm, royalties are sometimes negotiable (a company's guidelines will indicate if they pay royalties). Payment for a poem is more, about $200 on the average, for all rights.

Because greeting card companies are as individual as the people who run them, payment varies. The companies that give royalties are indeed a minority, and flat-fee is the norm, on acceptance or on publication, for all rights. While most companies do not allow the writer to retain rights to his work, there are a few that do. Your contract will tell you if you are selling all rights to an idea.

7. Some companies will indicate that they wish to hold an idea for further consideration. This generally means it must pass a review board

before they decide to accept or reject it. In this case, do not submit the idea elsewhere until the company has made its final decision. Sometimes they will hold an idea up to six months; after sixty days, however, you may send a polite letter with SASE, inquiring about its status. If they decide not to purchase your idea, you are then free to submit it to another company.

8. I'm often asked, "How can I keep a company from 'stealing' my ideas?" You must keep in mind the old saying, "There is nothing new under the sun." Maybe someone, somewhere, has already come up with your idea and has beaten you to the punch. Editors have reputations to maintain, and it is highly unlikely that they will steal your idea. You may submit your idea anywhere you choose (following guidelines, of course). If your work is rejected, it is because an editor simply cannot use it or may already have something similar; if it is rejected a number of times, consider discarding or reworking it. Editors want to accept new ideas; that's their job.

Some other tips:

• Always enclose a self-addressed stamped envelope with the proper postage with any correspondence to a greeting card company.

• Always be polite when you write to an editor. I once sent a thank-you note to an editor for purchasing an idea, and she remembered me the next time she needed a one-liner for a card. Now she regularly faxes me cartoon cards that need inside gags.

• Diversify. Some companies may want punchy one-liners or thoughtful poetry for plaques, magnets, buttons, mugs, key chains, and "softline" items like T-shirts and aprons. Keep in mind that "brevity is the soul of wit." It's a tiny space you're trying to fill, so conserve your words, but pack them with wit.

• There's always a market for humor of various types: risqué, studio, juvenile, cute, silly, contemporary, or laugh-out-loud.

• Keep in mind that women purchase 85% to 90% of all greeting cards.

• Do not telephone an editor. Mail or fax is preferable.

• Don't take rejections personally. Relax, have fun, and fine-tune your rejected work, especially if editors offer encouragement and tell you to keep at it.

Some of the larger greeting card companies, like Hallmark (and some of the small ones just starting out), do not accept work from free lancers and use only staff writers. Do not let this deter you. Keep sending to other companies for guidelines and you may find one that likes your writing style.

❑ 61

PROFILES TAKE COURAGE

BY BOB SCHULTZ

THE NERVOUS MAN IN THE RUMPLED SPORTS COAT PICKED UP THE handgun from its place near the microphone, lifted one slat of the mini-blind, and watched as the slow-moving car disappeared around the corner. "Can't be too careful after all those death threats," he said. "Now, what else does your magazine want to know about me?"

All articles on interviewing stress how to put the person you're interviewing at ease, but none of them told me how to put myself at ease as I jumped every time I heard the slightest noise outside for the rest of that interview. Some profiles take courage.

Interviewing locally famous, or notorious, characters like this conservative talk-show host has been one of my more regular sources of bylines and income. The skills I have acquired interviewing a small-town mayor or the local handwriting analyst are the same skills I've used to interview celebrities. What skills do you need to start seeing your byline on profiles? Here are the steps I follow:

Find an interesting subject. Where can you find people interesting enough to profile in local newspapers and regional magazines? Everywhere! Look in the phone book for unusual businesses, and you may find people like the owner of the Used Car Factory, who turns out "new" roadsters or brings that old Chevy back to life so it looks as good, or better, than it did when it rolled off the assembly line. If Halloween or New Year's is coming up, that store with all the old costumes might make an interesting story, with some great photo possibilities.

Follow local news articles and watch for those little human interest pieces. A handwriting analyst in a local fraud trial turned out to be an expert on Elvis Presley's handwriting. An arresting officer in another case turned out to be a singer in a rock and roll band comprised of uniformed officers.

Do your research. Before you ask your first question, you need to know something about the person you're interviewing, or about the career or activity that makes the person noteworthy. If he's a radio talk show host, tape a few shows and listen to them to become familiar with his favorite themes and strongest opinions. If she's a handwriting expert, pick up a book on handwriting analysis or on crime investigation to get enough background to ask relevant questions. If he's a famous author, read a book or two along with book reviews of his work to see what the critics think of his work.

Respect your subject. You don't have to fall in love with or agree with everything the person you're profiling says, but you do have to respect him or her enough to write an article that is accurate and fair. If you look down on your subject, your arrogance will show through, diminishing the reader's respect and interest in the person.

You don't have to believe in psychics to write good articles on a local psychic. Your job is to get to know the person well enough to illuminate the qualities that will make this person interesting to readers.

Hook your reader. Once you have the background you need, start writing. You need a lead paragraph that will hook readers and keep them reading till the end. They may never have heard of the person you're profiling and never thought about doing whatever it is that the person does, so you have to work to draw them into the article. Here is an opening paragraph to an article I wrote on a local boudoir photographer:

Considering what she isn't wearing, perhaps she just stepped out of a shower. Reclining in peace and apparent solitude, she takes a bite from a juicy red apple. Slowly, a huge serpent slithers up from behind her.

Wonder what happens next? I hope so. If you don't entice readers with your opening paragraph, they're probably already skipping on to the next article, so the hook is critical.

Use anecdotes and interesting quotes. If you think the person you're interviewing should be in the hall of fame, just telling readers your opinion probably won't carry much weight. You are much more likely to be convincing by describing an activity or a comment that illustrates your opinion.

As I interviewed a woman with multiple sclerosis confined to a wheelchair, I noticed that she didn't have any "handicap" plates on her van. "Oh, I don't ever use those parking places," she said. "Those are for people who'd have breathing trouble or other problems if they couldn't park close. Remember, I'm not disabled." And, of course, she isn't disabled, because she refuses to see herself that way. But, she said it better than I could.

Letting a person you disagree with speak his or her mind will give readers information that will help them form their own opinions. In an article about a basketball coach, I acknowledged that the coach felt that his being labeled a blatant sexist was due to some out-of-context quotes. I found his original statement and quoted it in its entirety. When readers had a chance to read his complete statement, the coach came across as "blatantly sexist," but he did it in his own words!

Surprise the reader. Anecdotes and quotes that surprise readers usually keep them reading for more, as do anecdotes that reveal the humanity in larger-than-life people.

During an interview with Ray Bradbury, he showed me the autographs of people like Jean Harlow and W.C. Fields that he collected when he was a youngster in Los Angeles. But the note he seemed to treasure most was from someone much less famous—his daughter: "Mom, I don't know what time I'll be home, but I will be safe. P.S. One of the cats threw up on the stairs." That simple quote brought home the fact that my profile was about Ray Bradbury, father and husband, not just Ray Bradbury, author.

Be positive, but don't "puff." Those too-good-to-be-true articles about celebrities are often called "puff" pieces. The magazine or newspaper generally looks for a positive article about someone from an industry that advertises in the publication, or a famous person. The trick is to show the person's good qualities without making your profile sound like a nomination for sainthood.

To make it clear that a local TV news anchorman had not let his fame go to his head, he closed his interview with these words: "Don't tell my mother I'm a newsman. She thinks I'm a piano player in a whorehouse." I used that quote as the ending of my profile.

Wrap it up. Second in importance only to the hook that draws readers in, is an ending that will keep them thinking about your article after they finish it. An illustration of giving your profile a big finish comes from an article I wrote on Robin Cook. I had ended a review of one of Mr. Cook's medical thrillers by mentioning that I was going in to have two wisdom teeth taken out the next day and I was grateful that Cook hadn't written any books to scare me out of that surgery. After reading my review, Mr. Cook wrote to me, saying, "I wanted you to know that my next book will be called *Tooth* . . . a thriller about wisdom teeth!"

Fictionalize it. Take the real-life characters you've interviewed and profiled and mix and match them to create characters for your fiction. Change that conservative talk show host into a liberal talk show hostess. Create a series sleuth out of that handwriting analyst. Keep track of the comments, the habits, the eccentricities of the fascinating people you profile, and then recycle revised versions of those people into your short stories and novels.

There are many good reasons to write profiles. They get you away from your solitary word processor and out interacting with interesting people; they give you experience conducting interviews, connect you with local experts you can call on later, and provide you with bits and pieces for creating memorable fictional characters that are deeply rooted in reality.

There are plenty of interesting people out there just waiting to tell their stories. They might as well tell them to you. Just ask them to check their guns at the door.

❏ 62

WRITING MEDICAL ARTICLES

BY JAN ROADARMEL LEDFORD

GOOD NEWS, WRITERS! THERE'S A TOPIC THAT'S ALWAYS HOT. EVERY-one wants to read about it. It's time-honored, yet on the leading edge of technology. It's medicine!

The surprising news is that you don't need a medical degree to write many types of medical articles. Naturally, it helps to be working in the medical field in some capacity. But any writer who is interested enough to do careful research can turn out good, solid articles on medical topics. Your best investments are a medical terminology class at your local vocational-technical school, an illustrated medical dictionary, a drug reference book, and a basic text on medicine, such as *The Merck Manual.*

The two cardinal rules for writing medical articles are the same for any type of writing: Know your audience and know your target publication. There are basically two types of audiences: the lay and the professional. The markets, however, are vast.

Writing for the lay audience

The usual purpose of lay-oriented medical writing is to inform. Answering questions is what this type of material is all about. To organize your thinking, ask yourself: What does the patient (reader) need/want to know? What do care-givers want the patient to know? What action do we want the reader to take?

With answers in hand, you can formulate an outline that includes an introduction (scenarios and statistics work very well here), a definition of the problem, cause(s) of the problem, treatment options, and the expected outcome. This outline will fit almost any medical condition that you care to write about. Depending on your slant, you may want to concentrate more on one area than another. For example, an exposé on the side effects of a specific treatment would dwell more heavily on the "expected outcome."

As always, you must write on a level appropriate for your audience. If you are approaching a newspaper, you will use a simpler vocabulary and shorter sentences than when writing for a trade journal. In any case, be sure to define medical terms or replace them with common lay terms. (For example, say "gum" instead of "gingiva.") An anatomical drawing is often helpful in introducing terms and in orienting your readers.

While you do not need medical credentials to write for the average reader, you may need someone with medical credentials to add credibility to your article. This might be accomplished by interviewing, then quoting, a person in the field. Or, you might consider writing as a coauthor or ghost author for a medical professional. You know the writer's admonition to "write what you know." Your reader (and editor) is going to ask, "*How* do you know?" Associating your work with someone who has medical credentials will answer that question.

If you understand medical terms and statistics, you can search through medical journals and "translate" technical research into lay-oriented articles. Find someone (well-known, if possible) who has a stake in the research to add human drama and interest to your story. Be sure to get your numbers right. Case studies in such journals make for interesting reading as well. (Wouldn't your readers be fascinated to learn about a procedure in which a surgeon used a piece of donor sclera [white of the eye] as a framework on which to rebuild someone's external *ear?*)

Your local newspaper and health magazines are not the only markets for your lay-oriented medical articles. Many general-interest magazines have a health-related column or use medical information. Parenting magazines are a good market because parents are extremely concerned about their children's health. Scientific magazines are interested in new technology. There are support groups or foundations for many diseases, widening your market to newsletters. Or, you could turn your article into a brochure and offer the copy to physicians or interested organizations. The American Academy of Ophthalmology, for example, has patient education brochures on all types of eye disorders. (Note: this might be a one-time sale or a work-for-hire situation.)

Depending on your topic, you may want to market the piece to appropriate non-medical trade journals. Suppose you've written a great article on carpal tunnel syndrome (CTS). Who would be interested? Any professional whose work involves the wrist motion that aggravates the problem: athletes, mechanics, typists. The same goes for any other type of medical condition. Ask yourself: Who is affected by this condition? Every answer identifies a potential market.

Writing for medical professionals

The same approach can be used to write for professional medical trade journals. Before you start, consider the education level of your audience, and adjust your language and terminology appropriately. For example, a medical assistant may be trained at a vocational school or on the job. A physician's assistant has at least a four-year college degree. You must do meticulous research when writing for medical professionals, regardless of their education level. If you say something wrong, they'll know it!

Suggesting that you start out by writing for medical professionals with "lower" levels of credentials is like suggesting that a fiction writer start out by writing for children. Writing for children is *not* easier: It's different. But it *is* true that the higher the level of medical professional that you're writing for, the greater your need for medical credentials personally, or for an association with someone who has the credentials. • This "associate" may agree to pay you for your work if his or her name is given as the primary or sole author. However, your payment will probably come in the form of copies. It is considered an obligation and a privilege to share medical knowledge with your colleagues; hence, monetary reimbursements are not usually offered.

The trades, however, may offer regular pay or an honorarium. And don't limit your market or your slant. You might sell your article on carpal tunnel syndrome to *RDH* (a trade journal for dental hygienists), but by changing your slant a little, you might place the piece in the *Professional Medical Assistant* (a journal of the American Association of Medical Assistants). *PMA* has a feature called "The Two-Minute Clinic" and might be interested in an informational article that would help readers learn more about CTS.

If you move into writing for regular medical journals, you'll receive one of a writer's greatest rewards: editorial feedback. In journals that select articles by peer review, the reviewer is required to give the reason(s) that an article is rejected. What a wonderful way to learn the craft! A physician-client hired me to write an article on a unique surgical procedure he'd used. I told him from the outset that because the technique was controversial, we might have trouble placing it. He wanted me to go ahead, so I wrote the piece and then made a list of medical journals that published related surgical cases. I sent the article to the first (and most prestigious) journal on the list. As I feared, the article came back. But with it came the reviewer's comments and suggestions I used to make the article stronger and sent it to journal Number Two. This journal also rejected it . . . but also sent comments, which I again utilized. Journal Number Three published the twice-improved piece. Not only was the physician happy, but I had learned and grown as a writer. This type of feedback doesn't often come in fiction writing. Or in most types of nonfiction writing, for that matter.

Additional research sources

Besides using a good medical dictionary and general medical text as part of your research, don't overlook your local physicians and other health care workers as references. Not only can you interview them, but you also may be able to use their extensive personal libraries. In addition, you can ask them for patient education brochures. Virtually every practice in all branches of medicine uses handouts to inform their patients.

Earlier I mentioned organizations that deal exclusively with certain diseases and conditions. Check your local library's reference shelf for the *Encyclopedia of Organizations* published by Gale Research, Inc. Not only are these organizations good potential markets, but they can also supply a wealth of information. Some of these organizations run local support groups. These, in turn, may be able to put you in touch with individuals who are experts on the condition or who actually have the disorder themselves.

The National Library of Medicine offers on-line information via MedLine. Using appropriate key words, you can search the NLM computer banks for journal articles related to your topic. You must specify if you want to search back prior to the last several years. But in medical writing, you usually won't want to use a reference over five years old, anyway, unless you are doing a historical piece. The program can retrieve the abstracts for you. Often the abstract alone gives enough information for a lay-oriented article. Or, you can order the full article on-line or through your library. The reference list at the end of any medical article may supply further resources to check into.

Medical writing is challenging and extremely rewarding. You have the potential to reassure, to encourage, and to offer hope through your words. For more information about this branch of writing, contact the American Medical Writers Association, 9650 Rockville Pike, Bethesda, MD 20814–3998.

❏ 63

BECOMING A BIOGRAPHER

BY WILLIAM SCHOELL

TO BECOME A BIOGRAPHER, YOU MUST FIRST BE INTRIGUED BY OTHER people's lives. You must have a good understanding of human nature and a willingness to ask the tough questions, both of yourself, your subject, and the people who knew him or her. You must understand the difference between biography and memoir, and know the right approach to take to your biography depending on the subject and related factors.

Of course, first, you must choose your subject. An important basic factor is your enthusiasm level; there's nothing worse than spending months or years writing about somebody you have no deep interest in. Is there a particular historical figure or a contemporary celebrity whose life or work you admire, whose background you'd like to explore? If you find yourself wondering what kind of childhood this person had, what kind of relationship he or she had with his spouses and children and coworkers, what went on behind the scenes, then it's a good bet other people have the same curiosity. Then finding the answers to your questions will not be a chore to you, but rather a welcome revelation.

Next, you must decide if you are truly the right person to write this biography. A genuine interest in the subject and writing talent are, of course, prerequisites and the ones that matter the most. But today's publishers also like their authors to have some background related to the subject's, or even a vague connection. (Keep in mind that if by any chance you knew your subject personally or had some kind of relationship with him or her, you'll be writing what might more appropriately be called a *memoir,* that is, your personal recollections of the subject. This is the difference between a straight biography, of, say, Tennessee Williams by an author who may or may not ever have met him, and a book on the playwright written by his brother or a close friend who knew him well.)

You do not need to know or have known your subject personally to write a good biography about him. However, if you want to write about a filmmaker, an actor, or a director, it would be helpful to have written a few film reviews or filmmaker profiles, even if only for a local paper. If your subject is a composer, singer, or conductor, then some background in music will indicate you will have a better understanding than the rest of us as to what drives this person. If you've written an interview or an article about one of today's celebrities, it will certainly help sell a biography of him.

When you've decided on your subject, the next step is to think seriously about the subject's marketability. If the person is very obscure, it might be better to try first to sell a magazine article rather than a book. Then again, perhaps this person's obscurity is entirely undeserved. Perhaps there is something "special" about this person that gives him or her historical validity and therefore contemporary interest. For instance, the bestseller lists in recent years have featured biographies of women who were feminists long before the word was in fashion, and African-Americans whose contribution to society had never before been fully explored. There have also been successful biographies published about people whose sole claim to fame is the people they knew and worked with.

If you're uncertain how publishers might react to your subject, test the waters by querying a magazine or two. A published piece enclosed with your book proposal will show the editor that others thought your subject would be interesting to a mass audience. Your proposal should make clear that there's much more to say about the person, that there's plenty of room to develop things you only mentioned in the article.

Suppose you have a strong interest in chronicling someone's life, but there really is no special "hook" on which to hang your proposal. The person was not ahead of his time in any particular way; she does not fit neatly into any modern trends. Query a smaller firm or publisher, one less concerned with the bottom line. Trade publishers—that is, publishers whose books are sold in bookstores—are understandably concerned with sales potential, and frankly, a biography of an obscure person who did not do anything *very* significant, will not get past the sales representative who sits in at all editorial board meetings.

Even a small press, however, will want subjects who have done *something* significant: Your Uncle Joe may have been a marvelous character, but if he's never painted, written, composed, made a film, or left some kind of unique achievement behind, there probably isn't a book in him.

Also remember that most small firms pay tiny advances if they pay any at all, so if you need to take a leave of absence from your job to do research for your biography, you might, regrettably, have to move on to a more commercial subject.

As for historical subjects, publishers want a fresh approach to major figures, books that reveal, rather than rehash. If your subject is not internationally famous, you must explain why he is important and what his contribution was, and especially, *why* people might be interested in reading about him. When it comes to modern-day celebrities, there is one basic rule of thumb. Are people talking about him or her? There's little point in trying to market to a major trade publisher a biography of a film or rock star who hasn't worked or been in the public eye (or gossip columns) in years—unless he or she has reached cult status like Elvis or Marilyn.

After choosing your subject, you have to decide on the tone and style of your book. Largely, these will be set by the subject's achievement: A book on major figures like Beethoven, or Winston Churchill, whose life played out across an international arena in a fascinating, frenetic time period, will require a very serious, profound approach. On the other hand, books on Brad Pitt, Leonardo DiCaprio, or the Spice Girls, whose accomplishments and fame are recent and don't have a large body of work, and whose fans are primarily teenagers, should be comparatively light and breezy. An artist like Laurence Olivier would require an in-depth approach; a movie star like Marilyn Monroe with her much narrower range should get a much lighter treatment. However, because Monroe was involved with world-famous men (and because recent biographers have created such a "mystery" about her death), some biographers feel an intense approach to her life is the only way to go. Look at your subject with an objective eye and then decide on the appropriate tone and style. Sometimes it's not the subject but the events she was embroiled in and the people she knew that determine what kind of book you should write.

Your proposal should consist of an introduction mentioning the highlights of your subject's life, the things that make him memorable, and any fresh theories you have regarding his life and work. The rest should be a chapter-by-chapter outline showing that you have knowledge of his life and times and can effectively organize the material. If you've never published a book before, the publisher or agent will probably want to see a sample chapter or two. These do not necessarily have to be the first two chapters but could be a part of your subject's life or career that particularly intrigues you and information that you have special access to and develop in later chapters.

By this time, you should have read everything you could find on your subject. As you read, make a note of published "facts" that bother you or seem inconsistent. Biographers often make conjectures about their subjects that may or may not be supported by facts. Make a list of questions about your subject that you'll want to answer in your book. Is this person's public reputation (good or bad) deserved? What areas of her life and work have never been adequately explored? In addition to books and magazines available in the public library, remember that there may be collections in special libraries or museums—personal letters, private papers, notes and diaries—that relate to your subject.

When you've exhausted the books and files in the library, make a list of every living person (or their offspring) who might have known or worked with your subject. Famous people can often be contacted through professional organizations like Actors Equity, the Screen Actors Guild, the Authors Guild, and Mystery Writers of America; others may be in the phone book or can be reached via their employers or universities. Sometimes the best anecdotes and information come not from other big names, who may have reasons for putting a "spin" on their memories, but from ordinary people who have crossed paths with your subject in interesting ways. Each person you speak to may be able to provide the names and phone numbers of others who knew or have some information about your subject.

If the person you're writing about has already been the subject of several biographies, or one good recent one, you might want to consider a different, non-chronological approach. When I did my book on Al Pacino, I found that a pretty comprehensive biography about him had already been published. I decided to have a biographical section up front in my book and then to concentrate on the actor's career—one chapter for each film—with a final section on his stage work. In this way, I was able to analyze his films and acting style more intensely than would have been possible in a regular biography. When several Steven Spielberg adult biographies were published just as I was putting together a proposal for one, I decided to target mine for the young adult market. Sometimes it's a good idea to expand upon or refocus your original plan, as my coauthor and I did when we found that several Frank Sinatra books were coming out at once. We decided, therefore, to do a book on the entire Rat Pack—Sinatra, Dean Martin, Sammy Davis, Jr., Peter Lawford, Joey Bishop—instead.

To organize your material better, use file folders, one for each chapter, that will include. photocopies, tear sheets, phone numbers, transcripts, and a list of other material too large to fit in the folder—books, videos, audio cassettes—that you will need to refer to when you do the writing. Give yourself at least several months to complete your research (although you can work on certain chapters as you gather the material). Keep in mind that busy people—whether it's the director of a Rat Pack movie or a college professor who wrote a thesis on a classical composer—can take months to answer your letters or return your phone calls.

Whether your book winds up in the bookstore or on the library shelf, you'll have the satisfaction of knowing that as a biographer you've helped illuminate the lives and careers of people that the world should know more about.

❑ 64

FROM FOOD PROCESSOR TO WORD PROCESSOR

BY SUSAN KELLY

I BEGAN WRITING ABOUT FOOD FOR TWO REASONS: FIRST, I LIKE TO cook as much as I like to eat; second, I wanted a break from what I usually write about, which is crime. (Let me note here that many mystery authors manage to combine corpses and cuisine, à la Katherine Hall Page and Robert B. Parker. For myself, I'd just as soon keep the two separate.)

The first thing I noticed when I began researching the field is the enormous editorial appetite (first awful but irresistible pun) for articles about food and cooking. I was staggered by the number of journals devoted to the culinary arts. On my local grocery store's magazine rack, which is by no means either huge or comprehensive, I counted three publications devoted just to Italian cuisine. I couldn't begin to count the other special interest journals: vegetarian, light, country, ethnic, heart-safe, etc., or the large number of general magazines that publish articles on food.

Newspapers, daily or weekly, big city or small town, print vast numbers of articles on food and cooking. (The larger papers devote whole sections to the subject.) Most newspapers will consider free-lance work. Rates vary widely. You may not get paid much—or indeed anything by a very small publication—but you will have garnered a byline and a clip to add to your store of credentials.

The market for articles on food is a thriving one. And why not? Aside from sex and death, I can't think of a greater human interest subject than food.

Here is my own personal recipe for writing about food and cooking, one that I have checked in my test kitchen. The ingredients are given in order of assembly, but feel free to rearrange them or make substitutions—as any innovative cook would do.

302

1. **Go with your particular interest and expertise.** This is especially important for the beginner. After you've established yourself, you can branch out into other areas. But for the time being, if you have the world's best recipe for gefilte fish, or *caldo verde,* or cassoulet, or pot roast, or linguine with clam sauce, or if your grandmother was the best German cook in recent history, the world wants to hear about it.

2. **Decide the focus of your piece and then pare (second awful but irresistible pun) that down as much as possible.** It's no good trying to dash off a 2,000-word piece on "Italian Food." There are thousands of *books* on this subject already, and many others to come. Editors need articles with narrowly focused topics and with fresh slants.

To provide focus as well as originality, it helps to think in terms of categories. The following lists are by no means all-inclusive, but may be extensive enough to inspire you to create your own:

Ethnic: Thai, French, Italian, Jewish, Polish, Irish, Creole, African, Portuguese, Caribbean, Mexican, Swedish, Chinese

Provincial/Regional: Southern, New England, Southwestern, Pacific Rim, Tuscan, Provençal, Mediterranean, Iberian, Cantonese

Holiday: Thanksgiving, Passover, Easter, Christmas, Asian New Year, Chanukah, Kwanzaa

Seasonal: spring, summer, fall, winter (or by month)

Occasional: wedding, birthday, anniversary, graduation, bar mitzvah/bas mitzvah, christening, bridal or baby shower, cocktail party

Meal Type: breakfast, brunch, lunch, tea, dinner, late supper

Health/Vegetarian: Low fat/low cholesterol, low salt, low sugar or sugar-free, meatless, non-dairy

Food Types: appetizers, soups, main courses, salads, desserts

Clearly, you don't have to consider all those categories. A choice of three is a good start. To illustrate my point: If you want to write about Italian cooking, why not do a piece on an Italian Christmas Eve dinner? Or, since the traditional Italian Christmas Eve dinner involves twelve fish dishes, refine the topic further by considering a fourth category, that of the food group. If your interest—or expertise—is Jewish cooking, think of writing an article about a seder dinner. There you have ethnicity, holiday, and meal type established for you. Once your imagination starts rolling, the possibilities are endless. A vegetarian Thai summer luncheon; a Scottish brunch for New Year's Day; a Provençal birthday picnic for two; a low-fat Mexican dinner.

3. **Write *articles* about food and cooking, not recipe files.** Your articles should offer helpful practical information beyond lists of ingredients and cooking times. Editors and their readers want serving suggestions, menu plans, and whatever other instruction and guidance you can offer. Tips about table decoration are always welcome, as are suggestions about wine appropriate to the food.

4. **Articles about food and cooking benefit from background.** In addition to giving instructions, include anecdotes. These can be personal— how *you* became interested in cooking such and such; first time you cooked it; your guests' reactions to it.

If you have no personal anecdotes, historical and cultural ones will do fine. If you are writing about veal Marengo, for instance, you might want to mention that the dish was invented to celebrate Napoleon's victory over Austria in the Italian town of Marengo. If you are writing about champagne, you might recount the legend that the bowl-shaped champagne glass (from which, incidentally, one should never drink) was formed from the mold of the breast of the mistress of the French king. Or that *puttanesca* sauce is alleged to have been the invention of Italian prostitutes seeking to whip up a quick snack for their clients. Such stories add real spice (third awful but irresistible pun) to a piece.

5. **Bear in mind that food and travel overlap.** Think of the Korean produce markets of New York. And the Polish sausage-makers of the Pioneer Valley in Massachusetts. Or the chowder specialists of coastal Maine. Or the Italian immigrant fishermen of San Francisco, who invented *cioppino*. Readers enjoy local color along with a recipe.

6. **Always get exact quantities of ingredients for recipes—and then test them yourself.** Make sure the instructions you give your readers are as clear and exact as possible. Be precise—even though anyone

who cooks knows that exact times and measurements are absolutely essential only in certain kinds of baking. I suppose everyone's heard the story about the published recipe that called for a can of condensed milk to be placed in a crockpot along with the rest of the ingredients. Now, common sense would dictate that one would *pour* the condensed milk from the can *into* the crockpot. Unfortunately, some readers, not explicitly *told* to do so, *didn't*. The results of that omission were . . . explosive!

If you offer recipes with variations or substitutions for ingredients, be sure to check out all those as well. Fat-free unflavored yogurt seems like a perfectly acceptable replacement for sour cream, and many times it is. In other cases—ugh. You can't predict with assurance. Don't take someone else's word. Perform your own taste-test.

7. **If you are writing about a professional chef, be sure to interview him or her.** This means going beyond accumulating the basic biographical and career data. Get permission to watch the chef in action. Request (no, insist on) written copies of any recipes the chef is willing to share. Ask for the chef's own personal serving and wine suggestions. Get the menu, whether the chef is an independent caterer or the employee/owner of a restaurant, so you can refer to it while you write. Talk to the chef's colleagues and competitors.

A real bonus of a thorough interview is that you will probably be invited to sample the chef's art.

8. **Time your article appropriately.** This is of special importance to a free lancer. Allow a lead time of a month for a small newspaper, two months for bigger ones, and up to a year for magazines. Publishers plan each issue well in advance for a number of reasons—the tightness of printing schedules is the foremost. No publisher is willing to incur the expense involved to disrupt the deadlines except for a drastic reason. Don't submit an article on fourteenth-century English Valentine's Day treats to a magazine in December and expect to see it in print in February. A year from that February is more like it.

9. **Finally, read at least a year's back issues of the magazine you're interested in querying about an article idea.** This will give you a clear sense of what particular publications seek and the tone and style in which your article should be written.

Some magazines look for pieces with a light or humorous touch. Others demand a more serious, almost scientific, approach. Still others want a definite historical, cultural, regional, or social orientation. Also, bear in mind a magazine's audience. A journal whose typical reader is a college graduate, a resident of an upscale city neighborhood or affluent suburb, and a professional earning in excess of $150,000 a year will not be interested in an article on the manifold culinary uses of Fritos.

Do not worry if the publication you've targeted for your article on "low-fat pasta salads for an informal June wedding" published a similar-sounding piece five years ago. Yours, because it's yours, will be different. And in any case, such ideas are always recycled.

□ 65

MILITARY MONEY:
CASHING IN ON OLD WAR STORIES

BY LANCE Q. ZEDRIC

IF YOU'VE ALWAYS WANTED TO WRITE FOR MILITARY MAGAZINES, BUT never considered yourself an expert, relax—you don't have to be an expert or even a veteran to break into this well-paying free-lance market. It's easier than you think, and often the best material can be found in an old history book or even right next door.

There are plenty of topics bivouacked out there. All you have to do is ask. Everyone knows a family member, friend or neighbor who served in the military. And they all have an old war story to tell. The kind old man next door might have been a celebrated war hero or a Medal of Honor winner! Your grandfather, father, aunt or uncle might have served aboard a ship with Admiral Nimitz, eaten Christmas dinner with General Patton, or participated in a historic event. Millions of stories are waiting to be told.

After you've blown the dust off *U.S. History 101,* turn to the sections on World War I, World War II, Korea, the Vietnam War, and even the more recent military ventures, and you will find accounts of important battles, commanders, or military events that, with a little research and a fresh angle, will provide ideal material for an interesting article.

Recon the market. Research military publications, and become familiar with their readership. A sound battle plan will prevent having your article become a rejection slip casualty.

The military market ranges from general to specific. For example, *VFW Magazine* (Veterans of Foreign Wars) and *American Legion Magazine* have readerships of more than two million veterans from every branch of the military. They publish various articles on training, weaponry, tactics, veterans legislation, active and former units, military personalities and nostalgia. Publications with such large readerships prefer articles that appeal to as many of their readers as possible.

They focus on events involving large military units, such as Army and Marine divisions, Navy fleets, and Air Force Squadrons. Smaller publications, on the other hand, cater to more defined audiences. *Behind The Lines: The Journal of U.S. Special Operations,* specializes in articles on elite U.S. units, such as the Green Berets and Navy SEALs; others focus on respective branches of the military. *Army Magazine* appeals to Army veterans; *All Hands* and *Navy Times* to the Navy; and *Air Force Times* to the Air Force. Magazines like *Civil War Illustrated, World War II* and *Vietnam,* among others, appeal to enthusiasts of a particular war.

Editors are always on the lookout for articles offering new insights on prominent military leaders and for anniversary articles commemorating notable battles and events. But most publications prefer articles on major anniversaries, such as the fifth, tenth, twenty-fifth, fiftieth, and one-hundredth.

But military publications aren't limited to anniversary themes. Anything to do with the home front is also desirable. Whether it's an article on industrial war production, sending care packages to a family member overseas, or collecting "sweetheart pins," the possibilities are endless. Read past issues and look for a theme.

It will save time and effort to consult a calendar. Since most magazines require at least four months' lead time, allow ample time to query, research, and write an article. If you're writing a 50th-anniversary article on the armistice during the Korean War, which occurred in June 1953, send your query or article to the editor by February 2003.

But be careful. War recollections can be a professional minefield. Here are a couple of tips to remember when interviewing a war veteran for an article:

Never write a military article based solely on a personal recollection. As years pass, war stories tend to be exaggerated and important details omitted. Whether intentional or not, veterans often "embellish" their experiences and recollections. What might have been a five-minute skirmish with a squad of enemy troops armed with pistols in 1944, may, more than fifty years later, become a bloody, year-long siege against two divisions of crack troops armed with automatic rifles! So, beware. Ask the veteran you're interviewing for specific times, dates, locations, books, articles, documents, and for the name of anyone who could "help verify" the account.

Use tact when interviewing a veteran. War is often the most traumatic event in a person's life, and it can be an ongoing source of great
pain. Don't begin an interview with "how many people did you kill?"
or "tell me what it's like to kill somebody." Insensitivity will guarantee
failure. Ease into the interview, and allow the person time to relax and
learn more about you. For example, ask an open question, such as
"tell me what you were doing before you left for military service." As
your subjects relax, ask specific questions. But steer clear of potentially sensitive questions until a solid rapport is established. Always
put the veteran's feelings first.

If you want to research a specific military unit, but can't find anyone
who served in it, don't give up. Most units have a veterans' association
and are listed with the Office of the Chief of Military History in Washington, D.C. Another approach is to consult reunion announcements
listed in military magazines; these usually provide a phone number to
call for information. Explain that you are researching an article on
their unit, and chances are a membership roster will be in the mail.

When you need detailed accounts of a particular unit, government
institutions are the best source. The National Archives at Suitland,
Maryland, contains enough information for the most ambitious military
article. The United States Military History Institute at Carlisle Bar-
racks, Pennsylvania, is an outstanding repository for unit histories and
contains the personal papers of some of the country's most outstanding
military figures. Service academy libraries at West Point, Annapolis,
and Colorado Springs, along with military post libraries across the
nation, also have extensive unit histories and rare documents. But call
first and obtain clearance. Admittance is not guaranteed.

Good photographs can sell an article. In many cases, military photographs are easy to obtain. Most veterans have a few snapshots and
will eagerly show them or lend them to you to be copied. With luck, a
rare one-of-a-kind photo might turn a reluctant would-be editor into an
eager, all-too-happy-to-write-you-a-check editor!

Photographs can also be purchased from several government
sources. The Still Photo Branch of the National Archives in College
Park, Maryland, is one. It will research its photo files and provide a
partial listing on three topics. You then select a commercial contractor
from a list to produce the photographs.

Other government sources in the Washington, D.C., area maintain extensive photo files and offer similar services. The Department of Defense Still Media Records Center provides Army, Navy, Air Force, and Marine Corps photographs from 1954 to the present. The Smithsonian's National Air and Space Museum has Air Force photographs prior to 1954. Coast Guard photographs are available through the Commandant at Coast Guard Headquarters.

If time is short, consult the ad sections of military magazines. Military photo catalogues are available from a number of private suppliers. The photos might cost more, but they will arrive much faster than if they were ordered from Uncle Sam. And an 8 x 10 B&W photo may sell a $500 article.

After concluding your research and obtaining photographs, it's time to write. Here are a few more helpful tips:

1. Write tight and factually. The military audience is knowledgeable and will not be won over with flowery prose or fluffy writing. They appreciate facts and hate filler. Most readers are veterans and know how to cut through fat to get to the point.

2. Use quotes from participants when possible. Put the reader in a muddy foxhole alongside a bedraggled infantryman. Put him or her in the cockpit of a bullet-ridden F-14 screaming toward a Soviet MIG at mach 1 with guns blazing! Let the reader take part in the action.

3. Extol duty, honor and country. Patriotism sells, especially with readers of military magazines. Don't be afraid to wave the flag responsibly.

Whether you write about an elite unit fighting its way out from behind enemy lines against insurmountable odds, recount the monumental invasion of Normandy, or retell the sad story of a soldier's loneliness far from home, if you do your homework and follow a few simple rules, you should be well on your way to breaking into this lucrative market. Salute!

□ 66

WHEN YOU WRITE A PERSONAL EXPERIENCE ARTICLE

BY JUDY BODMER

SOMETHING HAS HAPPENED TO YOU AND YOU WANT TO WRITE ABOUT it. Does that mean it's marketable? Not necessarily. Many people who take my creative writing class do so because they've been through a divorce, had a child die, experienced a life-threatening illness, or have come to a place in their lives at which they want to pass on what they've learned to another generation and would like to write about their experiences.

Some of them get published. Others don't. Those who do have learned the basic principles of writing a marketable personal experience article: They slant their idea to a specific audience, choose one of the three types of articles that will tell their story best, use all four of the basic elements of a personal experience article, and target the right market. The secret to getting a personal experience article published is to use your experience as a stepping-stone to help others who have faced similar situations. Writing about a tragic event, such as the death of a child, probably won't sell until the writer understands what he or she learned while going through the experience. A couple of angles one could use are: 1) how to cope with the death of a child or 2) how to help a friend grieve.

The experience you write about doesn't have to be tragic. It can be as simple as baking cookies with your grandchildren, watching your son play baseball, or writing thank-you notes. It may take you quite a while to process and find the right slant. Keep asking yourself, what did I learn that will help someone else? When you've finally found the message in your experience, describe it in one sentence or phrase; it will keep your article on track. You won't be tempted to go off on interesting but irrelevant sidetracks that may have really happened but have nothing to do with the theme. Your phrase should read something like this:

- Six steps that helped me forgive.
- Ways to cope with an empty nest.
- How to handle stress.

Don't skimp on taking this step. One of the main reasons articles are rejected is that they aren't focused.

THREE KINDS OF PERSONAL EXPERIENCE ARTICLES

Once you know the theme, you are ready to choose the type of article you want to write. Basically there are three: *straight narration, partial frame,* and *full frame.*

Straight narration

This type of article reads like a short story: It has a beginning, a middle, and an end. You set scenes, use dialogue, and action. As in a good short story, the tension should mount until it is resolved. The message woven throughout the piece is driven home with a powerful ending. The straight narration approach is best used to describe a dramatic event: a daring rescue off a mountaintop; surviving an airplane crash; or having a baby in the middle of a snowstorm. This is where you should let your personality and the personality of the people involved shine through. Use strong nouns and active verbs. Show the action. Don't just say you and your husband had a fight, show it.

Partial frame

This type of article is used most frequently. It usually opens with an anecdote and then makes a transition into the body of the article. For example, a taxi driver picks up a fare in New York City. In the body of the article you show how that fateful day changed the taxi driver's life forever. Or you open with a description of taking your three young children grocery shopping. The body of the article then discusses the simple trick you learned that helped turn a sometimes frustrating chore into a game your children all love.

Full frame

Here you first set a scene of your article using description, dialogue, and action. You then move into the body and list the points you plan to cover; for instance, the five things your mother never told you about sex. Each point is then expanded, sometimes quoting experts, statistics, or anecdotes. In the end, you shift back to the opening scene to wrap up your discussion.

An article I wrote for a parenting magazine on why I watch my son play baseball opens as I sit in the stands. I describe being cold, burning my mouth on hot coffee, and seeing my son strike out. In the body of the article I discuss the reasons parents put themselves through this often painful experience. For the ending, I returned to my opening scene describing my son asking for money to buy a hamburger and the coach coming up and talking to me. Through action and dialogue I answer the question that I presented in my opening.

THE FOUR ELEMENTS OF
A PERSONAL EXPERIENCE ARTICLE

Before you begin to write, make a rough outline using the following four elements of a personal experience article.

1. *The opening.* Choose an aspect of your story that will catch the reader's attention. It can be an anecdote, a quotation, an intriguing situation or a question that must be answered. One of my articles opened with an anecdote about a minister who counseled a couple. The wife wanted to leave her husband because she couldn't take the black book any more. The black book turned out to be a list that the husband was keeping of everything she'd done wrong since the day they married.

2. *The transition.* Transition statements that are pretty straightforward and sound almost trite tell the reader where you are going.

In "Helping Friends Who Grieve," which appeared in *Reader's Digest,* Lois Duncan describes the fatal shooting of her daughter. After opening with the tragic event, she uses the following transition statement: "Here is some advice I wish I'd been given when heartbreak was a stranger." The transition for my black book article was, "If you are keeping a similar list, what I learned may help you."

Writing a good transition statement is probably the most important step in writing personal experience articles. If you've processed your theme, it should be easy to write. It will also help you focus your article to a specific audience.

3. *The body.* In the body, you discuss what you learned from your

experience. You can use bullets, numbers, headings (remember readers and editors love white space), or just develop the idea in narrative form. Each point can be enhanced with more details, examples from other people, quotes from experts, statistics, or another example from your life. In my black book article, I talked about the steps needed to achieve forgiveness.

4. *The ending*. In the end, drive home your message. Here you can summarize the points you've made, quote an expert or someone famous, challenge your reader, or project the future. Whenever I'm stuck, I look back at my opening. Is there some element there that you can draw on to help you wrap up your article? In the transition statement of my baseball article, I asked, "Why do I do this?" For the ending I answer with the question, "Where else can I watch my son grow into a man?"

THE MARKET

Many magazines are looking for personal experience pieces; the trick is to match your theme with the right magazine. Once you've found a promising market, study a couple of issues. (The library is a good source for periodicals, or write for a sample copy.) Look at the cover, the table of contents, and the ads. Read the articles. Try to get a feel for the reader.

An author I know sold an article on her Hawaiian camping trip to the *Seattle Times* and then rewrote her camping experience from a different angle and sold it to *Seattle's Child*. One of my students wrote a piece about the ways she has made her long commute fun. She sold it to a newspaper in Seattle, which has a terrible traffic problem. Another young author sold a piece to *Seventeen* about how to make the most of being grounded—something she had experienced a lot of growing up.

Timeliness is also a factor. Seasonal material should be submitted six to twelve months ahead of the holiday or special celebration. (Check your market list for individual magazine requirements.) During the Christmas season, collect ideas and write about them while you're still under the influence of the season. Then starting in January send them out. If the idea hasn't sold by June, put it away, rework it if necessary, and try again the following year.

Magazines receive lots of submissions for the major holidays, but they are constantly looking for articles about some of the lesser known ones such as Arbor Day, St. Patrick's Day, or Martin Luther King's Birthday. They want stories about swimming for summer, skiing in winter. My baseball article was set in May and was just right for the next Mother's Day.

After choosing a market, you will save time by querying magazines to see if they'd be interested in your idea. Most magazines reply to queries within two weeks to a month. (Again, check your market lists. Some magazines want to see only the completed article.)

Once you receive a positive response to your query, try to picture a typical reader sitting across from you at lunch and write to him or her. This will help give your reader a truly personal experience.

With planning and persistence, personal experience articles can be a good way to break into publishing. They take little research, are in great demand, and pay anywhere from $15 to $2,000. Another benefit of these articles: There's nothing more rewarding than touching someone's heart.

❑ 67

SNOOPING IN THE PAST: WRITING HISTORICAL BIOGRAPHIES

BY LAURIE WINN CARLSON

THE PAST FEW YEARS HAVE SEEN BIOGRAPHIES OF PEOPLE FROM THE past propelled onto bestseller lists across the country: *Undaunted Courage,* Stephen Ambrose's biography of Meriwether Lewis; *Unredeemed Captive,* by John Demos, the story of Eunice Williams and the French and Indian War; *No Ordinary Time,* the story of Franklin and Eleanor Roosevelt by Doris Kearns Goodwin, and several biographies of Jane Austen, to name only a few.

The spectacular sales of historical biographies prove that the public wants stories about heroes and heroines, whether their lives involved statesmanship, exploration, or writing literature. People read biographies for many of the same reasons they read novels: to be entertained, to be informed, to be comforted or inspired, to identify with successful people, to live somebody else's life for a while. There's every reason to write historical biographies if you like historical research, enjoy learning about people, and can master the elements of good storytelling.

How does a writer go about retelling the life of a historical person in a way that grabs first an editor, then the reader? Even the most intriguing person's life can be incredibly boring unless presented with creativity and skill. Writing historical biographies requires a combination of techniques from nonfiction and fiction writing, and like the novelist, the first decision the biographer makes is, "Whose story can I tell?" Just like creating a main character in a novel, choosing the subjects for biographies is all-important. Who they are, the times they lived in, and the choices they made are what keeps the narrative going.

The main character

The person you choose to write about must be someone with whom readers will want to identify. That doesn't mean they have to be saints—readers like to read about "bad guys," too, and biographies of history's villains can make compelling reading. Just be careful to select someone whose life and character pique your interest. I decided to write about women missionaries in the West because they were different from our commonly held perceptions—they were feminists rather than conventional nineteenth-century wives and mothers—and that makes their story intriguing and interesting to today's readers.

Avoid stereotypes: They are too boring. Challenge your preconceptions, search for people who tried to break the mold society had created for them, who strived to do something different and worthwhile, even if they made poor decisions or met with failure. Similar to a protagonist in a novel, good biographies follow the "hero's journey." Writers need to examine a person's life, the hurdles and obstructions he or she met, and how that person overcame them. If he or she failed miserably, perhaps that failure can be understood better or differently from today's perspective.

Like the novelist, as a biographer you want to reveal a person's character bit by bit, showing rather than telling. Using the subject's own writings (diaries, letters) as well as what others wrote or said about the person can be very revealing, but, of course, other people's opinions can be biased, based on personal resentments or jealousies. How you interpret the facts determines whether or not your biography will have true depth and dimension. You'll want to reveal details about your subject's life throughout your book, looking for ways to stir readers' emotions by creating drama and tension, even some suspense, to propel them forward.

Setting

For historical biographies, time and place are extremely important to the picture of the subject's life. What best-selling biographies have in common is that they examine lives of people who lived in periods of turmoil and action, and are carefully researched and scrupulously accurate. In addition, they are written in a lively narrative style that engages and holds readers' interest.

As you choose the person to write about, look at the geographic setting and the time period and social class in which they lived. Time and place achieve a symbolic importance in a biography, as they do in a novel. In biographies, the setting is another character of sorts; it provides hurdles the protagonist must overcome. An impoverished childhood, geographic isolation, ramifications of social class—these all become part of the setting in a biography. When writing about a woman of the early nineteenth century, it makes a great deal of difference whether she lived in a settled New England village or on the Ohio frontier. Where and when she lived is part of her life's story.

When you're casting about for a particular subject for your biography, look for people who lived in exciting times. That will make the entire story much more interesting and provide conflicts outside the person's inner character.

Other characters

Biographies, like novels, have antagonists or villains. Your subject may be young, idealistic, duty-bound; the "bad guys" can be treacherous weather, distance, rugged terrain, armed and dangerous dissidents, time running out, lack of funds, or simply the dark side of human nature. You will also need to identify and include people who helped the protagonist: lovers, mentors, siblings, rescuers, friends, or confidants. Adding these elements will enrich the biography—you will not simply be retelling chronological events in a dead person's life—and will eventually give the biography a sort of climactic resolution.

When you choose a suitable subject to write about, be careful not to choose someone you're in love with—and be sure not to fall in love with the subject as you write. Be alert for evidence of character failings in even the most righteous subject's life: Those natural flaws, mistakes, and weaknesses make the character more well-rounded and real.

Theme

Once you've selected the subject for your biography, ask yourself: Why do I want to write about this person? It's an important question because it gives you the theme for the book. What topics, besides the facts of the person's life, will you include? What broader issues will you address as you tell about this particular person and the times he or she lived in? The theme is really the story you are telling, whether it's about an ordinary person trying to save the farm, a business, society, or whether the theme is one of family devotion, escape from intolerable conditions, or how to overcome adversity and become a leader. These are the overall themes you should really be exploring when you write a person's life from the past.

Study psychological motivation, and place the person's life within the times in which he or she lived. Don't judge his or her efforts (or lack of them) by today's social standards, but determine the expectations of the period in which your subject lived and how he or she did or did not live up to them.

Structure

Most biographies are pretty much chronological, because that's how lives are lived. But you can jump around or diverge somewhat to keep the narrative dramatic as well as realistic. What you're trying to do is to write in scenes, like a playwright. Plan your story around the incidents or events with the most dramatic potential. Select scenes that are visual, full of conflict, danger, failure, suffering, turning points, beginnings, discoveries, and successes. You can't recount all the events in the person's life, but only the most important, dramatic ones; perhaps limit the scope of the book to a span of only a few years or a decade, rather than an entire lifetime. Omit details of childhood, education, old age, or other times when your subject's life held little conflict or excitement. Focus your narrative on the times and events that shaped the subject's life.

Research

Research strongly affects your selection of a subject. You certainly can't select someone about whom there's practically nothing known, because then you have to invent the facts, in which case you should switch from writing a biography to writing a historical novel.

If you want to write about someone with an extensive written record—diaries, court records, letters, and military records—you'll have no problem with research. If, however, you choose a female subject who wasn't famous enough to have left behind lots of written records (and most women in history would fall into this category), you'll need to search harder for information, and can perhaps write a group biography, as I did. This will enable you to use what several women wrote about each other, and by comparing and contrasting their lives, you'll be able to produce a strong narrative.

Researching the biography is all-important in giving your writing authenticity; the use of specialized jargon of the day, and specific details gleaned from your research will help make your book credible. The foods people ate, the fabric used in the clothing they wore, the specific illnesses and medicines they were subject to—these all help the reader become more involved in the story you are telling and make your words ring true. This research takes time, but these tiny details makes the subject's life become more real to you, too. The words I found in missionary hymns of the 1830s made me see how women connected becoming a missionary with going to far-off lands for adventure. I would have never discovered that fact if I'd simply accepted that they sang "generic" church hymns. The exact words in the hymns provided a rich resource for understanding the people who sang them. As you do your research, you should at times be surprised, or else you simply aren't digging enough.

A last question to ask as you set about writing a biography: Why would anyone else want to read about this person? Your answer will help you identify your theme and focus, and maintain the energy and effort it takes to complete a project as time-consuming and difficult as writing a historical biography. A satisfying mix of personality, historical setting, and human nature, moving along a chronological continuum, gives you (and your readers) a story to enjoy and remember.

If there's one other thing a historical biographer needs, it's a passion for digging into the lives of people, finding out all you can about them and the times in which they lived—along with the drive to tell others about it. An unquenchable desire for gossip (backed up by research, mind you) goes a long way, too!

❑ 68

THE BUSINESS OF WRITING ABOUT BUSINESS

BY CHRISTINE M. GOLDBECK

WALL STREET REPORTERS AREN'T THE ONLY WRITERS MAKING MONEY from the business community. Most business journals and regional weekly or monthly publications dealing with issues and information important to business people depend on free-lance writers, and pay well for the articles they receive or assign.

Step one to breaking into this market is to tell yourself that business is not intimidating or boring. That you aren't an M. B. A., that you flunked high school economics, that you don't know the difference between a mutual fund and a certificate of deposit—none of this really matters. The business community is not an ogre, and all business people are not stuffed shirts who are too busy with the bottom line to talk about their industry or their enterprise. Nor is business writing non-creative and rigidly routine.

In fact, many business owners and operators like to share their expertise and experiences. So, not only will you get bylines and make money writing about business, you will learn a lot.

Call the local Chamber of Commerce or any other business support agency to inquire whether there is a business journal published in your area, and check your newspaper to see whether it has a business page. Bigger daily papers usually run such a page in each issue. Smaller dailies often publish a business page on a weekly basis.

Business story subjects run the gamut: new businesses, profiles of business people, the grand opening of a business, a store reopening a year after it was destroyed by fire, trends in an industry, affirmative action contracts, a bankrupt bagel shop, a new product sold in the area, college bookstores selling quarts of milk for continuing education students . . . as long as it relates to doing business and you can write it for business people, you're in.

A newspaper editor will want samples of your published works in order to assess your ability to write interesting business copy. Business journals usually have writer's guidelines and on request, will mail them to you, along with a sample issue. Therefore, that byline might be but a telephone call to an editor away.

Let's say you've received a go-ahead from a business editor on an article about a business in your community. Now what?

You will of course want to set up an appointment to interview the owner, and to be prepared for that interview by learning something about him or her, the company, and the industry. Your local community library, as well as area university libraries, are great places to obtain information on the businesses and types of industries in the area. Take time to familiarize yourself with all the information that is available.

These are some of the references you should consult for background information on a company or a business executive:

• **Annual reports.** A public company's annual report contains helpful information (in addition to the stuff they write for stockholders). Look for statistics that reveal financial information about the company.

• **Trade journals** (magazines and newspapers devoted to a specific industry).

• **Local chambers of commerce and business associations.** Staffs at such agencies are usually good about giving you some information about their member companies, many of which are small- to medium-size private enterprises. So, if you need to know the identity of the president of Aunt Mabel's Meatballs, call the Chamber of Commerce nearest to the location of the business.

• **Commercial on-line services, the Internet, and the World Wide Web.** Here you'll find a wealth of information about industry trends and specific companies and business leaders. (For a recent piece on how high paper prices are affecting profit in a number of industries, I went to an on-line newsstand, searched under the key words "paper," "costs," and "paper prices," and got more information than I was able to use. But, it certainly gave me a lot of background, which I used to formulate questions for my interviews.) Dun & Bradstreet and other business references can also be contacted via the Internet.

Like a typical newspaper or magazine article, a business feature is built on the five Ws (*who, what, where, when,* and *why*—and don't forget *how*), answering such questions as:

What is the business: What does it make or what services does it provide for sale? Where is it located? How long has the company been in business? How does it market its product or service?

Once you have that vital information, you will need to focus on the people who run the business, asking every interviewee from whom you need information the following kinds of questions:

- What is your business strategy?
- How are you marketing your product?
- How much did you invest to start the business? Did you get loans, and if so, what kind?
- Who is your competition and how do you try to stay ahead of them?
- How much do you charge for your product?
- Is this a sole proprietorship, a privately held company, or a public operation?
- What are your annual sales?
- How many employees do you have?

Let's say you're going to write about your neighbor who makes meatballs and sells them to local supermarkets. If your piece is for a mainstream newspaper, the editor will probably instruct you to take what is called a "general assignment approach," which simply means you will have to use a style the average newspaper reader will understand and find satisfying. You won't use business lingo, and you will find something interesting, even homey, about your subject or topic and center your story on that specific point.

You will ask your subject how, when, and where she got started, why she wanted to sell her meatballs, and what made her think this business could be profitable. What did she do before making meatballs?

Your lead might read:

Up to her elbows in ground beef, Susan Tucker fondly recalls the times she and her Aunt Mabel made meatballs for the Saint Mary's Church socials. A year ago, Tucker gave up her 7-to-3 job sewing collars on coats to sell "Aunt Mabel's Meatballs." "Too bad Mabel isn't here to see how good business has been," she says.

This type of human interest piece, extolling personal success, the local church, and good old Aunt Mabel, sells mainstream newspapers.

If your piece is for a business journal, you'll need to handle it a little differently, since you are writing for a different audience—business people.

Something like this might work:

An Olive County businesswoman last year used a recipe for homemade meatballs to launch a business that currently employs ten people. Susan Tucker, the owner of Aunt Mabel's Meatballs, started the business in the kitchen of her Brownsville home. Within six months, she had made enough money to purchase and renovate an old restaurant located in Brownsville's commercial district, where she and her employees now make meatballs for wholesale and retail sales. They package and ship their product to a number of supermarkets and restaurants in the region and sell hot meatball hoagies to downtown shoppers, as well.

"I started out making and selling meatballs wholesale to places like Acme Market and Joe's Spaghetti House," Tucker says. "After we moved into this building, I thought it would be a good idea to sell the product retail, so I started selling sandwiches and fresh meatballs from here. That proved to be a good decision, too."

Tucker invested no capital when she launched the business. She says there was little overhead cost, and she quickly recouped what she paid for beef, eggs, and the other ingredients by selling the meatballs for $2.99 per pound.

See the difference? It's the same story, but tailored for a different readership.

This method of getting the information and writing a business journal piece can be used for any type of business or industry. Here's another example, using a service industry executive as the source:

The president of Bridgetown Health Services Inc. says his company now sells medical insurance to small businesses that have fewer than five employees. Owen Johnson says that the small business health plan was created in order to stay competitive in the ever-evolving health industry. The new policy was put on the market October 1, and within two months, the company had signed up 500 small businesses.

"There are major competitors trying to break into this marketplace. We wanted to get a jump on them. By selling our 'Small Business Health Plan,' we believe we have entrenched ourselves in the Northeast Pennsylvania medical insurance field," Johnson said. "It proved to be a good business decision."

Reporting on business is not difficult when you know your subject, get the vital information, then ask those extra questions specific to doing business in a particular field. If you were writing a piece about a fire, a murder, a local church yard sale, a visit from the Pope, you would ask questions specific to that event or person. This is really all you will do in business writing: You will write the story so that your readers—business people—will be informed and entertained. Also, you'll build up your publication credits, make new contacts, and learn interesting things about the people in your area.

Reference materials I recommend and which you may want to have on hand include *The Associated Press Stylebook and Libel Manual,* which contains a section on business writing, and *BusinessSpeak,* compiled by Dick Schaaf and Margaret Kaeter (Warner Books). Both should be available through a local bookstore or in a good public or business library.

Trade groups with information about business journals include the Association of Area Business Publications, 5820 Wilshire Blvd., Suite 500, Los Angeles, CA 90036, (213) 937-5514, and The Network of City Business Journals, 128 S. Tryon St., Suite 2350, Charlotte, NC 28202, (800) 433-4565.

There are also professional societies for business writers. Write the Society of American Business Editors and Writers, University of Missouri, 76 Gannett Hall, Columbia, MO 65211, or the American Business Press, 675 Third Ave., Suite 415, New York, NY 10017.

❑ 69

TRUE CRIME WRITING:
A DYNAMIC FIELD

BY PETER A. DEPREE

FEW GENRES IN JOURNALISM TODAY ARE AS EXCITING AND PROFITable as true crime, whether article or book. Although this piece focuses on the true crime article, many of the techniques and methods discussed in the following six steps are readily applicable to the true crime book.

STEP ONE: *Researching the field.* Buy several true crime magazines and spend a rainy afternoon getting a feel for the slant and depth of the articles. Jot down what you liked and didn't like about them. Then, dash off a request to the editorial office of one or two of the magazines for the writers guidelines (include the requisite SASE).

STEP TWO: *Finding a crime.* Visit your local library and look in the index of the biggest newspaper in your area under the heading Murder/ Manslaughter, going back about four years, and photocopy those index pages. (Most crimes more than four or five years old are too stale to fit the slant of true detective magazines.) Highlight the crimes that seem most likely to make interesting true crime pieces. The few sentences describing each article will give you a good feel for the highlights of the case. Select about half a dozen cases that look promising. As you peruse them, you will whittle down the group for one reason or another until you're left with one or two that have all the elements you need for an effective true crime piece. Most detective magazine guidelines will help you narrow them down: The crime is always murder; the "perp" (police parlance for perpetrator) has been convicted; there was a substantial investigation leading to the arrest; the crime took place reasonably near your area (important, since you'll have to go to the court to gather research); and photos are available for illustration.

STEP THREE: *Doing the research.* First, with the index as a guide, collect all available newspaper articles on the crime you've selected so you can make an outline before reading the trial transcript. Your library should have either back issues or microfilm (provided you followed Step One and picked a case no more than four years old). If there are two or more newspapers in your area that covered the crime, get copies of all of them. Often, pertinent details were printed by one paper but not the other.

STEP FOUR: *Reading the trial transcript.* Call the clerk's office of the court where the trial took place and ask for the case number on the crime and whether the transcript is available to the public (it usually is). By now you should have a three- or four-page outline based on all the articles you've read. Take your outline and a lot of paper and pens to the courthouse, and be prepared to spend a whole day reading the trial record; even a trial that lasted only three or four days can fill several bound volumes. (When I was doing research for a book on the Nightstalker serial killer case in Los Angeles, the court record was 100,000 pages long and filled three shopping carts!) Skim and make notes of the quotes and material you'll need; this will be a lot easier if you've prepared your outline carefully, since you'll already know the key names to watch for—the lead detective, prosecutor, defense attorney, victim, witnesses, responding officer, and so forth. You'll need to look for material on several different levels simultaneously: details for accuracy, dramatic quotes, colorful background, etc. There will usually be far more of these elements than you could possibly pack into an article, so you have the luxury of choosing only the very best. You may discover a brand-new form of writing frustration when you have to slash all those dramatic prosecutorial summations and subplots down to the required word count.

Use whatever form of research you're comfortable with. I find a combination of scribbling notes in my own pseudo-shorthand and dictating into a hand-held recorder suits me. (Pack enough spare batteries and tapes!) I can mumble into my recorder faster than I can write. Having photocopies made at the court is usually prohibitively expensive, so copy very selectively. As a rule of thumb, the parts of a transcript that yield the most important factual information are the opening remarks of both attorneys; the questioning of the lead detective; the testimony of expert witnesses such as forensic technicians; and the summing up of both attorneys. A couple of tips: Dates are especially important, and so are names.

Almost as important as the transcript is the court file. Specify to the court clerk that you would like that as well as the transcript.

STEP FIVE: *Writing the article.* Reread the writers guidelines for the magazine to which you're submitting your piece, then write the kind of article *you* would find exciting and surprising (or shocking) to read. Chances are that if a particular detail, scene, or quote piques your interest, it belongs in your piece. Don't get lost in boring minutiae, but do remember that sprinkling in telling details seasons the piece and sharpens the focus.

If your detective used a K9 dog to search for evidence, you might mention that it was a Rottweiler named Butch, with a mangled ear. If the ballistics expert test-fired the gun, you could throw in that detail, noting that he fired it into a slab of gel, then retrieved the bullet and viewed it under a comparison microscope for tell-tale striations, and so on. The trial transcript is packed with details like these that make your article stand out from a "made-up" detective story.

As you're writing, watch your length. Editors are not impressed with articles that run a few thousand words over their suggested length.

STEP SIX: *Secondary wrap-up research.* True crime editors are picky about certain details, especially names (check those writers guidelines again!). If you mention "Mr. Gordon," you should specify that he is Commissioner John Gordon of the Gotham City Police Department. Change the names of witnesses or family members, for obvious reasons. Go back to the library to check the details that will give your writing authority. For instance, if the crime was committed with a shotgun and you don't know a pump-action from an over-&-under, you need to do some minor research to find out. If your crime involves DNA fingerprinting, you'll need to spend no more than an hour in the library to find enough useful facts to give your article a little snap. I recently wrote an article on a killer who was suffering from paranoid schizophrenia. In just four pages in two college psych textbooks— twenty minutes' investment of my time—I came up with more than enough facts for my piece.

What to watch out for

There are at least four articles in my computer that are almost completely written, but went nowhere. Why? Because I made stupid, unnecessary mistakes—mistakes that *you* would never make if you follow a few simple rules. The following three are non-negotiable:

1) *Never start on an article without querying the magazine first.* Nothing is quite as frustrating as writing twenty detailed pages on the Longbow rapist, only to discover that Joe Bland already sold that piece to your target magazine a year ago. You now have a pile of perfectly good kindling.

2) *Always make doubly sure the trial transcript is available.* You should never have to invest more than one or two full days in researching the transcript and court file, but that doesn't help when on the day you need it you learn that the whole file was shipped five hundred miles away so the appeals judges could study it at their leisure. (We're talking *months* here.)

3) *Never start an article without making sure photos are available.* Etch this in stone. No true crime magazine will run an article without *at least* three photos. The minimum basics are a photo of the perp; one of the victim; one of the crime scene. These can be what I call "documentary-grade"; sometimes, even a particularly sharp photo clipped from a newspaper will suffice. But query your target magazine first, and always make sure the picture is in the public domain (i.e., a high school yearbook photo of the killer, a photo of the victim distributed to all the papers, a snapshot of the bank building where an armed robbery took place).

True crime writing might be called entry-level journalism. If you can write a tightly researched and entertaining piece following these suggestions, you'll have a better chance of success.

❏ 70

FREE-LANCING FOR YOUR LOCAL NEWSPAPER

BY DAN RAFTER

EVER DREAM OF WRITING FOR *THE NEW YORK TIMES* OR *THE WASHington Post*, or reviewing movies for *Entertainment Weekly?* The writers whose names are atop the biggest stories and features didn't just show up one day and start typing. Most of them worked their way up from small beginnings.

One way to get started in the world of nonfiction writing is to freelance for a local community newspaper. Most towns, even most big cities, have at least one. You might find in their pages a story about winners of the high school's science fair, or the results of the Little League baseball playoffs.

Free-lancing for these papers may not be glamorous, but it's an excellent way for beginning writers to learn the basics of nonfiction writing. You'll also learn a lot, even when writing for the smallest local papers. You'll experience the thrill of having your name in print. And if you prove to be a reliable reporter, you'll get to write something every week. If you want to move up in the world of nonfiction writing, free-lance reporting gives you the most important tool of all: a portfolio of published stories. You won't get paid much, generally about $20 to $30 an assignment. But writing for the local paper can give a young writing career a big boost. Here's how to get started.

Making contact

First, buy a copy of your local paper and study it carefully, noting the various bylines on the stories. The paper probably uses a number of free-lance writers. If the same writer's name keeps popping up, it means the paper relies on a staff writer for most of the material.

Learn the types of stories the paper features, and figure out what is missing. Maybe, for instance, the staff reporters aren't covering the high school's track team. That might be something you can do. If you've had experience working with the chamber of commerce, who better to write about the local business climate?

Once you've studied the paper, call the editor. You can find his or her name on the masthead located near the front of the paper, usually on the editorial page. At small papers, the editor assigns stories to free-lancers, so don't waste your time talking to anyone else. Keep in mind that editors at small newspapers don't have a lot of time. Before you call them, make sure you know exactly what you want to say. If you're nervous, write a script for yourself. Tell the editors you're familiar with the paper and would like to report for it on a free-lance basis. If you have writing experience, mention it. If there are any areas you'd most like to cover, such as sports or feature writing, mention this, too.

Most editors will ask for a cover letter, resume, and writing samples. Send exactly what the editor requests. If you don't hear anything within two to three weeks, don't take it personally: give the editor another call. Editors are notorious for not following up on letters or phone calls. If you send a professionally written cover letter with strong writing samples, you're more than likely on your way to your first assignment.

Standing out from the crowd

A lot of writers want free-lance reporting jobs, even at the weeklies. That means editors sift through a stream of cover letters and resumes each week. They look first for strong clips, published samples of your writing. They'll spare little more than a glance at your resume if you don't send some writing samples with it.

If you've never been published, don't panic. There are several ways to get into print.

Do you belong to an association, church or club that has a newsletter? Write some stories for them. Your chamber of commerce may publish a community newspaper of its own. Volunteer to write for it. If you're a college student, or even if you're just taking classes part-time, write for your school newspaper. You probably won't get paid for any of this when you're just getting started, but getting published is more important at this stage than making money.

You can also write a letter to the editor of your local newspaper. While not a true example of reporting, a well-crafted letter speaks volumes about your writing skills.

If you're really ambitious, attend the next meeting of your local city council, park or school board. Interview the important people after the meeting, and write a piece on it and send it to your local paper. Your style may appeal to the editor, and your story could show up in the news section.

Drafting the irresistible cover letter

Samples aren't the only thing editors look at. Your resume is important, and should list your special skills. But the cover letter is even more important. Here's your chance to show some clean and efficient prose, the traits of good newspaper writing. An effective cover letter details your background, explains why you want the job, and lists your qualifications, all on one sheet of paper. A good cover letter can make up for other flaws, such as a limited number of writing samples.

Rich Parmeter, editor of the *Regional News,* a weekly based in the southwest suburbs of Chicago, is no pushover. His paper has won more than 200 writing awards. His standards are high. One free-lancer Parmeter hired didn't send him a single writing sample. What made the difference?

A great cover letter, that's what.

"She wrote a wonderful letter," Parmeter says. "It was direct and to the point. It showed no bad habits. She said she never thought about writing for a newspaper, but was fascinated by the chance to do some reporting in her own community. I appreciated that enthusiasm."

What sets one cover letter apart from the next? The ability to tell editors exactly what you can do for them.

Have you lived in your community for decades? This gives you a special insight into the way your town works. Mention this in your cover letter. Did you play high school basketball? That makes you a perfect candidate to cover local sports. If you have a financial background you'll do a great job writing about the city council's budget planning.

The cover letter is your chance to show editors everything you can do. It's no time to be modest.

The more you can do . . .

Newspaper budgets leave little room for new hires these days, especially at weeklies. The cost of newsprint continues to rise, and the growing field of electronic publishing lures scores of advertisers from newspapers. At many community papers, editors have fewer dollars than ever to spend on free-lancers. That's the case at the *Harbor County News,* based in southwest Michigan. The paper employes just three steady free-lancers. Editor Phyllis Kelly keeps an eye out for one thing when she's hiring new free-lancers: diversity. In these penny-pinching days, the ability to do several things well has become more important than ever.

"It's always better if you can do double duty," Kelly says. "We don't have any staff photographers, for instance, so we prefer writers who can also take photos."

If you have a skill besides writing, let editors know it. If you've done proofreading, mention it in your cover letter. If you've worked in sales, put that in there, too; you may get a side job selling ads for the paper. And, by all means, let the editor know if you can take photos.

The world of free-lancing is a tough one. A National Writers Union study a few years ago found that only 16 percent of free-lance writers earned more than $30,000 a year. But the study didn't show how much fun you can have free-lancing . . . and it didn't measure the satisfaction you get from seeing your name in print.

So give it a shot. After all, writing for a community paper might be the first step toward that 16 percent club.

❏ POETRY

❑ 71

Becoming a Poet

By Diana O'Hehir

Talking becomes poetry as walking becomes dancing," wrote poet Josephine Miles in her introduction to *The Poem, A Critical Anthology* (Prentice-Hall). "It takes on form to give shape to a mood or an idea."

Yes. We've all felt that. During those moments of pure felicity when poetry welled up and became our natural medium, when writing seemed loving and straightforward, a natural activity. But what about those other times when writing was difficult? How do you not only become a poet, but how do you keep on being one?

It's the first day of a fall course I'm teaching called "Creative Writing. Poetry." "How many of you," I ask, "are poets?"

My naïve question produces only three raised hands. I don't ask how many of the others here would *like* to be poets; instead, I start inquiring about what difficulties are imagined. And in no time I have a long list, most of its items familiar:

"How do I get started?"

"I used to write. Now I can't."

"How do I know I'm any good?"

Yes, almost everyone in this varied group (the ages range from seventeen to fifty-five) would like to be a poet. But fear of poetry—"because it's so difficult . . . so important . . . so different . . ." is a major complaint of this class.

"I don't have any ideas. When my life's not dramatic, I don't know what to write about."

"Somebody said, write your dreams. But I don't remember my dreams." At this point I ask everyone to grab a sheet of paper and list seven objects she really hates. "Objects, artifacts from ordinary life that irritate you, gizmos that won't do their job or get in your way. Things you really feel strongly about. Stuff that springs to mind when

337

I say *hate*. You can see them clearly. Remember, you're listing objects, not human beings, not events. Things you can touch and see—clock-radio, television set, purple scarf, leaky ballpoint pen."

The class settles in with enthusiasm to list stuff they hate. "No," I answer a question, "your list isn't a poem, though it looks something like it on the page. But if you choose one of those hated items—the one you see most vividly, whose physical details you know best—you'll probably be able to write about it. And maybe that's the beginning of a poem."

A hand goes up. "Somebody said that if I wrote a poem that rhymed you wouldn't let me stay in the class."

This question produces such enormous issues of craft, discipline, originality, and control, calls for such a long lecture on form, its use and abuse, that I move on completely. "Now," I announce enthusiastically, "we're going to look at some poems by professional poets, poems that will give you a lift; you'll notice that one of the most beautiful and moving of these is rhymed throughout."

I've been writing poetry all my life and some of the students are just about to begin, but our problems are much the same. We face issues of self-worth and of dogged application, questions of how to keep going. (Remember that Emily Dickinson had only five poems published in her lifetime; William Blake printed his own poems by hand and died a pauper.) At home now, after my class, I'm drawing up a mental list, a list for myself. It's short and stupid and obvious; it includes a series of instructions to myself and a list of recipes to overcome block.

The recipes at least are specific and direct. They sound simple-minded; they don't always work, but they're a place to begin.

First, here's an anti-block measure that we all know: Find a friend, at least one friend to whom you can show your work. This person should ideally be another writer with whom you trade reactions. And it helps if the friend (a) likes your work; (b) is not too competitive; and (c) writes a lot, so that he or she is eager for you to show up with your poems.

And second (related and also simple-minded), get yourself into a group of writers. Choose this group with enormous care. Not too large a group, one with some people your own age, people whose work you respect, and at least one of whom is a better poet than you. Writers who offer genuine criticism but aren't destructive. Not at all. Not the least little bit!

There are lots of small anti-block devices. Sometimes these work; often they don't.

Vary your routine. If you use a computer, try a yellow pad. Pen instead of pencil. Different chair, different table, back to light instead of facing the view, etc.

Vary your routine *dramatically.* Leave home, go to San Francisco or Hoboken and sit in a park. Claim a table in a coffeehouse. Public libraries are great for composition; if you're like me, you feel enclosed and comforted by public libraries.

Imitate. Read voraciously and then shamelessly imitate a poet whom you really respect. After a while, you may get the surprise of finding you sound like that poet, but different, good in your own way.

Imitate *other* **art (not writing).** Music, painting, sculpture, architecture? I don't mean to write *about* these arts, but to try to reinterpret them. What would a poetic version of the *Nabucco* Hebrew Chorus be like? Of the Vietnam Memorial?

Use a newspaper headline as a first line of a poem. (Or a quote. Or someone else's first line. Or a line of instruction for your computer/shampoo/pancake mix.)

And so on, and on. Look out your window and react, in poetry, to the first thing you see. Write about your dreams. If you don't remember dreams, get a reproduction of a surrealist painting—Dali, di Chirico, Chagall, or whoever—and try to describe it. Write a letter in poetry to someone you hate, to somebody you used to love, or to someone you loved too late. *From* someone you've wronged. Obviously, all these devices are tricks to get you started. Maybe some of them will produce meaningful work, maybe none will, but you *will* be writing, if only briefly.

So, what good are tricks? Well, anything that works, works. But beyond such questions as "How do I get some words on the page *today?*" are fundamental issues of commitment and address: Why are we doing this? How do I make myself feel like a poet?

Back home in my room, I translate my class's questions into a more simple catch-all question for myself: How do I keep going?

Read, I tell myself. Read poetry, lots of it, poems that are strange
and thorny, that make my scalp prickle. (That's how Alice B. Toklas
knew she was in the presence of genius.) Read many other works, too,
the more difficult and challenging, the better. I'm lazy; I like to ignore
this straightforward instruction. But on the few occasions when I follow it I'm really happiest, glowing with a sense of Calvinist rightness,
fighting with ideas that stretch my mind. Not knowledge I can copy or
imitate, but astronomy, geology, physics (I don't understand that one
at all), philosophy. Beside me is a stack of books that I need to review
each time I pick them up.

Difficult reading can lead to poetry; exotic flotsam can surface unexpectedly. "Almost always my poems begin with a small scrap of language," William Matthews says, "—a few words or an image."* And
he goes on to make a comparison between deep-sea diving and poetic process.

A second instruction to myself involves honesty. It sounds feebleminded to say *try to be completely honest with yourself; don't tell lies
to yourself.* Of course we're honest; who fakes inside the safe haven
of her own writing? Well, I do. I'm not talking about creative invention
and imagination, which are absolutely necessary. I'm talking about
dishonesty in recognizing my own true attitudes. I pretend I can write
in a fashionable style that's not mine. Or I pretend to a point a view,
not mine, which might get me published. Oddly enough, these efforts
never work; poems written that way are bad and weak, imitations of
imitations; I know this and so does the editor of the magazine I'm
hoping to fool.

Editors of magazines? Publication? How do you get published?
There are, of course, simple rules about the way a manuscript should
look, about knowing the magazine you're submitting your poems to.
But, if you want to keep going, to think of yourself as a poet, do that
sending out automatically and then forget it. Ridiculous? Impossible?
Yes, almost. But watching the mailbox is highly destructive. Maybe
you can trade duties with a friend: "I'll send yours, you send mine."
This friend who reads your work *is* publication; remind yourself of that.
And that thrill from getting published lasts only about ten minutes.

My final instruction to myself is one some poets don't agree with,

---

*From *50 Contemporary Poets: The Creative Process.* Alberta T. Turner, Editor.
(David McKay and Co.)

but I find it essential. Edit. Everyone has an editorial personality as well as a creative, intuitive one. Don't let that editorial personality interfere with your original creative process. At the time of inspiration, the editorial self can be an anti-muse that stops you before you start. But go back later, after a month, a year, and review rigorously, with all the honesty and judgment you have. Be thorough and incisive. Forgive nothing. There's a liberating sense of rightness that comes when a poem finally meets your own exact standards. Marvin Bell says, "I remember carrying a draft of the poem, at first on yellow sheets, later, ironically, a Xerox of a draft—on trips, finally, all the way to Europe. I let it lie, awaiting a clear perspective. . . . I wanted the poem to speak as the objects and occasions had spoken to me: haltingly, correctingly, without a posed moment to make famous."

We're back to Josephine Miles's statement about poetry, that it gives shape or mood to an idea. What a simple, unassuming concept, and what a fantastically ambitious and disturbing one. No wonder we poets are excited and disturbed by our job.

❏ 72

THE POET'S CHOICE:
LYRIC OR NARRATIVE

BY GREGORY ORR

POETS ARE HAUNTED BY THE DREAM OF PERFECTION IN A WAY THAT writers in no other literary art form are. And unity is one of those mysterious elements interwoven with poetry's fatal dream of its own perfection.

Unity is something almost all poets and those writing about poetry have insisted upon as an essential element. But things become complicated when we decide to define unity, because there are many definitions leading to many different kinds of poems.

Suppose we begin with two kinds of poems and the distinct kind of unity each might aspire to: *lyric poems* and *narrative poems*. They aren't different kinds of poems; they actually exist on a spectrum with (pure) lyric on one end and (pure) narrative on the other. I've put the adjective "pure" in parentheses because there is no such beast; every lyric has some element of narrative in it, even if it is only an implied dramatic context for its words. Similarly, every narrative has some lyric element, if only a metaphor placed at a crucial point or the heightening of its rhythmic texture, as it approaches its narrative climax. Lyric and narrative are part of a continuum, and it is extremely interesting to take a number of your poems and try to locate them along this spectrum. Ask yourself: Is this sonnet more lyric than narrative? And how does it compare with any of my other poems in terms of lyric and narrative elements? Which is dominant?

Lyrics and narratives are the products of different sensibilities or of the same sensibility operating in two distinct ways. These differences can be understood by comparing them with the making of a sculpture. There are two basic ways of making a piece of sculpture: carving and modeling.

The carving method involves taking a piece of stone or wood and cutting away toward some desired or intuited shape *within* the original block. The finished piece emerges as the extra material is stripped away.

The modeling method requires the sculptor to construct a skeletal structure out of wood or metal that essentially defines the shape of the piece, much as our skeleton defines the shape of our bodies. This structure is called an armature. Once the armature is constructed, the sculptor proceeds by slapping lumps of clay or plaster on it to flesh out the shape. This modeling technique is one of accretion: The sculptor has added material to make his piece, and the finished piece is larger than what he or she began with. Also, the carving technique results in a piece that is smaller than the original stone the sculptor began with.

What do these two techniques have to do with poetry? They correspond to the lyric and narrative modes. The lyric poem is created like the carved sculpture—the poet intuits a hidden, compelling shape within the language of the first draft. The secret is to carve away, to eliminate the excess as you work your way toward the lyric's secret center. The motto of the lyric is somewhat mystical: "Less is more."

The author of narrative, on the other hand, has a different purpose: If the lyric poet seeks a hidden center, then the narrative poet wants to tell a story—this happened, and then that happened. He or she wants to add material, to keep moving, to find out what is over the next hill. The narrative poem is a kind of journey, and it needs to add action to action, event to event, line to line. Narrative poems get longer as they are rewritten, because the narrative poet discovers his or her meanings by asking, "What next?" and pushing a poem's protagonist further by adding one line to the next. One of the cleverest definitions of narrative thinking comes from contemporary poet Frank O'Hara, who spoke of his work as his "I-did-this-and-then-I-did-that" poems. O'Hara's remark sounds almost glib, but he's articulating the secret of how a narrative gets made. The narrative poet's motto is the sensible: "More is more."

The narrative poem wanders across a landscape, propelled by verbs and unified by the need to have a beginning, middle, and end that relate to each other. The narrative poem is searching for something and won't be happy (complete, unified) until it has found it. The lyric poem has a different shape—it *constellates* around a single center, usually an emotional center: a dominant feeling. If the shape of a narrative is a line meandering down the page, then the shape of a lyric is that of a snowflake or crystal. The lyric is not searching, because it already knows what it knows, what it feels. Browning caught this already-knowing when he said "the lyric poet digs where he stands." The lyric poet digs into his or her emotion, a single, centered thing.

Needless to say, neither the narrative nor the lyric is "right"; each can be merely a direction a poet might take a poem. But they also reflect inclinations a poet has, and as such, they can be more deeply rooted in the dominant psychology of a poet.

Robert Frost is a prime modern example of a narrative temperament—not that his poems contain no lyric moments, but that the lyric was seldom his aim, and lyric unity was not what he usually sought. William Carlos Williams would be my candidate for a poet whose primary temperament is lyric.

What do I mean by lyric and narrative unity? Aristotle, who in the fifth century B.C. became the first poet-friendly critic with his *Poetics,* knew that unity was essential to the dramatic effectiveness of poetry. His idea of poetry was essentially narrative, and he proposed that what could unify narrative poetry was this: that it describe a single action. He further insisted that there had to be a beginning, a middle, and an end to this action, and that these three parts should be in a harmonious relationship.

When Robert Frost writes his poem "Directive," he is giving us a quintessential narrative poem, which will take the form of a journey, the poet-speaker offering himself to us as a guide. We travel over a landscape toward the ruins of a vanished village (we are also, in a sense, traveling backward in time). It is the narrative as journey, the narrative as a series of actions where *verbs,* those action words, move us forward from one sentence to the next. How will Frost's "Directive" achieve narrative unity? By arriving at a significant location (the village, the spring behind the deserted house) and making a significant discovery (the cup hidden in the hollow tree). We have journeyed a long way, we have journeyed from being "lost" and disoriented to being "found" and located.

Here is Edmund Waller's 17th-century lyric "On a Girdle." The girdle he celebrates is an embroidered sash or belt women then wore around their waists, not the "foundation garment" in modern use:

On a Girdle

That which her slender waist confined
Shall now my joyful temples bind;
No monarch but would give his crown
His arms might do what this had done.

It was my heaven's extremest sphere,
The pale which held that lovely deer;
My joy, my grief, my hope, my love
Did all within this circle move.

A narrow compass! and yet there
Dwelt all that's good, and all that's fair.
Give me but what this ribband bound,
Take all the rest the sun goes round.
(1664)

Waller's poem achieves lyric unity through two methods. One is through the single emotion that motivates and animates the poem: praise of the beloved. The poet is at pains to tell us how enraptured he is at the thought of his beloved: He'd rather have her in his arms than the whole world in his possession. Notice that Waller sticks with the single emotion and takes it all the way through the poem. Lyrics tend to do that—locate their single, central emotion and take it to the limit.

The second unifying element in Waller's poem is "technical," i.e., the recurring use of circle images and metaphors. Almost everything is a circle starting (and ending) with the sash that encircles his beloved's waist. He puts the sash around his head, and that reminds him of the circle of a king's crown and arms around a woman's waist. In stanza two he thinks of heavenly spheres and the circle of fence (pale) that might confine a deer; in stanza three, he thinks of her waist again, and (the final line) the giant orbit of the sun around the earth (here he's using the old earth-centered cosmic scheme).

The reason I chose Waller's poem rather than, say, a William Carlos William lyric is this: The very technique that unifies Waller's lyric—a series of metaphors—would work *against* narrative unity.

Why? How? Simply this: Metaphors slow a poem down. The more metaphors, the slower the going. The reader has to stop and think about (and savor) the comparisons. But narrative poems thrive on momentum; they need to keep moving. A good narrative poet knows to beware of metaphors and use them sparingly. Metaphors are a lyric poet's friend, but they can disrupt narrative unity, which is based on unfolding action.

A lyric poem can go wrong in many ways: Most commonly, the first draft has not sufficiently surrounded its emotional or imagistic character. (In this situation, when the sculptor revises by carving the block of wood, he ends up with no more than a toothpick, or even less.)

Similarly, when a narrative poem goes wrong, it can get completely lost and wander aimlessly. Remember that in Frost's poem, the speaker/poet/guide knows exactly where his poem is taking readers, even if they don't.

If a poem you're working on is giving you trouble, try to locate it on the spectrum that goes from lyric to narrative. If your poem aspires to narrative, then keep it moving with verbs and action, and ask yourself where this story best begins, how it develops, how it is resolved. If your poem aspires to lyric, ask where its emotional or imagistic center is, and see if you can strengthen it by stripping away extra material.

❑ 73

WHAT IS A POEM?

BY DIANA DER-HOVANESSIAN

WHAT IS A POEM EXACTLY? HOW CAN YOU TELL A PIECE OF WRITING is a poem? Should it rhyme? Those are the questions most often asked to me as a poetry workshop leader.

There could be flip answers: You know the writing is a poem if it bites. Or, poetry is that stuff printed with wide margins. My favorite definition is simply: *Poetry is made of words and magic.* And I like how W. H. Auden described the presence of magic. He said he would never shave while reading a real poem because he'd cut himself. Poetry is writing that gives the reader goose bumps.

Of course, some prose has that magic, too. During the 15 years that I was a visiting poet in the Massachusetts schools, the first thing that children wanted to know was, "What's the difference between poetry and prose? Poetry and verse? "

A poem has the magic to zing into your heart or the pit of your stomach or wherever goose bumps begin. Verse, on the other hand, can be defined more specifically. The word comes from the French *vers,* meaning to turn. Verse refers to measured lines that end, or turn, on the rhyme. Poetry can be in verse, but all verse is not poetry. If we say, "Mary owned a small pet lamb with snow white wool," that would be prose, of course, the ordinary way of talking. But if we say "Mary had a little lamb / Its fleece was white as snow. / And everywhere that Mary went / the lamb was sure to go," we have measured lines and rhymes, verse, but no goose bumps.

I like to compare prose to walking and verse to dancing, because dance is measured. "If you were going from one end of this room to the other with an ordinary stride," I say to my students, "we could compare that to prose. But if you danced, turning and turning, say in waltz time, we could compare that to verse. *However,* if you could *fly* from here to there, then we would have poetry." Poetry is magic.

Then I give specific examples of each. For instance, here are three little pieces about an onion. The dictionary definition is in prose, of course: "The onion is a pungent vegetable of the allium sepia family which can be eaten raw or cooked." In verse we could say:

> The dictionary does not describe
> your translucent clothes
> nor does it tell the way
> you tickle eyes and nose . . .

Or in a poem:

> I peel off
> layers and layers
> of meaning
> all of them
> add up to tears.

Verse always rhymes, poetry can be rhymed or free. And a poem, as in the last example, is a way of saying two things at once. Two or more. That's why poetry that is dense with meaning can be read and reread many times, offering up new interpretations each time. But too much density, too much opaqueness, hinders communication. And the first aim of any kind of writing is communication.

Can poetry be taught?

Technique can be taught. Poets in the schools transfer enthusiasm for poetry, and that in itself is a big thing. They also show that the fun of playing with words should not be confined to experts. Anyone can enjoy the process: writing out pain, telling a story, your story, giving your take on the world. But to make the poem into art is another matter. Art takes skill. A facility with words might be a gift, or the result of practice, skillful rewriting, or both.

I'm a great believer in revision. Rewrite, rewrite, rewrite is my credo.

How can you tell when a poem is finished?

Robert Frost said poems are never finished, they are abandoned. He would change poems even after publication. You will find different versions of his poems in different editions.

I have my advanced students put their poems into forms . . . making a villanelle (19 lines in six stanzas), using two repeating lines from a poem they have already written. But for beginners I don't stress forms. I tell them to use the length of the line as punctuation. I tell them to have a line stop when they want to take a breath. When rhymes and meter are used, the lines, of course, end with the rhyme.

It is good exercise for more advanced students to use rhyme patterns in sonnets, etc. Forms are fun. It's sometimes helpful to put a poem into form, then take it out, to make sure it has the right shape. Rarely does a poem arrive full blown on the page, a gift from your word processor.

In my own family, poetry was a way of life. Both my parents recited poems all the time in several languages, my mother in English, my father in Armenian, French, Russian. And it was natural for us children to learn poems by heart and recite them.

I recommend constant reading. And beginning poets should memorize great poems. A good exercise for them is to write poems using work they admire as models. Poets more advanced in their craft should try to find a workshop group. Sometimes just hearing yourself read your poem to others will give you ideas on how to improve it. And getting a poem ready to take to a workshop will help finish it as much as the feedback you'll get. If you do not have a group, it is helpful to read your work aloud to yourself.

When it's time to send it off for publication, when you think the poem is polished enough, when you have a batch of four or five good ones, enclose a short note to the editor. List some places you've published or the name of the poet with whom you've studied. A short note. Keep a log or card index of what poem is where so that you will not submit a poem to the same magazine twice.

When I started publishing my poetry, I did not know one was expected to submit cover letters. I thought that was apple-polishing. I thought each poem stood on its own merit—as it does, but a note will sometimes get a good poem past the first reader.

I had been writing since I was twelve, and started publishing very young. I had not taken poetry workshops as an undergraduate; I just learned the protocol of submission, the layout of a poem on a page, the obligatory SASE, from a magazine—most likely *The Writer*—I saw in a library.

Nowadays there is a growing outlet for the spoken poem, at poetry cafés in most large cities. There are also open readings at schools and poetry societies and centers. The so-called slam poets are part of a popular movement of poetry performers who memorize their work, as did troubadours of old, to recite them as dramatically as possible, sometimes for prizes. Some of these poems hold up on the page, some do not. But the movement has brought new audiences to "the word." The most rewarding experience remains seeing your poem in a publication you can hold in your hand. A poem, after all, is an object you've made, and you should be able to see it, touch it. Here are some of my exercises to help you get started:

1. Since poetry is a way of holding onto the past and making time palpable, write down your very first memory. Were you in a crib? Was it a bath, a train ride? Do you remember who was with you? Write a short paragraph about it. If you are blocking out the past, just make up something. You might find it's a true memory *after* you get it on the page. Rewrite it with shorter lines, cutting any extraneous words until it feels like a poem or a real evocation of the past.

2. Write a riddle describing a vegetable or fruit or something you might find in the refrigerator: clam, potato, cauliflower, pepper, watermelon, for instance. Read poems that are riddles, such as "A Narrow Fellow in the Grass," by Emily Dickinson.

3. Write a poem about yourself, listing what you like and dislike. Lists and chants are among the oldest poetry forms in the world. Read the "Song of Solomon," then do a chant poem.

4. Write a poem describing yourself from the point of view of your mother or a sibling.

5. Read "The Ball Turret Gunner," by Randall Jarrell, which is a "mask poem," the putting on of another persona. Write a poem from the point of view of a homeless woman, a first-grader who doesn't know English, a cash register clerk.

6. Look in the mirror and imagine yourself at age 85 looking back on your life.

7. Write a couplet—two lines that rhyme—about the biggest surprise at a school reunion.

8. Now take those two lines and use them as the repeating lines in a villanelle.

9. Write a paragraph about what you would do if you had only six months to live. Now change it into a poem, taking out the excess words. Don't use rhymes this time.

10. Write a poem using colors, various shades of gray, for instance, to describe a street.

11. Write a short poem comparing the blindness of lovers to various blind objects.

12. Use a lot of fragrances or smells in a poem about a place, such as Tagliabue's poem about the man carrying a fish on the subway.

13. Write an angry poem about dieting and the use of skinny models in fashion magazines.

❏ 74

FINDING THE RIGHT FORM
FOR YOUR POEM

BY N. I. CLAUSSON

AS A POET AND TEACHER, WHAT I NOTICE MOST ABOUT THE POEMS of beginning poets (in addition to the lack of concreteness and specificity) is that their form seems arbitrary, that there is no reason for a poem to have the number of lines it does, for the line breaks to come where they do, or for the poem to be long and narrow, short and wide, or divided into four-line stanzas (quatrains) with one extra line at the end. I often get the impression that I could rearrange the lines and stanzas without affecting the poem's meaning. In short, the poet has not mastered form.

Form is not a convenient container into which you can pour your meaning. Trying to define form so it is instantly intelligible to beginning poets (or even to experienced ones) is very difficult. It is much easier to say what form is *not*.

When you jot down a note to a friend asking her to take out the garbage and phone Mary to invite her to the barbecue, it really doesn't matter how many sentences you use or where you end one line and start another. But poems are not notes (as anyone who has read William Carlos Williams' "This Is Just to Say" will know). Poetry is a field of writing in which how you say it is just as important as what you say. But even that definition doesn't nail down what I'm trying to get across. Poetry is an area of writing in which meaning is determined by form. In the successful poem, form creates meaning.

The best way to explain this concept is with an example. I've chosen Linda Pastan's "love poem." (If you haven't read any of Pastan's poetry, you have a real treat in store for you.) Here's the poem:

love poem
I want to write you
a love poem as headlong
as our creek
after thaw
when we stand
on its dangerous
banks and watch it carry
with it every twig
every dry leaf and branch
in its path
every scruple
when we see it
so swollen
with runoff
that even as we watch
we must grab each
other or
get our shoes
soaked we must
grab each other

If the meaning of this poem were simply *in the words* Pastan has brilliantly chosen, then we could rearrange them into a different configuration and the meaning should not change, or change so little as to be insignificant. Let's do that. Here is my "rearrangement" (of course, it is one of many possible versions):

I want to write you a love poem
as headlong as our creek after thaw

when we stand on its dangerous banks
and watch it carry with it every twig,
every dry leaf and branch in its path,
    every scruple;

when we see it so swollen with runoff
that even as we watch
we must grab each other and step back.

We must grab each other,
or get our shoes soaked.
We must grab each other.

In one sense, the two versions say the same thing. I have not added or deleted a single word, or changed the order of any words, although

Linda Pastan's "love poem" is reprinted here from *The Imperfect Paradise*, © 1988 by Linda Pastan, and published by permission of the publishers, W. W. Norton & Company.

I have added punctuation. But the difference between the two poems is enormous. It is the difference between a successful poem and a stillborn one. And that difference is a difference of form.

What is most noticeable about the form of Pastan's poem is that it enacts or duplicates in language both the movement of the creek during spring thaw and the emotional release of the speaker. Like many love poems, this one is organized around a controlling metaphor, which here compares being in love to being swept down a creek during spring thaw; being in love is like being in the power of an uncontrollable natural force. The lover can no more control her or his feelings than the objects in the stream (twig, leaf, and branch) can control their movement. That feeling of being in the power of an uncontrollable force somehow has to get into the poem; and the only way for this to happen in poetry is for the form of the poem in some way to embody that feeling. The meaning of the words alone cannot convey that experience; it's the form the words take on the page that convey the speaker's state of mind.

But the poem is not just saying that love is like a powerful force of nature. It is also saying that *the poem itself* is "as headlong / as our creek / after thaw." The poem has to be like the creek. The problem is how, in language, to create the experience of being carried headlong along a creek like a branch or a leaf. The only way to do this is through the movement of the words on the page—that is, through *form*. In reading Pastan's poem, the reader experiences—through the form of the poem—the headlong feeling of the speaker. The reader moves headlong through the poem, unable to pause at any point to catch his or her breath. The reason for this is that there are no periods or capital letters separating the three sentences of the poem; there are no pauses at the end of any of the lines (they are all enjambed); and the poem is printed on the page as one long, narrow stanza without breaks or subdivisions. The words rush past the reader just as the turbulent creek rushes past the speaker.

But what about my version? What's wrong with it? There is a contradiction at the heart of the poem: The words are saying one thing (that love is an irresistible natural force and that a love poem must carry the reader along like the victim of this force), but the form of the poem is saying just the opposite: that one can talk about the headlong, uncontrolled force of love in language as controlled and logical as the language of a chemistry textbook. Notice how my line and stanza breaks neatly coincide with grammatical and syntactic units. It isn't that my poem lacks form; it's that the form is inappropriate for *this* poem. In short, I have not solved the problem of how to make the form of the poem consistent with the propositions that the words are making about love and about love poems. My poem is stillborn.

Is there any other form that Pastan could have chosen to gain the effect she wants? Perhaps, but I doubt it. True, she could have written the poem in long lines that go almost from margin to margin. The first line of such a version might be: "I want to write you a love poem as headlong as our creek after thaw . . ." Such a poem would of course create a strong sense of irresistible forward movement, but something would be missing. In Pastan's poem the short enjambed lines create a sense of jerky disorientation that is perfect to covey the sense of the jerky, unpredictable movements of the objects in the stream. Long lines would create a sense of steady, predictable forward movement. But that is not the feeling Pastan wants to create. It still would not have been the best form for her poem.

To a large extent the problem of writing poetry is the problem of how to solve similar problems of form. Once you realize this fact, you will find that you are writing much better poems because what you say and how you say it will be inseparable. The proof will be in the noticeable decline in rejection letters in your mailbox.

Of course, writing a good poem is much more than a matter of form. For a poem to be good, the poet has to have something worthwhile to say: If you find the perfect form in which to say something that should have been left unsaid, you will not have written a successful poem. Nor will having something worthwhile to say in itself make you a poet. Only saying something significant in the most significant form will make you a significant poet.

❑ 75

POETS SPEAK IN MANY VOICES

BY GEORGE KEITHLEY

WRITERS OF THE PERSONA POEM—A DRAMATIC MONOLOGUE SPOKEN in the voice of a character created by its author—often find it one of the most rewarding of poetic forms. And often for the same reasons that delight readers: At its best, the poem may be surprising, insightful, and dramatic, all at the same time.

While *persona* may refer to the speaker of any poem, the term *persona poem,* in current usage, refers to a poem spoken by a central character other than the author. Immediately you see one of its attractions: It invites us to enter the consciousness of a creature other than oneself. Who hasn't, at some time, wondered what it would be like to be someone else? Or tried to understand how the world might look when viewed from a perspective other than our own? Well, for the duration of each persona poem, the poet thinks and feels and speaks as someone else; perhaps a person of a different sex, age, nationality, or culture.

Because of this different perspective, in which the poet assumes the role of someone else, the persona poem differs essentially from a lyric poem (in which the speaker is the author) or a narrative poem (written in the third person about other people and their experiences).

Among the best-known examples of the persona poem are some of the most admired poems in the English language: Robert Browning's "My Last Duchess," T.S. Eliot's "Journey of the Magi," W.B. Yeats's "Crazy Jane Talks with the Bishop," and Hart Crane's "Repose of Rivers" (a monologue in the mind of the Mississippi River).

As that last example suggests, the *persona,* or speaking-consciousness of the poem, needn't be a person. Poems in this form have also been written from the imagined intelligence of rain, snow, fog, fire, sheep, frogs, bears, horses, whales, characters from fairy tales, and the constellations in the night sky.

Whether they are historical figures or fictional ones, human or non-human, the speakers of these poems bring to both the poet and the reader many voices that might otherwise have remained silent, not only in the world around us, but also within ourselves.

A few of the many successful persona poems written by modern poets are Linda Pastan's "Old Woman," Galway Kinnell's "The Bear," Louise Bogan's "Cassandra," James Wright's "Saint Judas," and Gwendolyn Brooks's "We Real Cool" and "Big Bessie Throws her Son into the Street." The telling nature of these titles is no accident. The reader of a persona poem should learn from the title or the first lines of the poem exactly who is speaking, and perhaps—something of the situation that has moved the speaker to address us.

Keep the identity of the speaker clear and direct. Since you're asking the reader to embark on a journey into the consciousness of another being, often one in inner turmoil, let the identity of that figure be clear from the start. The poem's essential mystery lies in what the speaker reveals to readers, and in the language in which the revelation is expressed. In one of the most famous persona poems, Browning offers the title "My Last Duchess," and the speaker, the Duke, begins:

> That's my last Duchess painted on the wall,
> Looking as if she were alive. I call
> That piece a wonder now...

Immediately the reader knows that the Duchess has died, and her widowed husband cares more about her portrait than he cared for her.

In my book, *Earth's Eye,* I included a poem, "Waiting for Winter," which begins:

> I think of my name, Julia Grahm,
> and hold my hands so in a circle,
> making my mind obey my mind.

In the first line the speaker gives readers her name and invites them to see that introspection and self-restraint are her significant features. (She'll go on to reveal that, in her forties, living alone, she's keenly attuned to the promptings of her body and soul.)

Similarly, in the same book, my poem, "In Early Spring," begins with a young woman saying:

> In early spring I felt the weight
> of his legs
> upon my own. I undid my dress,
> we watched the wind row
> across the water . . .

At this point, I hope the poem has established the voice of its central character and has suggested her situation.

About the speaker's situation—remember that the persona poem is a *dramatic* monologue. Ask yourself: What is it about this situation that causes my character to experience an intensity of insight and emotion? What is the urgency that compels this person to speak? What makes us eager to reveal ourselves to others? When you can answer these questions, you're ready to write the poem and hope to see it published.

Once the nature of your central character is apparent to you, and the figure has begun to reveal itself, you then have the speaking-consciousness that is vital to the persona poem, and you're ready to move on, within the life of that character. I often visit a diner where a waitress, as she places food before her customers, smiles, and says: "There you go!" As if she's recognizing our hunger, our anticipation, and our readiness to begin. That feeling of release, of freedom to explore, is typical of the poet and the reader, meeting each other in the persona poem. For the poem offers a wide range of physical and psychological experience not often accessible to us. Writing it, or reading it, we inhabit another life—or perhaps a part of our own consciousness of which we're usually unaware.

I tend to write the persona poem for two different purposes. One is to allow myself to enter a state of feeling, a state of being, and to speak from within that context, which previously had been unknown to me. It might mean empathizing with a character of a far different nature, but by assuming the thoughts and feelings of that speaker, to the extent that I give voice to them, I might come to a better understanding of the "character" of that figure. On the other hand, the persona might be very compatible, but I find it difficult to write about myself in the first person, so the dramatic figure, the persona, is a mask that allows me to speak, free of an otherwise stifling inhibition.

A word of caution. Much has been said about the ethics of appropriating someone else's culture or history: a poet pretending to be someone he or she is not, in order to capitalize on a history of suffering that the writer hasn't endured. The rule is simple: Don't do it. You write with your head and your heart. Your conscience will tell you if your empathy is authentic. Or not. A virtue of the persona poem is that it affords both poet and reader an opportunity for understanding and compassion.

A second reason for writing the persona poem is that often the central figure is involved in a dramatic situation or story. Taking on the character of the figure is a way of entering the story. The speaking figure is itself our invitation to enter the poem.

So the persona poem will be most compelling if the main figure, the speaking-consciousness, is at the center of a dramatic situation, for the moral and psychological pressures of a conflict will bring thought and feeling into focus. Why is that persona compelling to us? Why at this particular moment? If the poem's central character, its speaking voice, is encountered at a moment of dramatic tension, or moral consequence, or significant insight, the answer will be evident to the poet and the reader alike.

The drama that compels our interest may or may not be apparent from the character's actions. What's vitally important is the poet's understanding of the character's inner nature at the moment when it's revealed to the reader. In "The Pleading Child," another poem in *Earth's Eye,* I tried to evoke the troubled joy a young boy experiences one winter night with his parents and his sister, in what might otherwise seem a very peaceful environment:

> After Christmas Mass the strains
> of carols call us to the flesh
> and blood figures in the stable crèche:
> "Joy to the world! the Savior reigns..."
>
> Joseph, Mary, and the Child in white.
> Kneeling, the Kings set down their pomp
> and gifts. We troop into the night—
> <u>Moon, lift up your little lamp.</u>
>
> The stone bridge straddles the stiff creek.
> Skate blades slung back, two sharp boys slip
> off the ice. Beyond the bridge we grip
> each other's hands to climb the bleak
> hill. My sister whispers, "Look!"
> Fresh tracks pock the snow, dogs romp
> down the road in a ragged pack—
> <u>Moon, lift up your little lamp.</u>

Something more than the snow or chill
makes my mother stop and weep.
Something her heart had hidden deep
within the winter pulses still:
Silent in the sparkling dark,
lovers bundle past the pump
house and pause. Only their eyes speak—
Moon, lift up your little lamp.

Father shoulders Julia over
a steep drift. Why do I cry?
Mother's singing, ". . . the sounding joy,
Repeat the sounding joy." I shiver
in my short coat and she stoops to fold
her arms around me. Gladly we tramp
home across the glittering cold—
Moon, hold up your happy lamp!

Whether the resulting persona poem is a character study or the evolving of a story, there is, at the heart of the poem, a figure who compels our attention. The writer's interest in this figure might be an impulse toward compassion, or humor, or the desire to come to understand different aspects of human nature or the natural world. Or it might be a desire to explore the drama of the character's situation.

Each of these is a fundamental motive for writing, and the persona poem results from the combination of introspection, examination, and drama. It is a dramatic form, and a poetic medium, but it is also, and essentially, a poem. So it must live and prosper according to those qualities of language, rhythm, tension, and imagery that we give it.

The possibilities for subjects in the persona poem are limited only by our imagination and our willingness to take risks—which is another way of saying that it's time to get to work. Now, for however long it takes to write the poem, you find yourself becoming (and giving voice to):

• A teacher facing her third-grade class on the first morning of the school year.

• A man watching a baseball game with his father who is recovering from a stroke.

• The almost silent snowfall that settles upon a pine forest.

• A parent attending the military funeral of an only son, killed in combat.

• A woman riding the subway home to her apartment while she considers a recent marriage proposal that she's not quite willing to accept. Or reject.

• A river flowing swiftly under a fine spring rain.

• A child walking thoughtfully through the dappled shade of a fruit orchard on a summer morning.

• A man who stands in a public parking lot looking at his red pickup truck, while two police officers pull his arms behind his back and handcuff his wrists.

• An owl gliding over a frozen field at twilight.

• A stand-up comic waiting to go on stage in a small theater.

• An elderly woman picking her way through a city park, a bag of groceries in her arms, while her granddaughter skips ahead of her into the deepening dusk.

• A colt running through a field of grass glossy with sunlight.

"There you go!"

❑ 76

WHAT MAKES GOOD POETRY?

BY PETER MEINKE

WHAT MAKES GOOD POETRY? IS ONE OF THOSE SUBJECTS THAT MAKES me (and most poets) groan: It's amorphous, subjective, and potentially endless. But like many vague questions, it *does* force you to think and take a stand; in fact several stands, as the ankle bone's connected to the foot bone. In a recent discussion, here's the stand I wound up on, for you to look at and consider from wherever *you're* standing. It's an important question, after all, one that we're constantly deciding as we pick up and put down poems, choose which books to buy out of the unlimited choices, and tell our friends, "You have to read *this!*"

A serious and talented young writer asked, "How can you tell when a poem is *really* good?," the unspoken corollary question being, "How can we make our own poems better?"

Although everyone has thought about this, many people tend to answer along the lines of "I know it when I see it." This is unhelpful because intelligent and sophisticated people like different poems and different poets: Many readers admire John Ashbery, Howard Nemerov, Gwendolyn Brooks, Charles Simic, language poets, new formalists (make any random list)—but these are seldom the same people. So, unless we simply believe that good poetry is the kind we write ourselves, it could be helpful for us to use whatever definition we come up with as a way to measure the poems we're working on.

Our tastes are probably "set" when we're very young, by the first poems that moved us, by our first real teachers (academic or not). Nevertheless, it seems to me that there are some useful things to say on this subject, even though there's no agreement on how to apply them; so I've broken my definition into six intertwining parts, as follows.

We've all had the experience of being bowled over (goosebumps, tears, laughter, gasps) from reading or hearing a poem. But a truly good poem is as good or better upon rereading. Unlike novels or even short stories, our favorite poems tend to be those we read over and over again. "Age cannot wither her, nor custom stale / Her infinite variety." This suggests something about the nature of poetry: 1) *It withholds something from us at first,* yielding its secrets slowly, like a lover. In our poems, it's almost always a mistake to tell too much, to supply "answers." A poem isn't a sermon or a lecture. "Let us go then, you and I," is the (English) beginning of "The Love Song of J. Alfred Prufrock." Who is "you"? Who is "I"? After all this time, scholars still disagree.

I think a good poem performs two opposite functions at once: 2) *It surprises and satisfies.* Without both of these qualities, a poem either doesn't work, or doesn't work *for long.* (I take for granted that one aspect of good poems is that they *repay* this rereading.)

A poem can surprise in lots of different ways. It can surprise by vocabulary: "Buffalo Bill's / defunct / who used to / ride a watersmooth-silver / stallion" (E. E. Cummings). Or by image: "Dumb / As old medallions to the thumb" (Archibald MacLeish). Or by idea: "My little horse must think it queer / To stop without a farmhouse near / Between the woods and frozen lake / The darkest evening of the year" (Robert Frost).

But after the surprise, a good poem also seems *inevitable.* A typical reaction to a good poem, expressed in various ways, is, "I knew that, but didn't know I knew it." You don't learn things from poetry the way you do from geography (the capital of Costa Rica is San José) or history (the battle of Blenheim was in 1704). Rather, poetry satisfies an inner sensibility (linked to that early-formed "taste") which, though varying from reader to reader, is real and particular.

This feeling of inevitability is connected to the poem's music, its interesting sounds. 3) *A good poem sounds special,* either melodious like T. S. Eliot, homespun like Robert Frost, jumpy like William Carlos Williams, etc. A poem sets up a rhythm: the insouciant in-your-face tone of "Buffalo Bill's / defunct" is matched perfectly by its ending: "how do you like your blueeyed boy / Mister Death." The hint of formal rhythms in the beginning of "Prufrock" culminates in the iambic pentameter of its last lines:

> We have lingered in the chambers of the sea
> By sea-girls wreathed with seaweed red and brown
> Till human voices wake us, and we drown.

And the problem of how to end his stanzas of triple rhymes, with one unrhymed line, in Frost's "Stopping by Woods" is solved by his repeating his last line: "And miles to go before I sleep, / And miles to go before I sleep," making a quadruple rhyme and a perfect stop.

As writers, we have to learn to follow the poem's music, and hope that the sense follows along. When Wallace Stevens begins, "Chieftain Iffucan of Azcan in caftan / of tan with henna hackles, halt!" we know he's drunk on the delights of sound, not sense (though it *does* make sense, sort of). "Follow the music and not the meaning" is generally good advice when you're rewriting your poems. It will hardly ever be your idea that's original: If anything, it will be your voice. Sonnets by Shakespeare, Donne, Wordsworth, Frost, Millay, Wilbur, Dove don't sound at all alike, even though they might have the exact same rhyme schemes and number of syllables.

4) *A good poem is memorable.* It becomes part of our mental/emotional landscape: Every line we remember changes us as every leaf changes the skyline. The key word here is *line:* Looking through our own poems, we should try to make each line memorable. Why should anyone read this? Why should anyone read this *twice?* I remember that John Donne was the first one to affect me that way: "Come live with me, and be my love," "She, she is dead; she's dead," "For God's sake hold your tongue, and let me love." I wanted to memorize (and did) line after line. This, by the way, is one advantage of formal poetry—it's easier to memorize—but that's another topic!

5) *Poems speak to the unanswerable questions.* By moving primarily through images rather than logical constructions, poems address the essentially mysterious aspects of life: Why are we here, who am I, what's true or false, what is the good life? These are the important questions, and the very act of asking them is as close to a definitive answer as we're likely to get. This is why even people who dislike poetry embrace it at the major turnings of their lives: birth, death, love, celebration and mourning.

This doesn't mean a poem has to be murky or unfathomable. Rather it means, like that rare thing, a clear and pure lake, a good poem has depth. The strange thing about "clear" poems like "Stopping by Woods on a Snowy Evening" or "A Red Wheelbarrow" is that they are less clear on rereading, i.e., they can go in many directions, all kinds of "meanings" are suggested. (To say a poem has many meanings is far from saying that it's meaningless.) Even a simple love poem means something different to a high school girl, a farm boy, a widow, a grandfather. Your idea of what dire event Yeats is predicting in "The Second Coming" will depend on your religion, personality, and life experience. But that poem is plenty clear enough!

My last definition is this: 6) *A good poem fulfills its promises.* What it sets out to do—musically, visually, emotionally—it accomplishes. At the end of a poem, we feel we have arrived. "A poem should not mean / but be," "And Richard Cory, one calm summer night, / Went home and put a bullet through his head," "Without a tighter breathing / And Zero at the Bone—," "And the heaviest nuns walk in a pure floating / Of dark habits, / keeping their difficult balance." These last lines, whether formal or free, are set up by what has gone before, and click into place like the last piece of a puzzle. They seem in retrospect, as I said before, inevitable.

In some ways, these are vague descriptions—but if you apply these to your own poems, they can become quite specific. I hope they help. In the end, of course, good poems resist definition and explication: Like the natural things of this world, they are what they are.

I'll conclude here with a short poem of my own. Normally I'd just read or print this poem without elaborating on it—but this is a poem in which I've tried to capture what it feels like to want and/or need to write poetry, and what elements are necessary for its creation. I think, with careful and friendly rereadings, these elements will make themselves clear. But it's also a love poem. It is the nature of poetry, and of the world, to be more than one thing at once.

The Shells of Bermuda

First the wind through the window lifting
this room with breath tugging the curtains waking
the flowers turning one by one slowly
the pages of old books Then the sun
through the windows glinting in corners
warming the tops of tables The cicadas'
shrill vibrations the woodpecker's percussion
even the high whine of Mrs. Rheinhold
as she scolds her children *Pamela! Paul!*
All necessary: but the window most of all

There are moments in every day
when a hunger seizes and the hands

tremble and a wall turns transparent
or a cup speaks   Suddenly
bright as the shells of Bermuda
the combs for your long hair blaze on the desk
(from *Night Watch on the Chesapeake* by Peter Meinke, U. of
Pittsburgh Press, 1987)

❑ 77

A Serious Look at Light Verse

By Rosemarie Williamson

I HAVE BEEN WRITING AND SELLING LIGHT VERSE FOR NEARLY THIRTY years. As an art school graduate (who had always enjoyed humorous writing), I had been undecided about my career choice until I enrolled in a creative writing course at a then-nearby New Jersey university. When my professor, who was both knowledgeable and enthusiastic, happened to spot a few of my verses lying around on the table beside my assignment pad, she got very excited. "These are great," she said. "Send them out—flood the market!"

I will never forget her words. I did indeed send my light verse out, to two of the markets she had suggested. To my utter amazement, within a week I received an acceptance from both *Good Housekeeping* magazine and *The Saturday Evening Post*. Hallelujah—I was hooked!

An early acceptance by *The Saturday Evening Post* was "Cost Plus":

> She sells
> Sea shells
> By the sea shore.
> Sam sells
> Clam shells
> For a bit more.

A sale to *Good Housekeeping* from the same period was "Mob Psychology":

> You join the bargain-hunting group,
> Grabbing and unfolding—
> Then find the only thing you want
> Is what some stranger's holding.

This is all well and good, you may be thinking, but how does the verse itself come about? Surely it doesn't evolve full-blown? Not at all. There are a few simple rules to remember, and within these confines, your creativity can run wild. First, you must have a funny idea. (If you find something amusing, chances are others will, too.) Everyday events provide one of the richest sources for humor; the office, supermarket, church, sporting events, shopping mall—all can produce laughable situations.

Possibly the easiest and most common poetic form for humor is the four-line verse, called the quatrain. The quatrain is a neat little package whose length makes it ideal for use as a magazine filler, or for other spots where space is limited. Its brevity is particularly suited to telling a "joke in rhyme," which essentially defines light verse. Making each word count, the first three lines build up to the fourth line, the all-important punch line.

Second in importance is the title, which can serve one or more functions. Titles can provide background material, act as lead-ins, or simply be relevant wordplay. Remember that a clever title is your first chance to catch an editor's eye.

Following are two favorite titles of mine—which may have been instrumental in selling the verses:

Of All the Gauls!

Caesar's legions, so we're told,
Were famous for their marches.
Which may account for Rome today
Being full of fallen arches.

(The Wall Street Journal)

Handwriting on the Cave

A caveman's life was fraught with fear,
His world was full of predators,
And it's much the same for modern man,
Except we call them creditors.

(The American Legion Magazine)

A word about meter

In a humorous poem the meter (or rhythm or beat) should be regular and simple, to make sure that readers' (or listeners') attention will focus on the words and not be distracted by unexpected changes in rhythm. Otherwise, double entendres and other forms of wordplay could easily be missed. Irregular and even innovative meter certainly has a place in the poetic scheme of things. Long, rambling epics, elegiac stanzas, and free verse are all perfectly acceptable forms, but they're *not* light verse—whose format is quite different.

Two examples of uncomplicated metric lines come to mind. Familiar to most of us, the first line is from a nursery rhyme, and the second from a Christmas carol:

MAry, MAry, QUITE conTRAry

and its inverse

it CAME upON a MIDnight CLEAR

You will notice that I have capitalized the accented or "stressed" syllables; the unaccented or "unstressed" syllables are in lower case. The first line starts with a stressed syllable, the second with an unstressed one. Either would be a splendid vehicle for light verse. (No need, here, to go into the intricacies of "iambic tetrameter," etc. Life is complicated enough! I just remembered that years ago I wrote a short verse called "They Trod on My Trochee"—which remains unsold!)

So far we have a boffo title and a knee-slapping punch line, but what about the other lines? Not to mention the rhyme scheme—what is appropriate for light verse? The first three lines of a humorous quatrain should provide fodder for the grand finale in the fourth line. If the last line concerns a dog, the build-up lines could be full of canine humor—"Dry Bones," old sayings, puppy puns, etc. When my children were growing up, we had a family dog. Kids-plus-dog inspired the following poem, which ran in *The Saturday Evening Post*:

Dog Days

School is out, the weather's nippy—
They forecast snow; the kids yell "Yippee!"
And greet the flakes with eager glance,
But Fido views the scene askance—
"Although for kids it has its assets,
It's enough to BURY us poor bassets!"

I had more to say about the subject than usual, so I extended it into a set of three couplets.

The most common rhyme scheme for a quatrain is to have the second and fourth lines rhyme. Frequently, the first and third lines also rhyme (but with a different end-rhyme sound from lines #2 and #4). The following verse (which I sold to *The Wall Street Journal*) demonstrates the most common rhyme scheme:

Gag Rule

> While dental work for some is painful,
> And frequently induces squawking,
> My complaint is somewhat different—
> It means I have to give up talking!

While you'll be aware of the second/fourth line rhyme in this poem (a copy of which hangs in my dentist's office!), there are other things going on as well. You'll note the dentist-related wordplay of the title. The word "squawking" is funny-sounding—even more so when associated with supposedly mature adults. The last line, however, is the real clincher, with its surprise ending.

Endowed with a good sense of humor, you're already halfway there, and the rest of the trip is fun.

Markets

An investment that's sure to pay long-term dividends is the purchase of a few books: an introduction to poetry that explains basic terms and concepts, as well as that perennial poet's pal, a rhyming dictionary. Public libraries are virtual wellsprings of information about and examples of light verse by well-known humor writers—from the amiable Robert Benchley to the tart-tongued Dorothy Parker.

Several of the so-called slick magazines are good markets for light verse. This can be an off again-on again situation, however, so it's best to check recent issues to determine their current editorial policy.

Literary and college magazines can be good markets for beginning as well as established verse writers. *Cimarron Review,* a publication of Oklahoma State University, bought two of my verses, one of which follows:

From "A" to Zebra

> Our kids described their zoo trip to us,
> Excitedly, at home that night:
> "We saw most animals in color—
> But the striped one was in black and white."

A real plus in writing light verse is the fact that the entire process can be just plain FUN! Not many professions can offer such an enticing "perk." With practice, you can learn to view life's little annoyances as raw material for humor—it becomes positively addictive. After writing—and selling—light verse for nearly thirty years, I find the challenge just as exciting today as when I started out, and that's saying quite a bit.

❏ 78

In Praise of Rhyme

By Jennifer Shepherd

AFTER MY LACK OF SUCCESS IN RECEIVING PUBLICATION FOR RHYMED poetry, I decided to test the "audience" of real people out in the world, not just higher-ups in the literary community. Where I live, we have a lot of coffeehouses where there are regular poetry readings.

I read some of my work for an audience of about 100 people, and I found their response to be very warm. They didn't treat my poems as if they were less important or more superficial because they were in rhyme form. In fact, listeners that evening said that the rhyme actually helped them focus on the various pieces they heard, allowing them to analyze and retain the poems better.

This got me thinking about the exclusionary nature of many poetry editors, how rhyming is just not considered "cool" these days. I can't help wondering if, in the universal rebellion against rhyme, the literary community has been missing out on a heck of a lot of fun.

Ideas that pour forth naturally from a poet's brain in rhyme form do so for reasons of their own. Should rhyming poetry automatically be categorized as less profound, less worthy of consideration, than the non-rhyming kind? To do so excludes a large number of thoughtful rhymers from even receiving attention from both audience and peers.

Poetry used to be romantic and playful entertainment, conveyed primarily via storytellers' presentations. Anecdotes, songs, and tall tales anchored themselves more easily in the listener's mind when they were expressed through rhyme. Rhyme allowed people to carry the poet's sentiments home with them, because the words became fixed in their brains.

We now live in a much more literate age, and almost anyone can pick up a volume of poetry and begin to read. But we also live in an era of information and entertainment overload. Commercial jingles, news report sound bites, and the latest overplayed hit song on the radio flood us with far too much stimuli. Time seems to be speeding up, while our memories and attention spans get shorter. Most people remember very little of what they hear or see these days. And poetry, foremost among all artistic forms, is getting lost in the shuffle.

Meanwhile, poets from all over the world do their best to raise their voices above this cacophony. They continue to express ideas that they feel have value to an audience consisting of 1) themselves; 2) a hand-picked "worthy" few; or 3) as many people of the general public as possible.

All of them want essentially the same thing. The greatest poets of both past and present have sought to create doorways through which others can enter into a thought-provoking, reality-shifting experience.

Rhyme need not detract from creating this experience. Quite often, rhyme can actually enhance the balance and impact of a poem. Rhyme serves as a framing device for the poet's thoughts—the wooden beams, if you will, of a writer's doorway to reality. If the linguistic carpenter is at all skilled, rhyme can perform its task well.

Shakespeare's most affecting work still stimulates and captivates us, "in spite of" its iambic pentameter. And his work remains portable, readily available to the average memory, not just because of its age, but because it is structured in rhyme.

Yes, it's true—clumsy young poets sometimes fasten upon rhyme with a death grip, refusing to let go until they have created poetry destined to make readers (and listeners) scream with terror. But just because the occasional poem has imprinted itself indelibly upon your memory doesn't mean that you should greet each new rhymed poem with a visceral gasp, its very appearance causing you distress.

Don't berate rhyme. It has no power to harm you, in spite of the rumors circulating among many contemporary poets. Content that is vague or vacuous deserves blame; the rhyme form in itself does not.

So try stepping beyond the current literary norms. Be open to creating and enjoying poetry of all kinds. And the next time you encounter a rhyme, let it linger and possibly carve out a few neural pathways. That way, the piece might remain locked in your memory box and filed under "fun."

And who among us couldn't use a bit more fun?

❑ 79

THE WISDOM OF
A WISHY-WASHY POET

BY RACHEL HADAS

IN THINKING ABOUT WHAT I WOULD WRITE THAT WOULD BE HELPFUL
to aspiring authors, I thought I'd steer a middle course between the
Scylla and Charybdis of too grand and too pedestrian. I will, therefore,
not attempt to inspire the reader with transcendent words of wisdom
about the beauty of poetry (I'm principally a poet and have more
confidence in my wisdom regarding poetry than, say, fiction); neither
will I remind readers to keep copies of all their work, be sure to have
their name on every page, and enclose self-addressed envelopes with
their submissions, sound as such reminders would be.

Instead, I'm offering a list. Not DO's and DON'TS, but rather, something closer to the way my own zig-zaggy mind and wishy-washy temperament seem to operate. People often find themselves teetering
dizzily between opposing instincts and options; certainly, writers, and
perhaps especially beginning writers, do. Very often there is something
to be said for both sides, even if the two seem in blatant contradiction.
Finally you have to decide; but for the dedicated writer, there's always
another chance, another way to tackle the problem, another way to go
about getting this particular poem or manuscript done.

I am not guaranteeing success or even enlightenment, but I hope to
provide some food for thought and perhaps spark some recognition
along the way. Writers need to remember that they are not alone. And
finally, I append to my list of ON THE ONE HAND/ON THE OTHER HAND
a small dessert tray of quotes I've come across recently, from writers
I admire, which are (I hope) both entertaining and enlightening.

• Autonomy
On the one hand—You can't help learning from the work of other writers, and you should do just that. Read all you can; you can't be a good

writer unless you are familiar with literature. Furthermore, ask the advice of other writers/readers regarding your own work.

On the other hand—You need to make sure that what you are writing comes from you and is not just an imitation of or a homage to some other writer. Reading too much may even interfere with the development of your own voice. You are alone in this business and need to make your own decisions; don't depend on the advice of others, which is fallible anyway.

• Consistency

On the one hand—Develop your own individual style, tone, or voice and stick to it! Your work will be more distinctive and recognizable that way.

On the other hand—Don't lock yourself into a single mode because it has worked for you once or because you're afraid to stray from one style. Be wily, restless, experimental, dialogic. Have the courage of your own wishy-washiness.

• Scale: universality

On the one hand—Don't be afraid to tackle immense topics: love, death, the meaning of life, what's wrong with the world today.

On the other hand—Don't be afraid of what may seem very limited, even miniature topics.

• Obscurity

On the one hand—Avoid pretension and obscurity. If you don't know what you're saying, how can anyone else be expected to? And even if you do know, since people can't read your mind, they may well be puzzled by sudden allusions, leaps, or discontinuities.

On the other hand—Poetry is better at flying than any other literary form, so don't be afraid to leap, glide, and skip steps. Also, it's all right not to understand everything one writes or reads; like dreams, poems can be both enigmas and solutions.

• Poetry

On the one hand—Poetry can do anything from exhort, pray, sing, lament, insult, or narrate to telling a joke, cursing an enemy, or depicting a scene. What you attempt to do in poetry shouldn't be limited by a narrow sense of the limits of genre.

On the other hand—Poetry is better at some things than others. Are you sure that what you're writing isn't really a story or article, a cartoon or editorial, a personal letter, photo, or painting? There's also the historical aspect to be aware of; at certain times in the past, treatises on farming or astronomy or philosophy were often in verse. Nowadays, they rarely are. Do you want to buck this trend? Can or should you? Maybe. . . .

• Your audience

On the one hand—Be aware of your audience. Who are you writing for? Who are they likely to be? Who do you want them to be?

On the other hand—All you can do is write as well as you can, be persistent, be adaptable within your aesthetic limits, and get published; the audience will take care of itself. Furthermore, certain poets we now think of as great—Emily Dickinson and Cavafy are two who come to mind—published little or no work during their lifetimes.

• Writer

On the one hand—Remember to ask yourself such questions as what gives you the right to be called an author? Why do you want to be an author in the first place? Why do you want to publish?

On the other hand—If you are writing, then you're a writer, and naturally you want to publish.

• Perfectionism

On the one hand—Poems (this is true for all writing, of course, but even more so of poetry) are made of words, and every word counts. Revise, revise, cut, polish, expand, move things around, until the poem is as good as you can possibly make it. One good poem is worth a thousand sloppy ones.

On the other hand—Endless fussing over details can undermine your confidence in your own work and leave you unable to finish anything, whether it's a poem or a manuscript, so you can move on to the next thing.

• Inspiration

On the one hand—Try to have a regular schedule for writing, at the same time every day if possible, whether or not you feel inspired on a given day. Waiting for the Muse to descend is a romantic holdover, childish and self-defeating more often than not.

On the other hand—Grinding away at your writing whether you feel like it or not is a recipe for boredom—the reader's as well as yours. Writing on a regular schedule is, at least for poets, obsessive and unnecessary. Be free, spontaneous, untrammeled.

• Teaching

On the one hand—You can learn to be a better poet in all sorts of ways: courses, workshops, conferences, writing groups, and, of course, reading.

On the other hand—Writing cannot be taught.

* * *

To anchor you after that dose of dialectics, here are a few wise words I've turned up in my magpie-like pokings:

"All objects await human sympathy. It is only the human that can humanize." (Louise Bogan)

"The subconscious, when dredged up without skill or imagination, can be every bit as tiresome as the conscious." (Louise Bogan)

"How can a person not personify?" (James Merrill)

"There is nothing in the human predicament that is truly sectarian, parochial, narrow, foreign, of 'special' or 'limited' or 'minority' interest; all subjects are universal." (Cynthia Ozick)

"Precocious adolescents make do with whatever odd conglomerate of wave-worn diction the world washes up at their feet. Language at this stage uses them; years must pass before the tables turn, if they ever do." (James Merrill)

"Last year's writers are routinely replaced by this year's; the baby carriages are brimming over with poets and novelists." (Cynthia Ozick)

❏ 80

CREATE YOUR OWN POET'S LIBRARY

BY DAVID KIRBY

MOST WRITERS I KNOW HAVE A COLLECTION OF TOTEMS ON OR NEAR their desks: a photo of Whitman, a strand of heather from the Brontés' parsonage, a fortune-cookie slip promising great success. These are our power objects, the ritual devices we gaze at, touch, even talk to as we prepare to shoulder the mantle of authorship. Where would we be without them?

Well, we'd probably be right there at our desks anyway, doing the best we can. But good writing comes more easily when it takes place within a rich, familiar environment that not only locates us in a sympathetic time and space but also reminds us of a larger context, that realm where the immortals dwell. A friendly physical setting is a point of departure for a writer as well as a source of continuous encouragement during that long journey we make every day through an often-strange landscape of fresh feelings and new ideas.

I've got my gadgets and gizmos—postcards, mementoes, strange things I've put on my desk unthinkingly but for some reason never removed—yet books are the things that help me the most with my own writing. I always use the same coffee cup, a chipped, badly stained object that my sons gave me years ago, though in a pinch I suppose I could drink my morning jolt of "rocket fuel" from some other vessel. But there are certain books I find indispensable. One person's lifesaver is another's dust trap, of course, so I trust you'll edit this list to meet your own requirements as you compile or revise your poet's bookshelf. Some of these items are available on CD-ROM or come already included in a computer's hard drive. However, even the most computer-centric writers I know still surround themselves with their favorite books.

Personally, I couldn't get along without:

(1) A dictionary, probably two. Almost any dictionary will do for

378

daily use as long as it is comprehensive enough to be useful and small enough so that you can handle it comfortably. After that, it's nice to have *Webster's Third New International Dictionary* (Merriam-Webster), or, even better, the *Oxford English Dictionary* (Oxford University Press), which comes in a compact (i.e., small-print version). Mark Twain said that the difference between the right word and the one that is almost right is the difference between "lightning" and "lightning bug," and certainly the dictionary's principal purpose is to steer the writer toward the most precise expression. But it can also be used as a aid to inspiration. The poet Carolyn Knox writes a poetry that is so lush and word-drunk that I once asked her, "Do you just look through the dictionary sometimes for interesting words?" Her answer was, "Of course. Don't you?" I didn't then, but I do now.

(2) The Bible. The Judeo-Christian tradition permeates the whole of Western culture. But our ordinary lives are shaped by religious language as well; just listen to what a self-described atheist says when he pounds his thumb with a hammer and you'll see what I mean. The Garden of Eden, the Flood, the Marriage of Cana: these are timeless stories of innocence, righteousness, and love, chapters in a rich anthology that addresses our deepest sorrows and our highest hopes. From Dante to Dickinson, writers have always borrowed from the Bible and always will.

As with the dictionary, any standard version will do, though an index is essential. The Bible is a big book in more ways than one, and if you're looking for the story of Abraham and Isaac, you won't want to spend hours wandering in the desert with Moses and the Chosen People.

(3) A real thesaurus. I say "real" because these days, every computer comes equipped with a thesaurus of sorts, but to date there is no substitute for *Roget's International Thesaurus* (HarperCollins). For instance, if I want to consider synonyms for "totem," which occurs in the first sentence of this article, I can hit the Alt-F1 keys on my keyboard, but then the screen tells me "Word Not Found" in my computer thesaurus. On the other hand, if I look up "totem" in *Roget's,* I can choose from "earmark," "emblem," "token," and "badge" as well as "genius," "demon," "good angel," and a dozen other choices. This is one more case of the computer being faster but not better than the book.

Besides, computer tools don't really encourage serendipity. Again, imagine you're looking up "totem." Your computer may tell you there's no such word, but on the way to looking it up in *Roget's,* you may (as I just did) stumble across "stiacciato," which can be used in place of "mask," "plague," "medallion," "cameo," etc. A real thesaurus reminds us of the richness of our language in a way that the more efficient if single-minded computer cannot.

(4) A one-volume encyclopedia. Of course a multi–volume set would be ideal, but something along the lines of *The Columbia Encyclopedia* (Columbia University Press) is ideal for most purposes, especially when you take shelf space into account as well as cost.

(5) *Bartlett's Familiar Quotations* (Little, Brown). Did Samuel Johnson say "A little knowledge is a dangerous thing" or "A little learning is a dangerous thing"? You often hear the former, but the latter is correct. And by the way, Alexander Pope said it, not Johnson.

(6) A current edition of an almanac, such as the *World Almanac* (World Almanac). Recently I was writing a poem about rhythm and blues and I needed to find out when Fats Domino was born, and that's not the kind of thing you're going to find in the encyclopedia. (Answer: February 26, 1928.)

(7) Langford Reed's *The Writer's Rhyming Dictionary,* with an introduction by John Holmes (The Writer, Inc.). Even a free-verse poet will from time to time want to find a word with a very particular sound, and this or a similar book will lead you to the right one. It will also surprise you: how else would you learn that the rhymes for "Christmas" include "anabasse," "contrabass," "octobass," "Boreas," "isinglass," and "galloglass," as well as a bunch of words you already know?
Yes, the version of Windows on my computer has a rhymer, but I value it more for its speed than for its usefulness. For as with the dictionary and the thesaurus, the rhyming dictionary permits the kind of happy accident of which wonderful poems are made. Speaking of which . . .

(8) Jack Elster's *There's a Word for It!* (Pocket Books) is an engrossing guide to all those words you know exist even if you don't know what they are. Thanks to Elster, I found out that I am a "cruciver-

balist." No, not someone who nails grammar books to boards—a cruci-verbalist is a devotee of crossword puzzles.

More seriously, suppose you want to describe someone who hates men. Everyone knows that a woman hater is a "misogynist." "Misanthrope" isn't the word you want, because a misanthrope hates everyone. But a "misandrist" is someone who hates men only.

(9) *The Oxford Companion to American Literature* and *The Oxford Companion to English Literature* (Oxford University Press). These two books, like the next item on this list, keep me out of trouble because through them I stay connected with the great tradition out of which all writing flows. After all, you can't do something new unless you have an idea of what has already been done.

Right now I'm working on a poem about my recent trip to Venice, so before I began to write I reminded myself of what Shakespeare said about that city in *The Merchant of Venice* and *Othello.* I don't plan to outdo Shakespeare, of course, but I do want to say something different from what he said.

(10) At least one anthology of classic poetry. This can range from such manageable volumes as Oscar Williams' *Immortal Poems* (Pocket Books) or William Harmon's *The Concise Columbia Book of Poetry* (Columbia University Press), which contains the 100 poems included most often in more than 400 anthologies, to the thousand-plus-page textbook you kept from your college days. Again, the point is to be able to connect with the best of the past and use it in the best way.

(11) Half a dozen current poetry collections. Obviously a poet's connection with the past is essential, but it is equally clear that poets need to learn from their contemporaries. Right now I'm looking at the spines of recent books by Primo Levi, Marilyn Hacker, Reginald Shepherd, and Dorothy Barresi; I also see two anthologies, the *Coffeehouse Poetry Anthology* edited by June King and Larry Smith (Bottom Dog Press), which emphasizes the oral tradition, and *The Party Train: A Collection of North American Prose Poetry,* edited by Robert Alexander, Mark Vinz, and C. W. Truesdale (New Rivers Press). A sumptuous feast is served 24 hours a day within the modest space these books occupy, and whenever I pick up one of these collections, I am certain of getting my Recommended Daily Allowance of Vitamin P.

As with the older poetry, this new writing is not something I want either to duplicate or deny. What I seek in these pages is inspiration, an inkling of what has been done and what remains for me to do. This is the part of my poet's bookshelf that changes most frequently, and it is the part least likely to be cloned by any other poet. Vitamin P takes many different forms, and you know which poets are best for you.

(12) A book from The Wild Card Category. You have a further chance to personalize your poet's bookshelf by including something so outlandish that only you would find it useful. One of my favorite books in this category is *The Romance Writers' Phrase Book* by Jean Kent and Candace Shelton (Berkley Publishing Group). This is a book of over 3,000 "tags" or one-line descriptions used to convey emotion—or passion, actually, since romance heroes and heroines seem never to do anything halfway.

In the "Eyes" chapter, for example, you will find such headings as "Expression," "Color," "Movement," and so on, with dozens of tags under each, such as (from "Expression") "her wide-eyed innocence was merely a smoke screen," "his eyes were cold and proud," and "his eyes glowed with a savage inner fire." I love to dip into this book whenever I think I'm being too stiff or pedantic. Then my own eyes begin to glow with a savage inner fire as I return—no, swagger—to my task.

Are these the books you need to make your own poetry the best it can be? Many of them are, no doubt, whereas others may strike you as unimportant. The idea is to create your own poet's bookshelf and stock it with works that will, like old friends, gaze down upon you and murmur silent encouragement as you pursue your craft.

□ 81

WRITING POETRY FOR CHILDREN AND YOUNG ADULTS

BY PAT LOWERY COLLINS

FOR YOUNG CHILDREN, A POEM IS A DEEPLY SATISFYING WAY OF LOOKing at the world. Fascinated at first by rhyme for its own sake, they soon begin to appreciate poetry that deals with simple concepts. They love slapstick, the wildly impossible, the ridiculous, word play, fanciful questions, clever and unexpected conclusions, twists and turns. They dote on repetition, used to great effect in *A Fine Fat Pig,* by Mary Anne Hoberman, in which the word abracadabra, used as an exclamation, precedes each line describing a zebra.

They revel in the action rhymes, finger play, and later, jump rope games, that depend on onomatopoeia, hyperbole and alliteration, as well as in such farcical verse as *Merry Merry FIBruary,* by Doris Orgel. Using these last two devices and the fun of a deliberate fib, the claim is made that "On the first of FIBruary/Setting out from Hackensack/ My Aunt Selma, in a seashell/ Sailed to Samarkand and back."

Poetry books for this age group are heavily illustrated, not only to complement the words, but also sometimes to explain them. And since poets are usually very visual writers, they will often provide the artist with exciting possibilities for illustrations without really trying.

The combined *Hector Protector* and *As I Went Over the Water* by Maurice Sendak is an unusual case in which poems and illustrations are all of one piece. Words emphasizing the text pepper the illustrations, and much of the action is in the pictures instead of the words. But in most cases, poems, even for the very young, rhymed or unrhymed, should be able to stand on their own.

Sometimes a single poem is used as the entire text for a picture book, illustrated so as to enhance or help to develop a concept or story. The text of my nonfiction book, *I Am an Artist,* is actually one long poem conveying the concept, through the finely detailed paintings of Robin Brickman, that art is a process which begins with our experiences in the natural world.

It's been my observation that children in the middle grades (ages 9–12) are no longer as fascinated by rhyme. To some degree they want a poem to be as profound as what they are experiencing in life, something that takes them seriously. Yet, they still look for poetry that is simple and unlabored. *Haiku,* three unrhymed lines (in Japanese they must consist of 17 syllables) offering an unusual perspective on a spark of reality, is a perfect vehicle. Writing in this form is not as easy as it sounds. To provide an example, I struggled to produce: "Evening/is quietly stitching/the seam of night."

Children of this age are intrigued by the subtlety of haiku, and its shortness is irresistible to those just learning to put their own thoughts on paper.

But humorous, silly verse, either in such traditional forms as the limerick or in new and inventive ways, still holds great appeal. Thus the information that "Oysters/are creatures/without/any features," provided by John Ciardi in *Zoo Doings,* may be better remembered than the multiplication tables.

It is also a good time for books such as *Alice Yazzie's Year,* by Ramona Maher, in which unrhymed poems, each one complete in itself, taken together tell a story of a year in the life of a Navajo girl, a year that holds such mysteries as the birth of a lamb. We are told that "The new lamb sucks/The pinyon burns low/The lamb goes to sleep/ His nose is a black star."

Poems about parents quarrelling or grandparents dying are often interspersed with poetry in a lighter vein in collections for this age group. One that does this effectively is *Knock at A Star,* collected by X. J. Kennedy and Dorothy M. Kennedy.

Language for its own sake becomes the focus again for readers about eleven to twelve, when communication with peers, intrigue, and secrets are important. Poetry is then a vehicle to express feelings without exposing them. Tools for this are found in nonsense sounds, obscure meanings, double meanings, rhyme, and, of course, humor. The mystery of nonsense—even an entire made-up language—seems to hold the same allure as it had for the four-year-old. Young readers are all too willing to accept the special logic of Lewis Carroll's "Jabberwocky" and will have no trouble figuring out that when the Jabberwock "came whiffling through the tulgey wood/And burbled as it came," the "beamish boy" slays him as his "vorpal blade went snicker-snack!"

But these same children are also looking for poets able to look at life in the ways that they do. The poetry of Walter de la Mare has a timeless appeal because he affirms feelings that are universal. His book *Peacock Pie* was first published in 1913 and has been in print ever since. I'm currently illustrating a collection for Atheneum called *Sports, Power and Dreams of Glory, Poems Starring Girls,* edited by Isabel Joshlin Glaser, that affirms the dreams and aspirations of young women in such poems as "Abigail," by Kaye Starbird*, which ends by saying, "And while her mother said, 'Fix your looks,'/ Her father added, 'Or else write books.'/ And Abigail asked, 'Is that a dare?' And wrote a book that would curl your hair."

Teenagers may establish a passionate identification with one particular poet as they look for role models, a sense of history, a way to understand the world as it changes in and around them. By this time, they have probably been made aware of the mechanics and craft of poetry and are intrigued by experimentation. They can appreciate any poet whose vision is not too obscure. Because of the need of adolescents to deal with strong feelings and disturbing issues such as death and suicide, they are often attracted to poets with dysfunctional lives, for example, Sylvia Plath and Anne Sexton.

Most poetry for this age group appears in anthologies related to a single theme, to a city or to some historical period.

My own feeling is that even though the poetry you are compelled to write may turn out to have a special appeal for this age group, you will be competing with Shakespeare, T. S. Eliot, Walt Whitman, Emily Dickinson, and a cast of thousands. Of course, there is a lot of wonderful poetry out there for young children too, but not enough of it. And here I think the masters of today are a good match for those of yesterday and have an edge because they speak to the familiar.

But knowing your audience is only a beginning. There are a number of other things you should bear in mind in writing poetry for young people.

Don't fall victim to the mistaken notion that writing poetry for children of any age is easier than writing for adults. Your perspectives and

---

*Excerpted from "Abigail," in *The Pheasant on Route Seven,* by Kaye Starbird. Copyright ©1968 by Kaye Starbird. Reprinted by permission of Marian Reiner for the author.

topics may be different, but the skills you must bring to task are the same, skills honed through years of reading good poetry and working to develop your craft. Your most important assets will be a good memory and a strong awareness of the child within you.

It is a common misconception that almost anyone can write poetry for children. It's true we can get away with serving them peanut butter sandwiches for dinner, but it better be creamy peanut butter or the kind with just the right amount of nuts. Just so, the quality of poetry we give our children should be the best available, from the very beginning of their awareness of language.

Another misconception is that almost any idea for a children's book should be written in rhymed verse. Quite the opposite is true. Although there are exceptions, even reasonably good verse will not necessarily make for a more compelling text, and bad verse can, in fact, be deadly. So many "first" manuscripts in verse are submitted to editors that there is almost a universal resistance to them. Here I must admit to being an offender myself with my first book for children, *My Friend Andrew.* Looking back, I realize that any advantage I may have had was somehow knowing enough to keep it simple.

Things I personally object to, not under the control of the poet, are anthologies that include bad poems simply because they're by "good" poets, and minor poems by major poets because they're short; uneven collections by one poet or many; and anthologists who completely overlook contemporary poems and poets. The inability of some editors to recognize good poetry or to appreciate a child's ability to understand abstract concepts is a real problem.

Besides being as meticulous when writing poetry for children as you would be in writing for adults, you should, under penalty of a one-way trip down the rabbit hole, avoid all of the following:

• Poetry that talks down to the reader or is used as a vehicle to deliver a moral or message, unless it is written with good humor, as when Shel Silverstein, in his *Where the Sidewalk Ends,* admonishes readers to "Listen to the Mustn'ts."

• Near rhymes. They stop children in their tracks and detract from the flow of the poem. An example would be "lion's" rhymed with "defiance" and "cat" with "hate" in the poem "My Old Cat," by Hal Summers. *(Knock at A Star)*

• Rhymes that are too cute, convenient, or overused. "Rain" rhymed with "Spain" comes to mind.

• Lazy images. Even well-known poets sometimes do this, settling for the most obvious image, metaphor, or simile as in "wide as the sky."

• Rhyme for rhyme's sake, not because it will assist in saying what you want to say in the most interesting way. If, as with the book, *Madeline,* by Ludwig Bemelmans, it would be hard to imagine your own story being told in any other way, then, by all means, go for it. (I felt this way about *Andrew.*)

• Subject matter inappropriate for the intended age group, sometimes directed more to the parent than the child, or dealing with subjects outside the child's experience.

• Distorted rhyme that's hard to read aloud. Always read your own work aloud to avoid this.

• Poetry that is florid and old-fashioned, written in the accepted style of an earlier period.

• Poetry that is too complex or obscure. Young readers won't want to struggle to understand what may be very personal imagery.

• Writing presented in the form of a poem that isn't poetry by any stretch of the imagination and isn't even good prose.

• Writers who believe they must write like another poet in order to be published.

There was only one Dr. Seuss. If he had insisted on being another Edward Lear, we would have missed his unique vision and voice. If you aren't sure enough of your own voice, keep studying the work of poets you admire—their pace, rhyme schemes and structure—and keep writing until you find how to say what you want to in ways uniquely yours.

Like Valerie Worth, in her *All the Small Poems,* you may have wonderful, quiet perceptions to express about everyday objects and happenings. Borrow her microscope if you must, but wear your prescription lenses and present the world through your observations and special talents, having in mind that building a poem is much like building a block tower: You will be balancing one word or line against another; arranging and rearranging; dropping one word, adding another, until the poem begins to say what you had in mind all along or what may never before have occurred to you. When a poem really comes together, really "happens," it is a moment like no other. You will feel like the child whose tower at long last has reached the sky.

Today, the market for children's poetry is quite different from what it was in the inhospitable 1980s. Then, there were a few poets who had cracked the barrier somewhat earlier and continued to be published, but a limited number of new names came on the scene. Thanks to the firmer financial footing of most book departments for young readers, to some editors who realize that poetry rounds out a list, and to the demand by teachers and librarians, there is currently greater opportunity for new poets. A number of publishing houses are actively seeking poetry for children, but they are highly selective and still apt to overlook a talented newcomer in favor of a poet more likely to turn a profit.

But the field of poetry has never been considered a lucrative one. There are exceptions, as with any art form, and for some poets, who continue to put their words down on paper napkins and laundry lists, there is really no escape.

❏ PLAYWRITING

□ 82

THE DEVIL'S IN THE REWRITE

BY JULIE JENSEN

REWRITING IS LIKE MILK OR EXERCISE—EITHER YOU LIKE IT OR YOU don't. Also like milk and exercise, it's necessary. So it's best if we all learn to like it. Better yet, if we all learn to love it.

Because theater is a collaborative art form, writing for the stage is full of rewriting: Directors, actors, designers all play a part. They all have opinions, and they all affect the play, either overtly or covertly. Some of them will actually tell you how to rewrite; others will just make choices that make the text changes necessary.

It's wise to be open-minded about rewrites. The best playwrights listen, cull the suggestions, and make the changes they find genuinely helpful. Unwise playwrights take all suggestions and try to incorporate them. Foolish playwrights listen to no one and make no changes at all.

Here are a few suggestions, things to keep in mind during the rewriting process.

The first concerns **plot**. Ask yourself this question: What's the difference between the character at the beginning of the play and at the end? In other words, did something happen? Think back on your favorite plays. Compare the leading character at the beginning with the one at the end. Look at Romeo and Juliet when we first meet them. By the end, of course, they are dead. But they have done more than just die. They've been through a lot. And that's good. One sign of a good plot.

The second test concerns **structure**. Are the events in an arc? Arc implies an arch. But arc is also more elastic than that. Arc is a bubble in the wind, stretching. It's a good shape for a play.

Next, make sure you've written **beats**. Beats are the small units of a play. Beats in a play correspond to paragraphs in prose. They should have beginnings, middles, and ends. It's easiest to define a beat as the time between a character's starting to pursue a goal and the point at which he achieves it, changes it, or stops. That section or segment is a beat.

Can a beat be short? Of course. Sometimes a piece of stage business is a whole beat. The character reads the note, thinks a second, wads it up, and tosses it into the fire. That's a beat. A beat might also be a page or two long. A woman wants her husband to wrap a present for their child. Her pursuit of that goal is a beat. Her reasons compose the element of the beat. She's running late, she's got to change her clothes, and the child will be home at any moment. When she grabs the box, tosses it on the couch, and decides to wrap it herself, that's the end of the beat.

The reason you write in beats is simple: You want your play to be made up of sections rather than isolated lines. It's also easy for actors to play beats. They understand them instinctively and will endeavor to supply them if you don't. The structure of the action is also easier to apprehend if it's divided into beats. Could you have a good piece of prose in which there were no paragraphs? Well, perhaps, but I doubt it. We think in sections. We feel in sections. Sections help us divide up an experience.

Now then, a radical suggestion: Don't think about *expanding* your play. Think about *cutting* it. If expansion is really a goal, think about adding events, not expanding dialogue. In general, playwrights worry entirely too much about their work being too short. Most people in the audience worry about a play being too long. Try packing a lot of events into a small section of time rather than scattering a few events over a long period of time.

Recently, I was standing in a theater lobby, waiting to see a new play. Someone came out with news that the play was only 95 minutes long, with one intermission. We were buoyant. And yet, I'll bet anything that the playwright had tormented herself about whether the play was long enough.

I had a similar experience at the opening of a college production of a musical. "It's three hours and twenty minutes long," someone said. We were all disappointed. I myself was inconsolable. One couple frowned and left.

Theater experiences need to be intense and, in general, shorter than they were in the past. Audiences just won't put up with a lot of talk. They certainly can't put up with the boredom. And overlong plays threaten both.

My best advice is to rewrite the play to please the audience and yourself. Examine your own responses to experiences in the theater. Then go ahead and be ruthless. Cut any scene not necessary to the story, even if it contains some of your favorite bits, lines, or ideas. *Especially* if it contains your favorite bits, lines, or ideas, cut it. If it doesn't further the story, it sticks out as "writerly," calls attention to itself, to the writing. And that is a no-no, the writer equivalent to a show-off child. Embarrassing rather than impressive.

Cut also any repeated beats. That means any beats in which the character repeats the same tactics in pursuit of a goal. Say, for example, that a character wants his sister to leave the room. His first tactic is to lure her out, his second is to threaten her, his third is to insult her. If he threatens her twice, it is less effective than if he threatens her only once.

Now we are at the micro-editing stage. Pare down the individual lines. Make sure they're economical. What if a character says something like, "Oh, hell, Bill, how many times do I have to tell you? You just don't understand anything." All right. But check to see if the line would be better if it read, "Hell, Bill, you just don't understand anything." Then take a look at that version. Maybe it would be better yet if it read, "You understand nothing." Make sure you've tested every line every possible way. Almost always, the most economical version is the best.

A writer with a particularly good ear will often imitate speech, and that can be wonderful. But it can also lead to extra beats in a line, especially at the beginning. For example, a character will say something like, "Well, yes, I know, but I also like horses." Far better if the character says, "I also like horses." It's cleaner, sharper, in some way more surprising. But most of all, it moves the scene along. It steps forward rather than marching in place, and then stepping forward.

You can also sharpen the individual lines by letting a character go on the offensive. What if the line reads, "I don't know. I don't think you understand." We know already that the lead-in sentence is unnecessary. But the second sentence is inert. What if, instead, it reads, "You. What do you understand?" You've said the same thing, you've shortened the speech, and you've also issued a challenge. The line is sharper, cleaner, better. And probably the scene is, too.

On the other hand, the character might surprise you, and say, "It smells like Campbell's Vegetable Soup in here." Good for him. Surprises are wonderful. Most plays have too few of them.

That leads me to another suggestion. Note the images you're using. (Images are figures of speech that appeal to one of the five senses.) Quite consciously, make sure that your images are interesting, subtle, fun. And while you're at it, check to see if they appeal to at least four of the five senses. Of the senses—sight, touch, smell, taste, and hearing—we tend to overdo images of sight and neglect all the others.

This next suggestion is quite radical: If you're having trouble with a section you've rewritten several times, try using iambics (a two-syllable foot, the first unaccented, the second accented). They are very easy rhythm structures, quite natural to English. They make the language rock, give it a sense of momentum. (By the way, you need not worry about the pentameter part or any other number of feet to the line. The important thing is the iambic.)

Practice some lines. Don't worry about meaning. Pay attention only to the rhythm: Ta-DUM, ta-DUM, ta-DUM. Here's an example: "In fact, the words are in my mind. But God himself could hardly give them voice." Good old iambic. Write more lines, just for practice. "You can't believe I'm dead tonight. I've gone and said too much." Language is pure sound and rhythm. Just practice the rocking motion.

Now take a look at some of your awkward lines. See if letting them rock back and forth will help you move the scene along.

One final suggestion (I like to apply this one after I've been playing with the details, the mechanics, because it is a marked contrast): Test your play for truth. Is what you're saying true? Is what this character says and does true? You can learn to finesse anything, but make sure you don't lose your soul in the process. All the technical expertise in the world can't compensate for a play that lies.

❏ 83

WHEN THE WELL RUNS DRY

BY KENT R. BROWN

YOU'VE FINISHED THAT SCATHING DIATRIBE AGAINST SOMETHING OR other, and that hysterical comedy about the time you and three long-time women friends from Cape May, New Jersey, were stranded in a country 'n western bar in Amarillo, Texas. Now what? Your audience is hungry for something new, original, daring, funny but not silly, silly but not stupid, serious but not a complete downer, and your blank computer screen is daring you to knock its socks off. And nothing's coming. You've run dry!

It's a fact. As storytellers, you sometimes get stuck, run out of steam. Or perhaps you find yourself writing the same play over and over again, using similar themes, situations, and characters. You need to expand your skills by varying your plots and characterizations. Where then do you go for artistic stimulation? The answer? Everywhere. History, myth, biographies, diaries, letters, newspapers, obituaries, and the yellow pages—all are possible sources of inspiration.

Reading history, whether ancient or current, places us at the center of the social, political, scientific, and military revolutions that left their mark on human development. We can explore the public and private lives of Jefferson, Lincoln, Madame Curie, or Louis XIV. We can research the Ming Dynasty, Alexander's conquest of the western world, the Great Depression, the role of women in science or the influence of immigration on the social fabric of America. The possibilities are endless. We can continue our fascination with whatever our favorite themes might be, but we must draw our characters, accurately or with artistic embellishments, from the fabric of history.

History is full of fascinating people, but perhaps you don't have the time or, truthfully, the interest to wade through scholarly analyses. You're willing to be enriched and all that, but you really want to write the five- to six-character play with no more than one or two settings.

If so, start reading the newspaper. You do read the newspaper, you say, but nothing leaps out at you. Why would it? *You* have to improvise, speculate.

Over several mornings, with *The New York Times* and two local newspapers before me, I decided to see what plots and characters might be hiding within the articles I read. I tried to keep an eye out for conflict, that situation in which two energies go up against one another. Without conflict, without making choices, there is little drama. Here goes.

• **Article:** The opening of a new art gallery. The drama: A photographer/artist who "sees" life as a set of flat planes and surfaces has difficulty communicating his/her own heart. Maybe a parent is dying and the artist tries to convey emotion through drawings or photographs. But the parent is blind. The play takes place in the gallery, perhaps, or in the summer cottage where the artist, estranged over the years, has come to say goodbye. What might happen? The possibilities are endless.

• **Article:** A biographer has elected to focus on embarrassing/sexual behavior engaged in by the subject of the biography. The drama: The biographer is approached by the subject's last surviving family member and is asked to expunge this unflattering period/episode/event in the subject's background. But the biographer needs the publication to break into an august circle of celebrity biographers. The issues are fascinating. Does any singular action actually reflect the essence of an individual? Are reputations built upon truths or fiction? Is honesty really the best policy?

• **Article:** The need to establish an investment strategy at an early age to insure that a child's college tuition will be fully funded. The drama: A single father/mother, having made disastrous financial decisions, resolves to take money from a teen-age child's education fund to cover loans or bad debts. Where is the play set? In the living room, fine, but how about a playground? On a teeter-totter? It might be dynamic to see an adult and fully-grown child coming to terms with the parent's flaws, surrounded by toys of symbolic innocence and hope. Maybe this is really a play for young people focusing on two children who set out to help their father/mother who is ill at home and has lost his/her job. How might they help out? What difficulties might they encounter?

• **Article:** Legal vs. emotional claim to items in an estate. The drama: A niece or long-distant relative appears after a funeral claiming title to an object that has been willed to her sister with whom she has had a stormy relationship. What rights do the sisters really have? What evidence will they each produce? What do they know about the family, the deceased, each other? What are the *real* stakes here?

• **Article:** A longtime social club has been meeting in an old house that is up for sale. The members face displacement. The drama: One of the club members is the buyer but does not want the others to continue meeting there. Why? I don't know yet, but if I started to explore the energy inherent in the situation, something would emerge.

• **Article:** A mother and two sick children are stranded by the side of the road in bad weather. The drama: A grown daughter, her ailing mother, and her two teen-age children are stranded at a roadside picnic rest stop. Two men approach and offer their assistance, which requires one of the stranded family members to go with one of the men while the second man stays with the family. I'm intrigued.

• **Article:** A retrospective piece looking at the Mars Rover and efforts of the engineers and scientists. The drama: What must it be like to devote one's life effort to a machine? Is it to benefit the human race, or is it motivated by a desire for celebrity? What about the scientists' families and the time the scientists spent away from loved ones? Perhaps a scientist tries to excite his children to share his enthusiasm for the work, but the children rebel because of his absence. Maybe this play is set in the backyard in a tent or a lean-to the father helped build. And the children refuse to come inside the house.

For a little comedy, try the absurd:

• **Article:** Older children in greater numbers seek money and financial assistance from their parents. The comedy: A scruffy, slightly degenerate father seeks financial aid from his grown child. But the grown child is such a poor manager of money that the father moves in with him or her and tries to manage not only the child's financial life but the child's love life as well.

• **Article:** A feature on an unfamous writer of famous jingles. The comedy: A quiet, unassuming writer of greeting cards and jingles is approached by a mobster/unsavory character to write a tribute for the

mob/gang's boss on the eve of . . . something or other. I haven't figured
it out quite yet, but maybe the writer falls in love with the gangster's
daughter or wife or mistress!

At the core of these speculations must always be the search for an
energy opposite to that generated by the protagonist. And don't require
all the questions you may have about the material to be fully known
before you begin to write. Many writers launch into their work letting
the impulse and energy guide their inquiry. Often, too, the ending is
not what they originally thought it was going to be. That's not necessarily bad. The exploration most likely will unearth future plot or character possibilities.

I used several issues of *USA Today* in writing my play, *The Phoenix
Dimension*. The inciting event was actually supplied by a friend who
answered his phone one morning and heard a woman's voice plead,
"Help me." My friend didn't recognize the voice, thought it was a
prank, and hung up. But he couldn't get back to sleep. What if the plea
was genuine, what if he had stayed on the phone longer? Concurrently,
I had become increasingly fed up with America's obsession with violence. Indulgent and confessional talk shows, depressing nightly news,
and hundreds of articles about how we damage ourselves in so many
ways in this country—all this had been fueling my frustration. *The
Phoenix Dimension* fused together these two separate but thematically
related states.

A ringing telephone is heard in the dark. A man in his 50s answers
it. A woman's voice is heard. He hangs up. She calls back. He is
hooked. She has a seductive voice and seems to know a great deal
about his life, even warning him that his job is in jeopardy. A man of
simple means, his full identity has been invested in his work. He becomes wary. She calls him at his office, but he never gave out his work
number. His world begins to come apart. Younger employees want his
job, and the boss seems eager to see the man leave the company. By
the end of the play, and without ever having met her directly, the
woman has persuaded him to kill his boss, who happens to be the
woman's husband.

To create the impression of being off-center and no longer in control
of a stable environment, I wrote a series of sound bites influenced by
jingles, discount and grocery store announcements, radio and television talk shows, and predominantly, from those thumbnail news

items *USA Today* lists under the heading of each state. These were interspersed throughout the play, between scenes, as my central character dressed, went to work, stared out the window, sat in a bar, and so on. Also, I never allowed him to leave the stage, thus intensifying his sense of being assaulted by the frantic and often absurd dimensions of life. For several months, I read these news snippets to learn about murders, bizarre marital difficulties, gang killings, killer bee attacks, and a host of other actual events. Each was tailored to underscore specific moments in the play, or to serve as ironic counterpoints to the action. I don't believe I could have made up all the items I used. In this instance, truth was stranger than fiction but served my fictional needs perfectly.

Besides history, biography, personal observations, and journalism, what's left? Obituaries. Here's what you'll find:

• A rural farmer who fought in W.W. II, fathered seven children, lost his farm in a major Midwest flood, played Santa Claus at annual Rotary Christmas festivities, sang with a barbershop quartet, survived three wives, and lived to be ninety-seven years of age. And that's just what was printed in the obituary! What influence might his W.W. II experiences have had on his attitude toward life? What made him want to play Santa Claus?

• A single mother in the south, with three adopted children of mixed heritage, who earned her living as a professional mourner, a tutor in Italian, a nurse, and a choir singer who often sang at ten church services per week. She served on the state's Welfare Commission and generated funding initiatives for the Special Olympics. What conflicts did she have with her children, her employers? How did she spend whatever quiet time came her way, or was she driven to prove something to herself or to someone else?

• A Ph.D. university scholar of hard sciences who was a sports photographer and National Science Foundation Fellowship recipient, a Formula 1 race car driver, and loved ballet and classical music. Was this a man who valued control and precision but enjoyed dealing with risky variables as he raced around the track?

Finally, if you are really pressed for time, and are fed up with the alcoholic fathers, insensitive psychiatrists, and arrogant teachers that always seem to turn up in your cast lists, try this: Open a telephone book and turn to the yellow pages. You'll be amazed at the countless occupations, associations, and businesses that keep this country moving but seldom walk the stage: air conditioning contractors, termite controllers, animal welfare directors, antique dealers, architects, auto supply owners/workers/secretaries, bank examiners, birth center directors, private bodyguards, billiard parlor owners, bookbinders, burial vault salespersons, caterers, chiropractors, ministers, crane operators, kitchen designers, elevator inspectors—I'll stop here.

Imagine the options! You can mix and match your characters as you do your wardrobe. How about a crane operator father who is an opera buff? Why not? Or a chiropractor who studied film in college and knows the dialogue to all the films by John Ford and plays out a different scene each time he's working on a client. Or maybe there's a play about a burial vault salesperson who meets an antique dealer/ mortician/bookbinder who wants to be buried in a specially designed vault that plays Dixie whenever the doors are opened. Well, this last idea may or may not fly, but give it a try. The point here is that what we do and how we elect to spend our time and our energy tells volumes about our values—and our characters' values, as well.

To develop a rich appreciation for how fascinating people's lives can be, read the oral histories compiled by Studs Terkel: *The Good War, Hard Times, Working,* and *American Dreams.* The personal tales of fear, joy, aspiration, and regret are riveting, superior tributes to human tenacity. Also, for a personal perspective on history, take a look at *Eyewitness to History,* edited by John Carey, for examples of life as it was lived from the siege of Jerusalem in 70 A.D. to the fall of Ferdinand Marcos in 1986.

To see how history and nonfiction can inform the theatrical imagination, take a good look at Robert Bolt's *A Man for All Seasons;* Robert Schenkkan's *The Kentucky Cycle;* James Goldman's *The Lion in Winter; Clarence Darrow,* by David Rintels; *Becket,* by Jean Anouilh; the musical *Quilters,* by Molly Newman (book) and Barbara Damashek (book, music and lyrics); and *Across the Plains,* by Sandra Fenichel Asher.

Root your work in reality, but remember, fact alone is not drama. You have to push it, shape it, tease it into a dramatic work that can be more truthful to the spirit of human condition than the facts that created it.

❑ 84

CREATING EFFECTIVE STAGE CHARACTERS

BY DAVID COPELIN

ONE OF THE GREATEST REWARDS OF WRITING PLAYS LIES IN CRAFTING memorable characters. I love those wonderful moments in the process when characters you've invented start developing traits you never imagined for them, changing in ways that make them seem almost autonomous, creating *themselves.*

Although such moments can't be guaranteed, you can prepare for them by choosing those techniques of characterization that will help you jump-start the souls of the diverse citizens of your imagination.

How do you do this? Let's look at three areas of character creation: the *verbal,* the *non-verbal,* and the *relational.*

To dramatize the world is to unmask it. A novelist can describe characters at length, telling us who they are, what they look like, what they think and feel, and even how we should react to them. But a playwright's characters must unmask *themselves*—and quickly. Characters reveal who they are through their stage behavior: their words, their interaction with other characters, their strategic silences, their presence or absence in a particular scene. Stage characters also comment on each other. Some of that commentary is credible, some is not. Part of the role of the audience, part of their pleasure, is to figure out which part is which.

Since plays are so compressed in time and space, a little has to stand for a lot. So, to the extent that you can sketch a character's "character" with a few lines of dialogue, or through a minimal number of gestures, you will be a master of dramatic economy. In the most successful plays, such economy exposes both character and the world that surrounds that character in a theatrically involving way.

Dialogue is a primary means of communication in the theater. The first thing to remember about dialogue is that you can do quite a lot with very little. For example, take Tom Stoppard's provocative comedy *Travesties*. At one point in the play, mention is made of an imminent world-wide social revolution. A British Embassy bureaucrat inquires, "A *social* revolution? Unaccompanied women smoking at the opera, that sort of thing?"

We laugh, and we instantly understand who the character is, the nature of the society he's used to, and his utter incomprehension of a radically changing world. Stoppard tells us everything we need to know *in one line*.

Depending on who they are and what they want, characters will have different strategies of communication. In David Mamet's *Sexual Perversity in Chicago,* a young woman has just begun a love affair and has been with her new boyfriend for several days. When she returns to the apartment she shares with a woman friend, her roommate greets her laconically: "Your plants died."

In that brief moment, we learn a good deal about the roommate's personality, the women's relationship, the passage of time, domestic responsibility, jealousy, and cynicism. In performance, this moment is both funny and poignant.

Some characters don't talk much, but are devastatingly powerful. (Check out Ruth in Harold Pinter's *The Homecoming*.) Some characters chatter on and on, but are of little consequence in a play's power scheme. Such chatter can be quite useful as a source of comic relief, or it can be a convincing mannerism of disguise for a character who needs to conceal something from other characters and from the audience.

Audiences tend to believe whatever stage characters say. You can use this credulity in many ways. One of your most interesting options is to have characters *lie*—to themselves, to other characters, and to the audience. Moreover, characters who sometimes lie may also sometimes tell the truth! This is a situation ripe for dramatic exploitation.

Characters who reveal small truths win an audience's confidence; they can then conceal the larger truths you're *really* writing about until late in the play, and the audience will forgive you—and the characters—the deception.

Have you noticed that direct audience address has become quite commonplace in contemporary plays? Have you noticed how mixed the results are? If you have one of your characters confide in the audience, make sure that the character *has* to do so. Don't use this technique simply because it appears to be easier than juxtaposing characters with different agendas. Such appearances deceive the audience.

It's usually unwise to have a character state the theme of your play. Focus instead on what the characters *want* and on what actions they take to get it. The audience will then have all the information they need to perceive the theme on their own.

Try not to have your characters explain their own or each other's motivations. Plays in which every character speaks as though she or he has had years of psychotherapy tend to be dramatically inert, because they do too much of the audience's work, too little of their own.

How do you choose one mode of verbal communication over another? Think of your cast of characters as an orchestra—whether chamber, full, or jug band doesn't matter. Much of your play's "music" comes from the permutations and combinations of characters as they speak and interact, so mixing speakers with different voices and rhythms automatically creates a theatrical "score." Of course, you may be writing a play in which all the characters *need* to sound alike. If so, go ahead. But this is not a choice to be made *unconsciously.* Your choice must reveal the *interplay* between plot and character, the *tension* between individual personalities and the situations they find themselves in. That's what's important dramatically.

As a play evolves, any kind of change in a character is permissible, as long as he or she behaves consistently within the parameters that you set. Altering a character's age, class or gender can have a positive impact on both the story and the other characters in the play, especially if the change makes your character less stereotypical, more idiosyncratic—and *raises the stakes.* This criterion also applies to adding, deleting and combining characters. Each such change will force you to review your dialogue, and probably to revise and tighten it.

Once your characters are established verbally, with their conflicting personalities revealed by their particular and unique ways of speaking, remember that, on stage, they also exist visually. That raises a whole different set of challenges—the *non-verbal.* Since you're writing for performance, you need to think about *people*, not just about words on a page; about non-verbal communication; and about communication in three dimensions.

Be aware that while words are important, visual elements, silence, and non-verbal sound all must be part of your playwriting strategy. Words express only what characters need to *say*. A character's tone of voice, body language, and the like express the emotions that underlie those words more complexly. This is what actors call "subtext." What's *between* the lines may reinforce what's being said out loud, or contradict it. In either case, what isn't spoken may well be more important to the persuasiveness of your play than what *is*.

The 18th-century diarist Samuel Pepys often wrote of going to the theater "to hear a play." We don't do that anymore; nowadays, we go to *see* a play. The difference is crucial. For modern people, seeing is believing. Therefore, in the theater, where the entire visual and aural context can be manipulated for effect, lighting and non-verbal sound can contribute to an audience's understanding of character as strongly as do your words. You need to appreciate what non-verbal communication can and cannot do to help you define your characters. How do they walk? What radio station do they listen to? Should the lighting make them look innocuous or sinister? Do they belch? And so on.

You can combine verbal and non-verbal means to present character far more effectively than you can express it with either mode alone. In Marie Irene Fornes's play, *The Conduct of Life,* an overworked, exploited domestic servant in the household of a Latin American fascist talks to us as she goes about her chores. She lists a number of things she does as soon as she wakes up, adding, "Then I start the day." After another list of chores, she repeats, "Then I start the day." After a third list, she says it again. And we're exhausted!

We understand, we *feel,* the dreariness of the character's life, and the oppression of her situation, even as we see her do her chores quickly and efficiently. The playwright's words and the actress's physicality combine to create an unforgettable character and theater with a powerful political sensibility.

You must also consider the *relational* aspects of character.

What do I mean by that?

I've been talking about character as if each personality in a play were an individual, distinct from other characters and more or less independent of them. But characters in plays are even less autonomous than human beings are in the "real" world. Whatever may be the rules of the dramatic universe you've created, chances are that *relationships* between characters are more important to the play's energy and forward motion than the individual characters you create one by one can ever be.

Try thinking about your characters in pairs, in triangles, in the context of their society, as well as individually. You can create character groupings that illustrate the workings of social forces without being too obvious about it, without losing the charm of the immediate and personal. If you need to, you can alter audience expectations of time, space, blood ties, cause and effect, or anything else that they usually take for granted. It's fun, and it stops conventional thinking in its tracks—one of the reasons we have theater in the first place.

For example, look at Caryl Churchill's *Cloud 9*. This justly celebrated play subverts commonplace notions of what character is in the theater and in the world. Churchill's highly economical method, which only a truly imaginative playwright could use so effectively, explodes received ideas about gender and its immutability. By having men play female characters and women play male characters, by having them interact in highly provocative ways, Churchill dramatizes complex issues that range from patriarchy and imperialism, to domestic violence and sexual pleasure. The play is exhilarating, because Caryl Churchill has the wit and the craft to turn our expectations of character upside down—and make us like it.

You will probably not want or be able to use every technique for presenting character that you run across, but your own arsenal of ways to make the people "work" is bound to grow, whether you write kitchen-sink realism, post-neo-futurist cabaret sketches, playlets for children, or any other dramatic form that puts human beings on a stage.

Remember, the wide variety of character-revealing techniques is there to serve your purposes. If you can't find contemporary techniques that fulfill your needs, feel free to invent (or revive!) those that do. Whatever makes your characters memorable makes *you* a better playwright.

❑ 85

FINDING A THEME
FOR YOUR PLAY

BY PETER SAGAL

USUALLY WHEN PEOPLE ASK ME WHAT MY PLAYS ARE ABOUT, I HEM
and haw and squint off into the sky and then come up with something
like, "Well, there's this guy, and he has this dog . . . . and then this
army invades. . . . well, it's really kind of a love story, in the end." I
feel silly, and my questioner hasn't learned anything, which may be
right, because if he wants to know what the play is about, he should
see the thing. I mean, we write immortal works of dramatic literature,
not slogans.

But I recently wrote a play that could be summarized in a single
sentence.* This was a first for me, and because of this, and because
the sentence in question invoked some political and moral questions,
I became instantly known as a Dramatist of Serious Theme. This makes
me bristle, because like every other normal writer, I resent any praise
that is not universal. What are my comedies, chopped liver?

Nonetheless, I'm now known as a guy with something to say, and
I've been asked here to give some tips on how to say it, that is, how
to approach the problem of Theme in playwriting. (That raises the
ancillary question of how you write a play when you have *nothing* to
say, which is a problem I face daily.) Somebody—I think it was Woody
Allen quoting Samuel Goldwyn—said that people go to the theater for
entertainment; if you want to send a message, call Western Union. But
the theater has changed a lot and seems to be surviving only because
of its toehold in Meaning; i.e., movies and TV may give you cleavage
and explosions, etc., but if you want to learn something, come to the
theater. Somebody else said—and this time I know, it was the actor

---

*"A Jewish lawyer defends the First Amendment rights of a man who says the Holo-
caust did not happen." (*Denial,* Long Wharf Theater, Dec. 1995)

406

Simon Callow—that in this day and age, going to the theater for "entertainment" is like going to a restaurant for indigestion.

So how to approach the theme play, the political or "problem" play? First of all, it seems to me that the playwright should always begin not from a statement, but a question. It is boring to be told an opinion, but it is interesting to be asked for your own. Thus, a writer who sets off to tell us, "Racism is bad!," for example, will probably ultimately irritate the audience, because they know that racism is bad and they're sorry, but frankly they don't feel that they had to pay $20 or whatever to be told again. But a writer who asks the audience, "Why is racism bad?" or even "Is racism ever justified?" will hold the playgoers' attention, because they may never have thought about it before, and their answers may surprise or please or horrify the playwright.

Once you have framed your question in an interesting and provocative way, how do you dramatize it? Here we fall into the great Unknown, because the answer depends on your particular vision of drama and the theater, and my answer may not suit you and your purposes. For example, if you're Brecht, you'll pose your question by writing it on a banner and hanging it upstage center. What I do is try to make the Thematic Problem into a personal one.

Sometimes it's obvious how to do this, sometimes it's not. If you're writing about True Love, then clearly your play will need some lovers. If it's about racism, then a racist or two will be in order. More complicated questions require more complicated solutions, but part of your job as a dramatist (some would say your *whole* job) is to find that telling situation, that moment of crisis and decision plucked from the entire span of an infinite number of imaginary lifetimes, that perfectly distills the essence of the question you're addressing. For example, let's say you want to write about the tension between duty to self and duty to country. You want to write about a solider. But which solider, in which war? An Englishman fighting in World War I? A Jew fighting in World War II? An Asian American fighting in Vietnam? Any situation will give different emphases to different sides of your question. How do you choose?

In considering this choice, remember that the worst sin the dramatist can commit is to lie to an audience. In this context, it means putting a question out there and then making the answer easy or simple when it's not. There's a great temptation when asking an important question—"Will True Love Always Triumph?"—to go immediately for the best and most comforting answer—"Yes!"—and ignore all the evidence to the contrary that's in the world, in your heart, in your own play. Consider *King Lear*. Its answer to that particular question would be a resounding *No*, so during the 17th century, the play was rewritten by Nahum Tate to answer *Yes*: Cordelia, quite alive at the end, united with Edmund and her loving father. That rewritten version was rejected by history for, among other things, being a lie.

So if you are going to ask a tough question, and you should, you must be merciless in your search for the answer. Let the situation of the play be rife with ambiguity and doubt. Let your characters be contradictory, holding both bad and good within them. Let the most horrible opinions be held by the most pleasant and attractive people. Let good people do terrible things to one another; let them react to kindness with anger and to attacks with fear. Because that's what happens in the real world, and if by chance you do want to say, ultimately, something good—that Love will triumph, that freedom is precious and worth fighting for—it won't help your case to set your play in a fantasy world where these things come easier than they actually are.

What I've often done is to take a character I admire and like, and then either put that character in a very difficult position, or cause him or her to do something rather unpleasant and then have to deal with the results. In my play *Denial* I took a character who was very confident in her support of free speech and confronted her with another character—very charming, by the way—who made her want to scream and strike out every time he opened his mouth. In *Angels in America*, by Tony Kushner, a lead character, who is charming and sympathetic and funny, abandons his lover in time of crisis, so we are left to ask ourselves—we, who think of ourselves as charming and sympathetic and funny—if when the time came, we might do the same thing.

The second worst sin in the theater, after lying, is to be boring. In fact, it's often in the pursuit of not being boring that we end up telling our worst lies. There's a strong temptation—driven by the market and our own inclination to be cheerful—to preach to the choir. The theater of today desperately wants to say something Useful and Good about the world; it wants to condemn what needs condemning and praise what needs praising, according to the mores of the day. But the problem is that unless you do that from a deeply informed, dramatically charged, almost universally comprehending place, you're going to bore the heck out of your audience.

How do you achieve that kind of aesthetic Buddha-nature, where you comprehend everything, where all forces balance, where the true strengths and faultlines of the universe reveal themselves?

Work hard, write every day, and tell the truth. It may not work, but nothing else will.

❏ JUVENILE AND YOUNG ADULT

□ 86

HANDS-ON RESEARCH: FINDING A BAGPIPER

BY ELOISE MCGRAW

I ENJOY RESEARCH. I LOVE FINDING OUT ALL ABOUT A PLACE AND time and the people who lived then and how they dressed and what they believed, and then recreating it all in fiction. The search for accuracy has led me into some long and arduous paper chases through interlibrary loan, but I've never minded. Sound book research can not only expand your education in all directions; it can keep you from making a fool of yourself. The local library can be a writer's best friend.

But how can you find out things no book ever tells you?

Imagine yourself standing on the roof of Notre Dame Cathedral. How much—if any—could you see of a house across the street? Now transfer yourself down to the street in front of such a house. How well—if at all—could you see a person standing on the cathedral roof? Imagination isn't going to give you those answers; there's too much you don't know. Guess at matters of hard fact, and you're sure to expose your ignorance. But how to find out more about that cathedral roof? Not one solitary guidebook provides a clue.

To many writers, the element of *place*—the setting—is not as important as other elements of the story. To some of us it is fundamental. When I write, the inner process is like watching a movie—in living color—with sound. If I have no clear mental picture of where and when everything is happening, and a reliable inner map of the landscape, I'm stymied. My characters are, too. They either stumble around in a sort of fog or just sit there, mum.

There are a number of ways to find out what you're writing about. You can go to Paris—or wherever—yourself. Frequently, this is not possible. I hadn't the leisure or the money to travel to the Nile Valley during the years I was writing three novels about Egypt. In any case, my setting was *ancient* Egypt, and no traveler can go there except via

413

the library shelves, the museum collections, and his own powers of visualization. Years later, when I finally did go to Egypt, I found that these three approaches had not let me down; in fact, the research I had done enabled me to see ancient Egypt right through the modern overlay.

Historical novels aren't the only books that require research. Twelve of my nineteen novels have contemporary settings, but there wasn't one that didn't require a little research into *something*. I've had to find out about knots, codes, World War II fighter planes, sleight-of-hand tricks, parrots, logging, old stagecoach schedules, company mergers, fox-hunting lingo, pioneer gravestones, and so-called antique stores that sell toys and ice-picks and buttonhooks just like the ones I grew up with. But first—most memorably—circuses.

I took my initial plunge into real research only because my editor gave me a shove. It was my very first book—already written, already accepted and awaiting (though I was unaware of it) the back-and-forthing between editor and author that grooms a manuscript for publication. I knew nothing about this process. I knew almost nothing about circuses or bareback riders, either—though that's what my book was about. It must have read convincingly, because when my editor inquired if I had, myself, worked in a circus, she seemed taken aback when I said no. "I've read three books about them, though," I assured her. Whereupon my education, in circuses *and* research, began, and has continued to this day.

There are times when nobody can answer your question. Faced with a well-documented historical fact—a baffling suicide, an inexplicable disappearance or usurping, a war that led nowhere—how do you discover the cause behind the effect, the powerful human motivations, that nobody has documented at all? And here's a more prosaic sort of poser: How many days would it take, by what route, to travel from Egypt to Babylon in 1500 B.C.? How many miles to walk from Hastings to Canterbury in 1067, through what sort of countryside?

To answer such questions you must use plain ingenuity, a kind of labor-intensive jigsaw puzzle technique (to gather and fit together various unrelated scraps of information), and some leaps of imagination (to fill in the picture they suggest).

I managed to solve the Hastings-to-Canterbury puzzle by such means. Other questions immediately arose, all having to do with the creation of the Bayeux Tapestry, on which my main character was going to work. How long would it take her to embroider one figure, one sail? Would the work hurt her fingers or tire her back? I wasted time asking people who didn't know. The hands-on method was the only one left.

I had to learn from a book how to do the three stitches used on the Tapestry. That done, I selected one scene and drew it on linen (using the old art school squaring-off method) to exact size, 40 by 20 inches. Using my drawing table—minus its board—as a stretcher I settled down to embroider the scene in a wool thread similar to the handspun original, keeping track of the hours and my sensations. It took me 200 hours, working two to three hours a day during one spring—writing the book in the mornings and embroidering in the afternoons. It's not your back that gets sore; it's your fingertips—but only on the outline stitch.

Now, as research this was going overboard. I know that, but I enjoyed every minute—and learned to embroider, besides.

The historical past—even the dimmest, most distant past—at least concerns the real world. What about the worlds you invent yourself?

Fantasy—dreaming them up or writing them down—seems easy and is anything but. It is a brave (or naive) beginner who tackles it. Consider Flannery O'Connor's comment: ". . . when one writes a fantasy, reality is the proper basis of it. . . . I would even go so far as to say that the person writing the fantasy has to be even more strictly attentive to the concrete detail than someone writing in a naturalistic vein—because the more convincing the properties in it have to be."

In short, fantasy must seem even more real than real. The strange landscapes, the smell and color of the dragons, the squeaky voice of the talking mouse, the details of every chair and mantle ornament in the old rabbit's living room, must be clearly visualized and sharply described.

Visualizing—that's the hard part. When I was planning *The Moorchild*—a fantasy—my first worst hurdle was getting the visual landscape in my mind. This is not a problem with a historical novel, because you've read up on your chosen place and period until you feel more solidly oriented in, say, 17th-century London than you do in your own neighborhood. Obviously, it is not a problem with a modern-day setting. But with a fantasy, where are you?

The Moorchild was based on elements of British and European folk-lore—that is, on a well-established body of *traditional* fantasy. Because of this matrix, I did not feel wholly free. I had two places to invent—one an isolated human village at the edge of a non-specific moor in a non-real time similar to the early Middle Ages. The other place, hidden under the nearby moor, would be the Mound, the parallel world of my (also invented) non-human creatures, the Moorfolk.

The landscape inside the Mound gave me very little trouble. Lodged in a far corner of my mind, just waiting, was the memory of a salt mine I visited as a child—a vast, glittering cavern where sound drifted eerily without echo, where on a slope I'd judged only a short walk away a donkey and cart looked the size of toys, where an hour flew by like an instant and yet stood still, all these years later, in vivid recollection. Once I'd thought of that salt mine my imagination took off, and I had my Mound. But a wholly fanciful setting for my human characters seemed wrong for a story based on elements of real folklore. I wanted to give my village solid, pseudo-historical reality based on the real world. Yet I didn't want to use an identifiable country because I wanted to keep this a fantasy. Deadlock.

I had to work my way out of it, using trial and error with no idea what would work. From the beginning, I had thought of a countryside and climate reminiscent of (perhaps) northwest England or the Scottish Highlands—so I started with that, and read up on the medieval use of such lands, the woods, the common fields, the "waste land," the shared plows and animals, what kind of houses, which crops. Then I mentally situated my village in such surroundings—feeling as though I were constructing a cardboard stage with a painted backdrop—and gave it the few craftsmen such a village would need: a miller, a blacksmith, a potter.

With nearly total lack of confidence, I started my characters moving through this jerry-built environment. And astonishingly—as if each character carried a magic wand—the details came alive; the place became real and substantial to me, feature by feature, as the villagers moved through it. The vaguely mentioned hillside apple orchard a child climbed past took solid root and was there for good. Once a woman hurried up the village street I could see the street—grassy and crooked, with the well halfway along, and old Fiach with his dog sitting in the sun. Soon I knew where everybody lived, and the ways to the fields and the moor and the woods, and the whole place was mine. I can't guarantee that this method will work for you, but unpromising as it feels while you're doing it, it's worth a try.

I went through a similar process to invent my Moorfolk—who are *not* elves, nor fairies, nor brownies, nor any other of those remarkably well-documented traditional beings. I drew some qualities and habits from such creatures, especially their non-human emotions and attitudes, but my Moorfolk are themselves. And this painted me into another corner; for unlike the sprites of folklore, who all play fiddles, Moorfolk play bagpipes.

So I suddenly needed to know what bagpipes look like up close, how all those tubes and tassels and straps are hung together, how you hold bagpipes when you play, which bit you blow into. Is the conglomeration heavy to carry, where do you feel the pressure, how do you work that bag when both hands are busy fingering stops, what's the hardest trick in playing it, could an undersized child of nine or ten ever manage it at all . . . ? My questions, like my ignorance, were endless, and called for some hands-on answers. But how to find a bagpiper, just like that? The nearest I'd ever come to one was in northern Scotland.

I was dwelling hopelessly on the air fare to the Highlands or even to Indianapolis, home of an old friend's ex-son-in-law, who, I thought, used to play the pipes. My daughter then reminded me of the Highland Games held annually on a nearby college campus—always accompanied by an entire—and undoubtedly local—bagpipe band. I phoned my suburban chamber of commerce and learned the name of an expert high-school-age piper who lived just a few blocks away. I got enthusiastic cooperation, all my answers, and a hands-on, ear-splitting hour I'll never forget.

In that instance, the hopeless turned out to be easy. But that doesn't always happen. You have to be prepared to go the extra mile. No matter; it's that mile that's often the most rewarding.

❏ 87

FORGET THE ALAMO:
WRITING HISTORY FOR CHILDREN

BY SYLVIA WHITMAN

GROWING UP, I FELT THE SAME WAY ABOUT HISTORY AS I DID ABOUT spinach: Everybody said it was good for me, and I detested it. Elections, treaties, dates, and more dates—what a bore! Luckily, I loved to read. Just as I managed to meet my minimum RDA of vitamins with frozen peas and grape juice, I got a rough sense of the past through biographies and novels like *Johnny Tremaine* (1943), Esther Forbes's award-winning story of an apprentice silversmith on the eve of the American Revolution. The last thing I ever expected, though, was that I would end up writing history books that teachers could inflict upon kids.

I first started to enjoy history in college in the early 1980s. By then "social history" had moved into the academic mainstream. Although it would seem that social historians should be poring over the guest list of the Boston Tea Party, they are more likely to be studying the propaganda of rebellion or 18th-century perceptions of Native Americans. Social historians are the "big picture" people: They tend to highlight change instead of chronology; to focus on processes rather than events; to think in terms of decades instead of weeks or months; to follow the transmutations of ideas as they trickle down from the intelligentsia and trickle up from popular culture. Also, in the 1980s, stirrings of multiculturalism were beginning to influence scholarship, and women's studies was gaining respectability. I had long taken an interest in the activities of my mother and grandmothers, my personal links to the past. At last, academia was encouraging me to place family history in a broader context.

Developments at the university level have influenced elementary and secondary school curricula. Time lines are now merely a springboard in many history classes. Teachers searching for books and periodicals to enrich textbook fare and stimulate research projects have helped feed a boom in nonfiction of all kinds for children. If you're interested in writing about the past you have a captive audience.

Fact vs. fiction

Most of the biographies I devoured as a child read like novels. I remember in particular one about Clara Barton, founder of the American Red Cross. In the opening chapter, Clara is celebrating her sixth birthday. As she divides up her cake, she forgets to leave herself a piece. Although the scene skillfully makes a point about Clara's selflessness, the author would never get away with all that embellishment today. It's historical fiction, not history.

Teachers and publishers expect authors to adhere to certain scholarly conventions. You can conjecture from the evidence; you can contrast opposing viewpoints; you can report conversations documented in journals or letters or tape recordings. But you can never invent characters or recreate dialogue. Writing "pure" history requires a sort of collage mentality. You have to search out the juiciest facts, then juxtapose them to support your points.

Going to the sources

Some authors avoid putting any of their own words into the collage by compiling anthologies of first-person quotes. This cut-and-paste approach asks young readers to extrapolate a lot. I prefer to blend primary and secondary sources—combining accounts by people who lived through or witnessed events with analysis and reports by academics or journalists. By paraphrasing, quoting, and interpreting, you can give more structure to the collage. You can also scale history down to an elementary reading level.

Before I begin a first draft, I survey the topic in the library to find out what's on the shelf, what's in print, and what might be available through interlibrary loan. My proposals always include an outline and a bibliography. Neither is considered binding, but they force me to think early about structure, about themes, and especially about the variety of my sources.

Cast your net widely. Researching *Hernando de Soto and the Explorers of the American South,* I relied on four published accounts. Luis Hernandez de Biedma described the group's wanderings. Although both de Soto's secretary and a Portuguese nobleman documented the

ruthlessness of the Spaniards, the latter also admired his leader's pa-
nache. Garcilaso de la Vega, a 16th-century mestizo historian who
nicknamed himself "the Inca," didn't travel with the expedition, but
his romantic version based on interviews with survivors stands out for
its sympathetic portrayal of Native Americans. Instead of designating
one chronicle as the "true" version, I juggled all four. I let my readers
see the seams of history—the biases of the winesses, and the "facts"
on which they disagreed.

With secondary sources, try to draw on recent work by young historians as well as classics by old masters. Essential to my book *This
Land Is Your Land: The American Conservation Movement* was William Cronon's *Changes in the Land: Indians, Colonists, and the Ecology of New England* (1983). Each generation rewrites history. It's not
coincidence that Cronon published his groundbreaking study about the
colonial deforestation and economic exploitation of the Atlantic coast
after Earth Day 1970. Even if you're writing about Pilgrims, make sure
you've skimmed titles from the past three decades.

And don't overlook related works in other disciplines—art history,
literature, anthropology, sociology, even science. To find out about
Native American trail building for *Get Up and Go! The History of
American Road Travel,* for instance, I consulted several anthropologi-
cal studies of the Iroquois. A balanced bibliography always results in
a better book.

Don't limit your search for lively details to books, either. I love
leafing through old magazines to get a feel for an era through ads,
advice columns, radio shows, and lyrics. I often use song titles as
section headings, such as "You'd Be So Nice To Come Home To"
(a WWII era hit) or "Fifteen Kisses on a Gallon of Gas" (an early
car tune).

As Studs Terkel has demonstrated in his many collections of interviews, oral history brings the past to life. I've used personal reminiscences in all of my "People's History" books. In addition to quoting
from Terkel's *The Good War* and other first-person accounts, I always
try to do some original research. Posting notes on the bulletin board
at a local senior center produced a lode of informants on WWII, including a charming saxophone player who had joined the Marines in order
to play in the band and had ended up a Japanese POW. Most newspapers list community meetings, and I added some color to *This Land*

Is Your Land by attending a local reunion of the Civilian Conservation Corps. To track down a talkative trucker, I started with a phone call to a garage listed in the Yellow Pages. If you have access to the Internet, you can easily contact people beyond your neighborhood. From a small town in New York, I arranged interviews with transportation engineers on the West Coast by posting a note in a cyberspace discussion group. Eloquent or unpolished, these voices add texture to the collage. Their conversational tone makes history more accessible to young readers.

Nothing beats photographs for pulling the past out of the mist. Much admired authors like Russell Freedman (*Franklin Delano Roosevelt,* 1990) and Jerry Stanley (*Children of the Dust Bowl,* 1992) write books that are almost photo essays. Although most publishers, like mine, handle all the layout and illustration, editors always appreciate ideas. If you come across an exciting photo, make a photocopy—with credit information—to submit with your manuscript. Because color is expensive to print and stock photo agencies often charge hefty fees, black-and-white "public domain" snapshots from libraries, historical societies, and government agencies are usually more attractive. A small publisher might expect you to round up illustrations yourself. If you don't find appropriate pictures in published material and don't have time to comb through archives, you could hire a photo researcher.

These are a few major archives:

*Library of Congress, Prints and Photographs Division, Washington, DC 20540

*National Archives and Records Administration, Still Picture Branch, 8601 Adelphi Road, College Park, MD 20740

*International Museum of Photography, George Eastman House, 900 East Avenue, Rochester, NY 14618

The three C's

Although most authors present history as a narrative, it may take other forms, too. In *Ticket to the Twenties: A Time Traveler's Guide* (1993), Mary Blocksma breaks down the decade into flashy chapters on everything from jive talk to breakfast. Did you know the first electric pop-up toaster hit the market in 1926? Instead of merely listing the presidents, consult *How the White House Really Works* (1989), George Sullivan's "upstairs, downstairs" tour of 1600 Pennsylvania

Avenue. While most titles fall into the categories of biography, survey, or "issue" book, your imagination is the only limit.

Once I begin writing, I stick to the three C's—*clarity, context,* and *cohesion.* Although the vocabulary you use may be simple, writing for children is often harder than writing for adults. Just try summarizing the causes of World War II in a paragraph or two for someone with no knowledge of European history. To the degree possible, keep background brief, points clear; write straightforward topic sentences, and leave the nuance to the details.

To aid the reader in evaluating an event or a person, try to include context about the period. This is the sort of low-key background that often appears in popular histories for adults, from Frederick Allen's *Only Yesterday: An Informal History of the 1920s* (1931) to David Brinkley's *Washington Goes To War* (1988). Whether you write about Earth Day or Ralph Nader or highway planning in the '60s and '70s, remind your readers that in those decades, Americans were beginning to "question authority." Since many children today have working moms, they may not appreciate the change in women's roles that "Rosie the Riveter" represented during the 1940s. Therefore, in *"V" Is for Victory: The American Home Front During World War II,* I discuss the public relations efforts of the government Office of War Information and the ads that defense plants ran to encourage people to apply for wartime work. Make it real. Describe the smell of Main Street in the heyday of horse-drawn wagons or the pastimes of Sunday afternoons before the advent of television and the NFL.

Finally, focus on themes. In a biography, you might want to trace the influence of a particular trait or skill over a lifetime—for instance, Rachel Carson's keen observation. Describing the World War II home front, I emphasized Americans' shared sense of purpose, despite racial and ethnic tensions. Since authors for young people face strict limits (in some cases, several centuries compressed into 60 pages of manuscript), they have to cull their research ruthlessly. The key-concept method gives you criteria for deciding what to keep and what to discard. Writing history, after all, is the art of pulling facts out of a grab bag and turning them into a story worth remembering.

❏ 88

WRITING BIOGRAPHIES FOR YOUNG PEOPLE

BY JAMES CROSS GIBLIN

THERE WAS A TIME WHEN IT WAS ACCEPTED PRACTICE FOR YOUNG people's biographies to whitewash their subjects to a certain extent. For example, juvenile biographies either ignored or gave a once-over-lightly treatment to personal failings like a drinking problem, and they scrupulously avoided any mention of complications in their subjects' sex lives.

Such whitewashing was intended to serve several different purposes. It protected the subject's reputation and made him or her a more suitable role model, one of the main goals of juvenile biographies in earlier periods. At the same time it shielded young readers from some of life's harsher realities.

All this has changed in the last twenty-five or thirty years as an increased openness in the arts and the media has spread to the field of children's literature. Young people who watch TV talk shows after school and dip into celebrity tell-all books expect more realism in the biographies that are written expressly for them. As a consequence, juvenile biographies of Franklin D. Roosevelt now acknowledge that he had a mistress, and young adult studies of John F. Kennedy frankly discuss his health problems and womanizing.

Today, the chief goal of a young people's biography is not to establish a role model but rather to provide solid, honest information about a man or woman worth knowing for one reason or another. However, a children's writer still has to make judgments about what facts to include in the biography and how much emphasis to give them. These judgments aren't always easy to arrive at, as I've discovered with the biographies I've written for young people. Each book presents its own unique problems, for which unique solutions must be found.

Much depends on the age of the intended audience. For example, when I was writing a picture book biography of George Washington for ages six to nine, I felt it was important to describe Washington's changing attitude toward slavery, from easy acceptance in youth to rejection as he grew older. With that background in place, I was confident even quite young readers could grasp the significance of Washington's will, which specified that his slaves would be freed after the death of his wife, Martha.

A picture book biography of Thomas Jefferson presented a much more complex set of problems. Although Jefferson had written in the Declaration of Independence that "all men are created equal," he never rejected the concept of slavery as Washington did. How could he? The very existence of his beloved Monticello depended on slave labor. After much thought, I decided there was no way I could avoid discussing Jefferson's conflicted position. But I tried to present it as clearly and simply as possible and was careful not to let the discussion overshadow Jefferson's many accomplishments.

The role of the slave Sally Hemings proved harder to deal with. Whenever I mentioned in talks with writers that I was doing a biography of Jefferson, African-Americans in the audience invariably asked how I was going to treat Sally. I told them I intended to incorporate items from the historical record in the main text—that Sally had come into Jefferson's household as part of his wife's inheritance from her father; had accompanied Jefferson's younger daughter to Paris when Jefferson was the American ambassador to France; and had become one of the most trusted house slaves at Monticello in her later years.

In the back matter, along with other additional information, I said I'd include the story that one of Sally's sons, Madison Hemings, told an Ohio journalist in the mid-19th century. According to Madison, Jefferson had made Sally his mistress after his wife's death and had fathered her seven children, five of whom lived to adulthood and three of whom "passed" as white.

My editor felt that the latter story, aside from being controversial, would be too complicated for six-to-nine-year-olds to absorb. She urged me to leave it out, and in the end I decided she was right. If the book had been directed toward an upper elementary or young adult readership, I would have insisted on the story's retention. But I decided it was probably too involved for a younger audience.

However, the references to Sally Hemings remain in the body of the book, letting readers know that a slave by that name figured in Thomas Jefferson's life. When those same readers grow older, they can read about Sally in greater detail in other books about Jefferson. Meanwhile, my book—while not going deeply into the matter—will at least have introduced Sally to them instead of pretending she didn't exist.

Biographies for older children confront the writer with a different set of difficulties. What sort of balance do you aim for between the subject's achievements and his failings? This question was brought home to me in a particularly vivid way when I was working on a biography of Charles A. Lindbergh for ages ten to fourteen. Rarely in American history has there been such a sharp dichotomy between a subject's accomplishments—in Lindbergh's case his almost incredible solo flight to Paris in 1927, along with his other contributions to aviation—and his errors, namely his flirtation with fascism in the 1930s and his open admiration of Nazi Germany.

If I'd been writing a biography for adults, I might well have focused more intently on the part Lindbergh played in bringing about the appeasement of Adolf Hitler at Munich and his subsequent speeches urging the United States to take an isolationist stand with regard to the war in Europe. But while I went into this phase of Lindbergh's life in some detail, I decided it was my duty as a biographer for young people to "accentuate the positive," as the old song lyric goes.

An adult biographer may choose to expose or debunk his subject, assuming that readers will be able to compare his version of the person's life with other, more favorable accounts. I don't believe that option is open to the juvenile biographer, whose readers will most likely have little or no prior knowledge of the subject and thus will be unable to make comparisons. Such readers deserve a more even-handed introduction to the person.

Of course, that wouldn't be possible if one were writing about a destructive personality like Adolf Hitler, Joseph Stalin, or Senator Joseph McCarthy. But even in the portrayal of someone as reviled as these men, the juvenile biographer would have the responsibility of trying to help young readers understand how a human being could be capable of such inhuman acts. In other words, the writer wouldn't simply wallow in the person's excesses, as some adult biographers might be tempted to do, but instead would try to offer a full-scale portrait and locate the sources of the person's evil actions.

If you're thinking about writing a biography for young people, here are a few questions you would do well to ask yourself. Having the answers in hand should save you time when you're researching and writing the project.

Depending on the age group of the readers, how best can you convey an accurate, three-dimensional picture of the subject in ways that the intended audience can comprehend?

If the book is for younger children, should you discuss the seamier aspects of the subject's life, or merely hint at them and leave a fuller treatment to biographers for older children?

If you're writing for an older audience, how much space should you devote to the darker side of the subject's life and experience? In a biography of sports star Magic Johnson, for example, should you go into detail about the promiscuous behavior that, by Johnson's own account, was responsible for his becoming infected with the AIDS virus, or should you merely mention it in passing?

As you seek answers to these questions, you'll have to rely ultimately on your own good taste and judgment, combined with your knowledge of the prevailing standards in the children's book field. Perhaps the most decisive factor of all, though, will be your feeling for the subject.

Jean Fritz, the author of many award-winning biographies for young people, once said that she had to like a subject tremendously before she could write about the person. I'd amend that to say I must be *fascinated* by a subject in order to invest the time and energy needed to discover what makes the person tick.

The intensity of your fascination with your subject should be of great help as you decide how much weight to give the person's positive and negative aspects. It should also communicate itself to young people, making them want to keep on reading about the intriguing man or woman at the center of your biography.

❑ 89

BRINGING HISTORY TO LIFE
FOR CHILDREN

BY DEBORAH M. PRUM

DID YOU KNOW PETER THE GREAT PRACTICED DENTISTRY ON HIS SUB-jects? That Botticelli means "little barrel"? Or that Ivan III's new wife was so heavy, she broke her bed the first night she stayed at the Czar's palace?

With marvelous facts like these at our disposal, there is no excuse for subjecting children to boringly written history. Of course, the primary purpose of writing history for kids is to instruct, not to entertain. However, once you lose a child's interest, you risk losing your audience. A good writer achieves a balance, presenting facts and concepts in a way that will entice a young reader to read on cheerfully and willingly.

Keep them awake with verbs

Nothing puts someone to sleep faster than the use of boring verbs. Granted, when you are writing about past events, you naturally tend to use verbs like "was, were, had been," but entangling your prose in passive constructions will slow down forward movement in your piece.

Whenever you can, use active image verbs. Consider these two sentences:

By the mid-sixteenth century, the unhappy serfs were hungry and became violent.
Starving serfs stormed the palace, destroying furnishings and attacking the royal guards.

Make them laugh

Use humor liberally in your writing. Catchy subtitles help, especially when you have to discuss subjects that ordinarily may not appeal to children. The subtitle "The Burning of the Papal Bull—*Not* a Barbecue!" will attract more interest than "Martin Luther Rebels."

When appropriate, include a cartoon. A cartoon will draw a child's eyes to a page. You can use a cartoon to poke fun with your material (i.e. a picture of Botticelli dressed in a barrel, apropos of his nickname). Or, you can use a cartoon to make a point. A cartoon depicting the disputing political parties prior to the Civil War may serve to inform your reader as effectively as a paragraph on the subject.

Highlighting an amusing fact makes children more likely to plow through less interesting information. For example, in a discussion of the Gutenberg press, you can start by mentioning that Johann Gutenberg started out life as "John Gooseflesh" (Gensfleisch). Once you have grabbed their attention, then you can go on to talk about the somewhat drier details of your topic.

Be careful when using humor. Avoid the temptation to distort fact in order to be funny.

Using sidebars

Not all factual information or lists may fit smoothly into your text, and may slow the pacing of your piece. For material that is tangential to your primary point, sidebars are a useful way to handle these problems.

A sidebar enables you to include greater detail on a topic without disrupting your narrative flow. Sidebars can give your reader an in-depth view of the period you are discussing. For a piece on the Civil War, you might include a few recipes of the dishes popular at the time. Or, if you are discussing Leonardo Da Vinci, you might include a list of all his inventions. Every once in a while, it doesn't hurt to include a nonsensical sidebar, like this one:

Places Marco Polo did *not* explore:
1. Lizard Lick, North Carolina
2. Walla Walla, Washington
3. Newark, New Jersey

When writing about history for children, you can easily get bogged down in confusing details. Good organization of your material is essential. A young child reading about the first few centuries of Russian history will be tempted to think that every last Russian of importance was named Ivan or Fedor. Of course, that's not true. But, you have to provide a way to sort through potentially confusing material. There are several ways to help your readers:

One is to show a detailed family tree at the beginning of your chapter, including dates, actions for which the person is famous, and nicknames (i.e. Ivan the Great, Ivan the Terrible, Fedor the Feebleminded).

If you must discuss many events occurring over several years, consider using a time line to show the "who, what, and when" of any era in a clear and simple way.

Another way to help a child understand some of the forces contributing to an event is to tell a story. How did a lightning storm change Martin Luther's life? Talk about the time Borgia betrayed the Duke of Urbino: Borgia borrowed, then used the Duke's own weapons to attack his city. Mention that Peter III played with lead soldiers and dolls, and ultimately lost the Russian Empire to his wife, Catherine the Great. By telling these stories, you will make your material far more interesting and you will give children a better sense of history.

Controversy

Don't shy away from controversy. Make it your ally. Use the tension controversial issues create to add excitement to your text. When possible, tell both sides of the story. Readers know that historians disagree. Help your readers form their own opinions by including direct quotes from the controversial figures, quotes of correspondence, or transcripts of debates. Give the children a chance to hear both sides and an opportunity to develop their critical thinking skills.

Not all historians agree, but you can make controversy work for you. That statement will not come as a shock to most adults, yet it does pose a problem for writers. Which side of the story do you present to young readers? Maybe the "facts" are clear (although, not always), but one historian may slant a discussion in a completely different way from another.

For example, what about Machiavelli? Was he an ogre, an opportunist with dangerous political ideas? Was he a practical political scientist who merely described reality? Does the answer lie somewhere in between? Those are good questions, debated by one and all. How should you present the topic to children?

Fascinating beginnings

You must capture your young reader's attention at the beginning of a chapter and end it in a way that will make that child want to go on to the next chapter.

Begin with an interesting fact or a question: "What does the word 'Medici' mean to you? 1) an interesting pasta dish, 2) a new foreign convertible, 3) a deadly tropical disease, or 4) none of the above."

Capture your reader's attention by opening a chapter with a scene from everyday life at the time your book takes place. (Make it clear that this event "might" have happened but don't veer from accepted fact.) For example, you could start a chapter on Thomas Jefferson by describing him playing his violin for some guests in his drawing room at Monticello.

Ending your chapter well is just as important as beginning well. You want your reader to finish your book. Make a statement that will pique the child's curiosity.

Insofar as possible, make your book a visual pleasure. If you are writing about Ben Franklin, see if you can find museum photographs of his pot-bellied stove. Look for pictures of Catherine the Great's crown or Galileo's telescope. If you are discussing a war or an explorer, include colorful maps.

When writing history for children, be certain that you know your audience. Spend some time around the age group for whom you are writing. Listen to the words they use. Pay attention to how they form their sentences. Figure out what they think is funny. Then, in your own writing, use syntax slightly more complex than what they used. Include a few unfamiliar terms, but be certain to highlight and define any new word. When you are presenting a concept that is foreign to your readers, compare it with one they already understand.

Once your material is written, test it on a child you know. Find a curmudgeonly person who is a reluctant reader. You will be sure to get some valuable comments. A grumpy child will provide a good first test for your material. Then, if you have the opportunity, read your manuscript in front of a classroom of kids. Are your words greeted with excitement and interest, or just yawns and glassy-eyed stares? If you see tired looks and drooping eyelids, enliven your prose accordingly. However, if the children want to know more, you've got a winner.

❑ 90

WHEN YOU WRITE HUMOR FOR CHILDREN

BY JULIE ANNE PETERS

CHILDREN ARE BORN TO LAUGH. IN FACT, HUMOR IS THOUGHT TO BE the first expressive form of communication. Good writers understand the value of humor when they write for children. Not only does humor entertain and amuse them, but it lures the most reluctant reader.

When my first book, *The Stinky Sneakers Contest,* was selected by third-grade children in Greater Kansas City as their favorite book of 1995, I was delighted—and shocked. Humorous books rarely win awards. In the kingdom of exalted literature, humor is relegated to serfdom. But the award confirmed my belief that even though funny books infrequently win prestigious literary prizes, they do become children's favorites.

Writers often tell me, "I'm not a funny person. I can't write humor." Piffle! Betsy Byars, grandmistress of humorous children's books, reveals the secret. "The funniest word in the vocabulary of a second grader," she says, "is 'underwear.'" Use it liberally. "Poo poo" works for preschoolers. Or you can rise above so-called potty humor and choose one of the standard humor devices that follow.

Surprise

Writers and illustrators of picture books are guaranteed laughter or smiles by springing the unexpected on their young readers. Books are the perfect vehicle for creating humor through surprise. James Stevenson demonstrates this very effectively in his book, *Quick! Turn the Page.*

To bring about surprise, take an expected event or consequence and create the unexpected. A boy bounces a ball. He expects it to go up and come down. Page one: Ball goes up. Page two: A wild monkey in a banyan tree snatches the ball and steals off to . . . ? Next page.

Surprise can delight page after page, intermittently, or just once, with a surprise ending. Read Judith Viorst's poem, "Mother Doesn't Want a Dog," for a classic example of a surprise ending.

Exaggeration

The earliest American humor used exaggeration in its purest form: larger-than-life heroes performing superhuman feats. Remember Pecos Bill, Paul Bunyan, and John Henry? The American tall tale is still a favored form of humor for children. Anne Isaac's *Swamp Angel* moves this classic genre into the 1990s with her female superheroine. Not only does Swamp Angel fend off Thundering Tarnation, the marauding bear, she has to prove herself to taunting backwoodsmen who'd have her stay at home, quilting.

Transcendental toasters, madcap Martians, and articulate animals are all examples of truth stretching. My favorite mouthy mammal is the mutt, Martha, in Susan Meddaugh's *Martha Speaks*. After Martha dog eats a bowl of alphabet soup, she becomes quite the loquacious pooch. "You people are so bossy. COME! SIT! STAY! You never say please."

Journey beyond the bounds of possibility to create exaggerated humor. How about a plucky petunia? A daring doormat? Even preschool children can differentiate between the real and unreal as they gleefully embrace the fun in make-believe.

Word and language play

With wordplay, language is key to the rhythm, sound, and rhyme that carries your story forward. Readers become reciters. Jack Prelutsky, Shel Silverstein, and Joyce Armor are wizards of wordplay in their witty poetry. Nancy Shaw's "Sheep" books are shear joy (yes, pun intended).

If you're not a poet and you know it, try your hand at literal translation. *Amelia Bedelia* books by Peggy Parish teach you how. Amelia Bedelia, the indomitable maid, takes every order, every conversation, every suggestion literally, and sets herself up for catastrophe. Children love trying to predict the consequences of Amelia's misunderstandings.

Role reversal

Eugene Trivizas chose role reversal to retell a classic fairy tale in his *The Three Little Wolves and the Big Bad Pig*. To make the most effective use of role reversal, choose familiar characters acting out of character. Turn everyday events topsy-turvy. Harry Allard uses children's perceptions about substitute teachers (whether true or not) when he changes meek, mild Miss Nelson into bleak, vile Viola Swamp. You may choose to switch family members, as Mary Rodgers did with her mother/daughter exchange in *Freaky Friday,* or people and their pets, aliens with automobiles, princes and paupers. Stay away from twins, though. It's been done and done and done.

Nonsense

Nonsense includes incongruity and absurdity, ridiculous premises, and illogical series of events. What makes a nonsense book funny is its weirdness. *Imogene's Antlers,* by David Small, is the story of a young girl who wakes up one day to find she's grown antlers. This is a problem. Imogene has trouble getting dressed; she can't fit through narrow doorways; her antlers get caught in the chandelier. Even worse, her mother keeps fainting at the sight of her. Though children recognize the absurdity of Imogene's situation, they also see how well she copes with her sudden disability. This book speaks to children's physical differences, which is a fundamental value of humor.

Literary humor helps children grow. It offers distancing from pain, from change and insecurity, from cruelty, disaster and loss. Children are not always sophisticated or mature enough emotionally to laugh at themselves. Humorous books with subtle serious themes offer children ways to deal positively with life's inequities. They offer a magic mirror, through which children's problems—and their solutions—can be reflected back.

Slapstick

Farce and horseplay have been part of the American humor scene since vaudeville—maybe before. Who knows what Neanderthals did for fun? Physical humor appeals to the child in all of us. Hectic, frenetic chases and bumbling, stumbling characters cause chaos in the pages of children's books. Your plot will immediately pick up pace if you include a frantic fiasco or two. Check out Betsy Byars' *Golly Sisters.* May-May and Rose's calamitous capers are rip-roaring fun. Avi used slapstick masterfully in his book *Romeo and Juliet Together (And*

Alive) At Last! His high schoolers' rendition of Shakespeare's master-piece would make The Bard weep (with tears of laughter).

Satire

You can achieve humor by poking fun at human vices, human foibles or the general social order, which rarely makes sense to children, so they love to see it pulverized on paper. My favorite satirical series is "The Stupids," by Harry Allard. I swear these people lived next door to me when I was growing up. James Marshall's illustrations add hilar-ity to the humor.

To write effective satire for children, you must recognize the ridicu-lous in youngsters' lives. Make fun of uppity people's pretensions, lampoon restrictions, and spoof the silly societal mores children are expected to embrace. Create characters who teeter on the edge, who challenge the status quo—and thrive. Read Sid Fleischman's *The Whipping Boy* for a lesson in writing satire.

Adolescent angst

Family and school stories, growing up and coming-of-age novels make up the bulk of children's humorous fiction. Adolescence just seems to lend itself to humor. Laughter helps older children deal with life's larger dilemmas: death, divorce, disability, senility, loss, and un-welcome change. Reading about characters who successfully and hu-morously overcome obstacles provides children with painless lessons on how to handle their own problems.

For my book *B.J.'s Billion-Dollar Bet,* I started with a troublesome topic—betting. Frequently, I overhear conversations between kids who are placing bets: "Oh, sure. I bet you," or "Wanna bet? Come on, let's bet on it." And they bet away valuable items—clothing, sports card collections, lunch money. To show the consequences of betting, I cre-ated B.J. Byner, a compulsive gambler who bets and loses all of his possessions, then begins to bet away his family's belongings. When B.J. loses his mother's lottery ticket in a wager, then finds out the ticket is a fifty-million-dollar winner, he has to get that ticket back!

I hope young readers will see that the risks of gambling are consider-able; the losses more than they may be willing or able to pay. Betting can result in loss of friendship, family conflict, and, as with any addic-tion, loss of control and self-respect. If I hadn't chosen a humorous premise for this book, it would have been too preachy.

Middle-grade and young adult novels include more urbane, cerebral humor. These young people are developing their own individual views of the world, and social relationships take on a major role.

For my middle-grade novel, *How Do You Spell Geek?*, I began with a funny, offbeat character, Lurlene Brueggemeyer, the geek, and built the story around her. The issues are serious ones—judging people by their appearance, shifting alliances between friends, peer pressure, and self-examination, but I gave my main character, Ann, a sarcastic sense of humor and a wry way of watching her world get weird, which seems to lighten the load.

Read the masters of middle-grade humor: Ellen Conford, Barbara Park, Beverly Cleary, Betsy Byars, Daniel Pinkwater, and Jerry Spinelli, among many, many others.

There are humor writers who defy classification; they relate to their audiences through rebellion, radicalism, and general outrageousness. Three young adult authors who fall into this special category are M.E. Kerr, Richard Peck, and Paul Zindel. Their books validate an emerging adult's individuality, passion, and self-expression.

If you plan to try your hand at humor, steer clear of targeting a specific age group. I've received letters from eight-year-olds who are reading my junior high novel, *Risky Friends*. And I'm sure you know high schoolers who still get a hoot out of Dr. Seuss. Even though sense of humor evolves as we grow older, we never lose appreciation for the books that made us laugh when we were younger.

Humor writing is a spontaneous act. It comes from deep within, from your own wacky way of looking at the world. One word of caution: Humor has power. What we laugh at, we make light of. What we laugh at, we legitimize and condone. Cruelty is never funny. Violence isn't funny. Torture, torment, neglect, war, hatred, and preying on others' misfortunes are not subjects for children's humor. There's a fine line between sarcasm and cynicism; between light-spirited and mean-spirited. So be aware. If you do write humor for children, observe the limits.

There's more than one way to connect with children through humor (beyond using "underwear"). In fact, with all the techniques available, and given the fact that children laugh easily, your chances of eliciting gleeful responses are excellent.

❏ 91

DYNAMIC DETAILS
MAKE A DIFFERENCE IN
CHILDREN'S FICTION

BY BEVERLY J. LETCHWORTH

Marcy edged closer to the lake, amazed at the large number of snow geese. She stood quietly, not wanting to disturb them. But despite her caution, an alarm jetted through the flock, and they rose together in a mob of blurred white, their flapping wings sounding like the clattering of a thousand clapping hands. Marcy gasped as the rising mass spewed into the air and spread quickly across the fields.

WHAT MADE THIS PARAGRAPH SO EFFECTIVE? DETAILS—DETAILS THAT worked. Specific, well-chosen details that wove in sensory perceptions, imagery, and a simile helped make the scene come alive and made the setting real, believable. Readers could see the geese, hear their wings, and feel Marcy's wonderment. They felt involved.

That's the goal of good storytelling: Involve your readers so they feel they're part of the action. Readers must feel connected to your characters, settings, even to objects, or they'll lose interest in the story. This holds true for any fiction writing, whether for adults or children.

But in writing children's fiction, you must consider more restrictions, because children are bored by long descriptions about settings or characters. Therefore, details must be limited and chosen with care. Opt for those details that convey only the most significant aspects of a setting, character, or object.

Also, keep in mind that the younger the reader, the fewer details should be used. For young children whose attention span is short, details must be strictly limited. In a description about an attic, you may choose to say only, "The attic was dim and dusty. Cobwebs hung in the corners. Bulging boxes and broken furniture lined the walls." These few details offer readers definite sensory images that bring the scene to life. Sometimes, a single detail is enough to set the tone: "An owl hooted low and loud, making her shiver."

As children mature, they can grasp more details and appreciate the many layers of a character or setting; and, indeed, they can absorb some of the subtleties.

Let's go back to the attic and add more details suitable for older readers.

The attic lay dim and dusty before her—a small room with a low ceiling that seemed a perfect size for an Alice-in-Wonderland escape. Bulging boxes overflowing with old clothes sat like curled-up sleepers, and a torn overstuffed chair seemed a fat lady at rest beside them. From all corners cobwebs hung in tattered white streamers, looking soft and gauzy in the dusky light.

More depth has been added, but you'd better stop here or the description will become tedious. Even for teenagers, don't overdo the details. The detailed style of Charles Dickens is passé today; children of the computer age with its easy access to quick information won't keep reading a book that's verbose.

You can achieve a fast-paced, stimulating style by using methods for selecting and using effective details. It takes practice, but it's worth the effort.

1. Establish what age group you're writing for to determine how many details to include.

2. Select the most telling details to describe the particular situation and connote specific aspects of the setting or character.

For physical description of a character, choose only one of two details, rather than a whole paragraph to reveal the essence of that character. For example: "Straight-backed, her head high, she strode into the room." Or, "He didn't bother to push the long, greasy hair from his eyes as he lurched down the steps."

To convey an emotional reaction without becoming wordy, you may show your character's sadness by simply saying, "Again she felt the familiar sharp sting of tears behind her eyes."

An individual object may often merit some detail. Again, choose the best detail to make it real to the reader. "The satin dress lay across the bed, as smooth and soft as melted gold." Or, "Amid the jumble of plastic glasses and shriveled plants, the silver bell glinted like a jewel on the sunny kitchen windowsill." Or, "The fern hung from the ceiling and dripped its lacy fronds onto the floor."

3. Use the five senses to bring your scene to life. Sight is vital in descriptions, but don't neglect the other senses. Bring in sound, smell, taste, and touch whenever possible, for they add depth and realism. And don't forget color.

4. Use specific details so readers can see and feel the scene. First, envision the setting you want to describe, and make a list of its specific qualities. A run-down bookstore may include details such as: water stains on the ceiling, books piled haphazardly on shelves and in corners, a cat meowing from a shelf, a crooked wood floor, cobwebs in the windows, musty smell, dust and grit on books. From this list, choose three details that would set the ambiance of the scene without becoming tiresome.

5. If you can't visualize a setting adequately, visit the type of place you have in mind. A wealth of details will present themselves, some you never expected. For example: When you envision a boat dock, you can see water, fishing boats, nets and rods, heavy ropes. What you couldn't imagine was the slap of water against the boats, the gentle sway of the dock beneath your feet, the cloying fish smell, gulls. These sensory details will add the realism needed to make readers feel they are there.

Of course, it's not always possible to visit a place. Not many of us can take a quick trip to a rainforest or go to a circus whenever we want to. If you can't visit, then read, read, read about the setting you want to use. Study pictures that will give you a better sense of the sights, sounds, maybe even the smells of the particular locale.

6. Create similes and metaphors when appropriate. Remember the satin dress and the silver bell. Figures of speech enhance details, but for young readers, use details cautiously. Young minds can't always grasp the comparisons, so use them sparingly, and keep them simple and easy to understand. For older readers, figures of speech can be used more frequently.

7. Occasionally, allow your characters to describe the details of a setting or object. This technique offers a change of pace and gives the reader the benefit of a character's feelings and opinions about a place or object.

8. Break up descriptions in order to incorporate more appropriate details as interestingly as possible. Sprinkle details throughout the scene so there are no long stretches of solid text. One of my stories for middle-grade readers, set in 1850, features Lithia Ann, a free black girl who dreams of getting an education so she can become a teacher. Her walk into town with her brother Roan needed to include many details. I tried to scatter them in between dialogue, thoughts, and action to make the following scene more appealing.

As they walked, the smell of the river wafted around them. It flowed on their right, a wide ribbon of currents, always moving, always changing. Lithia Ann felt its strength and it always revived her. Some of her worry dropped away, and she took deep breaths of the river's scent.

In the distance blared a deep mournful steamboat whistle. The *James Hawthorne,* thought Lithia Ann. She could always tell the steamboat by its deep haunting sound, just as she could identify other steamboats by their particular-sounding whistles.

As they passed shops and stores, Lithia Ann called out the names of various businesses. It was still exciting to be able to read the names and signs in the windows.

"Some day you'll be able to read too, Roan," she said enthusiastically. "Then you'll know what everything is." She remembered the first time she had realized that a group of letters spelled a word: C-A-T. . . .

Soon they reached the bustling wharf. Noises pushed aside Lithia Ann's thoughts. Grunts and yells, thuds, and bangs filled the streets as men unloaded cargo from flatboats and steamboats tied at the pier. Dogs barked, horses snorted, mules brayed. . . .

Lithia Ann and Roan rested on the wooden boardwalk in front of the hotel. A fishmonger with his cart of fresh fish called to passersby, "Fresh fish, fresh fish, fit for the pan!"

An old woman pushed a wheelbarrow filled with strawberries. "Straaaawberrrrries!" she shouted. Lithia Ann's mouth watered.

Roan dashed up to the cart and held out his hand to the old woman. "No money, no berries," she said harshly, pushing past him.

"I only wanted one," Roan said sadly, when Lithia Ann took him by the hand.

I hope that these specific details help you visualize the sights, sounds, and smells of a river town in the 1850s and make you feel as if you are walking the dirt streets with the characters.

Details are vital elements of any story, for they picture the world of the characters. Like yarn in a rug, details woven throughout the plot, ever-changing in color and pattern, offer readers a way to "belong" to the story. As a writer, you must strive to bring out this involvement. Only by presenting the most effective details can you make this happen.

□ 92

CAPTURING THE
YOUNG ADULT READER

BY CHERYL ZACH

TRYING TO CAPTURE THE YOUNG ADULT READER IS A BIT LIKE ALICE'S pursuit of the White Rabbit; these young people are almost as elusive and as hard to pin down. So who's really reading young adult books, and how do we write for them? There's no simple answer.

The young adult books you find on library or bookstore shelves run the gamut from innocent first-kiss stories to accounts of the much more serious consequences of an unintended pregnancy, from lighthearted running-for-class-president tales to suspenseful live-or-die mysteries.

Librarians were the first to search for young adult books that would be of interest to high school or mature junior high students. But as the concept of books aimed especially at this age group became common, bookstores stepped in to define the label "young adult." Some of the confusion may have been caused when booksellers and publishers, perhaps in an attempt to broaden the market, perhaps in recognizing that children like to "read up"—that is, read about characters slightly older than themselves—lowered the age levels of YA to include readers as young as ten or eleven.

At the same time, some editors and librarians feel that readers 16 to 22 are underserved. Many readers that age are turning to adult books, but do adult authors address their particular concerns?

Obviously, the subject matter portrayed in books for pre-teens won't be the same as in novels for older teens. To make the equation even harder to solve, the age at which teenagers and adolescents experience physical, emotional, and mental maturation varies widely.

So defining the YA reader depends partly on whom you ask. Yet despite this problem of definition, the YA novel is too important a genre to be ignored. The coming-of-age novel chronicling a young person's first experiences with romance, with death, with adult actions and consequences, with personal responsibility is too significant to be considered only as a marketing ploy.

As a result, authors and publishers strive for meaningful YA books, while sometimes targeting different age groups. Junior high students often enjoy Lois Lowry's perceptive, humorous Anastasia books and also feel the tug of Lurlene McDaniel's poignant novels of critically ill adolescents.

Older teens may be drawn to the darker threads of a Lois Duncan mystery, such as *Killing Mr. Griffin,* or to Christopher Pike's or R.L. Stine's more graphic horror novels. Novels such as my own *Runaway* and *Family Secrets* also deal with more mature themes—a pregnant teen on the run; an adopted teenager seeking her birth parents and discovering a dark secret in her family's past.

Some books seem to span the age groups; historical novels like my *Carrie's Gold* or *Southern Angel,* a Civil War saga, or fantasy novels such as Lloyd Alexander's Prydain Chronicles or Anne McCaffrey's Dragonsinger books, seem to attract readers from a wide age group, sometimes including adults. These books often have significant themes, but the fact that the stories are presented in another time or place, free of the restraints of modern costume and slang and social traditions, perhaps contributes to their ageless appeal.

Although topics and treatments may vary in books for younger or older teens, fortunately other aspects will not. Readers of any age will respond to well-drawn, three-dimensional characters, a significant problem that the protagonist (not a helpful adult) will resolve or come to terms with, realistic dialogue, and a fast-paced plot with compelling scenes.

In addition, modern readers expect a quick beginning that sweeps them immediately into the story. They want to be introduced to the main character right away, to see at least a hint of the problem this young person faces, and they want to care enough about his or her character to guarantee that they will hang around to see what happens.

How does the YA author create likable, yet vulnerable characters? Go into their backgrounds; examine their families, and their position in the family (the oldest child is often expected to be more responsible; the youngest may be more indulged). Look at their relationships with their parents, with their siblings, with school friends and teachers, with the neighbor next door, the neighborhood or school bully, the part-time employer. Consider a character's earlier experiences—even a child has a past!—and see what has helped make him into the person he is today. Your characters may not be perfect, but make sure they're basically decent; you have to like your characters first, if you want your readers to like them, too.

The protagonist should have a real problem, an age-appropriate problem that young people will identify with. Try to be honest with your readers; never condescend to them. I know that to a ten-year-old, getting the wrong teacher on the first day of school can be a real disaster; that a fifteen-year-old may really be in love, no pat-on-the-head infatuation here; that a sixteen-year-old could be in a life or death situation if he defies the local gang. Keep up with what's happening in real life, and keep in mind that adolescence today is not the same as it was twenty years ago. Watch the news, read teen magazines and listen to teen music. Make sure the setting and the dialogue are up-to-date. I get some of my best ideas from newspaper or news stories. (The plot of *Runaway* evolved from a short article in the back pages of my local paper.)

Also, remember that just as the novel itself has a shape, a rise and fall and rise to an ultimate climax, scenes also have their own shape and purpose. A scene that does not move the story forward, provide more understanding of the character, create suspense or humor, or provide information about the setting has no place in your YA novel. Test every line of dialogue and every paragraph of narrative to make sure it is absolutely necessary. For today's impatient readers, you must write cleanly and succinctly, in graceful prose. Make every word count.

Finally, be sure the climax is truly the most exciting part of the book. Show how your young protagonist rises to the most difficult challenge he or she has faced, and meets it head-on in a scene that is played to its emotional, physical, and intellectual zenith, so that your readers will sit on the edge of their seats and be unable to put the book down until they know what the resolution will be. And then, we writers—along with teachers and parents—will hope that kids, no matter what their ages, will be eager to read another YA novel, and another, and another.

❑ 93

TEN TIPS ON WRITING
PICTURE BOOKS

BY DIANE MAYR

AS A CHILDREN'S LIBRARIAN, I DO STORY HOURS FOR PRESCHOOLERS ages 3 to 5. Children this age have developed language skills, but aren't yet able to read on their own. After more than 1,500 story hours, I know what these children like. By sharing this knowledge I hope to improve the chances of my wowing young patrons with some great picture book—yours.

Tip #1: READ. When wannabe writers tell me they have written a book for children, I ask them to compare their book to something already in print. I'm usually met with a blank stare, or "I haven't read many children's books." If you haven't read what's out there, how do you know if your book is better than—or as good as—the rest? How do you know your version of "The Three Little Pigs" is different enough from the traditional one to attract a child's (or publisher's) attention? [Suggestions of titles to "study" will be shown in brackets.]

Tip #2: BE BRIEF. Good books for preschoolers run 800 words or less—sometimes considerably less. Look at the word counts of some of the "classics": *The Very Hungry Caterpillar* (Eric Carle)—225; *If You Give A Mouse A Cookie* (Laura Joffe Numeroff)—291; *The Snowy Day* (Ezra Jack Keats)—319; and *Corduroy* (Don Freeman)—708.

Don't use a lot of description, the illustrator will fill in the details. (You may, though, wish to provide notes, separate from the text, about illustrative elements crucial to your story.) A balance of dialogue and narration works best.

Tip #3: TELL A GOOD STORY. If your forte is "mood" pieces, then you're not aiming for the preschool audience. For them, something has to happen, and the story must have a beginning, a middle, and an end. The ending must not be ambiguous; predictability is expected.

Have you heard of the "rule of three"? The main character must complete three tasks, or face three foes, before winning the day. The rule has worked for generations of talespinners; try letting your heroine face the monster under the bed three times before she develops the courage to banish it. [Read: *The Wolf's Chicken Stew*, by Keiko Kasza]

Tip #4: KNOW THE PRESCHOOL PSYCHE. Preschoolers are strongly tied to their homes and family. They enjoy hearing about situations they're familiar with such as the arrival of a new baby. It's your task to develop a twist on a familiar theme, but make the twist believable. [Read: *Julius, The Baby Of The World*, by Kevin Henkes]

As adults, we have a tendency to dismiss a preschooler's fears and "problems" as inconsequential, but they're very real. They need to be addressed and dealt with reassuringly. [Read: *Rosie's Baby Tooth*, by Maryann Macdonald]

The problems adults see as significant—death, divorce, abuse, etc.—are topics for bibliotherapy; such books have a place, but are not for the general audience. Nor are 3-to 5-year-olds the audience for a picture book that tries to explain the Holocaust. Childhood is short but critical in the development of character. Preschoolers deserve to feel secure.

Animals often appear as the characters in picture books, but don't allow the talking animals in your stories to do things a child wouldn't do. For example, don't have Baby Monkey cross a busy street by herself. If you do, preschoolers will invariably ask, "Where's the Mommy?" If Baby Monkey needs to cross the street without Mom in order to advance your plot, leave it in, but don't arbitrarily dismiss a young monkey's (child's) need to depend on responsible adults. [Read: *Baby Duck And the Bad Eyeglasses*, by Amy Hest]

Tip #5: SUREFIRE PLEASERS. Preschoolers love humor! But, they're not looking for subtlety. Think pratfalls without pain. Sophisticated punning is out, but nonsense words draw a laugh. [Read: FROGGIE GETS DRESSED, by Jonathan London; *Contrary Mary*, by Anita Jeram; *Tacky The Penguin*, by Helen Lester; *Mother Makes A Mistake*, by Ann Dorer]

Noises are always a hit. Preschoolers will "moo" and "quack" along with the reader—and love doing it! [Read: *Is This A House For Hermit Crab?*, by Amy McDonald; *Peace At Last*, by Jill Murphy; *Small Green Snake*, by Libba Moore Gray]

Allow the audience to discover a "secret" before the main character does. Little kids, so frequently put down by older siblings, more advanced peers, and even by adults, appreciate the opportunity to feel "smarter" than someone else. This device is often used by puppeteers who have the audience see the villain before the lead puppet does. If you've ever heard the gleeful screams, "Look behind you! He's behind you!", then you know how successful this can be with preschoolers. [Read: any of Frank Asch's books about Bear. Two good examples: *Mooncake* and *Bread And Honey*]

Questions scattered throughout the story—for example, "Should he look under the bed?"—allow interaction between the child and the story. Kids love to interact! [Read: *The Noisy Book,* by Margaret Wise Brown]

Tip #6: PICTURES ARE ESSENTIAL. If your story makes sense without out visual clues, then it is not a picture book. Text and pictures must contribute equally to telling the story. (One note of caution: Unless you are an accomplished artist/illustrator, do not attempt to illustrate your own work if you plan to submit it to a trade publisher. You need not seek out an illustrator, the illustrator will be selected by your publisher.) [Read: *King Bidgood's In The Bathtub,* by Audrey Wood, illustrated by Don Wood]

Tip #7: WATCH YOUR LANGUAGE! Preschoolers tend to take what you say literally. If I read aloud—"'Look, it's snowing!' he cried."—without a doubt, a child will interrupt me to ask, "Why is he crying?" Use "he said" or "he shouted."

Nothing destroys the flow of a story like having to stop to explain an unfamiliar term. Use language with which today's children are comfortable. Don't use "frock" for dress or "dungarees" for jeans.

Tip #8: LEARN THE 3 "R's." Repetition, rhythm, and rhyme work well with the younger set. Traditional folktales like "The Little Red Hen" still appeal to them because of the repetition. Rhyme, unfortunately, can kill a story if it's not done well. Rather than write a story entirely in rhyme, try a few repetitive rhyming sentences. [Read: *Millions Of Cats,* by Wanda Gag; *A Cake For Barney,* by Joyce Dunbar]

Tip #9: READ ALOUD. Read your story out loud and listen. If you stumble, nine times out of ten, there's something wrong with the writing. When it finally sounds right to you, try reading it to someone else for continuity and clarity.

Tip #10: MAKE A DUMMY. Fold eight pieces of paper in half and staple at the fold. You now have a 32-page dummy. Cut and paste your words onto the pages, leaving the first three pages blank for front matter. You'll need to make decisions on length. Is the story too short? Too long? Does it flow smoothly? You may want to make notes about the pictures you envision for each page or spread. The suspense in a story could be jeopardized by raising a problem in the text on a left-hand page and having a picture on the right-hand page provide the solution. Remember, preschoolers are "reading" the illustrations as you're reading the words. It's preferable to have a page turn before providing resolutions or answers.

Bonus Tip: Make Friends with Your Children's Librarian. She can introduce you to the classic picture books, as well as to the best of what's currently being published. She'll have review journals and publishers' catalogues for you to look at, and she can double as a critical reader.

I've been waiting more than ten years for the perfect picture book to share with my story hour kids; I can wait a little longer for you to write it!

❑ 94

WRITING FOR CHILDREN'S MAGAZINES

BY DONNA FREEDMAN

NOT EVERYONE CAN WRITE FOR CHILDREN, BUT EVERYONE SHOULD want to: Children's magazines can be a lucrative market. I've been paid as much as $350 for a 150-word article. And there are hundreds of free-lance opportunities, from Sunday-school papers to glitzy, high-tech skateboard 'zines. The market has grown markedly in recent years: In 1985, the Institute of Children's Literature identified 354 free-lance markets; today, ICL lists 582 such markets.

Writing for kids isn't easy. You have a small space in which to pack a lot of information. You have to write in language they can understand, and you need ideas that will grab the attention of youngsters who are increasingly distracted by CD-ROM, cable television, video games, and other competing entertainment.

Most important of all, you need to put aside any preconceived notions about childhood. Children are a lot more sophisticated than they were in your own childhood years, and they want articles and stories that are relevant to their world. Children's publications now call for writing that reflects the realities of modern life: latchkey kids, for example, or single-parent families.

Pastimes and hobbies may be a lot different from those you remember. Small-town kids may still go to the old swimming hole in the summer, but suburban and urban youngsters today are more likely to play soccer or spend their free time on their skateboards. Therefore, you need to familiarize yourself with what they are doing if you want to write for them. Borrow a friend's children, teach a Sunday-school class, coach a sports team, or eavesdrop at McDonald's. Do anything to get an idea of what kids are like today.

Although juvenile magazines publish a fair number of short stories, you're much more likely to sell nonfiction: articles that paint vivid pictures of historical events or use colorful, down-to-earth imagery to explain a scientific or technological phenomenon. Profiles of famous people can no longer be dry as dust: Readers want to feel the wind on Amelia Earhart's face, or hear the crash as Thomas Edison's prototype light bulb shatters on the floor.

Editors are looking for more biography, history, and hard science. Nature is a perennial favorite, but most magazines already have backlogs of articles about Really Interesting Animals or Fascinating Natural Phenomena. It's not that these ideas can't make good reading, it's that they need a new approach.

For example, *Highlights for Children* recently published an article about a tiger in an animal sanctuary. Normally, the magazine doesn't use pieces set in zoos or sanctuaries, but this piece was different because the writer used her senses to create a picture of the sleekness of the tiger's fur, the roughness of its tongue, its ever-changing moods. It worked because it was evocative. If it had been encyclopedic— "Tigers live in Asia. They are endangered."—it would have been boring, and not held the attention of young readers.

Even an article that has a lot of information needs to be written in an exciting, attention-getting style. Since slang or jargon tends to sound phony when used by adults, concentrate on unusual details and the newest research you can find. Intrigue readers and show them how much you care about the subject, whether it's tiger fur or in-line skating.

You don't need to be a rocket scientist to write about the space program, or an entomologist to write about dung beetles. All you really need is a dedication to research, an ability to write clearly and concisely, and a respect for your young audience.

One of the most common mistakes writers make is writing "down" to children—being too sweet, too jaunty, or too didactic. Children don't want to be patronized or preached at.

The worst crime of all is to try to shoehorn in some moral. If there's a lesson to be learned, you should show it, not tell it. Your average nine-year-old isn't going to have an epiphany like, "Guess I should have listened to what the Sunday-school teacher/Grandma/my dad said." If he read anything preachy or boring, he'd groan out loud: "Give me a break!" Like most of us, kids read magazines to be entertained.

Articles and stories need to fit into very small spaces in the magazines. Even if a magazine specifies 800 to 1,200 words, don't feel compelled to use up all the allotted space. Editors love tight writing, because children, particularly beginning readers, are more likely to finish a short piece than a daunting 1,200-worder.

Marketing skills are as important as writing skills. There's no sense writing a piece on the maternal instincts of wolverines only to find that there's no market for such an article. And if you're sending out ideas blindly, without the slightest bit of market research, you're not just wasting postage, you're wasting an editor's time.

A little market research would show, for instance, that *Cricket* doesn't publish horror stories; that *Highlights* steers clear of pop culture; that the editors at the Children's Better Health Institute don't like stories that feature junk food.

Also, it's not enough to know what kind of articles the editors want; you also need to know what kind of writing they prefer. It's almost impossible to get a sense of a magazine's voice from writer's guidelines. The only way to do that is to read several issues of the magazine to give you an idea of what you might be able to sell.

The stories and articles in children's publications may be slangy and colorful, or written in a graceful, literary style. Not a single word is wasted; each is carefully chosen for maximum impact.

You might consider subscribing to a few magazines, such as *Highlights, Cricket,* and *Cobblestone.* Or spend a couple of hours each month in the local library, reading as many children's magazines as possible. Go through back issues, too.

The Writer Magazine is a good place to find other outlets for your work. So are specialty publications, such as *Children's Writer* (published by the Institute of Children's Literature) or the Society of Children's Book Writers and Illustrators *Bulletin.*

Sunday-school papers and other religious periodicals are always hungry for good writing, and they publish up to 52 times a year. They tend to pay less than mainstream children's magazines, but they're a good place for beginners to hone their writing skills, learn to work with editors, and compile some clips.

It's a lot tougher to sell to a high-profile magazine. The best-known publications may get as many as 1,000 unsolicited manuscripts each month. One way to break in is through the "front of the book" sections found in many magazines. These are made up of very short items about interesting or newsworthy children's activities. Your local newspaper is a great resource for front-of-book items. Did a youngster in your town start a recycling program, climb a mountain, break a 10k record in his age group? Other kids want to know about it.

Juvenile magazines devote a lot of space to puzzles, crafts, hidden pictures, dot-to-dot, and word finds. This can be another good way to break into the market. Your experience with children might also help you sell a story or an article. For example, you might package an article on Halloween with an easy-to-do crossword puzzle using lots of spooky words. Or a story about friendship could go hand-in-hand with a craft page on how to make friendship bracelets.

Some writers believe they can get away with lazy research or substandard writing because it's "only" for kids. Nothing could be further from the truth. Editors will accept only the very best for their young readers.

□ 95

WRITING MYSTERIES FOR YOUNG PEOPLE

BY PEG KEHRET

PART OF THE JOY OF WRITING FOR CHILDREN IS THE LETTERS THEY send me. One of my favorite letters said, "It took my teacher two weeks to read *Nightmare Mountain* to our class. You wrote it in three days. Wasn't that hard to do?"

I have never written a book in three days! *Nightmare Mountain* took me nine months, and then my editor asked for revisions. Writing mysteries for children is not easy or fast, but it is fun and enormously satisfying. Here are some hints to help you write a mystery that will satisfy young readers.

*Begin the novel in an exciting place. Sometimes this means rearranging your material after the book is written. I wrote *Nightmare Mountain* in chronological order, but when it was finished, I realized there was too much background information at the beginning of the book. Although it was necessary information, it gave the story a slow start.

I took a letter from the middle of the novel and made it my opening. Now the book begins: "Dear Mom, Someone's trying to kill me." The letter is less than a page long; it became my whole first chapter. Chapter two starts at the true beginning, with the necessary background information. At the end of chapter six, Molly finally picks up her pen and writes to her mother, but meanwhile that letter has generated suspense throughout the first five chapters.

When you finish your first draft, read through it to see if there is a more exciting scene with which to open your novel. If so, try moving that scene to the beginning of the story.

Another good way to open a mystery is with intriguing dialogue. A fourth-grade teacher told me that she once read the first paragraph of six novels to her class and then let them vote on which book she would read aloud to them. My book, *Horror at the Haunted House,* was the students' choice. Here is my beginning: "Hey, Ellen! I'm going to get my head chopped off."

Such an opening makes the readers curious. They will want to read on, to see where the opening leads.

*Be sure all of the dialogue is appropriate to the character. A young child does not speak the same way his parents do; a belligerent teenager will sound different from one who is trying to please. The funny kid should get the laugh lines.

I try not to use current slang, even in dialogue. It dates a book too quickly. These days, kids say *awesome.* Several years ago, it was *rad* and before that, *groovy* was in. A book for children will often stay in print a long time; don't make it seem old-fashioned by using language that doesn't last.

*Give your protagonist a personal problem in addition to the main story problem. This will add depth to your story and will help you create a more believable and sympathetic character. For example: In *Night of Fear,* the main story problem is that T.J. is abducted. The personal problem is his unhappiness over the changes in his grandmother, who has Alzheimer's disease. Grandma Ruth, through T.J.'s memories, becomes a major character and her disease creates reader sympathy. Tension is also increased as readers wait to find out if Grandma Ruth got home safely after T.J. was forced to leave her alone. Because T.J. cares deeply about his grandma, the readers care, too.

*The title of any book for children must grab young readers and create curiosity; for a mystery, the title should also hint at danger. My working title for *Terror at the Zoo* was *Zoo Night,* but that title did not suggest any danger or conflict. (The editor said it sounded like a nonfiction title.) *Terror at the Zoo* makes it clear that the book is a suspense novel, and it arouses the curiosity of potential readers who wonder what scary event happens at the zoo.

Another editor once suggested that I try to use an action verb in every title. I have done so several times, with good results.

*Provide new information. Kids like to learn interesting facts, and if you weave the information in as a natural part of the plot, your readers learn easily and naturally. In *Horror at the Haunted House,* a

collection of antique Wedgwood is important to the plot, as are historical scenes about Joan of Arc.

The characters in *Backstage Fright* find a stolen Van Gogh painting.
I could have used a fictitious artist, but by using Van Gogh I introduced
young readers to a great artist, thus broadening the learning experience
of the students and the classroom usefulness of the book.

In *Race To Disaster,* the children take their dog, Bone Breath, to do
pet therapy at a nursing home where they realize that an elderly patient
has witnessed a murder. A subplot involves a patient who is drawn out
of a shock-induced silence by continued exposure to the dog. Children
who read that book get a mystery about a pair of diamond thieves,
and also information about pet therapy and how it works.

When I am writing the first draft of a book, I ask myself, "What will
children learn from this book? What new topic can I introduce?"
Often, unusual information adds a plot twist that I would not have
thought of otherwise.

*Put some humor in every book. If your mystery involves a serious
problem, humor will give a much-needed lightening of mood. It does
the same in a suspense book in which the tension is high page after
page. A character who makes kids laugh will quickly become a favorite, and readers will beg for more books about him. But make it genuine
humor, not bathroom jokes or put-down jokes that make fun of
someone.

*End every chapter with a cliffhanger. I've had children complain,
"Why do you always quit at the good parts?" These are the same kids
who then say they loved the book and couldn't put it down. The chapter ending makes the reader want to continue.

Sometimes while I'm writing I'll come up with a sentence that I
realize would make a good chapter ending. When that happens, I space
down a couple of lines to remind myself that this would be a good spot
for a break. Other times, I need to rewrite until I have a good cliffhanger sentence for the end of each chapter. Here is an example of a
chapter ending from *Danger at the Fair:*

Corey couldn't let the man get away. Forgetting his promise to stay with Ellen,
he took off across the fairgrounds after the thief.

*Make the first paragraph of each chapter short and compelling. At the end of a chapter, readers will usually peek ahead, to see what happens next. If they see a long narrative, they may decide to put the book aside and go play soccer. But if the next chapter begins, "Hey, Ellen!" Corey waved from the sidewalk. "We got a video of you on fire!", chances are they'll keep reading.

*Let your book reflect who you are and what you stand for. This will help with that all-important quality, voice.

Certain themes surface over and over in my mysteries: kindness to all creatures; violence is not a solution; each of us is responsible for our own actions. My main characters are outraged by people who dump unwanted pets (*Desert Danger*).

The antiviolence message is strong in *Night of Fear* when Grandma Ruth tells T.J. to "win with your wits, not with your fists," and in *Race to Disaster* when Rosie and Kayo organize Goodbye Guns Day at their school.

You can't write from a soapbox; you need to write stories, not sermons. But if your characters deal with social and ethical problems, your mystery has a definite plus.

*Don't mimic what's already popular. For several years, the juvenile mystery market has been flooded with Goosebumps wannabes, but editors look for fresh ideas and new voices.

It's far better to risk writing a mystery that reflects your unique vision, than to attempt to imitate what some other writer did. Be true to yourself. Write what you love to write, and your writing will attract like-minded readers.

*Ask authorities to check your book for accuracy. There's nothing worse than having a reader point out that you have made an error. (Unfortunately, I know this from personal experience.) If you are dealing with factual information, double-check everything. *Terror at the Zoo* was read by two people from the education department of Seattle's Woodland Park Zoo, where the story is set. Whatever flaws the book may have, I know the information about the zoo and its animals is correct. My latest novel, *The Volcano Disaster,* deals with the eruption of Mount St. Helens. I did extensive research, but I also had the manuscript read by the Lead Interpreter at the Mount St. Helens Visitors' Center.

I have never had anyone turn down my request to check a manuscript. Actually, they seem delighted to share their knowledge. I do include their names on my acknowledgments page, and, of course, I see that each person who has helped me receives a signed copy of the book on publication.

*Make your mystery an appropriate length. If it's too long (more than 200 pages) it may be intimidating to all but the most enthusiastic young reader. A good length for juvenile mysteries is 125 to 150 double-spaced manuscript pages.

*Read current award-winning juvenile mysteries to become familiar with the best style and content. The Mystery Writers of America presents an Edgar each year to a juvenile mystery novel.

Many states have annual children's book award programs, in which students are encouraged to read selected titles and then vote for their favorite. A glance at the master list from any of these programs shows a large number of mysteries, which are often the books that win the prize.

School Library Journal and *The Horn Book* are magazines that review children's books and announce awards. Look for mysteries that have won a state children's book award, such as the Iowa Children's Choice Award, the Indiana Young Hoosier Award, or the Pacific Northwest Young Readers Choice Award. These books are recommended by librarians and are popular with young readers. Study them to see how the authors did it.

*Last, but most important of all, put the words on paper. Write until you have a first draft of at least 125 pages. Then go back and, using these hints, revise and polish your manuscript. You may end up with an award-winning mystery and wonderful letters such as this: "Dear Peg Kehret, Can I start helping you write your storys? I aldredy have an idea. It is called Atack of the Killer Strawberries. Your $nu1 fan, Melissa."

❏ 96

When You Write a Biography for Children

By Ruth Turk

Is writing a biography for children different from writing one for adults?

As a writer of seven published biographies for young readers, I must admit that while some of the basics are similar, there are enough differences to make this undertaking a challenging and rewarding experience.

From the outset it is important to keep in mind that the subject you choose must be attractive, not only to you, the writer, but to your young readers. While your primary goal is to impart authentic biographical information, you will write more convincingly if you have respect for your subject. When I researched the life of blind singer Ray Charles, I was impressed by the courage he manifested in dealing with blindness, racism, poverty, and a serious drug problem. As a result, I did not minimize these aspects of his life, but portrayed them with the clarity and honesty they deserved.

Whether the age level you are targeting is primary or middle grade, do not "talk down" to your readers. While your writing must be straightforward and uncomplicated, young readers will resent oversimplification. If you use technical terms, it makes sense to include a glossary. Equally important is the use of lively verbs and adjectives that jump from the page, maintain a brisk pace, and help create glowing visual images in the young mind. Conditioned by rock music, skateboards, television, and computers, young people today march to a different drum from those in previous generations. How to compete? The best way is to hook that juvenile with the opening paragraph, then follow through with the complete biography.

Author Lillie Patterson's young adult biography of Martin Luther King, Jr. opens with a dramatic account of the Rosa Parks incident in

Montgomery, Alabama, in 1955. When Rosa refuses to give up her seat for a white passenger, the driver stops the bus.

"Look, woman, I told you I wanted the seat. Are you going to stand up?"

"No," said Parks.

"Well, if you don't, I am going to have you arrested."

"Go on and have me arrested," said Rosa Parks.

After starting her book with the story of the Montgomery Bus Boycott, the author proceeded to introduce her subject, Martin Luther King, Jr. in chapter two, and followed through with the chronological development of his life.

If your subject is not alive, there are advantages and disadvantages. One advantage is the fact that the subject cannot object to what or how you write. Still another is that the last chapter ends with the subject's death and rarely has to be updated. Research on any subject, living or dead, starts with your reading everything written about her or him, including articles in newspapers and other periodicals, as well as history books concerning the relevant time periods. Reading the work of other biographers will help to determine your own insights and points of departure.

Reference librarians are particularly helpful in helping you find memoirs, journals, and letters of both deceased and living subjects. Browsing in secondhand bookshops and museums will often unearth nuggets of information that don't always turn up in public libraries or large bookstores. In researching the lives of Louisa May Alcott and Edith Wharton I was able to locate literary foundations in New England in areas where both women lived and wrote their timeless masterpieces. These organizations forwarded books, pamphlets, and photos that helped me create a composite portrait for each biography.

Incidentally, as you conduct your research, keep track of good photographs that you can later recommend to your publisher's photography department. An editor or publisher seriously considering a manuscript may appreciate photo sources, even though the photo staff usually tracks down their own. My experience with pictures for a juvenile biography of playwright Lillian Hellman was atypical, but rewarding.

When my editor informed me that a photograph of Hellman in her early childhood could not be located, I did a bit of detective work on my own. After learning the name of the playwright's last personal secretary, I surmised that she might still be living in the same city where she had worked years ago. I got her phone number and called to persuade her how meaningful it would be for young readers to see Lillian as a little girl. Did she know where such a picture could be found? She did. A week later the photograph was in the hands of my delighted editor. Moral of the story? Don't hesitate to go beyond authorship limits if it will enhance the quality of your work.

If your subject is alive, you may encounter a few frustrations on the road to success, such as his or her refusal to be interviewed personally. You may have to rely on friends, relatives, or possibly enemies (the third category is one I cannot recommend!). If you are fortunate enough to set up interviews, prepare a list of carefully thought-out questions, and plan to use a tape recorder. If your subject won't agree to being taped, be prepared to jot down notes you can incorporate later on. When you use quotations, be sure to cite accurate sources and dates; your publisher will require you to include these credits in the finished biography. Though it is comforting and convenient to have the subject's approval, it is not mandatory to obtain permission to write the story of someone's life.

Before you undertake comprehensive research about your subject, be certain to consult *Books in Print* to find what other books of a similar nature are available. There could be a half dozen or more authors who have chosen to write about the same subject. In that case if you are still determined to go ahead, you will need to come up with a different approach or format, or both.

For a children's biography, plan the number of chapters before you begin to write (ordinarily from six to twelve, depending on your organization of the material). As you accumulate dates, facts, and incidents, keep them in separate folders so they will be easily accessible as you develop the different chapters. Occasionally, you will come across items about the subject that appear to be unrelated, for example, an account about a friend or member of the subject's family. Don't discard these references; you may use one when you least expect it.

Scan current periodicals for mention of your subject's awards or citations for past achievements. If your accepted manuscript is already in its final publishing stage, your editor may suggest a brief epilogue to bring the biography up to date. For instance, when I learned that

Amy Carter was getting married, I was able to insert that fact on the last page of my biography of former first lady Rosalynn Carter. What happens to the family members in your subject's life will be of interest to young readers, especially when it is a famous family.

When the first draft of your manuscript is completed, try testing parts of it on a few willing listeners, preferably those at the age level for whom you're writing—but do not include close friends or relatives! Most young people will be objective and will react quickly and honestly, which is what you want. If you belong to a writer's critique group, ask for their comments and make use of those that are constructive. Most writers, particularly those who write for children, will benefit from an impartial sounding board. Sometimes when a manuscript is read aloud, nuances may be picked up more readily than when the same material is read silently. If a human sounding board is not available, read what you've written into a tape recorder, then play it several times. You will be surprised at the changes you might make as a result of listening.

Another way to receive valuable feedback is to arrange visits to elementary school classes. Many teachers will welcome a local writer willing to read her work to children and then discuss it with them. Insights and reactions from unbiased young listeners are usually constructive and gratifying.

Researching and writing a biography for children is not a quick or easy project. It takes time, dedication, and discipline. It also means always keeping in mind the young person for whom you are writing. An adult reader may struggle a bit longer with a boring biography before he gives up; ten-year-olds will continue to read only as long as the first page unless you, the author, hook them immediately and hold them for the duration.

Exciting fiction can stimulate a child's imagination, but a carefully researched and well-written biography can present accurate information, intriguing insights, historical perspective, and unforgettable role models. Children's biographies do more than record facts. As the author, you are documenting creative human goals and achievements that young people will remember long after they grow into busy and sophisticated adults.

As a biographer for children you are performing a special service for coming generations. When you complete that first biography, you might be understandably weary, but you'll also feel proud. I know.

❑ 97

WRITING NONFICTION FOR YOUNG READERS

BY NANCY WARREN FERRELL

AS A PUBLISHED AUTHOR OF NONFICTION FOR YOUNG READERS, I'VE often been approached by people who say they have a great idea and want to write a book, but they are not sure where to start.

First, go to your public library and study the type of books you want to write. See how other authors handle their material, and get a sense of the different grade and age levels of the books in print. Check *Books in Print* to see how many books have already been written on your topic. Obviously, if several have been published for the same age group in recent years, it might be best to turn to another topic, unless your slant is fresh.

Note the names of the publishers who bring out certain kinds of books. It's a waste of time and postage to submit nonfiction to a company that publishes only fiction. You can also locate marketing information in the Book Publishers section of this book. In addition, consult current publishers' catalogues found in the children's department of the library. Or you can write for catalogues and guidelines from the publishers themselves.

While at the library, locate books on creative writing and check references in them. Take a few home to study writing techniques. If you find one or two books you really like, order them from the publishers or buy them from the bookstore to start your home library.

After completing some preliminary research on your topic, write a one-page query letter to an appropriate publisher to see if their house is interested in your subject. In the letter, describe what you have in mind and how you plan to approach the material. Be sure to indicate if you have special knowledge of your topic, such as work experience. You might also write a brief outline of your proposed book to include with your query.

If you have photographs or know they are available, mention that in your query. Ordinarily, an author is not responsible for illustrations or photographs in books. Nevertheless, some writers who take good pictures should indicate their credentials. Arrangements for publication and payment are made in the final contract.

Send your proposal to about five publishers, including an SASE (self-addressed, stamped envelope) with each one. Note this information on a file card so you know to whom and when you submitted the queries.

Usually, you receive responses to your queries—yes or no. Let's say a publisher likes your idea, and after some talk and negotiation, you sign a contract. You will often receive comments and suggestions from your editor to help you shape your book to fit the publisher's needs. Now the serious work begins.

Check out a number of books on your topic from the library—both adult and juvenile. Read and make copies of specific magazine articles you can locate. Surf the Internet for additional material.

On 4″ × 6″ file cards, note such information as the title, author, where located, etc., for each book, article, or contact you may consult. Keeping a record of this data will help you build a bibliography if you should need one; it also gives a specific reference point if you wish to add information to your manuscript or check facts during the revision process. Otherwise, you could be frantically looking through piles of books and papers trying to find a quote or a fact that your editor has questioned. Taking time for these reference cards at the start of your research proves its worth over and over.

If it's important as part of your research to interview people in an agency or business, go to the top. Make appointments beforehand. As an example, when I researched my book on the U.S. Coast Guard, I arranged an appointment with the Alaskan commander, a rear admiral. I described my project, and he in turn sent a memo to the local offices explaining who I was, and requesting their cooperation. This clearance proved invaluable. Everyone I met took me seriously, and was willing to help.

As you read and digest your subject material, you might find that distant locations have valuable information or photographs you need. Write letters so that data can be coming back to you as you get farther into your project. Be sure to write a quick "thank you" when you receive the material.

Arrange for any on-scene experiences you know would be interesting. This can be the most fun, because you are actively doing, feeling, and understanding the excitement you want to convey to young readers. If, for example, you are writing a book about fishing, go fish; if writing about a historical site, visit that location to get a true-life experience, and then pass as much as you can on to your readers.

My most exciting hands-on experience was going up in a Coast Guard search-and-rescue helicopter to take photographs. Again, this experience was cleared through the rear admiral first. At Sitka Air Station, the flight mechanic fitted me out in an orange mustang suit. I was briefed beforehand, and up we went. When the chopper flew high above Sitka harbor, a crew member wrapped a gunner's belt around my waist, hooked me onto a strap, and opened the cabin doors. There I was, breathless, the toes of my shoes clamped to the door sill, with nothing but air in front and beneath me! "There you are," a crew member said, "take all the pictures you want."

At this point, you should be aware of the one universal warning that flashes like a red light: Do not talk down to young readers; this is not a writing mistake, but a way of thinking—you cannot correct it with a comma or a paragraph break. Respect your readers, show them you have something fascinating to tell them, and give them credit for absorbing the information.

What I've found helpful in writing for elementary-grade readers is to conjure up, say, some eight-year-olds and figuratively plunk them down in front of me. Then I begin writing with them in mind. If I sense they are getting restless or do not seem to understand, I'm not doing my job.

While you are absorbing information on your subject, keep an eye out for unusual facts and anecdotes to include in your final version. For instance, while doing research for *U.S. Air Force,* I learned that when the first U.S. air force was formed in 1907, the division had no aircraft, and only three men—none of whom could fly a plane! To me that was a startling, amazing fact that had to be shared with young readers.

During this research-gathering stage, you have only a general idea of how to handle your material. Normally, it does not come in a rush, but in bits and pieces until a smooth, balanced manuscript emerges. There are changes, reorganization, insertions, deletions. It takes time and work.

Then when you actually begin writing, keep certain techniques in mind:

Make your verbs active, appeal to the five senses, and use dialogue to give life to your words. If possible, use actual dialogue from journals and letters, keeping in mind that youngsters can be experts in certain fields, too. Experts give authority to your writing. When I needed an expert role-model for my *Alaska: A Land in Motion* geography book, I located a 12-year-old boy who was the first young person to climb the highest mountain in North America—Mt. McKinley.

Make your chapter headings and openings as interesting as possible. One chapter heading in my book, *Battle of the Little Bighorn,* for example, was the Sioux Indian battle cry, "It is a good day to die!" In my book, *The New World of Amateur Radio,* I told of the strange behavior of cattle several hours before an Alaska earthquake. Grab your readers from the start, and pull them in.

Use newspaper headlines, actual cassette tape dialogues, bumper stickers, etc. in your narrative. In my *Fishing Industry* book, for instance, I duplicated actual boat radio talk. For my diplomacy book, *Passports to Peace,* I used authentic secret code phrases, and added excitement to *U.S. Air Force* by including video dialogue of a real intercept of a Russian fighter plane entering U.S. air space. Besides adding drama, these short units help break up text, catch the reader's eye and hold his or her interest.

Make adult role-models real; show your young readers that even successful adults, with all their accomplishments, have weaknesses, too. I found that a cadet in the first U.S. Coast Guard Academy class, who later became national commander, had trouble with seasickness. Mentioning this human frailty gave this role model another dimension.

When possible, relate your writing to the interest of young readers. For instance, when I focused on the devastation of an earthquake, I described it and found a photograph of an elementary school affected by the disaster. When I related the public's reaction to George Custer's death in *Battle of the Little Bighorn,* I mentioned school students in Custer's hometown. Such material personalizes the text for your readers.

Take care with your paragraphs. If you want real punch, use one-word or one-sentence paragraphs. But use this technique sparingly, or the "punch" will lose its power from overuse. And in the reverse, do not make your paragraphs too long. Lengthy paragraphs suggest detailed description, which often turns off the young reader. Breaking up paragraphs makes the material more inviting.

During this whole process of writing and working with an editor, remember that writing is a business. Meet your deadlines. Do not promise something you cannot deliver. Be sensitive to suggested changes. Proving that you are reliable and reasonable shows you can handle another project.

Once your book is published, good things may happen: You may receive letters from young readers and may be asked to speak to school or community groups, and publishers may prove to be more receptive to your new book ideas. So, if you are inspired to write, write. Remember, if your ideas remain in your head, or your written drafts remain in a drawer, nothing will happen at all. Send your manuscripts out. To quote my 12-year-old McKinley mountain climber, "Go for it!"

Practical Advice

You might locate a local writer's organization. Members of such groups give encouragement, critique creative work, and help with marketing information. They are, so to speak, your personal cheering section.

For a broader view, join a national organization such as the Society of Children's Book Writers and Illustrators; you do not have to be a published author to join. Their monthly bulletins not only present practical information to members, but the Society also prints materials that deal with marketing, manuscript format, how-to books on writing, copyright and tax data, and much more—mostly for the price of postage. Becoming a member gives newcomers a sense of purpose. (Society of Children's Book Writers and Illustrators, 345 N. Maple Dr., #296, Beverly Hills, CA 90210. Yearly membership is $50.00.)

❑ EDITING AND MARKETING

❏ 98

THE AUTHOR/EDITOR CONNECTION

BY EVE BUNTING

AT A WRITERS' CONFERENCE ONCE, I HEARD AN AUTHOR STATE: "Make no mistake. The writer and the editor are enemies. He's always on the side of the publisher and not on yours." I was astonished and appalled. This has never been my experience. Never.

As a children's book writer who "publishes around," I have several editors, male and female, young and older. Since I don't work through an agent, my contacts are directly author to editor. I have always been treated fairly and have always had the assurance that we are a team, striving for the best possible book.

This is not to say there have not been disagreements. Of course there have. But with compromise on both sides we have always been able to work a problem out.

To establish and keep a good relationship, there are some things the author should bear in mind.

1) Be prepared to listen when your editor suggests changes. Yes, the book is yours. Yes, every word is as perfect as you have been able to make it. But the editor has had a lot of experience, knows what works and what doesn't, and is as anxious as you are for a quality book. **But,** be prepared to take a stand if you feel you are right. Present your case. Be factual. Be reasonable. Chances are she (I'm using the generic "she" because I have more female editors than male) will come around to your thinking. Be gracious if you are proven wrong. The best editors during discussion will be careful to ask: "Do you agree?" and will often say: "Of course, you have the last word." That may not be exactly true, but it leaves room for further discussion.

2) Try to realize that your editor is a person who works hard. Do not burden her with unnecessary questions and complaints. Yes, you want to know how your book is coming along. It's O.K. to ask. But

not every week. When it's finally published, you want to know how it is selling. Call the royalty department. Yes, you are upset that you can't find a copy in your local bookstore. Call the sales department and ask if they know why.

You don't think your work has been promoted with enough enthusiasm? (A lot of us feel that way. I was going to say *most* of us, but perhaps many authors are totally satisfied. I don't know any of them!) Talk to the Promotions Department to suggest what they might do, as well as what you are willing to do: bookstore signings, school visits, visits to your local library. Perhaps it can be a joint project between you and the publisher.

3) If you submit a new manuscript to your editor, try not to be irate if she doesn't get back to you right away. Understand that she has a workload that allows only a small percentage of her time to be spent reading manuscripts—even yours. She has meetings coming out of her ears!

4) If your editor tells you that your book will not be published this year, and possibly not until the following fall, or the spring after that, bite the bullet. Publishers' lists fill up, and you have to realize that you are going to have your book scheduled where (a), there is a slot for it, or (b), where the publisher feels it will sell best. There's no point in ranting and raving in your very understandable impatience. Your editor will bless you for not being difficult.

5) When you are asked to make corrections on a manuscript or galleys, do them promptly. The editor is making deadlines herself. Being on time can determine whether or not your book makes that list where it's slotted. If your manuscript is not ready, another book may replace yours.

6) Be absolutely certain of your facts. An error in a nonfiction book is unforgivable, and it is equally unforgivable in fiction. A reader or reviewer is going to pick up on it. Children's books are particularly open to scrutiny. The embarrassment of an error falls on the editor and copy editor, but yours is the primary accountability. A mistake will not endear you to anyone. In my very first middle-grade novel, I made an incredible blunder: I put the Statue of Liberty in New York Harbor a year before it was actually there! Horrors! No one caught it, except an astute librarian who challenged me on it while I stood at a

podium, talking about the book. Double horrors! I will never forget that moment nor the lesson I learned. Since I was a fairly recent immigrant from Ireland, I managed to exclaim, "Oh! Forgive me! I thought that wonderful statue was always there, welcoming the tired and the poor as she welcomed me." That got applause instead of boos! It was corrected in the next printing.

7) For picture book writers who are not fortunate enough to be able to illustrate their books, the key words are "be reasonable." Of course, we want the very best artists in the country—in the world—to illustrate our books. Surely, this is not too much to ask! You pine for Trina Schart Hyman. You know she'd do an exquisite job. You lust after Barbara Cooney. Her style would be just perfect for your book. And how about Chris Van Allsburg? But if you are reasonable, you will know that every picture book author wants those illustrators and others equally wonderful, equally famous. The reality is that we are probably not going to get any one of them. It is all right to ask, but don't be aggrieved or petulant if it doesn't happen. Usually the artist is chosen by the editor in consultation with the art department and after much perusal of sample art and already published picture books. They are usually very good at choosing just the right artist. Perhaps they come up with a "first time" artist, and your first reaction is likely to be, "Oh, no! Not for *my* book!" But all wonderful illustrators start somewhere. I personally have discovered the thrill of having newish, relatively unknown artists turn out to be smash hits and lift my books beyond the ordinary to the extraordinary. I thank them. And I thank my editors. They know I trust them.

8) Try to accept the fact that you are not your editor's only author. She is juggling four, six, eight other writers and illustrators, too. She can't give you her undivided attention. You may think another author is getting more than her fair share of attention. That may be true. But that author may have paid her dues in many years of good books. One of her books may have made a million dollars for the company. It may have earned a lot of money and prestige-making awards. It's been said that 20% of a publisher's list supports the other 80%. Another author's book and the attention it gets may be making it possible for your book to get published.

9) If, by unfortunate chance, your editor has to turn down your

next manuscript, take a deep breath and swallow your disappointment. When she says she's sorry, she probably is. An editor does not easily reject a book, especially if she has worked with the author before. It is easier to be the bearer of pleasant news. Your editor may have fought for your book with a publishing committee and lost. Say, "I'm sorry, too. Can you give me any idea why you decided against it?" Listen to what she says. You may want to make changes before you submit it elsewhere. And remember, you may want to try her with another manuscript in the future, so keep that relationship cordial.

10) Remember that your editor is human. Show appreciation for her efforts in making your book the thing of beauty that it is. Flowers, candy, or other gifts are unnecessary. A simple thank-you note is sufficient.

Ten points about how to keep that author/editor relationship warm and cordial. A word or two about the editor/author relationship. What should an author expect to get from her editor?

- As quick a reading of a new manuscript as possible.
- As quick a response as possible.
- Enthusiasm.
- Open-mindedness.
- Support of the book with the sales and publicity departments.
- Attentiveness to your misgivings, if any.
- A commitment to keep in touch. Not to hear what is happening to your book is horrible, and since you would be out of line to bug her, she should be courteous and keep you informed.
- Praise. Insecure as we are, we need a certain amount of TLC.
- The assurance that author and editor are in this together. It's *your* book.
- To be a person of her word. If she says she'll call, write, see you, then you have the right to assume she is dependable, as you are.

So . . . we have a good author/editor relationship, and a good book. Working together, with consideration for one another, we've done it!

❑ 99

What Do Agents Want?

By Nancy Love

AGENTS SAY THEY WANT NEW WRITERS, BUT WHEN YOU SEND A QUERY or a proposal, they fire back, "No thanks!" What are you to make of this mixed message? Aside from those agents who really do not welcome new clients, the rest of us need a continuous supply of fresh offerings to submit to publishers, but since we are in the publishing business to sell books, we are constantly trying to select those we think publishers want. The question we ask is: *What do publishers want?*

Death by mid-list

The conventional wisdom these days is, *Publishers do not want mid-list books*. The term "mid-list" refers to the place a book has in a publishing house catalogue. It is a book that is not "front-list" (books listed in the first few pages of the catalogue and declared thereby best-seller material), and it is not "back-list" (perennials listed in the back of the catalogue and kept in print season after season). Translation: Only best sellers need apply. That leaves high and dry the nice, little literary or commercial novel with no break-out potential. And what about first novels?

The reality is, mid-list and first novels *do* get published, often by smaller publishing houses, many of which have fine reputations for discriminating taste, and then the authors are poached by the mainstream houses that didn't have the guts to take a chance themselves. Or they are championed by stubborn editors at the larger houses who want to nurture a talented writer or who have enough clout to bulldoze through the disapproval of sales and marketing departments.

Another reality is that it is often easier to get a first novel accepted than a second if the first one bombed. Enter the Dread Sales Record. Once you have a sales history documented in bookstore computers everywhere, it will follow you around for the rest of your publishing life, and can be amended only by subsequent successes that balance out the failures, or by changing your name.

One of the dirty little secrets of agentry is that many agents will avoid novels with either of the above potential problems (i.e., a mid-list book or a second book that follows a wipe-out first book), but might be less than candid about sharing these reasons for rejection.

Appetite for nonfiction

Sure, publishers want front-list nonfiction titles, too, but are more welcoming to a mid-list book that has a potential of being back-listed. Most fiction is here today, gone tomorrow, but a nonfiction title that yields even modest, but steady, revenue may be kept around for a number of years. Many publishers will take on a "small" book they believe will not only earn out, but will generate income in the long run.

But before you rejoice prematurely, remember that today publishers have an insatiable appetite for credentials attached to nonfiction books. Backing by an authority or institution is important, and for some books, essential. A health book needs a genuine medical (doctor, hospital, or health organization) imprimatur, foreword, or co-authorship. A cookbook needs a food establishment tie-in (restaurateur, chef, or TV or print food personality. For large publishers, credentials are a must for an offer of even a minimal advance on a nonfiction book. To really hit pay dirt, you might need more than credentials; it will also help if you have a "platform"—a following or a guaranteed promise of advance sales. In this scenario, the author is not just a gardening authority, but she can also attach the name of the Garden Clubs of America to her book and a promise that the organization will offer it as a premium to their members.

The agent connection: Do you even want one?

If you write short fiction or articles, academic or textbooks, or poetry, you don't need or want an agent. Often, writers of literary fiction also do better on their own when approaching smaller publishers or college presses that agents may not deal with because of slow response time and low or non-existent advances.

I know writers of both fiction and nonfiction who—initially, anyhow—like to represent themselves and do well at it. But be prepared to spend a lot of downtime with the nitty-gritty of that process. You might also come out ahead if you have connections and are more comfortable being in control.

Getting in the agent's door

What makes the difference?

Agents often specialize. First, research your target. Find out if you are in the right place before you waste your stamp and everyone's time. Use listings in authors' source books. Scan books that are similar to yours for an acknowledgment of an agent. Use the name of the workshop leader or fellow writer who referred you. Go to writers' conferences where you might meet appropriate agents. Collect their cards and use the connection when you are querying.

Winning queries and proposals

There are whole books devoted to this subject, so I will stress just a few points:

• Queries need to be positive, succinct, yet contain the facts about who you are and what the book is about. A query is like a short story in which every word has to count. A novel can ramble a bit, but short stories and queries don't have that luxury.

• There is no excuse for bad spelling or grammar. If you and your computer can't be counted on to proofread, ask a friend to read your work.

• Proposals and summaries of novels can be more expansive, but they also should be professionally crafted. Your writing ability and skills are being judged in everything you submit.

• There is nothing in a nonfiction proposal more important than a marketing plan. Make suggestions for how the publisher can promote the book, and even more essential, tell the publisher how you can help. Do you have media contacts? Are you an experienced speaker? Do you have lists of newsletters in your field that might review or write about the book? Do you lecture at meetings where the book can be sold or flyers can be distributed? Do you have a web site or belong to an organization that does and will promote your book? You get the idea.

Authors frequently respond to a request for this information by saying, "I write the book. That's my job. Selling the book is the job of the publisher." Unfortunately, while that might have been true at one time, it is no longer. Even when large advances are involved, I have discovered that publishers need and expect input from authors, and their cooperation and willingness to pitch in with ideas and commitment.

As an agent, I have to be sensitive to that point of view, so I find myself making decisions on whether or not to take on an author based not only on what she has to say and how well she says it, but on her credentials, her visibility, and on her ability to promote and become involved in publicity. Also, if you are able to put aside some of your advance to pay for publicity and perhaps a publicist, be sure to let the agent know this.

A marketing plan is not usually expected from a novelist, but it is a pleasant and welcome surprise if one is forthcoming. Fiction is promoted, too, by in-store placement, author appearances, book jacket blurbs. Sales of mysteries are helped by authors who are active in such organizations as the Mystery Writers of America (regional branches), Sisters in Crime, and other mystery writer organzations that support their members and boost their visibility. All novelists can start a minor groundswell by making themselves known at local bookstores, by placing items in neighborhood newspapers, and by using other local media. Some writers have reached out to store buyers with mailings of postcards, bookmarks or reading copies. Signal your readiness to participate, and make known what contacts you have, when you are approaching an agent.

Start out by writing the big, the bold, the grabber novel every agent is going to want. This works only if an author feels that option is viable. I strongly believe a writer has to have a passion for the book she is writing, whether it is fiction or nonfiction, or it probably isn't going to work.

Till death do us part

You've succeeded in attracting an agent; now what? I would advise waiting until an agent indicates an interest before plunging in with such nuts-and-bolts questions as, What is your commission? Which other writers do you represent? Do you use a contract?

I'm in favor of author-agent contracts, because they spell out the understanding and obligations of the two parties, not the least of which is how either one can end the relationship. Basically, unless an agent commits a serious breach, she is on the contract with the publisher for the life of the contract. There should be, however, an agreed-upon procedure for dissolving the author-agent contract.

After all, the author-agent relationship is the business equivalent of a marriage. Attracting the partner is just the beginning.

□ 100

BEATING THE ODDS OF REJECTION

BY DENNIS E. HENSLEY

BEGINNING WRITERS HAVE OFTEN SHOWN ME THEIR REJECTED MANU-scripts to which the editor has attached a small note reading, "Thank you for your manuscript, but this does not meet our current editorial needs." What does that mean? Understandably, these aspiring writers, having studied the market and submitted a competently written article, wonder what had gone wrong.

My first response is that all writers get rejection slips, including me. Pearl Buck received a rejection for one of her short stories the very week she was notified she had won the Nobel Prize for Literature! It's part of the writing business: If you aren't getting rejected, you aren't attempting to break into new markets or explore new writing options. To risk rejection is to grow. In the long run, it's something positive. Of course, in the short run, it hurts. Writers put their heart and soul on paper. The manuscript becomes their "baby," and nobody wants someone saying, "Your baby has big ears." In essence, that's what a rejection letter sounds like. Since your manuscript cannot get published if you don't submit it, you must risk rejection by sending it out again. But there are better ways of coping with rejection and even of reducing the odds of ever having it happen.

First, a rejection slip isn't necessarily a sign that your writing is poor. A lot of superb manuscripts come across editors' desks that they wish they could publish, but sometimes factors unrelated to the writing make publishing them impossible. The editor may have just accepted a manuscript on the same topic from another author. He may have paid such a large advance on one project, his budget won't allow him to accept any new submissions for a few months. Or she may admire a writer's talent, but her publishing house has decided not to publish textbooks or cookbooks or children's novels any longer. Hence, the decision to reject isn't always related to writing talent.

Sometimes editors' personal lives get in the way. An editor may have a bias against the position an article is taking and reject it; another who agrees with your point of view may accept it. One editor may like the article, but may worry that it might offend one of the magazine's advertisers, so the article gets nixed. The editor may have a headache or may have had a fight with his or her spouse and everything gets rejected that day because of the editor's bad mood. After all, editors *are* human.

On occasion editors can be wrong in rejecting a manuscript. One editor might be too old to realize the high interest in techno games, so he rejects an article about it. Another editor might not like your staccato, short-sentenced style, so she rejects the manuscript, not realizing that a generation reared on MTV and split-screen images can readily relate to writing such as this. Just because one editor rejects a manuscript, it doesn't mean the topic or the writing style is not worthy of publication. It's a good idea to try your manuscript on several editors.

Understanding what an editor is saying in a rejection letter is also important. If you receive a form rejection slip, it probably means that the publisher has no real interest in your manuscript or in establishing a working relationship with you. But if you receive a rejection slip with a personal note from the editor, take heart. That can mean that while the manuscript is not what the editor needs, you, the writer, have caught the editor's eye. You should feel encouraged to send other material to that publication or publishing house.

On the other hand, don't read more into a rejection letter than is really there. When an editor says, "Thank you for submitting . . .," don't take it as enthusiasm when it is really just courtesy. Similarly, when an editor writes, "Perhaps you'll have more success with another periodical . . .," that is not an invitation for you to write back and say, "Please give me a list of those places you think I should be submitting my manuscript."

Rejection letters are good starting places for manuscript revisions. If two or three editors say that your stories have good plots but weak characters, then retain the plot ideas but work on making your characters more three-dimensional. Likewise, if several editors like your article concepts but say your writing mechanics require too much revision, then learn to do copyediting yourself.

Here are several other suggestions on how to reduce the odds of getting your manuscript rejected:

1. *Let it sit a while.* Don't try to edit your material as soon as you finish writing, because you will be too emotionally attached to it and too familiar with its contents. Let it "cool" for a few days or more, then go back to see if it still seems the best you can make it.

2. *Gauge your timing.* Send Christmas articles in the summer, not in December. Give editors plenty of lead time.

3. *Work your way up.* Before trying to compete in the mass market, get some experience by writing for smaller-circulation trade journals, specialty periodicals, or even your hometown newspaper. Editors of these publications often have more time to help you improve your writing and marketing skills. As you improve, you can expand your market outreach.

4. *Hone your mechanics.* Most editors do not have time to do a thorough copyediting job of your manuscript, then fax or mail it back to you, and wait for you to revise and then resubmit it. Instead, sharpen your writing skills so that your manuscripts do not have comma splices, sentence fragments, spelling errors, or grammar problems. If you need help in these areas, have someone in your writing group go over your work.

5. *Don't underestimate the impact of the query letter and book proposal.* Too often writers just "dash off" a query letter to obtain a go-ahead for submission from an editor. You may think that even if your query letter isn't very persuasive, it's OK. It's the manuscript that really counts, right? *Wrong!* The query letter is the equivalent of a job interview. If an editor receives a query letter or book proposal that is weak, poorly written and unprofessional, the editor will assume the manuscript will be more of the same. So, put as much effort into your query as you do with the manuscript itself.

6. *Know your topic thoroughly.* If you are writing a novel, know the genre. For example, if you want to write a romance, read a lot of romances—both the classics and more contemporary works. If you are writing nonfiction, do exhaustive reseearch. Talk to experts, read whatever is available on the topic, and become something of a walking authority on the topic yourself.

7. Finally, *give networking a try.* Make contacts in the world of publishing by attending writers' conferences and meeting editors face to

face. Bring your manuscript and schedule an appointment so that you can talk to an editor about your ideas, current writing projects, and finished works. Weeks later, when you write a query letter, you can begin with, "Thanks again for meeting with me at the summer writers' conference. I've used your suggestions on preparing this article and hope you will find it acceptable." This pre-established relationship with an editor can work in your favor; you are no longer a blank face.

Although getting a rejection letter is never uplifting, it doesn't have to be devastating, either. One of the secrets of coping with both rejection and success is momentum. Keep several manuscripts in the mail at all times. In that way, if a rejection letter comes in, you can comfort yourself with the knowledge that you have four other manuscripts out there that could get accepted any day. (Conversely, if you receive an acceptance, bear in mind that any of the four other manuscripts out there could get rejected.) That being the case, you'd better stay at your typewriter or word processor. This sort of thinking keeps a writer balanced.

❑ 101

How to Get a Literary Agent

By Lewis Burke Frumkes

Each year at the writers' conference I run at Marymount Manhattan College in New York City, the most popular panel is always the one on literary agents.

The reason for this popularity is that writers think they may be able to secure a good agent by attending the panel, or at the very least, that they will learn just what agents are looking for. Maybe, if a writer is lucky, he will be able to strike up a relationship with one of the agents on the panel and convince him or her to take him on as a new client. Maybe the agent will sense the writer's talent and potential and ask to see his or her work. By this time the writer is already fantasizing about being the next Saul Bellow or Barbara Taylor Bradford or Patricia Cornwell or John Grisham, because the agents on the panel all represent clients of this caliber. The writer imagines the millions he will receive from the auction of his manuscript: *Simon & Schuster offers 3 million for Sanguine Rudebaker's first novel . . . No, wait! HarperCollins offers 5 million . . . Simon & Schuster ups the bid to 7 million.* Instant fame and fortune are there for the taking: All the writer has to do is get an agent.

Is this realistic? "Of course not," says Eugene Winnick, the president of McIntosh and Otis, a leading literary agency that represents, for example, Mary Higgins Clark, one of the world's most successful mystery writers. "The odds against the beginning writer's becoming a best-selling author are astronomical. Nor should the writer be concerned with just fame and glory. Those who have the Hollywood starlet mentality and pursue only glitz and glamour as an end seldom produce anything of consequence. Writers who do become successful authors usually do so because they feel compelled to write, to follow their muse. They are passionate about their work and *must* write because it's what they love to do. The writer who is serious about writing must surrender his image of being rich and famous and be true to his craft."

Nevertheless, agents are important. While they cannot guarantee you sales, they certainly have a better shot at making a sale than you do. Agents know just which publishing houses would be interested in your book; they don't send out your manuscript randomly. And when they do send it out under their imprimatur, they usually send it to an editor who is senior at the publishing house. If you send your manuscript to the publisher, over the transom, it will probably be read by a low-level reader who may return it to you, never having shown it to anyone higher up.

Consider too that in the event a sale is made, your agent is the perfect person to negotiate the contract for you. Your agent regards you as a professional and will fight for the highest possible payment for your work. Your agent believes in you or he wouldn't be representing you. After all, he doesn't make any money unless he can sell your book. Think about that: The agent may charge you fifteen percent, but he won't receive his percentage unless he sells your book. Any way you look at it, fifteen percent of nothing is still nothing. However, if your agent manages to sell your book for a million dollars, you will most likely feel comfortable paying him fifteen percent for his hard work. (Curious how generous we become when we are counting millions!)

According to literary agent Tom Wallace of the Wallace Agency, "In negotiating with the publisher, your agent will retain certain rights you never dreamed of, never even knew existed." On the off chance that your book becomes a fabulous bestseller and sells umpteen-gazillion copies, you will appreciate that your agent did not sell Internet rights or the rights for Togoland, and Mauritius, and the intergalactic airwaves. "Your agent understands the importance of these rights," says Wallace, "and will exploit your manuscript to its maximum potential either by retaining certain subsidiary rights, or making sure the publisher pays top dollar to get them."

Also, in addition to being your agent/lawyer, he may also act as your financial consultant. Writers, by and large, are notoriously inept when it comes to finances, and often need advice in this area. Also, working together in close collaboration over a period of years, writers and agents often become close friends. It is a wonderful but underappreciated aspect of the agent/writer relationship.

Naturally, friendship is not the most important thing you are seeking from an agent, at least not initially; it is a byproduct. You are seeking an advocate who believes in you and will represent you in the best possible manner to publishers—and that is what you generally get. An agent who takes you on as a client believes in your work; he believes he can sell your work; he truly thinks you are talented, or he wouldn't agree to represent you. This already says something terrific about your agent . . . he has good taste.

At this point I assume we agree that having an agent is worthwhile. So when do you begin looking for an agent? Well, not when you are trying to sell your first essay or short story to a magazine; no agent will try to sell one short story, or an essay, or article for you. There is not enough money in it, and besides, it is something you can do yourself. In fact, it's very good experience for you to get to know the magazine markets, and to learn how to deal with editors. Book projects are different. Many publishers today won't even look seriously at an unagented book, so this is the time you need an agent. For their part, agents generally want to handle a book, because it will potentially involve a larger amount of money, perhaps an auction, and also because it really reflects your work in a more serious way.

O.K., so how do you find the agent? One of the most common ways is to ask writer-friends to recommend a good one. If you don't know any professional writers with agents, you should probably get in touch with The Association of Authors' Representatives (10 Astor Pl., 3rd Floor, New York, NY 10003), which will send you a list of their members for a $7 check or money order and a 55¢ SASE (self-addressed, stamped envelope). And there are many other organizations, some quite specific, such as The Screen Actors Guild, or The Romance Writers of America, which will also send you lists. Finally, you can consult this book's list of first-rate agents who don't charge reading fees, or any of the books on agenting that can be found in the reference section of the library, or possibly, in a good bookstore.

Tom Wallace suggests another way. "One overlooked method of obtaining an agent or an editor," he says, "is to pick up a book by an author you admire and whose work is similar in type to your own, then comb the author's acknowledgments. This may yield the names of his agent and his editor."

Now that you've narrowed the field and zeroed in on the agent or agents you want to represent you . . . how do you make your approach?

"Send a query letter first, with an SASE," says Robin Rue of the Writers House. "If the agent is interested, he or she will get back to you, asking to see more of your work."

Jonathan Dolger, of the Jonathan Dolger Literary Agency, says, "Usually I can tell quickly from a query—whether the author writes fiction or nonfiction—if it is worth following up. If fiction, I prefer a synopsis and a couple of chapters, and if nonfiction, I want to know why the book is different from all the other books on that subject now on the market. This also helps me in my presentation to the publishers."

Good agents are highly sought after for all the reasons I have outlined earlier and because everyone wants to be represented by a top agent—someone who represents successful writers and brings in the big-dollar contracts. This is only natural. People have heard that Amanda Urban, Andrew Wylie, Molly Friedrich, Ginger Barber, Lynn Nesbit, and Mort Janklow are "super-agents" who represent celebrity clients, big-time writers. It's as if the provenance of the agent accrues to you. Thus it is not uncommon to hear a writer subtly drop into a conversation that his agent represents Norman Mailer or John Updike or Tom Wolfe or Cynthia Ozick, or whoever the fashionable writer at the time is. However, beginning writers must keep in mind that what is more important than who the agent represents is that he love your work, and believe in you, and be willing to get out there and be an advocate for you. It won't do you any good if your agent represents only the most distinguished writers but leaves you at the gate, and pushes only the work of his star clients. You are better served by an agent who will give you and your work the attention it deserves, not put you on a back burner and leave you to deal with his secretary when she has the time.

"Put another way," says Carol Mann, a literary agent who has a mix of high-profile clients as well as unknowns, "it's only common sense that an agent with a lot of high-profile clients will not have as much time for you and your work. You are clearly better off with an agent who has an intuitive feeling for your work and will personally pick up the phone for you when you need her."

Suppose after approaching several agents, more than one is interested in your work. What do you do? Clearly, you are in a good position. You must realize that while personality is important, you are not marrying the agent. You obviously will want to go with the agent who convinces you she can do the best for you in terms of selling your work and managing your career. But it won't hurt for you and the agent to be compatible. If you live in New York, take the agent to lunch. You can meet face to face and ask any questions you may have. After you have lunched with your various prospects . . . go with your gut feeling. It is that simple. There probably will not even be a formal contract between you. Your contract is a handshake. Clearly, no agent can compel you to give her your work, and conversely, you cannot force an agent to represent you well if she doesn't wish to.

Never question the agent who thinks you have talent. Probably you have, and probably the agent who recognizes it is someone you should think seriously about having represent you; you don't want to pursue an agent who doesn't want you.

❑ 102

Negotiating the Book Contract

By Sherri L. Burr

YOUR DREAM IS ABOUT TO BE REALIZED. YOUR FIRST BOOK CONTRACT arrives in the mail. You go directly to the advance clause. It is exactly as you agreed. You look no further, sign the contract, and return it, confident of your great deal.

You are deliriously happy, until one day you run into an experienced writing friend. She's unhappy because she has not received a single royalty from her publisher since her advance.

"How could that happen?" you ask.

"I never read the fine print that said royalties were paid on net proceeds. I thought I'd be paid on the gross sales price. Instead, the publisher is paying me a percentage based on the amount that is received from booksellers, minus a few deductions for shipping costs and other overhead charges. My current statement says I owe the publisher money."

"That's terrible," you reply, secretly wondering if the same thing could happen to you. You rush home, take out your contract, and begin to read it. You are appalled by what you find and wonder what to do.

While this may never have happened to you, it serves as a reminder to review your contract carefully before signing. It is easy to understand why writers do not read their book contracts carefully. Contracts are usually written in "legal garbage-ese" and printed in the smallest type that the best computer scientists can design. The saying, "The big print giveth and the small print taketh away," is particularly appropriate to book contracts.

But don't despair; all contracts are negotiable. You just need to invest some time in determining what rights you should keep, and what rights the publisher will want. Here are some important issues to consider when reviewing your contract:

Manuscript clause

Many book contracts begin with a standard clause dealing with the specifics of the manuscript: the title, the name of the author, the length, the due date, how many copies you must deliver in hard copy and on disk. Sometimes, in this clause the publisher reserves the right to reject the final manuscript as unacceptable or unpublishable.

A savvy negotiator may be able to get the publisher to waive this clause, but don't count on it. Instead, try to insert that the publisher's right of rejection must be "reasonably exercised," which is often implied in the contract. Publishers rarely reject a manuscript at the final stages, unless they think that it is unpublishable.

What makes a manuscript unpublishable? The final draft may not be as well written as the initial proposal. Or the subject of the book has become dated: A psychological profile of Bob Dole that might have sold in 1992 would not be acceptable today. Or the manuscript may contain damaging information about a prominent family, and the publisher becomes worried about potential libel suits. For these and other reasons, the publisher will insist on keeping an "out" clause in the contract, permitting the return of all rights to the author.

If a publisher does exercise its "out" clause, what happens to your advance? Often, the advance is tied to the production of an acceptable manuscript. Under most contracts, if the publisher deems your manuscript unacceptable, you must refund the advance.

In Joan Collins' well-publicized dispute with Random House, however, a jury ruled that she did not have to return her advance—even though Random House found her manuscript unacceptable—and that the company had to pay her part of the additional monies due on her contract. Instead of the usual clause that the author must produce an "acceptable" manuscript, Ms. Collins' contract merely required her to produce a "completed" manuscript. Although this case has been unusual for the publicity it generated, there have been other instances where the publisher, as an act of good will, has permitted the author to keep the advance.

Copyright issues

Ideally, the contract should provide that the publisher will register the copyright *in the name of the author*. Some contracts, particularly those from university and small presses, state that the publisher will register the copyright *in the name of the publisher,* but this clause is negotiable.

The "Rights and Royalties" clauses are critical for you to understand. If your publisher has only the capacity to publish your book in English and distribute it in Canada and the United States, why grant the publisher all the rights to your book, including the right to publish it in any translation throughout the world? Instead, tell the publisher that you want to sell the rights only to the English-language edition in specific countries. Also, consider selling the publisher audio and electronic rights only if the company has these divisions. If not, retain the rights for sales at a later date.

If your publisher is a major conglomerate with movie divisions and your book has movie potential, consider granting the publisher the movie rights, but only if you are sure that you or your agent could not sell the movie rights yourselves for more profit. Ask your agent about his contacts with Hollywood and whether he has sub-agency relations with Hollywood agents.

You should also be aware that the publisher may ask to split the movie rights 50–50. Try to negotiate to a more profitable (60–40, 75–25, 85–15) split, because the publisher will be acting as your agent.

Royalty provisions

Traditional publishers typically offer a royalty fee of 10% to 15% on the retail price for hardcover books, but less for paperback. On mass market paperback books, publishers may print 500,000 copies or more, offer authors a 5% royalty, and sell the books in discount markets such as K-Mart and Wal-Mart. Writers or their agents can propose a royalty schedule. For example, after the first 10,000 or 50,000 or 100,000 or so in sales, the royalty fee increases according to an agreed-upon scale.

Some smaller presses offer payment on net proceeds because they sell fewer copies and therefore receive less money. Make sure the term "net proceeds" is concretely defined in your contract; it is important to specify that net proceeds include the money that the publisher receives from its sales. In a net profit deal, you should be able to negotiate a higher royalty percentage payment, at least 10% to 15% or more.

Accounting provisions

Accounting provisions indicate when you can expect to receive royalty checks. Most trade publishers have semiannual accountings; most academic and small presses have annual accountings. Payments are made within 30 to 90 days following the close of the accounting period.

These provisions may be difficult to negotiate because they often depend on the publisher's overall accounting practices. However, trade publishers have been known to provide shorter accounting periods for their best-selling authors who are generating a great deal of revenue. You can ask for a similar arrangement, but if you do not yet fall into this category, do not be surprised if your publisher resists setting up a different system for you.

Warranties

Almost impossible to negotiate, these clauses require the author to guarantee to the publisher that:
- the author is the sole creator and owner of the work.
- the work has not been previously published.
- the work does not violate another work's copyright.
- the work does not violate anyone's right of privacy.
- the work does not libel or defame anyone.
- the work does not violate any government regulation.

If you or your work violates the above warranties, the publisher has a right to cancel the contract.

Warranty clauses are often accompanied by an indemnity provision, requiring the author to indemnify, or repay, the publisher, should the work violate a warranty provision. If the publisher is sued because of the author's work, the author must defend the lawsuit and reimburse the publisher for any related expenses.

Expenses, permissions, and fair use

Publishers may grant authors budgets to cover certain expenses, such as those connected with travel or interviews. This is obviously a negotiable point, though it may be difficult for a first-time book author to negotiate reimbursement for such expenses.

If you plan to quote from copyrighted works, you should get the permission of the copyright holder (usually either the author or the publisher) to do so. Sometimes the publisher will grant a budget for permission fees; other times, you must cover the cost of such permissions.

In some cases, authors claim a fair-use privilege to use other people's work, such as when critiquing it, in which case permission is not needed. Determining whether the fair-use privilege applies requires authors to use their best judgment. However, you should be aware that if the copyright owner sues, you have to pay to defend both yourself and the publisher.

New editions, author's copies, out of print

The contract may also specify that the publisher has the first right to publish further editions of the work. This should be a negotiable item. Authors of a continuing series (such as mysteries) and textbook publications should beware of such clauses, because they may give the publisher the right to name other writers to produce additional editions. Obviously, the original author would want to retain this right.

The author's copies clause specifies how many free copies of your book you will receive, and the cost of any additional copies you may want to purchase. Sometimes these clauses specify that you cannot resell reduced-price copies. Try to strike this portion of the clause or spell out circumstances where resale would be permitted, such as when you sell copies at a lecture, conference, or book signing.

Also, make sure that the contract provides that when the book goes out of print, all rights revert to the author.

Assignment

A clause that has become standard in the era of mergers and acquisitions is the assignment clause, granting the publisher the right to assign the contract to another publisher. You could easily sell your book to Publisher A only to have Publisher Q purchase or merge with Publisher A soon thereafter. With an assignment clause, Publisher Q would assume the responsibility for publishing your book. You would be protected because the book would still be published.

Your contract may contain fewer clauses than those mentioned here, or it may be more extensive. Whether it's long or short, in large or small print, you should read your contract carefully! You will not only avoid royalty payment shock, but also prevent your book contract dreams from becoming nightmares should some unforeseen disaster strike. Having read your contract, you will know that the price of a magnifying glass could prove a good investment!

❏ 103

KILLING OFF CHARACTERS . . . AND OTHER EDITORIAL WHIMS

BY LOUISE MUNRO FOLEY

EDITORIAL COMMENTS ARE SELDOM GREETED WITH ENTHUSIASM BY writers, but most writers drag themselves—however ungraciously—back to the keyboard to make the changes requested by the editors. Over the years I have often gnashed my teeth as I capitulated to editors' suggestions, but found that in most cases the points they made were valid. Furthermore, the editors' advice aided me on future books as well, helping me to identify recurring pitfalls of my own making—sort of a signal to keep me from repeating errors over and over again.

Did I learn from my mistakes? Yes, indeed.

My first mistake was selling the first book I ever wrote. After dropping over half a dozen transoms and being promptly being shipped back to me, it finally sold to Random House. That was the good news. The bad news was my attitude. This is a snap, right? Knock out a book, persevere in sending it out, and you'll eventually get a check in the mail. Not quite. My next three book manuscripts and their numerous form rejection slips still reside in my filing cabinet, silent reminders against getting too cocky.

Lesson 1: Respect the craft and the competition.

I learned something else from that first book: The letter I received from Random House expressing their interest led off with a mysterious line. "Several of us have enjoyed reading this chapter. When may we see the rest of the book?"

Well! Obviously there was a difference of opinion here about what age group I was writing for. I was thinking in terms of a picture book, but the vocabulary I had used prompted the editor to see it as a book for older readers. I did what any anxious writer would do: Using the same characters, I sat down and wrote more "books" (to me), "chapters" (to them), and sent them off.

Lesson 2: Know the age level you're writing for.

O.K. I was learning to follow the rules, and one piece of advice we've all heard repeatedly is *write what you know*. I could do that. With two sports-playing sons, I set out to cash in on those hot-dusty—cold-rainy (take your seasonal pick) hours I had spent on bleachers in local parks. I wrote a picture book about baseball. This time, I had the language level right, but the opening was all wrong. Delacorte expressed an interest. An editor called me, saying, "Your story starts out on page eleven." The first ten pages were cut before *Somebody Stole Second* was published, with my page eleven as page one.

I still tend to go through a narrative "warming-up" process when I start a new book, but a sign on my office wall—"Your story starts on page 11"—reminds me to do some heavy editing before sending out a manuscript.

Lesson 3: Introduce the protagonist and the problem quickly.

If you think that losing ten pages is bad, listen up. Figuring that I was on a sports roll, I turned my attention to football. (*Tackle 22*, Delacorte) This time the editor didn't stop at cutting pages. "You don't need this many kids," he groused. "Young readers will get confused." He killed off characters. Three of them. And had the survivors deliver the dialogue of my three excised players. In retrospect, I felt he was right.

Lesson 4: Don't overpopulate your book.

My next editorial lesson came when an editor I had previously worked with invited me to write a story about sibling rivalry. Would I give it a try? Would I?! Piece of cake! As the middle daughter in a family of three girls, I knew everything there was to know about sibling rivalry.

I wrote the book. Five-year-old Sammy finds restrictions are imposed on his lifestyle after the arrival of his baby sister: He doesn't go to the park as often; he has to curtail noisy activities during her naps; he gets less attention from neighbors and family.

But even with a relatively satisfying ending—after he came to grips with the changes—the book was a hard sell. Although the idea had been suggested by the editor, the folks at Western Publishing sensed there was something wrong with my manuscript. Several editors had a go at it, and the rewrites were drudgery. Finally, the correct diagnosis was made: The problem was with the flashbacks. In making comparisons, Sammy would think back to what it was like before baby sister's arrival. And picture-book kids don't handle flashbacks very well.

I solved the problem by introducing Grandma and a friend who could talk (in the present) with Sammy, about how it used to be, thus eliminating the flashbacks.

Lesson 5: Avoid flashbacks in books for readers eight years old or younger.

Then there was was my "now you see it, now you don't" picture book—the vanishing act of my repertoire. By the time the editor got through writing her "suggestions," my locale was changed from rural to suburban; neighbors became family friends; a brother was now a neighbor; and a number of plot elements were dumped and replaced. The editor's letter ran over half as long as the book; I shelved my manuscript and wrote *her* book.

A cop-out? No, for this compelling reason. The editor had a slot in a series for the book she outlined, and I wanted to make the sale.

She hadn't asked me to write something to which I was philosophically or ethically opposed; "her" book wasn't better or worse than mine, it was just different.

Lesson 6: If you get an assignment, write it to spec.

Should we, as writers, always be compliant? Should we just roll over and play dead when editorial fingers snap? No, of course not. But be aware that putting up a fight doesn't always assure a win. Here's my horror story.

After teaching a class for six years on "Writing and Selling Non-Sexist Books for Children" at the university and community college level, I considered that I knew the language and nuances of sexism that creep into books for kids, sending subtle but lasting skewed messages. And I conscientiously kept them out of my work . . . unless I deliberately wanted them there for a good reason.

Such was the case with *Ghost Train* (Bantam), in which one of my male characters uttered a sentence that upset the editor (the third one to work on the book, thanks to the transient nature of publishing people).

The storyline goes like this: In a desperate attempt to salvage some of the peach crop when a trucker's strike halts shipping in the Okanagan Valley, my character suggests they have a Peach Festival to lure tourists.

Harry, the orchard owner, excited about the idea, says: "I'll get some of my lady friends to bake pies. . . ."

"No," says the editor. "Delete 'lady.' It's sexist."

"Wait a minute," I argued. "Harry's fifty years old. A bachelor. A farmer. He doesn't know any *men* who bake pies. It's perfectly logical for him to say 'lady friends.' This is the way he would normally talk. It has to do with the integrity of his character."

I lost. In the published book, the editor has Harry saying that his housekeeper can get some of her friends together to bake pies . . . a statement that has its own sexist connotation.

Lesson 7: Fight to keep your character's dialogue in sync with his or her personality, and don't willingly sacrifice a persona in order to suit the editor.

The most puzzling piece of advice I've ever had from an editor came when I was working on book four in *The Vampire Cat Series* (TOR) for middle-aged readers.

In my outline, I had the villainous vampire come down with chicken pox, transmitted by the little brother of the girl protagonist.

"I don't think so," said the editor.

"Why not?" I asked.

"It's not realistic," she replied.

"Oh. Realistic," I repeated.

I hung up the phone, promising to give it some thought.

In a series that featured a talking cat, a host of vampires, and a feline underground spy network, her response called for some intense deliberation on my part. I'm still working on it.

Lesson 8: Don't ever lose your sense of humor.

❑ INTERVIEWS

□ 104

A Conversation with P.D. James

By Lewis Burke Frumkes

Lewis Burke Frumkes: P.D. James is probably the most famous living writer of mystery novels. Let me begin by asking you, Phyllis Dorothy James, why did you choose to use initials rather than your name?

P.D. James: I made this decision as soon as I finished my first novel. Of course, I didn't know then that it would be published. I could have used Phyllis Dorothy James or my married name, Phyllis Dorothy White, or I could have P.D. James, and I wanted my maiden name rather than my married name. I thought it was important to write under my own genes, and, well, P.D. James is short, slightly mysterious. So P.D. James it was. I certainly wasn't attempting to hide my sex, which would have been foolish anyway, because as soon as a book is published, everyone knows you're a woman. I never wanted to pretend otherwise. Now, when I have to sign so many books, it's rather an advantage that I'm not Phyllis Dorothy James White.

LBF: Your novels have an incredibly complex array of characters. Do you think of yourself as a novelist, as a mystery writer, or both?

PDJ: I suppose both. I would describe myself as a novelist writing within the constraints of a classical detective story. I have at least two novels which haven't been detective stories. I like to think of myself as a novelist, but then I'm not in the least ashamed of writing mysteries. So, I suppose, crime novelist.

LBF: *A Certain Justice,* your fourteenth novel, is an extremely fine piece of work. It's set in the chambers in the British jurisprudence system, and shows a wealth of knowledge of that system. How did you do the research for it?

PDJ: I have a quite useful preliminary knowledge of the British legal system because I worked in the British Home Office, and I was concerned with criminal law. I'm interested in trials, and I have a complete set of notable British trials in my library. Of course, as I began researching the book, I realized how much I didn't know. I had immense help from lawyers, went to many trials, had lunch with judges, spent time in chambers, and wandered around the Middle Temple, where the book is mostly set.

LBF: Are female barristers as common as male?

PDJ: No, but there are far more of them than there used to be. I'm not sure there are equal numbers of them, but they're certainly growing in numbers. Not many of them become judges.

LBF: Can we say, without giving too much of the plot away, that there is a certain female barrister in this novel who is defending an unlikable character, and ultimately becomes a victim herself, and then in the rest of the novel we try to find out who did her in? Why did you choose a female barrister lead for this? Have you any particular animus against female barristers?

PDJ: No, no, not in the slightest. Readers will see from the clues and what happens to her daughter, that it was natural for the victim to be a woman. I was very much interested in her past and what made her the kind of woman she was. She fascinated me. I think I enjoyed writing about her more than I would have had I been writing solely about a male barrister, but of course I do explore the lives, the motives, the compulsions, and the professional concerns of the male barristers who are in chambers with her.

LBF: When you have as complicated a story as *A Certain Justice,* do you plot it out beforehand? Do you come up with your main character, then develop her character, and then fill in other characters around her? How does it work for you?

PDJ: It takes quite a long time. Often, it takes as long to plot and plan the book as it does to write it. It begins with a setting, with an idea that I have murder coming right into the heart of chambers, into offices of distinguished lawyers and the striking down of a distinguished criminal lawyer. I had the main idea, which was the setting. Then, of course, Venetia came next: her childhood, her life, her relationship with her daughter, with her ex-husband, with her lover, who feels that as a politician it's expedient to return to his wife before the general election. Venetia's relationship with other lawyers with whom she works. She really is at the heart of the book. Then, indeed, come all the people whose lives touch hers.

LBF: Venetia and Octavia. Both are interesting names ending with a, kind of a certain type. How come they weren't named Carolyn or Margaret or Elizabeth?

PDJ: Naming is very important and very interesting to me. It's odd you should have asked that because I left something out of the book, something about Venetia's father. I had intended to say in the book that he was fake. He ran a boys' school and everything about it was a big fake. The cops weren't really cops, and the staff weren't really qualified. He used to say, 'My daughter Venetia, she was conceived when we were in Venice,' and his daughter knew he'd never been to Venice, so that even her name seemed to her a little false. And in the book, her daughter Octavia is born. One of the other lawyers, when talking to the detective about her daughter, said, "She's called Octavia because she was born in the first minute of the first day of October." Her mother, Venetia, is always rational. It was, in my mind, a contrast. She was named Octavia because of the day on which she was born.

LBF: Who were some of the writers who inspired you when you were growing up? Which ones did you read that may have led you to write mysteries?

PDJ: I think where mystery writing is concerned, it was the women who were writing when I was an adolescent, the time between the wars, specifically, Dorothy L. Sayers. But apart from her, certainly Graham Greene and Evelyn Waugh, as far as style is concerned. I think he was probably the greatest stylist of his generation. I've learned a lot from my enthusiasm for Evelyn Waugh—and Jane Austen.

LBF: They were wonderful models! There is something about mystery writing—you are a charming, intelligent woman, and yet you also love murder and gore. What, do you think, makes a writer in this genre so in love with crime? Is it the murder, is it the mystery, like a game or a puzzle to solve, or is it the acts of violence and crime in itself that you find most fascinating?

PDJ: I don't think it's the acts of violence, and it certainly isn't the gore as gore. Very rarely in my books do I actually describe the act of murder. Nearly always the body is discovered by someone, and that can be very horrific because I try to make that very realistic. The person who discovers the body is horribly shocked.

LBF: How the blood is drained from the face of the person who discovers the body.

PDJ: Absolutely. I would like to think the blood drains from the faces of the readers as they observe this scene. So I don't think it's horror for horror. I couldn't write a book about the torture of one human being by another. And I can't see that on television or on film; I'm repelled by it. I think it is the *mystery,* it's the construction, it's the form, the structure of it. It's bringing order out of disorder, using this unique crime and the disruption it always brings, as an opportunity for exploring characters. Just providing a credible mystery in itself is, for me, absolutely fascinating. I think that on a more psychological level I'm aware that I'm very frightened of violence, both physical and psychological. Writing about it is one way in which one can deal with it. I think that for some readers it's a very reassuring form because it does suppose we live in a rational, comprehensible universe, and it is the duty of human beings to try to achieve some kind of justice, however imperfect that justice is.

LBF: It's been said that you have a truncheon, or something like it, near your bed, so that should anyone break into your room, you would be prepared—and unhesitatingly . . .

PDJ: (Laughs). Well it's one of those things that journalists make up. It isn't a truncheon, it's a little policeman's club. What had happened, actually, just before I was setting out for a major American tour years ago, was that someone downstairs hurled a brick through my drawing room window. The glass was 19th century glass, very thick. I was awakened in the middle of the night by this astonishing noise—it was as if a tank had driven into the house, let alone a smashed window. So, of course, I went downstairs to investigate, and then I called the police. It was highly inconvenient because I had to get a friend to get the window patched up, because I was flying off from Heathrow the next morning. People said I shouldn't have gone down to investigate, but, I thought, it's absolute human nature to investigate. I'm not likely to cower in my bedroom. I had this policeman's club, and I thought,

I'll just keep it by the bed, so if it happens again, I'll still go down, but at least I'll have something in my hand.

LBF: When you are not writing or reading Dorothy Sayers or Evelyn Waugh, do you read any contemporary work? Whose books do you enjoy?

PDJ: On the whole, I enjoy contemporary writers like A.S. Byatt and Margaret Drabble. I prefer today's women authors to men. Maybe an odd thing, and one I'm not particularly pleased or proud about, I find that as I get older, I do read less contemporary fiction. I regularly reread old fiction, novelists who were difficult for me. Henry James was one, and now I'm reading his novels quite seriously. I love biography, autobiography, and history. So really, I'm rereading fiction or going back to the classics.

LBF: Have you discerned any difference between American mystery writing and British?

PDJ: There's probably less difference now than there used to be. I'm not really an expert on mystery writing. It seems to me that when I first started reading it, there was a great difference. The American writers—you have some absolutely magnificent novelists who wrote mysteries, and of course, one is thinking of Hammett and Raymond Chandler and Ross MacDonald. They're wonderful novelists. Generally, they have private eyes who worked as much against officialdom as they did against the murderer. Sometimes quite violent, whereas in England they were somewhat domestic, really. British police may have been totally inefficient, but they were virtuous. However inefficient they were, they were somewhat class-ridden in the 1930s. Not particularly notable as novels on the whole. When you think of the big names, you think of Dick Francis. He's always got a bit of violence in his books, but it's not a violent society, really, nor is it with Colin Dexter's Inspector Morse. The differences, I think, are still there.

LBF: Do you write longhand, do you write on a computer or type-writer?

PDJ: I certainly don't write on the computer or word processor, because no machine devised by man is user-friendly to me. It's partly my age. I do like writing by hand. I like the feeling of words almost coming down from the brain and the arm, onto paper. But my handwriting is atrocious, and of course it gets worse as I write more quickly. So when I've done that I dictate what I've written onto tape while I can still read it. Then my secretary types it. In a sense, that's the first draft on which I work. I have an old electric portable which I'm rather fond of, and I bash away happily at that. But of course when that gives out, I'll be in trouble because those typewriters can't be replaced. Now, everything's on the screen. Everything's a word processor.

LBF: Do you work at night, during the day? Do you work every day?

PDJ: Once I begin writing, as opposed to plotting and planning, I do try to work every day. Whether I'm feeling like it or not, I get up early and write. I move into the world of the book, and I move in with these characters.

LBF: What advice would you give to young writers starting out?

PDJ: I would say develop your use of language by reading good writers, not so that you can copy their style, because writers need to develop their own style. But when you meet an unusual word, get used to it, write it down, find out what it means. Try to increase your vocabulary, because a good writer needs a good vocabulary. You need to read, you need to practice writing, and you need to go through the world with all your senses alert to what is around you: the natural world, the world of men and women, the world of work. For a writer, nothing that happens is ever wasted. It's developing that sensitivity to life, and at the same time trying to hone the craft, thinking of it as a craft.

□ 105

A CONVERSATION WITH
RUSSELL BANKS

BY LEWIS BURKE FRUMKES

Lewis Burke Frumkes: Russell Banks is one of this country's best writers. You probably read him previously in *Rule of the Bone,* or saw the movie version of his book, *The Sweet Hereafter.* Russell has split the clouds with his new blockbuster novel, *Cloudsplitter,* published by HarperCollins. Where should we begin with this, Russell? John Brown is getting a lot of attention these days. What brought you to him as the basis of a big novel?

Russell Banks: I think of him as a door that opened into a whole world for me, which is one reason I suppose the book is as long as it is. John Brown was very important to me when I was a college kid in the sixties, and was politically active in the civil rights and anti-war movements. And Brown's face would be on the wall of an S.D.S. office alongside Che Guevara and Jimi Hendrix. He was very much connected to literary figures that I was obsessed with at the time: the New England transcendentalists like Emerson and Thoreau. All that was in the back of my brain, and then it kind of faded out as the sixties faded out, until I moved into upstate New York and bought a house in the Adirondacks. It turned out that Brown and eleven of his cohorts from the Harpers Ferry raid were buried down the road, where he'd had a farm for many years.

LBF: Is it near Mirror Lake?

RB: It isn't very far from Mirror Lake and Lake Placid. It's North Elbow, just over the hill, and faces Mt. Marcy (the highest mountain in New York), an Indian name meaning "cloudsplitter," thus the title of my novel.

LBF: A great title.

RB: Brown became suddenly a ghostly presence in my life, at the same time very tangible and real, because these were the hills he walked over, the place he lived, and the place where he ran slaves north into Canada. It's from that house that he launched the famous raid on Harpers Ferry.

LBF: You tell the story through the eyes or the memory of his son, Owen—an unusual device. Why did you choose Owen?

RB: It's not really an original device. Basically there's the same situation in *Moby Dick,* in which an apparently minor character tells a story about a larger-than-life character. It was a necessary route for this charismatic, larger-than-life, emblematic figure of John Brown, since I wanted to tell his story from inside and up close. I wanted to tell a domestic story, a relational story, and I wanted to humanize him, and make him real—to me and to others. So his son, Owen, in the 1840s and 1850s, was perfect, because he was present at all the most important moments in his father's public life. And he was at Harpers Ferry and escaped—and lived to tell about it. And to make the story perfect for a novelist, he never told about it. He disappeared into the equivalent then of the abolitionist underground after Harpers Ferry. He was a wanted man, and reappeared on a mountaintop in California.

LBF: Psychologically, what are the resonances in this story for you with your own father?

RB: I think the father-son story, in all its various shapes and permutations, has fascinated me since the beginning of my writing life, and since the beginning of my life, for that matter. But it was an approach that I had never quite entertained before. What happens in a relationship between a father and son, for instance, in which the father is a dominating, controlling figure, but also happens to be right? John's an idealistic man, not a brute, not a sadist, not a psychopath, but something more complicated and seductive. To me, it's the Abraham and Isaac story, but told from the point of view of Isaac, the son. In Sunday school, that story was always told from the point of view of Abraham; it was a test of Abraham's faith: Would he sacrifice his son for his God? I always identified with Isaac, the son. This is tough: Your father takes you out onto the mountain and sharpens his knife. It always chilled me. Why did they tell this story after all? Was it meant to scare kids? It's a story I wanted finally to go to the heart of and see from the point of view of the son.

LBF: And well you did. *Cloudsplitter* is a big book in every sense, and it's getting such good reviews that it has almost moved you to another level. Are you getting different kinds of attention?

RB: My audience is much larger, but it has also changed. My books are being read increasingly by younger people, people in their twenties and teens who are serious readers; that's incredibly gratifying to me. I'm 58 now, but I can still remember that when I was young, a book could change my life. Whatever I read could turn my head in an important way. So it's very gratifying to know that my book is being read by people whose lives—in their minds—are at stake when they read. But it has changed my life in other ways as well. Naturally, it's changed it economically. It means that I don't have to teach any longer and I'm pleased by that, as much as I like teaching.

LBF: Your other novel, *The Sweet Hereafter,* has been getting a lot of attention because of the film.

RB: It's a brilliant film, a marvelous piece of work: very imaginative and serious without being somber. Then, to my astonishment, it's also been well-received by the public, Academy Award nominations for Best Director and Best Screenplay, and it's even making money.

LBF: You've had other books that were made into films.

RB: Yes, *Affliction* has been making the festival circuit. It's a terrific movie, I think. It's a brutal movie, a wonderfully powerful movie.

LBF: *Cloudsplitter* will undoubtedly be a big film.

RB: I hope so. If properly done, that'll be the difficulty. It could easily be ruined.

LBF: While most of the literary community knows your work, where did you come from? How did you originally get into writing?

RB: I kind of back-doored my way in. I came out of a blue-collar world in upstate New Hampshire, where the idea of being a writer was like the idea of being a butterfly or something. And so I didn't take myself seriously as a writer for the longest time. In my early twenties

I tried college for about six weeks and fled. I worked as a plumber. My father and my grandfather were plumbers, and I had been a plumber's helper as a boy; it was the only thing I knew. I was writing at night, because I was falling in love with books. When I was 24, my wife's mother, bless her soul, decided that this boy should go to college, and she paid for my bachelor's degree at the University of North Carolina at Chapel Hill.

LBF: That school is considered one of the best.

RB: It's a great school, and it was fabulous in the sixties. It was so exciting to be there, it really politicized me in a way I never understood before. Up to then my politics had been basically an adolescent fantasy. But suddenly in the middle of the civil rights movement and the anti-war movement, it was fish-or-cut bait time, and it really changed me. When I got out of Chapel Hill in 1968, I was publishing fairly widely and was able to get a position teaching freshman English.

LBF: You have a lot of rough-edged stuff in your books. How much were you involved in?

RB: You mean troubled, turbulent youth? I grew up an angry boy and became an angry young man, in some ways self-destructive. Someone once asked me, "If you hadn't become a writer, what would you have become?" And I thought about that for a while, and I said I think I would have become dead on a parking lot outside a bar in Lakeland, Florida, by the time I was 22 or 23. I had a lot of rough edges. I was trying to blast free of what I felt to be a constricting past or family background. I was lucky, very lucky, that I escaped alive and didn't injure or maim anyone else in the process.

LBF: How do you actually work on a book? When you get an idea, do you get right down to writing? Do you do research?

RB: *Cloudsplitter* required a good deal more research than anything else I'd ever written, mainly because I was working outside my turf, 150 years into the past. I needed to know what it was like to lead a daily life in rural America in the 1840s, so I had to do a great deal of research, and I did that first. In a way, the John Brown story is a given: Every school kid knows it ends at Harpers Ferry. The characters were not givens: I had to find them and invent a few. But I basically spent a year and a half doing nothing but research, till I reached a point where I wondered, "Now, how do I enter this story? How do I tell this story?" And I discovered Owen Brown, by tracking down a footnote to the dusty shelves of the Rare Book Room at Columbia University to research materials that had been accumulated at the turn of the century, including interviews with the surviving children of John Brown, by then elderly men and women. And I thought, "Now, that's the way. I'll have Brown's son, Owen, as an old man, telling the story at the turn of the century to a young woman research assistant of an historian. He will recount what happened, and he'll get so carried away by his tale, that before he knows it he'll be telling his own most inner feelings to this woman."

LBF: Do you write every day?

RB: Pretty much.

LBF: On a word processor?

RB: Whatever works. Some days I can write better on a word processor, and the language seems to flow, and then it'll all get bottled up, and I'll start to feel strangled, and I have to switch to a yellow-lined pad and a pencil and continue that way. That'll work for a while, and then I'll start to feel strangled again, and I'll switch again.

LBF: What's your advice to young writers starting out?

RB: Going back to what you were saying earlier about things changing with this book, and the scale of my career, in a sense, changing. It won't have much effect on my writing because it's happening to me in my middle fifties. Had it happened to me in my middle thirties, it could have had a disastrous effect on me, before my habits were set, before my routines and my values were set. I would say to any young writer, "Don't confuse your career with your work. Your work is the one thing you can have control over, and you must have control over it, but your career you can't control. You just have to let it happen to you."

❏ 106

A CONVERSATION WITH ARUNDHATI ROY

By LEWIS BURKE FRUMKES

Lewis Burke Frumkes: Arundhati Roy's novel, *The God of Small Things,* published by Random House, has received extraordinary notices in this country and around the world. *The New York Times* called it "a dazzling and brilliant novel." Arundhati, is this very heady stuff for you? Are you able to keep this in perspective?

Arundhati Roy: I haven't found it that difficult to deal with what has happening. It *has* been a big surprise. It took me four and a half years of solitary work to write this book, and I think to do something over such a long period of time and then to get such a positive reaction is very rewarding.

LBF: I would imagine. Why don't you introduce us to the book? What is it about, from your perspective?

AR: I'm always tempted to say that it's about everything. It's not as if I had a three-point program and then wrote a story around it. I've always believed that a story is the simplest way of presenting a complex world. It's a way of making sense of the world.

LBF: Through the small things?

AR: Yes, through the small things. Technically, the book is set in Kerala, south India, but it isn't really a book about India or about Kerala. It's a book about how, over years, human society continues to behave in very similar ways, even though the details may be different.

LBF: Human nature is human nature, a thousand years ago or today?

AR: Exactly. Kerala, the southernmost state in India, where I grew up, is a unique place and an incredible backdrop for a novel, because it's the only place in the world, I think, in which four of the world's five big religions live together. Against this sort of backdrop human drama plays itself out, and you realize in the long run it really doesn't make such a huge difference because human society continues to divide itself up, it continues to make war across those divisions.

LBF: You speak English fluently. Do you speak English in India? Do you speak Hindi, Bengali? Urdu?

AR: Almost all educated Indians will speak at least two, if not three, languages. I speak three: Hindi, Malayalam—which is the language we speak in Kerala—and English.

LBF: And what language do you think in?

AR: I think and write in English.

LBF: Tell us about yourself, how your career developed.

AR: I grew up in Kerala on the banks of this little river, sticking labels on my grandmother's pickle bottles. She runs a pickle factory there.

LBF: As does someone in the book.

AR: Yes. I finished school partly in Kerala. My mother started the school, and I studied there. I was the guinea pig; the only person in the class. Then I went away to boarding school and came back.

After school, all I wanted really was to leave. I found Kerala in many ways a very terrifying place to grow up. When I was admitted to the School of Architecture in Delhi, I left home, and I didn't go back again for many years. I lived on my own with a group of young people. We were all teenagers with no supervision, nobody to order our lives for us. I think that's not as unusual here as it is in India. In India, it's unheard of that somebody would be in that situation, especially a woman. I lived in what we call a slum colony within the walls of an old monument in New Delhi. I actually enjoyed myself immensely. We had no money but we had a lot of fun. When you're that young, somehow the future doesn't scare you, you just live from day to day. When I graduated, I decided I was going to be a flower child. So I went off to Goa, where I used to make cake and sell it on the beach. After a bit, I came back to Delhi and met my husband. He was making a film, which he asked me to act in. Acting wasn't something I ever wanted to do, but I felt it was a good way to observe the process of filming. So I did act, and then became a screenplay writer. I wrote and designed the films I worked on.

LBF: As a former filmwriter and actress, do you want to be involved with the film of *The God of Small Things?*

AR: Nothing that I've done in film has been remotely as satisfying as writing my novel, and I continue to think of it as a visual but unfilmable book. I don't know if I want it to be a film. I don't really see cinema as the last stop for literature. The language, the narrative, the characters would have to be somehow broken apart and made again to be a film. Even translating the book into different languages—though it's been translated into many—is difficult to do, it has to be reimagined in some way.

LBF: Your book was written in English, but where was it first published?

AR: It was first published in India. I was very keen for it to be published in India first.

LBF: In Hindi?

AR: No, in English. There are more people in India who speak English than there are in England. It's the only common language.

LBF: Your use of language is wonderful. Do you have favorite words—words that you use more often than other words, or words that do something for you, are very special to you, musical?

AR: Because Indians tend to speak more than one language—in my case, as I said, three languages—I think that sort of revitalizes the language that I write in. I try to make my language do what I want it to do; I don't like to do what the language wants me to do. Sometimes that process is so instinctive that I don't think about it.

LBF: What advice would you give to other writers starting out?

AR: I'm very suspicious of free advice.

LBF: Do you want to charge me for it? (Laughs)

AR: No. By free advice, I mean people who just advise people unnecessarily. Each person has to do it in his way. The way I worked was not to open my work up to opinions until it was finished. I worked for four and a half years without discussing it or showing it to anyone. Sometimes when you start soliciting opinions, your work just gets up and walks away. You have to be focused enough to know that you have to do it regardless of whether it's published or not, or whether it's successful or not.

❏ 107

A Conversation with Joyce Christmas

By Claire E. White

Claire White: Joyce Christmas is the author of 11 mysteries, eight featuring Lady Margaret Priam, expatriate Brit living in Manhattan. Her second series stars retired office manager, Betty Trenka. Joyce, let me begin by asking you what inspires you when you write.

Joyce Christmas: Finishing what I'm working on. And the money. I don't think a professional writer has to be inspired. It's a job.

CW: How do you write: computer, dictation, or longhand?

JC: Mostly on the computer. But I do drafts on a good old electronic typewriter and lacking that, in longhand.

CW: Do you write every day?

JC: I try to, but I have a full-time job, so sometimes work obligations get in the way. But I try to write early in the morning and in the evenings, and when I have a deadline, as much as I can get away with at work.

CW: You must have an understanding boss!

JC: He is my best friend and my Constant Reader.

CW: That helps, certainly. Do you ever get writer's block? What is your "cure" for it?

JC: Sometimes. Lying down and watching old sitcoms or going someplace different, like a museum, or buying something. Out of the writing life for a while usually cures it.

CW: How did you make your first sale of a book you wrote?

JC: My very first book was a ghostwriting job, and I was asked to help the author. She didn't quite know what a book was, and even though it was nonfiction, it had to have a beginning, middle and an end. My first novel, now out of print, was *Hidden Assets,* and a writing partner and I were asked by an editor to write it. (For whatever reason, she wanted a book about a male stripper. Go figure.) Because I had a dozen ghostwritten books behind me, I guess it was assumed that I could write a novel.

CW: Did you use an agent?

JC: Yes. I have a wonderful agent. But it is not easy to get one. Again, because I had a track record of completing books, I didn't have a problem.

CW: What is the hardest part about writing in the mystery genre?

JC: The competition, thinking of plots that are as good as other people's. Mysteries really are highly competitive, and there are a lot of them out there. It's a real challenge.

CW: Lady Margaret has an on-again, off-again romance with New York detective Sam De Vere. Is it difficult to integrate romance into a mystery?

JC: Yes. The genre isn't really suited to romance unless it's an integral part of the plot. But I think the protagonist needs an emotional partner to rely on. You know, writing a book means filling up pages with something happening, and it can't always be a murder.

CW: Yes, true. How do you create your characters?

JC: First I think of what kind of character I need. A society lady, a suburban neighbor, and so forth, and then I start thinking of qualities and likes and dislikes, maybe basing them somewhat on people I know—but I do not base any character completely on a real person. The characters do take on a kind of life of their own, and then you think of something you can add to make them more realistic and often more valuable to the plot.

CW: How much research is involved with writing the Lady Margaret Priam books?

JC: I try not to say anything wrong, so for the books not set in New

York, I either "research" by going to the place where they are set—Caribbean (although I lived there for many years), Harrods, Beverly Hills, and Forest Lawn, etc. I walk about New York to look at the streets and buildings that I'm writing about, I read the gossip columns, and I formerly did public relations work for various charities, so I absorbed a lot of information that I put to use. It's not heavy-duty research, but as I noted, I try not to say anything really wrong. Traffic has to travel in the right direction on one-way streets, stuff like that.

CW: In mystery writing, which do you believe is more important—plot or character—and why?

JC: Plot and character are equally important to make a good book. Some readers prefer character-driven books, others like plot-driven. And writers are either character or plot people, and their books reflect which they are.

CW: Your newer sleuth is Betty Trenka, an older, retired office manager. What does she like to do in her spare time? What are her pet peeves? What music does she like? Where does she shop?

JC: Betty was forced to retire in her sixties, and she hates having spare time after years of comfortable routine. She's busy trying to make a life for herself after retirement. Peeves? Being forced to do anything domestic, and of course that damned cat someone left on her doorstep. (Actually, she and Tina the cat have reached a detente. I think Betty would miss her if she were gone.) I've never mentioned it, but I think Betty likes Frank Sinatra, music from her girlhood during and just after World War Two. She buys her clothes at the mall and from L.L. Bean catalogues. Betty likes the wine chosen by her neighbor Ted Kelso, who also cooks her favorite meals. She is without vices (so far).

CW: Does she have a sense of humor? What are her best qualities?

JC: She sees the absurdity of things, and her best quality is common sense and determination. Finishing a job once started.

CW: How did you create Betty?

JC: My editor asked me to start a new series, and I had had a number of older characters in my books, so I thought a senior sleuth would be fun. Then it turned out that senior sleuths were Hot!! I have a lot of friends who are in their 70s and 80s, so they provided role models.

CW: You were Associate Editor at *The Writer* Magazine for a number of years. What did that position entail?

JC: Editing articles for the magazine, and for the company's other publication, *Plays,* one-act plays for children (I wrote a few). Writing letters to authors, getting market information and writing it up, proofreading, layout of the magazines, and editing books of plays, seeing them through the press, buying paper, specifying type. Everything. And my bosses, Sylvia Burack, still the Editor, and the late Abe Burack, Editor, were better than a college education in publishing. True publishers of the old school, which are fast disappearing. I learned about writing, and the whole business.

CW: What is the difference between the "old school" of publishing and the new?

JC: I don't think the Buracks, or the rest of us, went out to a lengthy business lunch more than once a year. The old school cared more about what they were publishing, and didn't have an eye out for the "mega-deal." They cared about helping new authors along; they wouldn't dream of paying a has-been a million bucks because they knew the market, and knew whether they would make the money back. They believed in "the profession" and they weren't bottom-line-oriented in the way today's publishing conglomerates are. They didn't think of books as the equivalent of toothpaste. Books were not just a bunch of units to be sold. Mind you, there are wonderful, caring editors today, like mine. But the book business is Big Business, but alas, not every good book is a blockbuster, ready to be sold to be the movies. I still avoid business lunches.

CW: What were the biggest mistakes you saw in submissions to *The Writer?*

JC: Most submissions were by invitation, but I was always surprised that famous fiction writers had trouble writing articles about writing. Many of them were not always good at writing straightforward expository prose. But I confess, it's not easy to write meaningfully about fiction writing. A plug for a friend: Mystery novelist Meg Chittenden's book, *How to Write Your Novel,* is excellent (and was published by The Writer, Inc.).

CW: Does being an editor affect the way you write?

JC: Definitely. It helps greatly in doing revisions; you know that the passage you *absolutely love!* should probably be removed. I guess the critical eye for things like sense and grammar comes from my editing days.

CW: It seems that over the years the mystery genre has gotten a lot more violent and grisly in the storylines (plots about serial killers, etc.) Do you see a trend toward gore in this genre?

JC: Again, there are readers who adore serial killer books. I read them only occasionally because I don't like grisly stories, but yes, I do think publishers are asking for them because there's an audience for them. I can't begin to analyze why. I won't blame it on TV, but America has this romance with violence that doesn't sit well with me.

CW: Do you find the Internet useful?

JC: I *love* the Internet. I love e-mail, I love reading Dorothy L, I love finding sites that talk about things I'm interested in. I like being able to find news stories from a few days ago that I missed. It's a terrific resource that I use for entertainment, writing and for company business. Long may it wave!

CW: We love the Internet, too! Now, for the aspiring authors out there . . . how useful are writers' groups and conventions ?

JC: Conventions are great fun. Writers get a chance to meet fans, and fans get a chance to see us make fools of ourselves on panels. Bouchercon is very large, but there are lots of smaller conventions (Cluefest in Dallas, Malice Domestic in Washington, Mid-Atlantic in Philadelphia, Left Coast Crime in San Diego, to name a few) that are easier to handle. I belong to a number of writers organizations. Mystery Writers of America helps foster a sense of fellowship with other mystery writers. In the recent past, there have been problems reported with MWA, but every organization has problems, and MWA's were blown out of proportion. It's a good organization. I also belong to International Association of Crime Writers, which gives me a chance to meet overseas colleagues, and Sisters in Crime is a terrific group for both writers and fans.

CW: What is your best advice to the aspiring mystery novelist?

JC: Read, read, read in the genre. Write, write, write, everything you can. Writing is like being a professional musician. You have to practice the scales over and over so that when you sit down to perform, you don't have to think about where the notes are. I've never had any experience with writing critique groups, but if you trust your colleagues, it's very helpful to have astute readers who can help if you go astray or get stuck, or don't understand what you're trying to say. Publications, electronic or otherwise, that talk about writing can be helpful by giving you ideas you might not have thought of, and help with technique. I find Dorothy L very helpful in getting a sense of what readers care about, what they hate or find trite. My agent is helpful, too, but I think he's probably too kind.

❏ 108

A Conversation with
Elmore Leonard

By Lewis Burke Frumkes

Lewis Burke Frumkes: I'd like to begin by asking Elmore Leonard to tell us a little bit about how his novel, *Riding the Rap,* differs from any of his other books.

Elmore Leonard: I'm not sure that it is different, because it still has my cast of characters, or at least, the type of characters I like to work with; I spend at least half the time with the antagonist. Every year or so, while I'm writing a book, I get a letter from a friend who's in the business. He says, "Well, has your first chapter become your chapter three yet? Has your main character decided to do anything?" Because I'm so intrigued with the guys who are pulling the crime, whatever it is. I like their attitude. They never get along with each other. You always see that two of them are going to bump heads. You wonder which one might kill the other and be left then for the main character. I'm never sure myself, until I get to the scene where it's going to happen. Then I realize, it's got to be *this* guy, because my characters have to talk. In fact, they're auditioned. The characters are all auditioned in the early scenes so I can see how important they really are.

LBF: So you don't actually plot a novel out in detail before you begin?

EL: No, I don't. In *Riding the Rap,* Harry Arno, a character from my previous novel, *Pronto,* disappears. What happened to him? His former girlfriend Joyce asks her new boyfriend Raylan Givens, who's also the U.S. Deputy Marshall, "Would you look for Harry? What do you think happened to him?" Raylan, the lead character, isn't sure he cares what happened to Harry, because Joyce is so concerned with him, but he starts looking for him. That's the idea: What happened to Harry.

We see that Harry's been abducted, but not in the usual way. This is a scheme that was inspired by the hostage-taking in Beirut. Chip Ganz, the fellow who comes up with the idea, had watched stories on television about the hostage-taking and wondered, "Could there be any money in that? What if I took a hostage, blindfolded him and chained him to a wall in a filthy basement somewhere?" One of his accomplices says, "But, where are you going to find a filthy basement?" So, they end up holding the hostage in a fairly nice beachfront mansion. The idea is that instead of sending a ransom note to someone, they deal with just the hostage. "You tell us how you can get two million dollars to us without anyone knowing about it. If we like the idea, we'll let you go. If we don't like the idea, you're dead." These are the guys who are into money and manipulative with money. Harry Arno, for example, is a sports bookie. Another guy that they pick up is a savings-and-loan scoundrel who may have thirty million dollars hidden away somewhere—all his investors went broke, that kind of guy.

So, that's the scheme that I start with, and I develop it with different points of view. Among the bad guys, I have three points of view: Chip Ganz and the two fellows who work for him. Then I have Ben Rolins's point of view, Joyce's point of view, and Harry's point of view. So, in movie fashion, I can cut to anyone's point of view at any given time. That's the key—*point of view*—because I am always writing from the point of view of one of my characters, never from mine. I'm not the omniscient author. I don't know anything. If a character is looking out the window, and there's a reason to describe the weather, it will be as he sees the weather, not as I see the weather, not as I use imagery and fall on my face trying to be poetic in describing the weather. I avoid the difficult things in writing prose.

LBF: Do you always write that way?

EL: In studying Hemingway, I came upon this technique: letting the dialogue pull the story as much as possible. I've always been interested in dialogue, but I don't know that I work any harder at it than anyone else. I just have a good ear. I don't hang out wherever criminals hang out and listen. There's always the sound of a character. In some cases, it's more pronounced than others, but you never hear *me*. That's the main thing.

LBF: Now, it's no accident that you began by writing Westerns, right? The closing scene in *Riding the Rap* is like a Western thriller, with two men who could be called "fast guns" facing each other. It's an incredible scene. What in the Western do you take into the crime novel?

EL: Well, when I started writing in the 1950s the market for Westerns was tremendous. Almost all magazines except women's magazines were publishing Western stories, and Western movies were big. But, in the eight Western books and the thirty short stories that I wrote, I never once ended with that face-off in the street where they're going to draw, because that never happened. I would read the accounts in the *Tombstone Epitaph* of shootings. A guy is standing at a bar, and another guy walks in with a pistol, fires at him three or four times, and misses. The guy at the bar turns around, chases him out, and hits him once or twice as the guy's running across the street. That was a gunfight. Why would they stand waiting for somebody to count to three or for a twitch? Why would they do that? These men were not honorable, not like gentlemen in old French duels.

Now, in the climactic situation of *Riding the Rap,* there is a little dishonorability, and the reference, of course, is to Western movies when one character says, "I want to know what it's like to meet a guy like that, like in the movies, and draw."

LBF: In *Riding the Rap,* you deal with a psychic, the beautiful Reverend Navarro, who has a gift for reading Tarot. It was an interesting subplot.

EL: In a way, she's sort of a central character. A lot of the plot hinges on her. The guys in the book are attracted to her for different reasons. She practices her art—or her con; we are not always sure that she really is psychic. Sometimes she is. When she's talking to someone on the phone at night, and she says, "Turn the light on. I can't see," you wonder, "Hey, wait a minute." Or when she says to Raylan, "You're from West Virginia. No, you're from Kentucky originally, and you were a coal miner." How did she know that? She's holding his hands, but he could have been a dishwasher.

LBF: Who were your models when you were first starting out in crime writing?

EL: When I began to study writing, I studied Hemingway, Steinbeck,

A CONVERSATION WITH ELMORE LEONARD

and Richard Bissell—he wrote *7 1/2 Cents,* which became the play *The Pajama Game.* I loved Hemingway for his dialogue, but I realized I did not share his attitude about anything. He took himself and every-thing else so seriously. A writer's style really comes out of his attitude and how he sees things. So, I had to look around at other writers, including Mark Harris, who wrote *Bang the Drum Slowly,* John Steinbeck, and John O'Hara. I could never get into Faulkner. I could never read *Crime and Punishment;* there seemed to be too many words.

LBF: What do you read for pleasure when you're not writing?

EL: A book I enjoyed quite a bit was Stephen Hunter's *Dirty White Boys.* I like Pete Dexter. I like Ed McBain. I think you can't touch his police stuff. I like James Lee Burke, Jim Hall, and Carl Hiaasen. I don't read them all the time, but I think they are all pros.

LBF: Do you work on a word processor?

EL: No, I write in longhand, and then, I put it on the typewriter as I go along. I bought my first electric typewriter a few summers ago. For twenty years or so, I had been using a manual that I'd bought secondhand. Finally, I became tired of changing and hunting for the ribbons.

LBF: What's your writing schedule?

EL: When I'm writing a novel, I work from 9:30 a.m. to 6:00 p.m. every day and most of Saturday—unless it's summertime. I start a book in January and finish it by May. Then, I don't write anything for several months, and the time just flies by. By fall, I start thinking of the next book. About five years ago, I saw a picture of a female marshall in the paper. She was a good-looking woman in her early thirties, standing in front of a federal building in Miami with a shotgun on her hip. Just looking at this picture, I thought, "That is the next book." It wasn't the next book. I wrote a couple others first, but I kept the clipping. Finally, I used that character in a collection of short stories Otto Pen-zler put together for Delacorte, called *Out of Sight.* He asked me to write one, and I thought, "Well, I'll try out my female marshall, whose name is Karen Cisco. I'll get to know her in this short story."

LBF: What advice would you give to writers just starting out?

EL: Read. You read and study what the writer is doing. Find a writer you feel you have a rapport with, and study the paragraphing, study the punctuation, study everything. I think the paragraphing is extremely important. Learn how to paragraph to keep the story flowing. Find out by experimenting how you write most naturally. You may be a traditional prose writer, an omniscient author whose words and descriptions are the most important elements. Or, like me, you hide behind the characters and let them do all the work.

❏ 109

A CONVERSATION WITH JOAN DIDION

BY LEWIS BURKE FRUMKES

Lewis Burke Frumkes: Joan Didion is one of our finest writers. Her newest book, *The Last Thing He Wanted,* is a thriller, quite different from her earlier novels, like *Play It As It Lays.* I'd like to begin by asking her how she decided to write a thriller.

Joan Didion: In a real sense, *The Last Thing He Wanted* is a thriller— a political thriller and a love story. That surprised me. I hadn't expected it to be a love story, but it turned out to be one. It takes place in 1984, at the height of what we later came to know as Iran Contra, and is about a private person who becomes involved and gets in over her head.

LBF: You write literary novels. Why did you want to write a thriller?

JD: I had never written anything that depended totally on working out a plot, where everything has to mean something. It was a technical exercise. It is quite hard to do, but quite interesting.

LBF: Do you read thrillers?

JD: I read Conrad, of course.

LBF: What writers besides Conrad inspired you as a young person?

JD: Hemingway, because of his clear, clean sentences. It was exciting to me when I discovered them.

LBF: Many of your heroines, protagonists, are people who walk into situations. In one of your novels a woman walked across an air field. In another one, you imagined a plot out of seeing a woman in a particular place. Is that a stimulus?

JD: Absolutely. *Play It As It Lays* came out of my seeing a blonde woman in a white halter dress. I know who she was; she was a minor

525

actress who was paged in a casino at one o'clock in the morning. And, you just start wondering what brought her to that moment. There are a lot of moments that came out of actually observed things, but the most vivid was seeing a woman in a restaurant in the middle of the afternoon eating a chocolate parfait and bacon. This stayed with me.

LBF: While *The Last Thing He Wanted* is fiction and a thriller, as you describe it, there's a lot of non-fiction woven into the fiction. Could this possibly be described as roman à clef? Is Treat Morrison based on anyone we would know?

JD: No. He's based on a lot of people. There are threads of real people in him, and things he says are echoes of things others say. The situation did occur, however. In Central America during that period, there was the plot to attempt an assassination of an American Ambassador by people who wanted to increase American involvement.

LBF: Your husband, John Gregory Dunne, is also a writer. Do you ever edit each other?

JD: He reads everything I write. I read everything he writes. We might make suggestions of where something could go. A couple of years ago, for the first time in all the years that we've been married, we were simultaneously working on different projects. We never had this kind of sync before. And what it meant was that he finished his book the day before Christmas, and I finished mine the day after. But, from the end of August until Christmas, we never saw anyone. We didn't go out, we didn't do anything, we worked every night until eight or nine and would go to dinner in the neighborhood or build a fire. It was great. I think we would both like to duplicate that.

LBF: You love poetry. You write wonderful novels. You write essays. Is there some genre that you have not tackled that you would like to? Or was your new thriller an example of trying something new?

JD: Yes, I was trying something new. I have never wanted to write a play. I don't think I would like to write poetry because I like the long sustained format of a novel.

LBF: When do you do your writing?

JD: I used to write at night because when I was working at *Vogue*, that was the only time I had. But when I stopped working, I started to go to bed early and started writing at about 10:30 in the morning till 7:00 or 8:00 p.m. I now start writing late in the morning because there are certain household things I have to do, which I try to finish before 10:30. From then till about 5:00 p.m. I do rewrites, and then the rhythm starts kicking in for me, and I overcome my dislike of the things I have to do when I wake up every day.

LBF: What advice would you give to beginning writers?

JD: The most important and hardest thing for any writer to learn is the discipline of sitting down and writing even when you have to spend three days writing bad stuff before the fourth day, when you write something better. If you've been away from what you've been working on even for a day and a half, you have to put in those three days of bad writing to get to the fourth, or you lose the thread, you lose the rhythm. When you are a young writer, those three days are so unpleasant that you tend to think, "I'll go away until the mood strikes me." Well, you're out of the mood because you're not sitting there, because you haven't had that period of trying to push through till the fourth day when the rhythm comes.

LBF: What part of the writing process is the most exciting for you?

JD: When the rhythm comes and you go into overdrive. When a book starts to move and you know you can go with it. Between then and the time you finish it is a good period.

❑ 110

A Conversation with Peter Mayle

By Lewis Burke Frumkes

Lewis Burke Frumkes: I'm going to begin by asking Peter Mayle to tell us how his new book, *Chasing Cézanne,* which is kind of a mystery story, is different from his other books, and what it is about without giving too much away.

Peter Mayle: I guess it's slightly different because it does go beyond Provence for some of the action. Some of it takes place in New York, some in Paris, some in the Bahamas. It's about the art business, and what got me interested in that was a piece from *The Chicago Tribune,* I think, in which the journalist interviewed the head of the Scotland Yard Art & Antique Squad in London—which I didn't know existed. In the course of the interview this guy who makes a business of knowing what's happening in the art world said that the latest estimate of the value of stolen art around the world was over three billion dollars.

LBF: Stolen art? Three billion dollars?

PM: That's what he said. I wondered who had stolen it and where it had gone, because it wasn't destroyed. Somewhere, somebody has it. So I got interested in finding out a bit more about the art business. Through friends of friends of friends, I began to talk to some people who deal art in New York and London and asked about stolen art. They said it was probably a highly exaggerated journalistic story. That didn't ring very true to me. I then said I was trying to work out how I would steal a piece of art if I were a criminal.

The first thing I would need to know is the name of a good forger. "Now, maybe you can help me with the name of a good forger." And all these art dealers again said, "Forgers, no, we deal only with work of absolutely impeccable provenance. You'll have to go to one of these hole-in-corner dealers in Hong Kong or somewhere." They were all giving me a line that didn't seem to make any kind of sense, so I knew I was onto a reasonably good idea.

I was working out a scheme of stealing a famous painting, and I chose Cézanne because he's a local lad from Aix-en-Provence and I like his work very much. I thought, if I wanted to pick up a Cézanne, the current value of which is about $30 million, how would I set about doing it? The first thing I'd do, I decided, is I'd have it forged, and then, in the dead of night, I'd switch the forgery for the original. Then I had to work out how I'd get into people's houses or galleries or wherever the art was kept. That proved to be slightly more complicated, but I think I've come up with a fairly plausible way in which to persuade the rich, the wealthy and the art collectors of this world to open their doors to people and let them poke around with complete respectability.

LBF: Is *Chasing Cézanne* really a primer for an art thief?

PM: It could be. I don't think there's anything in there that isn't possible.

LBF: Will you feel awkward or untoward if you read in the newspaper one day, "Cézanne Stolen! Peter Mayle not Responding to Phone Calls."?

PM: It won't be the first time a Cézanne's been stolen, and having spoken to a lot of people—and jumped to several conclusions, which I like to do—I'm quite sure there are fakes hanging in the world's galleries and homes and collections, and people still think they're the real thing.

LBF: And there's a lot at stake. You're talking about a $30 million painting, and it's a major difference to a collector if it's real or it's fake.

PM: Oh, sure. But so many of these things are given the nod on the basis of one or two experts' opinion.

LBF: You also chose a photographer as your protagonist.

PM: He's essential to the plot of getting into people's houses. I don't want to give too much away, but what I've done is to invent a glossy magazine that does features on people's homes in various parts of the world, and reconnaisance is necessary to find out about security arrangements and that sort of thing.

LBF: Now, everyone knows you from *A Year in Provence* and *Hotel Pastis,* but in *Anything Considered,* you made a little bit of a foray into the mystery. Are you gradually making a transition to mystery writer?

PM: Not really. I'm always fascinated by nonviolent crime that's ingenious. I don't find anything at all attractive about guys who go into banks with submachine guns and blow everybody's head off. But when you get a criminal who's intelligent, who's imaginative, who does his homework and who pulls off an elegant crime, then I'm rather interested. Having said that, my next book, which I'm working on now, is a nonfiction book set in Provence, so I'm not continuing on a mystery run.

LBF: Peter, tell us how you started out. You've had a very interesting career.

PM: I started out in advertising. I got promoted and was made into an executive. I also had, at the time, some pretensions as to writing something a little bit more permanent than a commercial or newspaper ad, and so I wrote a little book for my children about the facts of life. And that did well enough to encourage me to think that I may have a future as a writer.

I left advertising at a time when my contract was coming up for renewal, and started ten years of acute financial shortage while I was working on my writing and doing everything that struggling writers do to get on. And then, after about ten years I sort of got back to where I was financially ten years before in the advertising business. My wife and I always wanted to live in France, and one day she said, "Look. You're a writer. We don't have to live in England to write. Why don't we go and try it?" So we did. I was going to write a novel, and I got distracted by the events of everyday life and started writing what turned into *A Year in Provence.*

LBF: How many copies has it sold?

PM: It's still going, remarkably. There are over four million copies around the world, in 22 languages, and I'm still astonished. And that's six years after publication. People want to know if there's some sort of secret for aging advertising men to get out of business, write bestsellers. . . .But maybe it comes from the fact that I've always regarded myself as the first person who ought to be amused by what I do, because I reckon that if I can't entertain me, how can I proceed to entertain anyone else? So I have fun. I don't write things I don't want to do.

LBF: Tell us about your writing habits. Did you start out writing longhand and now are on a computer? Did you always write on a computer?

PM: I always used to write on an automatic portable, one of those little tin things. I had one of those for twenty years. Then I broke my wrist and couldn't use a manual typewriter. So, struggling against progress I got hold of a Powerbook PC, and that's what I use now. It's wonderful, it makes writing so much easier because you can chop and change, you don't have to feed new bits of paper into the typewriter every five minutes. I use it as a typewriter and a filing cabinet.

LBF: Do you plot out your books carefully before you write them?

PM: Yes. For *Chasing Cézanne,* for instance, I did a 60-page outline before I started writing, because when I start writing I just want to concentrate on the words, rather than trying to think of the story at the same time. And so I do a long outline, chapter by chapter, working out what is going to happen in which chapter, which is quite fun. Also, the most fun of all for me, in researching a book, is deciding where a character is going to stop for lunch. And so in the outline, I'll sort of see places in the story and the plot where a conversation over a meal might be appropriate. I wonder where the characters are, if they're in New York or Paris or the South of France or wherever, and that is because I don't want them to eat anywhere I haven't tested myself. I go to these places.

LBF: You're obviously having a terrific career and enjoying it.

PM: I'm having a wonderful time. I feel very, very lucky. I can live where I want to live, write where I want to write, and people are kind enough to support my endeavors in this way. What makes people go for your books and not somebody else's, who may be every bit as hard-working, every bit as good a writer, might even have a better story, all sorts of things like that. I have to believe that a lot of it is work, obviously, but an awful lot of it is luck, for which one can take no credit at all. So I don't.

LBF: What authors do you read when you're not writing or when you're not reading your own work?

PM: I'm dying to read Tom Wolfe's newest book, *Ambush at Fort Bragg.* I also like E. B. White very much. I read and reread him. Also some of the mystery thriller writers that are so good in America— Nelson DeMille, Walter Mosley, James Lee Burke. I've really enjoyed *How the Irish Saved Civilization,* by Thomas Cahill. I'm reading Christopher Isherwood's diaries at the moment. I just read anything, really.

LBF: Can you give some advice to would-be writers?

PM: Write. There's no substitute for doing it. And you have to do it every day until it becomes a habit. It doesn't necessarily have to be a book. I think a lot of people are over-ambitious at the beginning and they try for too much. Try a short story or an article first and then gradually start writing longer and longer as you get your confidence. The thing to do is to write and to finish. There are so many books that are still in a state of half-completion in drawers all over the world. And they may be quite good, but if they never get finished nobody's ever going to know.

Where to Sell

Where to Sell

All information in these lists concerning the needs and requirements of magazines, book publishing companies, and theaters comes directly from the editors, publishers, and directors, but personnel and addresses change, as do requirements. No published listing can give as clear a picture of editorial needs and tastes as a careful study of several issues of a magazine or a book catalogue, and writers should never submit material without first thoroughly researching the prospective market. If a magazine is not available in the local library or on the newsstand, write directly to the editor for the price of a sample copy; contact the publicity department of a book publisher for an up-to-date catalogue, or a theater for a current schedule. Many companies also offer a formal set of writers guidelines, available for an SASE (self-addressed, stamped envelope) upon request.

While some of the more established markets may seem difficult to break into, especially for the beginner, there are thousands of lesser-known publications where editors will consider submissions from first-time free lancers.

All manuscripts must be typed double-space and submitted with self-addressed envelopes bearing postage sufficient for the return of the material. If a manuscript need not be returned, note this with the submission, and enclose an SASE or a self-addressed, stamped postcard for editorial reply. Use good white paper; onion skin and erasable bond are not acceptable. *Always* keep a copy of the manuscript, since occasionally material is lost in the mail. Magazines may take several weeks, or longer, to read and report on submissions. If an editor has not reported on a manuscript after a reasonable length of time, write a brief, courteous letter of inquiry.

Some publishers will accept, and may in fact prefer, work submitted on computer disk, usually noting the procedure and type of disk in their writers guidelines.

ARTICLE MARKETS

The magazines in the following list are in the market for free-lance articles in many categories. Unless listings state otherwise, a writer should submit a query first, including a brief description of the proposed article and any relevant qualifications or credits. A few editors want to see samples of published work, if available.

Submit photos or slides *only* if the editor has specifically requested them. A self-addressed envelope with postage sufficient to cover the return of the manuscript or the answer to a query should accompany all submissions.

GENERAL-INTEREST PUBLICATIONS

AIR & SPACE/SMITHSONIAN— 901 D St. S.W., 10th Fl., Washington, DC 20024-2518. George Larson, Ed. General-interest articles, 1,000 to 3,500 words, on aerospace experience, past, present, and future. Pays varying rates, on acceptance. Query.

AIR FORCE TIMES—See *Times News Service.*

AMERICAN HERITAGE— 60 Fifth Ave., New York, NY 10011. Richard F. Snow, Ed. Articles, 750 to 6,000 words, on U.S. history and background of American life and culture from the beginning to recent times. No fiction. Pays $300 to $1,500, on acceptance. Query.

AMERICAN JOURNALISM REVIEW— 8701 Adelphi Rd., Adelphi, MD 20783. Rem Rieder, Ed. Articles, 500 to 5,000 words, on print, broadcast, and electronic journalism. Pays 20¢ a word, on publication. Query.

THE AMERICAN LEGION—Box 1055, Indianapolis, IN 46206. Joe Stuteville, Ed. Articles, 750 to 2,000 words, on current world affairs, public policy, and subjects of contemporary interest. Payment is negotiable, on acceptance. Query.

AMERICAN VISIONS, THE MAGAZINE OF AFRO-AMERICAN CULTURE—1156 15th St. N.W., Suite 615, Washington, DC 20005. Joanne Harris, Ed. Articles, 1,500 words, and columns, 750 to 2,000 words, on African-American history and culture with a focus on the arts. Pays from $100 to $1,000, after publication. Query.

AMERICAS—OAS, 19th and Constitution Ave. N.W., Washington, DC 20006. James Patrick Kiernan, Dir. & Ed. Rebecca Read Medrano, Man. Ed. Features, 2,500 to 4,000 words, on Latin America and the Caribbean. Wide focus: anthropology, the arts, travel, science, and development. "We prefer stories that can be well illustrated." No political material. Pays from $400, on publication. Query.

ARMY TIMES—See *Times News Service.*

ASIAN PAGES—P.O. Box 11932, St. Paul, MN 55111-0932. Cheryl Weiberg, Ed.-in-Chief. Weekly newspaper tabloid. Profiles and news events, 500 words; short stories, 500 to 750 words; poetry, 100 words; and Asian-related fillers, 50 words. "All material must have a strong, non-offensive Asian slant." Pays $40 for articles, $25 for photos/cartoons, on publication.

THE ATLANTIC MONTHLY—77 N. Washington St., Boston, MA 02114. William Whitworth, Ed. Non-polemical, meticulously researched articles on public issues, politics, social sciences, education, business, literature, and the arts. Ideal length: 3,000 to 6,000 words, though short pieces, 1,000 to 2,000 words, are also welcome and longer text pieces will be considered. Pays excellent rates.

BON APPETIT—6300 Wilshire Blvd., Los Angeles, CA 90048. Barbara Fairchild, Exec. Ed. Articles on fine cooking (menu format or single focus), cooking classes, and gastronomically focused travel. Pays varying rates, on acceptance; buys all rights. Query with samples of published work.

BRAZZIL—P.O. Box 42536, Los Angeles, CA 90050-0536. Rodney Mello, Ed. Monthly. Articles, written in English, 800 to 5,000 words, on Brazil and its culture. Features include politics, economy, ecology, tourism, literature, and the arts. Pays $20 to $50, on publication.

CAPPER'S—1503 S.W. 42nd St., Topeka, KS 66609-1265. Ann Crahan, Ed. Articles, 500 to 700 words: human-interest, personal experience for family section, historical. Payment varies, on publication.

CHANGE—1319 18th St. N.W., Washington, DC 20036. Attn: Ed. Dept. Well-researched features, 2,500 to 3,500 words, on programs, people, and institutions of higher education; and columns, 700 to 2,000 words. "We can't usually pay for unsolicited articles."

THE CHRISTIAN SCIENCE MONITOR—One Norway St., Boston, MA 02115. Jane A. Lampmann, Features Ed. Articles, 800 words, for "Arts and Leisure," Jennifer Wolcott, Ed.; "Learning," Amelia Newcomb, Ed.; "Ideas," Jim Bencivengia, Ed.; "Home and Family," David Scott, Ed. Essays and poetry on the "Home Forum Page"; guest columns for "Opinion Page." Pay varies, on acceptance. Original material only, exclusive rights for 90 days.

CHRONICLES—The Rockford Institute, 934 N. Main St., Rockford, IL 61103. Thomas Fleming, Ed. "A Magazine of American Culture." Articles and poetry that displays craftsmanship and a sense of form. "Read the magazine first to get a feel for what we do." No fiction, fillers or jokes. Payment varies.

CIVILIZATION—Library of Congress, 575 Lexington Ave., 33rd floor, New York, NY 10022. Regan Solmo, Man. Ed. Thought-provoking nonfiction articles and essays; some book reviews and puzzles. "Writers should read the magazine to get a sense of our editorial needs." Guidelines are not available. Query. Payment varies.

COLUMBIA—1 Columbus Plaza, New Haven, CT 06510-3326. Richard McMunn, Ed. Journal of the Knights of Columbus. Articles, 500 to 1,500 words, on a wide variety of topics of interest to K. of C. members, their families, and the Catholic layman: current events, religion, education, art, etc., illustrated with color photos. Pays $250 to $500, on acceptance.

THE COMPASS—365 Washington Ave., Brooklyn, NY 11238. J.A. Randall, Ed. True stories, to 1,500 words, on the sea, sea trades, and aviation. Pays to $1,000, on acceptance. Query with SASE.

COSMOPOLITAN—224 W. 57th St., New York, NY 10019. Kate White, Ed. Steve Perrine, Exec. Ed. Articles, to 3,000 words, and features, 500 to 2,000 words, on issues affecting young career women. Query.

COUNTRY JOURNAL—4 High Ridge Park, Stamford, CT 06905. Josh Garskof, Man. Ed. Articles, 500 to 1,500 words, for country and small-town residents. Helpful, authoritative pieces; how-to projects, small-scale farming, and gardening. Pays $75 to $500, on acceptance. Send SASE for guidelines. Query with SASE.

DIVERSION MAGAZINE—1790 Broadway, New York, NY 10019. Tom Passavant, Ed.-in-Chief. Articles, 600 to 2,000 words, on travel, sports, hobbies, entertainment, food, etc., of interest to physicians at leisure. Photos. Pays from $500, on acceptance. Query.

EBONY—820 S. Michigan, Chicago, IL 60605. Lerone Bennett, Jr., Exec. Ed. "We do not solicit free-lance material."

THE ELKS MAGAZINE—425 W. Diversey Parkway, Chicago, IL 60614. Anna L. Idol, Man. Ed. Articles, 1,500 to 2,500 words, on technology, business, sports, and topics of current interest, for non-urban audience with above-average income. Pays 20¢ a word, on acceptance. Query with SASE.

EMERGE—BET Plaza, 1900 W. Place N.E., Washington, DC 20018. Florestine Purnell, Man. Ed. "Black America's Newsmagazine." Articles, 1,200 to 2,000 words, on current issues, ideas, or news personalities of interest to successful, well-informed African-Americans. Department pieces, 650 to 700 words, on a number of subjects. Pays 50¢ a word, on publication. Query.

ESQUIRE—250 W. 55th St., New York, NY 10019. David Granger, Ed.-in-Chief. Helene F. Rubinstein, Ed. Dir. Peter Griffin, Deputy Ed. Articles, 2,500 to 6,500 words, for intelligent adult audience. Pay varies, on acceptance. Query with published clips; complete manuscripts from unpublished writers. SASE required.

ESSENCE—1500 Broadway, New York, NY 10036. Susan L. Taylor, Ed.-in-Chief. Monique Greenwood, Exec. Ed. Provocative articles, 800 to 2,500 words, about black women in America today: self-help, how-to pieces, business and finance, work, parenting, health, celebrity profiles, and political issues. Pays varying rates, on acceptance. Query required.

EVERY WEDNESDAY—2519 N. Charles St., Baltimore, MD 21218. Avonie Brown, Ed. Illustrated feature articles, 750 to 1,000 words, on subjects covering the arts and entertainment of interests of African Americans. Pay varies, on publication. Query.

FAMILY CIRCLE—375 Lexington Ave., New York, NY 10017. Nancy Clark, Deputy Ed. Articles, to 2,000 words, on "women who make a difference," "profiles in courage/love" (dramatic narratives), opinion pieces on topic of general interest, humor essays. Pays top rates, on acceptance. Query required.

THE FUTURIST—World Future Society, 7910 Woodmont Ave., Suite 450, Bethesda, MD 20814. Cynthia Wagner, Man. Ed. Features, 1,000 to 5,000 words, on subjects pertaining to the future: environment, education, business, science, technology, etc. Submit complete manuscript with brief bio and SASE. Pays in copies.

GEIST—1014 Homer St., #103, Vancouver, BC, Canada V6B 2W9. Attn: Editorial Board. Quarterly. "The Canadian Magazine of Ideas and Culture."

Creative nonfiction, 200 to 1,000 words; excerpts, 300 to 1,500 words, from works in progress; long essays and short stories, 2,000 to 5,000 words. Payment varies, on publication. Query for longer pieces.

GLAMOUR—350 Madison Ave., New York, NY 10017. Bonnie Fuller, Ed.-in-Chief. Pamela Erens, Articles Ed. Editorial approach is "how-to" for women, 18 to 35. Articles on careers, health, psychology, interpersonal relationships, etc. Fashion, health, and beauty material staff-written. Pays from $1,000 for 1,500-to 2,000-word articles, from $1,500 for longer pieces, on acceptance.

GOOD HOUSEKEEPING—959 Eighth Ave., New York, NY 10019. Evelyn Renold, Articles Ed. Articles, 2,500 words, on a unique or trend-setting event; family relationships; personal medical pieces dealing with an unusual illness, treatment, and result; personal problems and how they were solved. Short essays, 750 to 1,000 words, on family life or relationships. Pays first-time writers $500 to $750 for short, essay-type articles; $1,500 to $2,000 for full-length articles, on acceptance. "Payment scale rises for writers with whom we work frequently." Buys all rights, though the writer retains the right to use material from the article as part of a book project. Queries preferred. Guidelines.

GRIT—1503 S.W. 42nd St., Topeka, KS 66609. Donna Doyle, Ed.-in-Chief. Articles, 500 to 1,200 words, on people, home, garden, lifestyle, friends and family, reminisces, grandparenting, Americana, American history and traditions, travel. Short fiction, 1,000 to 2,000 words (send to Fiction Ed.). SASE required. Pays 15¢ to 22¢ a word, extra for photos. Send complete manuscript with photos. Send for guidelines. Allow at least six months for review. Submissions will not be acknowledged, nor will status updates be given.

HARPER'S BAZAAR—1700 Broadway, 37th Fl., New York, NY 10019. Elizabeth Tilberis, Ed.-in-Chief. Articles for sophisticated women on current issues, books, art, film, travel, fashion and beauty. Send queries with one-to three-paragraph proposal; include clips and SASE. Rarely accepts fiction. Payment varies.

HARPER'S MAGAZINE— 666 Broadway, New York, NY 10012. Attn: Ed. Articles, 2,000 to 5,000 words. Query with SASE required. Very limited market.

HISPANIC MAGAZINE— 98 San Jacinto Blvd., Suite 1150, Austin, TX 78701. Managing Ed. General-interest English-language monthly covering career, business, politics, and culture. "We confront issues affecting the Hispanic community, but we prefer to emphasize solutions rather than problems." Features run 1,400 to 3,500 words; shorter pieces for "Hispanic Journal" and "Portfolio" sections. Features pay $450; shorter pieces, $200. Query.

HISTORIC PRESERVATION—1785 Massachusetts Ave. N.W., Washington, DC 20036. Robert Wilson, Ed. Feature articles from published writers, 1,500 to 4,000 words, on residential restoration, preservation issues, and people involved in preserving America's heritage. Query.

HOUSE BEAUTIFUL—1700 Broadway, New York, NY 10019. Elaine Greene, Features Ed. One personal memoir each month, "Thoughts of Home," with high literary standards. Pays 1¢ per word, on acceptance. Query with detailed outline and SASE. Guidelines.

IDEALS—P.O. Box 305300, Nashville, TN 37230. Lisa Ragan, Ed. Articles, 800 to 1,000 words; poetry, 12 to 50 lines. Light, nostalgic pieces. Payment varies. SASE for guidelines.

INQUIRER MAGAZINE—*Philadelphia Inquirer,* P.O. Box 8263, 400 N. Broad St., Philadelphia, PA 19101. Ms. Avery Rome, Ed. Local-interest features, 500 to 7,000 words. Profiles of national figures in politics, entertainment, etc. Pays varying rates, on publication. Currently overstocked; not accepting any free-lance submissions at this time.

ITALIAN AMERICA—219 E. St. N.E., Washington, DC 20002-4922. Anthony Mark Dalessandro, Ed. "The Official Publication of the Order Sons of Italy in America." Quarterly. Articles, 1,000 to 2,500 words, and fillers, 500 to 750 words, on people, institutions, and events of interest to the Italian-American community. Also book reviews. Payment varies, on publication. Queries preferred.

KIWANIS—3636 Woodview Trace, Indianapolis, IN 46268. Chuck Jonak, Man. Ed. Articles, 2,500 words, on home; family; international issues; the social, health, and emotional needs of youth (especially under age 6); career and community concerns of business and professional people. No travel pieces, interviews, profiles. Pays $500 to $1,000, on acceptance. Query. Send SASE for guidelines.

LADIES' HOME JOURNAL—125 Park Ave., New York, NY 10017. Pam O'Brien, Articles. Ed. Articles on contemporary subjects of interest to women. "See masthead for specific-topic editors and address appropriate editor." Query with SASE required.

LISTEN MAGAZINE—55 W. Oak Ridge Dr., Hagerstown, MD 21740. Lincoln Steed, Ed. Articles, 1,000 to 1,200 words, on problems of alcohol and drug abuse, for teenagers; personality profiles; self-improvement articles, and drug-free activities. Photos. Pays 5¢ to 7¢ a word, extra for photos, on acceptance. Guidelines. Sample issues available. Query.

MCCALL'S—375 Lexington Ave., New York, NY 10017. Attn: Articles Ed. Articles, 1,000 to 1,800 words, on current issues, human interest, family relationships. Payment varies, on acceptance. SASE.

MADEMOISELLE—350 Madison Ave., New York, NY 10017. Faye Haun, Man. Ed. Articles, 750 to 2,500 words, on subjects of interest to single, working women in their twenties. Reporting pieces, essays, first-person accounts, and humor; how-tos on personal relationships, work, and fitness. No fiction. Pays excellent rates, on acceptance. SASE required. Query with clips.

MANGAJIN—P.O. Box 77188, Atlanta, GA 30357-1188. Articles, profiles, and book reviews, 1,000 to 1,500 words on Japanese pop culture. Query the editors. Pays $150 to $500, on publication.

METROPOLITAN HOME—1633 Broadway, New York, NY 10019. Attn: Michael Lassell, Articles Dept. Service and informational articles for residents of houses, co-ops, lofts, and condominiums, on real estate, equity, wine and spirits, collecting, etc. Interior design and home furnishing articles with emphasis on lifestyle. Pay varies. Query with clips.

THE MOTHER EARTH NEWS—49 E. 21st St., 11th Fl., New York, NY 10010. Matthew Scanlon, Ed. Articles for rural and urban readers: home improvements, how-tos, indoor and outdoor gardening, family pastimes, health, food, ecology, energy, and consumerism. Pays varying rates, on acceptance.

MOTHER JONES—731 Market St., Suite 600, San Francisco, CA 94103. Jeffrey Klein, Ed. Investigative articles, political essays, cultural analyses, multicultural issues. "OutFront" pieces, 250 to 500 words. Query with SASE.

MS.—135 W. 50th St.,16th Fl., New York, NY 10020-1201. Attn: Manuscript Ed. Articles relating to feminism, women's roles, and social change; reporting, essays, theory, and analysis. No poetry or fiction. Pays market rates. Query with resumé, clips, and SASE.

NATIONAL ENQUIRER—Lantana, FL 33464. Attn: C. Montgomery. Mass audience: topical news, celebrities, how-to, scientific discoveries, human drama, adventure, medical news, personalities. Photos. Query (2 to 3 sentences, with source) with SASE.

NAVY TIMES—See *Times News Service.*

NEW WOMAN—2 Park Ave., 11th Fl., New York, NY 10016. Attn: Manuscripts and Proposals. Articles, 500 to 2,500 words, on relationships/sex and psychology, health news; book excerpts, essays, personal experience, and some travel. Submit seasonal material at least 5 months in advance. Simultaneous submissions. Reports in 3 months. Send #10 SASE for writer's guidelines. Pay varies.

THE NEW YORK TIMES MAGAZINE—229 W. 43rd St., New York, NY 10036. Attn: Articles Ed. Timely articles, approximately 3,000 words, on news items, forthcoming events, trends, culture, entertainment, etc. Pays to $2,500 for major articles, on acceptance. Query with clips.

THE NEW YORKER—20 W. 43rd St., New York, NY 10036. Send submissions to appropriate Editor (Fact, Fiction, or Poetry). Factual and biographical articles for "Profiles," "Reporter at Large," etc. Pays good rates, on acceptance. Query.

NEWSWEEK—251 W. 57th St., New York, NY 10019-1894. Attn: My Turn. Original personal (first person) opinion essays, 1,000 to 1,100 words, for "My Turn" column; must contain verifiable facts. Submit manuscript with SASE. Pays $1,000, on publication.

PARADE—711 Third Ave., New York, NY 10017. Articles Ed. National Sunday newspaper magazine. Factual and authoritative articles, 1,200 to 1,500 words, on subjects of national interest: social issues, common health concerns, sports, community problem-solving, and extraordinary acheivements of ordinary people. "We seek unique angles on all topics." No fiction, poetry, cartoons, games, nostalgia, quotes, or puzzles. Pays from $1,000. Query with two writing samples and SASE.

PENTHOUSE—277 Park Ave., 4th Fl., New York, NY 10172-0003. Peter Bloch, Ed. Lavada B. Nahon, Sr. Ed. General-interest or controversial articles, to 5,000 words. Pays to $1 a word, on acceptance.

PEOPLE WEEKLY—Time-Life Bldg., Rockefeller Ctr., New York, NY 10020. John Saar, Asst. Man. Ed. "Vast majority of material is staff-written." Will consider article proposals, 3 to 4 paragraphs, on timely, entertaining, and topical personalities. Pays good rates, on acceptance.

PLAYBOY—680 N. Lake Shore Dr., Chicago, IL 60611. Stephen Randall, Exec. Ed. Sophisticated articles, 4,000 to 6,000 words, of interest to urban men. Humor, satire. Pays on acceptance. Query.

PLAYGIRL—801 Second Ave., New York, NY 10017. Charlene Keel Razaek, Man. Ed. Articles, 1,500 to 3,000 words, on sexuality, relationships, and celebrities for women ages 18 and up. Query with clips. Mostly nonfiction. Pays negotiable rates, after acceptance.

QUEEN'S QUARTERLY—Queens Univ., Kingston, Ont., Canada K7L 3N6. Boris Castel, Ed. Articles, to 5,000 words, on a wide range of topics, and fiction, to 5,000 words. Poetry; send no more than 6 poems. B&W art. Pays to $400, on publication.

READER'S DIGEST—Pleasantville, NY 10570. Kenneth Tomlinson, Ed.-in-Chief. Unsolicited manuscripts will not be read or returned. General-interest articles already in print and well-developed story proposals will be considered. Send reprint or query to any editor on the masthead.

REAL PEOPLE—450 7th Ave., Suite 1701, New York, NY 10123-0073. Alex Polner, Ed. True stories, to 500 words, on interesting people, strange occupations and hobbies, eye opening stories about people, places and odd happenings. Pays $25 to $50, on publication; send submissions to "Real Shorts," Brad Hamilton, Ed. Query for interviews, 1,000 to 1,800 words, with movie or TV actors, musicians, and other entertainment celebrities. Pays $150 to $350, on publication. SASE.

REDBOOK—224 W. 57th St., New York, NY 10019. Pamela Lister, Sr. Ed. Toni Gerber Hope, Sr. Ed. Articles, 1,000 to 2,500 words, on subjects related to relationships, marriage, sex, current social issues, crime, human interest, health, psychology, and parenting. Payment varies, on acceptance. Query with clips.

ROLLING STONE—1290 Ave. of the Americas, 2nd Fl., New York, NY 10104. Attn: Ed. Magazine of American music, culture, and politics. No fiction. "We rarely accept free-lance material." Query.

THE ROTARIAN—1560 Sherman Ave., Evanston, IL 60201-3698. Charles W. Pratt, Ed. Articles, 1,200 to 2,000 words, on international social and economic issues, business and management, human relationships, travel, sports, environment, science and technology; humor. Pays good rates, on acceptance. Query.

RUSSIAN LIFE—89 Main St., #2, Montpelier, VT 05602-2948. Mikhail Ivanov, Ed. Articles, 1,000 to 3,000 words, on Russian culture, travel, history, politics, art, business and society. "We do not want stories about personal trips to Russia, editorials on developments in Russia, or articles that promote the services of a specific company, organization, or government agency." Query. Pays 7¢ to 10¢ a word; $20 to $30 per photo, on publication.

THE SATURDAY EVENING POST—1100 Waterway Blvd., Indianapolis, IN 46202. Ted Kreiter, Exec. Ed. Family-oriented articles, 1,500 to 3,000 words: humor, preventive medicine, destination-oriented travel pieces (not personal experience), celebrity profiles, the arts, and sciences. Pays varying rates, on publication. Queries preferred.

SMITHSONIAN MAGAZINE—900 Jefferson Dr., Washington, DC 20560. Marlane A. Liddell, Articles Ed. Articles on history, art, natural history, physical science, profiles, etc. Query with clips.

SPORTS ILLUSTRATED—1271 Ave. of the Americas, New York, NY 10020. Chris Hunt, Articles Ed. Query. Rarely uses free-lance material.

STAR—660 White Plains Rd., Tarrytown, NY 10591. Attn: Ed. Dept. Topical articles, 50 to 800 words, on show business and celebrities. Pays varying rates.

SUCCESS—733 Third Ave., 10th Fl., New York, NY 10017. Steven Sion, Ed.-in-Chief. Profiles of successful entrepreneurs; how-to articles on raising money and building a successful small business; science, psychology, behavior, and motivation articles, 500 to 3,500 words. Query.

TIMES NEWS SERVICE—Army Times Publishing Co., Springfield, VA 22159. Attn: R&R Ed. Articles, 500 to 750 words, that are informative, helpful, entertaining, and stimulating to a military audience for "R&R" newspaper section. Pays $75 to $100, on acceptance. Also, 1,000-to 1,200-word articles on careers after military service, travel, finance, and education for *Army Times, Navy Times,* and *Air Force Times.* Address Supplements Ed. Pays $125 to $275, on acceptance. Guidelines.

THE TOASTMASTER—P.O. Box 9052, Mission Viejo, CA 92690. Suzanne Frey, Ed. Articles, 1,500 to 2,500 words, on decision making, leadership, language, interpersonal and professional communication, humor, logical thinking, rhetorical devices, public speaking in general, profiles of great orators, speaking techniques, etc. Pays $100 to $250, on acceptance.

TOWN & COUNTRY—1700 Broadway, New York, NY 10019. Pamela Fiori, Ed.-in-Chief. Considers one-page proposals for articles. Include clips and resumé. Rarely buys unsolicited manuscripts.

TRAVEL & LEISURE—1120 Ave. of the Americas, New York, NY 10036. Nancy Novogrod, Ed.-in-Chief. Articles, 800 to 3,000 words, on destinations and travel-related activities. Regional pieces for regional editions. Pays varying rates, on acceptance. Query.

TROPIC—*The Miami Herald,* One Herald Plaza, Miami, FL 33132. Tom Shroder, Exec. Ed. Essays and articles, 1,000 to 4,000 words, on current trends and issues, light or heavy, for sophisticated audience. No short fiction (under 900 words) or poetry. Limited humor. Pays $200 to $1,000, on publication. SASE. Allow 4 to 6 weeks for response.

TV GUIDE—Radnor, PA 19088. Barry Golson, Exec. Ed. Short, light, brightly written pieces about humorous or offbeat angles of television and industry trends. (Majority of personality pieces are staff-written.) Pays on acceptance. Query.

URB—1680 N. Vine St., Suite 1012, Los Angeles, CA 90028-8836. Stacy Osbaum, Ed. Bimonthly. Features, varying lengths on dance and underground hip-hop music, featuring profiles of emerging musicians, singers, and groups. Pays about 10¢ a word, on publication. Query.

VANITY FAIR—350 Madison Ave., New York, NY 10017. Attn: Submissions (Specify News, Arts, or Culture). Pays on acceptance. Query.

VILLAGE VOICE—36 Cooper Sq., New York, NY 10003. Doug Simmons, Man. Ed. Articles, 500 to 2,000 words, on current or controversial topics. Pays $100 to $1,500, on acceptance. Query or send manuscript with SASE.

WASHINGTON POST MAGAZINE—*The Washington Post,* 1150 15th St. N.W., Washington, DC 20071. John Cotter, Sr. Ed. Essays, profiles, and Washington-oriented general-interest pieces, to 5,000 words, on business, arts and culture, politics, science, sports, education, children, relationships, behavior, etc. Pays from $1,000, after acceptance.

WOMAN'S DAY—1633 Broadway, New York, NY 10019. Stephanie Abarbanel, Sr. Articles Ed. Articles, 500 to 2,000 words, on subjects of interest to women: marriage, education, family health, child rearing, money management, interpersonal relationships, changing lifestyles, etc. Dramatic first-person narratives about women who have experienced medical miracles or other triumphs, or have overcome common problems, such as alcoholism. SASE required. Pays top rates, on acceptance. Query; unsolicited manuscripts not accepted.

WOMAN'S WORLD—270 Sylvan Ave., Englewood Cliffs, NJ 07632. Attn: Ed. Articles, 600 to 1,800 words, of interest to middle-income women between the ages of 18 and 60, on love, romance, careers, medicine, health, psychology, family life, travel; dramatic stories of adventure or crisis, investigative reports. Send SASE for guidelines. Pays $300 to $900, on acceptance. Query.

YANKEE—Yankee Publishing Co., P.O. Box 520, Dublin, NH 03444. Judson D. Hale, Ed. Articles, to 2,500 words, with New England angle. Photos. Pays $150 to $2,000 (average $800), on acceptance. Query required.

CURRENT EVENTS, POLITICS

THE AMERICAN LEGION—Box 1055, Indianapolis, IN 46206. Joe Stuteville, Ed. Articles, 750 to 2,000 words, on current world affairs, public policy, and subjects of contemporary interest. Pays $500 to $3,000, on acceptance. Query.

THE AMERICAN SCHOLAR—1811 Q St. N.W., Washington, DC 20009-9974. Joseph Epstein, Ed. Non-technical articles and essays, 3,500 to 4,000 words, on current affairs, the American cultural scene, politics, arts, religion, and science. Pays to $500, on acceptance.

THE AMICUS JOURNAL—Natural Resources Defense Council, 40 W. 20th St., New York, NY 10011. Kathrin Day Lassila, Ed. Investigative articles, profiles, book reviews, and essays, related to the environment, especially national and international environmental policy. Also poetry "rooted in nature." Pays varying rates, 30 days after acceptance. Queries required.

THE ATLANTIC MONTHLY—77 N. Washington St., Boston, MA 02114. William Whitworth, Ed. In-depth articles on public issues, politics, social sciences, education, business, literature, and the arts, with emphasis on information rather than opinion. Ideal length is 3,000 to 6,000 words, though short pieces, 1,000 to 2,000 words, are also welcome. Pays excellent rates, on acceptance.

BRIARPATCH—2138 McIntyre St., Regina, Saskatchewan, Canada S4P 2R7. George Manz, Man. Ed. "Saskatchewan's Independent Newsmagazine." Left-wing articles, 600 to 1,200 words, on politics, women's issues, environment, labor, international affairs for Canadian activists involved in social change issues. Pays in copies. Queries preferred.

CALIFORNIA JOURNAL—2101 K St., Sacramento, CA 95816. A.G. Block, Ed. "Independent analysis of politics and government." Balanced articles, 1,500 words, related to California government and politics. Advocacy pieces, 800 words. Pays $350 for articles, on publication. (No payment for advocacy pieces.) Query.

CAMPAIGNS & ELECTIONS—1511 K St. N.W., #941, Washington, DC 20005. Ron Faucheux, Ed. Feature articles, 700 to 4,000 words, related to the strategies, techniques, trends, and personalities of political campaigning. Campaign case studies, 1,500 to 3,000 words; how-to articles, 700 to 2,000 words, on specific aspects of campaigning; items, 100 to 800 words, for "Inside Politics"; and in-depth studies, 700 to 3,000 words, of public opinion, election results, and political trends that help form campaign strategy. Pays in subscriptions and free admission to certain public seminars.

CHURCH & STATE—1816 Jefferson Pl. N.W., Washington, DC 20036. Joseph L. Conn, Man. Ed. Articles, 600 to 2,600 words, on issues of religious liberty and church-state relations. Pays varying rates, on acceptance. Query.

COMMENTARY—165 E. 56th St., New York, NY 10022. Neal Kozodoy, Ed. Articles, 5,000 to 7,000 words, on contemporary issues, Jewish affairs, social sciences, community life, religious thought, culture. Serious fiction; book reviews. Pays on publication.

COMMONWEAL—475 Riverside Dr., New York, NY 10115. Margaret O'Brien Steinfels, Ed. Catholic. Articles, to 3,000 words, on political, social, religious, and literary subjects. Pays 3¢ a word, on acceptance.

COMMONWEALTH—177 Tremont St., 5th Fl., Boston, MA 02111. Dave Denison, Ed. Articles, 2,000 to 4,500 words, on politics, government, and public policy issues affecting Massachusetts citizens. Payment varies, on acceptance. Query.

CONSERVATIVE REVIEW—1307 Dolley Madison Blvd., Rm. 203, McLean, VA 22101. Fred Smith, Ed. Articles, ideally 300 to 500 words (longer is O.K., if subject warrants), that offer information on topics, not just conservative sermons. "Writers should be intimately familiar with their subject." Pays in copies.

COUNTRY CONNECTIONS—14431 Ventura Blvd., #407, Sherman Oaks, CA 91423. Catherine R. Leach, Ed. Bimonthly. Articles, to 2,500 words, and fiction, to 1,500 words. Poetry. Send 9" x 12" SASE with 78¢ postage for free sample; study journal before submitting. "We serve as a forum for public discourse about ethics, politics, social justice, community, animal rights and environmental issues, and life in the country." Pays in subscriptions or copies.

CULTUREFRONT—198 Broadway, 10th Fl., New York, NY 10038. Attn: Ed. "A Magazine of the Humanities." Fiction and articles, 2,500 words, related to theme. "News and a variety of views on the production, interpretation, and politics of culture." No payment. Query for current themes.

CURRENT HISTORY—4225 Main St., Philadelphia, PA 19127. William W. Finan, Jr., Ed. Country-specific political science and current affairs articles, to 20 pages. Hard analysis written in a lively manner. "We devote each issue to a specific region or country. Writers should be experts with up-to-date knowledge of the region." Queries preferred. Pays $300, on publication.

EMERGE—BET Plaza, 1900 W. Place N.E., Washington, DC 20018. Florestine Purnell, Man. Ed. "Black America's Newsmagazine." Articles, 1,200 to 2,000 words, on current issues, ideas, or news personalities of interest to successful, well-informed African-Americans. Department pieces, 650 to 700 words, on a number of subjects. Pays 50¢ a word, on publication. Query.

ENVIRONMENT—1319 18th St. N.W., Washington, DC 20036-1802. Barbara T. Richman, Man. Ed. Articles, 2,500 to 5,000 words, on environmental, scientific, and technological policy and decision-making issues, especially on a global scale. Pays $100 to $300, on publication. Query.

FIRST THINGS—156 Fifth Ave., #400, New York, NY 10010-7002. James Nuechterlein, Ed. Published 10 times a year. Essays and general social commentary, 1,500 words or 4,000 to 6,000 words, for academics and clergy members, on the role of religion in public life. Also, poetry, 4 to 40 lines. Pays $250 to $700, on publication.

FOREIGN SERVICE JOURNAL—2101 E St. N.W., Washington, DC 20037. Articles of interest to the Foreign Service and the US diplomatic community. Pays to 25¢ a word, on publication. Query.

THE FREEMAN—Foundation for Economic Education, 30 S. Broadway, Irvington-on-Hudson, NY 10533. Beth Hoffman, Man. Ed. Articles, to 3,500 words, on economic, political, and moral implications of private property, voluntary exchange, and individual choice. Pays 10¢ a word, on publication.

IN THESE TIMES—2040 N. Milwaukee Ave., Chicago, IL 60647. James Weinstein, Ed. Biweekly. Articles, 1,500 to 2,500 words, on politics, labor, women's issues, etc. "A magazine with a progressive political perspective. Please read before querying us." Payment varies, on publication. Query.

INQUIRER MAGAZINE—*Philadelphia Inquirer*, P.O. Box 8263, 400 N. Broad St., Philadelphia, PA 19101. Ms. Avery Rome, Ed. Local-interest features, 500 to 7,000 words. Profiles of national figures in politics, entertainment, etc. Pays varying rates, on publication. Query.

IRISH AMERICA— 432 Park Ave. S., Suite 1000, New York, NY 10016. Patricia Harty, Ed. Articles, 1,500 to 2,000 words, of interest to Irish-American audience; preferred topics include history, sports, the arts, and politics. Pays 10¢ a word, after publication. Query.

LABOR'S HERITAGE—10000 New Hampshire Ave., Silver Spring, MD 20903. Stuart Kaufman, Ed. Quarterly journal of The George Meany Memorial Archives. Publishes 15-to 30-page documented articles of original research for labor scholars, labor union members, and the general public. Pays in copies.

MIDSTREAM—110 E. 59th St., New York, NY 10022. Joel Carmichael, Ed. Articles of international and Jewish/Zionist concern. Pays 5¢ a word, after publication. Allow 3 months for response.

MOMENT MAGAZINE— 4710 41st St. N.W., Washington, DC 20016. Hershel Shanks, Ed. Sophisticated articles, 2,500 to 5,000 words, on Jewish culture, politics, religion, and personalities. Columns, to 1,500 words, with uncommon perspectives on contemporary issues, humor, strong anecdotes. Book reviews, 400 words. Pays $40 to $600.

MOTHER JONES—731 Market St., Suite 600, San Francisco, CA 94103. Jeffrey Klein, Ed. Investigative articles and political essays. Pays $1,000 to $3,000 for feature articles, after acceptance. Query with clips and SASE required.

THE NATION—72 Fifth Ave., New York, NY 10011. Katrina vanden Heuvel, Ed. Articles, 1,500 to 2,500 words, on politics and culture from a liberal/left perspective. Editorials, 750 to 1,000 words. Pays $75 per published page, to $300, on publication. Query.

THE NEW YORK TIMES MAGAZINE—229 W. 43rd St., New York, NY 10036. Attn: Articles Ed. Timely articles, approximately 4,000 words, on news items, trends, culture, etc. Pays $1,000 for short pieces, from $2,500 for major articles, on acceptance. Query with clips.

THE NEW YORKER—20 W. 43rd St., New York, NY 10036. Attn: Ed., "Comment." Political/social essays, 1,000 words. Payment on acceptance. Query.

ON THE ISSUES—Merle Hoffman Enterprises, Inc., 97-77 Queens Blvd., Suite 1120, Forest Hills, NY 11374-3317. Jan Goodwin, Ed. "The Progressive Woman's Quarterly." Articles, up to 2,000 words, on political or social issues.

Movie, music, and book reviews, 500 to 750 words. Query. Payment varies, on publication.

POLICY REVIEW—214 Massachusetts Ave. N.E., Washington, DC 20002. Attn: Articles Ed. Articles, 800 to 5,000 words, on reporting and analysis of domestic public policy issues. "We are the flagship journal of The Heritage Foundation, a conservative public policy research institute. We use articles that highlight private sector and local government alternatives to welfare state politics." Pays about $500, on publication.

THE PROGRESSIVE— 409 E. Main St., Madison, WI 53703. Matthew Rothschild, Ed. Articles, 1,000 to 3,500 words, on political and social problems. Pays $100 to $300, on publication.

PUBLIC CITIZEN MAGAZINE—1600 20th St. N.W., Washington, DC 20009. Melissa W. Kaye, Ed. Investigative reports and articles of timely political interest, for members of Public Citizen: consumer rights, health and safety, environmental protection, safe energy, tax reform, international trade, and government and corporate accountability. Photos, illustrations. Honorarium.

REASON—3415 S. Sepulveda Blvd., Suite 400, Los Angeles, CA 90034. Brian Doherty, Asst. Ed. "Free Minds and Free Markets." Articles, 850 to 5,000 words, on politics, economics, and culture "from a dynamic libertarian perspective." Pays varying rates, on acceptance. Query.

SATURDAY NIGHT—184 Front St. E., Suite 400, Toronto, Ont., Canada M5A 4N3. Kenneth Whyte, Ed. Canada's oldest magazine of politics, social issues, culture, and business. Features, 1,000 to 5,000 words, and columns, 800 to 1,000 words; fiction, to 3,000 words. Must have Canadian tie-in. Payment varies, on acceptance.

TIKKUN—26 Fell St., San Francisco, CA 94102. Michael Lerner, Ed. "A Bimonthly Jewish Critique of Politics, Culture & Society." Articles and fiction, 2,400 to 3,000 words. Poetry. "Read a copy to get a sense of what we publish. We are always interested in work pertaining to contemporary culture." Pays in copies.

VFW MAGAZINE— 406 W. 34th St., Kansas City, MO 64111. Richard K. Kolb, Ed. Articles, 1,000 words, related to current foreign policy and defense, American armed forces abroad, and international events affecting U.S. national security. Also, up-to-date articles on veteran concerns and issues affecting veterans. Pays to $500, on acceptance. Query. Guidelines.

THE WASHINGTON MONTHLY—1611 Connecticut Ave. N.W., Washington, DC 20009. Charles Peters, Ed. Helpful, informative articles, 1,000 to 4,000 words, on DC-related topics, including politics, and government and popular culture. Pays 10¢ a word, on publication.

WASHINGTON POST MAGAZINE—*The Washington Post,* 1150 15th St. N.W., Washington, DC 20071. Liza Mundy, Man. Ed. Essays, profiles, and general-interest pieces, to 5,000 words, on Washington-oriented politics and related issues. Pays from $1,000, after acceptance. SASE required.

REGIONAL AND CITY PUBLICATIONS

ADIRONDACK LIFE—P.O. Box 410, Jay, NY 12941. Elizabeth Folwell, Ed. Features, to 5,000 words, on outdoor and environmental activities and issues, arts, wilderness, wildlife, profiles, history, and fiction; focus is entirely on the Adirondack Park region of New York State. Pays to 25¢ a word, 30 days after acceptance. Query.

ALABAMA HERITAGE—The Univ. of Alabama, Box 870342, Tuscaloosa, AL 35487-0342. Suzanne Wolfe, Ed. Quarterly. Articles, to 5,000 words, on local, state, and regional history: art, literature, language, archaeology, music, religion, architecture, and natural history. Query, mentioning availability of photos and illustrations. Pays an honorarium, on publication, plus 10 copies. Guidelines.

ALASKA— 4220 B St., Suite 210, Anchorage, AK 99503. Bruce Woods, Ed. Articles, 1,500 words, on life in Alaska. Pays varying rates, on publication. Guidelines.

ALBERTA SWEETGRASS—Aboriginal Multi-Media Society of Alberta, 15001 112th Ave., Edmonton, Alberta, Canada T5M 2V6. Tabloid. Articles, 100 to 1,000 words (most often 500 to 800 words; briefs, 100 to 150 words): features, profiles, and community-based articles all with an Alberta angle.

ALOHA, THE MAGAZINE OF HAWAII AND THE PACIFIC—P.O. Box 3260, Honolulu, HI 96801. Lance Tominaga, Ed. Dir. Articles, 1,500 to 2,500 words, on the lifestyle, history, arts, sports, business, music, customs, and people of Hawaii and the Pacific. Poetry. Fiction. Pays $150 to $400 for full-length features, on publication. Query.

APPELLATION—1700 Soscol Ave., Suite 2, Napa, CA 94559. Colleen Daly, Ed.-in-Chief. Bimonthly. Articles, 900 to 1,500 words, on wine, food, gardens, and homes in wine country: The Napa and Sonoma valleys, California, the Pacific Northwest, and around the world. Pays on acceptance.

APPRISE—P.O. Box 2954, 1982 Locust Ln., Harrisburg, PA 17105. Jim Connor, Ed.-in-Chief. Articles, 1,500 to 3,500 words, of regional (central Pennsylvania) interest, including profiles of notable Pennsylvanians, and broadly based articles of social interest that "enlighten and inform." Pays 10¢ a word, on publication.

ARIZONA HIGHWAYS—2039 W. Lewis Ave., Phoenix, AZ 85009. Robert J. Early, Ed. Third-person experience articles, 1,200 to 1,800 words, on travel in Arizona; pieces on adventure, humor, lifestyles, nostalgia, history, archaeology, nature, etc. Departments also using personal experience pieces include "Mileposts," "Focus on Nature," "Along the Way," "Back Road Adventures," "Hiking," "Legends of the Lost," and "Arizona Humor." Pays 35¢ to 55¢ a word, on acceptance. Query required. Guidelines.

ASPEN MAGAZINE—P.O. Box G-3, Aspen, CO 81612-7452. Melissa Coleman, Man. Ed. Bimonthly. Articles, 500 to 1,000 words, of interest to readers in Aspen, Colorado. Payment varies, on publication. Query.

ATLANTA—1360 Peachtree St., Suite 1800, Atlanta, GA 30309. Lee Walburn, Ed. Articles, 1,500 to 5,000 words, on Atlanta subjects or personalities. Pays $300 to $2,000, on publication. Query.

ATLANTA HOMES AND LIFESTYLES—1100 Johnson Ferry Rd., #595, Atlanta, GA 30342-1746. Attn: Eds. Articles with a local angle. Department pieces for "Around Atlanta," "Design Takes," "Great Escapes," and "Quick Fix." Pays $50 to $300 for departments; $300 to $400 for features, on acceptance.

ATLANTIC CITY MAGAZINE—P.O. Box 2100, Pleasantville, NJ 08232. Michael Epifanio, Ed. Lively articles, 200 to 2,000 words, on Atlantic City and the southern New Jersey shore, for locals and tourists: entertainment, casinos, business, recreation, personalities, lifestyle, local color. Pays $50 to $600, on publication. Query.

BACK HOME IN KENTUCKY—P.O. Box 681629, Franklin, TN 37068-1629. Nanci P. Gregg, Man. Ed. Articles on Kentucky history, travel, craftsmen and artisans, Kentucky cooks, and "colorful" characters; limited personal nostalgia specifically related to Kentucky. Pays $25 to $100 for articles with B&W or color photos. Queries preferred.

BALTIMORE MAGAZINE—1000 Lancaster St., Suite 400, Baltimore, MD 21202. Ramsey Flynn, Ed. Articles, 500 to 3,000 words, on people, places, and things in the Baltimore metropolitan area. Consumer advice, investigative pieces, profiles, humor, and personal experience pieces. Payment varies, on publication. Query required.

THE BIG APPLE PARENTS' PAPER—36 E. 12th St., New York, NY 10003. Helen Rosengren Freedman, Man. Ed. Articles, 500 to 750 words, for New York City parents. Pays $35 to $50, on publication. Buys first NY-area rights.

BIG SKY JOURNAL—P.O. Box 1069, Bozeman, MT 59771. Michelle A. Orton, Man. Ed. Published 5 times a year. Articles, to 2,500 words, and fiction to 4,000 words, on Montana art and architecture, hunting and fishing, ranching and recreation. Payment varies, on publication. Query.

BLUE RIDGE COUNTRY—P.O. Box 21535, Roanoke, VA 24018. Kurt Rheinheimer, Ed. Bimonthly. Regional articles, 1,200 to 2,000 words, that "explore and extol the beauty, history, and travel opportunities in the mountain regions of VA, NC, WV, TN, KY, MD, SC, and GA." Color slides or B&W prints considered. Pays $200 for photo-features, on publication. Queries preferred.

BOCA RATON—JES Publishing, Amtec Ctr., Suite 100, 6413 Congress Ave., Boca Raton, FL 33487. Marie Speed, Ed. Articles, 800 to 3,000 words, on Florida topics, personalities, and travel. Pays $50 to $500, on acceptance. Query with clips required.

THE BOSTON GLOBE MAGAZINE—*The Boston Globe*, Boston, MA 02107. Evelynne Kramer, Ed. General-interest articles on regional topics and profiles, 2,500 to 5,000 words. Query and SASE required.

BOSTON MAGAZINE—300 Massachusetts Ave., Boston, MA 02115. Lisa Gerson, Ed. Asst. Informative, entertaining features, 1,000 to 3,000 words, on Boston-area personalities, institutions, and phenomena. Query. Pays to $2,000, on publication.

BOUNDARY WATERS JOURNAL—9396 Rocky Ledge Rd., Ely, MN 55731. Stuart Osthoff, Ed. Articles, 2,000 to 3,000 words, on wilderness, recreation, nature, and conservation in Minnesota's Boundary Waters Canoe Area Wilderness and Ontario's Quetico Provincial Park. Regular features include canoe-route journals, fishing, camping, hiking, cross-country skiing, wildlife and nature, regional lifestyles, history, and events. Pays $200 to $400, on publication; $50 to $150 for photos.

BUFFALO SPREE MAGAZINE—Box 38, Buffalo, NY 14226. Johanna Van De Mark, Ed./Pub. Articles, to 1,800 words, for readers in the western New York region. Pays $75 to $125, $25 for poetry, on publication.

BUSINESS IN BROWARD—P.O. Box 7375, Ft. Lauderdale, FL 33338-7375. Sherry Friedlander, Ed. Published 8 times a year. Articles, 1,000 words, on small business in eastern Florida county. Pay varies, on acceptance.

CANADIAN GEOGRAPHIC—39 McArthur Ave., Vanier, Ont., Canada K1L 8L7. Rick Boychuk, Ed. "Making Canada Better Known to Canadians and the World." Articles on interesting places, nature and wildlife in Canada. Payment varies, on acceptance. Query.

CAPE COD LIFE—P.O. Box 1385, Pocasset, MA 02559-1385. Nancy E. Berry, Man. Ed. Articles, to 2,000 words, on current events, business, art, history, gardening, and nautical lifestyle on Cape Cod, Martha's Vineyard, and Nantucket. Pays 15¢ a word, 30 days after publication. Query.

CARIBBEAN TRAVEL AND LIFE—P.O. Box 2456, Winter Park, FL 32790. Steve Blount, Ed. Articles, 500 to 3,000 words, on all aspects of travel, recreation, leisure, and culture in the Caribbean, the Bahamas, and Bermuda. Pays $75 to $750, on publication. Query with published clips.

CAROLOGUE—South Carolina Historical Society, 100 Meeting St., Charleston, SC 29401-2299. Stephen Hoffius, Ed. General-interest articles, to 10 pages, on South Carolina history. Queries preferred. Pays in copies.

CHESAPEAKE BAY MAGAZINE—1819 Bay Ridge Ave., Annapolis, MD 21403. Tim Sayles, Ed. Articles, to 3,000 words, on boating and fishing on Chesapeake Bay. No fiction or poetry. Photos. Pays $100 to $500, on acceptance. Query.

CHICAGO—500 N. Dearborn, Suite 1200, Chicago, IL 60610. Shane Tritsch, Man. Ed. Articles, 1,000 to 5,000 words, related to Chicago. Pays varying rates, on acceptance. Query.

CHICAGO HISTORY—Clark St. at North Ave., Chicago, IL 60614. Rosemary Adams, Ed. Articles, to 4,500 words, on Chicago's urban, political, social, and cultural history. Pays to $250, on publication. Query.

CINCINNATI MAGAZINE—One Centennial Plaza, 705 Central Ave., Suite 370, Cincinnati, OH 45202. Kitty Morgan, Ed. Articles, 500 to 3,500 words, on Cincinnati people and issues. Pays $50 to $500. Query with writing sample.

COLORADO BUSINESS—7009 S. Potomac, Englewood, CO 80112. Bruce Goldberg, Ed. Articles, varying lengths, on business, business personalities, and economic trends in Colorado. Preference given to Colorado residents. Pays on acceptance. Query.

COLORADO HOMES AND LIFESTYLES—7009 S. Potomac St., Englewood, CO 80112. Evalyn K. McGraw, Ed. Bimonthly. Articles, 1,300 to 1,500 words, with a Colorado focus. Department pieces, 1,100 to 1,300 words, cover architecture, artists, health, design trends, profiles, gardening, and travel. Pays $150 to $300, on acceptance. Guidelines. Query.

COMMON GROUND MAGAZINE—P.O. Box 99, McVeytown, PA 17051-0099. Ruth Dunmire and Pam Brumbaugh, Eds. Quarterly. General-interest articles, 500 to 5,000 words, related to central Pennsylvania's Juniata River Valley and its rural lifestyle. Related fiction, 1,000 to 2,000 words. Poetry, to 12 lines. Fillers, photos, and cartoons. Pays $25 to $200 for articles, $5 to $15 for fillers, and $5 to $25 for photos, on publication. Guidelines.

COMMONWEALTH—177 Tremont St., 5th Fl., Boston, MA 02111. Dave Denison, Ed. Articles, 2,000 to 4,500 words, on politics, government, and public policy issues affecting Massachusetts citizens. Payment varies, on acceptance. Query.

CONNECTICUT—35 Nutmeg Dr., Trumbull, CT 06611. Charles Monagan, Ed. Articles, 1,500 to 3,500 words, on Connecticut topics, issues, people, and lifestyles. Pays $500 to $1,200, within 30 days of acceptance.

CONNECTICUT FAMILY—See *New York Family.*

CRAIN'S DETROIT BUSINESS—1400 Woodbridge, Detroit, MI 48207. Cindy Goodaker, Exec. Ed. Business articles, 500 to 1,000 words, about Detroit, for Detroit business readers. Pays $10 per inch, on publication. Query required.

DELAWARE TODAY—P.O. Box 2800, Wilmington, DE 19805. Ted Spiker, Ed. Service articles, profiles, news, etc., on topics of local interest. Pays $150 for department pieces, $200 to $500 for features, on publication. Queries with clips required.

DOWN EAST—Camden, ME 04843. D.W. Kuhnert, Ed. Articles, 1,500 to 2,500 words, on all aspects of life in Maine. Photos. Pays on acceptance. Query.

EASTSIDE PARENT—Northwest Parent Publishing, 2107 Elliott Ave., #303, Seattle, WA 98121. Virginia Smyth, Ed. Articles, 300 to 2,500 words, for parents of children ages 14 and under. Pays $50 to $500, on publication. Queries preferred. Also publishes *Seattle's Child, Portland Parent, Puget Sound Parent, Snohomish County Parent,* and *South Sound Parent.*

ERIE & CHAUTAUQUA MAGAZINE—317 W. Sixth St., Erie, PA 16507. K. L. Kalvelage, Ed./Pub. Margaret Fisher Cutler, Assoc. Ed. Feature articles, to 2,500 words, on issues of interest to upscale readers in the Erie, Warren, and Crawford counties (PA), and Chautauqua (NY) county. Pieces with regional relevance. Pays after publication. Query preferred, with writing samples. Guidelines.

FAMILY TIMES—P.O. Box 932, Eau Claire, WI 54702. Ann Gorton, Ed. Articles, from 800 words, for parents in the Chippewa Valley, WI. Pays $35 to $50, on publication. Queries preferred. Guidelines.

FLORIDA TREND—Box 611, St. Petersburg, FL 33731-0611. Mark R. Howard, Exec. Ed. Articles on Florida business and businesspeople. Query with SASE required.

FLORIDA WILDLIFE—620 S. Meridian St., Tallahassee, FL 32399-1600. Attn: Ed. Bimonthly of the Florida Game and Fresh Water Fish Commission. Articles, 800 to 1,500 words, that promote native flora and fauna, hunting, fishing in Florida's fresh waters, outdoor ethics, and conservation of Florida's natural resources. Pays $50 per published page. SASE for guidelines and how-to-submit memo.

GEORGIA JOURNAL—The Indispensable Atlanta Co., Inc., P.O. Box 1604, Decatur, GA 30031-1604. David Osier, Ed./Pub. Conoly Hester, Man. Ed. Articles, 200 to 5,000 words, on Georgia's natural and human history and environment; also outdoor adventures, people, historical figures, places, events, travel in Georgia. Poetry, to 20 lines, and fiction, to 5,000 words, with Georgia settings; Georgia writers preferred. Pays $50 to $500, on publication. Query for nonfiction.

GOLDENSEAL—The Cultural Ctr., 1900 Kanawha Blvd. E., Charleston, WV 25305-0300. John Lilly, Ed. Quarterly. Articles, 1,000 and 3,000 words, on West Virginia history, folklife, folk art and crafts, and music of a traditional nature. Pays 10¢ a word, on publication. Guidelines.

GRAND RAPIDS—549 Ottawa N.W., Grand Rapids, MI 49503. Carole R. Valade, Ed. Service articles (dining guide, travel, personal finance, humor) and issue-oriented pieces related to Grand Rapids, Michigan. Pays $35 to $200, on publication. Query.

GULF COAST GOLFER—See *North Texas Golfer.*

HAWAII—1400 Kapiolani Blvd., A25, Honolulu, HI 96814. Jim Borg, Ed. Bimonthly. Articles, 1,000 to 2,500 words, related to Hawaii. Pays 10¢ and up a word, on publication. Query.

HIGH COUNTRY NEWS—Box 1090, Paonia, CO 81428. Betsy Marston, Ed. Biweekly. Articles, 2,000 words, and roundups, 750 words, on western environmental issues, public lands management, rural community, and natural resource issues; profiles of western innovators; pieces on western politics. "Writers must take regional approach." B&W photos. Pays 20¢ a word, on publication. Query.

ILLINOIS ENTERTAINER—124 W. Polk, Suite 103, Chicago, IL 60605. Michael C. Harris, Ed. Articles, 500 to 1,500 words, on local and national entertainment (emphasis on alternative music) in the greater Chicago area. Personality profiles; interviews; reviews. Photos. Pays varying rates, on publication. Query preferred.

THE ILLINOIS STEWARD—1102 S. Goodwin, W503 Turner Hall, Urbana, IL 61801. Phyllis Picklesimer, Ed. Mike Bolin, Man. Ed. Articles, 1,700 to 1,800 words, on Illinois history and heritage with a natural resource stewardship theme. No payment. Queries preferred.

INDIANAPOLIS MONTHLY—950 N. Meridian St., Suite 1200, Indianapolis, IN 46204. Sam Stall, Ed. Articles, 200 to 6,000 words, on health, sports, politics, business, interior design, personalities, controversy, and other topics. All material must have an Indianapolis/Indiana focus. Pays $50 to $500, on publication.

INQUIRER MAGAZINE—*Philadelphia Inquirer,* P.O. Box 8263, 400 N. Broad St., Philadelphia, PA 19101. Ms. Avery Rome, Ed. Articles, 1,500 to 2,000 words, and 3,000 to 4,500 words, on politics, science, arts and culture, business, lifestyles and entertainment, sports, health, psychology, education, religion, and humor. Pays varying rates. Query.

THE IOWAN MAGAZINE—108 Third St., Suite 350, Des Moines, IA 50309. Jay P. Wagner, Ed. Articles, 1,000 to 3,000 words, on business, arts, people, and history of Iowa. Essays on life in Iowa. Photos a plus. Payment varies, on acceptance. Query required.

ISLAND LIFE—P.O. Box 929, Sanibel Island, FL 33957. Joan Hooper, Ed. Articles, 500 to 1,200 words, with photos, on wildlife, flora and fauna, design and decor, the arts, shelling, local sports, historical sites, etc., directly related to the islands of Sanibel, Captiva, Marco, Estero, or Gasparilla. No first-person articles. Pays on publication.

JACKSONVILLE—White Publishing Co., 1032 Hendricks Ave., Jacksonville, FL 32207. Joseph White, Ed. Service pieces and articles, 1,500 to 2,500 words, on issues and personalities of interest to readers in the greater Jacksonville area. Department pieces, 1,200 to 1,500 words, on business, health, travel, personal finance, real estate, arts and entertainment, sports, dining out, food.

Home and garden articles on local homeowners, interior designers, remodelers, gardeners, craftsmen, etc., 1,000 to 2,000 words. Pays $200 to $500, on publication. Query required. Guidelines.

JOURNAL OF THE WEST—1531 Yuma, Box 1009, Manhattan, KS 66505-1009. Robin Higham, Ed. Articles, to 20 pages, on the history and culture of the West, then and now. Pays in copies.

KANSAS!—Kansas Dept. of Commerce, 700 S.W. Harrison, Suite 1300, Topeka, KS 66603-3957. Andrea Glenn, Ed. Quarterly. Articles, 1,000 to 1,250 words, on attractions and events of Kansas. Color slides. Pays to $300, on acceptance. Query.

KANSAS CITY MAGAZINE—7101 College Blvd., Suite 600, Overland Park, KS 66210. Zim Loy, Ed. Articles, 250 to 3,500 words, of interest to readers in Kansas City. Pays to 30¢ a word, on acceptance. Query.

KENTUCKY LIVING—P.O. Box 32170, Louisville, KY 40232. Paul Wesslund, Ed. Articles, 1,000 words, strong Kentucky angle a must: profiles (of people, places, events), history, biography, recreation, travel, leisure or lifestyle. Pays $125 to $350, on acceptance. Queries preferred. Guidelines.

LAKE SUPERIOR MAGAZINE—P.O. Box 16417, Duluth, MN 55816-0417. Paul Hayden, Ed. Articles with emphasis on Lake Superior regional subjects: historical and topical pieces that highlight the people, places, and events that affect the Lake Superior region. Pictorial essays; humor and occasional fiction. Quality photos enhance submission. "Writers must have a thorough knowledge of the subject and how it relates to our region." Pays to $600, extra for photos, on publication. Query.

LOS ANGELES MAGAZINE—11100 Santa Monica Blvd., 7th Fl., Los Angeles, CA 90025. Spencer Beck, Ed. Articles, to 3,000 words, of interest to sophisticated, affluent southern Californians, preferably with local focus on a lifestyle topic. Payment varies. Query.

LOUISVILLE—137 W. Muhammad Ali Blvd., Suite 101, Louisville, KY 40202. Larry Anas, Ed. Articles, 1,000 to 2,000 words, on community issues, personalities, and entertainment in the Louisville area. Photos. Pays from $50, on acceptance. Query; articles on assignment only. Limited market.

MEMPHIS—Contemporary Media, Box 256, Memphis, TN 38101. Tim Sampson, Ed. Articles, 1,500 to 4,000 words, on a wide variety of topics related to Memphis and the Mid-South region: politics, education, sports, business, history, etc. Profiles; investigative pieces. Pays $50 to $500, on publication. Query. SASE for guidelines.

METROKIDS—1080 N. Delaware Ave., Suite 702, Philadelphia, PA 19125. Nancy Lisagor, Ed. Tabloid. Features and department pieces, 500 to 1,000 words, on regional family travel, dining, and entertainment in the Philadelphia metropolitan region. Pays $25 to $50, on publication.

MIAMI METRO MAGAZINE—(formerly *South Florida Magazine*) 800 Douglas Rd., Suite 500, Coral Gables, FL 33134. Nancy Moore, Ed. Features, 1,100 to 2,000 words, and department pieces, 200 to 1,300 words, on news, profiles, and hot topics related to south Florida. Short, bright items, 200 to 400 words. Pays $75 to $700, within 30 days of acceptance. Query.

MICHIGAN LIVING—Auto Club of Michigan, 1 Auto Club Dr., Dearborn, MI 48126-9982. Ron Garbinski, Ed. Informative travel articles, 300 to 2,000 words, on U.S. and Canadian tourist attractions and recreational opportunities; special interest in Michigan. Pays $55 to $500 (rates vary for photos), on acceptance.

MID-WEST OUTDOORS—111 Shore Dr., Hinsdale, IL 60521-5885. Gene Laulunen, Ed. Articles, to 1,500 words, with photos, on where, when, and how to fish and hunt, within 600 miles of Chicago. Pays $25, on publication.

MILWAUKEE MAGAZINE—312 E. Buffalo, Milwaukee, WI 53202. John Fennell, Ed. Profiles, investigative articles, and service pieces, 2,000 to 4,000 words; local tie-in a must. No fiction. Pays $400 to $1,000, on publication. Query preferred.

MINNESOTA MONTHLY—Lumber Exchange Bldg., 10 S. Fifth St., Suite 1000, Minneapolis, MN 55402. David Mahoney, Ed. Articles, to 4,000 words, on people, places, events, and issues in Minnesota. Pays $50 to $1,000, on acceptance. Query.

MONTANA MAGAZINE—P.O. Box 5630, Helena, MT 59604. Beverly R. Magley, Ed. Recreation, travel, general-interest, regional profiles, photo-essays. Montana-oriented only. B&W prints, color slides. Pays 15¢ a word, on publication.

MPLS. ST. PAUL—220 S. 6th St., Suite 500, Minneapolis, MN 55402-4507. Brian E. Anderson, Ed. In-depth articles, features, profiles, and service pieces about the Minneapolis-St. Paul area, 300 to 4,000 words. Pays to $2,000.

NEBRASKA HISTORY—P.O. Box 82554, Lincoln, NE 68501. James E. Potter, Ed. Articles, 3,000 to 7,000 words, on the history of Nebraska and the Great Plains. B&W line drawings. Pays in copies. Cash prize awarded to one article each year.

NEVADA MAGAZINE—1800 Hwy. 50 East, Suite 200, Carson City, NV 89701. David Moore, Ed. Articles, 500 to 700 or 1,500 to 1,800 words, on topics related to Nevada: travel, history, recreation, profiles, humor, and attractions. Special section on Nevada events and shows. Photos. Pay varies, on publication.

NEW FRONTIERS OF NEW MEXICO—P.O. Box 1299, Tijeras, NM 87059. Wally Gordon, Ed./Pub. Fiction and in-depth nonfiction, to 3,000 words, related to New Mexico and the Southwest. Humor, to 1,000 words. Poetry, to 100 lines. Pays $25 to $200, on publication.

NEW HAMPSHIRE EDITIONS—100 Main St., Nashua, NH 03060. Rick Broussard, Ed. Lifestyle, business, and history articles with a New Hampshire angle, with sources from all regions of the state, for the company's statewide magazine, and specialty publications including *New Hampshire Legacy, The World Trader* and *New Hampshire Guide to the Internet.* Query. Payment varies, on publication.

NEW JERSEY MONTHLY—P.O. Box 920, Morristown, NJ 07963-0920. Jenny DeMonte, Ed. Articles, profiles, and service pieces, 1,500 to 3,000 words; department pieces on health, business, education, travel, sports, local politics, and arts with New Jersey tie-in, 750 to 1,500 words. Pays $25 to $100 for shorts, $400 to $700 for departments, $600 to $1,750 for features, on acceptance. Query with clips. Guidelines.

NEW MEXICO MAGAZINE—Lew Wallace Bldg., 495 Old Santa Fe Trail, Santa Fe, NM 87503. Attn: Ed. Articles, 250 to 2,000 words, on New Mexico subjects. No poetry or fiction. Pays about 30¢ a word, on acceptance. Query.

NEW YORK FAMILY—141 Halstead Ave., Suite 3D, Mamaroneck, NY 10543. Felice Shapiro, Susan Ross, Pubs. Betsy F. Woolf, Sr. Ed. Articles related to family life in New York City. Pays $50 to $200, on publication. Same requirements for *Westchester Family* and *Connecticut Family*.

NEWPORT LIFE—174 Bellevue Ave., Suite 207, Newport, RI 02840. Lynne Tungett, Jeffrey Hall, Pubs. John Pantalone, Ed. Quarterly. Annual City Guide. Articles, 500 to 2,500 words, on people, places, attractions of Newport County: general-interest, historical, profiles, international celebrities, social, and political issues. Departments, 200 to 750 words: sailing, dining, food and wine, home and garden, the arts in Newport County. Photos must be available for all articles. Query. SASE.

NORTH DAKOTA HORIZONS—P.O. Box 2639, Bismarck, ND 58502. Lyle Halvorson, Ed. Quarterly. Articles, about 2,500 words, on people, places, and events in North Dakota. Photos. Pays $75 to $300, on publication.

NORTH GEORGIA JOURNAL—P.O. Box 127, Roswell, GA 30077. Olin Jackson, Pub./Ed. History, travel, and lifestyle features, 2,000 to 3,000 words, on north Georgia; need human-interest approach and must be written in first person. Include interviews. Photos a plus. Pays $75 to $300, on acceptance. Query.

NORTH TEXAS GOLFER—9182 Old Katy Rd., Suite 212, Houston, TX 77055. David Widener, Man. Ed. Articles, 800 to 1,500 words, involving local golfers or related directly to north Texas. Pays from $50 to $425, on publication. Query. Same requirements for *Gulf Coast Golfer* (related to south Texas).

NORTHEAST MAGAZINE—*The Hartford Courant,* 285 Broad St., Hartford, CT 06115. Jane Bronfman, Ed. Asst. Articles and short essays, 750 to 3,000 words, that reflect the concerns of Connecticut residents. Pays $250 to $1,000, on acceptance.

NORTHERN LIGHTS—Box 8084, Missoula, MT 59807-8084. Attn: Deborah Clow. Articles, 500 to 3,000 words, about the contemporary West. "We look for finely crafted personal essays that illuminate what it means to live in the contemporary West. We're looking to bust the New York and Hollywood stereotypes." Pays 10¢ a word, on publication.

NORTHWEST REGIONAL MAGAZINES—P.O. Box 18000, Florence, OR 97439-0130. Attn: Jim Forst or Judy Fleagle. All submissions considered for use in *Oregon Coast, Oregon Outside* and *Northwest Travel.* Articles, 800 to 2,000 words, pertaining to travel, history, town/city profiles, events, outside activities, and nature. News releases, 200 to 500 words. Articles with photos (slides) preferred. Pays $50 to $300, after publication. Guidelines with SASE.

NORTHWEST TRAVEL—See *Northwest Regional Magazines.*

NOW & THEN—CASS/ETSU, P.O. Box 70556, Johnson City, TN 37614-0556. Jane Harris Woodside, Ed. Fiction and nonfiction, 1,500 to 3,000 words: short stories, articles, interviews, essays, memoirs, book reviews. Pieces must be related to theme of issue and have some connection to the Appalachian region. Also photos and drawings. SASE for guidelines and current themes. Pays $15 to $75, on publication.

OHIO MAGAZINE—62 E. Broad St., Columbus, OH 43215. Jean Kelly, Ed. Profiles of people, cities, and towns of Ohio; pieces on historic sites, tourist attractions, little-known spots. Lengths and payment vary. Query with clips.

OKLAHOMA TODAY—15 N. Robinson, Suite 100, Oklahoma City, OK 73102. Louisa McCune, Ed. Articles, 1,000 to 4,000 words: travel; profiles; history; nature and outdoor recreation; and arts. All material must have regional tie-in. Pays $75 to $750, on acceptance or publication. Queries preferred. Guidelines.

ORANGE COAST—3701 Birch St., Suite 100, Newport Beach, CA 92560. Patrick Mott, Ed. Articles, 2,000 to 3,000 words, of interest to educated Orange County residents. Pieces, 1,000 to 1,500 words, for regular departments, and 200-word pieces for "Short Cuts" (local phenomena). Query with clips. Pays $400 to $800 for features; $100 to $200 for departments; $25 to $50 for "Short Cuts," after acceptance. Guidelines.

ORANGE COUNTY WOMAN—3701 Birch St., #100, Newport Beach, CA 92660-2618. Janine Robinson, Ed. First-person fiction, 1,000 to 1,500 words, and articles, 500 to 1,500 words, for women living in Orange County, CA. "Our readers are highly educated, upscale women who are looking for information that will make their busy lives more efficient and gratifying. We cover everything from family issues to health and beauty." SASE for guidelines. Payment is $50 to $250, on acceptance.

OREGON COAST—See *Northwest Regional Magazines.*

OREGON OUTSIDE—Northwest Regional Magazines, Box 18000, 1525 12th St., Florence, OR 97439-0130. Judy Fleagle, Co-Ed. Quarterly. Articles, 1,000 to 1,500 words, on Oregon and the outdoors, "all kinds of adventure, from walks for families to extreme skiing." Prefers to receive manuscript/photo packages. Pays $100 to $350, on publication. Query.

ORLANDO MAGAZINE—260 Maitland Ave., Suite 2000, Altamonte Springs, FL 32701. Brooke Lange, Ed. Locally based articles and department pieces, lengths vary, for residents of Central Florida. Query with clips.

OUR STATE: DOWN HOME IN NORTH CAROLINA—P.O. Box 4552, Greensboro, NC 27404. Mary Ellis, Ed. Articles, 750 to 1,500 words, on people, history, and places in North Carolina. Photos. Pays on publication.

OUT WEST: THE NEWSPAPER THAT ROAMS—9792 Edmonds Way, Suite 265, Edmonds, WA 98020. Chuck Woodbury, Ed./Pub. Entertaining and informative articles, 150 to 500 words, and short pieces, 30 to 75 words, on the roadside West (not the old West): interesting people, unusual places to stay, offbeat attractions. "Send for a sample of the paper before you submit." Pays about 5¢ a word, on publication. Web site: http://www.outwestnewspaper.com.

OUTDOOR TRAVELER, MID-ATLANTIC—WMS Publications, Inc., P.O. Box 2748, Charlottesville, VA 22902. Marianne Marks, Ed. Tom Gillespie, Assoc. Ed. Quarterly. Articles, 1,500 to 2,000 words, on hiking/backpacking, canoeing/kayaking/rafting, camping, mountain biking, road cycling, travel, nature, and the environment from New York state to North Carolina. Travel articles on destinations and areas that offer recreational opportunities. Departments include "Destinations," 450 to 600 words, on practical and descriptive guides to sports destinations; book and product reviews. Pays $300 to $400 for features; payment varies for departments, on publication. Guidelines.

PALM SPRINGS LIFE—Desert Publications, 303 N. Indian Canyon Dr., P.O. Box 2724, Palm Springs, CA 92263. Stewart Weiner, Ed. Articles, 1,000 to 3,000 words, of interest to "wealthy, upscale people who live and/or play in the desert." Pays $150 to $500 for features, $25 to $75 for short profiles, on publication. Query required.

PENNSYLVANIA HERITAGE—P.O. Box 1026, Harrisburg, PA 17108-1026. Michael J. O'Malley III, Ed. Quarterly of the Pennsylvania Historical

Museum Commission. Articles, 3,000 to 4,000 words, relating to Pennsylvania fine and decorative arts, architecture, archaeology, history, industry and technology, travel, and folklore, written with an eye toward illustration. Photographic essays. Pieces should "introduce readers to the state's rich culture and historic legacy." Pays $300 to $500 for articles; up to $100 for photos and drawings, on publication.

PENNSYLVANIA MAGAZINE—Box 576, Camp Hill, PA 17001-0576. Matthew K. Holliday, Ed. General-interest features with a Pennsylvania focus. All articles must be accompanied by photocopies of possible illustrations. Query. Guidelines.

PERSIMMON HILL—1700 N.E. 63rd St., Oklahoma City, OK 73111. M.J. Van Deventer, Ed. Published by the National Cowboy Hall of Fame. Articles, 1,500 to 2,000 words, on Western history and art, cowboys, ranching, and nature. Top-quality illustrations a must. Pays from $100 to $250, on publication. Query.

PHOENIX MAGAZINE—5555 N. 7th Ave., Suite B200, Phoenix, AZ 85013. Beth Deveny, Ed. Articles, 1,000 to 3,000 words, on topics of interest to Phoenix-area residents. Pays $300 to $1,500, on publication. Query.

PITTSBURGH— 4802 Fifth Ave., Pittsburgh, PA 15213. Attn: Man. Ed. Profiles (to 800 words), feature stories and service pieces (1,200 to 3,000 words), and in-depth news features (to 5,000 words) geared to western Pennsylvania, eastern Ohio, northern West Virginia, and western Maryland readers. Pays from $300, on publication. Query with outline.

PITTSBURGH POST GAZETTE—34 Blvd. of the Allies, Pittsburgh, PA 15230. Mark S. Murphy, Ed. Sunday magazine. Well-written, well-organized, in-depth articles of regional interest, 1,000 to 3,500 words, on issues, personalities, human interest, historical moments. No fiction, hobbies, how-tos or "timely events" pieces. Pays from $350, on publication. Query.

PORTLAND MAGAZINE—578 Congress St., Portland, ME 04101. Colin Sargent, Ed. "Maine's City Magazine." Articles on local people, legends, culture, and trends. Fiction, to 750 words. Pays on publication. Query preferred.

PORTLAND PARENT—See *Eastside Parent.*

PROVINCETOWN ARTS— 650 Commercial St., Provincetown, MA 02657. Christopher Busa, Ed. Annual. Interviews, profiles, essays, 1,500 to 4,000 words. Mainstream fiction and novel excerpts, 500 to 5,000 words. Poems, submit up to 3 at a time. "We have a broad focus on the artists and writers who inhabit or visit Cape Cod." Pays from $125 for articles; $75 to $300 for fiction; $25 to $150 for poems, on publication.

PUGET SOUND PARENT—See *Eastside Parent.*

RANGE MAGAZINE—106 E. Adams, Suite 201, Carson City, NV 89706. C.J. Hadley, Ed. Quarterly. "The Cowboy Spirit on America's Outback." Articles, 500 to 2,000 words, on issues that threaten the West, its people, lifestyles, lands, and wildlife. "Our main purpose is to present public awareness of the positive presence of ranching operations on America's rangelands." Payment varies, on publication. Query preferred.

RECREATION NEWS—P.O. Box 32335, Washington, DC 20007-0635. Rebecca B. Heaton, Ed. Articles, 900 to 2,200 words, on recreation and travel around the mid-Atlantic region for government and private sector workers in the Washington, DC area. "Articles should have a conversational tone that's lean and brisk." Pays $50 for reprints, to $300 for cover articles, on publication. Queries preferred. Guidelines.

RHODE ISLAND MONTHLY—70 Elm St., Providence, RI 02903. Sarah Francis, Man. Ed. Features, 1,000 to 4,000 words, ranging from investigative reporting and in-depth profiles to service pieces and visual stories, on Rhode Island and southeastern Massachusetts. Seasonal material, 1,000 to 2,000 words. Fillers, 150 to 500 words, on Rhode Island places, customs, people, events, products and services, restaurants and food. Pays $250 to $1,000 for features; $25 to $50 for shorts, on publication. Query.

RURAL LIVING— 4201 Dominion Blvd., Suite 101, Glen Allen, VA 23060. Richard G. Johnstone, Jr., Ed. Features, 1,000 to 1,500 words, on people, places, historic sites in Virginia and Maryland's Eastern Shore. Queries preferred. Pays $150 to $200 for articles, on publication.

RURALITE—P.O. Box 558, Forest Grove, OR 97116. Attn: Ed. or Feature Ed. Articles, 800 to 2,000 words, of interest to a primarily rural and small-town audience in OR, WA, ID, WY, NV, northern CA, and AK. "Think pieces" affecting rural/urban interests, regional history and celebrations, self-help, profiles, etc. No fiction or poetry. Pays $30 to $400, on acceptance. Queries required. Guidelines.

SACRAMENTO MAGAZINE— 4471 D St., Sacramento, CA 95819. Krista Hendricks Minard, Ed. Features, 2,500 words, on a broad range of topics related to the region. Department pieces, 1,200 to 1,500 words, and short pieces, 400 words, for "City Lights" column. Pays $50 to $300, on publication. Query.

SAN DIEGO MAGAZINE— 4206 W. Point Loma Blvd., P.O. Box 85409, San Diego, CA 92138. Tom Blair, Ed. Virginia Butterfield, Exec. Ed. Ron Donoho, Man. Ed. Articles, 1,500 to 3,000 words, on local personalities, politics, lifestyles, business, history, etc., relating to San Diego area. Photos. Pays $250 to $750, on publication. Query with clips.

SAN DIEGO READER—P.O. Box 85803, San Diego, CA 92186. Jim Holman, Ed. Literate articles, 2,500 to 10,000 words, on the San Diego region. Pays $500 to $2,000, on publication.

SAN FRANCISCO—243 Vallejo, San Francisco, CA 94111. Dale Eastman, Ed. Service features, profiles of local newsmakers, and investigative pieces of local issues, 2,500 to 3,000 words. News items, 250 to 800 words, on subjects ranging from business to arts to politics. Payment varies, on acceptance. Query required.

SAN FRANCISCO EXAMINER MAGAZINE—*San Francisco Examiner*, 110 Fifth St., San Francisco, CA 94103. Attn: Ed. Articles, 1,200 to 3,000 words, on lifestyles, issues, business, history, events, and people in northern California. Query. Pays varying rates.

SASKATCHEWAN SAGE—Aboriginal Multi-Media Society of Alberta, 15001 112th Ave., Edmonton, Alberta, Canada T5M 2V6. Debora Lockyer, Man. Ed. Tabloid. Articles, 100 to 1,000 words, most often 500 to 800 words; briefs 100 to 150 words, features, profiles, and community-based articles with a Saskatchewan angle.

SAVANNAH MAGAZINE—P.O. Box 1088, Savannah, GA 31402. Mary Beth Kerdasha, Ed. Articles, 2,500 to 3,500 words, on people and events in and around Savannah and Chatham County. Historical articles, 1,500 to 2,500 words, of local interest. Reviews, 500 to 750 words, of Savannah-based books and authors. Short pieces, 500 to 750 words, on weekend getaways near Savannah. Pays $75 to $350, after acceptance. Submit complete manuscript. Guidelines.

SEATTLE—701 Dexter Ave. N., Suite 101, Seattle, WA 98109. Giselle Smith, Ed. City, local issues, home, and lifestyle articles, 500 to 2,000 words, relating directly to the greater Seattle area. Personality profiles. Pays $100 to $700, on publication. Guidelines.

SEATTLE WEEKLY—1008 Western, Suite 300, Seattle, WA 98104. Knute Berger, Ed. Articles, 250 to 4,000 words, from a Northwest perspective. Pays $25 to $800, on publication. Query. Guidelines.

SEATTLE'S CHILD—Northwest Parent Publishing, 2107 Elliott Ave., #303, Seattle, WA 98121. Ann Bergman, Ed. Articles, 400 to 2,500 words, of interest to parents, educators, and childcare providers of children 14 and under, and investigative reports and consumer tips on issues affecting families in the Puget Sound region. Pays $75 to $500, on publication. Query required.

SENIOR MAGAZINE—3565 S. Higuera St., San Luis Obispo, CA 93401. Attn: Ed. Articles, 600 to 900 words: personality profiles, travel pieces, articles about new things, places, business, sports, movies, television, and health; book reviews (of new or outstanding older books) of interest to seniors. Pays $1.50 per inch; $10 to $25 for B&W photos, on publication.

SILENT SPORTS—717 10th St., P.O. Box 152, Waupaca, WI 54981. Attn: Ed. Articles, 1,000 to 2,000 words, on canoeing, bicycling, cross-country skiing, running, hiking, backpacking, snowshoeing, inline skating, and other "silent" sports, in the upper Midwest region. "Articles must focus on the upper Midwest. No articles about places, people, or events outside the region." Pays $40 to $100 for features; $20 to $50 for fillers, on publication. Query.

SNOHOMISH COUNTY PARENT—See *Eastside Parent.*

SNOW COUNTRY—5520 Park Ave., Trumbull, CT 06611-0395. Lynn Prowitt, Assoc. Ed. Published 8 times a year. Features, 4,000 words, and articles, 1,000 to 2,000 words, on skiing, mountain biking, in-line skating, camping, rafting and other year-round mountain sports as well as lifestyle issues. First-person adventure articles, travel pieces, service-oriented articles, profiles of snow country residents. "Mountain Living," 100-to 700-word pieces on people and points of view, anecdotes, trends, issues. Query with clips and resumé. Pays 80¢ a word, on acceptance.

SOUTH CAROLINA HISTORICAL MAGAZINE—South Carolina Historical Society, 100 Meeting St., Charleston, SC 29401-2299. Stephen Hoffius, Ed. Scholarly articles, to 25 pages with footnotes, on all areas of South Carolina history. Pays in copies.

SOUTH CAROLINA WILDLIFE—P.O. Box 167, Columbia, SC 29202-0167. Attn: Man. Ed. Articles, 1,000 to 2,000 words, with regional outdoors focus: conservation, natural history and wildlife, recreation. Profiles. Pays from 15¢ a word. Query.

SOUTH FLORIDA MAGAZINE—See *Miami Metro Magazine.*

SOUTH SOUND PARENT—See *Eastside Parent.*

SOUTHERN CULTURES—Ctr. for the Study of the American South, CB #3355, Manning Hall, UNC-CH, Chapel Hill, NC 27599-3355. Laura Cotterman, Man. Ed. Articles, 15 to 25 typed pages, on folk, popular, and high culture of the South. "We're interested in submissions from a wide variety of intellectual traditions that deal with ways of life, thought, belief, and expression in the United States South." Pays in copies.

SOUTHWEST ART—5444 Westheimer, Suite 1440, Houston, TX 77056. Margaret L. Brown, Ed.-in-Chief. Articles, 1,200 to 1,800 words, on the artists, art collectors, museum exhibitions, gallery events and dealers, art history, and art trends west of the Mississippi River. Particularly interested in representational or figurative arts. Pays from $500, on acceptance. Query with at least 20 slides of artwork to be featured.

SUNSET MAGAZINE— 80 Willow Rd., Menlo Park, CA 94025. Rosalie Muller Wright, Ed. Western regional. Limited free-lance market, but some need for western travel. Query; include clips.

SUNSHINE: THE MAGAZINE OF SOUTH FLORIDA—*The Sun-Sentinel,* 200 E. Las Olas Blvd., Ft. Lauderdale, FL 33301-2293. Mark Gauert, Ed. Articles, 1,000 to 3,000 words, on topics of interest to south Floridians. Pays $300 to $1,200, on acceptance. Query. Guidelines.

SWEAT—736 E. Loyola Dr., Tempe, AZ 85282. Joan Westlake, Ed. "South West Exercise And Training." Articles, 500 to 1,200 words, on sports, wellness, and fitness with an Arizona angle. "No personal articles or tales. We want investigative pieces. Articles must relate specifically to Arizona or Arizonans." Pays $25 to $60 for articles; $15 to $70 for photos, on publication. Queries required; no unsolicited manuscripts.

TALLAHASSEE MAGAZINE—P.O. Box 1837, Tallahassee, FL 32302-1837. Kathy Grobe, Man. Ed. Articles, 800 to 1,500 words, on the life, people, and history of the north Florida-south Georgia area. Pays on acceptance. Query.

TEXAS HIGHWAYS MAGAZINE—P.O. Box 141009, Austin, TX 78714-1009. Jack Lowry, Ed. Texas travel, history, and scenic features, 200 to 1,800 words. Pays about 40¢ to 50¢ a word, $80 to $550 per photo. Query. Guidelines.

TEXAS MONTHLY—P.O. Box 1569, Austin, TX 78767-1569. Gregory Curtis, Ed. Features, 2,500 to 5,000 words, and departments, to 2,500 words, on art, architecture, food, education, business, politics, etc. "We like solidly researched pieces that uncover issues of public concern, reveal offbeat and previously unreported topics, or use a novel approach to familiar topics." Pays varying rates, on acceptance. Queries required.

TEXAS PARKS & WILDLIFE—3000 S. Interstate Hwy. 35, Suite 120, Austin, TX 78704. Articles, 800 to 1,500 words, promoting the conservation and enjoyment of Texas wildlife, parks, waters, and all outdoors. Features on hunting, fishing, birding, camping, and the environment. Photos a plus. Pays to $600, on acceptance; extra for photos.

TIMELINE—1982 Velma Ave., Columbus, OH 43211-2497. Christopher S. Duckworth, Ed. Articles, 1,000 to 6,000 words, on history of Ohio (politics, economics, social, and natural history) for lay readers in the Midwest. Pays $100 to $900, on acceptance. Queries preferred.

TROPIC—*The Miami Herald,* One Herald Plaza, Miami, FL 33132. Tom Shroder, Exec. Ed. General-interest articles, 750 to 3,000 words, for south Florida readers. Pays $200 to $1,000, on acceptance. SASE.

TUCSON LIFESTYLE—Old Pueblo Press, 7000 E. Tanque Verde, Tucson, AZ 85715. Sue Giles, Ed.-in-Chief. Local slant to all articles on businesses, lifestyles, the arts, homes, fashion, and travel in the Southwest. Payment varies, on acceptance. Query preferred.

VERMONT—20½ Main St., P.O. Box 800, Middlebury, VT 05753. Julie Kirgo, Man. Ed. Articles on all aspects of contemporary Vermont: its people, culture, politics, and special places. Pays $200 to $1,000, on publication. Query.

VERMONT LIFE— 6 Baldwin St., Montpelier, VT 05602. Tom Slayton, Ed.-in-Chief. Articles, 500 to 3,000 words, on Vermont subjects only. Pays 20¢ a word, extra for photos. Query preferred.

VIRGINIA BUSINESS— 411 E. Franklin St., Suite 105, Richmond, VA 23219. James Bacon, Ed. Articles, 1,000 to 2,500 words, related to the business scene in Virginia. Pays varying rates, on acceptance. Query required.

VIRGINIA WILDLIFE—P.O. Box 11104, Richmond, VA 23230-1104. Attn: Ed. Articles, 1,000 to 1,500 words, with Virginia tie-in, on fishing, hunting, wildlife management, outdoor safety and ethics, etc. Articles may be accompanied by color photos. Pays from 15¢ a word, extra for photos, on publication. Query.

WASHINGTON POST MAGAZINE—*The Washington Post*, 1150 15th St. N.W., Washington, DC 20071. Tom Frail, Man. Ed. Personal-experience essays, profiles, and general-interest pieces, to 6,000 words, on business, arts and culture, politics, science, sports, education, children, relationships, behavior, etc. Articles should be of interest to people living in Washington, DC, area. Pays from $750, on acceptance. Limited market.

THE WASHINGTONIAN—1828 L St. N.W., Suite 200, Washington, DC 20036. John Limpert, Ed. Helpful, informative articles, 1,000 to 4,000 words, on DC-related topics. Pays 50¢ a word, on publication.

WESTCHESTER FAMILY—See *New York Family.*

WESTERN SPORTSMAN—140 Ave. F N., Saskatoon, Sask., Canada S7L 1V8. George Gruenefeld, Ed. Informative articles, to 2,500 words, on hunting, fishing, and outdoor experiences in British Columbia, Alberta, Saskatchewan, and Manitoba. How-tos, where-tos, cartoons. Photos. Pays $75 to $300.

WESTWAYS—P.O. Box 25001, Santa Ana, CA 92799-5001. Attn: Ed. Articles, 1,000 to 2,500 words, on travel in California, western U.S., greater U.S., and overseas. Pays from 50¢ a word, on acceptance. Query.

WINDSPEAKER—Aboriginal Multi-Media Society of Alberta, 15001 112th Ave., Edmonton, Alberta, Canada T5M 2V6. Debora Lockyer, Ed. Tabloid. Features, news items, sports, op-ed pieces, columns, etc., 200 to 1,000 words, concerning Canada's Aboriginal peoples. Pays from $3 per published inch, after publication. Query. Guidelines.

WINDY CITY SPORTS—1450 W. Randolph, Chicago, IL 60607. Jeff Banowetz, Ed. Articles, to 1,000 words, on amateur sports in the Chicago area. Queries required. Pays $100, on publication.

WISCONSIN TRAILS—P.O. Box 5650, Madison, WI 53705. Howard Mead, Ed./Pub. Articles, 1,500 to 3,000 words, on regional topics: outdoors, lifestyle, events, history, arts, adventure, travel; profiles of artists, craftspeople, and regional personalities. Pays 25¢ per word, on publication. Query.

WYOMING RURAL ELECTRIC NEWS—P.O. Box 380, Casper, WY 82606-0380. Kris Wendtland, Ed. Articles, 500 to 900 words, on issues relevant to rural Wyoming. Articles should support Wyoming's personal and economic growth, social development, and education. Wyoming writers given preference. Pays $20 to $50, on publication.

YANKEE—Yankee Publishing Co., P.O. Box 520, Dublin, NH 03444. Judson D. Hale, Ed. Articles and fiction, 500 to 2,500 words, on New England and New England people. Pays $500 to $2,500 for features, on acceptance. Query required.

YANKEE MAGAZINE'S TRAVEL GUIDE TO NEW ENGLAND—33 Union St., Boston, MA 02108. Mike Campbell, Ed. Articles, 500 to 2,000 words, on activities, attractions, places to visit in New England. Photos. Pays on acceptance. Query with outline and writing samples required.

YIPPY YI YEA WESTERN LIFESTYLES— 8393 E. Holly Rd., Holly, MI 48442-8819. Nicole Brown, Ed. Articles, 1,200 words, on Western subjects, including artisans, galleries, decorating, travel, history, and celebrities. Pays $250, on publication.

TRAVEL ARTICLES

AAA TODAY—378 Whooping Loop, Suite 1272, Altamonte Springs, FL 32701. Margaret Cavanaugh, Ed. Bimonthly. Articles, 1,000 to 1,200 words, on travel in Pennsylvania, West Virginia, New York, New York, Massachusetts, and Ohio. Color photos. Pays $300 to $400, on publication.

ADVENTURE JOURNAL—(formerly *Adventure West*) 650 S. Orcas St., Suite 103, Seattle, WA 98108. Kristina Schreck, Man Ed. Bimonthly. Travel articles, 2,500 to 3,000 words, on risky wild adventures; 700 to 2,000 words, on shorter trips with information on where to stay and what to do. Profiles and essays also used. Emphasis on both domestic and international travel. Pays 15¢ a word, for unsolicited submissions, within 30 days of publication.

ADVENTURE WEST—See *Adventure Journal.*

AIR FORCE TIMES—See *Times News Service.*

ARIZONA HIGHWAYS—2039 W. Lewis Ave., Phoenix, AZ 85009. Richard G. Stahl, Sr. Ed. Informal, well-researched personal-experience and travel articles, 1,600 to 1,800 words, focusing on a specific city or region in Arizona. Also articles dealing with nature, environment, flora and fauna, history, anthropology, archaeology, hiking. Departments for personal-experience pieces include "Focus on Nature," "Along the Way," "Back Road Adventures," "Hiking," and "Arizona Humor." Pays 35¢ to 55¢ a word, on acceptance. Query with published clips only. Guidelines.

ARMY TIMES—See *Times News Service.*

BIG WORLD—P.O. Box 8743-A, Lancaster, PA 17604. Jim Fortney, Ed. Quarterly. Articles, 500 to 4,000 words, that offer advice on working and studying abroad, humorous anecdotes, first-person experiences, or other "down-to-earth" travel information. "For people who prefer to spend their traveling time responsibly discovering, exploring, and learning, in touch with locals and their traditions, and in harmony with their environment." Pays $10 to $20 for articles, $5 to $20 for photos, on publication. Web page: www.bigworld.com

BLUE RIDGE COUNTRY—P.O. Box 21535, Roanoke, VA 24018. Kurt Rheinheimer, Ed. Regional travel articles, 750 to 1,200 words, on destinations and backroads drives in the mountain regions of VA, NC, WV, TN, KY, MD, SC, and GA. Color slides and B&W prints considered. Pays to $200 for photo-features, on publication. Queries preferred.

BREW MAGAZINE—1120 Mulberry St., Des Moines, IA 50309. Beverly Walsmith, Ed. "Traveling America's Brewpubs and Microbreweries." Bimonthly. Articles, 1,500 to 1,800 words, on new brewpubs around the country. "Our focus is on the brewpub and the community where it is located." Pays 10¢ a word, on publication. Query preferred.

CANADIAN DIVER & WATERSPORT—See *Diver Magazine.*

CAR & TRAVEL—1000 AAA Dr., Heathrow, FL 32746-5063. Marianne T. Camas, Ed. Articles, 600 to 1,500 words, on consumer automotive and travel concerns. Pays $200 to $800, on acceptance. Query with writing samples required. Articles by assignment only.

CARIBBEAN TRAVEL AND LIFE—330 W. Canton Ave., Winter Park, FL 32790. Steve Blount, Ed. Lively, informative articles, 500 to 2,500 words, on all aspects of travel, leisure, recreation, and culture in the Caribbean, Bahamas, and Bermuda, for upscale, sophisticated readers. Photos. Pays $75 to $750, on acceptance. Query.

CHILE PEPPER—1227 W. Magnolia Ave., Fort Worth, TX 76104. Joel Gregory, Pub. First-person food and travel articles, 1,000 to 1,500 words, about spicy world cuisine. Queries required. Payment varies, on publication.

CONDE NAST TRAVELER—360 Madison Ave., New York, NY 10017. Alison Humes, Features Ed. Uses very little free-lance material.

CRUISE TRAVEL—990 Grove St., Evanston, IL 60201. Robert Meyers, Ed. Charles Doherty, Man. Ed. Ship-, port-, and cruise-of-the-month features, 800 to 2,000 words; cruise guides; cruise roundups; cruise company profiles; travel suggestions for one-day port stops. "Photo-features strongly recommended." Payment varies, on acceptance. Query with sample color photos.

DIVER MAGAZINE—230-11780 Hammersmith Way, Richmond, B.C., Canada V7A 5E3. Stephanie Bold, Ed. Illustrated articles, 500 to 1,000 words, on dive destinations. Shorter pieces are also welcome. "Travel features should be brief and accompanied by excellent slides and/or prints and a map. Unsolicited articles will be reviewed only from August to October and will be considered for *Diver Magazine* and *Canadian Diver & Watersport.*" Guidelines. Limited market.

ENDLESS VACATION—Box 80260, Indianapolis, IN 46280. Laurie D. Borman, Ed. Travel features, to 1,500 words; primarily on North American destinations, some international destinations. Pays on acceptance. Query preferred. Send SASE for guidelines. Limited market.

FAMILY CIRCLE—110 Fifth Ave., New York, NY 10011. Sylvia Barsotti, Sr. Ed. Travel articles, to 1,500 words. Concept travel pieces should appeal to a national audience and focus on affordable activities for families; prefer service-filled, theme-oriented travel pieces or first-person family vacation stories. Payment varies, on acceptance. Query.

FRIENDLY EXCHANGE—P.O. Box 2120, Warren, MI 48090-2120. Dan Grantham, Ed. Articles, 700 to 1,500 words, offering readers "news you can use," on lifestyle issues, such as home, health, personal finance, and travel. Photos. Pays $400 to $1,000, extra for photos. Query required. Guidelines.

GRAND TOUR: THE JOURNAL OF TRAVEL LITERATURE—P.O. Box 260, Haddonfield, NJ 08033. Jennifer Fisher, Man. Ed. Quarterly. Travel-related memoirs, essays, and articles, 1,000 to 7,000 words, that "combine the sharp eye of the reporter with the craft of the short story writer and the rhythm of the poet." Pays $50 to $200, on publication.

HISTORIC TRAVELER—6405 Flank Dr., Harrisburg, PA 17112. Tom Huntington, Ed. "The Guide to Great Historic Destinations." Bimonthly. Articles, 1,500 to 3,000 words, for upscale readers with a strong interest in history. "Accurate information on historic destinations. Possible topics: battlefields, museums, antique shows, events, hotels, inns, transportation, reenactments, preserved communities, and architectural wonders. No South Pacific Islands, Alpine skiing, or Mediterranean cruises." Guidelines. Pays from $300, on acceptance. Query with SASE and clips.

INTERLINE ADVENTURES: THE MAGAZINE FOR AIRLINE EMPLOYEES—211 E. 7th St., #1100, Austin, TX 78701. Scherry Sweeney, Ed. Travel Articles, 1,800 to 2,500 words, with photos, on shopping, sightseeing, dining, and nightlife for airline employees. Prices, discount information, and addresses must be included. Pays $250 to $500, after publication.

INTERNATIONAL LIVING—105 W. Monument St., Baltimore, MD 21201. Kerstin Czarra, Man. Ed. Newsletter. Short pieces and features, 200 to 2,000 words, with useful information on real estate, retirement, investing, shopping, travel, employment, education, and lifestyles overseas. Pays $100 to $400, after publication.

ISLANDS—P.O. Box 4728, Santa Barbara, CA 93140-4728. Joan Tapper, Ed.-in-Chief. Destination features, 2,500 to 4,000 words, on islands around the world as well as department pieces and front-of-the-book items on island-related topics. Pays from 50¢ a word, on acceptance. Query with clips required. Guidelines.

JOURNEYS—5301 S. Federal Circle, Littleton, CO 80123. Kara Skruck, Ed. Annual. Departments, 800 words, and features, 1,800 words, on destinations. "Our readers are mature and well-traveled." Query with clips and list of potential cities/countries. Pays 50¢ per word, on acceptance.

MAIDEN VOYAGES—109 Minna St., Suite 240, San Francisco, CA 94105. Nanette C-Lee, Ed. Quarterly. "The Indispensable Guide to Women's Travel." Articles, to 1,500 words, and departments, to 600 words. "Heartfelt and transformative articles in a strong 'female' voice, and sweaty adventure tales." Pays $50 for articles, $35 for departments, on acceptance. Query.

MICHIGAN LIVING—Automobile Club of Michigan, 1 Auto Club Dr., Dearborn, MI 48126. Ron Garbinski, Ed. Informative travel articles, 300 to 2,000 words, on U.S. and Canadian tourist attractions and recreational opportunities; special interest in Michigan. Pays $55 to $500 (rates vary for photos), on acceptance.

MOUNTAIN LIVING MAGAZINE—7009 S. Potomac, Englewood, CO 80112. Robyn Griggs, Ed. Travel articles, 1,200 to 1,500 words, on cities, regions, establishments in the mountainous regions of the world. Pays $200 to $300, on acceptance.

NATIONAL GEOGRAPHIC—1145 17th St. N.W., Washington, DC 20036. William L. Allen, Ed. First-person articles on geography, exploration, natural history, archaeology, and science: 40% staff-written; 60% written by published authors. Does not consider unsolicited manuscripts.

NATIONAL MOTORIST—National Automobile Club, 1151 E. Hillside Blvd., Foster City, CA 94404. Jane Offers, Ed. Quarterly. Illustrated articles, 500 to 1,100 words, for California motorists, on motoring in the West, domestic and international travel, car care, roads, personalities, places, etc. Color slides. Pays from 10¢ a word, on acceptance. Pays for photos on publication. SASE required.

NAVY TIMES—See *Times News Service.*

NEW YORK DAILY NEWS— 450 W. 33rd St., New York, NY 10001. Gunna Bitee Dickson, Travel Ed. Articles, 700 to 900 words, on all manner of travel. Price information must be included. B&W or color photos or slides. Pays $100 to $200 (extra for photos), on publication.

THE NEW YORK TIMES—229 W. 43rd St., New York, NY 10036. Nancy Newhouse, Travel Ed. Query with SASE required; include writer's background, description of proposed article. Pays on acceptance.

NORTHWEST REGIONAL MAGAZINES—P.O. Box 18000, Florence, OR 97439. Attn: Judy Fleagle or Jim Forst. All submissions considered for use in *Oregon Coast* and *Northwest Travel*. Articles, 800 to 2,000 words, on travel, history, town/city profiles, outdoor activities, events, and nature. News releases, 200 to 500 words. Articles with slides preferred. Pays $50 to $300, after publication. Guidelines with SASE.

NORTHWEST TRAVEL—See *Northwest Regional Magazines.*

OREGON COAST—See *Northwest Regional Magazines.*

OREGON OUTSIDE—Northwest Regional Magazines, Box 18000, 1525 12th St., Florence, OR 97439-0130. Judy Fleagle, Jim Forst, Eds. Quarterly. Articles, 1,000 to 1,500 words, on Oregon and the outdoors, "all kinds of adventure, from walks for families to extreme skiing." Prefers to receive manuscript/photo packages. Pays $100 to $350, on publication. Query.

OUT WEST: THE NEWSPAPER THAT ROAMS— 9792 Edmonds Way, Suite 265, Edmonds, WA 98020. Chuck Woodbury, Ed./Pub. Entertaining and informative articles, 150 to 500 words, and short pieces, 30 to 75 words, on the rural West (not the old West): interesting people, unusual places to stay, offbeat attractions. "Send for a sample of the paper before you submit." Pays about 5¢ a word, on publication.

OUTDOOR TRAVELER, MID-ATLANTIC—WMS Publications, Inc., P.O. Box 2748, Charlottesville, VA 22902. Marianne Marks, Ed. Tom Gillespie, Assoc. Ed. Quarterly. Articles, 1,500 to 2,000 words, on hiking/backpacking, canoeing/kayaking/rafting, camping, mountain biking, road cycling, travel, nature, and the environment from New York state to North Carolina. Travel articles on destinations and areas that offer recreational opportunities. Departments include "Destinations," 450 to 600 words, on practical and descriptive guides to sports destinations; book and product reviews. Pays $300 to $400 for features; payment varies for departments, on publication. Guidelines.

ROUTE 66 MAGAZINE—326 W. Route 66, Williams, AZ 86046-2427. Paul Taylor, Ed. Articles, 1,500 to 2,000 words, on travel and life along Route 66 between Chicago and Los Angeles. Also, fillers, jokes, and puzzles, for the Children's Page. B&W photographs. Pays $20 per column, 45 days after publication. Query.

SACRAMENTO MAGAZINE— 4471 D St., Sacramento, CA 95819. Krista Hendricks Minard, Ed. Articles, 1,000 to 1,500 words, on destinations within a 6-hour drive of Sacramento. Pay varies, on publication. Query.

SPECIALTY TRAVEL INDEX—305 San Anselmo Ave., #313, San Anselmo, CA 94960. C. Steen Hansen, Co-Pub./Ed. Semiannual directory of adventure vacation tour companies, destinations, and vacation packages. Articles, 1,250 words, with special-interest, adventure type travel accounts and information. Pays 20¢ per word, on receipt of complete materials. Slides and photos considered. Queries preferred.

TEXAS HIGHWAYS MAGAZINE—P.O. Box 141009, Austin, TX 78714-1009. Jack Lowry, Ed. Travel, historical, cultural, scenic features on Texas, 200 to 1,800 words. Pays about 40¢ to 50¢ a word; photos $80 to $400. Guidelines.

TIMES NEWS SERVICE—Army Times Publishing Co., Springfield, VA 22159. Attn: R&R Ed. Travel articles, 700 words, on places of special interest to military people for use in "R&R" newspaper section. "We like travel articles to focus on a single destination but with short sidebar covering other things to see in the area." Pays $100, on acceptance. Pays $35 for original color slides or prints. Also, travel pieces, 1,000 words, for supplements to *Army Times*, *Navy Times*, and *Air Force Times*. Address Supplements Ed. Pays $125 to $200, on acceptance. Guidelines.

TRANSITIONS ABROAD—18 Hulst Rd., Box 1300, Amherst, MA 01004-1300. David Cline, Man. Ed. Articles for overseas travelers of all ages who seek an enriching, in-depth experience of the culture: work, study, travel, budget tips. Include practical, first-hand information. Emphasis on travel for personal enrichment. "Eager to work with inexperienced writers who want to share information not usually found in guidebooks. High percentage of material is from free lancers. Also seeking articles from writers with special expertise on cultural travel opportunites for specific types of travelers: seniors, students, families, etc." B&W photos a plus. Pays $1.50 per column inch, after publication. SASE required for guidelines and editorial calendar.

TRAVEL AMERICA—World Publishing Co., 990 Grove St., Evanston, IL 60201-4370. Randy Mink, Man. Ed. Robert Meyers, Ed. Features, 800 to 1,200 words, on U.S. vacation destinations. Pays up to $300, on acceptance. Top-quality color slides a must. Query.

TRAVEL & LEISURE—1120 Ave. of the Americas, New York, NY 10036. Nancy Novogrod, Ed.-in-Chief. Articles, 800 to 3,000 words, on destinations and travel-related activities. Short pieces for "Strategies" and "T&L Reports." Pays on acceptance: $2,500 to $5,000 for features; $750 to $1,500 for departments; $50 to $300 for short pieces. Query; articles on assignment.

TRAVEL SMART—Dobbs Ferry, NY 10522. Attn: Ed. Short pieces, 250 to 1,000 words, about interesting, unusual and/or economical places. Give specific details on hotels, restaurants, transportation, and costs. Pays on publication. "Send manila envelope with 2 first-class stamps for copy and guidelines." Query on longer pieces.

TRAVELERS' TALES, INC.—P.O. Box 610160, Redwood City, CA 94061. Attn: Ed. Personal travel stories and anecdotes, to 10 pages, for book anthologies focused on a particular country or theme. Payment varies, on publication. Guidelines.

WESTWAYS—P.O. Box 25001, Santa Ana, CA 92799-5001. Attn: Ed. Travel articles, 1,300 to 2,500 words, on southern California, the West, domestic and foreign destinations. Pays $1 a word, on acceptance.

INFLIGHT MAGAZINES

ABOARD—100 Almeria Ave., Suite 220, Coral Gables, FL 33134. Attn: Ed. Dept. Inflight magazine of 11 Latin American international airlines in Chile, Dominican Republic, Ecuador, Guatemala, El Salvador, Bolivia, Nicaragua, Honduras, Uruguay, and Paraguay. Articles, 1,200 to 1,500 words, with photos, on these countries and on science, sports, technology, adventure, wildlife, fashion, business, ecology, and gastronomy. No political stories. Pays $100 for articles; $100 for photos; $150 for articles with photos, on acceptance and on publication. Query.

ALASKA AIRLINES MAGAZINE—2701 First Ave., Suite 250, Seattle, WA 98121. Paul Frichtl, Ed. Articles, 250 to 2,500 words, on business, travel, and profiles of regional personalities for West Coast business travelers. Payment varies, on publication. Query.

AMERICA WEST AIRLINES MAGAZINE—Skyword Marketing Inc., 4636 E. Elwood St., Suite 5, Phoenix, AZ 85040-1963. Michael Derr, Ed. Business articles, destination pieces, arts and culture, 500 to 2,000 words; thoughtful but light essays. Pays from $250, on publication. Clips and SASE required. Guidelines. Very limited market.

AMERICAN WAY—P.O. Box 619640, Mail Drop 5598, DFW Airport, 4333 Amon Carter Blvd., Fort Worth, TX 76155. John Ostdick, Ed. American Airlines' inflight magazine. Send short stories, up to 2,500 words, to Fiction Ed. No unsolicited nonfiction material.

HEMISPHERES—1301 Carolina St., Greensboro, NC 27401. Randy Johnson, Ed. United Airlines inflight magazine. Articles, 1,200 to 1,500 words, on business, investing, travel, sports, family, food and wine, etc., that inform and entertain sophisticated, well-traveled readers. "The magazine strives for a unique global perspective presented in a fresh, strong, and artful graphic environment." Pays good rates, on acceptance. Query. Guidelines with SASE.

HORIZON AIR MAGAZINE—2701 First Ave., #250, Seattle, WA 98121-1123. Todd Powell, Ed. Business and travel articles on the companies, people, issues, and trends that define the Northwest. News items, 200 to 500 words, and profiles for "The Region" section. Other departments pieces, 1,600 words, cover corporate and industry profiles, regional issue analysis, travel, and community profiles. Pays $100 to $600, on publication.

US AIRWAYS ATTACHÉ—(formerly *USAIR Magazine*) 1301 Carolina St., Greensboro, NC 27401. Articles, 400 to 2,500 words, on "the finer things in life." Paragons department offers short pieces touting the best of the best; Informed Sources department contains experts' opinions and knowledge on a variety of topics. No politics or Hollywood issues. Pays $1 a word, on acceptance.

USAIR MAGAZINE—See *US Airways Attaché*.

WOMEN'S PUBLICATIONS

ASPIRE—107 Kenner Ave., Nashville, TN 37205. Jeanette Thomason, Ed.-in-Chief. Lifestyle magazine for Christian women. Articles, 500 to 2,000 words, on trends in health, career issues, parenting, and relationships, "inspiring and encouraging readers to incorporate faith into daily life." Pays 30¢ a word, on acceptance. Query with resumé and clips. SASE for guidelines.

BBW: BIG BEAUTIFUL WOMAN— 8484 Wilshire Blvd., Suite 900, Beverly Hills, CA 90211. Theresa Flynt-Gaerke, Pub. Dir. Articles, 1,500 words, of interest to women ages 25 to 50, especially large-size women, including interviews with successful large-size women and personal accounts of how to cope with difficult situations. Tips on restaurants, airlines, stores, etc., that treat large women with respect. Payment varies, on publication. Query.

BRIDAL GUIDE—Globe Communications Corp., 3 E. 54th St., New York, NY 10022. Diane Forden, Ed.-in-Chief. Laurie Bain Wilson, Travel Ed. Bimonthly. Articles, 1,500 to 3,000 words, on wedding planning, relationships, sexuality, health and nutrition, psychology, travel, and finance. No beauty, fashion articles; no fiction, essays, poetry. Pays on acceptance. Query with SASE.

BRIDE'S—140 E. 45th St., New York, NY 10017. Sally Kilbridge, Man. Ed. Articles, 800 to 3,000 words, for engaged couples or newlyweds, on wedding planning, relationships, communication, sex, decorating, finances, careers, remarriage, health, birth control, religion, in-laws. Major editorial subjects: home, wedding, and honeymoon (send honeymoon queries to Travel Dept.). No fiction or poetry. Pays from 50¢ a word, on acceptance.

COMPLETE WOMAN— 875 N. Michigan Ave., Suite 3434, Chicago, IL 60611. Bonnie L. Krueger, Ed. Lora Wintz, Sr. Ed. Articles, 1,000 to 2,000 words, with how-to sidebars, giving practical advice to women on love, sex, careers, health, personal relationships, etc. Also interested in reprints. Pays varying rates, on publication. Query with clips.

COSMOPOLITAN—224 W. 57th St., New York, NY 10019. Kate White, Ed. Betty Nichols Kelly, Fiction and Books Ed. Articles, to 3,000 words, and features, 500 to 2,000 words, on issues affecting young career women, with emphasis on jobs and personal life. Fiction on male-female relationships: short shorts, 1,500 to 3,000 words; short stories, 3,000 to 4,000 words; condensed published novels, 25,000 words. SASE required. Payment varies.

COUNTRY WOMAN—P.O. Box 989, Greendale, WI 53129. Kathy Pohl, Man. Ed. Profiles of country women (photo-feature packages), inspirational, reflective pieces. Personal-experience, nostalgia, humor, service-oriented articles, original crafts, and how-to features, to 1,000 words, of interest to country women. Pays $25 to $75 for crafts, humor, nostalgia; pays $150 for photo-features, on acceptance.

ELLE—1633 Broadway, New York, NY 10019. Amy Gross, Ed. Dir. Articles, varying lengths, for fashion-conscious women, ages 20 to 50. Subjects include beauty, health, fitness, travel, entertainment, and lifestyles. Pays top rates, on publication. Query required.

ESSENCE—1500 Broadway, New York, NY 10036. Susan L. Taylor, Ed.-in-Chief. Monique Greenwood, Exec. Ed. Provocative articles, 800 to 2,500 words, about black women in America today: self-help, how-to pieces, business and finance, work, parenting, health, celebrity profiles, art, travel, and political issues. Fiction, 800 to 2,500 words. Pays varying rates, on acceptance. Query for articles.

EXECUTIVE FEMALE—135 W. 50th St., New York, NY 10020. Fayne Erickson, President. Articles, 750 to 2,500 words, on managing people, time, money, companies, and careers, for women in business. Pays varying rates, on acceptance. Query.

FAMILY CIRCLE—375 Lexington Ave., New York, NY 10017. Nancy Clark, Deputy Ed. Articles, to 2,000 words, on "women who have made a difference," marriage, family, and child-care and elder-care issues; consumer affairs, psychology, humor, health, nutrition, and fitness. Pays top rates, on acceptance. Query required.

FIT PREGNANCY—21100 Erwin St., Woodland Hills, CA 91367-3712. Peg Moline, Ed. Articles, 500 to 2,000 words, on pregnant women's health, sports, and physical fitness. No fiction or poetry. Payment varies, on publication. Query.

GLAMOUR—350 Madison Ave., New York, NY 10017. Mary Hickey, Articles Ed. Bonnie Fuller, Ed.-in-Chief. Laurie Sprague, Man. Ed. Articles, from 1,000 words, on careers, health, psychology, politics, current events, interpersonal relationships, etc., for women ages 18 to 35. Fashion, entertainment, travel, food, and beauty pieces staff-written. Pays from $500, on acceptance. Query Articles Ed.

GOOD HOUSEKEEPING—959 Eighth Ave., New York, NY 10019. Evelyn Renold, Articles Ed. Lee Quarfoot, Fiction Ed. Articles, about 2,500 words, for married working women with children, 18 and younger. Social issues, dramatic personal narratives, medical news, marriage, friendship, psychology, crime, finances, work, parenting, and consumer issues. Best places to break in: "Better Way" (short, advice-driven takes on health, money, safety, and consumer issues) and profiles (short takes on interesting or heroic women or families). No submissions on food, beauty, needlework, or crafts. Short stories, 2,000 to 5,000 words, with strong identification for women. Unsolicited fiction not returned; if no response in 6 weeks, assume work was unsuitable. Pays top rates, on acceptance. Guidelines. Query with SASE for nonfiction.

HARPER'S BAZAAR—1700 Broadway, 37th Fl., New York, NY 10019. Elizabeth Tilberis, Ed.-in-Chief. Articles, 1,500 to 2,500 words, for active, sophisticated women: the arts, world affairs, travel, families, education, careers, health, and sexuality. Payment varies, on acceptance. No unsolicited manuscripts; query with SASE.

IRIS: A JOURNAL ABOUT WOMEN—The Women's Ctr., Box 323, HSC, Univ. of Virginia, Charlottesville, VA 22908. Susan K. Brady, Ed. Semiannual. Fiction, 2,500 to 8,000 words; book reviews, 900 words for a single book, 1,500 words for combined review; articles, 2,500 to 4,500 words; poetry, any length; personal essays to 2,500 words; photos and art essays and short humor. All material must focus on women's issues. Pays in subscription.

THE JOYFUL WOMAN—P.O. Box 90028, Chattanooga, TN 37412. Joy Rice Martin, Ed. Joanna Rice, Ed. Asst. Fiction, 500 to 1,000 words, for women with a "Christian commitment." Also first-person inspirational true stories, profiles of Christian women, practical and Bible-oriented how-to articles. Pays 3¢ to 4¢ a word, on publication. Queries required.

LADIES' HOME JOURNAL—125 Park Ave., New York, NY 10017. Myrna Blyth, Pub. Dir./Ed.-in-Chief. Articles of interest to women. Send queries to: Susan Crandell, Exec. Ed. (news/general interest); Elena Rover, Ed. (health/medical); Melina Gerosa, Sr. Ed. (celebrity/entertainment); Pamela Guthrie O'Brien, Features Ed. (sex/psychology); Lois Johnson, Beauty Dir. (beauty/fashion/fitness); Jan Hazard, Food Ed.; Shana Aborn, Features Ed. (personal experience); Mary Mohler, Sr. Ed. (children and families). Fiction accepted through literary agents only. True, first-person accounts, 1,000 words, "about the most intimate aspects of our lives" for anonymous "Woman to Woman": Submit typed, double-spaced manuscript with SASE to Box WW, c/o address above; pays $750. Guidelines.

MCCALL'S—375 Lexington Ave., New York, NY 10017. Attn: Articles Ed. Human-interest, self-help, social issues, and popular psychology articles, 1,200 to 2,000 words. Also publishes "Couples," first person essays, 1,400 words; "Families," how-to articles, 1,400 words; "Health Sense," short newsy items; and "Medical Report," health-related items, 1,200 words. Query with SASE. Payment varies, on acceptance.

MADEMOISELLE—350 Madison Ave., New York, NY 10017. Faye Haun, Man. Ed. Articles, 1,500 to 2,500 words, on work, relationships, health, and trends of interest to single, working women in their early to mid-twenties. Reporting pieces, essays, first-person accounts, and humor. No fiction. Submit query with clips and SASE. Pays excellent rates, on acceptance.

MAIDEN VOYAGES—109 Minna St., Suite 240, San Francisco, CA 94105. Nanette C-Lee, Ed. Quarterly. "The Indispensable Guide to Women's Travel." Articles, to 2,000 words, and departments, to 600 words. "Heartfelt and transformative articles in a strong 'female' voice, and sweaty adventure tales." Pays $75 for articles, $50 for departments, on acceptance. Query.

MIRABELLA—1633 Broadway, New York, NY 10019. Roberta Myers, Ed. Articles, varying lengths, for fashion-conscious women, ages 20 to 50. Subjects include beauty, health, fitness, travel, entertainment, and lifestyles. Pays top rates, on publication. Querywith clips.

MODERN BRIDE—249 W. 17th St., New York, NY 10011. Mary Ann Cavlin, Exec. Ed. Articles, 1,500 to 2,000 words, for bride and groom, on wedding planning, financial planning, juggling career and home, etc. Pays $600 to $1,200, on acceptance.

MODERNA—98 San Jacinto Blvd., Suite 1150, Austin, TX 78701. Valerie Menard, Sr. Ed. Bilingual quarterly. Articles, 1,200 to 3,000 words, on fashion, health and fitness, relationships, parenting, recipes, travel, and film and book reviews. Department pieces, 500 to 750 words, on travel, cards, health, food, and personal essays. No fiction or poetry. Pays $200 to $300 for features; $100 for department pieces, on publication.

MS.—135 W. 50th St., 16th Fl., New York, NY 10020-1201. Attn: Manuscript Ed. Articles relating to feminism, women's roles, and social change; national and international news reporting, profiles, essays, theory, and analysis. No fiction or poetry accepted, acknowledged, or returned. Query with resumé and published clips.

NA'AMAT WOMAN—200 Madison Ave., Suite 2120, New York, NY 10016. Judith A. Sokoloff, Ed. Articles on Jewish culture, women's issues, social and political topics, and Israel, 1,500 to 3,000 words. Short stories with a Jewish theme. Pays 10¢ a word, on publication.

NATURAL LIVING TODAY—175 Varick St., 9th Fl., New York, NY 10014. Attn: Ed. Dept. Bimonthly. Articles, 1,000 to 2,000 words, on all aspects of a natural lifestyle for women. Pays $75 to $200, on publication. Query.

NEW WOMAN—2 Park Ave., 11th Fl., New York, NY 10016. Attn: Manuscripts and Proposals. Articles for women ages 25 to 49, on self-discovery, self-development, and self-esteem. Features: relationships, careers, health and fitness, money, fashion, beauty, food and nutrition, travel features with self-growth angle, and essays by and about women pacesetters. Pays about $1 a word, on acceptance. Query with SASE.

ON THE ISSUES—Merle Hoffman Enterprises Ltd., 97-77 Queens Blvd., Suite 1120, Forest Hills, NY 11374-3317. Jan Goodwin, Ed. "The Progressive Woman's Quarterly." Articles, to 2,500 words, on political or social issues. Movie, music, and book reviews, 500 to 750 words. Payment varies, on publication. Query.

ORANGE COUNTY WOMAN—3701 Birch St., #100, Newport Beach, CA 92660-2618. Janine Robinson, Ed. First-person fiction, 1,000 to 1,500 words, and articles, 500 to 1,500 words, for women living in Orange County, CA. "Our readers are highly educated, upscale women who are looking for information that will make their lives more efficient and gratifying. We cover everything from family issues to health and beauty." SASE for guidelines. Payment is $50 to $250, on acceptance.

PLAYGIRL— 801 Second Ave., New York, NY 10017. Ceslie Armstrong, Ed.-in-Chief. Send queries to: Charlene Keel Razack, Man. Ed. Erotic entertainment for women. Insightful articles on sexuality and romance; sizzling fiction, humor, and in-depth celebrity interviews of interest to contemporary women. Pays varying rates, after acceptance. Query with clips. Guidelines.

RADIANCE: THE MAGAZINE FOR LARGE WOMEN—P.O. Box 30246, Oakland, CA 94604. Alice Ansfield, Ed./Pub. Quarterly. "A magazine for body acceptance." Articles, 1,500 to 3,500 words, that provide information, inspiration, and resources for women all sizes of large. Features include information on health, media, fashion, and politics that relate to issues of body size. Fiction and poetry also welcome. Pays $35 to $100, on publication.

REDBOOK—224 W. 57th St., New York, NY 10019. Pamela Lister, Susan Gifford, Sr. Eds. Dawn Raffel, Fiction Ed. Toni Hope, Sr. Ed. For mothers, ages 25 to 45. Short stories, 10 to 15 typed pages; dramatic inspirational narratives, 1,000 to 2,000 words. SASE required. Pays on acceptance. Query with writing samples for articles. Guidelines.

SAGEWOMAN—P.O. Box 641, Point Arena, CA 95468-0641. Anne Newkirk Niven, Ed. Quarterly. Articles, 200 to 5,000 words, on issues of concern to pagan and spiritually minded women. Material which expresses an earth-centered spirituality: personal experience, Goddess lore, ritual material, interviews, humor, and reviews. Accepts material by women only. Pays 2¢ a word, from $10, on publication.

SELF—350 Madison Ave., New York, NY 10017. Attn: Ed. "We no longer accept unsolicited manuscripts or queries."

TODAY'S CHRISTIAN WOMAN— 465 Gundersen Dr., Carol Stream, IL 60188. Ramona Cramer Tucker, Ed. Articles, 1,500 to 1,800 words, that are "warm and personal in tone, full of real-life anecdotes that deal with marriage, parenting, friendship, spiritual life, single life, health, work, and self." Humorous anecdotes, 150 words, that have a Christian slant. Payment varies, on acceptance. Queries required. Guidelines.

VIRTUE: HELPING WOMEN BUILD CHRIST-LIKE CHARACTER— (formerly *Virtue: The Christian Magazine for Women*) 4050 Lee Vance View, Colorado Springs, CO 80918-7102. Laura J. Barker, Ed. Articles and fiction, 200 to 1,400 words, on family, marriage, self-esteem, working women, humor, women's spiritual journeys, issues, relationship with family, friends and God. "Provocative, meaningful stories, especially those with bold messages shown in gracious ways." Pays 15¢ to 25¢ a word for articles; $25 to $50 for poetry, on publication. Submit up to 3 poems at a time. Query with SASE required.

VOGUE—350 Madison Ave., New York, NY 10017. Attn: Features Ed. Articles, to 1,500 words, on women, entertainment and the arts, travel, medicine, and health. General features. Pays good rates, on acceptance. Query; no unsolicited manuscripts.

WOMAN'S DAY—1633 Broadway, New York, NY 10019. Stephanie Abarbanel, Sr. Articles Ed. Human-interest or helpful articles, 750 to 1,200 words, on marriage, child-rearing, health, careers, relationships, money management. Dramatic first-person narratives of medical miracles, rescues, women's experiences, etc. "We respond to queries promptly; unsolicited manuscripts are returned unread." SASE. Pays top rates, on acceptance.

WOMAN'S TOUCH—1445 Boonville Ave., Springfield, MO 65802-1894. Peggy Musgrove, Ed. Aleda Swartzendruber, Man. Ed. Inspirational articles, 500 to 800 words, for Christian women. Pays on publication. Allow 3 months for response. Submit complete manuscript. Guidelines and editorial calendar.

WOMAN'S WORLD—270 Sylvan Ave., Englewood Cliffs, NJ 07632. Andrea Bien, Feature Ed. Articles, 600 to 1,800 words, of interest to middle-income women between the ages of 18 and 60, on love, romance, careers, medicine, health, psychology, family life, travel; dramatic stories of adventure or crisis, investigative reports. Fast-moving short stories, about 1,900 words, with light romantic theme. (Specify "short story" on outside of envelope.) Mini-mysteries, 1,200 words, with "whodunit" or "howdunit" theme. No science fiction, fantasy, horror, ghost stories, or gratuitous violence. Pays $300 to $900 for articles; $1,000 for short stories; $500 for mini-mysteries, on acceptance. Query for articles. Guidelines.

WOMEN IN BUSINESS—American Business Women's Assn., 9100 Ward Pkwy., Box 8728, Kansas City, MO 64114-0728. Elaine Minter, Ed.-in-Chief. Currently overstocked; not accepting any new material.

WOMEN'S SPORTS & FITNESS—2025 Pearl St., Boulder, CO 80302. Dagny Scott, Ed. Articles on fitness, nutrition, outdoor sports; how-tos; profiles; adventure travel pieces; and controversial issues in women's sports, 500 to 2,000 words. Pays on acceptance.

WORKING MOTHER—MacDonald Communications, 135 W. 50th St., 16th Fl., New York, NY 10020. Attn: Ed. Dept. Articles, to 2,000 words, that help women in their task of juggling job, home, and family. "We like pieces that solve or illuminate a problem unique to our readers." Payment varies, on acceptance.

WORKING WOMAN—135 W. 50th St., Suite 16, New York, NY 10020-1201. Articles, 200 to 1,500 words, on business and finance. "Our readers are high level executives and entrepreneurs who are looking for newsworthy information about the changing marketplace and its effects on their businesses and careers. Query. Pays from $300, on acceptance.

MEN'S PUBLICATIONS

ESQUIRE—250 W. 55th St., New York, NY 10019. David Granger, Ed.-in-Chief. Peter Griffin, Deputy Ed. Articles, 2,500 to 4,000 words, for intelligent audience. Pays varying rates, on acceptance. Query with clips and SASE.

FITNESS PLUS—12 W. 27th St., New York, NY 10001-6903. Steve Romondi, Ed. Bimonthly. Articles, 1,000 to 3,000 words, on serious health and fitness training for men. Payment varies, on publication. Queries preferred.

GALLERY— 401 Park Ave. S., New York, NY 10016-8802. Marc Medoff, Ed. Dir. Rich Friedman, Man. Ed. Articles, investigative pieces, interviews, profiles, to 2,500 words, for sophisticated men. Short humor, satire, service pieces, and fiction. Photos. Query. Guidelines.

GENRE—7080 Hollywood Blvd., Suite 1104, Hollywood, CA 90028. Mark Olmsted, Assoc. Ed. Fiction, 3,000 to 5,000 words, and articles, 750 to

3,000 words, of interest to gay men. "Feature articles should be national in scope and somehow related to the gay male experience." Pays $100 to $400 an article, on publication.

GQ—350 Madison Ave., New York, NY 10017. No free-lance queries or manuscripts.

MEN'S HEALTH—Rodale Press, 33 E. Minor St., Emmaus, PA 18098. Stephen Perrine, Deputy Ed. Articles, 1,000 to 2,500 words, on fitness, diet, health, relationships, sports, and travel for men ages 25 to 55. Pays from 50¢ a word, on acceptance. Query.

NEW MAN—600 Rinehart Rd., Lake Mary, FL 32746. Brian Peterson, Ed. No longer accepting unsolicited manuscripts.

PENTHOUSE—277 Park Ave., 4th Fl., New York, NY 10172-0003. Peter Bloch, Ed. Lavada B. Nahon, Sr. Ed. General-interest profiles, interviews, or investigative articles, to 5,000 words. No unsolicited fiction. Pays on acceptance.

PLAYBOY—680 N. Lake Shore Dr., Chicago, IL 60611. Stephen Randall, Ed. Articles, 3,500 to 6,000 words, and sophisticated fiction, 1,000 to 10,000 words (5,000 preferred), for urban men. (Address fiction to Attn: Fiction Ed.) Humor; satire. Science fiction. Pays to $5,000 for articles and fiction, $2,000 for short-shorts, on acceptance. SASE required.

PRIME HEALTH & FITNESS—21100 Erwin St., Woodland Hills, CA 91367. Bill Bush, Exec. Ed. Quarterly. Articles, 1,200 to 1,800 words, and department pieces, 600 to 800 words, on health and fitness challenges and lifestyle activities for men over 40.

ROBB REPORT—1 Acton Pl., Acton, MA 01720. Steven Castle, Ed. Upscale lifestyle magazine for the affluent. Feature articles and regular columns on investment opportunities, exotic cars, classic and collectible autos, yachts, fashion, travel, collectibles, technology, profiles, etc., emphasizing luxurious lifestyles. Pays on publication. Query with SASE and clips.

SENIORS MAGAZINES

AARP BULLETIN—601 E St. N.W., Washington, DC 20049. Elliot Carlson, Ed. Publication of the American Association of Retired Persons. Payment varies, on acceptance. Query required.

GET UP & GO!—(formerly *Senior Highlights*) 500 Fesler St., Ste. 101, El Cajon, CA 92020. Laura Impastato, Ed. Articles, 800 to 1,000 words, for active, older adults (50+); focus is on Southern California. Articles on local, state and national news. Features about celebrities, remarkable seniors, consumer interest, finance and investment, housing, sports, hobbies, collectibles, trends, travel, etc. Health and medicine articles emphasizing wellness, preventive care, and the latest on medical treatments. Pays $75 to $100, on publication. Limited freelance, mostly staff written.

GOOD TIMES—Senior Publications, Inc., 5148 Saint-Laurent Blvd., Montreal, Quebec, Canada H2T 1R8. Denise B. Crawford, Ed.-in-Chief. "The

Canadian Magazine for Successful Retirement." Celebrity profiles as well as practical articles on health, beauty, cuisine, hobbies, fashion, leisure activities, travel, taxes, legal rights, consumer protection, etc. Canadian content only. Payment varies. Query.

GOOD TIMES—Robert Morris Bldg., 100 N. 17th St., 9th Fl., Philadelphia, PA 19103. Karen Detwiler, Ed.-in-Chief. Mature lifestyle magazine for the 50 years and older population in Pennsylvania and Illinois. Articles, 1,500 to 2,000 words, on medical issues, health, travel, finance, fashion, gardening, fitness, legal issues, celebrities, lifestyles, and relationships. Payment varies, on publication. Query with samples and resumé.

LIFE LINES MAGAZINE—129 N. 10th St., Rm. 418, Lincoln, NE 68508-3627. Dena Rust Zimmer, Ed. Short stories, "Sports and Hobbies," "Remember When...," "Travels With...," and "Perspectives on Aging," to 450 words. Poetry, to 50 lines. Fillers and short humor, "the shorter the better." No payment.

MATURE LIFESTYLES—P.O. Box 44327, Madison, WI 53744. Sue Sveum, Ed. "South Central Wisconsin's Newspaper for the Active 50-Plus Population." Syndicated national coverage and local free lance.

MATURE LIVING—127 Ninth Ave. N., Nashville, TN 37234-0140. Al Shackleford, Ed. Fiction and human-interest articles, to 1,200 words, for senior adults. Must be consistent with Christian principles. Payment varies, on acceptance.

MATURE OUTLOOK—Meredith Corp., 1716 Locust St., Des Moines, IA 50309. Peggy Person, Ed. Bimonthly. Upbeat, contemporary articles, varying lengths, for readers 50 and older travel and leisure topics. Regular topics include health, money, food, travel, leisure, and stories of real people, 75 to 2,000 words. Pays $50 to $1,500, on acceptance. Query required. Guidelines.

MATURE YEARS—201 Eighth Ave. S., P.O. Box 801, Nashville, TN 37202. Marvin W. Cropsey, Ed. Articles of interest to older adults: health and fitness, personal finance, hobbies and inspiration. Anecdotes, to 300 words, poems, cartoons, jokes, and puzzles for older adults. "A Christian magazine that seeks to build faith. We always show older adults in a favorable light." Include name, address, and social security number with all submissions. Allow 2 months for response.

MILESTONES—246 S. 22nd St., Philadelphia, PA 19103. Robert Epp, Dir. Cathy Green, Ed. Tabloid published 10 times a year. News articles and features, 750 to 1,000 words, on humor, personalities, political issues, etc., for readers 50 and older. Articles are written by staff and local writers only.

MODERN MATURITY—601 E. St. N.W., Washington, DC 20049. J. Henry Fenwick, Ed. Articles, to 2,000 words, on careers, workplace, human interest, living, finance, relationships, and consumerism for readers over 50. Query. Pays $500 to $2,500, on acceptance.

NEW CHOICES: LIVING EVEN BETTER AFTER 50—28 W. 23rd St., New York, NY 10010. Greg Daugherty, Ed.-in-Chief. Service magazine for people ages 50 to retirement. Articles on health, personal finance, and travel. Payment varies, on acceptance. Query.

NEW JERSEY 50+ PLUS—1830 US Rt. 9, Toms River, NJ 08755-1210. Pat Jasin, Ed. Articles on finance, health, travel, and social issues for older readers. Pays in copies. Query required.

THE RETIRED OFFICER MAGAZINE—201 N. Washington St., Alexandria, VA 22314. Attn: Manuscripts Ed. Articles, 800 to 2,000 words, of interest to military members and their families. Current military/political affairs, recent military history (especially Vietnam and Korea), military family lifestyles, health, money, second careers. Photos a plus. Pays to $1,300, on acceptance. Queries required. Guidelines. E-mail: editor@troa.org.

SENIOR HIGHLIGHTS—See *Get Up & Go!*

SENIOR MAGAZINE—3565 S. Higuera St., San Luis Obispo, CA 93401. Attn: Ed. Articles, 900 to 1,200 words, of interest to men and women 40+; personality profiles, travel pieces, articles about new things, places, business, sports, movies, television, and health. Reviews of new or outstanding older books. Pays $1.50 per inch; $10 to $25 for B&W photos, on publication.

SENIOR TIMES—Suite 814, 1102 Pleasant St., Worcester, MA 01602-1232. Edwin H. Gledhill, Ed. Short stories, historial or people oriented, 500 to 1,200 words. Articles, 500 to 1,200 words, on arts, travel, local interest, entertainment, and positive role models for aging. Poetry, 10 to 200 words. No payment.

YESTERDAY'S MAGAZETTE—P.O. Box 18566, Sarasota, FL 34276. Ned Burke, Ed. Articles and stories, 500 to 1,000 words, set in the 1920s to '70s. Photos a plus. Traditional poetry, to 24 lines. Pays $5 to $25 for articles, on publication. Pays in copies for short pieces and poetry.

HOME & GARDEN/FOOD & WINE

THE AMERICAN COTTAGE GARDENER—P.O. Box 22232, Santa Fe, NM 87502-2232. Rand B. Lee, Ed. Quarterly. Articles, 750 to 3,000 words for cottage gardeners: how-to; plant profiles of specific genera or cultivars; interviews with noted or experienced cottage gardeners, plant breeders, and other specialists. "Topics we're always interested in: regional and ethnic cottage gardening, unusual plants adaptable to the cottage gardening style, fruits and vegetables in the ornamental plot." Pays $25 per printed page of article plus 3 copies. Queries required.

THE AMERICAN GARDENER—7931 E. Boulevard Dr., Alexandria, VA 22308-1300. David J. Ellis, Ed. Bimonthly. Articles, to 2,500 words, for American ornamental gardeners: profiles of prominent horticulturists, plant research and plant hunting, events and personalities in horticulture history, plant lore and literature, the politics of horticulture, etc. Humorous pieces for "Offshoots." "We run very few how-to articles." Pays $100 to $500, on publication. Query with SASE preferred.

AMERICAN HOMESTYLE & GARDENING—110 Fifth Ave., New York, NY 10011. Karen Saks, Ed.-in-Chief. Articles on interior design, remodeling, architecture, gardening, and the decorative arts. Payment varies, on acceptance. Query.

AMERICAN ROSE—P.O. Box 30,000, Shreveport, LA 71130. Beth Horstman, Man. Ed. Articles on home rose gardens: varieties, products, helpful advice, rose care, etc.

APPELLATION—1700 Soscol Ave., Suite 2, Napa, CA 94559. Colleen Daly, Ed.-in-Chief. Bimonthly. Articles, 500 to 1,500 words, on the wine, food, destinations, gardens, people, and landscapes of the international wine country regions. Pays on acceptance.

ATLANTA HOMES AND LIFESTYLES—1100 Johnson Ferry Rd., #595, Atlanta, GA 30342-1746. Attn: Eds. Articles with a local angle. Department pieces for "Around Atlanta," "Design Takes," "Great Escapes," and "Quick Fix." Pays $50 to $300 for departments; $300 to $400 for features, on acceptance.

BETTER HOMES AND GARDENS—1716 Locust St., Des Moines, IA 50309-3023. Jean LemMon, Ed. Articles, to 2,000 words, on money management, health, travel, and cars. Pays top rates, on acceptance. Query.

BON APPETIT—6300 Wilshire Blvd., Los Angeles, CA 90048. Barbara Fairchild, Exec. Ed. Articles on fine cooking (menu format or single focus), cooking classes, and gastronomically focused travel. Query with clips. Pays varying rates, on acceptance.

BRIDE'S—(formerly *Bride's & Your New Home*) 140 E. 45th St., New York, NY 10017. Sally Kilbridge, Man. Ed. Articles, 800 to 2,000 words, for engaged couples or newlyweds on wedding planning, home and decorating, and honeymoon. No fiction or poetry. Send travel queries to Travel Dept. Pay starts at 50¢ per word, on acceptance.

BRIDE'S & YOUR NEW HOME—See *Bride's*.

CANADIAN GARDENING—340 Ferrier St., Suite 210, Markham, Ont., Canada L3R 2Z5. Rebecca Hanes-Fox, Ed. Features, 1,200 to 2,500 words, that help avid home gardeners in Canada solve problems or inspire them with garden ideas; Canadian angle imperative. How-to pieces, to 1,000 words, on garden projects; include introduction and step-by-step instructions. Profiles of gardens, to 2,000 words. Department pieces, 200 to 400 words. Pays $75 to $700, on acceptance. Canadian angle imperative. Queries preferred.

CAROLINA GARDENER—P.O. Box 4504, Greensboro, NC 27404. L.A. Jackson, Ed. Bimonthly. Articles, 750 to 1,000 words, specific to southeast gardening: profiles of gardens in the southeast and of new cultivars or "good ol' southern heirlooms." Slides and illustrations should be available to accompany articles. Pays $150, on publication. Query required.

CHEF—Talcott Communications Corp., 20 N. Wacker Dr., Suite 1865, Chicago, IL 60606. Brent T. Frei, Ed.-in-Chief. "The Food Magazine for Professionals." Articles, 800 to 1,200 words, that offer professionals in the foodservice business ideas for food marketing, preparation, and presentation. Pays $200 to $300, on publication.

CHILE PEPPER—1227 W. Magnolia Ave., Fort Worth, TX 76104. Joel Gregory, Pub. Eddie Lee Rider, Jr., Exec. Ed. Food and travel articles, 1,000 to 1,500 words. "No general and obvious articles, such as 'My Favorite Chile Con Carne.' We want first-person articles about spicy world cuisine." No fillers. Payment varies, on publication. Queries required.

COFFEE JOURNAL—Suite 508, 123 3rd St. N., Minneapolis, MN 55401. Susan Bonne, Ed. Quarterly. Articles on gourmet coffee and tea, product profiles, tips on brewing and enjoying, travel features, and music reviews. Some literary fiction, to 3,000 words. Payment varies, on publication.

COLORADO HOMES AND LIFESTYLES—7009 S. Potomac St., Englewood, CO 80112. Evalyn K. McGraw, Ed. Bimonthly. Articles, 1,300 to 1,500 words, with a Colorado focus. Department pieces, 1,100 to 1,300 words, cover architecture, artists, health, design trends, profiles, gardening, and travel. Pays $150 to $300, on acceptance. Guidelines. Query.

CONTEMPORARY STONE DESIGN—299 Market St., 3rd Fl., Saddle Brook, NJ 07663-5312. Michael Reis, Ed. Quarterly. Articles, 1,500 words, on using stone in architecture and interior design. Photographs and drawings. Payment is $6 per column inch, on publication.

COOKING LIGHT—P.O. Box 1748, Birmingham, AL 35201. Doug Crichton, Ed. Articles on fitness, exercise, health and healthful cooking, nutrition, and healthful recipes. Query with clips and SASE.

COOK'S ILLUSTRATED—17 Station St., Brookline, MA 02146. Barbara Bourassa, Man. Ed. Bimonthly. Articles that emphasize techniques of home cooking with master recipes, careful testing, trial and error. Payment varies, within 60 days of acceptance. Query. Guidelines.

COUNTRY GARDENS—1716 Locust St., Des Moines, IA 50309-3023. LuAnn Brandsen, Ed. Bimonthly. Garden-related how-tos and profiles of gardeners, 750 to 1,500 words. Department pieces, 500 to 700 words, on garden-related travel, food, projects, decorating, entertaining. "The gardens we feature are informal, lush, old-fashioned rather than formal and manicured." Pays $250 to $400 for columns; $350 to $800 for features, on acceptance. Query required.

COUNTRY LIVING—224 W. 57th St., New York, NY 10019. Marjorie E. Gage, Features Ed. Articles, 800 to 1,200 words, on decorating, antiques, cooking, travel, home building, crafts, and gardens. "Most material is written in-house; limited free-lance needs." Payment varies, on acceptance. Query preferred.

DESIGN CONCEPT— 820 W. Jackson Blvd., #450, Chicago, IL 60607-3026. Rebecca Rolfes, Ed. Quarterly. "An Interior Design Magazine from Pier 1 Imports." Features for and interviews with professional interior designers, 800 to 1,200 words. Pays about 50¢ a word, on publication. Query.

FANCY FOOD—Talcott Communications Corp., 20 N. Wacker Dr., Suite 1865, Chicago, IL 60606. Carolyn Schwaar, Ed.-in-Chief. "The Business Magazine for Specialty Foods, Coffee and Tea, Natural Foods, Confections, and Upscale Housewares." Articles, 2,000 words, related to gourmet food. Pays $250 to $500, on publication.

FAST AND HEALTHY MAGAZINE—Pillsbury Co., 200 S. Sixth St., MS 28M7, Minneapolis, MN 55402. Betsy Wray, Ed. Bimonthly. Articles, 250 to 800 words, with recipes that can be prepared in 30 minutes or less. "We are open to proposals from experienced food writers or writer/recipe developers." Payment varies, on acceptance. Query.

FINE GARDENING—The Taunton Press, P.O. Box 5506, Newtown, CT 06470-5506. LeeAnne White, Ed. Bimonthly. Articles, 800 to 2,000 words, for readers with a serious interest in gardening: how-tos, garden design, as well as pieces on specific plants or garden tools. "Our primary focus is on ornamental gardening and landscaping." Picture possibilities are very important. Pays $300 to $1,200 per story story on a project basis, part on acceptance, part on completed galley. Photos, $75 to $500. Query. Guidelines.

FLOWER & GARDEN MAGAZINE—700 W. 47th St., Suite 810, Kansas City, MO 64112. Attn: Ed. Practical how-to articles, 500 to 1,500 words, on home gardening and landscaping. Photos a plus. Pays varying rates, on acceptance (on publication for photos). Query.

FOOD & WINE—1120 Ave. of the Americas, New York, NY 10036. Dana Cowin, Ed.-in-Chief. Mary Ellen Ward, Man. Ed. No unsolicited material.

GOURMET: THE MAGAZINE OF GOOD LIVING—Conde Nast, 360 Madison Ave., New York, NY 10017. Attn: Ed. No unsolicited manuscripts; query.

GROWERTALKS—P.O. Box 9, 335 N. River St., Batavia, IL 60510-0009. John Saxtan, Ed. Dir. Articles, 800 to 2,600 words, that help commercial greenhouse growers (not florist/retailers or home gardeners) do their jobs better: trends, successes in new types of production, marketing, business management, new crops, and issues facing the industry. Payment varies, on publication. Queries preferred.

THE HERB QUARTERLY—P. O. Box 689, San Anselmo, CA 94960. Linda Sparrowe, Ed. Articles, 2,000 to 4,000 words, on herbs: practical uses, cultivation, gourmet cooking, landscaping, herb tradition, medicinal herbs, crafts ideas, unique garden designs; profiles of herb garden experts; practical how-tos for the herb businessperson. Include garden design when possible. Pays on publication. Guidelines; send SASE.

HOME MAGAZINE—1633 Broadway, 44th Fl., New York, NY 10019. Gale Steves, Ed.-in-Chief. Linda Lentz, Articles Ed. Articles of interest to homeowners: architecture, remodeling, decorating, products, project ideas, landscaping and gardening, financial aspects of home ownership, home offices, home-related environmental and ecological topics. Pays varying rates, on acceptance. Query, with 50-to 200-word summary.

HOME MECHANIX—See *Today's Homeowner.*

HORTICULTURE—98 N. Washington St., Boston, MA 02114. Thomas C. Cooper, Ed. Published 10 times a year. Authoritative, well-written articles, 500 to 2,500 words, on all aspects of gardening. Pays competitive rates, on publication. Query.

HOUSE BEAUTIFUL—1700 Broadway, New York, NY 10019. Jane Margoues, Features Ed. Jane Margoues, Travel Ed. Service articles related to the home. Pieces on design, travel, and gardening. Query with detailed outline and photos if relevant. Guidelines.

KITCHEN GARDEN—P.O. Box 5506, Newtown, CT 06470-5506. Editorial. Bimonthly. Nonfiction articles, varying lengths, for home gardeners who "love to grow their own vegetables, fruits, and herbs and use them in cooking." Features include "Plant Profiles," "Garden Profiles," "Techniques," "Design," "Projects," and "Cooking." Pays $150 per page, half on acceptance, half on publication. Query.

LOG HOME LIVING—P.O. Box 220039, Chantilly, VA 20153. Janice Brewster, Exec. Ed. Articles, 1,000 to 1,500 words, on modern manufactured and handcrafted kit log homes: homeowner profiles, design and decor features. Pays $350 to $550, on acceptance.

THE MAINE ORGANIC FARMER & GARDENER—RR 2, Box 594, Lincolnville, ME 04849. Jean English, Ed. Quarterly. How-to articles and profiles, 100 to 2,500 words, for organic farmers and gardeners, consumers who care about healthful foods, and activists. Tips, 100 to 250 words. "Our readers want good solid information about farming and gardening, nothing soft." Pays about 6¢ a word, on publication. Queries preferred.

METROPOLITAN HOME—1633 Broadway, New York, NY 10019. Michael Lassell, Articles Dir. Service and informational articles for residents of houses, co-ops, lofts, and condominiums, on real estate, equity, wine and spirits, collecting, trends, etc. Interior design and home furnishing articles with emphasis on lifestyle. Payment varies. Query.

MOTHER EARTH NEWS—Sussex Publishers, 49 E. 21st St., 11th Fl., New York, NY 10010. Ed. Bimonthly featuring articles on organic gardening, building projects, holistic health, alternative energy projects, wild foods, and environment and conservation. "We are dedicated to helping our readers become more self-sufficient, financially independent, and environmentally aware." Photos and diagrams a plus. No fiction. Payment varies, on publication.

NATIONAL GARDENING MAGAZINE—180 Flynn Ave., Burlington, VT 05401. Michael MacCaskey, Ed.-in-Chief. Feature articles, 1,200 to 2,500 words, and departments, 800 to 1,000 words, for advanced and beginning gardeners: the latest on fruits, vegetables, and flowers; profiles of edible and ornamental plants; well-tested gardening techniques; news on how to use beneficial plants and creatures; information on soil improvement; and profiles of experienced gardeners. Include photos and slides if possible. Pay starts at 25¢ per word, on acceptance. Query only. Do not send original art.

ORGANIC GARDENING—33 E. Minor St., Emmaus, PA 18098. Sandra Weida, Office Coordinator. Published 9 times a year. How-to features and profiles of expert organic gardeners, 1,000 to 1,800 words, for home gardeners; also tips, techniques, and news, 100 to 600 words. "Organic methods only! Features must include variety recommendations as well as how to grow." Pays $25 to $125 for departments; $300 to $1,000 for features. Time of payment varies. Queries preferred.

TODAY'S HOMEOWNER—(formerly *Home Mechanix*) 2 Park Ave., New York, NY 10016. Paul Spring, Ed. Articles on home improvement and home-related topics including money management, home security, home care, home environment, home security, yard care, design and remodeling, tools, repair and maintenance, electronics, new products and appliances, building materials, lighting and electrical, home decor.

WINE SPECTATOR—387 Park Ave. S., New York, NY 10016. Jim Gordon, Man. Ed. Features, 600 to 2,000 words, preferably with photos, on news and people in the wine world, travel, food, and other lifestyle topics. Pays from $400, extra for photos, on publication. Query required.

WINES & VINES—1800 Lincoln Ave., San Rafael, CA 94901. Philip E. Hiaring, Ed. Articles, 2,000 words, on grape and wine industry, emphasizing marketing, management, and production. Pays 15¢ a word, on acceptance.

FAMILY & PARENTING MAGAZINES

ADOPTIVE FAMILIES MAGAZINE—2309 Como Ave., St. Paul, MN 55108. Linda Lynch, Ed. Bimonthly. Articles, 1,500 to 2,500 words, on living in an adoptive family and other adoption issues. Photos of families, adults, or children. Payment is negotiable. Query.

AMERICAN BABY—KIII Family & Leisure Group, 249 W. 17th St., New York, NY 10011. Judith Nolte, Ed. Articles, 1,000 to 2,000 words, for new or expectant parents on prenatal and infant care. Personal experience, 900 to 1,200 words, (do not submit in diary format). Department pieces, 50 to 350 words, for "Crib Notes" (news and feature topics). No fiction, fantasy pieces, dreamy musings, or poetry. Pays $500 to $1,000 for articles, $100 for departments, on acceptance. Guidelines.

ATLANTA PARENT—Suite 506, 4330 Georgetown Sq. II, Atlanta, GA 30338. Peggy Middendorf, Ed. Articles, 800 to 2,000 words, on parenting and baby topics. Related humor, 800 to 1,500 words. Photos of parents and/or children. Pays $15 to $30 an article; $15 for photos, on publication.

BABY MAGAZINE—124 E. 40th St., Suite 1101, New York, NY 10016. Jeanne Muchnick, Ed. Bimonthly. Parenting articles, 750 to 1,500 words, geared toward women in the last trimester of pregnancy and the first year of baby's life. "We want how-to and personal articles designed to smooth the transitions from pregnancy to parenthood." Payment varies, on acceptance. Query.

BABY TALK—1325 Avenue of the Americas, New York, NY 10019. Trisha Thompson, Fred Levine Eds. Articles, 1,000 to 3,000 words, by professionals, on pregnancy, babies, baby care, women's health, child development, work and family, etc. No poetry. Query by mail. Pays varying rates, on acceptance. SASE required.

BAY AREA BABY—See *Bay Area Parent.*

BAY AREA PARENT— 401 Alberto Way, Suite A, Los Gatos, CA 95032-5404. Mary Brence Martin, Ed. Articles, 1,200 to 1,400 words, on local parenting issues for readers in California's Santa Clara County and the South Bay area. Query. Mention availability of B&W photos. Pays 6¢ a word, $10 to $15 for photos, on publication. Also publishes *Valley Parent* for central Contra Costa County and the tri-valley area of Alameda County, *Bay Area Parent of Teens, Bay Area Baby, Preschool & Children's Finder,* and *Education and Enrichment Guide.*

BAY AREA PARENT OF TEENS—See *Bay Area Parent.*

BIG APPLE PARENT—36 E. 12th St., New York, NY 10003. Helen Rosengren Freedman, Man. Ed. Articles, 500 to 750 words, for NYC parents. Pays $35 to $50, on publication. Buys first NYC rights.

CATHOLIC PARENT—Our Sunday Visitor, Inc., 200 Noll Plaza, Huntington, IN 46750. Woodeene Koenig-Bricker, Ed. Features, how-tos, and general-interest articles, 800 to 1,000 words, dealing with the issues of raising children "with solid values in today's changing world. Keep it anecdotal and practical with an emphasis on values and family life." Payment varies, on acceptance. Guidelines.

CENTRAL CALIFORNIA PARENT—2037 W. Bullard, #131, Fresno, CA 93711. Sally Cook, Pub. Articles, 500 to 1,500 words, of interest to parents. Payment varies, on publication.

CHRISTIAN HOME & SCHOOL—3350 E. Paris Ave. S.E., Grand Rapids, MI 49512. Gordon L. Bordewyk, Ed. Articles for parents in Canada and the U.S. who send their children to Christian schools and are concerned about the challenges facing Christian families today. Pays $125 to $200, on publication. Send SASE for guidelines or 9"x12" SASE with 4 first-class stamps for guidelines and sample issue.

CHRISTIAN PARENTING TODAY— 4050 Lee Vance View, Colorado Springs, CO 80918. Erin Healy, Ed. Articles, 900 to 2,000 words, dealing with raising children with Christian principles. Departments: "Parent Exchange," 25 to 100 words, on problem-solving ideas that have worked for parents; "Life in our House," insightful anecdotes, 25 to 100 words, about humorous things said at home. Queries preferred for articles. Pays 15¢ to 25¢ a word, on publication. Pays $40 for "Parent Exchange," $25 for "Life in our House." Guidelines.

CONNECTICUT FAMILY—See *New York Family.*

DOVETAIL PUBLISHING—P.O. Box 19945, Kalamazoo, MI 49019. Joan C. Hawxhurst, Ed. Articles and essays, 800 to 1,000 words, on topics of interest to interfaith (Jewish/Christian) families. Related cartoons, humor, and photos also used. Payment varies.

EASTSIDE PARENT—Northwest Parent Publishing, 2107 Elliott Ave., #303, Seattle, WA 98121. Virginia Smytn, Ed. Articles, 300 to 2,500 words, for parents of children under 14. Readers tend to be professional, two-career families. Queries preferred. Pays $50 to $600, on publication. Also publishes *Seattle's Child, Portland Parent, Puget Sound Parent, Snohomish County Parent,* and *Pierce County Parent.*

EDUCATION AND ENRICHMENT GUIDE—See *Bay Area Parent.*

EXCEPTIONAL PARENT—555 Kinderkamack Rd., Oradell, NJ 07649-1517. Maxwell J. Schleifer, Ed.-in-Chief. Articles, to 1,500 words, for parents and professionals caring for children and young adults with disabilities. Practical ideas and techniques on parenting, technology, research, legislation, and rehabilitation. Query. Pays $50, 60 days after publication.

EXPECTING—*See Parents Expecting.*

FAMILY— 169 Lexington Ave., New York, NY 10016. Stacy P. Brassington, Ed. Articles, 1,000 to 2,000 words, of interest to women with children. Topics include: military lifestyle, home decorating, travel, moving, food, personal finances, career, relationships, family, parenting, health and fitness. Pays to $200, on publication.

FAMILYFUN—Walt Disney Publishing Group, 244 Main St., Northampton, MA 01060. Jon Adolph, Exec. Ed. Articles, to 1,500 words, on family activities. Payment varies, on acceptance.

FAMILY LIFE— 1633 Broadway, 41st Floor, New York, NY 10019. Peter Herbst, Ed.-in-Chief. Published 10 times a year. Articles for parents of children ages 3 to 12. Payment varies (generally $1 a word), on acceptance. Limited market. Query required.

FAMILY TIMES—P.O. Box 932, Eau Claire, WI 54702. Ann Gorton, Ed. Articles, from 800 words, on children and parenting issues: health, education, raising children, how-tos, new studies and programs for educating parents. Pays $35 to $50, on publication. Query preferred. Guidelines.

GROWING CHILD/GROWING PARENT—22 N. Second St., P.O. Box 620, Lafayette, IN 47902-0620. Nancy Kleckner, Ed. Articles, to 1,500 words, on subjects of interest to parents of children under 6. No personal experience pieces or poetry. Guidelines.

HOME LIFE— 127 Ninth Ave. N., Nashville, TN 37234. Ivey Harrington, Man. Ed. Southern Baptist. Articles, to 1,500 words, on Christian marriage, parenting, and family relationships. Query with SASE required. Pays from $75 for articles, on acceptance.

JOYFUL CHILD MAGAZINE— 6224 E. Portia St., Mesa, AZ 85215. Peggy Jenkins, Ed. Quarterly. Fiction and nonfiction, 500 to 1,000 words, that "explore how society and education can more effectively nurture children (and adults) to express their fullest potential, thus releasing their inner joy. Articles on educating and parenting the whole child (body, mind, and spirit)." Pays in copies. Queries preferred. Guidelines available.

L.A. PARENT—See *Wingate Enterprises, Ltd.*

METROKIDS— 1080 N. Delaware Ave., Suite 702, Philadelphia, PA 19125. Sharon Cohen, Man. Ed. Tabloid for Delaware Valley families. Features and department pieces, 500 to 1,000 words, on parenting, regional travel, local kids' programs, nutrition, and product reviews. Pays $25 to $50, on publication.

MINNESOTA PARENT— 401 N. Third St., #550, Minneapolis, MN 55401-1387. Jeannine Ouellette-Howitz, Ed. Tabloid. Articles, 2,000 to 2,500 words, and features, 4,500 words, on family concerns and events: parenting, health, learning, pregnancy/birth/infants, family life. Personal essays related to parenting. Department pieces, 1,000 words, on infants, teens, finance, food, home, books and travel. Short fiction, 2,000 to 3,000 words, poetry, and B&W photos. Pays $150 to $350 for articles; $75 for departments; $25 for reprints, on publication.

MOSAICA DIGEST— P.O. Box 340272, Brooklyn, NY 11234-0272. Attn: Submission Dept. Joseph Ginberg, Pres. Fiction, 1,500 to 4,000 words; articles, 1,500 to 3,000 words; fillers, 100 to 300 words, of interest to Jewish families. First-person pieces, humor, travel, and history. Articles of Jewish interest are preferred (not articles about religion or religious issues). "We are a family-oriented magazine, and everything must be squeaky clean! No profanity, etc." Reprints are preferred. Pays to $50, on publication.

MOTHERING— P.O. Box 1690, Santa Fe, NM 87504. Ashisha, Sr. Ed. Bimonthly. Articles, to 2,000 words, on natural family living, covering topics such as pregnancy, birthing, parenting, etc. "We're looking for articles that have a strong point of view and come from the heart." Also poetry, 3 to 20 lines. Pays $150 to $300, on publication. Query.

NEW YORK FAMILY— 141 Halstead Ave., Suite 3D, Mamaroneck, NY 10543. Felice Shapiro, Susan Ross Benamram, Pubs. Betsy F. Woolf, Sr. Ed. Articles related to family life in New York City and general parenting topics. Pays $50 to $200. Same requirements for *Westchester Family* and *Connecticut Family.*

PARENTGUIDE NEWS— 419 Park Ave. S., 13th Fl., New York, NY 10016. Jenine M. DeLuca, Ed.-in-Chief. Articles, 1,000 to 1,500 words, related to families and parenting issues: trends, profiles, health, education, travel, fashion, calendar of events, seasonal topics, reader's opinions, kid's page, special programs, products, etc. Humor and photos also considered.

PARENTING—See *Wingate Enterprises, Ltd.*

PARENTING— 1325 Avenue of the Americas, New York, NY 10019. Attn: Articles Ed. Articles, 500 to 3,000 words, on education, health, fitness, nutrition, child development, psychology, and social issues for parents of young children. Query.

PARENTLIFE— MSN 140, 127 Ninth Ave. N., Nashville, TN 37234. Attn: Ed. Articles on Christian family issues. Resumés only.

PARENTS— 685 Third Ave., New York, NY 10017. Ann Pleshette Murphy, Ed. Articles, 1,500 to 2,500 words, on parenting, family, women's and community issues, etc. Informal style with quotes from experts. Pays from $1,000, on acceptance. Query.

PARENT'S DIGEST—100 Park Ave., New York, NY 10017. Mary E. Mohler, Ed.-in-Chief. Published 3 times a year by *Ladies' Home Journal*. Articles, 250 to 2,500 words, for parents; frequently uses reprints. Payment varies, on acceptance. Query.

PARENTS EXPECTING—(formerly *Expecting*) 375 Lexington Ave., New York, NY 10017. Maija Johnson, Ed. Not buying any new material in the foreseeable future.

PARENTS EXPRESS—921 South St., Philadelphia, PA 19147. Sharon Sexton, Ed. Articles on children and family topics for Philadelphia-area parents. Pays $120 to $250 for first rights, $25 to $35 for reprints, on publication.

PIERCE COUNTY PARENT—See *Eastside Parent.*

PORTLAND PARENT—See *Eastside Parent.*

PRESCHOOL & CHILDREN FINDER—See *Bay Area Parent.*

PUGET SOUND PARENT—See *Eastside Parent.*

SAN DIEGO PARENT—See *Wingate Enterprises, Ltd.*

SCHOLASTIC PARENT & CHILD—555 Broadway, New York, NY 10012-3919. Andrea Barbalich, Exec. Ed. Bimonthly. Articles, 600 to 900 words, on childhood education and development. "We are the learning link between home and school." Payment varies, on acceptance. Query; no unsolicited manuscripts. SASE.

SEATTLE'S CHILD—Northwest Parent Publishing, 2107 Elliott Ave., #303, Seattle, WA 98121. Ann Bergman, Ed. Articles, 400 to 2,500 words, of interest to parents, educators, and childcare providers of children under 12, plus investigative reports and consumer tips on issues affecting families in the Puget Sound region. Pays $75 to $400, on publication. Query.

SESAME STREET PARENTS—One Lincoln Plaza, New York, NY 10023. Articles, 800 to 2,500 words. Articles on health to P.J. Tanz, Assoc. Ed.; articles on family finance to Arleen Love, Asst. Ed.; articles on education, computer, review material to Linda Bernstein, Features Ed. Personal essays and other articles of interest to any editor. "Covers parenting issues for families with young children (to 8 years old)." Pays $1 per word, up to 6 weeks after acceptance. SASE for guidelines.

SNOHOMISH COUNTY PARENT—See *Eastside Parent.*

TOLEDO AREA PARENT NEWS—1120 Adams St., Toledo, OH 43624. Veronica Hughes, Ed. Articles on parenting, child and family health, and other family topics, 1,100 to 1,200 words. Writers must be from Northwest Ohio and Southern Michigan. Pays $75 to $100 per article, on acceptance. Query required.

TWINS—The Magazine for Parent of Multiples, 5350 S. Roslyn St., Suite 400, Englewood, CO 80111. Susan J. Alt, Ed.-in-Chief. Send submissions to Heather White, Asst. Ed. Features, 1,100 to 1,300 words, third person. Departments, 750 to 950 words, first person. "Articles must be multiples specific and focus on every day issues parents of twins, triplets, and more face. Features should have 2 to 3 professional and/or parental experience sources." Payment is $75 to $250, on publication. Query or send complete manuscript.

VALLEY PARENT—See *Bay Area Parent.*

WESTCHESTER FAMILY—See *New York Family.*

WINGATE ENTERPRISES, LTD.—P.O. Box 3204, 443 E. Irving Dr., Burbank, CA 91508. Attn: Eds. Publishes city-based parenting magazines with strong "service-to-parent" slant. Articles, 1,200 words, on child development, health, nutrition, and education. *San Diego Parent* covers San Diego area; *Parenting* covers the Orange County, CA, area; *L.A. Parent* is geared toward parents of children to age 10. Pays $100 to $350, on acceptance. Query.

WORKING MOTHER—MacDonald Communications, 135 W. 50th St., New York, NY 10020. Attn: Ed. Dept. Articles, to 2,000 words, that help women juggle job, home, and family. Payment varies, on acceptance.

LIFESTYLE MAGAZINES

ACCENT ON LIVING—P.O. Box 700, Bloomington, IL 61702-0700. Betty Garee, Ed. Quarterly. Articles, 800 to 1,000 words, for physically disabled consumers, mostly mobility impaired. Topics include travel, problem solving, and accessibility. "We like articles on devices or how-to information that make tasks easier." Pays 10¢ a word, on publication. Query.

AMERICAN HEALTH FOR WOMEN—28 W. 23rd St., New York, NY 10010. Attn: Ed. Dept. Lively, authoritative articles, 1,000 to 2,000 words, on women's health and lifestyle aspects of health and fitness; 100-to 500-word news reports. Payment varies for news stories and features, on acceptance. Query with clips.

AQUARIUS: A SIGN OF THE TIMES—1035 Green St., Roswell, GA 30075. Dan Liss, Ed. Articles, 800 words (with photos or illustrations), on New Age lifestyles and positive thought, holistic health, metaphysics, spirituality, environment. No payment.

AVATAR JOURNAL—237 N. Westmonte Dr., Altamonte Springs, FL 32714. Miken Chappell, Ed. Bimonthly. Articles, 500 words, on self-development, awakening consciousness, and spiritual enlightenment. "Spiritual in nature. Pieces that teach a lesson, paradigm shifts, epiphany experiences, anecdotes with theme of obtaining enlightenment, healing, inspiration, metaphysics." Pays $100 for articles; $50 for poems, on publication.

BACKHOME—P.O. Box 70, Hendersonville, NC 28793. Lorna K. Loveless, Ed. Articles, 800 to 2,500 words, on alternative buildling methods, renewable energy, organic gardening, livestock, home schooling, home business, healthful cooking. "We hope to provide readers with ways to gain more control over their lives by becoming more self-sufficient: raising their own food, making their own repairs, using alternative energy, etc. We do not promote 'dropping out' of society, but ways to become better citizens and caretakers of the planet." Pays $25 per page; $20 for photos, on publication. Queries preferred.

CAPPER'S—Editorial Dept., 1503 S.W. 42nd St., Topeka, KS 66609-1265. Ann Crahan, Ed. Human-interest, personal-experience, historical articles, 300 to 700 words. Poetry, to 15 lines, on nature, home, family. Novel-length fiction for serialization. Letters on women's interests, recipes, and hints for "Heart of the Home." Jokes. Children's writing and art section. Pays varying rates, on publication.

THE CHRISTIAN SCIENCE MONITOR—One Norway St., Boston, MA 02115. Jane A. Lampmann, Features Ed. Newspaper. Articles on lifestyle trends, women's rights, family, and parenting. Pays varying rates, on acceptance.

COMMON BOUNDARY—5272 River Rd., Suite 650, Bethesda, MD 20816. Attn: Manuscript Ed. Bimonthly. Feature articles, 3,000 to 4,000 words, exploring the connections between psychology, spirituality, and creativity. Essays, book reviews, department pieces (1,500 to 1,800 words), and 500-word news items. Readers are mental health professionals, pastoral counselors, spiritual directors, and lay readers.

COUNTRY—5400 S. 60th St., Greendale, WI 53129. Dan Matel, Man. Ed. Pieces, 500 to 1,500 words, on interesting rural and country people who have unusual hobbies; liberal use of direct quotes. Good candid, color photos required. Pays on publication.

COUNTRY AMERICA—1716 Locust St., Des Moines, IA 50309-3023. Bill Eftink: general inquiries. Roberta Peterson: country people, country lifestyle, almanac, travel, comedy; Neil Pond: country entertainment, entertainers' lifestyles and events; Jody Garlock: general interest, personalities, country essays, travel; Diane Yanney: foods, recipes, country crafts; Bob Ehlert: heritage and traditions, country places, country people. Articles should be light on copy with potential for several color photos. Queries preferred.

COUNTRY CONNECTIONS—14431 Ventura Blvd., #407, Sherman Oaks, CA 91423. Catherine R. Leach, Ed. Bimonthly. Articles, to 2,000 words, and fiction, to 1,000 words. Poetry. "We serve as a forum for public discourse about ethics, politics, social justice, community, democracy, animal and environmental issues." Pays from $25 to $50.

CURIO—P.O. Box 522, Bronxville, NY 10708-0522. Mickey Z., Ed. Quarterly. Articles, to 3,000 words; essays, to 2,000 words; reviews, to 300 words; interviews, in Q & A format. Features "lively coverage and analysis of arts, politics, health, entertainment, and lifestyle issues." No fiction. Payment varies, on publication.

DIALOGUE: A WORLD OF IDEAS FOR VISUALLY IMPAIRED PEOPLE OF ALL AGES—P.O. Box 5181, Salem, OR 97304-0181. Carol McCarl, Ed. Quarterly. Articles, 800 to 1,200 words, and poetry, 20 lines, for visually impaired youth and adults. Career opportunities, educational skills, and recreational activities. "We want to give readers an opportunity to learn about interesting and successful people who are visually impaired." Payment varies, on publication. Queries are preferred. SASE.

EARTH STAR—P.O. Box 1033, Cambridge, MA 02140. Cody Bideaux, Ed. Bimonthly. Articles, 200 to 3,000 words, on health, metaphysical subjects, environment, celebrity interviews, music. Pieces on local Boston arts and entertainment. "Our readers are interested in spirituality, personal growth, social responsibility, contemporary social issues, and holistic health." Pays $50 to $300, on acceptance. Query.

FELLOWSHIP—Box 271, Nyack, NY 10960-0271. Richard Deats, Ed. Bimonthly published by the Fellowship of Reconciliation, an interfaith, pacifist organization. Features, 1,500 to 2,000 words, and articles, 750 words, "dealing with nonviolence, opposition to war, and a just and peaceful world community." Photo-essays (B&W photos, include caption information). SASE required. Pays in copies and subscription. Queries preferred.

FRIENDLY EXCHANGE—P.O. Box 2120, Warren, MI 48090-2120. Dan Grantham, Ed. Articles, 700 to 1,500 words, offering readers "news you can use," on lifestyle issues such as home, health, personal finance, and travel. Photos. Pays $400 to $1,000, extra for photos. Query required. Guidelines.

GENRE—7080 Hollywood Blvd., Suite 1104, Hollywood, CA 90028. Mark Olmsted, Assoc. Ed. Fiction, 3,000 to 5,000 words, and articles, 750 to 3,000 words, of interest to gay men. "Feature articles should be national in scope and somehow related to the gay male experience." Pays $100 to $400, on publication.

GERMAN LIFE—Zeitgeist Publishing, 226 North Adams St., Rockville, MD 20850-1829. Heidi Whitesell, Ed. Bimonthly. Articles, 500 to 2,500 words, on German culture, its past and present, and how America has been influenced by its German element: history, travel, people, the arts, and social and political issues. Fillers, 50 to 200 words. Pays $300 to $500 for full-length articles, to $80 for short pieces and for fillers, on publication. Queries preferred.

GNOSIS—P.O. Box 14217, San Francisco, CA 94114. Richard Smoley, Ed. Articles, to 4,000 words, on esoteric and mystical traditions of the West; 1,000-word news items related to current events in esoteric spirituality; book reviews, 250 to 1,000 words; interviews with spiritual leaders, authors, and scholars. Pays $100 to $250 per article, on publication. Query for current themes.

GOOD TIMES—Robert Morris Bldg., 100 N. 17th St., 9th Fl., Philadelphia, PA 19103. Karen Detwiler, Ed.-in-Chief. Mature lifestyle magazine for people 50 years and older. Articles, 1,500 to 2,000 words, on medical issues, health, travel, finance, fashion, gardening, fitness, legal issues, celebrities, lifestyles, and relationships. Guidelines. Payment varies, on publication. Query.

THE GREEN MAN—See *Pan Gaia*.

HEALTH QUEST—200 Highpoint Dr., Suite 215, Chalfont, PA 18914. Tamara Jeffries, Ed. "The Publication of Black Wellness." Articles, 500 to 1,500 words, on health issues of interest to African-American men and women. "We focus on total health, so articles cover mind, body, spirit, and cultural wellness." Payment varies, on publication. Query preferred.

HEART & SOUL—Rodale Press, Inc., 733 Third Ave., 15th Fl., New York, NY 10017. Stephanie Stokes Oliver, Ed.-in-Chief. Articles, 800 to 1,500 words, on health, beauty, fitness, nutrition, and relationships for African-American women. "We aim to be the African-American woman's ultimate guide to total well-being-body, mind, and spirit." Payment varies, on acceptance. Queries preferred.

INSIDE MAGAZINE—226 S. 16th St., Philadelphia, PA 19102-3392. Jane Biberman, Ed. Jewish lifestyle magazine. Articles, 1,500 to 3,000 words, on Jewish issues, health, finance, and the arts. Pays $75 to $600 for departments; $600 to $1,200 for features, after publication. Queries required; send clips if available.

INSIDER MAGAZINE—4124 W. Oakton, Skokie, IL 60076. Rita Cook, Ed. Dir. Articles, 750 to 1,500 words, on issues, career, politics, sports, and entertainment. "We are mainly a college publication, but to appeal to college readers you must write above them." Pays 1¢ to 5¢ a word, on publication. Queries preferred.

INTERRACE—2870 Peachtree Rd., Suite 264, Atlanta, GA 30305. Candy Mills, Ed. Articles, 800 words, with an interracial, intercultural, or interethnic theme: news event, commentary, personal account, exposé, historical, interview, etc. No fiction. "Not limited to black/white issues. Interaction between blacks, whites, Asians, Latinos, Native Americans, etc., is also desired." No payment.

INTUITION—P.O. Box 460773, San Francisco, CA 94146. Colleen Mauro, Ed. Bimonthy. Articles, 750 to 6,000 words, on intuition, creativity, and spiritual development. Departments, 750 to 2,000 words, include profiles; "Frontier Science," breakthroughs pertaining to parapsychology, creativity, etc.; "Intuitive Tools," history and application of a traditional approach to accessing information. Pays $25 for book reviews to $1,200 for cover articles.

JEWISH CURRENTS—22 E. 17th St., #601, New York, NY 10003. Morris U. Schappes, Ed. Articles and book reviews, 2,400 to 3,000 words, on progressive Jewish culture or history: Holocaust resistance commemoration, Black-Jewish relations, Yiddish literature and culture, Jewish labor struggles. "We are a secular Jewish magazine." No fiction. No payment.

THE JEWISH HOMEMAKER—391 Troy Ave., Brooklyn, NY 11213. Avi Goldstein, Ed. Published 4 times a year. Articles, 1,200 to 2,000 words, for a traditional/Orthodox Jewish audience. Humor. Payment varies, on publication. Query.

LEFTHANDER MAGAZINE—P.O. Box 8249, Topeka, KS 66608-0249. Kim Kipers, Ed. Bimonthly. Articles, 1,500 to 1,800 words, related to left-handedness: profiles of left-handed personalities; performing specific tasks or sports as a lefty; teaching left-handed children. Personal experience pieces for "Perspective." SASE for guidelines. Pays $80 to $100, on publication. Buys all rights. Query.

LINK: THE COLLEGE MAGAZINE—The Soho Bldg., 110 Greene St., Suite 407, New York, NY 10012. Jeff Howe, Ed.-in-Chief. News, lifestyle, and issues for college students. Short features, 300 to 500 words, on college culture. Well-researched, insightful, authoritative articles, 2,000 to 3,000 words, on academics, education news, breaking stories, lifestyle, and trends; also how-to and informational pieces. Pays $500 to $1,500, on publication. Query. Guidelines.

MAGICAL BLEND—133½ Broadway St., Chico, CA 95928-5317. Jerry Snider, Ed. Nonfiction; positive, uplifting articles, to 3,000 words, on spiritual exploration, lifestyles, occult, white magic, New Age thought.

MOMENT MAGAZINE— 4710 41st St. N.W., Washington, DC 20016. Attn: Sr. Ed. Sophisticated articles, 2,500 to 5,000 words, on Jewish culture, politics, religion, and personalities. Columns, to 1,500 words, with uncommon perspectives on contemporary issues, humor, strong anecdotes. Book reviews, 400 words. Pays $40 to $600.

MOUNTAIN LIVING MAGAZINE—7009 S. Potomac, Englewood, CO 80112. Robyn Griggs, Ed. Articles, 1,200 to 1,500 words, on topics related to mountains: travel, home design, architecture, gardening, art, cuisine, sports, and people. Pays $50 to $400, on acceptance.

NATIVE PEOPLES MAGAZINE—The Arts and Lifeways, 5333 N. 7th St., Suite C-224, Phoenix, AZ 85014-2804. Gary Avey, Pub. Ben Winton, Assoc. Ed. Quarterly. Authentic and positive articles, 1,800 to 2,800 words, featuring portrayals of present traditional and cultural practices. Pays 25¢ a word, on publication. Query; include availability of photos. Guidelines and sample copy. SASE.

NEW AGE, THE JOURNAL FOR HOLISTIC LIVING— 42 Pleasant St., Watertown, MA 02172-2312. Joan Duncan Oliver, Ed. Articles for readers who take an active interest in social change, personal growth, health, and contemporary issues. Features, 2,000 to 4,000 words; columns, 750 to 1,500 words; short news items, 150 words; and first-person narratives, 750 to 1,500 words. Pays varying rates, after acceptance.

NEW CHOICES: LIVING EVEN BETTER AFTER 50—28 W. 23rd St., New York, NY 10010. Greg Daugherty, Ed.-in-Chief. News and service magazine for people ages 50 to 65. Articles on retirement planning, financial strategies, housing options, as well as health and fitness, travel, leisure pursuits, etc. Payment varies, on acceptance.

THE NEW YORK TIMES MAGAZINE—229 W. 43rd St., New York, NY 10036. Topical, personal pieces, 900 words, for "Lives." Pays $1,000, on acceptance.

NEWPORT LIFE—174 Bellevue Ave., Suite 207, Newport, RI 02840. Lynne Tungett, Jeffrey Hall, Publishers. John Pantalone, Ed. Quarterly. Annual City Guide. Articles, 500 to 2,500 words, on people, places, attractions of Newport County: general-interest, historical, profiles, international celebrities, and social and political issues. Departments, 200 to 750 words: sailing, dining, food & wind, home & garden, the arts in Newport County. Photos must be available for all articles. Query. SASE.

OUT—The Soho Bldg., 110 Greene St., Suite 600, New York, NY 10012. James Collard, Ed.-in-Chief. Articles, 50 to 8,000 words, on various subjects (current affairs, culture, fitness, finance, etc.) of interest to gay and lesbian readers. Payment varies, on publication. Query. Guidelines.

OUT YOUR BACKDOOR— 4686 Meridian Rd., Williamston, MI 48895. Jeff Potter, Ed. Articles and fiction, 2,500 words, for thrifty, down-to-earth culture enthusiasts. "Budget travel especially by bike and boat, second-hand treasure, and homespun but high-quality culture all combine to yield an energetic, practical, folksy post-modern magazine." Study sample issue before submitting. Pays in copies.

PALM SPRINGS LIFE—Desert Publications, 303 N. Indian Canyon Dr., Palm Springs, CA 92262. Stewart Weiner, Ed. Articles, 1,000 to 3,000 words, of interest to "wealthy, upscale people who live and/or play in the desert." Pays $150 to $500 for features, $25 to $75 for short profiles, on publication. Query required.

PAN GAIA—(formerly *The Green Man*) P.O. Box 641, Point Arena, CA 95468-0641. Diane Conn Darling, Ed. "Living the Pagan Life." Articles, 1,500 to 3,000 words. Pays 1¢ per word. Query for guidelines.

THE PHOENIX—7152 Unity Ave. N., Brooklyn Ctr., MN 55429. Pat Samples, Ed. Tabloid. Articles, 800 to 1,500 words, on recovery, renewal, and growth. Department pieces for "Bodywise," "Family Skills," or "Personal Story." "Our readers are committed to physical, emotional, mental, and spiritual health and well-being. Read a sample copy to see what we publish." Pays 3¢ to 5¢ a word, on publication. Guidelines and calendar. SASE.

ROBB REPORT—1 Acton Pl., Acton, MA 01720. Steven Castle, Ed. Consumer magazine for the high-end/luxury market. Features on lifestyles, home interiors, boats, travel, investment opportunities, exotic automobiles, business, technology, etc. Payment varies, on publication. Query with SASE and published clips.

SAGEWOMAN—P.O. Box 641, Point Arena, CA 95468-0641. Anne Newkirk Niven, Ed. Quarterly. Articles, 200 to 5,000 words, on issues of concern to pagan and spiritually minded women. Material which expresses an earth-centered spirituality: personal experience, Goddess lore, ritual material, interviews, humor, and reviews. Accepts material by women only. Pays 2¢ a word, from $10, on publication.

SCIENCE OF MIND—P.O. Box 75127, Los Angeles, CA 90075. Jim Shea, Asst. Ed. Articles, 1,500 to 2,000 words, that offer a thoughtful perspective on how to experience greater self-acceptance, empowerment, and meaningful life. "Achieving wholeness through applying Science of Mind principles is the primary focus." Inspiring first-person pieces, 1,000 to 2,000 words. Interviews with notable spiritual leaders, 3,500 words. Poetry, to 28 lines. Pays $25 per page. Queries required (except for poetry).

SWING—342 Madison Ave., #1402, New York, NY 10017. Megan Liberman, Exec. Ed. Articles, 800 to 3,000 words, on issues of interest to readers in their 20s. Pays 50¢ to $1 a word, on publication. Query with clips.

T'AI CHI—P.O. Box 26156, Los Angeles, CA 90026. Marvin Smalheiser, Ed. Articles, 1,200 to 4,000 words, on T'ai Chi Ch'uan, other internal martial arts and related topics such as qigong, Chinese medicine and healing practices, Chinese philosophy and culture, health, meditation, fitness, self-improvement, as well as news about teachers and schools. Pays $75 to $500, on publication. Query required. Guidelines. SASE.

TROIKA—P.O. Box 1006, Weston, CT 06883. Rachel Parker, Ed. Quarterly. Articles, 2,000 to 2,500 words, and columns, 750 to 1,400 words, for arts, health, science, human interest, international interests, business, leisure, ethics, and personal finance. "For educated, affluent baby-boomers, who are seeking to balance their personal achievements, family commitments, and community involvement." Pays $250 to $1,000, on publication. Query.

TURNING WHEEL—P.O. Box 4650, Berkeley, CA 94704. Susan Moon, Ed. Quarterly. Articles, poetry, fillers, and artwork. "Magazine is dedicated to the development of engaged Buddhism, engaged spirituality and spiritual politics." No payment.

US AIRWAYS ATTACHÉ—(formerly *USAIR Magazine*) 1301 Carolina St., Greensboro, NC 27401. Articles, 400 to 2,500 words, on "the finer things in life." Paragons department offers short pieces touting the best of the best; Informed Sources department contains experts' opinions and knowledge on a variety of topics. No politics or Hollywood issues. Pays $1 a word, on acceptance.

USAIR MAGAZINE—See *US Airways Attaché*.

VEGETARIAN VOICE—P.O. Box 72, Dolgeville, NY 13329. Maribeth Abrams-McHenry, Man. Ed. Quarterly. Informative, well-researched and/or inspiring articles, 600 to 1,800 words, on lifestyles and consumer concerns, health, nutrition, animal rights, the environment, world hunger, etc. "Our underlying philosophy is total vegetarian; all our recipes are vegan and we do not support the use of leather, wool, silk, etc." Guidelines. Pays in copies.

VENTURE INWARD—67th and Atlantic Ave., P.O. Box 595, Virginia Beach, VA 23451. A. Robert Smith, Ed. Articles, to 4,000 words, on metaphysical and spiritual development subjects. Prefer personal experience. Opinion pieces, to 800 words, for "Guest Column." "Turning Point," to 800 words, on an inspiring personal turning point experience. "The Mystical Way," to 1,500 words, on a personal paranormal experience. "Holistic Health," brief accounts of success using Edgar Cayce remedies. Book reviews, to 500 words. Pays $30 to $300, on publication. Query.

VIRTUE: HELPING WOMEN BUILD CHRIST-LIKE CHARACTER— (formerly *Virtue: The Christian Magazine for Women*) 4050 Lee Vance View, Colorado Springs, CO 80918-7102. Laura J. Barker, Ed. Articles and fiction, 200 to 1,400 words, on family, marriage, self-esteem, working women, humor, women's spiritual journeys, issues, relationship with family, friends and God. "Provocative, meaningful stories, especially those with bold messages shown in gracious ways." Pays 15¢ to 25¢ a word for articles; $25 to $50 for poetry, on publication. Submit up to 3 poems at a time. Query with SASE required.

WE—372 Central Park West, Suite 6-B, New York, NY 10025-8205. Charles A. Riley II, Ed.-in-Chief. Monthly. Fiction, 1,500 to 2,000 words, and nonfiction, varying lengths, for people with disabilities "celebrating their lives in sports and the arts, spotlighting foreign travel, and dining out in major American cities." Some fillers and photographs. Payment varies, on publication. Query.

WEIGHT WATCHERS MAGAZINE—2100 Lakeshore Dr., Birmingham, AL 35209. Exec. Ed. Articles on fashion, beauty, food, health, nutrition, fitness, and weight-loss motivation and success. Pays on acceptance. Query with clips required. Guidelines.

WHOLE LIFE TIMES—21225 Pacific Coast Hwy., Suite B, P.O. Box 1187, Malibu, CA 90265. S.T. Alcantara, Sen. Ed. Tabloid. Feature articles, 2,000 words, with a holistic perspective. Departments and columns, 800 words. Well-researched articles on the environment, current political issues, women's issues, and new developments in health, as well as how-to, humor, new product information, personal growth, and interviews. Pays 5¢ to 10¢ a word for features only, 30 days after publication.

WIRED—520 Third St., San Francisco, CA 94107-1427. Patricia Reiley, Ed. Asst. Lifestyle magazine for the "digital generation." Articles, essays, profiles, fiction, and other material that discusses the "meaning and context" of digital technology in today's world. Guidelines. Payment varies, on acceptance.

YIPPY YI YEA WESTERN LIFESTYLES— 8393 E. Holly Rd., Holly, MI 48442-8819. Nicole Brown, Ed. Articles, 1,200 words, on Western subjects, including artisans, galleries, decorating, travel, history, and celebrities. Pays $250, on publication.

YOGA JOURNAL—2054 University Ave., Berkeley, CA 94704. Rick Fields, Ed. Articles, 1,200 to 4,000 words, on holistic health, spirituality, yoga, and transpersonal psychology; New Age profiles; interviews. Pays $100 to $3,000, on acceptance.

SPORTS & RECREATION

ADVENTURE CYCLIST—Adventure Cycling Assn., P.O. Box 8308, Missoula, MT 59807. Daniel D'Ambrosio, Ed. Articles, 1,200 to 2,500 words: accounts of bicycle tours in the U.S. and overseas, interviews, personal-experience pieces, humor, and news shorts. Pays $25 to $65 per published page.

ADVENTURE JOURNAL—(formerly *Adventure West*) 650 S. Orcas St., Suite 103, Seattle, WA 98108. Kristina Schreck, Man. Ed. Bimonthly. Recreational travel articles, 2,500 to 3,500 words, on risky wild adventures; 700 to 1,200 words, on shorter trips that offer a high degree of excitement; and service pieces, 700 to 1,200 words, on short excursions. Profiles and essays also used. Pays 15¢ a word, on publication. Include clips.

ADVENTURE WEST—See *Adventure Journal.*

AKC GAZETTE—51 Madison Ave., New York, NY 10010. Mark Roland, Features Ed. "The official journal for the sport of purebred dogs." Articles, 1,000 to 2,500 words, relating to purebred dogs, for serious fanciers. Pays $200 to $450, on acceptance. Queries preferred.

THE AMERICAN FIELD—542 S. Dearborn, Chicago, IL 60605. B.J. Matthys, Man. Ed. Yarns about hunting trips, bird-shooting; articles to 1,500 words, on dogs and field trials, emphasizing conservation of game resources. Pays varying rates, on acceptance.

AMERICAN HUNTER—NRA Publications, 11250 Waples Mill Rd., Fairfax, VA 22030. John Zent, Ed. Articles, 1,400 to 2,000 words, on hunting. Photos. Pays on acceptance. Guidelines.

AMERICAN MOTORCYCLIST—American Motorcyclist Assn., 33 Collegeview Rd., Westerville, OH 43081-1484. Greg Harrison, Ed. Articles and fiction, to 3,000 words, on motorcycling: news coverage, personalities, tours. Photos. Pays varying rates, on publication. Query with SASE.

THE AMERICAN RIFLEMAN—11250 Waples Mill Rd., Fairfax, VA 22030. Mark Keefe, Man. Ed. Factual articles on use and enjoyment of sporting firearms. Pays on acceptance.

AMERICAN SQUAREDANCE MAGAZINE—P.O. Box 777, N. Scituate, RI 02857. Ed and Pat Juaire, Eds. Articles and fiction, 1,000 to 1,500 words, related to square dancing. Poetry. Fillers, to 100 words. Pays $1.50 per column inch.

AQUA-FIELD PUBLISHING COMPANY—39 Ave. at the Commons, Shrewsbury, NJ 07702. Attn: the Eds. Publishes 17 magazines. How-to features, 2,000 to 3,000 words, on hunting, fishing, fly-fishing, gardening, outdoor adventure, woodworking, and deck building. "Especially interested in new approaches to activities or embellishments of tried-and-true methods." Occasionally use shorter pieces, 500 to 1,500 words. Articles should be accompanied by color slides or B&W prints. Pays $300 to $400 for features. Query.

ATLANTIC SALMON JOURNAL—P.O. Box 429, St. Andrews, N.B., Canada E0G 2X0. Jim Gourlay, Ed. Articles, 1,500 to 3,000 words, related to Atlantic salmon: fishing, conservation, ecology, travel, politics, biology, how-tos, anecdotes. Pays $100 to $400, on publication.

BACKPACKER MAGAZINE—Rodale Press, 33 E. Minor St., Emmaus, PA 18098. Thom Hogan, Exec. Ed. Articles, 250 to 3,000 words, on self-propelled backcountry travel: backpacking, kayaking/canoeing, mountaineering; technique, nordic skiing, health, natural science. Photos. Pays varying rates. Query.

THE BACKSTRETCH—P.O. Box 7065, Louisville, KY 40257-0065. Melissa McIntosh, Ed. United Thoroughbred Trainers of America. Feature articles, with photos, on subjects related to thoroughbred horse racing. Pays after publication. Sample issue and guidelines on request.

BACKWOODSMAN—P.O. Box 627, Westcliffe, CO 81252. Charlie Richie, Ed. Articles for the twentieth-century frontiersman: muzzleloading, primitive weapons, black powder cartridge guns, woodslore, survival, homesteading, trapping, etc. Historical and how-to articles. No payment.

BASEBALL FORECAST, BASEBALL ILLUSTRATED—See *Hockey Illustrated.*

BASKETBALL FORECAST—See *Hockey Illustrated.*

BASSIN'—NatCom, Inc., 5300 CityPlex Tower, 2448 E. 81st St., Tulsa, OK 74137-4207. Mark Chesnut, Exec. Ed. Articles, 1,200 to 1,400 words, on how and where to bass fish, for the amateur fisherman. Pays $350 to $500, on acceptance. Query.

BASSMASTER MAGAZINE—B.A.S.S. Publications, P.O. Box 17900, Montgomery, AL 36141. Dave Precht, Ed. Articles, 1,500 to 2,000 words, with photos, on freshwater black bass and striped bass. "Short Casts" pieces, 400 to 800 words, on news, views, and items of interest. Pays $200 to $500, on acceptance. Query.

BC OUTDOORS—300-780 Beatty St., Vancouver, B.C., Canada V6B 2M1. Karl Bruhn, Ed. Articles, to 1,500 words, on fishing, hunting, conservation, and all forms of non-competitive outdoor recreation in British Columbia. Photos. Pays from 20¢ to 27¢ a word, on publication.

BICYCLE GUIDE—See *Bicyclist.*

BICYCLING—135 N. 6th St., Emmaus, PA 18098. Stan Zukowski, Man. Ed. Articles, 500 to 2,500 words, for serious cyclists, on recreational riding, fitness training, nutrition, bike maintenance, equipment, racing and touring, covering all aspects of the sport: road, mountain biking, track racing, etc. Photos, illustrations. Pays $50 to $2,000, on acceptance. Guidelines.

BICYCLIST—(formerly *Bicycle Guide*) 6420 Wilshire Blvd., Los Angeles, CA 90048-5515. Attn: Ed. Articles on cycling history, personality profiles, and photos for all-road cycling enthusiasts. Pays varying rates, on publication. Buys all rights. Query with clips.

BIRD WATCHER'S DIGEST—P.O. Box 110, Marietta, OH 45750. William H. Thompson, III, Ed. Articles, 600 to 2,500 words, for bird watchers: first-person accounts; how-tos; pieces on endangered species; profiles. Pays from $50, on publication. Submit complete manuscript. SASE for guidelines.

BLACK BELT—P.O. Box 918, Santa Clarita, CA 91380-9018. Attn: Ed. Articles related to self-defense: how-tos on fitness and technique; historical, travel, philosophical subjects. Pays $100 to $300, on publication. Guidelines.

BOUNDARY WATERS JOURNAL—9396 Rocky Ledge Rd., Ely, MN 55731. Stuart Osthoff, Ed. Articles, 2,000 to 3,000 words, on wilderness, recreation, nature, and conservation in Minnesota's Boundary Waters Canoe Area Wilderness and Ontario's Quetico Provincial Park. Regular features include canoe-route journals, fishing, camping, hiking, cross-country skiing, wildlife and nature, regional lifestyles, history, and events. Pays $200 to $400, on publication; $50 to $150 for photos.

BOW & ARROW HUNTING—265 S. Anita, Suite 120, Orange, CA 92868. Bob Torres, Ed. Articles, 1,200 to 2,500 words, with color slides, B&W or color photos, on bowhunting; profiles and technical pieces, primarily on deer hunting. Pays $100 to $300, on acceptance. Same address and mechanical requirements for *Gun World.*

BOWHUNTER MAGAZINE—6405 Flank Dr., Harrisburg, PA 17112. M.R. James, Ed.-in-Chief. Dwight Schuh, Ed. Informative, entertaining features, 500 to 2,000 words, on bow- and-arrow hunting. Fillers. Photos. "Study magazine first." Pays $100 to $400, on acceptance.

BOWLING—5301 S. 76th St., Greendale, WI 53129. David Yeghiaian, Ed. Articles, to 1,500 words, on all aspects of bowling, especially human interest. Profiles. "We're looking for unique, unusual stories about bowling people and places, and occasionally publish business articles." Pays varying rates, on publication. Query required.

BUCKMASTERS WHITETAIL MAGAZINE—P.O. Box 244022, Montgomery, AL 36124-4022. Russell Thornberry, Exec. Ed. Semiannual. Articles and fiction, 2,500 words, for serious sportsmen. "Big Buck Adventures" articles capture the details and the adventure of the hunt of a newly discovered trophy. Fresh, new whitetail hunting how-tos; new biological information about whitetail deer that might help hunters; entertaining deer stories; and other department pieces. Photos a plus. Pays $250 to $400 for articles, on acceptance. Guidelines.

BUGLE—Rocky Mountain Elk Foundation, P.O. Box 8249, Missoula, MT 59807-8249. Lee Cromrich, Ed. Asst. Bimonthly. Fiction and nonfiction, 1,500 to 4,000 words, on elk and elk hunting. Department pieces, 1,000 to 3,000 words, for: "Thoughts and Theories"; "Situation Ethics"; and "Women in the Outdoors." Pays 20¢ a word, on acceptance.

CANADIAN DIVER & WATERSPORT—See *Diver Magazine.*

CANOE AND KAYAK MAGAZINE—P.O. Box 3146, Kirkland, WA 98083. Jan Nesset, Ed.-in-Chief. Features, 1,600 to 2,500 words; department pieces, 500 to 1,000 words. Topics include canoeing or kayaking adventures, destinations, boat and equipment reviews, techniques and how-tos, short essays, camping, environment, safety, humor, health, history, etc. Pays 12½¢ a word, on publication. Query preferred. Guidelines.

CAR AND DRIVER—2002 Hogback Rd., Ann Arbor, MI 48105. Csaba Csere, Ed.-in-Chief. Articles, to 2,500 words, for enthusiasts, on new cars, classic cars, industry topics. "Ninety percent staff-written. Query with clips. No unsolicited manuscripts." Pays to $2,500, on acceptance.

CAR CRAFT—6420 Wilshire Blvd., Los Angeles, CA 90048. David Freiburger, Ed. Articles and photo-features on high performance street machines, drag cars, racing events; technical pieces; action photos. Pays from $150 per page, on publication.

CASCADES EAST—716 N.E. Fourth St., P.O. Box 5784, Bend, OR 97708. Geoff Hill, Ed./Pub. Articles, 1,000 to 2,000 words, on outdoor activities (fishing, hunting, golfing, backpacking, rafting, skiing, snowmobiling, etc.), history, special events, and scenic tours in central Oregon Cascades. Photos. Pays 5¢ to 10¢ a word, extra for photos, on publication.

CHESAPEAKE BAY MAGAZINE—1819 Bay Ridge Ave., Annapolis, MD 21403. Tim Sayles, Ed. Articles, to 1,500 words, on boating, fishing, destinations and people on the Chesapeake Bay. Photos. Pays $100 to $700, on acceptance. Query.

CROSS COUNTRY SKIER—P.O. Box 50120, Minneapolis, MN 55405. Jim Chase, Ed. Published October through February. Articles, to 2,000 words, on all aspects of cross-country skiing. Departments, 1,000 to 1,500 words, on ski maintenance, skiing techniques, health and fitness. Pays $300 to $700 for features, $100 to $350 for departments, on publication. Query.

CURRENTS—212 W. Cheyenne Mountain Blvd., Colorado Springs, CO 80906. Greg Moore, Ed. Quarterly. "Voice of the National Organization for Rivers." Articles, 500 to 2,000 words, for kayakers, rafters, and river canoeists, pertaining to whitewater rivers and/or river running. Fillers. B&W action photos. Pays from $40 for articles, $30 to $50 for photos, on publication. Queries preferred.

CYCLE WORLD—1499 Monrovia Ave., Newport Beach, CA 92663. David Edwards, Ed.-in-Chief. Technical and feature articles, 1,500 to 2,500 words, for motorcycle enthusiasts. Photos. Pays on publication. Query.

CYCLING U.S.A.—U.S. Cycling Federation, One Olympic Plaza, Colorado Springs, CO 80909. Frank Stanley, Ed. Articles, 500 to 1,000 words, on bicycle racing. Pays 10¢ a word, on publication. Query.

DANCE DRILL—1212 Ynez Ave., Redondo Beach, CA 90277. Kay Crawford, Ed. Quarterly. Articles, fiction, poetry, fillers, and humor related to the pep arts (dance drill, flags, cheerleading, majorettes, or pom pon girls). Payment varies, on publication.

THE DIVER—P.O. Box 28, St. Petersburg, FL 33731-0028. Bob Taylor, Ed. Articles on divers, coaches, officials, springboard and platform techniques, training tips, etc. Pays $15 to $50, extra for photos ($5 to $10 for cartoons), on publication.

DIVER MAGAZINE—230-11780 Hammersmith Way, Richmond, B.C., Canada V7A 5E3. Stephanie Bold, Ed. Illustrated articles, 500 to 1,000 words, on dive destinations. Shorter pieces are also welcome. "Travel features should be brief and accompanied by excellent slides and/or prints and a map. Unsolicited articles will be reviewed only from August to October and will be considered for *Diver Magazine* and *Canadian Diver & Watersport*." Pays $2.50 per column inch, on publication. Guidelines. Limited market.

EQUUS—Fleet Street Corp., 656 Quince Orchard Rd., Gaithersburg, MD 20878. Laurie Prinz, Exec. Ed. Articles, 1,000 to 3,000 words, on all breeds of horses, covering their health, care, the latest advances in equine medicine and research. "Attempt to speak as one horseperson to another." Pays $100 to $400, on publication.

FAMILY MOTOR COACHING—8291 Clough Pike, Cincinnati, OH 45244-2796. Robbin Gould, Ed. Articles, 1,500 to 2,000 words, on technical topics and travel routes and destinations accessible by motorhome. Payment varies, on acceptance. Query preferred.

FIELD & STREAM—2 Park Ave., New York, NY 10016. Duncan Barnes, Ed. Articles, 1,500 to 2,000 words, with photos, on hunting, fishing. Short articles, to 1,000 words. Fillers, 75 to 500 words. Cartoons. Pays from $800 for feature articles with photos, $75 to $500 for fillers, $100 for cartoons, on acceptance. Query for articles.

FLIGHT—Air Age Publishing, 100 E. Ridge, Ridgefield, CT 06877-4606. Tom Atwood, Ed. Articles, 2,500 to 3,000 words, on "the history, the hardware, and the human heart of aviation." Send one-page outline to Dana Donia, Ed. Asst. Payment is $600.

FLY FISHERMAN—6405 Flank Dr., Harrisburg, PA 17112. Philip Hanyok, Man. Ed. Query.

FLY ROD & REEL—P.O. Box 370, Camden, ME 04843. James E. Butler, Ed. Fly-fishing pieces, 2,000 to 2,500 words, and occasional fiction; articles on the culture and history of the areas being fished. Pays on acceptance. Query.

FOOTBALL DIGEST—Century Publishing Co., 990 Grove St., Evanston, IL 60201. Kenneth Leiker, Ed. Steve Greenberg, Assoc. Ed. Nonfiction articles, 1,500 to 2,500 words, for the hard-core football fan: profiles of pro and college stars, nostalgia, trends in the sport. Pays on publication. Query.

FOOTBALL FORECAST—See *Hockey Illustrated*.

FUR-FISH-GAME—2878 E. Main St., Columbus, OH 43209. Mitch Cox, Ed. Illustrated articles, 800 to 2,500 words, preferably with how-to angle, on hunting, fishing, trapping, dogs, camping, or other outdoor topics. Some humorous or where-to articles. Pays to $150, on acceptance.

GAME AND FISH PUBLICATIONS—P.O. Box 741, Marietta, GA 30061. Attn: Ed. Dept. Publishes 30 monthly outdoor magazines for 48 states. Articles, 1,500 to 2,500 words, on hunting and fishing. How-tos, where-tos, and adventure pieces. Profiles of successful hunters and fishermen. No hiking, canoeing, camping, or backpacking pieces. Pays $125 to $175 for state-specific articles, $200 to $250 for multi-state articles, before publication. Pays $25 to $75 for photos.

GOLF DIGEST—5520 Park Ave., Trumbull, CT 06611. Jerry Tarde, Ed. Instructional articles and features on players, to 2,500 words. Fiction, 1,000 to 2,000 words. Fillers, photos. Pays varying rates, on acceptance. Query preferred.

GOLF FOR WOMEN—125 Park Ave., 22nd Fl., New York, NY 10017. Susan Comolli, Sr. Ed. Leslie Day, Ed.-in-Chief. Timely, news-oriented pieces; new products and services; human interest stories concerning women, golf, and business. Query; include resumé and clips.

GOLF JOURNAL—Golf House, P.O. Box 708, Far Hills, NJ 07931-0708. Brett Avery, Ed. Official publication of the United States Golf Association. A general-interest magazine on the game with articles on a variety of contemporary and historic topics. Pays varying rates, on publication.

GOLF TIPS—Werner Publishing Corp., 12121 Wilshire Blvd., #1200, Los Angeles, CA 90025-1175. John Ledesma, Man. Ed. Articles, 500 to 1,500 words, for serious golfers: unique golf instruction, golf products, interviews with pro players. Fillers: short "shotmaking" instruction tips. Queries preferred. Pays $200 to $600, on publication.

THE GREYHOUND REVIEW—National Greyhound Assn., Box 543, Abilene, KS 67410. Tim Horan, Man. Ed. Articles, 1,000 to 10,000 words, pertaining to the greyhound racing industry: how-to, historical nostalgia, interviews. Pays $85 to $150, on publication.

GULF COAST GOLFER—See *North Texas Golfer*.

GUN DIGEST—Krause Publications, Inc., 700 E. State St., Iola, WI 54990. Ken Warner, Ed. Well-researched articles, to 5,000 words, on guns and shooting, equipment, etc. Photos. Pays from 10¢ a word, on acceptance. Query.

GUN DOG—P.O. Box 35098, Des Moines, IA 50315. Rick Van Etten, Man. Ed. Features, 1,000 to 2,500 words, with photos, on bird hunting: how-tos, where-tos, dog training, canine medicine, breeding strategy. Fiction. Humor. Pays $150 to $300 for fillers and short articles, $150 to $450 for features, on acceptance.

GUN WORLD—See *Bow & Arrow Hunting*.

GUNGAMES—Box 516, Moreno Valley, CA 92556. Roni Toldanes, Ed. Bimonthly. Articles and fiction, 1,200 to 1,500 words, about "the fun side of guns and shooting. No self-defense articles." Related poetry, to 300 words. Pays $250 to $350, on publication.

HANG GLIDING—U.S. Hang Gliding Assn., P.O. Box 1330, Colorado Springs, CO 80901-1330. Gilbert Dodgen, Ed. Articles, 2 to 3 pages, on hang gliding. Pays to $50, on publication. Query.

HOCKEY ILLUSTRATED—Lexington Library, Inc., 233 Park Ave. S., New York, NY 10003. Stephen Ciacciarelli, Ed. Articles, 2,500 words, on hockey players and teams. Pays $125, on publication. Query. Same address and requirements for *Baseball Illustrated, Wrestling World, Pro Basketball Illustrated, Pro Football Illustrated, Baseball Forecast, Pro Football Preview, Football Forecast,* and *Basketball Forecast.*

HORSE & RIDER—1597 Cole Blvd., Suite 350, Golden, CO 80401. Sue M. Copeland, Ed. Articles, 500 to 2,000 words, with photos, on western riding and training. and general horse care geared to the performance horse. Pays varying rates, on publication. Buys one-time rights. Guidelines.

HORSEMEN'S YANKEE PEDLAR—83 Leicester St., N. Oxford, MA 01537. Kelley R. Small, Pub. News and feature-length articles, about horses and horsemen in the Northeast. Photos. Pays $2 per published inch, on publication. Query.

HOT BOAT—Sport Publications, 8484 Wilshire Blvd., #900, Beverly Hills, CA 90211. Brett Bayne, Ed. Family-oriented articles, 600 to 1,000 words, on motorized water sport events and personalities: general-interest, how-to, and technical features. Pays $85 to $300, on publication. Query.

HUNTING—6420 Wilshire Blvd., Los Angeles, CA 90048-5515. Todd Smith, Ed. How-to/where-to articles on practical aspects of hunting. At least 15 photos required with articles. Query required. Guidelines. Pays $300 to $500 for articles with B&W photos, extra for color photos. Manuscripts are paid on acceptance; photos, on publication.

INSIDE SPORTS—990 Grove St., Evanston, IL 60201. Kenneth Leiker, Ed. In-depth, insightful nonfiction sports articles, player profiles relating to baseball, football, basketball, hockey, auto racing, and boxing. Payment varies, on publication. Query.

INSIDE TEXAS RUNNING—9514 Bristlebrook Dr., Houston, TX 77083-6193. Joanne Schmidt, Ed. Articles and fillers on running in Texas. Pays $35 to $100 for articles; $10 for short fillers; $10 to $25 for photos, on acceptance.

JOURNAL OF ASIAN MARTIAL ARTS—821 W. 24th St., Erie, PA 16502. Michael A. DeMarco, Ed. Quarterly. Articles, 2,000 to 10,000 words, on martial arts and Asian culture: interviews (with scholars, master practitioners, etc.) and scholarly articles based on primary research in recognized disciplines (cultural anthropology, comparative religion, etc.). Reviews, 1,000 words, of related books and audiovisual material. Pays $150 to $500 for articles, on publication; pays in copies for reviews.

KITPLANES—1000 Quail St., Suite 190, Newport Beach, CA 92660. Dave Martin, Ed. Articles, 1,000 to 4,000 words, on all aspects of design, construction, and performance of aircraft built from kits and plans by home craftsmen. Pays $60 per page, on publication.

LAKELAND BOATING—1560 Sherman Ave., Suite 1220, Evanston, IL 60201-5047. Randall W. Hess, Ed. Articles for powerboat owners on the Great Lakes and other area waterways, on long-distance cruising, short trips, maintenance, equipment, history, regional personalities and events, and environment. Photos. Pays on publication. Query. Guidelines.

MEN'S HEALTH—Rodale Press, 33 E. Minor St., Emmaus, PA 18098. David Zinczenko, Sr. Ed. Articles, 1,000 to 2,500 words, on sports, fitness, diet, health, nutrition, relationships, and travel, for men ages 25 to 55. Pays from 50¢ a word, on acceptance. Query.

MICHIGAN OUT-OF-DOORS—P.O. Box 30235, Lansing, MI 48909. Dennis Knickerbocker, Ed. Features, 1,000 to 1,500 words, on hunting, fishing, camping, hiking, sailing, wildlife, and conservation in Michigan. Pays $90 to $180, on acceptance.

MID-WEST OUTDOORS—111 Shore Dr., Hinsdale, IL 60521-5885. Gene Laulunen, Ed. Articles, 1,000 to 1,500 words, with photos, on where, when, and how to fish and hunt in the Midwest. No Canadian material. Pays $15 to $35, on publication.

MOTOR BOATING & SAILING—250 W. 55th St., 4th Fl., New York, NY 10019-5905. Peter A. Janssen, Ed./Pub. Articles, 1,500 words, on buying, maintaining, and enjoying boats. Hard-core, authoritative how-to. Query. Payment varies, on acceptance.

MOTOR TREND—6420 Wilshire Blvd., Los Angeles, CA 90048-5515. C. Van Tune, Ed. Articles, 250 to 2,000 words, on autos, racing, events, histories, and profiles. Color photos. Pay varies, on acceptance. Query.

MOTORHOME MAGAZINE—2575 Vista Del Mar, Ventura, CA 93001. Barbara Leonard, Ed. Dir. Articles, to 2,000 words, with color slides, on motorhomes. Also travel and how-to pieces. Pays to $600, on acceptance.

MUSHING—P.O. Box 149, Ester, AK 99725-0149. Todd Hoener, Ed. Dog-driving how-tos, profiles, and features, 1,500 to 2,000 words; and department pieces, 500 to 1,000 words, for competitive and recreational dogsled drivers, weight pullers, dog packers, and skijorers. International audience. Photos. Pays $20 to $175, on publication. Queries preferred. Guidelines and sample issue on request.

MUZZLE BLASTS—P.O. Box 67, Friendship, IN 47021-0067. Terri Trowbridge, Dir. of Pub. Articles, 500 to 1,500 words, on hunting with muzzleloading rifles, technical aspects of the rifles, historical pieces. Pays $50 to $400, on publication. Send for guidelines.

NATIONAL PARKS MAGAZINE—1776 Massachusetts Ave. N.W., Washington, DC 20036. Leslie Happ, Ed.-in-Chief. Articles, 1,500 to 2,000 words, on areas in the National Park System, proposed new areas, threats to parks or park wildlife, new trends in park use, legislative issues, and endangered species of plants or animals relevant to national parks. No fiction, poetry, personal narratives, "My trip to...," or straight travel pieces to individual parks. Also, articles, 1,500 words, on "low-impact" travel to national park sites. Pays $400 to $1,000, on acceptance. Query with clips. Guidelines with SASE.

NEW YORK OUTDOORS—Allsport Publishing Corp., 51 Atlantic Ave., Floral Park, NY 11001. Scott Shane, Ed.-in-Chief. Features, to 1,500 words, with B&W prints or color transparencies, on any aspect of outdoor sports travel or adventure in northeast U.S. Pays to $250 for major features. Queries preferred.

NORTH TEXAS GOLFER—9182 Old Katy Rd., Suite 212, Houston, TX 77055. Bob Gray, Pub. Articles, 800 to 1,500 words, of interest to golfers in north Texas. Pays $50 to $250, on publication. Queries required. Same requirements for *Gulf Coast Golfer* (for golfers in south Texas).

NORTHEAST OUTDOORS—Woodall Publishing Corp., 13975 W. Polo Trail Dr., Lake Forest, IL 60045-5000. Brent Peterson, Ed. Articles, 1,000 to 2,000 words, preferably with B&W photos, on camping and recreational vehicle (RV) touring in northeast U.S.: camp cookery, recreational vehicle hints. Stress how-to, where-to. Cartoons. Pay varies. Guidelines.

OFFSHORE—220-9 Reservoir St., Needham Heights, MA 02194. Suzanne Althoff, Man. Ed. Articles, 1,200 to 2,500 words, on boats, people, places, maritime history, and events along the New England, New York, and New Jersey coasts. Writers should be knowledgeable boaters. Photos a plus. Pays $250 to $500.

OPEN WHEEL— 65 Parker St., #2, Newburyport, MA 01950. Dick Berggren, Ed. Articles, to 6,000 words, on open wheel drivers, races, and vehicles. Photos. Pays to $400 on publication.

OUTDOOR AMERICA—707 Conservation Ln., Gaithersburg, MD 20878-2983. Attn: Articles Ed. Quarterly publication of the Izaak Walton League of America. Articles, 1,250 to 2,000 words, on natural resource conservation issues and outdoor recreation, with emphasis on IWLA member/chapter tie-in; especially fishing, hunting, and camping. Also, short items, 500 to 750 words. Pays 30¢ a word. Query with clips. No unsolicited manuscripts.

OUTDOOR CANADA—703 Evans Ave., Suite 202, Toronto, Ont., Canada M9C 5E9. James Little, Ed. Published 8 times yearly. Articles, 1,500 to 3,000 words, on fishing, camping, hiking, canoeing, hunting, and wildlife. Pays $500 and upwards, on publication.

OUTDOOR LIFE—2 Park Ave., New York, NY 10016. Todd W. Smith, Ed.-in-Chief. Articles, 1,400 to 1,700 words, and short, instructive items, 900 to 1,100 words, on hunting, fishing, boats, outdoor equipment, and related subjects. Pays $300 to $550, on acceptance. Query.

PADDLER MAGAZINE—P.O. Box 775450, Steamboat Springs, CO 80477. Eugene Buchanan, Ed. Dir. Articles on canoeing, kayaking, rafting, sea kayaking. "Best way to break in is to target a specific department, i.e. 'Hotlines,' 'Paddle People,' etc." Pays $5 an inch, on publication. Query preferred. Guidelines.

PENNSYLVANIA ANGLER AND BOATER—Pennsylvania Fish and Boat Commission, P.O. Box 67000, Harrisburg, PA 17106-7000. Attn: Art Michaels, Ed. Articles, 500 to 3,000 words, with photos, on freshwater fishing in Pennsylvania. Pays $50 to $400, on acceptance. Must send SASE with all material. Query. Guidelines.

PENNSYLVANIA GAME NEWS—Game Commission, 2001 Elmerton Ave., Harrisburg, PA 17110-9797. Bob Mitchell, Ed. Articles, to 2,500 words, on hunting, wildlife, and other outdoor subjects, except fishing and boating. Photos. Pays from 6¢ a word, extra for photos, on acceptance.

PETERSEN'S BOWHUNTING— 6420 Wilshire Blvd., Los Angeles, CA 90048-5515. Jay Michael Strangis, Ed. How-to articles, 2,000 to 2,500 words, on bowhunting. Also pieces on where to bowhunt, unusual techniques and equipment, and profiles of successful bowhunters will also be considered. Photos must accompany all manuscripts. Pays $300 to $400, on acceptance. Query with SASE.

PETERSEN'S HUNTING— 6420 Wilshire Blvd., 14th Fl., Los Angeles, CA 90048-5515. Todd Smith, Ed. How-to articles, 2,250 words, on all aspects of sport hunting. B&W photos; color slides. Pays $300 to $500, on acceptance. Query with SASE.

PGA MAGAZINE— 888 W. Big Beaver Rd., Suite 600, Troy, MI 48084-4737. Attn: Ed. Articles, 1,500 to 2,500 words, on golf-related subjects. Pays $300 to $500, on acceptance. Query.

PLANE & PILOT—12121 Wilshire Blvd., #1200, Los Angeles, CA 90025-1175. Steve Werner, Ed. Aviation related articles, 1,500 to 2,500 words, targeted to the single engine, piston powered recreational pilot. Training, maintenance, travel, equipment, pilot reports. Occasional features on antique, classic, and kit- or home-built aircraft. Payment varies, on publication. Query preferred.

POWER AND MOTORYACHT—249 W. 17th St., New York, NY 10011. Diane M. Byrne, Sr. Ed. Articles, 1,000 to 2,000 words, for owners of powerboats, 24 feet and larger. Seamanship, ship's systems, maintenance, sportfishing news, travel destinations, profiles of individuals working to improve the marine environment. "For our readers, powerboating is truly a lifestyle, not just a hobby." Pays $500 to $1,000, on acceptance. Query required.

POWERBOAT—1691 Spinnaker Dr., Suite 206, Ventura, CA 93001. Eric Colby, Ed. Articles, to 2,000 words, with photos, for high performance powerboat owners, on outstanding achievements, water-skiing, competitions; technical articles on hull and engine developments; how-to pieces. Pays $300 to $1,000, on publication. Query.

PRACTICAL HORSEMAN—Box 589, Unionville, PA 19375. Mandy Lorraine, Ed. How-to articles conveying experts' advice on English riding, training, and horse care. Pays on acceptance. Query with clips.

PRIVATE PILOT MAGAZINE—265 S. Anita Dr., Suite 120, Orange, CA 92868-3310. Bill Fedorko, Exec. Ed. Fly-in destinations, hands-on, how-to, informative articles, 1,500 to 3,000 words, for general aviation pilots, aircraft owners, and aviation enthusiasts. Quality photos. Pays $300 to $650, on publication. Query.

PRO BASKETBALL ILLUSTRATED—See *Hockey Illustrated.*

PRO FOOTBALL ILLUSTRATED, PRO FOOTBALL PREVIEW—See *Hockey Illustrated.*

RESTORATION—P.O. Box 50046, Dept. TW, Tucson, AZ 85703-1046. W.R. Haessner, Ed. Articles, 1,200 to 1,800 words, on restoration projects in general, as well as restoration of autos, trucks, planes, trains, etc., and related building (bridges and structures). Photos. Pays from $25 per page, on publication. Queries required.

RIDER—2575 Vista Del Mar, Ventura, CA 93001. Mark Tuttle Jr., Ed. Articles, to 2,000 words, with slides, on travel, touring, commuting, and camping motorcyclists. Pays $100 to $750, on publication. Query.

ROCK & ICE MAGAZINE— 603A S. Broadway, Boulder, CO 80303. Dougald MacDonald, Ed. Bimonthly. Articles, 500 to 4,000 words, for technical rock and ice climbers: sport climbers, mountaineers, alpinists, and other adventurers. Slides and B&W photos considered. Query. Pays $300 per published page.

RUNNER TRIATHLETE NEWS—P.O. Box 19909, Houston, TX 77224. Lance Phegley, Ed. Articles on running for road racing and multi-sport enthusiasts in TX, OK, NM, LA, and AR. Payment varies, on publication.

RUNNER'S WORLD—Rodale Press, 33 E. Minor St., Emmaus, PA 18098. Bob Wischnia, Sr. Ed. Articles for "Human Race" (submit to Eileen Shovlin), "Finish Line" (to Cristina Negron), and "Health Watch" (to Adam Bean) columns. Send feature articles or queries to Bob Wischnia. Payment varies, on acceptance. Query.

RV TRAVELER—Woodall Publishing Co., P.O. Box 5000, Lake Forest, IL 60045-5000. Brent Peterson, Ed. RV-related travel articles, 1,000 to 1,200 words, for Midwest camping families.

SAFARI—4800 W. Gates Pass Rd., Tucson, AZ 85745. William Quimby, Publications Dir. Lisa M. Ludy, Manuscripts Ed. Articles, 2,000 words, on worldwide big game hunting and/or conservation projects of Safari Club International's local chapters. Pays $200, extra for photos, on publication.

SAILING—125 E. Main St., Port Washington, WI 53074. M. L. Hutchins, Ed. Features, 700 to 1,500 words, with photos, on cruising and racing; first-person accounts; profiles of boats and regattas. Query for technical or how-to pieces. Pays varying rates, 30 days after publication. Guidelines.

SALT WATER SPORTSMAN—77 Franklin St., Boston, MA 02110. Barry Gibson, Ed. Articles, 1,200 to 1,500 words, on how anglers can improve their skills, and on new places to fish off the coast of the U.S. and Canada, Central America, the Caribbean, and Bermuda. Photos a plus. Pays $350 to $700, on acceptance. Query.

SEA, AMERICA'S WESTERN BOATING MAGAZINE—17782 Cowan, Suite C, Irvine, CA 92614. Bart Ortberg, Man. Ed. Features, 800 to 1,500 words, and news articles, 200 to 250 words, of interest to West Coast power boaters: cruise destinations, analyses of marine environmental issues, technical pieces on navigation and seamanship, news from western harbors. No fiction, poetry, or cartoons. Pays varying rates, on publication.

SEA KAYAKER—P.O. Box 17170, Seattle, WA 98107-0870. Christopher Cunningham, Ed. Articles, 400 to 4,500 words, on ocean kayaking. Related fiction. Pays about 12¢ a word, on publication. Query with clips and international reply coupons.

SHOTGUN SPORTS—P.O. Box 6810, Auburn, CA 95604. Frank Kodl, Ed. Articles with photos, on trap and skeet shooting, sporting clays, hunting with shotguns, reloading, gun tests, and instructional shooting. Pays $25 to $200, on publication.

SILENT SPORTS—717 10th St., P.O. Box 152, Waupaca, WI 54981-9990. Attn: Ed. Articles, 1,000 to 2,000 words, on bicycling, cross country skiing, running, canoeing, hiking, backpacking, and other "silent" sports. Must have regional (upper Midwest) focus. Pays $50 to $100 for features; $20 to $50 for fillers, on publication. Query.

SKI MAGAZINE—929 Pearl St., Suite 200, Boulder, CO 80302. Andy Bigford, Ed. Articles, 1,300 to 2,500 words, for experienced skiers: profiles, and destination articles. Short, 100-to 300-word, news items for "Ski Life" column. Equipment instruction and racing articles are staff-written. Query (with clips) for articles. Pays from $50, on acceptance.

SKI RACING INTERNATIONAL—Box 1125, Rt. 100, Waitsfield, VT 05673. Tim Etchells, Ed. Articles by experts on race techniques and conditioning secrets. Coverage of World Cup, pro, collegiate, and junior ski and snowboard competition. Comprehensive results. Photos. Rates vary.

SKYDIVING MAGAZINE—1725 N. Lexington Ave., DeLand, FL 32724. Sue Clifton, Ed. Timely news articles, 300 to 800 words, relating to sport and military parachuting. Fillers. Photos. Pays $25 to $200, extra for photos, on publication.

SNOW COUNTRY—5520 Park Ave., Trumbull, CT 06611-0395. Kathleen Ring, Sr. Ed. Published 8 times a year. Features, 2,500 to 4,000 words, and articles, 1,000 to 2,000 words on skiing, mountain biking, in-line skating, camping, rafting and other year-round mountain sports as well as lifestyle issues. First-person adventure articles, travel pieces, service-oriented articles, profiles of snow country residents. "Mountain Living," 100-to 700-word pieces on people and points of view, anecdotes, trends, issues. Query with clips and resumé. Pays 80¢ a word, on acceptance.

SNOWBOARDER—P.O. Box 1028, Dana Point, CA 92629. Rob Campbell, Man. Ed. Doug Palladini, Pub. Bimonthly. Articles, 1,000 to 1,500 words, on snowboarding personalities, techniques, and adventure; color transparencies or B&W prints. Limited fiction market, 1,000 to 1,500 words. Pays $150 to $800, on acceptance and on publication.

SNOWEST—520 Park Ave., Idaho Falls, ID 83402. Lane Lindstrom, Ed. Articles, 1,200 words, on snowmobiling in the western states. Pays to $100, on publication.

THE SNOWSHOER—Box 458, Washburn, WI 54891. Jim Radtke, Ed. Fiction and articles on snowshoeing, 1,000 to 1,500 words. Pays 5¢ a word, on publication. Queries preferred.

SOCCER JR.—27 Unquowa Rd., Fairfield, CT 06430. Joe Provey, Ed. Articles, fiction, and fillers related to soccer for readers in 5th and 6th grade. Pays $450 for features; $250 for department pieces, on acceptance. Query.

SOUTH CAROLINA WILDLIFE—P. O. Box 167, Columbia, SC 29202-0167. John E. Davis, Ed. Articles, 1,000 to 2,000 words, with state and regional outdoor focus: conservation, natural history, wildlife, and recreation. Profiles, how-tos. Pays on acceptance.

SPORT MAGAZINE— 6420 Wilshire Blvd., Los Angeles, CA 90048. Cam Benty, Ed. Dir. No fiction, poetry, or first person. Query with clips.

SPORTS ILLUSTRATED—1271 Ave. of the Americas, New York, NY 10020. Chris Hunt, Articles Ed. Query.

SPORTS ILLUSTRATED FOR KIDS—1271 Ave. of the Americas, New York, NY 10020. Steve Malley, Asst. Man. Ed. Articles, 1,000 to 1,500 words, (submit to Bob Der) and short features, 500 to 600 words, (submit to Erin Egan) for 8-to 13-year-olds. "Most articles are staff-written. Department pieces are the best bet for free lancers." (Read magazine and guidelines to learn about specific departments.) Puzzles and games (submit to Nick Friedman). No fiction or poetry. Pays $500 for departments, $1,000 to $1,250 for articles, on acceptance. Query required.

STOCK CAR RACING— 65 Parker St., #2, Newburyport, MA 01950. Dick Berggren, Feature Ed. Articles, to 6,000 words, on stock car drivers, races, and vehicles. Photos. Pays to $400, on publication.

SWEAT—736 E. Loyola Dr., Tempe, AZ 85282. Joan Westlake, Ed. Articles, 500 to 1,200 words, on sports or fitness with an Arizona angle. "No personal articles or tales. We want investigative pieces. Articles must relate specifically to Arizona or Arizonans." Pays $25 to $60 for articles; $12 to $70 for photos, on publication. Queries required; no unsolicited manuscripts.

T'AI CHI—P.O. Box 26156, Los Angeles, CA 90026. Marvin Smalheiser, Ed. Articles, 800 to 4,000 words, on T'ai Chi Ch'uan, other internal martial arts and related topics such as qigong, Chinese medicine and healing practices, Chinese philosophy and culture, health, meditation, fitness, and self-improvement. Pays $75 to $500, on publication. Query required. Guidelines.

TENNIS—5520 Park Ave., P. O. Box 0395, Trumbull, CT 06611-0395. Donna Doherty, Ed. Instructional articles, features, profiles of tennis stars, grassroots articles, humor, 800 to 2,000 words. Photos. Payment varies, on publication. Query.

TENNIS WEEK—341 Madison Ave., #600, New York, NY 10017-3705. Eugene L. Scott, Pub. Kim Kodl, Heather Holland, Randy Master, Man. Eds. In-depth, researched articles, from 1,000 words, on current issues and personalities in the game. Pays $125, on publication.

TRAILER BOATS—20700 Belshaw Ave., Carson, CA 90746-3510. Randy Scott, Ed. Lifestyle, technical and how-to articles, 500 to 2,000 words, on boat, trailer, or tow vehicle maintenance and operation; skiing, fishing, and cruising. Fillers, humor. Pays $100 to $700, on acceptance.

VELONEWS—1830 N. 55th St., Boulder, CO 80301. John Wilcockson, Ed. John Rezell, Sr. Ed. Articles, 500 to 1,500 words, on competitive cycling, training, nutrition; profiles, interviews. No how-to or touring articles. "We focus on the elite of the sport." Pay varies, on publication.

THE WALKING MAGAZINE—9-11 Harcourt, Boston, MA 02116. Seth Bauer, Ed. Articles, 1,500 to 2,000 words, on fitness, health, equipment, nutrition, travel, and adventure, famous walkers, and other walking-related topics. Shorter pieces, 500 to 1,500 words, and essays for "Ramblings" page. Photos welcome. Pays $750 to $2,500 for features, $100 to $600 for department pieces, on acceptance. Guidelines.

THE WATER SKIER—799 Overlook Dr., Winter Haven, FL 33884. Samantha Clark, Man. Ed. Feature articles on water skiing. Pays varying rates, on publication.

WATERSKI—World Publications, Inc., 330 W. Canton Ave., Winter Park, FL 32789. Rob May, Ed. Features, 1,250 to 2,000 words, on boating and water skiing. Instructional features, 1,350 words, including sidebars; quick tips, 350 words. (Travel pieces and profiles are done on assignment only.) Pays $35 for fillers; $125 to $500 for columns and features, after acceptance. Guidelines. Query.

THE WESTERN HORSEMAN—P.O. Box 7980, Colorado Springs, CO 80933-7980. Pat Close, Ed. Articles, about 1,500 words, with photos, on care and training of horses; farm, ranch, and stable management; health care and veterinary medicine. Pays to $800, on acceptance.

WESTERN OUTDOORS—3197-E Airport Loop, Costa Mesa, CA 92626. Attn: Ed. Timely, factual articles on fishing, 1,200 to 1,500 words, of interest to western sportsmen. Pays $400 to $500, on acceptance. Query. Guidelines.

WESTERN SPORTSMAN—140 Ave. F N., Saskatoon, Sask., Canada S7L 1V8. George Gruenefeld, Ed. Articles, to 2,500 words, on hunting and fishing in British Columbia, Alberta, Saskatchewan, and Manitoba; how-to pieces. Photos. Pays $75 to $300, on publication.

WINDY CITY SPORTS—1450 W. Randolph, Chicago, IL 60607. Jeff Banowetz, Ed. Articles, 1,000 words, on amateur sports in Chicago. Pays $100, on publication. Query required.

WOMEN'S SPORTS & FITNESS—2025 Pearl St., Boulder, CO 80302. Dagny Scott, Ed. Articles on fitness, nutrition, outdoor sports; how-tos; profiles; adventure travel pieces; and controversial issues in women's sports, 500 to 2,000 words. Pays on publication.

WRESTLING WORLD—See *Hockey Illustrated.*

YACHTING—20 E. Elm St., Greenwich, CT 06830. Charles Barthold, Ed. Articles, 1,500 words, on upscale recreational power and sail boating. How-to and personal-experience pieces. Photos. Pays $350 to $1,000, on acceptance. Queries preferred.

AUTOMOTIVE MAGAZINES

AMERICAN MOTORCYCLIST—American Motorcyclist Assn., 33 Collegeview Rd., Westerville, OH 43081-1484. Greg Harrison, Ed. Articles and fiction, to 3,000 words, on motorcycling: news coverage, personalities, tours. Photos. Pays varying rates, on publication. Query with SASE.

CAR AND DRIVER—2002 Hogback Rd., Ann Arbor, MI 48105. Steve Spence, Man. Ed. Articles and profiles, to 2,500 words, on unusual people or manufacturers involved in cars, racing, etc. "Ninety-five percent staff-written. Query with clips. No unsolicited manuscripts." Pays to $2,500, on acceptance.

CAR & TRAVEL—1000 AAA Dr., Heathrow, FL 32746-5063. Douglas Damerst, Ed. Automobile and travel concerns, including automotive travel, purchasing, and upkeep, 750 to 1,500 words. Pays $300 to $600, on acceptance. Query with clips; articles are by assignment only.

CAR CRAFT—6420 Wilshire Blvd., Los Angeles, CA 90048. David Freiburger, Ed. Articles and photo-features on high performance street machines, drag cars, racing events; technical pieces; action photos. Pays from $150 per page, on publication.

CYCLE WORLD—1499 Monrovia Ave., Newport Beach, CA 92663. David Edwards, Ed.-in-Chief. Technical and feature articles, 1,500 to 2,500 words, for motorcycle enthusiasts. Photos. Pays $100 to $200 per page, on publication. Query.

MOTOR TREND—6420 Wilshire Blvd., Los Angeles, CA 90048-5515. C. Van Tune, Ed. Articles, 250 to 2,000 words, on autos, auto history, racing, events, and profiles. Photos required. Pay varies, on acceptance. Query.

OPEN WHEEL—See *Stock Car Racing.*

RESTORATION—P.O. Box 50046, Dept. TW, Tucson, AZ 85703-1046. W.R. Haessner, Ed. Articles, 1,200 to 1,800 words, on restoration of autos, trucks, planes, trains, etc., and buildings (bridges, structures, etc.). Photos. Pays from $25 per page, on publication. Queries required.

RIDER—2575 Vista Del Mar Dr., Ventura, CA 93001. Mark Tuttle Jr., Ed. Articles, to 2,000 words, with color slides, on travel, touring, commuting, and camping motorcyclists. Pays $100 to $750, on publication. Query.

ROAD & TRACK—1499 Monrovia Ave., Newport Beach, CA 92663. Ellida Maki, Man. Ed. Short automotive articles, to 450 words, of a "timeless nature" for knowledgeable car enthusiasts. Pays on publication. Query.

ROAD KING—Hammock Publishing, 3322 W. End Ave., Suite 700, Nashville, TN 37203. Tom Berg, Ed. Bill Hudgins, Ed. Dir. Bimonthly. Articles, 300 to 1,500 words, on business of trucking from a driver's point of view; profiles of drivers and their rigs; technical aspects of trucking equipment; trucking history; travel destinations near major interstates; humor; fillers. No fiction. Include clips with submission. Pays negotiable rates, on acceptance.

STOCK CAR RACING—65 Parker St., #2, Newburyport, MA 01950. Dick Berggren, Ed. Features, technical automotive pieces, and profiles of interesting racing personalities, to 6,000 words, for oval track racing enthusiasts. Fillers. Pays $75 to $350, on publication. Same requirements for *Open Wheel*.

FITNESS MAGAZINES

AMERICAN FITNESS—15250 Ventura Blvd., Suite 200, Sherman Oaks, CA 91403. Peg Jordan, R.N., Ed. Rhonda Wilson, Man. Ed. Articles, 500 to 1,500 words, on exercise, health, research, trends, research, nutrition, alternative paths, etc. Illustrations, photos.

COOKING LIGHT—P.O. Box 1748, Birmingham, AL 35201. Melissa Aspell, Fitness Ed. Articles on fitness, exercise, health and healthful cooking, nutrition, and healthful recipes. Query.

FIT MAGAZINE—1700 Broadway, New York, NY 10019. Lisa Klugman, Ed. Lively, readable service-oriented articles, 800 to 1,200 words, on exercise, nutrition, lifestyle, and health for women ages 18 to 35. Writers should have some background in or knowledge of sports, fitness, and/or health. Also considers 500-word essays for "Finally Fit" column by readers who have lost weight and kept it off. Pays $300 to $500, on publication. Query.

FITNESS—Gruner & Jahr USA Publishing, 375 Lexington Ave., New York, NY 10017-5514. Sally Lee, Ed. Articles, 500 to 2,000 words, on health, exercise, sports, nutrition, diet, psychological well-being, alternative therapies, sex, and beauty for readers around 30 years old. Queries required. Pays approximately $1 per word, on acceptance.

FITNESS PLUS—12 W. 27th St., New York, NY 10001-6903. Steve Romondi, Ed. Articles, 1,000 to 3,000 words, on serious health and fitness training for men. Payment varies, on publication. Queries preferred.

IDEA HEALTH & FITNESS SOURCE—(formerly *Idea Today*) 6190 Cornerstone Ct. E., Suite 204, San Diego, CA 92121-3773. Ed. Practical articles, 1,000 to 3,000 words, on new exercise programs, business management, nutrition, sports medicine, dance-exercise, and one-to-one training techniques. Articles must be geared toward the aerobics instructor, exercise studio owner or manager, or personal trainer. No consumer or general health articles. Payment is negotiable, on acceptance. Query preferred.

IDEA PERSONAL TRAINER—6190 Cornerstone Ct. E., Suite 204, San Diego, CA 92121-3773. Ed. Association publication for personal fitness trainers. Articles on exercise science; program design; profiles of successful trainers; business, legal, and marketing topics; tips for networking with other trainers and with allied medical professionals; client counseling; and training tips. "What's New" column includes industry news, products, and research. Query. Payment varies, on acceptance.

IDEA TODAY—See *Idea Health & Fitness Source*.

INSIDE TEXAS RUNNING— 9514 Bristlebrook Dr., Houston, TX 77083-6193. Joanne Schmidt, Ed. Articles and fillers on running in Texas. Pays $35 to $100 for articles; $10 to $25 for photos and short fillers, on acceptance.

MEN'S FITNESS—21100 Erwin St., Woodland Hills, CA 91367. Jerry Kindela, Ed.-in-Chief. Features, 1,500 to 1,800 words, and department pieces, 1,200 to 1,500 words, dealing with fitness. Pay varies, 6 weeks after acceptance. Limited market.

MEN'S HEALTH—Rodale Press, 33 E. Minor St., Emmaus, PA 18098. Lou Schuler, Fitness Ed. Articles, 1,000 to 2,500 words, on fitness, diet, health, relationships, sports, and travel, for men ages 25 to 55. Pays from 50¢ a word, on acceptance. Query.

THE PHYSICIAN AND SPORTSMEDICINE— 4530 W. 77th St., Minneapolis, MN 55435. Susan Hawthorne, Exec. Ed. News and feature articles. Clinical articles must be co-authored by physicians. Sports medicine angle necessary. Pays $300 to $1,600, on acceptance. Query. Guidelines.

PRIME HEALTH & FITNESS—21100 Erwin St., Woodland Hills, CA 91367. Bill Bush, Exec. Ed. Quarterly. Articles, 1,200 to 1,800 words, and department pieces, 600 to 800 words, on health and fitness challenges and lifestyle activities for men over 40.

SHAPE—21100 Erwin St., Woodland Hills, CA 91367-3772. Peg Moline, Ed. Dir. Articles, 1,200 to 1,500 words, with new and interesting ideas on the physical and mental side of getting and staying in shape; reports, 300 to 400 words, on journal research. Payment varies, on publication. Guidelines. Limited market.

SWEAT—736 E. Loyola Dr., Tempe, AZ 85282. Joan Westlake, Ed. Articles, 500 to 1,200 words, on amateur sports, outdoor activities, wellness, or fitness with an Arizona angle. "No self-indulgent or personal tales. We want investigative pieces. Articles must relate specifically to Arizona or Arizonans." Pays $25 to $60 for articles; $15 to $70 for photos, on publication. Queries required; no unsolicited manuscripts. Web site: Westwoman@aol.com

VIM & VIGOR— 1010 E. Missouri Ave., Phoenix, AZ 85014. Jenn Woolson, Ed. Positive articles, with accurate medical facts, on health and fitness, 1,200 to 2,000 words, by assignment only. Writers may submit qualifications for assignment. Pays $500, on acceptance. Guidelines with SASE.

THE WALKING MAGAZINE— 9-11 Harcourt, Boston, MA 02116. Seth Bauer, Ed. Articles, 1,500 to 2,500 words, on fitness, health, equipment, nutrition, travel and adventure, and other walking-related topics. Shorter pieces, 150 to 800 words, and essays for "Ramblings" page. Photos welcome. Pays $750 to $1,800 for features, $100 to $500 for department pieces, within a week of acceptance. Guidelines.

WEIGHT WATCHERS MAGAZINE—2100 Lakeshore Dr., Birmingham, AL 35209. Articles on health, nutrition, fitness, and weight-loss motivation and success. Pays from $500, on acceptance. Query with clips required. Guidelines.

WOMEN'S SPORTS & FITNESS—2025 Pearl St., Boulder, CO 80302. Dagny Scott, Ed. Articles on fitness, nutrition, outdoor sports; how-tos; profiles; adventure travel pieces; and controversial issues in women's sports, 500 to 2,000 words. Pays on publication.

YOGA JOURNAL—2054 University Ave., Berkeley, CA 94704. Rick Fields, Ed. Articles, 300 to 6,000 words, on holistic health, meditation, conscious living, spirituality, and yoga. Pays $75 to $300, on acceptance.

CONSUMER/PERSONAL FINANCE

BLACK ENTERPRISE—130 Fifth Ave., New York, NY 10011. Earl G. Graves, Ed. Articles on money management, careers, political issues, entrepreneurship, high technology, and lifestyles for black professionals. Profiles. Pays on acceptance. Query.

COMPLETE WOMAN— 875 N. Michigan Ave., Suite 3434, Chicago, IL 60611. Bonnie Krueger, Ed. Lora Wintz, Sr. Ed. Articles, 1,000 to 2,000 words, with how-to sidebars, giving advice to women. Also interested in reprints. Pays varying rates, on publication. Query with clips.

ESSENCE—1500 Broadway, New York, NY 10036. Susan L. Taylor, Ed.-in-Chief. Monique Greenwood, Ed. Articles, 800 to 2,500 words, for black women in America today, on business and finance, as well as health, art, travel, politics, and celebrity profiles, self-help pieces, how-tos. Payment varies, on acceptance. Query.

FAMILY CIRCLE—375 Lexington Ave., New York, NY 10017. Ann Matturo, Jennifer Pirtle, Editors-Writers. Enterprising, creative, and practical articles, 1,000 to 1,500 words, on investing, smart ways to save money, secrets of successful entrepreneurs, and consumer news on smart shopping. Pays $1 a word, on acceptance. Query with clips.

GOOD HOUSEKEEPING— 959 Eighth Ave., New York, NY 10019. Lisa Benenson, Better Way Ed. Short advice-driven articles on money, finances, consumer issues, health, and safety for "Better Way" section. Pays good rates, on acceptance. Guidelines.

HOME MECHANIX—See *Today's Homeowner.*

KIPLINGER'S PERSONAL FINANCE MAGAZINE—1729 H St. N.W., Washington, DC 20006. Attn: Ed. Dept. Articles on personal finance (i.e., buying insurance, mutual funds). Pays varying rates, on acceptance. Query required.

KIWANIS—3636 Woodview Trace, Indianapolis, IN 46468. Chuck Jonak, Man. Ed. Articles, 2,500 words, on financial planning for younger families and retirement planning for older people. Pays $500 to $1,000, on acceptance. Query required.

MODERN BRIDE—249 W. 17th St., New York, NY 10011. Mary Ann Cavlin, Exec. Ed. Articles, 1,500 to 2,000 words, for bride and groom, on wedding planning, financial planning, juggling career and home, etc. Pays $600 to $1,200, on acceptance.

THE MONEYPAPER—1010 Mamaroneck Ave., Mamaroneck, NY 10543. Vita Nelson, Ed. Financial news and money-saving ideas; particularly interested in information about companies with dividend reinvestment plans. Brief, well-researched articles on personal finance, money management: saving, earning, investing, taxes, insurance, and related subjects. Pays $75 for articles, on publication. Query with resumé and writing sample.

NEW CHOICES: LIVING EVEN BETTER AFTER 50—28 W. 23rd St., New York, NY 10010. Greg Daugherty, Ed.-in-Chief. News and service magazine for people ages 50 to 65. Articles on retirement planning, financial strategies, housing options, as well as health and fitness, travel, leisure pursuits, etc. Payment varies, on acceptance.

OUT—The Soho Bldg., 110 Greene St., Suite 600, New York, NY 10012. James Collard, Ed.-in-Chief. Articles, 50 to 8,000 words, on arts, politics, fashion, finance and other subjects for gay and lesbian readers. Guidelines. Query.

ROBB REPORT—1 Acton Pl., Acton, MA 01720. Steven Castle, Ed. Features on investment opportunities for high-end/luxury market. Lifestyle articles, home interiors, boats, travel, exotic automobiles, business, technology, etc. Payment varies, on publication. Query with SASE and clips.

TODAY'S HOMEOWNER—(formerly *Home Mechanix*) 2 Park Ave., New York, NY 10016. Paul Spring, Ed.-in-Chief. Home improvement articles, remodeling, maintenance, home finances. Time- or money-saving tips for the home and yard. Pays from $900 for features. Up to 15% free-lance written.

WOMAN'S DAY—1633 Broadway, New York, NY 10019. Stephanie Abarbanel, Sr. Articles Ed. Articles, 750 to 2,000 words, on financial matters of interest to a broad range of women. Pays to $750, on acceptance. Query with SASE. No unsolicited manuscripts.

YOUR MONEY—8001 N. Lincoln Ave., Skokie, IL 60077. Dennis Fertig, Ed. Informative, jargon-free personal finance articles, to 2,500 words, for the general reader, on investment opportunities and personal finance. Pays 50¢ a word, on acceptance. Query Deborah Rogus, Assoc. Ed., with clips for assignment. (Do not send manuscripts on disks.)

BUSINESS & TRADE PUBLICATIONS

ABA JOURNAL—American Bar Assn., 750 N. Lake Shore Dr., Chicago, IL 60611. Gary A. Hengstler, Ed./Pub. Articles, to 3,000 words, on law-related topics: current events in the law and ideas that will help lawyers practice better and more efficiently. Writing should be in an informal, journalistic style. Payment varies; buys all rights. Limited market.

ACROSS THE BOARD—845 Third Ave., New York, NY 10022. Melissa Master, Asst. to the Ed. Articles, 1,000 to 4,000 words, on a variety of topics of interest to business executives; straight business angle not required. Payment varies, on publication.

ALTERNATIVE ENERGY RETAILER—P.O. Box 2180, Waterbury, CT 06722. David Johnston, Ed. Feature articles, 1,000 words, for retailers of hearth products, including appliances that burn wood, coal, pellets, and gas, and hearth accessories and services. Interviews with successful retailers, stressing the how-to. B&W photos. Pays $200, extra for photos, on publication. Query.

AMERICAN BANKER—One State Street Plaza, New York, NY 10004. Phil Roosevelt, Ed. Articles, 1,000 to 3,000 words, on banking and financial services, technology in banking, consumer financial services, investment products. Pays varying rates, on publication. Query preferred.

AMERICAN COIN-OP—500 N. Dearborn St., Chicago, IL 60610-9988. Paul Partika, Ed. Articles, to 2,500 words, with photos, on successful coin-operated laundries: management, promotion, decor, maintenance, etc. Pays from 8¢ a word, $8 per B&W photo, 2 weeks prior to publication. Query. Send SASE for guidelines.

AMERICAN DEMOGRAPHICS—P.O. Box 68, Ithaca, NY 14851-9989. Shannon Dortch, Sr. Ed. Articles, 500 to 2,000 words, on the 4 key elements of a consumer market (its size, its needs and wants, its ability to pay, and how it can be reached), with specific examples of how companies market to consumers. Readers include marketers, advertisers, and strategic planners. Pays $100 to $500, on acceptance. Query.

AMERICAN LAUNDRY NEWS—500 N. Dearborn St., Room 1100, Chicago, IL 60610. Larry K. Ebert Articles, 500 to 1,500 words, on the institutional laundering trade as practiced in hotels, hospitals, correctional facilities, and nursing homes. Infection control, government regulation, new technology, major projects, industrial accidents, litigation, and mergers and acquisitions. Query. Pays $100 to $300, on publication.

AMERICAN MEDICAL NEWS—515 N. State St., Chicago, IL 60610. Wayne Hearn, Topic Ed. Articles, 900 to 1,500 words, on socioeconomic developments in health care of interest to physicians across the country. No pieces on health, clinical treatments, or research. Pays $500 to $1,500, on acceptance. Query required. Guidelines.

AMERICAN SCHOOL & UNIVERSITY—P.O. Box 12901, 9800 Metcalf, Overland Park, KS 66212-2216. Joe Agron, Ed. Articles and case studies, 1,200 to 1,500 words, on design, construction, operation, and management of school and university facilities. Queries preferred.

ARCHITECTURE—1130 Connecticut Ave. N.W., Suite 625, Washington, DC 20036. Deborah Dietsch, Ed. Articles, to 3,000 words, on architecture, building technology, professional practice. Pays 50¢ a word.

AREA DEVELOPMENT MAGAZINE— 400 Post Ave., Westbury, NY 11590. Geraldine Gambale, Ed. Articles for top executives of industrial companies on sites and facility planning. Pays 25¢ a word. Query.

ART BUSINESS NEWS—270 Madison Ave., 6th Fl., New York, NY 10016. Sarah Seamark, Ed. Articles, 1,000 words, for art dealers and framers, on trends and events of national importance to the art and framing industry, and relevant business subjects. Payment varies, on publication. Query preferred.

AUTOMATED BUILDER— 1445 Donlon St., Suite 16, Ventura, CA 93003. Don Carlson, Ed. Articles, 500 to 750 words, on various types of home manufacturers and dealers with slides or color prints. Pays $300, on acceptance, for articles with photos. Query required.

BARRON'S—200 Liberty St., New York, NY 10281. Edwin A. Finn, Jr., Ed. Investment-interest articles. Query.

BARTENDER—P.O. Box 158, Liberty Corner, NJ 07938. Jaclyn W. Foley, Pub./Ed. Quarterly. Articles, 100 to 1,000 words, emphasizing liquor and bartending for bartenders, tavern owners, and owners of restaurants with full-service liquor licenses. Department pieces, 200 to 1,000 words, and related fillers, 25 to 100 words. Pays $50 to $200 for articles, $5 to $25 for fillers, on publication.

BEAUTY EDUCATION—3 Columbia Cir., Albany, NY 12212. Catherine Frangie, Pub. Articles, 750 to 1,000 words, that provide beauty educators, trainers, and professionals in the cosmetology industry with information, skills, and techniques on such topics as hairstyling, makeup, aromatherapy, retailing, massage, and beauty careers. Send SASE for editorial calendar and themes. Articles on assignment only. Pays in copies. Query.

BOATING INDUSTRY—National Trade Publications, 13 Century Hill Dr., Latham, NY 12110-2197. Anne Dantz, Man. Ed. Articles, 1,000 to 2,500 words, on recreational marine products, management, merchandising and selling, for boat dealers and marina owners/operators. Photos. Pays varying rates, on publication. Query.

BOOKPAGE—ProMotion, Inc., 2501 21st Ave. S., Suite 5, Nashville, TN 37212. Ann Meador Shayne, Ed. Book reviews, 500 words, for a consumer-oriented tabloid used by booksellers to promote new titles and authors. Query with writing samples and areas of interest; Editor will make assignments for reviews. Pays $20 per review. Guidelines.

BUILDER—Hanley-Wood, Inc., One Thomas Cir. N.W., Suite 600, Washington, DC 20005. Boyce Thompson, Ed. Articles, to 1,500 words, on trends and news in home building: design, marketing, new products, etc. Pays negotiable rates, on acceptance. Query.

BUSINESS AND COMMERCIAL AVIATION— 4 International Dr., Rye Brook, NY 10573. Attn: Ed. Articles, 2,500 words, with photos, for pilots, on use of private aircraft for business transportation. Pays $100 to $500, on acceptance. Query.

BUSINESS MARKETING—740 N. Rush St., Chicago, IL 60611. Karen Egolf, Ed. Articles on marketing, advertising, and promoting products and services to business buyers. Pays competitive rates, on acceptance. Queries required.

BUSINESS START-UPS—2392 Morse Ave., Irvine, CA 92614-6234. Karen Axelton, Man. Ed. Monthly. Articles, 1,200 to 1,500 words, on all aspects of entrepreneurship, particularly, starting up a new business and motivational ideas. Pays $400 and up, on acceptance. Guidelines. Query.

BUSINESS TIMES—P.O. Box 580, 315 Peck St., New Haven, CT 06513. Joel MacClaren, Ed. Articles on Connecticut-based businesses and corporations. Query.

CAMPGROUND MANAGEMENT—P.O. Box 5000, Lake Forest, IL 60045-5000. Mike Byrnes, Ed. Detailed articles, 500 to 2,000 words, on managing recreational vehicle campgrounds. Photos. Pays $50 to $200, after publication.

CHEF—Talcott Communications Corp., 20 N. Wacker Dr., Suite 1865, Chicago, IL 60606. Brent T. Frei, Ed.-in-Chief. "The Food Magazine for Professionals." Articles, 600 to 1,200 words, that offer professionals in the foodservice business ideas for food marketing, preparation, and presentation. Pays $100 to $300, on publication.

CHIEF EXECUTIVE—733 Third Ave., 21st Fl., New York, NY 10017. J.P. Donlon, Ed. CEO bylines. Articles, 2,500 to 3,000 words, on management, financial, or business strategies. Departments, 1,200 to 1,500 words, on investments, amenities, and travel. Features on CEOs at leisure, Q&A's with CEOs, other topics. Pays varying rates, on acceptance. Query required.

CHINA, GLASS & TABLEWARE—See *Tableware Today.*

CLEANING AND MAINTENANCE MANAGEMENT MAGAZINE—13 Century Hill Dr., Latham, NY 12110-2197. Dominic Tom, Man. Ed. Articles, 500 to 1,200 words, on managing efficient cleaning and custodial/maintenance operations; profiles, photo-features, or general-interest articles directly related to the industry; also technical/mechanical how-tos. Photos encouraged. Pays to $300 for features, on publication. Query. Guidelines.

CLUB MANAGEMENT— 8730 Big Bend Blvd., St. Louis, MO 63114. Tom Finan, Pub. The official magazine of the Club Managers Assn. of America.

Features, to 2,000 words, and news items from 100 words, on management, budget, cuisine, personnel, government regulations, etc., for executives who run private clubs. "Writing should be tight and conversational, with liberal use of quotes." Color photos usually required with manuscript. Query preferred. Guidelines.

COLORADO BUSINESS—7009 S. Potomac, Englewood, CO 80112. Bruce Goldberg, Ed. Articles, varying lengths, on business, business personalities, and economic trends in Colorado. Preference given to Colorado residents. Pays on acceptance. Query.

COMMERCIAL CARRIER JOURNAL—Chilton Way, Radnor, PA 19089. Paul Richards, Exec. Ed. Thoroughly researched articles on private fleets and for-hire trucking operations. Pays from $50, on acceptance. Queries required.

COMPUTER GRAPHICS WORLD—10 Tara Blvd., Suite 500, Nashua, NH 03062-2801. Phil LoPiccolo, Ed. Articles, 1,000 to 3,000 words, on computer graphics technology and its use in science, engineering, architecture, film and broadcast, and interactive entertainment. Computer-generated images. Pays $600 to $1,000 per article, on acceptance. Query.

THE CONSTRUCTION SPECIFIER—Construction Specifications Institute, 601 Madison St., Alexandria, VA 22314. Anne Scott, Ed. Technical articles, 1,000 to 3,000 words, on the "nuts and bolts" of nonresidential construction, for owners/facility managers, architects, engineers, specifiers, contractors, and manufacturers. Pays 15¢ per word, on publication.

CONVENIENCE STORE NEWS—233 Park Ave. S., 6th Fl., New York, NY 10003. Maureen Azzato, Ed.-in-Chief. Features and news items, 750 to 1200 words, for convenience store owners and operators. Photos, with captions. Pays negotiated price for features; extra for photos, on publication. Query.

COOKING FOR PROFIT—P.O. Box 267, Fond du Lac, WI 54936-0267. Colleen Phalen, Pub./Ed.-in-Chief. Articles, of varying lengths, for foodservice professionals: profiles of successful restaurants, chains, and franchises, schools, hospitals, nursing homes, or other "institutional feeders"; also case studies on successful energy management within the foodservice environment. Business to business articles of interest to foodservice professionals. Payment varies, on publication.

CRAIN'S CHICAGO BUSINESS—740 Rush St., Chicago, IL 60611. David Snyder, Ed. Business articles about the Chicago metropolitan area exclusively.

DEALERSCOPE CONSUMER ELECTRONICS MARKETPLACE—North American Publishing Co., 401 N. Broad St., Philadelphia, PA 19108. Jane Pinkerton, Ed. Articles up to 1,000 words, on new consumer electronics, computer and major electronics products, and any associated new technologies, coming to retail. Pays varying rates, on publication. Query with clips.

DENTAL ECONOMICS—P.O. Box 3408, Tulsa, OK 74101. Dick Hale, Ed. Articles, 1,200 to 3,500 words, on business side of dental practice, patient and staff communication, personal investments, etc. Pays $100 to $400, on acceptance.

DIVIDENDS—Imagination Publishing, 820 W. Jackson, Suite 450, Chicago, IL 60607. Shannon Watts, Ed. Features, 1,000 to 1,500 words, of interest to small business owners; small-business profiles, 500 to 600 words. Pays 50¢ to 75¢ a word, on acceptance. Query.

DRAPERIES & WINDOW COVERINGS— 666 Dundee Rd., Suite 807, Northbrook, IL 60062-2769. Katie Sosnowchik, Ed. Articles, 1,000 to 2,000 words, for retailers, wholesalers, designers, and manufacturers of draperies and window, wall, and floor coverings. Profiles, with photos, of successful businesses in the industry; management and marketing related articles. Pays $150 to $250, after acceptance. Query.

EMERGENCY— 6300 Yarrow Dr., Carlsbad, CA 92009-1597. Doug Fiske, Ed. Articles, to 3,000 words, of interest to paramedics, emergency medical technicians, flight nurses, and other prehospital personnel; disaster management, advanced and basic life support, assessment, treatment. Pays $100 to $400 for features, $50 to $300 for departments. Photos are a plus. Guidelines and editorial calendar available.

EMPLOYEE SERVICES MANAGEMENT—NESRA, 2211 York Rd., Suite 207, Oak Brook, IL 60523. Cynthia M. Helson, Ed. Articles, 1,200 to 2,500 words, for human resource and employee service professionals on work/life issues, employee services, wellness, management and personal development. Pays in copies.

THE ENGRAVERS JOURNAL—26 Summit St., P.O. Box 318, Brighton, MI 48116. Rosemary Farrell, Man. Ed. Articles, of varying lengths, on topics related to the engraving industry or small business. Pays $150 to $300, on acceptance. Query.

ENTREPRENEUR—2392 Morse Ave., Irvine, CA 92614. Rieva Lesonsky, Ed.-in-Chief. Articles for small business owners, on all aspects of running a business. Pay varies, on acceptance. Query required.

EXECUTIVE FEMALE—135 W. 50th St., New York, NY 10020. Fayne Erickson, President. Articles, 750 to 2,500 words, on managing people, time, money, companies, and careers, for women in business. Pays varying rates, on acceptance. Query.

FANCY FOOD—Talcott Communications Corp., 20 N. Wacker Dr., Suite 1865, Chicago, IL 60606. Carolyn Schwaar, Ed.-in-Chief. "The Business Magazine for Specialty Foods, Confections, and Upscale Housewares." Articles, 2,000 words, related to gourmet food. Pays $250 to $500, on publication.

FARM JOURNAL—Centre Sq. W., 1500 Market St., Philadelphia, PA 19102-2181. Sonja Hillgren, Ed. Practical business articles, 500 to 1,500 words, with photos, on growing crops and raising livestock. Pays 20¢ to 50¢ a word, on acceptance. Query required.

FINANCIAL WORLD—1328 Broadway, New York, NY 10001. Seth E. Hoyt, Pres./Pub., Steven Taub, Ed.-in-Chief. Features and profiles of large companies and financial institutions and the people who run them. Pays varying rates, on publication. Query required.

FIRE CHIEF—35 E. Wacker Dr., Suite 700, Chicago, IL 60601-2198. Scott Baltic, Ed. Monthly. Articles, 1,000 to 5,000 words and department pieces, 1,200 to 1,800 words, for "Training Perspectives," "EMS Viewpoint," and "Sound Off," for fire officers. SASE for guidelines. Pays up to 30¢ per word, on publication.

FISHING TACKLE RETAILER MAGAZINE—P.O. Box 17151, Montgomery, AL 36141-0151. Dave Ellison, Ed. Deborah Johnson, Man. Ed. Articles, 300 to 1,250 words, for merchants who carry angling equipment. Business focus is required, and writers should provide practical information for improving management and merchandising. Pays varying rates, on acceptance.

FITNESS MANAGEMENT—P.O. Box 1198, Solana Beach, CA 92075. Ms. Ronale Tucker, Ed., Edward H. Pitts, Co-Publisher. Authoritative features, 750 to 2,500 words, and news shorts, 100 to 750 words, for owners, managers, and program directors of fitness centers. Content must be in keeping with current medical practice; no fads. Pays 8¢ a word, on publication. Query.

FLORIST—P.O. Box 250455, Franklin, MI 48025-0455. Barbara Koch, Man. Ed. Articles, to 1,500 words, on retail florist shop management.

FLOWERS &—11444 W. Olympic Blvd., Los Angeles, CA 90064. Joanne Jaffe, Ed.-in-Chief. Articles, 500 to 1,500 words, with how-to information for retail florists. Pays 50¢ a word, on acceptance. Query with clips.

FOOD MANAGEMENT—1100 Superior Ave., Cleveland, OH 44114. John Lawn, Ed. Articles on food service in hospitals, nursing homes, schools, colleges, prisons, businesses, and industrial sites. Trends, legislative issues, and how-to pieces, with management tie-in. Query.

GARDEN DESIGN—100 Ave. of the Americas, 7th Fl., New York, NY 10013. Dorothy Kalins, Ed.-in-Chief. Douglas Brenner, Ed. Garden-related features, 500 to 1,000 words, on private, public, and community gardens; articles on art and history as they relate to gardens. Pays from 50¢ a word, on acceptance. Guidelines.

GENERAL AVIATION NEWS & FLYER—P.O. Box 39099, Tacoma, WA 98439-0099. Ben Sclair,Gen. Mgr. Articles, 500 to 2,500 words, of interest to "general aviation" pilots. Pays to $3 per column inch (approximately 40 words); $10 for B&W photos; to $50 for color photos; within a month of publication.

GLASS DIGEST—18 E. 41st St., New York, NY 10017-6222. Charles Cumpston, Ed. Articles, 1,200 to 1,500 words, on building projects and glass/metal dealers, distributors, storefront and glazing contractors. Pays varying rates, on publication.

GOLF COURSE NEWS—38 Lafayette St., Yarmouth, ME 04096. Hal Phillips, Ed. Features and news analyses, 500 to 1,000 words, on all aspects of golf course maintenance, design, building, and management. Pays $200, on acceptance.

GOVERNMENT EXECUTIVE—1501 M St. N.W., Washington, DC 20005. Timothy Clark, Ed. Articles, 1,500 to 3,000 words, for civilian and military government workers at the management level.

GREENHOUSE MANAGEMENT & PRODUCTION—P.O. Box 1868, Fort Worth, TX 76101-1868. David Kuack, Ed. How-to articles, innovative production and/or marketing techniques, 500 to 1,800 words, accompanied by color slides, of interest to professional greenhouse growers. Pays $50 to $300, on acceptance. Query required.

GROWERTALKS—P.O. Box 9, 335 N. River St., Batavia, IL 60510-0009. John Saxtan, Ed. Dir. Articles, 800 to 2,600 words, that help commercial greenhouse growers (not florist/retailers or home gardeners) do their jobs better: trends, successes in new types of production, marketing, business management, new crops, and issues facing the industry. Payment varies, on publication. Queries preferred.

HARDWARE TRADE—10617 France Ave. S., #225, Bloomington, MN 55431. Patt Patterson, Ed. Dir. Articles, 800 to 1,000 words, on unusual hardware and home center stores and promotions in the Northwest and Midwest. Photos. Query.

HARVARD BUSINESS REVIEW—Harvard Business School Publishing Corp., 60 Harvard Way, Boston, MA 02163. Request a copy of HBR's guidelines for authors, or query editors, in writing, on new ideas about management of interest to senior executives.

HEALTH FOODS BUSINESS—2 University Plaza, Suite 204, Hackensack, NJ 07601. Gina Geslewitz, Ed. Articles, 1,200 words, with photos, profiling health food stores. Pays on publication. Query. Guidelines.

HEALTH PROGRESS— 4455 Woodson Rd., St. Louis, MO 63134-3797. Judy Cassidy, Ed. Journal of the Catholic Health Assn. Features, 2,000 to 4,000 words, on hospital and nursing home management and administration, medical-moral questions, health care, public policy, technological developments in health care and their effects, nursing, financial and human resource management for health-care administrators, and innovative programs in hospitals and long-term care facilities. Payment negotiable. Query.

HEATING/PIPING/AIR CONDITIONING—1100 Superior Ave., Cleveland, OH 44114. Michael G. Ivanovich, Ed. Articles, to 5,000 words, on heating, piping, and air conditioning systems in industrial plants and large buildings; engineering information. Pays $60 per printed page, on publication. Query.

HOSPITALS & HEALTH NETWORKS—737 N. Michigan Ave., Chicago, IL 60611. Kevin Lumsdon, Man. Ed. Articles, 300 to 2,200 words, for health care executives. Query.

HUMAN RESOURCE EXECUTIVE—LRP Publications Co., 747 Dresher Rd., Horsham, PA 19044-0980. David Shadovitz, Ed. Profiles and case stories, 1,800 to 2,200 words, of interest to people in the human resource profession. Pays varying rates, on acceptance. Queries required.

INC.—38 Commercial Wharf, Boston, MA 02110. George Gendron, Ed. No free-lance material.

INCOME OPPORTUNITIES—1500 Broadway, Suite 600, New York, NY 10036-4015. Linda Molnar, Ed.-in-Chief. Articles on marketing, financing, and managing a small or home-based business, especially on a tight budget. Profiles of entrepreneurs who started their businesses on a shoestring. Pays varying rates, on acceptance. Query; no unsolicited manuscripts.

INDEPENDENT BUSINESS—125 Auburn Ct., Suite 100, Thousand Oaks, CA 91362. Maryann Hammers, Man. Ed. How-to articles, 1,200 to 2,000 words, of practical interest and value on all aspects of running a small business. Pays $550 to $1,500, on acceptance. Also, short fun profiles, about 400 words, on offbeat businesses; pays $50 to $100. Query. Guidelines.

INDEPENDENT LIVING PROVIDER—See *Today's Home Healthcare Provider.*

INDUSTRY WEEK—1100 Superior Ave., Cleveland, OH 44114-2518. Patricia Panchak, Ed. Biweekly. Articles, varying lengths, on business and management. Departments include "Executive Briefing," "Emerging Technologies," "Finance," "Economic Trends," and "Executive Life." Payment varies, on acceptance. Query.

INSTANT & SMALL COMMERCIAL PRINTER—P.O. Box 7280, Libertyville, IL 60048. Anne Marie Mohan, Ed. Articles, 3 to 6 typed pages, for operators and employees of printing businesses specializing in retail printing and/or small commercial printing: case histories, how-tos, technical pieces, small-business management. Pays $150 to $250, extra for photos, on publication. Query.

INTERNATIONAL BUSINESS— 9 E. 40th St., 10th Fl., New York, NY 10016. Linda Lynton, Ed.-in-Chief. Articles, 1,000 to 1,500 words, on global marketing strategies. Short pieces, 500 words, with tips on operating abroad. Profiles, 750 to 3,000 words, on individuals or companies. Pays 30¢ a word, on acceptance and on publication. Query with clips.

JEMS, JOURNAL OF EMERGENCY MEDICAL SERVICES—P.O. Box 2789, Carlsbad, CA 92018. John Becknell, Ed.-in-Chief. Articles, 1,500 to 3,000 words, of interest to emergency medical providers (EMTs, paramedics, nurses, and physicians) who work in the EMS industry worldwide.

LLAMAS— 46 Main St., Jackson, CA 95642. Cheryl Dal Porto, Ed. "The International Camelid Journal," published 5 times yearly. Articles, 300 to 3,000 words, of interest to llama and alpaca owners. Pays $25 to $300, extra for photos, on publication. Query.

LP-GAS MAGAZINE—131 W. First St., Duluth, MN 55802. Zane Chastain, Ed. Articles, 1,500 to 2,500 words, with photos, on LP-gas dealer operations: marketing, management, etc. Photos. Pays to 15¢ a word, extra for photos, on acceptance. Query.

LUXE—1515 Broadway, 12th Fl., New York, NY 10036-8901. Scotty Dupree, Ed. Quarterly. Business articles on marketing luxury items: 500-word pieces, 2,000-word profiles, 4,000-word features. "We will consider working with any experienced business writer." Pays $500 to $5,000, on acceptance.

MACHINE DESIGN—Penton Publishing Co., 1100 Superior Ave., Cleveland, OH 44114. Ronald Khol, Ed. Articles, to 10 typed pages, on mechanical and electromechanical design topics for engineers. Pays varying rates, on publication. Submit outline or brief description.

MAINTENANCE TECHNOLOGY—1300 S. Grove Ave., Barrington, IL 60010. Robert C. Baldwin, Ed. Technical articles with how-to information on increasing the reliability and maintainability of electrical and mechanical systems and equipment. Readers are managers, supervisors, and engineers in all industries and facilities. Payment varies, on acceptance. Query.

MANAGE—2210 Arbor Blvd., Dayton, OH 45439. Doug Shaw, Ed. Articles, 800 to 1,000 words, on management and supervision for first-line and middle managers. "Please indicate word count on manuscript and enclose SASE." Pays 5¢ a word.

MANAGING OFFICE TECHNOLOGY—1100 Superior Ave., Cleveland, OH 44114. Lura Romei, Ed. Articles, 3 to 4 double-spaced, typed pages, on new concepts, management techniques, technologies, and applications for management executives. Payment varies, on acceptance. Query preferred.

MANUFACTURING SYSTEMS—191 S. Gary, Carol Stream, IL 60188. Kevin Parker, Ed. Articles, to 2,000 words, on computer and information systems for managers and executives seeking to increase productivity in manufacturing firms. Pays 10¢ to 20¢ a word, on acceptance. Query required.

MARKETING NEWS—American Marketing Assn., 250 S. Wacker Dr., Chicago, IL 60606-5819. Lisa M. Keefe, Ed. Biweekly. Articles, 700 to 1,000 words, on every aspect of marketing, including advertising, sales promotion, direct marketing, telecommunications, consumer and business-to-business marketing, and market research. Pays $500 to $1,000, on publication. Query.

MIX MAGAZINE— 6400 Hollis St., Suite 12, Emeryville, CA 94608. Blair Jackson, Exec. Ed. Articles, varying lengths, for professionals, on audio, audio post-production, sound production, live sound, and music entertainment technology. Pay varies, on publication. Query.

MODERN HEALTHCARE—740 N. Rush St., Chicago, IL 60611. Clark Bell, Ed. News weekly covers management, finance, building design and construction, and new technology for hospitals, health maintenance organizations, nursing homes, and other health care institutions. Pays $200 to $400, on publication. Query; very limited free-lance market.

MODERN TIRE DEALER—P.O. Box 3599, Akron, OH 44309-3599. Lloyd Stoyer, Ed. Tire retailing and automotive service articles, 1,000 to 1,500 words, with photos, on independent tire dealers and retreaders. Pays $300 to $450, on publication. Query; articles by assignment only.

MUTUAL FUNDS—2200 S.W. 10th St., Deerfield Beach, FL 33442. Norman G. Fosback, Ed.-in-Chief. "Writers experienced in covering mutual funds for the print media should send resumé and clips." Pays to $1 a word, on acceptance.

NATIONAL FISHERMAN—121 Free St., P.O. Box 7438, Portland, ME 04112. Sam Smith, Ed. Articles, 200 to 2,000 words, aimed at commercial fishermen and boat builders. Pays $4 to $6 per inch, extra for photos, on publication. Query preferred.

NATION'S BUSINESS—1615 H St. N.W., Washington, DC 20062-2000. Articles on small-business topics, including management advice and success stories. Pays negotiable rates, on acceptance. Guidelines.

NEPHROLOGY NEWS & ISSUES—15150 N. Hayden Rd., Suite 101, Scottsdale, AZ 85260. Mark Neumann, Ed. News articles, human-interest features, and opinion essays on dialysis, kidney transplantation, and kidney disease.

THE NETWORK JOURNAL—333 Nostrand Ave., Brooklyn, NY 11216. Jacqueline Mitchell, Man. Ed. Monthly newspaper. Articles, 800 to 1,500 words, on small business, personal finance, and career management of interest to African American small business owners and professionals. Profiles of entrepreneurs; how-to pieces; articles on sales and marketing, managing a small business and personal finance. Pays $35 to $75, on acceptance.

NEW CAREER WAYS NEWSLETTER— 67 Melrose Ave., Haverhill, MA 01830. William J. Bond, Ed. How-to articles, 1,500 to 2,000 words, on new skills to use to move ahead at work in the 1990s. Pays varying rates, on publication. Query with outline and SASE. Same address and requirements for *Workskills Newsletter*.

NEW HAMPSHIRE EDITIONS— 100 Main St., Nashua, NH 03060. Rick Broussard, Ed. Lifestyle, business, and history articles with a New Hampshire angle, with sources from all regions of the state, for the company's statewide magazine and its specialty publication, *New Hampshire Legacy*. Payment varies, on publication.

NEW HAMPSHIRE LEGACY—See *New Hampshire Editions*.

THE NORTHERN LOGGER AND TIMBER PROCESSOR—Northeastern Logger's Assn., Inc., P.O. Box 69, Old Forge, NY 13420. Eric A. Johnson, Ed. Features, 1,000 to 2,000 words, of interest to the forest product industry. Photos. Pays 15¢ a word, on publication. Query preferred.

NSGA RETAIL FOCUS—National Sporting Goods Assoc., 1699 Wall St., Suite 700, Mt. Prospect, IL 60056. Brent Heathcott, Ed. Members magazine. Articles, 1,000 to 1,500 words, on sporting goods industry news and trends, the latest in new product information, and management and store operations. Payment varies, on publication. Query.

ON THE LINE—P.O. Box 1865, Lake Havasu City, AZ 86405. Mary Lougheed, Ed. Bimonthly. "The National Publication for Payphone Industry News." Articles, 500 to 1,000 words, on regulatory and legislative issues related to telecommunications. Payment varies, on publication. Queries preferred.

ONCE UPON A TIME—553 Winston Ct., St. Paul, MN 55118. Audrey B. Baird, Ed. "A 32-page magazine for Children's Writers and Illustrators." Quarterly. Articles, to 900 words: questions, insights, how-to articles, tips and experiences (no fiction) on the writing and illustrating life by published and unpublished writers. Also, short articles, 100 to 400 words. B&W artwork. No payment.

OPPORTUNITY MAGAZINE—18 E. 41st St., New York, NY 10017. Daniel Joelson, Ed. How-to articles for people who work at home, small business owners, and people interested in franchising and distributorships. Success stories. Payment varies, on publication. Query.

OPTOMETRIC ECONOMICS—See *Practice Strategies.*

PARTY & PAPER RETAILER—70 New Canaan Ave., Norwalk, CT 06850. Trisha McMahon Drain, Ed. Articles, 1,000 to 1,500 words, that offer employee, management, and retail marketing advice to the party or stationery store owner: display ideas, success stories; advertising, promotion, financial, and legal advice. "Articles grounded in facts and anecdotes are appreciated." Pay varies, on publication. Query with published clips.

PET BUSINESS—7-L Dundas Cir., Greensboro, NC 27407. Rita Davis, Ed. Brief, documented articles on animals and products found in pet stores; research findings; legislative/regulatory actions; business and marketing tips and trends. Pays 10¢ per word, on publication; pays $20 for photos.

PET PRODUCT NEWS—P.O. Box 6050, Mission Viejo, CA 92690. Stacy Hackett, Ed. Articles, 1,000 to 1,200 words, with photos, on pet shops, and pet and product merchandising. No fiction or news clippings. Pays $150 to $300, extra for photos. Query.

PHOTO MARKETING—3000 Picture Pl., Jackson, MI 49201. Gary Pageau, Exec. Ed. Business articles, 1,000 to 3,500 words, for owners and managers of camera/video stores or photo processing labs. Pays $150 to $500, extra for photos, on acceptance. Query; no unsolicited manuscripts.

PHYSICIAN'S MANAGEMENT—7500 Old Oak Blvd., Cleveland, OH 44130. Larry Frederick, Ed. Articles, 1,500 words, on finance, investments, malpractice, and office management for primary care physicians. No clinical pieces. Pays on acceptance. Query. SASE.

PIZZA TODAY—P.O. Box 1347, New Albany, IN 47151. Bruce Allar, Ed. Articles, to 2,500 words, on pizza business management for pizza entrepreneurs. Pizza business profiles. Pays $75 to $150 per published page, on publication. Query.

P.O.B.—Business News Publishing Co., 755 W. Big Beaver Rd., Suite 100, Troy, MI 48084. Beth Wierzbinski, Ed. Technical and business articles,

1,000 to 4,000 words, for professionals and technicians in the surveying and mapping fields. Technical tips on field and office procedures and equipment maintenance. Pays $150 to $500, on acceptance.

POLICE MAGAZINE— 6300 Yarrow Dr., Carlsbad, CA 92009-1597. Randall Resch, Ed. Articles and profiles, 1,000 to 3,000 words, on specialized groups, equipment, issues, and trends of interest to people in the law enforcement profession. Pays $100 to $400, on acceptance.

POOL & SPA NEWS—3923 W. Sixth St., Los Angeles, CA 90020. News articles for the swimming pool, spa, and hot tub industry. Pays from 10¢ to 20¢ a word, on publication. Query.

PRACTICE STRATEGIES—(formerly *Optometric Economics*) American Optometric Assn., 243 N. Lindbergh Blvd., St. Louis, MO 63141-7881. Gene Mitchell, Sr. Ed. Articles, 1,000 to 3,000 words, on private practice management for optometrists; direct, conversational style with how-to advice on how optometrists can build, improve, better manage, and enjoy their practices. Short humor and photos. Payment varies, on acceptance. Query.

PROGRESSIVE GROCER—263 Tresser Blvd., Stamford, CT 06901. Priscilla Donegan, Man. Ed. Articles related to retail food operations; ideas for successful merchandising, promotions, and displays. Short pieces preferred. Payment varies, on acceptance.

THE PROLIFIC FREELANCER—See *Today's $85,000 Freelance Writer.*

PUBLISH—Integrated Media, Inc., 501 Second St., San Francisco, CA 94107. Jake Widman, Ed. Features, 1,500 to 2,000 words, and reviews, 400 to 800 words, on all aspects of computerized publishing. Pays $400 to $600 for reviews, $850 to $1,200 for full-length features, on acceptance.

PUBLISHERS WEEKLY—245 W. 17th St., New York, NY 10011. Daisy Maryles, Exec. Ed. Articles, 900 words, on a current issue or problem facing publishing and bookselling for "My Say" column. Articles for "Booksellers' Forum" may be somewhat longer. Payment varies.

QUICK PRINTING—PTN Publishing Co., 445 Broad Hollow Rd., Melville, NY 11747. Gerald Walsh, Ed. Articles, 1,500 to 2,500 words, of interest to owners and operators of quick print shops, copy shops, and small commercial printers, on how to make their businesses more profitable; include photography/figures. Also, articles on using computers in graphic arts applications. Pays from $100, on publication.

REMODELING—Hanley-Wood, Inc., One Thomas Cir. N.W., Suite 600, Washington, DC 20005. Paul Deffenbaugh, Ed. Articles, 250 to 1,700 words, on remodeling and industry news for residential and light commercial remodelers. Pays on acceptance. Query.

RESTAURANTS USA—1200 17th St. N.W., Washington, DC 20036-3097. Jennifer Batty, Ed. Publication of the National Restaurant Assn. Articles, 1,000 to 2,500 words, on the foodservice and restaurant business. Restaurant experience preferred. Pays $350 to $800, on acceptance. Query.

ROOFER MAGAZINE—P.O. Box 7069, Troy, MI 48007. Melinda North, Ed. Technical and non-technical articles, 500 to 1,000 words, on roofing-related topics: new roofing concepts, energy savings, pertinent issues, roofing contractor profiles, industry concerns. Include photos. Pays negotiable rates, on publication. Guidelines.

THE RUSSIAN— 8621 Wilshire Blvd., Suite 700, Beverly Hills, CA 90211. Martha Little, Ed. Articles, 1,000 to 2,000 words, on business ventures in

Russia involving Western firms, Russian economic and political analysis, and business development in the U.S. pertaining to Russia. Also photographs, color slides, and drawings. Pays $150 to $500, up to 30 days after publication. Queries preferred.

RV BUSINESS—2575 Vista Del Mar Dr., Ventura, CA 93001. Sherman Goldenberg, Ed.-in-Chief. Articles, to 1,500 words, on RV industry news and product-related features. Articles on legislative matters affecting the industry. General business features rarely used. Pays varying rates.

SAFETY COMPLIANCE LETTER—24 Rope Ferry Rd., Waterford, CT 06386. Michele Rubin, Ed. Interview-based articles, 800 to 1,250 words, for corporate safety managers, on successful compliance-based safety and health programs and issues in the workplace. Pays to 20¢ a word, on acceptance. Query.

SAFETY MANAGEMENT—24 Rope Ferry Rd., Waterford, CT 06386. Shelley Wolf, Ed. Interview-based articles, 1,000 words, for safety professionals, on improving workplace safety and health. Pays to 15¢ a word, on acceptance. Query.

SIGN BUILDER ILLUSTRATED— 4905 Pine Cone Dr., #2, Durham, NC 27707-5258. James B. Hyatt, Ed. Bimonthly. How-to articles and editorials, 1,500 to 2,500 words, on the sign industry. Pays $300 to $500, on acceptance.

SMALL PRESS REVIEW—Dustbooks, P.O. Box 100, Paradise, CA 95967. Len Fulton, Ed./Pub. Reviews, 200 words, of small literary books and magazines; tracks the publishing of small publishers and small-circulation magazines. Query.

SOFTWARE MAGAZINE— One Research Dr., Westborough, MA 01581. Patrick Porter, Ed. Technical features, to 1,800 words, for computer-literate MIS audience, on how various software products are used. Pays about $1,000 to $1,200, on publication. Query required. Calendar of scheduled editorial features available.

SOUTHERN LUMBERMAN—P.O. Box 681629, Franklin, TN 37068-1629. Nanci P. Gregg, Man. Ed. Articles on sawmill operations, interviews with industry leaders, how-to technical pieces with an emphasis on increasing sawmill production and efficiency and new installations. "Always looking for 'sweetheart' mill stories; we publish one per month." Pays $100 to $250 for articles with B&W photos. Queries preferred.

SOUVENIRS, GIFTS, AND NOVELTIES MAGAZINE—(formerly *Souvenirs and Novelties*) 7000 Terminal Sq., Suite 210, Upper Darby, PA 19082. Attn: Ed. Articles, 1,500 words, on retailing and merchandising and collectible souvenir items for managers at zoos, museums, hotels, airports, and souvenir stores. Pays 12¢ a word, on publication.

STONE WORLD— 299 Market St., Third Floor, Saddle Brook, NJ 07663. Michael Reis, Ed. Articles, 750 to 1,500 words, on new trends in installing and designing with stone. For architects, interior designers, design professionals, and stone fabricators and dealers. Pays $6 per column inch, on publication. Query.

TABLEWARE TODAY—(formerly *China, Glass & Tableware*) 368 Essex Ave., Bloomfield, NJ 07003. Amy Stavis, Ed. Case histories and interviews, 1,500 to 2,500 words, with photos, on merchandising of tableware. Pays $100, per page, on publication. Query.

TANNING TRENDS—3101 Page Ave., Jackson, MI 49203-2254. Joseph Levy, Ed. Articles on small businesses and skin care for tanning salon owners. Scientific pro-tanning articles and "smart tanning" pieces. Query for profiles. "Our aim is to boost salon owners to the 'next level' of small business ownership. Focus is on business principles with special emphasis on public relations and marketing." Payment varies, on publication.

TEA & COFFEE TRADE JOURNAL—130 W. 42nd St., Suite 1050, New York, NY 10036. Jane P. McCabe, Ed. Articles, 3 to 5 pages, on trade issues of importance to the tea and coffee industry. Pays 20¢ per word, on publication. Query.

TEXTILE WORLD—6151 Powers Ferry Rd., Atlanta, GA 30339. Mac Isaacs, Ed. Articles, 500 to 2,000 words, with photos, on manufacturing and finishing textiles. Pays varying rates, on acceptance.

TODAY'S $85,000 FREELANCE WRITER—(formerly *The Prolific Freelancer*) P.O. Box 543, Oradell, NJ 07649. Brian Konradt, Ed. Bi-monthly. Articles, to 2,000 words, on operating a profitable free-lance commercial copywriting business and writing for downsized corporations, large and small businesses, ad agencies, and other commercial markets. No fiction. Pays 10¢ a word, on acceptance. Guidelines. SASE.

TODAY'S HOME HEALTHCARE PROVIDER—(formerly *Independent Living Provider*) 26 Main St., Chatham, NJ 07928-2402. Nancy DelPizzo, Ed. Articles, from 1,200 words, on the home healthcare market. "We're looking for good writers." Payment varies, on publication. Send query or resumé.

TOURIST ATTRACTIONS AND PARKS—7000 Terminal Sq., Suite 210, Upper Darby, PA 19082. Articles, 1,500 words, on successful management of parks and leisure attractions. News items, 250 and 500 words. Pays 10¢ a word, on publication. Query.

TRAILER/BODY BUILDERS—P.O. Box 66010, Houston, TX 77266. Paul Schenck, Ed. Articles on engineering, sales, and management ideas for truck body and truck trailer manufacturers. Pays from $100 per printed page, on acceptance.

TREASURY & RISK MANAGEMENT—111 W. 57th St., New York, NY 10019. Anthony Baldo, Ed. Eight issues per year. Articles, 200 to 3,000 words, on treasury management for corporate treasurers, CFOs, and vice presidents of finance. Pays 50¢ to $1 a word, on acceptance. Query.

UNIQUE OPPORTUNITIES—455 S. 4th Ave., #1236, Louisville, KY 40202. Bett Coffman, Assoc. Ed. Articles, 2,000 to 3,000 words, that cover the economic, business, and career-related issues of interest to physicians who are interested in relocating or entering new practices. Doctor profiles, 500 words. "Our goal is to educate physicians about how to evaluate career opportunities, negotiate the benefits offered, plan career moves, and provide information on the legal and economic aspects of accepting a position." Pays from 50¢ a word for features; $100 to $200 for profiles, on acceptance. Query.

WINES & VINES—1800 Lincoln Ave., San Rafael, CA 94901. Philip E. Hiaring, Ed. Articles, 2,000 words, on grape and wine industry, emphasizing marketing, management, and production. Pays 15¢ a word, on acceptance.

WOODSHOP NEWS—35 Pratt St., Essex, CT 06426-1185. Ian C. Bowen, Ed. Features, one to 3 typed pages, for and about people who work with wood: business stories, profiles, news. Pays from $40 to $250 minimum, on publication. Queries preferred.

WORKING WOMAN—230 Park Ave., New York, NY 10169. Articles, 350 to 2,500 words, on business and personal aspects of working women's lives. Pays from $300, on acceptance.

WORKSKILLS NEWSLETTER—See *New Career Ways Newsletter.*

THE WORLD TRADER—See *New Hampshire Editions.*

WORLD WASTES—6151 Powers Ferry Rd. N.W., Atlanta, GA 30339. Bill Wolpin, Ed./Pub. Case studies, market analysis, and how-to articles, 1,000 to 2,000 words, with photos of refuse haulers, recyclers, landfill operators, resource recovery operations, and transfer stations, with solutions to problems in the field. Pays from $125 per printed page, on publication. Query preferred.

IN-HOUSE/ASSOCIATION MAGAZINES

Publications circulated to company employees (sometimes called house magazines or house organs) and to members of associations and organizations are excellent, well-paying markets for writers at all levels of experience. Large corporations publish these magazines to promote good will, familiarize readers with the company's services and products, and advise them about the issues and events concerning a particular cause or industry.

AARP BULLETIN—601 E St. N.W., Washington, DC 20049. Elliot Carlson, Ed. Publication of the American Assn. of Retired Persons. Payment varies, on acceptance. Query required.

AMERICAN EDUCATOR—American Federation of Teachers, 555 New Jersey Ave. N. W., Washington, DC 20001. Liz McPike, Ed. Quarterly. Articles, 500 to 2,500 words, on politics and new trends in education; also well-researched news features on current problems in education, education law, professional ethics; "think" pieces and essays that explore current social issues relevant to American society. Pays from $300, on publication. Query.

THE AMERICAN GARDENER—7931 E. Boulevard Dr., Alexandria, VA 22308-1300. David J. Ellis, Ed. Bimonthly publication of the American Horticulture Society. Articles, to 2,500 words, for American ornamental gardeners: profiles of prominent horticulturists, plant research and plant hunting, events and personalities in horticulture history, plant lore and literature, the politics of horticulture, etc. Humorous pieces for "Offshoots." "We run very few how-to articles." Pays $100 to $400, on publication. Query preferred.

CALIFORNIA HIGHWAY PATROLMAN—2030 V St., Sacramento, CA 95818-1730. Carol Perri, Ed. Articles on the CHP, its personnel, programs, history and mission, or any true-life police-related story that is exciting, action-packed, of great human interest or humorous. Photos a plus. Buys one-time rights; pays 2½¢ a word, $5 for B&W photos, on publication. Guidelines and/or sample copy with 9x12 SASE.

CATHOLIC FORESTER—355 Shuman Blvd., P.O. Box 3012, Naperville, IL 60566-7012. Dorothy Deer, Ed. Official publication of the Catholic Order of Foresters, a fraternal life insurance organization for Catholics. General-interest articles and fiction, to 1,500 words, that deal with contemporary issues; no moralizing, explicit sex, or violence. Short, inspirational articles, to 500 words. "Need health and wellness, parenting, and financial articles." Pays 20¢ a word, on acceptance.

CATHOLIC LIBRARY WORLD—The Catholic Library Assn., 291 Springfield St., Chicopee, MA 01013-2839. Mary E. Gallagher, SSJ, Ed. Co-Chair. Articles for school librarians, academic librarians, and institutional archivists. No payment. Queries preferred.

COLUMBIA—1 Columbus Plaza, New Haven, CT 06510-0901. Richard McMunn, Ed. Journal of the Knights of Columbus. Articles, 1,500 words, for Catholic families. Must be accompanied by color photos or transparencies. No fiction. Pays to $500 for articles and photos, on acceptance.

THE COMPASS—365 Washington Ave., Brooklyn, NY 11238. J.A. Randall, Ed. True stories (no first-person accounts), to 2,000 words, on the sea, sea trades, and aviation. Pays $1,000, on acceptance. Query with SASE.

THE COSTCO CONNECTION—P.O. Box 34088, Seattle, WA 98124-1088. Anita Thompson, Man. Ed. Tabloid. Articles, 100 to 1,200 words, about small business and about Costco members. SASE for guidelines. The average pay is $300 to $400, on acceptance. Queries preferred.

THE ELKS MAGAZINE—425 W. Diversey Pkwy., Chicago, IL 60614. Tonya Harris, Ed. Asst. Articles, 1,500 to 2,500 words, on technology, sports, history, and topics of current interest; for non-urban audience with above-average income. Pays 15¢ to 20¢ a word, on acceptance. Query.

FIREHOUSE—PTN Publishing Co., 445 Broad Hollow Rd., Melville, NY 11747. Harvey Eisner, Ed.-in-Chief. Articles, 500 to 2,000 words: on-the-scene accounts of fires, trends in firefighting equipment, controversial fire-service issues, and lifestyles of firefighters. Query.

THE FURROW—Deere & Co., John Deere Rd., Moline, IL 61265. George R. Sollenberger, Exec. Ed. Specialized, illustrated articles on farming. Pays to $1,200, on acceptance.

FUTURIFIC—Foundation for Optimism, Inc., 305 Madison Ave., #10B, New York, NY 10165. Charlotte Kellar, Ed. Forecasts of what will be. "Only optimistic material will get published. Solutions, not problems. We track all developments giving evidence to our increasing life expectancy, improving international coexistence, the global tendency toward peace, and improving economic trends. We also report on all new developments, economic, political, social, scientific, technical, medical or other that are making life easier, better and more enjoyable for the greatest number of people." Pays in copies. Queries preferred.

HARVARD MAGAZINE—7 Ware St., Cambridge, MA 02138-4037. John Rosenberg, Ed. Articles, 500 to 5,000 words, with a connection to Harvard University. Pays from $100, on publication. Query required.

ITALIAN AMERICA—219 E. St. N.E., Washington, DC 20002-4922. Official publication of the Order Sons of Italy in America. Quarterly. Articles, 1,000 to 2,500 words, and fillers, 500 to 750 words, on people, institutions, and events of interest to the Italian-American community. Also book reviews. Payment varies, on publication. Queries preferred.

KIWANIS—3636 Woodview Trace, Indianapolis, IN 46268. Chuck Jonak, Man. Ed. Articles, 2,500 words (with 250-to 350-word sidebars), on lifestyle, relationships, world view, children's issues and concerns, education, trends, small business, religion, health, etc. No travel pieces, interviews, profiles. Pays $400 to $1,000, on acceptance. Query.

THE LION—300 22nd St., Oak Brook, IL 60523. Robert Kleinfelder, Sr. Ed. Official publication of Lions Clubs International. Articles, 800 to 2,000 words, and photo-essays, on club activities. Pays from $100 to $700, on acceptance. Query.

NEW HOLLAND NEWS—New Holland, Inc., P.O. Box 1895, New Holland, PA 17557. Attn: Ed. Articles, to 1,500 words, with strong color photo support, on agriculture and rural living. Pays on acceptance. Query.

OPTIMIST MAGAZINE— 4494 Lindell Blvd., St. Louis, MO 63108. Dena Hull, Man. Ed. Articles, to 1,000 words, on activities of local Optimist Clubs, and techniques for personal and club success. Pays from $100, on acceptance. Query.

RESTAURANTS USA—1200 17th St. N.W., Washington, DC 20036-3097. Jennifer Batty, Ed. Publication of the National Restaurant Assn. Articles, 1,000 to 2,500 words, on the foodservice and restaurant business. Restaurant experience preferred. Pays $350 to $800, on acceptance. Query.

THE RETIRED OFFICER MAGAZINE—201 N. Washington St., Alexandria, VA 22314. Address the Manuscripts Ed. Articles, 1,800 to 2,000 words, of interest to military retirees and their families. Current military/national affairs, recent military history, health/medicine, and second-career opportunities. No fillers. Photos a plus. Pays to $1,300, on acceptance. Query. Guidelines.

THE ROTARIAN—1560 Sherman Ave., Evanston, IL 60201-3698. Willmon L. White, Ed.-in-Chief. Charles W. Pratt, Ed. Publication of Rotary International, world service organization of business and professional men and women. Articles, 1,200 to 2,000 words, on international social and economic issues, business and management, human relationships, travel, sports, environment, science and technology; humor. Pays good rates, on acceptance. Query.

THE SCHOOL ADMINISTRATOR—American Assn. of School Administrators, 1801 N. Moore St., Arlington, VA 22209-1813. Jay P. Goldman, Ed. Articles related to school administration (K through 12). "We seek articles about school system practices, policies, and programs that have widespread appeal." Pays in copies. Guidelines.

VFW MAGAZINE— 406 W. 34th St., Kansas City, MO 64111. Richard K. Kolb, Ed. Articles, 1,000 words, related to current foreign policy and defense, American armed forces abroad, and international events affecting U.S. national security. Also, up-to-date articles on veteran concerns and issues affecting veterans. Pays to $500, on acceptance. Query. Guidelines.

RELIGIOUS MAGAZINES

AMERICA—106 W. 56th St., New York, NY 10019-3893. George W. Hunt, S.J., Ed. Articles, 1,000 to 2,500 words, on current affairs, family life, literary trends. Pays $75 to $150, on acceptance.

AMERICAN BIBLE SOCIETY RECORD—1865 Broadway, New York, NY 10023. Mike Maus, Man. Ed. Material related to work of American Bible Society: translating, publishing, distributing. All articles staff-written; accepts no free-lance material.

AMERICAN JEWISH HISTORY—American Jewish Historical Society, 2 Thornton Rd., Waltham, MA 02154. Dr. Marc Lee Raphael, Ed. Academic articles, 15 to 30 typed pages, on the settlement, history, and life of Jews in North and South America. Queries preferred. No payment.

AMIT MAGAZINE— 817 Broadway, New York, NY 10003-4761. Micheline Ratzersdorfer, Rita Schwalb, Eds. Patricia Israel, Man. Ed. Articles, 1,000 to 2,000 words, of interest to Jewish women: Middle East, Israel, history, holidays, travel, culture, food.

ANGEL TIMES—Angelic Realms Unlimited, Inc., Suite 110, 22 Perimeter Park, Atlanta, GA 30341. Linda Whitmon Vephula, Pub. Quarterly. Articles, 1,500 words, on true angelic experiences. No payment.

ANGLICAN JOURNAL— 600 Jarvis St., Toronto, Ont., Canada M4Y 2J6. Attn: Ed. National newspaper of the Anglican Church of Canada. Articles, to 1,000 words, on news and features of the Anglican Church across the country and around the world, including social and ethical issues and human-interest subjects in a religious context. Pays $50 to $300, on acceptance. Query required.

ANNALS OF ST. ANNE DE BEAUPRÉ—P.O. Box 1000, St. Anne de Beaupré, Quebec, Canada G0A 3C0. Roch Achard, C.Ss.R., Ed. Articles, 500 to 1,500 words, that promote devotion to St. Anne and Christian family values. "Write something inspirational, educational, objective, and uplifting." No poetry. Pays 3¢ to 4¢ a word, on acceptance.

ASPIRE—107 Kenner Ave., Nashville, TN 37205. Jeanette Thomason, Ed. Articles, 500 to 2,000 words, for Christian women on trends in health, career issues, parenting, and relationships that inspire and encourage readers to incorporate faith into daily life. Pays 25¢ a word, on acceptance. Query with resumé and clips.

THE BANNER—2850 Kalamazoo Ave. S.E., Grand Rapids, MI 49560. John D. Suk, Ed. Malcolm McBryde, Assoc. Ed. Fiction, to 2,500 words, nonfiction, to 1,800 words, and poetry, to 50 lines, for members of the Christian Reformed Church in North America. "The magazine's purpose is to inform, challenge, educate, comfort, and inspire members of the church." Also, some church-related cartoons. Pays $125 to $200 for articles, $40 for poetry, on acceptance. Query preferred.

BAPTIST LEADER—American Baptist Churches-USA, P.O. Box 851, Valley Forge, PA 19482-0851. D. Ng, Ed. Practical how-to or thought-provoking articles, 1,200 to 2,000 words, for local church lay leaders, pastors, and Christian education staff.

BIBLE ADVOCATE—P.O. Box 33677, Denver, CO 80233. Calvin Burrell, Ed. Articles, 1,000 to 2,000 words, and fillers, 100 to 500 words, on Bible passages and Christian living; also teaching articles. Some poetry, 5 to 25 lines, on religious themes. Opinion pieces, to 700 words. "Be familiar with the doctrinal beliefs of the Church of God (Seventh Day). For example, they don't celebrate a traditional Easter or Christmas." Pays $15 per page (to $35) for articles, $10 for poetry, on publication. Guidelines.

BRIGADE LEADER—Box 150, Wheaton, IL 60189. Deborah Christensen, Man. Ed. Inspirational articles, 1,000 words, for Christian men who lead boys in Christian service brigade programs. "Most articles are written on assignment by experts; very few free lancers used. Query with clips and we'll contact you if we need you for an assignment." Pays $60 to $150.

CATECHIST—330 Progress Rd., Dayton, OH 45449. Patricia Fischer, Ed. Informational and how-to articles, 1,200 to 1,500 words, for Catholic teachers, coordinators, and administrators in religious education programs. Pays $25 to $100, on publication.

CATHOLIC DIGEST—P.O. Box 64090, St. Paul, MN 55164-0090. Attn: Articles Ed. Articles, 1,000 to 3,500 words, on Catholic and general subjects. Fillers, to 300 words, on instances of kindness rewarded, for "Hearts Are Trumps"; accounts of good deeds, for "People Are Like That." Pays from $200 for original articles, $100 for reprints, on acceptance; $4 to $50 for fillers, on publication. Guidelines.

CATHOLIC NEAR EAST MAGAZINE—1011 First Ave., New York, NY 10022-4195. Michael La Civita, Exec. Ed. Bimonthly publication of CNEWA, a papal agency for humanitarian and pastoral support. Articles, 1,500 to 2,000 words, on people of the Middle East, northeast Africa, India, and eastern Europe: their faith, heritage, culture, and present state of affairs. Special interest in Eastern Christian churches. Color photos for all articles. Pays 20¢ a word. Query.

CATHOLIC PARENT—Our Sunday Visitor, Inc., 200 Noll Plaza, Huntington, IN 46750. Woodeene Koenig-Bricker, Ed. Features, how-tos, and general-interest articles, 800 to 1,000 words, for Catholic parents. "Keep it anecdotal and practical with an emphasis on values and family life. Don't preach." Payment varies, on acceptance.

CATHOLIC TWIN CIRCLE—33 Rossotto Dr., Hamden, CT 06514. Loretta G. Seyer, Ed. Features, how-tos, and interviews, 1,000 to 2,000 words, of interest to Catholic families; include photos. Opinion or inspirational columns, 600 to 800 words. Strict attention to Catholic doctrine required. Enclose SASE. Pays $75 to $300 for articles, $75 for columns, on publication.

CHARISMA & CHRISTIAN LIFE—600 Rinehart Rd., Lake Mary, FL 32746. Lee Grady, Ed. Dir. Charismatic/evangelical Christian articles, 1,500 to 2,500 words, for developing the spiritual life. News stories, 300 to 1,500 words. Photos. Pays varying rates, on publication.

THE CHRISTIAN CENTURY—407 S. Dearborn St., Chicago, IL 60605. James M. Wall, Ed. Ecumenical. Articles, 1,500 to 3,000 words, with a religious angle, on political and social issues, international affairs, culture, the arts. Poetry, to 20 lines. Photos. Pays about $50 per printed page, extra for photos, on publication.

CHRISTIAN EDUCATION COUNSELOR—1445 Boonville Ave., Springfield, MO 65802-1894. Sylvia Lee, Ed. Articles, 600 to 800 words, on teaching and administrating Christian education in the local church, for local Sunday school and Christian school personnel. Pays 5¢ to 10¢ a word, on acceptance.

CHRISTIAN EDUCATION JOURNAL—Trinity Evangelical Divinity School, 2065 Half Day Rd., Deerfield, IL 60015. Dr. Perry G. Downs, Ed. Articles, 10 to 25 typed pages, on Christian education topics. Guidelines.

CHRISTIAN EDUCATION LEADERSHIP—P.O. Box 2250, Cleveland, TN 37320-2250. Lance Colkmire, Ed. Quarterly. Articles, 500 to 1,200 words, that "encourage, inform, and inspire those who teach the Bible in the local church." No fiction, poetry, fillers, or artwork. Pays $25 to $55, on acceptance.

CHRISTIAN HOME & SCHOOL—3350 E. Paris Ave. S.E., Grand Rapids, MI 49512. Gordon L. Bordewyk, Ed. Articles for parents in Canada and the U.S. who send their children to Christian schools and are concerned about the challenges facing Christian families today. Pays $125 to $200, on publication. Send SASE for guidelines.

CHRISTIAN PARENTING TODAY—4050 Lee Vance View, Colorado Springs, CO 80918. Erin Healy, Ed. Articles, 900 to 2,000 words, dealing with raising children with Christian principles. Departments: "Train Them Up," 600 to 700 words, on child development (spiritual, moral, character building); "Healthy & Safe," 300-to 400-word how-to pieces on keeping children emotional and physically safe, home and away; "The Lighter Side," humorous essays on family life, 600 to 700 words; "Parent Exchange," 25 to 100 words on problem-solving ideas that have worked for parents; "Life in Our House," insightful anecdotes, 25 to 100 words, about humorous things said at home. (Submissions for "Parent Exchange" and "Life in our House" are not acknowledged or returned.) Pays 15¢ to 25¢ a word, on publication. Pays $25 to $125 for department pieces. Guidelines; send SASE.

CHRISTIAN SINGLE—127 Ninth Ave. N., Nashville, TN 37234-0140. Articles, 600 or 1,200 words, for single adults about leisure activities, issues related to single parents, inspiring personal experiences, humor, life from a Christian perspective. Payment varies, on acceptance. Query. Guidelines.

CHRISTIAN SOCIAL ACTION—100 Maryland Ave. N.E., Washington, DC 20002. Lee Ranck, Ed. Articles, 1,500 to 2,000 words, on social issues for concerned persons of faith. Pays $75 to $125, on publication.

CHRISTIANITY TODAY—465 Gundersen Dr., Carol Stream, IL 60188. Michael G. Maudlin, Man. Ed. Doctrinal social issues and interpretive essays, 1,500 to 3,000 words, from evangelical Protestant perspective. No fiction or poetry. Pays $200 to $500, on acceptance. Query.

CHURCH ADMINISTRATION—127 Ninth Ave. N., Nashville, TN 37234. Attn: Ed. Southern Baptist. How-to articles, 1,600 to 2,000 words, on administrative planning, staffing, pastoral ministry, organization, and financing. Pays 6½¢ a word, on acceptance. Query.

CHURCH & STATE—1816 Jefferson Pl. N.W., Washington, DC 20036. Joseph L. Conn, Ed. Articles, 600 to 2,600 words, on issues of religious liberty and church-state relations. Pays varying rates, on acceptance. Query.

CHURCH EDUCATOR—Educational Ministries, Inc., 165 Plaza Dr., Prescott, AZ 86303. Robert G. Davidson, Ed. How-to articles, to 1,750 words, on Christian education: activity projects, crafts, learning centers, games, bulletin boards, etc., for all church school, junior and high school programs, and adult study groups. Allow 3 months for response. Pays 3¢ a word, on publication.

THE CHURCH MUSICIAN—See *Church Musician Today.*

CHURCH MUSICIAN TODAY—(formerly *The Church Musician*) 127 Ninth Ave. N., Nashville, TN 37234. Jere Adams, Ed. Articles on choral techniques, instrumental groups, worship planning, music administration, directing choirs (all ages), rehearsal planning, music equipment, new technology, drama/pageants and related subjects, hymn studies, book reviews, and music-related fillers. Pays 5½¢ a word, on acceptance.

COLUMBIA—1 Columbus Plaza, New Haven, CT 06510-0901. Richard McMunn, Ed. Knights of Columbus. Articles, 1,500 words, for Catholic families. Must be accompanied by color photos or transparencies. No fiction. Pays to $500 for articles with photos, on acceptance.

COMMENTARY—165 E. 56th St., New York, NY 10022. Neal Kozodoy, Ed. Articles, 5,000 to 7,000 words, on contemporary issues, Jewish affairs, social sciences, religious thought, culture. Serious fiction; book reviews. Pays on publication.

COMMONWEAL— 475 Riverside Dr., New York, NY 10115. Margaret O'Brien Steinfels, Ed. Catholic. Articles, to 3,000 words, on political, religious, social, and literary subjects. Pays 3¢ a word, on acceptance.

THE COVENANT COMPANION—5101 N. Francisco Ave., Chicago, IL 60625. Donald L. Meyer, Ed. Articles, 1,200 words, with Christian implications published for members and attenders of Evangelical Church "seeking to inform, stimulate thought, and encourage dialogue on issues that impact the church and its members." Pays $25 to $50, on publication.

CRUSADER—P.O. Box 7259, Grand Rapids, MI 49510. G. Richard Broene, Ed. Fiction, 900 to 1,500 words, and articles, 400 to 1,000 words, for boys ages 9 to 14 that show how God is at work in their lives and in the world around them. Also, short fillers. Pays 4¢ to 6¢ a word, on acceptance.

DAILY MEDITATION—Box 2710, San Antonio, TX 78299. Ruth S. Paterson, Ed. Inspirational, self-improvement, nonsectarian religious articles "showing the way to greater spiritual growth," 300 to 1,650 words. Fillers, to 350 words; verse, to 20 lines. Pays 1½¢ to 2¢ a word for prose; 14¢ a line for verse, on acceptance. SASE required.

DECISION—Billy Graham Evangelistic Assn., 1300 Harmon Pl., P.O. Box 779, Minneapolis, MN 55440-0779. Roger C. Palms, Ed. Christian testimonies and teaching articles on evangelism and Christian nurturing, 1,200 to 1,500 words. Vignettes, 400 to 1,000 words. Pays varying rates, on publication.

DISCOVERIES—WordAction Publishing Co., 6401 The Paseo, Kansas City, MO 64131. Attn: Asst. Ed. Weekly take-home paper designed to correlate with Evangelical Sunday school curriculum. Fiction, 500 words, for 8-to 10-year-olds. Stories should feature contemporary, true-to-life characters and should illustrate character building and scriptural application. No poetry. SASE required. Pays 5¢ a word, on publication. Guidelines.

DREAMS & VISIONS—Skysong Press, 35 Peter St. S., Orillia, Ont., Canada L3V 5A8. Steve Stanton, Ed. New frontiers in Christian fiction. Eclectic fiction, 2,000 to 6,000 words, that "has literary value and is unique and relevant to Christian readers today." Pays ½¢ per word.

ENRICHMENT: A JOURNAL FOR PENTECOSTAL MINISTRY—1445 Boonville Ave., Springfield, MO 65802. Wayde I. Goodall, Ed. Articles, 1,200 to 1,500 words, slanted to ministers, on preaching, doctrine, practice; how-to features. Pays to 10¢ a word, on acceptance.

EVANGEL—Light and Life Press, Box 535002, Indianapolis, IN 46253-5002. Julie Innes, Ed. Free Methodist. Personal experience articles, 1,000 words; short devotional items, 300 to 500 words; fiction, 1,200 words, showing personal faith in Christ to be instrumental in solving problems. Send #10 SASE for sample and guidelines. Pays 4¢ a word for articles, $10 for poetry, on publication.

EVANGELIZING TODAY'S CHILD—Box 348, Warrenton, MO 63383-0348. Attn: Ed. Articles, 1,200 to 1,500 words, for Sunday school teachers, Christian education leaders, and children's workers. Feature articles should include teaching principles, instruction for the reader, and classroom illustrations. "Impact" articles, 700 to 900 words, show the power of the Gospel in or through the life of a child; "Resource Center," 200-to 300-word teaching tips. Also short stories, 800 to 1,000 words, of contemporary children dealing with problems; must have a scriptural solution. Pays 10¢ to 12¢ a word for articles; $15 to $25 for "Resource Center" pieces; 7¢ a word for short stories, 60 days after acceptance. Guidelines.

FAITH TODAY—M.I.P. Box 3745, Markham, Ontario, Canada L3R OY4. Marianne Meed Ward, Man. Ed. Articles, 1,500 words, on current issues relating to the church in Canada. Pays negotiable rates, on publication. Queries required.

THE FAMILY DIGEST—P.O. Box 40137, Fort Wayne, IN 46804. Corine B. Erlandson, Ed. Articles, 700 to 1,200 words, on family life, Catholic subjects, seasonal, parish life, prayer, inspiration, how-to, spiritual life, for the Catholic reader. Also publishes short humorous anecdotes drawn from personal experience and light-hearted cartoons. Pays $40 to $60 per article; $20 for personal anecdotes; $30 for cartoons, 4 to 6 weeks after acceptance.

FELLOWSHIP—Box 271, Nyack, NY 10960-0271. Richard Deats, Ed. Bimonthly published by the Fellowship of Reconciliation, an interfaith, pacifist organization. Articles, 750 and 1,500 to 2,000 words; B&W photo-essays, on active nonviolence, peace and justice, opposition to war. "Articles for a just and peaceful world community." SASE required. Pays in copies and subscription. Queries preferred.

FELLOWSHIP IN PRAYER—See *Sacred Journey: The Journal of Fellowship in Prayer.*

FIRST THINGS—156 Fifth Ave., #400, New York, NY 10010-7002. James Nuechterlein, Ed. Published 10 times a year. Essays and social commentary, 1,500 words or 4,000 to 6,000 words, for academics and clergy members, on the role of religion in public life. Pays $250 to $700, on publication.

FOURSQUARE WORLD ADVANCE—1910 W. Sunset Blvd., Suite 200, P.O. Box 26902, Los Angeles, CA 90026. Ronald D. Williams, Ed. Official publication of the International Church of the Foursquare Gospel. Religious fiction and nonfiction, 1,000 to 1,200 words, and religious poetry. Pays $75, on publication. Guidelines.

FRIENDS JOURNAL—1206 Arch St., Philadelphia, PA 19107. Vinton Deming, Ed. Articles, to 2,000 words, reflecting Quaker life today: commentary on social issues, experiential articles, Quaker history, world affairs. Poetry, to 25 lines, and Quaker-related humor and crossword puzzles also considered. Pays in copies. Guidelines.

THE GEM—Box 926, Findlay, OH 45839-0926. Evelyn Sloat, Ed. Articles, 300 to 1,600 words, and fiction, 1,000 to 1,600 words: true-to-life experiences of God's help, of healed relationships, and of growing maturity in faith. For adolescents through senior citizens. Pays $15 for articles and fiction, $5 to $10 for fillers, after publication.

GLORY SONGS—127 Ninth Ave. N., Nashville, TN 37234. Jere V. Adams, Ed. For volunteer and part-time music directors and members of church choirs. Very easy music and accompaniments designed specifically for the small church (4 to 6 songs per issue). Includes 8-page pull-out with articles for choir members on leisure reading, music training, and choir projects. Pays 5½¢ per word, on acceptance.

GROUP, THE YOUTH MINISTRY MAGAZINE—Box 481, Loveland, CO 80539. Rick Lawrence, Ed. Interdenominational magazine for leaders of junior and senior high school Christian youth groups. Articles, 500 to 1,700 words, about practical youth ministry principles, techniques, or activities. Short how-to pieces, to 300 words. Pays to $200 for articles, $35 for department pieces, on acceptance. Guidelines.

GUIDE—Review and Herald Publishing Assn., 55 W. Oak Ridge Dr., Hagerstown, MD 21740. Tim Lale, Ed. Stories, to 1,200 words, for Christian youth, ages 10 to 14. Pays 3¢ to 7¢ a word, on publication.

GUIDEPOSTS—16 E. 34th St., New York, NY 10016. Celeste McCauley, Features Ed. True first-person stories, 250 to 1,500 words, stressing how faith in God helps people cope with life. Anecdotal fillers, to 250 words. Pays $100 to $400 for full-length stories, $25 to $100 for fillers, on acceptance.

HOLINESS TODAY—6401 The Paseo, Kansas City, MO 64131. Attn: Man. Ed. Church of the Nazarene. Articles, 800 to 2,000 words, about distinctive Nazarenes, Christian family life and marriage, a Christian approach to social issues, seasonal material, and short devotional articles. Pays 4¢ to 5¢ a word, within 30 days of acceptance. Guidelines.

HOME LIFE—127 Ninth Ave. N., Nashville, TN 37234. Attn: Ed.-in-Chief. Southern Baptist. No longer accepts unsolicited manuscripts.

INDIAN LIFE—Box 3765, RPO Redwood Centre, Winnipeg, MB, Canada R2W 3R6. Attn: Acquisitions Ed. Christian teaching articles and testimonials of Native Americans, 1,000 to 1,200 words. "Our magazine is designed to help the North American Indian Church speak to the social, cultural, and spiritual needs of Native people." Writing should be at a seventh-grade reading level. "We prefer Native writers who write from within their culture. Read the magazine before submitting." Queries preferred.

INSIDE MAGAZINE—226 S. 16th St., Philadelphia, PA 19102-3392. Jane Biberman, Ed. Jewish lifestyle magazine. Articles, 1,500 to 3,000 words, on Jewish issues, health, finance, and the arts. Pays $75 to $600, after publication. Queries required; send clips if available.

JEWISH CURRENTS—22 E. 17th St., #601, New York, NY 10003-3272. Morris U. Schappes, Ed. Articles, 2,400 to 3,000 words, on Jewish history, Jewish secularism, progressivism, labor struggle, Holocaust and Holocaust-resistance, Black-Jewish relations, Israel, Yiddish culture. "We are pro-Israel though non-Zionist and a secular magazine; no religious articles." Overstocked with fiction and poetry. No payment.

THE JEWISH HOMEMAKER—391 Troy Ave., Brooklyn, NY 11213. Sara Levy, Ed. Bimonthly. Articles, 1,200 to 2,000 words, for a traditional/Orthodox Jewish audience. Humor. Payment varies, on publication. Query.

THE JEWISH MONTHLY—B'nai B'rith International, 1640 Rhode Island Ave. N.W., Washington, DC 20036. Eric Rozenman, Exec. Ed. Articles, 500 to 3,000 words, on politics, religion, history, culture, and social issues of Jewish concern with an emphasis on people. Pays 10¢ to 25¢ a word, on publication. Query with clips.

JOURNAL OF CHRISTIAN NURSING—P.O. Box 1650, Downers Grove, IL 60515. Judy Shelly, Sr. Ed. Articles, 8 to 12 double-spaced pages, that help Christian nurses view nursing practice through the eyes of faith: spiritual care, ethics, values, healing and wholeness, psychology and religion, personal and professional ethics, etc. Priority given to nurse authors, though work by non-nurses will be considered. Pays $25 to $80. Guidelines and editorial calendar.

THE JOYFUL WOMAN—P.O. Box 90028, Chattanooga, TN 37412. Joy Rice Martin, Ed. Articles and fiction, 500 to 1,200 words, for Christian women:

first-person inspirational true stories, profiles of Christian women, practical and biblically oriented how-to articles. Pays 3¢ to 4¢ a word, on publication. Queries required; no unsolicited manuscripts.

LEADERSHIP— 465 Gundersen Dr., Carol Stream, IL 60188. Kevin A. Miller, Ed. Articles, 500 to 3,000 words, on administration, finance, and/or programming of interest to ministers and church leaders. Personal stories of crisis in ministry. "We deal mainly with the how-to of running a church. We're not a theological journal but a practical one." Pays $50 to $350, on acceptance.

LIBERTY MAGAZINE—12501 Old Columbia Pike, Silver Spring, MD 20904-1608. Clifford R. Goldstein, Ed. Timely articles, to 2,500 words, and photo-essays, on religious freedom and church-state relations. Pays 6¢ to 8¢ a word, on acceptance. Query.

LIGHT AND LIFE—P.O. Box 535002, Indianapolis, IN 46253-5002. Doug Newton, Ed. Thoughtful articles about practical Christian living. Social and cultural analysis from an evangelical perspective. Pays 4¢ to 5¢ a word, on publication.

LIGUORIAN—Liguori, MO 63057-9999. Rev. Allan Weinert, Ed. Catholic. Articles and short stories, 1,500 to 2,000 words, on Christian values in modern life. Pays 10¢ to 12¢ a word, on acceptance.

THE LIVING LIGHT—U.S. Catholic Conference, Dept. of Education, Caldwell 345, The Catholic Univ. of America, Washington, DC 20064. Dr. Berard L. Marthaler, Office of the Exec. Ed. Theoretical and practical articles, 1,500 to 5,000 words, on religious education, catechesis, and pastoral ministry.

LIVING WITH TEENAGERS—127 Ninth Ave. N., Nashville, TN 37234. Articles, 400 to 1,200 words, told from a Christian perspective for parents of teenagers; first-person approach preferred. Queries welcome; SASE required. Pay is negotiable and made on acceptance.

THE LOOKOUT— 8121 Hamilton Ave., Cincinnati, OH 45231. David Faust, Ed. Articles, 500 to 1,800 words, on spiritual growth, family issues, applying Christian faith to current issues, and people overcoming problems with Christian principles. Inspirational or humorous shorts, 500 to 800 words. Pays 5¢ to 15¢ a word, on acceptance.

THE LUTHERAN— 8765 W. Higgins Rd., Chicago, IL 60631. Edgar R. Trexler, Ed. Articles, to 1,200 words, on Christian ideology, personal religious experiences, social and ethical issues, family life, church, and community of Evangelical Lutheran Church in America. Pays $100 to $500, on acceptance. Query required.

MARRIAGE PARTNERSHIP—Christianity Today, Inc., 465 Gundersen Dr., Carol Stream, IL 60188. Ron Lee, Ed. Articles, 500 to 2,000 words, related to marriage, for men and women who wish to fortify their relationship. Cartoons, humor, fillers. Pays $50 to $300, on acceptance. Query required.

MARYKNOLL—Maryknoll, NY 10545. Joseph Veneroso, M. M., Ed. Frank Maurovich, Man. Ed. Magazine of the Catholic Foreign Mission Society of America. Articles, 800 to 1,000 words, and photos relating to missions or missioners overseas. Pays $150, on acceptance. Payment for photos made on publication.

MATURE LIVING—127 Ninth Ave. N., Nashville, TN 37234. Al Shackleford, Ed. Fiction and human-interest articles, to 1,200 words, for senior adults. Must be consistent with Christian principles. Payment varies, on acceptance.

MATURE YEARS—201 Eighth Ave. S., P.O. Box 801, Nashville, TN 37202. Marvin W. Cropsey, Ed. Nondenominational quarterly. Articles, 1,500 to 2,000 words, on retirement or related subjects, inspiration. Humorous and serious fiction, 1,500 to 1,800 words. Travel pieces for seniors or with religious slant. Poetry, to 14 lines. Include social security number with manuscript. Guidelines.

MESSENGER OF THE SACRED HEART— 661 Greenwood Ave., Toronto, Ont., Canada M4J 4B3. Articles and short stories, about 1,500 words, for American and Canadian Catholics. Pays from 4¢ a word, on acceptance.

MIDSTREAM—110 E. 59th St., New York, NY 10022. Joel Carmichael, Ed. Jewish/Zionist-interest articles and book reviews. Fiction, to 3,000 words, and poetry. Pays 5¢ a word, after publication. Allow 3 months for response.

THE MIRACULOUS MEDAL— 475 E. Chelten Ave., Philadelphia, PA 19144-5785. Rev. William J. O'Brien, C.M., Ed. Dir. Catholic. Fiction, to 2,400 words. Religious verse, to 20 lines. Pays from 2¢ a word for fiction, from 50¢ a line for poetry, on acceptance.

MODERN LITURGY—160 E. Virginia St., #290, San Jose, CA 95112. Nick Wagner, Ed. Practical, imaginative how-to help for Roman Catholic liturgy planners. Pays in copies and subscription. Query required.

MOMENT MAGAZINE— 4710 41st St. N.W., Washington, DC 20016. Suzanne Singer, Man. Ed. Sophisticated, issue-oriented articles, 2,000 to 4,000 words, on Jewish topics. Nonfiction only. Pays $150 to $800, on publication.

MOMENTUM—National Catholic Educational Assn., 1077 30th St. N.W., Suite 100, Washington, DC 20007-3852. Patricia Feistritzer, Ed. Articles, 500 to 1,500 words, on outstanding programs, issues, and research in education. Book reviews. Pays $25 to $75, on publication. Query.

MOODY MAGAZINE— 820 N. La Salle Blvd., Chicago, IL 60610. Andrew Scheer, Man. Ed. Anecdotal articles, 1,200 to 2,000 words, on the evangelical Christian experience in the home, the community, and the workplace. Pays 15¢ to 20¢ a word, on acceptance. Query.

THE MUSIC LEADER—See *Plans & Pluses.*

NEW ERA—50 E. North Temple, Salt Lake City, UT 84150. Richard M. Romney, Man. Ed. Articles, 150 to 1,500 words, and fiction, to 2,000 words, for young Mormons. Poetry; photos. Pays 5¢ to 10¢ a word, 25¢ a line for poetry, on acceptance. Query.

NEW MAN— 600 Rinehart Rd., Lake Mary, FL 32746. Brian Peterson, Ed. Articles, to 2,000 words, that help men "in their quest for godliness and integrity." Profiles of everyday men who are doing something extraordinary, action-packed thrill and adventure articles, trend pieces that take an in-depth look at issues facing men today. Short items, 50 to 250 words, on unusual facts, motivational quotes, perspectives on news and events. Pays 10¢ to 35¢ per word, on publication.

NEW WORLD OUTLOOK— 475 Riverside Dr., Rm. 1470, New York, NY 10115. Alma Graham, Ed. Articles, 500 to 2,000 words, illustrated with color photos, on United Methodist missions and Methodist-related programs and ministries. Focus on national, global, and women's and children's issues, and on men and youth in missions. Pays on publication. Query.

OBLATES—9480 N. De Mazenod Dr., Belleville, IL 62223-1160. Mary Mohrman, Manuscripts Ed. Christine Portell, Man. Ed. Articles, 500 to 600 words, that inspire, uplift, and motivate through positive Christian values in everyday life. Inspirational poetry, to 16 lines. Pays $80 for articles, $30 for poems, on acceptance. Send 2 first-class stamps and SASE for guidelines and sample copy.

THE OTHER SIDE—300 W. Apsley, Philadelphia, PA 19144. Doug Davidson, Nonfiction Ed. Bob Finegan, Fiction Ed. Rod Jellema, Poetry Ed. Independent, ecumenical Christian magazine devoted to issues of peace, justice, and faith. Fiction, 500 to 5,000 words, that deepens readers' encounter with the mystery of God and the mystery of ourselves. Nonfiction, 500 to 4,000 words (most under 2,000 words), on contemporary social, political, economic, or racial issues in the U.S. or abroad. Poems, to 50 lines; submit up to 3 poems. Payment is 2 copies plus $20 to $350 for articles; $75 to $250 for fiction; $15 for poems, on acceptance. Guidelines.

OUR FAMILY—Box 249, Battleford, Sask., Canada S0M 0E0. Nestor Gregoire, Ed. Articles, 1,000 to 3,000 words, for Catholic families, on modern society, family, marriage, current affairs, and spiritual topics. Humor; verse. Pays 7¢ to 10¢ a word for articles, 75¢ to $1 a line for poetry, on acceptance. SAE with international reply coupons required with all submissions. Guidelines.

PARENTLIFE—MSN 140, 127 Ninth Ave. N., Nashville, TN 37234. Attn: Ed. Informative articles and personal experience pieces, 400 to 1,200 words, relating to family and the preschool child, written with a Christian perspective. Payment varies, on acceptance.

PASTORAL LIFE—Box 595, Canfield, OH 44406-0595. Anthony L. Chenevey, Ed. Articles, 2,000 to 2,500 words, addressing the problems of pastoral ministry. Pays 4¢ a word, on publication. Guidelines.

PENTECOSTAL EVANGEL—1445 Boonville Ave., Springfield, MO 65802. Hal Donaldson, Ed. Assemblies of God. Religious, personal experience, and devotional articles, 400 to 1,000 words. Pays 8¢ to 10¢ a word.

PERSPECTIVE—Pioneer Clubs, Box 788, Wheaton, IL 60189. Rebecca Powell Parat, Ed. Quarterly. Articles, 500 to 1,500 words, that provide growth for adult club leaders in leadership and relationship skills and offer encouragement and practical support. Readers are lay leaders of Pioneer Clubs for boys and girls (age 2 to 12th grade). "Most articles written on assignment; writers familiar with Pioneer Clubs who would be interested in working on assignment should contact us." Queries preferred. Pays $25 to $100, on acceptance. Guidelines.

PIME WORLD—17330 Quincy St., Detroit, MI 48221. Paul W. Witte, Man. Ed. Articles, 600 to 1,200 words, on Catholic missionary work in Asia, West Africa, and Latin America. Color photos. No fiction or poetry. Pays 6¢ a word, extra for photos, on publication.

PLANS & PLUSES—(formerly *The Music Leader*) Baptist Sunday School Board, 127 Ninth Ave. N., Nashville, TN 37234. Anne Trudel, Rhonda Edge Buescher, Eds. Annual. Dramas or programs, to 1,000 words, built around well-known hymns, for children in grades 3 to 6, and seasonal programs for children's choirs, to 1,000 words. Also, how-to articles, to 800 words, on organizing choir rehearsals for children, time savers and other tips for choir directors, and inspirational poetry. "Our readers are volunteer choir directors, and teachers in evangelical churches." Pays 5½¢ to 6½¢ a word, on acceptance. Send complete manuscript; no queries.

POWER AND LIGHT— 6401 The Paseo, Kansas City, MO 64131. Beula J. Postlewait, Preteen Ed. Fiction, 400 to 800 words, for grades 5 and 6, defining Christian experiences and demonstrating Christian values and beliefs. Pays 5¢ a word for multi-use rights, on publication.

THE PREACHER'S MAGAZINE—10814 E. Broadway, Spokane, WA 99206. Randal E. Denny, Ed. Scholarly and practical articles, 700 to 2,500 words, on areas of interest to Christian ministers: church administration, pastoral care, professional and personal growth, church music, finance, evangelism. Pays 3½¢ a word, on publication. Guidelines.

PRESBYTERIAN RECORD—50 Wynford Dr., North York, Ont., Canada M3C 1J7. John Congram, Ed. Fiction and nonfiction, 1,500 words, and poetry, any length. Short items, to 800 words, of a contemporary and often controversial nature for "Vox Populi." The purpose of the magazine is "to provide news, not only from our church but the church-at-large, and to fulfill both a pastoral and prophetic role among our people." Queries preferred. SAE with international reply coupons required. Pays about $50 (Canadian), on publication. Guidelines.

PRESBYTERIANS TODAY—100 Witherspoon, Louisville, KY 40202-1396. Eva Stimson, Ed. Articles, 1,200 to 1,500 words, of special interest to members of the Presbyterian Church (USA). Pays to $200, before publication.

THE PRIEST—200 Noll Plaza, Huntington, IN 46750-4304. Father Owen F. Campion, Ed. Viewpoints, to 1,500 words, and articles, to 5,000 words, on life and ministry of priests, current theological developments, etc., for priests, permanent deacons, and seminarians. Pays $75 to $250, on acceptance.

PURPOSE— 616 Walnut Ave., Scottdale, PA 15683-1999. James E. Horsch, Ed. Fiction, nonfiction, and fillers, to 750 words, on Christian discipleship and church-year related themes, with good photos; pieces of history, biography, science, hobbies, from a Christian perspective; Christian problem solving. First-person pieces preferred. Poetry, to 12 lines. "Send complete manuscript; no queries." Pays to 5¢ a word, to $2 a line for poetry, on acceptance.

QUEEN OF ALL HEARTS—26 S. Saxon Ave., Bay Shore, NY 11706-8993. J. Patrick Gaffney, S.M.M., Ed. Publication of Montfort Missionaries. Articles and fiction, 1,000 to 2,000 words, related to the Virgin Mary. Poetry. Pay varies, on acceptance.

THE QUIET HOUR— 4050 Lee Vance View, Colorado Springs, CO 80919. Gary Wilde, Ed. Short devotionals. Pays $15, on acceptance. By assignment only; query.

RECONSTRUCTIONISM TODAY—30 Old Whitfield Rd., Accord, NY 12404. Lawrence Bush, Ed. Articles on contemporary Judaism and Jewish culture. No fiction or poetry. Pays in copies and subscription.

REVIEW FOR RELIGIOUS—3601 Lindell Blvd., St. Louis, MO 63108. David L. Fleming, S.J., Ed. Informative, practical, or inspirational articles, 1,500 to 5,000 words, from a Catholic theological or spiritual point of view. Pays $6 per page, on publication. Guidelines.

SACRED JOURNEY: THE JOURNAL OF FELLOWSHIP IN PRAYER— (formerly *Fellowship in Prayer*) 291 Witherspoon St., Princeton, NJ 08542. Articles, to 1,500 words, relating to prayer, meditation, and the spiritual life as practiced by men and women of all faith traditions. Pays in copies. Guidelines.

ST. ANTHONY MESSENGER—1615 Republic St., Cincinnati, OH 45210-1298. Norman Perry, O.F.M., Ed. Articles, 2,000 to 3,000 words, on personalities, major movements, education, family, religious and church issues, spiritual life, and social issues. Human-interest pieces. Humor; fiction, 2,000 to 3,000 words. Articles and stories should have religious implications. Query for nonfiction. Pays 15¢ a word, on acceptance.

ST. JOSEPH'S MESSENGER—P.O. Box 288, Jersey City, NJ 07303-0288. Sister Ursula Maphet, Ed. Inspirational articles, 500 to 1,000 words, and fiction, 1,000 to 1,500 words. Verse, 4 to 40 lines. Payment varies, on publication.

SEEK—8121 Hamilton Ave., Cincinnati, OH 45231. Eileen H. Wilmoth, Ed. Articles and fiction, 400 to 1,200 words, on inspirational and controversial topics and timely religious issues. Christian testimonials. Pays 5¢ a word, on acceptance. 6" x 9" SASE for guidelines.

THE SENIOR MUSICIAN—127 Ninth Ave. N., Nashville, TN 37234. Jere V. Adams, Ed. Quarterly. For music directors, pastors, organists, pianists, choir coordinators. Easy choir music for senior adult choirs to use in worship, ministry, and recreation. Also includes leisure reading, music training, fellowship suggestions, and choir projects for personal growth. Pays 5½¢ a word, on acceptance.

SHARING THE VICTORY—Fellowship of Christian Athletes, 8701 Leeds Rd., Kansas City, MO 64129. John Dodderidge, Ed. Articles, interviews, and profiles, to 1,500 words, for co-ed Christian athletes and coaches in junior high, high school, college, and pros. Pays from $50, on publication. Query required.

SIGNS OF THE TIMES—P. O. Box 5353, Nampa, ID 83653-5353. Marvin Moore, Ed. Seventh-Day Adventists. Articles, 500 to 2,000 words: features on Christians who have performed community services; first-person experiences, to 1,000 words; health, home, marriage, human-interest pieces; inspirational articles. Pays to 20¢ a word, on acceptance. Send 9x12 SASE with 3 first-class stamps for sample and guidelines.

SISTERS TODAY—The Liturgical Press, St. John's Abbey, Collegeville, MN 56321-7500. Articles, 500 to 3,500 words, on theology, social justice issues, and religious issues for women and the Church. Poetry, to 34 lines. Pays $5 per printed page, $10 per poem, on publication; $50 for color cover photos and $25 for B&W inside photos. Send articles to: Sister Mary Anthony Wagner, O.S.B., Ed., St. Benedict's Monastery, St. Joseph, MN 56374-2099. Send poetry to: Sister Virginia Micka, C.S.J.,1884 Randolph Ave., St. Paul, MN 55105.

SOCIAL JUSTICE REVIEW—3835 Westminster Pl., St. Louis, MO 63108-3409. Rev. John H. Miller, C.S.C., Ed. Articles, 2,000 to 3,000 words, on social problems in light of Catholic teaching and current scientific studies. Pays 2¢ a word, on publication.

SPIRITUAL LIFE—2131 Lincoln Rd. N.E., Washington, DC 20002-1199. Edward O'Donnell, O.C.D., Ed. Professional religious journal. Religious essays, 3,000 to 5,000 words, on spirituality in contemporary life. Pays from $50, on acceptance. Guidelines.

STANDARD—6401 The Paseo, Kansas City, MO 64131. Articles and fiction, 300 to 1,700 words; poetry, to 20 lines; fiction with Christian emphasis but not overtly preachy; cartoons in good taste. Pays 3½¢ a word, on acceptance.

TEACHERS INTERACTION—3558 S. Jefferson Ave., St. Louis, MO 63118. Tom Nummela, Ed. Practical articles, 800 to 1,200 words, for Christian teachers and how-to pieces, to 100 words, specifically for Lutheran Church-Missouri Synod volunteer church school teachers. Pays $20 to $100, on publication. Freelance submissions accepted.

THEOLOGY TODAY—Box 29, Princeton, NJ 08542. Patrick D. Miller, Ed. Articles, 1,500 to 3,500 words, on theology, religion, and related social and philosophical issues. Literary criticism. Pays $50 to $200, on publication.

TIKKUN—26 Fell St., San Francisco, CA 94102. Michael Lerner, Ed. "A Bimonthly Jewish Critique of Politics, Culture, and Society." Articles and fiction, 2,400 to 3,000 words. Poetry. "Read a copy to get a sense of what we publish. We are always interested in work pertaining to contemporary culture." Pays in copies.

TODAY'S CHRISTIAN DOCTOR—P.O. Box 5, Bristol, TN 37621-0005. David B. Biebel, D. Min., Ed. Articles, 8 to 10 double-spaced pages, for Christian medical and dental professionals. Queries preferred. Guidelines.

TODAY'S CHRISTIAN WOMAN— 465 Gundersen Dr., Carol Stream, IL 60188. Ramona Cramer Tucker, Ed. Articles, 1,500 to 1,800 words, that are "warm and personal in tone, full of real-life anecdotes that deal with the following relationships: marriage, parenting, friendship, spiritual life, and self." Payment varies, on acceptance. Queries required. Guidelines.

THE UNITED CHURCH OBSERVER— 478 Huron St., Toronto, Ont., Canada M5R 2R3. Factual articles, 1,500 to 2,500 words, on religious trends, human problems, social issues. No poetry. Pays after publication. Query.

UNITED SYNAGOGUE REVIEW—155 Fifth Ave., New York, NY 10010. Lois Goldrich, Ed. Articles, 1,000 to 1,200 words, on issues of interest to Conservative Jewish community. Query.

UNITY MAGAZINE—1901 N.W. Blue Pkwy., Unity School of Christianity, Unity Village, MO 64065. Philip White, Ed. Religious and inspirational articles, 1,000 to 1,800 words, on spiritual growth, health and healing, metaphysical, Bible interpretation, and prosperity. Poems. Pays 20¢ a word, on acceptance.

VIRTUE: HELPING WOMEN BUILD CHRIST-LIKE CHARACTER— (formerly *Virtue: The Christian Magazine for Women*) 4050 Lee Vance View, Colorado Springs, CO 80918. Attn: Ed. Articles and fiction for Christian women. Journalistic reports on women's issues and women's lives and their spiritual journeys. Query for articles; SASE required. Guidelines.

VISTA MAGAZINE— 6060 Castleway Dr., Indianapolis, IN 46250-0434. Attn: Ed. Articles and adult fiction, on current Christian concerns and issues as well as fundamental issues of holiness and Christian living. Not accepting freelance material at this time.

THE WAR CRY—The Salvation Army, P.O. Box 269, Alexandria, VA 22313. Attn: Man Ed. Inspirational articles, to 800 words, addressing modern life and issues. Color photos. Pays 15¢ to 20¢ a word for articles, $150 to $200 for photos, on acceptance.

WARNER PRESS PUBLISHERS—P.O. Box 2499, Anderson, IN 46018. Jennie Bishop, Senior Ed. "Writers must send SASE for guidelines before submitting." Religious themes, sensitive prose, and inspirational verse for Sunday bulletins. Pays $20 to $35, on acceptance. Also accepts ideas for coloring and activity books.

WITH: THE MAGAZINE FOR RADICAL CHRISTIAN YOUTH—722 Main St., Box 347, Newton, KS 67114. Eddy Hall, Carol Duerksen, Eds. Fiction, 500 to 2,000 words; nonfiction, 500 to 1,600 words; and poetry, to 50 lines for Mennonite and Brethren teenagers. "Wholesome humor always gets a close read." B&W 8x10 photos accepted. Payment is 5¢ a word, on acceptance (3¢ a word for reprints).

WOMAN'S TOUCH—1445 Boonville, Springfield, MO 65802-1894. Peggy Musgrove, Ed. Aleda Swartzendruber, Man. Ed. Articles, 500 to 1,000 words, that provide help and inspiration to Christian women, strengthening family life, and reaching out in witness to others. Submit complete manuscript. Allow 3 months for response. Payment varies, on publication. Guidelines and editorial calendar.

WORLD VISION MAGAZINE—P.O. Box 9716, Federal Way, WA 98063-9716. Shelly Ngo, Man. Ed. Thoroughly researched articles, 1,200 to 2,000 words, on worldwide poverty, evangelism, the environment, and justice. Include reputable sources and strong anecdotes. "We like articles to offer positive ways Christians can make a difference." Query required. Payment negotiable, made on acceptance.

YOUNG SALVATIONIST—The Salvation Army, 615 Slaters Ln., P.O. Box 269, Alexandria, VA 22313. Attn: Lesa Davis, Man. Ed. Articles, 600 to 1,200 words, that teach the Christian view of everyday living, for teenagers. Short shorts, first-person testimonies, 600 to 800 words. Pays 15¢ a word (10¢ a word for reprints), on acceptance. SASE required. Send 8½x11 SASE (3 stamps) for theme list, guidelines, and sample copy.

YOUR CHURCH— 465 Gundersen Dr., Carol Stream, IL 60188. Richard Doebler, Ed. Articles, to 1,000 words, about church business administration. Pays about 15¢ a word, on acceptance. Query required. Guidelines.

HEALTH

ACCENT ON LIVING—P. O. Box 700, Bloomington, IL 61702. Raymond C. Cheever, Pub. Betty Garee, Ed. Articles, 250 to 1,000 words, about physically disabled people, including their careers, recreation, sports, self-help devices, and ideas that can make daily routines easier. Good photos a plus. Pays 10¢ a word, on publication. Query.

AMERICAN BABY—KIII Family & Leisure Group, 249 W. 17th St., New York, NY 10011. Judith Nolte, Ed. Articles, 1,000 to 2,000 words, for new or expectant parents on prenatal and infant care. Personal experience, 900 to 1,200 words (do not submit in diary format). Department pieces, 50 to 350 words, for "Crib Notes" (news and feature topics) and "Medical Update" (health and medicine). No fiction, fantasy pieces, dreamy musings, or poetry. Pays $500 to $1,000 for articles, $100 for departments, on acceptance. Guidelines.

AMERICAN FITNESS—15250 Ventura Blvd., Suite 200, Sherman Oaks, CA 91403. Peg Jordan, Ed. Rhonda Wilson, Man. Ed. Articles, 500 to 1,500 words, on exercise, health, trends, research, nutrition, alternative paths, etc. Illustrations, photos.

AMERICAN HEALTH FOR WOMEN—(formerly *American Health*) 28 W. 23rd St., New York, NY 10010. Attn: Editorial Dept. Lively, authoritative articles, 1,000 to 3,000 words, on women's health and lifestyle aspects of health and fitness; 100-to 500-word news reports. Query with clips. Pays on acceptance; fee is negotiated with assigning editor.

AMERICAN JOURNAL OF NURSING—555 W. 57th St., New York, NY 10019. Santa J. Crisall, Clinical and Ed. Dir. Articles, 1,500 to 2,000 words, with photos or illustrations, on nursing or disease processes. Query.

AQUARIUS: A SIGN OF THE TIMES—1035 Green St., Roswell, GA 30075. Dan Liss, Ed. Tabloid. Articles, 800 words (plus photo or illustration) on holistic health, metaphysics, spirituality, and the environment. "We are a great way for new writers to get clips." No payment. E-mail address: aquarius@atlanta.com.

ARTHRITIS TODAY—The Arthritis Foundation, 1330 W. Peachtree St., Atlanta, GA 30309. Cindy McDaniel, Ed. Research, self-help, how-to, general interest, general health, and lifestyle topics, and inspirational articles, 750 to 3,000 words, and briefs, 100 to 250 words. "The magazine is written to help people with arthritis live more productive, independent, and pain-free lives." Pays $500 to $2,000 for articles, $75 to $250 for briefs, on acceptance.

BABY TALK—1325 Ave. of the Americas, New York, NY 10019. Trisha Thompson, Ed. Articles, 1,000 to 1,500 words, by parents or professionals, on babies and baby care, etc. No poetry. Pay varies, on acceptance. SASE required.

BETTER HEALTH—1450 Chapel St., New Haven, CT 06511. Magaly Olivero, Pub. Dir. Wellness and prevention magazine published by The Hospital of Saint Raphael in New Haven. Upbeat articles, 2,000 to 2,500 words, that encourage a healthier lifestyle. Articles must contain quotes and narrative from healthcare professionals at Saint Raphael's and other local services. No first-person or personal experience articles. Pays $500, on acceptance. Query with SASE.

COPING: LIVING WITH CANCER—P.O. Box 682268, Franklin, TN 37068. Kay Thomas, Ed. Uplifting and practical articles for people living with cancer: medical news, lifestyle issues, and inspiring personal essays. No payment.

CURRENT HEALTH—900 Skokie Blvd., Suite 200, Northbrook, IL 60062-4028. Carole Rubenstein, Ed. Published 8 times a year. Articles, varying lengths, on drug education, nutrition, fitness and exercise, first aid and safety, and environmental awareness. Two editions: *Current Health 1,* for grades 4 to 7, and *Current Health 2,* for grades 7 to 12. Payment varies, on publication. Query; no unsolicited manuscripts.

DIABETES SELF-MANAGEMENT—150 W. 22nd St., New York, NY 10011. James Hazlett, Ed. Articles, 2,000 to 4,000 words, for people with diabetes who want to know more about controlling and managing it. Up-to-date and authoritative information on nutrition, pharmacology, exercise physiology, technological advances, self-help, and other how-to subjects. "Articles must be useful, instructive, and must have immediate application to the day-to-day life of our readers. We do not publish personal experience, profiles, exposés, or research breakthroughs." Query with one-page rationale, outline, writing samples, and SASE. Pays from $500, on publication. Buys all rights.

EATING WELL—823A Ferry Rd., Charlotte, VT 05445-1001. Marcelle DiFalco, Ed. Published 10 times per year. "A food book with a health perspective." Feature articles, 2,000 to 5,000 words, for readers who "know that what they eat directly affects their well-being, and believe that with the right approach, one can enjoy both good food and good health." Department pieces, 100 to 200 words, for "Nutrition News" and "Eating Well in America." "We look for strong journalistic voice; authoritative, timely coverage of nutrition issues; healthful recipes that emphasize good ingredients, simple preparation, and full flavor; and a sense of humor." Pays varying rates, 45 days after acceptance. Query.

FIT PREGNANCY—21100 Erwin St., Woodland Hills, CA 91367-3712. Peg Moline, Ed. Articles, 500 to 2,000 words, on pregnant women's health, sports, and physical fitness. Payment varies, on publication. Query.

FITNESS—Gruner & Jahr USA Publishing, 375 Lexington Ave., New York, NY 10017. Sally Lee, Ed. Articles, 500 to 2,000 words, on health, exercise, sports, nutrition, diet, psychological well-being, alternative therapies, and beauty. Average reader is 30 years old. Query required. Pays $1 a word, on acceptance.

FITNESS PLUS—12 W. 27th St., New York, NY 10001-6903. Steve Romondi, Ed. Bimonthly. Articles, 1,000 to 3,000 words, on serious health and fitness training for men. Payment varies, on publication. Queries preferred.

HEALTH QUEST—200 Highpoint Dr., Suite 215, Chalfont, PA 18914. Tamara Jeffries, Ed. "The Publication of Black Wellness." Articles, 500 to 1,000 words, on health issues of interest to African-American men and women. "We focus on total health, so articles cover mind, body, spirit, and cultural wellness." Payment varies, on publication. Query preferred.

HEART & SOUL—Rodale Press, Inc., 733 Third Ave., 15th Fl., New York, NY 10017. Stephanie Stokes Oliver, Ed.-in-Chief. Articles, 800 to 2,000 words, on health, beauty, fitness, nutrition, and relationships for African-American readers. Pays varying rates, on acceptance. Queries preferred.

HERBALGRAM—P.O. Box 201660, Austin, TX 78720. Barbara Johnston, Man. Ed. Quarterly. Articles, 1,500 to 3,000 words, on herb and medicinal plant research, regulatory issues, market conditions, native plant conservation, and other aspects of herbal use. Pays in copies. Query.

HOSPITALS & HEALTH NETWORKS—737 N. Michigan Ave., Chicago, IL 60611. Mary Grayson, Ed. Articles, 800 to 900 words, for hospital administrators, on financing, staffing, coordinating, and providing facilities for health care services. Query.

IDEA HEALTH & FITNESS SOURCE—(formerly *Idea Today*) 6190 Cornerstone Ct. E., Suite 204, San Diego, CA 92121-3773. Ed. Practical articles, 1,000 to 3,000 words, on new exercise programs, business management, nutrition, health, motivation, sports medicine, group-exercise, and one-to-one training techniques. Articles must be geared toward the exercise studio owner or manager, personal trainer and fitness instruction. No consumer or general health pieces. Payment negotiable, on acceptance. Query preferred. Guidelines.

IDEA PERSONAL TRAINER— 6190 Cornerstone Ct. E., Suite 204, San Diego, CA 92121-3773. Therese Hannon, Asst. Ed. Association publication for personal fitness trainers. Articles on exercise science; program design; profiles of successful trainers; business, legal, and marketing topics; tips for networking with other trainers and with allied medical professionals; client counseling; and training tips. "What's New" column includes industry news, products, and research. Payment varies, on acceptance. Query.

IDEA TODAY—See *Idea Health & Fitness Source*.

INDEPENDENT LIVING PROVIDER—1160 E. Jericho Tpke., Suite 200, Huntington, NY 11743. Anne Kelly, Ed. Articles, 1,500 words, on sales and service by home medical equipment providers. Topics: home health care business, managed care, health care reform, new products. Pays 15¢ a word, $15 per photo, on publication. Query.

LET'S LIVE—P.O. Box 74908, Los Angeles, CA 90004. Beth Salmon, Ed.-in-Chief. Articles, 1,000 to 1,500 words, on preventive medicine and nutrition, alternative medicine, diet, vitamins, herbs, exercise, recipes, and natural beauty. Pays about $500, on publication. Query.

MEDIPHORS—P.O. Box 327, Bloomsburg, PA 17815. Dr. Eugene D. Radice, Ed. "A Literary Journal of the Health Professions." Short stories, essays, and commentary, 4,500 words, related to medicine and health. Poetry, to 30 lines. "We are not a technical journal of science. We do not publish research or review articles, except of a historical nature." Pays in copies. Guidelines.

NURSING 97—1111 Bethlehem Pike, P.O. Box 908, Springhouse, PA 19477-0908. Patricia Nornhold, Exec. Dir. Most articles are clinically oriented, and written by nurses for direct caregivers. Also covers legal, ethical, management, and career aspects of nursing; narratives about personal nursing experiences. No poetry, cartoons, or puzzles. Pays $25 to $300, on publication. Query.

NUTRITION HEALTH REVIEW—P.O. Box 406, Haverford, PA 19041. Frank Ray Rifkin, Ed. Quarterly tabloid. Articles on medical progress, information relating to nutritional therapy, genetics, psychiatry, behavior therapy, surgery, pharmacology, animal health; vignettes relating to health and nutrition. "Vegetarian-oriented; we do not deal with subjects that favor animal testing, animal foods, cruelty to animals or recipes that contain animal products." Humor, cartoons. Pays on publication. Query.

PATIENT CARE—5 Paragon Dr., Montvale, NJ 07645. Deborah Kaplan, Ed. Articles on medical care, for primary-care physicians; mostly staff-written. Pays varying rates, on publication. Query; all articles assigned.

PERCEPTIONS—10736 Jefferson Blvd., Suite 502, Culver City, CA 90230. Judi V. Brewer, Ed. Articles, to 2,500 words, on government, alternative health, metaphysics. Reviews, to 500 words. Cartoons. "Broad-spectrum focus crossing barriers that separate ideologies, politics, etc." Sections include Political Slant (relevant information focusing on what we have in common); Healing Spiral (little-known facts and remedies); Concepts (a forum to broaden, awaken, and tickle the intellect). Pays in copies.

THE PHOENIX—7152 Unity Ave. N., Brooklyn Ctr., MN 55429. Pat Samples, Ed. Tabloid. Articles, 800 to 1,500 words, on recovery, renewal, and growth. Department pieces for "Bodywise," "Family Skills," or "Personal Story." "Our readers are committed to physical, emotional, mental, and spiritual health and well-being. Read a sample copy to see what we publish." Pays 3¢ to 5¢ a word, on publication. Send SASE for guidelines and calendar.

THE PHYSICIAN AND SPORTSMEDICINE— 4530 W. 77th St., Minneapolis, MN 55435. Susan Hawthorne, Exec. Ed. News and feature articles; clinical articles coauthored with physician. Sports medicine angle necessary. Pays $300 to $1,400, on acceptance. Query. Guidelines.

PREVENTION—33 E. Minor St., Emmaus, PA 18098. Marty Munson, Man. Ed. Query required. No guidelines available. Limited market.

PRIME HEALTH & FITNESS—21100 Erwin St., Woodland Hills, CA 91367. Bill Bush, Exec. Ed. Quarterly. Articles, 1,200 to 1,800 words, and department pieces, 600 to 800 words, on health and fitness challenges and lifestyle activities for men over 40.

PSYCHOLOGY TODAY—Sussex Publishing, 49 E. 21st St., New York, NY 10010. Anastasia Toufexis, Exec. Ed. Bimonthly. Articles, 2,000 words, on timely subjects and news. Pays varying rates, on publication.

RX REMEDY—120 Post Rd. W., Westport, CT 06880. Val Weaver, Ed. Bimonthly. Articles, 600 to 2,500 words, on health and medication issues for readers 50 and over. Regular columns include "Housecall" and "The Nutrition Prescription." Query. Pays $1 to $1.25 a word, on acceptance.

TANNING TRENDS—3101 Page Ave., Jackson, MI 49203-2254. Bonnie Gretzner, Ed. Articles on skin care and "smart tanning" for tanning salon owners. "We promote tanning clients responsibly and professionally." Payment varies, on publication.

TODAY'S SURGICAL NURSE—Slack, Inc., 6900 Grove Rd., Thorofare, NJ 08086. Frances R. DeStefano, Man. Ed. Clinical or general articles, from 2,000 words, of direct interest to surgical nurses.

TOTAL HEALTH—165 N. 100 E. #2, St. George, UT 84770. Katherine Hurd, Ed. Articles, 1,200 to 1,400 words, on preventative health care, fitness, diet, and mental health. Color or B&W photos. Pays $50 to $75, on publication.

VEGETARIAN TIMES— 4 High Ridge Park, Stamford, CT 06905. Toni Apgar, Ed. Dir. Articles, 1,200 to 2,500 words, on vegetarian cooking, nutrition, health and fitness, and profiles of prominent vegetarians. "News Items," to 500 words. "Herbalist" pieces, to 1,800 words, on medicinal uses of herbs. Queries required. Pays $75 to $1,000, on acceptance. Guidelines.

VEGETARIAN VOICE—P.O. Box 72, Dolgeville, NY 13329. Brian Graff, Assoc. Ed. Quarterly. Informative, well-researched and/or inspiring articles, 600 to 1,800 words, on health, nutrition, animal rights, the environment, world hunger, etc. Pays in copies. Guidelines.

VIBRANT LIFE—55 W. Oak Ridge Dr., Hagerstown, MD 21740. Attn: Larry Becker, Ed. Features, 750 to 1,500 words, on total health: physical, mental, and spiritual. Upbeat articles on the family and how to live happier and healthier lives, emphasizing practical tips; Christian slant. Pays $80 to $250, on acceptance.

VIM & VIGOR—1010 E. Missouri Ave., Phoenix, AZ 85014. Jake Poinier, Ed. Positive health and fitness articles, 1,200 to 2,000 words, with accurate medical facts. By assignment only; no queries or unsolicited manuscripts. Writers with feature- or news-writing ability may submit qualifications for assignment. Pays $500, on acceptance. Send SASE for guidelines.

THE WALKING MAGAZINE—9-11 Harcourt, Boston, MA 02116. Seth Bauer, Ed. Articles, 1,500 to 2,500 words, on fitness, health, equipment, nutrition, travel and adventure, famous walkers, and other walking-related topics. Shorter pieces, 150 to 800 words, and essays for "Ramblings" page. Photos welcome. Pays $750 to $1,800 for features, $100 to $500 for department pieces, on acceptance. Guidelines.

YOGA JOURNAL—2054 University Ave., Berkeley, CA 94704. Rick Fields, Ed. Articles, 300 to 6,000 words, on holistic health, meditation, conscious living, spirituality, and yoga. Pays $75 to $300, on acceptance.

YOUR HEALTH—5401 N.W. Broken Sound Blvd., Boca Raton, FL 33487. Susan Gregg, Ed.-in-Chief. Health and medical articles, 1,000 to 2,000 words, for a lay audience. Queries preferred. Pays $75 to $200, on publication.

EDUCATION

ACTIVITY RESOURCES—P.O. Box 4875, Hayward, CA 94540. Mary Laycock, Ed. Math educational material only for books geared to mathematics for grades K through 8. Submit complete book manuscript. Royalty.

AMERICAN EDUCATOR—American Federation of Teachers, 555 New Jersey Ave. N.W., Washington, DC 20001. Liz McPike, Ed. Quarterly. Articles, 500 to 2,500 words, on politics and new trends in education; also well-researched news features on current problems in education, education law, professional ethics; "think" pieces and essays that explore current social issues relevant to American society. Pays from $300, on publication. Query.

AMERICAN SCHOOL & UNIVERSITY—P.O. Box 12901, 9800 Metcalf, Overland Park, KS 66212-2215. Joe Agron, Ed. Articles and case studies, 1,200 to 1,500 words, on design, construction, operation, and management of school and university facilities. Queries preferred.

BEAUTY EDUCATION—3 Columbia Cir., Albany, NY 12212. Catherine Frangie, Pub. Articles, 750 to 1,000 words, that provide beauty educators, trainers, and professionals in the cosmetology industry with information, skills, and techniques on such topics as hairstyling, makeup, aromatherapy, retailing, massage, and beauty careers. Articles on assignment only. Send SASE for editorial calendar and themes. Pays in copies. Query.

BETTER VIEWING—141 Portland St., #7100, Cambridge, MA 02139-1937. Al Race, Ed. Bimonthly. Articles, 200 to 1,200 words, aimed at parents of children to age 16, on cable and broadcast programs, as well as strategies for gaining more control over TV use in their homes. Pays $100 to $500, on acceptance. Queries required.

BLACK ISSUES IN HIGHER EDUCATION—10520 Warwick Ave., Suite B-8, Fairfax, VA 22030-3136. Cheryl D. Fields, Exec. Ed. Biweekly. News and feature articles, 800 to 1,000 words, on blacks in post-secondary education. Also, fillers, to 250 words, on higher education and public policy. Pays about 25¢ per word, on publication. Query.

THE BOOK REPORT—Linworth Publishing, 480 E. Wilson Bridge Rd., Suite L, Worthington, OH 43085-2372. Carolyn Hamilton, Ed./Pub. "The Journal for Junior and Senior High Librarians." Articles, columns, and reviews by practicing educators about school libraries and librarians. Write for themes and guidelines. Also publishes *Library Talk*, "The Magazine for Elementary School Librarians," and *Technology Connection*, "The Magazine for Library and Media Specialists."

CABLE IN THE CLASSROOM—141 Portland St., #7100, Cambridge, MA 02139-1937. Al Race, Ed. Monthly. Articles, 200 to 1,200 words, for K through 12 teachers and media specialists, on upcoming educational cable television programs and creative ways to use those programs. Pays $100 to $500, on acceptance. Queries required.

CAREERS & THE DISABLED—See *Minority Engineer*.

CHANGE—1319 18th St. N.W., Washington, DC 20036. Attn: Man. Ed. Columns, 700 to 2,000 words, and in-depth features, 2,500 to 3,500 words, on programs, people, and institutions of higher education. "We can't usually pay for unsolicited articles."

CHRISTIAN EDUCATION JOURNAL—Trinity Evangelical Divinity School, 2065 Half Day Rd., Deerfield, IL 60015. Dr. Perry G. Downs, Ed. Articles, 10 to 25 typed pages, on Christian education topics. Guidelines.

CHRISTIAN EDUCATION LEADERSHIP—P.O. Box 2250, Cleveland, TN 37320-2250. Lance Colkmire, Ed. Quarterly. Articles, 500 to 1,200 words, that "encourage, inform, and inspire those who teach the Bible in the local church." No fiction, poetry, fillers, or artwork. Pays $25 to $55, on acceptance.

EARLY CHILDHOOD NEWS—330 Progress Road, Dayton, OH 45449. Megan Shaw, Ed. Bimonthly. Fiction, 400 to 600 words and nonfiction 600 to 2,200 words, and poetry, 400 to 600 words, for child care professionals. "Our purpose is to provide child care professionals with practical information, based upon educational theory, for use inside the classroom." Photographs. Pays $100 to $200, on publication. Query or send complete manuscript.

EARLY CHILDHOOD TODAY—Scholastic, Inc., 555 Broadway, 5th Fl., New York, NY 10012. Andrea Barbalich, Exec. Ed. Articles, 500 to 900 words, for teachers, offering practical information, strategies, and tips on child development and education. Also personal stories and program spotlights. Write to Article Submissions. Payment varies, on publication.

EQUAL OPPORTUNITY—See *Minority Engineer.*

GIFTED EDUCATION PRESS QUARTERLY—P.O. Box 1586, 10201 Yuma Ct., Manassas, VA 20108. Maurice Fisher, Pub. Articles, to 4,000 words, written by educators, laypersons, and parents of gifted children, on the problems of identifying and teaching gifted children and adolescents. "Interested in incisive analyses of current programs for the gifted and recommendations for improving the education of gifted students. Particularly interested in advocacy for gifted children, biographical sketches of highly gifted individuals, and the problems of teaching humanities, science, ethics, literature, and history to the gifted. Looking for highly imaginative and knowledgeable writers." Query required. Pays in subscription.

THE HISPANIC OUTLOOK IN HIGHER EDUCATION—210 Rt. 4 East, Paramus, NJ 07652. Attn: Ed. Articles, 1,500 to 2,000 words, on the issues, concerns, and potential models for furthering the academic results of Hispanics in higher education. Queries are preferred. Payment varies, on publication.

THE HORN BOOK MAGAZINE—11 Beacon St., Suite 1000, Boston, MA 02108. Roger Sutton, Ed.-in-Chief. Articles, 600 to 2,800 words, on books for young readers and related subjects for librarians, teachers, parents, etc. Payment varies, on publication. Send complete manuscript.

INDEPENDENT LIVING PROVIDER—See *Minority Engineer.*

INSTRUCTOR MAGAZINE—Scholastic, Inc., 555 Broadway, New York, NY 10012. Mickey Revenaugh, Ed. Articles, 300 to 1,500 words, for teachers in grades K through 8. Payment varies, on acceptance.

ITC COMMUNICATOR—International Training in Communication, P.O. Box 1809, Sutter Creek, CA 95685. JoAnn Levy, Ed. Educational articles, 200 to 800 words, on leadership, language, speech presentation, procedures for meetings, personal and professional development, written and spoken communication techniques. SASE required. Pays in copies.

JOURNAL OF SCHOOL LEADERSHIP—211 Hill Hall, College of Education, Univ. of Missouri-Columbia, Columbia, MO 65211. Dr. Paula M. Short,

Ed. Bimonthly. Articulate, accurate, and authoritative articles on educational administration, particularly on translating research and theory into practice. No payment.

JOYFUL CHILD MAGAZINE— 6224 E. Portia St., Mesa, AZ 85215. Peggy Jenkins, Ed. Quarterly. Fiction and nonfiction, 500 to 1,000 words, that "explore how society and education can more effectively nurture children (and adults) to express their fullest potential, thus releasing their inner joy. Articles on educating and parenting the whole child (body, mind, and spirit)." Some short poetry. Queries preferred. Guidelines. Pays in copies.

LEADERSHIP PUBLISHERS, INC.—P.O. Box 8358, Des Moines, IA 50301-8358. Attn: Dr. Lois F. Roets. Educational materials for talented and gifted students, grades K to 12. Send SASE for catalogue and guidelines before submitting. Pays in royalty for books, and flat fee for booklets.

LEARNING—3515 W. Market St., Greensboro, NC 27403. Attn: Manuscript Submissions. Bimonthly. Articles, 50 to 1,500 words, that help K-6 teachers deal with issues such as stress, motivation, burnout, and other self-improvement topics; successful teaching strategies to reach today's kids; and ideas to get parents involved. SASE required. Pays from $10 to $300, on acceptance. Allow 9 months for response.

LIBRARY TALK—See *The Book Report.*

MEDIA & METHODS—1429 Walnut St., Philadelphia, PA 19102. Michele Sokoloff, Ed. Dir. Articles, 800 to 1,000 words, on media, technologies, and methods used to enhance instruction and learning in K through 12th-grade classrooms. Pays $50 to $200, on publication. Query required.

MINORITY ENGINEER—1160 E. Jericho Turnpike, Suite 200, Huntington, NY 11743. James Schneider, Ed. Articles, 1,000 to 1,500 words, for college students, on career opportunities; techniques of job hunting, and role-model profiles of professional minority engineers. Interviews. Pays 10¢ a word, on publication. Query. Also publishes: *Equal Opportunity*; *Careers & the DisABLED*, query James Schneider; *Woman Engineer* and *Independent Living Provider*, query Editor Anne Kelly.

MOMENTUM—National Catholic Educational Assn., 1077 30th St. N.W., Suite 100, Washington, DC 20007-3852. Patricia Feistritzer, Ed. Articles, 500 to 1,500 words, on outstanding programs, issues, and research in education. Book reviews. Query or send complete manuscript. No simultaneous submissions. Pays $25 to $75, on publication.

THE MUSIC LEADER—See *Plans & Pluses.*

PLANS & PLUSES—(formerly *The Music Leader*) Baptist Sunday School Board, 127 Ninth Ave. N., Nashville, TN 37234. Anne Trudel, Rhonda Edge Buescher, Eds. Annual. Dramas or programs built around well-known hymns, designed for children in grades 3 to 6, to 1,000 words. Seasonal programs for children's choirs, to 1,000 words. How-to articles, to 800 words, on organizing choir rehearsals for children; also time savers and other tips for choir directors. Inspirational poetry for challenge of teaching children. "Our readers are volunteer choir directors and teachers in evangelical churches. Articles should be encouraging, not too academic, and practical." Pays 5½¢ to 6½¢ a word, on acceptance. Send complete manuscript; no queries.

PHI DELTA KAPPAN— 408 N. Union St., Box 789, Bloomington, IN 47402-0789. Pauline Gough, Ed. Articles, 1,000 to 4,000 words, on educational research, service, and leadership; issues, trends, and policy. Rarely pays for manuscripts.

REACHING TODAY'S YOUTH—National Education Service, P.O. Box 8, Bloomington, IN 47402. Alan Blankstein, Sr. Ed. Articles, 1,500 to 2,500 words, that provide an interdisciplinary perspective on positive approaches to reaching and educating youth who are troubled, angry, or disconnected from school, peers, or family. Readers are educators, parents, youth care professionals, residential treatment staff, juvenile justice professionals, police, researchers, youth advocates, child and family psychologists, community members and students. Send SASE for guidelines and current themes.

SCHOLASTIC PARENT & CHILD—555 Broadway, New York, NY 10012-3919. Andrea Barbalich, Exec. Ed. Bimonthly. Articles, 600 to 900 words, on children's education and development. "We are the learning link between home and school." Payment varies, on acceptance. Query; no unsolicited manuscripts. SASE.

SCHOOL ARTS MAGAZINE—50 Portland St., Worcester, MA 01608. Dr. Eldon Katter, Ed. Articles, 800 to 1,000 words, on art education with special application to the classroom: successful and meaningful approaches to teaching art, innovative art projects, uncommon applications of art techniques or equipment, etc. Photos. Pays varying rates, on publication. Guidelines.

SCHOOL SAFETY—National School Safety Ctr., 4165 Thousand Oaks Blvd., Suite 290, Westlake Village, CA 91362. Ronald D. Stephens, Exec. Ed. Published 8 times during the school year. Articles, 2,000 to 3,000 words, of use to educators, law enforcers, judges, and legislators on the prevention of drugs, gangs, weapons, bullying, discipline problems, and vandalism; also on-site security and character development as they relate to students and schools. No payment.

TECH DIRECTIONS—3970 Varsity Drive,, Ann Arbor, MI 48107-8623. Tom Bowden, Man. Ed. Articles, one to 10 double-spaced typed pages, for teachers and administrators in industrial, technology, and vocational educational fields, with particular interest in classroom projects, computer uses, and legislative issues. Pays $10 to $150, on publication. Guidelines.

TECHNOLOGY & LEARNING—Peter Li, Inc., 222 Front St., #401, San Francisco, CA 94111. Judy Salpeter, Ed. Articles, to 3,000 words, for administrators and teachers of grades K through 12, about uses of computers and related technology in the classroom: human-interest and philosophical articles, how-to pieces, software reviews, and hands-on ideas. Payment varies, on acceptance.

TECHNOLOGY CONNECTION—See *The Book Report.*

TODAY'S CATHOLIC TEACHER—330 Progress Rd., Dayton, OH 45449. Mary Noschang, Ed. Articles, 600 to 800 words, 1,000 to 1,200 words, and 1,200 to 1,500 words, on education, parent-teacher relationships, innovative teaching, teaching techniques, etc., of use to educators in Catholic schools. Pays $65 to $250, on publication. SASE required. Query. Guidelines.

WOMAN ENGINEER—See *Minority Engineer.*

FARMING & AGRICULTURE

AMERICAN BEE JOURNAL—51 N. Second St., Hamilton, IL 62341. Joe M. Graham, Ed. Articles on beekeeping, for professionals. Photos. Pays 75¢ a column inch, extra for photos, on publication.

BEE CULTURE— 623 W. Liberty St., Medina, OH 44256. Mr. Kim Flottum, Ed. Basic how-to articles, 500 to 2,000 words, on keeping bees and selling bee products. Slides or B&W prints. Payment varies, on acceptance and on publication. Queries preferred. E-mail address: bculture@aol.com

THE BRAHMAN JOURNAL—P.O. Box 220, Eddy, TX 76524-0220. Joe Brockett, Ed. Articles on Brahman cattle only. Photos. Pays $150 to $300, on publication. Queries preferred.

BUCKEYE FARM NEWS— Ohio Farm Bureau Federation, 2 Nationwide Plaza, Box 479, Columbus, OH 43216-0479. Lynn Echelberger, Copy Ed. Articles, to 600 words, related to agriculture. Pays on publication. Query. Limited market.

DAIRY GOAT JOURNAL—P.O. Box 10, Lake Mills, WI 53551. Dave Thompson, Ed. Articles, to 1,500 words, on successful dairy goat owners, youths and interesting people associated with dairy goats. "Especially interested in practical husbandry ideas." Photos. Pays $50 to $150, on publication. Query.

FARM AND RANCH LIVING—5400 S. 60th St., Greendale, WI 53129. Nick Pabst, Ed. Articles, 1,000 words, on rural people and situations; nostalgia pieces; profiles of interesting farms and farmers, ranches and ranchers. Pays $15 to $300, on acceptance and on publication.

FARM INDUSTRY NEWS—7900 International Dr., Minneapolis, MN 55425. Joe Degnan, Ed. Articles for farmers, on new products, machinery, equipment, chemicals, and seeds. Pays $350 to $500, on acceptance. Query required.

FARM JOURNAL— Centre Sq. W., 1500 Market St., Philadelphia, PA 19102-2181. Sonja Hillgren, Ed. Articles, 500 to 1,500 words, with photos, on the business of farming. Pays 20¢ to 50¢ a word, on acceptance. Query.

FLORIDA GROWER & RANCHER—1555 Howell Branch Rd., Suite C-204, Winter Park, FL 32789. Frank Garner, Ed. Articles and case histories on Florida citrus and vegetable growers. Pays on publication. Query; buys little free-lance material.

THE FURROW—Deere & Co., John Deere Rd., Moline, IL 61265. George Sollenberger, Exec. Ed. Specialized, illustrated articles on farming. Pays to $1,200, on acceptance.

THE LAND—P.O. Box 3169, Mankato, MN 56002-3169. Randy Frahm, Ed. Articles on Minnesota agriculture and rural issues. Pays $25 to $45, on acceptance. Query required.

NATIONAL CATTLEMEN—5420 S. Quebec St., Englewood, CO 80111-1904. Curt Olson, Ed. Articles, 1,200 words, related to the cattle industry. Payment varies, on publication.

NEW HOLLAND NEWS—New Holland, Inc., P.O. Box 1895, New Holland, PA 17557-0903. Attn: Ed. Articles, to 1,500 words, with strong color photo support, on agriculture and rural living. Pays on acceptance. Query.

ONION WORLD—P.O. Box 9036, Yakima, WA 98909-9036. D. Brent Clement, Ed. Production and marketing articles, to 1,500 words (preferred length 1,200 words), for commercial onion growers and shippers. "Research oriented articles are of definite interest. No gardening articles." Pays about $5 per column inch, on publication. Query preferred.

PEANUT FARMER—3000 Highwoods Blvd., Suite 300, Raleigh, NC 27604-1029. Mary Evans, Man. Ed. Articles, 500 to 2,000 words, on production and management practices in peanut farming. Pays $50 to $350, on publication.

PENNSYLVANIA FARMER—P.O. Box 4475, Gettysburg, PA 17325. John R. Vogel, Ed. Articles on farmers in PA, DE, MD, and WV; timely business-of-farming concepts and successful farm management operations. Short pieces on humorous experiences in farming. Payment varies, on publication.

PROGRESSIVE FARMER—2100 Lakeshore Dr., Birmingham, AL 35209. Jack Odle, Ed. Articles, to 5 double-spaced pages (3 pages preferred), on farmers or new developments in agriculture; rural communities; and personal business issues concerning the farmstead, home office, relationships, worker safety, finances, taxes, and regulations. Pays $50 to $400, on publication. Query.

RURAL HERITAGE—281 Dean Ridge Ln., Gainesboro, TN 38562. Gail Damerow, Ed. How-to and feature articles, 800 to 1,200 words, related to the present-day use of work horses, mules, and oxen. Pays 5¢ a word, $10 for photos, on publication. SASE for guidelines.

SHEEP! MAGAZINE—P.O. Box 10, Lake Mills, WI 53551. Dave Thompson, Ed. Articles, to 1,500 words, on successful shepherds, woolcrafts, sheep raising, and sheep dogs. "Especially interested in people who raise sheep successfully as a sideline enterprise." Photos. Pays $80 to $150, extra for photos, on publication. Query.

SMALL FARM TODAY—3903 W. Ridge Trail Rd., Clark, MO 65243-9525. Paul Berg, Man. Ed. Agriculture articles, 800 to 1,800 words, on preserving and promoting small farming, rural living, and "agripreneurship." How-to articles on alternative crops, livestock, and direct marketing. Pays 3½¢ a word, on publication. Query.

SMALL FARMER'S JOURNAL—P.O. Box 1627, Dept. 106, Sisters, OR 97759. Address the Eds. How-tos, humor, practical work horse information, livestock and produce marketing, gardening information, and articles appropriate to the independent family farm. Pays negotiable rates, on publication. Query.

SUCCESSFUL FARMING—1716 Locust St., Des Moines, IA 50309-3023. Gene Johnston, Man. Ed. Articles on farm production, business, and families; also farm personalities, health, leisure, and outdoor topics. Pays varying rates, on acceptance.

TOPICS IN VETERINARY MEDICINE—Pfizer Animal Health, 812 Springdale Dr., Exton, PA 19341. Kathleen Etchison, Ed. Technical articles, 1,200 to 1,500 words, and clinical features, 500 words, on veterinary medicine. Photos. Pays $300, $150 for shorter pieces, extra for photos, on publication.

THE WESTERN PRODUCER—Box 2500, Saskatoon, Saskatchewan, Canada S7K 2C4. Address Man. Ed. Articles, to 800 words (prefer under 600 words), on agricultural and rural subjects, preferably with a Canadian slant. Photos. Pays from 20¢ a word; $20 to $45 for B&W photos; $35 to $100 for color photos, on publication.

WYOMING RURAL ELECTRIC NEWS—P.O. Box 380, Casper, WY 82606-0380. Kris Wendtland, Ed. Articles, 500 to 900 words, on issues relevant to rural Wyoming. Articles should support Wyoming's personal and economic growth, social development, and education. Wyoming writers given preference. Pays $20 to $50, on publication.

ENVIRONMENT & CONSERVATION

ALTERNATIVES JOURNAL—Faculty of Environmental Studies, Univ. of Waterloo, Waterloo, Ontario, Canada N2L 3G1. Nancy Doucet, Man. Ed. Quarterly. Feature articles, 4,000 words; notes, 200 to 500 words; and reports, 750 to 1,000 words, that focus on Canadian content in areas of environmental thought, policy, and action. No payment.

THE AMERICAN FIELD—542 S. Dearborn, Chicago, IL 60605. B.J. Matthys, Man. Ed. Yarns about hunting trips, bird-shooting; articles, to 1,500 words, on dogs and field trials, emphasizing conservation of game resources. Pays varying rates, on acceptance.

AMERICAN FORESTS—910 17th St., Suite 600, Washington, DC 20006. Michelle Robbins, Ed. Looking for skilled science writers for well-documented articles on the use, enjoyment, and management of forests. Send clips. Query.

THE AMICUS JOURNAL—Natural Resources Defense Council, 40 W. 20th St., New York, NY 10011. Kathrin Day Lassila, Ed. Quarterly. Articles and book reviews on local, national and international environmental topics. (No fiction, speeches, or product reports accepted.) Pays varying rates, 30 days after acceptance. Query with SASE required.

ANIMALS—350 S. Huntington Ave., Boston, MA 02130. Joni Praded, Dir./Ed. Informative, well-researched articles, to 2,500 words, on animal protection, national and international wildlife, pet care, conservation, and environmental issues that affect animals. No personal accounts or favorite pet stories. Pays from $350, on acceptance. Query.

ATLANTIC SALMON JOURNAL—P.O. Box 429, St. Andrews, N.B., Canada E0G 2X0. Jim Gourlay, Ed. Articles, 1,500 to 3,000 words, related to Atlantic salmon: fishing, conservation, ecology, travel, politics, biology, how-tos, anecdotes. Pays $100 to $400, on publication.

AUDUBON—700 Broadway, New York, NY 10003. Roger Cohn, Exec. Ed. Bimonthly. Articles, 300 to 4,000 words, on conservation and environmental issues, natural history, ecology, and related subjects. Payment varies, on acceptance. Query with clips.

THE BEAR ESSENTIAL—P.O. Box 10342, Portland, OR 97296. Thomas L. Webb, Ed. Semiannual. Unique environmental articles, 750 to 3,500 words; essays, 250 to 2,500 words; artist profiles, 750 to 1,500 words; product watch, 250 to 1,000 words; and reviews, 100 to 1,000 words. Fiction, 750 to 4,500 words (2,500 is ideal). Poetry. Pays 5¢ a word, after publication. Query for non-fiction.

BIRD WATCHER'S DIGEST—P.O. Box 110, Marietta, OH 45750. William H. Thompson, III, Ed. Articles, 600 to 2,500 words, for bird watchers: first-person accounts; how-tos; pieces on endangered species; profiles. Pays from $50, on publication. Write for guidelines. Submit complete manuscript with SASE.

BUGLE—Rocky Mountain Elk Foundation, P.O. Box 8249, Missoula, MT 59807-8249. Lee Cromrich, Ed. Asst. Bimonthly. Fiction and nonfiction, 1,500 to 4,000 words, on wildlife conservation, elk ecology and hunting. Department pieces, 1,000 to 3,000 words, for: "Thoughts and Theories"; "Situation Ethics"; and "Women in the Outdoors." Pays 20¢ a word, on acceptance.

CALIFORNIA WILD—(formerly *Pacific Discovery*) California Academy of Sciences, Golden Gate Park, San Francisco, CA 94118-4599. Gordy Slack, Assoc. Ed. Quarterly. Well-researched articles, 1,500 to 3,000 words, on natural history and preservation of the environment. Pays 25¢ a word, before publication. Query.

CANADIAN WILDLIFE—11450 Albert Hudon, Montreal North, Quebec, Canada H1G 3J9. Martin Silverstone, Ed. Articles, 1,500 to 2,500 words, on national and international wildlife issues: wild areas, nature-related research, endangered species, wildlife management, land use issues, character profiles, and science and politics of conservation. Department pieces, 150 to 500 words, for "Backyard Habitat," "Last Call," and "Species at Risk." Pays $500 to $1,600 (Canadian) for features; $50 to $100 for departments and book reviews, on publication.

E: THE ENVIRONMENTAL MAGAZINE—Earth Action Network, Inc., P.O. Box 5098, Westport, CT 06881. Jim Motavalli, Ed. Environmental features, 4,000 words, and news for departments: 400 words for "In Brief"; and 1,000 words for "Currents." Pays 20¢ a word, on publication. Query.

EQUINOX—11450 Albert Hudon Blvd., Montreal North, Quebec, Canada H1G 3J9. Alan Morantz, Ed., Sylvia Barrett, Man. Ed. Articles, 2,000 to 5,000 words, on popular geography, science, wildlife, natural history, the arts, travel, and adventure. Department pieces, 250 to 400 words, for "Nexus" (science and medicine). Pays $1,500 to $3,500 for features, $150 to $350 for short pieces, on acceptance.

FLORIDA WILDLIFE— 620 S. Meridian St., Tallahassee, FL 32399-1600. Attn: Ed. Bimonthly of the Florida Game and Fresh Water Fish Commission. Articles, 800 to 1,200 words, that promote native flora and fauna, hunting, fishing in Florida's fresh waters, outdoor ethics, and conservation of Florida's natural resources. Pays $50 a page, on publication. SASE for "how to submit" memo.

HERBALGRAM—P.O. Box 201660, Austin, TX 78720. Barbara Johnston, Man. Ed. Quarterly. Articles, 1,500 to 3,000 words, on herb and medicinal plant research, regulatory issues, market conditions, native plant conservation, and other aspects of herbal use. Pays in copies. Query.

INTERNATIONAL WILDLIFE—National Wildlife Federation, 8925 Leesburg Pike, Vienna, VA 22184. Jonathan Fisher, Ed. Articles, 2,000 words, that make nature, and human use and stewardship of it, understandable and interesting; covers wildlife and related issues outside the U.S. Pays $2,000 for full-length articles, on acceptance. Query with writing samples. SASE for guidelines.

MOTHER EARTH NEWS—Sussex Publishers, 49 E. 21st St., 11th Fl., New York, NY 10010. Ed. Bimonthly featuring articles on organic gardening, building projects, holistic health, alternative energy projects, wild foods, and environment and conservation. "We are dedicated to helping our readers become more self-sufficient, financially independent, and environmentally aware." Photos or diagrams a plus. No fiction. Payment varies, on publication.

NATIONAL GEOGRAPHIC—1145 17th St. N.W., Washington, DC 20036. William Allen, Ed. First-person, general-interest, heavily illustrated articles on science, natural history, exploration, and geographical regions. Written query required.

NATIONAL PARKS MAGAZINE—1776 Massachusetts Ave. N.W., Washington, DC 20036. Leslie Happ, Ed.-in-Chief. Articles, 1,500 to 2,000 words, on areas in the National Park System, proposed new areas, threats to parks or park wildlife, new trends in park use, legislative issues, and endangered species of plants or animals relevant to national parks. No fiction, poetry, personal narratives, "My trip to...," or straight travel pieces on individual parks. Articles, 1,500 words, on "low-impact" travel to 4 or 5 national park sites. Pays $400 to $1,000, on acceptance. Query with clips (original slant or news hook is essential to successful query). Guidelines with SASE.

NATIONAL WILDLIFE— 8925 Leesburg Pike, Vienna, VA 22184. Mark Wexler, Ed. Articles, 1,000 to 2,500 words, on wildlife, conservation, environment; outdoor how-to pieces. Photos. Pays on acceptance. Query.

NEW HAMPSHIRE WILDLIFE—P.O. Box 239, Concord, NH 03302-0239. Mary Shriver, Ed. Bimonthly tabloid. Fiction and nonfiction, 1,700 to 2,000 words. "Dedicated to preserving and protecting hunting, fishing, and trapping and for the conservation of fish and wildlife habitat." No payment.

THE NEW YORK STATE CONSERVATIONIST—50 Wolf Rd., Rm. 548, Albany, NY 12233-4502. R.W. Groneman, Ed. "The official magazine of the New York State Department of Environmental Conservation." Bimonthly. Articles, varying lengths, on environmental/conservation programs and policies of New York. Pays $50 to $100 for articles; $15 for photos; and $50 for original artwork, on publication.

OUTDOOR AMERICA—707 Conservation Ln., Gaithersburg, MD 20878-2983. Attn: Articles Ed. Quarterly publication of the Izaak Walton League of America. Articles, 1,250 to 2,000 words, on natural resource conservation issues and outdoor recreation, with emphasis on IWLA member/chapter tie-in; especially fishing, hunting, and camping. Short items, 500 to 750 words. Pays 30¢ a word. Query with clips.

OUTDOOR TRAVELER, MID-ATLANTIC—WMS Publications, Inc., P.O. Box 2748, Charlottesville, VA 22902. Marianne Marks, Ed. Tom Gillespie, Assoc. Ed. Quarterly. Articles, 1,500 to 2,000 words, on hiking/backpacking, canoeing/kayaking/rafting, camping, mountain biking, road cycling, travel, nature, and the environment from New York state to North Carolina. Travel articles on destinations and areas that offer recreational opportunities. Departments include "Destinations," 450 to 600 words, practical and descriptive guides to sports destinations; book and product reviews. Pays $300 to $400 for features; payment varies for departments, on publication. Guidelines.

PACIFIC DISCOVERY—See *California Wild.*

SIERRA— 85 2nd St., San Francisco, CA 94105. Joan Hamilton, Ed.-in-Chief. Articles, 750 to 2,500 words, on environmental and conservation topics, travel, hiking, backpacking, skiing, rafting, cycling. Photos. Pays from $500 to $2,000, extra for photos, on acceptance. Query with clips.

SMITHSONIAN MAGAZINE— 900 Jefferson Dr., Washington, DC 20560. Marlane A. Liddell, Articles Ed. Articles on history, art, natural history, physical science, profiles, etc. Query with clips. SASE.

SPORTS AFIELD—250 W. 55th St., New York, NY 10019. John Atwood, Ed.-in-Chief. Articles, 500 to 2,000 words, with quality photos, on hunting, fishing, nature, survival, conservation, ecology, personal experiences. How-to pieces; humor, fiction. Payment varies, on acceptance.

TEXAS PARKS & WILDLIFE—Fountain Park Plaza, 3000 S. Interstate Hwy. 35, Suite 120, Austin, TX 78704. David Baxter, Ed. Articles, 800 to 1,500 words, promoting the conservation and enjoyment of Texas wildlife, parks, waters, and all outdoors. Features on hunting, fishing, birding, camping, and the environment. Photos a plus. Pays to $600, on acceptance; extra for photos.

VIRGINIA WILDLIFE—P.O. Box 11104, Richmond, VA 23230-1104. Attn: Ed. Articles, 1,250 to 1,750 words, on fishing, hunting, wildlife management, outdoor safety, ethics, etc. All material must have Virginia tie-in and may be accompanied by color photos. Pays from 15¢ a word, extra for photos, on acceptance. Query.

WHOLE EARTH—(formerly *Whole Earth Review*) 1408 Mission Ave., San Rafael, CA 94901. Attn: Ed. Quarterly. Articles and book reviews. "Good article material is often found in passionate personal statements or descriptions of the writer's activities." Pays $40 for reviews; payment varies for articles, on publication.

WILD OUTDOOR WORLD—Box 1249, Helena, MT 59624. Carolyn Cunningham, Ed. Dir. Articles, 600 to 800 words, on North American wildlife, for readers ages 8 to 12. Pays $100 to $500, on acceptance. Query. SASE.

WILDLIFE CONSERVATION—The Wildlife Conservation Society, Bronx, NY 10460. Nancy Simmons, Sr. Ed. First-person articles, 1,500 to 2,000 words, on "popular" natural history, "based on author's research and experience as opposed to textbook approach." Payment varies, on acceptance. Guidelines.

MEDIA & THE ARTS

THE AMERICAN ART JOURNAL—730 Fifth Ave., New York, NY 10019-4105. Jayne A. Kuchna, Ed. Scholarly articles, 2,000 to 10,000 words, on American art of the 17th through the early 20th centuries. Photos. Pays $200 to $500, on acceptance.

AMERICAN INDIAN ART MAGAZINE—7314 E. Osborn Dr., Scottsdale, AZ 85251. Roanne P. Goldfein, Ed. Detailed articles, 10 to 20 double-spaced pages, on American Indian arts: painting, carving, beadwork, basketry, textiles, ceramics, jewelry, etc. Pays varying rates, on publication. Query.

AMERICAN JOURNALISM REVIEW—8701 Adelphi Rd., Adelphi, MD 20783. Rem Rieder, Ed. Articles, 500 to 5,000 words, on print or electronic journalism, ethics, and related issues. Pays 20¢ a word, on publication. Query.

AMERICAN THEATRE—355 Lexington Ave., New York, NY 10017. Jim O'Quinn, Ed. Features, 250 to 2,500 words, on the theater and theater-related subjects. Departments include "Profiles," "Books," "Commentary," and "Media." Payment varies, on publication. Query.

AMERICAN VISIONS, THE MAGAZINE OF AFRO-AMERICAN CULTURE—1156 15th St. N.W., Suite 615, Washington, DC 20005. Joanne Harris, Ed. Articles, 1,500 to 2,500 words, and columns, 1,000 words, on African-American culture with a focus on the arts. Pays from $100 to $600, on publication. Query.

ART & ANTIQUES—3 E. 54th St., 11th Fl., New York, NY 10022. Paula Rackow, Ed. Investigative pieces, overviews, or personal narratives, 1,500 to 2,000 words, and news items, 250 to 350 words, on art or antiques. Pays 75¢ to $1 a word, on publication. Query with resumé and clips.

THE ARTIST'S MAGAZINE—1507 Dana Ave., Cincinnati, OH 45207. Sandra Carpenter, Ed. How-to features, 1,200 to 1,800 words, and department pieces for the working artist. Pays $150 to $350 for articles. Guidelines. Query.

BACK STAGE—1515 Broadway, 14th Fl., New York, NY 10036-8901. Sherry Eaker, Ed.-in-Chief "The Performance Arts Weekly." Service features only, dealing with succeeding in the business. Payment varies, on publication. Queries required.

BACK STAGE WEST—5055 Wilshire Blvd., 6th Fl., Los Angeles, CA 90036. Robert Kendt, Ed. Weekly. Articles and reviews for actor's trade paper for the West Coast. Query required. Pays 10¢ to 15¢ a word, on publication.

BETTER VIEWING—141 Portland St., #7100, Cambridge, MA 02139-1937. Al Race, Ed. Bimonthly. Articles, 200 to 1,200 words, aimed at parents of children to age 16, on quality cable and broadcast programs, as well as strategies for gaining more control over TV use in their homes. Pays $100 to $500, on acceptance. Queries required.

BLUEGRASS UNLIMITED—Box 111, Broad Run, VA 20137-0111. Peter V. Kuykendall, Ed. Articles, to 3,500 words, on bluegrass and traditional country music. Photos. Pays 8¢ to 10¢ a word, extra for photos.

BOMB—594 Broadway, Suite 905, New York, NY 10012. Editor Quarterly. Articles, varying lengths, on artists, musicians, writers, actors, and directors. Some fiction and poetry. Pays $100, on publication. Send complete manuscript.

CABLE IN THE CLASSROOM—141 Portland St., #7100, Cambridge, MA 02139-1937. Al Race, Ed. Monthly. Articles, 200 to 1,200 words, for K through 12 teachers and media specialists, on upcoming educational cable television programs and creative ways to use those programs. Pays $100 to $500, on acceptance. Queries required.

THE CHURCH MUSICIAN—See *Church Musician Today.*

CHURCH MUSICIAN TODAY—(formerly *The Church Musician*) 127 Ninth Ave. N., Nashville, TN 37234. Jere V. Adams, Ed. Articles on choral techniques, instrumental groups, worship planning, music administration, directing choirs (all ages), rehearsal planning, music equipment, new technology, drama/pageants and related subjects, hymn studies, book reviews, and music-related fillers. Pays 5½¢ a word for articles on hard copy; 6¢ per word for articles on diskette, on acceptance.

CINEASTE—200 Park Ave. S., Suite 1601, New York, NY 10003-1503. Attn: Eds. Quarterly. Articles, 2,000 to 3,000 words, on the art and politics of the cinema. "Articles should discuss a film, film genre, a career, a theory, a movement, or related topic, in depth." Interviews with people in filmmaking. Department pieces, 1,000 to 1,500 words. Pays $75 to $100, on publication.

DANCE MAGAZINE—33 W. 60th St., New York, NY 10023. Richard Philp, Ed.-in-Chief. Articles on dancers, companies, history, professional concerns, health, current events, and news. Photos. Query; limited free-lance market.

DANCE TEACHER NOW—3101 Poplarwood Ct., Suite 310, Raleigh, NC 27604-1010. Neil Offen, Ed. Articles, 1,000 to 3,000 words, for professional dance educators, senior students, and other dance professionals on practical information for the teacher and/or business owner; economic and business issues related to the profession. Profiles of schools, methods, and people who are leaving their mark on dance. Must be thoroughly researched. Photos a plus. Pays 10¢ per word, on publication. Query. Web site: http://www.danceteacher.com E-mail: DancEditor@aol.com

DECORATIVE ARTIST'S WORKBOOK—1507 Dana Ave., Cincinnati, OH 45207. Anne Hevener, Ed. How-to articles, 1,000 to 1,500 words, on decorative painting. "Painting projects only, not crafts." Profiles, 500 words, of up-and-coming painters for "The Artist of the Issue" column. Pays $150 to $300 for features; $100 to $150 for profiles, on acceptance. Query required.

DRAMATICS—Educational Theatre Assoc., 3368 Central Pkwy., Cincinnati, OH 45225-2392. Don Corathers, Ed. Articles, interviews, how-tos, 750 to 4,000 words, for high school students of the performing arts with an emphasis on theater practice: acting, directing, playwriting, technical subjects. Prefer articles that "could be used by a better-than-average high school teacher to teach students something about the performing arts." Also publishes plays. Pays $25 to $300 honorarium. Complete manuscripts preferred; graphics and photos accepted.

EMMY—5220 Lankershim Blvd., N. Hollywood, CA 91601-2800. Gail Polevoi, Man. Ed. Bimonthly. Articles, 2,000 words, related to the television industry: contemporary issues and trends in broadcast and cable; VIPs, especially those behind the scenes; and new technology. Pays from $900, on publication. "It is easier for newcomers to break in with shorter pieces rather than full-length articles. These items can run 500 to 700 words; pay starts at $250." Query.

THE ENGRAVERS JOURNAL—26 Summit St., P. O. Box 318, Brighton, MI 48116. Rosemary Farrell, Man. Ed. Articles, varying lengths, on topics related to the engraving industry and small business operations. Pays $75 to $225, on acceptance. Query.

FILM COMMENT—70 Lincoln Ctr. Plaza, New York, NY 10023-6595. Richard T. Jameson, Ed. Bimonthly. Articles, 1,000 to 5,000 words, on films (new and old, foreign and domestic), as well as performers, writers, cinematographers, studios, national cinemas, genres. Opinion and historical pieces also used. Pays 33¢ a word, on publication.

FILM QUARTERLY—Univ. of California Press Journals, 2120 Berkeley Way, Berkeley, CA 94720. Ann Martin, Ed. Historical, analytical, and critical articles, to 6,000 words; film reviews, book reviews. Guidelines.

FLUTE TALK—Instrumentalist Publishing Co., 200 Northfield Rd., Northfield, IL 60093. Kathleen Goll-Wilson, Ed. Articles, 6 to 12 double-spaced pages, on flute performance, music, and pedagogy; fillers; photos and line drawings. Thorough knowledge of music or the instrument a must. Pays honorarium, on publication. Queries preferred.

GUITAR PLAYER MAGAZINE— 411 Borel Ave., Suite 100, San Mateo, CA 94402. Attn: Ed. Articles, from 200 words, on guitars and related subjects. Pays $100 to $600, on acceptance. Buys one-time and reprint rights.

INDIA CURRENTS—P.O. Box 21285, San Jose, CA 95151. Vandana Kumar, Managing Ed. Fiction, to 2,000 words, and articles, to 1,000 words, on Indian culture in the United States and Canada. Articles on Indian arts, entertainment, and dining. Also music reviews, 500 words; book reviews, 500 words;

commentary on national or international events affecting the lives of Indians, 800 words. Pays in subscriptions.

INDIAN ARTIST—1807 Second St., #61, Santa Fe, NM 87505-3510. Michael Hice, Ed. Quarterly. Articles on contemporary Native American art and interviews with Native American artists, 200 to 2,300 words. Some fillers and photographs. Payment varies, on acceptance. Query.

INTERNATIONAL MUSICIAN—Paramount Bldg., 1501 Broadway, Suite 600, New York, NY 10036. Attn: Ed. Articles, 1,500 to 2,000 words, for professional musicians. Pays varying rates, on acceptance. Query.

KEYBOARD MAGAZINE—Suite 100, 411 Borel Ave., San Mateo, CA 94402. Marvin Sanders, Ed. Articles, 300 to 5,000 words, on keyboard instruments, MIDI and computer technology, and players. Photos. Pays $200 to $600, on acceptance. Query.

LIVING BLUES—Hill Hall, Room 301, Univ. of Mississippi, University, MS 38677. David Nelson, Ed. Articles, 1,500 to 10,000 words, about living African-American blues artists. Interviews. Occasional retrospective/historical articles or investigative pieces. Pays $75 to $200, on publication; $25 to $50 per photo. Query.

MODERN DRUMMER—12 Old Bridge Rd., Cedar Grove, NJ 07009. Ronald L. Spagnardi, Ed. Articles, 500 to 2,000 words, on drumming: how-tos, interviews. Pays $50 to $500, on publication.

NEW ENGLAND ENTERTAINMENT DIGEST—P.O. Box 88, Burlington, MA 01803. Julie Ann Charest, Ed. News and features on the arts and entertainment industry in New England and New York. Pays $15 to $75, on publication.

OPERA NEWS—The Metropolitan Opera Guild, 70 Lincoln Ctr. Plaza, New York, NY 10023-6593. Rudolph S. Ranch, Ed. Articles, 600 to 2,500 words, on all aspects of opera. Payment varies, on publication. Query.

PERFORMANCE—1101 University Dr., Suite 108, Fort Worth, TX 76107. Jane Cohen, Ed.-in-Chief. The leading publication on the touring industry: concert promoters, booking agents, concert venues and clubs, as well as support services, such as lighting, sound, and staging companies.

PETERSEN'S PHOTOGRAPHIC— 6420 Wilshire Blvd., Los Angeles, CA 90048-5515. Ron Leach, Ed. Articles and how-to pieces, with photos, on travel, portrait, action, and digital photography, for beginners, advanced amateurs, and professionals. Pays $125 per printed page, on publication.

PEI (PHOTO ELECTRONIC IMAGING) MAGAZINE—229 Peachtree St. NE, Suite 2200, International Tower, Atlanta, GA 30303. E. Sapwater, Exec. Ed. Articles, 1,000 to 3,000 words, on electronic imaging, computer graphics, desktop publishing, pre-press and commercial printing, multimedia, and web design. Material must be directly related to professional imaging trends and techniques. Query required; all articles on assignment only. Payment varies, on publication.

PLAYBILL—52 Vanderbilt Ave., New York, NY 10017. Judy Samelson, Ed. No unsolicited manuscripts. Provides information necessary to the understanding and enjoyment of each Broadway production, certain Lincoln Center and Off-Broadway productions and regional attractions served. Features articles by and about theatre personalities, fashion, entertainment, dining, etc.

POPULAR PHOTOGRAPHY—1633 Broadway, New York, NY 10019. Jason Schneider, Ed.-in-Chief. Illustrated how-to articles, 500 to 2,000 words, for serious amateur photographers. Query with outline and photos.

ROLLING STONE—1290 Ave. of the Americas, 2nd Fl., New York, NY 10104. Attn: Ed. Magazine of American music, culture, and politics. No fiction. Query; no unsolicited manuscripts. Rarely accepts free-lance material.

THE SENIOR MUSICIAN—127 Ninth Ave. N., Nashville, TN 37234. Jere V. Adams, Ed. Quarterly music periodical. Easy choir music for senior adult choirs to use in worship, ministry, and recreation. Also includes leisure reading, music training, fellowship suggestions, and choir projects for personal growth. For music directors, pastors, organists, pianists, choir coordinators. Pays 5½¢ a word, on acceptance.

SOUTHWEST ART—5444 Westheimer, Suite 1440, Houston, TX 77056. Margaret L. Brown, Ed. Articles, 1,200 to 1,800 words, on the artists, art collectors, museum exhibitions, gallery events and dealers, art history, art trends, and Western American art. Particularly interested in representational or figurative arts. Pays from $400, on acceptance. Query with at least 20 slides of artwork to be featured.

STAGE DIRECTIONS—SMW Communications, Inc., 3101 Poplarwood Ct., Suite 310, Raleigh, NC 27604. Stephen Peithman, Ed.-in-Chief. Neil Offen, Ed. How-to articles, to 2,000 words, on acting, directing, costuming, makeup, lighting, set design and decoration, props, special effects, fundraising, and audience development for readers who are active in all aspects of community, regional, academic, or youth theater. Short pieces, 400 to 500 words, "are a good way to approach us first." Pays 10¢ a word, on publication. Guidelines.

STORYTELLING MAGAZINE—116 W. Main St., Jonesborough, TN 37659. Attn: Eds. Features, 1,000 to 3,000 words, related to the oral tradition. News items, 200 to 400 words, and photos reflecting unusual storytelling events/applications. Query. "Limited free-lance opportunities." Pays in copies.

THEATRE CRAFTS INTERNATIONAL—32 W. 18th St., New York, NY 10011. Jacqueline Tien, Pub. David Johnson, Ed. Articles, 500 to 2,500 words, on design, technical, and management aspects of theater, opera, dance, television, and film for those in performing arts and the entertainment trade. Pays on acceptance. Query.

U.S. ART—220 S. Sixth St., Suite 500, Minneapolis, MN 55402. Sara Gilbert, Ed. Features and artist profiles, 1,200 words, for collectors of limited-edition art prints. Query. Pays $300 to $450, within 30 days of acceptance.

VIDEOMAKER—P.O. Box 4591, Chico, CA 95927. Stephen Muratore, Ed. Authoritative, how-to articles geared to hobbyist and professional video camera/camcorder users: instructionals, editing, desktop video, audio and video production, innovative applications, tools and tips, industry developments, new products, etc. Pays varying rates, on publication. Queries preferred.

WATERCOLOR—1515 Broadway, New York, NY 10036-8901. M. Stephen Doherty, Ed. Quarterly. How-to articles, varying lengths, on watercolor and other water media, such as gouache, casein, acrylic, etc. Payment varies, on publication. Query.

WEST ART—P.O. Box 6868, Auburn, CA 95604-6868. Martha Garcia, Ed. Features, 350 to 700 words, on fine arts and crafts. No hobbies. Photos. Pays 50¢ per column inch, on publication. SASE required.

WILDLIFE ART—Sculpture Forum, P.O. Box 16246, St. Louis Park, MN 55416-0246. Robert J. Koenke, Ed. Informative, thought-provoking articles, 500 to 2,500 words, on wildlife and art topics. All media, including wood, bronze, stone, glass, and metal. Many features spotlight individual artists; query with photos or slides of artist's work. Guidelines. Payment varies, on acceptance. Query required.

HOBBIES, CRAFTS, COLLECTING

AMERICAN HOW-TO—12301 Whitewater Dr., Suite 260, Minnetonka, MN 55343. Tom Sweeney, Ed. No unsolicited material.

AMERICAN WOODWORKER—Rodale Press, 33 E. Minor St., Emmaus, PA 18098. Tim Snyder, Exec. Ed. "A how-to bimonthly for the woodworking enthusiast." Technical or anecdotal articles, to 2,000 words, relating to wood-working or furniture design. Fillers, drawings, slides and photos considered. Pays from $150 per published page, on publication; regular contributors paid on acceptance. Queries preferred. Guidelines.

ANCESTRY—P.O. Box 476, Salt Lake City, UT 84110. Loretto Szucs, Exec. Ed. Bimonthly for Professional Family Historian and hobbyists who are interested in getting the most out of their research. Articles, 1,500 to 4,000 words, that instruct (how-tos, research techniques, etc.) and inform (new research sources, new collections, etc.). No family histories, genealogies, or pedigree charts. Pays $50 to $150, on publication. Guidelines.

THE ANTIQUE TRADER WEEKLY—Box 1050, Dubuque, IA 52004. Kyle Husfloen, Ed. Articles, 1,000 to 2,000 words, on all types of antiques and collectors' items. Photos. Pays from $25 to $200, on publication. Query preferred. Buys all rights.

ANTIQUES & AUCTION NEWS—P.O. Box 500, Mount Joy, PA 17552. Attn: Ed. Weekly newspaper. Factual articles, 600 to 1,500 words, on antiques, collectors, collections, and places of historic interest. Photos. Query required. Pays $5 to $20, after publication.

ANTIQUEWEEK—P.O. Box 90, Knightstown, IN 46148. Tom Hoepf, Ed., Central Edition; Connie Swaim, Ed., Eastern Edition. Weekly antique, auction, and collectors' newspaper. Articles, 500 to 1,500 words, on antiques, collectibles, restorations, genealogy, auction and antique show reports. Photos. Pays from $40 to $150 for in-depth articles, on publication. Query. Guidelines.

AOPA PILOT—421 Aviation Way, Frederick, MD 21701. Thomas B. Haines, Ed. Magazine of the Aircraft Owners and Pilots Assn. Articles, to 2,500 words, with photos, on general aviation for beginning and experienced pilots. Pays to $750.

THE AUCTION EXCHANGE—P.O. Box 57, Plainwell, MI 49080-0057. Attn: Ed. Weekly tabloid. Articles, 500 to 700 words, on auctions, antiques, collectibles, and Michigan history. "We have 9,000 subscribers who collect all sorts of things." Queries preferred.

AUTOGRAPH COLLECTOR MAGAZINE—510-A S. Corona Mall, Corona, CA 91719. Ev Phillips, Ed. Articles, 1,000 to 2,500 words, on all areas of autograph collecting: preservation, framing, and storage, specialty collections, documents and letters, collectors and dealers. Queries preferred. Guidelines. Payment varies.

BECKETT BASEBALL CARD MONTHLY—15850 Dallas Pkwy., Dallas, TX 75248. Mike McAllister, Ed. Articles, 500 to 2,000 words, geared to baseball card collecting, with an emphasis on the pleasures of the hobby. "We accept no stories with investment tips." Query. Pays $150 to $250, on acceptance. Guidelines.

BECKETT BASKETBALL CARD MONTHLY—15850 Dallas Pkwy., Dallas, TX 75248. Mike McAllister, Man. Ed. Articles, 400 to 1,000 words, on the sports-card hobby, especially basketball card collecting for readers 10 to 40. Query. Pays $100 to $250, on acceptance. Also publishes *Beckett Baseball Card Monthly, Beckett Sports Collectibles & Autographs, Beckett Football Card Monthly, Beckett Hockey Card Monthly,* and *Beckett Racing Monthly.* SASE for guidelines.

BIRD TALK—Box 6050, Mission Viejo, CA 92690. Melissa Kauffman, Ed. Articles for pet bird owners: care and feeding, training, safety, outstanding personal adventures, exotic birds in their native countries, profiles of celebrities' pet birds, travel to bird parks or shows. Good transparencies a plus. Pays up to 10¢ a word, after publication. Query required.

BIRD WATCHER'S DIGEST—P.O. Box 110, Marietta, OH 45750. William H. Thompson III, Ed. Articles, 600 to 3,000 words, on bird-watching experiences and expeditions: information about rare sightings; updates on endangered species; interesting backyard topics and how-tos. Pays from $50, on publication. Allow 8 weeks for response.

BIRDER'S WORLD—44 E. 8th St., Suite 410, Holland, MI 49423. Eldon D. Greij, Ed. Bimonthly. Articles, 2,200 to 2,400 words, on all aspects of birding, especially on a particular species or the status of an endangered species. Tips on birding, attracting birds, or photographing them. Personal essays, 1,000 to 1,500 words. Book reviews, to 500 words. Pays $350 to $450, on publication. Query preferred.

BREW MAGAZINE—1120 Mulberry St., Des Moines, IA 50309. Beverly Walsmith, Ed. "Traveling America's Brewpubs and Microbreweries." Bimonthly. Articles, 1,500 to 1,800 words, on new brewpubs around the country. "Our focus is on the brewpub and the community where it is located." Pays 10¢ a word, on publication. Query preferred.

BREW YOUR OWN—Niche Publications, 216 F St., Suite 160, Davis, CA 95616. Craig Bystrynski, Ed. Practical how-to articles, 800 to 2,500 words, for homebrewers. Pays $50 to $150, on publication. Query.

CANADIAN STAMP NEWS—103 Lakeshore Rd., Suite 202, St. Catharines, Ont., Canada L2N 2T6. Ellen Rodger, Ed. Biweekly. Articles, 1,000 to 2,000 words, on stamp collecting news, rare and unusual stamps, and auction and club reports. Special issues throughout the year; send SASE for guidelines. Photos. Pays from $70, on publication.

CARD PLAYER—3140 S. Polaris #8, Las Vegas, NV 89102. Linda Johnson, Pub. "The Magazine for Those Who Play to Win." Articles on poker events, personalities, legal issues, new casinos, tournaments, and prizes. Also articles on strategies, theory and game psychology to improve poker play. Occasionally uses humor, cartoons, puzzles, or anecdotal material. Pays $35 to $100, on publication; $15 to $35 for fillers. Guidelines.

THE CAROUSEL NEWS & TRADER— 87 Park Ave. W., Suite 206, Mansfield, OH 44902. Attn: Ed. Features on carousel history and profiles of amusement park operators and carousel carvers of interest to band organ enthusiasts, carousel art collectors, preservationists, amusement park owners, artists, and restorationists. Pays $50 per published page, after publication. Guidelines.

CHESS LIFE—3054 NYS Rte. 9W, New Windsor, NY 12553-7698. Glenn Petersen, Ed. Articles, 500 to 3,000 words, for members of the U.S. Chess Federation, on news, profiles, technical aspects of chess. Features on all aspects of chess: history, humor, puzzles, etc. Fiction, 500 to 2,000 words, related to chess. Photos. Pays varying rates, on acceptance. Query; limited freelance market.

CLASSIC TOY TRAINS—21027 Crossroads Cir., Waukesha, WI 53187. Attn: Ed. Articles, with photos, on toy train layouts and collections. Also toy train manufacturing history and repair/maintenance. Pays $75 per printed page, on acceptance. Query.

COLLECTOR EDITIONS—170 Fifth Ave., New York, NY 10010. Joan Muyskens Pursley, Ed. Articles, 750 to 1,500 words, on collectibles, mainly contemporary limited-edition figurines, plates, and prints. Pays $150 to $350, within 30 days of acceptance. Query with photos.

COLLECTORS JOURNAL—P.O. Box 601, Vinton, IA 52349. Connie Gewecke, Ed. Weekly tabloid. Features, to 2,000 words, on antiques and collectibles. Pays $10 for articles, $15 for articles with photos, on publication.

COLLECTORS NEWS—P.O. Box 156, Grundy Ctr., IA 50638. Linda Kruger, Ed. Articles, to 1,000 words, on private collections, antiques, and collectibles, especially modern limited-edition collectibles, 20th-century nostalgia, Americana, glass and china, music, furniture, transportation, timepieces, jewelry, farm-related collectibles, and lamps; include quality color or B&W photos. Pays $1 per column inch; $25 for front-page color photos, on publication.

COMBO—5 Nassau Blvd. S., Garden City S., NY 11530. Ian M. Feller, Ed. Articles, from 800 words, related to non-sports cards (comic cards, TV/movie cards, science fiction cards, etc.) and comic books; collecting and investing; fillers. Queries preferred. Pays to 10¢ a word, on publication.

COUNTRY FOLK ART MAGAZINE— 8393 E. Holly Rd., Holly, MI 48442-8819. Attn: Ed. Dept. Articles on decorating, artisans, collectibles; how-to pieces, 750 to 1,000 words, with a creative slant on American folk art. Pays $150 to $300, on acceptance. Submit pieces on seasonal topics one year in advance.

COUNTRY HANDCRAFTS —See *Crafting Traditions.*

CRAFT SUPPLY MAGAZINE—225 Gordons Corner Rd., P.O. Box 420, Manalapan, NJ 07726-0420. John Tracey, Ed. Bimonthly. Articles, 800 to 1,500 words, of interest to professional crafters; also general small business advice. Pays $75 to $200, on publication.

CRAFTING TRADITIONS—(formerly *Country Handcrafts*) 5400 S. 60th St., Greendale, WI 53129. Kathleen Anderson, Ed. All types of craft designs (needlepoint, quilting, woodworking, etc.) with complete instructions and full-size patterns. Pays from $25 to $250, on acceptance, for all rights.

CRAFTS 'N THINGS—2400 Devon, Suite 375, Des Plaines, IL 60018-4618. Marie Clapper, Ed. How-to articles on all kinds of crafts projects, with instructions. Send manuscript with instructions and photograph of the finished item. Pays $50 to $250, on acceptance.

DOG FANCY—P.O. Box 6050, Mission Viejo, CA 92690. Attn: Ed. Articles, 900 to 1,500 words, on dog care, health, grooming, breeds, activities, events, etc. Photos. Payment varies, on publication.

DOLL WORLD—306 E. Parr Rd., Berne, IN 46711. Cary Raesner, Ed. Vicki Steensma, Assoc. Ed. Informational articles about dollmaking and doll collecting. Patterns for original doll and clothing designs. Original paper dolls. Doll history, nostalgic stories, doll crafters and artists, doll accessories. Bios.

DOLLHOUSE MINIATURES—(formerly *Nutshell News*) 21027 Crossroads Cir., P.O. Box 1612, Waukesha, WI 53187. Kay Melchisedech Olson, Ed. Articles, 1,200 to 1,500 words, for dollhouse-scale miniatures enthusiasts, collectors, craftspeople, and hobbyists. Interested in artisan profiles and how-to projects. "Writers must be knowledgeable of scale miniatures." Color slides or B&W prints required. Payment varies, on acceptance. Query.

DOLLS, THE COLLECTOR'S MAGAZINE—170 Fifth Ave., New York, NY 10010. Stephanie Finnegan, Ed. Articles, 500 to 2,500 words, for knowledgeable doll collectors; sharply focused with a strong collecting angle, and concrete information (value, identification, restoration, etc.). Include high quality slides or transparencies. Pays $100 to $350, within 30 days of acceptance. Query.

FIBERARTS—50 College St., Asheville, NC 28801. Ann Batchelder, Ed. Published 5 times yearly. Articles, 400 to 2,000 words, on contemporary trends in fiber sculpture, weaving, surface design, quilting, stitchery, papermaking, felting, basketry, and wearable art. Query with photos of subject, outline, and synopsis. Pays varying rates, on publication.

FIGURINES & COLLECTIBLES—Cowles Enthusiast Media, 6405 Flank Dr., Harrisburg, PA 17112. Mindy Kinsey, Man. Ed. Not currently accepting material. Articles, 1,000 to 1,500 words, for collectors of modern collectibles (Hummel, Cherished Teddies, Precious Moments, etc.): artists and manufacturer profiles, collector profiles, some travel pieces. "We do not cover plates, prints, steins, or other non-figural pieces. No fiction or personal experience." Pays 20¢ to 25¢ a word, on publication. Query preferred.

FINE LINES—P.O. Box 718, Ingomar, PA 15127. Deborah A. Novak, Ed. Publication of the Historic Needlework Guild. Articles, 500 to 1,500 words, about historic needlework, museums, famous historic needlework, or themes revolving around stitching (samplers, needlework tools, etc.). Pays varying rates, on acceptance. Queries required.

FINE WOODWORKING—63 S. Main St., Newtown, CT 06470. Timothy Schreiner, Ed. Bimonthly. Articles on woodworking: basics of tool use, stock preparation and joinery, specialized techniques and finishing, shop-built tools, jigs and fixtures; or any stage of design, construction, finishing and installation of cabinetry and furniture. "We look for high-quality workmanship, thoughtful designs, safe and proper procedures." Departments: "Methods of Work," "Q&A," "Master Class," "Finish Lines" "Tools & Materials," and "Notes and Comments." Pays $150 per page, on publication; pays from $10 for short department pieces. Query.

FINESCALE MODELER—P.O. Box 1612, Waukesha, WI 53187. Bob Hayden, Ed. How-to articles for people who make nonoperating scale models of aircraft, automobiles, boats, figures. Photos and drawings should accompany articles. One-page model-building hints and tips. Pays from $45 per published page, on acceptance. Query preferred.

FLOWER & GARDEN CRAFTS EDITION—700 W. 47th St., Suite 810, Kansas City, MO 64112. Roberta Schneider, Ed. Instructions and models for original knit, crochet, tat, quilt, cross stitch and crafts. Also includes gardening features and recipes which are assigned by staff. Send photos with manuscript. Pays on acceptance; negotiable rates for instructional items.

GAMES—P.O. Box 184, Ft. Washington, PA 19034. R. Wayne Schmittberger, Ed.-in-Chief. "The magazine for creative minds at play." Features and short articles on games and playful, offbeat subjects. Visual and verbal puzzles, pop culture quizzes, brainteasers, contests, game reviews. Pays top rates, on publication. Send SASE for guidelines; specify writer's, crosswords, variety puzzles, or brainteasers.

HERITAGE QUEST—American Genealogical Lending Library, P.O. Box 329, Bountiful, UT 84011. Leland Meitzler, Ed. Bimonthly. Genealogy how-to articles, 2 to 4 pages; national, international, or regional in scope. Pays $30 per published page, on publication.

THE HOME SHOP MACHINIST—2779 Aero Park Dr., Box 1810, Traverse City, MI 49685. Joe D. Rice, Ed. How-to articles on precision metalworking and foundry work. Accuracy and attention to detail a must. Pays $40 per published page, extra for photos and illustrations, on publication. Guidelines.

KITPLANES—1000 Quail St., Suite 190, Newport Beach, CA 92660. Dave Martin, Ed. Articles geared to the growing market of aircraft built from kits and plans by home craftsmen, on all aspects of design, construction, and performance, 1,000 to 4,000 words. Pays $60 per page, on publication.

LOST TREASURE—P.O. Box 451589, Grove, OK 74345. Patsy Beyerl, Man. Ed. How-to articles, legends, folklore, and stories of lost treasures. Also publishes *Treasure Cache* (annual): articles on documented treasure caches with sidebar telling how to search for cache highlighted in article. Pays 4¢ a word, $5 for photos, $100 for cover photos.

THE MIDATLANTIC ANTIQUES MAGAZINE—P.O. Box 908, Henderson, NC 27536. Lydia Stainback, Ed. Articles, 500 to 2,000 words, on antiques, collectibles, and related subjects. "We need show and auction reporters." Queries are preferred. Payment varies, on publication.

MILITARY HISTORY—741 Miller Dr. S.E., #D2, Leesburg, VA 20175. Jon Guttman, Ed. Bimonthly. Features, 4,000 words with 500-word sidebars, on the strategy, tactics, and personalities of military history. Department pieces, 2,000 words, on intrigue, weaponry, and perspectives; book reviews. No fiction. Pays $200 to $400, on publication. Query. SASE for guidelines.

MINIATURE COLLECTOR—30595 Eight Mile Rd., Livonia, MI 48152-1761. Ruth Keessen, Pub. Articles, 800 to 1,200 words, with photos, on outstanding $\frac{1}{12}$-scale (dollhouse) miniatures and the people who make and collect them. Original, illustrated how-to projects for making miniatures. Pays varying rates, within 30 days of acceptance. Query with photos.

MINIATURE QUILTS—See *Traditional Quiltworks.*

MODEL RAILROADER—21027 Crossroads Cir., P.O. Box 1612, Waukesha, WI 53187. Andy Sperandeo, Ed. Articles on model railroads, with photos of layout and equipment. Pays $90 per printed page, on acceptance. Query.

NEW ENGLAND ANTIQUES JOURNAL— 4 Church St., Ware, MA 01082. Jody Young, Gen. Mgr. Jamie Mercier, Man. Ed. Well-researched articles, usually by recognized authorities in their field, 2,000 to 5,000 words, on antiques of interest to dealers or collectors; antiques market news, to 500 words; photos required. Pays from $100 to $250, on publication. Query or send manuscript. Reports in 2 to 4 weeks.

NUTSHELL NEWS—See *Dollhouse Miniatures*.

PETERSEN'S PHOTOGRAPHIC—6420 Wilshire Blvd., Los Angeles, CA 90048. Ron Leach, Ed. How-to articles on all phases of still photography of interest to the amateur and advanced photographer. Pays about $100 per printed page for article accompanied by photos, on publication.

POPULAR MECHANICS—224 W. 57th St., New York, NY 10019. Sarah Deem, Man. Ed. Articles, 300 to 1,500 words, on latest developments in mechanics, industry, science, telecommunications; features on hobbies with a mechanical slant; how-tos on home and shop projects; features on outdoor adventures, boating, and electronics. Photos and sketches a plus. Pays to $1,500; to $500 for short pieces, on acceptance. Buys all rights.

POPULAR WOODWORKING—1507 Dana Ave., Cincinnati, OH 45207. Steve Shanesy, Ed. Project articles, to 3,000 words; techniques pieces, to 1,500 words, for the "modest production woodworker, small shop owner, wood craftsperson, intermediate hobbyist and woodcarver." Pays $500 to $1,000 for large, complicated projects; $100 to $500 for small projects and other features; pays on acceptance. Query with brief outline and photo of finished project.

QUILTING TODAY—See *Traditional Quiltworks*.

RAILROAD MODEL CRAFTSMAN—P.O. Box 700, Newton, NJ 07860-0700. William C. Schaumburg, Ed. How-to articles on scale model railroading; cars, operation, scenery, etc. Pays on publication.

RENAISSANCE MAGAZINE—Phantom Press Publications, 13 Appleton Rd., Nantucket, MA 02554. Kim Guarnaccia, Ed. Feature articles on jousting, history, costuming, Renaissance faires; interviews; and reviews of Renaissance books, music, movies, and games. Pays 4¢ a word, on publication.

RESTORATION—P.O. Box 50046, Dept. TW, Tucson, AZ 85703-1046. W.R. Haessner, Ed. Articles, 1,200 to 1,800 words, on restoring and building machines, boats, autos, trucks, planes, trains, buildings, toys, tools, etc. Photos and art required. Pays from $25 per page, on publication. Query.

REUNIONS MAGAZINE—P.O. Box 11727, Milwaukee, WI 53211-0727. Edith Wagner, Ed. Positive and instructive articles related to reunions (family, class, military reunions, searching, and some genealogy). "The magazine is reunion organizers speaking to reunion organizers. No class reunion catharsis stories." Pays honoraria and copies. www.reunionsmag.com

RUG HOOKING MAGAZINE—Stackpole Magazines, 500 Vaughn St., Harrisburg, PA 17110. Patrice Crowley, Ed. How-to and feature articles on rug hooking for beginners and advanced artists. Payment varies.

SCHOOL MATES—U.S. Chess Federation, 3054 NYS Rt. 9W, New Windsor, NY 12553-7698. Jay Hastings, Publications Dir. Articles and fiction, 250 to 800 words, and short fillers, related to chess for beginning chess players (primarily children, 8 to 15). "Primarily instructive material, but there's room for fun puzzles, cartoons, anecdotes, etc. All chess related. Articles on chess-playing celebrities are always of interest to us." Pays from $20, on publication. Query; limited free-lance market.

73 AMATEUR RADIO—70 Rte. 202N, Peterborough, NH 03458. F.I. Marion, Assoc. Pub. Articles, 1,500 to 3,000 words, for electronics hobbyists and amateur radio operators. Pays $50 to $250.

SEW NEWS—P.O. Box 1790, News Plaza, Peoria, IL 61656. Linda Turner Griepentrog, Ed. Articles, to 3,000 words, "that teach a specific technique, inspire a reader to try new sewing projects, or inform a reader about an interesting person, company, or project related to sewing, textiles, or fashion." Emphasis is on fashion (not craft) sewing. Pays $25 to $400, on acceptance. Queries required; no unsolicited manuscripts accepted.

SPORTS COLLECTORS DIGEST—Krause Publications, 700 E. State St., Iola, WI 54990. Tom Mortenson, Ed. Articles, 750 to 2,000 words, on old baseball card sets and other sports memorabilia and collectibles. Pays $50 to $100, on publication.

TEDDY BEAR REVIEW—Collector Communications Corp., 170 Fifth Ave., New York, NY 10010. Stephen L. Cronk, Ed. Articles on antique and contemporary teddy bears for makers, collectors, and enthusiasts. Pays $100 to $300, within 30 days of acceptance. Query with photos.

TRADITIONAL QUILTWORKS—Chitra Publications, 2 Public Ave., Montrose, PA 18801. Attn: Ed. Team. Specific, quilt-related how-to articles, 700 to 1,500 words. Patterns, features, and department pieces. Completed manuscripts preferred. Pays $75 per published page, on publication. Also publishes *Quilting Today* and *Miniature Quilts*.

TREASURE CACHE—See *Lost Treasure*.

WATERCOLOR—1515 Broadway, New York, NY 10036-8901. M. Stephen Doherty, Ed. Quarterly. How-to articles, varying lengths, on watercolor and other water media, such as gouache, casein, acrylic, etc. Pays varying rates, on publication. Query.

WEST ART—Box 6868, Auburn, CA 95604-6868. Martha Garcia, Ed. Features, 350 to 700 words, on fine arts and crafts. No hobbies. Photos. Pays 50¢ per column inch, on publication. SASE required.

WESTERN & EASTERN TREASURES—P.O. Box 1598, Mercer Island, WA 98040-1598. Rosemary Anderson, Man. Ed. Illustrated articles, to 1,500 words, on treasure hunting and how-to metal-detecting tips. Pays 2¢ a word, extra for photos, on publication.

WILDFOWL CARVING AND COLLECTING—Stackpole Magazines, 500 Vaughn St., Harrisburg, PA 17110. Cathy Hart, Ed.-in-Chief. How-to and reference articles, of varying lengths, on bird carving; collecting antique and contemporary carvings. Query. Pays varying rates, on acceptance.

WOODENBOAT MAGAZINE—P.O. Box 78, Brooklin, ME 04616. Matthew Murphy, Ed. How-to and technical articles, 4,000 words, on construction, repair, and maintenance of wooden boats; design, history, and use of wooden boats; and profiles of outstanding wooden boat builders and designers. Pays $150 to $200 per 1,000 words. Query preferred.

WOODWORK— 42 Digital Dr., Suite 5, Novato, CA 94949. John Lavine, Ed. Bimonthly. Articles for woodworkers on all aspects of woodworking (simple, complex, technical, or aesthetic). Pays $150 per published page; $35 to $75 for "Techniques," on publication. Queries or outlines (with slides) preferred.

YELLOWBACK LIBRARY—P.O. Box 36172, Des Moines, IA 50315. Gil O'Gara, Ed. Articles, 300 to 2,000 words, on boys'/girls' series literature

(Hardy Boys, Nancy Drew, Tom Swift, etc.) for collectors, researchers, and dealers. "Especially welcome are interviews with, or articles by past and present writers of juvenile series fiction." Pays in copies.

YESTERYEAR—P.O. Box 2, Princeton, WI 54968. Michael Jacobi, Ed. Articles on antiques and collectibles for readers in WI, IL, IA, MN, and surrounding states. Photos. Will consider regular columns on collecting or antiques. Pays from $20, on publication. Limited market.

ZYMURGY—Box 1679, Boulder, CO 80306-1679. Dena Nishek, Ed. Articles appealing to beer lovers and homebrewers. Pays after publication. Guidelines. Query.

SCIENCE & COMPUTERS

AD ASTRA—National Space Society, 922 Pennsylvania Ave. S.E., Washington, DC 20003-2140. Pat Dasch, Ed.-in-Chief. Lively, non-technical features, to 3,000 words, on all aspects of international space exploration. Particularly interested in "Living in Space" articles; space settlements; lunar and Mars bases. Pays $150 to $200, on publication. Query. Guidelines.

AMERICAN HERITAGE OF INVENTION & TECHNOLOGY— 60 Fifth Ave., New York, NY 10011. Frederick Allen, Ed. Quarterly. Articles, 2,000 to 5,000 words, on history of technology in America, for the sophisticated general reader. Pays on acceptance. Query.

THE ANNALS OF IMPROBABLE RESEARCH—AIR, P.O. Box 380853, Cambridge, MA 02238. Marc Abrahams, Ed. Science humor, science reports and analysis, one to 4 pages. Brief science-related poetry. B&W photos. "This journal is the place to find the mischievous, funny, iconoclastic side of science." Guidelines. No payment.

ARCHAEOLOGY—135 William St., New York, NY 10038. Peter A. Young, Ed.-in-Chief. Articles on archaeology by professionals or lay people with a solid knowledge of the field. Pays $250 to $500, on publication. Query required.

ASTRONOMY—P.O. Box 1612, Waukesha, WI 53187. Bonnie Gordon, Ed. Dave Eicher, Man. Ed. Articles on astronomy, astrophysics, space programs, recent discoveries. Hobby pieces on equipment and celestial events; short news items. Pays varying rates, on acceptance.

CLOSING THE GAP—526 Main St., Box 68, Henderson, MN 56044. Megan Hagen, Man. Ed. Bimonthly tabloid. Articles, 700 to 1,500 words, that describe a particular microcomputer product that affects the education, vocation, recreation, mobility, communication, etc., of persons who are handicapped or disabled. Non-product related articles also used. Web site: http://www.closingthegap.com

COMPUTERSCENE MAGAZINE—3507 Wyoming Blvd. N.E., Albuquerque, NM 87111. Greg Hansen, Man. Ed. Noel Hansen, Bus. Mgr. Computer-related articles and fiction, 800 to 1,500 words. "We provide New Mexico computer users with entertaining and informative articles on all aspects of computers: hardware, software, technology, productivity, advice, personal experience, even computer-related fiction." Fillers, 400 to 800 words. Pays $40 to $75, on publication. Send SASE for guidelines and editorial calendar.

ELECTRONICS NOW—500 Bi-County Blvd., Farmingdale, NY 11735. Carl Laron, Ed. Technical articles, 1,500 to 3,000 words, on all areas related to electronics. Pays $50 to $500 or more, on acceptance.

ENVIRONMENT—1319 18th St. N.W., Washington, DC 20036-1802. Barbara T. Richman, Man. Ed. Factual and analytical articles, 2,500 to 5,000 words, on scientific, technological, and environmental policy and decision-making issues, especially on a global scale. Pays $100 to $300. Query.

FINAL FRONTIER—1017 S. Mountain Ave., Monrovia, CA 91016. Dave Cravotta, Ed. Articles, 1,500 to 2,500 words; columns, 800 words; and shorts, 250 words, about people, events, and new concepts of opening up the space frontier. Pays about 40¢ a word, on acceptance. Query with clips, mentioning availability of art and photos.

FOCUS—Turnkey Publishing, Inc., P.O. Box 200549, Austin, TX 78720. J. Todd Key, Ed. Articles, 700 to 4,000 words, on Data General computers. Photos a plus. Pays to $50, on publication. Query required.

HOBSON'S CHOICE: SCIENCE FICTION AND TECHNOLOGY—The Starwind Press, P.O. Box 98, Ripley, OH 45167. Attn: Submissions Ed. Articles and literary criticism, 1,000 to 5,000 words, for readers interested in science and technology. Also science fiction and fantasy, 2,000 to 10,000 words. Pays 1¢ to 4¢ a word, on acceptance. Query for nonfiction.

HOMEPC—CMP Publications, 600 Community Dr., Manhasset, NY 11030-5772. Andrea Linne, Features Ed. Articles that help home computer users get the most out of their PCs. Payment varies, on acceptance. Query with clips and resumé required.

LINK-UP—2222 River Rd., King George, VA 22485. Loraine Page, Ed. Dir. Articles about online services, the Internet, and CD-ROM for the computer owner who uses this technology for business, home, and educational use. Pays $90 to $220 for articles, on publication. Photos a plus.

NATURAL HISTORY—American Museum of Natural History, Central Park W. at 79th St., New York, NY 10024. Bruce Stutz, Ed.-in-Chief. Informative articles, to 3,000 words, on anthropology and natural sciences. "Strongly recommend that writers send SASE for guidelines and read our magazine." Pays from $1,000 for features, on acceptance. Query.

OMNI INTERNET—General Media International, 277 Park Ave., 4th Fl., New York, NY 10172-0003. Pamela Weintraub, Ed. Monthly on-line (electrical) version. Articles, 750 to 1,000 words, on scientific aspects of the future: space colonies, cloning, machine intelligence, ESP, origin of life, future arts, lifestyles, etc. Address fiction, 2,000 to 10,000 words, to Ellen Datlow, Fiction Ed., *OMNI Internet* at above address. Pays $800 to $3,500 for articles; $150 for shorter items, on acceptance. Query.

PC GRAPHICS & VIDEO—201 E. Sandpointe Ave., Suite 600, Santa Ana, CA 92707. Frank Moldstad, Ed. Applications of graphics and video on pc-compatible computers for professionals and enthusiasts. Pays flat rate. Query; unsolicited manuscripts not accepted.

POPULAR ELECTRONICS—500 Bi-County Blvd., Farmingdale, NY 11735. Julian Martin, Ed. Features, 1,500 to 2,500 words, for electronics hobbyists and experimenters. "Our readers are science and electronics oriented, understand computer theory and operation, and like to build electronics projects." Fillers and cartoons. Pays $25 to $500, on acceptance.

POPULAR SCIENCE—2 Park Ave., New York, NY 10016. Fred Abatemarco, Ed.-in-Chief. Articles, with photos, on developments in science and technology. Short illustrated articles on new inventions and products; photo-essays, book excerpts. Payment varies, on acceptance.

PUBLISH—Integrated Media, Inc., 501 Second St., San Francisco, CA 94107. Jake Widman, Ed. Features, 1,500 to 2,000 words, and reviews, 400 to 800 words, on all aspects of computerized publishing. Pays $400 to $600 for reviews, $850 to $1,200 for full-length features, on acceptance.

RESELLER MANAGEMENT MAGAZINE—275 Washington St., Newton, MA 02158. Tony Strattner, Ed.-in-Chief. Articles, 500 to 1,200 words, that emphasize profitable strategies for value-added resellers, systems, integrators, software developers, and VAR-consultants. "Magazine sections include how-tos for selling, marketing, customer, technology, business, and verticals." Payment varies. Query.

THE SCIENCES—2 E. 63rd St., New York, NY 10021. Peter G. Brown, Ed. Essays and features, 2,000 to 4,000 words, and book reviews, on all scientific disciplines. Pays honorarium, on publication. Query.

SCIENCEWORLD—Scholastic, Inc., 555 Broadway, New York, NY 10012-3999. Rex Roberts, Ed. Science articles, 750 words, and science news articles, 200 words, on life science, earth science, physical science, environmental science technology, and/or health for readers in grades 7 to 10 (ages 12 to 15). "Articles should include current, exciting science news. Writing should be lively and show an understanding of teens' perspectives and interests." Pays $100 to $125 for news items; $300 to $750 for features. Query with a well-researched proposal, suggested sources, 2 to 3 clips of your work, and an SASE.

SKY & TELESCOPE—Sky Publishing Corp., P.O. Box 9111, Belmont, MA 02178-9111. Timothy Lyster, Man. Ed. Articles for amateur and professional astronomers worldwide. Department pieces for "Amateur Astronomers," "Astronomical Computing," "Astronomical Imaging," "Telescope Techniques," "Observer's Log," and "Gallery." Also, 1,000-word opinion pieces, for "Focal Point." Mention availability of diagrams and other illustrations. Pays 10¢ to 25¢ a word, on publication. Query required.

TECHNOLOGY & LEARNING—Peter Li, Inc., 600 Harrison St., San Francisco, CA 94107-1370. Judy Salpeter, Ed. Articles, to 3,000 words, for teachers of grades K through 12, about uses of computers and related technology in the classroom: human-interest and philosophical articles, how-to pieces, software reviews, and hands-on ideas. Payment varies, on acceptance.

TECHNOLOGY REVIEW—MIT, W59-200, Cambridge, MA 02139. John Benditt, Ed. General-interest articles on technology and innovation. Payment varies, on acceptance. Query.

ANIMALS

ANIMAL PEOPLE—P.O. Box 960, Clinton, WA 98236-0906. Attn: Ed. "News for People Who Care About Animals." Tabloid published 10 times a year. Articles and profiles, "especially of seldom recognized individuals of unique and outstanding positive accomplishment, in any capacity that benefits animals or illustrates the intrinsic value of other species. No atrocity stories, essays on why animals have rights, or material that promotes animal abuse, including hunting, fishing, trapping, and slaughter." No fiction or poetry. Pays honorarium, on acceptance. Query.

ANIMALS—350 S. Huntington Ave., Boston, MA 02130. Joni Praded, Dir./Ed. Informative, well-researched articles, to 2,500 words, on animal protection, national and international wildlife, pet care, conservation, and environmental issues that affect animals. No personal accounts or favorite pet stories. Pays from $350, on acceptance. Query.

BIRD TALK—Box 6050, Mission Viejo, CA 92690. Melissa Kauffman, Ed. Articles for pet bird owners: care and feeding, training, safety, outstanding personal adventures, exotic birds in their native countries, profiles of celebrities' birds, travel to bird parks or bird shows. Pays 7¢ to 10¢ a word, after publication. Query required; good transparencies a plus.

CAT FANCY—P.O. Box 6050, Mission Viejo, CA 92690. Jane Calloway, Ed. Nonfiction, to 2,500 words, on cat care, health, grooming, etc. Pays 5¢ to 10¢ a word, on publication. Query with SASE required.

CATS—Box 1790, Peoria, IL 61656. Annette Bailey, Ed. Monthly, with one annual issue. Nonfiction articles, 1,200 to 3,200 words, on the health and welfare of cats. Photos. Pays $50 to $600, on acceptance. SASE for guidelines. Query.

CATSUMER REPORT—P.O. Box 10069, Austin, TX 78766. Judith Becker, Ed. Articles, 800 to 1,100 words, for cat owners and cat lovers. "Do not 'speak' in the voice of a cat!" No fiction or poetry. Small payment, on publication.

DAIRY GOAT JOURNAL—P.O. Box 10, Lake Mills, WI 53551. Dave Thompson, Ed. Articles, to 1,500 words, on successful dairy goat owners, youths and interesting people associated with dairy goats. "Especially interested in practical husbandry ideas." Photos. Pays $50 to $150, on publication. Query.

DOG WORLD—Primedia Special Interest Publications, 29 N. Wacker Dr., Chicago, IL 60606-3298. Donna L. Marcel, Ed. Articles, to 3,000 words, for breeders, pet owners, exhibitors, kennel operators, veterinarians, handlers, and other pet professionals on all aspects of pet care and responsible ownership: health care, training, legal rights, animal welfare, etc. Queries required. Allow 4 months for response. Pays $50 to $500, on acceptance. Guidelines.

EQUUS—Fleet Street Corp., 656 Quince Orchard Rd., Suite 600, Gaithersburg, MD 20878. Laurie Prinz, Exec. Ed. Articles, 1,000 to 3,000 words, on all breeds of horses, covering their health and care as well as the latest advances in equine medicine and research. "Attempt to speak as one horseperson to another." Pays $100 to $400, on publication.

THE FLORIDA HORSE—P.O. Box 2106, Ocala, FL 34478. Dan Mearns, Ed. Articles, 1,500 words, on Florida thoroughbred breeding and racing. Also veterinary articles, financial articles, and articles of general interest. Pays $100 to $200, on publication.

FRESHWATER AND MARINE AQUARIUM—P.O. Box 487, Sierra Madre, CA 91024. Don Dewey, Ed. "The Magazine Dedicated to the Tropical Fish Enthusiast." How-to articles, varying lengths, on anything related to basic, semi-technical, and technical aspects of freshwater and marine aquariology. Payment is $50 to $350 for features, $50 to $250 for secondary articles, $50 to $150 for columns, and $25 to $75 for fillers. Guidelines.

GOOD DOG!—P.O. Box 10069, Austin, TX 78766-1069. Judi Sklar, Ed. Bimonthly. "The Consumer Magazine for Dog Owners." Articles, one to 2 pages, that are informative and fun to read. No fiction. No material "written" by the dog. Small payment, on publication.

HORSE & RIDER—1597 Cole Blvd., Suite 350, Golden, CO 80401. Sue M. Copeland, Ed. Articles, 500 to 3,000 words, with photos, on western training and general horse care: feeding, health, grooming, etc. Pays varying rates, on acceptance. Guidelines.

HORSE ILLUSTRATED—P.O. Box 6050, Mission Viejo, CA 92690. Moira C. Harris, Ed. Articles, 1,500 to 2,500 words, on all aspects of owning and caring for horses. Photos. Pays $200 to $300, on publication. Query.

HORSEMEN'S YANKEE PEDLAR—83 Leicester St., N. Oxford, MA 01537. Kelley R. Small, Pub. News and feature-length articles, about horses and horsemen in the Northeast. Photos. Pays $2 per published inch, on publication. Query.

I LOVE CATS—450 7th Ave., Suite 1701, New York, NY 10123. Lisa Allmendinger, Ed. Fiction, preferably 500 to 700 words, about cats. Articles, to 1,000 words. No poetry, puzzles, or humor. "Read the magazine, then request guidelines with SASE." Pays $50 to $250; $20 to $25 for fillers, on publication.

LLAMAS—P.O. Box 250, Jackson, CA 95642. cheryl Dal Porto, Ed. "The International Camelid Journal," published 5 times yearly. Articles, 300 to 3,000 words, of interest to llama and alpaca owners. Pays $25 to $300, extra for photos, on publication. Query.

MUSHING—P.O. Box 149, Ester, AK 99725-0149. Todd Hoener, Pub. How-tos, innovations, history, profiles, interviews, and features related to sled dogs, 1,500 to 2,000 words, and department pieces, 500 to 1,000 words, for competitive and recreational dog drivers and skijorers. International audience. Photos. Pays $20 to $250, on publication. Send SASE for guidelines.

PETLIFE MAGAZINE—1227 W. Magnolia Ave., Ft. Worth, TX 76104. Jana Murphy, Man. Ed. Bimonthly. How-to pieces and human interest features, 500 to 1,500 words, for pet owners and pet lovers. No first-person pieces. Pays $150 to $300, on acceptance.

PRACTICAL HORSEMAN—Box 589, Unionville, PA 19375. Mandy Lorraine, Ed. How-to articles on English riding, training, and horse care. Payment varies, on acceptance. Query with clips.

REPTILE & AMPHIBIAN MAGAZINE—RD #3, Box 3709-A, Pottsville, PA 17901. Erica Ramus, Ed./Pub. Bimonthly. Articles, 1,500 to 2,500 words, for "devoted, advanced amateur herpetologists." Book reviews, 750 words. Pays $100 for features, $50 for reviews, on acceptance.

THE WESTERN HORSEMAN—P.O. Box 7980, Colorado Springs, CO 80933-7980. Pat Close, Ed. Articles, 1,500 to 2,500 words, with photos, on care and training of horses; farm, ranch, and stable management; health care and veterinary medicine. Pays to $600, on acceptance.

WILDLIFE CONSERVATION—The Wildlife Conservation Society, Bronx, NY 10460. Nancy Simmons, Sr. Ed. Articles, 1,500 to 2,000 words, that "probe conservation controversies to search for answers and help save threatened species." Payment varies, on acceptance. Guidelines.

YOUNG RIDER—Box 8237, Lexington, KY 40383. Lesley Ward, Ed. Bimonthly. Stories, 1,200 words, about horses and children. Photos. Query or send manuscript. Pays $120, on publication.

TRUE CRIME

DETECTIVE CASES—See *Globe Communications Corp.*

DETECTIVE DRAGNET—See *Globe Communications Corp.*

DETECTIVE FILES—See *Globe Communications Corp.*

GLOBE COMMUNICATIONS CORP.—1350 Sherbrooke St. W., Suite 600, Montreal, Quebec, Canada H3G 2T4. Dominick A. Merle, Ed. Factual accounts, 3,500 to 6,000 words, of "sensational crimes, preferably sex crimes, either pre-trial or after conviction." All articles will be considered for *Startling Detective, True Police Cases, Detective Files, Headquarters Detective, Detective Dragnet*, and *Detective Cases*. Query with pertinent information, including dates, site, names, etc. Pays $250 to $350, on acceptance; buys all rights.

HEADQUARTERS DETECTIVE—See *Globe Communications Corp.*

P.I. MAGAZINE: AMERICA'S PRIVATE INVESTIGATION JOURNAL—755 Bronx Ave., Toledo, OH 43609. Bob Mackowiak, Ed. Profiles of professional investigators containing true accounts of their most difficult cases. Pays $75 to $100, plus copies, on publication.

STARTLING DETECTIVE—See *Globe Communications Corp.*

TRUE POLICE CASES—See *Globe Communications Corp.*

MILITARY

AIR FORCE TIMES—See *Times News Service.*

AMERICAN SURVIVAL GUIDE—Y-Visionary, L.P., Ste. 120, 2655 Anita Dr., Orange, CA 92868-3310. Jim Benson, Ed. Articles, 1,500 to 2,000 words, with photos, on human and natural forces that pose threats to everyday life, all forms of preparedness, food production and storage, self defense and weapons, etc. All text must be accompanied by photos (and vice versa). Pays $80 per published page, on publication. Query.

AMERICA'S CIVIL WAR—Cowles History Group, 741 Miller Dr. S.E., Suite D-2, Leesburg, VA 20175. Roy Morris, Jr., Ed. Articles, 2,000 to 4,000 words, on the strategy, tactics, personalities, arms and equipment of the Civil War. Department pieces, 2,000 words. Query with illustration ideas. Pays from $150 to $300, on publication. Guidelines. SASE.

ARMY MAGAZINE—Box 1560, Arlington, VA 22210-0860. Mary B. French, Ed.-in-Chief. Features, 1,000 to 1,500 words, on military subjects. Essays, humor, history (especially World War II), news reports, first-person anecdotes. Pays 12¢ to 18¢ a word, $25 to $50 for anecdotes, on publication. Guidelines.

ARMY TIMES—See *Times News Service.*

COAST GUARD—Commandant (G-CP-2m),U.S. Coast Guard, 2100 2nd St. S.W., Washington, DC 20593-0001. Kenneth Arbogast, Ed. Articles on maritime topics, including search and rescue, law enforcement, maritime safety, protection of the marine environment, and related topics. Photos a plus. Pays in copies.

COMMAND—P.O. Box 4017, San Luis Obispo, CA 93403. Ty Bomba, Ed. Bimonthly. Articles, 800 to 10,000 words, on any facet of military history or current military affairs. "Popular, not scholarly, analytical military history." Pays 5¢ a word, on publication. Query.

FAMILY—169 Lexington Ave., New York, NY 10016. Don Hirst, Ed. Articles, 1,000 to 2,000 words, of interest to military women with children. Pays to $200, on publication. Guidelines.

MARINE CORPS GAZETTE—Box 1775, Quantico, VA 22134. Col. John E. Greenwood, Ed. Military articles, 500 to 2,000 words; features, 2,500 to 5,000 words; book reviews, 300 to 750 words. "Our magazine serves primarily as a forum for active duty officers to exchange views on professional, Marine Corps-related topics. Opportunity for 'outside' writers is limited." Queries preferred.

MILITARY—2122 28th St., Sacramento, CA 95818. Lt. Col. Michael Mark, Ed. Articles, 600 to 2,500 words, on firsthand experience in military service: World War II, Korea, Vietnam, and all current services. "Our magazine is about military history by the people who served. They are the best historians." No payment.

MILITARY HISTORY—741 Miller Dr. S.E., #D2, Leesburg, VA 20175. Jon Guttman, Ed. Bimonthly. Features, 4,000 words with 500-word sidebars, on strategy and tactics of military history. Department pieces, 2,000 words, on intrigue, personality, weaponry, perspectives, and travel. Pays $200 to $400, on publication. Query with illustration ideas. Guidelines. SASE.

NAVAL AVIATION NEWS—157-1 Washington Navy Yard, 901 M St. S.E., Washington, DC 20374-5059. Cdr. Jim Carlton, Ed. Bimonthly. Articles on Naval aviation history, technology, and news. No payment.

NAVY TIMES—See *Times News Service.*

OFF DUTY MAGAZINE—3505 Cadillac Ave., Suite O-105, Costa Mesa, CA 92626. Tom Graves, Man. Ed. Travel articles, 1,800 to 2,000 words, for active-duty military Americans (age 20 to 40) and their families worldwide. Must have wide scope; no out-of-the-way places. Military angle essential. Photos. Pays from 20¢ a word, extra for photos, on acceptance. Query required. Guidelines. Limited market.

THE RETIRED OFFICER MAGAZINE—201 N. Washington St., Alexandria, VA 22314. Attn: Manuscripts Ed. Articles, 1,800 to 2,000 words, of interest to military retirees and their families. Current military/political affairs, military history, health, money, military family lifestyles, and second-career job opportunities. Photos a plus. Pays to $1,300, on acceptance. Queries required; no unsolicited manuscripts. Guidelines.

TIMES NEWS SERVICE—Army Times Publishing Co., Springfield, VA 22159. Attn: R&R Ed. Free-lance material for "R&R" newspaper section. Articles about military life and its problems, as well as interesting things people are doing. Travel articles, 700 words, on places of interest to military people. Profiles, 600 to 700 words, on interesting members of the military community. Personal-experience essays, 750 words. No fiction or poetry. Pays $75 to $100, on acceptance. Also articles, up to 1,200 words, for supplements to *Army Times*, *Navy Times*, and *Air Force Times*. Address Supplements Ed. Pays $125 to $350, on acceptance. Guidelines.

VIETNAM—Cowles History Group, 741 Miller Dr. S.E., Suite D-2, Leesburg, VA 20175. Col. Harry G. Summers, Jr., Ed. Articles, 2,000 to 4,000 words, on the strategy, tactics, personalities, arms, and equipment of the Vietnam War. Pays from $150 to $300, on publication. Query with illustration ideas. Guidelines. SASE.

WORLD WAR II—Cowles History Group, 741 Miller Dr. S.E., Leesburg, VA 20175. Michael Haskew, Ed. Articles, 2,000 to 4,000 words, on the strategy, tactics, personalities, arms, and equipment of World War II. Department pieces, 2,000 words. Pays from $100 to $200, on publication. Query with illustration ideas. Guidelines. SASE.

HISTORY

ALABAMA HERITAGE—The Univ. of Alabama, Box 870342, Tuscaloosa, AL 35487-0342. Suzanne Wolfe, Ed. Quarterly. Articles, to 5,000 words, on local, state, and regional history: art, literature, language, archaeology, music, religion, architecture, and natural history. Pays an honorarium, on publication, plus 10 copies. Query, mentioning availability of photos and illustrations. Guidelines.

AMERICAN HERITAGE— 60 Fifth Ave., New York, NY 10011. Richard F. Snow, Ed. Articles, 750 to 5,000 words, on U.S. history and background of American life and culture from the beginning to recent times. No fiction. Pays from $300 to $1,500, on acceptance. Query.

AMERICAN HERITAGE OF INVENTION & TECHNOLOGY— 60 Fifth Ave., New York, NY 10011. Frederick Allen, Ed. Quarterly. Articles, 2,000 to 5,000 words, on history of technology in America, for the sophisticated general reader. Query. Pays on acceptance.

AMERICAN HISTORY— 6405 Flank Dr., Harrisburg, PA 17112. Attn: Ed. Articles, 3,000 to 5,000 words, soundly researched. Style should be popular, not scholarly. No travelogues, fiction, or puzzles. Pays $300 to $650, on acceptance. Query. No unsolicited manuscripts.

AMERICAN JEWISH HISTORY—American Jewish Historical Society, 2 Thornton Rd., Waltham, MA 02154. Dr. Marc Lee Raphael, Ed. Articles, 25 to 35 typed pages, on American Jewish history. Queries preferred. No payment.

AMERICA'S CIVIL WAR—Cowles History Group, 741 Miller Dr. S.E., Suite D-2, Leesburg, VA 20175-8920. Roy Morris, Jr., Ed. Articles, 3,500 to 4,000 words, on the strategy, tactics, personalities, arms and equipment of the Civil War. Department pieces, 2,000 words. Query with illustration ideas. Pays from $150 to $300, on publication. SASE. Visit website: www.thehist orynet.com.

ANCESTRY—P.O. Box 476, Salt Lake City, UT 84110. Loretto Szucs, Exec. Ed. Bimonthly for professional family historians and hobbyists who are interested in getting the most out of their research. Articles, 1,500 to 4,000 words, that instruct (how-tos, research techniques, etc.) and inform (new research sources, new collections, etc.). No family histories, genealogies, or pedigree charts. Pays $50 to $150, on publication. Guidelines.

AVIATION HISTORY—Cowles History Group, 741 Miller Dr. S.E., Suite D-2, Leesburg, VA 20175-8920. Attn: Eds. Bimonthly. Articles, 3,500 to 4,000 words with 500-word sidebars and excellent illustrations, on aeronautical history. Department pieces, 2,000 words. Pays $150 to $300, on publication. Query. SASE for guidelines. Visit website: www.thehistorynet.com.

THE BEAVER— 167 Lombard Ave., #478, Winnipeg, Manitoba, Canada R3B 0T6. A. Greenberg, Ed. Articles, 500 to 3,000 words, on Canadian history, "written to appeal to general readers." Payment varies, on publication. Queries preferred.

CAROLOGUE—South Carolina Historical Society, 100 Meeting St., Charleston, SC 29401-2299. Stephen Hoffius, Ed. General-interest articles, to 10 pages, on South Carolina history. Queries preferred. Pays in copies.

CHICAGO HISTORY—Clark St. at North Ave., Chicago, IL 60614. Rosemary Adams, Ed. Articles, to 4,500 words, on political, social, and cultural history of Chicago. Pays to $250, on publication. Query.

CIVIL WAR TIMES—6405 Flank Dr., Harrisburg, PA 17112. James Kushlan, Ed. Articles, 2,500 to 4,000 words, on the Civil War. "Accurate, annotated stories with strong narrative relying heavily on primary sources and the words of eyewitnesses. We prefer gripping, top-notch accounts of battles in the Eastern Theater of the war, and eyewitness accounts (memoirs, diaries, letters) and common soldier photos." Pays $400 to $650 for features, on acceptance. Query.

COMMAND—P.O. Box 4017, San Luis Obispo, CA 93403. Ty Bomba, Ed. Bimonthly. Articles, 800 to 10,000 words, on any facet of military history or current military affairs. "Popular, not scholarly, analytical military history." Pays 5¢ a word, on publication. Query.

EARLY AMERICAN HOMES—6405 Flank Dr., Harrisburg, PA 17112. Mimi Handler, Ed. Articles, 1,000 to 3,000 words, on early American life: arts, crafts, furnishings, history, and architecture before 1850. Pays $50 to $500, on acceptance. Query.

EIGHTEENTH-CENTURY STUDIES—Dept. of English, CB 3520, Greenlaw Hall, Univ. of North Carolina, Chapel Hill, NC 27599. Attn: Eds. Quarterly. Articles, to 6,500 words, on all aspects of the eighteenth century, especially those that are interdisciplinary or that are of general interest to scholars working in other disciplines. Blind submission policy: Submit 2 copies of manuscript; author's name and address should appear only on separate title page. No payment.

GOLDENSEAL—The Cultural Ctr., 1900 Kanawha Blvd. E., Charleston, WV 25305-0300. John Lilly, Ed. Features, 3,000 words, and shorter articles, 1,000 words, on traditional West Virginia culture and history. Oral histories, old and new B&W photos, research articles. Pays 10¢ a word, on publication. Guidelines.

THE GOLDFINCH—State Historical Society of Iowa, 402 Iowa Ave., Iowa City, IA 52240-1806. Millie Frese, Ed. Quarterly. Articles, 200 to 800 words, and short fiction on Iowa history for young people. "All articles must correspond to an upcoming theme." Pays $25 per article, on acceptance. Query for themes.

GOOD OLD DAYS—306 E. Parr Rd., Berne, IN 46711. Ken Tate, Ed. True stories (no fiction), 500 to 1,200 words, that took place between 1900 and 1955. Departments include: "Good Old Days on Wheels," about period autos, planes, trolleys, and other transportation; "Good Old Days in the Kitchen," favorite foods, appliances, recipes; "Home Remedies," hometown doctors, herbs and poultices, harrowing kitchen table operations, etc. Pays $15 to $75, on publication.

THE HIGHLANDER—P.O. Box 22307, Kansas City, MO 64113. Crennan M. Wade, Ed. Bimonthly. Articles, 1,300 to 2,200 words, related to Scottish history. "We do not use any articles on modern Scotland or current problems in Scotland." Pays $100 to $150, on acceptance. Photos must accompany manuscripts.

HISTORIC TRAVELER— 6405 Flank Dr., Harrisburg, PA 17112. Tom Huntington, Ed. Bimonthly. Articles, 800 to 2,500 words, for upscale readers with a strong interest in history and historic sites. "Accurate information on historic destinations. Possible topics: battlefields, museums, antique shows, events, hotels, inns, transportation, reenactments, preserved communities, and architectural wonders. No South Pacific Islands, Alpine skiing, or Mediterranean cruises." Pays $300 to $500, on acceptance. Query with SASE and clips. Guidelines.

JOURNAL OF THE WEST—1531 Yuma, Box 1009, Manhattan, KS 66505-1009. Robin Higham, Ed. Articles, to 15 pages, devoted to the history and the culture of the West, then and now. B&W photos. Pays in copies or subscription.

KENTUCKE: THE MAGAZINE OF BLUEGRASS STATE HERITAGE— P.O. Box 1873, Ashland, KY 41105. William E. Ellis, Ed. Bimonthly. Articles, to 2,500 words, on local, regional, and state heritage, including agricultural, architectural, literary, military, natural, pioneer and political history. Pays honorarium plus copies, on publication. Query with clips mentioning availability of photos.

LABOR'S HERITAGE— 10000 New Hampshire Ave., Silver Spring, MD 20903. Quarterly journal of The George Meany Memorial Archives. Articles, 80 pages, for labor scholars, labor union members, and the general public. Pays in copies.

MILITARY HISTORY—741 Miller Dr. S.E., #D2, Leesburg, VA 20175-8920. Jon Guttman, Ed. Bimonthly. Features, 4,000 words with 500-word sidebars, on the strategy, tactics, and personalities of military history. Department pieces, 2,000 words, on espionage, weaponry, personalities, perspectives, and travel. Pays $200 to $400, on publication. Query. SASE for guidelines. Visit website: www.thehistorynet.com.

MONTANA JOURNAL—P.O. Box 4087, Missoula, MT 59806. Mike Haser, Ed. Bimonthly tabloid. Human-interest articles, to 1,000 words, about the people, places, and events that helped build Montana. Pays 2¢ a word, on publication. Query preferred.

MONTANA, THE MAGAZINE OF WESTERN HISTORY—225 N. Roberts St., Box 201201, Helena, MT 59620-1201. Charles E. Rankin, Ed. Authentic articles, 3,500 to 5,500 words, on the history of the American and Canadian West; new interpretive approaches to major developments in western history. Footnotes or bibliography must accompany article. "Strict historical accuracy is essential." No fiction. Queries preferred. No payment made.

NEBRASKA HISTORY—P.O. Box 82554, Lincoln, NE 68501. James E. Potter, Ed. Articles, 3,000 to 7,000 words, relating to the history of Nebraska and the Great Plains. B&W line drawings. Allow 60 days for response. Pays in copies. Cash prize awarded to one article each year.

NOW & THEN—CASS/ETSU, P.O. Box 70556, Johnson City, TN 37614-0556. Jane Harris Woodside, Ed. Fiction and nonfiction, 1,500 to 3,000 words: short stories, articles, interviews, essays, memoirs, book reviews. Pieces must be related to theme of issue and have some connection to the Appalachian region. Also photos and drawings. SASE for guidelines and current themes. Pays $15 to $75, on publication.

OLD WEST—P.O. Box 2107, Stillwater, OK 74076. Marcus Huff, Ed. Thoroughly researched and documented articles, 1,500 to 4,500 words, on the history of the American West. B&W 5x7 photos to illustrate articles. Queries are preferred. Pays 3¢ to 6¢ a word, on acceptance.

PENNSYLVANIA HERITAGE—P.O. Box 1026, Harrisburg, PA 17108-1026. Michael J. O'Malley III, Ed. Quarterly of the Pennsylvania Historical and Museum Commission and the Pennsylvania Heritage Society. Articles, 2,500 to 3,500 words, that "introduce readers to the state's rich culture and historic legacy. Seeks unusual and fresh angle to make history come to life, including pictorial or photo essays, interviews, travel/destination pieces." Prefers to see complete manuscript. Pays to $500, up to $100 for photos or drawings, on acceptance.

PERSIMMON HILL—1700 N.E. 63rd St., Oklahoma City, OK 73111. M.J. Van Deventer, Ed. Published by the National Cowboy Hall of Fame. Articles, 1,500 words, on western history and art, cowboys, ranching, and nature. Top-quality illustrations with captions a must. Pays from $150 to $250, on publication.

PROLOGUE—National Archives, NPOL, 8601 Adelphi Rd., College Park, MD 20740-6001. Quarterly. Articles, varying lengths, based on the holdings and programs of the National Archives, its regional archives, and the presidential libraries. Query. Pays in copies.

RENAISSANCE MAGAZINE—Phantom Press Publications, 13 Appleton Rd., Nantucket, MA 02554. Kim Guarnaccia, Ed. Feature articles on Renaissance and Medieval history, reenactment roleplaying, and Renaissance faires. Interviews, reviews of Medieval and Renaissance books, music, movies, and games. Pays 4¢ a word, on publication.

RUSSIAN LIFE— 89 Main St., #2, Montpelier, VT 05602-2948. Mikhail Ivanov, Ed. Articles, 1,000 to 3,000 words, on Russian culture, travel, history, politics, art, business, and society. "We do not want stories about personal trips to Russia, editorials on developments in Russia, or articles that promote the services of a specific company, organization, or government agency." Pays 7¢ to 10¢ a word; $20 to $30 per photo, on publication. Query.

SCOTTISH JOURNAL—P.O. Box 3165, Barrington, IL 60011. Angus J. Ray, Ed. Articles, 1,500 to 2,000 words, on Scottish history, famous Scots, clans, battles. Travel pieces on specific areas in Scotland. Queries preferred. Pays $150 to $200, on acceptance.

SOUTH CAROLINA HISTORICAL MAGAZINE—South Carolina Historical Society, 100 Meeting St., Charleston, SC 29401-2299. Stephen Hoffius, Ed. Scholarly articles, to 25 pages including footnotes, on South Carolina history. "Authors are encouraged to look at previous issues to be aware of previous scholarship." Pays in copies.

TRUE WEST—P.O. Box 2107, Stillwater, OK 74076-2107. Marcus Huff, Ed. True stories, 500 to 4,500 words, with photos, about the Old West to 1930. Some contemporary stories with historical slant. Source list required. Pays 3¢ to 6¢ a word, extra for B&W photos, on acceptance.

VIETNAM—Cowles History Group, 741 Miller Dr. S.E., Suite D-2, Leesburg, VA 20175-8920. Col. Harry G. Summers, Jr., Ed. Articles, 2,000 to 4,000 words, on the strategy, tactics, personalities, arms, and equipment of the Vietnam War. Pays $150 to $300, on publication. Query with illustration ideas. SASE. Visit website: www.thehistorynet.com.

THE WESTERN HISTORICAL QUARTERLY— Utah State Univ., Logan, UT 84322-0740. Anne M. Butler, Ed. Original articles about the American West, the Westward movement from the Atlantic to the Pacific, twentieth-century regional studies, Spanish borderlands, Canada, northern Mexico, Alaska, and Hawaii. No payment made.

WILD WEST—741 Miller Dr., S.E., #D-2, Leesburg, VA 20175-8920. Gregory Lalire, Ed. Bimonthly. Features, to 4,000 words, with 500-word side-bars, and department pieces, 2,000 words, on Western history from the earliest North American settlements to the end of the 19th century. Pays $150 to $300, on publication. Query with SASE. Visit website: www.thehistorynet.com.

WORLD WAR II— Cowles History Group, 741 Miller Dr. S.E., Suite D-2, Leesburg, VA 20175-8920. Michael Haskew, Ed. Articles, 3,500 to 4,000 words, on the strategy, tactics, personalities, arms, and equipment of World War II. Pays $100 to $200, on publication. Query with illustration ideas. SASE for editorial guidelines. Website: www.thehistorynet.com.

YESTERDAY'S MAGAZETTE—P.O. Box 18566, Sarasota, FL 34276. Ned Burke, Ed. Articles and fiction, to 1,000 words, on the 1920s to the 1970s, nostalgia and memories of people, places, and things. Traditional poetry, to 24 lines. Pays $5 to $25, on publication. Pays in copies for poetry and short pieces. Guidelines.

COLLEGE, CAREERS

THE BLACK COLLEGIAN—140 Carondelet St., New Orleans, LA 70130. James Perry, Ed. Articles, to 1,600 words, on entry-level career oppor-tunities, the job search process, how-to prepare for entry-level positions, what to expect as an entry-level professional, and culture and experiences of African-American collegians. Audience: African-American juniors and se-niors. Pays on publication. Query.

BYLINE—Box 130596, Edmond, OK 73013. Marcia Preston, Ed.-in-Chief. General fiction, 2,000 to 4,000 words. Nonfiction: 1,500-to 1,800-word features and 300-to 750-word special departments. Poetry, 10 to 30 lines pre-ferred. Nonfiction and poetry must be about writing. Humor, 200 to 600 words, about writing. "We seek practical and motivational material that tells writers how they can succeed, not why they can't. Overdone topics: writers' block, the muse, rejection slips." Pays $5 to $10 for poetry; $15 to $35 for depart-ments; $50 for features and $100 for short fiction, on acceptance.

CAMPUS LIFE— 465 Gundersen Dr., Carol Stream, IL 60188. Harold Smith, V.P./Ed. Articles reflecting Christian values and world view, for high school and college students. Humor, general fiction, and true, first-person ex-periences. "If we have a choice of fiction, how-to, and a strong first-person story, we'll go with the true story every time." Photo-essays, cartoons. Pays 15¢ to 20¢ a word, on acceptance. Query.

CAREER DIRECTIONS—21 N. Henry St., Edgerton, WI 53534. Diane Everson, Pres. and Pub. Tabloid. "Current News & Career Opportunities for Students." Career-related articles, 500 to 1,500 words, especially how-to. Pays $50 to $150, on acceptance. Also publishes the newsletter *Career Waves*, for career development professionals.

CAREER WAVES— See *Career Directions*.

CAREER WORLD—GLC., 900 Skokie Blvd., Suite 200, Northbrook, IL 60062-4028. Carole Rubenstein, Sr. Ed. Published 7 times a year, September through April/May. Gender-neutral articles about specific occupations and career awareness and development for junior and senior high school audience. Query with clips and resumé. Payment varies, on publication.

CAREERS AND...—See *Careers and the College Grad.*

CAREERS AND THE COLLEGE GRAD—201 Broadway, Cambridge, MA 02139. Kathleen Grimes, Pub. Annual. Career-related articles, 1,500 to 2,000 words, for junior and senior liberal arts students. Career-related fillers, 500 words and line art or color prints. Queries preferred. No payment. Same address and requirements for *Careers and the MBA* (semiannual) for first- and second-year MBA students; *Careers and the Engineer* (semiannual) for junior and senior engineering students; *Careers and the Minority Lawyer* (semiannual) for law school students; *Careers and the International MBA; Careers and the Woman MBA; Careers and the Minority MBA*; and *Careers and the Minority Undergraduate.*

CAREERS & THE DISABLED—See *Minority Engineer.*

CIRCLE K—3636 Woodview Trace, Indianapolis, IN 46268-3196. Nicholas K. Drake, Exec. Ed. Serious and light articles, 1,500 to 1,700 words, on careers, college issues, trends, leadership development, self-help, community service and involvement. Pays $200 to $400, on acceptance. Queries preferred.

COLLEGE BOUND MAGAZINE—2071 Clove Rd., Suite 206, Staten Island, NY 10304. Gina LaGuardia, Ed. Features, 600 to 1,000 words, and department pieces, 50 to 300 words, that offer high school students a view of college life. Especially interested in personal accounts by current college students. Pays $25 to $100, on publication.

EQUAL OPPORTUNITY—See *Minority Engineer.*

FLORIDA LEADER—c/o Oxendine Publishing, P.O. Box 14081, Gainesville, FL 32604-2081. Kay Quinn, Man. Ed. Published 3 times a year. Articles, 800 to 1,000 words, for Florida college students. "Focus on leadership, college success, profiles of growth careers in Florida and the Southeast." Pays $35 to $75, on publication.

INSIDER MAGAZINE—4124 W. Oakton, Skokie, IL 60201. Rita Coole, Ed. Dir. Articles, 700, 1,500, and 2,100 words, on issues, careers, politics, sports, and entertainment for readers ages 18 to 34. Pays 1¢ to 3¢ a word, on publication. Query for themes.

LINK: THE COLLEGE MAGAZINE—The Soho Building, 110 Greene St., Suite 407, New York, NY 10012. Ty Wenger, Ed.-in-Chief. News, lifestyle, and issues for college students. Informational how-to and short features, 300 to 500 words, on education news, finances, academics, employment, lifestyles, and trends. Well-researched, insightful, authoritative articles, 2,000 to 3,000 words. Pays $500 to $1,500, on publication. Queries preferred. Guidelines.

MINORITY ENGINEER—1160 E. Jericho Turnpike, Suite 200, Huntington, NY 11743. James Schneider, Ed. Articles, 1,000 to 1,500 words, for college students, on career opportunities; techniques of job hunting; developments in and applications of new technologies. Interviews. Profiles. Pays 10¢ a word, on publication. Query. Same address and requirements for *Woman Engineer* (address Anne Kelly), and *Equal Opportunity* and *Careers & the DisABLED* (address James Schneider).

STUDY BREAKS MAGAZINE—600 W. 28th St., #103, Austin, TX 78705. Gal Shweiki, Pub. Fillers, humor, jokes, etc., of interest to students at The Univ. of Texas at Austin, Texas Tech. Univ., Texas A & M Univ., Southwest Texas State Univ., and The Univ. of North Texas. Pays $15.

UCLA MAGAZINE—10920 Wilshire Blvd., Suite 1500, Los Angeles, CA 90024. Jeffrey Hirsch, Ed. Quarterly. Articles, 2,000 words, must be related to UCLA through research, alumni, students, etc. Pays to $2,000, on acceptance. Queries required.

UNIQUE OPPORTUNITIES—455 S. 4th Ave., #1236, Louisville, KY 40202. Bett Coffman, Assoc. Ed. Articles, 2,000 to 3,000 words, that cover economic, business, and career-related issues of interest to physicians who are looking for their first practice or looking to make a career move. Doctor profiles, 500 words. "Our goal is to educate physicians about how to evaluate career opportunities, negotiate the benefits offered, plan career moves, and provide information on the legal and economic aspects of accepting a position." Pays 50¢ a word for features; $200 for profiles, on acceptance. Query.

WOMAN ENGINEER—See *Minority Engineer.*

OP-ED MARKETS

THE ARGUS LEADER—P.O. Box 5034, Sioux Falls, SD 57117-5034. Pam Terrell, Editorial Page Ed. Articles, to 850 words, on a wide variety of subjects for "Readers' Forum" column. "We very rarely accept out-of-state columns." No payment. Guidelines.

THE ATLANTA CONSTITUTION—P.O. Box 4689, Atlanta, GA 30302. Teresa Weaver, Op-Ed Ed. Articles related to the Southeast, Georgia, or the Atlanta metropolitan area, 200 to 800 words, on a variety of topics: law, economics, politics, science, environment, performing and manipulative arts, humor, education; religious and seasonal topics. Pays $75 to $125, on publication. Submit complete manuscript.

THE BALTIMORE SUN—P.O. Box 1377, Baltimore, MD 21278-0001. Hal Piper, Opinion-Commentary Page Ed. Articles, 600 to 1,500 words, on a wide range of topics: politics, education, foreign affairs, lifestyles, etc. Humor. Payment varies, on publication. Exclusive rights: MD and DC.

THE BOSTON GLOBE—P.O. Box 2378, Boston, MA 02107-2378. Marjorie Pritchard, Ed. Articles, to 700 words, on economics, education, environment, foreign affairs, and regional interest. Pays $100, on publication. Send complete manuscript. Exclusive rights: New England.

BOSTON HERALD—One Herald Sq., Boston, MA 02106. Attn: Editorial Page Ed. Pieces, 600 to 800 words, on economics, foreign affairs, politics, regional interest, and seasonal topics. Prefer submissions from regional writers. Payment varies, on publication. Exclusive rights: MA, RI, and NH.

THE CHARLOTTE OBSERVER—P.O. Box 30308, Charlotte, NC 28230-0308. Jane Pope, Deputy Ed., Editorial Pages. Well-written, thought-provoking articles, to 700 words. "We are only interested in articles on local (Carolinas) issues or that use local examples to illustrate other issues." Pays $50, on publication. No simultaneous submissions in NC or SC.

THE CHICAGO TRIBUNE—435 N. Michigan Ave., Chicago, IL 60611. Marcia Lythcott, Op-Ed Page Ed. Pieces, 800 words, on domestic and international affairs, environment, regional interest, and personal essays. SASE required.

THE CHRISTIAN SCIENCE MONITOR—One Norway St., Boston, MA 02115. Clara Germani, Opinion Page Ed. Pieces, 400 to 900 words, on domestic and foreign affairs, economics, education, environment, law, media, politics, and cultural commentary. Pays up to $250, on acceptance. Retains all rights for 90 days after publication.

THE CLEVELAND PLAIN DEALER—1801 Superior Ave., Cleveland, OH 44114. Gloria Millner, Assoc. Ed. Pieces, 700 to 800 words, on a wide variety of subjects. Pays $75, on publication.

DALLAS MORNING NEWS—Communications Ctr., P.O. Box 655237, Dallas, TX 75265. Bob Moos, "Viewpoints" Ed. Pieces, 750 words, on politics, education, foreign and domestic affairs, cultural trends, seasonal and regional issues. Pay averages $75, on publication. SASE required. Exclusive rights: Dallas/Ft. Worth area.

DENVER POST—P.O. Box 1709, Denver, CO 80201. Bob Ewegen, Ed. Articles, 400 to 700 words, with local or regional angle. No payment for freelance submissions. Query.

DES MOINES REGISTER—P.O. Box 957, Des Moines, IA 50304. Attn: "Opinion" Page Ed. Articles, 500 to 750 words, on all topics. Prefer Iowa subjects. Pays $50 to $75, on publication. Exclusive rights: IA.

DETROIT FREE PRESS—321 W. Lafayette Blvd., Detroit, MI 48226. Attn: Op-Ed Ed. Opinion pieces, to 800 words, on domestic and foreign affairs, economics, education, environment, law, politics, and regional interest. Priority given to local writers or topics of local interest. Pays $50 to $100, on pulication. Query. Exclusive rights: MI and northern OH.

THE DETROIT NEWS—615 W. Lafayette Blvd., Detroit, MI 48226. Attn: Richard Burr. Pieces, 500 to 750 words, on a wide variety of subjects. Pays $75, on publication.

THE FLINT JOURNAL—200 E. First St., Flint, MI 48502-1925. Carlton Winfrey, Opinion Dept. Ed. Articles, 650 words, of regional interest by local writers. Non-local writers should query. No payment. Limited market.

FRESNO BEE—1626 E St., Fresno, CA 93786-0001. James Boren, Editorial Page Editor. Articles, 750 words, by central California writers only.

INDIANAPOLIS STAR—P.O. Box 145, Indianapolis, IN 46206-0145. John H. Lyst, Ed. Articles, 700 to 800 words. Pays $40, on publication. Exclusive rights: IN.

LONG BEACH PRESS-TELEGRAM—604 Pine Ave., Long Beach, CA 90844. Larry Allison, Ed. Articles, 750 to 900 words, on regional topics. Pays $75, on publication. Exclusive rights: Los Angeles area.

LOS ANGELES TIMES—Times Mirror Sq., Los Angeles, CA 90053. Bob Berger, Op-Ed Ed. Commentary pieces, 650 to 700 words, on many subjects. "Not interested in nostalgia or first-person reaction to faraway events. Pieces must be exclusive." Payment varies, on publication. Limited market. SASE required.

THE NEW YORK TIMES—229 W. 43rd St., New York, NY 10036. Attn: Op-Ed Ed. Opinion pieces, 650 to 800 words, on any topic, including public policy, science, lifestyles, and ideas, etc. Include your address, daytime phone number, and social security number with submission. "If you haven't heard from us within 2 weeks, you can assume we are not using your piece. Include SASE if you want work returned." Pays on publication. Buys first North American rights.

NEWSDAY—"Viewpoints," 235 Pinelawn Rd., Melville, NY 11747. Noel Rubinton, "Viewpoints" Ed. Pieces, 700 to 800 words, on a variety of topics. Pays $150, on publication.

THE ORANGE COUNTY REGISTER—P.O. Box 11626, Santa Ana, CA 92711. Cathy Taylor, Ed. Dir. Articles on a wide range of local and national issues and topics. Pays $50 to $100, on publication.

THE OREGONIAN—1320 S.W. Broadway, Portland, OR 97201. Attn: Opinion & Commentary Ed. Articles, 900 to 1,000 words, of news analysis from Pacific Northwest writers or on regional topics. Pays $100 to $150, on publication. Send complete manuscript.

PITTSBURGH POST GAZETTE—34 Blvd. of the Allies, Pittsburgh, PA 15222. John Allison, Contributions Ed. Articles, to 1,000 words, on a variety of subjects. No whimsy. Pays $60 to $150, on publication. SASE required.

THE REGISTER GUARD—P.O. Box 10188, Eugene, OR 97440. Don Robinson, Editorial Page Ed. All subjects; regional angle preferred. Pays $25 to $50, on publication. Very limited use of non-local writers.

THE SACRAMENTO BEE—2100 Q St., Sacramento, CA 95852. Jewel A. Reilly, Op-Ed Ed. Op-ed pieces, to 750 words; state and regional topics preferred. Pays $150, on publication.

ST. LOUIS POST-DISPATCH—900 N. Tucker Blvd., St. Louis, MO 63101. Donna Korando, Commentary Ed. Articles, 700 words, on economics, education, science, politics, foreign and domestic affairs, and the environment. Pays $70, on publication. "Goal is to have at least half of the articles by local writers."

ST. PAUL PIONEER PRESS—345 Cedar St., St. Paul, MN 55101. Ronald D. Clark, Ed. Articles, to 750 words, on a variety of topics. Strongly prefer authors or topics with a connection to the area. Pays $75, on publication.

ST. PETERSBURG TIMES—Box 1121, 490 First Ave. S., St. Petersburg, FL 33731. Jon East, "Perspective" Section Ed. Authoritative articles, to 2,000 words, on current political, economic, and social issues. Payment varies, on publication. Query.

THE SAN FRANCISCO CHRONICLE—901 Mission St., San Francisco, CA 94103. Dean Wakefield, Open Forum Ed. Articles, 400 and 650 words, "that represent lively writing, are pertinent to public policy debates, and move the debate forward." Pays to $150 (usually $75 to $100 for unsolicited pieces), on publication.

SAN FRANCISCO EXAMINER—110 5th St., San Francisco, CA 94103. Attn: Op-Ed Ed. Well-written articles, 500 to 650 words, double-spaced; preference given to local and state issues and to subjects bypassed by most news media. No sports. No first-run movies. Payment varies, on publication.

SEATTLE POST-INTELLIGENCER—P.O. Box 1909, Seattle, WA 98111. Joann Byrd, Editorial Page Ed. Articles, 750 to 800 words, on foreign and domestic affairs, environment, education, politics, regional interest, religion, science, and seasonal material. Prefer writers who live in the Pacific Northwest. Pays $75 to $150, on publication. SASE required. Very limited market.

USA TODAY—1000 Wilson Blvd., Arlington, VA 22229. Juan J. Walte, Ed./Columns. Articles, 700 to 1,000 words, that cover American culture, politics, economics and "the real lives people live with the twist of strong opinion." No unnamed sources or composite anecdotes. Pays $300, on publication. Send complete manuscript to Op-Ed Editor.

THE WALL STREET JOURNAL—Editorial Page, 200 Liberty St., New York, NY 10281. David B. Brooks, Op-Ed Ed. Articles, to 1,500 words, on politics, economics, law, education, environment, humor (occasionally), and foreign and domestic affairs. Articles must be timely, heavily reported, and of national interest by writers with expertise in their field. Pays $150 to $300, on publication.

WASHINGTON TIMES—3600 New York Ave. N.E., Washington, DC 20002. Frank Perley, Articles and Opinion Page Ed. Articles, 800 to 1,000 words, on a variety of subjects. No pieces written in the first-person. "Syndicated columnists cover the 'big' issues; find an area that is off the beaten path." Pays $150, on publication. Exclusive rights: Washington, DC, and Baltimore area.

ADULT MAGAZINES

CHIC—8484 Wilshire Blvd., Suite 900, Beverly Hills, CA 90211. Scott Schalin, Lisa Jenio, Exec. Eds. Sex-related articles, interviews, erotic fiction, 2,500 words. Query for articles. Pays $150 for brief interviews, $350 for fiction, on acceptance.

GENESIS—210 Route 4 E., Suite 401, Paramus, NJ 07652. Paul Gambino, Ed. Dir. Dan Davis, Man. Ed. Sexually explicit fiction and nonfiction features, 800 to 2,000 words. Celebrity interviews, photo-essays, product and film reviews. Pays on publication. Query with clips.

PENTHOUSE—277 Park Ave., 4th Fl., New York, NY 10172-0003. Peter Bloch, Ed. Lavada B. Nahon, Sr. Ed. Articles, to 5,000 words: general-interest profiles, interviews (with introduction), and investigative pieces. Pays on acceptance.

PLAYBOY—680 N. Lake Shore Dr., Chicago, IL 60611. Stephen Randall, Exec. Ed. Articles, 3,500 to 6,000 words, and sophisticated fiction, 1,000 to 10,000 words (5,000 preferred), for urban men. Humor; satire. Science fiction. Pays to $5,000 for articles and fiction, $2,000 for short-shorts, on acceptance.

PLAYGIRL—801 Second Ave., New York, NY 10017. Charlene Keel Razaek, Man. Ed. Articles, 1,500 to 4,000 words, for women 18 and older. Pays varying rates, on acceptance.

VARIATIONS, FOR LIBERATED LOVERS—277 Park Ave., New York, NY 10172. V. K. McCarty, Ed. Dir./Assoc. Pub. First-person true narrative descriptions of "a couple's enthusiasm, secrets, and exquisitely articulated sex scenes squarely focused within one of the magazine's pleasure categories." Pays $400, on acceptance.

FICTION MARKETS

This list gives the fiction requirements of general-and special-interest magazines, including those that publish detective and mystery, science fiction and fantasy, romance and confession stories. Other good markets for short fiction are the *College, Literary, and Little Magazines* where, though payment is modest (usually in copies only), publication can bring the work of a beginning writer to the attention of editors at the larger magazines. Juvenile fiction markets are listed under *Juvenile, Teenage, and Young Adult Magazines.* Publishers of book-length fiction manuscripts are listed under *Book Publishers.*

GENERAL FICTION

ABORIGINAL SF—P.O. Box 2449, Woburn, MA 01888-0849. Charles C. Ryan, Ed. Stories, 2,500 to 7,500 words, with a unique scientific idea, human or alien character, plot, and theme of lasting value; "must be science fiction; no fantasy, horror, or sword and sorcery." Pays $200. Send SASE for guidelines.

AFRICAN VOICES—270 W. 96th St., New York, NY 10025. Carolyn A. Butts, Exec. Ed. Quarterly. Humorous, erotic, and dramatic fiction, 500 to 2,500 words, by ethnic writers. Nonfiction, 500 to 1,500 words: investigative articles, artist profiles, essays, and first-person narratives. Poetry, to 50 lines. Pays $25 for fiction, on publication, plus 5 copies of magazine. (Payment varies for nonfiction.)

AIM MAGAZINE—P.O. Box 1174,, Maywood,, IL 60153. Myron Apilado, Ed. Short stories, 800 to 3,000 words, geared to proving that people from different backgrounds are more alike than they are different. Story should not moralize. Pays from $15 to $25, on publication. Annual contest. $100 prize.

ALFRED HITCHCOCK MYSTERY MAGAZINE—1270 Ave. of the Americas, New York, NY 10020. Cathleen Jordan, Ed. Well-plotted, plausible mystery, suspense, detection and crime stories, to 14,000 words; "ghost stories, humor, futuristic or atmospheric tales are all possible, as long as they include a crime or the suggestion of one." Pays 8¢ a word, on acceptance. Guidelines with SASE.

ALOHA, THE MAGAZINE OF HAWAII AND THE PACIFIC—P.O. Box 3260, Honolulu, HI 96801. Cheryl Tsutsumi, Ed. Fiction to 2,000 words, with a Hawaii focus. Pays $150 to $300, on publication. Query.

THE AMERICAN VOICE—332 W. Broadway, Suite 1215, Louisville, KY 40202. Frederick Smock, Ed. Avant-garde, literary fiction, nonfiction, and well-crafted poetry, any length (shorter works are preferred). "Please read our journal before attempting to submit. Interested in work from all the Americas; translations, new writers, etc." Payment varies, on publication.

ANALOG SCIENCE FICTION AND FACT—1270 Ave. of the Americas, New York, NY 10020. Stanley Schmidt, Ed. Science fiction, with strong characters in believable future or alien setting: short stories, 2,000 to 7,500 words; novelettes, 10,000 to 20,000 words; serials, to 70,000 words. Include SASE. Pays 5¢ to 8¢ a word, on acceptance. Query for novels.

ASIMOV'S SCIENCE FICTION MAGAZINE—1270 Ave. of the Americas, New York, NY 10020. Gardner Dozois, Ed. Short science fiction and fantasies, to 15,000 words. Pays 6¢ to 8¢ a word, on acceptance. Guidelines. Website: www.asimovs.com

THE ATLANTIC MONTHLY—77 N. Washington St., Boston, MA 02114. William Whitworth, Ed. Short stories, 2,000 to 6,000 words, of highest literary quality, with "fully developed narratives, distinctive characterization, freshness in language, and a resolution of some kind." SASE. Pays $2,500, on acceptance.

THE BELLETRIST REVIEW—Marmarc Publications, P.O. Box 596, Plainville, CT 06062. Marlene Dube, Ed. Semiannual. Fiction, 1,500 to 5,000 words: adventure, contemporary, erotica, psychological horror, humor, literary, mainstream, suspense, and mystery. No fantasy, juvenile, westerns, overblown horror, or confessional pieces. Annual fiction contest; send SASE for guidelines. Pays in copies.

THE BOSTON GLOBE MAGAZINE—*The Boston Globe*, Boston, MA 02107. Evelynne Kramer, Ed. Short stories, to 3,000 words. Include SASE. Pays on acceptance.

BOYS' LIFE—1325 W. Walnut Hill Ln., P.O. Box 152079, Irving, TX 75015-2079. Shannon Lowry, Fiction Ed. Publication of the Boy Scouts of America. Humor, mystery, science fiction, adventure, 1,200 words, for 8- to 18-year-old boys; study back issues. Pays from $750, on acceptance. Send SASE for guidelines. Send complete manuscript; no queries.

BUFFALO SPREE MAGAZINE—Box 38, Buffalo, NY 14226. Johanna Van De Mark, Ed./Pub. Fiction and humor, to 2,000 words, for thoughtful, intelligent readers in the western New York region. Pays $125 to $150, on publication.

BYLINE—Box 130596, Edmond, OK 73013. Marcia Preston, Ed.-in-Chief. Kathryn Fanning, Man. Ed. General fiction, 2,000 to 4,000 words. Nonfiction: 1,500- to 1,800-word features and 300- to 750-word special departments. Poetry, 10 to 30 lines preferred. Nonfiction and poetry must be about writing. Humor, 100 to 600 words, about writing. "We seek practical and motivational material that tells writers how they can succeed, not why they can't. Overdone topics: writers' block, the muse, rejection slips." Pays $5 to $10 for poetry; $15 to $35 for departments; $50 for features; and $100 for short fiction, on acceptance. SASE for guidelines or see Web page: http://www.bylinemag.com.

CAPPER'S—1503 S.W. 42nd St., Topeka, KS 66609-1265. Ann Crahan, Ed. Fiction, 7,500 to 40,000 words (12,000 to 20,000 words preferred), for serialization. No profanity, violence, or explicit sex. Pays $75 to $300, on publication.

CATHOLIC FORESTER—355 Shuman Blvd., P.O. Box 3012, Naperville, IL 60566-7012. Dorothy Deer, Ed. Official publication of the Catholic Order of Foresters. Fiction, to 1,200 words (prefer shorter); "looking for more contemporary, meaningful stories dealing with life today." No sex, violence, romance, or "preachy" stories; religious angle not required. Pays 20¢ a word, on acceptance.

CHESS LIFE—3054 NYS Rte. 9W, New Windsor, NY 12553-7698. Glenn Petersen, Ed. Fiction, 500 to 2,000 words, related to chess for members of the U.S. Chess Federation. Also, articles, 500 to 3,000 words, on chess news, profiles, technical aspects of chess. Pays varying rates, on acceptance. Query; limited market.

COBBLESTONE: DISCOVER AMERICAN HISTORY—30 Grove St., Suite C, Peterborough, NH 03458-1454. Meg Chorlian, Ed. Historical fiction, 500 to 800 words, for children aged 8 to 14 years; must relate to theme. Pays 20¢ to 25¢ a word, on publication. Send SASE for guidelines.

COMMON GROUND MAGAZINE—P.O. Box 99, McVeytown, PA 17051-0099. Ruth Dunmire and Pam Brumbaugh, Eds. Quarterly. Fiction, 1,000 to 2,000 words, related to Central Pennsylvania's Juniata River Valley. Pays $25 to $200, on publication. Guidelines.

COSMOPOLITAN—224 W. 57th St., New York, NY 10019. Alison Broner, Senior Books Ed. Novel excerpts; submissions must be sent by a publisher or agent. Payment rates are negotiable. SASE.

COUNTRY WOMAN—P.O. Box 989, Greendale, WI 53129. Kathy Pohl, Man. Ed. Fiction, 750 to 1,000 words, of interest to rural women; protagonist must be a country woman. "Stories should focus on life in the country, its problems and joys, as experienced by country women; must be upbeat and positive." Pays $90 to $125, on acceptance.

CRICKET—P.O. Box 300, Peru, IL 61354-0300. Marianne Carus, Ed.-in-Chief. Fiction, 200 to 2,000 words, for 9- to 14-year-olds. Pays to 25¢ a word, on publication. SASE.

DISCOVERIES—WordAction Publishing Co., 6401 The Paseo, Kansas City, MO 64131. Attn: Asst. Ed. Weekly take-home paper designed to correlate with Evangelical Sunday school curriculum. Fiction, 500 words, for 8- to 10-year-olds. Stories should feature contemporary, true-to-life characters and should illustrate character building and scriptural application. No poetry. Pays 5¢ a word, on publication. Send SASE for guidelines and theme list.

DOGWOOD TALES MAGAZINE—P.O. Box 172068, Memphis, TN 38187. Attn: Ed. Bimonthly "for the fiction lover in all of us." Short stories, 250 to 4,500 words (prefer no more than 3,000 words), in any genre except religion or pornography. "Stories should be fresh, well-paced, and have strong endings." Pays on acceptance. Contests. SASE for guidelines.

ELLERY QUEEN'S MYSTERY MAGAZINE—1270 Ave. of the Americas, 10th Fl., New York, NY 10020. Janet Hutchings, Ed. High-quality detective, crime, and mystery stories, 1,500 to 10,000 words. Also "Minute Mysteries," 250 words, short verses, limericks, and novellas, to 17,000 words. "We like a mix of classic detection and suspenseful crime." "First Stories" by unpublished writers. Pays 3¢ to 8¢ a word, occasionally higher for established authors, on acceptance.

ESQUIRE—250 W. 55th St., New York, NY 10019. David Granger, Ed.-in-Chief. Send finished manuscript of short story; submit one at a time. No full-length novels. No pornography, science fiction, poetry, or "true romance" stories. Include SASE.

EVANGEL—Light and Life Communications, P.O. Box 535002, Indianapolis, IN 46253-5002. Julie Innes, Ed. Free Methodist. Fiction and nonfiction, to 1,200 words, with personal faith in Christ shown as instrumental in solving problems. Pays 4¢ a word, on publication. SASE for guidelines.

FAMILY CIRCLE—375 Lexington Ave., New York, NY 10017. Kathy Sagan, Sr. Ed. Fiction is no longer being considered.

FICTION INTERNATIONAL—English Dept., San Diego State Univ., San Diego, CA 92182-8140. Harold Jaffe, Ed. Formally innovative and politically committed fiction and theory. Query for themes. Submit between September 1st and December 15th.

FLY ROD & REEL—P.O. Box 370, Camden, ME 04843. James E. Butler, Ed. Occasional fiction, 2,000 to 3,000 words, related to fly fishing. Special annual fiction issue published in summer. Payment varies, on acceptance.

GALLERY— 401 Park Ave. S., New York, NY 10016-8802. Barry Janoff, Ed. Dir. Rich Friedman, Man. Ed. Fiction, to 3,000 words, for sophisticated men. "We are not looking for science fiction, mystery, 40s-style detective, or stories involving aliens from other planets. We do look for interesting stories that enable readers to view life in an off-beat, unusual, or insightful manner: fiction with believable characters and actions. We encourage quality work from unpublished writers." Pays $500, on publication. SASE for guidelines.

GLIMMER TRAIN PRESS—710 S.W. Madison St., #504, Portland, OR 97205. Susan Burmeister-Brown, Ed. Fiction, 1,200 to 7,500 words. "Eight stories in each quarterly magazine." Pays $500, on acceptance. Submit material in January, April, July, and October; allow 3 months for response. "Send SASE for guidelines before submitting."

GOOD HOUSEKEEPING— 959 Eighth Ave., New York, NY 10019. Lee Quarfoot, Fiction Ed. Short stories, 1,000 to 3,000 words, with strong identification figures for women, by published writers and "beginners with demonstrable talent." Novel condensations or excerpts from about-to-be-published books only. Query; no longer accepts unsolicited manuscripts.

GRIT—1503 S.W. 42nd St., Topeka, KS 66609. Donna Doyle, Ed.-in-Chief. Short stories, 1,000 to 2,000 words; also historical, mystery, western, adventure, and romance serials (15,000 or more words in 1,000-word installments with cliff-hangers). Should be upbeat, inspirational, wholesome and interesting to mature adults. No reference to drinking, smoking, drugs, sex, or violence. Also publishes true-story nostalgia. Pays up to 22¢ a word, on publication. All fiction submissions should be marked "Fiction Dept." Send $4 for sample copy. SASE for guidelines. Allow at least 6 months for review. Submissions will not be acknowledged, nor will status updates be given.

GUIDEPOSTS FOR KIDS—P.O. Box 638, Chesterton, IN 46304. Mary Lou Carney, Ed. Value-centered bimonthly for 7- to 12-year-olds. Problem fiction, mysteries, historicals, 1,000 to 1,400 words, with "realistic dialogue and sharp imagery. No preachy stories about Bible-toting children." Pays $300 to $500 for all rights, on acceptance. No reprints.

HARDBOILED—Gryphon Publications, P.O. Box 209, Brooklyn, NY 11228-0209. Gary Lovisi, Ed. Hard, cutting-edge crime fiction, to 3,000 words, "with impact." "It's a good idea to read an issue before submitting a story." Payment varies, on publication. Query for articles, book and film reviews.

HARPER'S MAGAZINE— 666 Broadway, New York, NY 10012. Attn: Eds. Will consider unsolicited fiction manuscripts. Query for nonfiction (very limited market). No poetry. SASE required.

HIGHLIGHTS FOR CHILDREN— 803 Church St., Honesdale, PA 18431-1824. Christine French Clark, Man. Ed. Fiction on sports, humor, adventure, mystery, folktales, etc., 900 words, for 8- to 12-year-olds. Easy rebus form, 100 to 120 words, and easy-to-read stories, to 500 words, for beginning readers. "We are partial to stories in which the protagonist solves a dilemma through his or her own resources." Pays from 14¢ a word, on acceptance. Buys all rights.

THE JOYFUL WOMAN—P.O. Box 90028, Chattanooga, TN 37412. Joy Rice Martin, Ed. First-person inspirational true stories and sketches, 500 to

1,000 words; occasionally uses some fiction. Pays 3¢ to 4¢ a word, on publication.

LADIES' HOME JOURNAL—125 Park Ave., New York, NY 10017. Fiction; only accepted through agents.

THE MAGAZINE OF FANTASY AND SCIENCE FICTION—Box 1806, Madison Sq. Station, New York, NY 10159. Gordon Van Gelder, Ed. Fantasy and science fiction stories, to 25,000 words. Pays 5¢ to 8¢ a word, on acceptance.

MATURE LIVING—127 Ninth Ave. N., Nashville, TN 37234. Al Shackleford, Ed. Fiction, 900 to 1,200 words, for senior adults. Must be consistent with Christian principles. Pays $75, on acceptance.

MIDSTREAM—110 E. 59th St., New York, NY 10022. Joel Carmichael, Ed. Fiction with a Jewish/Zionist reference, to 3,000 words. Pays 5¢ a word, after publication. Allow one month for response.

NA'AMAT WOMAN—200 Madison Ave., 21st Fl., New York, NY 10016. Judith A. Sokoloff, Ed. Short stories, approximately 2,500 words, with Jewish theme. Pays 10¢ a word, on publication.

NEW MYSTERY MAGAZINE—The Flatiron Bldg., 175 Fifth Ave., Suite 2001, New York, NY 10010-7703. Charles Raisch, Ed. Quarterly. Mystery, crime, detection, and suspense short stories, 2,000 to 6,000 words, with "sympathetic characters in trouble and visual scenes." Book reviews, 250 to 2,000 words, of upcoming or recently published novels. Pays 3¢ to 10¢ a word, on publication. No guidelines; study back issues.

THE NEW YORKER—20 W. 43rd St., New York, NY 10036. Attn: Fiction Dept. Short stories, humor, and satire. Payment varies, on acceptance.

PLAYBOY—680 N. Lake Shore Dr., Chicago, IL 60611. Alice K. Turner, Fiction Ed. Limited market.

PLAYGIRL—801 Second Ave., New York, NY 10017. Judy Cole, Ed.-in-Chief. Contemporary, erotic fiction, from a female perspective, 3,000 to 4,000 words. "Fantasy Forum," 1,000 to 2,000 words. Pays from $200; $25 to $100 for "Fantasy Forum", after acceptance.

POWER AND LIGHT—6401 The Paseo, Kansas City, MO 64131. Beula J. Postlewait, Preteen Ed. Fiction, 500 to 800 words, for grades 5 to 6, defining Christian experiences and values. Pays 5¢ a word for multiple-use rights, on publication.

PURPOSE—616 Walnut Ave., Scottdale, PA 15683-1999. James E. Horsch, Ed. Fiction, up to 750 words, on problem solving from a Christian point of view. Poetry, 3 to 12 lines. Pays to 5¢ a word for fiction; to $1 per line for poetry, on acceptance.

QUEEN'S QUARTERLY—Queens Univ., Kingston, Ont., Canada K7L 3N6. Attn: Fiction Ed. Fiction, to 5,000 words, in English and French. Pays to $300, on publication.

RANGER RICK—8925 Leesburg Pike, Vienna, VA 22184. Deborah Churchman, Fiction Ed. Action-packed nature-and conservation-related fiction, to 900 words, for 7- to 12-year-olds. No anthropomorphism. "Especially interested in very short fiction and multicultural stories." Pays to $550, on acceptance. Buys all rights. Guidelines.

ST. ANTHONY MESSENGER—1615 Republic St., Cincinnati, OH 45210-1298. Norman Perry, O.F.M., Ed. Barbara Beckwith, Man. Ed. Fiction that makes readers think about issues, lifestyles, and values. Pays 15¢ a word, on acceptance. Queries or manuscripts accepted.

SCHOOL MATES—U.S. Chess Federation, 3054 NYS Rt. 9W, New Windsor, NY 12553-7646. Jay Hastings, Publications Dir. Fiction and articles, 250 to 800 words, and short fillers, related to chess for beginning chess players (primarily children, ages 6 to 15). "Instructive, but there's room for fun puzzles, anecdotes, etc. All chess related." Pays from $20, on publication. Query; limited free-lance market.

SEA KAYAKER—P.O. Box 17170, Seattle, WA 98107-0870. Christopher Cunningham, Ed. Short stories exclusively related to ocean kayaking, 1,000 to 3,000 words. Pays on publication.

SEVENTEEN— 850 Third Ave., New York, NY 10022. Ben Schrank, Fiction Ed. High-quality, literary short fiction, to 4,000 words. Pays on acceptance.

SPORTS AFIELD—250 W. 55th St., New York, NY 10019. John Atwood, Ed-in-Chief. Occasional fiction, 1,500 words maximum, on outdoor sports and nature-related topics. Humor. Payment varies, on acceptance.

STRAIGHT— 8121 Hamilton Ave., Cincinnati, OH 45231. Heather E. Wallace, Ed. Well-constructed fiction, 1,000 to 1,500 words, showing Christian teens using Bible principles in everyday life. Contemporary, realistic teen characters a must. Most interested in school, church, dating, and family life stories. Pays 5¢ to 7¢ a word, on acceptance. Guidelines.

'TEEN— 6420 Wilshire Blvd., Los Angeles, CA 90048-5515. Attn: Fiction Dept. Short stories, 2,500 to 4,000 words: mystery, teen situations, adventure, romance, humor for teens. Pays from $200, on acceptance.

TEEN LIFE—1445 Boonville Ave., Springfield, MO 65802-1894. Tammy Bicket, Ed. Fiction, to 1,200 words, for 13- to 19-year-olds. Articles, 500 to 1,000 words. Strong evangelical emphasis a must: believable characters working out their problems according to biblical principles. Buys first rights; pays on acceptance. Reprints considered.

TRUE CONFESSIONS—233 Park Ave. S., New York, NY 10003. Pat Byrdsong, Ed. Timely, emotional, first-person stories, 2,000 to 10,000 words, on romance, family life, and problems of today's young blue-collar women. Pays 5¢ a word, after publication.

VIRTUE: HELPING WOMEN BUILD CHRIST-LIKE CHARACTER— (formerly *Virtue: The Christian Magazine for Women*) 4050 Lee Vance View, Colorado Springs, CO 80918-7102. Laura J. Barker, Ed. Fiction, 1,200 to 1,400 words, with a Christian slant; inspirational, women's spiritual journeys, women's perspectives. Pays 15¢ to 25¢ a word, on publication. Query with SASE for articles.

WESTERN PEOPLE—Box 2500, Saskatoon, Sask., Canada S7K 2C4. Attn: Ed. Short stories, 1,200 to 2,500 words, on subjects or themes of interest to rural readers in western Canada. Pays $100 to $200, on acceptance. Enclose international reply coupons and SAE.

WOMAN'S WORLD—270 Sylvan Ave., Englewood Cliffs, NJ 07632. Attn: Fiction Dept. Fast-moving short stories, no more than 1,500 words, with realistic relationship theme. (Specify "romance" on outside of envelope.) Mini-mysteries, to 1,000 words, with "whodunit" or "howdunit" theme. (Specify "mini mystery" on envelope. No science fiction, fantasy, or historical romance and no horror, ghost stories, or gratuitous violence. "Dialogue-driven romances help propel the story." Pays $1,000 for romances, $500 for mini-mysteries, on acceptance. SASE for guidelines and manuscript return.

YANKEE—Yankee Publishing Co., P.O. Box 520, Dublin, NH 03444. Judson Hale, Ed. Edie Clark, Fiction Ed. High-quality, literary short fiction, to 3,000 words (shorter preferred), with New England setting; no sap buckets or lobster pot stereotypes. Pays $1,000, on acceptance.

DETECTIVE & MYSTERY

ALFRED HITCHCOCK'S MYSTERY MAGAZINE—1270 Ave. of the Americas, New York, NY 10020. Cathleen Jordan, Ed. Well-plotted, previously unpublished mystery, detective, suspense, and crime short stories, to 14,000 words. Submissions by new writers strongly encouraged. Pays 8¢ a word, on acceptance. No simultaneous submissions, please. (Submissions sent to *AHMM* are not considered for, or read by, *Ellery Queen's Mystery Magazine*, and vice versa.) Guidelines with SASE.

ARMCHAIR DETECTIVE—549 Park Ave., Suite 252, Scotch Plains, NJ 07076-1705. Elizabeth Foxwell, Ed.-in-Chief. Articles on mystery and detective fiction; biographical sketches, reviews, etc. No fiction. Pays $12 a printed page; reviews are unpaid. SASE for guidelines.

COZY DETECTIVE MYSTERY MAGAZINE—686 Jake Ct., McMinnville, OR 97128. David Rowell Workman, Sr. Ed. Mystery and suspense, fiction and nonfiction, to 5,000 words. Poems, to 20 lines. Pays in copies.

ELLERY QUEEN'S MYSTERY MAGAZINE—1270 Ave. of the Americas, 10th Fl., New York, NY 10020. Janet Hutchings, Ed. Detective, crime, and mystery fiction, approximately 1,500 to 10,000 words. Occasionally publishes novelettes, to 20,000 words, by established authors and humorous mystery verse. No sex, sadism, or sensationalism. Particularly interested in new writers and "first stories." Pays 3¢ to 8¢ a word, occasionally higher for established authors, on acceptance.

HARDBOILED—Gryphon Publications, P.O. Box 209, Brooklyn, NY 11228-0209. Gary Lovisi, Ed. Hard, cutting-edge crime fiction (suspense, noir, private eye) to 3,000 words. Payment varies, on publication. Query for articles, book and film reviews, and longer fiction.

MURDEROUS INTENT—P.O. Box 5947, Vancouver, WA 98668-5947. Margo Power, Ed./Pub. Quarterly. Mystery and suspense stories and mystery-related articles, 2,000 to 4,000 words; fillers, to 750 words; poems, to 30 lines. "We love humor in mysteries. Surprise us!" Pays $10, on acceptance. Query for nonfiction.

MYSTERY TIME—P.O. Box 2907, Decatur, IL 62524. Linda Hutton, Ed. Semiannual. Suspense, 1,500 words, and poems about mysteries, up to 16 lines. "We prefer female protagonists. No gore or violence." Pays $5, on acceptance.

NEW MYSTERY MAGAZINE—The Flatiron Bldg., 175 Fifth Ave., Suite 2001, New York, NY 10010-7703. Charles Raisch, Ed. Mystery, crime, detection, and suspense short stories, 2,000 to 6,000 words. No true crime. Book reviews, 250 to 2,000 words, of upcoming or recently published novels. Pays $15 to $500, on publication. No guidelines; study back issues.

SLEUTHHOUND MAGAZINE—P.O. Box 890294, Oklahoma City, OK 73189-0294. Peggy Farris, Ed. Quarterly. Articles, 500 to 2,000 words. How-to articles; book reviews; interviews with well-known writers. "No explicit sex, gore or extreme violence." Pays 3¢ to 6¢ a word, on publication.

WHISPERING WILLOW MYSTERIES—P.O. Box 890294, Oklahoma City, OK 73189-0294. Darlene Hoffman, Acquisitions Ed. Quarterly. Mystery and mystery/suspense, 500 to 5,000 words. Nonfiction, 500 to 1,250 words: mysterious personal experiences and interviews with police officers and detectives about their on-the-job experiences. "No explicit sex, gore, or extreme violence." Pays 4¢ a word, on publication.

SCIENCE FICTION & FANTASY

ABERRATIONS—P.O. Box 460430, San Francisco, CA 94146. Richard Blair, Man. Ed. Science fiction, horror, and fantasy, to 8,000 words. "Experimental, graphic, multi-genre is O.K. with science fiction/fantasy/horror tie-in." Pays ½¢ a word, on publication. Guidelines.

ABORIGINAL SF—P.O. Box 2449, Woburn, MA 01888-0849. Charles C. Ryan, Ed. Short stories, 2,500 to 7,500 words, and poetry, one to 2 typed pages, with strong science content, lively, unique characters, and well-designed plots. No sword and sorcery, horror, or fantasy. Pays $200 for fiction, $15 for poetry, $4 for science fiction jokes, and $20 for cartoons, on publication.

ABSOLUTE MAGNITUDE—P.O. Box 910, Greenfield, MA 01302-0910. Warren Lapine, Ed. Quarterly. Character-driven technical science fiction, 1,000 to 25,000 words. No fantasy, horror, satire, or funny science fiction. Pays 1¢ to 5¢ a word (1¢ a word for reprints), on publication. Guidelines.

ADVENTURES OF SWORD & SORCERY—P.O. Box 285, Xenia, OH 45385. Randy Dannenfelser, Ed. Quarterly. High fantasy and heroic fantasy, 1,000 to 8,000 words. Pays 3¢ to 6¢ a word, on acceptance.

ANALOG SCIENCE FICTION AND FACT—1270 Ave. of the Americas, New York, NY 10020. Stanley Schmidt, Ed. Science fiction with strong characters in believable future or alien setting: short stories, 2,000 to 7,500 words; novelettes, 10,000 to 20,000 words; serials, to 80,000 words. Also uses future-related articles. Pays to 7¢ a word, on acceptance. Query for serials and articles.

ASIMOV'S SCIENCE FICTION MAGAZINE—1270 Ave. of the Americas, New York, NY 10020. Gardner Dozois, Ed. Short, character-oriented science fiction and fantasy, to 15,000 words. Pays 5¢ to 8¢ a word, on acceptance. Guidelines.

DRAGON MAGAZINE—1801 Lind Ave. S.W., Renton, WA 98055. Dave Gross, Ed. Articles, 1,500 to 7,500 words, on fantasy and science fiction role-playing games. Fantasy, 1,500 to 8,000 words. Pays 5¢ to 8¢ a word for fiction, on acceptance. Pays 4¢ a word for articles, on publication. All submissions must include a disclosure form. Guidelines.

DREAMS OF DECADENCE—P.O. Box 910, Greenfield, MA 03102-0013. Angela Kessler, Ed. Quarterly digest devoted to vampire poetry and fiction. Atmospheric, well-written stories, 1,000 to 7,000 words, with the emphasis on dark fantasy rather than horror. Poetry, "the less horrific and more explicitly vampire, the better." Pays 1¢ to 5¢ a word for fiction, on publication. Pays in copies for poetry.

FANGORIA— 475 Park Ave. S., 8th Fl., New York, NY 10016. Anthony Timpone, Ed. Published 10 times yearly. Movie, TV, and book previews, reviews, and interviews, 1,800 to 2,500 words, in connection with upcoming horror films. "A strong love of the genre and an appreciation and understanding of the magazine are essential." Pays $175 to $225, on publication.

FANTASY MACABRE—P.O. Box 20610, Seattle, WA 98102. Jessica Salmonson, Ed. Fiction, to 3,000 words, including translations. "We look for a tale that is strong in atmosphere, with menace that is suggested and threatening rather than the result of dripping blood and gore." Pays 1¢ a word, to $30 per story, on publication. Also publishes *Fantasy & Terror* for poetry-in-prose pieces.

HADROSAUR TALES—Hadrosaur Productions, P.O. Box 8468, Las Cruces, NM 88006. David Summers, Ed. Semiannual. Literary science fiction and fantasy, 1,500 to 6,000 words. Science fiction-or fantasy-based poetry, one to 2 pages. No graphic horror or violence. Pays $6 for fiction; $2 per poem, on acceptance, plus copies.

HEROINES OF FANTASY—See *Shadow Sword.*

HOBSON'S CHOICE: SCIENCE FICTION AND TECHNOLOGY—The Starwind Press, P.O. Box 98, Ripley, OH 45167. Attn: Submissions Ed. Science fiction and fantasy, 2,000 to 10,000 words. Articles and literary criticism, 1,000 to 5,000 words, for readers interested in science and technology. Query for nonfiction. Pays 1¢ to 4¢ a word, on acceptance.

IN DARKNESS ETERNAL—Stygian Vortex Publications, 113 Highland Park Dr., Athens, GA 30605-3577. Glenda Woodrum, Ed.-in-Chief. T'shai K., Fiction and Poetry Ed. Annual. Stories from 3,000 words, articles, and artwork by and for vampire enthusiasts. No stories about serial killers, prostitutes, or anything involving people becoming vampires from the bite of a vampire; no Dracula or other media related vampire tales. Payment is 50¢ per printed page; $1 to $3 for poetry. Query. Guidelines.

THE LEADING EDGE—3163 JKHB, Provo, UT 84602. David Burnett, Ed. Semiannual. Science fiction and fantasy, 3,000 to 12,000 words; poetry, to 600 lines; and articles, to 8,000 words, on science, scientific speculation, and literary criticism. No excessive profanity, overt violence, or excessive sexual situations. No simultaneous submissions. Pays $10 to $100, on publication. Guidelines.

THE MAGAZINE OF FANTASY AND SCIENCE FICTION—Box 1806, Madison Sq. Station, New York, NY 10159-1806. Gordon Van Gelder, Ed. Fantasy and science fiction stories, to 15,000 words. Pays 5¢ to 7¢ a word, on acceptance.

MARION ZIMMER BRADLEY'S FANTASY MAGAZINE—P.O. Box 249, Berkeley, CA 94701. Marion Zimmer Bradley, Ed. Quarterly. Well-plotted stories, 3,500 to 4,000 words. Action and adventure fantasy "with no particular objection to modern settings." Send SASE for guidelines before submitting. Pays 3¢ to 10¢ a word, on acceptance.

NIGHT TERRORS—1202 W. Market St., Orrville, OH 44667-1710. Mr. D. E. Davidson, Ed. Stories of psychological horror, the supernatural or occult, from 2,000 to 5,000 words. Pays in copies and by arrangement with professional writers.

OF UNICORNS AND SPACE STATIONS—P.O. Box 97, Bountiful, UT 84011-0097. Gene Davis, Ed. Science fiction and fantasy, to 5,000 words. Poetry related to science fiction, science, or fantasy. "Do not staple or fold long manuscripts." Pays 1¢ per word for fiction; $5 for poems, on publication.

OMNI INTERNET—General Media International, 277 Park Ave., 4th Fl., New York, NY 10172-0003. Ellen Datlow, Fiction Ed. On-line magazine. Strong, realistic science fiction, 2,000 to 10,000 words, with good characterizations. "We want to intrigue our readers with mindbroadening, thought-provoking stories that will excite their sense of wonder." Some fantasy. No horror, ghost, or sword and sorcery tales. Pays $1,300 to $2,250, on acceptance. SASE. http: //www.omnimag.com

PIRATE WRITINGS: TALES OF FANTASY, MYSTERY & SCIENCE FICTION—P.O. Box 329, Brightwaters, NY 11718-0329. Edward J. McFadden, Pub./Ed. Tom Piccirilli, Assoc. Ed. Mystery, science fiction, fantasy, 250 to 6,000 words. Poetry, to 20 lines. Pays 1¢ to 5¢ a word.

SCAVENGER'S NEWSLETTER—519 Ellinwood, Osage City, KS 66523-1329. Janet Fox, Ed. Flash fiction, 1,200 words, in the genres of science fiction, fantasy, horror, and mystery. Articles, 1,000 words, pertaining to writing and art in those genres. Poems, to 10 lines, and humor, 500 to 700 words, for writers and artists. "Most of the magazine is market information." Pays $4 for fiction, articles, and cover art; $2 for humor, poems, and inside art, on acceptance.

SCIENCE FICTION CHRONICLE—P.O. Box 022730, Brooklyn, NY 11202-0056. Andrew Porter, Ed. News items, 300 to 800 words, for science fiction and fantasy readers, professionals, and booksellers. Interviews with authors, 3,000 to 5,000 words. No fiction. Pays 3½¢ to 5¢ a word, on publication. Query. E-mail: SF—Chronicle@Compuserve.com

SHADOW SWORD—Stygian Vortex Publications, 113 Highland Park Dr., Athens, GA 30605-3577. Glenda J. Woodrum, Ed. Annual. Stories, from 3,000 words, and artwork for fantasy enthusiasts: heroic fantasy, sword & sorcery. "No 'cute' stories or fantasies set in a version of the real technological world. We would like to see more non-human characters." Also sword & sorcery and heroic fantasy with female protagonists for *Heroines of Fantasy*. Pays 50¢ per printed page, $1 to $3 for poetry, and one copy, on publication. Query for stories over 8,500 words. Guidelines.

SHAPESHIFTER!—Stygian Vortex Publications, 113 Highland Park, Athens, GA 30605-3577. Coyote Osborne, Ed. Annual. Stories and artwork on lycanthropes, shape-changers, and partly human creatures. Query for stories over 9,000 words. "We prefer stories in which the shapeshifters are the heroes/protagonists, not stories in which they ravage a small town, etc." Pays one copy plus 50¢ per printed page; $1 to $3 per poem, on publication. Guidelines.

TALEBONES—Fairwood Press, 10531 S.E. 250th Pl., #104, Kent, WA 98031. Patrick and Honna Swenson, Eds. Science fiction and dark fantasy, to 6,000 words. Articles, to 3,000 words, on the state of speculative fiction. Poetry. Cartoons with science fiction or fantasy themes. "I'm looking for science fiction and dark fantasy with strong characters and entertaining story lines. Fiction should be more toward the darker side, without being pure horror." Pays 1¢ a word for fiction and $7 per poem, on acceptance.

THE ULTIMATE UNKNOWN—Combs Press, P.O. Box 219, Streamwood, IL 60107-0219. David D. Combs, Ed. Fiction and nonfiction on horror, science fiction, and the future, to 3,000 words. Related poetry, to 20 lines. Payment is one copy.

THE URBANITE: SURREAL & LIVELY & BIZARRE—Box 4737, Davenport, IA 52808. Mark McLaughlin, Ed. Published 3 times a year. Dark fantasy, horror (no gore), surrealism, reviews, and social commentary, to 3,000 words. Free verse poems, to 2 pages. Pays 2¢ to 3¢ a word; $10 for poetry, on acceptance. Query for themes.

WEIRD TALES—(formerly *Worlds of Fantasy & Horror*) 123 Crooked Ln., King of Prussia, PA 19406-2570. George Scithers, Pub. Darrell Schweitzer, Ed. Quarterly. Fantasy and horror (no science fiction), to 8,000 words. Pays about 3¢ per word, on acceptance. Guidelines.

WORLDS OF FANTASY & HORROR —See *Weird Tales.*

CONFESSION & ROMANCE

BLACK CONFESSIONS—See *Black Romance.*

BLACK ROMANCE—233 Park Ave. S., New York, NY 10003. Marcia Y. Mahan, Ed. Romance fiction, 4,500 to 5,000 words, and relationship articles. Queries preferred. Pays $100 to $125, on publication. Also publishes *Black Secrets, Bronze Thrills, Black Confessions,* and *Jive.* Guidelines.

BLACK SECRETS—See *Black Romance.*

BRONZE THRILLS—See *Black Romance.*

INTIMACY—233 Park Ave. S., 7th Fl., New York, NY 10003. Marcia Y. Mahan, Ed. Fiction, 5,000 to 5,800 words, for black women ages 18 to 45; must have contemporary plot and contain 2 romantic and intimate love scenes. Pays $100 to $125, on publication. Guidelines.

JIVE—See *Black Romance.*

ROMANTIC HEARTS—P.O. Box 450669, Westlake, OH 44145. Debra Krauss, Ed./Pub. Short romantic fiction, 1,500 to 4,000 words; related how-to articles and essays with a romantic theme, 500 to 1,500 words; love poems, to 25 lines. "We are looking for heartwarming tales of love and romance that are rich with emotion and strong characterization." Pays in copies. Guidelines.

TRUE CONFESSIONS—233 Park Ave. S., New York, NY 10003. Pat Byrdsong, Ed. Timely, emotional, first-person stories, 1,000 to 9,000 words, on romance, family life, and problems of today's young blue-collar women. Pays 5¢ a word, after publication.

TRUE EXPERIENCE—233 Park Ave. S., New York, NY 10003. Rose Bernstein, Ed. Heather Young, Assoc. Ed. Realistic first-person stories, 1,000 to 12,000 words, on family life, single life, love, romance, overcoming hardships, mysteries. Pays 3¢ a word, after publication.

TRUE LOVE—233 Park Ave. S., New York, NY 10003. Alison Way, Ed. Fresh, young, true-to-life stories, on love and topics of current interest. Must be written in the past tense and first person. Pays 3¢ a word, after publication. Guidelines.

TRUE ROMANCE—233 Park Ave. S., New York, NY 10003. Pat Vitucci, Ed. True or true-to-life, dramatic and/or romantic first-person stories, 3,000 to 10,000 words. All genres: tragedy, mystery, peril, love, family struggles, etc. Topical themes. Love poems. "We enjoy working with new writers." Reports in 3 to 5 months. Pays 3¢ a word, a month after publication.

POETRY MARKETS

As the following list attests, the market for poetry in general magazines is rather limited: There aren't many general-interest magazines that use poetry, and in those that do, the competition to break into print is stiff, since editors use only a limited number of poems in each issue. In addition to the magazines listed here, writers may find their local newspapers receptive to poetry.

While poetry may be scant in general-interest magazines, it is the backbone of a majority of the college, little, and literary magazines (see page 691). Poets will also find a number of competitions offering cash awards for unpublished poems in the *Literary Prize Offers* list.

ALOHA, THE MAGAZINE OF HAWAII AND THE PACIFIC—P.O. Box 3260, Honolulu, HI 96801. Lance Tominaga, Ed. Poetry relating to Hawaii. Pays $30 per poem, on publication.

AMERICA—106 W. 56th St., New York, NY 10019. Patrick Samway, S.J., Literary Ed. Serious poetry, preferably in contemporary prose idiom, 10 to 25 lines. Occasional light verse. Submit 2 or 3 poems. Pays $1.40 per line, on publication. Guidelines.

THE AMERICAN SCHOLAR—1811 Q St. N.W., Washington, DC 20009-9974. Anne Fadiman, Ed. Highly original poetry for college-educated, intellectual readers. Pays $50, on acceptance.

ASIAN PAGES—P.O. Box 11932, St. Paul, MN 55111-0932. Cheryl Weiberg, Ed.-in-Chief. Poetry, 100 words, with "a strong, non-offensive Asian slant." Pays on publication.

THE ATLANTIC MONTHLY—77 N. Washington St., Boston, MA 02114. Peter Davison, David Barber, Poetry Eds. Previously unpublished poetry of highest quality. Limited market; only 2 to 3 poems an issue. Interested in new poets. Occasionally uses light verse. "No simultaneous submissions; we make prompt decisions." Pays excellent rates, on acceptance.

CAPPER'S—1503 S.W. 42nd St., Topeka, KS 66609-1265. Nancy Peavler, Ed. Free verse, light verse, traditional, nature, and inspirational poems, 4 to 16 lines, with simple everyday themes. Submit up to 6 poems at a time, with SASE. Pays $10 to $15, on acceptance.

CHILDREN'S PLAYMATE—P.O. Box 567, Indianapolis, IN 46206. Terry Harshman, Ed. Poetry for children, 6 to 8 years old, on good health, nutrition, exercise, safety, seasonal and humorous subjects. Pays from $25, on publication. Buys all rights.

THE CHRISTIAN SCIENCE MONITOR—One Norway St., Boston, MA 02115. Elizabeth Lund, Poetry Ed. Finely crafted poems that celebrate the extraordinary in the ordinary. Seasonal material always needed. No violence, sensuality, racism, death and disease, helplessness, hopelessness. Short poems preferred; submit no more than 5 poems at a time. SASE required. Pays varying rates, on publication.

COUNTRY WOMAN—P.O. Box 989, Greendale, WI 53129. Kathy Pohl, Man. Ed. Traditional rural poetry and light verse, 4 to 30 lines, on rural experiences and country living; also seasonal poetry. Poems must rhyme. Pays $10 to $25, on acceptance.

EVANGEL—Light and Life Communications, Box 535002, Indianapolis, IN 46253-5002. Julie Innes, Ed. Free Methodist. Devotional or nature poetry, 8 to 16 lines. Pays $10, on publication.

MATURE YEARS—201 Eighth Ave. S., P.O. Box 801, Nashville, TN 37202. Marvin W. Cropsey, Ed. United Methodist. Poetry, to 14 lines, on preretirement, retirement, Christianity, inspiration, seasonal subjects, aging. No "saccharine" poetry. Submit up to 6 poems at a time. Pays 50¢ to $1 per line.

MIDSTREAM—110 E. 59th St., New York, NY 10022. Attn: Poetry Ed. Poetry of Jewish/Zionist interest. "Brevity highly recommended." Pays $25, on publication. Allow 3 months for response.

THE MIRACULOUS MEDAL—475 E. Chelten Ave., Philadelphia, PA 19144-5785. William J. O'Brien, C.M., Ed. Catholic. Religious verse, to 20 lines. Pays 50¢ a line, on acceptance.

MODERN BRIDE—249 W. 17th St., New York, NY 10011. Mary Ann Cavlin, Exec. Ed. Short verse of interest to bride and groom. Pays $25 to $35, on acceptance.

THE NATION—72 Fifth Ave., New York, NY 10011. Grace Schulman, Poetry Ed. Poetry of high quality. Pays after publication. SASE requried.

NATIONAL ENQUIRER—Lantana, FL 33464-0002. Kathy Martin, Fillers Ed. Short poems, to 8 lines, with traditional rhyming verse, of an amusing, philosophical, or inspirational nature. No experimental poetry. Original epigrams, humorous anecdotes, and "daffynitions." Submit seasonal/holiday material at least 2 months in advance. Pays $25, after publication. Material will not be returned; do not send SASE.

THE NEW YORKER—20 W. 43rd St., New York, NY 10036. Attn: Poetry Ed. First-rate poetry. Pays top rates, on acceptance. Include SASE.

PURPOSE—616 Walnut Ave., Scottdale, PA 15683-1999. James E. Horsch, Poetry Ed. Poetry, to 8 lines, with challenging Christian discipleship angle. Pays 50¢ to $1.65 a line, on acceptance.

RADIANCE: THE MAGAZINE FOR LARGE WOMEN—P.O. Box 30246, Oakland, CA 94604. Alice Ansfield, Ed./Pub. Quarterly. Poetry, fiction, and essays for women about issues of size, self-esteem, and body. Payment varies, on publication. Web site: http://www.radiancemagazine.com.

ST. JOSEPH'S MESSENGER—P.O. Box 288, Jersey City, NJ 07303-0288. Sister Ursula Maphet, Ed. Light verse and traditional poetry, 4 to 40 lines. Pays $5 to $20, on publication.

THE SATURDAY EVENING POST—P.O. Box 567, Indianapolis, IN 46206. Steven Pettinga, Post Scripts Ed. Light verse and humor. No conventional poetry. SASE required. Pays $15, on publication.

WARRIOR POETS—P.O. Box 7616, Wantagh, NY 11793. R.J. Erbacher, Ed.-in-Chief. Published 3 times per year. "The Magazine of Medieval Poetry." Poetry, any length; stories, 2,000 words, dealing with swords and chivalry, knights and maidens, love and bravery, sorcery and dragons, warriors, and poets. "Ancient stuff that rings with clashing swords, dragon roars, damsel's screams, and wizard's incantations." Payment is in copies, on publication. Guidelines.

WESTERN PEOPLE—P.O. Box 2500, Saskatoon, Sask., Canada S7K 2C4. Michael Gillgannon, Man. Ed. Short poetry with Western Canadian themes. Pays on acceptance. Send international reply coupons.

YANKEE—Yankee Publishing Co., P.O. Box 520, Dublin, NH 03444. Jean Burden, Poetry Ed. Serious poetry of high quality, to 30 lines. Pays $50 per poem for all rights, $35 for first rights, on publication. SASE required.

YESTERDAY'S MAGAZETTE—P.O. Box 18566, Sarasota, FL 34276. Ned Burke, Ed. Traditional poetry, to 24 lines. Pays in copies for poetry and short pieces.

COLLEGE, LITERARY, & LITTLE MAGAZINES

The thousands of literary journals, little magazines, and college quarterlies published today welcome work from novices and pros alike; editors are always interested in seeing traditional and experimental fiction, poetry, essays, reviews, short articles, criticism, and satire, and as long as the material is well-written, the fact that a writer is a beginner doesn't adversely affect his or her chances for acceptance.

Most of these smaller publications have small budgets and staffs, so they may be slow in their reporting time; several months is not unusual. In addition, they usually pay only in copies of the issue in which published work appears and some (particularly college magazines) do not read manuscripts during the summer.

Publication in the literary journals can, however, lead to recognition by editors of large-circulation magazines, who read the little magazines in their search for new talent. There is also the possibility of having one's work chosen for reprinting in one of the prestigious annual collections of work from the little magazines.

Because the requirements of these journals differ widely, it is always important to study recent issues before submitting work to one of them. Large libraries may carry a variety of journals, or a writer may send a postcard to the editor and ask the price of a sample copy.

For a complete list of literary and college publications and little magazines, writers may consult such reference works as *The International Directory of Little Magazines and Small Presses*, published annually by Dustbooks (P.O. Box 100, Paradise, CA 95967).

ABOUT SUCH THINGS— 420 W. Walnut Ln., Philadelphia, PA 19144. Laurel Webster, Man. Ed. Semiannual. Essays and reviews of arts and cultural topics. Free verse poetry. Fiction, to 3,000 words. "The magazine is intended to be a voice for Christian writers but not an evangelistic tool." Pays in 2 copies.

AFRICAN AMERICAN REVIEW—Dept. of English, Indiana State Univ., Terre Haute, IN 47809. Joe Weixlmann, Ed. Essays on African American literature, theater, film, art, and culture; interviews; poems; fiction; and book reviews. Submit up to 6 poems. Pays an honorarium and copies. Query for book review assignments; send 3 copies of all other submissions. Responds in 3 months.

AFRICAN VOICES—270 W. 96th St., New York, NY 10025. Carolyn A. Butts, Exec. Ed. Quarterly. Humorous, erotic, and dramatic fiction, 500 to 2,500 words, by ethnic writers. Nonfiction, 500 to 1,500 words, including investigative articles, artist profiles, essays, and first-person narratives. Pays in copies. SASE.

AGNI—Boston Univ., Creative Writing Program, 236 Bay State Rd., Boston, MA 02215. Askold Melnyczuk, Ed. Valerie Duff, Man. Ed. Short stories, poetry, and reviews. Manuscripts read October 1 to January 31.

ALABAMA LITERARY REVIEW—Troy State Univ., Smith 253, Troy, AL 36082. Theron Montgomery, Chief Ed. Annual. Contemporary, literary fiction and nonfiction, 3,500 words; short drama, to 25 pages; and poetry, to 2 pages. Thought-provoking B&W photos. Pays in copies (honorarium when available). Responds within 3 months.

ALASKA QUARTERLY REVIEW—Univ. of Alaska Anchorage, 3211 Providence Dr., Anchorage, AK 99508. Attn: Eds. Short stories, novel excerpts, short plays, and poetry (traditional and unconventional forms). Submit manuscripts between August 15 and May 15. Pays in subscription (and honorarium when funding is available).

ALBATROSS—P.O. Box 7787, North Port, FL 34287-0787. Richard Smyth, Richard Brobst, Eds. High-quality poetry; especially interested in ecological and nature poetry written in narrative form. Interviews with well-known poets. Submit 3 to 5 poems with brief bio. Pays in copies.

AMELIA—329 E St., Bakersfield, CA 93304. Frederick A. Raborg, Jr., Ed. All types of fiction, to 5,000 words, including science fiction, western, and romance. Pays $35, plus 2 copies. Annual contest.

THE AMERICAN BOOK REVIEW—Unit for Contemporary Literature, Illinois State Univ., Campus Box 4241, Normal, IL 61790-4241. Tara Reeser, Man. Ed. Literary book reviews, 700 to 1,200 words. Pays $50 or 2-year subscription and copies. Query with clips of published reviews.

AMERICAN LITERARY REVIEW—Univ. of North Texas, P.O. Box 13827, Denton, TX 76203-6827. Lee Martin, Ed. Short fiction and creative nonfiction, to 30 double-spaced pages, and poetry (submit 3 to 5 poems). Pays in copies.

THE AMERICAN POETRY REVIEW—1721 Walnut St., Philadelphia, PA 19103. Attn: Eds. Highest quality contemporary poetry. Responds in 10 weeks.

THE AMERICAN SCHOLAR—1811 Q St. N.W., Washington, DC 20009-9974. Anne Fadiman, Ed. Articles, 3,500 to 4,000 words, on science, politics, literature, the arts, etc. Book reviews. Pays up to $500 for articles, $100 for reviews, on publication.

AMERICAN SHORT FICTION—Parlin Hall 108, Univ. of Texas, Austin, TX 78712-1164. Joseph E. Kruppa, Ed. Literary fiction only, any length. Pays $400 per story, on acceptance. Manuscripts read September 1 through May 31.

THE AMERICAN VOICE—332 W. Broadway, Suite 1215, Louisville, KY 40202. Frederick Smock, Ed. Published 3 times per year. Avant-garde, literary fiction, nonfiction, and well-crafted poetry, any length (shorter works are preferred). "Please read our journal before attempting to submit." Payment varies, on publication.

AMERICAN WRITING— 4343 Manayunk Ave., Philadelphia, PA 19128. Alexandra Grilikhes, Ed. Semiannual. "We encourage experimentation, new writing that takes risks with form, point of view, and language. We're interested in the voice of the loner, states of being, and initiation. We strongly suggest reading a copy of the magazine before submitting your work." Fiction and nonfiction, to 3,500 words, and poetry. Pays in copies.

ANOTHER CHICAGO MAGAZINE—3709 N. Kenmore, Chicago, IL 60613. Attn: Ed. Semiannual. Fiction, essays on literature, and poetry. "We want writing that's urgent, new, and lives in the world." Pays in copies on acceptance, and small honorarium when possible.

ANTHOLOGY—P.O. Box 4411, Mesa, AZ 85211-4411. Sharon Skinner, Exec. Ed. Bimonthly. Stories, 1,500 words, and nonfiction, 1,000 to 5,000 words, any genre. Poetry, any style, to 100 lines. "We also accept stories based in the fictional city of Haven, where people make their own heroes." Payment is one copy.

ANTIETAM REVIEW— 41 S. Potomac St., Hagerstown, MD 21740. Susanne Kass and Ann Knox, Eds.-in-Chief. Fiction and nonfiction (interviews, essays), to 5,000 words; poetry and photography. Submissions from natives or residents of MD, PA, WV, VA, DE, or DC only. Pays from $20 to $100. Guidelines. Manuscripts read September through January.

THE ANTIGONISH REVIEW— St. Francis Xavier Univ., P.O. Box 5000, Antigonish, NS, Canada B2G 2W5. George Sanderson, Ed. Poetry; short stories, essays, book reviews, 1,800 to 2,500 words. Pays in copies.

ANTIOCH REVIEW—P.O. Box 148, Yellow Springs, OH 45387-0148. Robert S. Fogarty, Ed. Timely articles, 2,000 to 8,000 words, on social sciences, literature, and humanities. Quality fiction. Poetry. No inspirational poetry. Pays $10 per printed page, on publication. Poetry considered from September to May; other material considered year-round.

APALACHEE QUARTERLY—Apalachee Press, 401 Ravenna Blvd., Suite 152, Seattle, WA 98115. k. Margaret Grossman, Cathy Fallon, Roslyn Solomon, Michael Waters, Eds. Fiction, nonfiction, poetry, reviews, art, photos, interviews, criticism, and parts-of-novels for our upcoming issue *The New Millennium*. All styles and subject matter will be considered, from literary to experimental, from traditional forms to the truly eccentric. Our only criteria is excellence. We are extremely selective about what goes in AQ. Be selective in submitting. Pays $5 per published page on publication.

APPALACHIA—5 Joy St., Boston, MA 02108. Parkman Howe, Poetry Ed. Semiannual publication of the Appalachian Mountain Club. Oldest mountaineering journal in the country covers nature, conservation, climbing, hiking, canoeing, and ecology. Poems, to 30 lines. Pays in copies.

ARACHNE—2363 Page Rd., Kennedy, NY 14747-9717. Susan L. Leach, Ed. Semiannual. Fiction, to 1,500 words. Poems (submit up to 7). "We are looking for rural material." Pays in copies. Manuscripts read in January and July.

ARIZONA QUARTERLY—Univ. of Arizona, Main Library B-541, Tucson, AZ 85721. Edgar A. Dryden, Ed. Criticism of American literature and culture from a theoretical perspective. No poetry or fiction. Pays in copies.

ART TIMES—P.O. Box 730, Mt. Marion, NY 12456. Raymond J. Steiner, Ed. Fiction, to 1,500 words, and poetry, to 20 lines, for literate, art conscious readers (generally over 40 years old). Feature essays on the arts are staff-written. Pays $25 for fiction, in copies for poetry, on publication.

ARTFUL DODGE—College of Wooster, Wooster, OH 44691. Daniel Bourne, Ed. Annual. Fiction, to 20 pages. Literary essays, especially those involving personal narrative, to 15 pages. Poetry, including translations of contemporary poets; submit 3 to 6 poems at a time; long poems encouraged. Pays $5 per page, on publication, plus 2 copies. Manuscripts read year-round.

AURA LITERARY/ARTS REVIEW—P.O. Box 76, Univ. Center, UAB, Birmingham, AL 35294. Hunter Bell, Ed.-in-Chief. Fiction and essays on literature, to 5,000 words; poetry; B&W photos. Pays in copies. Guidelines.

BEACON STREET REVIEW—WLP Div., Emerson College, 100 Beacon St., Boston, MA 02116. Attn: Ed. Semiannual. Fiction, poetry, memoir, essays, to 20 pages. "Produced and edited by graduate students. We publish primarily writing by students in MFA programs." Send 3 copies of submission, short bio, and SASE. No payment.

THE BEAR ESSENTIAL—P.O. Box 10342, Portland, OR 97296. Thomas L. Webb, Ed. Semiannual. Unique environmental articles, 750 to 2,250 words; essays, 100 to 2,500 words; artist profiles, 750 to 1,000 words; product watch, 250 to 1,500 words; and reviews, 100 to 1,000 words. Fiction, 750 to 4,500 words (2,500 is ideal). Poetry. Pays 5¢ a word, after publication. Query for nonfiction.

BELLES LETTRES—1243 Maple View Dr., Charlottesville, MD 22902-8779. Janet Mullaney, Ed. Published 3 times a year; devoted to literature by or about women. Articles, 250 to 2,000 words: reviews, interviews, rediscoveries, and retrospectives; columns on publishing news, reprints, and nonfiction titles. Annual contest. Query required. Payment varies.

THE BELLINGHAM REVIEW—The Signpost Press, MS 9053, Western Washington Univ., Bellingham, WA 98225. Robin Hemley, Ed. Semiannual. Fiction and nonfiction, to 10,000 words, and poetry, any length. Pays in copies and subscription. Manuscripts read October to April. Contests. Guidelines.

BELLOWING ARK—P.O. Box 45637, Seattle, WA 98145. Robert R. Ward, Ed. Bimonthly. Short fiction that portrays life as a positive, meaningful process. Pays in copies. Manuscripts read year-round.

BELOIT POETRY JOURNAL—RFD 2, Box 154, Ellsworth, ME 04605. Attn: Ed. Strong contemporary poetry, of any length or in any mode. Pays in copies. Guidelines. No simultaneous submissions.

BIG SKY STORIES—P.O. Box 477, Choteau, MT 59422. Happy Jack Feder, Ed. Bimonthly. Fiction, 1,000 to 5,000 words and 600 to 800 words, set in Montana or Wyoming before 1950. "Know your history. Our readers know theirs." Payment varies, on publication.

THE BITTER OLEANDER— 4983 Tall Oaks Dr., Fayetteville, NY 13066-9776. Paul B. Roth, Ed./Pub. Short stories, 2,000 to 3,000 words. Poems, one to 100 lines. "Only highly imaginative poems and stories will suffice." Pays in copies. SASE.

BLACK BEAR REVIEW—Black Bear Publications, 1916 Lincoln St., Croydon, PA 19021-8026. Ave Jeanne, Ed. Semiannual. Contemporary poetry and art work. "We publish poems with social awareness, originality, and strength." Pays in one copy. Web site: http:members.aol.com/bbreview/index.htm

BLACK DIRT—(formerly *Farmer's Market*) Elgin Community College, 1770 Spartan Dr., Elgin, IL 60123-7193. Attn: Ed. Short stories, to 30 pages, and poetry. Pays in copies and subscription.

BLACK MOON: POETRY OF IMAGINATION—233 Northway Rd., Reistertown, MD 21136. Alan Britt, Ed. Imaginative poetry, long or short. Payment is one copy. Query. Guidelines.

THE BLACK WARRIOR REVIEW—The Univ. of Alabama, P.O. Box 862936, Tuscaloosa, AL 35486-0027. Christopher Chambers, Ed. Fiction, poetry, essays. Pays $75 to $100 for stories; $35 to $45 for poems, on publication. Reads in summer.

BLOOD & APHORISMS—P.O. Box 702, Toronto, Ont., Canada M5S 2Y4. Michelle Alfano, Ed. Fiction, 500 to 5,000 words, and literary reviews, essays, and interviews. "No exploitative or violent genres, pornography, mystery, or romance." Pays $35 per page, on publication. Query for nonfiction.

THE BLOOMSBURY REVIEW—1762 Emerson St., Denver, CO 80218. Tom Auer, Ed. Marilyn Auer, Assoc. Ed. Book reviews, publishing features, interviews, essays, poetry. Pays $5 to $25, on publication.

BLUE UNICORN—22 Avon Rd., Kensington, CA 94707. Attn: Ed. Published in October, February, and June. "We are looking for originality of image, thought, and music; we rarely use poems over a page long." Submit up to 5 poems. Artwork used occasionally. Pays in one copy. Guidelines. Contest. SASE.

BLUELINE—English Dept., SUNY, Potsdam, NY 13676. Rick Henry, Ed. Fiction, to 2,500 words, on Adirondack region or similar areas. Also poetry and essays. Manuscripts read September through November.

BORDERLANDS: TEXAS POETRY REVIEW—1501 W. 5th St., Suite E-2, Austin, TX 78703. Attn: Ed. Semiannual. "Outward-looking" poetry of a political, spiritual, ecological, or social nature. Bilingual poems and translations of original poetry (both translation and original poem by the same author). Send up to 5 poems. Interviews and essays, to 3,000 words, on contemporary poets, especially those from the Southwest. Pays one copy. Query for essays and contest.

BOSTON REVIEW—E53-407, 30 Wadsworth, MIT, Cambridge, MA 02139. Matthew Howard, Man. Ed. Reviews and essays, 800 to 3,000 words, on politics, literature, art, music, film, photography. Original fiction, to 5,000 words. Poetry. Pays $40 to $100. Manuscripts read year-round.

BOTTOMFISH—De Anza College, 21250 Stevens Creek Blvd., Cupertino, CA 95014. David Denny, Ed. Annual. Short stories, short-shorts, poetry, creative nonfiction, interviews, photography. Pays in copies. Manuscripts read September to February. (Decisions made in March. Magazine published in April.)

BOULEVARD— 4579 Laclede Ave., #332, St. Louis, MO 63108-2103. Richard Burgin, Ed. Published 3 times a year. High quality fiction, to 30 pages. Pays to $150, on publication. Pieces often reprinted in books and anthologies. No submissions read from April 1 through October 1.

BRIAR CLIFF REVIEW—Briar Cliff College, 3303 Rebecca St., Sioux City, IA 51104. Tricia Currans-Sheehan, Ed. Prose, to 5,000 words: fiction, humor/satire, Siouxland history, thoughtful nonfiction. Also poetry, book reviews, and art. "We're an eclectic literary and cultural magazine focusing on, but not limited to, Siouxland writers and subjects." Pays in copies. Manuscripts read August through October.

THE BRIDGE—14050 Vernon St., Oak Park, MI 48237. Jack Zucker, Ed. Helen Zucker, Fiction Ed. Mitzi Alvin, Poetry Ed. Semiannual. Fiction, to 20 pages, and poetry to 200 lines. "Serious, realistic work with style." Pays in copies.

BUCKNELL REVIEW—Bucknell Univ., Lewisburg, PA 17837. Attn: Ed. Interdisciplinary journal in book form. Scholarly articles on arts, science, and letters. Pays in copies.

CALLALOO—Univ. of Virginia, Dept. of English, 322 Bryan Hall, Charlottesville, VA 22903. Charles H. Rowell, Ed. Fiction, poetry, drama, and popular essays by, and critical studies and bibliographies on Afro-American, Caribbean, and African artists and writers. Payment varies, on publication.

CALLIOPE—Creative Writing Program, Roger Williams Univ., Bristol, RI 02809-2921. Martha Christina, Ed. Poetry. Pays in copies and subscription. No submissions April through July.

CALYX, A JOURNAL OF ART & LITERATURE BY WOMEN—P.O. Box B, Corvallis, OR 97339. M. Reaman, Man. Ed. Fiction, 5,000 words; book reviews, 1,000 words (please query about reviews); poetry, to 6 poems. Include short bio. Pays in copies and subscription. Guidelines. SASE. Submissions accepted March 1 to April 15 and October 1 to November 15.

THE CANDLELIGHT POETRY JOURNAL—P.O. Box 6815, Scarborough, ME 04070-6815. Carl and Robin Heffley, Eds. Quarterly. Poetry, to 30 lines. (Submit no more than 5 poems.) Articles, 1,000 to 1,500 words, about poetry. Contests. Payment varies. Query required for articles.

THE CAPE ROCK—Dept. of English, Southeast Missouri State Univ., Cape Girardeau, MO 63701. Harvey E. Hecht, Ed. Semiannual. Poetry, to 70 lines, and B&W photography. (One photographer per issue; pays $100.) Pays in copies and $200 for best poem in each issue. Manuscripts read August to April.

THE CAPILANO REVIEW—Capilano College, 2055 Purcell Way, N. Vancouver, B.C., Canada V7J 3H5. Robert Sherrin, Ed. Experimental and literary fiction, 4,000 words; drama; poetry; photos and drawings. Pays $50 to $200, on publication.

THE CARIBBEAN WRITER—Univ. of the Virgin Islands, RR 02, Box 10,000, Kingshill, St. Croix, USVI 00850. Erika J. Waters, Ed. Annual. Fiction, to 15 pages (submit no more than 2 stories at a time), poems (no more than 5), and personal essays (no more than 2); the Caribbean should be central to the work. Blind submissions policy: place title only on manuscript; name, address, and title on separate sheet. Pays in copies. Annual deadline is September 30.

THE CAROLINA QUARTERLY—Greenlaw Hall CB#3520, Univ. of North Carolina, Chapel Hill, NC 27599-3520. Robert West, Ed. Poetry and fiction, to 7,000 words, by new or established writers.

THE CENTENNIAL REVIEW—312 Linton Hall, Michigan State Univ., East Lansing, MI 48824-1044. R.K. Meiners, Ed. Articles, 3,000 to 5,000 words, on sciences, humanities, and interdisciplinary topics. Pays in copies.

THE CHARITON REVIEW—Truman State Univ., Kirksville, MO 63501. Jim Barnes, Ed. Highest quality poetry and fiction, to 6,000 words. Modern and contemporary translations. "The only guideline is excellence in all matters."

CHATTAHOOCHEE REVIEW—DeKalb Community College, 2101 Womack Rd., Dunwoody, GA 30338-4497. Lawrence Hetrick, Ed. Quarterly. Fiction, essays, interviews, book reviews, and poetry. Pays from $15 per page, on publication. Send SASE for guidelines.

CHELSEA—Box 773, Cooper Sta., New York, NY 10276. Richard Foerster, Ed. Alfredo de Palchi, Sr. Assoc. Ed. Andrea Lockett and Eric Miles Williamson, Assoc. Eds. Fresh, original fiction and nonfiction, to 25 manuscript pages. Poems (submit 4 to 6). Translations welcome. "We are an eclectic literary magazine serving a sophisticated international audience. No racist, sexist, pornographic, or romance material." Query for book reviews. Pays $15 per page, on publication. Contests. Guidelines.

CHICAGO REVIEW—5801 S. Kenwood Ave., Chicago, IL 60637. Andrew Rathmann, Ed. Neda Ulaby, Fiction Ed. Fiction. Pays in copies plus one year subscription. Manuscripts read year-round; replies in 4 to 5 months.

CICADA—329 "E" St., Bakersfield, CA 93304. Frederick A. Raborg, Jr., Ed. Quarterly. Fiction, to 2,500 words, related to haiku or Japan. Limited fiction market; publishes one story each issue. Pays $10 and copies.

CIMARRON REVIEW—205 Morrill Hall, Oklahoma State Univ., Stillwater, OK 74078-0135. Peter Donahue, Assoc. Ed. Fiction. Seeks an individual style that focuses on contemporary themes. Pays $50 for stories and essays; $15 for poems. Manuscripts read year-round.

CITIES AND ROADS—P.O. Box 10886, Greensboro, NC 27404. Tom Kealey, Ed. Short fiction, to 6,000 words, by North Carolina writers, any genre. Pays in copies.

CLOCKWATCH REVIEW—Dept. of English, Illinois Wesleyan Univ., Bloomington, IL 61702-2900. James Plath, Zarina Mullan Plath, Eds. Semiannual. Fiction, to 4,000 words, and poetry, to 36 lines. "Our preference is for fresh language, a believable voice, a mature style, and a sense of the unusual in the subject matter." Pays $25 for fiction, $5 for poetry, on acceptance, plus copies. Manuscripts read year-round.

COLLAGES & BRICOLAGES—P.O. Box 360, Shippenville, PA 16254. Marie-José Fortis, Michael Kressley, Eds. Annual. Fiction and nonfiction, plays, interviews, book reviews, and poetry. Surrealistic, feminist, and expressionistic drawings in ink. "I seek innovation and honesty. The magazine often focuses on one subject; query for themes." B&W photos; photo-collages. Pays in copies. Manuscripts read August through November.

COLORADO REVIEW—English Dept., Colorado State Univ., Fort Collins, CO 80523. David Milofsky, Ed. Short fiction on contemporary themes. Manuscripts read September to April 30. Send for guidelines and upcoming contests.

COLUMBIA: A JOURNAL OF LITERATURE & ART—(formerly *Columbia: A Magazine of Poetry & Prose*) 404 Dodge, Columbia Univ., New York, NY 10027. Attn: Ed. Semiannual. Fiction. SASE for guidelines. Poetry; submit up to 5 poems. Nonfiction. Pays in copies. SASE required. Manuscripts read September to May. Upcoming theme sections: Fall 1998, "Reinventing Tales of Old: A New Look at Fairy Tales, Legends, Parables, and Fables." Spring

1999, "Spectatorship, Exhaustion, Competition: Athletics Beyond Sports Reporting." Address submissions to Fall or Spring Theme.

THE COMICS JOURNAL—Fantagraphics, Inc., 7563 Lake City Way, Seattle, WA 98115. Attn: Man. Ed. "Looking for freelancers with working knowledge of the diversity and history of the comics medium." Reviews, 2,500 to 5,000 words; domestic and international news, 500 to 7,000 words; commentaries, 500 to 1,500 words; interviews; and features, 2,500 to 5,000 words. Query for news and interviews. Pays 2¢ a word, on publication. Guidelines.

CONCHO RIVER REVIEW—Angelo State Univ., English Dept., San Angelo, TX 76909. James A. Moore, Ed. Semiannual. Fiction, essays, and book reviews, 1,500 to 5,000 words. Poetry, 500 to 1,500 words. "We tend to publish traditional stories with a strong sense of conflict, finely drawn characters, and crisp dialogue. Critical papers, articles, and personal essays with a Texas or Southwestern literary slant preferred. Query for book reviews." Payment is one copy.

CONFLUENCE—P.O. Box 336, Belpre, OH 45714-0336. David B. Prather, Poetry Ed. Daniel Born, Fiction Ed. Published annually by Marietta College and the Ohio Valley Literary Group. Poetry and short fiction. Pays in copies. Manuscripts read September through March.

CONFRONTATION—Dept. of English, C.W. Post of L.I.U., Brookville, NY 11548. Martin Tucker, Ed. Serious fiction, 750 to 6,000 words. Pays $15 to $200, on publication.

THE CONNECTICUT POETRY REVIEW—P.O. Box 818, Stonington, CT 06378. J. Claire White and Harley More, Eds. Poetry, 5 to 20 lines, and reviews, 700 words. Pays $5 per poem, $10 per review, on acceptance. Manuscripts read September to January and April to June.

CONNECTICUT RIVER REVIEW—35 Lindsley Pl., Stratford, CT 06497. Norah Christianson, Ed. Semiannual. Poetry. Submit up to 3 poems. Pays in one copy. Guidelines.

CONTRABAND: THE JOURNAL OF FUGITIVE THOUGHT—(formerly *L'ouverture: The Black Marketplace of Ideas*) P.O. Box 8565, Atlanta, GA 30306. Bill Campbell, Ed. Quarterly. Fiction, any genre; satire, essays. Cultural and political commentary. Poetry. "We're a multicultural publication hoping to provoke thought in our readership, to build a cacophony of dialogue." Pays in copies. Manuscripts read year-round.

CQ/CALIFORNIA STATE POETRY QUARTERLY—California State Poetry Society, Box 7126, Orange, CA 92863. Attn: Ed. Board. Poetry, to 60 lines. All poets welcome. Payment is one copy. Responds within 4 months.

CRAZY QUILT—P.O. Box 632729, San Diego, CA 92163-2729. Attn: Eds. Fiction, to 4,000 words, poetry, one-act plays, literary criticism, and author interviews. Also B&W art, photographs. Pays in copies. Fiction read January through March. Other submissions read year-round.

CRAZYHORSE—English Dept., Univ. of Arkansas, Little Rock, AR 72204. Address Poetry Ed. or Criticism Ed. Mainstream poetry, nonfiction prose, and criticism.

THE CREAM CITY REVIEW—English Dept., Box 413, Univ. of Wisconsin, Milwaukee, WI 53201. Staci Leigh O'Brien, Ed. Semiannual. "We serve a national audience interested in a diversity of writing (in terms of style, subject, genre) and writers (gender, race, class, publishing history, etc.). Both well-known and newly published writers of fiction, poetry, and essays are featured, along with B&W artwork." Pays in copies. Manuscripts read September 1 to April 30.

CREATIVE NONFICTION—5501 Walnut, Suite 202, Pittsburgh, PA 15232. Lee Gutkind, Ed. "No length requirements; seeking well-written prose, attentive to language, rich with detail and distinctive voice on any subject." Pays from $5 per published page.

THE CRESCENT REVIEW—P.O. Box 15069, Chevy Chase, MD 20825. J.T. Holland, Ed. Short stories only. Pays in copies. Manuscripts read July through October and January through April.

CRITICAL INQUIRY—Univ. of Chicago Press, 202 Wieboldt Hall, 1050 E. 59th St., Chicago, IL 60637. W. J. T. Mitchell, Ed. Critical essays that offer a theoretical perspective on literature, music, visual arts, and popular culture. No fiction, poetry, or autobiography. Pays in copies. Manuscripts read year-round.

CUMBERLAND POETRY REVIEW—P.O. Box 120128, Acklen Sta., Nashville, TN 37212. Attn: Eds. High-quality poetry and criticism; translations. Send up to 6 poems with brief bio. No restrictions on form, style, or subject matter. Pays in copies.

CUTBANK—English Dept., Univ. of Montana, Missoula, MT 59812. Attn: Eds. Semiannual. Fiction, to 40 pages (submit one story at a time), and poems (submit up to 5 poems). All manuscripts are considered for the Richard Hugo Memorial Poetry Award and the A.B. Guthrie, Jr. Short Fiction Award. Pays in copies. Guidelines. Manuscripts read August 15 to March 15.

DENVER QUARTERLY—Dept. of English, Univ. of Denver, Denver, CO 80208. Bin Ramke, Ed. Fiction and poetry. Pays $5 per printed page, after publication.

THE DEVIL'S MILLHOPPER—The Devil's Millhopper Press, USC/ Aiken, 171 University Pkwy., Aiken, SC 29801-6309. Stephen Gardner, Ed. Poetry. Send SASE for guidelines and contest information. Pays in copies.

THE DISTILLERY—Motlow State Community College, P.O. Box 88100, Tullahoma, TN 37388. Stuart Bloodworth, Ed. Semiannual. Fiction, 4,000 words; poetry, submit 4 to 6 poems; critical essays; photos and drawings. Responds in 2 to 3 months. Pays in copies.

DOUBLE DEALER REDUX—632 Pirate's Alley, New Orleans, LA 70116. Rosemary Jams, Ed. Quarterly. Fiction, essays, and poetry. "We showcase the work of promising writers." No payment. Query. Contest.

DREAMS & VISIONS—Skysong Press, 35 Peter St. S., Orillia, Ontario, Canada L3V 5A8. Steve Stanton, Ed. Eclectic fiction, 2,000 to 6,000 words, that is "in some way unique and relevant to Christian readers today." Pays ½¢ per word.

EARTH'S DAUGHTERS—P.O. Box 41, Central Park Sta., Buffalo, NY 14215. Attn: Ed. Published 3 times a year. Fiction, to 1,000 words, poetry, to 40 lines, and B&W photos or drawings. "Finely crafted work with a feminist theme." Pays in copies. SASE for guidelines and themes.

ECLECTIC RAINBOWS—1538 Tennessee Walker Dr., Roswell, GA 30075. Linda T. Dennison, Ed./Pub. Annual. Essays (no nostalgia), articles, celebrity interviews, 1,000 to 4,000 words. Poetry, to 30 lines. Limited fiction (no science fiction or horror). "New Age emphasis is on personal and planetary growth and transformation. Be positive in approach; humorous point-of-view always welcome." Pays to $25, on publication. Guidelines. Contests.

EDGE CITY REVIEW—10912 Harpers Sq. Ct., Reston, VA 20191. T.L. Ponick, Ed. Literary fiction, to 3,500 words; essays, to 2,500 words; formal, metrical poetry. Reviews of small press books. "Prefer metrical poetry to free verse and coherent short fiction to self-consciously styled work. Political slant is to the right." Pays in copies.

ELF: ECLECTIC LITERARY FORUM—P.O. Box 392, Tonawanda, NY 14150. C. K. Erbes, Ed. Fiction, 3,500 words. Essays on literary themes, 3,500 words. Poetry, to 30 lines. Allow 4 to 8 weeks for response. Pays in one copy. Guidelines.

EPOCH—251 Goldwin Smith Hall, Cornell Univ., Ithaca, NY 14853-3201. Michael Koch, Ed. Serious fiction and poetry. Pays $5 a page for fiction and poetry. No submissions between April 15 and September 21. Guidelines.

EUREKA LITERARY MAGAZINE—Eureka College, P.O. Box 280, Eureka, IL 61530. Loren Logsdon, Ed. Nancy Perkins, Fiction Ed. Semiannual. Fiction, 25 to 30 pages, and poetry, submit up to 4 poems at a time. "We promote no specific political agenda or literary theory." Pays in copies.

EVENT—Douglas College, Box 2503, New Westminster, BC, Canada V3L 5B2. Calvin Wharton, Ed. Short fiction. Pays $22 per printed page, on publication.

EXPRESSIONS—P.O. Box 16294, St. Paul, MN 55116. Sefra Kobrin Pitzele, Ed. Semiannual, nonprofit. Literature and art by people with disabilities and ongoing illnesses. Fiction and articles, to 2,000 words. Poetry, to 64 lines. B&W artwork. "We hope to be a place where talented people who may have limited energy, finances, or physical ability can be published." Pays in copies. Guidelines. Contests.

EXQUISITE CORPSE—P.O. Box 25051, Baton Rouge, LA 70894. Andrei Codrescu, Ed. Fiction, nonfiction, and poetry for "a journal of letters and life." B&W photos and drawings. Read the magazine before submitting. Payment is 10 copies and one-year subscription. Manuscripts read year-round.

FARMER'S MARKET—See *Black Dirt.*

FEELINGS POETRY JOURNAL—See *Poets' Paper.*

FICTION—c/o English Dept., City College of New York, Convent Ave. at 138th St., New York, NY 10031. Mark Jay Mirsky, Ed. Semiannual. Short stories and novel excerpts, to 5,000 words. "Read the magazine before submitting." Payment varies, on acceptance. Manuscripts not read in the summer.

FICTION INTERNATIONAL—English Dept., San Diego State Univ., San Diego, CA 92182-8140. Harold Jaffe, Ed. Innovative and politically committed fiction and theory. Query for annual themes. Pays in copies. Manuscripts read from September 1 to December 15.

THE FIDDLEHEAD—Campus House, Univ. of New Brunswick, Fredericton, NB, Canada E3B 5A3. Attn: Ed. Serious fiction, 2,500 words. Pays about $10 per printed page, on publication. Include international reply coupons with submissions.

FIELD—Rice Hall, Oberlin College, Oberlin, OH 44074. Pamela Alexander, Martha Collins, David Walker, David Young, Eds. Serious poetry, any length, by established and unknown poets; essays on poetics by poets. Translations by qualified translators. Payment varies, on publication. Manuscripts read year-round.

FIVE FINGERS REVIEW—P.O. Box 12955, Berkeley, CA 94712-3955. Annual. "Writing with a sense of experimentation, an awareness of tradition, and a willingness to explore artistic boundaries." Pays in copies.

THE FLORIDA REVIEW—English Dept., Univ. of Central Florida, Orlando, FL 32816. Russell Kesler, Ed. Semiannual. Mainstream and experimental fiction and nonfiction, to 7,500 words. Poetry, any style. Pays in copies.

FLYWAY—203 Ross Hall, Iowa State Univ., Ames, IA 50011-1201. Stephen Pett, Ed. Poetry, fiction, creative nonfiction, and reviews. Pays in copies. Manuscripts read September through May.

FOLIO—Dept. of Literature, American Univ., Washington, DC 20016. Attn: Ed. Semiannual. Fiction, poetry, translations, and essays. Photos and drawings. Pays in 2 copies. Submissions read September through March. Contest.

FOOTWORK, THE PATERSON LITERARY REVIEW—See *The Paterson Literary Review.*

THE FORMALIST—320 Hunter Dr., Evansville, IN 47711. William Baer, Ed. Metrical poetry. "Well-crafted poetry in a contemporary idiom which uses meter and the full range of traditional poetic conventions in vigorous and interesting ways. Especially interested in sonnets, couplets, tercets, ballads, the French forms, etc." Howard Nemerov Sonnet Award ($1,000); SASE for details.

THE FRACTAL—George Mason Univ., 4400 University Dr., MS 2D6, Fairfax, VA 22030. Christopher Elliot, Jessica Darago, Sr. Eds. Fantastic fiction, poetry, art, and nonfiction. Guidelines. Pays $25 for fiction; $50 for nonfiction; $5 for poetry, on publication. Send complete manuscript.

FREE INQUIRY—P.O. Box 664, Buffalo, NY 14226. Paul Kurtz, Ed. Tim Madigan, Exec. Ed. Articles, 500 to 5,000 words, for "literate and lively readership. Focus is on criticisms of religious belief systems, and how to lead an ethical life without a supernatural basis." Pays in copies.

FUGUE—Univ. of Idaho, English Dept., Brink Hall, Room 200, Moscow, ID 83844-1102. Address Exec. Ed. Fiction and nonfiction to 6,000 words. Poetry, any style, 100 lines. Open to new writers. Include SASE. Pays in copies and small honorarium.

GEORGETOWN REVIEW—P.O. Box 6309 SS, Hattiesburg, MS 39406. John Fulmer, Ed. Semiannual. Fiction and poetry; new exciting voices. Guidelines. Contest.

THE GEORGIA REVIEW—Univ. of Georgia, Athens, GA 30602-9009. Stanley W. Lindberg, Ed. Stephen Corey, Assoc. Ed. Janet Wondra, Asst. Ed. Self-contained short fiction. No novel excerpts. Subject matter, style, and length are unrestricted. "All manuscripts receive serious consideration." Pays $35 per printed page, plus one-year subscription. No simultaneous submissions. Manuscripts read September through May.

THE GETTYSBURG REVIEW—Gettysburg College, Gettysburg, PA 17325. Peter Stitt, Ed. Quarterly. Poetry, fiction, essays, and essay reviews, 1,000 to 20,000 words. Pays $2 a line for poetry; $25 per printed page for prose. Allow 6 months for response. No simultaneous submissions.

GLIMMER TRAIN PRESS—710 S.W. Madison St., #504, Portland, OR 97205. Susan Burmeister-Brown, Ed. Quarterly. Fiction, 1,200 to 7,500 words. Eight stories in each issue. Pays $500, on acceptance. Submit material in January, April, July, and October. Allow 3 months for response. Short story award for new writers; SASE for details.

GOTHIC JOURNAL—P.O. Box 6340, Elko, NV 89802-6340. Kristi Lyn Glass, Pub. Bimonthly. News and reviews for readers, writers, and publishers of romantic suspense; romantic mystery; and gothic, supernatural, and woman-in-jeopardy romance novels. Articles, 1,000 to 2,000 words, on gothic and romantic suspense topics; author profiles, 3,000 to 4,000 words; book reviews, 250 to 500 words. Pays $20 for articles, $30 for author profiles, on publication. Web site: http://gothicjournal.com/romance/.

GRAIN—Box 1154, Regina, Sask., Canada S4P 3B4. J. Jill Robinson, Ed. Short stories, to 30 typed pages; poems, send up to 8; visual art. Pays $30 to $100 for stories and poems, $100 for cover art, $30 for other art. SAE with international reply coupons required. Manuscripts read year-round. Web site: www.skwriter.com.

GRAND STREET—131 Varick St., #906, New York, NY 10013. Jean Stein, Ed. Quarterly. Poetry, any length. Pays $3 a line, on publication. Will not read unsolicited fiction or essays.

GRAND TOUR: THE JOURNAL OF TRAVEL LITERATURE—P.O. Box 66, Thorofare, NJ 08086. Jennifer Fisher, Man. Ed. Quarterly. Travel-related memoirs, essays, and articles, 1,000 to 7,000 words, that "combine the sharp eye of the reporter with the craft of the short story writer and the rhythm of the poet." Pays $50 to $200, on publication.

GRASSLANDS REVIEW—P.O. Box 626, Berea, OH 44017. Laura Kennelly, Ed. Semiannual. Short stories, 1,000 to 3,500 words. Poetry, any length. "We seek imagination without sloppiness, ideas without lectures, and delight in language. Our purpose is to encourage new writers." Pays in copies. Manuscripts read in March and October only.

GREEN MOUNTAIN REVIEW—Johnson State College, Johnson, VT 05656. Neil Shepard, Poetry Ed. Tony Whedon, Fiction Ed. Fiction and creative nonfiction, including literary essays, book reviews, and interviews, to 25 pages. Poetry. Manuscripts read September through April. Payment varies (depending on funding), on publication.

GREEN'S MAGAZINE—P.O. Box 3236, Regina, Sask., Canada S4P 3H1. David Green, Ed. Fiction for family reading, 1,500 to 4,000 words. No simultaneous submissions. Pays in copies. Submissions from US must include international reply coupons.

THE GREENSBORO REVIEW—English Dept., 134 McIver Bldg., UNCG, P.O. Box 26170, Greensboro, NC 27402-6170. Jim Clark, Ed. Semiannual. Poetry and fiction. Submission deadlines: September 15 and February 15. Pays in copies. Guidelines.

GULF COAST—English Dept., Univ. of Houston, Houston, TX 77204. Attn: Ed. Semiannual. Fiction (no genre fiction), nonfiction, poetry (submit up to 5), and translations. No payment.

HABERSHAM REVIEW—Piedmont College, Demorest, GA 30535-0010. Frank Gannon, Ed. Emory Lavender, Asst. Ed. Stephen R. Whited, Poetry Ed. Short stories, essays, satire, reviews, poetry. "Approximately two-thirds of each issue will have a southern focus." Pays in copies.

HALF TONES TO JUBILEE—Pensacola Junior College, English Dept., 1000 College Blvd., Pensacola, FL 32504. Walter F. Spara, Ed. Fiction, to 1,500 words, and poetry, to 60 lines. Pays in copies. Manuscripts read August 15 to May 15. Contest.

HAPPY—240 E. 35th St., Suite 11A, New York, NY 10016. Bayard, Ed. Quarterly. Fiction, to 6,000 words. "No previously published work. No pornography. No racist/sexist pandering. No bourgeois boredom." Pays $5 per 1,000 words, on publication, plus one copy.

HARP-STRINGS—P.O. Box 640387, Beverly Hills, FL 34464. Madelyn Eastlund, Ed. Poems, 14 to 80 lines, on a variety of topics and in many forms. No light verse, "prose masquerading as poetry," confessions, or raw guts poems. Pays in copies.

HAWAII REVIEW—Dept. of English, Univ. of Hawaii, 1733 Donagho Rd., Honolulu, HI 96822. Malia E. Gellert, Ed.-in-Chief. Quality fiction, poetry, interviews, and essays. Manuscripts read year-round.

HAYDEN'S FERRY REVIEW—Box 871502, Arizona State Univ., Tempe, AZ 85287-1502. Attn: Ed. Semiannual. Fiction, essays, and poetry (submit up to 6 poems). Include brief bio and SASE. Deadline for Spring/Summer issue is September 30; Fall/Winter issue, February 28. Pays in copies.

THE HEARTLANDS TODAY—Firelands Writing Ctr. of Firelands College, Huron, OH 44839. Larry Smith and Nancy Dunham, Eds. Fiction, 1,000 to 4,500 words, and nonfiction, 1,000 to 3,000 words, about the contemporary Midwest. Poetry (submit 3 to 5 poems). "Writing must be set in the Midwest, but can include a variety of themes." B&W photos. Pays $10 to $20 honorarium, plus copies. Query for current themes. Contest. Manuscripts read January 1 to June 15.

HEAVEN BONE—P.O. Box 486, Chester, NY 10918. Steve Hirsch, Ed. Annual. "The Bridge Between Muse & Mind." Fiction, to 5,000 words. Magazine and book reviews, 250 to 2,500 words. Poetry (submit no more than 10 pages at a time). "Alternative-cultural, post-beat, surrealist, and yogic/anti-paranoiac." Allow 6 months for response. Pays in copies.

HEROES FROM HACKLAND—1225 Evans, Arkadelphia, AR 71923. Mike Grogan, Ed. Quarterly. Nostalgic articles, 750 to 1,500 words, on B-movies (especially westerns and serials), comic books, grade school readers, juvenile series books, cartoons, vintage autos, country music and pop music before 1956, and vintage radio and television. "We believe in heroes, especially those popular culture icons that serious critics label 'ephemera.'" Pays in copies.

HIGH PLAINS LITERARY REVIEW—180 Adams St., Suite 250, Denver, CO 80206. Robert O. Greer, Ed. Fiction, 3,000 to 6,500 words, as well as poetry, essays, reviews, interviews. "Designed to bridge the gap between the academic quarterlies and commercial reviews." Pays $10 a page for poetry; $5 a page for fiction, on publication.

THE HIGHLANDER—P.O. Box 22307, Kansas City, MO 64113. Crennan Wade, Ed. Bimonthly. Articles, 1,300 to 1,900 words, related to Scottish history. "We do not want articles on modern Scotland." Pays $100 to $150, on acceptance.

THE HOLLINS CRITIC—P.O. Box 9538, Hollins College, Roanoke, VA 24020. R.H.W. Dillard, Ed. Published 5 times a year. Features an essay on a contemporary fiction writer, poet or dramatist, cover sketch, brief biography, and book list. Also, book reviews and poetry. Pays $25 for poetry, on publication.

HOME PLANET NEWS—P.O. Box 415, Stuyvesant Sta., New York, NY 10009. Enid Dame and Donald Lev, Eds. Quarterly art tabloid. Fiction, to 8 typed pages; reviews, 3 to 5 pages; and poetry, any length. Query for nonfiction. Pays in copies and subscription. Manuscripts read February through May.

THE HUDSON REVIEW— 684 Park Ave., New York, NY 10021. Frederick Morgan and Paula Deitz, Eds. Quarterly. Fiction, to 10,000 words. Essays, to 8,000 words. Poetry, submit up to 10. Payment varies, on publication. Guidelines. Reading periods: Nonfiction read January through April. Poetry read April through July. Fiction read June through November.

HURRICANE ALICE: A FEMINIST QUARTERLY—Dept. of English, Rhode Island College, Providence, RI 02908. Attn: Joan Dagle Fiction, poetry, and nonfiction, 500 to 3,500 words, with feminist perspective. Pays in copies.

ILLYA'S HONEY— 432 Greenridge, Coppell, TX 75019. Stephen W. Brodie, Ed. Quarterly. Short fiction, any subject, any style, to 1,000 words; poetry, to 60 lines. "No forced rhyme or overly religious verse." Manuscripts read year-round.

INDIANA REVIEW—Ballantine 465, Indiana Univ., Bloomington, IN 47405. Laura McCoid, Ed. Brian Leung, Assoc. Ed. We look for daring stories that integrate theme, language, character, and form. We like polished writing, humor, and fiction which has consequence beyond the world of its narrator. Please read the magazine before submitting. Also publish poetry. Pays $5 per page. Manuscripts read year-round.

INK—P.O. Box 52558, 264 Bloor St. W., Toronto, Ontario, Canada M5S 1V0. John Degen, Ed. Quarterly. Poetry. Fiction, to 3,000 words. Query for interviews, reviews, and articles on the arts. No payment.

INTERIM—Dept. of English, Univ. of Nevada, Las Vegas, NV 89154-5034. James Hazen, Ed. Semiannual. Poetry, any form or length; fiction, to 7,500 words (uses up to 2 stories per issue). Pays in copies and 2-year subscription. Responds in 2 months.

INTERNATIONAL POETRY REVIEW—Dept. of Romance Languages, Univ. of North Carolina, Greensboro, NC 27412. Attn: Ed. Semiannual. Book reviews, interviews, and short essays, to 1,500 words. Original English poems and contemporary translations of poems. "We prefer material with cross-cultural or international dimension." Pays in copies.

INTERNATIONAL QUARTERLY—P.O. Box 10521, Tallahassee, FL 32302. Van K. Brock, Ed. Fiction and nonfiction, to 5,000 words; poetry. Pays in copies and subscription.

THE IOWA REVIEW—EPB 308, Univ. of Iowa, Iowa City, IA 52242. David Hamilton, Mary Hussmann, Eds. Essays, poems, stories, reviews. Pays $10 a page for prose; $1 a line for poetry, on publication. Manuscripts read September through January.

IRIS: A JOURNAL ABOUT WOMEN—The Women's Ctr., Box 323, HSC Univ. of Virginia, Charlottesville, VA 22908. Susan K. Brady, Ed. Semiannual. Fiction, 2,500 to 8,000 words; personal essays, to 2,500 words; poetry. "Our readers are mostly women; very diverse in age and interests." Pays in subscription.

THE JAMES WHITE REVIEW—P.O. Box 3356, Butler Quarter Sta., Minneapolis, MN 55403. Phil Willkie, Pub. "A Gay Men's Literary Quarterly." Short stories, to 9,000 words, and poetry, to 250 lines. Book reviews. Responds in 3 months.

JAPANOPHILE—P.O. Box 7977, Ann Arbor, MI 48107. Susan Lapp, Ed. Fiction, to 4,000 words, with a Japanese setting and at least one Japanese and at least one non-Japanese character. Articles, 2,000 words, that celebrate Japanese culture. "We seek to promote Japanese-American understanding. We are not about Japan-bashing or fatuous praise." Pays to $25, on publication. Annual short story contest; deadline December 31.

JOURNAL OF NEW JERSEY POETS—County College of Morris, 214 Center Grove Rd., Randolph, NJ 07869-2086. Sander Zulauf, Ed. Semiannual. Serious contemporary poetry by current and former New Jersey residents. "Although our emphasis is on poets associated with New Jersey, we seek work that is universal in scope." Pays in copies.

KALEIDOSCOPE—United Disability Services, 701 S. Main St., Akron, OH 44311-1019. Darshan Perusek, Ph.D., Ed.-in-Chief. Semiannual. Fiction, essays, interviews, articles, and poetry relating to disability and the arts, to 5,000 words. Photos a plus. "We present balanced, realistic images of people with disabilities and publish pieces that challenge stereotypes." Submissions accepted from writers with or without disabilities. Pays $10 to $125. Guidelines recommended. Manuscripts read year-round; response may take up to 6 months.

KALLIOPE: A JOURNAL OF WOMEN'S ART—Florida Community College at Jacksonville, 3939 Roosevelt Blvd., Jacksonville, FL 32205. Attn: Ed. Fiction, to 2,500 words; poetry; interviews of women writers, to 2,000 words; and B&W photos of fine art. Query for interviews only. Pays $10 or in copies.

KARAMU—Dept. of English, Eastern Illinois Univ., Charleston, IL 61920. Olga Abella, Lauren Smith, Eds. Annual. Contemporary or experimental fiction. Creative nonfiction prose, personal essays, and memoir pieces. Poetry. Pays in copies. Manuscripts read year-round; best time to submit is January to May.

KELSEY REVIEW—Mercer County Community College, P.O. Box B, Trenton, NJ 08690. Robin Schore, Ed. Fiction and nonfiction, to 2,000 words, and poetry by writers living or working in Mercer County, NJ. Pays in copies.

THE KENYON REVIEW—Kenyon College, Gambier, OH 43022. David H. Lynn, Ed. Published 3 times a year. Fiction, poetry, essays, literary criticism, and reviews. Pays $10 a printed page for prose, $15 a printed page for poetry, on publication. Manuscripts read September through March.

KIOSK—c/o English Dept., 306 Clemens Hall, SUNY Buffalo, Buffalo, NY 14260. Paula Melton, Ed. Kevin Grauke, Fiction Ed., Sheri Weinstein and Loren Goodman, Poetry Eds. Fiction, to 20 pages, with a "strong sense of voice, narrative direction, and craftsmanship." Poetry "that explores boundaries, including the formally experimental." Address appropriate editor. Pays in copies. Manuscripts read September 1 to December 1.

LAMBDA BOOK REPORT—1773 T St., N.W., Suite One, Washington, DC 20009. Kanani Kanka, Sr. Ed. Reviews and features, 250 to 1,500 words, of gay and lesbian books. Pays $10 to $75, 30 days after publication. Queries preferred.

LATINO STUFF REVIEW—P.O. Box 440195, Miami, FL 33144. Nilda Cepero-Llevada, Ed./Pub. Short stories, 3,000 words; poetry, to one page; criticism and essays on literature, the arts, social issues. Bilingual publication focusing on Latino topics. Pays in copies.

THE LAUREL REVIEW—Northwest Missouri State Univ., Dept. of English, Maryville, MO 64468. William Trowbridge, David Slater, Beth Richards, Eds. Semiannual. Fiction, nonfiction, and poetry. Pays in copies and subscription.

THE LEADING EDGE—3163 JKHB, Provo, UT 84602. David Burnett, Ed. Semiannual. Science fiction and fantasy, 3,000 to 12,000 words; poetry, to 600 lines; and articles, to 8,000 words, on science, scientific speculation, and literary criticism. No excessive profanity, overt violence, or excessive sexual situations. No simultaneous submissions. Pays ¼¢ per word, on publication. Guidelines.

THE LEDGE—78-44 80th St., Glendale, NY 11385. Timothy Monaghan, Ed. Poetry; submit 3 to 5 poems at a time. "We publish provocative, well-crafted poems by well-known and lesser-known poets. Excellence is our main criterion." Pays in copies.

LIGHT—Box 7500, Chicago, IL 60680. John Mella, Ed. Semiannual. Light verse. Also fiction, reviews, and essays, to 2,000 words. Fillers, humor, jokes, quips. "If it has wit, point, edge, or barb, it will find a home here." Cartoons and line drawings. Pays in copies. Query for nonfiction.

LILITH, THE INDEPENDENT JEWISH WOMEN'S MAGAZINE—250 W. 57th St., New York, NY 10107. Susan Weidman Schneider, Ed.-in-Chief. Faye Moskowitz, Fiction Ed. Fiction, 1,500 to 2,000 words, on issues of interest to Jewish women.

LITERAL LATTE— 61 E. 8th St., Suite 240, New York, NY 10003. Jenine Gordon Bockman, Ed./Pub. Bimonthly distributed to cafés and bookstores. Fiction and personal essays, to 6,000 words; poetry, to 2,000 words; art. Pays in subscription, honorarium, and copies. Contests and awards.

LITERARY MAGAZINE REVIEW—Dept. of English Language and Lit., Univ. of Northern Iowa, 117 Baker Hall, Cedar Falls, IA 50614-0502. Grant Tracey, Ed. Reviews and articles concerning literary magazines, 1,000 to 1,500 words, for writers and readers of contemporary literature. Pays in copies. Query.

THE LITERARY REVIEW—Fairleigh Dickinson Univ., 285 Madison Ave., Madison, NJ 07940. Walter Cummins, Ed.-in-Chief. Martin Green, Harry Keyishian, William Zander, Eds. Serious fiction. Open to a variety of imaginative approaches, including translations. Pays in copies.

LONG SHOT—P.O. Box 6238, Hoboken, NJ 07030. Danny Shot, Nancy Mercado, Lynne Breitfeller, Andy Clausen, Eds. Fiction, poetry, and nonfiction, to 10 pages. B&W photos and drawings. Pays in copies.

THE LONG STORY—18 Eaton St., Lawrence, MA 01843. Attn: Ed. Stories, 8,000 to 20,000 words; prefer stories about common folks and a thematic focus. Pays in copies.

L'OUVERTURE: THE BLACK MARKETPLACE OF IDEAS—See *Contraband: The Journal of Fugitive Thought.*

LYNX EYE— c/o Scribblefest Literary Group, 1880 Hill Dr., Los Angeles, CA 90041. Pam McCully, Kathryn Morrison, Eds. Quarterly. Short stories, vignettes, novel excerpts, one-act plays, essays, belle lettres, satires, and reviews, 500 to 5,000 words; poetry, to 30 lines. Pays $10, on acceptance.

THE MACGUFFIN—Schoolcraft College, Dept. of English, 18600 Haggerty Rd., Livonia, MI 48152. Arthur J. Lindenberg, Ed. General, mainstream, and experimental fiction and nonfiction, 400 to 5,000 words. Poetry. "No religious, inspirational, confessional, romance, horror, or pornography." Pays in copies.

THE MALAHAT REVIEW—Univ. of Victoria, P.O. Box 1700, Victoria, BC, Canada V8W 2Y2. Derk Wynand, Ed. Fiction and poetry, including translations. Pays from $25 per page, on acceptance.

MANOA—English Dept., Univ. of Hawaii, Honolulu, HI 96822. Frank Stewart, Ed. Ian MacMillan, Fiction Ed. Lisa Ottiger, Book Reviews Ed. Fiction, to 30 pages; essays, to 25 pages; book reviews, 4 to 5 pages; and poetry (submit 4 to 6 poems). "Writers are encouraged to read the journal carefully before submitting." Pays $25 for poetry and book reviews; $20 to $25 per page for fiction, on publication.

MANY MOUNTAINS MOVING— 420 22nd St., Boulder, CO 80302. Naomi Horii, Marilyn Krysl, Eds. Semiannual. Fiction, nonfiction, and poetry by writers of all cultures. Pays in copies.

MASSACHUSETTS REVIEW—South College, Univ. of Massachusetts, Amherst, MA 01003. Attn: Ed. Short fiction, 15 to 25 pages. Pays $50, on publication. SASE required. Manuscripts read October through May.

THE MAVERICK PRESS—Rt. 2, Box 4915, Eagle Pass, TX 78852-9605. Carol Cullar, Ed. Short stories, to 1,500 words, and unrhymed poetry. Pays in copies. Query with SASE for themes.

MEDIPHORS—P.O. Box 327, Bloomsburg, PA 17815. Eugene D. Radice, MD, Ed. "A literary journal of the health professions." Short stories, essays, and commentary, 4,500 words. "Topics should have some relation to medicine and health, but may be quite broad." Poems, to 30 lines. Humor. Pays in copies. Guidelines. Web site: www.mediphors.org.

MESSAGES FROM THE HEART—P.O. Box 64840, Tucson, AZ 85728. Lauren B. Smith, Ed. Quarterly. Heartfelt letters, diary excerpts, poems, or essays, to 800 words, that contain an element of hope. Drawings and B&W photos. Manuscripts read year-round. Pays in copies.

MICHIGAN HISTORICAL REVIEW—Clarke Historical Library, Central Michigan Univ., Mt. Pleasant, MI 48859. Attn: Ed. Semiannual. Scholarly articles related to Michigan's political, social, economic, and cultural history; articles on American, Canadian, and Midwestern history that directly or indirectly explore themes related to Michigan's past. Manuscripts read year-round.

MID-AMERICAN REVIEW—Dept. of English, Bowling Green State Univ., Bowling Green, OH 43403. George Looney, Ed. High-quality fiction, poetry, articles, translations, and reviews of contemporary writing. Fiction, to 5,000 words, (query for longer work). Reviews, articles, 500 to 2,500 words. Pays to $50, on publication (pending funding). Manuscripts read September through May.

MIDWEST QUARTERLY—Pittsburg State Univ., Pittsburg, KS 66762. James B. M. Schick, Ed. Scholarly articles, 2,500 to 5,000 words, on contemporary academic and public issues; poetry. Pays in copies. Manuscripts read year-round.

THE MINNESOTA REVIEW—Dept. of English, Univ. of Missouri, Columbia, MO 65211. Attn: Ed. Politically committed fiction, 1,000 to 6,000 words; nonfiction, 5,000 to 7,500 words; and poetry, to 3 pages, for readers committed to social issues, including feminism, neomarxism, etc. Pays in copies. Responds in 2 to 4 months.

MISSISSIPPI MUD—7119 Santa Fe Ave., Dallas, TX 75223. Joel Weinstein, Ed. Short stories, to 50 pages, and novel excerpts, 50 to 100 pages; poetry, any length. Pays $25 for poems; $50 to $100 for fiction, on publication.

MISSISSIPPI REVIEW—Ctr. for Writers, Univ. of Southern Mississippi, Box 5144, Hattiesburg, MS 39406-5144. Frederick Barthelme, Ed. Serious fiction. Pays in copies.

THE MISSOURI REVIEW—1507 Hillcrest Hall, Univ. of Missouri-Columbia, Columbia, MO 65211. Greg Michalson, Man. Ed. Speer Morgan, Ed. Evelyn Somers, Nonfiction Ed. Fiction. Also poetry, essays, interviews, and book reviews. Pays $20 per printed page, on contract. Manuscripts read year-round.

MODERN HAIKU—P.O. Box 1752, Madison, WI 53701-1752. Robert Spiess, Ed. Haiku and articles about haiku. Pays $1 per haiku, $5 a page for articles. Manuscripts read year-round.

MONTHLY REVIEW—122 W. 27th St., New York, NY 10001. Paul M. Sweezy, Harry Magdoff, Ellen Meiksins Wood, Eds. Analytical articles, 5,000 words, on politics and economics, from independent socialist viewpoint. Pays $25 for reviews, $50 for articles, on publication.

MOOSE BOUND PRESS—P.O. Box 111781, Anchorage, AK 99511-1781. Sonia Walker, Ed. Quarterly. Short stories, to 2,000 words. Poetry, to 30 lines. Essays, to 500 words. "Wholesome, energetic, and uplifting writing. We are kind to beginning writers." Send for annual themes. Payment varies, on publication.

MUDDY RIVER POETRY REVIEW—28 Wessex Rd., Newton Centre, MA 02159. Zvi A. Sesling, Michael D. Sesling, Eds. Annual. Poems. "While free verse is preferred, nothing will be rejected if it is quality." No previously published poems. Payment is one copy.

MYSTERY TIME—P.O. Box 2907, Decatur, IL 62524. Linda Hutton, Ed. Semiannual. Suspense, 1,500 words, and poems about mysteries, up to 16 lines. "We prefer female protagonists. No gore or violence." Pays $5, on acceptance.

THE NAPLES REVIEW—626 Third St. N., Naples, FL 34102-5537. Mr. Leslie Waller, Ed. Quarterly. Articles, essays, short stories, novel excerpts, and plays, to 10 pages. Poetry, to 2 pages. Preference given to residents of Southwest Florida or subject matter related to the area. Pays in copies.

NEBO: A LITERARY JOURNAL—Dept. of English, Arkansas Tech. Univ., Russellville, AR 72801-2222. Attn: Ed. Mainstream fiction, to 3,000 words. (Poetry; submit up to 5 poems.) Pays in one copy. SASE for guidelines.

NEBRASKA REVIEW—Writer's Workshop, FAB 212, Univ. of Nebraska at Omaha, Omaha, NE 68182-0324. James Reed, Ed. Susan Aizenberg, Poetry Ed. Short stories and personal essays, to 7,500 words. Poetry. Pays in copies and subscription.

NEGATIVE CAPABILITY— 62 Ridgelawn Dr. E., Mobile, AL 36608. Sue Walker, Ed. Fiction and poetry. Annual contest, $500 prize; send SASE for guidelines.

NEOLOGISMS—Box 869, 1102 Pleasant St., Worcester, MA 01602. Jim Fay, Pub. Short stories, essays, and criticism, to 10 pages. Poetry, all styles "except love-oriented mush." Submit up 5 pages of poetry. Payment is one copy.

NEW DELTA REVIEW—c/o Dept. of English, Louisiana State Univ., Baton Rouge, LA 70803-5001. Attn: Eds. Semiannual. Fiction and nonfiction, to 5,000 words. Submit up to 4 poems, any length. Also essays, interviews, and reviews. "We want to see your best work." Pays in copies. Also awards prize for best poem and short story for each issue. Manuscripts read September through May.

NEW ENGLAND REVIEW—Middlebury College, Middlebury, VT 05753. Stephen Donadio, Ed. Jodee Stanley Rubins, Man. Ed. Fiction, nonfiction, and poetry of varying lengths. Also, speculative and interpretive essays, critical reassessments, statements by artists working in various media, interviews, testimonials, letters from abroad. "We are committed to exploration of all forms of contemporary cultural expresssion." Pays $10 per page ($20 minimum), on publication. Manuscripts read September through May.

NEW ENGLAND WRITERS' NETWORK—P.O. Box 483, Hudson, MA 01749-0483. Glenda Baker, Ed.-in-Chief. Short stories and novel excerpts, to 2,000 words. All genres except pornography. Personal and humorous essays, to 1,000 words. Up beat, positive poetry, to 32 lines. Pays $10 for stories; pays in copies for other material. Guidelines. Submit fiction, poetry, and essays June 1 to August 31 only.

NEW LAUREL REVIEW— 828 Lesseps St., New Orleans, LA 70117. Lee Meitzen Grue, Ed. Annual. Fiction, 10 to 20 pages; nonfiction, to 10 pages; poetry, any length. Library market. No inspirational verse. International readership. Read journal before submitting. Pays in one copy.

NEW LETTERS—Univ. House, Univ. of Missouri-Kansas City, 5101 Rockhill Rd., Kansas City, MO 64110-2499. James McKinley, Ed.-in-Chief. Fiction, 3,500 to 5,000 words. Poetry, submit 3 to 6 poems at a time. SASE for literary awards guidelines. Manuscripts read October 15 to May 15.

NEW ORLEANS REVIEW—Box 195, Loyola Univ., New Orleans, LA 70118. Ralph Adamo, Ed. Serious fiction, especially short fiction; also poetry and essays. Experimental work welcome.

THE NEW YORK QUARTERLY—P.O. Box 693, Old Chelsea Sta., New York, NY 10113. William Packard, Ed. Published 3 times a year. Poems of any style and persuasion, well written and well intentioned. Pays in copies. Manuscripts read year-round.

NEXUS—Wright State Univ., W016A Student Union, Dayton, OH 45435. Larry Sawyer, Ed. Jos Ampleforth, Contributing Ed. Poetry, fiction, plays, essays, interviews, reviews, photography, and art. Specializes in experimental, avant-garde work, and topics that transform the world. Pays in 2 copies.

NIGHTMARES—Box 587, Rocky Hill, CT 06067-0587. Ed Kobialka, Ed. Published 3 times a year. Horror fiction, to 7,000 words, for readers 13 and older (preferred length is 3,000 words). Ghost stories, dark science fiction/ fantasy, mystery, even romance, "but all stories must be scary." Related poetry. No explicit sex or excessive blood. Pays $10 for fiction, $5 to $10 per page for poetry, on acceptance.

NIGHTSUN—School of Arts & Humanities, Frostburg State Univ., Frostburg, MD 21532-1099. Brad Barkley, Barbara Hurd, Karen Zealand, Eds. Annual. Short stories, about 12 pages, and poems, to 40 lines. Payment is 2 copies. Manuscripts read September through April.

NIMROD INTERNATIONAL JOURNAL—Univ. of Tulsa, 600 S. College Ave., Tulsa, OK 74104-3189. Dr. Francine Ringold, Ed.-in-Chief. Quality fiction, experimental and traditional. Also poetry. Publishes 2 issues annually, one awards, one thematic. Pays $6,000 in awards annually. Send SASE for contest (or general) guidelines.

96 INC.—P.O. Box 15559, Boston, MA 02215. Attn: Ed. Annual. Fiction, 1,000 to 7,500 words; interviews; and poetry of varying length. Pays in subscription, 4 copies, and modest payment, if funding is available.

THE NORTH AMERICAN REVIEW—Univ. of Northern Iowa, Cedar Falls, IA 50614-0516. Peter Cooley, Poetry Ed. Poetry of high quality. Pays from $20 per poem, on publication. Manuscripts read year-round.

NORTH ATLANTIC REVIEW—15 Arbutus Ln., Stony Brook, NY 11790-1408. John Gill, Ed. Annual. Fiction and nonfiction, to 5,000 words; fillers, humor, photographs and illustrations. A special section on social or literary issues is a part of each issue. No poetry. Pays in copies. Responds in 6 months.

THE NORTH DAKOTA QUARTERLY—Univ. of North Dakota, Grand Forks, ND 58202-7209. Attn: Ed. Essays in the humanities and social sciences; fiction; reviews; and poetry. Limited market. Pays in copies.

NORTHEASTARTS—P.O. Box 94, Kittery, ME 03904. Mr. Leigh Donaldson, Ed. Fiction and nonfiction, to 750 words; poetry, to 30 lines; and short essays and reviews. "Both published and new writers are considered. No obscene or offensive material." Payment is 2 copies.

NORTHEAST CORRIDOR—Beaver College, 450 S. Easton Rd., Glenside, PA 19038. Susan Balée, Ed. Semiannual. Literary fiction, personal essays, and interviews, 10 to 20 pages. Poetry, to 40 lines (submit 3 to 5). "We seek the work of writers and artists living in or writing about the Northeast Corridor of America." Pays $25 for stories or essays, $10 for poems, on publication.

NORTHWEST REVIEW—369 PLC, Univ. of Oregon, Eugene, OR 97403. John Witte, Ed. Janice MacRae, Fiction Ed. Published 3 times a year. Serious, original, and vital fiction. "We are very proud of our reputation as a forum for the most talented upcoming young writers." Pays in copies. Send SASE for guidelines.

NORTHWOODS JOURNAL—P.O. Box 298, Thomaston, ME 04861. Robert W. Olmsted, Ed. Articles of interest to writers; fiction, 2,500 words. Poetry, any length. "Read guidelines first." Pays $5 per page, on acceptance.

NOTRE DAME REVIEW—Creative Writing Program, English Dept., Univ. of Notre Dame, Notre Dame, IN 46556. Attn: Man. Ed. Semiannual. Fiction, 10 to 15 pages. Essays, reviews, and poetry, 3 to 5 pages. Manuscripts read September through April. Payment varies, on publication.

OASIS—P.O. Box 626, Largo, FL 33779. Neal Storrs, Ed. Short fiction and literary essays, to 7,000 words, poetry, and translations from French,

German, Italian, or Spanish. Any subject. "Style is paramount." Pays $15 to $50 for prose, $5 per poem, on publication. Guidelines. Responds promptly.

OF UNICORNS AND SPACE STATIONS—P.O. Box 97, Bountiful, UT 84011-0097. Gene Davis, Ed. Science fiction and fantasy, to 5,000 words. Poetry related to science fiction, science, or fantasy. "Do not staple or fold long manuscripts." Pays 1¢ per word for fiction; $5 for poems, on publication.

OFFERINGS—P.O. Box 1667, Lebanon, MO 65536. Velvet Fackeldey, Ed. Quarterly. Poetry, to 30 lines, traditional and free verse. Students and unpublished writers encouraged. No payment.

THE OHIO REVIEW—Ellis Hall, Ohio Univ., Athens, OH 45701-2979. Wayne Dodd, Ed. Short stories. Pays $5 per page, plus copies, on publication. Manuscripts read September 15th through May 30th.

OLD CROW—FKB Press, P.O. Box 403, Easthampton, MA 01027. John Gibney, Ed. Semiannual. Fiction and nonfiction, 200 to 6,000 words. Poetry, to 500 lines. "International readership. Our purpose is to publish new and established writers who have something true to say which might raise the hairs on the backs of our readers' necks." Pays in copies. Rotating reading period.

THE OLD RED KIMONO—Humanities Div., Floyd College, Box 1864, Rome, GA 30162. Jeff Mack, Jacob Sullins, Eds. Annual. Fiction, to 1,200 words. Poetry, submit 3 to 5 poems. "Poems and stories should be concise and imagistic. Nothing sentimental or didactic." Pays in copies.

100 WORDS—473 EPB, Univ. of Iowa, Iowa City, IA 52242. Carolyn Brown, Ed. Bimonthly. Prose and poetry, to 100 words. Translations with original text. Send SASE for guidelines and themes.

ONIONHEAD—Arts on the Park, Inc., 115 N. Kentucky Ave., Lakeland, FL 33801-5044. Attn: Ed. Council. Short stories, to 4,000 words; essays, to 2,500 words; and poetry, to 60 lines; on provocative social, political, and cultural observations and hypotheses. Pays in copies. Send SASE for Wordart poetry contest information. Manuscripts read year-round; responds in 12 weeks.

OSIRIS—Box 297, Deerfield, MA 01842. Andrea Moorhead, Ed. Multilingual poetry journal, publishing poetry in English, French, German, and other languages in a translation/original format. Pays in copies.

OTHER VOICES—Univ. of Illinois at Chicago, Dept. of English (M/C 162), 601 S. Morgan St., Chicago, IL 60607-7120. Lois Hauselman, Ed. Fresh, accessible short stories and novel excerpts, to 5,000 words. Pays in copies and/or modest honorarium. Manuscripts read October to April.

OUTERBRIDGE—College of Staten Island, English Dept. 2S-218, 2800 Victory Blvd., Staten Island, NY 10314. Charlotte Alexander, Ed. Annual. Well-crafted stories, about 20 pages, and poetry, to 4 pages, "directed to a wide audience of literate adult readers." Pays in 2 copies. Manuscripts read September to June.

THE OXFORD AMERICAN—P.O. Box 1156, Oxford, MS 38655. Marc Smirnoff, Ed. Quarterly. Short fiction and nonfiction of a Southern nature. "Strong interest in good nonfiction." Cartoons, photos, and drawings. Pays from $50 for poetry and art; from $100 for nonfiction, on publication.

PAINTBRUSH: A JOURNAL OF POETRY AND TRANSLATION—Language & Literature Div., Truman State Univ., Kirksville, MO 63501. Ben Bennani, Ed. Annual. Poetry, translations, interviews, and book reviews.

Periodically publishes special monograph issues highlighting the work of individual writers. Query.

PALO ALTO REVIEW—Palo Alto College, 1400 W. Villaret, San Antonio, TX 78224-2499. Ellen Shull, Ed. Semiannual. Fiction and articles, 5,000 words. "We look for wide-ranging investigations of historical, geographical, scientific, mathematical, artistic, political, and social topics, anything that has to do with living and learning." Interviews; 200-word think pieces for "Food for Thought"; poetry, to 50 lines (send 3 to 5 poems at a time); reviews, to 500 words, of books, films, videos, or software. "Fiction shouldn't be too experimental or excessively avant-garde." Pays in copies.

PANGOLIN PAPERS—P.O. Box 241, Nordland, WA 98358. Pat Britt, Ed. Literary fiction, 100 to 7,000 words. Pays in copies

PANHANDLER—English Dept., Univ. of W. Florida, Pensacola, FL 32514-5751. Laurie O'Brien, Ed. Semiannual. Fiction, 1,500 to 3,000 words; poetry, any length. Pays in copies. Responds within 6 months.

PARABOLA: THE MAGAZINE OF MYTH AND TRADITION— 656 Broadway, New York, NY 10012. Attn: Eds. Quarterly. Articles, to 4,000 words, and fiction, 500 words, retelling traditional stories, folk and fairy tales. "All submissions must relate to an upcoming theme. We are looking for a balance between scholarly and accessible writing devoted to the ideas of myth and tradition." Send SASE for guidelines and themes. Payment varies, on publication.

THE PARIS REVIEW—541 E. 72nd St., New York, NY 10021. Attn: Fiction and Poetry Eds. Fiction and poetry of high literary quality. Pays on publication.

PARNASSUS—205 W. 89th St., Apt. 8F, New York, NY 10024-1835. Herbert Leibowitz, Ed. Critical essays and reviews on contemporary poetry. International in scope. Pays in cash and copies. Manuscripts read year-round.

PARTING GIFTS—3413 Wilshire, Greensboro, NC 27408. Robert Bixby, Ed. Fiction, to 1,000 words, and poetry, to 100 lines. Pays in copies. Manuscripts read January to June.

PARTISAN REVIEW—Boston Univ., 236 Bay State Rd., Boston, MA 02215. William Phillips, Ed.-in-Chief. Edith Kurzweil, Ed. Serious fiction, poetry, and essays. Payment varies. No simultaneous submissions. Manuscripts read September through to May.

PASSAGER: A JOURNAL OF REMEMBRANCE AND DISCOVERY— c/o Univ. of Baltimore, 1420 N. Charles St., Baltimore, MD 21201-5779. Mary Azrael, Kendra Kopelke, Eds. Fiction and essays, 3,000 words, of "remembrance and discovery." Poetry, to 40 lines. "We publish writers of all ages, but with an emphasis on new older writers." Pays in copies.

PASSAGES NORTH—Northern Michigan Univ., Dept. of English, 1401 Presque Isle Ave., Marquette, MI 49855. Anne Ohman Youngs, Ed. Semiannual. Poetry, fiction, interviews, and literary nonfiction. Pays in copies. Manuscripts read September to May.

THE PATERSON LITERARY REVIEW—(formerly *Footwork, The Paterson Literary Review*) Passaic County Comm. College, College Blvd., Paterson, NJ 07505-1179. Maria Mazziotti Gillan, Ed. High-quality fiction and poetry, to 10 pages. Pays in copies. Manuscripts read January through May.

PEARL—3030 E. Second St., Long Beach, CA 90803. Marilyn Johnson, Ed. Fiction, 500 to 1,200 words, and poetry, to 40 lines. "We are interested in accessible, humanistic poetry and fiction that communicates and is related to real life. Along with the ironic, serious, and intense, humor and wit are welcome." Pays in copies.

PEREGRINE: THE JOURNAL OF AMHERST WRITERS AND ARTISTS PRESS—P.O. Box 1076, Amherst, MA 01004. Nancy Rose, Man. Ed. Annual. Fiction, poetry, book reviews. "Unpretentious and memorable writing by new and established authors. We welcome work reflecting diversity of voice." Guidelines.

PERMAFROST—English Dept., Univ. of Alaska Fairbanks, P.O. Box 755720, Fairbanks, AK 99775. Ryan M. Johnson, Ed. Poetry, up to 5 poems; fiction and nonfiction, to 30 pages. Contests. Reading period: September through March 15.

PIG IRON PRESS—P.O. Box 237, Youngstown, OH 44501-0237. Jim Villani, Ed. Fiction, to 8,000 words. Pays $5 per published page, on publication. Current theme: "Religion in Modernity." Deadline for submissions: December 31, 1999. Send SASE for additional information.

THE PIKEVILLE REVIEW—Humanities Div., Pikeville College, 214 Sycamore St., Pikeville, KY 41501. James Alan Riley, Ed. Annual. Contemporary fiction, poetry, creative essays, and book reviews. Payment varies on publication.

PIVOT—250 Riverside Dr., #23, New York, NY 10025. Martin Mitchell, Ed. Annual. Poetry, to 75 lines. Pays 2 copies. Manuscripts read January through May.

PLEIADES—Dept. of English and Phil., Central Missouri State Univ., Warrensburg, MO 64093. R. M. Kinder, Kevin Prufer, Eds. Traditional and experimental poetry, fiction, criticism, translations, and reviews. Cross-genre especially welcome. Pays $10 for prose; $3 for poetry, on publication.

PLOUGHSHARES—Emerson College, 100 Beacon St., Boston, MA 02116-1596. Attn: Ed. Serious fiction, to 6,000 words, and poetry (submit up to 3 poems at a time). Pays $25 per page ($50 to $250), on publication. Guidelines available with SASE. Manuscripts read August 1st through March 31st.

POEM—c/o English Dept., U.A.H., Huntsville, AL 35899. Nancy Frey Dillard, Ed. Serious lyric poetry. Pays in copies. Manuscripts read year-round; best to submit December to March or June to September.

POETRY—60 W. Walton St., Chicago, IL 60610. Joseph Parisi, Ed. Poetry of highest quality. Submit 3 to 4 poems. Allow 10 to 12 weeks for response. Pays $2 a line, on publication.

POETRY EAST—DePaul Univ., English Dept., 802 W. Belden Ave., Chicago, IL 60614-3214. Richard Jones, Ed. Brian Hayes, Man. Ed. Semiannual. Poetry, essays, and translations. "Please send a sampling of your best work. Do not send book-length manuscripts without querying first." Pays in copies.

THE POET'S PAGE—P.O. Box 372, Wyanet, IL 61379. Ione K. Pence, Ed./Pub. Quarterly. Poetry, any length, style, and topic. Articles and essays on poetry and poetic forms, poets, styles, etc. Pays in copies.

POETS' PAPER—(formerly *Feelings Poetry Journal*) Anderie Poetry Press, P.O. Box 85, Easton, PA 18044-0085. Carole J. Heffley, Harriett Hunt, Eds. Semiannual. "Contemporary poetry that conveys an immediate, clear sense of recognition and thought." Rhymed metered verse as well as free verse. Submit up to 3 poems, any length. Contests. Responds in 4 to 6 weeks.

PORTLAND REVIEW—c/o Portland State Univ., P.O. Box 751, Portland, OR 97207. Misty Sturgeon, Ed. Semiannual. Short fiction, essays, poetry, reviews, photography, and artwork. Include bio. Payment is one copy.

POTOMAC REVIEW—P.O. Box 354, Port Tobacco, MD 20677. Eli Flam, Ed. Regionally rooted quarterly: to inform, entertain, and seek deeper values. Fiction and literary essays, to 3,000 words. Poetry,, submit 3 poems (to 5 pages total). Pays in copies.

POTPOURRI—P.O. Box 8278, Prairie Village, KS 66208. Polly W. Swafford, Ed. Quarterly. Short stories, to 3,500 words. Literary essays, travel pieces, and humor, to 2,500 words. Poetry and haiku, to 75 lines. "We like clever themes that avoid reminiscence, depressing plots, and violence." Original B&W illustrations. Pays in one copy.

PRAIRIE SCHOONER—201 Andrews Hall, Univ. of Nebraska, Lincoln, NE 68588-0334. Hilda Raz, Ed. Short stories, poetry, essays, book reviews, and translations. Pays in copies. Manuscripts read September through May; responds in 3 months. Annual contests.

PRESS QUARTERLY—125 W. 72nd St., Suite 3-M, New York, NY 10023. Daniel Roberts, Ed. Short stories and poems that "deliver an invigorating dose of clear, humanized storytelling." Payment varies, on publication.

PRIMAVERA—Box 37-7547, Chicago, IL 60637. Attn: Ed. Board. Annual. Fiction that focuses on the experiences of women; "author need not be female." No simultaneous submissions. SASE required. Pays in 2 copies.

PRISM INTERNATIONAL—E462-1866 Main Mall, Creative Writing Program, Univ. of British Columbia, Vancouver, B.C., Canada V6T 1Z1. Attn: Ed. High-quality fiction, poetry, drama, creative nonfiction, and literature in translation, varying lengths. Include international reply coupons. Pays $20 per published page. Annual short fiction contest.

THE PROSE POEM—English Dept., Providence College, Providence, RI 02198. Peter Johnson, Ed. Prose poems. Book reviews, 4 to 6 pages. Pays in copies. Query for book reviews. Manuscripts read January through March.

PUCKERBRUSH REVIEW—76 Main St., Orono, ME 04473-1430. Constance Hunting, Ed. Semiannual. Literary fiction, criticism, and poetry of various lengths, "to bring literary Maine news to readers." Pays in 2 copies. Manuscripts read year-round.

PUDDING MAGAZINE: THE INTERNATIONAL JOURNAL OF APPLIED POETRY—c/o Pudding House Writers Resource Ctr., Bed & Breakfast for Writers, Johnstown, OH 43031. Jennifer Bosveld, Ed. Poems on popular culture, social concerns, personal struggle; articles/essays on poetry in the schools and in human services. Manuscripts read year-round; responds promptly.

PUERTO DEL SOL—New Mexico State Univ., Box 3E, Las Cruces, NM 88003-0001. K. West, Kevin McIlvoy, Antonya Nelson, Eds. Short stories and personal essays, to 30 pages; novel excerpts, to 65 pages; articles, to 45 pages, and reviews, to 15 pages. Poetry, photos. Pays in copies. Manuscripts read September through February.

QUARTER AFTER EIGHT—Ellis Hall, Ohio Univ., Athens, OH 45701. Attn: Eds. Annual. Avant-garde short fiction, novel excerpts, essays, criticism, investigations, and interviews, to 10,000 words. Submit no more than 2 pieces. Prose poetry (submit up to 5 poems); no traditional poetry. Pays in copies. Manuscripts read September through March. Guidelines.

QUARTERLY WEST—317 Olpin Union, Univ. of Utah, Salt Lake City, UT 84112. Margot Schilpp, Ed. Fiction, short-shorts, poetry, essays, translations, and reviews. Pays $25 to $50 for stories, $15 to $50 for poems. Manuscripts read year-round. Biennial novella competition in even-numbered years.

RAG MAG—P.O. Box 12, Goodhue, MN 55027-0012. Beverly Voldseth, Ed. Semiannual. Eclectic fiction and nonfiction, art, photos. Poetry, any length. No religious writing. Pays in copies. SASE for guidelines and themes.

RAMBUNCTIOUS REVIEW—1221 W. Pratt Blvd., Chicago, IL 60626. Richard Goldman, Nancy Lennon, Beth Hausler, Eds. Fiction, to 12 pages; poems, submit up to 5 at a time. Pays in copies. Manuscripts read September through May. Contests. Guidelines.

READER'S BREAK—Pine Grove Press, P.O. Box 85, Jamesville, NY 13078. Gertrude S. Eiler, Ed. Semiannual. Fiction, to 3,500 words, about relationships, tales of action, adventure, science fiction and fantasy, suspense, and mystery. Themes and plots may be historical, contemporary, or futuristic. Emphasis is on fiction but will consider nonfiction in story form. Poems, to 75 lines. Pays in one copy.

RE:AL, THE JOURNAL OF LIBERAL ARTS—Stephen F. Austin State Univ., P.O. Box 13007, SFA Sta., Nacogdoches, TX 75962. Attn: Eds. Experimental, genre, and historical fiction; reviews and scholarly nonfiction, 250 to 5,000 words. Poetry, to 10 pages. Pays in copies.

RED CEDAR REVIEW—Dept. of English, 17-C Morrill Hall, Michigan State Univ., E. Lansing, MI 48824-1036. Carrie Preston, Poetry Ed. David Sheridan, Fiction Ed. Fiction, to 5,000 words; and poems, submit up to 5. Pays in copies. Manuscripts read year-round.

RED ROCK REVIEW—Dept. of English, Community College of Southern Nevada, 3200 E. Cheyenne Ave., N. Las Vegas, NV 89030. Dr. Richard Logsdon, Ed. Semiannual. Short fiction, to 5,000 words; book reviews, to 1,000 words; poetry, to 2 pages. "We're geared toward publishing the work of already established writers. No taboos." Payment varies, on acceptance.

REED MAGAZINE—Dept. of English, San Jose State Univ., One Washington Sq., San Jose, CA 95192-0090. Address Man. Ed. Fiction, personal essays, and reminiscences, to 4,000 words; submit no more than 2 stories or essays at a time. Poetry, to 40 lines, on any subject; submit up to 3 at a time. "We want material of a literary nature, addressing the human condition." B&W photos. Payment is one copy. Manuscripts read to January 31.

RESPONSE: A CONTEMPORARY JEWISH REVIEW—114 W. 26th St., Suite 1004, New York, NY 10001-6812. David R. Adler, Michael Steinberg, Charita Baumhaft, Eds. Pearl Gluck, Fiction and Poetry Ed. Fiction, to 25 double-spaced pages, that explores Jewish experience in an unconventional fashion. Articles, to 25 pages, with a focus on Jewish issues. Poetry, to 80 lines, and book reviews. Pays in copies.

REVIEW: LATIN AMERICAN LITERATURE AND ARTS—Americas Society, 680 Park Ave., New York, NY 10021. Alfred J. MacAdam, Ed. Semiannual. Work in English translation, 1,000 to 1,500 words, by and about young and established Latin American writers; essays and book reviews. Payment varies, on acceptance. Query.

RIVER CITY—Dept. of English, Univ. of Memphis, Memphis, TN 38152. Paul Naylor, Ed. Poems, short stories, essays, and interviews. No novel excerpts. Pay varies according to grants. Manuscripts read September through April. Guidelines. Contests.

RIVER OAK REVIEW—P.O. Box 3127, Oak Park, IL 60303. Semiannual. Address Fiction, Poetry, or Nonfiction Ed. No criticism, reviews, or translations. Limit prose to 20 pages; poetry to batches of no more than 4. Pays in copies, and small honorarium, as funding permits.

RIVER STYX—3207 Washington Ave., St. Louis, MO 63103. Attn: Ed. Published 3 times a year. Poetry, fiction, personal essays, literary interviews, B&W photos, and color cover artwork. Payment is $8 per printed page plus subscription. Manuscripts read May through October; reports in 2 to 3 months.

RIVERSIDE QUARTERLY—Box 12085, San Antonio, TX 78212. Leland Sapiro, Ed. Science fiction and fantasy, to 3,500 words; reviews, criticism, any length; poetry and letters. Send poetry to Sheryl Smith, 515 Saratoga, #2, Santa Clara, CA 95050. Pays in copies.

ROANOKE REVIEW—Roanoke College, Salem, VA 24153. Robert R. Walter, Ed. Fiction, to 5,000 words, and poetry, to 100 lines. Pays in copies.

ROCKFORD REVIEW—P.O. Box 858, Rockford, IL 61105. David Ross, Ed.-in-Chief. Published 3 times a year. Fiction, essays, and satire, 250 to 1,300 words. Experimental and traditional poetry, to 50 lines (shorter works preferred). One-act plays and other dramatic forms, to 10 pages. "We prefer genuine or satirical human dilemmas with coping or non-coping outcomes that ring the reader's bell." Submit up to 3 works at a time. Pays in copies; two $25 Editor's Choice Prizes awarded each issue.

ROSEBUD—P.O. Box 459, Cambridge, WI 53523. Rod Clark, Ed. Quarterly. Fiction, articles, profiles, 1,200 to 1,800 words, and poems; love, alienation, travel, humor, nostalgia, and unexpected revelation. Pays $45 plus copies, on publication. Guidelines.

ROSWELL LITERARY REVIEW—P.O. Box 2412, Roswell, NM 88202-2412. Harvey Stanbrough, Ed. Quarterly. Fiction, to 6,000 words, personal essays, and poetry. Pays from ½¢ a word for prose; from ¼¢ a word for reprints; from $1 per poem.

SALAMANDER— 48 Ackers Ave., Brookline, MA 02146. Jennifer Barber, Ed. Semiannual. "A magazine for poetry, fiction, and memoir." Short stories, including translations and works in progress; creative nonfiction and memoirs. Poetry, any length. "No criticism or essays (unless autobiographical). No science fiction." Pays an honorarium if funding is available, on publication.

SAN FERNANDO POETRY JOURNAL—18301 Halstead St., Northridge, CA 91325. Richard Cloke, Ed. Quality poetry, 20 to 100 lines, with social content; scientific, philosophical, and historical themes. Pays in copies.

SANSKRIT LITERARY/ART PUBLICATION—Cone Ctr., Univ. of North Carolina/Charlotte, Charlotte, NC 28223-0001. Attn: Ed. Annual. Poetry, short fiction, photos, and fine art. Pays in copies. Manuscripts read in fall only; deadline October 30.

SANTA BARBARA REVIEW—P.O. Box 808, Summerland, CA 93067-0808. P.S. Leddy, Ed. Short stories; occasionally plays. Biographies and essays, to 6,500 words. Poems. Translations. B&W art and photos. Pays in copies.

SCANDINAVIAN REVIEW—725 Park Ave., New York, NY 10021. Attn: Ed. Published 3 times a year. Poetry or prose translated from Nordic languages for a lay audience with interest in Nordic countries for annual translation prize competition; write for submission rules. Feature articles on culture, politics, and lifestyle of Scandinavia. Pays from $100, on publication.

SCRIVENER—McGill Univ., 853 Sherbrooke St. W., Montreal, Quebec, Canada H3A 2T6. Attn: Eds. Poems, submit 5 to 15; prose, to 20 pages; reviews, to 5 pages. Photography and graphics. Pays in copies.

THE SEATTLE REVIEW—Padelford Hall, Box 354330, Univ. of Washington, Seattle, WA 98195. Colleen J. McElroy, Ed. Stories, to 20 pages; poetry; essays on the craft of writing; and interviews with northwest writers. Payment varies. Manuscripts read October through May.

SENECA REVIEW—Hobart & William Smith Colleges, Geneva, NY 14456. Deborah Tall, Ed. Poetry, translations, and essays on contemporary poetry. Pays in copies and 2-year subscription. Manuscripts read September through April.

SHENANDOAH—Washington and Lee Univ., Troubadour Theatre, 2nd Fl., Lexington, VA 24450-0303. R.T. Smith, Ed. Quarterly. Highest quality fiction, poetry, criticism, essays and interviews. "Read the magazine before submitting." Pays $25 per page for prose; $2.50 per line for poetry, on publication.

SING HEAVENLY MUSE! WOMEN'S POETRY & PROSE—P.O. Box 13320, Minneapolis, MN 55414. Attn: Ed. Short stories and essays, to 5,000 words. Poetry. Query for themes and reading periods. Pays in copies.

SKYLARK—2200 169th St., Hammond, IN 46323-2094. Pamela Hunter, Ed. "The Fine Arts Annual of Purdue Calumet." Fiction and articles, to 4,000 words. Poetry, to 21 lines. B&W prints and drawings. Pays in one copy. Manuscripts read November through April for fall publication.

SLIPSTREAM—Box 2071, Niagara Falls, NY 14301. Attn: Ed. Contemporary poetry, any length. Pays in copies. Query for themes. Guidelines. Fiction overstocked.

THE SMALL POND MAGAZINE—P.O. Box 664, Stratford, CT 06497-0664. Napoleon St. Cyr, Ed. Published 3 times a year. Fiction, to 2,500 words; poetry, to 100 lines. Pays in copies. Query for nonfiction. Include short bio. Manuscripts read year-round.

SMALL PRESS REVIEW—Box 100, Paradise, CA 95967. Len Fulton, Ed. Reviews, 200 words, of small literary books and magazines; tracks the publishing of small publishers and small-circulation magazines. Query.

SNAKE NATION REVIEW—Snake Nation Press, 110 #2 W. Force, Valdosta, GA 31601. Roberta George, Ed. Quarterly. Short stories, novel chapters, and informal essays, 5,000 words, and poetry, to 60 lines. Pays in copies and prizes.

SNOWY EGRET—P.O. Box 9, Bowling Green, IN 47833. Philip Repp, Ed. Poetry, fiction, and nonfiction, to 10,000 words. Natural history from artistic, literary, philosophical, and historical perspectives. Pays $2 per page for prose; $2 to $4 for poetry, on publication. Manuscripts read year-round.

SONORA REVIEW—Dept. of English, Univ. of Arizona, Tucson, AZ 85721. Attn: Fiction, Poetry, or Nonfiction Ed. (Address appropriate genre editor.) Annual contests; send for guidelines. Simultaneous submissions accepted (except for contest entries). Manuscripts read year-round.

THE SOUTH CAROLINA REVIEW—Dept. of English, Clemson Univ., Clemson, SC 29634-1503. Wayne Chapman, Ed. Semiannual. Fiction, essays, reviews, and interviews, to 4,000 words. Poems. Send complete manuscript. Pays in copies. Response time is 6 to 9 months. Manuscripts read September through May (but not in December). No multiple submissions.

SOUTH DAKOTA REVIEW—Box 111, Univ. Exchange, Vermillion, SD 57069-2390. Brian Bedard, Ed. Exceptional fiction, 3,000 to 5,000 words, and poetry, 10 to 25 lines. Critical articles, especially on American literature, Western American literature, theory and esthetics, creative nonfiction, 3,000 to 5,000 words. Pays in copies. Manuscripts read year-round; slower response time in the summer.

THE SOUTHERN CALIFORNIA ANTHOLOGY—c/o Master of Professional Writing Program, WPH 404, Univ. of Southern California, Los Angeles, CA 90089-4034. James Ragan, Ed.-in-Chief. Fiction, to 20 pages, and poetry, to 5 pages. Pays in copies. Manuscripts read September to January.

SOUTHERN EXPOSURE—P.O. Box 531, Durham, NC 27702. Chris Kromm, Ed. Quarterly forum on "Southern movements for social change." Short stories, to 3,600 words, essays, investigative journalism, and oral histories, 500 to 3,600 words. Pays $25 to $250, on publication. Query.

SOUTHERN HUMANITIES REVIEW—9088 Haley Ctr., Auburn Univ., AL 36849. Dan R. Latimer, Virginia M. Kouidis, Eds. Short stories, essays, and criticism, 3,500 to 15,000 words; poetry, to 2 pages. Responds within 3 months. No simultaneous submissions.

SOUTHERN POETRY REVIEW—Advancement Studies, Central Piedmont Community College, Charlotte, NC 28235. Ken McLaurin, Ed. Poems. No restrictions on style, length, or content. Manuscripts read September through May.

THE SOUTHERN REVIEW— 43 Allen Hall, Louisiana State Univ., Baton Rouge, LA 70803-5005. Dave Smith, James Olney, Eds. Emphasis on highest quality contemporary literature in United States and abroad and with special interest in southern culture and history. Fiction, 4,000 to 8,000 words. Pays $12 a page for fiction, $20 a page for poetry, on publication. No manuscripts read in the summer.

SOUTHWEST REVIEW—307 Fondren Library W., Box 750374, Southern Methodist Univ., Dallas, TX 75275-0374. Elizabeth Mills, Sr. Fiction Ed. Fiction, essays, poetry, and interviews with well-known writers, 3,000 to 7,500 words. Pays varying rates.

SOU'WESTER—Southern Illinois Univ. at Edwardsville, Edwardsville, IL 62026-1438. Fred W. Robbins, Ed.; Nancy Avdoian, Assoc. Ed. Susan Garrison, Fiction Ed. Fiction, to 5,000 words. Poetry. Pays in copies. Manuscripts not read in August.

THE SOW'S EAR POETRY REVIEW—19535 Pleasant View Dr., Abingdon, VA 24211-6827. Attn: Ed. Quarterly. Eclectic poetry and art. Submit one to 5 poems, any length, plus a brief biographical note. Interviews, essays, and articles, any length, about poets and poetry are also considered. B&W photos and drawings. Payment is one copy. Poetry and chapbook contests. Guidelines.

SPECTACLE—Pachanga Press, 101 Middlesex Turnpike, Suite 6, Box 155, Burlington, MA 01803. Richard Aguilar, Ed. Semiannual exploring American life, art, and passion. Personal essays on a theme. Send SASE for themes. Pays $30, on publication.

SPECTRUM—Univ. of California/ Santa Barbara, Box 14800, Santa Barbara, CA 93107. Attn: Ed. Annual. Novel excerpts, short stories, various narrative, poetry, nonfiction essays, slides of art. Annual deadline is February 1.

SPELUNKER FLOPHOUSE—P.O. Box 617742, Chicago, IL 60661. Chris Kubica, Wendy Morgan, Eds. Annual. "We especially like work that is high in language/technique and deals with the micro-details of everyday life. We dislike religious, political, socially 'un-rested,' or genre work." Submit up to 3 short stories, 100 to 10,000 pages total, or up to 5 poems, each one page or less. Pays in copies. http://members.aol.com.spelunkerf/

SPOON RIVER POETRY REVIEW—Dept. of English, Stevenson Hall, Illinois State Univ., Normal, IL 61790-4240. Lucia Cordell Getsi, Ed. Poetry, any length. Pays in copies.

SPRING FANTASY—Women in the Arts, P.O. Box 2907, Decatur, IL 62524-2907. Linda Hutton, Ed. Fiction for adults and children; personal essays, to 1,500 words. Poetry, to 32 lines. Payment is one copy.

SPSM&H—329 E St., Bakersfield, CA 93304. Frederick A. Raborg, Jr., Ed. Single sonnets, sequences, essays about the sonnet form, short fiction in which the sonnet plays a part, books, and anthologies. Pays $10, plus copies, for fiction and essays; "best of issue" sonnets, $14.

STAND MAGAZINE—Dept. of English, Hibbs Bldg., 900 Park Ave., Richmond, VA 23284-2005. David Latané, U.S. Ed. (179 Wingrove Rd., Newcastle upon Tyne NE4 9DA UK) British quarterly. Fiction, 2,000 to 5,000 words, and poetry to 100 lines (submit up to 6 poems). No formulaic verse.

STORY QUARTERLY—P.O. Box 1416, Northbrook, IL 60065. Anne Brashler, Marie Hayes, Eds. Short stories. Pays in copies.

THE STYLUS—9412 Huron Ave., Richmond, VA 23294. Roger Reus, Ed. Annual. Articles on writers ("no scholarly, heavily footnoted, dull literary theses"). Original fiction and author interviews. Pays in copies.

THE SUN—The Sun Publishing Co., 107 N. Roberson St., Chapel Hill, NC 27516. Sy Safransky, Ed. Essays, interviews, and fiction, to 7,000 words; poetry; photos, illustrations, and cartoons. "We're interested in all writing that makes sense and enriches our common space." Pays $300 to $500 for fiction; $300 to $750 for nonfiction; $50 to $200 for poetry, on publication.

SYCAMORE REVIEW—Purdue Univ., Dept. of English, West Lafayette, IN 47907. Sarah Griffiths, Ed.-in-Chief. Semiannual. Poetry, short fiction (no genre fiction), personal essays, drama, and translations. Pays in copies. Manuscripts read September to April.

TALE SPINNER—P.O. Box 336, Bedford, IN 47421. Joe Glasgow, Ed. Semiannual. Commercial fiction, 800 to 4,000 words, and poems, to 20 lines. No erotic material.

TALKING RIVER REVIEW—Lewis-Clark State College, 500 8th Ave., Lewiston, ID 83501. Attn: Eds. Semiannual. Short stories, novel excerpts, and essays, to 7,500 words. Poetry, any length or style; submit up to 5 poems. "We publish emerging writing alongside established writers." Pays in copies and subscription. Manuscripts read September through February.

TALUS AND SCREE—P.O. Box 851, Waldport, OR 97394. Carla Perry, Ed. Semiannual. Poetry (no length limit), short fiction (including novel excerpts), memoir vignettes, interviews, reviews, line drawings, photos, and cartoons. Prefer e-mail submissions: talus@webjacks.com. Pays in copies.

TAR RIVER POETRY—Dept. of English, East Carolina Univ., Greenville, NC 27858-4353. Peter Makuck, Ed. Poetry and reviews. "We prefer poems with strong imagery and figurative language. No trite, worn-out phrases, vague abstractions, or cliché situations." Pays in copies. Submit September through April.

THEMA—Box 74109, Metairie, LA 70033-4109. Virginia Howard, Ed. Theme-related fiction, to 20 pages, and poetry, to 2 pages. Pays $25 per story; $10 per short-short; $10 per poem; $10 for B&W art/photo, on acceptance. Send SASE for themes and guidelines.

32 PAGES—Rain Crow Publishing, 2127 W. Pierce Ave., Apt. 2B, Chicago, IL 60622-1824. Michael S. Manley, Pub. Bimonthly. Poetry, short fiction, creative nonfiction, drama, and graphical narrative, to 8,000 words. Pays $5 per published page, on publication. Guidelines.

360 DEGREES: ART & LITERARY REVIEW— 880 Catalina Cir., Vallejo, CA 94589. Karen Kinnison, Ed. Quarterly art and literary review, featuring fiction and poetry (any length), and artwork. Send photocopies and photographs only. Payment is one copy.

THE THREEPENNY REVIEW—P.O. Box 9131, Berkeley, CA 94709. Wendy Lesser, Ed. Fiction, to 5,000 words. Poetry, to 100 lines. Essays, 1,500 to 3,000 words, on books, theater, film, dance, music, art, television, and politics. Pays to $200, on acceptance. Limited market. Guidelines. Manuscripts read September through May.

TIGHTROPE—323 Pelham Rd., Amherst, MA 01002. Ed Rayher, Ed. Limited-edition, letterpress semiannual. Poetry, any length. Pays in copies. Manuscripts read year-round.

TOMORROW MAGAZINE—P.O. Box 148486, Chicago, IL 60614-8486. Tim W. Brown, Ed. Poetry with an underground sensibility. Pays in copies.

TOMORROW: SPECULATIVE FICTION—See *www.tomorrowsf.com*

TONGUES—Bard College, Annandale-on-Hudson, NY 12504-5000. Raman Frey, Ed. Fiction, to 4,000 words; essays and interviews, to 16 pages; poetry. "We prefer to work with international motif or global perspective." Pays an honorarium, on publication, and in copies. Web site: http://tongues.base.org.

TRIQUARTERLY—Northwestern Univ., 2020 Ridge Ave., Evanston, IL 60208-4302. Attn: Ed. Serious, aesthetically informed and inventive poetry and prose, for an international and literate audience. Payment varies. Manuscripts read October through March. Allow 10 to 12 weeks for reply.

2AM MAGAZINE—P.O. Box 6754, Rockford, IL 61125-1754. Gretta Anderson, Ed. Poetry, articles, reviews, and personality profiles, 500 to 2,000 words, as well as fantasy, horror, and some science fiction/sword-and-sorcery short stories, 500 to 5,000 words. Pays ½¢ a word, on acceptance. Manuscripts read year-round.

TWO RIVERS REVIEW—Anderie Poetry Press, 215 McCartney St., Easton, PA 18042. Philip Memmer, Ed. Semiannual. Excellent contemporary poetry, any style, from established poets and astonishing newcomers. Submit up to 3 poems, any length. Responds in one month.

THE URBANITE: SURREAL & LIVELY & BIZARRE—Box 4737, Davenport, IA 52808. Mark McLaughlin, Ed. Published 3 times a year. Dark fantasy, horror (no gore), surrealism, reviews, and social commentary, to 3,000 words. Free verse poems, to 2 pages. Pays 2¢ to 3¢ a word; $10 for poetry, on acceptance. Query for themes.

URBANUS MAGAZINE—P.O. Box 192921, San Francisco, CA 94119. Peter Drizhal, Ed. Published 3 times a year. Fiction and nonfiction, 1,000 to 6,000 words, and poetry, to 40 lines, that reflect contemporary and urban influences for a "readership generally impatient with the mainstream approach." B&W photos and drawings. Pays $25 to $150 for articles, $15 to $20 for poems, on acceptance.

VERMONT INK—P.O. Box 3297, Burlington, VT 05401-3297. Donna Leach, Ed. Quarterly. Short stories, 2,000 words, that are well-written, entertaining, and "basically G-rated": adventure, historical, humor, mainstream, mystery and suspense, regional interest, romance, science fiction, and westerns. Poetry, to 25 lines, should be upbeat or humorous. Pays to $25 for stories; to $10 for poetry, on acceptance. Send complete manuscript with short bio and SASE.

VERSE UNTO US—907 Oak Lane Dr., Joshua, TX 76058. Alan Steele, Ed. Quarterly. Fiction, 500 to 2,750 words, any subject. Poetry, to 30 lines, any style or subject. Pays $5 for fiction; $5 for best poem in magazine, on publication.

VERVE—P.O. Box 3205, Simi Valley, CA 93093. Ron Reichick, Ed. Contemporary fiction and nonfiction, to 1,000 words, that fit the theme of the issue. Poetry, to 2 pages; submit up to 5 poems. Pays in one copy. Query for themes.

VINCENT BROTHERS REVIEW—4566 Northern Cir., Riverside, OH 45424-5733. Kimberly Willardson, Ed. Published 3 times a year. Fiction, nonfiction, poetry, fillers, and B&W art. "Read sample copies/back issues before submitting." Pays from $15 for fiction and nonfiction; $5 for poems; $10 for poetry used in "Page Left" feature. Guidelines.

VIRGINIA QUARTERLY REVIEW—One W. Range, Charlottesville, VA 22903. Attn: Ed. Quality fiction and poetry. Serious essays and articles, 3,000 to 6,000 words, on literature, science, politics, economics, etc. Pays $10 per page for prose, $1 per line for poetry, on publication.

VISIONS INTERNATIONAL—Black Buzzard Press, 1007 Ficklen Rd., Fredericksburg, VA 22405. Bradley R. Strahan, Ed. Published 3 times a year. Poetry, to 50 lines, and B&W drawings. (Query for art.) Read magazine before submitting. Pays in copies (or honorarium when funds available). Manuscripts read year-round.

WASCANA REVIEW—c/o Dept. of English, Univ. of Regina, Regina, Sask., Canada S4S 0A2. Kathleen Wall, Ed. Short stories, 2,000 to 6,000 words. Pays $3 per page, after publication.

WASHINGTON REVIEW—P.O. Box 50132, Washington, DC 20091-0132. Clarissa Wittenberg, Ed. Poetry; articles on literary, performing and fine arts in the Washington, D.C., area. Fiction, 1,000 to 2,500 words. Area writers preferred. Pays in copies. Responds in 3 months.

WEBER STUDIES—Weber State Univ., 1214 University Cir., Ogden, UT 84408-1214. Sherwin W. Howard, Ed. "An Interdisciplinary Humanities Journal." Fiction, to 4,500 words; nonfiction, to 5,000 words; poetry, to 3 pages (submit no more than 3 poems). "High quality submissions only, please." Pays $25 to $100, on publication.

WEST BRANCH—Bucknell Hall, Bucknell Univ., Lewisburg, PA 17837. Karl Patten, Robert Taylor, Eds. Fiction and poetry. Pays in copies and subscriptions. SASE required.

WESTERN HUMANITIES REVIEW—Univ. of Utah, Salt Lake City, UT 84112. Dawn Corrigan, Man. Ed. Quarterly. Fiction and essays, to 30 pages, and poetry. Pays $35 for poetry, $100 for short stories and essays, on publication. Manuscripts read October through May; responds in 3 to 6 months.

WHETSTONE—P.O. Box 1266, Barrington, IL 60011. Attn: Eds. Fiction and creative nonfiction, to 20 pages. Poems, submit up to 7. Payment varies, on publication.

WHISKEY ISLAND—Dept. of English, Cleveland State Univ., Cleveland, OH 44115. Pat Stansberry, Ed. Fiction with a literary dimension, to 6,500 words. Multi-dimensional and complex poetry, to 10 pages. "We like to experiment with tone, point of view, etc., as long as the piece has something significant to say." Pays in copies.

THE WILLIAM AND MARY REVIEW—P.O. Box 8795, College of William and Mary, Williamsburg, VA 23187-8795. Adriana X. Tatum, Ed. Annual. Fiction, critical essays, and interviews, 2,500 to 7,500 words; poetry, all genres (submit 4 to 6 poems); and art, all media. Pays in copies. Manuscripts read September through March. Responds in 3 months.

WILLOW SPRINGS—MS-1, Eastern Washington Univ., 705 W. First, Spokane, WA 99204. Attn: Ed. Fiction, poetry, translation, and art. Length and subject matter are open. No payment. Manuscripts read September 15 to May 15.

WIND MAGAZINE—P.O. Box 24548, Lexington, KY 40524. Charlie Hughes and Leatha Kendrick, Eds. Semiannual. Short stories, poems, and essays. Reviews of books from small presses and news of interest to the literary community. Pays in copies. Contests. Manuscripts read year-round. Web site: http://www.lit-arts.com/wind.

WINDSOR REVIEW—Dept. of English, Univ. of Windsor, Windsor, Ont., Canada N9B 3P4. Attn: Ed. Short stories, poetry, and original art. Pays $15 for poetry; $50 for fiction, on publication. Responds in one to 3 months.

THE WORCESTER REVIEW—6 Chatham St., Worcester, MA 01609. Rodger Martin, Ed. Poetry (submit up to 5 poems at a time), fiction, and critical articles about poetry with a New England connection. Pays in copies. Responds within 6 months.

WRITERS FORUM—Univ. of Colorado, 1420 Austin Bluffs Pkwy., Colorado Springs, CO 80933-7150. C. Kenneth Pellow, Ed. Annual. Mainstream and experimental fiction, 1,000 to 8,000 words. Emphasis on Western themes and writers. Up to five poems by one author considered. Manuscripts read year-round. Pays in copies.

WRITERS' INTERNATIONAL FORUM and WRITERS' INTERNATIONAL FORUM FOR YOUNG AUTHORS—P.O. Box 516, Tracyton, WA 98393-0516. Sandra Haven, Ed. Fiction and essays, to 1,000 words; all genres except horror. Articles on the craft of writing. Pays from $10, on acceptance. Guidelines. Contest.

WRITERS ON THE RIVER—P.O. Box 40828, Memphis, TN 38174-0828. Mick Denington, Ed. Florence Bruce, Asst. Ed.; Russell Strauss, Prose Ed.;

Wanda Rider, Poetry Ed. Family oriented. Publishes poetry, one page; fiction and nonfiction: adventure, fantasy, historical and regional, mainstream, humor, mystery/suspense, to 2, 500 words. Accepts submissions only from states bordering the Mississippi River. Pays in copies.

WWW.TOMORROWSF.COM—(formerly *Tomorrow: Speculative Fiction*) P.O. Box 6038, Evanston, IL 60204. Algis Budrys, Ed. Bimonthly. Electronic magazine. Fiction and nonfiction, any length. Science fiction, fantasy, horror, and science. Also, some cartoons and poetry. Pays 4¢ to 7¢ per word for fiction and nonfiction; $25 for cartoons; and 50¢ per line for poetry.

YARROW—English Dept., Lytle Hall, Kutztown State Univ., Kutztown, PA 19530. Harry Humes, Ed. Semiannual. Poetry. "Just good, solid, clear writing. We don't have room for long poems." Pays in copies. Manuscripts read year-round.

ZOETROPE: ALL STORY—260 Fifth Ave., Suite 1200, New York, NY 10001. Adrienne Brodeur, Ed.-in-Chief. Stories and one-act plays, under 7,000 words. Pays good rates, on acceptance. No submissions from June 1 to August 31. Allow 5 months for response.

ZYZZYVA—41 Sutter, Suite 1400, San Francisco, CA 94104. Howard Junker, Ed. Publishes work of West Coast writers only: fiction, essays, and poetry. Pays $50, on acceptance. Manuscripts read year-round.

GREETING CARDS & NOVELTY ITEMS

Companies selling greeting cards and novelty items (T-shirts, coffee mugs, buttons, etc.) often have their own specific requirements for the submission of ideas, verse, and artwork. In general, however, each verse or message should be typed double-space on a 3x5 or 4x6 card. Use only one side of the card, and be sure to put your name and address in the upper left-hand corner. Keep a copy of every verse or idea you send. (It's also advisable to keep a record of what you've submitted to each publisher.) Always enclose an SASE, and do not send out more than ten verses or ideas in a group to any one publisher. Never send original artwork unless a publisher indicates a definite interest in using your work.

AMBERLEY GREETING CARD COMPANY—11510 Goldcoast Dr., Cincinnati, OH 45249-1695. Dave McPeek, Ed. Humorous ideas for cards: birthday, illness, friendship, anniversary, congratulations, "miss you," etc. Send SASE for market letter before submitting ideas. Pays $150. Buys all rights.

AMERICAN GREETINGS—One American Rd., Cleveland, OH 44144. Kathleen McKay, Ed. Recruitment. Send #10 SASE to receive Humorous Writing guidelines. Currently seeking humor only.

BLUE MOUNTAIN ARTS, INC.—P.O. Box 1007, Boulder, CO 80306. Attn: Editorial, Dept. TW. Poetry and prose about love, friendship, family, philosophies, etc. Also material for special occasions and holidays: birthdays, get well, Christmas, Valentine's Day, Easter, etc. Submit seasonal material 5 months in advance of holiday. No artwork. Include SASE. Pays $200 per poem.

BRILLIANT ENTERPRISES—117 W. Valerio St., Santa Barbara, CA 93101-2927. Ashleigh Brilliant, Ed. Illustrated epigrams. Send SASE and $2 for a catalogue and samples. Pays $40, on acceptance.

COMSTOCK CARDS—600 S. Rock, Suite 15, Reno, NV 89502-4115. David Delacroix, Ed. Adult humor, outrageous or sexual, for greeting cards. SASE for guidelines. Payment varies, on publication.

CURRENT, INC.—Box 2559, Colorado Springs, CO 80901-2559. Ed. Dept. Non-risqué birthday, woman-to-woman cards, and Post-It notes.

DAYSPRING GREETING CARDS—P.O. Box 1010, Siloam Springs, AR 72761. Attn: Freelance Editor. Inspirational material for everyday occasions and most holidays. Currently only accepting free-lance copy submissions from published greeting card authors. Qualified writers should send samples of their published greeting cards (no more than 5 cards or copies). Also, the words "Previously Published" must be written on the lower left corner of the mailing envelopes containing copy submissions. Payment is $50 on acceptance. Send SASE for guidelines, or email to: info@dayspring.com, and type in the word "write" for guidelines.

DESIGN DESIGN, INC.—P.O. Box 2266, Grand Rapids, MI 49501-2266. Tom Vituj, Creative Dir. Short verses for both humorous and sentimental concepts for greeting cards. Everyday (birthday, get well, just for fun, etc.) and seasonal (Christmas, Valentine's Day, Easter, Mother's Day, Father's Day, Graduation, Halloween, Thanksgiving) material. Flat fee payment on publication.

DUCK & COVER—P.O. Box 21640, Oakland, CA 94620. Jim Buser, Ed. Outrageous, off the wall, original one-liners for buttons and magnets. SASE for guidelines. Pays $25, on publication.

EPHEMERA, INC.—P.O. Box 490, Phoenix, OR 97535. Attn: Ed. Provocative, irreverent, and outrageously funny slogans for novelty buttons and magnets. Submit typed list of slogans with SASE. Pays $35 per slogan, on publication. SASE for guidelines; also available from website: www.ephemera-inc.com

FREEDOM GREETING CARD COMPANY—774 American Drive, Bensalem, PA 19020. Jay Levitt, Ed. Dept. Traditional and humorous verse and love messages. Inspirational poetry for all occasions. Pays negotiable rates, on acceptance. Query with SASE.

HALLMARK CARDS, INC.—Box 419580, Mail Drop 288, Kansas City, MO 64141. No unsolicited submissions.

KATE HARPER DESIGNS—P.O. Box 2112, Berkeley, CA 94703. Attn: Guidelines TW. Quotes, to 20 words, about work, life, technology, political themes, current social issues, etc., from everyday people for hand-assembled "quotation" cards that take a lighthearted look at life in the 90s. Submit original quotes on index card, one quote per card. No drawings, artwork, or visuals. Send SASE for guidelines before submitting. Pays $25, on acceptance. Also accepting submissions from children under 13. Send SASE for guidelines format. Pays $25 per quote accepted.

LAFFS BY MARCEL—Schurman Design, 101 New Montgomery, 6th Fl., San Francisco, CA 94110. Attn: Deanne Quinones. Humorous birthday, everyday, and seasonal ideas.

OATMEAL STUDIOS—Box 138 TW, Rochester, VT 05767. Attn: Ed. Humorous, clever, and new ideas needed for all occasions. Send legal-size SASE for guidelines.

PANDA INK—P.O. Box 5129, West Hills, CA 91308-5129. Ruth Ann Epstein, Ed. Judaica, metaphysical, cute, whimsical, or beautiful sentiment for greeting cards, bookmarks, clocks, and pins. Submit ideas typed on 8½ x 11 paper, include SASE. "Best time to submit is beginning of the year; decisions are made in January." Payment varies, on acceptance.

PARAMOUNT CARDS—P.O. Box 6546, Providence, RI 02940-6546. Attn: Editorial Freelance. Humorous and traditional card ideas for birthday, relative's birthday, friendship, romance, get well, Christmas, Valentine's Day, Easter, Mother's Day, Father's Day, and Graduation. Submit each idea (5 to 10 per submission) on 3x5 card with name and address on each, along with an SASE. Payment varies, on acceptance.

PLUM GRAPHICS—P.O. Box 136, Prince Station, New York, NY 10012. Yvette Cohen, Ed. Editorial needs change frequently; write for guidelines (new guidelines 3 times per year). Queries required. Pays $40 per card, on publication.

RED FARM STUDIO—1135 Roosevelt Ave., P.O. Box 347, Pawtucket, RI 02862. Attn: Production Coord. Traditional cards for birthday, get well, wedding, anniversary, friendship, new baby, sympathy, congrats, and Christmas; also light humor. Pays $4 a line. Send SASE.

ROCKSHOTS, INC.— 632 Broadway, New York, NY 10012. Bob Vesce, Ed. Adult, provocative, humorous gag lines for greeting cards. Submit on 4x5 cards with SASE. Pays $50 per line, on acceptance. SASE for guidelines.

SUNRISE PUBLICATIONS, INC.—P.O. Box 4699, Bloomington, IN 47402-4699. Attn: Text Ed. Original copy for holiday and everyday cards. "Submit up to 15 verses, one to 4 lines, on 3x5 cards; simple, to-the-point ideas that could be serious, humorous, or light-hearted, but sincere, without being overly sentimental. Rhymed verse not generally used." Allow 3 months for response. SASE for guidelines and for return of your submission. Pays standard rates.

VAGABOND CREATIONS, INC.—2560 Lance Dr., Dayton, OH 45409. George F. Stanley, Jr., Ed. Greeting cards with graphics only on cover (no copy) and short punch line inside: birthday, everyday, Valentine's Day, Christmas, and graduation. Mildly risqué humor with double entendre acceptable. Ideas for illustrated theme stationery. Pays $15, on acceptance.

WEST GRAPHICS PUBLISHING—1117 California Dr., Burlingame, CA 94010. Attn: Production Dept. Outrageous humor concepts, all occasions (especially birthday) and holidays, for photo and illustrated card lines. Submit on 3x5 cards: concept on one side; name, address, and phone number on other. Pays $100, 30 days after publication.

HUMOR, FILLERS, & SHORT ITEMS

Magazines noted for their filler departments, plus a cross-section of publications using humor, short items, jokes, quizzes, and cartoons, follow. However, almost all magazines use some type of filler material from time to time, and writers can find dozens of markets by studying copies of magazines at a library or newsstand.

THE AMERICAN FIELD—542 S. Dearborn, Chicago, IL 60605. B.J. Matthys, Man. Ed. Short fact items and anecdotes on hunting dogs and field trials for bird dogs. Pays varying rates, on acceptance.

AMERICAN SPEAKER—Attn: Current Comedy, 1101 30th St. N.W., Washington, DC 20007. Aram Bakshian, Ed.-in-Chief. Original, funny, performable jokes on news, fads, topical subjects, business, etc., for "Current Comedy" section of *American Speaker* Magazine. Jokes for roasts, retirement dinners, and for speaking engagements. Humorous material specifically geared for public speaking situations such as microphone feedback, introductions, long events, etc. Also interested in longer original jokes and anecdotes that can be used by public speakers. No poems, puns, ethnic jokes, or sexist material. Pays $12, on publication. Guidelines.

THE ANNALS OF IMPROBABLE RESEARCH—AIR, P.O. Box 380853, Cambridge, MA 02238. Marc Abrahams, Ed. Science humor, science reports and analysis, one to 4 pages. B&W photos. "This journal is the place to find the mischievous, funny, iconoclastic side of science. An insider's journal that lets anyone sneak into the company of wonderfully mad scientists." Guidelines. No payment.

ARMY MAGAZINE—2425 Wilson Blvd., Arlington, VA 22210-0860. Mary B. French, Ed.-in-Chief. True anecdotes on military subjects. Pays $25 to $50, on publication.

ASIAN PAGES—P.O. Box 11932, St. Paul, MN 55111-0932. Cheryl Weiberg, Ed.-in-Chief. Profiles and news events, 500 words; short stories, 500 to 750 words; poetry, 100 words; and Asian-related fillers, 50 words. "All material must have a strong, non-offensive Asian slant." Pays $40 for articles, $25 for photos/cartoons, on publication.

THE ATLANTIC MONTHLY—77 N. Washington St., Boston, MA 02114. Attn: Ed. Sophisticated humorous or satirical pieces, 1,000 to 3,000 words. Some light poetry. Pays from $500 for prose, on acceptance.

ATLANTIC SALMON JOURNAL—P.O. Box 429, St. Andrews, N.B., Canada E0G 2X0. Jim Gourlay, Ed. Fillers, 50 to 100 words, on salmon politics, conservation, and nature. Pays $25 for fillers, on publication.

BICYCLING—135 N. 6th St., Emmaus, PA 18098. Attn: Eds. Anecdotes, helpful cycling tips, and other items for "Bike Shorts" section, 150 to 250 words. Pays $25 to $50, on acceptance.

BYLINE—Box 130596, Edmond, OK 73013. Kathryn Fanning, Man. Ed. Humor, 200 to 400 words, about writing. Pays $15 to $25 for humor, on acceptance.

CAPPER'S—1503 S.W. 42nd St., Topeka, KS 66609-1265. Ann Crahan, Ed. Letters, to 300 words, sharing heartwarming experiences, nostalgic accounts, household hints, poems, and recipes, for "Heart of the Home." Poetry to 16 lines. Pays on acceptance. Freelance articles on historical, informational, unusual items to 700 words. Pays on publication. Query only for serial fiction. Jokes, submit up to 6 at a time. Pays varying rates (and in gift certificates), on publication.

CASCADES EAST—716 N. E. 4th St., P. O. Box 5784, Bend, OR 97708. Geoff Hill, Ed. Fillers related to travel, history, and recreation in central Oregon. Pays 5¢ to 15¢ a word, extra for photos, on publication.

CATHOLIC DIGEST—P.O. Box 64090, St. Paul, MN 55164-0090. Attn: Filler Ed. Articles, 200 to 500 words, on instances of kindness, for "Hearts Are Trumps." Stories about conversions, for "Open Door." Reports of tactful remarks or actions, for "The Perfect Assist." Accounts of good deeds, for "People Are Like That." Humorous pieces, 50 to 300 words, on parish life, for "In Our Parish." Amusing signs, for "Signs of the Times." Jokes; fillers. No fiction. Pays $2 per line, on publication.

CHICKADEE—179 John St., Suite 500, Toronto, Ont., Canada M5T 3G5. Kat Mototsune, Ed. Juvenile poetry, 10 to 15 lines. Fiction, 800 words. Pays on acceptance. Enclose $2.00 money order and IRC for reply.

CHILDREN'S PLAYMATE—1100 Waterway Blvd., P.O. Box 567, Indianapolis, IN 46206. Terry Harshman, Ed. Articles and fiction, puzzles, games, mazes, poetry, crafts, and recipes for 6- to 8-year-olds, emphasizing health, fitness, sports, safety, and nutrition. Pays to 17¢ a word (varies on puzzles), on publication.

THE CHURCH MUSICIAN—127 Ninth Ave. N., Nashville, TN 37234-0160. Jere V. Adams, Ed. Humorous fillers with a music slant for church music leaders, pastors, organists, pianists, and members of the music council or other planning groups. (No clippings.) Pays 5½¢ a word, on publication.

COLUMBIA JOURNALISM REVIEW—Columbia Univ., 700 Journalism Bldg., New York, NY 10027. Gloria Cooper, Man. Ed. Amusing mistakes in news stories, headlines, photos, etc. (original clippings required), for "Lower Case." Pays $25, on publication.

COMBO—5 Nassau Blvd. S., Garden City South, NY 11530. Ian M. Feller, Ed. Fillers related to non-sports cards (comic cards, TV/movie cards, science fiction cards, etc.) and comic books. Pays 10¢ a word, on publication.

COUNTRY WOMAN—P. O. Box 989, Greendale, WI 53129. Kathy Pohl, Man. Ed. Short rhymed verse, 4 to 20 lines, seasonal and country-related. All material must be positive and upbeat. Pays $10 to $15, on acceptance.

CRACKED—Globe Communications, Inc., 3 E. 54th St., 15 Fl., New York, NY 10022-3108. Lou Silverstone, Andy Simmons, Eds. Cartoon humor, one to 5 pages, for 10- to 15-year-old readers. "Queries are not necessary, but read the magazine before submitting material!" Pays from $100 per page, on acceptance.

CYCLE WORLD—1499 Monrovia Ave., Newport Beach, CA 92663. David Edwards, Ed.-in-Chief. News items on motorcycle industry, legislation, trends. Pays on publication.

FACES—Cobblestone Publishing, 30 Grove St., Suite C, Peterborough, NH 03458-1454. Elizabeth Crooker, Ed. Puzzles, mazes, crosswords, and picture puzzles for children. Send SASE for list of monthly themes before submitting.

FAMILY CIRCLE—375 Lexington Ave., New York, NY 10017. Uses some short humor, 750 words. No fiction. Payment varies, on acceptance.

THE FAMILY DIGEST—P.O. Box 40137, Fort Wayne, IN 46804. Corine B. Erlandson, Ed. Family-or Catholic parish-oriented anecdotes, 10 to 125 words, of funny or unusual real-life parish and family experiences. Pays $20, 4 to 6 weeks after acceptance.

FARM AND RANCH LIVING—5400 S. 60th St., Greendale, WI 53129. Nick Pabst, Ed. Fillers on rural people and living, 200 words. Pays from $15, on acceptance and publication.

FATE—P.O. Box 64383, St. Paul, MN 55164-0383. Attn: Ed. Factual fillers, to 300 words, on strange, psychic, or paranormal happenings. True personal stories, to 500 words, on proof of mystic experiences. Pays 10¢ a word for fillers (minimum $10), $25 for personal accounts. SASE for guidelines. E-mail: fate@llewellyn.com

FIELD & STREAM—2 Park Ave., New York, NY 10016. Duncan Barnes, Ed. Fillers on hunting, fishing, camping, etc., to 500 words. Cartoons. Pays $75 to $250, sometimes more, for fillers; $100 for cartoons, on acceptance.

FINESCALE MODELER—P.O. Box 1612, Waukesha, WI 53187. Bob Hayden, Ed. One-page hints and tips on building nonoperating, scale models. Payment varies, on acceptance.

GAMES—P.O. Box 184, Ft. Washington, PA 19034. R. Wayne Schmittberger, Ed.-in-Chief. Pencil puzzles, visual brainteasers, and pop culture tests. Humor and playfulness a plus; quality a must. Pays top rates, on publication.

GERMAN LIFE—Zeitgeist Publishing, 226 North Adams St., Rockville, MD 20850-1829. Heidi Whitesell, Ed. Fillers, 50 to 200 words, on German culture, its past and present, and how America has been influenced by its German element: history, travel, people, the arts, and social and political issues; also humor and cartoons. Articles, 500 to 2,000 words. Pays to $80 for fillers; $300 to $500 for articles, on publication. Queries preferred for articles.

GLAMOUR—350 Madison Ave., New York, NY 10017. Attn: Viewpoint Ed. Articles, 1,000 words, for "Viewpoint" section: opinion pieces for women. Pays $500, on acceptance.

GUIDEPOSTS—16 E. 34th St., New York, NY 10016. Celeste McCauley, Features Ed. Inspirational anecdotes, to 250 words. Pays $10 to $75, on acceptance.

MAD MAGAZINE—1700 Broadway, 5th Fl., New York, NY 10019. Attn: Eds. Humorous pieces on a wide variety of topics. Two- to 8-panel cartoons (not necessary to include sketches with submission). Pays top rates, on acceptance. Guidelines strongly recommended.

MATURE LIVING—127 Ninth Ave. N., MSN 140, Nashville, TN 37234. Attn: Ed. Brief, humorous, original items. "Grandparents Brag Board" items; Christian inspirational pieces for senior adults, 125 words. Pays $15 to $25.

MATURE YEARS—201 Eighth Ave. S., P.O. Box 801, Nashville, TN 37202. Marvin W. Cropsey, Ed. Poems, cartoons, puzzles, jokes, anecdotes, to 300 words, for older adults. Allow 2 months for manuscript evaluation. "A Christian magazine that seeks to build faith. We always show older adults in a favorable light." Include name, address, social security number with all submissions.

MID-WEST OUTDOORS—111 Shore Dr., Hinsdale, IL 60521-5885. Gene Laulunen, Man. Ed. Where to and how to fish and hunt in the Midwest, 700 to 1,500 words, with 2 photos. Pays $15 to $30, on publication.

MODERN BRIDE—249 W. 17th St., New York, NY 10011. Mary Ann Cavlin, Exec. Ed. Humorous pieces, 500 to 1,000 words, for brides. Pays on acceptance.

NATIONAL ENQUIRER—Lantana, FL 33464. Kathy Martin, Fillers Ed. Short, humorous or philosophical fillers, witticisms, anecdotes, jokes, tart comments. Original items only. Short poetry, 8 lines or less, with traditional rhyming verse, amusing, philosophical, or inspirational in nature. No obscure or artsy poetry. Submit seasonal/holiday material at least 3 months in advance. Pays $25, after publication.

NEW HUMOR MAGAZINE—P.O. Box 216, Lafayette Hill, PA 19444. Edward Savaria, Jr., Ed. Humorous stories, 500 to 1,500 words; short humorous poetry; and fillers, 25 to 400 words. "Odd humor with an edge. Keep it clean and tasteful." Pays $40 to $85 for stories, $5 to $15 for fillers, on publication.

THE NEW YORKER—20 W. 43rd St., New York, NY 10036. Attn: Newsbreaks Dept. Amusing mistakes in newspapers, books, magazines, etc. Pays $10, on acceptance.

OPTOMETRIC ECONOMICS—See *Practice Strategies*.

OUTDOOR LIFE—2 Park Ave., New York, NY 10016. Todd W. Smith, Ed. Short instructive items, 900 to 1,100 words, on hunting, fishing, boating, and outdoor equipment; regional pieces on lakes, rivers, specific geographic areas of special interest to hunters and fishermen. Not soliciting materials at present.

PLAYBOY—680 N. Lake Shore Dr., Chicago, IL 60611. Attn: Party Jokes Ed. or After Hours Ed. Jokes; short original material on new trends, lifestyles, personalities; humorous news items. Pays $100 for jokes; $50 to $350 for "After Hours" items, on publication.

PLAYGIRL—801 Second Ave., New York, NY 10017. Attn: Man. Ed. Humorous pieces, 800 to 1,500 words, on romance and relationships with a sexual twist, from male or female perspective, 800 to 1,000 words, for "Playgirl Punchline." Pays varying rates, after acceptance. Query.

PRACTICE STRATEGIES—(formerly *Optometric Economics*) Amer. Optometric Assn., 243 N. Lindbergh Blvd., St. Louis, MO 63141. Gene Mitchell, Man. Ed. Short humor for optometrists; writers should have some knowledge of optometry. Pay varies, on acceptance.

READER'S DIGEST—Pleasantville, NY 10570. Consult "Contributor's Corner" page for guidelines. No submissions acknowledged or returned.

REAL PEOPLE—450 7th Ave., Suite 1701, New York, NY 10123-0073. Brad Hamilton, Ed. True stories, to 500 words, about interesting people for "Real Shorts" section: strange occurrences, everyday weirdness, occupations, etc.; may be funny, sad, or hair-raising. Also humorous items, to 75 words, taken from small-circulation newspapers, etc. Pays $25 to $50, on publication.

RHODE ISLAND MONTHLY—70 Elm St., Providence, RI 02903. Paula M. Bodah, Ed. Short pieces, to 500 words, on Rhode Island and southeastern Massachusetts: places, customs, people and events. Pays $50 to $150. Query.

ROAD KING—Hammock Publishing, 3322 W. End Ave., Suite 700, Nashville, TN 37203. Attn: Fillers Ed. Trucking-related cartoons and fillers. Payment is negotiable, on publication.

THE ROTARIAN—1560 Sherman Ave., Evanston, IL 60201-3698. Charles W. Pratt, Ed. Occasional humor articles. Payment varies, on acceptance. No payment for fillers, anecdotes, or jokes.

SACRAMENTO MAGAZINE— 4471 D St., Sacramento, CA 95819. Krista Minard, Ed. "City Lights," interesting and unusual people, places, and behind-the-scenes news items, to 400 words. All material must have Sacramento tie-in. Payment varies, on publication.

THE SATURDAY EVENING POST—P.O. Box 567, Indianapolis, IN 46206. Steven Pettinga, Post Scripts Ed. Humor and satire, to 100 words, that is upbeat and postive. No lurid references. Light verse, cartoons, jokes, for verse. Original material only. SASE required. Pays $15 for verse; $125 for cartoons, on publication.

SKI MAGAZINE— 929 Pearl St., Suite 200, Boulder, CO 80302. Andrew Bigford, Ed.-in-Chief. Short, 100- to 300-word items on news, events, and people in skiing for "Ski Life" department. Pays on acceptance.

SLICK TIMES—P.O. Box 1710, Valley Center, CA 92082. Michael Johnson, Ed. Political humor, 1,000 to 2,000 words, "poking fun at the Clintons." Pays $250 to $375, on publication.

SPORTS AFIELD—250 W. 55th St., New York, NY 10019. Attn: Almanac Ed. Unusual, useful tips and information, 100 to 300 words, for "Almanac" section: on camping, hiking, hunting, fishing, skiing, mountain biking, rock climbing, boating, and natural history. Photos. Pays on publication.

STAR— 660 White Plains Rd., Tarrytown, NY 10591. Attn: Ed. Topical articles, 50 to 800 words, on show business and celebrities. Pays varying rates.

STITCHES, THE JOURNAL OF MEDICAL HUMOUR—16787 Warden Ave., R.R. #3, Newmarket, Ont., Canada L3Y 4W1. Simon Hally, Ed. Humorous pieces, 250 to 2,000 words, for physicians. "Most articles have something to do with medicine." Short humorous verse and original jokes. Pays 30¢ to 40¢ (Canadian) a word; $50 (Canadian) for cartoons, on publication. Fax: (416) 853-6565

TECH DIRECTIONS—3970 Varsity Dr., Box 8623, Ann Arbor, MI 48107-8623. Tom Bowden, Man. Ed. Cartoons, puzzles, brainteasers, and humorous anecdotes of interest to technology and industrial education teachers and administrators. Pays $20 for cartoons; $25 for puzzles, brainteasers, and other short classroom activities; $5 for humorous anecdotes, on publication.

THOUGHTS FOR ALL SEASONS: THE MAGAZINE OF EPIGRAMS— 478 N.E. 56th St., Miami, FL 33137. Michel P. Richard, Ed. Epigrams and puns, one to 4 lines, and poetry, to one page. "Writers are advised not to submit material until they have examined a copy of the magazine." Payment is one copy.

TOUCH—Box 7259, Grand Rapids, MI 49510. Carol Smith, Man. Ed. Puzzles based on the NIV Bible, for Christian girls ages 8 to 14. Pays $10 to $15 per puzzle, on publication. Send SASE for theme update.

TRAVEL SMART—Dobbs Ferry, NY 10522. Attn: Ed. Interesting and useful travel-related tips. Practical, specific, information for vacation or business travel. Fresh, original material. Pays $5 to $150. Query for over 250 words.

TRUE CONFESSIONS—233 Park Ave. S., New York, NY 10003. Pat Byrdsong, Ed. Warm, inspirational first-person fillers, to 300 words, about love, marriage, family life, prayer for "Woman to Woman," "My Moment with God," "My Man," and "Incredible But True." Also, short stories, 1,000 to 2,000 words. Pays after publication. Buys all rights.

WISCONSIN TRAILS—P.O. Box 5650, Madison, WI 53705. Attn: Ed. Short articles/fillers, 300 words, about Wisconsin: places to go, things to do, etc. Query. No clippings or phone calls. E-mail: info@wistrails.com.

JUVENILE & YOUNG ADULT MAGAZINES

JUVENILE MAGAZINES

AMERICAN GIRL—8400 Fairway Pl., P.O. Box 998, Middleton, WI 53562-0998. Attn: Asst. to the Magazine Dept. Bimonthly. Articles, to 800 words, and contemporary or historical fiction, to 3,000 words, for girls ages 8 to 12. "We do not want 'teenage' material, i.e. articles on romance, make-up, dating, etc." Payment varies, on acceptance. Query for articles; include photo leads with historical queries.

BABYBUG—P.O. Box 300, Peru, IL 61354. Marianne Carus, Ed.-in-Chief. Paula Morrow, Ed. Stories, to 4 sentences; poems, and action rhymes, to 8 lines, for infants and toddlers, 6 months to 2 years. Pays from $25, on publication. Guidelines.

BOYS' QUEST—P.O. Box 227, Bluffton, OH 45817-4610. Attn: Ed. Bimonthly. Fiction and nonfiction, 500 words, for boys ages 6 to 12. "We are looking for articles, stories, and poetry that deal with timeless topics such as pets, nature, hobbies, science, games, sports, careers, simple cooking, etc." B&W photos a plus. Pays 5¢ a word, on publication. Send SASE for guidelines.

CALLIOPE: WORLD HISTORY FOR YOUNG PEOPLE—Cobblestone Publishing, Inc., 30 Grove St., Peterborough, NH 03458. Rosalie Baker and Charles Baker, Eds. Theme-based magazine, published 9 times yearly. Articles, 750 to 1,000 words, with lively, original approach to world history (East/West) through the Renaissance. Shorts, 200 to 750 words, on little-known information related to issue's theme. Fiction, to 1,200 words: historical, biographical, adventure, or retold legends. Activities for children, to 800 words. Puzzles and games. Pays 20¢ to 25¢ a word, on publication. Guidelines and themes.

CHICKADEE MAGAZINE—179 John St., Suite 500, Toronto, Ont., Canada M5T 3G5. Kat Mototsune, Ed. Adventure, folktale, and humorous stories and poems for 6- to 9-year-olds. Also puzzles, activities, and observation games. No religious material. Pays varying rates, on acceptance. Submit complete manuscript with $2.00 check or money order for return postage. Send $4.28 (Canadian dollars) for guidelines.

CHILD LIFE—1100 Waterway Blvd., P.O. Box 567, Indianapolis, IN 46206. Lise Hoffman, Ed. Nostalgia and some health-related material, the latter generated in-house or assigned, for 9- to 11-year-olds. Currently not accepting manuscripts for publication.

CHILDREN'S DIGEST—1100 Waterway Blvd., P.O. Box 567, Indianapolis, IN 46206. Layne Cameron, Ed. Not considering new material at this time. Health and general-interest publication for preteens. Informative articles, 500 to 1,200 words, and fiction (especially realistic, adventure, mystery, and humorous), 500 to 1,500 words. Historical and biographical articles. Poetry and activities. Pays from 12½¢ a word, from $15 for poems, on publication.

CHILDREN'S PLAYMATE—1100 Waterway Blvd., P.O. Box 567, Indianapolis, IN 46206. Terry Harshman, Ed. General-interest and health-related short stories (health, fitness, nutrition, safety, and exercise), 500 to 600 words, for 6- to 8-year-olds. Easy recipes and how-to crafts pieces with simple instructions. Poems, puzzles, dot-to-dots, mazes, hidden pictures. Pays to 17¢ a word, from $25 for poetry, on publication. Buys all rights.

CLICK—332 S. Michigan Ave., Suite 2000, Chicago, IL 60604. Attn: Ed. Bimonthly. Articles, to 850 words for readers 3 to 7, about natural, physical, or social sciences, the arts, technology, math, and history. Fiction, if the goal of the story is to address a question about the world. Pays 25¢ a word, on publication.

CLUBHOUSE—Box 15, Berrien Springs, MI 49103. Krista Phillips, Ed. Currently overstocked; not considering new material at this time. Action-oriented Christian stories, 800 to 1,200 words. Children in stories should be wise, brave, funny, kind, etc. Pays $25 to $35 for stories.

COBBLESTONE: DISCOVER AMERICAN HISTORY—30 Grove St., Suite C, Peterborough, NH 03458-1454. Meg Chorlian, Ed. Theme-related articles, biographies, plays, and short accounts of historical events, 700 to 800 words, for 8- to 15-year-olds; also supplemental nonfiction, 300 to 600 words. Fiction, 700 to 800 words. Activities (crafts, recipes, etc.) that can be done either by children alone or with adult supervision. Poetry, to 100 lines. Crossword and other word puzzles using the vocabulary of the issue's theme. Pays 20¢ to 25¢ a word, on publication. (Payment varies for activities and poetry.) Send SASE for guidelines and themes.

CONTACT KIDS—(formerly *3-2-1 Contact*) 1 Lincoln Plaza, Children's Television Workshop,, New York, NY 10023. Curtis Slepian, Ed. Entertaining and informative articles, 600 to 1,000 words, for 8- to 14-year-olds, on all aspects of science, computers, scientists, and children who are learning about or practicing science. Pays $75 to $500, on acceptance. No fiction. Query.

CRAYOLA KIDS—Meredith Custom Publishing, 1912 Grand Ave., Des Moines, IA 50309-3379. Barbara Hall Palar, Ed. Bimonthly for families with children 3 to 8 years old. Hands-on crafts and seasonal activities, one to 4 pages. Puzzle ideas related to issue themes. Pays $50 to $250, on acceptance. Send SASE for themes. Query with resumé and work samples.

CRICKET—P.O. Box 300, Peru, IL 61354-0300. Marianne Carus, Ed.-in-Chief. Articles and fiction, 200 to 2,000 words, for 9- to 14-year-olds. (Include bibliography with nonfiction.) Poetry, to 30 lines. Pays to 25¢ a word, to $3 a line for poetry, on publication. Guidelines.

DISCOVERIES—WordAction Publishing Co., 6401 The Paseo, Kansas City, MO 64131. Attn: Asst. Ed. Weekly designed to correlate with Evangelical Sunday school curriculum. Fiction, 500 words, for 8- to 10-year-olds should feature contemporary, true-to-life characters and illustrate character building and scriptural application. No poetry. Pays 5¢ a word, on publication. Guidelines.

THE DOLPHIN LOG—The Cousteau Society, 61 East 8th St., Box 112, New York, NY 10003. Lisa Rao, Ed. Articles, 400 to 600 words, on a variety of topics related to our global water system: marine biology, ecology, natural history, and water-related subjects, for 7- to 13-year-olds. No fiction. Pays $50 to $200, on publication. Query.

FACES—Cobblestone Publishing, 30 Grove St., Suite C, Peterborough, NH 03458-1454. Elizabeth Crooker, Ed. In-depth feature articles, 800 words, with an anthropology theme. Shorts, 300 to 600 words, related to themes. Fiction, to 800 words, on legends, folktales, stories from around the world, etc., related to theme. Activities, to 700 words, including recipes, crafts, games, etc., for children. Published monthly, September through May. Pays 20¢ to 25¢ a word. Write for guidelines and themes.

THE FLICKER MAGAZINE—P.O. Box 660544, Birmingham, AL 35266-0544. Ann Dorer, Assoc. Ed. Bimonthly. Articles, to 500 words, for 10- to 12-year-olds; stories, 800 to 850 words. Short poems and jokes. Based on Christian values and principles, encourages balanced growth in all areas of life: physical, mental, spiritual, social, and emotional. Pays 10¢ a word on acceptance. SASE for guidelines.

THE FRIEND—50 E. North Temple, 23rd Fl., Salt Lake City, UT 84150. Vivian Paulsen, Man. Ed. Stories and articles, 1,000 to 1,200 words. Stories, to 250 words, for younger readers and preschool children. Pays from 9¢ a word, from $25 per poem, on acceptance. Prefers completed manuscripts. Guidelines.

GIRLS' LIFE—Monarch Avalon, Inc., 4517 Harford Rd., Baltimore, MD 21214. Kelly White, Sr. Ed. Features of various lengths and one-page departments that entertain and educate girls ages 7 to 14. Payment varies, on publication. Query with resumé and clips. Send SASE for guidelines.

THE GOLDFINCH—State Historical Society of Iowa, 402 Iowa Ave., Iowa City, IA 52240-1806. Quarterly. Articles, 200 to 800 words, and short fiction on Iowa history for young people. "All articles must correspond to an upcoming theme." Pays $25 per article, on acceptance. Query for themes.

GUIDEPOSTS FOR KIDS—P.O. Box 638, Chesterton, IN 46304. Mary Lou Carney, Ed. Issue-oriented, thought-provoking articles, 1,000 to 1,500 words. "Things kids not only need to know, but want to know." Fiction: historicals and mysteries, 700 to 1,300 words, and contemporary stories, 1,000 words. "Not preachy. Dialogue-filled and value-driven." Pays competitive rates, on acceptance. Query for articles.

HIGHLIGHTS FOR CHILDREN— 803 Church St., Honesdale, PA 18431-1824. Beth Troop, Manuscript Coord. Easy-to-read stories, to 500 words for 6- to 8-year-olds; and fiction, to 900 words, for 8-year-olds and up. Humor, adventure, mystery, fantasy, folktales, and talking animal stories. "We'd also like to see stories that don't fit in any of those categories, but are good, meaningful stories for children." Pays from 14¢ a word, on acceptance. SASE for guidelines.

HOPSCOTCH, THE MAGAZINE FOR GIRLS—P.O. Box 164, Bluffton, OH 45817-0164. Marilyn Edwards, Ed. Bimonthly. Articles and fiction, 600 to 1,000 words, and short poetry for girls ages 6 to 12. Special interest in articles, with photos, about girls involved in worthwhile activities. "We believe young girls deserve the right to enjoy a season of childhood before they become young adults; we are not interested in such topics as sex, romance, cosmetics, hairstyles, etc." Pays 5¢ a word, on publication. Send SASE for guidelines.

HUMPTY DUMPTY'S MAGAZINE—1100 Waterway Blvd., P.O. Box 567, Indianapolis, IN 46206. Nancy Axelrad, Ed. General-interest publication with an emphasis on health and fitness for 4- to 6-year-olds. Easy-to-read fiction, to 500 words, with health and nutrition, safety, exercise, or hygiene as theme; humor and light approach preferred. Creative nonfiction, including photo-stories. Crafts with clear, brief instructions. No-cook recipes using healthful ingredients. Short verse, narrative poems. Pays to 22¢ a word, from $25 for poems, on publication. Buys all rights.

JACK AND JILL—1100 Waterway Blvd., P.O. Box 567, Indianapolis, IN 46206. Daniel Lee, Ed. Articles, 500 to 800 words, for 7- to 10-year-olds, on sports, fitness, health, nutrition, safety, exercise. Features, 500 to 700 words, on history, biography, life in other countries, etc. Fiction, to 700 words. Short poems, games, puzzles, projects, recipes. Photos. Pays 10¢ to 20¢ a word, extra for photos, on publication.

JUNIOR SCHOLASTIC—Scholastic, Inc., 555 Broadway, New York, NY 10012. Lee Baier, Ed. On-the-spot reports from countries in the news. Payment varies, on acceptance. Query.

JUNIOR TRAILS—1445 Boonville Ave., Springfield, MO 65802-1894. Sinda Zinn, Ed. Fiction, 1,000 to 1,500 words, with a Christian focus, believable characters, and moral emphasis. Articles, 300 to 500 words, on science, nature, biography. Pays 4¢ to 7¢ a word, on acceptance.

KID CITY—Children's Television Workshop, 1 Lincoln Plaza, New York, NY 10023. We do not accept any free-lance work.

KIDS TRIBUTE—71 Barber Greene Rd., Don Mills, Ont., Canada M3C 2A2. Maureen Littlejohn, Ed. Quarterly. Movie- or entertainment-related articles, 500 words, for 8- to 13-year-olds. Pays $50 to $75 (Canadian), on acceptance. Query required.

LADYBUG—P.O. Box 300, Peru, IL 61354-0300. Marianne Carus, Ed.-in-Chief. Paula Morrow, Ed. Picture stories and read-aloud stories, 300 to 750 words, for 2- to 6-year-olds; poetry, to 20 lines; songs and action rhymes; crafts, activities, and games. Pays 25¢ a word for stories; $3 a line for poetry, on publication. Guidelines.

MUSE—The Cricket Magazine Group, 332 S. Michigan Ave., Suite 2000, Chicago, IL 60604. Submissions Ed. Bimonthly. Articles, 1,000 to 2,500 words, on problems connected with a discipline or area of practical knowledge, for children ages 8 to 14. Guidelines. Query with resumé, writing samples, list of possible topics, and SASE. Pays 50¢ a word, within 60 days of acceptance. Guidelines.

MY FRIEND—Pauline Books & Media, Daughters of St. Paul, 50 St. Pauls Ave., Boston, MA 02130. Sister Kathryn James Hermes, Ed. "The Catholic Magazine for Kids." Fun stories, 150 to 900 words, with Christian values for 6- to 12-years-olds. Buys first rights. Pays $35 to $100 for stories, $5 for fillers. Query for artwork. Guidelines.

NATIONAL GEOGRAPHIC WORLD—1145 17th St. N.W., Washington, DC 20036-4688. Susan Tejada, Ed. Picture magazine for young readers, ages 8 and older. Natural history, adventure, archaeology, geography, science, the environment, and human interest. Proposals for picture stories only. No unsolicited manuscripts.

NEW MOON, THE MAGAZINE FOR GIRLS AND THEIR DREAMS— P.O. Box 3620, Duluth, MN 55803-3620. Barbara Stretchberry, Man. Ed. "Our goal is to celebrate girls and support their efforts to hang on to their voices, strengths, and dreams as they move from being girls to becoming women." Profiles of girls and women, 300 to 1,000 words. Science and math experiments, 300 to 600 words. Submissions from both girls and adults. Queries preferred. Pays 8¢ to 12¢ a word, on publication. Also publishes companion letter, *New Moon Network: For Adults Who Care About Girls.*

ODYSSEY: SCIENCE THAT'S OUT OF THIS WORLD— Cobblestone Publishing, 30 Grove St., Suite C, Peterborough, NH 03458. Elizabeth Lindstrom, Ed. Features, 750 words, on astronomy, space science, and other related physical sciences for 8- to 14-year-olds. Science-related fiction, myths, legends, and science fiction stories. Experiments and games. Pays 20¢ to 25¢ a word, on publication. Guidelines and themes.

ON THE LINE— 616 Walnut, Scottdale, PA 15683-1999. Mary Clemens Meyer, Ed. Monthly magazine for 9- to 14-year-olds. Nature, general nonfiction, and how-to articles, 350 to 500 words; fiction, 1,000 to 1,800 words; poetry, puzzles, cartoons. Pays to 5¢ a word, on acceptance.

OWL— The Owl Group, 179 John St., Suite 500, Toronto, Ont., Canada M5T 3G5. Keltie Thomas, Ed. Articles, 500 to 1,000 words, for 8- to 12-year-olds, about animals, science, people, technology, new discoveries, activities. Pays varying rates, on acceptance. Enclose $2.00 money order and SAE for reply. Guidelines.

PLAYS, THE DRAMA MAGAZINE FOR YOUNG PEOPLE— 120 Boylston St., Boston, MA 02116-4615. Elizabeth Preston, Man. Ed. Wholesome one-act comedies, dramas, skits, satires, farces, and creative dramatic material suitable for school productions at junior high, middle, and lower grade levels. Plays with modern settings preferred. Also uses dramatized classics, folktales and fairy tales, puppet plays. No religious plays or musicals. Pays good rates, on acceptance. Buys all rights. Query for classics, folk and fairy tales. Guidelines.

POCKETS— 1908 Grand Ave., Box 189, Nashville, TN 37202-0189. Janet Knight, Ed. Ecumenical magazine for 6- to 12-year-olds. Fiction and scripture stories, 600 to 1,500 words; short poems; games and family communication activities; role model stories; and stories about children involved in justice and environmental projects. Pays from 14¢ a word, $2 per line for poetry, on acceptance. Guidelines and themes. Annual fiction contest; send SASE for details.

POWER AND LIGHT— 6401 The Paseo, Kansas City, MO 64131. Beula J. Postlewait, Preteen Ed. Fiction, 500 to 800 words, for grades 5 and 6, with Christian emphasis. Pays 5¢ a word for multi-use rights, 1¾¢ a word for reprints. Pays $15 for cartoons and puzzles.

R-A-D-A-R— Standard Publishing, 8121 Hamilton Ave., Cincinnati, OH 45231. Gary Thacker, Ed. Weekly Sunday school take-home paper. Articles, 400 to 500 words, on nature, hobbies, crafts. Short stories, 900 to 1,000 words: mystery, sports, school, family, with 10-year-old as main character; serials, 2,000 words. Christian emphasis. Poems. Pays to 7¢ a word, to 50¢ a line for poetry, on acceptance. SASE for guidelines.

RANGER RICK—National Wildlife Federation, 8925 Leesburg Pike, Vienna, VA 22184. Gerald Bishop, Ed. Articles, to 900 words, on wildlife, conservation, natural sciences, and kids in the outdoors, for 7- to 12-year-olds. Nature-related fiction, mysteries, fantasies, and science fiction welcome. Games (no crosswords or word-finds), crafts, humorous poems, outdoor activities, and puzzles. For nonfiction, query with sample lead, list of references, and names of experts you plan to contact. Guidelines. Pays to $600, on acceptance.

SCIENCEWORLD—Scholastic, Inc., 555 Broadway, New York, NY 10012-3999. Mark Bregman, Ed. Science articles, 750 words, and news articles, 200 words, on life science, earth science, physical science, technology, environmental science and/or health for readers in grades 7 to 10 (ages 12 to 15). "Articles should include current, exciting science news. Writing should be lively and show an understanding of teens' perspectives and interests." Pays $100 to $125 for news items; $200 to $650 for features. Query with a well-researched proposal, suggested sources, 2 to 3 clips of your work, and an SASE.

SHOFAR—43 Northcote Dr., Melville, NY 11747. Gerald H. Grayson, Ed. Short stories and articles, 500 to 1,000 words; poetry, to 50 lines; short fillers, games, puzzles, and cartoons for Jewish children, 8 to 13. All material must have a Jewish theme. Pays 10¢ a word, on publication. Submit holiday pieces at least 6 months in advance.

SKIPPING STONES—P.O. Box 3939, Eugene, OR 97403. Arun N. Toké, Exec. Ed. "A Multicultural Children's Magazine." Articles, approximately 500 to 750 words, relating to support groups, networking and community, cross cultural communications and living abroad, humor unlimited, religions, nature, traditions, and cultural celebrations in other countries, for 8- to 16-year-olds. "Especially invited to submit are youth from diverse backgrounds and/or those with physical challenges. We print art, poetry, songs, games, stories, and photographs from around the world and include many different languages (with English translation)." Payment is one copy, on publication. Annual Youth Honor Awards; send SASE for guidelines.

SOCCER JR.—27 Unquowa Rd., Fairfield, CT 06430. Joe Provey, Ed. Fiction and fillers about soccer for readers ages 8 and up. Pays $450 for a feature or story; $250 for department pieces, on acceptance. Query.

SPIDER—P.O. Box 300, Peru, IL 61354. Attn: Submissions Ed. Fiction, 300 to 1,000 words, for 6- to 9-year-olds: realistic, easy-to-read stories, fantasy, folk and fairy tales, science fiction, fables, myths. Articles, 300 to 800 words, on nature, animals, science, technology, environment, foreign culture, history (include short bibliography with articles). Serious, humorous, or nonsense poetry, to 20 lines. Puzzles, activities, and games, to 4 pages. Pays 25¢ a word, $3 per line for poetry, on publication.

SPORTS ILLUSTRATED FOR KIDS—Time & Life Bldg., 1271 Ave. of the Americas, New York, NY 10020. Stephen Malley, Asst. Man. Ed. Articles, 1,000 to 1,500 words (submit to Bob Der), and short features, 500 to 600 words (submit to Nick Friedman), for 8- to 13-year-olds. "Most articles are staff-written. Department pieces are the best bet for free lancers." Read magazine and guidelines to learn about specific departments. Puzzles and games (submit to Nick Friedman). No fiction or poetry. Pays $500 for departments, $1,000 to $1,250 for articles, on acceptance. Query required.

STONE SOUP, THE MAGAZINE BY YOUNG WRITERS AND ARTISTS—Box 83, Santa Cruz, CA 95063-0083. Gerry Mandel, Ed. Stories, free-verse poems, plays, book reviews by children under 14. "Preference given to writing based on real-life experiences." Pays $10. Web site: www.stonesoup.com.

STORY FRIENDS—Mennonite Publishing House, Scottdale, PA 15683. Rose Stutzman, Ed. Stories, 350 to 800 words, for 4- to 9-year-olds, on Christian faith and values in everyday experiences. Poetry. Pays to 5¢ a word, to $10 per poem, on acceptance.

SUPERSCIENCE—Scholastic, Inc., 555 Broadway, New York, NY 10012. Attn: Ed. Science news and hands-on experiments for grades 4 through 6. Article topics are staff-generated and assigned to writers; send resumé and children's and science writing clips. Include large SASE for editorial calendar and sample issue. Pays $50 to $650, on acceptance.

SURPRISES—1200 N. 7th St., Minneapolis, MN 55411. Tim Drake, Ed. Bimonthly. Articles, 50 to 250 words, for readers 5 to 11. Puzzles, games, artwork. Pays $25 to $100, on publication.

3-2-1 CONTACT—See *Contact Kids*.

TOUCH—Box 7259, Grand Rapids, MI 49510. Carol Smith, Man. Ed. Upbeat fiction and features, 500 to 1,000 words, for Christian girls ages 8 to 14: personal life, nature, crafts. Poetry, puzzles. Pays 2½¢ a word, extra for photos, on publication. Query with SASE for theme update.

TURTLE MAGAZINE FOR PRESCHOOL KIDS—1100 Waterway Blvd., Box 567, Indianapolis, IN 46206. Terry Harshman, Ed. Heavily illustrated articles with an emphasis on health and nutrition for 2- to 5-year-olds. Humorous, entertaining fiction. Also, crafts, recipes, activities, and simple science experiments. Simple poems. Action rhymes and read-aloud stories, to 300 words. Pays to 22¢ a word for stories; from $15 for poems; payment varies for activities. Pays on publication. Buys all rights. Send SASE for guidelines.

U.S. KIDS, A WEEKLY READER MAGAZINE—P.O. Box 567, Indianapolis, IN 46206. Jeff Ayers, Ed. Articles, 500 to 1,000 words, for readers 5 to 10, on real children involved in health, fitness, sports, nutrition activities. Also interested in kids' community efforts, fun hobbies, science, nature, etc. Fiction 500 to 900 words (no fantasy); some poetry.

WILD OUTDOOR WORLD—Box 1249, Helena, MT 59624. Carolyn Cunningham, Ed. Dir. Articles, 600 to 800 words, on North American wildlife, for readers ages 8 to 12. Pays $100 to $500, on acceptance. Query.

WONDER TIME—6401 The Paseo, Kansas City, MO 64131. Todd Forrest, Asst. Ed. Stories, 250 to 350 words, for 6- to 8-year-olds, with Christian emphasis to correlate with Sunday school curriculum. Pays $25 for stories, on production. Send SASE for guidelines, themes, and sample issue.

YOUNG JUDEAN—50 W. 58th St., New York, NY 10019. Deborah Neufeld, Ed. Quarterly. Articles, 500 to 1,000 words, with photos, for 9- to 12-year-olds, on Israel, Jewish holidays, Jewish-American life, Jewish history. Fiction, 800 to 1,000 words, on Jewish themes. Fillers, humor, reviews. No payment.

ZILLIONS—Consumers Union of the United States, 101 Truman Ave., Yonkers, NY 10703-9925. Karen McNulty, Man. Ed. Bimonthly. Articles, up to 1,000 words, on consumer education (money, product testing, health, etc.), for kids ages 8 to 12. "We are the *Consumer Reports* for kids." Pays $500 to $2,000, on publication. Guidelines.

YOUNG ADULT MAGAZINES

ALIVE NOW!—P.O. Box 189, Nashville, TN 37202. Attn: Ed. Short essays, 250 to 400 words, with Christian emphasis for adults and young adults. Poetry, one page. B&W photos. Pays $20 to $30, on publication. Query with SASE for themes.

ALL ABOUT YOU—6420 Wilshire Blvd., Los Angeles, CA 90048-5515. Roxanne Camron, Ed. Dir. Beth Mayall, Ed. Articles, 1,000 to 1,500 words, on issues of interest to middle school girls. Payment varies, on acceptance. Queries.

BLUE JEAN MAGAZINE—7353 Pittsford-Victor Rd., Suite 201-203, Victor, NY 14564-9790. Victoria E. Nam, Exec. Ed. Alternative to teen fashion and beauty magazines. Publishes fiction, nonfiction, artwork, poetry. Profiles of girls and women who are "changing the world," and articles, 700 to 1,400 words, on the environment, health, sports and popular culture. Mostly written and produced by teens. No fashion spreads, supermodels, or dieting tips. Send SASE for guidelines.

BOYS' LIFE—1325 W. Walnut Hill Ln., P.O. Box 152079, Irving, TX 75015-2079. Monthly publication of the Boy Scouts of America. Articles and fiction, 500 to 1,500 words, for 8- to 18-year-old boys. Pays from $350 for major articles, $750 for fiction, on acceptance. Query for articles; send complete manuscript for fiction. SASE.

CAMPUS LIFE—465 Gundersen Dr., Carol Stream, IL 60188. Harold Smith, V.P./Ed. Articles reflecting Christian values and world view, for high school and college students. Humor, general fiction, and true, first-person experiences. "If we have a choice of fiction, how-to, and a strong first-person story, we'll go with the true story every time." Photo-essays, cartoons. Pays 15¢ to 20¢ a word, on acceptance. Query.

CHALLENGE—4200 North Point Parkway, Alpharetta, GA 30022-4176. Joe Conway, Ed. Southern Baptist. Articles, to 800 words, for 12- to 18-year-old boys, on teen issues, current events. Photo-essays on Christian sports personalities. Pays 10¢ a word, extra for photos, on acceptance.

CRACKED—Globe Communications, Inc., 3 E. 54th St., 15 Fl., New York, NY 10022-3108. Lou Silverstone, Andy Simmons, Eds. Humor, one to 5 pages, for 10- to 15-year-old readers. Cartoons/comic book style work; no short stories or poetry. "Read magazine before submitting." Pays $100 per page, on acceptance.

EDGE, THE HIGH PERFORMANCE ELECTRONIC MAGAZINE FOR STUDENTS—4905 Pine Cone Dr., Suite 2, Durham, NC 27707. Greg Sanders, Ed. Magazine for bright high school students available only on the Web. Features, 1,200 to 1,500 words. Departments include "News to Use," 400 to 500 words; "Performance," 750 words; "Mindstuff," 500-word reviews of older books; "What's Hot Now," 250 to 400 words, on interesting, worthwhile products. "The magazine is not about school; it's about teenagers living the learning lifestyle. Our readers are sophisticated. Don't write anything elementary, preachy, or thoughtless. Especially interested in literary journalism/creative nonfiction." Pays $400 to $500 for features, $25 to $300 for department pieces, on acceptance. Queries preferred. Guidelines. Web site: http://www.jayi.com/edge.

EXPLORING—P.O. Box 152079, 1325 W. Walnut Hill Ln., Irving, TX 75015-2079. Scott Daniels, Exec. Ed. Publication of Boy Scouts of America.

Articles, 500 to 1,500 words, for 14- to 21-year-old boys and girls, on teenage trends, college, computer games, music, education, careers, "Explorer" activities (hiking, canoeing, camping), and program ideas for meetings. No controversial subjects. Pays $250 to $1,000, on acceptance. Query. Guidelines.

KEYNOTER—3636 Woodview Trace, Indianapolis, IN 46268. Julie A. Carson, Exec. Ed. Articles, 1,300 to 1,500 words, for high school leaders: general-interest features; self-help; contemporary teenage problems. No fillers, poetry, first-person accounts, or fiction. Pays $150 to $350, on acceptance. Query preferred.

LISTEN MAGAZINE—55 W. Oak Ridge Dr., Hagerstown, MD 21740. Lincoln Steed, Ed. Articles, 1,200 to 1,500 words, providing teens with "a vigorous, positive, educational approach to the problems arising from the use of tobacco, alcohol, and other drugs." Pays $30 to $200, on acceptance.

MERLYN'S PEN: FICTION, ESSAYS, AND POEMS BY AMERICA'S TEENS—P.O. Box 1058, Dept. WR, East Greenwich, RI 02818. R. James Stahl, Ed. Writing by students in grades 6 through 12. Short stories and essays, to 5,000 words; reviews; travel pieces; and poetry, to 200 lines. Responds in 10 weeks. Pays $10 to $125, plus copies. Guidelines.

NEW ERA—50 E. North Temple, Salt Lake City, UT 84150. Richard M. Romney, Ed. Articles, 150 to 1,500 words, and fiction, to 2,000 words, for young Mormons. Poetry. Photos. Pays 5¢ to 20¢ a word, 25¢ a line for poetry, on acceptance. Query.

REACT—Parade Publications, 711 Third Ave., New York, NY 10017. Attn: Man. Ed. Weekly. Articles, to 800 words, on national and international news, entertainment, sports, social issues related to teenagers, and profiles of notable young people for readers 12 to 17. Payment varies, on acceptance. Query with related clips.

SCIENCE WORLD—Scholastic, Inc., 555 Broadway, New York, NY 10012-3999. Attn: Eds. Articles, 750 words, on life science, earth science, physical science, environmental science, or health science for 7th to 10th graders (ages 12 to 15). Science news pieces, 200 words. Submit well-researched proposal, including suggested sources, 2 to 3 clips of your work, and SASE. Pays $100 to $125 for news items; $200 to $650 for features.

SEVENTEEN—850 Third Ave., New York, NY 10022. Susan Brenna, Features Ed. Articles, to 2,500 words, on subjects of interest to teenagers. Sophisticated, well-written fiction, 1,000 to 4,000 words, for young adults. Personal essays, to 1,200 words, by writers 23 and younger for "Voice." Pays varying rates, on acceptance.

SISTERS IN STYLE—233 Park Ave. S., 5th Fl., New York, NY 10003. Cynthia Marie Horner, Ed. Dir. Bimonthly. "For Today's Young Black Woman." Articles. No fiction or poetry. Beauty, fashion, quizzes, and advice for African-American teens. Payment varies, on publication. Query.

STRAIGHT—8121 Hamilton Ave., Cincinnati, OH 45231. Heather E. Wallace, Ed. Articles on current situations and issues for Christian teens. Humor. Well-constructed fiction, 1,000 to 1,500 words, showing teens using Christian principles. Poetry by teenagers. Photos. Pays about 5¢ to 7¢ a word, on acceptance. Guidelines.

'TEEN—6420 Wilshire Blvd., Los Angeles, CA 90048-5515. Attn: Ed. Short stories, 2,500 to 4,000 words: mystery, teen situations, adventure, romance, humor for teens. Pays from $200 to $600, on acceptance. Buys all rights.

TEEN LIFE—1445 Boonville Ave., Springfield, MO 65802-1894. Tammy Bicket, Ed. Not currently accepting material. Articles, 500 to 1,000 words, and fiction, to 1,200 words, for 13- to 19-year-olds; strong evangelical emphasis. Interviews with Christian athletes and other well-known Christians; true stories; up-to-date factual articles. Send SASE for current topics. Pays on acceptance.

TEEN VOICES—P.O. Box 120-027, Boston, MA 02112-0027. Alison Amoroso, Ed.-in-Chief. Quarterly. Fiction and nonfiction, 200 to 400 words; and poetry, any length. Submissions by teenage girls only. Pays in copies.

TIGER BEAT—Sterling/MacFadden Partnership, 233 Park Ave. S., New York, NY 10003. Louise Barile, Ed. Articles, to 4 pages, on young people in show business and the music industry. Pays varying rates, on acceptance. Query.

WHAT! A MAGAZINE—108-93 Lombard Ave., Winnipeg, Manitoba, Canada R3B 3B1. Stuart Slayen and Leslie Malkin, Eds. Published 5 times a year and distributed in high schools. Articles, 650 to 2,000 words, on contemporary issues for teenaged readers. Pays $100 to $500 (Canadian), on publication. Queries preferred.

YM—685 Third Ave., New York, NY 10017. Maria Baugh, Man. Ed. Articles, to 2,500 words, on entertainment, lifestyle, fashion, beauty, relationships, health, for women ages 14 to 19. Payment varies, on acceptance. Query with clips.

YOU!—31194 La Baya Dr., Suite 200, Westlake Village, CA 91362. Attn: Submissions Ed. Articles, 200 to 1,000 words, on topics related to teenagers, especially moral issues, faith, and contemporary pop culture viewed from the Catholic/Christian perspective. No payment.

YOUNG AND ALIVE—4444 S. 52nd St., Lincoln, NE 68506. Richard J. Kaiser, Man. Ed. Gaylena Gibson, Ed. Quarterly. Feature articles, 800 to 1,400 words, for blind and visually impaired young adults on adventure, biography, camping, careers, health, history, hobbies, holidays, marriage, nature, practical Christianity, sports, and travel. Photos. Pays 3¢ to 5¢ a word, $5 to $20 for photos, on acceptance. Guidelines.

YOUNG SALVATIONIST—The Salvation Army, 615 Slaters Ln., P.O. Box 269, Alexandria, VA 22313. Attn: Lesa Davis, Man. Ed. Articles for teens, 800 to 1,200 words, with Christian perspective; fiction, 800 to 1,200 words; short fillers. Pays 10¢ to 15¢ a word, on acceptance.

YOUTH UPDATE—*St. Anthony Messenger Press,* 1615 Republic St., Cincinnati, OH 45210. Attn: Ed. Articles on timely topics for Catholic teens. Avoid cuteness, glib phrases and clichés, academic or erudite approaches, preachiness. Pays 14¢ a word, on acceptance. Query with outline and SASE.

THE DRAMA MARKET

Community, regional, and civic theaters and college dramatic groups offer the best opportunities today for playwrights to see their work produced, whether on the stage or in dramatic readings. Indeed, aspiring playwrights will be encouraged to hear that many well-known playwrights received their first recognition in the regional theaters. Payment is generally nominal, but regional and university theaters usually buy only the right to produce a play, and all further rights revert to the author. Since most directors like to work closely with authors on any revisions necessary, theaters will often pay the playwright's expenses while in residence during rehearsals. The thrill of seeing your play come to life on the stage is one of the pleasures of being on hand for rehearsals and performances. In addition to producing plays and giving dramatic readings, many theaters also sponsor competitions or new play festivals.

Aspiring playwrights should query college and community theaters in their region to find out which ones are interested in seeing original scripts. Dramatic associations of interest to playwrights include the Dramatists Guild (1501 Broadway, Suite 701, New York, NY 10036), and Theatre Communications Group, Inc. (355 Lexington Ave., New York, NY 10017), which publishes the annual *Dramatists Sourcebook*. *The Playwright's Companion*, published by Feedback Theatrebooks (305 Madison Ave., Suite 1146, New York, NY 10165), is an annual directory of theaters, play publishers, and prize contests seeking scripts. See the *Organizations for Writers* list for details on dramatists' associations.

Some of the theaters on this list require that playwrights submit all or some of the following with scripts—cast list, synopsis, resumé, recommendations, return postcard—and with scripts and queries, SASEs must always be enclosed.

While the almost unlimited television offerings on commercial, educational, and cable TV stations, in addition to the hundreds of films released yearly, may lead free-lance writers to believe that opportunities to sell movie and television scripts are infinite, unfortunately, this is not true. With few exceptions, TV and film producers and programmers will read scripts and queries submitted only through recognized agents. (For a list of agents, see page 855.) Writers who want to try their hand at writing directly for this very limited market should be prepared to learn the special techniques and acceptable format of scriptwriting, either by taking a workshop through a university or at a writers conference, or by reading one or more of the many books that have been written on this subject. Also, experience in playwriting and a knowledge of dramatic structure gained through working in amateur, community, or professional theaters can be helpful.

REGIONAL & UNIVERSITY THEATERS

ACTORS THEATRE OF LOUISVILLE—316 W. Main St., Louisville, KY 40202. Michael Bigelow Dixon, Lit. Mgr. Ten-minute comedies and dramas, to 10 pages. Longer one-act and full-length plays accepted from literary agents, and from playwrights with letter of recommendation from another professional theatre. SASE. Annual contest. Guidelines.

A. D. PLAYERS—2710 W. Alabama, Houston, TX 77098. Attn: Lit. Mgr. Jeannette Clift George, Artistic Dir. Full-length or one-act comedies, dramas, musicals, children's plays, and adaptations with Christian world view. Submit synopsis and cast list with SASE. Readings. Pays negotiable rates.

ALABAMA SHAKESPEARE FESTIVAL—The State Theatre, #1 Festival Dr., Montgomery, AL 36117-4605. Jennifer Hebblethwaite, Lit. Assoc. Full-length scripts with southern and/or African-American themes, issues, or history; and scripts with southern and/or African-American authors. One work per author; query.

ALLIANCE THEATRE COMPANY—1280 Peachtree St. N.E., Atlanta, GA 30309. Attn: Lit. Dept. Dramas, comedies, and musicals, especially those that speak to a culturally diverse community; plays with compelling stories and engaging characters, told in adventurous or stylish ways. No unsolicited manuscripts, or telephone inquiries. Letter of inquiry with synopsis and no more than 10 pages of sample dialogue accepted only with SASE for reply.

AMERICAN LITERATURE THEATRE PROJECT—Fountain Theatre, 5060 Fountain Ave., Los Angeles, CA 90029. Simon Levy, Prod. Dramaturg. One-act and full-length stage adaptations of classic and contemporary American literature. Sets and cast size are unrestricted. Send synopsis and SAS postcard. Rate of payment is standard, as set by the Dramatists Guild.

AMERICAN LIVING HISTORY THEATER—P.O. Box 752, Greybull, WY 82426. Dorene Ludwig, Artistic Dir. One-act, (one or 2 characters preferred) historically accurate (primary source materials only) dramas dealing with marketable American historical and literary characters and events. Submit treatment and letter with SASE. Responds within 6 months. Pays varying rates.

AMERICAN PLACE THEATRE—111 W. 46th St., New York, NY 10036. Martin Blank, Artistic Assoc. "No unsolicited manuscripts accepted. Agent submission only. We seek challenging, innovative works and do not favor obviously commercial material."

AMERICAN THEATRE OF ACTORS—314 W. 54th St., New York, NY 10019. James Jennings, Artistic Dir. Full-length dramas for a cast of 2 to 6. Submit complete play and SASE. Reports in one to 2 months.

ARENA STAGE—1101 Sixth St. S.W., Washington, DC 20024. Cathy Madison, Lit. Mgr. No unsolicited manuscripts; send synopsis, first 10 pages of dialogue, and bio.

ARKANSAS REPERTORY THEATRE COMPANY—601 S. Main, P.O. Box 110, Little Rock, AR 72203-0110. Brad Mooy, Lit. Mgr. Full-length comedies, dramas, and musicals; prefer up to 8 characters. Send synopsis, cast list, resumé, and return postage; do not send complete manuscript. Reports in 3 months.

BARTER THEATER—P.O. Box 867, Abingdon, VA 24212-0867. Richard Rose, Artistic Dir. Full-length dramas, comedies, adaptations, and children's plays. Submit synopsis, dialogue sample, and SASE. Allow 6 to 8 months for report. Royalty policies consistent with industry standard.

BERKSHIRE THEATRE FESTIVAL—Box 797, Stockbridge, MA 01262. Kate Maguire, Producing Dir. Full-length comedies, musicals, and dramas; cast to 8. Submit through agent only.

BOARSHEAD THEATER— 425 S. Grand Ave., Lansing, MI 48933. John Peakes, Artistic Dir. Full-length comedies and dramas with simple sets and cast of up to 10. Send precis, 5 to 10 pages of dialogue, and cast list with descriptions; do not send complete manuscript. SAS postcard for reply.

BRISTOL RIVERSIDE THEATRE— Box 1250, Bristol, PA 19007. Susan D. Atkinson, Producing/Artistic Dir. Full-length plays with up to 15 actors and a simple set.

CALIFORNIA UNIVERSITY THEATRE— California, PA 15419. Dr. Richard J. Helldobler, Chairman. Unusual, avant-garde, and experimental one-act and full-length comedies and dramas, children's plays, and adaptations. Cast size varies. Submit synopsis with short, sample scene(s). Payment available.

CENTER STAGE— 700 N. Calvert St., Baltimore, MD 21202. James Magruder, Resident Dramaturg. Full-length comedies, dramas, translations, adaptations. No unsolicited manuscripts. Send synopsis, a few sample pages, resumé, cast list, and production history. Allow 8 to 10 weeks for reply.

CHILDSPLAY, INC.— Box 517, Tempe, AZ 85280. David Saar, Artistic Dir. Multigenerational plays running 45 to 120 minutes: dramas, musicals, and adaptations for family audiences. Productions may need to travel. Submissions accepted July through December. Send synopsis and 10-page dialogue sample. Reports in 2 to 6 months.

CIRCLE IN THE SQUARE/UPTOWN— 1633 Broadway, New York, NY 10019-6795. Michael Breault, Artistic Assoc. Accepts agented material only. SASE.

CITY THEATRE COMPANY— 57 S. 13th St., Pittsburgh, PA 15203. Literary Dept. Full-length cutting-edge comedies and dramas; especially interested in women and minorities. Cast to 10; simple sets. Query September to May. Royalty.

CLASSIC STAGE COMPANY— 136 E. 13th St., New York, NY 10003. Mary Esbjornson, Exec. Dir. David Esbjornson, Artistic Dir. Full-length adaptations and translations of existing classic literature. Submit synopsis with cast list and 12 pages of sample dialogue, September to May. Offers readings. Pays on royalty basis.

THE CONSERVATORY THEATRE ENSEMBLE— c/o Tamalpais High School, 700 Miller Ave., Mill Valley, CA 94941. Daniel Caldwell, Artistic Dir. Comedies, dramas, children's plays, adaptations, and scripts addressing high school issues for largely female cast (about 3 women per man). "One-act plays of approximately 30 minutes are especially needed, as we produce 40 short plays each season using teenage actors." Send synopsis and resumé to Attn: Susan Brashear, Assoc. Art. Dir.

CROSSROADS THEATRE CO.— 7 Livingston Ave., New Brunswick, NJ 08901. Ricardo Khan, Artistic Dir. Full-length and one-act dramas, comedies, musicals, and adaptations; issue-oriented experimental plays that offer honest, imaginative, and insightful examinations of the African-American experience. Also interested in African and Caribbean plays and plays exploring cross-cultural issues. No unsolicited scripts; queries only, with synopsis, cast list, resumé, and SASE.

DELAWARE THEATRE COMPANY— 200 Water St., Wilmington, DE 19801-5030. Cleveland Morris, Artistic Dir. Full-length comedies, dramas, and musicals. Prefer cast of no more than 10. SASE required. Reports in 6 months.

No longer accepting unsolicited manuscripts, except from local authors. Agent submissions in the form of synopses or letters of inquiries will be considered. The "Connections" competition has been suspended for the time being.

DENVER CENTER THEATRE COMPANY—1050 13th St., Denver, CO 80204. Attn: Bruce K. Sevy, Associate Artistic Dir./New Play Development. New play festival in June. Primus prize to female playwright. Send SASE; request guidelines and information.

DETROIT REPERTORY THEATRE—13103 Woodrow Wilson Ave., Detroit, MI 48238. Barbara Busby, Lit. Mgr. Full-length comedies and dramas. Scripts accepted October to April. Enclose SASE. Pays royalty.

STEVE DOBBINS PRODUCTIONS— 650 Geary Blvd., San Francisco, CA 94102. Alan Ramos, Lit. Dir. Full-length comedies, dramas, and musicals. Cast of up to 12. Query with synopsis and resumé. No unsolicited manuscripts. Reports in 6 months. Offers workshops and readings. Pays 4% to 6% of gross.

DORSET THEATRE FESTIVAL—Box 519, Dorset, VT 05251. Jill Charles, Artistic Dir. Full-length comedies, musicals, dramas, and adaptations for up to 8 cast members; simple set preferred. Query with synopsis, cast size, and SAS postcard. Pays varying rates. Residencies at Dorset Colony House for Writers available September to November, March to May; inquire. E-mail: theatre@sover.net. Web site http://www.theatredirectories.com

EAST WEST PLAYERS—244 S. San Pedro St., # 301, Los Angeles, CA 90012. Tim Dang, Artistic Dir. Ken Narasaki, Lit. Mgr. Produces 4 to 5 new plays annually. Original plays, translations, adaptations, musicals, and youth theater, "all of which must illuminate the Asian or Asian-American experience, or resonate in a significant fashion if cast with Asian-American actors." Readings. Prefer to see query letter with synopsis and 10 pages of dialogue; complete scripts also considered. Reports in 5 to 6 weeks for query; 6 months for complete script.

ENSEMBLE STUDIO THEATRE—549 W. 52nd St., New York, NY 10019. Attn: Lit. Mgr. Send full-length or one-act comedies and dramas with resumé and SASE, September to April. Rarely pays for scripts. Fifteen readings of new plays per year.

FLORIDA STUDIO THEATRE—1241 N. Palm Ave., Sarasota, FL 33577. Chris Angermann, New Play Development. Innovative plays with universal themes. Query with synopsis and SASE. Also accepting musicals and musical revues.

WILL GEER THEATRICUM BOTANICUM—Box 1222, Topanga, CA 90290. Attn: Lit. Dir. All types of scripts for outdoor theater, with large playing area. Submit synopsis with SASE. Pays varing rates.

THE GOODMAN THEATRE—200 S. Columbus Dr., Chicago, IL 60603. Susan V. Booth, Lit. Mgr. Queries from recognized literary agents or producing organizations required for full-length comedies or dramas. No unsolicited scripts.

THE GUTHRIE THEATER—725 Vineland Pl., Minneapolis, MN 55403. Attn: Lit. Dept. Full-length dramas and adaptations of world literature, classic masterworks, oral traditions, and folktales. No unsolicited scripts; professional recommendation or letter of inquiry from playwright/agent. SASE. Reports in 3 to 4 months.

HIPPODROME STATE THEATRE—25 S.E. Second Pl., Gainesville, FL 32601. Tamerin Dygert, Dramaturg. Full-length plays with unit sets and casts of up to 8. Agent submissions and professional recommendations only; no unsolicited material. Submissions accepted May through August. Send synopsis only, with reviews and professional recommendation.

HOLLYWOOD THESPIAN COMPANY—12838 Kling St., Studio City, CA 91604-1127. Rai Tasco, Artistic Dir. Full-length comedies and dramas for integrated cast. Include cast list and SAS postcard with submission.

HORIZON THEATRE COMPANY—P. O. Box 5376, Station E, Atlanta, GA 31107. Jeff and Lisa Adler, Artistic Dirs. Full-length comedies, dramas, and satires. Encourages submissions by women writers. Cast of no more than 10. Submit synopsis with cast list, resumé, and recommendations. Pays percentage. Readings. Reports in 6 months.

HUNTINGTON THEATRE COMPANY—264 Huntington Ave., Boston, MA 02115. Scott Edmiston, Lit. Assoc. Full-length comedies and dramas. Query with synopsis, cast list, and resumé.

ILLINOIS THEATRE CENTER— 400 Lakewood Blvd., Park Forest, IL 60466. Attn: Producing Dir. Full-length comedies, dramas, musicals, and adaptations, for unit/fragmentary sets, and up to 8 cast members. Send summary and SAS postcard. No unsolicited manuscripts. Pays negotiable rates. Workshops and readings offered.

ILLUSTRATED STAGE COMPANY—Box 640063, San Francisco, CA 94164-0063. Steve Dobbins, Artistic Dir. Full-length comedies, dramas, and musicals for a cast of up to 18. Query with synopsis and SASE. No unsolicited manuscripts. Offers workshops and readings.

INVISIBLE THEATRE—1400 N. First Ave, Tucson, AZ 85719. Deborah Dickey, Lit. Mgr. Letter of introduction from theatre professional must accompany submissions for full-length comedies, dramas, musicals, and adaptations. Submit after October 2000. Cast of up to 10; simple set. Also one-act plays. Pays royalty.

JEWISH REPERTORY THEATRE—1395 Lexington Ave., New York, NY 10128. Ran Avni, Artistic Dir. Full-length comedies, dramas, musicals, and adaptations, with up to 10 cast members, relating to the Jewish experience. Pays varying rates. Enclose SASE.

KUMU KAHUA THEATRE, INC.— 46 Merchant St., Honolulu, HI 96813. Harry Wong III, Artistic Dir. Full-length plays especially relevant to life in Hawaii. Prefer simple sets for arena and in-the-round productions. Submit resumé and synopsis January through April. Pays $50 per performance. Readings. Contests.

LIVE OAK THEATRE—719 Congress Ave., Austin, TX 78701. Full-length plays and adaptations, but not currently soliciting new works.

LOS ANGELES DESIGNERS' THEATRE—P.O. Box 1883, Studio City, CA 91614-0883. Richard Niederberg, Artistic Dir. Full-length comedies, dramas, musicals, fantasies, or adaptations. Religious, political, social, and controversial themes encouraged. Nudity, "adult" language, etc., O.K. "Please detail in the cover letter what the writer's proposed involvement with the production would be beyond the usual. Do not submit material that needs to be returned." Send proposals. Payment varies. E-mail: LADESIGNERS @Juno.com.

THE MAGIC THEATRE—Fort Mason Ctr., Bldg. D, San Francisco, CA 94123. Kent Nicholson, Lit. Mgr. Comedies and dramas. "Special interest in political, non-linear, and multicultural work for mainstage productions." Query with synopsis, resumé, first 10 to 20 pages of script, and SASE; no unsolicited manuscripts. Pays varying rates.

MANHATTAN THEATRE CLUB—311 W. 43rd St., New York, NY 10036. Attn: Kate Loewald. Full-length and one-act comedies, dramas, and musicals. No unsolicited manuscripts or queries; agent submissions only.

METROSTAGE—P.O. Box 329, Alexandria, VA 22313. Carolyn Griffin, Prod. Dir. Full-length comedies, dramas, and children's plays; casts of no more than 8. Send synopsis, 10 page dialogue sample, resumé, and return post card. Responds in 2 months.

MILL MOUNTAIN THEATRE—One Market Sq., Second Fl., Roanoke, VA 24011-1437. Jack Parrish, Lit. Mgr. One-act comedies and dramas, 25 to 35 minutes. For full-length plays, send letter, resumé, and synopsis. Send SASE for guidelines for new play competition. Payment varies.

MISSOURI REPERTORY THEATRE— 4949 Cherry St., Kansas City, MO 64110. Felicia Londré, Dramaturg. Full-length comedies and dramas. Query with synopsis, cast list, resumé, and SAS postcard. Royalty. Allow 6 months for response. New scripts seldom produced.

MUSICAL THEATRE WORKS— 440 Lafayette St., New York, NY 10003. Lonny Price, Art. Dir. Please call or write for submission guidelines.

NATIONAL BLACK THEATRE—2033 Fifth Ave., Harlem, NY 10035. Attn: Tunde Samuel. Drama, musicals, and children's plays. "Scripts should reflect African and African-American lifestyle. Historical, inspirational, and ritualistic forms appreciated." Workshops and readings.

NATIONAL PLAYWRIGHTS CONFERENCE, EUGENE O'NEILL THE-ATRE CENTER—234 W. 44th St., Suite 901, New York, NY 10036. Mary F. McCabe, Man. Dir. Annual competition to select new stage plays and teleplays/screenplays for development during the summer at organization's Waterford, CT, location. Submission deadline: December 1. Send #10-size SASE in the fall for guidelines. Pays stipend, plus travel/living expenses during conference.

NEW ENSEMBLE ACTORS THEATRE PROJECT OF SALT & PEPPER MIME CO.—320 E. 90th St., #1B, New York, NY 10128. Ms. Scottie Davis, Dir. One-acts, all genres, conducive to "nontraditional" casting, surreal sets with mimetic concepts. One-or 4-person cast. Send resumé to 250 W. 65th St., New York, NY 10023. Scripts reviewed from May to December. Works also considered for readings, critiques, storyplayers, and experimental development. Logging fee/Application required.

NEW THEATRE, INC.—P.O. Box 173, Boston, MA 02117-0173. Attn: NEWorks Submissions Program. New full-length scripts for readings, workshop, and main stage productions. Include SASE.

NEW TUNERS/THE THEATRE BUILDING—1225 W. Belmont Ave., Chicago, IL 60657. Warner Crocker, Artistic Dir. Full-length musicals only, for cast to 15; no wing/fly space. Send query with brief synopsis, cassette tape of score, cast list, resumé, SASE, and SAS postcard. Pays on royalty basis.

NEW YORK SHAKESPEARE FESTIVAL/JOSEPH PAPP PUBLIC THE-ATER— 425 Lafayette St., New York, NY 10003. Shirley Fishman, Mervin P. Antonio, Lit. Mgrs. Wiley Hausam, musicals. Plays and translations, and adaptations. Submit sample dialogue with synopsis, cassette (for musicals), and SASE. Allow 4 to 6 months for response.

NEW YORK STATE THEATRE INSTITUTE—155 River St., Troy, NY 12180. Attn: Patricia Di Benedetto Snyder, Producing Artistic Dir. Emphasis on new, full-length plays and musicals for family audiences. Query with synopsis and cast list. Payment varies.

ODYSSEY THEATRE ENSEMBLE—2055 S. Sepulveda Blvd., Los Angeles, CA 90025. Ron Sossi, Artistic Dir. Full-length comedies, dramas, musicals, and adaptations: provocative subject matter, or plays that stretch and explore the possibilities of theater. Query Sally Essex-Lopresti, Lit. Mgr., with synopsis, 8 to 10 pages of sample dialogue, and resumé. Pays variable rates. Allow 2 to 6 months for reply to script; 2 to 4 weeks for queries. Workshops and readings.

OLDCASTLE THEATRE COMPANY—Bennington Center for the Arts, P.O. Box 1555, Bennington, VT 05201. Eric Peterson, Dir. Full-length comedies, dramas, and musicals for a small cast (up to 10). Submit synopsis and cast list in the winter. Reports in 6 months. Offers workshops and readings. Pays expenses for playwright to attend rehearsals. Royalty.

PENGUIN REPERTORY COMPANY—Box 91, Stony Point, Rockland County, NY 10980. Joe Brancato, Artistic Dir. Full-length comedies and dramas with cast size to 5. Submit script, resumé, and SASE. Payment varies.

PEOPLE'S LIGHT AND THEATRE COMPANY—39 Conestoga Rd., Malvern, PA 19355. Alda Cortese, Lit. Mgr. Full-length comedies, dramas, adaptations. No unsolicited manuscripts; query with synopsis, 10 pages of script required. Reports in 6 months. Payment negotiable.

PIER ONE THEATRE—Box 894, Homer, AK 99603. Lance Petersen, Lit. Dir. Full-length and one-act comedies, dramas, musicals, children's plays, and adaptations. Submit complete script; include piano score with musicals. Pays 8% of ticket sales for mainstage musicals; other payment varies.

PLAYHOUSE ON THE SQUARE—51 S. Cooper in Overton Sq., Memphis, TN 38104. Jackie Nichols, Artistic Dir. Full-length comedies, dramas; cast of up to 15. Contest deadline is April for fall production. Pays $500.

PLAYWRIGHTS HORIZONS—416 W. 42nd St., New York, NY 10036. Address Literary Dept. Full-length, original comedies, dramas, and musicals by American authors. No one-acts or screenplays. Synopses discouraged; send script, resumé and SASE, include tape for musicals. Off Broadway contract.

PLAYWRIGHTS' PLATFORM—164 Brayton Rd., Boston, MA 02135. Attn: Lit. Dir. Script development workshops and public readings for New England playwrights only. Full-length and one-act plays of all kinds. No sexist or racist material. Residents of New England send scripts with short synopsis, resumé, SAS postcard, and SASE. Readings conducted at Massachusetts College of Art (Boston).

POPLAR PIKE PLAYHOUSE—7653 Old Poplar Pike, Germantown, TN 38138. Frank Bluestein, Artistic Dir. Full-length and one-act comedies, dramas, musicals, and children's plays. Submit synopsis with SAS postcard and resumé. Pays $300.

PORTLAND STAGE COMPANY—Box 1458, Portland, ME 04104. Attn: Lit. Dir. Not accepting unsolicited material at this time.

PRINCETON REPERTORY COMPANY—44 Nassau St., Suite 350, Princeton, NJ 08542. Victoria Liberatori, Artistic Dir. One-act and full-length comedies and dramas for a cast of up to 10. "We are dedicated to the production of unusual plays, new and reinterpreted, which promote a greater awareness of contemporary issues especially those focusing on women." Submit synopsis with resumé, cast list, and 3-page dialogue sample. Consideration for reading and/or production. Responds within one year.

THE PUERTO RICAN TRAVELING THEATRE—141 W. 94th St., New York, NY 10025. Miriam Colon Valle, Artistic Dir. Full-length and one-act comedies, dramas, and musicals; cast of up to 8; simple sets. "We prefer plays based on the contemporary Hispanic experience, material with social, cultural, or psychological content." Payment negotiable.

THE REPERTORY THEATRE OF ST. LOUIS—Box 191730, St. Louis, MO 63119. Attn: Lit. Dir. Query with brief synopsis, technical requirements, and cast size. Unsolicited manuscripts will be returned unread.

ROUND HOUSE THEATRE—12210 Bushey Dr., Silver Spring, MD 20902. Attn: Production Office Mgr. Full-length comedies, dramas, and adaptations; cast of up to 10; prefer simple set. Send one-page synopsis with 3 or 4 sample pages, cast list, and technical requirements. No unsolicited manuscripts.

SEATTLE REPERTORY THEATRE—155 Mercer St., Seattle, WA 98109. Sharon Ott, Artistic Dir. Full-length comedies, dramas, and adaptations. Submit synopsis, 10-page sample, SAS postcard, and resumé to Kurt Beattie, Associate Artistic Dir. New plays series with workshops each spring.

SOCIETY HILL PLAYHOUSE—507 S. 8th St., Philadelphia, PA 19147. Walter Vail, Dramaturg. Full-length dramas, comedies, and musicals with up to 6 cast members and simple set. Submit synopsis and SASE. Reports in 6 months. Nominal payment.

SOUTH COAST REPERTORY—P. O. Box 2197, Costa Mesa, CA 92628. John Glore, Lit. Mgr. Full-length comedies, dramas, musicals, juveniles. Query with synopsis and resumé. Payment varies.

SOUTHERN APPALACHIAN REPERTORY THEATRE—P.O. Box 1720, Mars Hill, NC 28754. James W. Thomas, Artistic Dir. Full-length comedies, dramas, musicals, and plays including (but not limited to) scripts with Appalachian theme. Submit resumé, recommendations, full script, and SASE. Send SASE for information on Southern Appalachian Playwright's Conference (held in April each year). Pays $500 royalty if play is selected for production during the summer season. Deadline for submissions is October 31 each year.

THE SPUYTEN DUYVIL THEATRE CO.—P.O. Box 1024, New York, NY 10024. Attn: Lit. Dir. Full-length comedies and dramas with single set and cast size to 10. SASE required.

STAGE ONE: PROFESSIONAL THEATRE FOR YOUNG AUDIENCES— (formerly *Stage One: The Louisville Children's Theatre*) 5 Riverfront Plaza, 501 W. Main Street , Louisville, KY 40202. J. Daniel Herring, Assoc. Dir. Adaptations of classics and original plays for young audiences ages 4 to 18. Submit script with resume and SASE. Reports in 4 to 5 months.

STAGE ONE: THE LOUISVILLE CHILDREN'S THEATRE—See *Stage One: Professional Theatre for Young Audiences*.

STAGES REPERTORY THEATRE—3201 Allen Pkwy., #101, Houston, TX 77019. Rob Bundy, Artistic Dir. Currently accepting plays for Children's Theatre Playwright Festival, Texas Playwrights' Festival, Women's Repertory Project, and Hispanic Playwrights' Festival. Send for guidelines on each theme.

MARK TAPER FORUM—135 N. Grand Ave., Los Angeles, CA 90012. Pier Carlo Talenti, Lit. Assoc. Full-length comedies, dramas, musicals, juveniles, adaptations. Query.

THE TEN MINUTE MUSICALS PROJECT—Box 461194, W. Hollywood, CA 90046. Michael Koppy, Prod. One-act musicals. Include audio cassette, libretto, and lead sheets with submission. "We are looking for complete short musicals." Pays $250.

THEATER OF THE FIRST AMENDMENT—George Mason University, Institute of the Arts MSN 3E6, Fairfax, VA 22030. Rick Davis, Artistic Dir. Full-length and one-act comedies, drama, and adaptations. Send synopsis and resumé with return post card.

THEATRE AMERICANA—Box 245, Altadena, CA 91003-0245. Attn: Playreading Chair. Full-length comedies and dramas, preferably with American theme. No children's plays or musicals. Language and subject matter should be suitable for a community audience. Send bound manuscript with cast list, resumé, and SASE, by February 1. No payment. Allow 3 to 6 months for reply. Submit no more than 2 entries per season.

THEATRE ON THE SQUARE—450 Post St., San Francisco, CA 94102. Jonathan Reinis, Artistic Dir. Full-length comedies, dramas, and musicals for 15-person cast. Submit cast list and script with SASE. Reports in 30 days.

THEATRE/TEATRO—Bilingual Foundation of the Arts, 421 N. Ave., #19, Los Angeles, CA 90031. Agustin Coppola, Lit. Mgr. Margarita Galban, Artistic Dir. Full-length plays about the Hispanic experience; small casts. Submit manuscript with SASE. Pays negotiable rates.

THEATREWORKS—1100 Hamilton Court, Menlo Park, CA 94025. Attn: Lit. Dept. Full-length comedies, dramas, and musicals. Submit complete script or synopsis with SAS postcard and SASE, cast list, theatre resumé, and production history. For musicals, include cassette of up to 6 songs and lyrics for all songs. Responds in 4 months for submissions made March to July; 5 months for submissions August to January. Payment is negotiable.

THEATREWORKS/USA—151 W. 26th St., 7th Fl., New York, NY 10001. Barbara Pasternack, Lit. Mgr. One-hour children's musicals and plays with music for 5-person cast. Playwrights must be within commutable distance to New York City. Submit outline or treatment, sample scenes, and music in spring, summer. Pays royalty and commission.

WALNUT STREET THEATRE COMPANY—825 Walnut St., Philadelphia, PA 19107. Beverly Elliott, Lit. Mgr. Mainstage: Full-length comedies, dramas, musicals, and popular, upbeat adaptations; also, one-to 4-character plays for studio stage. Submit 10 to 20 sample pages with SAS postcard, character breakdown, and synopsis. Musical submissions must include an audio cassette. Reports in 6 months. Payment varies.

THE WESTERN STAGE—156 Homestead Ave., Salinas, CA 93901. Joyce Lower, Dramaturg. Harvey Landa, Exec. Dir. Ongoing submissions; send query. Prefers adaptations of works of literary significance and/or large cast shows. Two or more shows chosen to workshop yearly.

GARY YOUNG MIME THEATRE—23724 Park Madrid, Calabasas, CA 91302. Gary Young, Artistic Dir. Comedy monologues and vignettes, for children and adults. Currently overstocked; not seeking new material.

PLAY PUBLISHERS

ALABAMA LITERARY REVIEW—Troy State Univ., 253 Smith Hall, Troy, AL 36082. Theron Montgomery, Ed. Full-length and one-act comedies and dramas, to 50 pages. Query preferred. Responds to queries in 2 weeks; 2 to 3 months for complete manuscripts. Do not submit material in August. Payment is in copies; honorarium when available.

AMELIA—329 E St., Bakersfield, CA 93304. Frederick A. Raborg, Jr., Ed. One-act comedies and dramas; no longer than 45 minutes running time. Responds in 2 to 3 months. Payment is $35, on acceptance.

ANCHORAGE PRESS—Box 8067, New Orleans, LA 70182. Attn: Ed. Plays and musicals that have been proven in multiple production, for children ages 6 to 18. "We publish 8 to 10 new playbooks and one to 3 new hardcover books each year." Royalty.

ART CRAFT PUBLISHING COMPANY—See *Heuer Publishing Company.*

BAKER'S PLAYS—100 Chauncy St., Boston, MA 02111. Ray Pape, Assoc. Ed. Full-length plays, one-act plays for young audiences, musicals, chancel dramas. Prefers produced plays; plays suitable for high school, community and regional theaters; "Plays from Young Authors" division features plays by high school playwrights. Send resumé; include press clippings if play has been produced. Responds within 2 to 6 months. E-mail: info@bakers plays.com. Web site: www.bakersplays.com

BLIZZARD PUBLISHING—73 Furby St., Winnipeg, Manitoba, Canada R3C 2A2. Peter Atwood, Man. Ed. One-act and full-length dramas, children's plays, and adaptations. Queries preferred. Responds in 3 to 4 months. Royalty.

CALLALOO—Dept. of English, Univ. of Virginia, Charlottesville, VA 22903. Charles H. Rowell, Ed. One-act dramas by and about African-American, Caribbean, and African writers. Scripts read September through May. Responds in 3 to 6 months. Payment varies, on publication.

I. E. CLARK PUBLICATIONS—P.O. Box 246, Schulenburg, TX 78956. Donna Cozzaglio, Ed. One-act and full-length plays and musicals, for children, young adults, and adults. Serious drama, comedies, classics, fairytales, melodramas, and holiday plays. "We seldom publish a play that has not been produced." Responds in 2 to 6 months. Royalty.

COLLAGES & BRICOLAGES—P.O. Box 360, Shippenville, PA 16254. Marie-José Fortis, Ed. Michael Kressley, Art Ed. One-act avant-garde comedies and dramas. Manuscripts read August through November; responds in one to 3 months. Payment is in copies.

CONFRONTATION—Dept. of English, C.W. Post of L.I.U., Greenvale, NY 11548. Martin Tucker, Ed. One-act comedies, dramas, and adaptations. Manuscripts read September through May. Responds in 6 to 8 weeks. Pays $25 to $100, on publication.

CONTEMPORARY DRAMA SERVICE—Meriwether Publishing Co., Box 7710, 885 Elkton Dr., Colorado Springs, CO 80903. Arthur Zapel, Ed. Easy-to-stage comedies, skits, one-acts, large-cast musicals, and full-length comedy plays for schools and churches. (Junior high through college level; no elementary level material.) Adaptations of classics and improvised material for classroom use. Character education plays and comedy monologues and duets. Chancel drama for Christmas and Easter church use. Enclose synopsis.

Books on theater arts subjects, scene books, and anthologies. Textbooks for speech and drama. Pays by fee arrangement or royalty.

DRAMATIC PUBLISHING COMPANY—311 Washington St., Woodstock, IL 60098. Linda Habjan, Ed. Full-length and one-act plays and musicals for the professional, stock, amateur, and children's theater market. Send SASE. Royalty. Responds within 4 to 6 months. E-mail: 75712.3621@compus erve.com. Web site: www.dramaticpublishing.com.

DRAMATICS—Educational Theatre Assoc., 3368 Central Pkwy., Cincinnati, OH 45225-2392. Don Corathers, Ed. One-act and full-length plays for high school production. Pays $100 to $400 for one-time, non-exclusive publication rights, on acceptance.

ELDRIDGE PUBLISHING COMPANY—P. O. Box 1595, Venice, FL 34284. Nancy Vorhis, Ed. Dept. One-act and full-length plays and musicals suitable for performance by schools, churches, and community theatre groups. Comedies, tragedies, dramas, skits, spoofs, and religious plays (all holidays). Submit complete manuscript with cover letter, biography, and SASE. Responds in 2 months. Flat fee for one-act and religious plays, paid on publication; royalties for full-length plays. E-mail: info@histage.com. Web site: http.// www.histage.com

SAMUEL FRENCH, INC.— 45 W. 25th St., New York, NY 10010. Lawrence Harbison, William Talbot, Eds. Full-length plays and musicals for dinner, community, stock, college, and high school theaters. One-act plays, 20 to 45 minutes. Children's plays, 45 to 60 minutes. Royalty.

HEUER PUBLISHING COMPANY—(merged with *Art Craft Publishing Company*) P.O. Box 248, Cedar Rapids, IA 52406. C. Emmett McMullen, Ed. One-act comedies and dramas for contest work; two-and three-act comedies, mysteries, or farces, and musicals, with one interior setting, for middle school and high school production. Pays royalty or flat fee. E-mail: editor@hit plays.com. Web site: www.hitplays.com

LYNX EYE—c/o Scribblefest Literary Group, 1880 Hill Dr., Los Angeles, CA 90041. Pam McCully, Kathryn Morrison, Co-Eds. One-act plays, 500 to 5,000 words, for thoughtful adults who enjoy interesting reading and writing. Also, short stories, vignettes, novel excerpts, essays, satires; poetry, to 30 lines. Pays $10, on acceptance.

NATIONAL DRAMA SERVICE—MSN 170, 127 Ninth Ave. N., Nashville, TN 37234. Attn: Ed. Scripts, 2 to 7 minutes long: drama in worship, puppets, clowns, Christian comedy, mime, movement, readers theater, creative worship services, and monologues. "We publish dramatic material that communicates the message of Christ. We want scripts that will give even the smallest church the opportunity to enhance their ministry with drama." Payment varies, on acceptance. Guidelines.

PIONEER DRAMA SERVICE—P. O. Box 4267, Englewood, CO 80155. Attn: Ed. Full-length and one-act plays as well as musicals, melodramas, and children's theatre. No unproduced plays or plays with largely male casts or multiple sets. Query preferred. Royalty. E-mail: piodrama@aol.com. Web site: www.pioneerdrama.com

PLAYERS PRESS, INC.—P.O. Box 1132, Studio City, CA 91614-0132. Robert W. Gordon, Ed. One-act and full-length comedies, dramas, and musicals. "No manuscript will be considered unless it has been produced." Query with manuscript-size SASE and 2 #10 SASEs for correspondence. Include resumé and/or biography. Responds in 3 to 12 months. Royalty.

PLAYS, THE DRAMA MAGAZINE FOR YOUNG PEOPLE—120 Boylston St., Boston, MA 02116-4615. Elizabeth Preston, Man. Ed. One-act plays, with simple contemporary sets, for production by young people, 7 to 17: comedies, dramas, farces, skits, holiday plays. Also adaptations of classics, biography plays, puppet plays, and creative dramatics. No musicals or plays with religious themes. Maximum lengths: lower grades and skits, 10 double-spaced pages; middle grades, 15 pages; junior and senior high, 20 pages. Guidelines. Pays good rates, on acceptance. Query for adaptations of folk tales and classics. Buys all rights.

PRISM INTERNATIONAL—Dept. of Creative Writing, Univ. of British Columbia, Buch E462, 1866 Main Mall, Vancouver, BC, Canada V6T 1Z1. Attn: Ed. One-act plays and translations of contemporary work. Responds in 4 to 6 months. Pays $20 per page, on publication, $10 per page web rights. Send request with SASE for rules to register for new drama contest. E-mail: prism@unixg.ubc.ca. Web Site: http://www.arts.ubc.ca/prism

RAG MAG—P.O. Box 12, Goodhue, MN 55027. Beverly Voldseth, Ed. Semiannual. Full-length and one-act comedies and dramas. SASE for guidelines. Send complete play. No plays read May through August. No themes beginning 1999. Pays in copies.

ROCKFORD REVIEW—P.O. Box 858, Rockford, IL 61105. David Ross, Ed. One-act comedies, dramas, and satires, to 1,300 words. "We prefer genuine or satirical human dilemmas with coping or non-coping outcomes that illuminate the human condition." Publishes one to 2 plays per issue. Pays in copies (plus invitation to attend reading-reception in the summer). Two $25 Editor's Choice Prizes awarded each issue.

SINISTER WISDOM—P.O. Box 3252, Berkeley, CA 94703. Margo Mercedes Rivera, Ed. Quarterly. One-act (no longer than 15 pages) lesbian drama. "We are particularly interested in work that reflects the diversity of our experiences: as lesbians of color, ethnic lesbians, Jewish, old, young, working class, poor, disabled, fat. Only material by born-woman lesbians is considered." Responds in 3 to 9 months; write for upcoming themes. Payment is in 2 copies, on publication. SASE.

SMITH AND KRAUS, INC.—P.O. Box 127, Main St., Lyme, NH 03768. Marisa Smith, Pres. Original plays and teaching texts for the K to 12 market; some material for adults including history, biography. Does not accept full-length and one-act plays unless the play in question has been produced within the year and is therefore eligible for the "Best Scene and Monologue Series for the Year." Does not return manuscripts. Response time is 3 months. Pays on publication.

BOOK PUBLISHERS

The following list includes the major book publishers for adult and juvenile fiction and nonfiction and a representative number of small publishers from across the country, as well as a number of university presses.

Before submitting a complete manuscript to an editor, it is advisable to send a brief query letter describing the proposed book, and an SASE. The letter should also include information about the author's special qualifications for dealing with a particular topic and any previous publication credits. An outline of the book (or a synopsis for fiction) and a sample chapter may also be included.

While it is common practice to submit a book manuscript to only one publisher at a time, it is becoming more and more acceptable to submit the same query or proposal to more than one editor simultaneously. When sending multiple queries, *always* make note of it in each submission.

Book manuscripts may be packaged in typing paper boxes (available from a stationery store) and sent by first-class mail, or, more common and less expensive, by "Special Fourth Class Rate—Manuscript." For rates, details of insurance, and so forth, inquire at your local post office. With any submission to a publisher, be sure to enclose sufficient postage for the manuscript's return.

Royalty rates for hardcover books usually start at 10% of the retail price of the book and increase after a certain number of copies have been sold. Paperbacks generally have a somewhat lower rate, about 5% to 8%. It is customary for the publishing company to pay the author a cash advance against royalties when the book contract is signed or when the finished manuscript is received. Some publishers pay on a flat-fee basis.

While most of the publishers on this list consider either unsolicited manuscripts or queries, an increasing number now read only agented submissions. Since finding an agent is not an easy task, especially for newcomers, writers are advised to try to sell their manuscripts directly to the publisher first.

Writers seeking publication of their book-length poetry manuscripts are encouraged to enter contests that offer publication as the prize (see *Literary Prize Offers,* page 799); many presses that once considered unsolicited poetry manuscripts by emerging or unpublished writers now limit their reading of such manuscripts to those entered in their contests for new writers.

ABBEVILLE PRESS—22 Cortlandt St., New York, NY 10007. Attn: Submissions Ed. Illustrated adult nonfiction books on art, architecture, gardening, fashion, interior design, decorative arts, cooking, and travel, as well as illustrated children's books. Submit outline, sample illustrations, and sample chapters to Meredith Schizer. For juveniles, submit complete manuscript to Thomas Sand. Do not send original art or transparencies. Royalty.

ABINGDON PRESS—P.O. Box 801, Nashville, TN 37202. Joseph A. Crowe, Ed. General-interest books: mainline, social issues, marriage/family, self-help, exceptional people. Query with outline and one or 2 sample chapters. Guidelines.

ACADEMIC PRESS—Harcourt Brace, 525 B St., Suite 1900, San Diego, CA 92101. Attn: Ed. Dept. Scientific and technical books and journals for research-level scientists, students, and professionals; upper-level undergraduate and graduate science texts.

ACE BOOKS —200 Madison Ave., New York, NY 10016. Susan Allison, V.P., Ed.-in-Chief. Science fiction and fantasy. Query with first 3 chapters and outline to Anne Sowards, Ed. Royalty.

ACTIVITY RESOURCES—P.O. Box 4875, Hayward, CA 94540. Mary Laycock. Math educational material only. "Our main focus is on grades K through 8." Submit complete manuscript. Royalty.

ADAMS-BLAKE PUBLISHING— 8041 Sierra St., Fair Oaks, CA 95628. Monica Blane, Ed. Books on business, careers, and technology. Query or send complete manuscript. Multiple submissions accepted. Royalty. See www.adams-blake.com for guidelines.

ADAMS-HALL PUBLISHING—11661 San Vicente Blvd., Suite 210, Los Angeles, CA 90049. Sue Ann Bacon, Marketing Dir. Business and personal finance books with wide market appeal. Query with proposed book idea, a listing of current competitive books, author qualifications, and the reason that the book is unique. Royalty.

ADAMS MEDIA COPORATION—260 Center St., Holbrook, MA 02343. Edward Walters, Ed.-in-Chief. Nonfiction trade books on business and careers, financial planning, self-improvement, family and parenting, relationships, pets, humor, inspiration, and historical biography. Query with outline, at least 2 sample chapters, and SASE. Royalty.

ALABASTER—See *Multnomah Publishers.*

ALASKA NORTHWEST BOOKS—2208 N.W. Market St., Suite 406, Seattle, WA 98107. Ellen Harkins Wheat, Sr. Ed. Nonfiction, 50,000 to 100,000 words, with an emphasis on natural world and history of Alaska and the Pacific Northwest: travel books; cookbooks; field guides; children's books; outdoor recreation; natural history; native culture; lifestyle. Send query or sample chapters with outline. Guidelines.

ALLWORTH COMMUNICATIONS, INC.— 10 E. 23rd St., Suite 400, New York, NY 10010. Ted Gachot, Ed. Helpful books for professional artists, designers, writers, and photographers. Query with outline and sample chapters. Royalty.

ALPINE PUBLICATIONS—225 S. Madison Ave., Loveland, CO 80537. B.J. McKinney, Pub. Nonfiction books, 35,000 to 60,000 words, on dogs and horses. Submit outline and sample chapters or complete manuscript. Royalty.

ALYSON PUBLICATIONS—P.O. Box 4371, Los Angeles, CA 90078. Attn: Ed. Gay and lesbian adult fiction and nonfiction books, from 65,000 words. *Alyson Wonderland* imprint: Children's picture books with gay and lesbian themes; young adult titles, from 65,000 words. Query with outline only. Royalty. See www.alyson.com for guidelines.

AMERICAN PARADISE PUBLISHING—P.O. Box 37, St. John, USVI 00831. Gary M. Goodlander, Ed. "We are interested in 'hopelessly local' books, between 80 and 300 pages. We need useful, practical books that help our Virgin Island readers lead better and more enjoyable lives." Guidebooks, cookbooks, how-to books, books on sailing, yacht cruising, hiking, snorkeling, sportfishing, local history, and West Indian culture, specifically aimed at Caribbean readers/tourists. Query with outline and sample chapters. Royalty.

THE AMERICAN PSYCHIATRIC PRESS—1400 K St. N.W., Washington, DC 20005. Carol C. Nadelson, M.D., Ed.-in-Chief. Books that interpret scientific and medical aspects of psychiatry for a lay audience and that address specific psychiatric problems. Authors must have appropriate credentials to write on medical topics. Query required. Royalty.

ANCHOR BOOKS—Imprint of Doubleday and Co., 1540 Broadway, New York, NY 10036. Martha K. Levin, Pub. Adult trade paperbacks and hardcovers. Nonfiction, multicultural, sociology, psychology, philosophy, women's interest, etc. No unsolicited manuscripts.

ANCHORAGE PRESS—Box 8067, New Orleans, LA 70182. Attn: Acquisitions Ed. Dramatic publishers. Plays for children ages 4 to 18. "We publish 8 to 10 new playbooks and one to 3 new hardcover books each year." Royalty.

AND BOOKS—702 S. Michigan, South Bend, IN 46601. Janos Szebedinsky, Ed. Adult nonfiction. Topics include computers, fine arts, health, philosophy, regional subjects, and social justice.

ANHINGA PRESS—P.O. Box 10595, Tallahassee, FL 32302-0595. Rick Campbell, Ed. Poetry books. (Publishes 3 books a year.) Query or send complete manuscripts. Flat fee. Annual poetry prize of $2,000 plus publication; send #10 SASE for details.

ANTIQUE TRADER BOOKS—See *Landmark Specialty Books.*

APPALACHIAN MOUNTAIN CLUB BOOKS—5 Joy St., Boston, MA 02108. Attn: Ed. Dept. Regional (New England) and national nonfiction titles, 250 to 400 pages, for adult audience; juvenile and young adult nonfiction. Topics include guidebooks on non-motorized backcountry recreation, nature, outdoor recreation skills (how-to books), mountain history/biography, search and rescue, conservation, and environmental management. Query with outline and sample chapters. Multiple queries considered. Royalty.

ARCADE PUBLISHING—141 Fifth Ave., New York, NY 10010. Richard Seaver, Pub./Ed., Jeannette Seaver, Assoc. Pub., Cal Barksdale, Timothy Bent, Sean McDonald, Eds. Fiction and nonfiction. No unsolicited manuscripts. Query.

ARCHON BOOKS—See *Shoe String Press.*

ARCHWAY/MINSTREL BOOKS—Pocket Books, 1230 Ave. of the Americas, New York, NY 10020. Patricia MacDonald, V.P./ Ed. Dir. Young adult contemporary fiction (suspense thrillers, romances) and nonfiction (popular current topics), for ages 12 to 16. *Minstrel Books*: young reader fiction including thrillers, adventure, fantasy, humor, animal stories, for ages 6 to 11. Send query, outline, sample chapters to Attn: Manuscript Proposals.

AVALON BOOKS—401 Lafayette St., New York, NY 10003. Wilhelm H. Mickelsen, Pres. Marcia Markland, VP/Pub. Hardcover books, 40,000 to 50,000 words: romances, mysteries, and westerns. No explicit sex. Query with first 3 chapters and outline; nonreturnable. SASE for guidelines.

AVERY PUBLISHING GROUP—120 Old Broadway, Garden City Park, NY 11040. Attn: Man. Ed. Nonfiction, from 40,000 words, on health, childbirth, child care, healthful cooking. Query. Royalty.

AVISSON PRESS, INC.—3007 Taliaferro Rd., Greensboro, NC 27408. Martin L. Hester, Exec. Ed. Helpful nonfiction books on health, lifestyle, finance, etc., for older Americans; books on teenage issues, teen problems, and parenting; young adult biography (for readers 10 to 18). Query with outline or sample chapter, bio and SASE. Royalty.

AVON BOOKS—1350 Ave. of the Americas, Room 231, New York, NY 10019. Attn: Avon Editorial. Genre fiction, general fiction and nonfiction. Send one-to two-page query letter describing book and up to 35 sample pages with SASE. *Avon Hardcover*: adult commercial fiction and nonfiction. *Avon Eos*: science fiction, fantasy, 75,000 to 100,000 words. *Avon Romance*: historical or contemporary romance, 100,000 words. *Camelot*: fiction and nonfiction for 7- to 10-year-olds. No picture books. *Flare*: fiction and nonfiction for ages 12 and up.

BAEN BOOKS—Baen Publishing Enterprises, P.O. Box 1403, Riverdale, NY 10471-1403. Jim Baen, Pres./Ed.-in-Chief. Strongly plotted science fiction; innovative fantasy. Query with synopsis and manuscript. Advance and royalty. Guidelines available for letter-sized SASE.

BAKER BOOK HOUSE—P. O. Box 6287, Grand Rapids, MI 49516-6287. Rebecca Cooper, Ed. Asst. Religious nonfiction: books for trade, clergy, seminarians, collegians. Religious fiction. Royalty.

BALBOA BOOKS—See *Tiare Publications*.

BALLANTINE BOOKS—201 E. 50th St., New York, NY 10022. Attn: Ed.-in-Chief. General fiction and nonfiction. Query.

BALSAM PRESS—36 E. 22nd St., 9th Fl., New York, NY 10010. Barbara Krohn, Exec. Ed. General and illustrated adult nonfiction. Query. Royalty.

BANKS CHANNEL BOOKS—P.O. Box 4446, Wilmington, NC 28406. Attn: Book Ed. Books of regional interest by North Carolina writers only. Query for nonfiction of special interest in southeastern NC. Fiction through biennial contest only (guidelines available with SASE).

BANTAM BOOKS—1540 Broadway, New York, NY 10036. Irwyn Applebaum, Pres./Pub. Adult fiction and nonfiction. Mass-market titles, submit queries to the following imprints: *Crime Line*, crime and mystery fiction; *Domain*, frontier fiction, historical sagas, traditional westerns; *Fanfare*, women's fiction, historical and contemporary romance; *Spectra*, science fiction and fantasy; *Bantam Nonfiction*, wide variety of commercial nonfiction, including true crime, health and nutrition, sports, reference. Agented queries and manuscripts only.

BANTAM SPECTRA BOOKS—1540 Broadway, New York, NY 10036. Anne Lesley Groell, Ed. Patrick LoBrutto, Sr. Ed. Science fiction and fantasy, with emphasis on storytelling and characterization. First three chapters and synopsis with SASE; no unsolicited manuscripts. Royalty.

BARRON'S EDUCATIONAL SERIES, INC.—250 Wireless Blvd., Hauppauge, NY 11788. Grace Freedson, Acquisitions Dir. Juvenile nonfiction (science, nature, history, hobbies, and how-to) and picture books for ages 3 to 6. Adult nonfiction (business, pet care, childcare, sports, test preparation, cookbooks, foreign language instruction). Query with SASE. Guidelines.

BAUHAN, PUBLISHER, WILLIAM L.—Box 443, Dublin, NH 03444. William L. Bauhan, Ed. Biographies, fine arts, gardening, architecture, and history books with an emphasis on New England. Submit query with outline and sample chapter.

BAYLOR UNIVERSITY PRESS—P.O. Box 97363, Baylor Univ., Waco, TX 76798-7363. Janet L. Burton, Academic Publications Coordinator. Scholarly nonfiction, especially oral history and church-state issues. Query with outline. Royalty.

BEACON PRESS—25 Beacon St., Boston, MA 02108. Attn: Camille Andrews. General nonfiction: world affairs, women's studies, anthropology, history, philosophy, religion, gay and lesbian studies, nature writing, African-American studies, Latino studies, Asian-American studies, Native-American studies. Series: "Concord Library" (nature writing); "Barnard New Women Poets." Query. Agented manuscripts only.

BEAR & COMPANY, INC.—P.O. Drawer 2860, Santa Fe, NM 87504. John Nelson, Ed. Nonfiction "that will help transform our culture philosophically, environmentally, and spiritually." Query with outline, sample chapters, and SASE. Royalty.

BEHRMAN HOUSE—235 Watchung Ave., W. Orange, NJ 07052. Adult and juvenile nonfiction, varying lengths, in English and in Hebrew, on Jewish subject matter. Query with outline and sample chapters. Flat fee or royalty.

BELLWETHER-CROSS PUBLISHING—765 Cedar Cross Rd., Dubuque, IA 52003. Jill Crow, Ed. Educational materials in most disciplines from preschool through college. Also, trade nonfiction in a variety of topics. For educational materials, query with proposed book idea, list of current competitive books, and bio. For trade nonfiction, query with outline and sample chapters. SASE. Royalty.

BENCHMARK BOOKS—99 White Plains Rd., Tarrytown, NY 10591-9001. Judith Whipple, Ed. Dir. Books, 3,000 to 30,000 words, for young readers (grades 3 up) on science, sports, the arts, wildlife, math, and health. Series include: "Cultures of the World," "Cultures of the Past," "Biomes of the World," "Life Issues," "Discovering Math," and others. Query with outline. Royalty or flat fee. No single title submissions.

BERKLEY PUBLISHING GROUP —200 Madison Ave., New York, NY 10016. General-interest fiction and nonfiction; science fiction, suspense, and mystery novels; romance. Submit through agent only. Publishes both reprints and originals. Paperback books, except for some hardcover mysteries and science fiction. Young adult books: Laura Anne Gilman, Ed. Horror, suspense, adventure, and romance. Query required.

THE BESS PRESS—3565 Harding Ave., Honolulu, HI 96816. Revé Shapard, Ed. Nonfiction books about Hawaii, Asia, and the Pacific for adults, children, and young adults. Query. Royalty.

BETHANY HOUSE PUBLISHERS—11300 Hampshire Ave. S., Minneapolis, MN 55438. Attn: Ed. Dept. Religious fiction and nonfiction. Query with sample chapters. Royalty.

BETTER HOMES AND GARDENS BOOKS—See *Meredith Corp. Book Publishing*.

BEYOND WORDS PUBLISHING—20827 N.W. Cornell Rd., Suite 500, Hillsboro, OR 97124. Attn: Adult Acquisitions Ed. or Children's Acquisitions Ed. Books on personal growth, women, and spiritual issues. Adult nonfiction books, 150 to 250 pages. Children's picture books, 32, 48, 60, or 80 pages. Submit outline and sample chapters for adult titles; complete manuscript for juvenile titles. Royalty.

BICK PUBLISHING HOUSE—307 Neck Rd., Madison, CT 06443. Dale Carlson, Ed. Books, 64 to 250 pages, on wildlife rehabilitation, special needs/ disabilities, psychology. Submit outline and sample chapters. Royalty.

BINFORD & MORT PUBLISHING—5245 N.E. Elam Young Pkwy., Suite C, Hillsboro, OR 97124. P.L. Gardenier, Ed. Books on subjects related to the Pacific Coast and the Northwest. Lengths vary. Query. Royalty.

BIRCH LANE PRESS—See *Carol Publishing Group.*

BLACK BELT PRESS—Black Belt Publishing, LLC, P.O. Box 551, Montgomery, AL 36101. Randall Williams, Ed.-in-Chief. Southern fiction, biography, history, and folklore. Query with cover letter, synopsis or outline, author bio, and SASE for reply. Royalty varies.

BLACK BUZZARD PRESS—Vias, Visions-International, 1007 Ficklen Rd., Fredericksburg, VA 22405. Bradley R. Strahan, Ed. Poetry manuscripts, to 30 pages. Query first. Royalty.

BLAIR, PUBLISHER, JOHN F.—1406 Plaza Dr., Winston-Salem, NC 27103. Carolyn Sakowski, Pres. Books, 70,000 to 100,000 words: biography, history, folklore, and guidebooks, with southeastern tie-in. Query. Royalty.

BLOOMBERG PRESS—P.O. Box 888, Princeton, NJ 08542-0888. Melissa Hafner, Ed. Nonfiction, varying lengths, on topics such as business, finance, and small business. Query with outline and sample chapter or send complete manuscript. SASE. Pays varying rates. Royalty.

BLUE DOLPHIN PUBLISHING, INC.—P.O. Box 8, Nevada City, CA 95959. Paul M. Clemens, Ed. Books, 200 to 300 pages, on comparative spiritual traditions, lay and transpersonal psychology, self-help, health, healing, and "whatever helps people grow in their social awareness and conscious evolution." Query with outline, sample chapters, and SASE. Royalty.

BLUE HERON PUBLISHING—24450 N.W. Hansen Rd., Hillsboro, OR 97124. Dennis Stovall, Ed. Adult nonfiction for series on writing/publishing. Also literary nonfiction. Query. Royalty. Accepting no proposals in 1998.

BOA EDITIONS, LTD.—260 East Ave., Rochester, NY 14604. Steven Huff and Thomas Ward, Eds. Books of poetry, approximately 70 pages. Query or send complete manuscript. Royalty.

BONUS BOOKS—160 E. Illinois St., Chicago, IL 60611. Andrea Lacko, Man. Ed. Nonfiction; topics vary widely. Query with sample chapters and SASE. Royalty.

BOTTOM DOG PRESS, INC.—c/o Firelands College, Huron, OH 44839. Larry Smith, Dir. Collections of personal essays, stories, 50 to 200 pages, and poetry for combined chapbook publication (30 to 50 poems). Subjects should be midwestern or working class in focus. "Interested writers should query." Royalty.

BOYDS MILLS PRESS—815 Church St., Honesdale, PA 18431. Beth Troop, Manuscript Coord. Hardcover trade books for children. Fiction: picture books; middle-grade fiction with fresh ideas and involving story; young adult novels of literary merit. Nonfiction should be "fun, entertaining, and informative." Send outline and sample chapters for young adult novels and nonfiction, complete manuscripts for all other categories. Royalty.

BRANDEN PUBLISHING COMPANY—17 Station St., Box 843, Brookline Village, MA 02147. Attn: Ed. Dept. Novels, biographies, and autobiographies. Especially books by or about women, 250 to 350 pages. Also considers queries on history, computers, business, performance arts, and translations. Query only with SASE. Royalty. Website: www.branden.com

BRASSEY'S, INC.—22883 Quicksilver Dr., Dulles, VA 20166. Don McKeon, Ed. Dir. Nonfiction books, 75,000 to 130,000 words: national and international affairs, history, foreign policy, defense, military and political biography, sports. No fiction. Query with synopsis, author bio, outline, sample chapters, and SASE. Royalty. E-mail: Brasseys@aol.com.

BRAZILLER PUBLISHERS, GEORGE—171 Madison Ave., Suite 1103, New York, NY 10016. Attn: Ed. Dept. Fiction and nonfiction. Art history, collections of essays and short stories, anthologies. Send art history manuscripts to Art Ed.; others to Fiction Editor. Send outline with sample chapters.

BREAKAWAY BOOKS—336 W. 84th St., #4, New York, NY 10024. Garth Battista, Pub. Literary sports novels or collections of essays or stories. "Our goal is to bring to light literary writing on the athletic experience." Royalty.

BRETT BOOKS, INC.—P.O. Box 290-637, Brooklyn, NY 11229-0637. Barbara J. Brett, Pres./Pub. Nonfiction for adult trade market. "Submit a query letter of no more than 2 pages, stating your professional background and summarizing your book proposal in 2 to 4 paragraphs." SASE. Royalty.

BRIDGE WORKS—Box 1798, Bridgehampton, NY 11932. Barbara Phillips, Pres./Ed. Dir. Mainstream adult literary fiction and nonfiction, 50,000 to 75,000 words. Royalty.

BRISTOL PUBLISHING ENTERPRISES—P.O. Box 1737, San Leandro, CA 94577. Jennifer L. Newens, Ed. Cookbooks. Query with outline, sample chapters, resumé, and SASE. Royalty.

BROADMAN AND HOLMAN PUBLISHERS—127 Ninth Ave. N., Nashville, TN 37234. Richard P. Rosenbaum, Jr., V. P. Trade, academic, religious and inspirational nonfiction. Query with SASE. Royalty. Guidelines.

BROADWAY BOOKS—A Div. of Bantam, Doubleday, Dell, 1540 Broadway, New York, NY 10036. John Sterling, Ed.-in-Chief. Adult nonfiction; small and very selective fiction list. No unsolicited submissions.

BROWNDEER PRESS—Imprint of Harcourt Brace Children's Books, 9 Monroe Pkwy., Suite 240, Lake Oswego, OR 97035-1487. Linda Zuckerman, Ed. Dir. Picture books, humorous fiction for middle-grade readers and young adults. Also easy readers. Considers submissions from agents, published authors, or members of SCBWI only. Query for nonfiction with cover letter, resumé, and sample chapter; send complete manuscript for picture books (avoid rhyming text). For longer fiction, send first 3 chapters, synopsis, and short cover letter including list of published works. SASE required for all correspondence.

BULFINCH PRESS—3 Center Plaza, Boston, MA 02108. Attn: Ed. Dept. Illustrated fine art and photography books. Query with outline or proposal, sample artwork, vita, and SASE.

BURFORD BOOKS—(formerly part of *Lyons & Burford, Publishers*) P.O. Box 388, Short Hills, NJ 07078. Peter Burford, Pub. Books, 100 to 300 pages, related to the outdoors. Query with outline. Royalty.

BYRON PREISS VISUAL PUBLICATIONS—24 W. 25th St., New York, NY 10010. Attn: Ed. Dept. Book packager. "We are primarily interested in seeing samples from established authors willing to work to specifications on firm deadlines." Genres: science fiction, fantasy, horror, juvenile, young adult, nonfiction. Pays competitive advance against royalties for commissioned work.

C&T PUBLISHING—P.O. Box 1456, Lafayette, CA 94549. Barbara Kuhn, Ed.-in-Chief. Quilting books, 64 to 200 finished pages. "Our focus is how-to, although we will consider picture, inspirational, or history books on quilting." Send query, outline, or sample chapters. Multiple queries considered. Royalty.

CALYX BOOKS—P.O. Box B, Corvallis, OR 97339. Margarita Donnelly, Micki Reaman, Eds. Feminist publisher. Novels, short stories, poetry, nonfiction, translations, and anthologies by women. Accepts submissions for books from June 15 to August 15, 1998 and from January 1 to March 1, 1999. Send SASE for guidelines before submitting, or e-mail calyx@proaxis.com for guidelines.

CAMELOT BOOKS—See *Avon Books.*

CANDLEWICK PRESS—2067 Massachusetts Ave., Cambridge, MA 02140. Elizabeth Bicknell, Ed.-in-Chief. No unsolicited material.

CAPSTONE PRESS, INC.—P.O. Box 669, Mankato, MN 56001-0669. Attn: Ed. Dept. High interest/low-reading level and early reader nonfiction for children, specifically, reluctant and new readers. Send SASE for catalogue of series themes. Resumé and query required; no manuscripts will be accepted. Flat fee.

CAROL PUBLISHING GROUP—120 Enterprise Ave., Secaucus, NJ 07094. Allan J. Wilson, Ed. General nonfiction. *Citadel Press*: biography (celebrity preferred), autobiography, film, history, and self-help, 70,000 words. *Birch Lane Press*: adult nonfiction, 75,000 words. *Lyle Stuart*: adult nonfiction, 75,000 words, of a controversial nature, gaming, etc.; address Hillel Black, Ed. Also *University Books*. Query with SASE required. Royalty.

CAROLRHODA BOOKS—241 First Ave. N., Minneapolis, MN 55401. Rebecca Poole, Ed. Complete manuscripts for ages 4 to 12: biography, science, nature, history, photo-essays; historical fiction. Guidelines. Hardcover.

CAROUSEL PRESS—P.O. Box 6038, Berkeley, CA 94706-0038. Carole T. Meyers, Ed. Travel guides, especially family-oriented. Send letter, table of contents, and sample chapter. "We publish one or 2 new books each year and will consider out-of-print books that the author wants to update." Modest advance and royalty.

CARROLL AND GRAF PUBLISHERS, INC.—19 W. 21st St., Suite 601, New York, NY 10001. Kent E. Carroll, Exec. Ed. General fiction and nonfiction. No unagented submissions.

CARTWHEEL BOOKS—Scholastic, Inc., 555 Broadway, New York, NY 10012. Picture, novelty, and easy-to-read books, to about 1,000 words, for children, preschool to third grade. No novels or chapter books. Royalty or flat fee. Query; no unsolicited manuscripts.

CASSANDRA PRESS—P.O. Box 150868, San Rafael, CA 94915. Attn: Ed. Dept. New age, holistic health, metaphysical, and psychological books. Query with outline and sample chapters, or complete manuscript. Include SASE. Royalty (no advance).

THE CATHOLIC UNIVERSITY OF AMERICA PRESS— 620 Michigan Ave. N.E., Washington, DC 20064. David J. McGonagle, Dir. Scholarly nonfiction: American and European history (both ecclesiastical and secular); Irish studies; American and European literature; philosophy; political theory; theology. Query with prospectus, annotated table of contents, or introduction and resumé. Royalty.

CELESTIAL ARTS—See *Ten Speed Press.*

CHAPTERS BOOKS—Imprint of Houghton Mifflin, 222 Berkeley St., Boston, MA 02116. Barry Estabrook, Rux Martin, Eds. Nonfiction books on gardening, nature, health and nutrition, and cooking. Query with outline, sample chapters, and resumé; include SASE. Royalty.

CHARLESBRIDGE PUBLISHING— 85 Main St., Watertown, MA 02172. Attn: Submissions Ed. Children's picture books, primarily nonfiction. Send complete manuscript. Exclusive submissions only: must indicate on envelope and cover letter. Pays royalty or flat fee. Web site: www.charlesbridge.com.

CHATHAM PRESS—P. O. Box A, Old Greenwich, CT 06870. Roger H. Lourie, Man. Dir. Books on the Northeast coast, gardening, New England maritime subjects, and the ocean. Large photography volumes. Query with outline, sample chapters, illustrations, and SASE. Royalty.

CHELSEA GREEN PUBLISHING CO.—P.O. Box 428, White River Junction, VT 05001. Jim Schley, Ed.-in-Chief. Nonfiction: natural history, environmental issues, energy and shelter, organic agriculture, and ecological lifestyle books with strong backlist potential. Query with outline and SASE. Royalty.

CHELSEA HOUSE PUBLISHERS—1974 Sproul Rd., Broomall, PA 19008. Attn: Acquisitions Ed. Juvenile books (for ages 8 up) for publication in a series format. Series include: "Black Americans of Achievement"; "Indians of North America"; "Life in America 100 Years Ago," among others. No unsolicited manuscripts. Query with writing sample for consideration of assignments. SASE required. Flat fee.

CHICAGO REVIEW PRESS— 814 N. Franklin St., Chicago, IL 60610. Cynthia Sherry, Ed. Nonfiction: activity books for young children, project books for ages 10 to 18, general nonfiction, architecture, pregnancy, how-to, popular science, and regional gardening and other regional topics. Query with outline and sample chapters.

CHILDREN'S BOOK PRESS—246 First St., Suite 101, San Francisco, CA 94105. Submissions Ed. Bilingual and multicultural picture books, 750 to 1,500 words, for children in grades K through 6. "We publish folktales and contemporary stories reflecting the traditions and culture of the emerging majority in the U.S. and worldwide. Ultimately, we want to help encourage a more international, multicultural perspective on the part of all young people." Query. Pays advance on royalties.

CHILDREN'S LIBRARY PRESS—P.O. Box 1919, Joshua Tree, CA 92252. Attn: Acquisitions Ed. Texts for picture books. Submit complete manuscript. Royalty.

CHILDREN'S PRESS—Sherman Turnpike, Danbury, CT 06816. Attn: Submissions Ed. Science and biography, 10,000 to 25,000 words, for supplementary use in libraries and classrooms. Picture books, 50 to 1,000 words. Royalty or outright purchase. Currently overstocked; not accepting unsolicited manuscripts.

CHINA BOOKS—2929 24th St., San Francisco, CA 94110. Wendy K. Lee, Sr. Ed. Books relating to China or Chinese culture. Adult nonfiction, varying lengths. Juvenile picture books, fiction, nonfiction, and young adult books. Query. Royalty. Manuscript guidelines available on the web at www.chinabooks.com.

CHRONICLE BOOKS— 85 Second St., San Francisco, CA 94105. Attn: Ed. Dept. Fiction, art, photography, architecture, design, nature, food, gift-books, regional topics. Children's books. Send proposal or complete manuscript for fiction with SASE.

CHRONIMED PUBLISHING—P.O. Box 59032, Minneapolis, MN 55459. Jeff Braun, Ed. Man. Consumer books (50,000 to 60,000 words) on nutrition, cooking, general health, and chronic diseases from expert writers. Send proposal with outline and sample chapters. Royalty.

CITADEL PRESS—See *Carol Publishing Group.*

CLARION BOOKS—215 Park Ave. S., New York, NY 10003. Attn: Ed., Fiction, nonfiction, and picture books: short novels and lively stories for ages 6 to 10 and 8 to 12, historical fiction, humor; picture books for infants and children to age 7; biography, natural history, social studies, American and world history for readers 5 to 8, and 9 up. Royalty. Hardcover. Currently overstocked; no unsolicited manuscripts.

CLARK CITY PRESS—P.O. Box 1358, Livingston, MT 59047. Attn: Ed. Dept. Collections of poems, short stories, and essays; novels, biographies. Royalty. Currently overstocked; not accepting any new submissions.

CLEIS PRESS—P.O. Box 14684, San Francisco, CA 94114. Frédérique Delacoste, Ed. Fiction and nonfiction, 200 pages, by women. No poetry. Send SASE with 2 first-class stamps for catalogue before querying. Royalty.

CLOVER PARK PRESS—P.O. Box 5067-T, Santa Monica, CA 90409-5067. Martha Grant, Acquisitions Ed. Nonfiction adult books on California (history, natural history, travel, culture, or the arts), biography of extraordinary women, nature, travel, exploration, scientific/medical discovery, travel, adventure. Query with outline, sample chapter, author bio, and SASE.

COFFEE HOUSE PRESS—27 N. 4th St., Suite 400, Minneapolis, MN 55401. Attn: Chris Fischbach. Literary fiction (no genres). Query with SASE.

COLLIER BOOKS—See *Macmillan Reference USA.*

CONARI PRESS—2550 Ninth St., Suite 101, Berkeley, CA 94710. Claudia Schaab, Ed. Assoc. Adult nonfiction: women's issues, personal growth, parenting, and spirituality. Submit outline, sample chapters, and 6½″ x 9½″ SASE. Royalty.

CONCORDIA PUBLISHING HOUSE—3558 S. Jefferson Ave., St. Louis, MO 63118. Attn: Book Development. Practical family books and devotionals. Children's fiction with explicit Christian content. No poetry. Query. Royalty.

CONFLUENCE PRESS—Lewis-Clark State College, 500 8th Ave., Lewiston, ID 83501-2698. James R. Hepworth, Dir. Literary fiction, essay collections, literary criticism, regional history, natural history, biography, and poetry. SASE for guidelines. Royalty.

COPPER BEECH BOOKS—See *The Millbrook Press.*

COPPER CANYON PRESS—P.O. Box 271, Port Townsend, WA 98368. Sam Hamill, Ed. Poetry books only. No unsolicited manuscripts. Send SASE for guidelines. Royalty.

CORNELL UNIVERSITY PRESS—Box 250, Sage House, 512 E. State St., Ithaca, NY 14851. Frances Benson, Ed.-in-Chief. Scholarly nonfiction, 80,000 to 120,000 words. Query with outline. Royalty.

COTLER BOOKS, JOANNA—See *HarperCollins Children's Books.*

CRAFTSMAN BOOK COMPANY— 6058 Corte del Cedro, P.O. Box 6500, Carlsbad, CA 92018. Laurence D. Jacobs, Ed. How-to construction and estimating manuals and software for professional builders, 450 pages. Query. Royalty. Paperback.

CREATIVE ARTS BOOK CO.— 833 Bancroft Way, Berkeley, CA 94710. Donald S. Ellis, Pub. Adult nonfiction and fiction: women's issues, music, African-American and Asian, and California topics. Query with outline, sample chapters, SASE. Royalty.

CRIME LINE—See *Bantam Books.*

THE CROSSING PRESS—P.O. Box 1048, Freedom, CA 95019. Elaine Goldman Gill, Pub. Jill Schettler, Acq. Ed. Health and nutrition, holistic health, women's interests, spiritual growth and healing, new age topics, empowerment, cookbooks. Royalty.

CROWN BOOKS FOR YOUNG READERS—201 E. 50th St., New York, NY 10022. Simon Boughton, Pub. Dir. Children's nonfiction (science, sports, nature, music, and history) and picture books for ages 3 and up. Query for nonfiction. Send complete manuscript for picture books to: Submissions Ed. Guidelines.

CUMBERLAND HOUSE PUBLISHING—2200 Abbott Martin Rd., Suite 102, Nashville, TN 37215. Mary Sanford, Ed. Adult nonfiction, to 100,000 words and mysteries. Query with outline and sample chapters. Royalty.

CURBSTONE PRESS—321 Jackson St., Willimantic, CT 06226. Alexander Taylor, Pub./Ed. Fiction, nonfiction, poetry books, and picture books that reflect a commitment to social change, with an emphasis on contemporary writing from Latin America and Latino communities in the U.S. Agented material only. Royalty.

DANIEL AND COMPANY, JOHN—P.O. Box 21922, Santa Barbara, CA 93121. John Daniel, Pub. Books, to 200 pages, in the field of belles lettres and literary memoirs; stylish and elegant writing; essays and short fiction dealing with social issues; one poetry title per year. Send synopsis or outline with no more than 50 sample pages and SASE. Allow 6 to 8 weeks for response. Royalty.

DAVIES-BLACK PUBLISHING—3803 E. Bayshore Rd., Palo Alto, CA 94303. Melinda Adams Merino, Acquisitions Ed. Books, 250 to 400 manuscript pages. Professional and trade titles in business and careers.

DAVIS PUBLICATIONS, INC.—50 Portland St., Worcester, MA 01608. Books, 100 to 300 manuscript pages, for the art education market; mainly for teachers of art, grades K through 12. Must have an educational component. Grades K through 8, address Claire M. Golding; grades 9 through 12, address Helen Ronan. Query with outline and sample chapters. Royalty.

DAW BOOKS, INC.—375 Hudson St., 3rd Fl., New York, NY 10014-3658. Elizabeth R. Wollheim, Pres. & Pub. Sheila E. Gilbert, Exec. V.P. & Pub. Peter Stampfel, Submissions Ed. Science fiction and fantasy, 85,000 words and up. No short stories, collections, or anthologies. Royalty.

DAWN PUBLICATIONS— 14618 Tyler Foote Rd., Nevada City, CA 95959. Glenn J. Hovemann, Ed. Dept. Nature awareness books for children. Children's picture books with a positive, uplifting message to awaken a sense of appreciation and kinship with nature. For children's works, submit complete manuscript and specify intended age. SASE for guidelines. Royalty.

DEARBORN FINANCIAL PUBLISHING, INC.—155 N. Wacker Dr., Chicago, IL 60606-1719. Carol Luitjens, V.P. Cynthia Zigmund, Ed. Dir. Professional and Consumer books and courses on financial services, real estate, banking, small business, investing, etc. Query with outline and sample chapters. Royalty and flat fee.

DEE PUBLISHER, INC., IVAN R.—1332 N. Halsted St., Chicago, IL 60622-2637. Ivan R. Dee, Pres. Nonfiction books on history, politics, biography, literature, and theater. Query with outline and sample chapters. Royalty.

DEL REY BOOKS—201 E. 50th St., New York, NY 10022. Shelly Shapiro, Exec. Ed. Veronica Chapman and Steve Saffel, Sr. Eds. Science fiction and fantasy, 60,000 to 120,000 words; first novelists welcome. Fantasy with magic basic to plotline. Query with outline and 3 sample chapters. Include manuscript-size SASE. Royalty.

DELACORTE PRESS—1540 Broadway, New York, NY 10036. Leslie Schnur, Jackie Cantor, Tom Spain, Eds. General adult fiction and nonfiction. Accepts material from agents only.

THE DELACORTE PRESS BOOKS FOR YOUNG READERS—(formerly *Laurel-Leaf*) 1540 Broadway, New York, NY 10036. Attn: Ed. Dept. Unsolicited young adult manuscripts are accepted only for the Delacorte Press Prize for a first young adult novel. This must be a work of fiction written for ages 12 to 18, by a previously unpublished author. Send SASE for rules and guidelines.

DELL BOOKS—1540 Broadway, New York, NY 10036. Commercial fiction (including romance, mystery, and westerns) and nonfiction (including health, war, and spirituality). Agented submissions only.

DELTA BOOKS—1540 Broadway, New York, NY 10036. Attn: Ed. Dept., Book Proposal. General-interest nonfiction, submit detailed chapter outline with sample chapters and fiction, submit full manuscript with narrative synopsis (no more than 10 pages). Poetry not considered. Allow 3 months for reply. SASE.

DEVIN-ADAIR PUBLISHERS, INC.—P.O. Box A, Old Greenwich, CT 06870. J. Andrassi, Ed. Books on conservative affairs, Irish topics, photography, Americana, self-help, health, gardening, cooking, and ecology. Send outline, sample chapters, and SASE. Royalty.

DI CAPUA BOOKS, MICHAEL—See *HarperCollins Children's Books.*

DIAL PRESS—1540 Broadway, New York, NY 10036. Susan Kamil, Ed. Dir. Quality fiction and nonfiction. No unsolicited material.

DIMI PRESS—3820 Oak Hollow Ln. S.E., Salem, OR 97302-4774. Dick Lutz, Pres. Books on visual things in nature, e.g., unique animals, different cultures, astonishing natural events or disasters. Also, books on travel (no travel guides). Query. Royalty.

DK INK—Imprint of Dorling Kindersley, 95 Madison Ave., New York, NY 10016. Neal Porter, Pub. Picture books and fiction for middle-grade and older readers. Submit complete manuscript. Royalty.

DOMAIN—See *Bantam Books.*

DOUBLEDAY AND CO.—1540 Broadway, New York, NY 10036. Stephen Rubin, Pub./Pres. Proposals from literary agents only. No unsolicited material.

DUNNE BOOKS, THOMAS—175 Fifth Ave., New York, NY 10010. Thomas L. Dunne, Ed. Adult fiction (mysteries, trade, etc.) and nonfiction (history, biographies, science, politics, humor, etc.). Query with outline, sample chapters, and SASE. Royalty.

DUQUESNE UNIVERSITY PRESS— 600 Forbes Ave., Pittsburgh, PA 15282. Attn: Ed. Dept. Scholarly publications in the humanities and social sciences; creative nonfiction (book-length only) by emerging writers. Guidelines.

DUTTON ADULT—375 Hudson St., New York, NY 10014. Arnold Dolin, Sr. V.P./Assoc. Pub. Fiction and nonfiction books. Manuscripts accepted only from agents or on personal recommendation.

DUTTON CHILDREN'S BOOKS—375 Hudson St., New York, NY 10014. Lucia Monfried, Assoc. Pub. & Ed.-in-Chief. Picture books, easy-to-read books; fiction and nonfiction for preschoolers to young adults. Submit outline and first 3 chapters with query for fiction and nonfiction, complete manuscripts for picture books and easy-to-read books. Manuscripts should be well written with fresh ideas and child appeal. Include SASE.

EAKIN PRESS—P.O. Drawer 90159, Austin, TX 78709-0159. Melissa Roberts, Sr. Ed. Adult nonfiction, 60,000 to 80,000 words: Texana, regional cookbooks, Mexico and the Southwest, WWII, military. Children's books: history, culture, geography, etc., of Texas and the Southwest. Juvenile picture books, 5,000 to 10,000 words; fiction, 20,000 to 30,000 words; young adult fiction, 25,000 to 40,000 words. Currently overstocked; query. Royalty.

EASTERN WASHINGTON UNIVERSITY PRESS—Mail Stop 14, Eastern Washington Univ., 526 5th St., Cheney, WA 99004-2431. Attn: Eds. Literary essays, history, social commentary, and other academic subjects. Limited fiction and well-researched historical novels (one title every 2 years or so). One or 2 books of poetry, 60 to 150 pages, each year. "We are a small regional university press, publishing titles that reflect our regional service, our international contacts, our strong creative writing program, and research and interests of our exceptional faculty." Send complete manuscript, query with outline, or Mac-compatible diskette. Royalty.

THE ECCO PRESS—100 W. Broad St., Hopewell, NJ 08525. Daniel Halpern, Ed.-in-Chief. Literary fiction, general nonfiction, poetry, memoirs, cooking, and sports-related books. No unsolicited poetry or manuscripts. Queries only.

EERDMANS PUBLISHING COMPANY, INC., WM. B.—255 Jefferson Ave. S.E., Grand Rapids, MI 49503. Jon Pott, Ed.-in-Chief. Protestant, Roman Catholic, and Orthodox theological nonfiction; religious history and biography; ethics; philosophy; literary studies; spiritual growth. For children's religious books, query Judy Zylstra, Children's Book Ed. Royalty.

ELEMENT BOOKS—160 North Washington St., 4th Floor, Boston, MA 02114. Roberta Scimone, Acquisitions Ed. Books on world religions, ancient wisdom, astrology, meditation, women's studies, and alternative health and healing. Study recent catalogue. Query with outline and sample chapters. Royalty.

ELLIOTT & CLARK—Black Belt Publishing, LLC, P.O. Box 551, Montgomery, AL 36101. Attn: Submissions Ed. Illustrated books on history, photography, gardening, health, music. Query with cover letter, synopsis or outline, author bio, and SASE for reply. Royalty varies.

ENSLOW PUBLISHERS, INC.—P.O. Box 699, 44 Fadem Rd., Springfield, NJ 07081. Brian D. Enslow, Ed./Pub. No fiction; nonfiction books for young people only. Areas of emphasis are children's and young adult books for ages 10 to 18 in the fields of social studies, science, and biography. Also reference books for all ages and easy reading books for teenagers.

EPICENTER PRESS—P.O. Box 82368, Kenmore, WA 98028. Kent Sturgis, Pub. Quality nonfiction trade books, contemporary western art and photography titles, and destination travel guides emphasizing Alaska and the West Coast. "We are a regional press whose interests include but are not limited to the arts, history, environment, and diverse cultures and lifestyles of the North Pacific and high latitudes."

ERIKSSON, PUBLISHER, PAUL S.—P.O. Box 62, Forest Dale, VT 05745. Attn: Ed. Dept. General nonfiction (send outline and cover letter); some fiction (send 3 chapters with query). Royalty.

EVANS & CO., INC., M.—216 E. 49th St., New York, NY 10017. Attn: Ed. Dept. Books on health, self-help, popular psychology, and cookbooks. Limited list of commercial fiction. Query with outline, sample chapter, and SASE. Royalty.

EVENT HORIZON PRESS—P.O. Box 867, Desert Hot Springs, CA 92240. Joseph Cowles, Pub. Adult fiction and nonfiction. Currently overstocked; no unsolicited manuscripts.

EXCALIBUR PUBLICATIONS—Box 36, Latham, NY 12110-0036. Alan M. Petrillo, Ed. Books on military history, firearms history, antique arms and accessories, military personalities, tactics and strategy, history of battles. Query with outline and 3 sample chapters. SASE. Royalty or flat fee.

FABER AND FABER—53 Shore Dr., Winchester, MA 01890. Attn: Man. Ed. Nonfiction books on topics of popular culture and general interest, including history, biography, women's interest, film, and gay and lesbian interest. Query (no more than two pages); publisher will contact author if interested; no calls please. Royalty.

FACTS ON FILE, INC.—11 Penn Plaza, New York, NY 10001. Reference and trade books on science, health, literature, language, history, the performing arts, ethnic studies, popular culture, sports, etc. (No fiction, poetry, computer books, technical books or cookbooks.) Query with outline, sample chapter, and SASE. Royalty. Hardcover.

FAIRVIEW PRESS—2450 Riverside Ave. S., Minneapolis, MN 55454. Lane Stiles, Sr. Ed. (Adult). Jessica Thoreson, Children's Book Ed. Adult books, 80,000 words, that offer advice and support on relationships, parenting, domestic violence, divorce, family activities, aging, health, self-esteem, social issues, addictions, etc. Children's picture books, about 1,000 words, for readers 4 to 9, on related subjects. Query with outline and sample chapters for adult books. Submit complete manuscript for picture books. Royalty.

FANFARE—1540 Broadway, New York, NY 10036. Beth de Guzman, Wendy McCurdy, Sr. Eds. Cassie Goddard, Assoc Ed. Stephanie Kip, Ed. Historical and contemporary women's fiction, about 90,000 to 150,000 words. Study field before submitting. Query. Paperback and hardcover.

FARRAR, STRAUS & GIROUX—19 Union Sq. W., New York, NY 10003. Adult and juvenile literary fiction and nonfiction.

THE FEMINIST PRESS AT THE CITY UNIVERSITY OF NEW YORK—City College; Wingate Hall Convent Ave. at 138th St., New York, NY 10031.

Florence Howe, Pub. Reprints of significant "lost" fiction, original memoirs, autobiographies, biographies; multicultural anthologies; handbooks; bibliographies. "We are especially interested in international literature, women and peace, women and music, and women of color." Royalty.

FIREBRAND BOOKS—141 The Commons, Ithaca, NY 14850. Nancy K. Bereano, Ed. Feminist and lesbian fiction and nonfiction. Royalty. Paperback and library edition cloth.

FIRESIDE BOOKS—1230 Ave. of the Americas, New York, NY 10020. No unsolicited manuscripts.

FLARE BOOKS—See *Avon Books.*

FODOR'S TRAVEL GUIDES—201 E. 50th St., New York, NY 10022. Karen Cure, Ed. Dir. Travel guides for both foreign and US destinations. "For our Gold Guides, our flagship series, we generally hire writers who live in the area they will write about or who have a very intimate knowledge of the area they will cover; we're open to new ideas beyond our Gold Guides as well." Gold Guides follow established format. Send writing sample, and, for proposals for new books, a sample chapter, outline, and statement about your guide's intended audience.

FONT & CENTER PRESS—P.O. Box 95, Weston, MA 02193. Ilene Horowitz, Ed./Pub. Cookbooks. How-to books. Alternative history for adults and young adults. Send proposal, outline, and sample chapter(s). Responds in 3 months. SASE required. Royalty.

FORGE—Tom Doherty Associates, 175 Fifth Ave., 14th Fl., New York, NY 10010. Melissa Ann Singer, Sr. Ed. General fiction; limited nonfiction, from 80,000 words. Also interested in literary fiction, particularly women's. Query with complete synopsis and first 3 chapters to Jennifer Hogan, Asst. Ed. Advance and royalty.

FORTRESS PRESS—Box 1209, Minneapolis, MN 55440. Dr. Henry French, Ed. Dir. Books in the areas of biblical studies, theology, ethics, professional ministry, and church history for academic and professional markets, including libraries. Query.

FORUM—c/o Prima Publishing, 3875 Atherton Rd., Rocklin, CA 95765. Steven Martin, Ed. Serious nonfiction books on current affairs, public policy, libertarian/conservative thought, high level management, individual empowerment, and historical biography. Submit outline and sample chapters. Royalty.

THE FREE PRESS—See *Macmillan Reference USA.*

FREE SPIRIT PUBLISHING— 400 First Ave. N., Suite 616-W, Minneapolis, MN 55401-1724. Lisa Leonard, Ed. Asst. Nonfiction self-help for kids, with an emphasis on school success, self-awareness, self-esteem, creativity, social action, lifeskills, and special needs. Creative classroom activities for teachers; adult books on raising, counseling, or educating children. Queries only. Request free catalog and guidelines. Advance and royalty.

FRONT STREET BOOKS, INC.—20 Battery Park Ave., #403, Asheville, NC 28801. Stephen Roxburgh, Pres./Pub. Fiction, poetry, and picture books for children. Query with sample chapters. Royalty.

FULCRUM PUBLISHING—350 Indiana St., Suite 350, Golden, CO 80401. Attn: Submissions Dept. Adult trade nonfiction: gardening, travel, nature, history, education, and Native American culture. No fiction. Send cover letter, sample chapters, table of contents, author credentials, and market analysis. Royalty.

GENESIS PUBLISHING CO., INC.—1547 Great Pond Rd., N. Andover, MA 01845-1216. Gerard M. Verschuuren, Ed. Adult fiction and nonfiction, especially religion and philosophy books. Query. Royalty.

GIBBS SMITH, JUNIOR—P.O. Box 667, Layton, UT 84041. Theresa Desmond, Ed. Juvenile books: western/cowboy; activity; how-to; nature/environment; and humor. Fiction picture books, to 1,000 words; nonfiction books, to 10,000 words, for readers 4 to 12. Royalty.

GIBBS SMITH PUBLISHER—P.O. Box 667, Layton, UT 84041. Madge Baird, Ed. Dir. Adult nonfiction. Query. Royalty.

GINIGER CO. INC., THE K.S.—250 W. 57th St., Suite 414, New York, NY 10107. Attn: Ed. Dept. General nonfiction. Query with SASE; no unsolicited manuscripts. Royalty.

GLENBRIDGE PUBLISHING LTD.— 6010 W. Jewell Ave., Lakewood, CO 80232. James A. Keene, Ed. Nonfiction books on a variety of topics, including business, history, and psychology. Query with sample chapter and SASE. Royalty.

GLOBE PEQUOT PRESS, THE— 6 Business Park Rd., Box 833, Old Saybrook, CT 06475. Elizabeth Taylor, Submissions Ed. Nonfiction with national and regional focus; travel; outdoor recreation; home-based business. Query with sample chapter, contents, and one-page synopsis. SASE required. Royalty or flat fee.

GODINE PUBLISHER, DAVID R.— 9 Hamilton Place, Boston, MA 02108. No unsolicited manuscripts. Royalty.

GOLD EAGLE—See *Worldwide Library.*

GOLD 'N' HONEY—See *Multnomah Publishers.*

GOLDEN BOOKS FAMILY ENTERTAINMENT— 888 Seventh Ave., New York, NY 10106-4100. Patty Sullivan, Exec. V.P./Pub., children's publishing group. Children's fiction and nonfiction: picture books, storybooks, concept books, novelty books. Adult nonfiction. No unsolicited manuscripts. Royalty or flat fee.

GOLDEN WEST PUBLISHERS— 4113 N. Longview, Phoenix, AZ 85014. Hal Mitchell, Ed. Cookbooks and nonfiction Western history and travel books. Currently seeking writers for state and regional cookbooks. Query. Royalty or flat fee.

GRAYWOLF PRESS—2402 University Ave., Suite 203, St. Paul, MN 55114. Attn: Ed. Dept. Literary fiction (short story collections and novels), poetry, and essays.

GREAT QUOTATIONS—1967 Quincy Ct., Glendale Heights, IL 60139. Patrick Caton, Ed. General adult titles, 80 to 365 pages, with strong, clever, descriptive titles and brief, upbeat text. "We publish small, quick-read gift books." Query with outline and sample chapters or send complete manuscript. Royalty.

GREENWILLOW BOOKS—1350 Ave. of the Americas, New York, NY 10019. Susan Hirschman, Ed.-in-Chief. Children's books for all ages. Picture books.

GROSSET AND DUNLAP, INC.—200 Madison Ave., New York, NY 10016. Jane O'Connor, Pub. Mass-market children's books. Currently not accepting unsolicited manuscripts. Royalty.

GROVE/ATLANTIC MONTHLY PRESS—841 Broadway, 4th Fl., New York, NY 10003-4793. Morgan Entrekin, Pub. Distinguished fiction and nonfiction. Query; no unsolicited manuscripts. Royalty.

GRYPHON HOUSE, INC.—P.O. Box 207, Beltsville, MD 20705. Kathy Charner, Ed.-in-Chief. Resource books, 150 to 500 pages, for parents and teachers of young children from birth to 8 years old. Query with outline and sample chapters. Royalty.

GULLIVER BOOKS—See *Harcourt Brace & Co. Children's Book Div.*

GULLIVER GREEN—See *Harcourt Brace & Co. Children's Book Div.*

HACHAI PUBLISHING—156 Chester Ave., Brooklyn, NY 11218. Dina Rosenfeld, Ed. Full-color children's picture books, 32 pages, for readers ages 2 to 8; Judaica, Bible tales. Query or send complete manuscript. Flat fee. Web site: www.hachai.com.

HANCOCK HOUSE PUBLISHERS, LTD.—1431 Harrison Ave., Blaine, WA 98230. Attn: Ed. Dept. Adult nonfiction: guidebooks, biographies, natural history, popular science, conservation, animal husbandry, falconry, and sports. Some juvenile nonfiction. Query with outline and sample chapters or send complete manuscript. Multiple queries considered. Royalty.

HARCOURT BRACE & CO.—525 B St., Suite 1900, San Diego, CA 92101. Attn: Ed. Dept. Adult trade nonfiction and fiction. No unsolicited manuscripts. Queries accepted with SASE.

HARCOURT BRACE & CO. CHILDREN'S BOOK DIV.—525 B St., Suite 1900, San Diego, CA 92101-4495. Attn: Manuscript Submissions. Juvenile fiction and nonfiction for beginning readers through young adults under the following imprints: *Browndeer Press, Gulliver Books, Red Wagon Books, Odyssey Classics, Silver Whistle, Magic Carpet Books, Libros Viajeros, Harcourt Brace Big Books, Gulliver Green, Harcourt Brace Young Classics, Harcourt Brace Paperbacks,* and *Voyager Books.* Query with SASE; manuscripts accepted from agents.

HARCOURT BRACE PROFESSIONAL PUBLISHING—525 B St., Suite 1900, San Diego, CA 92101-4495. Attn: Sidney Bernstein, V.P. & Pub. Professional books for practitioners in accounting, auditing, tax and financial planning. Query. Royalty and work-for-hire.

HARDSCRABBLE BOOKS—See *University Press of New England.*

HARLEQUIN BOOKS/CANADA—225 Duncan Mill Rd., Don Mills, Ont., Canada M3B 3K9. Randall Toye, Ed. Dir. *Mira Books*: Dianne Moggy, Sr. Ed. Contemporary women's fiction, 100,000 words. Query. *Harlequin Superromance*: Paula Eykelhof, Sr. Ed. Contemporary romance, 85,000 words, with a mainstream edge. Query. *Harlequin Temptation*: Birgit Davis-Todd, Sr. Ed. Sensuous, humorous contemporary romances, 60,000 words. *Love and Laughter*: Malle Vallik, Assoc. Sr. Ed. The lighter side of love, 55,000 words. Query.

HARLEQUIN BOOKS/U.S.—300 E. 42nd St., 6th Fl., New York, NY 10017. Debra Matteucci, Sr. Ed. Contemporary romances, 70,000 to 75,000 words. Send for tip sheets. *Harlequin American Romances*: bold, exciting romantic adventures, "where anything is possible and dreams come true."

Harlequin Intrigue: set against a backdrop of mystery and suspense, world-wide locales. Query. Paperback.

HARPER SAN FRANCISCO—(formerly *HarperCollins San Francisco*) 353 Sacramento St., Suite 500, San Francisco, CA 94111-3653. Attn: Acquisitions Ed. Books on spirituality and religion. No unsolicited manuscripts; query required.

HARPERCOLLINS CHILDREN'S BOOKS—10 E. 53rd St., New York, NY 10022-5299. Picture books, chapter books, and fiction and nonfiction for middle-grade and young adult readers. "Our imprints (*HarperTrophy* paperbacks, *Joanna Cotler Books, Michael di Capua Books*, and *Laura Geringer Books*) are committed to producing imaginative and responsible children's books. All publish from preschool to young adult titles." Guidelines. Royalty.

HARPERCOLLINS PUBLISHERS—10 E. 53rd St., New York, NY 10022-5299. Adult Trade Department: Address Man. Ed. Fiction, nonfiction (biography, history, etc.), reference. Submissions from agents only. College texts: Address College Dept. No unsolicited manuscripts; query only.

HARPERCOLLINS SAN FRANCISCO—See *Harper San Francisco.*

HARPERPAPERBACKS—HarperCollins, 10 E. 53rd St., New York, NY 10022-5299. Carolyn Marino, Ed. Dir. John Silbersack, Science Fiction/Fantasy Ed.-in-Chief. John Douglas, Exec. Ed. Jessica Lichtenstein, Sr. Ed. Laura Cifelli, Caitlin Blasdell, Eds. Leslie Stern, Assoc. Ed.

HARPERPRISM—10 E. 53rd St., New York, NY 10022-5299. John Silbersack, Sr. V.P./Pub. Dir. John Douglas, Exec. Ed. Caitlin Blasdell, Ed. Science fiction/fantasy. No unsolicited manuscripts; query.

HARPERTROPHY—See *HarperCollins Children's Books.*

HARVARD COMMON PRESS—535 Albany St., Boston, MA 02118. Bruce Shaw, Ed. Adult nonfiction: cookbooks, travel guides, books on childcare and parenting, health, small business, etc. Send outline, analysis of competing books, and sample chapters or complete manuscript. SASE. Royalty.

HARVARD UNIVERSITY PRESS—79 Garden St., Cambridge, MA 02138-1499. No free-lance submissions: "We hire no writers."

HARVEST HOUSE PUBLISHERS—1075 Arrowsmith, Eugene, OR 97402. LaRae Weikert, Ed. Mgr. No longer accepts unsolicited material.

HAWORTH PRESS, INC.—10 Alice St., Binghamton, NY 13904-1580. Bill Palmer, Ed. Scholarly press interested in research-based adult nonfiction: psychology, social work, gay and lesbian studies, women's studies, family and marriage; some recreation and entertainment. Send outline with sample chapters or complete manuscript. Royalty.

HAY HOUSE—P.O. Box 5100, Carlsbad, CA 92018-5100. Attn: Ed. Dir. Self-help books on health, self-awareness, spiritual growth, astrology, psychology, philosophy, women's and men's issues, metaphysics, and the environment. Query with outline, a few sample chapters, and SASE. Royalties.

HAZELDEN EDUCATIONAL MATERIALS—Box 176, Center City, MN 55012. Kate Kjorlien, Trade Asst. Self-help books, 100 to 400 pages, relating to addiction, recovery, spirituality, and wholeness. Query with outline and sample chapters. Multiple queries considered. Royalty.

HEALTH COMMUNICATIONS, INC.—3201 S.W. 15th St., Deerfield Beach, FL 33442. Christine Belleris, Ed. Dir. Books, 250 pages, on self-help, recovery, inspiration, and personal growth for adults. Query with outline and 2 sample chapters and SASE. Royalty.

HEALTH INFORMATION PRESS— 4727 Wilshire Blvd., #300, Los Angeles, CA 90010. Kathryn Swanson, Ed. Books, 250 pages, that "simplify complicated health and medical issues so that consumers can make informed decisions about their health and medical care." Query with outline and sample chapters. Royalty.

HEALTH PRESS—P.O. Box 1388, Santa Fe, NM 87504. K. Schwartz, Ed. Health-related adult and children's books, 100 to 300 pages. "We're seeking cutting-edge, original manuscripts that will excite, educate, and help readers." Author must have credentials, or preface/intro must be written by M.D., Ph.D., etc. Controversial topics are desired; must be well researched and documented. Submit outline, table of contents, and first chapter with SASE. Royalty.

HEARST BOOKS —See *William Morrow and Co., Inc.*

HEARTSONG PRESENTS—P.O. Box 719, Uhrichsville, OH 44683. Rebecca Germany, Man. Ed. Contemporary and historical romances, 50,000 to 55,000 words, that present a conservative, evangelical Christian world view. Pays flat fee.

HEBREW UNION COLLEGE PRESS—3101 Clifton Ave., Cincinnati, OH 45220. Barbara Selya, Ed. Scholarly books, 200 pages, on very specific topics in Judaic studies. "Our usual print run is 500 books, and our target audience is mainly rabbis and professors." Query with outline and sample chapters. No payment.

HEINEMANN—361 Hanover St., Portsmouth, NH 03801. Attn: Ed. Dept. Practical theatre, world literature, and literacy education. Query.

HEMINGWAY WESTERN STUDIES SERIES—Boise State University, 1910 University Dr., Boise, ID 83725. Tom Trusky, Ed. Artists' and eccentric format books (multiple editions) relating to Rocky Mountain environment, race, religion, gender and other public issues. Guidelines.

HIGGINSON BOOK COMPANY—148 Washington St., Salem, MA 01970. Attn: Ed. Dept. Nonfiction genealogy and local history only, 20 to 1,000 pages. Specializes in reprints. Query. Royalty.

HIGHSMITH PRESS—P.O. Box 800, Fort Atkinson, WI 53538-0800. Donald Sager, Pub. Adult books, 80 to 360 pages, on professional library science, education, and reference. Teacher activity and curriculum resource books, 48 to 240 pages, for pre-K through 12. Query with outline and sample chapters. Royalty. Guidelines available at web site: www.hpress.high smith.com.

HIPPOCRENE BOOKS—171 Madison Ave., New York, NY 10016. George Blagowidow, Ed. Dir. Language instruction books and foreign language dictionaries, international cookbooks, travel guides, military history, Polish interest books. Send outline and sample chapters with SASE for reply. Multiple queries considered. Royalty.

HOLIDAY HOUSE, INC.— 425 Madison Ave., New York, NY 10017. Regina Griffin, V. P. Lisa Hopp, Assoc. Ed. General juvenile fiction and nonfiction. Submit complete manuscript for picture book or 3 sample chapters and summary for novel; enclose SASE. Royalty. Hardcover only.

HOLT AND CO., HENRY—115 W. 18th St., New York, NY 10011. Distinguished works of biography, history, fiction, and natural history; humor; child activity books; parenting books; books for the entrepreneurial business person; and health books. "Virtually all submissions come from literary agents or from writers whom we publish."

HOME BUILDER PRESS—National Assoc. of Home Builders, 1201 15th St. N.W., Washington, DC 20005-2800. Doris M. Tennyson, Sr. Ed. How-to and business management books, 150 to 200 manuscript pages, for builders, remodelers, developers, other building industry professionals, and consumers. Writers should be experts in homebuilding, remodeling, land development, sales, marketing, or related aspects of the building industry. Query with outline and sample chapter. Royalty.

HOMESTEAD PUBLISHING—P.O. Box 193, Moose, WY 83012. Carl Schreier, Pub. Guidebooks, fiction, art, history, and biography. Royalty.

HOUGHTON MIFFLIN COMPANY—222 Berkeley St., Boston, MA 02116-3764. Attn: Ed. Dept. Fiction: literary, historical. Nonfiction: history, biography, psychology. No unsolicited submissions. Children's book division, address Children's Trade Books: picture books, fiction, and nonfiction for all ages. Query. Royalty.

HOWARD UNIVERSITY PRESS—2225 Georgia Ave. N.W., Washington, DC 20017. Ed Gordon, Dir. Nonfiction books, 300 to 500 manuscript pages, on African diaspora, history, political science, literary criticism, biography, women's studies. Query with outline and sample chapters. Royalty.

HP BOOKS—200 Madison Ave., New York, NY 10016. Attn: Ed. Dept. How-tos on cooking, automotive topics. Query with SASE.

HUMANICS PUBLISHING GROUP—P.O. Box 7400, Atlanta, GA 30357. W. Arthur Bligh, Acquisitions Ed. Inspiring trade books, 100 to 300 pages: self-help, spiritual, instructional, philosophy, and health for body, mind, and soul. Also, children's educational books/teacher resource guides for grades K through 6. "We are interested in books that people go to for help, guidance, and inspiration." Query with outline and SASE required. Royalty.

HUNGRY MIND PRESS—1648 Grand Ave., St. Paul, MN 55105. David Unowsky, Ed. Pearl Kilbride, Ed. Fiction; memoirs; contemporary affairs; cultural criticism; nature writing; spiritual reflection; travel essays; nonfiction. "Books that examine the human experience, encourage reflection, and enrich everyday life. We want to involve writers in the planning and marketing of their books and build a strong relationship with booksellers." Query with outline and sample chapters. Royalty.

HUNTER PUBLISHING, INC.—130 Campus Dr., Edison, NJ 08818. Kim André, Acquisitions Dept. Travel guides to the U.S., South America, and the Caribbean.

HYPERION—114 Fifth Ave., New York, NY 10011. Material accepted from agents only. No unsolicited manuscripts or queries considered.

HYSTERIA PUBLICATIONS—P.O. Box 8581, Bridgeport, CT 06605. Lysbeth Guillorn, Ed. Humorous books that are "progressive, provocative, liberating, funny, and insightful," 96 to 112 finished pages. Also publishes nonfiction women's trade hardcover books under the *Rose Communications* imprint. Query with sample chapters or complete manuscript. SASE for guidelines. Royalty.

IMPACT PUBLISHERS, INC.—P.O. Box 910, San Luis Obispo, CA 93406. Attn: Acquisitions Ed. Popular psychology books, from 200 pages, on personal growth, relationships, families, communities, and health for adults. Children's books for "Little Imp" series on issues of self-esteem. "Writers must have advanced degrees and professional experience in human-service fields." Query with outline and sample chapters. Royalty.

INDIANA UNIVERSITY PRESS— 601 N. Morton St., Bloomington, IN 47404-3797. Attn: Ed. Dept. Scholarly nonfiction, especially cultural studies, literary criticism, music, history, women's studies, African-American studies, science, philosophy, African studies, Middle East studies, Russian studies, anthropology, regional, etc. Query with outline and sample chapters. Royalty.

INNER TRADITIONS INTERNATIONAL, INC.—One Park St., Rochester, VT 05767. Jon Graham, Acquisitions Ed. Books representing the spiritual, cultural, and mythic traditions of the world, focusing on inner wisdom and the perennial philosophies and alternative modalities of healing. Query. Royalty.

INSTRUCTOR BOOKS—See *Scholastic Professional Books.*

INTERNATIONAL MARINE—A Div. of McGraw-Hill, Box 220, Camden, ME 04843. Jonathan Eaton, Ed. Dir. Books on boating (sailing and power).

INTIMATE MOMENTS—See *Silhouette Books.*

ISLAND PRESS—1718 Connecticut Ave. N.W., Suite 300, Washington, DC 20009. Dan Sayre, Ed.-in-Chief. Nonfiction focusing on natural history, literary science, the environment, and natural resource management. "We want solution-oriented material to solve environmental problems. For our imprint, *Shearwater Books*, we want books that express new insights about nature and the environment." Query or send manuscript. SASE required.

ITHACA BOOKS, INC.—246 Mero, La Canada, CA 91011. Christopher J. Husa, Man. Dir. Books, 10,000 to 12,000 words, for children ages 8 to 13, based on true stories of adventure, exploration, and discovery. "Accuracy is critical; research is essential." Royalty.

JAI PRESS, INC.—55 Old Post Rd., #2, P.O. Box 1678, Greenwich, CT 06836. Herbert Johnson, Ed. Research and technical reference books on such subjects as business, economics, management, sociology, political science, computer science, life sciences, and chemistry. Query or send complete manuscript. Royalty.

JALMAR PRESS—24426 S. Main St., Suite 702, Carson, CA 90745. Dr. Bradley L. Winch, Pub. Nonfiction books for parents, teachers, and caregivers. "Our emphasis is on helping children and adults live from the inside/out so that they become personally and socially responsible." Special interest in peaceful conflict resolution and whole brain learning. Multiple queries considered. Submit outline. Royalty.

JAMES BOOKS, ALICE—Univ. of Maine at Farmington, 98 Main St., Farmington, ME 04938. Peg Peoples, Program Dir. "Shared-work cooperative" publishes books of poetry (48 to 64 pages) by writers through two annual competitions. The New England/New York Competition publishes manuscripts by writers living in New England (deadline is September); authors become active collective members. The Beatrice Hawley Competition is open to poets nation-wide (deadline is December); authors do not become members. "We emphasize the publication of poetry by women and poets of color, but also welcome and publish manuscripts by men." Authors paid with 100 copies of their books. Request guidelines with SASE.

JIST WORKS—720 N. Park Ave., Indianapolis, IN 46202. Attn: Submissions Ed. Career and "life decision" books for people all reading and academic levels. Also business, welfare-to-work titles, and trade topics for consumers. Query with outline and sample chapters. Payment made on a royalty or flat fee basis.

JOHNSON BOOKS, INC.—1880 S. 57th Ct., Boulder, CO 80301. Stephen Topping, Ed. Dir. Nonfiction: environmental subjects, archaeology, geology, natural history, astronomy, travel guides, outdoor guidebooks, fly fishing, regional. Query. Royalty.

JONA BOOKS—P.O. Box 336, Bedford, IN 47421. Joe Glasgow, Ed. Nonfiction: biographies, Native American history, old west, and military history. Fiction: action adventure, alternative history, historical fiction, mysteries, and military science fiction. Contracts negotiated; no advances.

JONATHAN DAVID PUBLISHERS, INC.— 68-22 Eliot Ave., Middle Village, NY 11379. Alfred J. Kolatch, Ed.-in-Chief. General nonfiction (how-to, sports, cooking and food, self-help, etc.) and books on Judaica. Query with outline, sample chapter, resumé, and SASE. Royalty or outright purchase.

JOVE BOOKS—200 Madison Ave., New York, NY 10016. Fiction and nonfiction. No unsolicited manuscripts.

KALMBACH BOOKS—21027 Crossroads Cir., Waukesha, WI 53187. Terry Spohn, Sr. Acquisitions Ed. Adult nonfiction, 18,000 to 50,000 words, on scale modeling, railroading, model railroading, miniatures, and amateur astronomy. Send outline with sample chapters. Accepts multiple queries. Royalty.

KAR-BEN COPIES— 6800 Tildenwood Ln., Rockville, MD 20852. Judye Groner, Ed. Books on Jewish themes for preschool and elementary children (to age 9): picture books, fiction, and nonfiction. Complete manuscript preferred; SASE. Royalty. Web site: http://www.karben.com

KEATS PUBLISHING, INC.—27 Pine St., Box 876, New Canaan, CT 06840. Richard Gallen, Pub. Health, nutrition, alternative and complimentary medicine, and preventive health care. Royalty.

KENSINGTON PUBLISHING CORP.— 850 Third Ave., New York, NY 10022. Paul Dinas, Ed.-in-Chief. Ann LaFarge, Exec. Ed. Popular fiction; historical and contemporary romance; *Splendor Romances* (110,000 words); Arabesque (African American) romances; regencies (80,000 words); westerns; nonfiction. Agented material only.

KENT PRESS—P.O. Box 1169, Stamford, CT 06904-1169. Katie DeVito, Man. Ed. Books on legal issues relating to intellectual property and licensing. Query with outline. Royalty.

KENT STATE UNIVERSITY PRESS—Kent State Univ., Kent, OH 44242. John T. Hubbell, Dir. Julia Morton, Ed.-in-Chief. Interested in scholarly works in history and literary criticism of high quality, any titles of regional interest for Ohio, scholarly biographies, archaeological research, the arts, and general nonfiction.

KNOPF BOOKS FOR YOUNG READERS, ALFRED A.—201 E. 50th St., New York, NY 10022. Distinguished juvenile fiction and nonfiction. Query; no unsolicited manuscripts. Royalty. Guidelines.

KNOPF, INC., ALFRED A.—201 E. 50th St., New York, NY 10022. Attn: Sr. Ed. Distinguished adult fiction and general nonfiction. Query for nonfiction. Royalty.

KODANSHA AMERICA, INC.—114 Fifth Ave., New York, NY 10011. Attn: Ed. Dept. Nonfiction books, 50,000 to 200,000 words, on cross-cultural, Asian and other international subjects. Query with outline, sample chapters, and SASE. Royalty.

KRAUSE PUBLICATIONS, INC.—700 E. State St., Iola, WI 54990-0001. Paul Kennedy, Acq. Ed. Antiques and collectibles, sewing and crafts, antique automotive topics, numismatics, sports, philatelics, outdoors, guns and knives, toys, records and comics.

LANDMARK SPECIALTY BOOKS—(formerly *Antique Trader Books*) 150 W. Brambleton Ave., Norfolk, VA 23510. Allan W. Miller, Man. Ed. Collector guides and reference books, 200 pages, on antiques and collectibles. Query with outline and sample chapter. Royalty.

LARK BOOKS—50 College St., Asheville, NC 28801. Carol Taylor, Pub. Distinctive books for creative people in crafts, how-to, leisure activities, and "coffee table" categories. Query with outline. Royalty.

LAUREL-LEAF—See *The Delacorte Press Books for Young Readers.*

LEADERSHIP PUBLISHERS, INC.—P.O. Box 8358, Des Moines, IA 50301-8358. Dr. Lois F. Roets, Ed. Educational materials for talented and gifted students, grades K to 12, and teacher reference books. No fiction or poetry. Send SASE for catalogue and writer's guidelines before submitting. "We're getting too many manuscripts that have nothing to do with our area of publication." Query or outline. Royalty for books; flat fee for booklets.

LEE & LOW BOOKS—95 Madison Ave., New York, NY 10016. Philip Lee, Pub. Elizabeth Szabla, Ed.-in-Chief. Focus is on fiction and nonfiction picture books for children ages 4 to 10. "Our goal is to meet the growing need for books that address children of color and to provide books on subjects and stories they can identify with. Of special interest are stories set in contemporary America. Folklore and animal stories not considered." Include SASE. Advance/royalty.

LIBROS VIAJEROS—See *Harcourt Brace & Co. Children's Book Div.*

LIFETIME BOOKS, INC.—2131 Hollywood Blvd., Hollywood, FL 33020. Callie Rucker, Sr. Ed. Nonfiction (200 to 300 pages): general interest, how-to, self-help, cooking, hobby, business, health, and inspiration. Query with letter or outline and sample chapter, SASE. Royalty. Send 9x12 SASE with 5 first-class stamps for catalogue.

LIMELIGHT BOOKS—See *Tiare Publications.*

LINCOLN-HERNDON PRESS, INC.—818 S. Dirksen Pkwy., Springfield, IL 62703. Shirley A. Buscher, Asst. Pub. American humor that reveals American history. Humor collections. Query.

LINNET BOOKS, LINNET PROFESSIONAL BOOKS—See *Shoe String Press.*

LITTLE, BROWN & CO.—3 Center Plaza, Boston, MA 02108. Attn: Ed. Dept. Fiction, general nonfiction, sports books. Query only.

LITTLE, BROWN & CO. CHILDREN'S BOOK DEPT.—3 Center Plaza, Boston, MA 02108. Attn: Ed. Dept. Juvenile fiction and nonfiction and picture books. No unsolicited manuscripts. Accepts agented material only.

LITTLE SIMON—See *Simon & Schuster Books for Young Readers.*

LITTLE TIGER PRESS—N16 W23390 Stoneridge Dr., Waukesha, WI 53188. Acquisitions Ed. Picture books, 500 to 1,500 words, for the preschool to 8-year-old range. Send complete manuscript with cover letter and SASE. Do not send original artwork. Request guidelines with SASE.

LLEWELLYN PUBLICATIONS—P.O. Box 64383, St. Paul, MN 55164-0383. Nancy J. Mostad, Acquisitions Mgr. Books, from 75,000 words, on subjects of self-help, how-to, alternative health, astrology, metaphysics, new age, and the occult. Metaphysical/occult fiction. "We're interested in any kind of story (mystery, historical, gothic, occult, metaphysical adventure), just as long as the theme is authentic occultism, and the work is both entertaining and educational." Query with sample chapters. Multiple queries considered. Royalty.

LONGSTREET PRESS—2140 Newmarket Pkwy., Suite 122, Marietta, GA 30067. Melanie Lasoff, Asst. Ed. Nonfiction, varying lengths, that appeals to a general audience. Query with outline and sample chapters. Accepts very little fiction, and only through an agent. SASE. Allow 5 months for response. Royalty.

LOTHROP, LEE & SHEPARD BOOKS—1350 Ave. of the Americas, New York, NY 10019. Susan Pearson, Ed.-in-Chief. Juvenile fiction and nonfiction, picture books. Does not review unsolicited material. Royalty.

LOVE AND LAUGHTER—See *Harlequin Books/Canada.*

LOVESWEPT—1540 Broadway, New York, NY 10036. Susann Brailey, Sr. Ed. Joy Abella, Administrative Ed. Adult contemporary romances, approximately 55,000 to 60,000 words. Study field before submitting. Query required. Paperback only.

LUCENT BOOKS—P.O. Box 289011, San Diego, CA 92198-9011. Bonnie Szumski, Man. Ed. David Haugen, Ed. Books, 18,000 to 25,000 words, for junior high/middle school students. "Overview" series: current issues (political, social, historical, environmental topics). Other series include "World History," "Importance Of" (biography), "The Way People Live" (exploring daily life and culture of communities worldwide, past and present). No unsolicited material; work is by assignment only. Flat fee. Query for guidelines and catalogue.

LYLE STUART—See *Carol Publishing Group.*

LYONS PRESS—(formerly *Lyons & Burford, Publishers*) 31 W. 21st St., New York, NY 10010. Bryan Oettel, Ed. Books, 100 to 300 pages, on cooking, gardening, sports, woodworking, natural history, and science. Query with outline. Royalty.

MCCLANAHAN BOOK CO.—23 W. 26th St., New York, NY 10010. Kenn Goin, Ed. Dir. Mass-market books for children, preschool to third grade. "Most books published as part of a series." Majority of work is done on a "Work for Hire" basis. Flat fee. Query.

MCELDERRY BOOKS, MARGARET K.—1230 6th Ave., New York, NY 10020. Margaret K. McElderry, Ed.-at-Large. Emma Dryden, Sr. Ed. Childrens and young adult books, including picture books; quality fiction; fantasy; beginning chapter books; humor; realism; and nonfiction. Request guidelines before querying.

MCFARLAND & COMPANY, INC., PUBLISHERS—Box 611, Jefferson, NC 28640. Robert Franklin, Pres./Ed.-in-Chief. Steve Wilson and Virginia Tobiassen, Eds. Scholarly and reference books, from 225 manuscript pages, in many fields, except mathematical sciences. Particularly interested in general reference, performing arts, sports, women's studies, and African American studies. No new age, inspirational, children's, poetry, fiction, or exposés. Submit complete manuscripts or query with outline and sample chapters. Royalty.

MCGREGOR PUBLISHING—118 S. Westshore Blvd., Suite 233, Tampa, FL 33609. Lonnie Herman, Pub. Fiction and nonfiction, especially biography, sports, self-help. Query with outline and sample chapters or send complete manuscript. Royalty.

MACMILLAN REFERENCE USA—1633 Broadway, New York, NY 10019. Attn: Ed. Dept. General Book Division: Religious, sports, science, travel, and reference books. No fiction. Paperbacks: *Collier Books,* history, psychology, contemporary issues, sports, popular information, childcare, health. *The Free Press,* college texts and professional books in social sciences, humanities. Query. Royalty.

MACMURRAY & BECK, INC.—1649 Downing St., Denver, CO 80218. Frederick Ramey, Exec. Dir. Quality fiction and narrative nonfiction.

MADISON BOOKS—4720 Boston Way, Lanham, MD 20706. James E. Lyons, Pub. Full-length nonfiction: history, biography, contemporary affairs, trade reference. Query required. Royalty.

MADLIBS—See *Price Stern Sloan, Inc.*

MAGIC ATTIC PRESS—373 Park Ave. S., 8th Fl., New York, NY 10016. Jay Brady, Man. Ed. Series fiction for young girls, ages 7 to 12. Submit writing samples only: a portion of a work in progress or a chapter from a finished book (to 10 pages); include resumé, and SASE.

MAGIC CARPET BOOKS—See *Harcourt Brace & Co. Children's Book Div.*

MAGINATION PRESS—750 First St., N.E., Washington, DC 20002. Darcie Conner Johnston, Ed. Children's picture books dealing with the psychotherapeutic treatment or resolution of serious childhood problems. Picture books for children 4 to 11; nonfiction for children 8 to 18. Most books are written by mental health professionals. Submit complete manuscript. Royalty.

MEADOWBROOK PRESS—5451 Smetana Dr., Minnetonka, MN 55343. Attn: Submissions Ed. Upbeat, useful books, 60,000 words, on pregnancy, childbirth, and parenting; shorter works of humor, party planning, and children's activities; fiction anthologies and humorous poetry for children. Send for guidelines. Royalty or flat fee.

MEGA-BOOKS, INC.—240 E. 60th St., New York, NY 10022. Toni Ann Scaramuzzo, Man. Ed. Book packager. Young adult books, 150 pages, children's books. Query for guidelines. Flat fee.

MEREDITH CORP. BOOK PUBLISHING—(*Better Homes and Gardens Books* and *Ortho Books*) 1716 Locust St., Des Moines, IA 50309-3023. James D. Blume, Ed.-in-Chief. Books on gardening, crafts, decorating, do-it-yourself, cooking, health; mostly staff-written. "Interested in free-lance writers with expertise in these areas." Limited market. Query with SASE.

MESSNER, JULIAN—Simon & Schuster Educational Group, Silver Burdett Press, 299 Jefferson Rd., P.O. Box 480, Parsippany, NJ 07054-0480. Susan Eddy, Pub. Curriculum-oriented nonfiction. General nonfiction, for ages 8 to 14: science, nature, biography, history, social issues, and hobbies. Lengths vary. Royalty.

THE MICHIGAN STATE UNIVERSITY PRESS—1405 S. Harrison Rd., Suite 25, E. Lansing, MI 48823-5202. Scholarly nonfiction, with concentrations in history, regional history, women's studies, African-American history, contemporary culture; also Native American Series, Rhetoric Series, and Lotus Poetry Series. Submit prospectus, table of contents, and sample chapters to Acquisitions Ed. Authors should refer to *The Chicago Manual of Style, 14th Edition*, for formats and styles.

MIDDLE PASSAGE PRESS—5517 Secrest Dr., Los Angeles, CA 90043-2029. Barbara Bramwell, Ed. Small press. Nonfiction that focuses on African-American experience in the historical, social, and political context of American life. Query with sample chapters. Royalty.

MID-LIST PRESS— 4324 12th Ave. S., Minneapolis, MN 55407-3218. Marianne Nora, Assoc. Pub. Collections of short fiction and poetry, novels, and creative nonfiction. Interested in publishing "high literary merit and fresh artistic vision by new and emerging writers and by writers ignored, marginalized, or excluded from publication by commercial and mainstream publishers." Query. Royalty.

MILKWEED EDITIONS— 430 First Ave. N., Suite 400, Minneapolis, MN 55401-1743. Emilie Buchwald, Ed. "We publish excellent award-winning fiction, poetry, essays, and nonfiction, the kind of writing that makes for good reading." Publishes about 15 books a year. Send SASE for guidelines before submitting manuscript. Royalty. Also publishes *Milkweeds for Young Readers*: high quality novels for middle grades.

THE MILLBROOK PRESS—2 Old New Milford Rd., Brookfield, CT 06804. Meghann Hall, Ed. Asst. Nonfiction for early elementary grades through grades 7 and up, appropriate for the school and public library or trade market, encompassing curriculum-related topics and extracurricular interests. Some picture books. Imprint: *Copper Beech Books*. Query with outline and sample chapter. Royalty.

MIRA BOOKS—See *Harlequin Books/Canada*.

THE MIT PRESS—5 Cambridge Center, Cambridge, MA 02142. Larry Cohen, Ed.-in-Chief. Books on computer science/artificial intelligence; cognitive sciences; economics; finance; architecture; aesthetic and social theory; linguistics; technology studies; environmental studies; and neuroscience.

MONDO PUBLISHING—One Plaza Rd., Greenvale, NY 11548. Attn: Submissions Ed. Picture books, nonfiction, and early chapter books for readers ages 4 to 10. "We want to create beautiful books that children can read on their own and find so enjoyable that they'll want to come back to them time and time again." Query. Royalty.

MONTANA HISTORICAL SOCIETY—225 N. Roberts, Helena, MT 59620. Martha Kohl, Ed. Books on Montana history. Query. Royalty.

MOON HANDBOOKS—Moon Publications, Inc., P.O. Box 3040, Chico, CA 95927-3040. Taran March, Exec. Ed. Travel guides, 400 to 500 pages. Will consider multiple submissions. Query. Royalty.

MOREHOUSE PUBLISHING— 4775 Linglestown Rd., Harrisburg, PA 17112. Debra Farrington, Ed. Dir. Theology, pastoral care, church administration, spirituality, Anglican studies, history of religion, books for children, youth, elders, etc. Query with outline, contents, and sample chapter. SASE required. Royalty.

MORROW AND CO., INC., WILLIAM—1350 Ave. of the Americas, New York, NY 10019. Attn: Eds. Adult fiction and nonfiction: no unsolicited manuscripts. *Mulberry Books* (children's paperbacks), Amy Cohn, Ed. Dir.; *Hearst Books* (general nonfiction).

MOUNTAIN PRESS PUBLISHING—1301 S. 3rd W., P.O. Box 2399, Missoula, MT 59806. Attn: Kathleen Ort, Ed.-in-Chief Nonfiction, 300 pages: natural history, field guides, geology, horses, Western history, Americana, and outdoor guides. Query with outline and sample chapters; multiple queries considered. Royalty.

THE MOUNTAINEERS BOOKS—1001 S.W. Klickitat Way, Suite 201, Seattle, WA 98134. Margaret Foster, Ed.-in-Chief. Nonfiction books on non-competitive aspects of outdoor sports such as mountaineering, backpacking, walking, trekking, canoeing, kayaking, bicycling, skiing; independent adventure travel. Field guides, how-to and where-to guidebooks, biographies of outdoor people; accounts of expeditions. Natural history and conservation. Submit sample chapters and outline. Royalty.

MUIR PUBLICATIONS, JOHN—P.O. Box 613, Santa Fe, NM 87504-0613. Cassandra Conyers, Acq. Ed. Travel guidebooks for adults. Alternative health topics for adults and children. Send manuscript or query with sample chapters. No fiction. Royalty or work for hire.

MULBERRY BOOKS—See *William Morrow and Co., Inc.*

MULTNOMAH PUBLISHERS—(formerly *Questar Publishers*) 204 W. Adams Ave., P.O. Box 1720, Sisters, OR 97759. Attn: Ed. Evangelical, Christian publishing house with 3 imprints: *Multnomah Books*, message-driven, clean, moral, uplifting fiction (not necessarily religious), and nonfiction; address Ed. Dept. *Alabaster*, contemporary women's fiction that upholds strong Christian values; address Karen Ball, Ed. *Gold 'n' Honey*, developmentally appropriate stories for children; address Lois Keffer, Ed. Submit 2 or 3 sample chapters with outline, cover letter, and SASE. Royalty.

MUSTANG PUBLISHING CO., INC.—Box 3004, Memphis, TN 38173. Rollin A. Riggs, Ed. Nonfiction for 18-to 40-year-olds, specializing in travel, humor, and how-to. Send queries for 100-to 300-page books, with outlines and sample chapters. No phone calls. Royalty. SASE required.

THE MYSTERIOUS PRESS—Time and Life Bldg., 1271 Ave. of the Americas, New York, NY 10020. William Malloy, Ed.-in-Chief. Mystery/suspense novels. Agented manuscripts only.

NAIAD PRESS, INC.—Box 10543, Tallahassee, FL 32302. Barbara Grier, Ed. Adult fiction, 48,000 to 50,000 words, with lesbian themes and characters: mysteries, romances, gothics, ghost stories, westerns, regencies, spy novels, etc. Query with letter and one-page précis only. Royalty.

NATUREGRAPH PUBLISHERS—P.O. Box 1047, Happy Camp, CA 96039. Barbara Brown, Ed. Nonfiction: Native-American culture, natural history, outdoor living, land, gardening, Indian lore, and how-to. Query. Royalty.

THE NAVAL INSTITUTE PRESS—Annapolis, MD 21402. Attn: Acquisitions Dept. Nonfiction, 60,000 to 100,000 words: military histories; biographies; ship guides. Occasional military fiction, 75,000 to 110,000 words. Query with outline and sample chapters. Royalty.

NEW CANAAN PUBLISHING COMPANY—P.O. Box 752, New Canaan, CT 06840. Kathy Mittelstadt, Ed. Juvenile fiction, to 40,000 words, for readers ages 5 to 16. "We want children's books with strong educational and moral content." Submit complete manuscript. No multiple queries. Royalty.

NEW HORIZON PRESS—P.O. Box 669, Far Hills, NJ 07931. Joan Dunphy, Ed.-in-Chief. True stories, 96,000 words, dealing with contemporary issues, especially true crime, that revolve around a hero or heroine. Royalty. Query.

NEW LEAF PRESS, INC.—P.O. Box 726, Green Forest, AR 72638. Jim Fletcher, Acquisitions Ed. Nonfiction, 100 to 400 pages, for Christian readers: how to live the Christian life, devotionals, gift books. Query with outline and sample chapters. Royalty.

THE NEW PRESS— 450 W. 41st St., New York, NY 10036. Andre Schifrin, Dir. Serious nonfiction: history, economics, education, politics. Fiction in translation. Query required.

NEW RIVERS PRESS— 420 N. 5th St., Suite 910, Minneapolis, MN 55401. James Cihlar, Man. Ed. Collections of short stories, essays, and poems from emerging writers in upper Midwest. "Most of our books are published through the Minnesota Voices Project competition. SASE for guidelines."

NEW VICTORIA PUBLISHERS—P.O. Box 27, Norwich, VT 05055. ReBecca Béguin, Ed. Lesbian feminist fiction and nonfiction, including mystery, biography, history, fantasy; some humor and education. Guidelines. Query with outline and sample chapters; SASE. Royalty.

NEW WORLD LIBRARY—14 Pamaron Way, Novato, CA 94949. Attn: Submissions Ed. Inspirational and practical nonfiction books and audio cassettes on spirituality, personal growth, health and wellness, business and prosperity, religion, recovery, multicultural studies, and women's studies. "Dedicated to awakening individual and global potential." Query with outline, sample chapter, and SASE. Multiple queries accepted. Royalty.

NEWCASTLE PUBLISHING—13419 Saticoy St., N. Hollywood, CA 91605. Daryl Jacoby, Pub. Nonfiction manuscripts, 200 to 250 pages, for older adults on personal health, health care issues, psychology, and relationships. "We are not looking for fads or trends. We want books with a long shelf life." Multiple queries considered. Royalty.

NEWMARKET PRESS—18 E. 48th St., New York, NY 10017. Keith Hollaman, Exec. Ed. Nonfiction on health, psychology, self-help, child care, parenting, music, film, and personal finance. Query required. Royalty.

NORTH COUNTRY PRESS—RR 1, Box 1395, Unity, ME 04988. Patricia Newell, Mary Kenney, Eds. Nonfiction with a Maine and/or New England tie-in with emphasis on the outdoors; also limited fiction (Maine-based mystery). "Our goal is to publish high-quality books for people who love New England." Query with SASE, outline, and sample chapters. No unsolicited manuscripts. Royalty.

NORTHEASTERN UNIVERSITY PRESS—360 Huntington Ave., 416 CP, Boston, MA 02115. Scott Brassart, Ed. Nonfiction, 50,000 to 200,000 words: trade and scholarly titles in music, criminal justice, women's studies, ethnic studies, law, sociology, environmental studies, American history, and literary criticism. Submit query with outline and sample chapter or complete manuscript. Royalty.

NORTHERN ILLINOIS UNIVERSITY PRESS—DeKalb, IL 60115. Mary L. Lincoln, Dir. Books, 250 to 450 typescript pages, for scholars and informed general readers. Submit history, regional topics, literature and Russian studies topics to Mary Lincoln; philosophy, politics, anthropology, economics, and other social sciences to Martin Johnson. Query with outline. Royalty.

NORTHLAND PUBLISHING—P.O. Box 1389, Flagstaff, AZ 86002. Erin Murphy, Ed.-in-Chief. Nonfiction books on Western arts; Native American culture, myth, art, and crafts; Western regional nonfiction; and cookbooks. Unique children's picture books, 350 to 1,500 words, and middle reader chapter books, approximately 20,000 words, with American West/Southwest regional themes. Potential market for proposed adult and middle reader books. Query with outline, sample chapters. For children's books, send complete manuscript. "Include SASE with all submissions and queries. No queries by phone or fax." Royalty.

NORTHWORD PRESS, INC.—5900 Green Oak Dr., Minnetonka, MN 55343. Barbara K. Harold, Man. Ed. Nonfiction nature and wildlife books for children and adults. Send SASE with 7 first-class stamps for catalogue and SASE for guidelines. Royalty or flat fee.

NORTON AND CO., INC., W.W.—500 Fifth Ave., New York, NY 10110. Attn: Ed. High-quality literary fiction and nonfiction. No occult, paranormal, religious, genre fiction (formula romance, science fiction, westerns), arts and crafts, young adult, or children's books. No unsolicited manuscripts.

NTC/CONTEMPORARY PUBLISHING GROUP—4255 W. Touhy Ave., Lincolnwood, IL 60646. John T. Nolan, Ed. Dir. Trade nonfiction, 100 to 400 pages, on health, fitness, sports, cooking, humor, business, popular culture, finance, women's issues, quilting, and crafts. Query with outline, sample chapter, and SASE. Royalty.

ODYSSEY CLASSICS—See *Harcourt Brace & Co. Children's Book Div.*

OHIO UNIVERSITY PRESS/SWALLOW PRESS—Scott Quadrangle, Athens, OH 45701. David Sanders, Dir. Scholarly nonfiction, 350 to 450 manuscript pages, especially literary criticism, regional studies, African studies. *Swallow Press*: general interest and western Americana. Query with outline and sample chapters. Royalty.

THE OLIVER PRESS—Charlotte Square, 5707 W. 36th St., Minneapolis, MN 55416. Teresa Faden, Ed. Collective biographies for young adults. Submit proposals for books, 20,000 to 25,000 words, on people who have made an impact in such areas as history, politics, crime, science, and business. Flat fee (approximately $1,000).

OPEN COURT PUBLISHING CO.—332 S. Michigan Ave., Suite 2000, Chicago, IL 60604. Attn: Acquisitions Dept. Scholarly books on philosophy, Jungian psychology, psychology, personal stories of development, religion, eastern thought, history, public policy, feminist thought, education, science, social issues, contemporary culture, and related topics. Send sample chapters with outline and resumé. Royalty.

ORCHARD BOOKS—95 Madison Ave., New York, NY 10016. Sarah Caguiat, Ed. Ana Cerro, Ed. Dominic Barth, Assoc. Ed. Juvenile fiction. Picture books and middle-grade fiction, 100 to 150 pages. Limited amount of nonfiction. No unsolicited manuscripts. Query only.

ORCHISES PRESS—P.O. Box 20602, Alexandria, VA 22320-1602. Roger Lathbury, Ed. Nonfiction books, 128 to 500 pages; and intellectually sophisticated, technically expert poetry books, 48 to 128 pages. No fiction. Query with sample chapters. Royalty.

OREGON STATE UNIVERSITY PRESS—101 Waldo Hall, Corvallis, OR 97331. Attn: Ed. Dept. Scholarly books in a limited range of disciplines and books of particular importance to the Pacific Northwest, especially dealing with the history, natural history, culture, and literature of the region or with natural resource issues. Query with summary of manuscript.

ORTHO BOOKS—See *Meredith Corp. Book Publishing.*

OSBORNE/MCGRAW HILL—2600 Tenth St., Berkeley, CA 94710. Scott Rogers, Ed.-in-Chief. Computer books for general and technical audience. Query. Royalty.

OUR SUNDAY VISITOR PUBLISHING—200 Noll Plaza, Huntington, IN 46750. Jacquelyn M. Lindsey, Jim Manney, Acquisitions Eds. Catholic-oriented books of various lengths. No fiction. Query with outline and sample chapters. Royalty.

THE OVERLOOK PRESS—386 W. Broadway, 4th Fl., New York, NY 10012. Tracy Carns, Pub. Dir. Literary fiction, some fantasy/science fiction, foreign literature in translation, general nonfiction, including art, architecture, design, film, history, biography, crafts/lifestyle, martial arts, Hudson Valley regional interest, and children's books. Query with outline, sample chapters and SASE. Royalty.

OWEN PUBLISHERS, INC., RICHARD C.—Dept. TW, P.O. Box 585, Katonah, NY 10536. Janice Boland, Ed. Fiction and nonfiction. Brief story-books, approximately 45 to 100 words, suitable for 5- and 7-year-old beginning readers for the "Books for Young Learners" collection. Also, short stories that interest, inform, inspire, fascinate, and entertain, for 7- and 8-year olds for "Books for Fluent Readers" collection. Royalties for writers. Flat fee for illustrators. Writers must send SASE for guidelines before submitting.

OXFORD UNIVERSITY PRESS—198 Madison Ave., New York, NY 10016. Attn: Ed. Dept. Authoritative books on literature, history, philosophy, etc.; college textbooks, medical, scientific, technical and reference books. Query. Royalty.

PAGES PUBLISHING—801 94th Ave. N., St. Petersburg, FL 33702. Acquisitions Ed. Novels, 20,000 to 24,000 words, and nonfiction, to 20,000 words for children in grades 5 to 8; middle-grade fiction, 14,000 words, for readers in grades 3 to 6; beginning chapter books, 500 to 2,000 words; and fiction and picture books, 250 to 800 words for younger readers. For picture books and shorter works, send complete manuscript; for novels, send 3 sample chapters and outline. Include bio, word count, and SASE with any submission.

PANTHEON BOOKS—201 E. 50th St., New York, NY 10022. Attn: Ed. Dept. Quality fiction and nonfiction. Query required. Royalty.

PAPIER-MACHE PRESS—627 Walker St., Watsonville, CA 95076. Sandra Martz, Ed. Theme anthologies; 6 to 8 books annually. "We emphasize, but are not limited to, the publication of books and related items for midlife and older women." Write for guidelines. Royalty.

PARA PUBLISHING—P.O. Box 8206-238, Santa Barbara, CA 93118-8206. Dan Poynter, Ed. Adult nonfiction books on parachutes and skydiving only. Author must present evidence of having made at least 1,000 jumps. Query. Royalty.

PARAGON HOUSE—2700 University Ave. W., Suite 200, St. Paul, MN 55114-1016. Gordon Anderson, Pub. Serious nonfiction, including philosophy, religion, and current affairs. Query. Royalty.

PASSPORT BOOKS— 4255 W. Touhy Ave., Lincolnwood, IL 60646-1975. Linda Gray, Ed. Adult nonfiction, 200 to 400 pages, picture books up to 120 pages, and juvenile nonfiction. Send outline and sample chapters for books on foreign language, travel, and culture. Multiple queries considered. Royalty and flat fee.

PAULIST PRESS—997 Macarthur Blvd., Mahwah, NJ 07430. Donald Brophy, Man. Ed. Adult nonfiction, 100 to 400 pages; and picture books, 8 to 10 pages, for readers 5 to 7 or 8 to 10. For adult books, query with outline and sample chapters. For juvenile books, submit complete manuscript to Karen Scialabba, Ed. Royalty.

PEACHPIT PRESS—1249 Eighth St., Berkeley, CA 94710. Cheryl Applewood, Man. Ed. Books on computer and graphic-design topics. Query with outline and sample chapters for manuscripts 100 to 1,100 words, or see proposal template on web site: http://www.peachpit.com.

PEACHTREE PUBLISHERS, LTD.— 494 Armour Cir. N.E., Atlanta, GA 30324. Attn: Ed. Dept. Wide variety of children, juvenile, and young adult books, fiction and nonfiction. No religious material, science fiction/fantasy, romance, mystery/detective, and historical fiction; no business, scientific, or technical books. Send outline and sample chapters. SASE required. Royalty.

PELICAN PUBLISHING CO., INC.—P.O. Box 3110, Gretna, LA 70054. Nina Kooij, Ed.-in-Chief. General nonfiction: Americana, regional, architecture, travel, cookbooks. Royalty.

PENGUIN BOOKS—375 Hudson St., New York, NY 10014. Attn: Ed. Dept. Adult fiction and nonfiction paperbacks. Royalty.

THE PERMANENT PRESS—Noyac Rd., Sag Harbor, NY 11963. Judith Shepard, Ed. Original and arresting novels. Query. Royalty.

PERSPECTIVES PRESS—P.O. Box 90318, Indianapolis, IN 46290-0318. Pat Johnston, Pub. Nonfiction books on infertility, adoption, closely related reproductive health and child welfare issues (foster care, etc.). "Writers must read our guidelines before submitting." Query. Royalty. See web site for guidelines: www.perspectivespress.com.

PHILOMEL BOOKS—345 Hudson St., New York, NY 10014. Patricia Lee Gauch, Ed. Dir. Michael Green, Ed. Juvenile picture books, young adult fiction, and some biographies. Fresh, original work with compelling characters and "a truly childlike spirit." Query required.

PINEAPPLE PRESS—P.O. Box 3899, Sarasota, FL 34230. June Cussen, Ed. Serious fiction and nonfiction, Florida-oriented, 60,000 to 125,000 words. Query with outline, sample chapters, and SASE. Royalty.

PINNACLE BOOKS— 850 Third Ave., New York, NY 10022. Paul Dinas, Ed.-in-Chief. Nonfiction books: true crime, celebrity biographies, and humor. Unsolicited material not accepted.

PIPPIN PRESS—229 E. 85th St., Gracie Sta., Box 1347, New York, NY 10028. Barbara Francis, Pub. Small chapter books for children ages 7 to 10, with historical fiction and fantasy themes, as well as ethnic stories and humorous mysteries; imaginative nonfiction for children of all ages. Query with SASE only; no unsolicited manuscripts. Royalty.

PLANET DEXTER—One Jacob Way, Reading, MA 01867-3999. Nonfiction books for children ages 8 to 12. All product developed internally. No unsolicited submissions.

PLAYERS PRESS, INC.—P.O. Box 1132, Studio City, CA 91614. Robert Gordon, Ed. Plays and musicals for children and adults; juvenile and adult nonfiction related to theatre, film, television, and the performing arts. Lengths vary. Query. Royalty.

PLEASANT COMPANY— 8400 Fairway Pl., Middleton, WI 58562-0998. Jennifer Hirsch, Submissions Ed. Books, 10,000 to 40,000 words, for 8-to 12-year-old girls: historical mystery/suspense, contemporary fiction, and contemporary advice and activity. "We have a small 'concept-driven' list and do not use inexperienced writers." Query with outline and sample chapters or send complete manuscript. Pays on a flat fee or royalty basis.

PLENUM PUBLISHING CORP.—233 Spring St., New York, NY 10013. Linda Greenspan Regan, Exec. Ed. Trade nonfiction, approximately 300 pages, on popular science, criminology, psychology, social science, anthropology, and health. Query required. Royalty. Hardcover.

PLUME BOOKS—375 Hudson St., New York, NY 10014. Attn: Ed. Dept. Nonfiction: hobbies, business, health, cooking, child care, psychology, history, popular culture, biography, and politics. Fiction: serious literary and gay. Query.

POCKET BOOKS—1230 Ave. of the Americas, New York, NY 10020. Adult and young adult fiction and nonfiction. Mystery line: police procedurals, private eye, and amateur sleuth novels, 60,000 to 70,000 words. Royalty.

POPULAR PRESS—Bowling Green State Univ., Bowling Green, OH 43403. Ms. Pat Browne, Ed. Nonfiction, 250 to 400 pages, examining some aspect of popular culture. Query with outline. Flat fee or royalty.

POTTER, CLARKSON —201 E. 50th St., New York, NY 10022. Lauren Shakely, Ed. Dir. Illustrated trade books about such topics as cooking, gardening, and decorating. Submissions accepted through agents only.

PRAEGER PUBLISHERS— 88 Post Rd. W., Westport, CT 06880-4232. Attn: Pub. General nonfiction; scholarly and textbooks. Query with outline. Royalty.

PRESIDIO PRESS—505B San Marin Dr., Suite 300, Novato, CA 94945-1340. Attn: Ed. Dept. Nonfiction: military history and military affairs, from 90,000 words. Fiction: selected military and action-adventure works from 100,000 words. Query. Royalty.

PRICE STERN SLOAN, INC.—200 Madison Ave., New York, NY 10016. Lara Bergen, Ed. Dir. Witty or edgy middle grade fiction and nonfiction, calendars, and novelty juvenile titles. Imprints include *Troubador Press, Wee Sing, MadLibs.* Query with SASE required. Royalty.

PRIMA PUBLISHING—3875 Atherton Rd., Rocklin, CA 95765. Ben Dominitz, Pub. Steven K. Martin, Ed. Dir. Susan Silva, Jamie Miller, Eds. Nonfiction on variety of subjects, including business, health, self-help, entertainment, computers, inspiration, and cookbooks. "We want books with originality, written by highly qualified individuals." Advance against royalty.

PROMPT PUBLICATIONS—2647 Waterfront Pkwy. E. Dr., Indianapolis, IN 46214-2041. Attn: Acquisitions Ed. Nonfiction softcover technical books on electronics, how-to, troubleshooting and repair, electrical engineering, video and sound equipment, cellular technology, etc., for all levels of technical experience. Query with outline, sample chapters, author bio, and SASE. Royalty.

PRUETT PUBLISHING COMPANY—2928 Pearl St., Boulder, CO 80301. Jim Pruett, Pub. Nonfiction: outdoors and recreation, western U.S. history, travel, natural history and the environment, fly fishing. Query. Royalty.

PUTNAM'S SONS, G.P.—345 Hudson St., New York, NY 10014. Attn: Children's Ed. Dept. General trade nonfiction and fiction for ages 2 to 18. Mostly picture books and middle-grade novels. No unsolicited manuscripts. Royalty.

QED PRESS—155 Cypress St., Fort Bragg, CA 95437. Cynthia Frank, Ed. Health, gerontology, and psychology books. Query with outline and sample chapters. Royalty.

QUEST BOOKS—Theosophical Publishing House, 306 W. Geneva Rd., P. O. Box 270, Wheaton, IL 60189-0270. Brenda Rosen, Exec. Ed. Nonfiction books on Eastern and Western religion and philosophy, holism, healing, transpersonal psychology, men's and women's spirituality, creativity, meditation, yoga, ancient wisdom. Query. Royalty.

QUESTAR PUBLISHERS—See *Multnomah Publishers.*

QUILL TRADE PAPERBACKS—Imprint of William Morrow and Co., Inc., 1350 Ave. of the Americas, New York, NY 10019. Trade paperback adult fiction and nonfiction. Submit through agent only.

QUIXOTE PRESS—3544 Blakeslee St., Wever, IA 52658. Bruce Carlson, Pres. Adult fiction and nonfiction including humor, folklore, and regional cookbooks; some juvenile fiction. Query with sample chapters and outline. Royalty.

RAGGED MOUNTAIN PRESS—A Div. of McGraw-Hill, Box 220, Camden, ME 04843. Jonathan Eaton, Ed. Dir. Jeff Serena, Acquisitions Ed. Books on outdoor recreation.

RAINTREE STECK-VAUGHN PUBLISHERS—466 Southern Blvd., Chatham, NJ 07928. Walter Kossmann, Frank Sloan, Eds. Nonfiction books, 5,000 to 30,000 words, for school and library market: biographies for grades 3 and up; and science, social studies, and history books for primary grades through high school. Query with outline and sample chapters; SASE required. Flat fee or royalty.

RANDOM HOUSE, INC.—201 E. 50th St., New York, NY 10022. Attn: Ed. Dept. General fiction and nonfiction. Agented material only.

RANDOM HOUSE JUVENILE DIV.—201 E. 50th St., New York, NY 10022. Kate Klimo, Pub. Dir. Fiction and nonfiction for beginning readers; paperback fiction line for 7-to 9-year-olds. No unsolicited manuscripts. Agented material only.

RED CRANE BOOKS—2008 Rosina St., Suite B, Santa Fe, NM 87505. Marianne O'Shaughnessy, Ed. Art and folk art, bilingual material with Spanish and English, cookbooks, essays, gardening, herbal guides, natural history, novels, social and political issues and social history. No children's books. Send a short synopsis, 2 sample chapters, resumé, and SASE.

RED SAGE PUBLISHING, INC.—P.O. Box 4844, Seminole, FL 33775. Alexandria Kendall, Acquisitions Ed. Novella submissions for anthologies. Sensual romantic fiction, 20,000 to 30,000 words. "Love scenes should be sophisticated, erotic, and emotional. Push the envelope beyond the normal romance novel." Query with first 10 pages and synopsis. Royalty.

THE RED SEA PRESS—11-D Princess Rd., Suites D, E, F, Lawrenceville, NJ 08648. Kassahun Checole, Pub. Adult nonfiction, 360 double-spaced manuscript pages. "We focus on nonfiction material with a specialty on the Horn of Africa." Query. Royalty.

RED WAGON BOOKS—(Imprint of *Harcourt, Brace & Co. Children's Books*) 525 B St., Suite 1900, San Diego, CA 92101-4495. Attn: Acquisitions Ed. No unsolicited manuscripts. Query with SASE.

REGNERY PUBLISHING, INC.—One Massachusetts Ave., N.W., Washington, DC 20001. Attn: Ed. Dept. Nonfiction books. Query. Royalty.

RENAISSANCE HOUSE—541 Oak St., P. O. Box 177, Frederick, CO 80530. Eleanor H. Ayer, Ed. Regional guidebooks. Guidebooks on CO, AZ, CA, and the Southwest. "We use only manuscripts written to our specifications for new or ongoing series." "Not accepting unsolicited manuscripts at this time."

REPUBLIC OF TEXAS PRESS—See *Wordware Publishing*.

RISING TIDE PRESS—3831 N. Oracle Rd., Tucson, AZ 85705. Lee Boojamra, Ed. Books for, by, and about lesbians. Fiction, 60,000 to 80,000 words: romance, mystery, and science fiction/fantasy. Nonfiction, 40,000 to 60,000 words. Royalty. Reports in 3 months. SASE for guidelines.

RIZZOLI INTERNATIONAL PUBLICATIONS, INC.—300 Park Ave. S., New York, NY 10010. Manuela Soares, Children's Book Ed. Original manuscripts that introduce children to fine art, folk art, and architecture of all cultures for a small list. Nonfiction and fiction for all ages. Query with SASE or response card. Royalty.

ROC—375 Hudson St., New York, NY 10014. Laura Anne Gilman, Exec. Ed. Jennifer Heddle, Ed. Asst. Science fiction, fantasy. Send agented manuscripts to Laura Anne Gilman; unagented manuscripts to Jennifer Heddle.

ROCKBRIDGE PUBLISHING—P.O. Box 351, Berryville, VA 22611. Katherine Tennery, Ed. Book-length nonfiction on the Civil War, Virginia history, and travel guides to Virginia. Query. Royalty.

RODALE PRESS, INC.—400 S. 10th St., Emmaus, PA 18098. Pat Corpora, Pres. Books on health (men's, women's alternative, senior), gardening, cookbooks, spirituality, fitness, and pets. Query with resumé, table of contents/outline, and two sample chapters. Royalty and outright purchase. "We have a large in-house writing staff; the majority of our books are conceived and developed in-house. We're always looking for truly competent free lancers to write chapters for books." Payment on a work-for-hire basis; address Sally Reith, Asst. Acquisitions Ed.

ROSE COMMUNICATIONS—See *Hysteria Publications*.

ROYAL FIREWORKS PRESS—Box 399, First Ave., Unionville, NY 10988. Charles Morgan, Ed. Adult science fiction and mysteries. Juvenile and young adult fiction, biography, and educational nonfiction. Submit complete manuscripts with a brief plot overview. No multiple queries. Allow a three-week response time. Royalty.

RUNNING PRESS—125 S. 22nd St., Philadelphia, PA 19103. Attn: Asst. to Ed. Dir. Trade nonfiction: art, craft, how-to, self-help, science, lifestyles. Young adult books and interactive packages. Query with outline or table of contents and two-to three-page writing sample. Royalty for some projects; flat fee for others.

RUSSIAN HILL PRESS—1250 17th St., 2nd Fl., San Francisco, CA 94107. Kit Cooley, Asst. Ed. Books, 50,000 to 120,000 words. Literary and mainstream fiction, including thrillers and suspense. Nonfiction in the areas of politics, sociology, and literary biography. Royalty.

RUTGERS UNIVERSITY PRESS—100 Joyce Kilmer Ave., Piscataway, NJ 08854-8099. Paula Kantenwein, Editorial Asst. Nonfiction, 70,000 to 120,000 words. Query with outline and sample chapters. Royalty.

RUTLEDGE HILL PRESS—211 Seventh Ave. N., Nashville, TN 37219. Mike Towle, Ed. Market-specific nonfiction. Query with outline and sample chapters. Royalty.

ST. ANTHONY MESSENGER PRESS—1615 Republic St., Cincinnati, OH 45210-1298. Lisa Biedenbach, Man. Ed. Inspirational nonfiction for Catholics, supporting a Christian lifestyle in our culture; prayer aids, scripture, church history, education, practical spirituality, parish ministry, liturgy resources, Franciscan resources, family-based religious education program, and children's books. Query with 500-word summary. Royalty.

ST. MARTIN'S PRESS—175 Fifth Ave., New York, NY 10010. Attn: Ed. Dept. General adult fiction and nonfiction. Query. Royalty.

SAINT MARY'S PRESS—702 Terrace Heights, Winona, MN 55987-1320. Stephan Nagel, Ed.-in-Chief. Progressive Catholic publisher. Fiction, to 40,000 words, for young adults ages 14 to 17, "that gives insight into the struggle of teens to become healthy, hopeful adults and also sheds light on Catholic experience, history, or cultures." Query with outline and sample chapter. Royalty.

SANDLAPPER PUBLISHING, INC.—P.O. Drawer 730, Orangeburg, SC 29116-0730. Amanda Gallman, Book Ed. Nonfiction books on South Carolina history, culture, cuisine. Query with outline, sample chapters, and SASE. "No phone calls, please."

SASQUATCH BOOKS—615 2nd Ave., Suite 260, Seattle, WA 98104. Attn: Ed. Dept. Regional books on a wide range of nonfiction topics: travel, natural history, gardening, cooking, history, and public affairs. Books should have a Pacific Northwest and/or West Coast subject or theme. Query with SASE. Royalty.

SCARECROW PRESS—4720 Boston Way, Lanham, MD 20706. Shirley Lambert, Assoc. Pub. Reference works and bibliographies, from 150 pages, especially in the areas of library and information science, cinema, TV, radio, and theater, mainly for use by libraries. Query or send complete manuscript; multiple queries considered. Royalty.

SCHOCKEN BOOKS—201 E. 50th St., New York, NY 10022. Attn: Ed. Dept. General nonfiction: Judaica, women's studies, education, history, religion, psychology, cultural studies. Query with outline and sample chapter. Royalty.

SCHOLASTIC, INC.—555 Broadway, New York, NY 10012-3999. No unsolicited manuscripts.

SCHOLASTIC PROFESSIONAL BOOKS—555 Broadway, New York, NY 10012-3999. Attn: Shawn Richardson. Books by and for teachers of kindergarten through eighth grade. *Instructor Books*: practical, activity/resource books on teaching reading and writing, science, math, etc. *Teaching Strategies Books*: 64 to 96 pages on new ideas, practices, and approaches to teaching. Query with outline, sample chapters or activities, contents page, and resumé. Flat fee or royalty. Multiple queries considered. 8½" x 11" SASE for guidelines.

SCHWARTZ BOOKS, ANNE—Atheneum Publishers, 1230 Ave. of the Americas, New York, NY 10020. Anne Schwartz, Ed. Dir. Picture books through juvenile fiction and nonfiction as well as illustrated collections. Query; no unsolicited manuscripts.

SCOTT FORESMAN/ADDISON WESLEY—1900 E. Lake Ave., Glenview, IL 60025. Kathy Costello, Pres. Elementary and secondary textbooks. Royalty or flat fee.

SCRIBNER—1230 Ave. of the Americas, New York, NY 10020. Attn: Ed. Dept. No unsolicited manuscripts.

SEAL PRESS—3131 Western Ave., Suite 410, Seattle, WA 98121-1041. Jennie Goode, Man Ed. Feminist/women's studies books: popular culture and lesbian studies; parenting; domestic violence; health and recovery; sports and outdoors. Query. Royalty.

SEASIDE PRESS—See *Wordware Publishing*.

SEEDLING PUBLICATIONS— 4079 Overlook Dr. E., Columbus, OH 43214-2931. Lynn Salem, Ed. Picture books, fiction, and nonfiction for beginning readers. Books run no more than 300 words. "No stories in rhyme. Stories must have strong storyline or unique twist in events. Books must be for independent readers." Submit complete manuscript. Royalty or flat fee.

SEVEN STORIES PRESS—140 Watts St., New York, NY 10013. Dan Simon, Pub. Small press. Fiction and nonfiction. Query with SASE. Royalty.

SHAW PUBLISHERS, HAROLD—388 Gunderson Dr., Box 567, Wheaton, IL 60189. Lori McCullough, Ed. Asst. Nonfiction, 120 to 320 pages, with an evangelical Christian perspective. Some fiction and literary books. Query. Flat fee or royalty.

SHEARWATER BOOKS—See *Island Press*.

SHOE STRING PRESS—P.O. Box 657, 2 Linsley St., North Haven, CT 06473-2517. Diantha C. Thorpe, Ed./Pub. Books for children and teenagers, including juvenile nonfiction for ages 10 up. Resources for teachers and librarians that share high standards of scholarship and practical experience. Imprints include *Linnet Books, Archon Books,* and *Linnet Professional Publications.* Submit outline and sample chapters. Royalty.

SIERRA CLUB BOOKS— 85 Second St., San Francisco, CA 94105. Attn: Ed. Dept. Nonfiction: environment, natural history, the sciences, outdoors and regional guidebooks, nature photography; children's fiction and nonfiction. Query with SASE. Royalty.

SIGNAL HILL PUBLICATIONS—1320 Jamesville Ave., Box 131, Syracuse, NY 13210. Terrie Lipke, Ed. Asst. Fiction and nonfiction, 5,000 to 9,000 words for adults who read at low levels, for use in adult basic education and ESL programs, volunteer literacy organizations, and job training programs. Guidelines. Query; no unsolicited manuscripts. Royalty.

SILHOUETTE BOOKS—300 E. 42nd St., New York, NY 10017. Isabel Swift, V.P. Ed. Tara Gavin, Ed. Mgr. *Silhouette Romance*: Joan Marlow Golan, Sr. Ed. Contemporary romances, 53,000 to 58,000 words. *Special Edition*: Karen Taylor Richman, Sr. Ed. Sophisticated contemporary romances, 75,000 to 80,000 words. *Silhouette Desire*: Sensuous contemporary romances, 53,000 to 60,000 words. *Intimate Moments*: Leslie Wainger, Exec. Sr. Ed. Sensuous, exciting contemporary romances, 80,000 words. *Silhouette Yours Truly*: Leslie Wainger, Sr. Ed. Contemporary, fun romances, 50,000 words, with written word hook. Historical romance: 95,000 to 105,000 words, and more; query with synopsis and 3 sample chapters to Tracy Farrell, Sr. Ed. Query with synopsis and SASE to appropriate editor. Tipsheets available.

SILVER MOON PRESS—160 Fifth Ave., Suite 622, New York, NY 10010.

SILVER WHISTLE—See *Harcourt Brace & Co. Children's Book Div.*

SIMON & SCHUSTER—1230 Ave. of the Americas, New York, NY 10020. Adult books. No unsolicited material; manuscripts must be submitted by an agent.

SIMON & SCHUSTER BOOKS FOR YOUNG READERS—1230 Ave. of the Americas, New York, NY 10020. Stephanie Owens Lurie, Assoc. Pub./ V.P./Ed. Dir. Books for ages preschool through high school: picture books to young adult; nonfiction for all age levels. Hardcover only. Request guidelines before querying. SASE required for reply.

SINGER MEDIA CORP.—Seaview Business Park, 1030 Calle Cordillera, #106, San Clemente, CA 92673. Helen J. Lee, Acquisitions Dir. International literary agency and syndicate specializing in licensing foreign rights to books in the fields of business, management, celebrity biographies, self-help, occult, and fiction in all genres. Previously published books only. No poetry. Query first with SASE.

SKYLARK BOOKS—See *Yearling Books.*

THE SMITH—69 Joralemon St., Brooklyn, NY 11201-4003. Harry Smith, Pub./Ed. Michael McGrinder, Assoc Ed. Fiction, send up to 2 chapters (no synopsis); literary nonfiction, send outline and up to 2 chapters; and poetry, no more than 7 poems. "While publishing at a high level of craftsmanship, we have pursued the increasingly difficult, expensive, and now relatively rare policy of keeping our titles in print over the decades." Query; no complete manuscripts. Royalty. SASE.

SMITH AND KRAUS, INC.—P.O. Box 127, Main St., Lyme, NH 03768. Marisa Smith, Pres. Material of interest to the theatre community, collections of major American playwrights, annuals. Monologues, scenes, and plays that have been published in the current theatrical year. Plays and material for grades K through 12.

SOHO PRESS—853 Broadway, New York, NY 10003. Juris Jurjevics, Pub. Mysteries, thrillers, and contemporary fiction and nonfiction, from 60,000 words. Send SASE and complete manuscript. Royalty.

SOUNDPRINTS—353 Main Ave., Norwalk, CT 06851. Cassia Farkas, Ed. Factual children's books, 800 to 2,000 words, about oceanic and backyard animals, habitats, and history for young readers in preschool through fifth grade. No anthropomorphism. "Read one of our current stories in the relevant series before submitting or send SASE for guidelines." Pays flat fee.

SOURCEBOOKS—P.O. Box 372, Naperville, IL 60566. Todd Stocke, Ed. How-to and reference titles, including business, parenting, self-help, new age, gift-oriented, and health. Query with outline and sample chapters. Royalty.

SOUTHERN ILLINOIS UNIVERSITY PRESS—P.O. Box 3697, Carbondale, IL 62902-3697. James Simmons, Ed. Dir. Nonfiction in the humanities, 200 to 300 pages. Query with outline and sample chapters. Royalty.

SOUTHERN METHODIST UNIVERSITY PRESS—Box 415, Dallas, TX 75275. Kathryn Lang, Sr. Ed. Literary fiction. Nonfiction: scholarly studies in religion, medical ethics (death and dying); film, theater; scholarly works on

Texas or Southwest. No juvenile material, science fiction, or poetry. Query. Royalty.

SPECIAL EDITION—See *Silhouette Books.*

SPECTACLE LANE PRESS—Box 1237, Mt. Pleasant, SC 29465-1237. Attn: Ed. Dept. Humor books, 500 to 5,000 words, on subjects of strong, current interest, illustrated with cartoons. Buys text or text/cartoon packages. Occasional nonfiction, non-humor books on provocative subjects of wide concern. Royalty.

SPINSTERS INK—32 E. First St., #330, Duluth, MN 55802. Nancy Walker, Acquisitions Ed. Adult fiction and nonfiction books, 200-plus pages, that deal with significant issues in women's lives from a feminist perspective and encourage change and growth. Main characters and/or narrators must be women. Query with synopsis. Royalty.

SPLENDOR ROMANCES—See *Kensington Publishing Corp.*

STACKPOLE BOOKS—5067 Ritter Rd., Mechanicsburg, PA 17055. Judith Schnell, Ed. Dir. Books on the outdoors, nature, fishing, carving, woodworking, sports, sporting literature, cooking, gardening, history, and military reference. Query. Royalty; advance. Unsolicited materials will not be returned.

STA-KRIS, INC.—P.O. Box 1131, Marshalltown, IA 50158. Kathy Wagoner, Pres. Nonfiction adult-level gift books that portray universal feelings, truths, and values; or have a special-occasion theme. Query with bio, list of credits, complete manuscript, and SASE.

STANDARD PUBLISHING— 8121 Hamilton Ave., Cincinnati, OH 45231. Attn: Acquisitions Coord. Christian education resources and children's books. No unsolicited material except for Program books, which include material for special days such as Easter, Mother's Day, Father's Day, Thanksgiving, and Christmas. Guidelines.

STANFORD UNIVERSITY PRESS—Stanford University, Stanford, CA 94305-2235. Norris Pope, Dir. "For the most part, we publish academic scholarship." No original fiction or poetry. Query with outline and sample chapters. Royalty.

STARBURST PUBLISHERS—Box 4123, Lancaster, PA 17604. David A. Robie, Ed. Dir. Health, inspiration, Christian and self-help books. Query with outline for nonfiction book, synopsis for fiction book, and 3 sample chapters. Royalty. SASE. Web site: www.starburstpublisher.com.

STARRHILL PRESS—Black Belt Publishing, LLC, P.O. Box 551, Montgomery, AL 36101. Attn: Submission Ed. Affordable, succinct titles on American arts and letters. Query with cover letter, outline, author bio, and SASE for reply. Royalty varies.

STEMMER HOUSE PUBLISHERS, INC.—2627 Caves Rd., Owings Mills, MD 21117. Barbara Holdridge, Ed. Juvenile picture books and adult nonfiction. Specializes in art, design, cookbooks, children's, and horticultural titles. Query with SASE. Royalty.

STERLING PUBLISHING CO., INC.—387 Park Ave. S., New York, NY 10016. Sheila Anne Barry, Acquisitions Dir. How-to, hobby, woodworking, alternative health and healing, fiber arts, crafts, dolls and puppets, ghosts, wine, nature, oddities, new consciousness, puzzles, juvenile humor and activities, juvenile nature and science, medieval history, Celtic topics, gardening, alternative lifestyle, business, pets, recreation, sports and games books, reference, and home decorating. Query with outline, sample chapter, and sample illustrations. Royalty.

STONEYDALE PRESS—523 Main St., Box 188, Stevensville, MT 59870. Dale A. Burk, Ed. Adult nonfiction, primarily how-to, on outdoor recreation with emphasis on big game hunting. "We're a very specialized market. Query with outline and sample chapters essential." Royalty.

STOREY COMMUNICATIONS—Schoolhouse Rd., Pownal, VT 05261. Gwen Steege, Ed. Dir. How-to books for country living. Adult books, 100 to 350 pages, on gardening, animals, crafts, building, beer, and how-to. Royalty or flat fee.

STORY LINE PRESS—Three Oaks Farm, Brownsville, OR 97327-9718. Robert McDowell, Ed. Fiction, nonfiction, and poetry of varying lengths. Query. Royalty.

STRAWBERRY HILL PRESS—3848 S.E. Division St., Portland, OR 97202-1641. Carolyn Soto, Ed. Nonfiction: biography, autobiography, history, cooking, health, how-to, philosophy, performance arts, and Third World. Query with sample chapters, outline, and SASE. Royalty.

SUCCESS PUBLISHERS—Imprint of Markowski International Publishers, One Oakglade Cir., Hummelstown, PA 17036. Marjorie L. Markowski, Ed. Nonfiction, from 30,000 words: personal development, self-help, sales and marketing, leadership training, network marketing, motivation, and success topics. "We are interested in how-to, motivational, and instructional books of short to medium length that will serve recognized and emerging needs of society." Query with outline and 3 sample chapters. Royalty.

TAYLOR PUBLISHING CO.—1550 W. Mockingbird Ln., Dallas, TX 75235. Attn: Ed. Dept. Adult nonfiction: gardening, sports, health, popular culture, celebrity biographies, parenting, home improvement. Query with outline, sample chapter, author bio, and SASE. Royalty.

TEACHING STRATEGIES BOOKS—See *Scholastic Professional Books*.

TEMPLE UNIVERSITY PRESS—1601 N. Broad St., USB 306, Philadelphia, PA 19122-6099. Janet Francendese, Ed. Adult nonfiction. Query with outline and sample chapters. Royalty.

TEN SPEED PRESS—P.O. Box 7123, Berkeley, CA 94707. Attn: Ed. Dept. Self-help and how-to on careers, recreation, etc.; natural science, history, cookbooks. Imprints include: *Tricycle Press* and *Celestial Arts*. Query with outline, sample chapters, and SASE. Paperback. Royalty.

THIRD WORLD PRESS—P.O. Box 19730, Chicago, IL 60619. Attn: Ed. Board. "Progressive Black Publishing." Adult fiction, nonfiction, and poetry, as well juvenile fiction and young adult books. Query with outline. Royalty. E-mail twpress@aol.com for guidelines.

THUNDER'S MOUTH PRESS—841 Broadway, 4th Fl., New York, NY 10012. Neil Ortenberg, Pub. Jeri T. Smith, Ed. Mainly nonfiction: current affairs, popular culture, memoirs, and biography, to 300 pages. Royalty. Not currently publishing fiction.

TIA CHUCHA PRESS—P.O. Box 476969, Chicago, IL 60647. Luis Rodriguez, Ed. All types of poetry, approximately 60 to 100 pages. Annual deadline: June 30. Royalty.

TIARE PUBLICATIONS—P.O. Box 493, Lake Geneva, WI 53147. Gerry L. Dexter, Ed. General nonfiction, *Limelight* imprint; jazz discographies and commentaries, *Balboa* imprint. Query with outline and sample chapters. Royalties.

TILBURY HOUSE—132 Water St., Gardiner, ME 04345. Attn: Acquisitions Ed. Children's books that deal with cultural diversity or the environment; appeal to children and parents as well as the educational market; and offer possibilities for developing a separate teacher's guide. Adult books: nonfiction books about Maine or the Northeast. Query with outline and sample chapters.

TIMES BOOKS—201 E. 50th St., New York, NY 10022. Peter Bernstein, Pub. No unsolicited manuscripts or queries accepted.

TOPAZ—375 Hudson St., New York, NY 10014. Audrey LaFehr, Ed. Dir. Query.

TOR BOOKS—Tom Doherty Associates, 175 Fifth Ave., 14th Fl., New York, NY 10010. Patrick Nielsen Hayden, Sr. Ed. Science fiction and fantasy, from 80,000 words. Query with complete synopsis and first 3 chapters. Advance and royalty.

TOUCHSTONE—1230 Ave. of the Americas, New York, NY 10020. Attn: Ed. No unsolicited manuscripts.

TRANS NATIONAL GROUP—133 Federal St., Boston, MA 02110. Debra Lance, Book Development Mgr. Books for members of the Golf Society of the United States and the Adventure Club of North America. Subjects include golfing, backpacking, bicycling, camping, canoeing, fishing, hiking, mountain biking, outdoor photography, and skiing. Submit proposal with brief description of audience, resumé, and published clips. Pays a flat fee. Responds in 2 months.

TRICYCLE PRESS—Imprint of Ten Speed Press, P.O. Box 7123, Berkeley, CA 94707. Nicole Geiger, Ed. Children's books: Picture books, submit complete manuscripts. Activity books, submit about 20 pages and complete outline. "Real life" books that help children cope with issues. SASE required. Do not send original artwork. Responds in 12 weeks. Royalty.

TROUBADOR PRESS—See *Price Stern Sloan, Inc.*

TSR, INC.—P.O. Box 707, Renton, WA 98057-0707. Attn: Manuscript Ed. Epic game-related high fantasy, gritty, action-oriented fantasy, Gothic horror, some science fiction, about 100,000 words. Query. Advance royalty.

TUDOR PUBLISHERS, INC.—P.O. Box 38366, Greensboro, NC 27438. Pam Cox, Ed. Helpful nonfiction books for senior citizens, teenagers, and minorities. Young adult biographies and young adult novels. Reference library titles. High-quality adult fiction. Send proposal or query with sample chapters. Royalty.

TURTLE BOOKS— 866 United Nations Plaza, Suite 525, New York, NY 10017. John Whitman, Pub. Children's picture books only. Submit complete manuscript with SASE. Royalty.

TURTLE PRESS— 403 Silas Deane Hwy., Wethersfield, CT 06109. Cynthia Kim, Ed. Nonfiction, varying lengths, on all aspects of martial arts and Eastern philosophy. Query. Royalty.

TWENTY-FIRST CENTURY BOOKS—274 Madison Ave., Suite 1406, New York, NY 10016. Attn: Submissions Ed. Juvenile nonfiction, 10,000 to 30,000 words, for use in school and public libraries. Science, history, health, and social studies books for grades 5 and up. No fiction, workbooks, or picture books. Also accepts single titles for middle-grade and young adult readers. "Books are published primarily in series of 4 or more; not all titles in a series are necessarily by the same author." Submit outline and sample chapters. Royalty.

TYNDALE HOUSE—351 Executive Dr., Box 80, Wheaton, IL 60189. Ron Beers, V.P. Adult fiction and nonfiction on subjects of concern to Christians. Picture books with religious focus for preschool and early readers. No unsolicited manuscripts. Send 9 x 12 SASE with 9 first-class stamps for catalogue and guidelines.

UAHC PRESS—838 Fifth Ave., New York, NY 10021. Bennett Lovett-Graff, Man. Ed. Religious educational titles on or related to Judaism. Adult nonfiction; juvenile picture books, fiction, nonfiction, and young adult titles. Query with outline. Royalty.

UNIVERSITY BOOKS—See *Carol Publishing Group.*

UNIVERSITY OF ALABAMA PRESS—P.O. Box 870380, Tuscaloosa, AL 35487-0380. Attn: Ed. Dept. Scholarly and general regional nonfiction. Submit to appropriate editor: Nicole Mitchell, Ed. (history, public administration, political science, women's studies); Curtis Clark, Ed. (English, rhetoric and communication, Judaic studies); Judith Knight, Ed. (archaeology, anthropology). Send complete manuscript or proposal. Royalty.

UNIVERSITY OF ARIZONA PRESS—1230 N. Park Ave., Suite 102, Tucson, AZ 85719-4140. Stephen Cox, Dir. Christine R. Szuter, Ed.-in-Chief. Patti Hartmann, Acquiring Ed. Scholarly and popular nonfiction: Arizona, American West, anthropology, archaeology, behavioral sciences, environmental science, geography, Latin America, Native Americans, natural history, space sciences, women's studies. Query with outline, sample chapters, and current curriculum vitae or resume. Royalty.

UNIVERSITY OF GEORGIA PRESS—330 Research Dr., Athens, GA 30602-4901. Karen Orchard, Dir. Short story collections and poetry, scholarly nonfiction and literary criticism, Southern and American history, regional studies, biography and autobiography. For nonfiction, query with outline and sample chapters. Poetry collections considered in Sept. and Jan. only; short fiction in April and May only. A $15 fee is required for all poetry and fiction submissions. Royalty. SASE for competition guidelines.

UNIVERSITY OF ILLINOIS PRESS—1325 S. Oak St., Champaign, IL 61820. Richard L. Wentworth, Ed.-in-Chief. Scholarly and regional; nonfiction; and poetry, 70 to 100 pages. Rarely considers multiple submissions. Query. Royalty.

UNIVERSITY OF MINNESOTA PRESS—111 Third Ave. S., Suite 290, Minneapolis, MN 55401-2520. Nonfiction: literary and cultural theory, social and political theory; communications/media; anthropology; geography; international relations; Native American studies; regional titles, 50,000 to 225,000 words. Query with detailed prospectus or introduction, table of contents, sample chapter, and resumé. Royalty.

UNIVERSITY OF MISSOURI PRESS—2910 LeMone Blvd., Columbia, MO 65201-8227. Beverly Jarrett, Dir./Ed.in-Chief. Mr. Clair Wilcox, Acquisitions Ed. Scholarly books on American and European history; American, British, and Latin American literary criticism; political philosophy; intellectual history; regional studies; and short fiction.

UNIVERSITY OF NEBRASKA PRESS—312 N. 14th St., Lincoln, NE 68588-0484. Attn: Ed.-in-Chief. Specializes in the history of the American West, Native-American studies, literary and cultural nonfiction, fiction in translation, music, Jewish studies, and sports history. Send proposals with summary, a sample chapter, and resumé. Write for guidelines for annual North American Indian Prose Award.

UNIVERSITY OF NEW MEXICO PRESS—University of New Mexico, Albuquerque, NM 87131. Elizabeth C. Hadas, Ed. Dir. David V. Holtby, Larry Ball, Dana Asbury, and Barbara Guth, Eds. Scholarly nonfiction on social and cultural anthropology, archaeology, Western history, art, and photography. Query. Royalty.

UNIVERSITY OF NORTH TEXAS PRESS—P.O. Box 311336, Denton, TX 76203-1336. Frances B. Vick, Dir. Charlotte M. Wright, Assoc. Dir. Books on Western Americana, Texan culture, history (including regional), women's studies, multicultural studies, and folklore. Series include: "War and the Southwest" (perspectives, histories, and memories of war from authors living in the Southwest); "Western Life Series"; "Philosophy and the Environment Series"; and "Texas Writers" (critical biographies of Texas writers). Send manuscript or query with sample chapters; no multiple queries. Royalty.

UNIVERSITY OF OKLAHOMA PRESS—1005 Asp Ave., Norman, OK 73019-0445. John Drayton, Dir. Books, to 300 pages, on the history of the American West, Indians of the Americas, congressional studies, classical studies, literary criticism, natural history, and women's studies. Query. Royalty.

UNIVERSITY OF PITTSBURGH PRESS—3347 Forbes Ave., Pittsburgh, PA 15261. Attn: Eds. Scholarly nonfiction; poetry, for poets who have previously published full-length collections of poetry. Send manuscripts in September and October only; responds by late Spring. Send for rules.

UNIVERSITY OF SOUTH CAROLINA PRESS—937 Assembly St., Carolina Plaza, 8th Fl., Columbia, SC 29208. Fred Kameny, Ed.-in-Chief. Books on history, literature, rhetoric, religious studies, and international relations. No original fiction. Submit outline with sample chapters. Royalty.

UNIVERSITY OF TENNESSEE PRESS—293 Communications Bldg., Knoxville, TN 37996-0325. Attn: Joyce Harrison. Nonfiction, regional trade, and regional fiction, 200 to 400 manuscript pages. No poetry, translations, children's books, plays, or textbooks. Query with outline and sample chapters. Royalty.

UNIVERSITY PRESS OF COLORADO—P.O. Box 849, Niwot, CO 80544. Attn: Ed. Dept. Scholarly books in the humanities, social sciences, and applied sciences. Fiction for new series.

THE UNIVERSITY PRESS OF KENTUCKY—663 S. Limestone St., Lexington, KY 40508-4008. Nancy Grayson Holmes, Ed.-in-Chief. Scholarly books in the major fields. Serious nonfiction of general interest. Books related to Kentucky and the Ohio Valley, the Appalachians, and the South. No fiction, drama, or poetry. Query.

UNIVERSITY PRESS OF MISSISSIPPI—3825 Ridgewood Rd., Jackson, MS 39211-6492. Seetha Srinivasan, Ed.-in-Chief. Scholarly and trade titles in American literature, history, and culture; southern studies; African-American, women's and American studies; popular culture; folklife; art and architecture; natural sciences; health; and other liberal arts.

UNIVERSITY PRESS OF NEW ENGLAND—23 S. Main St., Hanover, NH 03755-2048. Attn: Ed. Dept. General and scholarly nonfiction. American history, literature, and cultural studies. Jewish studies, women's studies, studies of the New England region, and environmental studies, and performance studies. *Hardscrabble Books* imprint: fiction of New England, Wesleyen University Poetry Series.

VAN NOSTRAND REINHOLD—115 Fifth Ave., New York, NY 10003. Marianne Russell, CEO. Business, professional, scientific, and technical publishers of applied reference works. Hospitality, culinary, architecture, graphic and interior design, industrial and environmental health and safety, computer science, engineering, and technical management.

VANDAMERE PRESS—P.O. Box 5243, Arlington, VA 22205. Jerry Frank, Assoc. Acquisitions Ed. General trade, fiction and nonfiction, including history, military, parenting, healthcare/disability studies, and travel. Also books about the nation's capital for a national audience. Prefer to see outline with sample chapter for nonfiction; for fiction send 4 or 5 sample chapters. Multiple queries considered. Royalty. SASE required.

VIKING—375 Hudson St., New York, NY 10014. Barbara Grossman, Pub. Fiction and nonfiction. Nonfiction: psychology, sociology, child-rearing and development, cookbooks, sports, and popular culture. Query. Royalty.

VIKING CHILDREN'S BOOKS—345 Hudson St., New York, NY 10014. Attn: Ed. Dept. Fiction and nonfiction, including biography, history, and sports, for ages 7 to 14. Humor and picture books for ages 3 to 8. Query Children's Book Dept. with outline and sample chapter. For picture books, please send entire manuscript. SASE required. Advance and royalty.

VILLARD BOOKS—201 E. 50th St., New York, NY 10022. Attn: Assoc. Ed. How-to, biography, humor, etc. "We look for authors who are promotable and books we feel we can market well." Royalty.

VINTAGE BOOKS—201 E. 50th St., New York, NY 10022. Attn: Ed. Dept. Quality fiction and serious nonfiction. Query with sample chapters for fiction; query for nonfiction.

VOYAGER BOOKS—See *Harcourt Brace & Co. Children's Book Div.*

VOYAGEUR PRESS—123 N. Second St., Stillwater, MN 55082. Todd R. Berger, Acquisitions Ed. Books, 15,000 to 100,000 words, on wildlife, travel, Americana, collectibles, natural history, hunting and fishing, regional topics; and Native American fiction, any length. "Photography is very important for most of our books." Guidelines. Query with outline and sample chapters. Royalty.

WALKER AND COMPANY—435 Hudson St., New York, NY 10014. Attn: Ed. Dept. Adult fiction: mysteries. Adult nonfiction: biography, history, science, natural history, health, psychology, popular science, and music. Juvenile nonfiction, including biography, science, history, music, and nature. Juvenile fiction: Middle grade and young adult novels. Query with synopsis and SASE. Guidelines. Royalty.

WARNER BOOKS—1271 Ave. of the Americas, New York, NY 10020. No unsolicited manuscripts or proposals.

WASHINGTON SQUARE PRESS—1230 Ave. of the Americas, New York, NY 10020. Nancy Miller, Dir. Paperback reprints only.

WASHINGTON STATE UNIVERSITY PRESS—Cooper Publications Bldg., P.O. Box 645910, Pullman, WA 99164-5910. Keith Petersen, Acquisitions

Ed. Glen Lindeman, Ed. Books on northwest history, prehistory, and culture, 200 to 350 pages. Query. Royalty.

WATTS, FRANKLIN—Sherman Turnpike, Danbury, CT 06813. Curriculum-oriented nonfiction for grades K to 12, including science, history, social studies, and biography. No unsolicited submissions.

WEE SING—See *Price Stern Sloan, Inc.*

WEISS ASSOCIATES, DANIEL—33 W. 17th St., New York, NY 10011. Alfred Nerz, Ed. Asst. Book packager. Young adult books, 45,000 words; middle grade books, 33,000 words; elementary books, 10,000 to 12,000 words. Query with outline and 2 sample chapters. Royalty and flat fee.

WESTMINSTER JOHN KNOX PRESS—100 Witherspoon St., Louisville, KY 40202. Richard Brown, Dir. Stephanie Egnotovich, Man. Ed. Books that inform, interpret, challenge, and encourage Christian faith and living. Royalty. Send SASE for guidelines.

WHISPERING COYOTE PRESS—300 Crescent Ct., Suite 860, Dallas, TX 75201. Ms. Lou Alpert, Ed. Picture books, 32 pages, for readers ages 4 to 12. Submit complete manuscript with SASE. Royalty.

WHITE PINE PRESS—10 Village Sq., Fredonia, NY 14063. Elaine La-Mattina, Ed. Novels, books of short stories, and essay collections, 250 to 350 pages. Query with outline and sample chapters. Royalty.

WHITECAP BOOKS—351 Lynn Ave., N. Vancouver, BC, Canada V7J 2C4. Robert McCullough, Dir. of Pub. Operations. Juvenile books, 32 to 84 pages, and adult books, varying lengths, on such topics as natural history, gardening, cookery, parenting, history and regional subjects. Query with table of contents, synopsis, and one sample chapter. Royalty and flat fee.

WHITMAN, ALBERT— 6340 Oakton, Morton Grove, IL 60053. Kathleen Tucker, Ed. Picture books for preschool children; novels, biographies, mysteries, and nonfiction for middle-grade readers. Send complete manuscript for picture books, 3 chapters and outline for longer fiction; query for nonfiction. Royalty.

WILDERNESS PRESS—2440 Bancroft Way, Berkeley, CA 94704. Caroline Winnett, Ed. Nonfiction: outdoor sports, recreation, and travel in the western U.S. Royalty.

WILEY & SONS, INC. JOHN— 605 Third Ave., New York, NY 10158-0012. Attn: Ed. Dept. Nonfiction: science/technology; business/management; travel; cooking; biography; psychology; computers; language; history; current affairs; health; finance. Send proposals with outline, author vita, market information, and sample chapter. Royalty.

WILEY CHILDREN'S BOOKS— 605 Third Ave., New York, NY 10158-0012. Kate Bradford, Ed. Nonfiction books, 96 to 128 pages, for 8-to 12-year-old children. Query. Royalty.

WILLIAMSON PUBLISHING CO.—P.O. Box 185, Charlotte, VT 05445. Attn: Nonfiction Ed. Active learning books for children and teachers. No children's picture books. Writers must send annotated table of contents, 2 sample chapters, and SASE.

WILLOW CREEK PRESS—9931 Hwy. 70 W., P.O. Box 147, Minocqua, WI 54548. Laura Evert, Man. Ed. Books, 25,000 to 50,000 words, on nature, wildlife, and outdoor sports. Query with sample chapters. Include SASE for return of materials. No fiction. Royalty.

WILLOWISP PRESS— 801 94th Ave. N., St. Petersburg, FL 33702. Attn: Acquisitions Ed. Beginning chapter books, 2,000 to 6,000 words. Juvenile books for children in grades pre-K through 8. Picture books, 300 to 800 words. Fiction, 14,000 to 18,000 words, for grades 3 through 5; 20,000 to 24,000 words for grades 5 through 8. Requirements for nonfiction vary. Query with outline, sample chapter, and SASE. Guidelines. Royalty or flat fee.

WILSHIRE BOOK COMPANY—12015 Sherman Rd., N. Hollywood, CA 91605-3781. Melvin Powers, Pub. Nonfiction: self-help, motivation/inspiration/spiritual, psychology, recovery, how-to, entrepreneurship, mail order, horsemanship, and Internet marketing; minimum, 60,000 words. Fiction: allegories that teach principles of psychological/spiritual growth. Send synopsis/detailed chapter outline, 3 chapters, and SASE. Royalty.

WINDSWEPT HOUSE PUBLISHERS—Mt. Desert, ME 04660. Jane Weinberger, Pub. Children's picture books; young adult novels; adult fiction and nonfiction. Query.

WOODBINE HOUSE— 6510 Bells Mill Rd., Bethesda, MD 20817. Susan Stokes, Ed. Books for or about people with disabilities only. No personal accounts, poetry, or novels. Query or submit complete manuscript with SASE. Guidelines. Royalty.

WORD PUBLISHING—545 Marriott Dr., Ste. 750, Box 141000, Nashville, TN 37214. Lee Gessner, Dep. Pub. Fiction and nonfiction, 65,000 to 95,000 words, dealing with the relationship and/or applications of biblical principles to everyday life. Query with outline and sample chapters. Royalty.

WORDWARE COMPUTER BOOKS—See *Wordware Publishing.*

WORDWARE PUBLISHING—2320 Los Rio Blvd., Suite 200, Plano, TX 75074. James S. Hill, Pub. *Wordware Computer Books.* Ginnie Bivona, Ed., *Republic of Texas Press:* Texana, Southwest regional, historical nonfiction including tales and legends of the old west and "legendary" characters, military history, women of the west and country humor. Ginnie Bivona, Ed., *Seaside Press*: Cities uncovered history/guidebooks, pet care, humor. Query with sample chapters, manuscript completion date, and author experience. Royalty.

WORKMAN PUBLISHING CO., INC.—708 Broadway, New York, NY 10003. Attn: Ed. Dept. General nonfiction. Normal contractual terms based on agreement.

WORLDWIDE LIBRARY—225 Duncan Mill Rd., Don Mills, Ont., Canada M3B 3K9. Randall Toye, Ed. Dir. Feroze Mohammed, Sr. Ed. Action adventure series for *Gold Eagle* imprint; mystery fiction reprints only. No unsolicited manuscripts.

WYNDHAM HALL PRESS—52857 C.R. 21, Bristol, IN 46507. Milton L. Clayton, Pub. Academic nonfiction. Submit complete manuscript. Royalty.

YEARLING BOOKS—1540 Broadway, New York, NY 10036. Attn: Ed. Dept. Not accepting unsolicited material for 1999.

ZONDERVAN PUBLISHING HOUSE—5300 Patterson S.E., Grand Rapids, MI 49530. Attn: Manuscript Review. Christian titles. General fiction and nonfiction; academic and professional books. Query with outline, sample chapter, and SASE. Royalty. Guidelines.

SYNDICATES

Syndicates buy material from writers and artists to sell to newspapers all over the country and the world. Authors are paid either a percentage of the gross proceeds or an outright fee. Of course, features by people well known in their fields have the best chance of being syndicated. In general, syndicates want columns that have been popular in a local newspaper or magazine. Since most syndicated fiction has been published previously in magazines or books, beginning fiction writers should try to sell their stories to magazines before submitting them to syndicates.

Always query syndicates before sending manuscripts, since their needs change frequently, and be sure to enclose SASEs with queries and manuscripts.

ARKIN MAGAZINE SYNDICATE—500 Bayview Dr., Suite F, N. Miami Beach, FL 33160. Mitzi Roberg, Ed. Dir. Articles, 750 to 2,200 words, for trade and professional magazines. Must have small-business slant, be written in layman's language, and offer solutions to business problems. Articles should apply to many businesses, not just a specific industry. No columns. Pays 3¢ to 10¢ a word, on acceptance. SASE required; query not necessary.

CONTEMPORARY FEATURES SYNDICATE—P. O. Box 1258, Jackson, TN 38302-1258. Lloyd Russell, Ed. Articles, 1,000 to 10,000 words: how-to, money savers, business, etc. Self-help pieces for small business. Pays from $25, on acceptance. Query.

HARRIS & ASSOCIATES FEATURES—15915 Caminito Aire Puro, San Diego, CA 92128. Dick Harris, Ed. Sports- and family-oriented features, to 1,200 words; fillers and short humor, 500 to 800 words. Queries preferred. Pays varying rates.

HISPANIC LINK NEWS SERVICE—1420 N St. N.W., Washington, DC 20005. Charles A. Ericksen, Ed. Trend articles, opinion and personal experience pieces, and general features with Hispanic focus, 650 to 700 words; editorial cartoons. Pays $25 for op-ed columns and cartoons, on acceptance. Send SASE for guidelines.

THE HOLLYWOOD INSIDE SYNDICATE—Box 49957, Los Angeles, CA 90049-0957. John Austin, Dir. Feature articles, 750 to 2,500 words, on TV and film personalities with B&W photo(s). Article suggestions for 3-part series. Pieces on unusual medical and scientific breakthroughs. Pays on percentage basis for features, negotiated rates for ideas, on publication. E-mail: hollywood@ce32.net

KING FEATURES SYNDICATE—235 E. 45th St., New York, NY 10017. Paul Eberhart, Exec. Ed. Columns, comics. "We do not consider or buy individual articles. We are interested in ideas for nationally syndicated columns." Submit cover letter, six sample columns of 650 words each, bio sheet and any additional clips, and SASE. No simultaneous submissions. Query with SASE for guidelines.

LOS ANGELES TIMES SYNDICATE—Times Mirror Sq., Los Angeles, CA 90053. Commentary, features, columns, editorial cartoons, comics, puzzles and games; news services and online products. Send SASE for submission guidelines.

NATIONAL NEWS BUREAU—P.O. Box 43039, Philadelphia, PA 19129. Harry Jay Katz, Ed. Articles, 500 to 1,500 words, interviews, consumer news, how-tos, travel pieces, reviews, entertainment pieces, features, etc. Pays on publication.

NEW YORK TIMES SYNDICATION SALES—122 E. 42nd St., New York, NY 10168. Gloria Brown Anderson, Pres. and Ed.-in-Chief. Carolee Morrison, International Ed. Previously published health, lifestyle, and entertainment articles only, to 1,500 words. Query with published article or tear sheet and SASE. No calls please. Pays 50% royalty on collected sales.

NEWSPAPER ENTERPRISE ASSOCIATION—200 Madison Ave., 4th Fl., New York, NY 10016. Robert Levy, Exec. Ed. Ideas for new concepts in syndicated columns. No single stories or stringers. Payment by contractual arrangement.

OCEANIC PRESS SERVICE—Seaview Business Park, 1030 Calle Cordillera, Unit #106, San Clemente, CA 92673. Peter Carbone, General Mgr. Buys reprint rights for foreign markets, on previously published novels, self-help, and how-to books; interviews with celebrities; illustrated features on celebrities, family, health, beauty, personal relationships, etc.; cartoons, comic strips. Pays on acceptance or half on acceptance, half on syndication. Query.

SINGER MEDIA CORP.—#106, 1030 Calle Cordillera, San Clemente, CA 92673. Helen J. Lee, V.P. International syndication, some domestic. Subjects must be of global interest. Features: celebrity interviews and profiles, women's, health, fitness, self-help, business, computer, etc., all lengths; psychological quizzes; puzzles (no word puzzles) and games for children or adults. Pays 50%.

TRIBUNE MEDIA SERVICES— 435 N. Michigan Ave., #1400, Chicago, IL 60611. Mark Mathes, Ed. Continuing columns, comic strips, features, electronic databases, puzzles and word games. Query with clips.

UNITED FEATURE SYNDICATE—200 Madison Ave., 4th Fl., New York, NY 10016-3903. Diana Loevy, V.P./Ed. Dir. No one-shots or series. Payment by contractual arrangement. Send samples with SASE.

LITERARY PRIZE OFFERS

Writers seeking the thrill of competition should review the extensive list of literary prize offers, many of them designed to promote the as-yet-unpublished author. All of the competitions listed here are for unpublished manuscripts and usually offer publication in addition to a cash prize. The prestige that comes with winning some of the more established awards can do much to further a writer's career, as editors, publishers, and agents are likely to consider the future work of the prize winner more closely.

There are hundreds of literary contests open to writers in all genres, and the following list covers a representative number of them. The summaries given below are intended merely as guides; since submission requirements are more detailed than space allows, writers should send an SASE for complete guidelines before entering any contest. Writers are also advised to check the monthly "Prize Offers" column of *The Writer* Magazine (120 Boylston St., Boston, MA 02116-4615) for additional contest listings and up-to-date contest requirements. Deadlines are annual unless otherwise noted.

ACADEMY OF AMERICAN POETS—Walt Whitman Award, 584 Broadway, Suite 1208, New York, NY 10012-3250. An award of $5,000 plus publication and a one-month residency at the Vermont Studio Center is offered for a book-length poetry manuscript by a poet who has not yet published a volume of poetry. Deadline: November 15. Entry fee.

ACADEMY OF MOTION PICTURE ARTS AND SCIENCES—The Nicholl Fellowships, 8949 Wilshire Blvd., Beverly Hills, CA 90211-1972. Up to five fellowships of $25,000 each are awarded for original screenplays that display exceptional craft and engaging storytelling. Deadline: May 1. Entry fee.

ACTORS THEATRE OF LOUISVILLE—Ten-Minute Play Contest, 316 W. Main St., Louisville, KY 40202-4218. A prize of $1,000 is offered for a previously unproduced ten-page script. Deadline: December 1.

AMERICAN ACADEMY OF ARTS AND LETTERS—Richard Rogers Awards, 633 W. 155th St., New York, NY 10032. Offers subsidized productions or staged readings in New York City by a nonprofit theater for a musical, play with music, thematic review, or any comparable work. Deadline: November 1.

AMERICAN ANTIQUARIAN SOCIETY—Fellowships for Historical Research, 185 Salisbury St., Worcester, MA 01609-1634. Attn: John B. Hench. At least three fellowships are awarded to creative and performing artists, writers, film makers, and journalists for research on pre-20th century American history. Residencies are four-to eight-weeks; travel expenses and stipends of $1,200 per month are offered. Deadline: October 5.

THE AMERICAN-SCANDINAVIAN FOUNDATION—Translation Prize, 725 Park Ave., New York, NY 10021. A prize of $2,000 is awarded for an outstanding English translation of poetry, fiction, drama, or literary prose originally written in Danish, Finnish, Icelandic, Norwegian, or Swedish. Second prize is $500. Deadline: June 1.

ANHINGA PRESS—Anhinga Prize for Poetry, P.O. Box 10595, Tallahassee, FL 32302-0595. A $2,000 prize will be awarded for an unpublished full-length collection of poetry, 48 to 72 pages, by a poet who has published no more than one full-length collection. Deadline: March 15. Entry fee.

ARMY MAGAZINE—Essay Contest, Box 1560, Arlington, VA 22210. Prizes of $1,000, $500, and $250 plus publication are awarded for essays on a given theme. Deadline: May 31.

THE ASSOCIATED WRITING PROGRAMS—Awards Series, Tallwood House, Mail Stop 1E3, George Mason Univ., Fairfax, VA 22030. In the categories of poetry, short fiction, the novel, and nonfiction, the prize is book publication and a $2,000 honorarium. Deadline: February 29. Entry fee.

ASSOCIATION OF JEWISH LIBRARIES—Sydney Taylor Manuscript Competition, 1327 Wyntercreek Ln., Dunwoody, GA 30338. Attn: Paula Sandfelder, Coordinator. Offers $1,000 for the best fiction manuscript, 64 to 200 pages, by an unpublished book author, writing for readers 8 to 11. Stories must have a positive Jewish focus. Deadline: January 15.

BAKER'S PLAYS—High School Playwriting Contest, 100 Chauncy St., Boston, MA 02111. Plays about the high school experience, written by high school students, are eligible for awards of $500, $250, and $100. Deadline: January 31.

BANTAM DOUBLEDAY DELL BOOKS FOR YOUNG READERS—Marguerite de Angeli Prize, Dept. BFYR, 1540 Broadway, New York, NY 10036. A prize of $1,500 and a $3,500 advance against royalties is awarded for a middle-grade fiction manuscript that explores the diversity of the American experience. Open to U.S. and Canadian writers who have not previously published a novel for middle-grade readers. Deadline: June 30.

BARNARD COLLEGE—New Women Poets Prize, Women Poets at Barnard, Columbia Univ., 3009 Broadway, New York, NY 10027-6598. Attn: Directors. A prize of $1,500 and publication by Beacon Press is offered for an unpublished poetry manuscript, 50 to 100 pages, by a female poet who has never published a book of poetry. Deadline: October 15.

THE BELLETRIST REVIEW—Fiction Contest, Marmarc Publications, P.O. Box 596, Plainville, CT 06062-0596. Prize of $200 plus publication is awarded for an unpublished short story, 2,500 to 5,000 words. Deadline: July 15. Entry fee.

THE BELLINGHAM REVIEW—Tobias Wolff Award in Fiction/49th Parallel Poetry Award, MS-9053, Western Washington Univ., Bellingham, WA 98225. Tobias Wolff Award in Fiction: Offers prizes of $500 plus publication, $250, and $100 for a short story or novel excerpt. Deadline: March 1. Annie Dillard Award in Nonfiction: Offers prizes of $500 plus publication, $250, and $100 for previously unpublished essays. Deadline: March 1. 49th Parallel Poetry Award: Offers publication and prizes of $500, $250, and $100 for individual poems. Deadline: November 30. Entry fees.

BEVERLY HILLS THEATRE GUILD/JULIE HARRIS PLAYWRIGHT AWARD—2815 N. Beachwood Dr., Los Angeles, CA 90068-1923. Attn: Marcella Meharg. Offers prize of $5,000, $2,000, and $1,000 for an unpublished full-length play. Deadline: November 1.

BIRMINGHAM-SOUTHERN COLLEGE—Hackney Literary Awards, Box 549003, Birmingham, AL 35254. A prize of $5,000 is awarded for an unpublished novel, any length. Deadline: September 30. Also, a $5,000 prize is shared for the winning short story, to 5,000 words, and poem of up to 50 lines. Deadline: December 31. Entry fees.

BLUE MOUNTAIN CENTER—Richard J. Margolis Award, 294 Washington St., Suite 610, Boston, MA 02108. A prize of $1,000 is awarded annually to a promising journalist or essayist whose work combines warmth, humor, wisdom, and a concern with social issues. Applications should include up to 30 pages of published or unpublished work. Deadline: June 1.

BOISE STATE UNIVERSITY—The Rocky Mountain Artists' Book Competition, Hemingway Western Studies Center, Boise, ID 83725. Tom Trusky, Ed. A prize of $500 and publication is awarded for up to 3 books; manuscripts (text and/or visual content) and proposals are considered for the short-run printing of books on public issues, especially the Inter-Mountain West. Deadline: year-round.

BOSTON REVIEW—Short Story Contest, E53-407, MIT, Cambridge, MA 02139. A prize of $300 plus publication is awarded for the best previously unpublished story of up to 4,000 words. Deadline: September 1. Entry fee.

BOX TURTLE PRESS, INC.—Mudfish Poetry Prize, 184 Franklin St., New York, NY 10013. Awards $500 plus publication in *Mudfish*. Deadline: April 30. Entry fee.

ARCH AND BRUCE BROWN FOUNDATION—P.O. Box 45231, Phoenix, AZ 85064. Offers $1,000 grants for gay and lesbian-positive fiction. Deadline: May 31.

BUCKNELL UNIVERSITY—The Philip Roth Residence in Creative Writing, Stadler Center for Poetry, Bucknell Univ., Lewisburg, PA 17837. Attn: Cynthia Hogue, Dir. The fall residency, which includes studio, lodging, meals, and a $1,000 stipend, may be used by a writer, over 21, not currently enrolled in a university, to work on a first or second book. The residency is awarded in odd-numbered years to a fiction writer, and in even-numbered years to a poet. Deadline: March 1.

CASE WESTERN RESERVE UNIVERSITY—Marc A. Klein Playwriting Award, Dept. of Theater Arts, 10900 Euclid Ave., Cleveland, OH 44106-7077. A prize of $1,000 plus production is offered for an original, previously unproduced full-length play by a student currently enrolled at an American college or university. Deadline: May 15.

CENTER FOR BOOK ARTS—Poetry Chapbook Prize, Center for Book Arts, 626 Broadway, 5th Floor, New York, NY 10012. Offers $1,000, publication and a public reading for poetry manuscript, to 500 lines. Deadline: December 31. Entry fee.

CHELSEA AWARD COMPETITION—P.O. Box 1040, York Beach, ME 03910. Attn: Ed. Prizes of $750 plus publication are awarded for the best unpublished short fiction and poetry. Deadlines: June 15 (fiction); December 15 (poetry). Entry fees.

THE CHICAGO TRIBUNE—Nelson Algren Awards, 435 N. Michigan Ave., Chicago, IL 60611. A first prize of $5,000 and three runner-up prizes of $1,000 are awarded for outstanding unpublished short stories, 2,500 to 10,000 words, by American writers. Deadline: February 1.

CLAREMONT GRADUATE SCHOOL—Kingsley Tufts Poetry Awards, 160 E. 10th St., Claremont, CA 91711. An award of $50,000 is given an American poet whose work is judged most worthy. An award of $5,000 is given an emerging poet whose work displays extraordinary promise. Books of poetry published or manuscripts completed in the calendar year are considered. Deadline: September 15.

CLAUDER COMPETITION—P.O. Box 383259, Cambridge, MA 02238-3259. Awards $2,500 plus professional production for a full-length play by a New England writer. Runner-up prizes of $500 and a staged reading also awarded. Deadline: June 30 (of odd-numbered years).

CLEVELAND STATE UNIVERSITY POETRY CENTER—Poetry Center Prize, Dept. of English, Rhodes Tower, Rm. 1815, 1983 E. 24th St., Cleveland, OH 44115-2440. Publication and $1,000 are awarded for a previously unpublished book-length volume of poetry. Deadline: March 1. Entry fee.

COALITION FOR THE ADVANCEMENT OF JEWISH EDUCATION—David Dornstein Memorial Creative Writing Contest, 261 W. 35th St., Floor 12A, New York, NY 10001. Publication and prizes of $700, $200, and $100 are awarded for the three best original, previously unpublished short stories, to 5,000 words, on a Jewish theme or topic, by writers age 18 to 35. Deadline: December 31.

COLONIAL PLAYERS, INC.—Promising Playwright Award, 98 Tower Dr., Stevensville, MD 21666. Attn: Fran Marchano. A prize of $750 plus possible production will be awarded for the best full-length play by a resident of MD, DC, VA, WV, DE, or PA. Deadline: December 31 (of even-numbered years).

COLORADO STATE UNIVERSITY—Colorado Prize for Poetry, Colorado Review, Dept. of English, Fort Collins, CO 80523. Attn: David Milofsky, Ed. Offers $1,500 plus publication for collection of original poems. Deadline: January 15. Entry fee.

COMMUNITY CHILDREN'S THEATRE OF KANSAS CITY—8021 E. 129th Terrace, Grandview, MO 64030. Attn: Mrs. Blanche Sellens, Dir. A prize of $500, plus production, is awarded for the best play, up to one hour long, to be performed by adults for elementary school audiences. Deadline: January 31.

COMMUNITY WRITERS ASSOCIATION—CWA Writing Contest, P.O. Box 12, Newport, RI 02840-0001. A prize of $500 plus free conference tuition is offered for short stories, to 2,000 words, and poetry, any length. Deadline: June 1. Entry fee.

EUGENE V. DEBS FOUNDATION—Bryant Spann Memorial Prize, Dept. of History, Indiana State Univ., Terre Haute, IN 47809. Offers a prize of $1,000 for a published or unpublished article or essay on themes relating to social protest or human equality. Deadline: April 30.

DEEP SOUTH WRITERS CONFERENCE—Contest Clerk, Drawer 44691, Univ. of Southwestern Louisianna, Lafayette, LA 70504-4691. Prizes ranging from $50 to $300 are offered for unpublished manuscripts in the following categories: Fiction (including science fiction); Novel; Nonfiction; Poetry; Drama; and French literature. Deadline: July 15. Miller Award: offers $500 for a play dealing with some aspect of the life of Edward de Vere (1550-1604), the 17th Earl of Oxford. Deadline: July 15 (of odd-numbered years). Entry fee.

DELACORTE PRESS—Prize for First Young Adult Novel, Bantam Doubleday Dell BFYR, 1540 Broadway, New York, NY 10036. A writer who has not previously published a young adult novel may submit a book-length manuscript with a contemporary setting suitable for readers ages 12 to 18. The prize is $1,500, a $6,000 advance, and hardcover and paperback publication. Deadline: December 31.

DRURY COLLEGE—Playwriting Contest, 900 N. Benton Ave., Springfield, MO 65802. Attn: Sandy Asher, Writer-in-Residence. Prizes of $300 and two $150 honorable mentions, plus possible production, are awarded for original, previously unproduced one-act plays. Deadline: December 1 (of even-numbered years).

DUBUQUE FINE ARTS PLAYERS—One-Act Playwriting Contest, 1321 Tomahawk Dr., Dubuque, IA 52003. Attn: Jennifer G. Stabenow, Coordinator. Prizes of $600, $300 and $200 plus possible production are awarded for unproduced, original one-act plays of up to 40 minutes. Deadline: January 31. Entry fee.

DUKE UNIVERSITY—Dorothea Lange-Paul Taylor Prize, Prize Committee, Center for Documentary Studies, Box 90802, Duke Univ., Durham, NC 27708-0802. A grant of up to $10,000 is awarded to a writer and photographer working together in the formative stages of a documentary project that will ultimately result in a publishable work. Deadline: January 31. Entry fee.

ELF: ECLECTIC LITERARY FORUM—Ruth Cable Memorial Prize, P.O. Box 392, Tonawanda, NY 14150. Awards of $500 and three $50 prizes are given for poems up to 50 lines. Short Fiction Prize awards $500 plus publication and two $50 prizes for stories, to 3,500 words. Deadline: March 31. Fiction deadline: August 31. Entry fee.

EMPORIA STATE UNIVERSITY—Bluestem Award, English Dept., Emporia State Univ., Emporia, KS 66801-5087. A prize of $1,000 plus publication is awarded for a previously unpublished book of poems by a U.S. author. Deadline: March 1. Entry fee.

THE FLORIDA REVIEW—The Editors Awards (specify Fiction, Nonfiction, or Poetry), Dept. of English, Univ. of Central Florida, Orlando, FL 32816-0001. Attn: Russell Kesler, Ed. Prizes of $500 plus publication are offered for short stories, essays, and creative nonfiction to 7,500 words, as well as groups of 3 to 5 poems, to 25 lines. Deadline: March 15. Entry fee.

THE FORMALIST—Howard Nemerov Sonnet Award, 320 Hunter Dr., Evansville, IN 47711. A prize of $1,000 plus publication is offered for a previously unpublished, original sonnet. Deadline: June 15. Entry fee.

FOUR WAY BOOKS—Intro Prize in Poetry, P.O. Box 535, Village Sta., New York, NY 10014. Attn: K. Clarke. Awards $3,500 ($2,000 honorarium plus $1,500 author tour money) and publication for a book-length collection of poems by a U.S. poet. Deadline: March 31. Entry fee.

GEORGE MASON UNIVERSITY—Greg Grummer Award in Poetry, *Phoebe: A Journal of Literary Arts*, 4400 Univ. Dr., Fairfax, VA 22030. A prize of $500 plus publication is offered for an outstanding previously unpublished poem. Deadline: December 15. Entry fee.

GEORGE WASHINGTON UNIVERSITY—Jenny McKean Moore Writer-in-Washington, Dept. of English, Washington, DC 20052. Attn: Prof. Christopher Sten. A salaried teaching position for two semesters is offered to a creative writer (of various mediums in alternate years) having "significant publications and a demonstrated commitment to teaching. The writer need not have conventional academic credentials." The Deadline: November 15.

THE GEORGETOWN REVIEW FICTION AND POETRY CONTEST—P.O. Box 6309, Southern Station, Hattiesburg, MS 39406-6309. A prize of $1,000 for a short story of no more than 25 pages or 6,500 words and $500 for a single poem, any length, plus publication and subscription. Deadline: October 1. Entry fee.

GLIMMER TRAIN PRESS—Semiannual Short Story Award for New Writers, 710 S.W. Madison St., #504, Portland, OR 97205. Writers whose fiction has never appeared in a nationally distributed publication are eligible to enter their stories of 1,200 to 7,500 words. Prizes are $1,200 plus publication, $500, and $300. Deadlines: March 31; September 30. Entry fee.

GREENFIELD REVIEW LITERARY CENTER—North American Native Authors First Book Awards, P.O. Box 308, 2 Middle Grove Rd., Greenfield Center, NY 12833. Attn: Joseph Bruchac, Dir. Native Americans of American Indian, Aleut, Inuit, or Metis ancestry who have not yet published a book are eligible to enter poetry, 64 to 100 pages, and prose, 200 to 300 pages (fiction or nonfiction) for $500 prizes plus publication. Deadline: March 15.

GROLIER POETRY PRIZE—6 Plympton St., Cambridge, MA 02138. Two $150 honorariums are awarded for poetry manuscripts of up to 10 double-spaced pages, including no more than five previously unpublished poems, by writers who have not yet published a book of poems. Deadline: May 1. Entry fee.

HEEKIN GROUP FOUNDATION—Fiction Fellowships Competition, Box 1534, Sisters, OR 97759. Awards the following fellowships to beginning career writers: two $1,500 Tara Fellowships in Short Fiction; two $3,000 James Fellowships for a Novel in Progress; one $2,000 Mary Molloy Fellowship for a Juvenile Novel in Progress (address H.G.F., P.O. Box 209, Middlebury, VT 05753; and one $2,000 Cuchulain Fellowhip for Rhetoric (Essay). Writers who have never published a novel, a children's novel, more than five short stories in national publication, or an essay are eligible to enter. Deadline: December 1. Entry fee.

HELICON NINE EDITIONS—Literary Prizes, 3607 Pennsylvania, Kansas City, MO 64111. Marianne Moore Poetry Prize: offers $1,000 for an original unpublished poetry manuscript of at least 48 pages. Willa Cather Fiction Prize: offers $1,000 for an original novella or short story collection, from 150 to 300 pages. Deadline: May 1. Entry fee.

LORIAN HEMINGWAY SHORT STORY COMPETITION—P.O. Box 993, Key West, FL 33041. Awards a $1,000 prize to an original, unpublished work short story, to 3,000 words by a writer whose fiction has never appeared in a nationally distributed publication. Deadline: June 1. Entry fee.

HIGHLIGHTS FOR CHILDREN—Fiction Contest, 803 Church St., Honesdale, PA 18431. Three $1,000 prizes plus publication are offered for stories on a given subject, up to 900 words. Deadline: February 28.

RUTH HINDMAN FOUNDATION—H.E. Francis Award, Dept. of English, Univ. of Alabama, Huntsville, AL 35899. A prize of $1,000 is awarded for a short story of up to 5,000 words. Deadline: December 31. Entry fee.

L. RON HUBBARD'S WRITERS OF THE FUTURE CONTEST—P.O. Box 1630, Los Angeles, CA 90078. Unpublished fiction writers are eligible to enter science fiction or fantasy short stories under 10,000 words, or novellas under 17,000 words. Quarterly prizes: $1,000, $750, and $500. Annual prize: $4,000. Deadlines: March 31; June 30; September 30; December 31.

INTERNATIONAL QUARTERLY—Crossing Boundaries Awards, P.O. Box 10521, Tallahassee, FL 32303-0521. Offers four prizes of $500 each plus publication for poetry, fiction, nonfiction, and "Crossing Boundaries," a category that includes "atypical work and innovative or experimental writing." Manuscripts, to 5,000 words; up to 5 poems per poetry submission. Deadline: March 1. Entry fee.

IUPUI CHILDREN'S THEATRE—Playwriting Competition, Indiana University-Purdue University at Indianapolis, 425 University Blvd., Suite 309, Indianapolis, IN 46202. Offers four $1,000 prizes plus staged readings for plays for young people. Deadline: September 1 (of even-numbered years).

ALICE JAMES BOOKS—Beatrice Hawley Award, Univ. of Maine at Farmington, 98 Main St., Farmington, ME 04938. A prize of publication plus 100 free copies is offered for the best poetry manuscript, 60 to 70 pages. Deadline: December 1. Entry fee.

JOE JEFFERSON PLAYERS ORIGINAL PLAY COMPETITION—P.O. Box 66065, Mobile, AL 36660. A prize of $1,000 plus production is offered for an original, previously unproduced play. Deadline: March 1.

JEWISH COMMUNITY CENTER THEATRE—Dorothy Silver Playwriting Competition, 3505 Mayfield Rd., Cleveland Heights, OH 44118. Attn: Elaine Rembrandt, Dir. Offers $1,000 and a staged reading for an original, previously unproduced full-length play, on some aspect of the Jewish experience. Deadline: December 15.

CHESTER H. JONES FOUNDATION—National Poetry Competition, P. O. Box 498, Chardon, OH 44024. Prizes of $1,000, $750, $500, $250, and $100, as well as several $50 and $10 prizes are awarded for original, unpublished poems of up to 32 lines. Deadline: March 31. Entry fee.

JAMES JONES SOCIETY—First Novel Fellowship, c/o Dept. of English, Wilkes Univ., Wilkes-Barre, PA 18766. An award of $2,500 is offered for a first novel-in-progress by an American. Deadline: March 1. Entry fee.

THE JOURNAL: THE LITERARY MAGAZINE OF O.S.U.—The Ohio State Univ. Press, 1070 Carmack Rd., Columbus, OH 43210-1002. Attn: David Citino, Poetry Ed. Awards $1,000 plus publication for at least 48 pages of original, unpublished poetry. Deadline: September 30. Entry fee.

KALLIOPE: A JOURNAL OF WOMEN'S ART—Sue Saniel Elkind Poetry Contest, Florida Community College at Jacksonville, 3939 Roosevelt Blvd., Jacksonville, FL 32205. Publication and $1,000 are awarded for the best poem, under 50 lines, written by a woman. Deadline: November 1. Entry fee.

KEATS/KERLAN MEMORIAL FELLOWSHIP—The Ezra Jack Keats Memorial Fellowship Committee, 109 Walter Library, 117 Pleasant St. S.E., Univ. of Minnesota, Minneapolis, MN 55455. A $1,500 fellowship is awarded to a talented writer and/or illustrator of children's books who wishes to use the Kerlan Collection for furtherance of his or her artistic development. Deadline: May 1.

KENT STATE UNIVERSITY PRESS—Stan and Tom Wick Poetry Prize, P.O. Box 5190, Kent, OH 44242-0001. Publication and $1,000 are offered for a book of poems, 48 to 68 pages, by a writer who has not previously published a collection of poetry. Deadline: May 1. Entry fee.

LODI ARTS COMMISSION—Drama Festival, 125 S. Hutchins St., Suite D, Lodi, CA 95240. A prize of $1,000 plus production is awarded for a full-length play; a prize of $500 plus production is awarded for a children's play. Deadline: April 1 (of odd-numbered years).

LOVE CREEK PRODUCTIONS—One-Act Play Festivals, 162 Nesbit St., Weehawken, NJ 07087-6817. One-act plays and theme-based plays are awarded production or staged readings. Deadlines vary.

AMY LOWELL POETRY TRAVELLING SCHOLARSHIP—Choate, Hall & Stewart, Exchange Pl., 53 State St., Boston, MA 02109-2891. Attn: F. Davis Dassori. A scholarship of approximately $29,000 is awarded for a poet to spend the year abroad to advance the art of poetry. Deadline: October 15.

THE MADISON REVIEW—Dept. of English, 600 N. Park St., Helen C. White Hall, Univ. of Wisconsin-Madison, Madison, WI 53706. Phyllis Smart Young Prize in Poetry: awards $500 plus publication for a group of three unpublished poems. Chris O'Malley Prize in Fiction: awards $500 plus publication for an unpublished short story. Deadline: September 30. Entry fees.

MIDDLEBURY COLLEGE—Katharine Bakeless Nason Prizes, c/o Bread Loaf Writers' Conference, Middlebury College, Middlebury, VT 05753. Attn: Carol Knauss. Publication and fellowships to the Bread Loaf Writers' Conference are offered for previously unpublished first books of poetry, fiction, and nonfiction. Deadline: March 1. Entry fee.

MID-LIST PRESS—First Series Awards, 4324 12th Ave. S., Minneapolis, MN 55407-3218. Publication and an advance against royalties are awarded for first books in the following categories: a novel in any genre, from 50,000 words; poetry, from 65 pages; short fiction, from 50,000 words; creative nonfiction, from 50,000 words. Deadline: February 1 (novel and poetry); July 1 (short fiction and creative nonfiction). Entry fees.

MIDWEST RADIO THEATRE WORKSHOP—MRTW Script Contests, 915 E. Broadway, Columbia, MO 65201. Workshop Script Contest: offers $800 in prizes, to be divided among two to four winners, and free workshop participation for contemporary radio scripts, 25 to 30 minutes long. Deadline: November 15. Entry fee.

MIDWEST THEATRE NETWORK—Biennial Rochester Playwright Festival, 5031 Tongen Ave. N.W., Rochester, MN 55901. Five to eight scripts of various lengths and types are chosen for festival production. Deadline: November 30 (of odd-numbered years).

MILL MOUNTAIN THEATRE—New Play Competition, 2nd Floor, One Market Square, Roanoke, VA 24011-1437. Attn: Jo Weinstein. Offers a $1,000 prize and staged reading, with possible full production, for an unpublished, unproduced, full-length or one-act play or musical. Cast size to ten. Deadline: January 1.

MISSISSIPPI REVIEW—Prize for Short Fiction and Poetry, The Center for Writers, Univ. of Southern Mississippi, Box 5144, Hattiesburg, MS 39406-5144. Attn: R. Fortenberry. Publication and $1,000 are offered for the best short story; $500 plus publication for the best poem. Deadline: May 31. Entry fee.

THE MISSOURI REVIEW—Editors' Prize, 1507 Hillcrest Hall, UMC, Columbia, MO 65211. Publication plus $1,500 is awarded for a short fiction manuscript (25 pages); $1,000 for an essay (25 pages); and $1,500 for poetry (10 pages). Deadline: October 15. Entry fee.

THE MOUNTAINEERS BOOKS—The Barbara Savage/"Miles from Nowhere" Memorial Award, 1001 S. W. Klickitat Way, Suite 201, Seattle, WA 98134. Offers a $3,000 cash award, plus publication and a $12,000 guaranteed advance against royalties for an outstanding unpublished, book-length manuscript of a nonfiction, personal-adventure narrative. Deadline: May 1 (of even-numbered years).

NATIONAL ENDOWMENT FOR THE ARTS—Nancy Hanks Center, 1100 Pennsylvania Ave. N.W., Room 720, Washington, DC 20506. Attn: Dir., Literature Program. Offers fellowships to writers and translators of poetry, fiction, plays, and creative nonfiction. Deadline: varies.

NATIONAL FEDERATION OF STATE POETRY SOCIETIES—Poetry Manuscript Contest, 3520 St. Rd. 56, Mechanicsburg, OH 43044. Attn: Amy Zook, Chairman. A prize of $1,000 is awarded for the best manuscript of poetry, 35 to 60 pages. Deadline: October 15. Entry fee.

NATIONAL POETRY SERIES—P.O. Box G, Hopewell, NJ 08525. Attn: Coordinator. Sponsors Annual Open Competition for unpublished book-length poetry manuscripts. Five manuscripts are selected for publication, and each winner receives a $1,000 award. Deadline: February 15. Entry fee.

NEW ENGLAND POETRY CLUB—Annual Contests, 11 Puritan Rd., Arlington, MA 02172. Attn: Virginia Thayer. Prizes range from $100 to $500 in various contests for members, nonmembers, and students. Deadline: April 15. Entry fee.

NEW ENGLAND THEATRE CONFERENCE—John Gassner Memorial Playwriting Award, c/o Dept. of Theatre, Northeastern Univ., 360 Huntington Ave., Boston, MA 02115. A $1,000 first prize and a $500 second prize are offered for unpublished, unproduced full-length plays written by New England residents or members of the NETC. Deadline: April 15. Entry fee.

NEW ISSUES PRESS/WESTERN MICHIGAN UNIVERSITY—New Issues Poetry Prize, Western Michigan Univ., Kalamazoo, MI 49008-5092. Attn: Herbert Scott, Ed. Awards $1,000 plus publication for a book-length collection of poetry by a poet who has never before published a full-length collection. Deadline: November 30. Entry fee.

NEW LETTERS—University of Missouri-Kansas City, 5100 Rockhill Rd., Kansas City, MO 64110-2499. Offers $750 for the best short story, to 5,000 words; $750 for the best group of three to six poems; $500 for the best essay, to 5,000 words. The work of each winner and first runner-up will be published. Deadline: May 15. Entry fee.

NEW YORK UNIVERSITY PRESS—New York University Press Prizes, 70 Washington Sq. S., 2nd Fl., New York, NY 10012-1091. Awards $1,000 plus publication to a book-length poetry manuscript and a book-length fiction manuscript. Deadline: May 1.

NIMROD/HARDMAN AWARDS—*Nimrod International Journal*, 600 S. College Ave., Tulsa, OK 74104-3189. Katherine Anne Porter Prize: offers prizes of $2,000 and $1,000 for fiction, to 7,500 words. Pablo Neruda Prize: offers prizes of $2,000 and $1,000 for one long poem or a selection of poems. Deadline: April 15. Entry fees.

NORTH CAROLINA WRITERS' NETWORK—International Literature Prizes, 3501 Hwy. 54 West, Studio C, Chapel Hill, NC 27516. Thomas Wolfe Fiction Prize: offers $500 for a previously unpublished short story or novel excerpt. Deadline: August 31. Paul Green Playwrights Prize: offers $500 for a previously unproduced, unpublished play. Deadline: September 30. Randall Jarrell Poetry Prize: offers $500 for a previously unpublished poem. Deadline: November 1. Entry fees.

NORTHEASTERN UNIVERSITY PRESS—Samuel French Morse Poetry Prize, English Dept., 406 Holmes Hall, Northeastern Univ., Boston, MA 02115. Attn: Prof. Guy Rotella, Chairman. Offers $500 plus publication for a full-length poetry manuscript by a U.S. poet who has published no more than one book of poems. Deadline: August 1 (for inquiries); September 15 (for entries). Entry fee.

NORTHERN KENTUCKY UNIVERSITY—Y.E.S. New Play Festival, Dept. of Theatre, FA 227, Nunn Dr., Highland Hts., KY 41099-1007. Attn: Sandra Forman, Project Dir. Awards three $400 prizes plus production for previously unproduced full-length plays and musicals. Deadline: October 31 (of even-numbered years).

NORTHERN MICHIGAN UNIVERSITY—Mildred & Albert Panowski Playwriting Competition, Forest Roberts Theatre, Northern Michigan Univ., 1401 Presque Isle Ave., Marquette, MI 49855-5364. Awards $2,000, plus production for an original, full-length, previously unproduced and unpublished play. Deadline: November 20.

O'NEILL THEATER CENTER—National Playwrights Conference, 234 W. 44th St., Suite 901, New York, NY 10036. Attn: Mary F. McCabe. Offers stipend, staged readings, and room and board at the conference, for new stage and television plays. Deadline: December 1. Entry fee.

OFF CENTER THEATER—Women Playwright's Festival, Tampa Bay Performing Arts Center, P.O. Box 518, Tampa, FL 33601. A $1,000 prize, production, and travel are offered for the best play about women, written by a woman; runner up receives staged reading. Deadline: September 15. Entry fee.

OLD DOMINION UNIVERSITY—Vassar Miller Prize in Poetry, c/o English Dept., Old Dominion University, Norfolk, VA 23529. Attn: Scott Cairns, Series Ed. Awards $1,000 plus publication by the University of North Texas Press for an original, unpublished poetry manuscript, 50 to 80 pages. Deadline: November 30. Entry fee.

PASSAGES NORTH—Elinor Benedict Poetry Prize, Dept. of English, Northern Michigan Univ., 1401 Presque Isle Ave., Marquette, MI 49855. $500 prize for unpublished poem. Deadline: December 1. Entry fee.

PATHWAY PRODUCTIONS—National Playwriting Contest, 9561 E. Daines Dr., Temple City, CA 91780. (Email: PathWayPro@aol.com) Awards $200 plus a workshop production to plays for and about teenagers. Deadline May 1.

PEN CENTER USA WEST—Grants for Writers with HIV/AIDS, 672 S. Lafayette Park Pl., #41, Los Angeles, CA 90057. Grants of $1,000 are awarded to writers with HIV/AIDS to continue and/or finish a current literary project. Writers living in the western U.S. who have been actively involved in creating literary work during the past three years are eligible to apply. Deadline: October 1.

PEN/JERARD FUND AWARD—PEN American Center, 568 Broadway, New York, NY 10012. Attn: John Morrone, Programs & Publications. Offers $4,000 to beginning female writers for a work-in-progress of general nonfiction. Applicants must have published at least one article in a national magazine or major literary magazine, but not more than one book of any kind. Deadline: January 1 (of odd-numbered years).

PEN WRITERS FUND—PEN American Center, 568 Broadway, New York, NY 10012. Attn: India Amos, Writers Fund Coordinator. Grants and interest-free loans of up to $500 are available to published writers or produced playwrights facing unanticipated financial emergencies. If the emergency is due to HIV- and AIDS-related illness, professional writers and editors qualify through the Fund for Writers and Editors with AIDS; all decisions are confidential. Deadline: year-round.

PEN WRITING AWARDS FOR PRISONERS—PEN American Center, 568 Broadway, New York, 10012. County, state, and federal prisoners are eligible to enter one unpublished manuscript, to 5,000 words, in each of these categories: fiction, drama, and nonfiction. Prisoners may submit up to 10 poems (any form) in the poetry category (to 20 pages total) in the poetry category. Prizes of $100, $50, and $25 are awarded in each category. Deadline: September 1.

PEREGRINE SMITH POETRY SERIES—Gibbs Smith, Publisher, P.O. Box 667, Layton, UT 84041. Offers a $500 prize plus publication for a previously unpublished 64-page poetry manuscript. Deadline: April 30. Entry fee.

PETERLOO POETS—Open Competition, 2 Kelly Gardens, Calstock, Cornwall PL18 9SA, U.K. Prizes totalling 5,100 British pounds, including a grand prize of £4,000 plus publication, are awarded for poems of up to 40 lines. Deadline: March 1. Entry fee.

PHILADELPHIA FESTIVAL OF WORLD CINEMA—"Set in Philadelphia" Screenwriting Competition, 3701 Chestnut St., Philadelphia, PA 19104-3195. A $5,000 prize is awarded for the best screenplay, 85 to 130 pages, set primarily in the greater Philadelphia area. Deadline: January 1. Entry fee.

PIG IRON PRESS—Kenneth Patchen Competition, P.O. Box 237, Youngstown, OH 44501. Awards paperback publication, $500, and 20 copies of the winning manuscript of fiction (in even-numbered years) and poetry (in odd-numbered years). Deadline: December 31. Entry fee.

PIONEER DRAMA SERVICE—Shubert Fendrich Memorial Playwriting Contest, P.O. Box 4267, Englewood, CO 80155-4267. A prize of publication plus a $1,000 advance is offered for a previously produced, though unpublished, full-length play suitable for community theater. Deadline: March 1.

PIRATE'S ALLEY FAULKNER SOCIETY—William Faulkner Creative Writing Competition, 632 Pirate's Alley, New Orleans, LA 70116. Prizes are $7,500 for an unpublished novel of fewer than 100,000 words; $2,500 for a novella of not more than 50,000 words; $1,500 for a short story, to 15,000 words; $1,500 for a personal essay to 2,500 words; and $750 for a single poem, to 750 words. All awards include prize money to be used as an advance against royalties to encourage publisher interest. Deadline: April 1. Entry fees.

PLAYBOY—College Fiction Contest, 680 N. Lakeshore Dr., Chicago, IL 60611. Prizes of $3,000 plus publication, and $500, are offered for a short story, up to 25 pages, by a college student. Deadline: January 1.

PLAYHOUSE ON THE SQUARE—New Play Competition, 51 S. Cooper, Memphis, TN 38104. Attn: Mr. Jackie Nichols, Exec. Dir. A stipend plus production is awarded for a full-length, previously unproduced play or musical. Deadline: April 1.

THE PLAYWRIGHTS' CENTER—Jerome Fellowships, 2301 Franklin Ave. E., Minneapolis, MN 55406. Five emerging playwrights are offered a $7,000 stipend and 12-month residency; housing and travel are not provided. Deadline: September 16.

POCKETS—Fiction Contest, c/o Lynn W. Gilliam, Assoc. Ed., P.O. Box 189, Nashville, TN 37202-0189. A $1,000 prize goes to the author of the winning 1,000-to 1,600-word story for children in grades 1 to 6. Deadline: August 15.

POETS AND PATRONS OF CHICAGO—Poets and Patrons of Chicago, 1206 Hutchings, Glenview, IL 60025. Attn: Agnes Wathall Tatera. Prizes are $75 and $25 for original, unpublished poems of up to 40 lines. Deadline: September 1.

POETS CLUB OF CHICAGO—130 Windsor Park Dr., C-323, Carol Stream, IL 60188. Attn: LaVone Holt. Shakespearean/Petrarchan Sonnet Contest, with prizes of $50, $35, and $15. Deadline: September 1.

PRISM INTERNATIONAL—Short Fiction Contest, Creative Writing Dept., Univ. of B.C., E462-1866 Main Mall, Vancouver, B.C., V6T 1Z1. Publication, a $2,000 first prize, and five $200 prizes are awarded for stories of up to 25 pages. Deadline: December 1. Entry fee.

PURDUE UNIVERSITY PRESS—Verna Emery Poetry Award, 1532 S. Campus Courts-E, W. Lafayette, IN 47907-1532. Unpublished collections of original poetry, 60 to 90 pages, are considered for an award of publication plus royalties. Deadline: April 15. Entry fee.

QUARTERLY WEST—Novella Competition, Univ. of Utah, 200 S. Central Campus Dr., Rm. 317, Salt Lake City, UT 84112-9109. Two $500 prizes plus publication will be awarded for novellas, 50 to 125 pages. Deadline: December 31. Entry fee.

RIVER CITY—Writing Awards in Fiction, Dept. of English, Univ. of Memphis, Memphis, TN 38152. Awards of $2,000 plus publication, $500, and $300 are offered for previously unpublished short stories, to 7,500 words. Deadline: December 1. Entry fee.

ROME ART & COMMUNITY CENTER—Milton Dorfman Poetry Prize, 308 W. Bloomfield St., Rome, NY 13440. Offers prizes of $500, $200, and $100 plus publication for the best original, unpublished poems. Deadline: November 1. Entry fee.

IAN ST. JAMES AWARDS—P.O. Box 60, Cranbrook, Kent TN17 2ZR, England. Attn: Merric Davidson. Offers 20 prizes of 200 to 2,000 British pounds plus publication for short stories. Deadline: April 30. Entry fee.

ST. MARTIN'S PRESS/MALICE DOMESTIC CONTEST—Thomas Dunne Books, 175 Fifth Ave., New York, NY 10010. Offers publication plus a $10,000 advance against royalties, for a best first traditional mystery novel. Deadline: October 15.

ST. MARTIN'S PRESS/PRIVATE EYE NOVEL CONTEST—PWA Contest, 175 Fifth Ave., New York, NY 10010. Co-sponsored by Private Eye Writers of America. The writer of the best first private eye novel, from 60,000 words, receives publication plus $10,000 against royalties. Deadline: August 1.

SARABANDE BOOKS—Poetry and Short Fiction Prizes, P.O. Box 4999, Louisville, KY 40204. Prizes are $2,000, publication, and a standard royalty contract in the competition for the Kathryn A. Morton Prize in Poetry (for a collection of poems, from 48 pages) and the Mary McCarthy Prize in Short Fiction (for a collection of short stories or novellas, 150 to 300 pages). Deadline: February 15. Entry fee.

SHENANARTS—Shenandoah International Playwrights Retreat, Rt. 5, Box 167-F, Staunton, VA 24401. Full fellowships are offered to playwrights to attend the four-week retreat held each August. Each year the retreat focuses on plays having to do with a specific region of the world. Deadline: February 1.

SIENA COLLEGE—International Playwrights' Competition, Siena College, 515 Loudon Rd., Loudonville, NY 12211-1462. Offers $2,000 plus campus residency expenses for the winning full-length script; no musicals. Deadline: June 30 (of even-numbered years).

SILVERFISH REVIEW PRESS—The Gerald Cable Poetry Contest, P.O. Box 3541, Eugene, OR 97403. Attn: Rodger Moody, Series Ed. Awards $1,000 plus publication to a book-length manuscript of poetry by an author who has not yet published a full-length collection. Deadline: November 1. Entry fee.

SNAKE NATION PRESS—Fiction and Poetry Contests, 110 #2 W. Force St., Valdosta, GA 31601. Attn: Nancy Phillips. Violet Reed Haas Prize: Offers publication plus $500 for a previously unpublished book of poetry, 50 to 75 pages. Deadline: January 15. *Snake Nation Review* Contest Issues: Prizes are publication plus $300, $200, and $100 for short stories; $100, $75, and $50 for poems. Deadlines: April 1; September 1. Entry fee.

SONORA REVIEW—Contests, Univ. of Arizona, Dept. of English, Tucson, AZ 85721. Poetry, Nonfiction Contest: offers $500 plus publication for the best poem; $150 plus publication for the best nonfiction. Deadline: July 1 for poetry and nonfiction. Short Story Contest: offers $500 plus publication for the best short story. Deadline: December 1. Entry fees.

SONS OF THE REPUBLIC OF TEXAS—Summerfield G. Roberts Award, 1717 8th St., Bay City, TX 77414. A prize of $2,500 is awarded for published or unpublished creative writing on the Republic of Texas, 1836-1846. Deadline: January 15.

THE SOUTHERN ANTHOLOGY—The Southern Prize, 2851 Johnston St., #123, Lafayette, LA 70503. A prize of $600 and publication are awarded for the best original, previously unpublished short story or novel excerpt, up to 7,500 words, or poem. Deadline: May 30. Entry fee.

SOUTHERN APPALACHIAN REPERTORY THEATRE—Playwrights' Conference, P.O. Box 1720, Mars Hill, NC 28754-0620. Attn: Dianne J. Chapman. Unproduced, unpublished scripts will be considered; up to 5 playwrights are selected to attend the conference and hear their plays read by professional actors; full production is possible. Deadline: October 30.

SOUTHERN POETRY REVIEW—Guy Owen Poetry Prize, Southern Poetry Review, Advancement Studies Dept., Central Piedmont Community College, Charlotte, NC 28235. Attn: Ken McLaurin, Ed. A prize of publication plus $500 is awarded for the best original, previously unpublished poem. Deadline: April 30. Entry fee.

THE SOW'S EAR PRESS—19535 Pleasant View Dr., Abingdon, VA 24211-6827. Chapbook Competition: offers a prize of $500 plus 50 published copies for the best poetry manuscript, as well as two $100 prizes. Deadline: April 30. Poetry Competition: offers prizes of $500, $100, and $50 for a previously unpublished poem of any length. Deadline: October 31. Entry fees.

SPOON RIVER POETRY REVIEW—Editors' Prize, 4240 Dept. of English, Illinois State Univ., Normal, IL 61790-4240. Publication and a $500 prize, as well as two $100 prizes, are awarded for single poems. Deadline: May 1. Entry fee.

STAND MAGAZINE—Short Story Competition, 179 Wingrove Rd., Newcastle upon Tyne, NE4 9DA, U.K. Prizes totalling 2,500 British pounds, including a £1,500 first prize, are awarded for previously unpublished stories under 6,000 words. Winning stories are published in *Stand Magazine*. Deadline: June 30 (of odd-numbered years). Entry fee.

STATE UNIVERSITY OF NEW YORK AT STONY BROOK—Short Fiction Prize, Dept. of English, Humanities Bldg., State Univ., Stony Brook, NY 11794-5350. Attn: Carolyn McGrath. A prize of $1,000 is offered for the best short story, up to 5,000 words, written by an undergraduate currently enrolled fulltime in an American or Canadian college. Deadline: February 28.

STORY LINE PRESS—Nicholas Roerich Prize, Three Oaks Farm, Brownsville, OR 97327-9718. A prize of $1,000 plus publication is awarded for an original book of poetry by a poet who has never before published a book of poetry. Deadline: October 15. Entry fee.

SUNY FARMINGDALE—Paumanok Poetry Award, Visiting Writers Program, Knapp Hall, SUNY Farmingdale, Farmingdale, NY 11735. Prizes of $1,000 and two $500 prizes are offered for entries of three to five poems. Deadline: September 15. Entry fee.

SYRACUSE UNIVERSITY PRESS—John Ben Snow Prize, 1600 Jamesville Ave., Syracuse, NY 13244-5160. Attn: Dir. Awards a $1,500 advance, plus publication, for an unpublished book-length nonfiction manuscript about New York State, especially upstate or central New York. Deadline: December 31.

TEN MINUTE MUSICALS PROJECT—Box 461194, W. Hollywood, CA 90046. Attn: Michael Koppy, Prod. Musicals of 7 to 20 minutes are eligible for a $250 advance against royalties and musical anthology productions at theaters in the U.S. and Canada. Deadline: August 31.

TENNESSEE MOUNTAIN WRITERS—The Tennessee Literary Awards, P.O. Box 4895, Oak Ridge, TN 37831-4895. Offers $250, $150, and $75 in two categories: Fiction and Poetry. Deadline: September 30. Entry fee.

THE THURBER HOUSE—Thurber House Residencies, 77 Jefferson Ave., Columbus, OH 43215. Attn: Michael J. Rosen, Lit. Dir. Three-month residencies and stipends of $5,000 each are awarded in the categories of writing, playwriting, and journalism. Winners have limited teaching responsibilities with The Ohio State University. Deadline: December 15.

TRITON COLLEGE—Salute to the Arts Poetry Contest, 2000 Fifth Ave., River Grove, IL 60171. Winning original, unpublished poems, to 60 lines, on designated themes, are published by Triton College. Deadline: April 1.

UNICO NATIONAL—Ella T. Grasso Literary Award Contest, 72 Burroughs Pl., Bloomfield, NJ 07003. A prize of $1,000 is awarded for the best essay or short story, 1,500 to 2,000 words, on the Italian-American experience; two $250 prizes also awarded. Deadline: April 1.

U.S. NAVAL INSTITUTE—Arleigh Burke Essay Contest, *Proceedings Magazine*, 118 Maryland Ave., Annapolis, MD 21402-5035. Attn: Bert Hubinger. Awards prizes of $3,000, $2,000, and $1,000 plus publication, for essays on the advancement of professional, literary, or scientific knowledge in the naval or maritime services, and the advancement of the knowledge of sea power. Deadline: December 1. Also sponsors several smaller contests; deadlines vary.

UNIVERSITIES WEST PRESS—Emily Dickinson Award in Poetry, P.O. Box 697, Williams, AZ 86046-0697. A prize of $500 plus publication is awarded for an unpublished poem. Deadline: July 31. Entry fee.

UNIVERSITY OF AKRON PRESS—The Akron Poetry Prize, 374B Bierce Library, Akron, OH 44325-1703. Publication and $500 are offered for a previously unpublished collection of poems. Deadline: June 30. Entry fee.

UNIVERSITY OF CALIFORNIA IRVINE—Chicano/Latino Literary Contest, Dept. of Spanish and Portuguese, UCI, Irvine, CA 92697-5275. Attn: Alejandro Morales, Dir. A first prize of $1,000 plus publication, and prizes of $500 and $250 are awarded in alternating years for poetry, drama, novels, and short stories. Deadline: April 30.

UNIVERSITY OF COLORADO—Nilon Award for Excellence in Minority Fiction, Fiction Collective Two, English Dept. Publications Ctr., Campus Box 494, Boulder, CO 80309-0494. Awards $1,000 plus joint publication for original, unpublished, book-length fiction, in English, by a U.S. citizen. Open to writers of the following ethnic minorities: African American, Hispanic, Asian, Native American or Alaskan Native, and Pacific Islander. Deadline: November 30.

UNIVERSITY OF GEORGIA PRESS—Flannery O'Connor Award for Short Fiction, Univ. of Georgia Press, 330 Research Dr., Athens, GA 30602-

4901. Two prizes of $1,000 plus publication are awarded for book-length collections of short fiction. Deadline: July 31. Entry fees.

UNIVERSITY OF GEORGIA PRESS CONTEMPORARY POETRY SERIES—Athens, GA 30602-4901. Offers publication of manuscripts from poets who have published at least one volume of poetry. Deadline: January 31. Publication of book-length poetry manuscripts is offered to poets who have never had a book of poems published. Deadline: September 30. Entry fee.

UNIVERSITY OF HAWAII AT MANOA—Kumu Kahua Playwriting Contest, Dept. of Drama and Theatre, 1770 East-West Rd., Honolulu, HI 96822. Awards $500 and $400 for full-length plays on the Hawaiian experience; $200 for plays on any topic. Also conducts contest for plays written by Hawaiian residents. Deadline: January 1.

UNIVERSITY OF IOWA—Iowa Publication Awards for Short Fiction, Iowa Writers' Workshop, 102 Dey House, Iowa City, IA 52242-1000. The John Simmons Short Fiction Award and the Iowa Short Fiction Award, both for unpublished full-length collections of short stories, offer publication under a standard contract. Deadline: September 30.

UNIVERSITY OF IOWA PRESS—The Iowa Poetry Prize, 100 Kuhl House, Iowa City, IA 52242-1000. Two $1,000 prizes, plus publication, are awarded for poetry manuscripts, 50 to 150 pages, by writers who have published at least one book of poetry. Deadline: May 31.

UNIVERSITY OF MASSACHUSETTS PRESS—Juniper Prize, Amherst, MA 01003. Offers a prize of $1,000 plus publication for a book-length manuscript of poetry; awarded in odd-numbered years to writers who have never published a book of poetry, and in even-numbered years to writers who have published a book or chapbook of poetry. Deadline: September 30. Entry fee.

UNIVERSITY OF NEBRASKA-OMAHA—Awards in Poetry and Fiction, *The Nebraska Review*, Univ. of Nebraska-Omaha, Omaha, NE 68182-0324. Offers $500 each plus publication to the winning short story (to 5,000 words) and the winning poem (or group of poems). Deadline: November 30. Entry fee.

UNIVERSITY OF NEBRASKA PRESS—North American Indian Prose Award, 312 N. 14th St., Lincoln, NE 68588-0484. Previously unpublished book-length manuscripts of biography, autobiography, history, literary criticism, and essays will be judged for originality, literary merit, and familiarity with North American Indian life. A $1,000 advance and publication are offered. Deadline: July 1.

UNIVERSITY OF PITTSBURGH PRESS—3347 Forbes Ave., Pittsburgh, PA 15261. Agnes Lynch Starrett Poetry Prize: offers $3,000 plus publication in the Pitt Poetry Series for a book-length collection of poems by a poet who has not yet published a volume of poetry. Deadline: April 30. Entry fee. Drue Heinz Literature Prize: offers $10,000 plus publication and royalty contract for an unpublished collection of short stories or novellas, 150 to 300 pages, by a writer who has previously published a book-length collection of fiction or at least three short stories or novellas in nationally distributed magazines. Deadline: June 30.

UNIVERSITY OF SOUTHERN CALIFORNIA—Ann Stanford Poetry Prize, Master of Professional Writing Program, WPH 404, Univ. of Southern California, Los Angeles, CA 90089-4034. Publication plus prizes of $750, $250, and $100 are awarded; submit up to five poems. Deadline: April 15. Entry fee.

UNIVERSITY OF WISCONSIN PRESS POETRY SERIES—114 N. Murray St., Madison, WI 53715. Attn: Ronald Wallace, Ed. Previously unpublished manuscripts, 50 to 80 pages, are considered for the Brittingham Prize in Poetry and the Felix Pollak Prize in Poetry, each offering $1,000 plus publication. Deadline: October 1. Entry fee.

THE UNTERBERG POETRY CENTER OF THE 92ND STREET Y—"Discovery"/*The Nation*, 1395 Lexington Ave., New York, NY 10128. Four prizes of $300, publication, and a reading are awarded for original 10-page manuscripts by writers who have not yet published a book of poetry. Deadline: February 1. Entry fee.

VETERANS OF FOREIGN WARS—Voice of Democracy Audio Essay Competition, VFW National Headquarters, 406 W. 34th St., Kansas City, MO 64111. Several national scholarships totalling over $120,000 are awarded to high school students for short, tape-recorded essays. Themes change annually. Deadline: November 1.

VILLA MONTALVO—Biennial Poetry Competition, P.O. Box 158, Saratoga, CA 95071. Residents of CA, NV, OR, and WA are eligible to enter poems in any style for prizes of: $1,000 plus an artist residency at Villa Montalvo, $500, and $300, as well as eight prizes of $25. Deadline: October 1 (of odd-numbered years). Entry fee.

WAGNER COLLEGE—Stanley Drama Award, Dept. of Humanities, 631 Howard Ave., Staten Island, NY 10301. Awards $2,000 for an original, previously unpublished and unproduced full-length play or musical or thematically related one-acts. Deadline: September 1.

TENNESSEE WILLIAMS/NEW ORLEANS LITERARY FESTIVAL—University of New Orleans, Lakefront, New Orleans, LA 70148. A $1,000 prize plus a staged reading and full production are offered for an original, unpublished one-act play. Deadline: December 1.

WRITERS AT WORK—Fellowship Competition, P.O. Box 1146, Centerville, UT 84014-5146. Prizes of $1,500 plus publication, and $500, in fiction and poetry categories, are awarded for excerpts of unpublished short stories, novels, essays, or poetry. Open to any writer who has not yet published a book-length volume of original work. Deadline: March 15. Entry fee.

THE WRITER'S VOICE—Annual Writing Awards, 5 W. 63rd St., New York, NY 10023. Capricorn Awards for writers over 40: $1,000 for a 48-to 68-page manuscript of poetry, and for the first 150 pages of a novel. Open Voice Awards: $500 each for published or unpublished writers of up to 10 pages of fiction or poetry. Deadline: December 31.

YALE UNIVERSITY PRESS—Yale Series of Younger Poets Prize, Box 209040, Yale Sta., New Haven, CT 06520-9040. Attn: Ed. Series publication is awarded for a book-length manuscript of poetry written by a poet under 40 who has not previously published a volume of poems. Deadline: February 29. Entry fee.

YOUNG PLAYWRIGHTS, INC.—Young Playwrights Festival, Dept. T, 321 W. 44th St., Suite 906, New York, NY 10036. Festival productions and readings are awarded for the best plays by writers 18 or younger. Deadline: December 1.

WRITERS COLONIES

Writers colonies offer solitude and freedom from everyday distractions so that writers can concentrate on their work. Though some colonies are quite small, with space for just three or four writers at a time, others can provide accommodations for as many as thirty or forty. The length of a residency may vary, too, from a couple of weeks to five or six months. These programs have strict admissions policies, and writers must submit a formal application or letter of intent, a resumé, writing samples, and letters of recommendation. As an alternative to the traditional writers colony, a few of the organizations listed offer writing rooms for writers who live nearby. Write for application information first, enclosing a stamped, self-addressed envelope. Residency fees are subject to change.

THE EDWARD F. ALBEE FOUNDATION, INC.
14 Harrison St.
New York, NY 10013
(212) 266-2020
David Briggs, *Foundation Secretary*
Located on Long Island, "The Barn," or the William Flanagan Memorial Creative Persons Center, is maintained by the Albee Foundation. "The standards for admission are, simply, talent and need." Twelve writers are accepted each season for one-month residencies, available from June 1 to October 1; applications, including writing samples, project description, and resumé, are accepted from January 1 to April 1. There is no fee, though residents are responsible for their own food and travel expenses.

ALTOS DE CHAVÒN
c/o Parsons School of Design
2 W. 13th St., Rm. 707
New York, NY 10011
(212) 229-5370
Stephen D. Kaplan, *Arts/Education Director*
Altos de Chavòn is a nonprofit center for the arts in the Dominican Republic committed to education, design innovation, international creative exchange, and the promotion of Dominican culture. Residencies average 12 weeks and provide the emerging or established artist an opportunity to live and work in a setting of architectural and natural beauty. All artists are welcome to apply, though writers should note there are no typewriters, the library is oriented more toward the design profession, and the apartments housing writers also accommodate university students. Two to three writers are chosen each year for the program. The fee is $350 per month for an apartment with kitchenette; linen and cleaning services are available at an extra cost. Applications include a letter of interest, writing sample, and resumé; deadline for application is July 15.

MARY ANDERSON CENTER FOR THE ARTS
101 St. Francis Dr.
Mount St. Francis, IN 47146
(812) 923-8602
Sarah Roberson Yates, *Executive Director*
Founded in 1989, the artists' residency and retreat is situated on the grounds of a Franciscan friary. Space is available for seven residents at a

time, including private rooms, working space, and a visual artists' studio; meals are provided. Two-week to three-month residencies are available and are granted based on project proposal and the artist's body of work; applications are accepted year-round. Fees are $30 per day, plus $15 to apply.

ATLANTIC CENTER FOR THE ARTS
1414 Art Center Ave.
New Smyrna Beach, FL 32168
(904) 427-6975
web site: www.atlantic-centerarts.org
Nicholas Conroy, *Program Director*

The center is located on the east coast of central Florida, with 67 acres of pristine hammockland on a tidal estuary. All buildings, connected by raised wooden walkways, are handicapped accessible and air conditioned. The center provides a unique environment for sharing ideas, learning, and collaborating on interdisciplinary projects. Master artists meet with talented artists for readings and critiques, with time out for individual work. Residencies are one to three weeks. Fees are $100 a week for tuition and $25 a day for housing; off-site, tuition-only plans are available; financial aid is limited. Application deadlines vary.

BERLINER KÜNSTLERPROGRAM
Artists-in-Berlin Program
Jägerstr. 23
D-10117 Berlin, Germany
030-2022080; fax: 030-2041267
e-mail: daad@daad.b.shuttle.de

One-year residencies are offered to well-known and emerging writers, filmmakers, and composers to promote cultural exchange. Up to 20 residencies are offered for periods beginning between January 1 and June 30. Room, board, travel, and living expenses are awarded. Application, project description, and copies of publications are due by January 1 of the year preceding the residency.

BLUE MOUNTAIN CENTER
Blue Mountain Lake, NY 12812-0109
(518) 352-7391
Harriet Barlow, *Director*

Hosts month-long residencies for artists and writers from mid-June to late October. Established fiction and nonfiction writers, poets, and playwrights whose work evinces social and ecological concern are eligible; 14 residents are accepted per session. Residents are not charged for their time at Blue Mountain, although all visitors are invited to contribute to the studio construction fund. There is no application form; apply by sending a brief biographical sketch, a plan for work at Blue Mountain, five to 10 slides or a writing sample of any length, an indication of preference for an early summer, late summer, or fall residence, and a $20 application fee, attention: *Admissions Committee*. Applications are due February 1.

BYRDCLIFFE ARTS COLONY
Artists' Residency Program
Woodstock Guild
34 Tinker St.
Woodstock, NY 12498
(914) 679-2079
e-mail: wguild@ulster.net web site: www.ulster.net/»wguild
Attn: *Director*
     The Villetta Inn, located on the 400-acre arts colony, offers private studios and separate bedrooms, a communal kitchen, and a peaceful environment for fiction writers, poets, playwrights, and visual artists. One-month residencies are offered from June to September. Fee is $500 per month. Submit application, resumé, writing sample, and two letters of recommendation; the deadline is April 1. Send SASE for application.

THE CAMARGO FOUNDATION
125 Park Square Ct.
400 Sibley St.
St. Paul, MN 55101-1982
Sheryl Mousley, *U.S. Secretariat*
     The Camargo Foundation maintains a center of studies in France for the benefit of nine scholars and graduate students each semester who wish to pursue projects in the humanities and social sciences relative to France and Francophone culture. In addition, one artist, one composer, and one writer are accepted each semester. The foundation offers furnished apartments and a reference library in the city of Cassis. Research should be at an advanced stage and not require resources unavailable in the Marseilles-Aix-Cassis region. Fellows must be in residence at the foundation; the award is exclusively a residential grant. Application materials include: application form, curriculum vitae, three letters of recommendation, and project description. Writers, artists, and composers are required to send work samples. Applications are due February 1.

CENTRUM
P.O. Box 1158
Port Townsend, WA 98368
(360) 385-3102
Marlene Bennett, *Program Facilitator*
     Writers are awarded one-month residencies between September and May. Applicants selected by a peer jury receive free housing and a $300 stipend. Previous residents may return on a space-available basis for a monthly fee. Applications are due October 1. The application fee is $15.

DJERASSI RESIDENT ARTISTS PROGRAM
2325 Bear Gulch Rd.
Woodside, CA 94062
(650) 747-1250; fax: (650) 747-0105
e-mail: drap@djerassi.org web site: www.djerassi.org
Judy Freeland, *Residency Coordinator*
     The Djerassi Program offers living and working spaces in a rural setting, for writers in the categories of prose (fiction), drama (playwrights, screenwriters), music (composers, librettists, lyricists), and poetry. Residencies are from four to five weeks. There are no fees other than the $25

application fee. The application deadline is February 15. Send an SASE for application packet.

DORLAND MOUNTAIN ARTS COLONY
Box 6
Temecula, CA 92593
(909) 676-5039
e-mail: dorland@ez2.net; web site: www.ez2.net/dorland/
Attn: *Admissions Committee*

Dorland is a nature preserve and "primitive retreat for creative people" located in the Palomar Mountains of Southern California. "Without electricity, residents find a new, natural rhythm for their work." Novelists, playwrights, poets, nonfiction writers, composers, and visual artists are encouraged to apply for residencies of one to two months. The fee of $300 a month includes cottage, fuel, and firewood. Send SASE for application; deadlines are March 1 and September 1.

DORSET COLONY HOUSE
Box 510
Dorset, VT 05251
(802) 867-2223
John Nassivera, *Director*

Writers and playwrights are offered low-cost room with kitchen facilities at the historic Colony House in Dorset, Vermont. Residencies are one week to one month, and are available in the fall and spring. Applications are accepted year-round, and up to eight writers stay at a time. The fee is $95 per week; financial aid is limited. For more information, send SASE.

FINE ARTS WORK CENTER IN PROVINCETOWN
24 Pearl St.
Provincetown, MA 02657
Hunter O'Hanian, *Executive Director*

Fellowships, including living and studio space and monthly stipends, are available at the Fine Arts Work Center on Cape Cod, for fiction writers and poets to work independently. Residencies are for seven months, October through May; apply before February 1 deadline. Five poets and five fiction writers are accepted. Send SASE for details; indicate that you are a writer in the request.

GLENESSENCE WRITERS COLONY
1447 West Ward Ave.
Ridgecrest, CA 93555
(760) 446-5894
Allison Swift, *Director*

Glenessence is a luxury villa located in the Upper Mojave Desert, offering private rooms with bath, pool, spa, courtyard, shared kitchen, fitness center, and library. Children, pets, and smoking are prohibited. Residencies are offered at $565 per month; meals are not provided. Reservations are made on a first-come basis. Seasonal: March through May; September through November.

THE TYRONE GUTHRIE CENTRE
Annaghmakerrig, Newbliss
County Monaghan
Ireland
(353) 47-54003; fax: (353) 47-54380
Bernard Loughlin, *Director*

Set on a 450-acre country estate, the center offers peace and seclusion to writers and other artists to enable them to get on with their work. All art forms are represented. One-to three-month residencies are offered throughout the year, at the rate of 2,000 pounds per month; financial assistance is available to Irish citizens only. A number of longer term self-catering houses in the old farmyard are also available at £300 per week. Writers chosen on the basis of c.v., samples of published work, and outline of intended project. Writers may apply for acceptance year-round.

THE HAMBIDGE CENTER
P.O. Box 339
Rabun Gap, GA 30568
(706) 746-5718; fax: (706) 746-9933
Judy Barber, *Director*

The Hambidge Center for Creative Arts and Sciences is located on 600 pristine acres of quiet woods in the north Georgia mountains. Eight private cottages are available for fellows. All fellowships are partially underwritten, residents are asked to contribute $125 per week. Two-week to six-week residencies, from March through December are offered to serious artists from all disciplines. Send SASE for application form. Application deadlines: November 1 and May 1.

HEADLANDS CENTER FOR THE ARTS
944 Fort Barry
Sausalito, CA 94965
(415) 331-2787

Programs at the Headlands Center, located on 13,000 acres of open coastal space, are available to residents of Ohio, North Carolina, and California. Application requirements vary by state. Decisions are announced in October for residencies beginning in February. There are no residency or application fees. Send SASE for more information.

HEDGEBROOK
2197 E. Millman Rd.
Langley, WA 98260
(360) 321-4786

Hedgebrook provides women writers, published or not, of all ages and from all cultural backgrounds, with a natural place to work. Established in 1988, the retreat is located on 30 acres of farmland and woods on Whidbey Island in Washington State. Each writer has her own cottage, equipped with electricity and woodstove. A bathhouse serves all six cottages. Writers gather for dinner in the farmhouse every evening and frequently read in the living room/library afterwards. Limited travel scholarships are available. Residencies range from one week to two months. April 1 is the application deadline for residencies from mid-June to mid-December; October 1 for mid-January to late May. Applicants are chosen by a selection committee composed of writers. There is a $15 fee to apply; send SASE for application.

KALANI OCEANSIDE RETREAT, INSTITUTE FOR CULTURE AND WELLNESS
Artist-in-Residence Program
RR2, Box 4500
Pahoa-Beach Road, HI 96778
(808) 965-7828; (800) 800-6886; fax: (808) 965-9613
e-mail: kalani@kalani.com; web site: www.kalani.com
Richard Koob, *Program Coordinator*

Located in a rural coastal setting of 113 botanical acres, Kalani Eco-Resort hosts and sponsors educational programs "with the aloha experience that is its namesake: harmony of heaven and earth." Residencies range from two weeks to two months and are available throughout the year. Fees range from $33 to $55 per day, meals available at additional fee. Applications accepted year-round.

LEIGHTON STUDIOS FOR INDEPENDENT RESIDENCIES
Office of the Registrar
The Banff Centre for the Arts
Box 1020, Station 28
107 Tunnel Mountain Dr.
Banff, Alberta T0L 0C0
Canada
(403) 762-6180; (800) 565-9989; fax: (403) 762-6345
e-mail: arts_info@banffcentre.ab.ca
web site: www.banffcentre.ab.ca/Leighton_Studios/
Attn: *Registrar*

The Leighton Studios are open year-round, providing time and space for artists to produce new work. Established writers, composers, musicians, and visual artists of all nationalities are encouraged to apply. Artists working in other mediums at the conceptual state of a project will also be considered. Weekly fees (Canadian dollars): $315 studio; $263 single room; $98.00 meals (optional). Reductions in the studio fee are available to applicants demonstrating financial need. Applications are accepted at any time. Space is limited; apply at least six months prior to preferred starting date. Write for application form or apply online.

THE MACDOWELL COLONY
100 High St.
Peterborough, NH 03458
(603) 924-3886
web site: www.macdowellcolony.org
Pat Dodge, *Admissions Coordinator*

Studios, room, and board are available for writers to work without interruption in a woodland setting. Selection is competitive. Apply by January 15 for stays May through August; April 15 for September through December; and September 15 for January through April. Residencies last up to eight weeks, and 80 to 90 writers are accepted each year. Send SASE for application.

THE MILLAY COLONY FOR THE ARTS
444 East Hill Rd.
P.O. Box 3
Austerlitz, NY 12017-0003
(518) 392-3103
Gail Giles, *Assistant Director*

At Steepletop, the former home of Edna St. Vincent Millay, writers are provided studios, universally accessible living quarters, and meals at no cost. Residencies last one month. Application deadlines are February 1, May 1, and September 1. Send SASE for more information and application. Applications can also be accessed by e-mail (application@millay colony.org).

MILLETT FARM: AN ART COLONY FOR WOMEN
295 Bowery
New York, NY 10003
Kate Millett, *Director*
Summer residencies are offered to women writers and visual artists at a picturesque tree farm in rural New York. In return for housing, all residents contribute four hours of work each weekday morning and contribute $80 a week toward meals. Preference is given to writers who can stay all summer or at least six weeks. For more information send an SASE.

MOLASSES POND WRITERS' RETREAT AND WORKSHOP
RR 1, Box 85C
Milbridge, ME 04658
(207) 546-2506
Martha Barron Barrett and Sue Wheeler, *Coordinators*
Led by published authors who teach writing at the University of New Hampshire. The one-week workshop is held in June and includes time set aside for writing, as well as manuscript critique and writing classes. Up to 10 writers participate, staying in a colonial farmhouse with private bed/work rooms for each participant and common areas for meals and classes. The $400 fee covers lodging, meals, and tuition. Applicants must be serious about their work. No children's literature or poetry. Submit statement of purpose and 15 to 20 pages of fiction or nonfiction between February 15 and March 1.

MONTANA ARTISTS REFUGE
Box 8
Basin, MT 59631
(406) 225-3525
Writers are offered low-cost apartment and studio space in a relaxed and unpretentious atmosphere, where they can work with other artists or in solitude. Residencies range from three months to one year, and rents range from $200 to $400 per month. Limited financial aid is available. Send SASE for information.

JENNY McKEAN MOORE WRITER-IN-WASHINGTON
Dept. of English
The George Washington University
Washington, DC 20052
Attn: Prof. Christopher Sten
The fellowship allows for a writer to teach two paid semesters (salary: $48,000) at The George Washington University. Teaching duties include a workshop each semester for students from the metropolitan community who may have had little formal education; and one class each semester for university students. Fiction and poetry alternate years. Applications include letter, indicating publications and other projects, extent of teaching experience, and other qualifications. The application must also include a resumé and a ten-to fifteen-page sample of your work. The application deadline is November 15.

NEW YORK MILLS ARTS RETREAT AND REGIONAL CULTURAL CENTER
24 N. Main Ave.
P.O. Box 246
New York Mills, MN 56567
(218) 385-3339
Kent Scheer, *Retreat Coordinator*

The Cultural Center, housed in a restored 1895 general store, is an innovative non-profit organization offering gallery exhibits, musical performances, theater, literary events, educational programs, the Great American Think-Off philosophy competition, and the Continental Divide Film and Music Festival. The Arts Retreat provides housing at the Whistle Stop Inn, a bed and breakfast located in an old, Victorian style home. Each artist receives financial assistance through a stipend, ranging from $750 for a two-week residency to $1,500 for four weeks, provided by the Jerome Foundation. Five to seven emerging artists, writers, filmmakers, or musicians are accepted during the nine month season. There is a review process twice a year; the deadlines are April 1 and October 1.

THE NORTHWOOD UNIVERSITY
Alden B. Dow Creativity Center
3225 Cook Rd.
Midland, MI 48640-2398
(517) 837-4478; fax: (517) 837-4468
Liz Drake, *Assistant Director*

The Fellowship Program allows individuals time away from their on-going daily routines to pursue their project ideas without interruption. A project idea should be innovative, creative, and have potential for impact in its field. Four ten-week residencies, lasting from early-June to mid-August, are awarded yearly. There is a $10 application fee. A $750 stipend plus room and board are provided. No spouses or families. Applications are due December 31.

OX-BOW
37 S. Wabash Ave.
Chicago, IL 60603
(312) 899-7455

One-week residencies are available mid-June to mid-August for writers who wish to reside and work in a secluded, natural environment. Recipients are required to pay $372 room and board, per week. Primarily a program for the visual arts, the mission of Ox-Bow is to nurture the creative process through instruction, example, and community. Resident writers are encouraged to present a reading of their work and to participate in the community life at Ox-Bow. For application form write or call. Application deadline is May 15.

RAGDALE FOUNDATION
1260 N. Green Bay Rd.
Lake Forest, IL 60045
(847) 234-1063
Sonja Carlborg, *Director*

Uninterrupted time and peaceful space allow writers a chance to finish works in progress, to begin new works, to solve thorny creative problems, and to experiment in new genres. The foundation is located 30 miles north of Chicago, on 55 acres of prairie. Residencies of two weeks to two months are available for writers, artists, and composers. The fee is $15 a day; some full and partial fee waivers available, based solely on financial need. Send SASE for deadline information. Application fee: $20.

SASKATCHEWAN WRITERS GUILD
Writers/Artists Colonies and Individual Retreats
P.O. Box 3986
Regina, Saskatchewan S4P 3R9
Canada
(306) 757-6310
Attn: *Colony Coordinator*

The Saskatchewan Colonies are at two locations: St. Peter's Abbey, near Humboldt, provides a six-week summer colony (July-August) and a two-week winter colony in February, for up to eight writers and artists at a time; applicant stays vary. Individual retreats of up to a month are offered year-round at St. Peter's, for up to three residents at a time. Emma Lake, near Prince Albert, is the site of a two-week residency in August. A fee of $125 (Saskatchewan Writers Guild members) or $175 (nonmembers) per week includes room and board. Submit application form, resumé, project description, two references, and a 10-page writing sample. Saskatchewan residents are given preference. Apply two to three months in advance.

THE JOHN STEINBECK ROOM
Long Island University
Southampton College Library
Southampton, NY 11968
(516) 287-8382
Robert Gerbereux, *Library Director*

The John Steinbeck Room at Long Island University provides a basic research facility to writers who have either a current contract with a book publisher or a confirmed assignment from a magazine editor. The room is available for a period of six months with one six-month renewal permissible. Send SASE for application.

THE THURBER HOUSE RESIDENCIES
c/o Thurber House
77 Jefferson Ave.
Columbus, OH 43215
(614) 464-1032; fax: (614) 228-7445
Michael J. Rosen, *Literary Director*

Residencies in the restored home of James Thurber are awarded to journalists, poets, and playwrights. Residents work on their own writing projects, and in addition to other duties, teach one class at the Ohio State University. A stipend of $5,000 per quarter is provided. A letter of interest and curriculum vitae must be received by December 15, at which time applications are reviewed for the upcoming academic year.

UCROSS FOUNDATION
Residency Program
2836 U.S. Hwy. 14-16 East
Clearmont, WY 82835
(307) 737-2291; fax: (307) 737-2322
Sharon Dynak, *Executive Director*

Residencies, two to eight weeks, in the foothills of the Big Horn Mountains in Wyoming, allow writers, artists, and scholars to concentrate on their work without interruption. Two residency sessions are scheduled annually: February to June and August to December. There is no charge for room, board, or studio space. Application deadlines are March 1 for the fall session and October 1 for the spring session. Send SASE for more information.

VERMONT STUDIO CENTER
P.O. Box 613NW
Johnson, VT 05656
(802) 635-2727; fax: (802) 635-2730;
e-mail: vscvt@pwshift.com
Attn: *Registrar*

The Vermont Studio Center offers two-week studio sessions for up to 12 writers from February through April, led by prominent writers and teachers focusing on fiction, creative nonfiction, and poetry. Independent writers' retreats from two to 12 weeks are available year-round for those seeking more solitude. Room, working studio, and meals are included in all programs. The fee is $2,900 for a month-long residency. Financial assistance is available based on both merit and need. Applications are accepted year-round. Application fee: $25.

VILLA MONTALVO ARTIST RESIDENCY PROGRAM
P.O. Box 158
Saratoga, CA 95071
(408) 961-5818
Kathryn Funk, *Artist Residency Program Director*

Villa Montalvo, in the foothills of the Santa Cruz Mountains south of San Francisco, offers one-to three-month residencies free of charge to writers. Several merit-based fellowships are available. The application deadlines are September 1 and March 1; send self-addressed label and 55¢ postage to receive brochure and application form. Application fee is $20.

VIRGINIA CENTER FOR THE CREATIVE ARTS
Sweet Briar, VA 24595
(804) 946-7236
Suny Monk, *Executive Director*

A working retreat for writers, composers, and visual artists in Virginia's Blue Ridge Mountains. Residencies from two weeks to two months are available year-round. Application deadlines are the 15th of January, May, and September; about 300 residents are accepted each year. A limited amount of financial assistance is available. Send SASE for more information.

THE WRITERS ROOM
10 Astor Pl., 6th Fl.
New York, NY 10003
(212) 254-6995; fax: (212) 533-6059
Donna Brodie, *Executive Director*

Located in the East Village, The Writers Room provides subsidized work space to all types of writers at all stages of their careers. "We offer urban writers a quiet place to escape from noisy neighbors, children, roommates, and other distractions of city life." The Room holds 30 desks separated by partitions, a typing room with five desks, a kitchen, and a library. Open 24 hours a day, 365 days a year. There is a one-time $50 application fee; fees for the three-month period include $175 for a "floater" desk. Part-time memberships at reduced rates are also available. Call, fax or write for application (no visits without appointment).

THE WRITERS STUDIO
The Mercantile Library Association
17 E. 47th St.
New York, NY 10017
(212) 755-6710
Harold Augenbraum, *Director*

The Writers Studio is a quiet place in which writers can rent space conducive to the production of good work. A carrel, locker, small reference collection, electrical outlets, and membership in the Mercantile Library of New York are available at the cost of $200 per three-month residency. Submit application, resumé, and writing samples; applications are considered year-round.

HELENE WURLITZER FOUNDATION OF NEW MEXICO
Box 545
Taos, NM 87571
(505) 758-2413; fax: (505) 758-2559

Rent-free and utility-free studios in Taos are offered to writers and creative artists in all media. "All artists are given the opportunity to be free of the shackles of a 9-to-5 routine." Length of residency varies from three to six months. The foundation is open from April 1 through September 30 and on a limited basis October through March. Residencies are assigned into the year 2001, but cancellations do occur. Write or fax for an application.

YADDO
Box 395
Saratoga Springs, NY 12866-0395
(518) 584-0746; fax: (518) 584-1312
e-mail: CHWAIT@aol.com
Candace Wait, *Program Coordinator*

Visual artists, writers, choreographers, film/video artists, performance artists, composers, and collaborators are invited for stays from two weeks to two months. Room, board, and studio space are provided. No stipends. Deadlines are January 15 and August 1. There is a $20 application fee; send SASE for form.

WRITERS CONFERENCES

Each year, hundreds of writers conferences are held across the country. The following list, arranged by state, represents a sampling of conferences; each listing includes the location of the conference, the month during which it is usually held, and the name and address of the person from whom specific information may be received. Writers are advised to write directly to conference directors for full details. Always enclose an SASE. Additional conferences are listed annually in the May issue of *The Writer* Magazine (120 Boylston St., Boston, MA 02116-4615).

ALABAMA

SPRING MINGLE '99—Gulf Shores, AL. February. Joan Broerman, Reg. Adv., Southern Breeze SCBWI, P.O. Box 26282, Birmingham, AL 35260.

WRITING TODAY—Birmingham, AL. March. Martha Andrews, Dir. of Special Events, Birmingham-Southern College, Box 549003, Birmingham, AL 35254.

SCBWI "WRITING & ILLUSTRATING FOR KIDS"—Birmingham, AL. October. Joan Broerman, Reg. Adv., Southern Breeze SCBWI, P.O. Box 26282, Birmingham, AL 35226.

ALASKA

SITKA SYMPOSIUM ON HUMAN VALUES & THE WRITTEN WORD—Sitka, AK. June. Carolyn Servid, Dir., The Island Institute, P.O. Box 2420, Sitka, AK 99835.

ARKANSAS

ARKANSAS WRITER'S CONFERENCE—Little Rock, AR. June. Peggy Vining, Dir., 6817 Gingerbread Ln., Little Rock, AR 72204.

CALIFORNIA

SAN DIEGO STATE UNIVERSITY ANNUAL WRITERS' CONFERENCE—San Diego, CA. January. Diane Dunaway, Coord., 5250 Campanile Dr., Room 2503, San Diego, CA 92182-1920.

JACK LONDON'S WRITERS' CONFERENCE—S. San Francisco, CA. March. Mariann M. Jackson, Dir., 327 "B" St., Redwood City, CA 94063.

IWWG EARLY SPRING IN CALIFORNIA CONFERENCE—Santa Cruz, CA. March. Hannelore Hahn, Dir., IWWG, P.O. Box 810, Gracie Station, New York, NY 10028.

WRITERS' FORUM—Pasadena, CA. March. Meredith Brucker, Dir., Pasadena City College, 1570 E. Colorado Blvd., Pasadena, CA 91106.

MOUNT HERMON CHRISTIAN WRITERS CONFERENCE—Mount Hermon, CA. March. David R. Talbott, Dir., P.O. Box 413, Mount Hermon, CA 95041.

FOOTHILL WRITERS' CONFERENCE—Los Altos Hills, CA. June. Kim Wolterbeek, Dir., Foothill College, 12345 El Monte Rd., Los Altos Hills, CA 94022.

GENE PERRET'S ROUND TABLE COMEDY WRITERS CONVENTION—Los Angeles, CA. July. Linda Perret, Dir., P.O. Box 786, Agoura Hills, CA 91376.

"WRITE-TO-BE-READ" WORKSHOP—Hume Lake, CA. July. Norman B. Rohrer, Dir., 260 Fern Lane, Hume Lake, CA 93628.

SQUAW VALLEY COMMUNITY OF WRITERS—Squaw Valley, CA. July-August. Brett Hall Jones, Dir., 10626 Banner Lava Cap, Nevada City, CA 95959.

CONFERENCE IN WRITING & ILLUSTRATING FOR CHILDREN—Los Angeles, CA. August. Lin Oliver, Dir., SCBWI, 345 N. Maple Dr., #296, Beverly Hills, CA 90210.

COLORADO

COLORADO CHRISTIAN WRITERS CONFERENCE—Estes Park, CO. May. Marlene Bagnull, Dir., 316 Blanchard Rd., Drexel Hill, PA 19026.

ASPEN WRITERS' FOUNDATION—Aspen, CO. June. Jeanne McGovern, Dir., Box 7726, Aspen, CO 81612.

18TH ANNUAL STEAMBOAT SPRINGS WRITERS CONFERENCE—Steamboat Springs, CO. July. Harriet Freiberger, Dir., P.O. Box 774284, Steamboat Springs, CO 80477.

24TH ANNUAL PUBLISHING INSTITUTE AT THE UNIVERSITY OF DENVER—Denver, CO. July-August. Elizabeth Geiser, Dir., 2075 S. Univ. Blvd., #D-114, Denver, CO 80210.

WOMEN & MOTHER EARTH CONFERENCE—Grand Junction, CO. August. Karla Vanderzanden, Exec. Dir., Canyonlands Field Institute, P.O. Box 68, Moab, UT 84532.

CONNECTICUT

SCBWI NEW ENGLAND CONFERENCE—Hartford, CT. May. Pegi Dietz Shea, Dir., 27 Fox Hill Dr., Rockville, CT 06066.

WESLEYAN WRITERS CONFERENCE—Middletown, CT. June. Anne Greene, Dir., Wesleyan Univ., Middletown, CT 06457.

DISTRICT OF COLUMBIA

WASHINGTON INDEPENDENT WRITERS SPRING CONFERENCE—Washington, DC. May. Rebecca Clay, Dir., 220 Woodward Bldg., 733-15th St. N.W., Washington, DC 20005.

EDPRESS—Washington, DC. June. Jeri Henorie, Dir., 201 Mullica Hill Rd., Glassboro, NJ 08028.

FLORIDA

17TH ANNUAL KEY WEST LITERARY SEMINAR: THE AMERICAN NOVEL—Key West, FL. January. Admin. Office, 9 Sixth St., Plum Island, MA 01951.

FLORIDA SUNCOAST WRITERS' CONFERENCE—St. Petersburg, FL. February. Steve Rubin, Dir., Univ. of South Florida, Dept. of English, Tampa, FL 33620.

19TH ANNUAL SOUTHWEST FLORIDA WRITERS' CONFERENCE— Ft. Myers, FL. February. Harold Hunt, Dir., GCCNWA, 2323 Del Prado Blvd., Suite 7, Cape Coral, FL 33990.

SLEUTHFEST '99—Fort Lauderdale, FL. March. Dianne N. Ell, Dir., 1432 S.E. 8th St., Deerfield Beach, FL 83441.

ERNEST HEMINGWAY LITERARY CONFERENCE—Sanibel Island, FL. June. Jeffry P. Lindsay, Dir., 2323 Del Prado Blvd., Suite 7, Cape Coral, FL 33990.

HEMINGWAY DAYS FESTIVAL & WRITER'S WORKSHOP—Key West, FL. July. K. Thurman, Dir., P.O. Box 4045, Key West, FL 33040.

FLORIDA REGION SCBWI CONFERENCE—Palm Springs, FL. September. Barbara Casey, Reg. Adv., 2158 Portland Ave., Wellington, FL 33414.

GEORGIA

SANDHILLS WRITERS CONFERENCE—Augusta, GA. March. Anthony Kellman, Dir., Augusta State Univ., Dept. of Lang, Lit. & Comm., 2500 Walton Way, Augusta, GA 30904.

SOUTHEASTERN WRITER'S ASSOC. WORKSHOP/CONFERENCE— St. Simons Island, GA. June. Cappy Hall Rearick, Pres., 114 Gould St., St. Simons Island, GA 31522.

ILLINOIS

MISSISSIPPI VALLEY WRITERS CONFERENCE—Rock Island, IL. June. David R. Collins, Dir., 3403-45th St., Moline, IL 61265.

WRITE-TO-PUBLISH CONFERENCE—Wheaton, IL. June. Lin Johnson, Dir., 9731 N. Fox Glen Dr., #6F, Niles, IL 60714.

"OF DARK & STORMY NIGHTS" WRITERS CONFERENCE—Rolling Meadows, IL. June. W.W. Spurgeon, Dir., P.O. Box 1944, Muncie, IN 47308.

19TH ANNUAL ROMANCE WRITERS OF AMERICA CONFERENCE— Chicago, IL. July-August. Allison Kelley, Dir., 13700 Veterans Memorial, #315, Houston, TX 77014.

AUTUMN AUTHORS' AFFAIR XVI—Schaumburg, IL. October. Nancy McCann, Dir., 1507 Burnham Ave., Calumet City, IL 60409.

INDIANA

BUTLER UNIVERSITY CHILDREN'S LITERATURE CONFERENCE— Indianapolis, IN. January. Valiska Gregory, Dir., c/o Shirley Daniel, Butler University, 4600 Sunset Dr., Indianapolis, IN 46208.

INDIANA UNIVERSITY WRITERS' CONFERENCE—Bloomington, IN. June-July. Maura Stanton, Dir., Ballantine 464, Bloomington, IN 47405.

MIDWEST WRITERS WORKSHOP—Muncie, IN. July. Earl Conn, Dir., Ball State Univ., Dept. of Journalism, Muncie, IN 47306.

IOWA

IOWA SUMMER WRITING FESTIVAL—Iowa City, IA. June, July. Peggy Houston, Dir., Univ. of Iowa, 116 International Center, Iowa City, IA 52242.

KANSAS

WRITERS WORKSHOP IN SCIENCE FICTION—Lawrence, KS. July. James Gunn, Dir., Univ. of Kansas, English Dept., Lawrence, KS 66045.

KENTUCKY

GREEN RIVER NOVELS-IN-PROGRESS WORKSHOP—Louisville, KY. March. Mary E. O'Dell, Dir., Green River Writers, Inc., 11906 Locust Rd., Middletown, KY 40243.

WRITERS RETREAT WORKSHOP—Erlanger, KY. May. Gail Provost, Dir., 9314 S. Evanston Pl., #1204, Tulsa, OK 74137.

GREEN RIVER WORKSHOP WEEKEND & WRITERS RETREAT— Louisville, KY. July. Mary E. O'Dell, Dir., Green River Writers, Inc., 11906 Locust Rd., Middletown, KY 40243.

TOUCH OF SUCCESS WRITING SEMINARS—Glendale, KY. October. Bill Thomas, Dir., Box 59, Glendale, KY 42740.

LOUISIANA

NORTH LOUISIANA ROMANCE WRITERS, INC., ROMANCE & MORE CONFERENCE—Shreveport, LA. March. Deborah McMartin, Dir., 2110 Surrey Ln., Bossier City, LA 71111.

TO WRITE—Lafayette, LA. March. Rosalind Foley, Dir., Writers' Guild of Acadiana, P.O. Box 51532, Lafayette, LA 70505-1532.

NEW ORLEANS POPULAR FICTION CONFERENCE—New Orleans, LA. November. Metsy Hingle, Dir., P.O. Box 740113, New Orleans, LA 70174.

MAINE

WELLS WEST—Borrego Springs, ME. January-March. Vic Levine, Dir., 69 Broadway, Concord, NH 03301.

IN CELEBRATION OF CHILDREN'S LITERATURE—Gorham, ME. July. Joyce Martin, Dir., Univ. of Southern Maine, 301 Bailey Hall, Gorham, ME 04038.

DOWNEAST MAINE WRITER'S WORKSHOPS—Stockton Springs, ME. July, August. Janet J. Barron, Dir., P.O. Box 446, Stockton Springs, ME 04981.

STONECOAST WRITERS' CONFERENCE—Freeport, ME. July-August. Barbara Hope, Dir., University of Southern Maine, Summer Session Office, 37 College Ave., Gorham, ME 04038.

59TH ANNUAL STATE OF MAINE WRITERS' CONFERENCE—Ocean Park, ME. August. Richard F. Burns, Dir., P.O. Box 7146, Ocean Park, ME 04063.

MARYLAND

SANDY COVE CHRISTIAN WRITERS' CONFERENCE—North East, MD. October. Jim Watkins, Dir., Sandy Cove Ministries, P.O. Box B, North East, MD 21901.

MASSACHUSETTS

TRURO CENTER FOR THE ARTS AT CASTLE HILL WRITERS WORKSHOPS—Truro, MA. Various dates. Mary Stackhouse, Dir., P.O. Box 756, Truro, MA 02666.

OUTWRITE CONFERENCE—Boston, MA. February. Karen Bollock-Jordan, Dir., BSEF, 29 Stanhope St., Boston, MA 02116.

LET YOUR IMAGINATION TAKE FLIGHT—Boston, MA. March. Terry Pino, Coord., P.O. Box 183, Wilmington, MA 01887.

SALTWINDS YANKEE BARN-BOOK ARTS WORKSHOPS—Kingston, MA. July. Lilla Ford, Dir., Box 52, Kingston, MA 02364.

CAPE COD WRITERS' CONFERENCE—Craigville Beach, MA. August. Don Ellis, Dir., Cape Cod Writers' Center, Inc., P.O. Box 186, Barnstable, MA 02630.

MICHIGAN

MARANATHA CHRISTIAN WRITERS SEMINAR—Muskegon, MI. August. Leona Hertel, Dir., 4759 Lake Harbor Rd., Muskegon, MI 49441.

38TH ANNUAL WRITERS' CONFERENCE, SPONSORED BY OAKLAND UNIVERSITY AND DETROIT WOMEN WRITERS—Rochester, MI. October. Gloria J. Boddy, Dir., Oakland Univ., 231 Varner Hall, Rochester, MI 48309.

MINNESOTA

SPLIT ROCK ARTS PROGRAM—Duluth, MN. July-August. Andrea Gilats, Dir., 314 Nolte Center, 315 Pillsbury Dr. S.E., Minneapolis, MN 55455.

"WRITING TO SELL"—Minneapolis, MN. August. Minneapolis Writers' Workshop, P.O. Box 24356, Minneapolis, MN 55424.

PETER DAVIDSON'S WRITERS SEMINAR—Coon Rapids, MN. September. Brenda Dickinson, Dir., 11200 Mississippi Blvd. N.W., Coon Rapids, MN 55433.

MISSISSIPPI

NATCHEZ LITERARY CELEBRATION—Natchez, MS. June. Carolyn Vance Smith, Dir., P.O. Box 894, Natchez, MS 39121.

MISSOURI

WRITING CAMP FOR TEENAGERS—Springfield, MO. June. Dr. John Bushman, Dir., Drury College, P.O. Box 664, Ottawa, KS 66067.

INVESTIGATIVE REPORTERS & EDITORS, INC. NATIONAL CONFERENCE—Kansas City, MO. June. Brant Houston, Dir., 138 Neff Annex, Columbia, MO 65211.

NEW LETTERS WEEKEND WRITERS CONFERENCE—Kansas City, MO. June. James McKinley, Dir., UMKC, Arts & Sciences Cont. Ed., 4825 Troost, Room 215, Kansas City, MO 64110.

CAT WRITERS' ANNUAL CONFERENCE—Kansas City, MO. November. Amy D. Shojai, Dir., Cat Writers' Assoc., P.O. Box 1904, Sherman, TX 75091.

MONTANA

YELLOW BAY WRITERS' WORKSHOP—Flathead Lake, MT. August. Shauna Miller, Program Man., Univ. of Montana, Cont. Ed., Missoula, MT 59812.

MOTHER LODE WRITERS WORKSHOP—Virginia City, MT. September. Gwen Petersen, Dir., Box 1255, Big Timber, MT 59011.

NEVADA

READING AND WRITING THE WEST—Reno, NV. July. Stephen Tchudi, Dir., Univ. of Nevada, Dept. of English/098, Reno, NV 89557.

NEW HAMPSHIRE

MOLASSES POND WRITER'S RETREAT/WORKSHOP—Wakefield, NH. June. Martha Barron Barrett, Dir., 36 Manning St., Portsmouth, NH 03801.

ODYSSEY: FANTASY WRITING WORKSHOP—Manchester, NH. June-July. Jeanne Cavelos, Dir., 20 Levesque Ln., Mont Vernon, NH 03057.

NEW ENGLAND WRITERS CONFERENCE—Hanover, NH. July. Frank Anthony, Dir., P.O. Box 483, Windsor, VT 05089.

SEACOAST WRITERS ASSOCIATION'S FALL CONFERENCE—Chester, NH. May, October. Paula Flanders, Dir., P.O. Box 6553, Portsmouth, NH 03802.

NEW JERSEY

THE COLLEGE OF NEW JERSEY WRITERS' CONFERENCE—Ewing, NJ. April. Jean Hollander, Dir., The College of New Jersey, Dept. of English, P.O. Box 7718, Ewing, NJ 08628.

NEW MEXICO

FREELANCERS MARKETPLACE—Various Locations & dates. Robert Spiegel, Dir., P.O. Box 20130, Albuquerque, NM 87154.

WRITING WOMEN'S LIVES—Santa Fe, NM. January. Robyn Jones, Dir., Recursos, 826 Camino de Monte Rey, Santa Fe, NM 87505.

MORENO VALLEY WRITERS GUILD—Angel Fire, NM. June. Jack C. Urban, Dir., P.O. Box 2000, Angel Fire, NM 87710.

TAOS SCHOOL OF WRITING—Taos Ski Valley, NM. July. Norman Zollinger, Dir., P.O. Box 20496, Albuquerque, NM 87154.

SANTA FE WRITERS' CONFERENCE—Santa Fe, NM. July-August. Stephen Lewis, Dir., Recursos, 826 Camino de Monte Rey, Santa Fe, NM 87505.

SOUTHWEST WRITERS WORKSHOP ANNUAL CONFERENCE—Albuquerque, NM. September. Carol Bruce-Fritz, Dir., 1338-B Wyoming Blvd., N.E., Albuquerque, NM 87112.

WRITING YOURSELF—Santa Fe, NM. October. Stephen Lewis, Dir., Recursos, 826 Camino de Monte Rey, Santa Fe, NM 87404.

GLORIETA CHRISTIAN WRITERS CONFERENCE—Glorieta, NM. November. Mona Gansberg Hodgson, Dir., P.O. Box 999, Cottonwood, AZ 86326.

NEW YORK

MEET THE AGENTS: BIG APPLE WRITING CONFERENCEE—New York, NY. April, October. Hannelore Hahn, Dir., IWWG, P.O. Box 810, Gracie Station, New York, NY 10028.

THE WRITERS' CENTER AT CHAUTAUQUA—Chautauqua, NY. June, August. Janette Martin, Dir., 953 Forest Ave. Ext., Jamestown, NY 14701.

INSTITUTE OF PUBLISHING & WRITING: CHILDREN'S BOOKS IN THE MARKETPLACE—Poughkeepsie, NY. June. Jean Marzollo, Dir., Vassar College, Box 300, 124 Raymond Ave., Poughkeepsie, NY 12604.

SEVENTH ANNUAL WRITER'S CONFERENCE '99—New York, NY. June. Lewis Burke Frumkes, Dir., Marymount Manhattan College, 221 E. 71st St., New York, NY 10021.

MANHATTANVILLE'S SUMMER WRITERS' WEEK—Purchase, NY. June. Ruth Dowd, Dir., Manhattanville College, 2900 Purchase St., Purchase, NY 10577.

CHENANGO VALLEY WRITER'S CONFERENCE—Hamilton, NY. June-July. Matthew Leone, Dir., Colgate Univ., Office of Summer Programs, 13 Oak Dr., Hamilton, NY 13346.

CATSKILL POETRY WORKSHOP—Oneonta, NY. July. Carol Frost, Dir., Hartwick College, Special Programs Office, Oneonta, NY 13820.

FEMINIST WOMEN'S WRITING WORKSHOPS—Geneva, NY. July. Margo Gumosky, Dir., P.O. Box 6583, Ithaca, NY 14851.

NEW YORK STATE SUMMER WRITERS INSTITUTE—Saratoga Springs, NY. July. Robert Boyers, Dir., Skidmore College, Saratoga Springs, NY 12866.

ROBERT QUACKENBUSH'S CHILDREN'S BOOK WRITING & ILLUS-TRATING WORKSHOPS—New York, NY. July. Robert Quackenbush, Dir., Quackenbush Studios, 460 E. 79th St., New York, NY 10021.

"REMEMBER THE MAGIC" ANNUAL CONFERENCE—Saratoga Springs, NY. August. Hannelore Hahn, Dir., IWWG, P.O. Box 810, Gracie Station, New York, NY 10028.

NORTH CAROLINA

NORTH CAROLINA WRITERS' NETWORK SPRING GALA—Chapel Hill, NC. June. Bobbie Collins-Perry, Dir., P.O. Box 954, Carrboro, NC 27510.

NORTH CAROLINA WRITERS' NETWORK'S ANNUAL FALL CON-FERENCE—Asheville, NC. November. Bobbi Collins-Perry, Dir., P.O. Box 954. Carrboro, NC 27510.

OHIO

HUDSON WRITERS MINI CONFERENCE—Hudson, OH. February. Lea Leever Oldham, Dir., 34200 Ridge Rd., #110, Willoughby, OH 44094.

8TH ANNUAL WESTERN RESERVE WRITERS MINI CONFERENCE— Kirtland, OH. March. Lea Leever Oldham, Dir., 34200 Ridge Rd., #110, Willoughby, OH 44094.

THE HEIGHTS WRITER'S CONFERENCE— Beachwood, OH. May. Lavern Hall, Dir., 35 N. Chillicothe Rd., Suite D, Aurora, OH 44202.

LORAIN COUNTY WRITERS MINI CONFERENCE— Elyria, OH. May. Lea Leever Oldham, Dir., 34200 Ridge Rd., #110, Willoughby, OH 44094.

VALLEY WRITERS CONFERENCE— Youngstown, OH. August. Nancy Christie, Dir., P.O. Box 4610, Youngstown, OH 44515.

SKYLINE WRITER'S CONFERENCE— N. Royalton, OH. August. Lili Kilburn, Dir., P.O. Box 33343, N. Royalton, OH 44133.

ANTIOCH WRITERS' WORKSHOP— Yellow Springs, OH. Summer. Gilah Rittenhouse, Dir., Antioch Writers' Workshop, P.O. Box 494, Yellow Springs, OH 45387.

16TH ANNUAL WESTERN RESERVE WRITERS CONFERENCE— Kirtland, OH. September. Lea Leever Oldham, Dir., 34200 Ridge Rd., #110, Willoughby, OH 44094.

COLUMBUS WRITERS CONFERENCE— Columbus, OH. September. Angela Palazzolo, Dir., P.O. Box 20548, Columbus, OH 43220.

CLEVELAND HEIGHTS/UNIVERSITY HEIGHTS WRITERS MINI CONFERENCE— Cleveland Heights, OH. October. Lea Leever Oldham, Dir., 34200 Ridge Rd., #110, Willoughby, OH 44094.

Oklahoma

8TH ANNUAL NORTHWEST OKLAHOMA WRITERS' WORKSHOP— Enid, OK. March. Bev Walton-Porter, Dir., Enid Writers Club, P.O. Box 5994, Enid, OK 73702.

SHORT COURSE ON PROFESSIONAL WRITING— Norman, OK. June. J. Madison Davis, Dir., Univ. of Oklahoma, 101 Copeland Hall, Norman, OK 73019.

THE OKLAHOMA FALL ARTS INSTITUTE'S WRITING WORKSHOP— Stillwater, OK. October. Mary Gordon Taft, Dir., Oklahoma Arts Institute, 720 N.W. 50th, P.O. Box 18154, Oklahoma City, OK 73154.

Oregon

FISHTRAP GATHERING & WORSHOPS— Wallowa Lake, OR. February, July. Rich Wandschneider, Dir., Fishtrap, P.O. Box 38, Enterprise, OR 97828.

OREGON CHRISTIAN WRITERS— Salem, OR. July. Duane Young, Dir., 3619 N.E. 91st Ave., Portland, OR 97220.

THE FLIGHT OF THE MIND, WOMEN WRITERS' WORKSHOPS— McKenzie Bridge, OR. June-July. Judith Barrington, Dir., Flight of the Mind, 622 S.E. 29th Ave., Portland, OR 97214.

WILLAMETTE WRITERS CONFERENCE— Portland, OR. August. Cherie Walters, Dir., 9045 S.W. Barbur, Suite 5A, Portland, OR 97219.

COOS BAY WRITERS CONFERENCE— Coos Bay, OR. Summer. Mary Scheirman, Dir., P.O. Box 4022, Coos Bay, OR 97459.

Pennsylvania

GREATER PHILADELPHIA CHRISTIAN WRITERS CONFERENCE— Dresher, PA. April. Marlene Bagnull, Dir., 316 Blanchard Rd., Drexel Hill, PA 19026.

PENNWRITERS ANNUAL CONFERENCE—Grantville, PA. May. C.J. Houghtaling, Dir., R.R. 2, Box 241, Middlebury Center, PA 16935.

ST. DAVID'S CHRISTIAN WRITERS CONFERENCE—Beaver Falls, PA. June. Susan Swan, Dir., c/o Audrey Stallsmith, Registrar, 87 Pines Rd. E., Hadley, PA 16130.

BUCKNELL SEMINAR FOR YOUNGER POETS—Lewisburg, PA. June. Cynthia Hogue, Dir., Bucknell Univ., Stadler Center for Poetry, Lewisburg, PA 17837.

LIGONIER VALLEY WRITERS CONFERENCE—Ligonier, PA. July. P.O. Box B, Ligonier, PA 15658.

MONTROSE CHRISTIAN WRITERS' CONFERENCE—Montrose, PA. July. Patti Souder, Dir., 5 Locust St., Montrose, PA 18801.

Rhode Island

EAST COAST WRITERS CONFERENCE—Bristol, RI. August. Eleyne Austen Sharp, Dir., Community Writers Assoc., P.O. Box 312, Providence, RI 02901.

NEW ENGLAND SCREENWRITERS CONFERENCE—Providence, RI. Summer. Robert Hofmann, Dir., P.O. Box 6705, Providence, RI 02940-6705.

South Carolina

SOUTH CAROLINA PLAYWRIGHTS CONFERENCE—Beaufort, SC. June. Bill Rauch, Dir., 1001 Bay St., Beaufort, SC 29902.

WRITER'S WEEKEND—Pendleton, SC. July. Wayne Link, Dir., Tri-County Tech. College, P.O. Box 587, Pendleton, SC 29670.

SOUTH CAROLINA WRITERS WORKSHOP ANNUAL CONFER-ENCE—N. Myrtle Beach, SC. October. Millard Howington, Dir., P.O. Box 7104, Columbia, SC 29202.

PALMETTO WRITER'S CONFERENCE—Pendleton, SC. November. Wayne Link, Dir., Tri-County Tech. College, P.O. Box 587, Pendleton, SC 29670.

Tennessee

AMERICAN CHRISTIAN WRITERS CONFERENCES—Various locations and dates. Reg A. Forder, Dir., Box 110390, Nashville, TN 37222.

NATIONAL FEDERATION OF PRESS WOMEN—Nashville, TN. June. Carol S. Pierce, Dir., Box 5556, Arlington, VA 22205.

SEWANEE WRITERS' CONFERENCE—Sewanee, TN. July-August. Wyatt Prunty, Dir., 310 St. Luke's Hall, 735 Univ. Ave., Sewanee, TN 37383.

TEXAS

UNIVERSITY OF MARY HARDIN-BAYLOR LITERARY FESTIVAL— Belton, TX. January. Donna Walker-Nixon, Dir., Box 8008, Belton, TX 76513.

WRITER'S ROUNDTABLE CONFERENCE—Dallas, TX. April. Deborah Morris, Dir., P.O. Box 461572, Garland, TX 75046.

AGENTS! AGENTS! AGENTS! & EDITORS TOO!—Austin, TX. July. Jim Bob McMillan, Dir., Austin Writers' League, 1501 W. 5th St., Suite E-2, Austin, TX 78703.

AGENTS! AGENTS! AGENTS! CONFERENCE—Austin, TX. Summer. Jim Bob McMilla, Dir., Austin Writers' League, 1501 W. 5th St., Suite E-2, Austin, TX 78703.

TELL ME A STORY: NORTH CENTRAL TEXAS SCBWI—Fort Worth, TX. October. Peggy Freeman, Dir., c/o Judith Bingahm, 517 N. Walnut Creek Dr., Mansfield, TX 76063.

UTAH

SAN JUAN WRITERS' WORKSHOP—Bluff, UT. March. Karla Vanderzanden, Exec. Dir., Canyonlands Field Institute, P.O. Box 68, Moab, UT 84532.

SOUTHERN UTAH WRITERS CONFERENCE—Cedar City, UT. July. David Lee, Dir., c/o Dean David Nyman, Southern Utah Univ., School of Cont. Ed., Cedar City, UT 84720.

DESERT WRITERS WORKSHOP—Moab, UT. November. Karla Vanderzanden, Exec. Dir., Canyonlands Field Institute, P.O. Box 68, Moab, UT 84532.

VERMONT

WILDBRANCH WORKSHOP IN OUTDOOR, NATURAL HISTORY, & ENVIRONMENTAL WRITING—Craftsbury Common, VT. June. David W. Brown, Dir., Wildbranch, Sterling College, Craftsbury Common, VT 05827.

BREAD LOAF WRITERS' CONFERENCE—Ripton, VT. August. Michael Collier, Dir., Middlebury College, Middlebury, VT 05753.

THE OLDERS' TRAVEL WRITING CONFERENCE—New England. Summer. Effin & Jules Older, Dirs., 3 New St., Albany, VT 05820.

THE OLDERS' CHILDREN'S WRITING WORKSHOP—Vermont. October. Effin & Jules Older, Dirs., 3 New St., Albany, VT 05820.

VIRGINIA

5TH ANNUAL NORTHERN VIRGINIA CHRISTIAN WRITERS' CONFERENCE—Springfield, VA. March. Jennifer Ferranti, Dir., P.O. Box 12390, Burke, VA 22009.

STEP BACK IN TIME—Williamsburg, VA. March. Sandra Greenman, Dir., 13 Woodlawn Ter., Fredericksburg, VA 22405.

22ND ANNUAL HIGHLAND SUMMER CONFERENCE—Radford, VA. June. Grace Toney Edwards, Dir., c/o Jo Ann Asbury, Radford Univ., Appalachian Reg. Studies Center., P.O. Box 7014, Radford, VA 24142.

SHENANDOAH INTERNATIONAL PLAYWRIGHTS RETREAT—Staunton, VA. August. Robert Graham Small, Dir., Pennyroyal Farm, Rt. 5, Box 167-F, Staunton, VA 24401.

WASHINGTON

WRITER'S WEEKEND AT THE BEACH—Ocean Park, WA. February. Birdie Etchison, Dir., P.O. Box 877, Ocean Park, WA 98640.

WASHINGTON STATE SCBWI CONFERENCE—Seattle, WA. April. D. Bergman, Dir., 4037-56th Ave. S.W., Seattle, WA 98116.

CLARION WEST SCIENCE FICTION & FANTASY WRITERS WORK-SHOP—Seattle, WA. June-July. Leslie Howle, Dir., 340-15th Ave. E., Suite 350, Seattle, WA 98112.

PORT TOWNSEND WRITERS' CONFERENCE—Port Townsend, WA. July. Sam Hamill, Dir., Box 1158, Port Townsend, WA 98368.

WISCONSIN

GREEN LAKE WRITERS CONFERENCE—Green Lake, WI. July. Blythe Ann Cooper, Dir., Green Lake Conference Ctr., W2511 Hwy. 23, Green Lake, WI 54941.

SOFER, THE JEWISH WRITERS' WORKSHOP—Oconomowoc, WI. August. Don Maseny, Coord., 555 Skokie Blvd., Suite 225, Northbrook, IL 60062.

SCBWI WRITER'S RETREAT FOR WORKING WRITERS—Green Bay, WI. October. Patricia Curtis Pfitsch, Dir., Rt. 1, Box 136, Gays Mills, WI 54631.

WYOMING

JACKSON HOLE WRITERS CONFERENCE—Jackson Hole, WY. July. Barbara Barnes, Dir., P.O. Box 3972, Laramie, WY 82071.

INTERNATIONAL

VOLCANOES & SCIENCE WRITING—Montserrat, BWI. Various dates. Bill Sargent, Dir., Earthwatch Expeditions, 680 Mt. Auburn St., Watertown, MA 02272.

ART WORKSHOPS IN LA ANTIGUA GUATEMALA—Antigua, Guatemala. Various dates. Liza Fourré, Dir., 4758 Lyndale Ave. S., Minneapolis, MN 55409.

19TH ANNUAL WRITERS' CONFERENCE—Winchester, Hampshire, England. June. Barbara Large, Dir., Chinook, Southdown Rd., Shawford, Hampshire, England SO21 2BY.

READING AND WRITING ABOUT LONDON—London, England. June-July. Stephen Tchudi, Dir., Univ. of Nevada, Dept. of English, Reno, NV 89557.

VICTORIA SCHOOL OF WRITING—Victoria, BC, Canada. July. Margaret Dyment, Dir., Box 8152, Victoria, B.C., Canada V8W 3R8.

STATE ARTS COUNCILS

State arts councils sponsor grants, fellowships, and other programs for writers. To be eligible for funding, a writer *must* be a resident of the state in which he is applying. Write or call for more information; 1-800 numbers are toll free for in-state calls only; numbers preceded by TDD indicate Telecommunications Device for the Deaf; TTY indicates Teletype-writer.

ALABAMA STATE COUNCIL ON THE ARTS
201 Monroe St., Suite 110
Montgomery, AL 36130
(334) 242-4076; fax: (334) 240-3269
Albert B. Head, *Executive Director*

ALASKA STATE COUNCIL ON THE ARTS
411 W. 4th Ave., Suite 1E
Anchorage, AK 99501-2343
(907) 269-6610; fax: (907) 269-6601
e-mail: info@aksca.org
Shannon Planchon, *Grants Officer*

ARIZONA COMMISSION ON THE ARTS
417 W. Roosevelt
Phoenix, AZ 85003
(602) 255-5882; fax: (602) 256-0282
Attn: Jill Bernstein, Public Information and Literature Dir.

ARKANSAS ARTS COUNCIL
1500 Tower Bldg.
323 Center St.
Little Rock, AR 72201
(501) 324-9766; fax: (501) 324-9154
e-mail: info@dah.state.ar.us
internet: http://heritage.state.ar.us
James E. Mitchell, *Executive Director*

CALIFORNIA ARTS COUNCIL
1300 I St., Suite 930
Sacramento, CA 95814
(916) 322-6555; fax: (916) 322-6575
e-mail: cac@cwo.com
internet: http://www.cac.ca.gov
Gay Carroll, *Public Information Officer*

COLORADO COUNCIL ON THE ARTS
750 Pennsylvania St.
Denver, CO 80203-3699
(303) 894-2617; fax: (303) 894-2615
Fran Holden, *Executive Director*

CONNECTICUT COMMISSION ON THE ARTS
1 Financial Plaza
Hartford, CT 06103
(860) 566-4770; fax: (860) 566-6462
John Ostrout, *Executive Director*

DELAWARE DIVISION OF THE ARTS
Carvel State Bldg.
820 N. French St.
Wilmington, DE 19801
(302) 577-8278; fax: (302) 577-6561
Barbara King, *Artist Services Coordinator*

FLORIDA ARTS COUNCIL
Dept. of State
Div. of Cultural Affairs
The Capitol
Tallahassee, FL 32399-0250
(850) 487-2980; fax: (850) 922-5259
TTY: (850) 488-5779
internet: www.dos.state.fl.us
Attn: Ms. Peyton Fearington

GEORGIA COUNCIL FOR THE ARTS
260 14th St. N.W., Suite 401
Atlanta, GA 30318
(404) 685-2787; fax: (404) 685-2788
Caroline Ballard Leake, *Executive Director*
Ann R. Davis, *Grants Manager, Literature*

HAWAII STATE FOUNDATION ON CULTURE AND THE ARTS
44 Merchant St.
Honolulu, HI 96813
(808) 586-0300; fax: (808) 586-0308
Holly Richards, *Executive Director*

IDAHO COMMISSION ON THE ARTS
Box 83720
Boise, ID 83720-0008
(208) 334-2119; fax (208) 334-2488
Attn: Cort Conley

ILLINOIS ARTS COUNCIL
James R. Thompson Center
100 W. Randolph, Suite 10-500
Chicago, IL 60601
(312) 814-6750; (800) 237-6994; fax: (312) 814-1471

INDIANA ARTS COMMISSION
8402 W. Washington St., Rm. 072
Indianapolis, IN 46204-2741
(317) 232-1268; TDD: (317) 233-3001; fax: (317) 232-5595
Dorothy Ilgen, *Executive Director*

IOWA ARTS COUNCIL
600 E. Locust
Des Moines, IA 50319-0290
(515) 282-6500; fax: (515) 242-6498
Attn: Stephen Poole

KANSAS ARTS COMMISSION
700 S.W. Jackson, Suite 1004
Topeka, KS 66603-3761
(913) 296-3335; fax: (913) 296-4989; TTY: (800) 766-3777
Robert T. Burtch, *Editor*
Eric Hayashi, *Executive Director*

KENTUCKY ARTS COUNCIL
31 Fountain Pl.
Frankfort, KY 40601
(502) 564-3757; fax: (502) 564-2839; TDD: (502) 564-3757
Attn: Gerri Combs, *Executive Director*

LOUISIANA STATE ARTS COUNCIL
Box 44247
Baton Rouge, LA 70804
(504) 342-8180; fax: (504) 342-8173
James Borders, *Executive Director*

MAINE ARTS COMMISSION
25 State House Station
Augusta, ME 04333-0025
(207) 287-2724; fax: (207) 287-2335; TDD: (207) 287-6740
internet: www.mainearts.com
Alden C. Wilson, *Director*

MARYLAND STATE ARTS COUNCIL
Arts-in-Education Program
601 N. Howard St.
Baltimore, MD 21201
(410) 333-8232; fax: (410) 333-1062
Linda Vlasak, *Program Director*
Pamela Dunne, *Artists-in-Education Program Coordinator*

MASSACHUSETTS CULTURAL COUNCIL
120 Boylston St., 2nd Floor
Boston, MA 02116-4802
(617) 727-3668; (800) 232-0960; TTY: (617) 338-9153
fax: (617) 727-0044
Attn: Michael Brady

MICHIGAN COUNCIL FOR ARTS AND CULTURAL AFFAIRS
1200 Sixth St., Suite 1180
Detroit, MI 48226-2461
(313) 256-3731; fax: (313) 256-3781
Betty Boone, *Executive Director*

MINNESOTA STATE ARTS BOARD
Park Square Court
400 Sibley St., Suite 200
St. Paul, MN 55101-1928
(651) 215-1600; (800) 8MN-ARTS; fax: (651) 215-1602
Lori Hindbjorgen, *Artist Assistance Program Associate*

COMPAS: WRITERS & ARTISTS IN THE SCHOOLS
304 Landmark Center
75 W. Fifth St.
St. Paul, MN 55102
(612) 292-3254; fax: (612) 292-3258
Daniel Gabriel, *Director*

MISSISSIPPI ARTS COMMISSION
239 N. Lamar St., Suite 207
Jackson, MS 39201
(601) 359-6030; fax: (601) 359-6008
Lynn Adams Wilkins, *Community Arts Director*

MISSOURI ARTS COUNCIL
Wainwright Office Complex
111 N. 7th St., Suite 105
St. Louis, MO 63101-2188
(314) 340-6845; fax: (314) 340-7215
Michael Hunt, *Program Administrator for Literature*

MONTANA ARTS COUNCIL
316 N. Park Ave., Suite 252
Helena, MT 59620-2201
(406) 444-6430; fax: (406) 444-6548
Arlynn Fishbaugh, *Executive Director*

NEBRASKA ARTS COUNCIL
3838 Davenport St.
Omaha, NE 68131-2329
(402) 595-2122; fax: (402) 595-2334
Jennifer Severin, *Executive Director*

NEVADA ARTS COUNCIL
602 N. Curry St.
Carson City, NV 89703
(702) 687-6680; fax: (702) 687-6688
Susan Boskoff, *Executive Director*

NEW HAMPSHIRE STATE COUNCIL ON THE ARTS
Phenix Hall
40 N. Main St.
Concord, NH 03301-4974
(603) 271-2789; fax: (603) 271-3584; TDD: (800) 735-2964
Audrey Sylvester, *Artist Services Coordinator*

NEW JERSEY STATE COUNCIL ON THE ARTS
Artist Services
CN 306
Trenton, NJ 08625
(609) 292-6130; fax: (609) 989-1440
Beth Vogel, *Manager Arts Education & Artists Services*

NEW MEXICO ARTS
228 E. Palace Ave.
Santa Fe, NM 87501
(505) 827-6490; fax: (505) 827-6043
Randy Forrester, *Local Arts Coordinator*

NEW YORK STATE COUNCIL ON THE ARTS
915 Broadway
New York, NY 10010
(212) 387-7022; fax: (212) 387-7164
Kathleen Masterson, *Director, Literature Program*

NORTH CAROLINA ARTS COUNCIL
Dept. of Cultural Resources
Raleigh, NC 27601-2807
(919) 733-2111 ext. 22; fax: (919) 733-4834
e-mail: dmcgill@ncacmail.dcr.state.nc.us
Deborah McGill, *Literature Director*

NORTH DAKOTA COUNCIL ON THE ARTS
418 E. Broadway, Suite 70
Bismarck, ND 58501-4086
(701) 328-3954; fax: (701) 328-3963
Patsy Thompson, *Executive Director*

OHIO ARTS COUNCIL
727 E. Main St.
Columbus, OH 43205-1796
(614) 466-2613; fax: (614) 466-4494
Bob Fox, *Literature Program Coordinator*

OKLAHOMA ARTS COUNCIL
P.O. Box 52001-2001
Oklahoma City, OK 73152-2001
(405) 521-2931; fax: (405) 521-6418
Betty Price, *Executive Director*

OREGON ARTS COMMISSION
775 Summer St. N.E.
Salem, OR 97310
(503) 986-0086; fax: (503) 986-0260;
e-mail: oregon.artscomm@state.or.us
internet: http://www.das.state.or.us/oac/
Attn: *Assistant Director*

PENNSYLVANIA COUNCIL ON THE ARTS
Room 216, Finance Bldg.
Harrisburg, PA 17120
(717) 787-6883; fax (717) 783-2538
James Woland, *Literature Program*
Attn: *Director, Education Program*

INSTITUTE OF PUERTO RICAN CULTURE
P.O. Box 4184
San Juan, PR 00902-4184
Luis E. Diaz Hernandez, *Executive Director*

RHODE ISLAND STATE COUNCIL ON THE ARTS
95 Cedar St., Suite 103
Providence, RI 02903
(401) 277-3880; fax: (401) 521-1351
Randall Rosenbaum, *Executive Director*

SOUTH CAROLINA ARTS COMMISSION
1800 Gervais St.
Columbia, SC 29201
(803) 734-8696; fax: (803) 734-8526
Sara June Goldstein, *Director, Literary Arts Program*

SOUTH DAKOTA ARTS COUNCIL
800 Governors Dr.
Pierre, SD 57501-2294
(605) 773-3131; fax: (605) 773-6962
e-mail: <sdac@stlib.state.sd.us>
Attn: Dennis Holub, *Executive Director*

TENNESSEE ARTS COMMISSION
401 Charlotte Ave.
Nashville, TN 37243-0780
(615) 741-1701; fax: (615) 741-8559
e-mail: aswanson@mail.state.tn.us
Attn: Alice Swanson

TEXAS COMMISSION ON THE ARTS
P.O. Box 13406
Austin, TX 78711-3406
(512) 463-5535; fax: (512) 475-2699

UTAH ARTS COUNCIL
617 E. South Temple
Salt Lake City, UT 84102-1177
(801) 533-5895; fax: (801) 533-6196
Guy Lebeda, *Literary Coordinator*

VERMONT ARTS COUNCIL
136 State St., Drawer 33
Montpelier, VT 05633-6001
(802) 828-3291; fax: (802) 828-3363
internet: http://www.state.vt.us/vermont-arts
Michele Bailey, *Artist Grants Coordinator*

VIRGINIA COMMISSION FOR THE ARTS
223 Governor St.
Richmond, VA 23219
(804) 225-3132; fax: (804) 225-4327
e-mail: pbaggett.arts@state.va.us
internet: www.artswire.org/~vacomm
Peggy J. Baggett, *Executive Director*

WASHINGTON STATE ARTS COMMISSION
234 E. 8th Ave.
P.O. Box 42675
Olympia, WA 98504-2675
(360) 753-3860 or (360)586-2421
internet: www.wa.gov/art
Bitsy Bidwell, *Community Arts Development Manager*

WEST VIRGINIA DIVISION OF CULTURE & HISTORY
WV Commission on the Arts
Culture and History Division
The Cultural Center, Capitol Complex
1900 Kanawha Blvd. E.
Charleston, WV 25305-0300
(304) 558-0220; fax: (304) 558-2779
Kate McComas, Program Coordinator

WISCONSIN ARTS BOARD
101 E. Wilson St., 1st Floor
Madison, WI 53702
(608) 266-0190; fax: (608) 267-0380
George Tzougros, *Executive Director*

WYOMING ARTS COUNCIL
2320 Capitol Ave.
Cheyenne, WY 82002
(307) 777-7742; fax: (307) 777-5499; e-mail: mshay@missc.state.wy.us
Michael Shay, *Literature Program Manager*

ORGANIZATIONS FOR WRITERS

ACADEMY OF AMERICAN POETS
584 Broadway, Suite 1208
New York, NY 10012
(212) 274-0343; fax: (212) 274-9427
Jonathan Galassi, *President*
    The Academy was founded in 1934 to support American poets at all stages of their careers and to foster the appreciation of contemporary poetry. The largest organization in the country dedicated specifically to the art of poetry, the Academy sponsors several national programs: an annual fellowship for distinguished poetic achievement; the Tanning prize, the largest annual literary award in the U.S.; the Lenore Marshall Poetry Prize; the James Laughlin Award; the Walt Whitman Award; the Harold Morton Landon Translation Award; poetry prizes at colleges and universities; and the American Poets Fund and the Atlas Fund, which provide financial assistance to poets and publishers of poetry. Readings, lectures, and symposia take place in New York City and throughout the United States. Membership is open to all. Annual dues: $25 and up.

AMERICAN SOCIETY OF JOURNALISTS AND AUTHORS, INC.
1501 Broadway, Suite 302
New York, NY 10036
(212) 997-0947
e-mail: ASJA@compuserve.com; web site: http://www.asja.org
Alexandra Owens, *Executive Director*
A nationwide organization of independent writers of nonfiction dedicated to promoting high standards of nonfiction writing through monthly meetings, annual writers' conferences, etc. The ASJA produces a free electronic bulletin board for free-lance writers on contract issues in the new-media age, and the organization offers extensive benefits and services including referral services, numerous discount services, and the opportunity to explore professional issues and concerns with other writers. Members also receive a monthly newsletter with confidential market information. Membership is open to professional free-lance writers of nonfiction; qualifications are judged by the membership committee. Call or write for application details.

THE ASSOCIATED WRITING PROGRAMS
Tallwood House, Mail Stop 1E3
George Mason University
Fairfax, VA 22030
(703) 993-4301; fax: (703) 993-4302
Attn: *Membership*
The AWP seeks to serve writers and teachers in need of community, support, information, inspiration, contacts, and ideas. Provides publishing opportunities, job listings, and an active exchange of ideas on writing and teaching, including an annual conference. Members receive six issues of *AWP Writer's Chronicle* and seven issues of *AWP Job List*. Publications include *The AWP Official Guide to Creative Writing Programs*. Annual dues: $57, *individual*; $37, *student*.

THE AUTHORS GUILD, INC.
330 W. 42nd St., 29th Fl.
New York, NY 10036-6902
(212) 563-5904; fax: (212) 564-5363
e-mail: staff@authorsguild.org
Attn: *Membership Committee*
As the largest organization of published writers in America, membership offers writers free reviews of publishing and agency contracts, access to group health insurance, and seminars on subjects of concern to authors. The Authors Guild also lobbies on behalf of all authors on issues such as copyright, taxation, and freedom of expression. A writer who has published a book in the last seven years with an established publisher, or has published three articles in periodicals of general circulation within the last eighteen months is eligible for active voting membership. An unpublished writer who has received a contract offer may be eligible for associate membership. All members of the Authors Guild automatically become members of its parent organization, the Authors League of America. First year annual dues: $90.

THE AUTHORS LEAGUE OF AMERICA, INC.
330 W. 42nd St.
New York, NY 10036-6902
(212) 564-8350; fax: (212) 564-5363
e-mail: Authors@pipeline.com
Attn: *Membership Committee*

A national organization representing over 14,000 authors and dramatists on matters of joint concern, such as copyright, taxes, and freedom of expression. Membership is restricted to authors and dramatists who are members of the Authors Guild and the Dramatists Guild. Matters such as contract terms and subsidiary rights are in the province of the two guilds.

THE DRAMATISTS GUILD
1501 Broadway, Suite 701
New York, NY 10036-3909
(212) 398-9366
Peter Stone, *President*; Christopher Wilson, *Acting Executive Director*

The national professional association of playwrights, composers, and lyricists, the guild was established to protect dramatists' rights and to improve working conditions. Services include use of the guild's contracts; a toll-free number for members in need of business advice; access to discount tickets; access to third-party health insurance programs and a group term life insurance plan; and numerous seminars. The Frederick Loew room is available to members for readings and rehearsals at a nominal fee. Publications currently include *The Dramatists Guild Quarterly*, *The Dramatists Guild Resource Directory*, and *The Dramatists Guild Newsletter*. All playwrights, produced or not, are eligible for membership. Annual dues: $125, *active*; $75, *associate*; $35, *student*.

INTERNATIONAL ASSOCIATION OF CRIME WRITERS (NORTH AMERICAN BRANCH)
P.O. Box 8674
New York, NY 10116-8674
(212) 243-8966
Jim Weikart, *Acting President*

This international association was founded in 1987 to promote communications among crime writers worldwide, encourage translation of crime writing into other languages, and defend authors against censorship and other forms of tyranny. The IACW sponsors a number of conferences, publishes a quarterly newsletter, *Border Patrol*, and annually awards the Hammett prize for literary excellence in crime writing to a work of fiction or nonfiction by a U.S. or Canadian author. Membership is open to published authors of crime fiction, nonfiction, and screenplays. Agents, editors, and booksellers in the mystery field are also eligible to apply. Annual dues: $50.

INTERNATIONAL ASSOCIATION OF THEATRE FOR CHILDREN AND YOUNG PEOPLE
Box 22365
Seattle, WA 98122-0365
(206) 392-2147; fax: (206) 443-0442
e-mail: ASSITEJ@aol.com
Dana Childs, *Office Manager*

The development of professional theater for young audiences and international exchange are the organization's primary mandates. Provides a link between professional theaters, artists, directors, training institutions, and arts agencies; sponsors festivals and forums for interchange among theaters and theater artists. Annual dues: $50, *individual*; $25, *student and retiree.*

THE INTERNATIONAL WOMEN'S WRITING GUILD
Box 810, Gracie Station
New York, NY 10028-0082
(212) 737-7536; fax: (212) 737-9469
e-mail: http://www.iwwg.com
Hannelore Hahn, *Executive Director & Founder*

Founded in 1976, serving as a network for the personal and professional empowerment of women through writing. Services include six issues of a 32-page newsletter, a list of literary agents, independent small presses, and publishing services, access to health insurance plans at group rates, access to writing conferences and related events throughout the U.S., including the annual "Remember the Magic" summer conference at Skidmore College in Saratoga Springs, NY, regional writing clusters, and year-round supportive networking. Any woman may join regardless of portfolio. Annual dues: $35; $45 *international.*

MIDWEST RADIO THEATRE WORKSHOP
KOPN
915 E. Broadway
Columbia, MO 65201
(314) 874-5676; fax: (314) 499-1662
e-mail: mrtw@mrtw.org
Sue Zizza, *Director*

Founded in 1979, the MRTW is the only national resource for American radio dramatists, providing referrals, technical assistance, educational materials, and workshops. MRTW coordinates an annual national radio script contest, publishes an annual radio scriptbook, and distributes a script anthology with primer. Send SASE for more information.

MYSTERIES FOR MINORS—(See *Sisters in Crime*)

MYSTERY WRITERS OF AMERICA, INC.
17 E. 47th St., 6th Fl.
New York, NY 10017
(212) 888-8171; fax: (212) 888-8107

The MWA exists for the purpose of raising the prestige of mystery and detective writing, and of defending the rights and increasing the income of all writers in the field of mystery, detection, and fact crime writing. Each year, the MWA presents the Edgar Allan Poe Awards for the best mystery writing in a variety of fields. The four classifications of membership are: *active*, open to any writer who has made a sale in the field of mystery, suspense, or crime writing; *associate*, for professionals in allied fields; *corresponding*, for writers living outside the U.S.; *affiliate*, for unpublished writers. Annual dues: $65; $32.50 *corresponding members.*

NATIONAL ASSOCIATION OF SCIENCE WRITERS, INC.
P.O. Box 294
Greenlawn, NY 11740
(516) 757-5664
Diane McGurgan, *Administrative Secretary*

The NASW promotes the dissemination of accurate information regarding science through all media, and conducts a varied program to increase the flow of news from scientists, to improve the quality of its presentation, and to communicate its meaning to the reading public. Anyone who has been actively engaged in the dissemination of science information is eligible to apply for membership. Active members must be principally involved in reporting on science through newspapers, magazines, TV, or other media that reach the public directly. Associate members report on science through limited-circulation publications and other media. Annual dues: $60.

NATIONAL CONFERENCE OF EDITORIAL WRITERS
6223 Executive Blvd.
Rockville, MD 20852
(301) 984-3015; fax: (301) 231-0026
e-mail: ncewhqs@erols.com
web site: www.ncew.org

A nonprofit professional organization established in 1947, NCEW exists to improve the quality of editorial pages and broadcast editorials, and to promote high standards among opinion writers and editors in North America. The association offers members networking opportunities, regional meetings, page exchanges, foreign tours, educational opportunities and seminars, an annual convention, and a subscription to the quarterly journal *The Masthead.* Membership is open to opinion writers and editors for general-circulation newspapers, radio or television stations, and syndicated columnists; teachers and students of journalism; and others who determine editorial policy. Annual dues are based on circulation or broadcast audience and range from $85 to $150 (journalism educators: $75; students: $50).

THE NATIONAL LEAGUE OF AMERICAN PEN WOMEN, INC.
The Pen Arts Building
1300 17th St. N.W.
Washington, DC 20036-1973
(202) 785-1997
Judith La Fourest, *National President,* Gail Dawson, *Exec. Administrator*

Founded in 1897, the league promotes development of the creative talents of professional women in the arts. Membership is through local branches, available by invitation from current members in the categories of Art, Letters, and Music.

THE NATIONAL WRITERS ASSOCIATION
1450 S. Havana, Suite 424
Aurora, CO 80012
(303) 751-7844; fax: (303) 751-8593
web site: www.nationalwriters.com
Sandy Whelchel, *Executive Director*

New and established writers, poets, and playwrights throughout the U.S. and worldwide may become members of the NWA, a full-time, customer-service- oriented association founded in 1937. Members receive a bimonthly newsletter, *Authorship*, and may attend the annual June conference. Annual dues: $85, *professional*; $65, *regular*; add $25 outside the U.S., Canada, and Mexico.

NATIONAL WRITERS UNION
113 University Place, 6th Fl.
New York, NY 10003
(212) 254-0279
Jonathan Tasini, *President*

Dedicated to bringing about equitable payment and fair treatment of free-lance writers through collective action. Membership is over 4,500 and includes book authors, poets, cartoonists, journalists, and technical writers in 14 chapters nationwide. The union offers its members contract and agent information, group health insurance, press credentials, grievance handling, a quarterly magazine, and sample contracts and resource materials. It sponsors workshops and seminars across the country. Membership is open to writers who have published a book, play, three articles, five poems, one short story or an equivalent amount of newsletter, publicity, technical, commercial, government, or institutional copy, or have written an equivalent amount of unpublished material and are actively seeking publication. Annual dues: $90 to $195.

NEW DRAMATISTS
424 W. 44th St.
New York, NY 10036
(212) 757-6960
Todd London, *Artistic Director*

New Dramatists is dedicated to finding gifted playwrights and giving them the time, space, and tools to develop their craft. Services include readings and workshops; a director-in-residence program; national script distribution for members; artist work spaces; international playwright exchange programs; script copying facilities; and a free ticket program. Membership is open to residents of New York City and the surrounding tri-state area. National memberships are offered to those outside the area who can spend time in NYC in order to take advantage of programs. Apply between July 15 and September 15. No annual dues.

NORTHWEST PLAYWRIGHTS GUILD
318 S.W. Palatine Hill Rd.
Portland, OR 97219
(503) 452-4778
e-mail: bjscript@teleport.com
Bill Johnson, *Office Manager*

The guild supports and promotes playwrights living in the Northwest through play development, staged readings, and networking for play competitions and production opportunities. Members receive monthly and quarterly newsletters. Annual dues: $25.

OUTDOOR WRITERS ASSOCIATION OF AMERICA, INC.
2155 E. College Ave.
State College, PA 16801
(814) 234-1011
Eileen King, *Meeting Director*

A non-profit, international organization representing professional communicators who report and reflect upon America's diverse interests in the outdoors. Membership, by nomination only, includes a monthly publication, *Outdoors Unlimited*; annual conference; annual membership directory; contests. The association also provides scholarships to qualified students.

PEN AMERICAN CENTER
568 Broadway
New York, NY 10012
(212) 334-1660
Michael Roberts, *Executive Director*
PEN American Center is one of more than 130 centers worldwide that compose International PEN. The 2,600 members of the American Center are poets, playwrights, essayists, editors, and novelists, as well as literary translators and those agents who have made a substantial contribution to the literary community. PEN American headquarters is in New York City, and branches are located in Boston, Chicago, New Orleans, Portland, Oregon, and San Francisco. Among the activities, programs, and services sponsored are literary events and awards, outreach projects to encourage reading, assistance to writers in financial need, and international and domestic human rights campaigns on behalf of many writers, editors, and journalists censored or imprisoned because of their writing. Membership is open to writers who have published two books of literary merit, as well as editors, agents, playwrights, and translators who meet specific standards; apply to membership committee.

THE PLAYWRIGHTS' CENTER
2301 Franklin Ave. E.
Minneapolis, MN 55406
(612) 332-7481
Carlo Cuesta, *Executive Director*
The Playwrights' Center fuels the theater by providing services that support playwrights and playwriting. Members receive applications for all programs, a calendar of events, eligibility to participate in special activities, including classes, outreach programs, and PlayLabs. For membership information, contact Jennifer Kane, Development and Communications Director. Annual dues: $40.

POETRY SOCIETY OF AMERICA
15 Gramercy Park
New York, NY 10003
(212) 254-9628; fax: (212) 673-2352
1-(800) USA-POEM, for a free brochure
e-mail: poetrysocy@aol.com; web site: www.poetrysociety.org
Elise Paschen, *Executive Director*
Founded in 1910, the PSA seeks to raise the awareness of poetry, to deepen the understanding of it, and to encourage more people to read, listen to, and write poetry. To this end, the PSA presents national series of readings including "Tributes in Libraries" and "Poetry in Public Places," mounts poetry posters on mass transit vehicles through "Poetry in Motion," and broadcasts an educational poetry series on cable television. The PSA also offers annual contests for poetry, seminars, poetry festivals, and publishes a newsletter. Annual dues: from $40 ($25 for students).

POETS AND WRITERS, INC.
72 Spring St.
New York, NY 10012
(212) 226-3586; fax: (212) 226-3963
web site: http://www.pw.org
Elliot Figman, *Executive Director*

Poets & Writers, Inc., was founded in 1970 to foster the development of poets and fiction writers and to promote communication throughout the literary community. A non-membership organization, it offers information for writers; *Poets & Writers Magazine* and other publications; as well as support for readings and workshops at a wide range of venues.

PUBLICATION RIGHTS CLEARINGHOUSE
National Writers Union
113 University Pl., 6th Fl.
New York, NY 10003
(212) 254-0279; fax: (212) 254-0673
e-mail: nwu@nwu.org
Naomi Zauderer, *Director*

Publication Rights Clearinghouse, the collective-licensing agency of the National Writers Union, was created in 1996 to help writers license and collect royalties for the reuse of their works in electronic databases and other new digital media. It is modeled after similar organizations that have long existed in the music industry. Enrollment is open to both NWU members and non-members. The one-time enrollment fee is $20 for NWU members and members of other writers' organizations that are associate sponsors of PRC; $40 for others.

ROMANCE WRITERS OF AMERICA
13700 Veterans Memorial Dr., Suite 315
Houston, TX 77014
(713) 440-6885; fax: (713) 440-7510
Allison Kelley, *Executive Director*

An international organization with over 150 local chapters across the U.S., Canada, Europe, and Australia; membership is open to any writer, published or unpublished, interested in the field of romantic fiction. Annual dues of $60, plus $10 application fee for new members; benefits include annual conference, contest, market information, and monthly professional journal, *Romance Writers' Report*.

SCIENCE-FICTION AND FANTASY WRITERS OF AMERICA, INC.
532 La Guardia Pl., #632
New York, NY 10012-1428
Robert J. Sawyer, Pres.

An organization whose purpose it is to foster and further the professional interests of science fiction and fantasy writers. Presents the annual Nebula Award for excellence in the field and publishes the *Bulletin* and *SFWA Handbook* for its members (also available to non-members).

Any writer who has sold a work of science fiction or fantasy is eligible for membership. Annual dues: $50, *active* ; $35, *affiliate*; plus $10 installation fee; send for application and information.

SISTERS IN CRIME
P.O. Box 442124
Lawrence, KS 66044-8933
e-mail: sistersincrime@juno.com
Sue Henry, *President*

Sisters in Crime was founded in 1986 to combat discrimination against women in the mystery field, educate publishers and the general public as to inequalities in the treatment of female authors, and raise the level of awareness of their contribution to the field. Membership is open to all and includes writers, readers, editors, agents, booksellers, and librarians. Publications include a quarterly newsletter and membership directory. Annual dues: $35, U.S.; $40, foreign. Members interested in mysteries for young readers may join Mysteries for Minors (Elizabeth James, Chair, P.O. Box 442124, Lawrence, KS 66044-8933) with no additional dues.

SOCIETY FOR TECHNICAL COMMUNICATION
901 N. Stuart St., #904
Arlington, VA 22203-1854
(703) 522-4114
web site: http://www.stc-va.org.
William C. Stolgitis, *Executive Director*

A professional organization dedicated to the advancement of the theory and practice of technical communication in all media. The 23,000 members in the U.S. and other countries include technical writers and editors, publishers, artists and draftsmen, researchers, educators, and audiovisual specialists. Annual dues: $95.

SOCIETY OF AMERICAN TRAVEL WRITERS
4101 Lake Boone Trail, Suite 201
Raleigh, NC 27607
(919) 787-5181; fax: (919) 787-4916
e-mail: cyoung@olson.mgmt.com
Cathy Young, CAE, *Executive Director*

The Society of American Travel Writers represents writers and other professionals who strive to provide travelers with accurate reports on destinations, facilities, and services. Membership is by invitation. Active membership is limited to travel writers and free lancers who have a steady volume of published or distributed work about travel. Application fees: $250, *active*; $500, *associate*. Annual dues: $130, *active*; $250, *associate*.

SOCIETY OF CHILDREN'S BOOK WRITERS & ILLUSTRATORS
345 N. Maple Dr., #296
Beverly Hills, CA 90210
web site: www.scbwi.org
Lin Oliver, *Executive Director*

A national organization of authors, editors, publishers, illustrators, librarians, and educators, the SCBWI offers a variety of services to people who write, illustrate, or share an interest in children's literature. Full memberships are open to those who have had at least one children's book or story published. Associate memberships are open to all those with an interest in children's literature. Annual dues: $50.

SOCIETY OF ENVIRONMENTAL JOURNALISTS
P.O. Box 27280
Philadelphia, PA 19118
(215) 836-9970; fax: (215) 836-9972
e-mail: SEJOffice@aol.com
web site: http://www.SEJ.org
Beth Parke, *Executive Director*

Dedicated to improving the quality, accuracy, and visibility of environmental reporting, the society serves 1,200 members with a quarterly newsletter, the *SEJournal*, national and regional conferences, World Wide Web (www.SEJ.org), and membership directory. Annual dues: $40; $30, *student*.

SOCIETY OF PROFESSIONAL JOURNALISTS
16 S. Jackson St.
Greencastle, IN 46135-0077
(765) 653-3333; fax: (765) 653-4631
web site: http://spj.org

With 13,500 members and 300 chapters, the Society seeks to serve the interests of print, broadcast, and wire journalists. Services include legal counsel on journalism issues, jobs-for-journalists career search newsletter, professional development seminars, and awards that encourage journalism. Members receive *Quill*, a monthly magazine that explores current issues in the field. SPJ promotes ethics and freedom of information programs. Annual dues: $70, *professional*; $35, *student*.

THE SONGWRITERS GUILD FOUNDATION
1560 Broadway, Suite 1306
New York, NY 10036
(212) 768-7902; fax: (212) 768-9048
Claudia Koal, *National Projects Director*

Open to published and unpublished songwriters, the Guild provides members with songwriter-publisher contracts, reviews contracts, collects royalties from publishers, offers group health and life insurance plans, conducts workshops and critique sessions, and provides a newsletter. Annual dues: $55, *associate*; $70 and up, *full member*.

THEATRE COMMUNICATIONS GROUP
355 Lexington Ave.
New York, NY 10017
(212) 697-5230
Ben Cameron, *Executive Director*

TCG, a national organization for the American theater, provides services to facilitate the work of playwrights, literary managers, and other theater professionals. Publications include the annual *Dramatists Sourcebook* and a line of theater books including plays. Individual members receive *American Theatre* magazine. Annual dues: $35, *individual*.

WESTERN WRITERS OF AMERICA, INC.
1012 Fair St.
Franklin, TN 37064
(615) 791-1444
James A. Crutchfield, *Secretary/Treasurer*

Membership is open to qualified professional writers of fiction and nonfiction related to the history and literature of the American West. Its chief purpose is to promote a more widespread distribution, readership, and appreciation of the West and its literature. Holds annual convention in the last week of June. Sponsors annual Spur Awards, Owen Wister Award, and Medicine Pipe Bearer's Award for published work and produced screenplays. Annual dues: $75.

WRITERS GUILD OF AMERICA, EAST, INC.
555 W. 57th St.
New York, NY 10019
(212) 767-7800; fax: (212) 582-1909
web site: http://www.wgaeast.org
Mona Mangan, *Executive Director*

WRITERS GUILD OF AMERICA, WEST, INC.
7000 W. 3rd St.
Los Angeles, CA 90048
(213) 951-4000; fax: (213) 782-4800
web site: www.wga.org
Brian Walton, *Executive Director*

The Writers Guild of America (East and West) represents writers in motion pictures, broadcast, cable and new media industries, including news and entertainment. In order to qualify for membership, a writer must fulfill current requirements for employment or sale of material in one of these fields.

The basic dues are $25 per quarter for both organizations. In addition, there are quarterly dues based on percentage of the member's earnings in any one of the fields over which the guild has jurisdiction. The initiation fee is $1,500 for WGAE, for writers living east of the Mississippi, and $2,500 for WGAW, for those living west of the Mississippi.

WRITERS INFORMATION NETWORK
P.O. Box 11337
Bainbridge Island, WA 98110
(206) 842-9103; fax: (206) 842-0536
e-mail: WritersInfoNetwork@juno.com
web site: http://www.bluejaypub.com/win/
Elaine Wright Colvin, *Director/Publisher*

W.I.N. was founded in 1983 to provide a link between Christian writers and the religious publishing industry. Offered are a bimonthly magazine, *The Win-Informer Magazine*, and market news, editorial services, advocacy and grievance procedures, referral services, and conferences. Annual dues: $30; $35, *foreign*.

LITERARY AGENTS

As the number of book publishers that will consider only agented submissions grows, more writers are turning to agents to sell their manuscripts. The agents in the following list handle both literary and dramatic material. Included in each listing are such important details as type of material represented, submission procedure, and commission. Since agents derive their income from the sales of their clients' work, they must represent writers who are selling fairly regularly to good markets. Nonetheless, many of the agents listed here note they will consider unpublished writers. Always query an agent first, and enclose a self-addressed, stamped envelope; most agents will not respond without it. Do not send any manuscripts until the agent has asked you to do so; and be wary of agents who charge fees for reading manuscripts. All of the following agents have indicated they do *not* charge reading fees, however some charge for copyright fees, manuscript retyping, photocopies, copies of books for use in the sale of other rights, and long distance calls.

To learn more about agents and their role in publishing, the Association of Authors' Representatives, Inc., publishes a canon of ethics as well as an up-to-date list of AAR members, available for $7 (check or money order) and a 55¢ legal-size SASE. Write to: Association of Authors' Representatives, Inc., 10 Astor Pl., 3rd Floor, New York, NY 10003.

Another good source which lists agents and their policies is *Literary Market Place*, a directory found in most libraries.

BRET ADAMS LTD.— 448 W. 44th St., New York, NY 10036. Attn: Bruce Ostler or Bret Adams. Screenplays, teleplays, stage plays, and musicals. Unproduced writers considered. Query with synopsis, bio, resumé, and SASE. Commission: 10%.

LEE ALLAN AGENCY—7464 N. 107 St., Milwaukee, WI 53224-3706. Attn: Mr. Lee A. Matthias. Adult genre fiction, nonfiction. Screenplays. Unpublished writers considered. Query with SASE. Commission: 15% books; 10% scripts. Fees: photocopying, overnight shipping, telephone. "Go to a bookstore and locate the exact place in the store where your book would be displayed. If it realistically fits a popular market niche, is not derivative or imitative, meets the size constraints, and you can't make it any better yourself, you are ready to find an agent."

JAMES ALLEN LITERARY AGENT—538 East Harford St., P.O. Box 909, Milford, PA 18337. Attn: James Allen. All types of adult fiction except Westerns; considers very few new authors. Query with 2-to 3-page synopsis; no multiple queries. Commission: 10% domestic; 20% foreign.

MICHAEL AMATO AGENCY—1650 Broadway, Rm. 307, New York, NY 10019. Attn: Michael Amato. Screenplays. Send query or complete manuscript. Commission: 10%.

MARCIA AMSTERDAM AGENCY— 41 W. 82nd St., #9A, New York, NY 10024. Attn: Marcia Amsterdam. Adult and young adult fiction; mainstream nonfiction. Screenplays and teleplays: comedy, romance, psychological suspense. Query with resumé; multiple queries O.K.; three-week exclusive for requested submissions. Commission: 15% books; 10% scripts.

AVATAR LITERARY AGENCY, INC.— 4611 S. University Dr., Suite 438, Davie, FL 33328. K. Lisa Brodsky, Agent. Fiction and nonfiction in all categories and genres, including collections of short stories and young adult novels. No other children's material; no poetry. Submit an e-mail query (ava tar@reps.net); send hard copy with SASE; or send entire manuscript on diskette with SASE. Commission: 10% domestic; 15% foreign.

THE AXELROD AGENCY—54 Church St., Lenox, MA 01240. Attn: Steven Axelrod. Adult fiction and nonfiction. Unpublished writers considered. Query; multiple queries O.K. Commission: 10% domestic; 20% foreign.

MALAGA BALDI LITERARY AGENCY—2112 Broadway, Suite #403, New York, NY 10023. Attn: Malaga Baldi. Adult fiction and nonfiction. Unpublished writers considered. Query first; "if I am interested, I ask for proposal, outline, and sample pages for nonfiction, complete manuscript for fiction." Multiple queries O.K. Commission: 15%. Response time: 10 weeks minimum.

THE BALKIN AGENCY—P.O. Box 222, Amherst, MA 01004. Attn: Rick Balkin. Adult nonfiction. Unpublished writers considered. Query with outline; no multiple queries. Commission: 15% domestic; 20% foreign. "Most interested in serious nonfiction."

VIRGINIA BARBER AGENCY—101 Fifth Ave., New York, NY 10003. Adult fiction and nonfiction. No unsolicited manuscripts. Query with outline, sample pages, bio/resumé and SASE. No multiple queries. Commission: 15% domestic; 20% foreign.

LORETTA BARRETT BOOKS—101 Fifth Ave., New York, NY 10003. Attn: Loretta Barrett. Adult fiction and nonfiction. Unpublished writers considered. Query with outline and 50 to 75 sample pages. Commission: 15%. Response time: 4 weeks.

REID BOATES LITERARY AGENCY—Box 328, 69 Cooks Crossroad, Pittstown, NJ 08867-0328. Attn: Reid Boates. Adult mainstream fiction and nonfiction. Unpublished writers rarely considered. Query with outline and sample pages; no multiple queries. Commission: 15%.

BOOK DEALS, INC.— Civic Opera Bldg., 20 N. Wacker Dr., Suite 1928, Chicago, IL 60606. Caroline Carney, President. General-interest adult fiction and nonfiction. Query with outline, first 20 pages, and bio. Commission: 15% domestic; 20% foreign.

GEORGES BORCHARDT, INC.—136 E. 57th St., New York, NY 10022. Adult fiction and nonfiction. Unpublished writers considered by recommendation only. No unsolicited queries or submissions. Commission: 15%.

BRANDT & BRANDT LITERARY AGENTS—1501 Broadway, New York, NY 10036. Adult fiction and nonfiction. Unpublished writers considered occasionally. Unsolicited query by letter only; no multiple queries. Commission: 15%.

THE HELEN BRANN AGENCY—94 Curtis Rd., Bridgewater, CT 06752. Attn: Carol White. Adult fiction and nonfiction. Unpublished writers considered. Commission: 15%.

ANDREA BROWN LITERARY AGENCY—P.O. Box 371027, Montana, CA 94037. Attn: Laura Rennert. Juvenile fiction and nonfiction only. Unpublished writers considered. Query with outline, sample pages, bio and resumé, and SASE; no faxes. Commission: 15% domestic; 20% foreign.

KNOX BURGER ASSOCIATES, LTD.—39½ Washington Square S., New York, NY 10012. Adult fiction and nonfiction. No science fiction, fantasy, or romance. Highly selective. Query with SASE; no multiple queries. Commission: 15%.

SHEREE BYKOFSKY ASSOCIATES, INC.—11 East 47th St., New York, NY 10017. Mostly adult nonfiction; some adult fiction. Unpublished writers considered. Query with outline, up to 3 sample pages or proposal, and SASE. Multiple queries O.K. if indicated as such. Commission: 15%.

MARTHA CASSELMAN—P.O. Box 342, Calistoga, CA 94515-0342. Martha Casselman, Agent. Darlene Dozier, Associate. Nonfiction, especially interested in cookbooks. Unpublished writers considered. Query with outline, bio/resumé, and SASE for return. Multiple queries O.K. if noted as such. Commission: 15%.

JULIE CASTIGLIA AGENCY—1155 Camino del Mar, Suite 510, Del Mar, CA 92014. Attn: Julie Castiglia. Fiction: commercial, ethnic and literary. Nonfiction: psychology, health, finance, women's issues, science, biography, spirituality, and Eastern religions. Query with outline, sample pages, bio and resumé. No multiple queries. Commission: 15%. "Please do not query on the phone. Attend workshops and writers' conferences before approaching an agent."

HY COHEN LITERARY AGENCY, LTD.—P.O. Box 43770, Upper Montclair, NJ 07043. Attn: Hy Cohen. Adult fiction, nonfiction, and juvenile. Unpublished writers considered. Unsolicited queries and manuscripts O.K., "with SASE, please!" Multiple submissions considered. Commission: 10% domestic; 20% foreign.

RUTH COHEN, INC.—P.O. Box 7626, Menlo Park, CA 94025. Attn: Ruth Cohen. Adult mysteries and women's fiction; quality juvenile fiction and nonfiction. Unpublished writers seriously considered. Query with first 10 pages, synopsis, bio and resumé, and SASE. Commission: 15%.

DON CONGDON ASSOCIATES, INC.—156 Fifth Ave., Suite 625, New York, NY 10010. Adult fiction and nonfiction. Query with outline; no multiple queries. Commission: 10% domestic.

THE DOE COOVER AGENCY—P.O. Box 668, Winchester, MA 01890. Attn: Doe Coover, Colleen Mohyde. Adult literary and commercial fiction and general nonfiction including social sciences, journalism, science, business, biography, memoir, and cookbooks. Unpublished writers considered. Query with outline and bio/resumé; no unsolicited manuscripts. Commission: 15%.

RICHARD CURTIS ASSOCIATES, INC.—171 E. 74th St., New York, NY 10021. Attn: Laura Tucker. Adult fiction and nonfiction. Unpublished writers considered. Query with outline, bio/resumé, and SASE; no multiple queries. Commission: 15% domestic; 20% foreign.

CURTIS BROWN LTD.—10 Astor Pl., New York, NY 10003. General trade fiction and nonfiction; also juvenile. Unpublished writers considered. Query; no multiple queries. Commission: unspecified.

SANDRA DIJKSTRA LITERARY AGENCY—1155 Camino del Mar, Suite 515C, Del Mar, CA 92014. Attn: Sandra Zane. Adult and children's fiction and nonfiction. Query with outline and bio/resumé. For fiction, submit first 50 pages and synopsis; for nonfiction, submit proposal. Commission: 15% domestic, 20% foreign. SASE.

THE JONATHAN DOLGER AGENCY— 49 E. 96th St., 9B, New York, NY 10128. Attn: Tom Wilson. Adult trade fiction and nonfiction. Considers unpublished writers. Query with outline and SASE. Commission: 15%. "No category mysteries, romance, or science fiction."

DOUGLAS, GORMAN, ROTHACKER & WILHELM, INC.—1501 Broadway, Suite 703, New York, NY 10036. Attn: Literary Office. Screenplays and full-length teleplays. Query with 10-page synopsis, bio/resumé. Commission: 10%.

DWYER & O'GRADY, INC.—P.O. Box 239, East Lempster, NH 03605. Attn: Elizabeth O'Grady. Branch office: P.O. Box 790, Cedar Key, FL 32625. Specialize in children's picture books for ages 6 to 12. Require strong story line, dialogue, and character development. Unpublished writers considered. Query with bio/resumé; no multiple queries. Commission: 15%. "Our primary focus is the representation of illustrators who also write their own stories; however, we represent authors who write for the children's market."

JANE DYSTEL LITERARY MANAGEMENT—One Union Square W., Suite 904, New York, NY 10003. Attn: Jane Dystel, Miriam Goderich, Todd Keithley. Adult fiction and nonfiction; some picture books and middle grade fiction. Unpublished writers considered. Query with bio/resumé, sample pages, and outline; no multiple queries. Commission: 15%.

EDUCATIONAL DESIGN SERVICES—P.O. Box 253, Wantaugh, NY 11793. Attn: Bertram L. Linder. Educational texts only. Unpublished writers considered. Query with outline, sample pages or complete manuscript, bio/resumé, and SASE. No multiple queries. Commission: 15% domestic, 25% foreign.

ETHAN ELLENBERG LITERARY AGENCY—548 Broadway, Suite #5E, New York, NY 10012. Ethan Ellenberg, Agent. Commercial and literary fiction and nonfiction. Specialize in first novels, thrillers, children's books, romance, science fiction, and fantasy. Nonfiction: health, new age/spirituality, pop-science, biography. No poetry or short stories. Query with first 3 chapters, synopsis, and SASE. "We respond within 2 weeks if interested." Commission: 15% domestic; 20% foreign.

ANN ELMO AGENCY—60 E. 42nd St., New York, NY 10165. Adult fiction, nonfiction, and plays. Juvenile for middle grades and up. No picture books. Unpublished writers considered. Please query first with outline, sample pages, and bio/resumé. No multiple queries. Commission: 15% domestic, 10% foreign.

FELICIA ETH—555 Bryant St., Suite 350, Palo Alto, CA 94301. Attn: Felicia Eth. Mostly adult nonfiction; some fiction. Unpublished writers considered. Query with outline, sample pages, and bio/resumé. Multiple queries O.K. if noted. Commission: 15% domestic; 20% foreign. "I am a small, very selective agent. My preference is for provocative, original subjects presented in a strong creative voice."

FARBER LITERARY AGENCY—14 E. 75th St., New York, NY 10021. Attn: Ann Farber. Adult fiction, nonfiction, and stage plays; juvenile books. Considers unpublished writers. Query with outline, sample pages, and SASE. Commission: 15% "with services of attorney."

JOYCE FLAHERTY—816 Lynda Ct., St. Louis, MO 63122. Attn: Joyce Flaherty. Adult fiction and nonfiction. Query with outline, sample chapter (first chapter for nonfiction), and bio. Commission: 15% domestic; 30% foreign.

FLANNERY LITERARY—1140 Wickfield Ct., Naperville, IL 60563-3303. Attn: Jennifer Flannery. Juvenile fiction and nonfiction, from board books through young adult novels. Unpublished writers considered. Query with SASE (no phone or fax queries); multiple queries O.K. Commission: 15%.

FOGELMAN LITERARY AGENCY—7515 Greenville Ave., Suite 712, Dallas, TX 75231. Attn: Linda M. Kruger. Adult romance. Commerical books of pop-culture. Query with SASE. Commission: 15% domestic; 10% foreign.

ROBERT A. FREEDMAN DRAMATIC AGENCY, INC.—1501 Broadway, Suite 2310, New York, NY 10036. Attn: Robert A. Freedman or Selma Luttinger. Screenplays, teleplays, and stage plays. Send query, outline, and bio/resumé; multiple queries O.K. Commission: 10%.

SAMUEL FRENCH, INC.— 45 W. 25th St., New York, NY 10010. Stage plays. Unpublished writers considered. Query with complete manuscript; unsolicited and multiple queries O.K.

GELFMAN SCHNEIDER—250 W. 57th St., Suite 2515, New York, NY 10107. Attn: Jane Gelfman. Adult fiction and nonfiction. Unpublished writers only considered if recommended by other writers or teachers. Query with outline, sample pages, and bio; no multiple queries. Commission: 15% domestic; 20% foreign.

GOLDFARB & GRAYBILL—See *Graybill & English, L.L.C.*

GOODMAN ASSOCIATES—500 West End Ave., New York, NY 10024. Attn: Elise Simon Goodman. Adult fiction and nonfiction. Unpublished writers considered. Query with outline, sample pages, and bio/resumé. Multiple queries O.K. Commission: 15% domestic; 20% foreign.

GRAYBILL & ENGLISH, L.L.C.—1920 N. St. N.W., Suite 620, Washington, DC 20036. Attn: Nina Graybill. Adult commercial and literary fiction and nonfiction. For nonfiction, query with outline; for fiction, query with outline and up to 3 sample chapters. Multiple queries O.K. Commission: 15% domestic, 20% foreign.

SANFORD J. GREENBURGER—55 Fifth Ave., 15th Fl., New York, NY 10003. Attn: Faith Hornby Hamlin. Nonfiction, including sports books, health, business, psychology, parenting, science, biography, gay; juvenile books. Unpublished writers with strong credentials considered. Query with outline, sample pages, bio, and SASE; multiple queries O.K. Commission: 15% domestic; 20% foreign.

MAIA GREGORY ASSOCIATES—311 E. 72nd St., New York, NY 10021. Adult nonfiction only. Query with sample pages and bio/resumé. No multiple queries. Commission: 15%.

THE CHARLOTTE GUSAY LITERARY AGENCY—10532 Blythe, Los Angeles, CA 90064. Adult literary fiction, nonfiction, and some young adult novels for film. Screenplays. Query with one-page outline, first 3 pages, bio/resumé, and SASE; multiple queries discouraged. Commission:10% dramatic, 15% literary.

HARDEN CURTIS ASSOCIATES— 850 Seventh Ave., Suite 405, New York, NY 10019. Attn: Mary Harden. Stage plays. Query with bio and resumé, SASE; no multiple queries. Commission: 10%.

JOY HARRIS LITERARY AGENCY, INC.—156 Fifth Ave., Suite 617, New York, NY 10010. Adult fiction and nonfiction. Unpublished writers considered. Query with outline, sample pages, and bio/resumé. No multiple queries. Commission: 15%.

HEACOCK LITERARY AGENCY, INC.—1523 Sixth St., Suite 14, Santa Monica, CA 90401. Attn: Rosalie Heacock, Pres. Adult fiction and nonfiction. Published and unpublished writers welcome to query with outline, bio/resumé, and SASE. No multiple queries. Commission: 15%.

FREDERICK HILL ASSOCIATES—1842 Union St., San Francisco, CA 94123. Attn: Irene Moore. Branch office: 8446½ Melrose Pl., Los Angeles, CA 90069. Adult fiction and nonfiction. Unpublished writers considered. Query with outline and bio/resumé; multiple queries O.K. Commission: 15% domestic, 20% foreign.

JOHN L. HOCHMANN BOOKS—320 E. 58th St., New York, NY 10022. Attn: John L. Hochmann. Nonfiction only: biography, social history, health and food, college textbooks. Unpublished writers considered, "provided they demonstrate thorough knowledge of thier subjects." Query with outline, sample pages, bio/resumé, and SASE. No multiple queries. Commission: 15% for domestic/Canadian; plus 15% foreign language and U.K. "Do not submit jacket copy. Submit detailed outlines and proposals that include evaluations of competing books."

BARBARA HOGENSON AGENCY—165 West End Ave., Suite 19-C, New York, NY 10023. Attn: Barbara Hogenson. Adult fiction, nonfiction. Screenplays and stage plays. Query with bio and synopsis, SASE; multiple queries O.K. Commission: 10% scripts; 15% books.

HULL HOUSE LITERARY AGENCY—240 E. 82nd St., New York, NY 10028. Attn: Lydia Mortimer. Nonfiction: biography, general history. Fiction, especially crime fiction. Query with SASE. Multiple queries O.K. Commission: 15% domestic; 10% foreign.

IMG BACH LITERARY AGENCY—22 E. 71st St., New York, NY 10021. Attn: Julian Bach, Carolyn Krupp. Adult fiction and nonfiction. Unpublished writers considered. Query with outline, sample pages, and bio/resumé. No multiple queries. Commission: 15% domestic.

SHARON JARVIS & CO.—Toad Hall, Inc., RR2, Box 16B, Laceyville, PA 18623. Adult fiction and nonfiction. Unpublished writers considered. Query with bio or resumé, and outline or synopsis. No unsolicited manuscripts. Commission: 15%. "Pay attention to what's selling and what's commercial."

JCA LITERARY AGENCY, INC.—27 W. 20th St., Suite 1103, New York, NY 10011. Adult fiction and nonfiction. Unpublished writers considered. Query with sample pages; multiple queries O.K. Commission: 15% domestic, 20% foreign.

NATASHA KERN LITERARY AGENCY, INC.—P.O. Box 2908, Portland, OR 97208-2908. Attn: Natasha Kern. Adult fiction and nonfiction. Query. Commission: 15% domestic; 10% foreign.

LOUISE B. KETZ AGENCY—1485 First Ave., Suite 4B, New York, NY 10021. Attn: Louise B. Ketz. Adult nonfiction on science, business, sports, history, and reference. Considers unpublished writers "with proper credentials." Query with outline, sample pages, and bio/resumé; multiple queries occasionally considered. Commission: 15%.

KIDDE, HOYT & PICARD—335 E. 51st St., New York, NY 10022. Attn: Katharine Kidde, Laura Langlie. Mainstream, literary, and romantic fiction; general nonfiction. Writers should have published articles to be considered. Query with 2 or 3 chapters and synopsis; also include past writing experience. Multiple queries O.K. Commission: 15%.

KIRCHOFF/WOHLBERG, INC. — 866 United Nations Plaza, Suite 525, New York, NY 10017. Attn: Liza Voges. Juvenile fiction and nonfiction only. Unpublished writers considered. Query; multiple submissions O.K. Commission: 15%.

HARVEY KLINGER, INC. — 301 W. 53rd St., New York, NY 10019. Attn: Harvey Klinger, Laurie E. Liss, David Dunton. Commercial and literary fiction and nonfiction. Unpublished writers considered. Query with outline and bio/resumé. No multiple queries. Commission: 15% domestic, 25% foreign.

BARBARA S. KOUTS — P.O. Box 560, Bellport, NY 11713. Attn: Barbara S. Kouts. Adult fiction, nonfiction, and juvenile for all ages. Unpublished writers considered. Query with bio/resumé. Multiple queries O.K. Commission: 10%.

PETER LAMPACK AGENCY, INC. — 551 Fifth Ave., Suite 1613, New York, NY 10176. Attn: Loren Soeiro, Assoc. Agent. Adult fiction and nonfiction including mainstream, mystery, suspense, thrillers, and literature. No romance, science fiction, horror, or Westerns. Unpublished writers considered. Query with synopsis/outline, up to 20 sample pages, and bio/resumé. Commission: 15% domestic; 20% foreign.

MICHAEL LARSEN/ELIZABETH POMADA — 1029 Jones St., San Francisco, CA 94109. Attn: M. Larsen, nonfiction; E. Pomada, fiction. Fiction: literary, commercial, and genre. Nonfiction: general, including biography, business, nature, health, history, arts, travel. Unpublished writers welcome. Query for fiction with first 30 pages, synopsis, SASE, and phone number; send #10 SASE for brochure. For nonfiction, query by phone: (415) 673-0939. Commission: 15%. For more information see web site: www.larsen/pomada.com

THE MAUREEN LASHER AGENCY — P.O. Box 888, Pacific Palisades, CA 90272. Attn: Ann Cashman. Adult fiction and nonfiction. Unpublished writers considered. Query with outline, sample pages, and bio/resumé. No multiple queries. Commission: 15%.

LEVANT & WALES, INC. — See *Wales Literary Agency.*

ELLEN LEVINE LITERARY AGENCY, INC. — 15 E. 26th St., Suite 1801, New York, NY 10010. Attn: Diana Finch, Louise Quayle. Adult fiction and nonfiction. Unpublished writers considered. Query with SASE. Commission: 15%.

LICHTMAN, TRISTER, SINGER & ROSS — 1666 Connecticut Ave. N.W., Suite 500, Washington, DC 20009. Attn: Gail Ross, Howard Yoon. Adult nonfiction. Unpublished writers considered. Query with outline, sample pages, resumé, and SASE. Multiple queries O.K. Commission: 15%.

NANCY LOVE LITERARY AGENCY — 250 E. 65th St., New York, NY 10021. Attn: Sherrie Sutton. Adult fiction: mysteries and thrillers; and nonfiction: health, parenting, inspirational, current affairs. Unpublished writers considered. For nonfiction, query with proposal; for fiction, query with first chapter. Commission: 15%.

DONALD MAASS LITERARY AGENCY — 157 W. 57th St., Suite 703, New York, NY 10019. Attn: Donald Maass, Pres. Jennifer Jackson, Associate. Adult fiction: science fiction, fantasy, mystery, suspense, horror, frontier, romance, mainstream, literary. Unpublished writers considered. Query with first 5 sample pages. Commission: 15% domestic; 20% foreign.

GINA MACCOBY LITERARY AGENCY — P.O. Box 60, Chappaqua, NY 10514. Adult fiction and nonfiction; juvenile for all ages. No computer books, horror, science fiction, diet books, or cookbooks. Unpublished writers considered. Query with SASE; multiple queries O.K. Commission: 15%. No unsolicited manuscripts.

CAROL MANN LITERARY AGENCY—55 Fifth Ave., New York, NY 10003. Attn: Carol Mann. 30% fiction; 70% nonfiction. Query with outline, sample pages, bio and resumé, and SASE. Commission: 15%.

MANUS ASSOCIATES, INC.— 417 E. 57th St., Suite 5D, New York, NY 10022. Attn: Janet Manus. Branch office: 430 Cowper St., Palo Alto, CA 94301. Adult fiction and nonfiction. No science fiction, category romance, or military books. Unpublished writers considered. Query with outline, sample pages, and bio/resumé. Multiple queries O.K. "on occasion." Commission: 15%.

ELISABETH MARTON AGENCY— One Union Square W., Rm. 612, New York, NY 10003-3303. Attn: Tonda Marton. Plays only. Not considering new work at this time. Commission: 10%.

JED MATTES, INC.—2095 Broadway, #302, New York, NY 10023-2895. Adult fiction and nonfiction. Unpublished writers considered. Query. Commission: 15% domestic; 20% foreign.

HELMUT MEYER LITERARY AGENCY—330 E. 79th St., New York, NY 10021. Attn: Helmut Meyer, Literary Agent. Adult nonfiction. Telephone query or query by mail with outline, sample pages, and bio/resumé. No multiple queries. Commission: 15%.

HENRY MORRISON, INC.—Box 235, Bedford Hills, NY 10507. Adult fiction and nonfiction; book-length only. Unpublished writers considered. Query with outline; multiple queries O.K. Commission: 15% domestic; 20% foreign. Fees: photocopying, shipping. "We are concentrating on a relatively small list of clients, and work toward building them in the U.S. and international marketplaces. We tend to avoid autobiographical novels and extremely literary novels, but always seek good nonfiction on major political and historical subjects."

MULTIMEDIA PRODUCT DEVELOPMENT— 410 S. Michigan Ave., Suite 724, Chicago, IL 60605. Jane Jordan Browne, Pres. Adult fiction and nonfiction, as well as juvenile fiction and nonfiction. "We are interested in commercial, overnight sellers in the areas of mainstream fiction and nonfiction." No short stories, poems, screenplays, articles, or software. Query with bio and SASE. Commission: 15% domestic; 20% foreign.

JEAN V. NAGGAR LITERARY AGENCY—216 E. 75th St., New York, NY 10021. Attn: Jean Naggar, Frances Kuffel, or Anne Engel (nonfiction). Adult mainstream fiction and nonfiction. Very few unpublished writers considered. Query with outline, SASE, bio, and resumé. Commission: 15% domestic, 20% foreign.

RUTH NATHAN AGENCY—53 E. 34th St., Suite 207, New York, NY 10016. Decorative arts, show business, biography. Selected historical fiction, pre-1500. No unsolicited queries. Commission: 15%. "To writers seeking an agent: Please note what my specialties are. Do not send science fiction, fantasy, children's books, or business books."

NEW ENGLAND PUBLISHING ASSOCIATES—P.O. Box 5, Chester, CT 06412. Adult nonfiction, especially women's studies, minority issues, literature, business, and reference. Unpublished writers considered. Query with outline, sample pages, and bio/resumé. Commission: 15% domestic; 20% foreign.

BETSY NOLAN LITERARY AGENCY—224 W. 29th St., 15th Fl., New York, NY 10001. Attn: Betsy Nolan. Adult nonfiction, especially popular psychology, child care, cookbooks, gardening, music books, African-American and Jewish issues. Query. Commission: 15%.

THE RICHARD PARKS AGENCY—138 E. 16th St., 5B, New York, NY 10003. Attn: Richard Parks. Adult nonfiction; fiction by referral only. Unpublished writers considered. Query with bio and resumé. Commission: 15% domestic; 20% foreign. "No phone calls or faxed queries, please."

PERKINS, RUBIE, AND ASSOCIATES—240 W. 35th St., New York, NY 10001. Attn: Lori Perkins or Peter Rubie. Adult fiction and nonfiction; some middle grade and young adult. Unpublished writers considered. Query with outline, sample pages, bio, and resumé; multiple queries O.K. Commission: 15% U.S.; 20% foreign.

JAMES PETER ASSOCIATES, INC.—P.O. Box 772, Tenafly, NJ 07670. Attn: Bert Holtje. Adult nonfiction. Unpublished writers considered. Query with outline, sample pages, and bio/resumé. No multiple queries. Commission: 15% domestic, 20% foreign.

ALISON PICARD, LITERARY AGENT—P.O. Box 2000, Cotuit, MA 02635. Attn: Alison Picard. Adult fiction, nonfiction, and juvenile. Unpublished writers considered. Query; multiple queries O.K. Commission: 15%.

PINDER LANE & GARON-BROOKE ASSOCIATES, LTD.—159 W. 53rd St., #14-E, New York, NY 10019. Attn: Jean Free. Adult fiction and nonfiction including thrillers, romance, contemporary, biography, lifestyle, and health. Unpublished writers considered. Query with outline, bio/resumé, and SASE; no multiple queries. Commission: 15% domestic, 30% foreign.

SUSAN ANN PROTTER—110 W. 40th St., Suite 1408, New York, NY 10018. Adult fiction and nonfiction only, specializing in mysteries, contemporary thrillers and science fiction, health, psychology, true crime, self-help, popular science, medicine, and parenting. Query by mail only, with description, bio/resumé, synopsis, and SASE. Commission: unspecified.

ROBERTA PRYOR, INC.—288 Titicus Rd., North Salem, NY 10560. Attn: Roberta Pryor. Adult fiction, nonfiction, current affairs, biographies, ecology. Unpublished writers considered. Query with outline, sample pages, and bio/resumé. Multiple queries O.K. Commission: 10% domestic; 10% foreign and film.

RAINES & RAINES—71 Park Ave., Suite 4A, New York, NY 10016. Attn: Keith Korman, Joan Raines, Theron Raines. Adult fiction, nonfiction, and juvenile for all ages. Query; no multiple queries. Commission: 15% domestic; 20% foreign. "Keep query to one page."

HELEN REES LITERARY AGENCY—308 Commonwealth Ave., Boston, MA 02115. Literary fiction and nonfiction. No short stories, science fiction, children's, religious, sports, occult, or poetry. Unpublished writers considered. Query with outline and bio/resumé. No multiple queries. Commission: 15%.

JODY REIN BOOKS, INC.—7741 S. Ash Ct., Littleton, CO 80122. Attn: Jody Rein. Literary and mainstream adult nonfiction and commercial nonfiction. Query with SASE. Commission: 15%.

RENAISSANCE/H.N. SWANSON, INC.—9220 Sunset Blvd., Suite 302, Los Angeles, CA 90069. Literary fiction and nonfiction. Screenplays and teleplays. Unpublished, unproduced writers considered. Query with bio and resumé. Commission: 10%.

JANE ROTROSEN AGENCY—318 E. 51st St., New York, NY 10022. Attn: Ruth Kagle. Adult fiction and nonfiction. Unpublished writers considered. Query with outline and bio; no unsolicited manuscripts. Commission: 15% U.S. and Canada; 20% foreign and film/TV.

PESHA RUBINSTEIN LITERARY AGENCY—1392 Rugby Rd., Teaneck, NJ 07666. Attn: Pesha Rubinstein. Commercial fiction: mysteries, romances, and thrillers; nonfiction; and juvenile. Unpublished writers considered. Query with first 10 pages, synopsis, and SASE. Commission: 15% domestic, 20% foreign.

RUSSELL & VOLKENING, INC.—50 W. 29th St., New York, NY 10001. Adult and juvenile fiction and nonfiction; specializing in literary fiction and narrative nonfiction. Queries for juvenile books should be addressed to Jennie Dunham. No screenplays, horror, romance, science fiction, or poetry. Unpublished writers considered. Query with letter and SASE. Commission: 10%.

RUSSELL-SIMENAUER LITERARY AGENCY, INC.—See *Jacqueline Simenauer Literary Agency, Inc.*

SANDUM & ASSOCIATES—144 E. 84th St., New York, NY 10028. Attn: Howard E. Sandum. Primarily nonfiction. Query with sample pages and bio/resumé. Multiple queries O.K. Commission: 15% domestic; 10% when foreign or TV/film subagents are used. "We do not consider manuscripts in genres such as science fiction, romance, or horror unless surpassing literary qualities are present."

SEBASTIAN AGENCY—333 Kearny St., Suite 708, San Francisco, CA 94108. Attn: Laurie Harper. Adult nonfiction only. Considers very few new writers. Query with outline, sample pages, and and bio/resumé. Commission: 15% domestic; 20% to 25% foreign.

BOBBE SIEGEL, RIGHTS LITERARY AGENT—41 W. 83rd St., New York, NY 10024. Attn: Bobbe Siegel. Adult fiction and nonfiction. Unpublished writers considered. Query; multiple queries O.K. SASE required. Commission: 15%.

JACQUELINE SIMENAUER LITERARY AGENCY, INC.—(formerly *Russell-Simenauer Literary Agency*) P.O. Box 43267, Upper Montclair, NJ 07043. Attn: Jacqueline Simenauer. Nonfiction: medical, pop psych, how-to/self-help, women's issues, health, alternative health concepts, fitness, diet, nutrition, current issues, true crime, business, celebrities, reference. Fiction: literary and mainstream commercial. Query with outline, synopsis, and SASE. Multiple queries O.K. Commission: 15% domestic; 25% foreign.

F. JOSEPH SPIELER LITERARY AGENCY—154 W. 57th St., Rm. 135, New York, NY 10019. Attn: F. Joseph Spieler. Branch office: Victoria Shoemaker, Agent, The Spieler Agency West, 1760 Solano Ave., Suite 300, Berkeley, CA 94707. Adult fiction and nonfiction; also juvenile for all ages. Unpublished writers considered. Query with sample pages; no multiple queries. Commission: 15%. No material will be returned if no SASE.

PHILIP G. SPITZER LITERARY AGENCY—50 Talmage Farm Ln., East Hampton, NY 11937. Attn: Philip Spitzer. Adult fiction and nonfiction. Query. Commission: 15% domestic; 20% foreign.

GLORIA STERN AGENCY—2929 Buffalo Speedway, #2111, Houston, TX 77098. Attn: Gloria Stern. Adult nonfiction, literary fiction. Query with short outline, bio/resume, one chapter, and SASE. Multiple queries O.K. Commission: 15%.

GUNTHER STUHLMANN, AUTHOR'S REPRESENTATIVE—P.O. Box 276, Becket, MA 01223. Attn: Barbara Ward. Literary fiction and nonfiction, especially biography, letters, and history. No mysteries, romance, science fiction, or adventure. Unpublished writers sometimes considered. Query with SASE; no multiple queries. Commission: 10% North America; 15% Britain and Commonwealth; 20% foreign.

THE TANTLEFF OFFICE—375 Greenwich St., Suite 700, New York, NY 10013. Attn: Charmaine Ferenczi, stage plays. Jill Bock, film and television. Stage plays, screenplays, teleplays. Unpublished writers considered. Query with synopsis, up to 10 sample pages, bio/resumé; multiple queries O.K. Commission: 10% scripts.

WALES LITERARY AGENCY, INC.—108 Hayes St., Seattle, WA 98109. E-mail: waleslit@aol.com Attn: Elizabeth Wales, Adrienne Reed. Mainstream and literary fiction and nonfiction, including women's, nature writing, multicultural stories, and animal stories. Unpublished writers considered. Query with outline, sample pages, and SASE. Multiple queries O.K. Commission: 15%.

JOHN A. WARE LITERARY AGENCY—392 Central Park W., New York, NY 10025. Attn: John Ware. Adult fiction and nonfiction. "Literate, accessible, noncategory fiction, plus thrillers and mysteries." Nonfiction: biography, history, current affairs, investigative journalism, social criticism, Americana and folklore, science, and reflective narratives. Unpublished writers considered. Query letter only, with SASE; multiple queries O.K. Commission: 15% domestic, 20% foreign.

WATKINS/LOOMIS AGENCY—133 E. 35th St., Suite One, New York, NY 10016. Attn: Tracy Smith. Adult fiction and nonfiction. Unpublished writers considered. Query with SASE; no multiple queries. Commission: 15%.

SANDRA WATT & ASSOCIATES—8033 Sunset Blvd., Suite 4053, Los Angeles, CA 90046. Attn: Sandra Watt. Adult fiction (mystery, thrillers, women's novels, detective) and nonfiction (spiritual, new age, animals, humor, anthropology, true crime, and gardening). Some middle grade, young adult, and picture books. Unpublished writers considered. Query with outline; multiple submissions O.K. Commission: 15%. "We're probably a bit old-fashioned in loving a great story."

WIESER & WIESER, INC.—118 E. 25th St.,7th Fl., New York, NY 10010. Attn: Olga Wieser. Adult fiction and nonfiction. Unpublished writers considered. Query with outline, sample pages, and bio/resumé. No multiple queries. Commission: 15%.

WITHERSPOON ASSOCIATES—235 E. 31st St., New York, NY 10016. Adult fiction and nonfiction. Unpublished writers considered. Query with sample pages; no multiple queries. Commission: 15%.

RUTH WRESCHNER, AUTHORS' REPRESENTATIVE—10 W. 74th St., New York, NY 10023. Attn: Ruth Wreschner. Adult fiction (mainstream novels, genre books, mysteries, romance) and nonfiction (by experts in a particular field); also young adult. No pornography or science fiction; very few children's books. Unpublished writers considered. Query with outline, sample pages, and bio/resumé. Multiple queries O.K. Commission: 15% domestic; 20% foreign.

ANN WRIGHT REPRESENTATIVES—165 W. 46th St., Suite 1105, New York, NY 10036-2501. Attn: Dan Wright. Adult fiction, screenplays, and teleplays. Query with bio/resumé and SASE. No multiple queries. Commission: 10% to 20%.

WRITERS HOUSE—21 W. 26th St., New York, NY 10010. Attn: Simon Lipskar, fiction. John Hodgeman, nonfiction; Alexa Lichtenstein, juvenile and young adult. Liza Landsman, multimedia. Adult fiction and nonfiction; juvenile for all ages; and young adult. Unpublished writers considered. "Query with one-page letter on why your project is excellent, what it's about, and why you're the wonderful author to write it." No multiple queries. Commission: 15% domestic; 20% foreign.

WRITERS' PRODUCTIONS—P.O. Box 630, Westport, CT 06881. Attn: David L. Meth. Adult fiction and nonfiction, both of literary quality. Children's books that fit into multimedia fantasies. Unpublished writers considered. Query with SASE. Commission: 15% domestic; 25% foreign, dramatic, multimedia, software sales, licensing, and merchandising.

ZACHARY SHUSTER LITERARY AGENCY—375 Riverside Dr., New York, NY 10025. Attn: Lane Zachary or Todd Shuster. Branch office: 45 Newbury St., Boston, MA 02116. Adult fiction and nonfiction. Juvenile fiction and nonfiction. Screenplays. Query with sample pages or submit complete manuscript. Commission: 15% domestic; 20% foreign.

SUSAN ZECKENDORF ASSOCIATES, INC.—171 W. 57th St., New York, NY 10019. Attn: Susan Zeckendorf. Fiction: literary fiction; mysteries; thrillers; women's commercial fiction. Nonfiction: science; music; biography; social history. Unpublished writers considered. Query with outline and bio/resumé. Commission: 15% domestic; 20% foreign.

Glossary

Advance—The amount a publisher pays a writer before a book is published; it is deducted from the royalties earned from sales of the finished book.

Agented material—Submissions from literary or dramatic agents to a publisher. Some publishing companies accept agented material only.

All rights—Some magazines purchase all rights to the material they publish, which means that they can use it as they wish, as many times as they wish. They cannot purchase all rights unless the writer gives them written permission to do so.

Assignment—A contract, written or oral, between an editor and writer, confirming that the writer will complete a specific project by a certain date, and for a certain fee.

B&W—Abbreviation for black-and-white photographs.

Book outline—Chapter-by-chapter summary of a book, frequently in paragraph form, allowing an editor to evaluate the book's content, tone, and pacing, and determine whether he or she wants to see the entire manuscript for possible publication.

Book packager—Company that puts together all the elements of a book, from initial concept to writing, publishing, and marketing it. Also called **book producer** or **book developer.**

Byline—Author's name as it appears on a published piece.

Clips—Copies of a writer's published work, often used by editors to evaluate the writer's talent.

Column inch—One inch of a typeset column; often serves as a basis for payment.

Contributor's copies—Copies of a publication sent to a writer whose work is included in it.

Copy —Manuscript pages before they are set into type.

Copy editing—Line-by-line editing to correct errors in spelling, grammar, and punctuation, and inconsistencies in style. Differs from **content editing**, which evaluates flow, logic, and overall message.

Copyright —Legal protection of creative works from unauthorized use. Under the law, copyright is secured automatically when the work is set down for the first time in written or recorded form.

Cover letter—A brief letter that accompanies a manuscript or book proposal. A cover letter is *not* a query letter (see definition, page 870).

Deadline —The date on which a written work is due at the editor's office, agreed to by author and editor.

Draft —A complete version of an article, story, or book. **First drafts** are often called **rough drafts**.

Fair use—A provision of the copyright law allowing brief passages of copyrighted material to be quoted without infringing on the owner's rights.

Feature —An article that is generally longer than a news story and whose main focus is an issue, trend, or person.

Filler—Brief item used to fill out a newspaper or magazine column; could be a news item, joke, anecdote, or puzzle.

First serial rights—The right of a magazine or newspaper to publish a work for the first time in any periodical. After that, all rights revert to the writer.

Galleys—The first typeset proofs of a manuscript, before they are divided into pages.

Ghostwriter—Author of books, articles, and speeches that are credited to someone else.

Glossy—Black-and-white photo with a shiny, rather than a matte, finish.

Hard copy—The printed copy of material written on a computer.

Honorarium—A modest, token fee paid by a publication to an author in gratitude for a submission.

International reply coupon (IRC)—Included with any correspondence or submission to a foreign publication; allows the editor to reply by mail without incurring cost.

Kill fee—Fee paid for an article that was assigned but subsequently not published; usually a percentage of the amount that would have been paid if the work had been published.

Lead time—Time between the planning of a magazine or book and its publication date.

Libel—A false accusation or published statement that causes a person embarrassment, loss of income, or damage to reputation.

Little magazines—Publications with limited circulation whose content often deals with literature or politics.

Mass market—Books appealing to a very large segment of the reading public and often sold in such outlets as drugstores, supermarkets, etc.

Masthead—A listing of the names and titles of a publication's staff members.

Ms—Abbreviation for manuscript; mss is the plural abbreviation.

Multiple submissions—Also called **simultaneous submissions**. Complete manuscripts sent simultaneously to different publications. Once universally discouraged by editors, the practice is gaining more acceptance, though some still frown on it. **Multiple queries** are generally accepted, however, since reading them requires less of an investment in time on the editor's part.

On speculation—Editor agrees to consider a work for publication "on speculation," without any guarantee that he or she will ultimately buy the work.

One-time rights—Editor buys manuscript from writer and agrees to publish it one time, after which the rights revert to the author for subsequent sales.

Op-ed—A newspaper piece, usually printed opposite the editorial page, that expresses a personal viewpoint on a timely news item.

Over-the-transom—Describes the submission of unsolicited material by a free-lance writer; the term harks back to the time when mail was delivered through the open window above an office door.

Payment on acceptance—Payment to writer when manuscript is submitted.

Payment on publication—Payment to writer when manuscript is published.

Pen name—A name other than his or her legal name that an author uses on written work.

Public domain—Published material that is available for use without permission, either because it was never copyrighted or because its copyright term is expired. Works published at least 75 years ago are considered in the public domain.

Q-and-A format—One type of presentation for an interview article, in which questions are printed, followed by the interviewee's answers.

Query letter—A letter —usually no longer than one page —in which a writer proposes an article idea to an editor.

Rejection slip—A printed note in which a publication indicates that it is not interested in a submission.

Reporting time—The weeks or months it takes for an editor to evaluate a submission.

Reprint rights—The legal right of a magazine or newspaper to print an article, story, or poem after it has already appeared elsewhere.

Royalty—A percentage of the amount received from retail sales of a book, paid to the author by the publisher. For hardcovers, the royalty is generally 10% on the first 5,000 copies sold; 12½% on the next 5,000 sold; 15% thereafter. Paperback royalties range from 4% to 8%, depending on whether it's a trade or mass-market book.

SASE—Self-addressed, stamped envelope, required with all submissions that the author wishes returned —either for return of material or (if you don't need material returned) for editor's reply.

Slush pile—The stack of unsolicited manuscripts in an editor's office.

Tear sheet—The pages of a magazine or newspaper on which an author's work is published.

Unsolicited submission—A manuscript that an editor did not specifically ask to see.

Vanity publisher—Also called **subsidy publisher.** A publishing company that charges author all costs of printing a book. No reputable book publisher operates on this subsidy basis.

Work for hire—When a work is written on a "for hire" basis, all rights in it become the property of the publisher. Though the work-for-hire clause applies mostly to work done by regular employees of a company, some editors offer work-for-hire agreements to free lancers. Think carefully before signing such agreements, however, since by doing so you will essentially be signing away your rights and will not be able to try to resell your work on your own.

Writers guidelines—A formal statement of a publication's editorial needs, payment schedule, deadlines, and other essential information.

INDEX TO MARKETS